W9-BUY-601

Francis A. Drexel
LIBRARY
Harvard Business School

Core Collection

1998

SAINT JOSEPH'S UNIVERSITY

FOURTH EDITION

PERSPECTIVES IN CONSUMER BEHAVIOR

Harold H. Kassarjian
Anderson School of Management
University of California, Los Angeles

Thomas S. Robertson
The Wharton School
University of Pennsylvania

HF
5415.32
.P47
RELEASE
1991

PRENTICE HALL, Englewood Cliffs, New Jersey 07632

Library of Congress Cataloging-in-Publication Data

Perspectives in consumer behavior / [edited by] Harold H. Kassarjian,
Thomas S. Robertson. -- 4th ed.
p. cm.
Previously published: Glenview, Ill. : Scott, Foresman, c1989.
Includes bibliographical references and index.
ISBN 0-13-660440-4
1. Consumer behavior. 2. Marketing
I. Kassarjian, Harold H. II. Robertson, Thomas S.
HF5415.32.P47 1991
658.8'342--dc20 90-40458
CIP

Editorial/production supervision and
interior design: Shelly Kupperman
Cover design: Mike Fender Design
Manufacturing buyer: Bob Anderson
Prepress buyer: Trudy Pisciotti

©1991, 1981, 1973, 1968 by Prentice-Hall, Inc.
A Division of Simon & Schuster
Englewood Cliffs, New Jersey 07632

All rights reserved. No part of this book may be reproduced, in any form or by any means, without permission in writing from the publisher.

Printed in the United States of America
10 9 8 7 6 5 4 3 2 1

ISBN 0-13-660440-4

PRENTICE-HALL INTERNATIONAL (UK) LIMITED, *London*
PRENTICE-HALL OF AUSTRALIA PTY. LIMITED, *Sydney*
PRENTICE-HALL CANADA INC., *Toronto*
PRENTICE-HALL HISPANOAMERICANA, S.A., *Mexico*
PRENTICE-HALL OF INDIA PRIVATE LIMITED, *New Delhi*
PRENTICE-HALL OF JAPAN, INC., *Tokyo*
SIMON & SCHUSTER ASIA PTE. LTD., *Singapore*
EDITORA PRENTICE-HALL DO BRASIL, LTDA., *Rio de Janeiro*

CONTENTS

PART TWO: LEARNING AND DECISION PROCESSES

PART THREE: AFFECT, MOTIVATION, AND PERSONALITY

PREFACE

This is the fourth edition of *Perspectives in Consumer Behavior* and the first under our new publisher, Prentice-Hall. The first edition of this book, published in 1968, was designed as a combined text and readings book since we felt both were needed at the time. Courses in consumer behavior were just coming into existence and text material was very limited. Myers and Reynolds had a short innovative paperback as did Zaltman but with a more specialized focus, and a few other volumes were in print. Instructors were often using social psychology texts and articles from the behavioral sciences.

The field of consumer behavior was emerging then as a distinct area of study within marketing, but the boundaries of the field had not yet been defined. There was little consensus on the topics that the field was to embrace. Our initial goal was to produce a volume of text and readings that would help delineate the field and that would meet the needs of our own students at UCLA as well as at other colleges and universities. Interestingly, simultaneously with the appearance of *Perspectives in Consumer Behavior,* Engel, Kollat and Blackwell published the first complete textbook in the field.

By the time the second edition was published, five years later, a field had emerged. An explosion of theories, propositions, concepts, methodologies and empirical studies had occurred. This was reflected in the content of *Perspectives in Consumer Behavior.* We were no longer dependent almost entirely on marketing and the core behavioral and social sciences—consumer behavior was developing a literature of its own. Again in that edition, text material was presented followed by review articles and empirical studies. One could see in those selections that it was the era of attitude research and the beginning of the cognitive approach to studies in consumer behavior.

Eight years later, in 1981, the third edition was published. Consumer behavior had come into its own. The *Journal of Consumer Research* had been launched and had become the premiere scientific medium. The Association for Consumer Research proceedings was publishing scores of articles each year, and marketing journals as well as psychology journals were publishing consumer behavior research. New textbooks had emerged and by then we felt that a smaller percentage of *Perspectives* should be devoted to text material. More empirical articles were presented and information processing research was beginning to overshadow attitude research.

Now we are at the fourth edition. A number of academic journals focusing on consumer behavior research are now available and some thirty full length books are in print from which an instructor can select material compatible with his or her approach to the subject. The problem of selecting classroom material has changed from one of paucity to an overwhelming array of excellent journal articles, monographs, textbooks, working papers, case books, and other materials.

Hence, the fourth edition again has evolved, consistent with developments in the field. Now, we present no text material at all. To do so would be redundant with the many fine textbooks on the market. Long introductions and explanations of concepts, theories and ideas are no longer needed. We feel, what is needed, is a collection of reprinted and original articles that present the best, or at least representative, research from the rich domain of what is available in consumer behavior in the 1990s. It is our intent to present a well-produced book of readings focusing on leading-edge articles as well as classics. Whenever possible, we have tried to design each chapter such that it contains a review paper that surveys the topic and presents the extant literature. Next, we have tried to include as many empirical articles as possible and, whenever feasible, to include a classic or theoretical article.

An aficionado of *Contents* will notice that many of the articles in this edition of *Perspectives,* have been published since the third edition. The field is indeed dynamic. What was new and exciting less than a decade ago is already incorporated in new research and the field moves on. This book has evolved over the decades much as the field has evolved. It has become far more empirical and research oriented in a traditional positivistic sense; yet, this edition has also made room for the newly developing topics of affect, mood, experiential behavior research, and naturalistic inquiry. Consumer behavior continues to be an intriguing field of study and we hope that we have been able to capture that interest and excitement in the articles to be presented.

A WORD OF THANKS

The process of selecting articles for this volume has involved many people. For example, we studied course syllabi from instructors across the country and in several other countries to gather a base of frequently assigned and important articles. We then sought the feedback of many colleagues and professors teaching consumer behavior to our initial set of selections. Similar to earlier editions of this book, we wanted this volume to lead the field and not merely follow it. Thus, the final set of articles reflects our judgments as editors as to which articles, within space limitations, are most likely to be of value to students in consumer behavior courses.

The process of completing this edition led to many debts of gratitude. Keith Hunt at Brigham Young University, a loyal friend and colleague was important to us at several points in the preparation of this volume. That wonderful scholar, Jim Bettman at Duke University, has had much influence on us individually, in the field, and now in the content of this book. Other important people include Carol Scott at UCLA, one of the most creative researchers in this field; Rich Lutz at Florida, a friend over the years and a key leader in the field; Bill Ross at Wharton, one of the emerging dynamic young scholars; Joel Cohen at the University of Florida, whose positive impact on the field has been felt for the past two-and-a-half decades; and Rich Oliver at Vanderbilt, with his high standards of excellence in his research and teaching.

In addition, Rich Lutz and Mary Jane Sheffet, a valued contributor to several editions, took the time to produce original materials for this edition. Bill Wilkie and Peter Dickson allowed us to publish their working paper before they could send it off to a journal. And, there are others who reviewed our various outlines, gave us valuable advice, and whom we may have overlooked: to them our apologies.

Therese Louie, graduate student and budding consumer behavior scholar, helped us in the clerical tasks involved; and Katrin Harich, at California State University, Fullerton, a friend and close colleague helped a great deal in the production of this volume. Our most sincere thanks go to Mary Ellen Roche at the Wharton School. Her concern, hard work, and charm has endeared her to us and has materially helped produce this book. Finally, we would like to express our appreciation to our production editor, Shelly Kupperman, at Prentice-Hall and to our acquiring editor Whitney Blake—a true professional in the world of publishing as well as Chris Treiber, the current acquisitions editor. That this fourth edition exists at all, is a tribute to these friends and colleagues and to the leading scholars whose work is represented in the papers that follow.

Harold H. Kassarjian
Thomas S. Robertson

1

SHOPPING FOR APPLIANCES: Consumers' Strategies and Patterns of Information Search*

William L. Wilkie
Peter R. Dickson

This paper reports the results of a national study of consumers' search and shopping for several major household appliances. A wide range of measures—some drawn from past work and some extending into new territory—were used. Interesting and sometimes puzzling results emerge, which lead to the proposal of a modified framework for conceptualizing consumer shopping behavior.

INTRODUCTION

Prepurchase information search has long been regarded as a significant element of a consumer's behavior. It is at this decision stage that consumers can learn more about their potential purchases. They can discover new brands, new product features, and/or new stores. In general, consumers at this stage undertake to match their personal desires with the external means of satisfying those desires.

In an economic sense, consumers' search for information represents a key basis of our competitive market system. The emphasis on freedom of consumer choice in this system stems from the belief that well-informed consumers are able to choose wisely. Informed consumer choice in turn rewards sellers who offer better marketing mixes, and stimulates other marketers to improve their offerings.

*MSI working paper, pp. 85–108. Copyright © 1985 by Marketing Science Institute, Cambridge, Massachusetts.

Research on the topic of consumer information search has direct implications for both public policy and marketing management decisions. Improving the availability and quality of consumer information is an attractive policy option in many situations. To implement this option well, however, a regulator should understand how and why consumers use such information. Similarly, marketing managers—including those in manufacturing, advertising, and retailing businesses—are deeply interested in how consumers decide to purchase a particular alternative at a particular store. Since information search represents the primary stage at which marketing can provide information and influence consumers' decisions, understanding this process becomes a significant topic for marketers as well.

This paper reports a national survey of consumers' information search for household durable goods. The extensive survey questionnaire included questions of direct interest to marketing strategists and public policymakers and was developed from the survey instruments used in such important prior studies as those of Katona and Mueller (1955), Newman and Staelin (1971), and Claxton, Fry, and Portis (1974). The resulting instrument thus represents what we believe is one of the most comprehensive measurements of consumer search and shopping behavior ever undertaken. The present paper focuses on providing a *descriptive* overview of the study's findings. Other articles will probe the most significant underpinnings of the findings detailed here.

Background

Consumer information search has received a reasonable degree of attention in the literature. Primary attention has been given to products for which information search might be especially useful: those which are purchased infrequently, are high in cost, and for which trial purchases or use experiences are not feasible, e.g., automobiles and household durables.

The first public study in this vein was published in 1953 by George Katona and Eva Mueller, who reported a nationwide survey of recent purchasers of major appliances. Since that study—which is still widely quoted 30 years later—several other major research efforts have been reported, including those by Newman and Staelin (1972) and Claxton, Fry, and Portis (1974). In addition, several comprehensive reviews of the research findings and issues in this area are also available (Granbois and Braden 1976; Newman 1977; and Dickson and Wilkie 1979).

Unlike the case in some other research areas, the results on consumer information search have been relatively consistent:

- A significant percentage of consumers show very little evidence of information-seeking behavior: A large number of consumers visit only *one* store, consider only *one* brand, and consult only a *few* information sources before buying durable goods.
- There is heterogeneity across consumers: Some consumers evidence a great deal of information search before purchase.
- On average, however, reported information search is surprisingly low.

These general findings have sparked considerable discussion and some speculation as to their causes. A number of methodological issues have been raised. First, it is difficult to specify what exactly "consumer information search" means. Among the measures included in past research, for example, are number of brands considered; number of stores shopped; number of information sources used; total purchase consideration time; and an overall index incorporating some or all of these measures. Second, it is difficult to compare results across research studies, as these have investigated different products, different samples, and different time periods, and may also have used different measures and analytical methods.

The typical use of a survey interview methodology has also been a subject of concern.

Because this type of method requires consumers to recall and report search activities which may have taken place as much as six to twelve months earlier, it is possible that these reports are systematically distorted toward indicating too little search. An interesting study by Newman and Lockeman (1976) compared observations of shoppers' behavior when they were purchasing shoes against their later reports of that same behavior. The observation method yielded considerably higher search scores than did the recall reports.[1]

In addition to the speculations that findings of low-search activities are attributable to data collection and measurement procedures (i.e., consumers do search more than we realize), there have been speculations about underlying explanations for low-search behavior. Some of these have focused on the costs of search versus its benefits, consumers' inability to search for more information because of limitations on information processing capabilities, and weaknesses in information availability. Among the most pressing research needs are more understanding of the consumer benefits achieved by search, as well as further details of the search process itself.

Positioning of This Study

The present study was intended to serve as a replication, update, and extension of prior work in this area. Given the stability of past results over times of great societal change and widely differing product categories, we did not expect that our results on measures comparable to those used in past studies would greatly differ from past findings. We were interested, however, in attempting to explain further why some such findings may occur, and to introduce further measures of shopping behavior and information search processes. The purpose of this paper, therefore, is to present an expanded picture of consumers' shopping and search behavior.

Figure 1.1 summarizes the important characteristics of the present study. In addition to the traditional measures of shopping behavior and information search behavior (Sector E in Figure 1.1) employed in past studies, we incorporated five other categories of measures in this study. Four of these (Sectors A–D) are expected to precede and affect each consumer's shopping and search behaviors. The fifth sector, "purchase and outcome measures," indicates the effects of shopping and search behaviors. Along

[1]The study reported in the present paper included purchases made from several days up to twelve months prior to the survey. To check for possible memory decay effects, elapsed time was cross-tabulated against all measures of search and shopping behavior. Of 120 chi-square tests, only three were significant at $p \leq .05$, and none of these showed a pattern of results consistent with a memory decay hypothesis. These results are consistent with the findings of a similar test reported by Punj and Staelin (1983).

FIGURE 1.1 Overview of the Measures

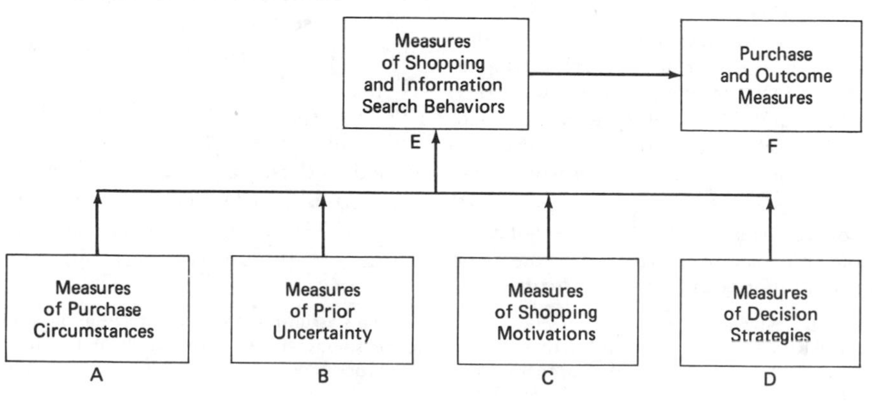

with the addition of the five new sectors, some new measures of shopping and search behavior were incorporated into Sector E.

As a set, then, these measures should allow us to address such major questions as:

- What circumstances or situations spark consumers' purchasing of durable goods? In what ways do differing circumstances affect shopping and search behaviors?
- How uncertain are consumers before beginning their search processes? About what are they uncertain?
- What are the shopping motivations of consumers as they begin their search and decision processes? How do these affect the processes themselves?
- How important are the various sources of consumer information?
- How much time is actually spent shopping for the purchase?
- How much does the shopping process change initial purchase intentions?
- How likely is it that consumers will purchase these products at a sale price?
- Why do shoppers stop searching for information?
- How satisfied are consumers with their durable goods purchases? Does this satisfaction depend on the type of shopping and search process they have employed?

METHOD

Following an extensive literature review, we undertook five stages of preliminary research:

1. Analysis of previous questionnaires. Questionnaires used in three earlier major studies (Katona and Mueller 1955; Newman and Staelin 1971; Claxton, Fry, and Portis 1974) were obtained from Professors Newman and Claxton and analyzed for content area and question wording.
2. Personal interviews with research management of the sponsoring firms. From these we obtained background information, insights into consumer behavior, and proprietary research instruments.[2]
3. A series of 20 in-depth personal interviews with appliance salespersons in two cities. These provided further insights on in-store salesperson/customer interactions and elicited salespersons' generalizations about consumers' behaviors.
4. Two focus group discussions with recent buyers of household durable goods. These discussions stressed the overall nature of the purchase process, with emphasis on the information search phase.
5. Questionnaire development in conjunction with the four preceding stages. Possible items were tested on recent purchasers at the end of the focus group sessions. When the questionnaire was close to completion, it was pretested in separate interviews with recent purchasers identified from the files of local appliance stores. The questionnaire underwent a final in-house pretest at the Home Testing Institute.

We chose the major domestic refrigeration and laundry appliances—refrigerators, freezers, clothes washers, and clothes dryers—as the focus of the research. These are important products in terms of household economics, energy consumption, and the lifestyle of the household. These appliances are well established, are in the maturity stage of their product life cycles, and have high penetration and replacement-purchase rates. We expected between-product differences in shopping behavior to be relatively minor within this set.[3]

The sample was obtained from the national consumer panel of the Home Testing Institute in a two-stage procedure. First, a brief postcard questionnaire was mailed to the entire panel of 5,000 households to identify those consumers who had purchased at least one of the target products within the prior year. This step yielded a qualifying sample of 700 households. The full four-page questionnaire was then mailed to these consumers; 585 responses were received back (84 percent response rate). Of these, 433 questionnaires reported purchases of the major appliances covered in this report.

[2]We would like to thank the following senior market researchers from the sponsoring companies for their advice and guidance: James J. Casey, C. Fred Purcell, Douglas A. Wattrick, and Marvin L. Cannon.

[3]This assumption was tested within the study and found to be sound. To explore search and shopping behavior differences depending on stage in the product life cycle, a sample of microwave oven purchasers was also studied and will be reported in a separate analysis (see Dickson 1981).

The demographic profile of the sample deviated slightly from U.S. Census population estimates in expected ways, reflecting different purchase rates for these appliances within different population groups. Larger families, for example, were slightly overrepresented, as were college-educated households. Low-income households (under $7,000) and older households (over age 55) were underrepresented by some five to ten percent.

In an effort to insure accuracy of reporting within a household, the questionnaire began with a "purchase participation" question; the household member having key involvement with the purchase was asked to complete the questionnaire. Background information on the consuming households was obtained from the panel firm.

EMPIRICAL FINDINGS

Traditional Search Measures

As noted above, the study took many measures of consumer information search and shopping behavior. In presenting the findings, we will begin with those measures commonly used in past research to describe information search.

Table 1.1 reports findings on four such measures of information search. When asked, "How long was it from the time you *first considered* purchasing your new appliance until you actually made the purchase?" respondents gave a wide range of times. Nine percent of the sample of purchasers reported same-day purchase, and one-third reported a total consideration time of less than one week. At the other extreme, nearly one-fourth of the sample considered buying for over three months. The modal and median response was the category of one to four weeks. An examination of this distribution suggests a greater possibility for information gathering activity than has generally been implied by past research.

The other three measures shown in Table 1.1 more directly report on the search process. The average *number of stores visited* was 2.5, but again this average hides high variability. One-fourth of the sample visited four or more stores, while three of every eight purchasers (37 percent) bought at the first and only store they visited. The average *number of brands considered* was 2.3, and again there was a wide range of responses. About one-third of the sample considered only one brand, while another one-sixth of consumers considered four or more brands.

Both the store visit and brand considered measures indicate that consumers undertake somewhat more search activity than was generally found in the earlier research literature. Interestingly, two other recent studies, by Westbrook and Fornell (1979) and Day and Deutscher (1982), have also found this somewhat higher level of shopping and search activity. It is possible, therefore, that the average level of consumer search has been *increasing* in recent years. Even if this is the case, of course, the high individual variability still remains, as do issues concerning the quality and impact of actual search behavior.

A fourth traditional measure, the types of information sources consulted by consumers, is also summarized in Table 1.1. "Independent" source types comprise two categories: friends and relatives, and *Consumer Reports* magazine. Even when they were prompted, thus encouraging an overstatement bias, *most consumers (52 percent) did not report consulting any independent sources of information.* Only one in nine purchasers (11 percent) reported consulting both types of sources. (A concern with recall and reporting difficulty and accuracy led us not to ask how many times each source type was consulted by a given consumer: several friends and/or relatives, for example, could have been called upon by a consumer reporting having consulted this source category.)

Consumers made somewhat more use of marketer-controlled information sources, with only 15 percent reporting no consultation with any type of marketer information. On average, however, respondents reported having consulted only two marketer source types before purchase. The nature of these sources and how they were used is discussed in the following section.

TABLE 1.1 Consumer Search and Shopping—Traditional Measures

A. Purchase Consideration Time

	Percent of Purchases (n = 433)	
Same day purchase	9%	
Within first week	24	Modal category = *1–4 Weeks*
1–4 weeks	*33*	Median category = *1–4 Weeks*
1–3 months	11	
3–6 months	11	
Over 6 months	13	

B. Number of Different Stores Visited

One	*37%*	Range = *0–12* Stores
Two	19	Mode = *1* Store
Three	19	
Four or more	25	Mean = *2.5* Stores

C. Number of Brands Considered

One	*32%*	Range = *1–8* Brands
Two	26	Mode = *1* Brand
Three	26	
Four or more	16	Mean = *2.3* Brands

D. Types of Information Sources Used

1. Number of independent source types (of two listed—friends and relatives, *Consumer Reports*)

Zero	52%	Range = *0–2* Sources used
One	37	Mode = *0* Sources used
Two	11	Mean = *.58* Sources used

2. Number of marketer source types (of seven listed—appliance salesperson, newspaper ad, catalog, brochures/labels, appliance repairperson, magazine ad, T.V. ad)

Zero	15%	Four	6%	Range = *0–7* Sources used
One	27	Five	5	Mode = *1* Sources used
Two	25	Six	2	
Three	19	Seven	—	Mean = *2.0* Sources used

Further Measures of Shopping and Information Search

Household Participation. Table 1.2 reports additional descriptors of the shopping and information search processes of purchasers. Part A of the table shows that women are far more influential than men in purchasing these major household appliances: in four out of every ten purchases, a woman was either solely or primarily responsible for the shopping and decision process. Just over half of the cases (52 percent) involved joint decision making with both wives and husbands involved. In less than ten percent of the cases, a male did the primary shopping and decision making.

Previous Purchase Experience. The second part of Table 1.2 reports respondents' previous purchases of the same appliance type. The sample split evenly on this measure: about one-third had never purchased the appliance before, one-third had made one purchase, and another third had made two or more purchases. While a significant number of consumers are thus entering an appliance purchase for the first time, two-thirds of the market have already gone through the process before and can presumably

TABLE 1.2 Consumer Search and Shopping—Further Measures

A. Household Participation		B. Previous Purchase Experience[a]	
Female Solely	29%	None	35%
Female Primarily	11	One	33
Joint effort w/ spouse	*52*	Two or more	32
Male primarily/solely	8		

C. Local Store Familiarity[b]		D. Actual Time Spent Shopping[c]	
None	4%	Less than two hours	*45%*
One to three stores	24	Two to four hours	28
Four or more stores	*72*	Five to eight hours	14
		More than eight hours	14

E. Store Visits vs. Brands Considered

	Number of Brands Considered					
Number of Stores	1	2	3	4+		
1[d]	*74%*	16%	6%	4%	100%	(n = 161, 37% of sample)
2	5	*63*	26	5	100	(n = 84, 19% of sample)
3	5	32	*53*	10	100	(n = 82, 19% of sample)
4+	7	8	38	*48*	100	(n = 102, 25% of sample)

F. Types of Stores Visited

1. Appliance store[e]	59%	5. Ward's	18%
2. Sears	57	6. Furniture store	15
3. Department store	27	7. Penney's	12
4. Discount store	25	8. K-Mart	9
		9. Other type	13

[a]Reflects number of previous purchases of same product.

[b]Reflects number of local stores selling appliances with which respondent was familiar.

[c]Reflects total household time spent shopping for the new appliance, including travel time.

[d]To be read: "Of all customers who visited only one store, 74% considered only a single brand, 16% considered two brands, etc."

[e]To be read: "59% of purchasers visited at least one specialty appliance store."

draw upon their past experience for the present purchase. Of course, purchases of related durable products provide further background experience with stores, brands, and salespersons that can be applied in making the present purchase.

Store Familiarity. Part C of Table 1.2 shows that before shopping for the new appliance, the vast majority of consumers were already quite familiar with a number of alternative stores at which they might purchase it. Only 4 percent of the sample was not familiar with any local stores, while over 70 percent was familiar with at least four retail outlets. This finding is supported by the results of a separate sample of persons who had recently moved their residences. In that analysis, only 12 percent of the sample was unfamiliar with any local stores, while over 60 percent was familiar with four or more appliance outlets (see Dickson 1981). Perhaps a great deal of this familiarity is attributable to the national chains, as well as to any shopping consumers might have had to do for other appliances immediately upon changing residence.

Total Shopping Time. Part D of Table 1.2 provides further interesting—and perhaps surprising—findings. When asked, "How much time in total did you (and/or members of your household) actually spend on the shopping for the new appliance (including traveling time to and from stores)?" almost half the sample (45 percent) indicated that they had spent less than two hours in total shopping for their appliance. Only one in eight consumers spent more than the equivalent of a day's work in shopping for the purchase.

This result is consistent with the findings on number of stores shopped, previous purchase experience, and local store familiarity. In addition, it appears to suggest a rapid culmination of the choice process once the shopping phase begins. When questioned as to whether the shopping times might be due to a factor, such as the presence of children, inhibiting search freedom, only one of ten respondents indicated this to have been the case. As to timing of the shopping, about half the sample reported doing most of their shopping for the appliance purchase on weekdays, with one-quarter on weeknights, and another quarter on weekends.

Brands Considered within Stores. Part E of Table 1.2 displays the frequency distribution of number of brands considered as purchase alternatives conditional on the number of stores visited. Results here indicate that *once consumers are in a given store, their shopping appears to be focused on a single brand rather than on comparisons of competing brands.*[4] Note, for example, that of those consumers who visited only one store, nearly three-quarters report that they considered only one brand for their purchase. Of those who visited two stores, moreover, over 60 percent considered just two brands.

Shopping at Different Types of Stores. Household durable goods are available at many types of outlets. The final section of Table 1.2 identifies these, together with the proportion of respondents who visited each. Note how the specialty appliance stores and the Sears chain together dominate this product-market in terms of store visits (and sales, which will be discussed later on). Over half of all buyers shopped at each of these store types. In addition, 13 percent obtained information by phoning specialty appliance stores, while 7 percent reported calling Sears.

When asked about their prior preferences, 60 percent of the consumers said that they had started out with a strong preference to shop at one particular store. There does not seem to be a clear pattern to shopping at different store types, however. A block-cluster analysis of store-shopping combinations revealed that 20 percent of the sample shopped only in specialty appliance outlets, while 17 percent shopped only at Sears. By comparison, a mere 2 percent shopped only at department stores, and 1 percent at discount outlets only. Only 1 in 12 consumers shopped at all four of the above-mentioned store types.

Consumers' Use of Information Sources

In theory, store visits may be a particularly costly mode of information gathering, so consumers may use out-of-store information sources beforehand to reduce the need for shopping visits. Our overall empirical results did not lend strong support to this expectation inasmuch as consumers typically used few sources before visiting stores. Across the consumer sample, however, a variety of types of sources were consulted by at least some purchasers. Table 1.3 displays the proportion of buyers who reported consulting each of nine different information sources.

The Salesperson as an Information Source. The left column of Table 1.3 shows that almost 60 percent of consumers reported consulting appliance salespersons as an information source, a figure that dominates by far any other source type. Previous research had not suggested that a salesperson would be so dominant an information source for consumers and in this sense the results are revealing.

On the other hand, given the nature of the retail purchase environment, why would 41 percent of consumers not report consulting this

[4]This is an inference from the pattern of data. In part this result is predetermined by the fact that Sears sells only the single brand name.

TABLE 1.3 Information Sources Consulted and Found Useful[a]

	Information Source	*Buyers Who Consulted*	*"Consulted If Considered Rate"*	*Buyers Who Found Source Useful*	*"Source Usefulness Rate"*	*Buyers' "Most Useful" Info Source*	*"Primacy Rate"*[b]
1.	Appliance salesperson	*59%*	*.94*	*49%*	.83	*41%*	*.61*
2.	Newspaper ad	39	.78	28	.72	13	.27
3.	Friend or relative	38	.84	31	.82	13	.28
4.	Catalog	35	.76	28	.80	9	.22
5.	Brochures/labels	28	.85	25	.89	9	.28
6.	*Consumer Reports*	20	.67	18	*.90*	9	.38
7.	Appliance repairperson	14	.78	10	.71	5	.28
8.	Magazine ad	12	.57	7	.58	1	.06
9.	T.V. ad	10	.53	5	.50	1	.05

[a]Column, 1, 3, and 5 are percentages of total sample; columns 2, 4, and 6 are calculated rates not based on total sample.

[b]"Primacy Rate" equals proportion of persons naming source as most useful, of all persons who consulted that source.

source? Two possibilities suggest themselves: (1) perhaps a significant minority of buyers see the salesperson as purely an exchange agent rather than as a source of advice and information and (2) our question was deliberately phrased so as to ask about consulting and "seeking out" information sources. Some respondents may not have sought out or initiated consultation with appliance salespersons, even though they may have obtained information and advice from such a source. If this is true, our results would understate the role of the appliance salesperson.

The remaining columns of Table 1.3 amplify the salesperson's role. The .94 "consulted if considered rate" reflects the very high proportion of persons who considered consulting the salesperson, then did so. This finding is not surprising given the structure of the retail environment. What may be more surprising, however, is the salesperson's very strong performance on buyers' ratings of "usefulness." Five out of every six consumers (83 percent) who reported consulting salespersons also reported finding them to be useful sources of information for their decision. Across the sample, therefore, almost half (49 percent) of consumers rated the salesperson as a useful information source.

Not only was the salesperson rated as "useful," but he or she was also chosen as the *single most useful* information source by 41 percent of the sample. Of course, this figure might be artificially high because of the large number of consumers who consulted only the salesperson. To partially account for this effect, we calculated a "Source Primacy Rate." This is the proportion of all buyers consulting a source who then named that source as the single most useful. As shown in Table 1.3, salespersons receive a *.61* rating on this measure, which is far above the rating for any other source of information. *Overall, then, the retail salesperson emerges in this study as by far the dominant information source in consumers' eyes,* notwithstanding questions of salespersons' image, possible bias, and expertise raised by some critical observers.

Other Sources. Table 1.3 reports some interesting statistics for the other information sources as well. Overall, the table does *not* suggest a consumer information search process in which the average buyer carefully considers all possible types of information sources and then, based on a cost-benefit or other criterion, decides not to consult some of them. Rather, the results show that *only a few information sources even "came to mind" as worthy of consultation.* This finding is contained in the "Consulted If Considered Rate," which is calculated as the number of consumers consulting a source as a proportion of all consumers who considered consulting that source.

For example, newspaper ads were consulted by only 39 percent of the buyers, a seemingly low number given the extensive use of retail advertising in this market. Part of the reason is a moderate consulted if considered rate of .78, indicating that 22 percent of the consumers who thought about consulting newspaper ads did not in fact go on to do so. Given the ads' easy physical availability, the more likely problem here is whether the timing of the ads fit well with the consumer's purchase decision timing. The 35 percent actual consultation rate for catalogs also appears to be low due to poor availability more than lack of awareness, although here the key problem is more likely to be the physical constraints of obtaining a catalog exactly at the desired consultation time.

Note how the consulted if considered rate differs across source types. For the least consulted sources, both consumer awareness and source availability appear to be problems. *Consumer Reports,* for example, was considered as a possible information source by only 30 percent of consumers: *70 percent of consumers did not even consider consulting this highly respected rating publication.* Moreover, only 20 percent of consumers report having actually consulted it, a result that would seem to stem from physical availability constraints more than timing. Availability difficulties are even more obvious in the cases of magazine and television ads, which finished last in the list of information sources consulted by buyers during their decision processes. Given this pattern of results, home videotext systems would appear to offer potential for supplementing several types of information sources.

As to consumers' ratings of information source usefulness, results are again interesting. Manufacturers' brochures and labels scored very high on this measure, almost reaching the impressive .90 "Source Usefulness Rate" achieved by *Consumer Reports.* Friends/relatives and catalogs also score well on this measure. Magazine and television ads again fare poorly, however: not only are they not consulted very often during a purchasing decision, but they apparently turn out to be helpful to consumers only on about half of the occasions when they are consulted.

The "Single Most Useful Source" rating generally contains few surprises beyond the salesperson's dominance. Of some note, however, is the falloff of *Consumer Reports* on this measure: although it was rated as "useful" by almost everyone who consulted it, the magazine was rated as the "most useful" source of information by only about one-third of these consumers. Magazine and television ads, meanwhile, maintained their dismal performance on these measures, with virtually no buyers reporting these sources of information to have been their most useful ones.

Purchase Circumstances

We now turn from direct measures of search and shopping to consider some conditions that are likely to affect how much search is attempted and where it might be directed. Our first set of conditions—"Purchase Circumstances"—refers to the *situational context* involved in the purchase. Table 1.4 displays three key purchase circumstances for major household appliances, as determined from our literature search and interviews with managers, salespersons, and consumers:

- "Failure" circumstance—an existing machine breaks down, necessitating new purchase.
- "Replacement" circumstance—a new machine replaces an existing working unit.
- "Residential Move" circumstance—a change in residence necessitates the acquisition of a new unit.

Each accounts for a significant proportion of major household appliance purchases. Their effects on search and shopping behavior, however, are quite distinct.

"Failure-Forced" Search. The case of "Failure-Forced" consumer purchases was the most common type in our study, accounting for 36 percent of the purchase situations. Consumers facing this circumstance already have an appliance; they therefore have usage experience available to contribute to their decisions regarding specific model features they desire and to

TABLE 1.4 Purchase Circumstances and Initial Consumer Uncertainty

A. Purchase Circumstances		*B. Perceived Time Pressure*	
Appliance failure	*36%*	Extreme	10%
Replacement of working unit		Great	10
—Needs some repair	24	Moderate	19
—Working well	14	Slight	22
Residential move	18	None	*40*
Other	8		

C. Initial Consumer Uncertainty

Dimension[a]	Proportion of Buyers Indicating Primarily: *Uncertanity*	*vs. Assurance*	*Segment Responding ("Very Sure")*	*Mean Rating*
At which stores to shop?	2%	*88%*	49%	6.1[b]
What brand to choose?	5	*80*	39	5.8
What model to choose?	6	*76*	31	5.7
The most important considerations you'll use for choice?	2	*88*	41	6.1
Features that are available?	3	*90*	34	5.9
Performance of different brands and models?	10	*74*	20	5.4

[a]Question asked: ". . . when you started seeking information and shopping for your new appliance, how sure were you about (dimension)?" Categories provided were: "Very, Moderately, Somewhat (Sure and Unsure)" and "Neither Sure nor Unsure" as a neutral response. The neutral category is deleted from this display: its magnitude can be ascertained as the difference between 100% and the sum of the percents given in each row.

[b]Where "Very Unsure" = 1, "Moderately Unsure" = 2, . . . and "Very Sure" = 7.

brand preference. They are likely to have prior search and shopping experience from their previous purchase(s), and to have lived in their community for at least a year, thereby acquiring considerable familiarity with stores at which they might purchase an appliance. They may also have already encountered a repairperson, from whom they may have obtained some information and advice.

All of these factors would tend to reduce the perceived need for search and shopping activity. Since these appliances have broken down, however, they are likely to have been older models. Their owners' experience base may not be current as to new product features, current brands and their performance, and store prices and specials. We would therefore expect search and shopping behavior to be geared toward these dimensions.

Primarily, of course, a product failure raises the question of the *timing* of the new purchase. The loss of any of these appliances can be a very disruptive event for a household. Overall, then, this situation should place relatively severe time constraints on the purchase process, and it may reduce overall search and shopping activity.

"Mobility" Situations. The "Residential Move" situation presents some interesting contrasts to the failure-forced purchase. To the extent that a move is planned well in advance, considerable lead time should be available for shopping and information search. When a household is moving, however, many other issues also require attention, and the opportunity costs for search might be fairly high.

Most moves in the U.S. are within the same county; consumers making such moves should be fairly familiar with the local stores selling appliances. A significant portion of moves, however, place consumers in new market areas (28 percent of the movers in this study moved 20 to 500 miles or more away from their previous residence). Long-distance moves are likely to be associated with less consumer knowledge of local stores, their locations, offerings, and policies. For some consumers, this unfamiliarity may lead to more store visits and higher shopping times. Conversely, some of these consumers might turn directly to those outlets familiar from their previous market area, such as Sears and other chains.

Other factors in a residence change can be significant as well: some moves are to new homes or rental dwellings where appliances are provided with the unit. These forms of consumer acquisition would likely require little or no shopping activity in the retail environment.[5]

"Replacement" Purchases. In contrast to either of the situations above, a "Replacement of Working Unit" circumstance would be likely to remove the constraint of having to obtain the machine by a specific point in time. In this situation, consumers would also be likely to possess a strong experience and knowledge base for search and shopping.

Our results showed, however, that the threat of product failure and repair bills constitutes an important factor in this circumstance as well as in the failure-forced purchase situation. As shown in Table 1.4, 63 percent of consumers in this category (24 percent of the entire sample) reported that their replaced appliance would have required some repairs in the near future, and that this eventuality was instrumental in their purchase of a new machine.

Those situations in which the machines were working well represent the most discretionary of the purchase circumstances. They account, however, for only 14 percent of all purchases. Consumers in this situation reported that desires for a larger machine (51 percent) and desires for new features (31 percent) were the primary reasons for their purchases. Again, however, these consumers represent relatively small segments of the total market, only 7 percent and 4 percent, respectively. Virtually no consumers reported that a remodeling project or desire for a more attractive style was the key reason for a replacement purchase.

[5]Because the present study focused on consumer information search and shopping behavior, such nonretail forms of acquisition were excluded from the study.

Of the three purchase circumstance categories, then, the replacement circumstance would seem to offer the best opportunities for a leisurely and deliberate consumer search process, as it essentially lifts the time constraints imposed by the other two circumstances.

Time Pressures on Purchase. Given that time pressure is theoretically a key dimension underlying the major purchase circumstances, it is interesting to examine what consumers reported about this measure. Part B of Table 1.4 summarizes these ratings. Again, as with most of the direct measures of search and shopping, consumers do not appear to be as strongly affected as theory might suggest. One-fifth of consumers did report "extreme" or "great" time pressure for their purchase decision. About the same number, however, reported only "slight" time pressure, and 40 percent—the modal response—reported having perceived no time pressure at all for their decision! As we found with most of the shopping and search measures, consumers display considerable heterogeneity, with many of them reporting low scores. For these people, at least, time pressure was not responsible for lower search levels.

Overall, this brief discussion of purchase circumstances is sufficient to indicate their potential significance in affecting consumer search. Discussion of these detailed findings is beyond the scope of the present paper but is available in Dickson (1981, 1984).

Initial Consumer Uncertainty

Theories of information have long held that information's basic role is to reduce uncertainty (e.g., Wilkie 1975). When applied to the consumer context, this theory leads to a hypothesis that a basic purpose of information search and shopping activity is to reduce decision uncertainty to some tolerable level (e.g., Howard and Sheth 1969; Hansen 1972). While this idea has intuitive appeal, there has been little, if any, research describing consumers' uncertainty and its effects on search behavior.

The present study asked purchasers how uncertain they were along six dimensions of their decision before they began the shopping process. Our results, summarized in Table 1.4C, again might be viewed as surprising.

Overall, *only very few consumers indicated that they had felt generally uncertain before beginning to seek information* for their specific purchase. Only 2 percent, for example, reported a feeling of uncertainty about which stores to shop at and the most important considerations they would use in making their choice. This figure increased only slightly for questions concerning which brand to choose, which model to choose, and knowledge about the appliance features available for purchase. Only in response to a question about performance of different brands and models—another measure of knowledge as opposed to a measure of choice uncertainty—did the proportion of uncertain consumers reach as high as 10 percent.

In sharp contrast, *substantial numbers of consumers reported being "very sure" on these same dimensions*. Consumers' certainty was strongest for the "stores to shop" and "most important considerations" items. The "performance" knowledge item elicited the fewest "very sure" responses, but even so there were twice as many consumers who were "very sure" as who were "somewhat, moderately, or very unsure." The mean ratings on the measures are provided in the right-hand column of Table 1.4C.

This pattern of results deserves some further elaboration. First, we should note that the phrasing of this question ("How sure . . .") logically allows for the expression of some degree of uncertainty within every option provided to the respondents in this study. Even the second strongest response ("Moderately Sure"), for example, implicitly suggests that the consumer may have been partially uncertain. The results, then, are not unambiguous regarding uncertainty. It is clear, however, that consumers were not experiencing strong feelings of uncertainty as they began their purchase processes. Instead, they seem to have felt, on average, to be well in control of the decision and its ramifications.

A second interesting result also emerges from this table. Our original construction of the six uncertainty dimensions was intended to reflect the various elements of a typical multiattribute model of consumer preference (e.g., Wilkie and Pessemier 1973). Implicit in this view was the assumption that consumers' decision process for durables is a "learning hierarchy" characteristic of high-involvement situations (e.g., Ray 1982). Specifically, we assumed that consumers' beliefs and evaluations would precede brand and model decisions. In a relative sense, therefore, we expected to see less uncertainty reported for knowledge items than for choice items, with the evaluation mechanism itself (e.g., "most important considerations") at a medium point.

The results, of course, did not reveal this pattern. Instead, it appears that consumers are most sure of their evaluation mechanisms and some of the attributes for the decision. They are least sure about the brand ratings on the attributes, but they are somewhat more sure about which brand they will choose. This puzzling result seems to suggest that either (1) consumers must view dimensions beyond product performance as being quite significant in their purchase decisions or (2) their decision processes differ from our assumption of a high-involvement learning model.

Finally, it should be noted that the questions involved uncertainty *before* the start of the shopping process. It is quite conceivable that a consumer's perceived uncertainty might *increase* during the process as a result of new information about brands, models, and/or store offerings. Considering the nature of salesperson/customer interactions, in fact, a sequence of increases and reductions in uncertainty is quite plausible. Our results, therefore, may understate the uncertainty experienced during the overall decision process, particularly for the consumers who changed their brand purchase intentions during the process. Nonetheless, our results do tie in well with the reports of the short duration of the actual shopping phase, and present an interesting picture for further consideration.

Consumers' Shopping Motivations

The primary purpose of information search presumably is to assist in making a "good" purchase. In attempting to better understand search and shopping behavior, however, we felt that studying additional consumer motivations and interests may be quite important. Part A of Table 1.5 summarizes our sample's reactions to six such shopping interests. The overall pattern of responses showed *primarily neutral reactions,* with average responses being only slight interest in most items. In general, then, it appears that while these additional search motives were present, for most consumers they did not exert a strong influence on search and shopping behaviors.

Again, however, there was substantial variability in the responses to the different items. Just over half the sample, for example, indicated that they wanted to find out about product drawbacks as well as benefits. While ap-

TABLE 1.5 Shopping Motivations and Decision Making

A. Consumers' Search Interests

Motive	*Percent of Consumers Who:* Agree	vs.	Disagree	*Neutral*[a]	*Mean Response*[b]
Enjoy Shopping	18%	vs.	*30%*	52%	3.7
Minimize time spent	*39*	vs.	15	46	4.7
Learn about product	*42*	vs.	11	47	5.0
Interest in technical aspects	29	vs.	20	51	4.3
Obtain most modern technology	*37*	vs.	8	55	4.9
Discover negatives	*52*	vs.	9	39	5.3
(Forced choice) "I was most interested in learning":	"As much as possible about appliance" vs. "Just enough to make a choice"				*69%* vs. 31
(Forced choice) "I was most interested in":	"Enjoying the search . . . because it was interesting" vs. "Spending as little time as possible"				32% vs. *68*

B. Overall Search and Choice Strategy Descriptions

Strategy Description	*Percent of Consumers Who:* Agree	vs.	Disagree	*Neutral*	*Mean Response*[b]
Strong reliance on experience and knowledge in search and purchase	*70%*	vs.	5%	25%	5.8
Strong reliance on new information from search	*35*	vs.	17	48	4.6
Reliance on knowledgeable others' advice	*40*	vs.	15	44	4.7
Strategy 1 vs. 2	Primary reliance on past experience and knowledge vs. Primary reliance on new information from search				*69%* vs. 31
Strategy 1 vs. 3	Primary reliance on past experience and knowledge vs. Primary reliance on knowledgeable others' advice				*68%* vs. 32

[a]"Agree" and "Disagree" include "Strong" and "Moderate" categories. Neutral includes "Somewhat" and "Neither Agree/Disagree."

[b]Where 1 = "Strongly Disagree," . . . 7 = "Strongly Agree" (ns range = 408–417 across these items).

proximately 40 percent of purchasers indicated that they had been interested in minimizing their time spent shopping, learning about appliances, and obtaining the most modern technology available, less than 30 percent indicated an interest in technical aspects of the purchase. The only potential shopping interest which received more negative reaction than positive was the desire to "enjoy" the shopping because the buyer felt it would be an interesting experience.

In reviewing the set of shopping interests, it becomes clear that several motives could potentially conflict for a given consumer. Within the questionnaire we therefore added a forced-choice item asking purchasers to select which of two motives had been the stronger for them. As shown in Table 1.5A, two-thirds of the purchasers chose "spending as little time as possible . . ." as more descriptive of their search and shopping desires than "enjoying the search because it was interesting."

A second forced choice item asked about the *degree* of learning desired by the sample during their search processes. Somewhat surprisingly (given the other results), two-thirds of the respondents reported that they had wanted to learn "as much as possible" about the appliance during search, while only one-third reported the more utilitarian, satisfying approach of "learning just enough to make my choice." To reconcile this finding with our other forced choice result, we surmise that most consumers want to pack as much learning as possible into a search process which takes as short a time as possible.

Consumers' Search and Decision Strategies

The final group of questions on search and shopping asked respondents to describe their overall search strategies during the purchase process. The results are summarized in Part B of Table 1.5, and offer some interesting insights.

In brief, three alternative strategies were described to respondents:

- reliance on personal experience and knowledge;
- reliance on new information from search;
- reliance on advice from knowledgeable others.

As shown in Table 1.5B, consumers were most likely to agree that the strategy of relying on one's past experience and personal knowledge described their purchase process. Although, on average, all three strategies received positive ratings, almost half the sample gave neutral responses for the second and third strategies.

Two forced-choice items then asked respondents to choose which member of a pair best described their purchase process. Again, past experience and personal knowledge emerged as playing the most important role in consumers' purchase processes. *Only about one-third of the purchasers said that they relied primarily on new information or advice obtained during their information search and shopping activities in making their purchase decisions.*

Purchase Behaviors and Consumer Satisfaction

The remaining empirical findings deal with the purchases themselves, and how they emerge from specific information search and shopping processes. Results are summarized in Table 1.6.

Purchase Characteristics. How many consumers buy appliances at reduced prices? As shown in Table 1.6, *over three-fourths of the sample (76 percent) reported having paid a special low price* for their new appliance. Most of the respondents (70 percent) did so by buying at a sale price. In addition, 17 percent—about one in every six purchasers—reported having negotiated with the salesperson, and arriving at a special price.[6] Thus, the norm for American buyers of appliances appears to be "buy it when it's on sale."

How likely are consumers to buy the same brand that they are replacing? Consistent with past results, our finding is that *less than one in three purchases is likely to be a "brand loyal" purchase.* Does such low brand loyalty primarily arise

[6]Eleven percent of the buyers negotiated a special price below the initial sale price.

TABLE 1.6 Consumer Purchases and Satisfaction

A. Characteristics of Purchases

	Percent of All Respondents		***Percent of Segment of Respondents***	
1. Purchased at special low price	*76%*	(n = 430)		
a. Appliance on sale	70			
b. Negotiated with salesperson	17			
2. Loyalty to same brand	*31*	(n = 377)		
3. Fulfilled initial brand intentions	*69*	(n = 427)		
a. Impact of brand loyalty:				
—Those brand loyal			87%[a]	(p < .001)
—Not brand loyal			63	
b. Impact of sale price:				
—Purchased on sale			67	(ns)
—Purchased at regular price			70	

B. Stores and Purchases

				Percent of Purchasers at That Store Type Who:			
Store Type	*Share of Market*	*Share of Visits*	*Sales Efficiency Ratio*[c]	*Bought On Sale*	*Negotiated Lower Price*	*Bought At First Store*	
Specialty appliance	37%	25%[b]	148	51%	*28%*	34%	(n = 155)
Sears	30	24	125	*89*	4	*46*	(n = 128)
Ward's	9	8	113	*92*	8	22	(n = 38)
Furniture	6	7	86	41	22	*48*	(n = 27)
Discount	5	11	45	80	20	30	(n = 20)
Department	4	11	36	69	13	38	(n = 16)
	(n = 423)	(n = 1020)					

C. Consumer Satisfaction

1. Search and shopping was a "pleasant experience":	
Strongly agree	14%
Mod/Somewhat agree	*42*
Neutral	24
Mod/somewhat disagree	12
Strongly disagree	8
	(n = 404)

2. Forced choice: why consumer stopped search and shopping:	
Cost/benefit rationale[d]	33%
vs.	
Exact match found[e]	*67*

3. Satisfaction with new appliance	
Very satisfied	*71%*
Satisfied	24
Neutral	3
Dissatisfied	2
Very dissatisfied	—
	(n = 432)

[a]To be read: 87% of brand loyal consumers fulfilled initial brand intentions.

[b]To be read: Of the 1020 store visits made in total by all consumers in the study, 25% were to specialty appliance stores.

[c]Reflects share of market over share of visits. N.B.: Requires caution in interpretation. Multiple store visits are likely in some categories but not others. Figures are likely inflated for specialty appliance, furniture, discount, and department store categories, but not for Sears and Ward's.

[d]Phrased: "I did not consider the benefits of further shopping worth the effort, so I made a choice from what I had seen already."

[e]Phrased: "I found exactly what I wanted."

during search and shopping, or is it due to other factors such as passage of time since the last purchase, dissatisfaction with a brand's performance in the later part of its useful life, or considerable incidental learning about other brands and their features since the last purchase? Our results on whether the purchase fulfilled initial brand intentions suggest that the other factors are quite significant and deserve further investigation. Only one-third of our sample reported having changed brand intentions during the shopping process. The majority of buyers purchased the brand and model they intended to buy when they started to shop.

This finding suggests that *brand loyalty is mostly lost before the shopping starts, rather than during the shopping process.* As shown in Table 1.6, seven out of eight consumers (87 percent) buying the same brand they were replacing had decided to do so before engaging in shopping and search activity. Shopping and search had a significantly greater impact on those who bought a different brand from the one they were replacing, but even here five in eight purchasers fulfilled their initial brand intentions.

How important, then, is a sale price in changing brand intentions? Surprisingly, a sale price reduction itself does not appear to shift brand shares. We found no significant difference in either brand loyalty or fulfillment of initial brand intentions as a function of purchasing at a special sale price. The impact of the sale price thus appears to be more geared to the timing—and perhaps store chosen—for the purchase than to the brand or model actually purchased (at least in the aggregate).

Where Consumers Buy. A consumer's search and shopping process inevitably involves a substantial degree of interaction and interdependence with the retailers contacted, their offerings, and their policies. Within the appliance industry there are many types of retail outlets available to consumers. As demonstrated in our earlier discussion of store visits, different types of retail outlets differ in their relative importance in the market. In addition, their effects on consumers' search and purchase processes should also be different, because of different policies regarding private labels versus national brands, number of brands carried, salesperson service versus self-service, and price-cutting and dealing. Our findings on these issues are summarized in Table 1.6, Part B.

A glance at that table makes it clear that the *market is dominated by specialty appliance stores and by Sears, which together account for two-thirds of all the purchases made by our sample. Sears' position is especially remarkable: the world's largest retailer appears to account for almost one in every three machines sold in these "white good" appliance categories!*

In-Store Sales Effectiveness. How did these outlets do so well? For example, is their main advantage in getting customers into their stores, or do they do a better job of "closing the sale" once buyers are there? Two columns of Table 1.6B are germane to this question: "Share of Visits" and "Sales-Efficiency Ratio."

With respect to the first measure, it is interesting to note that the specialty appliance stores and Sears maintain their lead: of respondents' visits to different store types, about one-fourth are directed to each of these leaders. Unfortunately, we did not gather detailed information on the number of stores *within* a type that were visited by each purchaser, so we cannot display the total visits made by consumers, or the exact share that each store type received. This means that the number of visits to those categories having multiple competing stores (e.g., specialty appliance, furniture, discount) is likely to be understated, while the number of visits to Sears or Ward's is likely to be more accurate.

Despite this bias, the store visit statistic is included in Table 1.6 because it yields some interesting results in the *opposite* direction from the statistic's deficiency. For example, we discover that the stores other than Sears and the specialty appliance stores are relatively more successful in attracting visits than they are in closing sales. This characteristic is quantified in our "Sales Efficiency Ratio," which reflects the share of market to share of visits for each store type. On this measure, the specialty stores lead with an index score of 148—that is, their share of market is almost 50 percent higher than we would expect solely on the basis of store-type visits. Sears follows on this measure with a score of 125, and is followed by Ward's with 113. The remaining store types all have efficiency ratios less than 100, indicating that they are relatively better at attracting shoppers than they are at closing the actual sales (whether because of differences in price, quality, sales effort, credit terms, or other factors cannot be determined from our data).

Because of the bias in the store visit statistic, the sales efficiency ratio is likely to overstate the actual performance of individual stores within certain of the categories. It is therefore difficult to reach a clear conclusion about specialty appliance stores, which furthermore undoubtedly vary in sales conversions from store to store. Sears and Ward's, however, are clearly strong on this dimension, with Sears showing special expertise in closing sales. According to other calculations with these data, in fact, Sears sells an appliance to over half of the consumers who step through its doors to shop there (and who go on to buy an appliance somewhere). The remaining store types evidence lower ratios even though these ratios are likely to be overstated. The in-store sales performance of both discounters and department stores is especially low in terms of converting a shopping visit into a sale.

Marketing Strategies and Purchase Outcomes. Do consumers who purchase at different types of stores show clear differences in their search processes and purchase behaviors? The remaining columns in Table 1.6, Part B, show that they do, and that these differences are likely to reflect the different marketing strategies adopted by various store types. For example, approximately 90 percent of Sears and Ward's buyers bought at a sale price—a sharp contrast with the 51 percent and 41 percent of sale purchases in specialty appliance and furniture store outlets, respectively. If we turn to negotiations about prices, however, these positions reverse themselves: about one in every four buyers reports having negotiated a special low price with an appliance store or furniture store salesperson, while almost no one (4 percent) reports having done so at Sears.

Other differences are interesting as well, and suggest that the information search and shopping paths to purchase are different depending on where one buys (whether these results stem from basic individual consumer differences or from interactions with the information and influence encountered during search is, of course, not entirely clear). *Sears and the furniture stores are especially effective at attracting consumers who purchase at the first store they visit. Given Sears' importance in terms of market share, this has to be considered as a major factor leading to the low levels of search and shopping activity encountered in past research as well as in the current study.* In an interesting competitive twist, Ward's emerges as the weakest store on this measure; its buyers are much more likely to shop elsewhere before ending up purchasing at Ward's.

Pathways to Purchase. The pathways to purchase are somewhat different as well. As reported earlier, salespersons were the information source most often consulted by our sample, followed by newspaper ads. These rankings did not hold up, however, when we analyzed which source buyers at the various store types consulted first. The source first consulted is an important measure of how initial search activity influences later behavior.

In brief, salespersons were most likely to be contacted first by consumers who bought at specialty appliance stores, but this observation did not hold for the remaining stores. Buyers at Sears and Ward's were most likely to begin by consulting either catalogs or newspaper ads, a result in keeping with their overwhelming tendency to purchase at sale prices. Buyers at furniture stores, on the other hand, were more likely to have begun with discussions with a friend or relative. The remaining store-type samples were too small to yield stable results.

Further findings of interest emerged when we analyzed the paths taken as a function of which source was first consulted. For example, a head-to-head analysis of Sears versus specialty appliance stores showed that, of those who began with:

Consumer Reports,	81% purchased at specialty stores.
Repairpersons,	73% purchased at specialty stores.
Salespersons,	63% purchased at specialty stores.
Friends/relatives,	There was no significant difference.
Newspaper ads,	61% purchased at Sears.
Catalogs,	72% purchased at Sears.

In conclusion, it is clear that there are substantial differences in the stores that sell appliances to the American public. These differences seem to attract segments of consumers who are interested in different marketing mixes. This positioning appears to be partially responsible for the low levels of search and shopping activity exhibited by many consumers. In order to more definitive, however, we need to investigate further this topic using other methodologies than the consumer survey employed in this study.

Consumer Satisfaction. After having gone through their purchase process and having owned the appliance for some time, how did consumers feel about the experience? Three dimensions of this question are reported in Part C of Table 1.6.

Again, substantial heterogeneity within the sample is evident with respect to customers' descriptions of the pleasure associated with the information search and shopping process itself. Only 14 percent of purchasers reported a strong positive on this measure; on the other hand, only 8 percent reacted with a strong negative. The modal response was a slight to moderately pleasant experience (42 percent). The remaining sample members were either neutral (24 percent) or slightly negative (12 percent). Overall, then, our results here were in keeping with those reported earlier on shopping interests and motivations—most consumers do not view the information search process as a painful process, but neither do they enjoy it as an end unto itself. Thus, there appears to be little drive to formally search and shop beyond the goal-oriented purpose of obtaining a product that meets the wants or needs that are salient at that time.

A lack of pleasure does not, of course, equate to a painful experience to be terminated at the soonest possible moment. To investigate the shopping termination issue further, a forced-choice measure asked purchasers why they had decided to stop shopping and purchase an appliance at the time they did, rather than continuing to shop. Given the modest consumer endorsements of search and shopping in the earlier sections of this paper, together with the very low absolute levels reported by many consumers in the study, we might well expect that their search would have been terminated as the result of an implicit cost-benefit calculation through which the consumer simply decides that the marginal costs of further search are not likely to yield benefits as large. In contrast, a consumer might also cease shopping and search if a purchase alternative arises which is so attractive that it should be purchased as soon as possible.

When confronted with these alternatives, our sample again provided surprising results: as shown in Table 1.6, Part C, *two-thirds of the purchasers responded that "I found exactly what I wanted."* For these persons, therefore, further search and shopping was presumably quite unnecessary, at least as they viewed the situation at the time.

Therefore, *low levels of search and shopping activity may, in fact, be indicators of efficiencies in the marketplace, rather than inefficiencies.* In order to accept this conclusion, of course, we need to accept that respondents' reactions to our measure are valid reflections of their thinking at the time of purchase, and that a consumer is typically capable of assessing accurately his or her ideal purchases and the returns to further search activity. These issues are difficult, and clearly require further research investigation. For the moment, at least, these findings should be viewed with caution.

Finally, after having owned their appliances for an average of just over one-half year, how satisfied were consumers with their purchases? The buyers' answer was: "Very Satisfied." As shown in Table 1.6C, 71 percent of buyers responded that they were "Very Satisfied" with their purchases, while another 24 percent responded "Satisfied." *In total, 95 percent of our sample reported being satisfied or very satisfied with their appliances. Only 2 percent registered any level of dissatisfaction.*

The time period covered is, of course, a relatively short one in terms of the entire useful life of these durable goods, and we would expect that some breakdowns and repair needs might well lower reported levels of satisfaction for these consumers in future years. However, as an indicator of short-to-intermediate-term effects of shopping and search behavior, this measure suggests that most consumers are quite pleased with the process they have gone through, and would likely adopt a similar mode of shopping for a similar appliance purchase in the future.

DISCUSSION

In its entirety, this set of results presents a rich and sometimes puzzling picture of consumer behavior leading to the purchase of a major household appliance. Many readers may have shared some of our reactions to the findings—that some results were unexpected and didn't "fit" well with our sense of the information search and shopping process for a major home product. We also wondered whether some of the results might not be artifactual—created by the types of measures we were using, and by the respondents' reactions to them.

Artifactual Explanations

Given that this type of study employs a retrospective survey methodology, several threats to the research immediately present themselves. These include pressures toward social desirability or "yea-saying," errors in recalling events from the past, and an increasing inability to recollect details about these events. Given the range of topics we covered within this survey, these potential biases would be likely to impact some areas more than others.

We have engaged in considerable thought and analysis attempting to evaluate the likely degree of such biases, but at present are still uncertain about their true impacts on our findings. Social desirability, for example, might help to explain some results, such as the low reported uncertainties or the desire to "learn as much as possible" during shopping, but the reports of low levels of *Consumer Reports* usage, perceived time pressure, number of sources consulted, stores shopped, etc., seem to go against a strong social desirability bias. Memory decay also seems plausible, but our test of whether measures differed as a function of elapsed time since the purchase convincingly demonstrated no differences.

While not discounting some effect of the threats described above, we do not conclude that they would account for the major portion of the strong results that did emerge. It thus appears that either the results are basically accurate or the main problems lie in: (1) our having missed measuring major sectors of the search and shopping process, (2) consumers' having systematically misperceived the process as they went through it, or (3) consumers' having systematically distorted their recollections of the process as they retrieved them from their memories.

There are reasonable arguments for each of the limiting explanations that remain. For example, all of our findings are consistent with the consumers' having developed considerable awareness, product knowledge, and feature, brand, and store predispositions prior to the point at which they perceived themselves to be "in the market" to purchase the appliance. To the extent that this preexisting awareness and knowledge is derived from environmental scanning (e.g., interest in what new developments exist in products and features) or "incidental learning" (e.g., having a friend demonstrate her new appliance while visiting her house), consumers may not code such learning as representing information search, and may not even be able to recall a specific episode of this type at a later point in time.

With respect to incorrect retrievals from memory, recent work in cognitive psychology has demonstrated that it is common for people to "misremember" prior states in a complex event after the eventual outcome has occurred.

This so-called hindsight bias or knew it all along effect stems from a process in which new information meshes with, and may modify or replace, older information about the process. Special questioning methods may need to be employed to try to tap the original perceptions more accurately (see, for example, Hasher, Attig, and Alba 1981).

Given the provocative nature of our findings, and the plausible rival hypotheses offered by these potential artifactual biases, future methodological work is clearly needed to assess the strength of the alternative hypotheses and to develop means to combat them. In the interim, however, we would also do well to consider the implications of the results as they have emerged. In this regard, we would propose a somewhat different framework to explain the patterns of our findings.

A New Framework for Information Search and Shopping Behavior

Most consumer behavior texts characterize buying behavior for major appliances as an extended and relatively complicated decision process. Consequently, research suggesting that many appliance buyers are rather casual shoppers and information seekers has somewhat surprised academics and consumer advocates. It has no doubt also triggered concern among marketing executives, advertising agencies, and the media, all of whom are interested in the effectiveness of manufacturers' and retailers' promotional strategies. With our confirmation and extension of previous research findings, a rethinking of some fundamental consumer shopping theory seems to be in order.

The following framework is proposed as an outflow of the findings of the present study. While not an extreme departure from conventional thinking, it does place greater weight on relatively less studied elements of consumer behavior, and may stimulate useful thought and debate.

I. Situational Determinants of Wants and Needs. All shoppers buy an appliance to fit a particular usage situation. In many cases, the purchase is precipitated by an external circumstance such as a product failure or residential move. The resulting physical, social, economic, and psychological situation severely constrains the choice. For example, the choice of refrigerator size is strongly affected by such factors as family size and space for the appliance in the kitchen. Physical features of the kitchen, food choice, the size and reach of family members, and income available will influence whether a side-by-side style is preferred over a conventional refrigerator/freezer. Beverage preferences and financial circumstances will affect the number and nature of specific features such as an icemaker or external beverage dispenser.

Appliance salespeople are well aware of the need to immediately "qualify" a customer, i.e., determine what are the most significant choice constraints, so that the sales interaction can proceed efficiently. While many consumers may not be certain about everything that they do want at the outset of the active purchase process, almost all consumers will be able to point to appliance models that they would *not* buy. This research suggests that consumers are fairly to very certain about what they want. This certainty reduces the need to search for information to help make the choice. It also dramatically reduces the number of appliance models that consumers will consider and shop for.

II. Prior Experience, Knowledge, and Predis-Positions. Initial uncertainty about where to shop and what brand to choose may well be low because the consumer frequently has prior experiences to draw upon, and has been engaged in incidental learning for some time. In addition, certain general inferences are reasonable, and consumers are likely to guide their shopping behaviors according to such beliefs (see Duncan and Olshavsky 1982). For example, most consumers are aware that millions of white appliances have been manufactured and sold over the last 60 years. They know that the major brands of appliances manufactured and sold today have withstood the test of time in the marketplace and are competitive in performance and price. The evidence that there is almost universal satisfaction with the performance of the major white appliances that were purchased provides a strong basis for a consumer's prior expectation that he or she will be happy with the choice. Hence, purchase risk is lower than we might otherwise expect it to be.

A similar "Economic Darwinism" inference can also be made about retailers, and could influence store choice. While the consumer may have specific brand and store loyalty that may have its origins as recently as the purchase of some other appliance, the consumer also knows that market forces act to keep manufacturers' and retailers' offerings within a comparable range. Hence, while consumers' brand and store familiarity is generally high, brand loyalty and store loyalty are not particularly needed as risk-reducing strategies for these products.

Consumers are also likely to have observed that retailers are frequently advertising home appliances at sale prices. Consequently, they intend to avail themselves of the savings that a special deal offers. In addition, they are likely to have a reasonably clear vision of several features that they do or do not wish to pay for in their appliance. The basic specifications for purchase are thus largely settled prior to overt shopping activity.

III. The Store Visit and Salesperson Interaction. A precipitating situation (e.g., breakdown) will stimulate overt information search and shopping activity. If time and circumstances allow, consumers may purposively seek out such sources as repairpersons, *Consumer Reports,* catalogs, or friends. Now that a purchase is to be made, the consumer asks, "Which alternative should I buy, and where?" If newspaper ads are available in a timely manner, the consumer may use them to identify stores, and brands and models that are at sale price.

Once the customer is in the first store, an initial "qualifying" phase serves to introduce the salesperson/customer interaction. Whether by default (because few or no other information sources have been consulted to this point), or because of the information, direction, and decision support they are able to bring to the shopping process, salespersons often become the dominant source of influence. Both the *importance* and the *role* of the salesperson have perhaps not been adequately appreciated to date.

Within our proposed framework, the salesperson performs several significant functions beyond providing information. First, he or she participates in, facilitates, and may de facto direct the (frequently joint husband-wife) decision-making process. Second, given the desires and price constraints of the consumer, the salesperson may guide a "respecification" process during the visit. Third, he or she will also provide for closure of the process and arrange for financing, payment, delivery, etc. Beyond these traditionally recognized functions, moreover, our framework stresses a fourth significant salesperson activity—participating in the consumer's decision regarding *further* search.

IV. A Key In-Store Decision: Further Search? In addition to the traditionally described aspects of a choice decision within the store (e.g., consideration of features, models, terms of sale), our framework highlights another decision that each consumer implicitly or explicitly makes during each store visit—whether to stop now or search further. If the consumer is assured by the information in the store, and particularly by the inputs of the salesperson, that there is little to be gained in undertaking further search, then the consumer and the salesperson are likely to close the purchase. The importance of beliefs concerning the marginal cost/benefit associated with further specific shopping activities (i.e., traveling two miles across town to another store, consulting *Consumer Reports,* or talking to a friend) emerges at this point in the process. We believe that this stage is best understood in the context of a dynamic-adaptive model of consumer behavior rather than the conventional search-process-choice model.

A Dynamic-Adaptive Approach to Shopping Behavior

A dynamic-adaptive model of consumer shopping behavior draws on Lewinian Field theory, Atkinson's behavioral tendency theory, and the economic marginal cost/benefit model. The essence of the approach is that consumer behavior *evolves* during the search and shopping process, which is itself a sequence of discrete behaviors. This characterization is distinctly different from the Dewey problem-solving model that is often used to characterize consumer behavior as discrete, noniterative stages such as problem recognition, information gathering, information processing, choice and behavior (see Engel and Blackwell 1982). As indicated in Figure 1.2, each search and shopping behavior (reading an ad, reading *Consumer Reports,* examining floor models, talking to a salesperson) ends with a consideration of the question "What is the next step?" For some consumers it may be abandonment or postponement of the process (See Dickson and Wilkie 1978).

For those who continue, the choice of the next step will be determined by the strengths of the competing behavioral drives (see Atkinson and Birch 1978). The direction of any further search drives depends on a *current* awareness (evoked set) of alternative sources of information, alternative appliance choices, and alternative retail outlets. The strength of such drives will depend on *current* marginal cost/benefit con-

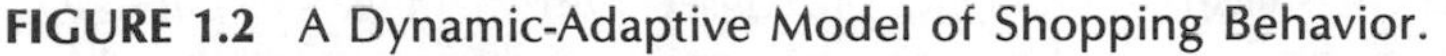

FIGURE 1.2 A Dynamic-Adaptive Model of Shopping Behavior.

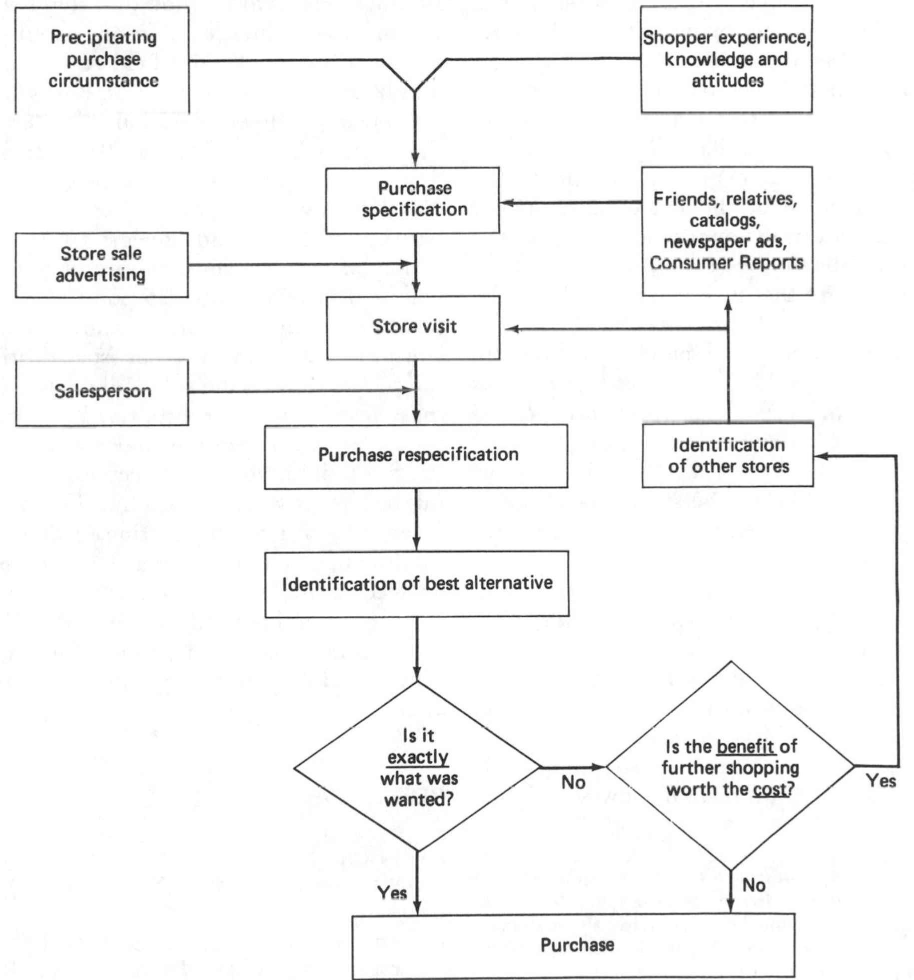

siderations. Consumer shopping is dynamic and adaptive in that search direction and strength changes as a result of previous search activity.[7]

The decision to stop and purchase versus continuing to search will depend primarily on two beliefs: (1) that better appliances may be available and/or (2) that a better value for the money can be found. If a salesperson confirms a consumer's prior opinions that the differences between the brands being considered are not great, or succeeds in convincing the consumer that he or she will not easily find a better brand, the consumer has only to decide whether he or she is likely to get a better price. The salesperson may provide some assurance on this point, by either "negotiating" or pointing to the sales price in effect at the time.

In addition, though, the consumer needs to decide how costly further search will be to him or her, and what benefits it likely will bring. When we realize that (1) many consumers will have little idea what the customary current price is for a desirable model and (2) that the direct and opportunity costs of further search may well require that it return a benefit in the order of $20–$50 to be worthwhile, it becomes more understandable that search and shopping are often not prolonged. Investigating this point, Ratchford (1980) used *Consumer Reports* ratings and the hedonic price function of model preference in a lab setting, and found that gains from search are likely to be small for refrigerators, washing machines, ranges, and air conditioners.

In a controversial paper, Olshavsky and Granbois (1979) concluded that for many purchases a decision process never occurs. While we observed evidence that a significant percentage of shoppers only considered one brand and model, it is our contention that a decision process *always* occurs in appliance shopping. The key to duration and direction, however, is the consumer's decision to search any further once an acceptable appliance is found.

Implications for Future Research

With respect to future research, it is useful to recognize that consumer researchers have tended to focus on the choice *among* brand alternatives, while generally overlooking the choice to search for *further* alternatives. New information can, of course, affect both of these choices. Given our results, we believe that future research should examine not only purchase choice but also "further information choice" and how it changes purchases. Our "pathways to purchase" findings represent a crude first step toward exploring the influence of prior search on later search behavior. Future field research, for example, might usefully focus on how salespeople influence the buyer's decision to undertake further search (see Olshavsky 1973). In such research, salespersons' perceptions of buyers' search behavior can provide very useful insights (see Furse, Punj, and Stewart 1984).

Beyond these issues, the findings that have emerged in this study also point to needed research on such substantive issues as "incidental learning," consumers' prior specifications for the purchase, and the role and contributions of the salesperson to the process. For more theoretical work on decision making, these results suggest that broadened conceptions of simplifying heuristics would be useful. The Marketing Science Institute is supporting further research into the nature of consumer demand under the auspices of its Durable Goods Steering Group. We are hopeful that this research will be helpful in resolving issues and gaining further understanding of this interesting and important topic area.

REFERENCES

ATKINSON, JOHN W., and DAVID BIRCH (1978), *Introduction to Motivation.* New York: D. Van Nostrand.

BRANDT, W. K., and G. S. DAY (1971), "Decision Process for Major Durables: An Empirical

[7]This low level of prestructured search plan is similar to the "muddling through" decision processes that Park (1982) found in his study of home-buying couples, although much of his emphasis was on a couple's joint decision making and treatment of housing features.

View," *AMA Conference Proceedings.* Chicago: American Marketing Association, pp. 381-385.

CLAXTON, JOHN D., JOSEPH N. FRY, and BERNARD PORTIS (1974), "A Taxonomy of Prepurchase Information Gathering Patterns," *Journal of Consumer Research,* 1 (December), pp. 35-42.

COX, ANTHONY, DONALD GRANBOIS, and JOHN SUMMERS (1983), "Planning, Search, Certainty and Satisfaction Among Durable Buyers; A Longitudinal Study," in Richard P. Bagozzi and Alice M. Tybout (Eds.), *Advances in Consumer Research,* Vol. X (Ann Arbor, MI: Association for Consumer Research), pp. 394-399.

DASH, J. F., L. G. SCHIFFMAN, and C. BERENSON (1976), "Information Search and Store Choice," *Journal of Advertising Research,* 16, pp. 35-40.

DAY, GEORGE S., and TERRY DEUTSCHER (1982), "Attitudinal Predictions of Choices of Major Appliance Brands," *Journal of Marketing Research,* 19 (May), pp. 192-198.

DICKSON, PETER R. (1981), "An Interactionist Study of Buyer Behavior," Unpublished Ph.D. dissertation, University of Florida.

DICKSON, PETER R. (1984), "An Interactionist Study of Buyer Behavior," College of Administrative Science Working Paper Series, The Ohio State University.

DICKSON, PETER R., and WILLIAM L. WILKIE (1978), "The Consumption of Household Durables: A Behavioral Review," Report No. 78-117, Marketing Science Institute, Cambridge, MA.

DOMMERMUTH, WILLIAM P. (1965), "The Shopping Matrix and Marketing Strategy," *Journal of Marketing Research,* 2 (May), pp. 129-132.

DUNCAN, CALVIN P., and RICHARD W. OLSHAVSKY (1982), "External Search: The Role of Consumer Beliefs," *Journal of Marketing Research,* 19 (February), pp. 32-43.

ENGEL, JAMES F., and ROGER D. BLACKWELL (1982), *Consumer Behavior.* Chicago: The Dryden Press.

FURSE, DAVID H., GIRISH, N. PUNJ, and DAVID W. STEWART (1984), "A Typology of Individual Search Strategies Among Purchasers of New Automobiles," *Journal of Consumer Research,* 10:6 (March), pp. 417-431.

GRANBOIS, DONALD H., and PATRICIA L. BRADEN (1976), "Good Consumership in Household Appliance Purchasing," *Journal of Business Research,* 4, pp. 103-116.

HANSEN, F. (1972), *Consumer Choice Behavior: A Cognitive Theory.* New York: The Free Press.

HASHER, LYNN, MARY ATTIG, and JOSEPH ALBA (1981), "I Knew It All Along: Or Did I?" *Journal of Verbal Learning and Verbal Behavior,* 20, pp. 86-96.

HOWARD, JOHN A., and JAGDISH N. SHETH (1969), *The Theory of Buyer Behavior.* New York: John Wiley.

KATONA, GEORGE, and EVA MUELLER (1955), "A Study of Purchasing Decisions," in Lincoln Clark (Ed.), *The Dynamics of Consumer Reaction. Consumer Behavior,* Vol. 1. New York: New York University Press.

NEWMAN, JOSEPH W. (1977), "Consumer External Search: Amount and Determinants," in Arch G. Woodside, Jagdish N. Sheth, and Peter D. Bennett (Eds.), *Consumer and Industrial Buying Behavior.* Amsterdam: North Holland.

NEWMAN, JOSEPH W., and B. D. LOCKEMAN (1975), "Measuring Prepurchase Information Seeking," *Journal of Consumer Research,* 2 (December), pp. 216-222.

NEWMAN, JOSEPH W., and RICHARD STAELIN (1971), "Multivariate Analysis of Differences in Buyer Decision Time," *Journal of Marketing Research,* 8 (May), pp. 192-198.

NEWMAN, JOSEPH W., and RICHARD STAELIN (1972), "Prepurchase Information Seeking for New Cars and Major Household Appliances," *Journal of Marketing Research,* 9 (August), pp. 249-257.

NEWMAN, JOSEPH W., and RICHARD STAELIN (1973), "Information Sources of Durable Goods," *Journal of Advertising Research,* 13, pp. 19-29.

OLSHAVSKY, R. W. (1973), "Consumer-Salesman Interaction in Appliance Retailing," *Journal of Marketing Research,* 10 (May), pp. 208-212.

OLSHAVSKY, RICHARD W., and DONALD H. GRANBOIS (1979), "Consumer Decision Making—Fact or Fiction?" *Journal of Consumer Research,* 6 (September), pp. 93-100.

PARK, C. WHAN (1982), "Joint Decisions in Home Purchasing: A Muddling-Through Process," *Journal of Consumer Research,* 9 (September), pp. 151-162.

PUNJ, G., and R. STAELIN (1983), "A Model of Consumer Information Search Behavior for New Automobiles," *Journal of Consumer Research,* 9 (March), pp. 366-380.

RATCHFORD, BRIAN T. (1980), "The Value of Information for Selected Appliances," *Journal of Marketing Research,* 17 (February), pp. 16–25.

RAY, MICHAEL L. (1982), *Advertising and Communication Management.* Englewood Cliffs, N.J.: Prentice-Hall.

ROTHE, J. T., and L. M. LAMONT (1973), "Purchase Behavior and Brand Choice Determinants for National and Private Brand Major Appliances," *Journal of Retailing,* 49 (Fall), pp. 19–33.

WESTBROOK, ROBERT A., and CLAES FORNELL (1979), "Patterns of Information Source Usage Among Durable Goods Buyers," *Journal of Marketing Research,* 16 (August), pp. 303–312.

WILKIE, WILLIAM L. (1975), *How Consumers Use Product Information: An Assessment of Research in Relation to Public Policy Needs.* Washington, DC: U.S. Government Printing Office.

WILKIE, WILLIAM L., and EDGAR A. PESSEMIER, "Issues in Marketing's Use of Multi-Attribute Attitude Models," *Journal of Marketing Research,* 10 (November), pp. 428–441.

2

CONSUMER PERCEPTIONS OF PRICE, QUALITY, AND VALUE: A Means-End Model and Synthesis of Evidence*

Valarie A. Zeithaml

Evidence from past research and insights for an exploratory investigation are combined in a conceptual model that defines and relates price, perceived quality, and perceived value. Propositions about the concepts and their relationships are presented, then supported with evidence from the literature. Discussion centers on directions for research and implications for managing price, quality, and value.

Though consumer perceptions of price, quality, and value are considered pivotal determinants of shopping behavior and product choice (Bishop 1984; Doyle 1984; Jacoby and Olson 1985, Sawyer and Dickson 1984; Schlechter 1984), research on these concepts and their linkages has provided few conclusive findings. Research efforts have been criticized for inadequate definition and conceptualization (Monroe and Krishnan 1985; Zeithaml 1983), inconsistent measurement procedures (Monroe and Krishnan 1985), and methodological problems (Bowbrick 1982; Olson 1977; Peterson and Wilson 1985). One fundamental problem limiting work in the area involves the meaning of the concepts: quality and value are indistinct and elusive constructs that often are mistaken for imprecise adjectives like "goodness, or luxury, or shininess, or weight" (Crosby 1979). Quality and value are not well differentiated from each other and from similar constructs such as perceived worth and utility. Because definition is difficult, researchers often depend on unidimensional self-report measures to capture the concepts (Jacoby, Olson, and Haddock 1973;

*Reprinted from the *Journal of Marketing,* 52 (July 1988), pp. 2–22. Published by the American Marketing Association, Chicago, Il, 60606.

McConnell 1968; Shapiro 1973) and thus must assume shared meanings among consumers.

What do consumers mean by quality and value? How are perceptions of quality and value formed? Are they similar across consumers and products? How do consumers relate quality, price, and value in their deliberations about products and services? This article is an attempt to provide answers to these questions by:

- defining the concepts of price, quality, and value from the consumer's perspective,
- relating the concepts in a model, and
- developing propositions about the concepts, examining the available evidence in support of the propositions, and suggesting areas where research is needed.

To accomplish these objectives, a review of previous research was augmented by an exploratory investigation of quality and value in the product category of beverages. Company interviews, a focus group interview, and 30 in-depth consumer interviews conducted by free-elicitation approaches generated qualitative data that supplemented previous research and served as the basis for 14 propositions.

THE EXPLORATORY STUDY

In the exploratory phase of the research, company, focus group, and in-depth consumer interviews were conducted to gain insight into consumer perceptions of quality and value. Cooperation was obtained from a national company that markets three distinct product lines of beverages: a line of 100 percent fruit-flavored children's drinks, a line of 100 percent fruit juices, and a line of tomato-based juices. In-depth interviews were held with the marketing research director, the senior product manager for juices, two company strategic planners, and the president of the company's advertising agency. Open-ended questions pertained to issues such as company knowledge about quality and value perceptions of consumers, ways the company determined those perceptions, and how quality and value were communicated to consumers.

A focus group interview on the topics of quality and value in beverages was held in a metropolitan area in the Southeast. The focus group was formed in accordance with guidelines traditionally followed in the marketing research field (Bellenger, Bernhardt, and Goldstucker 1976). Participants were recruited to fit the demographic profile of purchasers of fruit- and tomato-based beverages. All participants were women between the ages of 25 and 49 and all had at least one child younger than 10 years of age. Participants were screened to ensure current or recent usage of fruit- and tomato-based beverages. The identity of the participating firm was not revealed in the interview; discussion about price, quality, and value centered on consumer experiences and perceptions relating to beverages in general rather than to the specific brands of the sponsoring company. The moderator's questions covered such topics as the meaning of quality and value, and the role of price in quality and value judgments.

A total of 30 in-depth interviews with female consumers were held in three metropolitan areas (one in the Southwest, one on the East Coast, and one in the Midwest). Free-elicitation approaches recommended by Olson and Reynolds (1983) were used to obtain information about the cognitive structures of consumers. These techniques included triad sorts and laddering. In the triad sorts, similar brands in the beverage category were divided into sets of three and subjects were probed for distinctions among them. This initial process uncovered the important distinctions that respondents used to discriminate among products. The laddering process, which followed the triad sorts, involved a sequence of in-depth probes designed to force the consumer up the ladder of abstraction. As these procedures had successfully elicited the more important higher levels of abstraction in previous studies (Gutman and Alden 1985; Reynolds, Gutman, and Fiedler 1984; Reynolds and Jamieson 1985), they were used to reveal the links among product attributes, quality, and value. After these indirect methods, subjects responded to open-ended questions covering such topics as information needed to make judgments about quality and value, impact of related factors (e.g., advertising and packaging) on perceptions, and definitions of the concepts. Before debriefing, demographic and beverage usage data were collected from respondents.

As is typical in exploratory studies using means-end chains (e.g., Olson and Reynolds 1983), the data generated were not numerical. Instead, the data were in the form of protocols and means-end maps for individual consumers. Patterns of responses and observed similarities across individuals form the "results" of this type of exploratory study. When combined with the descriptive data from the executive and focus group interviews, the observations and insights provide a framework for speculating about the concepts and their relationships (Figure 2.1).

THE MODEL

Figure 2.1, an adaptation of a model first proposed by Dodds and Monroe (1985), affords an overview of the relationships among the concepts of price, perceived quality, and perceived value. In the following sections, relevant literature and evidence from the exploratory investigation are used to define and describe each concept in the model. To differentiate between proposed relationships and empirically supported relationships, discussion of each proposition is divided into two parts. First, propositions are developed on the basis of the qualitative data from the exploratory study and other conceptual work from the literature. Second, for each proposition, empirical evidence that supports and refutes the proposition is reviewed.

THE CONCEPT OF PERCEIVED QUALITY

Quality can be defined broadly as superiority or excellence. By extension, perceived quality can be defined as the consumer's judgment about a product's overall excellence or superiority.[1]

[1]Lewin's (1936) field theoretic approach to evaluating the instrumentality of actions and objects in achieving ends could be viewed as a foundation for this definition. In his view, instrumentality is the extent to which an object or action will achieve an end. In this case, quality could be viewed as instrumentality.

FIGURE 2.1 A Means-End Model Relating Price, Quality, and Value.

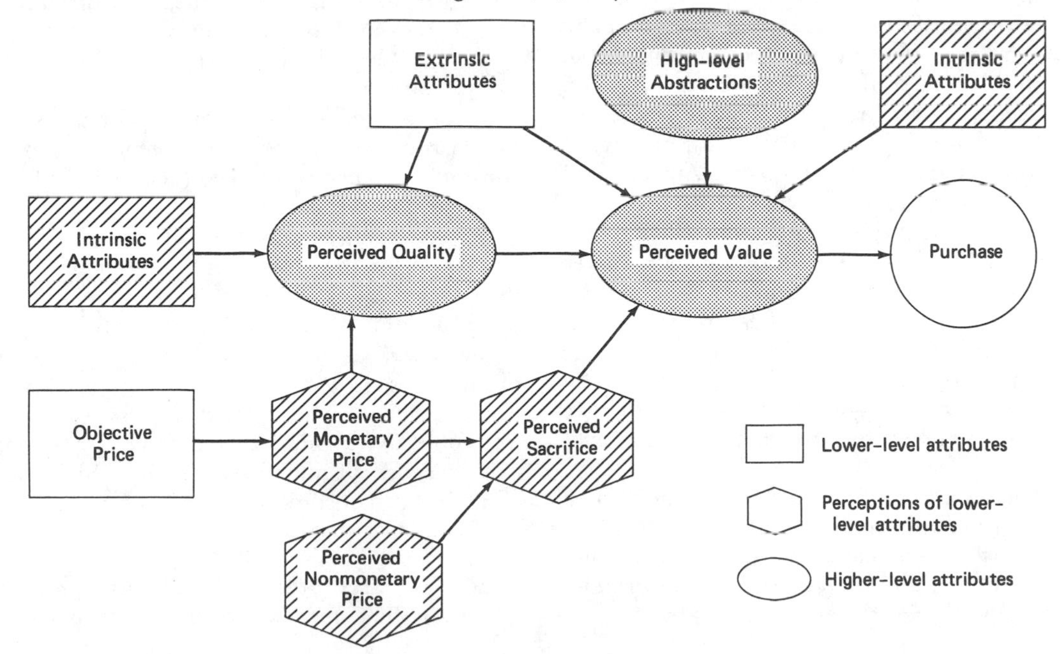

Perceived quality is (1) different from objective or actual quality, (2) a higher level abstraction rather than a specific attribute of a product, (3) a global assessment that in some cases resembles attitude, and (4) a judgment usually made within a consumer's evoked set.

Objective Quality versus Perceived Quality. Several researchers (Dodds and Monroe 1984; Garvin 1983; Holbrook and Corfman 1985; Jacoby and Olson 1985, Parasuraman, Zeithaml, and Berry 1986) have emphasized the difference between objective and perceived quality. Holbrook and Corfman (1985), for example, distinguish between mechanistic and humanistic quality: ". . . mechanistic [quality] involves an objective aspect or feature of a thing or event; humanistic [quality] involves the subjective response of people to objects and is therefore a highly relativistic phenomenon that differs between judges" (p. 33). "Objective quality" is the term used in the literature (e.g., Hjorth-Anderson 1984; Monroe and Krishnan 1985) to describe the actual technical superiority or excellence of the products.

As it has been used in the literature, the term "objective quality" refers to measurable and verifiable superiority on some predetermined ideal standard or standards. Published quality ratings from sources such as *Consumer Reports* are used to operationalize the construct of objective quality in research studies (see Curry and Faulds 1986). In recent years, researchers have debated the use of these measures of quality on methodological grounds (Curry and Faulds 1986; Hjorth-Anderson 1984, 1986; Maynes 1976; Sproles 1986). Concern centers on the selection of attributes and weights to measure objective quality; researchers and experts (e.g., *Consumer Reports*) do not agree on what the ideal standard or standards should be. Others (such as Maynes 1976) claim that objective quality does not exist, that all quality evaluations are subjective.

The term "objective quality" is related closely to—but not the same as—other concepts used to describe technical superiority of a product. For example, Garvin (1983) discusses product-based quality and manufacturing-based quality. Product-based quality refers to amounts of specific attributes or ingredients of a product. Manufacturing-based quality involves conformance to manufacturing specifications or service standards. In the prevailing Japanese philosophy, quality means "zero defects—doing it right the first time." Conformance to requirements (Crosby 1979) and incidence of internal and external failures (Garvin 1983) are other definitions that illustrate manufacturing-oriented notions of quality.

These concepts are not identical to objective quality because they, too, are based on perceptions. Though measures of specifications may be actual (rather than perceptual), the specifications themselves are set on the basis of what managers perceive to be important. Managers' views may differ considerably from consumers' or users' views. *Consumer Reports* ratings may not agree with managers' assessments in terms of either salient attributes or weights assigned to the attributes. In a research study for General Electric, Morgan (1985) points out striking differences between consumer, dealer, and manager perceptions of appliance quality. When asked how consumers perceive quality, managers listed workmanship, performance, and form as critical components. Consumers actually keyed in on different components: appearance, cleanability, and durability. Similarly, company researchers in the exploratory study measured beverage quality in terms of "flavor roundedness" and "astringency" whereas consumers focused on purity (100 percent fruit juice) and sweetness.

To reiterate, perceived quality is defined in the model as the consumer's judgment about the superiority or excellence of a product. This perspective is similar to the user-based approach of Garvin (1983) and differs from product-based and manufacturing-based approaches. Perceived quality is also different from objective quality, which arguably may not exist because all quality is perceived by someone, be it consumers or managers or researchers at *Consumer Reports*.

Higher Level Abstraction Rather than an Attribute. The means-end chain approach to understanding the cognitive structure of consumers holds that product information is retained in memory at several levels of abstraction (Cohen 1979; Myers and Shocker 1981; Olson and Reynolds 1983; Young and Feigin 1975). The simplest level is a product attribute; the most complex level is the value or payoff of the product to the consumer. Young and Feigin (1975) depicted this view in the "Grey benefit chain," which illustrates how a product is linked through a chain of benefits to a concept called the "emotional payoff."

Product → Functional Benefit → Practical Benefit → Emotional Payoff

Related conceptualizations (Table 2.1) pose the same essential idea: consumers organize information at various levels of abstraction ranging from simple product attributes (e.g., physical characteristics of Myers and Shocker 1981, defining attributes of Cohen 1979, concrete attributes of Olson and Reynolds 1983) to complex personal values. Quality has been included in multiattribute models as though it were a lower level attribute (criticisms of this practice have been leveled by Ahtola 1984, Myers and Shocker 1981, and others), but perceived quality is instead a second-order phenomenon: an abstract attribute in Olson and Reynold's (1983) terms, a "B" attribute (somewhat abstract, multidimensional but measurable) in Myers and Shockers' (1981) formulation.

Global Assessment Similar to Attitude. Olshavsky (1985) views quality as a form of overall evaluation of a product, similar in some ways to attitude. Holbrook and Corfman (1985) concur, suggesting that quality is a relatively global value judgment. Lutz (1986) proposes two forms of quality, "affective quality" and "cognitive quality." Affective quality parallels Olshavsky's and Holbrook and Corfman's views of perceived quality as overall attitude. Cognitive quality is the case of a superordinate inferential assessment of quality intervening between lower order case and an eventual overall product evaluation (Lutz 1986). In Lutz's view, the higher the proportion of attributes that can be assessed before purchase (search attributes)

TABLE 2.1 Selected Means-End Chain Models and Their Proposed Relationships with Quality and Value

Scheme	*Attribute Level*	*Quality Level*	*Value Level*	*Personal Value Level*
Young and Feigin (1975)	Functional benefits	Practical benefit	Emotional payoff	
Rokeach (1973) Howard (1977)	Product attributes	Choice criteria	Instrumental values	Terminal values
Myers and Shocker (1981)	Physical characteristics	Pseudophysical characteristics	Task or outcome referent	User referent
Geistfeld, Sproles, and Badenhop (1977)	Concrete, unidimensional, and measurable attributes (C)	Somewhat abstract, multidimensional but measurable (B)	Abstract, multidimensional, and difficult to measure attributes (A)	
Cohen (1979)	Defining attributes	Instrumental attributes		Highly valued states
Gutman and Reynolds (1979)	Attributes	Consequences	Values	
Olson and Reynolds (1983)	Concrete attributes	Abstract attributes	Functional consequences Psychosocial consequences Instrumental values	Terminal values

to those that can be assessed only during consumption (experience attributes), the more likely it is that quality is a higher level cognitive judgment. Conversely, as the proportion of experience attributes increases, quality tends to be an affective judgment. Lutz extends this line of reasoning to propose that affective quality is relatively more likely for services and consumer nondurable goods (where experience attributes dominate) whereas cognitive quality is more likely for industrial products and consumer durable goods (where search attributes dominate).

Judgment Made within the Consumer's Evoked Set. Evaluations of quality usually take place in a comparison context. Maynes (1976) claimed that quality evaluations are made within "the set of goods which . . . would in the consumer's judgment serve the same general purpose for some maximum outlay." On the basis of the qualitative study, and consistent with Maynes' contention, the set of products used in comparing quality appears to be the consumer's evoked set. A product's quality is evaluated as high or low depending on its relative excellence or superiority among products or services that are viewed as substitutes by the consumer. It is critical to note that the specific set of products used for comparison depends on the consumer's, not the firm's, assessment of competing products. For example, consumers in the exploratory study compared the quality of different brands of orange juice (which would be the comparison context of the firm), the quality of different forms (refrigerated vs. canned), and the quality of purchased versus homemade orange juice.

Figure 2.2 depicts the perceived quality component of the conceptual model in Figure 2.1.

P_{Q1}: Consumers use lower level attribute cues to infer quality.

FIGURE 2.2 The Perceived Quality Component.

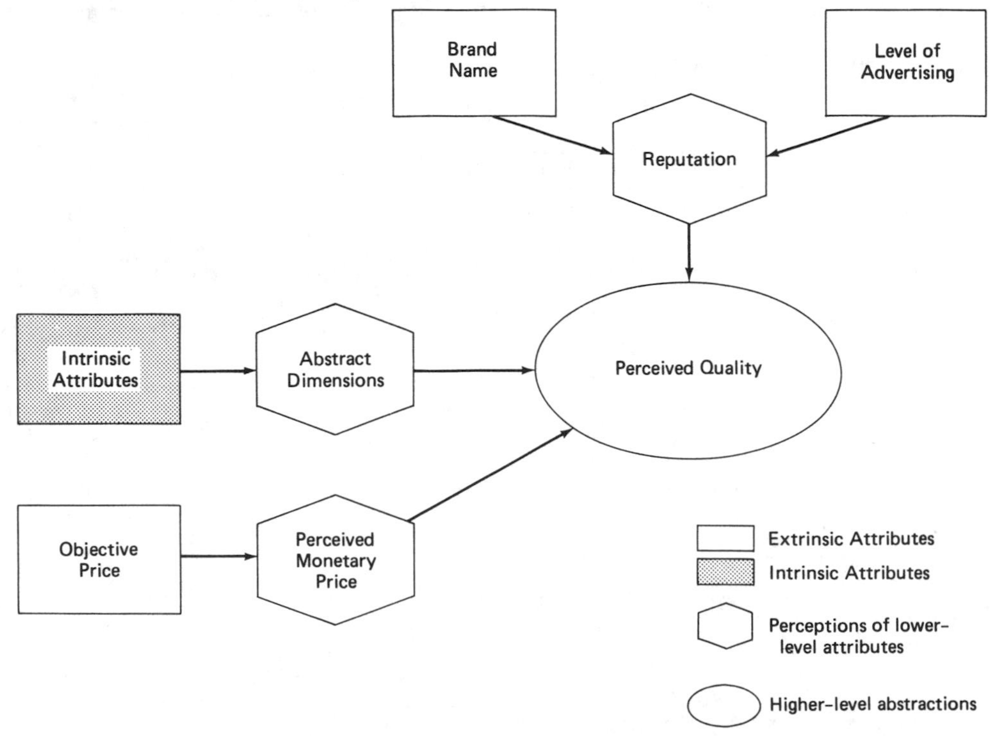

Holbrook and Corfman (1985) note that early philosophers used the word "quality" to refer to explicit features (i.e., properties or characteristics) of an object as perceived by a subject (e.g., Austin 1964, p. 44; Russell 1912). Olshavsky (1985) terms this tendency to infer quality from specific attributes "surrogate-based preference forming behavior" and cites examples of product categories in which a given surrogate is highly associated with quality (e.g., size signals quality in stereo speakers, style signals quality in cars and clothes). In the exploratory study, consumers repeatedly associated quality in fruit juices with purity (e.g., 100 percent fruit juice with no sugar added) or freshness. In these and other product categories, one or a few attributes from the total set of attributes appear to serve as reliable signals of product quality.

Attributes that signal quality have been dichotomized into intrinsic and extrinsic cues (Olson 1977; Olson and Jacoby 1972). Intrinsic cues involve the physical composition of the product. In a beverage, intrinsic cues would include such attributes as flavor, color, texture, and degree of sweetness. Intrinsic attributes cannot be changed without altering the nature of the product itself and are consumed as the product is consumed (Olson 1977; Olson and Jacoby 1972). Extrinsic cues are product-related but not part of the physical product itself. They are, by definition, outside the product. Price, brand name, and level of advertising are examples of extrinsic cues to quality.

The intrinsic-extrinsic dichotomy of quality cues is useful for discussing quality but is not without conceptual difficulties.[2] A small number of cues, most notably those involving the product's package, are difficult to classify as either intrinsic or extrinsic. Package could be considered an intrinsic or an extrinsic cue depending on whether the package is part of the physical composition of the product (e.g., a dripless spout in detergent or a squeezable ketchup container), in which case it would be an intrinsic cue, or protection and promotion for the product (e.g., a cardboard container for a computer), in which case it would be an extrinsic cue. For purposes of the model, package is considered an intrinsic cue but the information that appears on the package (e.g., brand name, price, logo) is considered an extrinsic cue.

Evidence. Researchers have identified key lower level attributes used by consumers to infer quality in only a few product categories. These lower level cues include price (Olson 1977; Olson and Jacoby 1972), suds level for detergents, size for stereo speakers (Olshavsky 1985), odor for bleach and stockings (Laird 1932), and produce freshness for supermarkets (Bonner and Nelson 1985).

> **P_{Q2}:** The intrinsic product attributes that signal quality are product-specific, but dimensions of quality can be generalized to product classes or categories.

Generalizing about quality across products has been difficult for managers and researchers. Specific or concrete intrinsic attributes differ widely across products, as do the attributes consumers use to infer quality. Obviously, attributes that signal quality in fruit juice are not the same as those indicating quality in washing machines or automobiles. Even within a product category, specific attributes may provide different signals about quality. For example, thickness is related to high quality in tomato-based juices but not in fruit-flavored children's drinks. The presence of pulp suggests high quality in orange juice but low quality in apple juice.

Though the concrete attributes that signal quality differ across products, higher level abstract dimensions of quality can be generalized to categories of products. As attributes become more abstract (i.e., are higher in the means-end

---

[2]Other methods of classification could have been used for these cues. Possible alternative classification schemes include (1) tangible/intangible, (2) distal/proximal (Brunswick 1956), and (3) direct/inferential. However, each of these dichotomies has the same "fuzzy set" problems that are inherent in the intrinsic/extrinsic dichotomy. Notably, with each scheme, some cues (particularly package) would be difficult to classify. Because the intrinsic/extrinsic dichotomy has a literature underpinning it, because it is widely used and recognized, and because it has clear managerial implications, it was retained in this review.

chains), they become common to more alternatives. Garvin (1987), for example, proposes that product quality can be captured in eight dimensions: performance, features, reliability, conformance, durability, serviceability, aesthetics, and perceived quality (i.e., image). Abstract dimensions that capture diverse specific attributes have been discussed by Johnson (1983) and Achrol, Reve, and Stern (1983). In describing the way consumers compare noncomparable alternatives (e.g., how they choose between such diverse alternatives as a stereo and a Hawaiian vacation), Johnson posited that consumers represent the attributes in memory at abstract levels (e.g., using entertainment value as the dimension on which to compare stereos and Hawaiian vacations). Similarly, Achrol, Reve, and Stern proposed that the multitude of specific variables affecting a firm in the environment can be captured in abstract dimensions. Rather than itemizing specific variables that affect particular firms in different industries under varying circumstances, they proposed conceptualizing the environment in terms of its abstract qualities or dimensions (e.g., homogeneity-heterogeneity, stability-instability, concentration-dispersion, and turbulence).

Olson (1978) pointed out that consumers may use informational cues to develop beliefs about products and that task response (i.e., choice or evaluation) may be a direct function of these mediating beliefs. According to Olson, these beliefs may be of two types: descriptive, which involve a restatement of the original information in more abstract terms (e.g., "accelerates from 0 to 60 in 5 seconds" generates the belief "high performance") and inferential, which involve an inference to information missing in the environment (e.g., "accelerates from 0 to 60 in 5 seconds" generates the belief "probably corners well, too"). This distinction roughly parallels Alba and Hutchinson's (1987) distinction between interpretive and embellishment inferences and both dichotomies illustrate the level at which dimensions of quality can be conceptualized.

Interviews with subjects in the exploratory study suggested that specific intrinsic attributes used to infer quality could not be generalized across beverages, but that higher level abstract dimensions could capture the meaning of perceived quality in whole categories or classes of beverages. Purity, freshness, flavor, and appearance were the higher level abstract dimensions subjects discussed in defining quality in the beverage category.

Evidence. In a study of quality in long distance telephone, banking, repair and maintenance, and brokerage services, Parasuraman, Zeithaml, and Berry (1985) found consistent dimensions of perceived quality across four consumer service industries. These abstract dimensions included reliability, empathy, assurance, responsiveness, and tangibles. Similarly, Bonner and Nelson (1985) found that sensory signals such as rich/full flavor, natural taste, fresh taste, good aroma, and appetizing looks—all higher level abstract dimensions of perceived quality—were relevant across 33 food product categories. Brucks and Zeithaml (1987) contend on the basis of exploratory work that six abstract dimensions (ease of use, functionality, performance, durability, serviceability, and prestige) can be generalized across categories of durable goods. Though empirical research has not verified the generalizability of dimensions for categories of packaged goods other than food products, for durable goods, or for industrial goods, abstract dimensions spanning these categories could be conceptualized, verified, and then used to develop general measures of quality in product categories.

> **P_{Q3}:** Extrinsic cues serve as generalized quality indicators across brands, products, and categories.

Extrinsic attributes (e.g., price, brand name) are not product-specific and can serve as general indicators of quality across all types of products. Price, brand name, and level of advertising are three extrinsic cues frequently associated with quality in research, yet many other extrinsic cues are useful to consumers. Of special note are extrinsic cues such as product warranties and seals of approval (e.g., Good Housekeeping). Price, the extrinsic cue receiving the most research attention (see Olson 1977 for a complete review of this literature), appears to function as a surrogate for quality when the consumer has inadequate information about intrinsic attributes. Similarly, brand name serves as a "shorthand" for quality by providing consumers with a bundle of information about the product (Jacoby et al. 1978; Jacoby, Szybillo, and Busato-Schach 1977). Level of advertising has been related to product quality by economists Nelson (1970, 1974), Milgrom and Roberts (1986), and Schmalensee (1978). The basic argument holds that for goods whose attributes are determined largely during use (experience goods), higher levels of advertising signal higher quality. Schmalensee argues that level of advertising, rather than actual claims made, informs consumers that the company believes the goods are worth advertising (i.e., of high quality). Supporting this argument is the finding that many subjects in the exploratory study perceived heavily advertised brands to be generally higher in quality than brands with less advertising.

The exploratory investigation of beverages provided evidence that form of the product (e.g., frozen vs. canned vs. refrigerated) is an additional important extrinsic cue in beverages. Consumers held consistent perceptions of the relative quality of different forms of fruit juice: quality perceptions were highest for fresh products, next highest for refrigerated products, then bottled, then frozen, then canned, and lowest for dry product forms.

Evidence. The literature on hedonic quality measurement (Court 1939; Griliches 1971) maintains that price is the best measure of product quality. Considerable empirical research has investigated the relationship between price and quality (see Olson 1977 for a review of this literature in marketing) and has shown that consumers use price to infer quality when it is the only available cue. When price is combined with other (usually intrinsic) cues, the evidence is less convincing.

In forming impressions about quality of merchandise, respondents in a study by Mazursky and Jacoby (1985) selected brand name more frequently than any other information. Gardner (1970, 1971) found significant main effects on quality perceptions due to brand name.

Kirmani and Wright (1987a,b) found empirical support for the relationship between level of spending on advertising and quality inferences. Manipulating expenditures on media budgets and on production elements in advertisements, they found significant effects of both on consumers' quality perceptions.

Bonner and Nelson (1985) confirm that product form relates to quality perceptions. An empirical study revealed the same hierarchy of quality in package form (fresh, refrigerated, frozen, bottled, canned, dried) as was found in the exploratory study. Bonner and Nelson conclude: "The sensory maintenance ability of packaging differs by type and those packaging forms that can best deliver a rich/full flavor, natural and fresh taste, good aroma, and an appetizing appearance, are likely to gain market share" (p. 75).

P_{Q4}: Consumers depend on intrinsic attributes more than extrinsic attributes
(a) at the point of consumption,
(b) in prepurchase situations when intrinsic attributes are search attributes (rather than experience attributes), and
(c) when the intrinsic attributes have high predictive value.

Which type of cue — intrinsic or extrinsic — is more important in signaling quality to the consumer? An answer to this question would help firms decide whether to invest resources in product improvements (intrinsic cues) or in marketing (extrinsic cues) to improve perceptions of quality. Finding a simple and definitive answer to this question is unlikely, but the exploratory study suggests the type of attribute that dominates depends on several key contingencies.

The first contingency relates to the point in the purchase decision and consumption process at which quality evaluation occurs. Consumers may evaluate quality at the point of purchase (buying a beverage) or at the point of consumption (drinking a beverage). The salience of intrinsic attributes at the point of purchase depends on whether they can be sensed and evaluated at that time, that is, whether they contain search attributes (Nelson 1970). Where search attributes are present (e.g., sugar content of a fruit juice or color or cloudiness of a drink in a glass jar), they may be important quality indicators. In their absence, consumers depend on extrinsic cues.

At the point of consumption, most intrinsic attributes can be evaluated and therefore become accessible as quality indicators. Many consumers in the exploratory study on beverages used taste as the signal of quality at consumption. If a beverage did not taste fresh or tasted "tinny" or too thin, the evaluation was that quality was low.

Consumers depend on intrinsic attributes when the cues have high predictive value (Cox 1962). Many respondents in the exploratory study, especially those expressing concern for their children's health and teeth, unequivocally stated that purity (100 percent juice, no sugar) was the criterion they used to judge quality across the broad fruit juice category. The link between quality and this intrinsic attribute was clear and strong: all fruit beverages with 100 percent juice were high quality beverages and all others were not.

Evidence. Researchers addressing this question (Darden and Schwinghammer 1985; Etgar and Malhotra 1978; Olson and Jacoby 1972; Rigaux-Bricmont 1982; Szybillo and Jacoby 1974) have concluded that intrinsic cues were in general more important to consumers in judging quality because they had higher predictive value than extrinsic cues. This conclusion does not account for the fact that many assessments about quality are made with insufficient information about intrinsic cues. Selected individual studies (e.g., Sawyer, Worthing, and Sendak 1979) have shown that extrinsic cues can be more important to consumers than intrinsic cues. Conflicting evidence about the importance of intrinsic and extrinsic cues becomes clearer if the conditions under which each type of cue becomes important are investigated.

P_{Q5}: Consumers depend on extrinsic attributes more than intrinsic attributes

(a) in initial purchase situations when intrinsic cues are not available (e.g., for services),

(b) when evaluation of intrinsic cues requires more effort and time than the consumer perceives is worthwhile, and

(c) when quality is difficult to evaluate (experience and credence goods).

Extrinsic cues are posited to be used as quality indicators when the consumer is operating without adequate information about intrinsic product attributes. This situation may occur when the consumer (1) has little or no experience with the product, (2) has insufficient time or interest to evaluate the intrinsic attributes, and (3) cannot readily evaluate the intrinsic attributes.

At point of purchase, consumers cannot always evaluate relevant intrinsic attributes of a product. Unless free samples are being provided, consumers cannot taste new food products before buying them. Consumers do not know for certain how long a washing machine or automobile will last until they purchase and consume it. In these and similar situations, the consumer relies on extrinsic attributes such as warranty, brand name, and package as surrogates for intrinsic product attributes.

At other times, intrinsic attributes on which to evaluate quality are available but the consumer is unwilling or unable to expend the time and effort to evaluate them. Working women, men, and single shoppers, for example, have been reported to use supermarket product information significantly less than other demographic segments (Zeithaml 1985), in part because these segments are more time-conscious than other segments (Zeithaml 1985; Zeithaml and Berry 1987). Working women interviewed in the exploratory study reported that they shopped quickly and could not study nutritional information carefully on beverage containers. They selected beverages on the basis of the freshness or quality conveyed by packages or brand names.

In other situations, intrinsic product attributes indicating quality are simply too difficult for the consumer to evaluate. Evaluation may be difficult prior to purchase, as with haircuts, restaurant meals, and other experience goods. Complex stereo equipment, insurance policies, and major auto repairs are examples of products that for many consumers are difficult to evaluate even after purchase and consumption. For these "credence goods" (Darby and Karni 1973), consumers may rely on extrinsic cues because they are simpler to access and evaluate.

Evidence. Research has shown that price is used as a quality cue to a greater degree when brands are unfamiliar than when brands are familiar (Smith and Broome 1966; Stokes 1985). Research also has shown that when perceived risk of making an unsatisfactory choice is high, consumers select higher priced products (Lambert 1972; Peterson and Wilson 1985; Shapiro 1968, 1973).

$\mathbf{P}_{Q6}$: The cues that signal quality change over time because of
- (a) competition,
- (b) promotional efforts of companies
- (c) changing consumer tastes, and
- (d) information.

As improved technology and increasing competition lead to the development of technically better products, the features that signal superiority change. The exploratory study suggested that the attribute cues signaling quality in beverages are not static, but instead change over time. The shift from canned orange juice to frozen orange juice to refrigerated orange juice is one example of the evolving standards of quality in beverages. The replacement of saccharin with Nutrasweet in beverages is another.

Harness (1978, p. 17) illustrates the forces of change and the responses made by Procter & Gamble to keep Tide detergent the highest quality brand in the packaged soap category:

> Since Tide was first introduced in 1947, consumers have changed, washing machines have changed, fabrics have changed, laundry habits have changed, and competition has changed. . . . These are just a few of the more significant changes in the household laundry market, and every one of these changes has a meaning for the performance and the marketing plans for Tide. The product which we are selling today is importantly different from the Tide product which we introduced in 1947. It is different in its cleaning performance, in sudsing characteristics, aesthetics, physical properties, packaging. In total, there have been 55 significant modifications in this one brand during its 30-year lifetime.

THE CONCEPT OF PERCEIVED PRICE

From the consumer's perspective, price is what is given up or sacrificed to obtain a product. This definition is congruent with Ahtola's (1984) argument against including monetary price as a lower level attribute in multiattribute models because price is a "give" component of the model, rather than a "get" component. Defining price as a sacrifice is consistent with conceptualizations by other pricing researchers (Chapman 1986; Mazumdar 1986; Monroe and Krishnan 1985).

Figure 2.1 delineates the components of price: objective price, perceived nonmonetary price, and sacrifice. Jacoby and Olson (1977) distinguished between objective price (the actual price of a product) and perceived price (the price as encoded by the consumer). Figure 2.1 emphasizes this distinction: objective monetary price is frequently not the price encoded by consumers. Some consumers may notice that the exact price of Hi-C fruit juice is $1.69 for a 6-pack, but others may encode and remember the price only as "expensive" or "cheap." Still others may not encode price at all.

A growing body of research supports this distinction between objective and perceived price (Allen, Harrell, and Hutt 1976; Gabor and Granger 1961; *Progressive Grocer* 1964). Studies reveal that consumers do not always know or remember actual prices of products. Instead, they encode prices in ways that are meaningful to them (Dickson and Sawyer 1985; Zeithaml 1982, 1983). Levels of consumer attention, awareness, and knowledge of prices appear to be considerably lower than necessary for consumers to have accurate internal reference prices for many products (Dickson and Sawyer 1985; Zeithaml 1982). Dickson and Sawyer reported that the proportions of consumers checking prices of four types of products (margarine, cold cereal, toothpaste, and coffee) at point of purchase ranged from 54.2 to 60.6 percent. Among the groups of consumers not checking prices in these studies, a large proportion (from 58.5 to 76.7 percent in the four product categories) stated that price was just not important. Another recent study indicates that price awareness differs among demographic groups, the greatest levels of awareness being in consumers who are female, married, older, and do not work outside the home (Zeithaml and Berry 1987). Attention to prices is likely to be greater for higher priced packaged goods, durable goods, and services than for low priced beverages, but other factors in these categories—complexity, lack of price information, and processing time required—may interfere with accurate knowledge of prices. An additional factor contributing to the gap between actual and perceived price is price dispersion, the tendency for the same brands to be priced differently across stores or for products of the same type and quality to have wide price variances (Maynes and Assum 1982).

> $\mathbf{P_{P1}}$: Monetary price is not the only sacrifice perceived by consumers.

Full price models in economics (e.g., Becker 1965) acknowledge that monetary price is not the only sacrifice consumers make to obtain products. Time costs, search costs, and psychic costs all enter either explicitly or implicitly into the consumer's perception of sacrifice. If consumers cannot find products on the shelf, or if they must travel distances to buy them, a sacrifice has been made. If consumers must expend effort to assemble durable products or time to prepare packaged goods, and if this time and effort does not provide satisfaction to the consumer in the form of recreation or a hobby, a sacrifice has been made.

Evidence. Research in economics, home economics, and marketing supports the proposition that other costs—time, effort, search, psychic—are salient to consumers (Down 1961; Gronau 1973; Leibowitz 1974; Leuthold 1981; Linder 1970; Mabry 1970; Mincer 1963; Nichols, Smolensky, and Tideman 1971; Zeithaml and Berry 1987).

THE PRICE-QUALITY RELATIONSHIP

Nearly 90 research studies in the past 30 years have been designed to test the general wisdom that price and quality are positively related. Despite the expectation of a positive relationship, results of these studies have provided mixed evidence.

> $\mathbf{P_{PQ1}}$: A general price-perceived quality relationship does not exist.

Price reliance is a general tendency in some consumers to depend on price as a cue to quality (Lambert 1972; Shapiro 1968, 1973). The body of literature summarized by Olson (1977) is based on the assumption that a general price-perceived quality relationship exists. Despite a multitude of experimental studies on the topic, however, the relationship has not surfaced clearly except in situations where methodological concerns such as demand artifacts (Sawyer 1975) could offer alternative explanations for the results (Monroe and Krishnan 1985; Olson 1977). Bowbrick (1982) questioned the universality of the price-perceived quality relationship, called the stream of studies on the topic "pseudoresearch," and claimed that the price-perceived quality hypothesis is too general and untestable to produce anything other than trivial results. Peterson and Wilson (1985) argue that the relationship between price and perceived quality is not universal and that the direction of the relationship may not always be positive.

Evidence. Monroe and Krishnan (1985) concluded that a positive price-perceived quality relationship does appear to exist despite the inconsistency of the statistical significance of the research findings. They also noted, however, that multiple conceptual problems and methodological limitations compromised previous research. Monroe and Dodds (1988) describe these limitations in greater detail and delineate a research program for establishing the validity of the price-quality relationship.

Many empirical studies have produced results that conflict with Monroe and Krishnan's assessment of a positive relationship. In several studies (Friedman 1967; Swan 1974), overall association between price and perceived quality is low. Other studies show the relationship to be nonlinear (Peterson 1970; Peterson and Jolibert 1976), highly variable across individuals (Shapiro 1973), and variable across products being judged (Gardner 1971). Other research, summarized by Olson (1977), shows that price becomes less important as a quality indicator when other product quality cues, such as brand name (Gardner 1971) or store image (Stafford and Enis 1969), are present. Exploratory and survey research (Bonner and Nelson 1985; Parasuraman, Zeithaml, and Berry 1985) indicates that price is among the least important attributes that consumers associate with quality.

Related studies (summarized by Hjorth-Anderson 1984) have consistently shown price to be correlated only weakly with objective (rather than perceived) quality. Typical of these studies is work by Sproles (1977), who correlated the prices of products with quality ratings obtained through *Consumer Reports* and *Consumers' Research Magazine*. Though a positive price-objective quality relationship was found in 51 percent of the 135 product categories, no relationship was found in 35 percent and a negative relationship was found in 14 percent. Similarly, Riesz found the mean rank correlation between price and objective quality to be .26 for 685 product categories reported in *Consumer Reports* between 1961 and 1975 and .09 for 679 brands of packaged foods (Riesz 1978). Geistfeld (1982) found variability among markets and across stores in the price-objective quality relationship. Most recently, Gerstner (1985) assessed the correlation between quality and price for 145 products and concluded that the relationship appeared to be product-specific and generally weak.

Both Peterson and Wilson (1985) and Olshavsky (1985) argue that the emphasis in price-quality studies should not be on documenting the general price-perceived quality relationship, but on the conditions under which price information is likely to lead to an inference about product quality. One possibility is that some individuals rely heavily on price as a quality signal whereas others do not. Peterson and Wilson sorted respondents into groups on the basis of their having a price-reliance schema and confirmed in an experiment that "schematics" perceive a stronger relationship between price and quality than "aschematics." This general tendency on the part of some consumers to associate price and quality has been examined in the context of covariation assessment by Roedder-John, Scott, and Bettman (1986), who confirmed that consumers differ in their beliefs about the association between the price and quality variables. These studies provide evidence that some consumers have a schema of price reliance, rather than indicating a generalized tendency in consumers to associate price and quality.

P_{PQ2}: The use of price as an indicator of quality depends on
(a) availability of other cues to quality,
(b) price variation within a class of products,
(c) product quality variation within a category of products,
(d) level of price awareness of consumers, and
(e) consumers' ability to detect quality variation in a group of products.

Monroe and Krishnan (1985) contend that most past price-perceived quality research has been exploratory and has not succeeded in resolving the question of when price is used to infer quality. Contingencies affecting the use of price as a quality indicator fit into three groups: informational factors, individual factors, and product category factors.

The first category of factors believed to affect the price-perceived quality relationship consists of other information available to the consumer. When intrinsic cues to quality are readily accessible, when brand names provide evidence of a company's reputation, or when level of advertising communicates the company's belief in the brand, the consumer may prefer to use those cues instead of price.

Several individual difference factors may account for the variation in the use of price as a quality signal. One explanatory variable is price awareness of the consumer: consumers unaware of product prices obviously cannot use price to infer quality. Another individual difference is consumers' ability to detect quality variation among products (Lambert 1972). If the consumer does not have sufficient product knowledge (or perhaps even interest) to understand the variation in quality (e.g., French, Williams, and Chance 1973), price and other extrinsic cues may be used to a greater degree.

Consumers appear to depend more on price as a quality signal in some product categories than in others. One explanation for this variation may be differences in price–objective quality relationships by category (e.g., the low price of Japanese automobiles does not diminish the well-established perception of quality in the category). Another explanation may be price variation in a category. In packaged goods categories (such as beverages) where products differ little in price, the consumer may not attribute higher quality to products that cost only a few cents more than those of competitors. Respondents in the exploratory study, for example, did not associate beverage price with quality. Still another category-specific contingency is quality variation: in categories where little variation is expected among brands (such as salt or paper sandwich bags), price may function only as an indication of sacrifice whereas in categories where quality variation is expected (such as canned seafood or washing machines), price may function also as an indication of quality.

Evidence. Olson (1977) showed that availability of intrinsic and extrinsic cues other than price typically results in weighting those factors (e.g., brand name) as more important than price. He concluded that brand name is a stronger cue than price for evaluating overall quality (Gardner 1971; Jacoby, Olson, and Haddock 1973; Smith and Broome 1966; Stokes 1985).

Studies have indicated that use of price as a quality indicator differs by product category. Except for wine and perfume, most positive links have been found in durable rather than in nondurable or consumable products (Gardner 1970; Lambert 1972; Peterson and Wilson 1985). In an experimental setting, Peterson and Wilson documented the relationship between price variation and price–perceived quality association: the greater the price variation, the greater the tendency for consumers to use price as a quality indicator.

In a recent meta-analysis of 41 studies investigating the association between price and perceived quality, Rao and Monroe (1987) found that the type of experimental design and the magnitude of the price manipulation significantly influenced the size of the price–perceived quality effects obtained. The number of cues manipulated and the price level were not found to have a significant effect. Because of constraints imposed by the meta-analysis, the reviewers included only consumer products and eliminated several studies as outliers, so the full range of prices and types of products was not investigated.

Considerable empirical research supports individual differences in consumer knowledge of prices. Consumers are not uniformly aware of prices and certain consumer segments (such as working women and men) are less aware of prices than other segments (Zeithaml 1985; Zeithaml and Berry 1987; Zeithaml and Fuerst 1983). Price awareness level has not been studied as it relates to quality perceptions, though Rao (1987) documented the impact of prior knowledge of products on the use of price as a quality cue.

THE CONCEPT OF PERCEIVED VALUE

When respondents in the exploratory study discussed value, they used the term in many different ways, describing a wide variety of attributes and higher level abstractions that provided value to them. What constitutes value—even in a single product category—appears to be highly personal and idiosyncratic. Though many respondents in the exploratory study agreed on cues that signaled quality, they differed considerably in expressions of value. Patterns of responses from the exploratory study can be grouped into four consumer definitions of value: (1) value is low price, (2) value is whatever I want in a product, (3) value is the quality I get for the price I pay, and (4) value is what I get for what I give. Each definition involves a different set of linkages among the elements in the model and each consumer definition has its counterpart in the academic or trade literature on the subject. The diversity in meanings of value is illustrated in the following four definitions and provides a partial explanation for the difficulty in conceptualizing and measuring the value construct in research.

Value is Low Price. Some respondents equated value with low price, indicating that what they had to give up was most salient in their perceptions of value. In their own words:

- Value is price—which one is on sale.
- When I can use coupons, I feel that the juice is a value.
- Value means low price.
- Value is whatever is on special this week.

In industry studies, Schechter (1984) and Bishop (1984) identified subsets of consumers that equate value with price. Other industry studies, including Hoffman's (1984), reveal the salience of price in the value equations of consumers.

Value is Whatever I Want in a Product. Other respondents emphasized the benefits they received from the product as the most important components of value:

- Value is what is good for you.
- Value is what my kids will drink.
- Little containers because then there is no waste.
- Value to me is what is convenient. When I can take it out of the refrigerator and not have to mix it up, then it has value.

This second definition is essentially the same as the economist's definition of utility, that is, a subjective measure of the usefulness or want satisfaction that results from consumption. This definition also has been expressed in the trade literature. Value has been defined as "whatever it is that the customer seeks in making decisions to buy" (*Chain Store Age* 1985). Schechter (1984) defines value as all factors, both qualitative and quantitative, subjective and objective, that make up the complete shopping experience. In these definitions, value encompasses all relevant choice criteria.

Value is the Quality I Get for the Price I Pay. Other respondents conceptualized value as a tradeoff between one "give" component, price, and one "get" component, quality:

- Value is price first and quality second.
- Value is the lowest price for a quality brand.
- Value is the same as quality. No—value is affordable quality.

This definition is consistent with several others that appear in the literature (Bishop 1984; Dodds and Monroe 1984; Doyle 1984; Shapiro and Associates 1985).

Value is What I Get for What I Give. Finally, some respondents considered all relevant "get" components as well as all relevant "give" components when describing value:

- Value is how many drinks you can get out of a certain package. Frozen juices have more because you can water them down and get more out of them.
- How many gallons you get out of it for what the price is.
- Whatever makes the most for the least money.
- Which juice is more economical.
- Value is what you are paying for what you are getting.
- Value is price and having single portions so that there is no waste.

This fourth definition is consistent with Sawyer and Dickson's (1984) conceptualization of value as a ratio of attributes weighted by their evaluations divided by price weighted by its evaluation. This meaning is also similar to the utility per dollar measure of value used by Hauser and Urban (1986), Hauser and Simmie (1981), Hauser and Shugan (1983), and others.

These four consumer expressions of value can be captured in one overall definition: perceived value is the consumer's overall assessment of the utility of a product based on perceptions of what is received and what is given. Though what is received varies across consumers (i.e., some may want volume, others high quality, still others convenience) and what is given varies (i.e., some are concerned only with money expended, others with time and effort), value represents a tradeoff of the salient give and get components.

Value and Quality. In the means-end chains, value (like quality) is proposed to be a higher level abstraction. It differs from quality in two ways. First, value is more individualistic and personal than quality and is therefore a higher level concept than quality. As shown in Table 2-1, value may be similar to the "emotional payoff" of Young and Feigin (1975), to "abstract, multi-dimensional, difficult-to-measure attributes" of Geistfeld, Sproles, and Badenhop (1977), and to "instrumental values" of Olson and Reynolds (1983). Second, value (unlike quality) involves a tradeoff of give and get components. Though many conceptualizations of value have specified quality as the only "get" component in the value equation, the consumer may implicitly include other factors, several that are in themselves higher level abstractions, such as prestige and convenience (see Holbrook and Corfman 1985 for a discussion of the difficulty involved in separating these abstractions in the value construct).

> **P_{V1}:** The benefit components of value include salient intrinsic attributes, extrinsic attributes, perceived quality, and other relevant high level abstractions.

Differences among the benefit or get components shown in the model and listed in P_{V1} can be illustrated by findings from the exploratory study of fruit juices. As discussed before, perceived quality in fruit juices was signaled by the attribute "100 percent fruit juice" plus sensory attributes such as taste and texture.

Some intrinsic attributes of fruit juices—other than those signaling quality—were cited as providing value to respondents. Color was one important intrinsic attribute. Most mothers knew which colors or flavors of juice their children would drink; only those flavors were considered to be acceptable to the child and therefore to have value for the mother. Other intrinsic attributes (e.g., absence of pulp and visible consistency of the drinks) also affected value perceptions.

In addition to perceived quality and these intrinsic attributes, other higher level abstractions contributed to perceptions of value. A frequently mentioned higher level abstraction for fruit juice was convenience. Some consumers did not want to reconstitute the juice. Others wanted self-serve containers so that children could get juice from the refrigerator by themselves. For this reason, small cans with difficult-to-open tops were not as convenient as little boxes with insertable straws. Fully reconstituted, ready-to-serve, and easy-to-open containers were keys to adding value in the category. These intrinsic and extrinsic lower level attributes added value through the higher level abstraction of convenience.

Another higher level abstraction important in providing value in children's fruit juices was appreciation. When children drank beverages the mothers selected, when they mentioned them to mother or evidenced thanks, the mothers obtained value. This particular psychological benefit was not evoked directly in any of the consumer interviews, but came through strongly in the laddering process. The value perceptions filtered through the higher level abstraction of appreciation and did not come directly through intrinsic or extrinsic attributes. This indirect inferencing process illustrates a major difficulty in using traditional multiattribute or utility models in measuring perceived value. The intrinsic attributes themselves are not always directly linked to value, but instead filter through other personal benefits that are themselves abstract.

Evidence. Though no empirical research has been reported on the pivotal higher level abstractions related to value, several dimensions have been proposed in selected categories. Bishop (1984), for example, claimed that value in supermarket shopping is a composite of the higher level abstractions of variety, service, and facilities in addition to quality and price. Doyle (1984) identified convenience, freshness, and time as major higher level abstractions that combine with price and quality to produce value perceptions in supermarket consumers.

> **P_{V2}:** The sacrifice components of perceived value include monetary prices and non-monetary prices.

Consumers sacrifice both money and other resources (e.g., time, energy, effort) to obtain products and services. To some consumers, the monetary sacrifice is pivotal: some supermarket shoppers will invest hours clipping coupons, reading food advertising in the newspaper, and traveling to different stores to obtain the best bargains. To these consumers, anything that reduces the monetary sacrifice will increase the perceived value of the product. Less price-conscious consumers will find value in store proximity, ready-to-serve food products, and home delivery—even at the expense of higher costs—because time and effort are perceived as more costly.

Evidence. Recent research reveals that saving time has become a pivotal concern of consumers in supermarket shopping and cooking. Supermarket shoppers have cited fast checkout as more important than low prices in selecting grocery stores (Food Marketing Institute 1985, 1986). Studies also show that consumers are willing to spend money to get more convenient packaging in food products (Morris 1985).

> **P_{V3}:** Extrinsic attributes serve as "value signals" and can substitute for active weighing of benefits and costs.

How carefully do consumers evaluate these components of products in making assessments of value? To judge from the product category of beverages, cognitive assessment is limited. Rather than carefully considering prices and benefits, most respondents depended on cues—often extrinsic cues—in forming impressions of value. A few respondents carefully calculated the cheapest brand in their set on a regular basis, but most seemed to follow Langer's (1978) notion of mindlessness: most respondents bought beverages with only minimal processing of available information. They repeatedly bought a brand they trusted or used extrinsic value cues to simplify their choice process.

These value triggers were present regardless of the way consumers defined value. Many consumers who defined value as low price reported using a coupon as a signal to low price without actually comparing the reduced price of the couponed brand with the prices of other brands, or they reported that "cents-off" or "everyday low price" signs or a private label brand triggered the value perception. Respondents who defined value in terms of what they wanted in products cited small containers, single-serving portions, and ready-to-serve containers. Consumers who defined value as the quality they get for the price they pay used signals such as 100 percent fruit juice on special or brand name on special. Finally, consumers who defined value as what they get for what they pay depended on form (frozen vs. canned juice) and economy-sized packages as signals.

Not all consumers responded in this mindless way—many saw their role as economical shopper to be important enough to spend time and effort to weigh carefully the give and get components in their own equations of value. Moreover, not all products are as simple or inexpensive as beverages. One would expect to find more rational evaluation in situations of high information availability, processing ability, time availability, and involvement in purchase.

Evidence. To date, no reported empirical

studies have investigated the potential of triggers that lead to perceptions of value.

> **P_{V4}:** The perception of value depends on the frame of reference in which the consumer is making an evaluation.

Holbrook and Corfman (1985) maintain that value perceptions are situational and hinge on the context within which an evaluative judgment occurs. This view may help explain the diversity of meanings of value. In the beverage category, for example, the frame of reference used by the consumer in providing meanings included point of purchase, preparation, and consumption. Value meant different things at each of these points. At the point of purchase, value often meant low price, sale, or coupons. At the point of preparation, value often involved some calculation about whether the product was easy to prepare and how much the consumer could obtain for what she paid. At consumption, value was judged in terms of whether the children would drink the beverage, whether some of the beverage was wasted, or whether the children appreciated the mother for buying the drinks.

Evidence. No empirical studies have been conducted to investigate the variation in value perceptions across evaluation contexts.

> **P_{V5}:** Perceived value affects the relationship between quality and purchase.

As Olshavsky (1985) suggested, not all consumers want to buy the highest quality item in every category. Instead, quality appears to be factored into the implicit or explicit valuation of a product by many consumers (Dodds and Monroe 1985; Sawyer and Dickson 1984). A given product may be high quality, but if the consumer does not have enough money to buy it (or does not want to spend the amount required), its value will not be perceived as being as high as that of a product with lower quality but a more affordable price. In other words, when $get_a - give_a > get_b - give_b$ but the shopper has a budget constraint, then $give_a >$ budget constraints $> give_b$ and hence b is chosen. The same logic may apply to products that need more preparation time than the consumer's time constraint allows.

The respondents in the beverage study illustrated this point as they discussed their typical purchasing behavior. For respondents with several children, beverages accounted for a large portion of their weekly food bill. Though most believed that pure fruit juice was of higher quality than fruit drinks, many of these respondents did not buy only pure fruit juice because it was too expensive. They tended to buy some proportion of pure fruit juice, then round out these more expensive purchases with fruit drinks. In their evaluation, high quality was not worth its expense, so lower levels of quality were tolerated in a portion of the weekly beverages. These consumers obtained more value from the lower quality juices because the low costs compensated for the reduction in quality.

Evidence. Several empirical studies have investigated the relationship between quality and purchase, but no empirical studies have investigated explicitly the role of value as an intervening factor between quality and purchase. However, studies on the use of unit price information (e.g., Aaker and Ford 1983; Dickson and Sawyer 1985; Zeithaml 1982) suggest that many consumers use unit price information (i.e., a measure of value) in making product choices in supermarkets.

RESEARCH IMPLICATIONS

The preceding propositions raise questions about ways in which quality and value have been studied in the past and suggest avenues for future research.

Current Practices in Measuring Quality

Academic research measuring quality has depended heavily on unidimensional rating scales, allowing quality to be interpreted in any way the respondent chooses. This practice does not ensure that respondents are interpreting quality similarly or in the way the researcher intends. Hjorth-Anderson (1984) claims that unidimensional scales are methodologically invalid by showing that the concept of overall quality has many dimensions. Holbrook and Corfman (1985) call for ambiguous quality measures to be replaced with scales based on conceptual definitions of quality. An example of the approach they recommended is illustrated by Parasuraman, Zeithaml, and Berry (1985), who investigated service quality in an extensive exploratory study, conceptualized it in dimensions based on that investigation, and operationalized it using the conceptual domain specified in the first phase (Parasuraman, Zeithaml, and Berry 1986). In that stream of research, quality was defined as a comparison between consumer expectations and perceptions of performance based on those dimensions, an approach that allows for individual differences across subjects in the attributes that signal quality.

The research approach used by Parasuraman, Zeithaml, and Berry (1985) could be used in different categories of products (e.g., packaged goods, industrial products, durable goods) to find the abstract dimensions that capture quality in those categories. Such an attempt is currently underway by Brucks and Zeithaml (1987) for durable goods. Studies also are needed to determine which attributes signal these dimensions, when and why they are selected instead of other cues, and how they are perceived and combined (see also Gutman and Alden 1985, Olson 1977, and Olson and Jacoby 1972 for similar expressions of needed research). Finally, the relationship between the constructs of attitude and quality should be examined. The instrumentality of a product feature (Lewin 1936) and the quality rating of such a feature in separately determining choice may be an interesting research issue. The convergent and discriminant validity of the constructs of attitude and quality also warrant investigation. Quality measurement scales remain to be developed and validated.

Current Practices in Modeling Consumer Decision Making

Three aspects of modeling consumer decision making can be questioned if the propositions prove to be accurate representations: the tendency to use actual attributes of products rather than consumer perceptions of those attributes, the practice of duplicating and commingling physical attributes with higher order attributes (Myers and Shocker 1981), and the failure to distinguish between the give and get (Ahtola 1984) components of the model.

Howard (1977, p. 28) clearly states the first problem.

> It is essential to distinguish between the attributes per se and consumers' perceptions of these attributes, because consumers differ in their perceptions. It is the perception that affects behavior, not the attribute itself. "Attribute" is often used to mean choice criteria, but this leads to confusion. To use "attribute" when you mean not the attribute itself but the consumer's mental image of it, is to reify what is in the consumer's mind.

Jacoby and Olson (1985) concur, claiming that the focus of marketers should not be objective reality but instead consumer perceptions, which may be altered either by changing objective reality or by reinterpreting objective reality for consumers.

Myers and Shocker (1981) point out that comingling quality, a higher level abstraction, with lower level physical attributes in models limits the validity and confounds the interpretation of many studies, especially when this practice duplicates lower level attributes. Therefore, it is necessary to use attributes from the same general classification or level in the hierarchy in modeling consumer decision making. Ahtola (1984) confirms that when the hierarchical nature of attributes is not recognized in consumer decision models, double and triple counting of the impact of some attributes results. Techniques to elicit and organize attributes, in his opinion, should precede modeling of the attributes. Myers and Shocker (1981) discuss different consumer decision models appropriate for the levels and ways attributes should be presented in research instruments and analyzed later. Huber and McCann (1982) reveal the impact of inferential beliefs on product evaluations and acknowledge that understanding consumer inferences is essential both in getting information from consumers and in giving information to consumers. Finally, Ahtola (1984) calls for expanding and revising models to incorporate the sacrifice aspects of price. Sacrifice should not be limited to monetary price alone, especially in situations where time costs, search costs, and convenience costs are salient to the consumer.

Methods Appropriate for Studying Quality and Value

The approach used in the exploratory investigation is appropriate for investigating quality in other product categories. Olson and Reynolds (1983) developed methods to aggregate the qualitative data from individual consumers. Aggregate cognitive mapping, structural analysis, cognitive differentiation analysis, and value structure mapping are all techniques designed especially to analyze and represent higher order abstractions such as quality. These techniques are more appropriate than preference mapping or multiattribute modeling for investigating concepts like quality and value (for a complete discussion and explication of these techniques, see Gutman and Alden 1985 or Reynolds and Jamieson 1985).

Several researchers have developed approaches to link product attributes to perceptions of higher level abstractions. Mehrotra and Palmer (1985) suggest a methodological approach to relating product features to perceptions of quality based on the work of Olson and Reynolds (1983). In their procedure, lists of cues and benefits are developed from focus groups or in-depth interviews with consumers, semantic differential scales are constructed to capture the benefits, a tradeoff procedure is used to determine the importance of the cues, and respondents match cues to product concepts. Through this type of analysis, degree of linkage (between cues and benefits), value of a cue, and competitive brand information are provided.

Mazursky and Jacoby (1985) also recognized the need for procedures to track the inference process from consideration of objective cues to the higher level image of quality. Instead of free-elicitation procedures, they used a behavioral processing simulation whereby they presented attribute information to respondents and asked them to form an impression of quality by choosing any information they wished. Though this method can be criticized as unrealistic, it provides insights into the types of information that consumers believe signal quality. Modifications of the method to make the environment more realistic (such as by Brucks 1985) are also possible.

Other researchers have described analytic procedures to link attributes with perceptions. Holbrook (1981) provides a theoretical framework and analytic procedure for representing the intervening role of perceptions in evaluative judgments. Neslin (1981) describes the superiority of statistically revealed importance weights over self-stated importance weights in linking product features to perceptions.

Researching Value

A major difficulty in researching value is the variety of meanings of value held by consumers. Building a model of value requires that the researcher understand which of many (at least of four) meanings are implicit in consumers' expressions of value. Utility models are rich in terms of methodological refinements (see Schmalensee and Thisse 1985 for a discussion of different utility measures and equations), but do not address the distinction between attributes and higher level abstractions. They also presume that consumers carefully calculate the give and get components of value, an assumption that did not hold true for most consumers in the exploratory study.

Price as a Quality Indicator

Most experimental studies related to quality have focused on price as the key extrinsic quality signal. As suggested in the propositions, price is but one of several potentially useful extrinsic cues; brand name or package may be equally or more important, especially in packaged goods. Further, evidence of a generalized price-perceived quality relationship is inconclusive. Quality research may benefit from a deemphasis on price as the main extrinsic quality indicator. Inclusion of other important indicators, as well as identification of situations in which each of those indicators is important, may provide more interesting and useful answers about the extrinsic signals consumers use.

MANAGEMENT IMPLICATIONS

An understanding of what quality and value mean to consumers offers the promise of improving brand positions through more precise market analysis and segmentation, product planning, promotion, and pricing strategy. The model presented here suggests the following strategies that can be implemented to understand and capitalize on brand quality and value.

Close the Quality Perception Gap

Though managers increasingly acknowledge the importance of quality, many continue to define and measure it from the company's perspective. Closing the gap between objective and perceived quality requires that the company view quality the way the consumer does. Research that investigates which cues are important and how consumers form impressions of quality based on those technical, objective cues is necessary. Companies also may benefit from research that identifies the abstract dimensions of quality desired by consumers in a product class.

Identify Key Intrinsic and Extrinsic Attribute Signals

A top priority for marketers is finding which of the many extrinsic and intrinsic cues consumers use to signal quality. This process involves a careful look at situational factors surrounding the purchase and use of the product. Does quality vary greatly among products in the category? Is quality difficult to evaluate? Do consumers have enough information about intrinsic attributes before purchase, or do they depend on simpler extrinsic cues until after their first purchase? What cues are provided by competitors? Identifying the important quality signals from the consumer's viewpoint, then communicating those signals rather than generalities, is likely to lead to more vivid perceptions of quality. Linking lower level attributes with their higher level abstractions locates the "driving force" and "leverage point" for advertising strategy (Olson and Reynolds 1983).

Acknowledge the Dynamic Nature of Quality Perceptions

Consumers' perceptions of quality change over time as a result of added information, increased competition in a product category, and changing expectations. The dynamic nature of quality suggests that marketers must track perceptions over time and align product and promotion strategies with these changing views. Because products and perceptions change, marketers may be able to educate consumers on ways to evaluate quality. Advertising, the information provided in packaging, and visible cues associated with products can be managed to evoke desired quality perceptions.

Understand How Consumers Encode Monetary and Nonmonetary Prices

The model proposes a gap between actual and perceived price, making it important to understand how consumers encode prices of products. Nonmonetary costs—such as time and effort—must be acknowledged. Many consumers, especially the 50 million working women in the U.S. today, consider time an important commodity. Anything that can be built into products to reduce time, effort, and search costs can reduce perceived sacrifice and thereby increase perceptions of value.

Recognize Multiple Ways to Add Value

Finally, the model delineates several strategies for adding value in products and services. Each of the boxes feeding into perceived value provides an avenue for increasing value perceptions. Reducing monetary and nonmonetary costs, decreasing perceptions of sacrifice, adding salient intrinsic attributes, evoking perceptions of relevant high level abstractions, and using extrinsic cues to signal value are all possible strategies that companies can use to affect value perceptions. The selection of a strategy for a particular product or market segment depends on its customers' definition of value. Strategies based on customer value standards and perceptions will channel resources more effectively and will meet customer expectations better than those based only on company standards.

REFERENCES

AAKER, DAVID A., and GARY T. FORD (1983), "Unit Pricing Ten Years Later: A Replication," *Journal of Marketing,* 47 (Winter), 118–122.

ACHROL, RAVI SINGH, TORGER REVE, and LOUIS STERN (1983), "The Environment of Marketing Channel Dyads: A Framework for Comparative Analysis," *Journal of Marketing,* 47 (Fall), 55–67.

AHTOLA, OLLI T. (1984), "Price as a 'Give' Component in an Exchange Theoretic Multicomponent Model," in *Advances in Consumer Research,* Vol. 11, Thomas C. Kinnear, Ed. Ann Arbor, MI: Association for Consumer Research, 623–626.

ALBA, JOSEPH W., and J. WESLEY HUTCHINSON (1987), "Dimensions of Consumer Expertise," *Journal of Consumer Research,* 14 (March), 411–454.

ALLEN, JOHN W., GILBERT D. HARRELL, and MICHAEL D. HUTT (1976), *Price Awareness Study.* Washington, DC: Food Marketing Institute.

ARCHIBALD, ROBERT B., CLYDE HAULMAN, and CARLISLE MOODY, JR. (1983), "Quality, Price, Advertising, and Published Quality Ratings," *Journal of Consumer Research,* 9 (4), 347–356.

AUSTIN, J. L. (1964), "A Plea for Excuses," in *Ordinary Language,* V. C. Chappell, Ed. New York: Dover, 41–63.

BECKER, GARY S. (1965), "Theory of the Allocation of Time," *Economic Journal,* 75 (September), 493–517.

BELLENGER, DANNY, KENNETH BERNHARDT, and JAC GOLDSTUCKER (1976), *Qualitative Research in Marketing.* Chicago: American Marketing Association.

BISHOP, WILLARD R., JR. (1984), "Competitive Intelligence," *Progressive Grocer* (March), 19–20.

BONNER, P. GREG, and RICHARD NELSON (1985), "Product Attributes and Perceived Quality: Foods," in *Perceived Quality,* J. Jacoby and J. Olson, Eds. Lexington, MA: Lexington Books, 64–79.

BOWBRICK, P. (1982), "Pseudoresearch in Marketing: The Case of the Price-Perceived-Quality Relationship," *European Journal of Marketing,* 14 (8), 466–470.

BRUCKS, MERRIE (1985), "The Effects of Product Class Knowledge on Information Search Behavior," *Journal of Consumer Research,* 12 (1), 1–16.

———, and VALARIE A. ZEITHAML (1987), "Price as an Indicator of Quality Dimensions," paper presented at Association for Consumer Research Annual Meeting, Boston, MA.

BRUNSWICK, EGON (1956), *Perception and the Representative Design of Psychological Experiments.* Berkeley, CA: University of California Press.

Chain Store Age (1985), "Consumers Say Value is More Than Quality Divided By Price" (May), 13.

CHAPMAN, JOSEPH (1986), "The Impact of Discounts on Subjective Product Evaluations," working paper, Virginia Polytechnic Institute and State University.

COHEN, JOEL B. (1979), "The Structure of Product Attributes: Defining Attribute Dimensions for Planning and Evaluation," in *Analytic Approaches to Product and Marketing Planning,* A. Shocker, Ed. Cambridge, MA: Marketing Science Institute.

COURT, ANDREW T. (1939), "Hedonic Price Indexes and Automotive Examples," in *The Dynamics of Automobile Demand.* New York: General Motors Corporation, 99–117.

COX, DONALD F. (1962), "The Measurement of Information Value: A Study in Consumer Decision Making," in *Proceedings,* Winter Conference. Chicago: American Marketing Association, 413–421.

CROSBY, PHILIP B. (1979), *Quality is Free.* New York: New American Library.

CURRY, DAVID J., and DAVID J. FAULDS (1986), "Indexing Product Quality: Issues, Theory, and Results," *Journal of Marketing,* 13 (June), 134-145.

DARBY, M. R., and E. KARNI (1973), "Free Competition and the Optimal Amount of Fraud," *Journal of Law and Economics,* 16 (April), 67-86.

DARDEN, WILLIAM R., and JOANN K. L. SCHWINGHAMMER (1985), "The Influence of Social Characteristics on Perceived Quality in Patronage Choice Behavior," in *Perceived Quality,* J. Jacoby and J. Olson, Eds. Lexington, MA: Lexington Books, 161-172.

DICKSON, PETER, and ALAN SAWYER (1985), "Point of Purchase Behavior and Price Perceptions of Supermarket Shoppers," Marketing Science Institute Working Paper Series.

DODDS, WILLIAM B., and KENT B. MONROE (1985), "The Effect of Brand and Price Information on Subjective Product Evaluations," in *Advances in Consumer Research,* Vol. 12, Elizabeth C. Hirschman and Morris B. Holbrook, Eds. Provo, UT: Association for Consumer Research, 85-90.

DOWN, S. A. (1961), "A Theory of Consumer Efficiency," *Journal of Retailing,* 37 (Winter), 6-12.

DOYLE, MONA (1984), "New Ways of Measuring Value," *Progressive Grocer-Value,* Executive Report, 15-19.

ETGAR, MICHAEL, and NARESH K. MALHOTRA (1978), "Consumers' Reliance on Different Product Quality Cues: A Basis for Market Segmentation," in *Research Frontiers in Marketing: Dialogues and Directions, 1978 Educators' Proceedings,* Subhash C. Jain, Ed. Chicago: American Marketing Association, 143-147.

Food Marketing Institute(1985), *Trends—Consumer Attitudes and the Supermarket, 1985 Update.* Washington, DC: Food Marketing Institute.

______(1986), *Trends—Consumer Attitudes and the Supermarket: 1986 Update.* Washington, DC: Food Marketing Institute.

FRENCH, N. D., J. J. WILLIAMS, and W. A. CHANCE (1983), "A Shopping Experiment on Price-Quality Relationships," *Journal of Retailing,* 48 (Spring), 3-16.

FRIEDMAN, L. (1967), "Psychological Pricing in the Food Industry," in *Prices: Issues in Theory, Practice, and Public Policy,* A. Phillips and O. Williamson, Eds. Philadelphia: University of Pennsylvania Press.

GABOR, ANDRE, and C. W. J. GRANGER (1961), "On the Price Consciousness of Consumers," *Applied Statistics,* 10 (2), 170-188.

GARDNER, D. M. (1970), "An Experimental Investigation of the Price-Quality Relationship," *Journal of Retailing,* 46 (Fall), 25-41.

______(1971), "Is There a Generalized Price-Quality Relationship?" *Journal of Marketing Research,* 8 (May), 241-243.

GARVIN, DAVID A. (1983), "Quality on the Line," *Harvard Business Review,* 61 (September-October), 65-73.

______(1987), "Competing on the Eight Dimensions of Quality," *Harvard Business Review,* 65 (November-December), 101-109.

GEISTFELD, LOREN V. (1982), "The Price-Quality Relationship-Revisited," *Journal of Consumer Affairs,* 14 (Winter), 334-346.

______, G. B. SPROLES, and S. B. BADENHOP (1977), "The Concept and Measurement of a Hierarchy of Product Characteristics," in *Advances in Consumer Research,* Vol. 4, W. D. Perreault, Jr., Ed. Ann Arbor, MI: Association for Consumer Research, 302-307.

GERSTNER, EITAN (1985), "Do Higher Prices Signal Higher Quality?" *Journal of Marketing Research,* 22 (May), 209-215.

GRILICHES, ZVI (1971), "Introduction: Hedonic Price Indexes Revisited," in *Price Indexes and Quality Change,* Zvi Griliches, Ed. Cambridge, MA: Harvard University Press, 3-15.

GRONAU, R. (1973), "The Intrafamily Allocation of Time: The Value of the Housewife's Time," *American Economic Review,* 63 (4), 634-651.

GUTMAN, JONATHAN, and SCOTT D. ALDEN (1985), "Adolescents' Cognitive Structures of Retail Stores and Fashion Consumption: A Means-End Chain Analysis of Quality," in *Perceived Quality,* J. Jacoby and J. Olson, Eds. Lexington, MA: Lexington Books, 99-114.

______, and THOMAS J. REYNOLDS (1979), "An Investigation of the Levels of Cognitive Abstraction Utilized by Consumers in Product Differentiation," in *Attitude Research Under the Sun,* J. Eighmey, Ed. Chicago: American Marketing Association.

HARNESS, EDWARD (1978), "Some Basic Beliefs About Marketing," speech to the Annual Marketing Meeting of the Conference Board, New York City.

HAUSER, J. R., and S. M. SHUGAN (1983), "Defensive Marketing Strategies," *Marketing Science,* 2 (Fall), 319–360.

———, and P. SIMMIE (1981), "Profit-Maximizing Perceptual Positions: An Integrated Theory for the Selection of Product Features and Price," *Management Science,* 27 (January), 33–56.

———, and GLEN URBAN (1986), "The Value Priority Hypotheses for Consumer Budget Plans," *Journal of Consumer Research,* 12 (March), 446–462.

HJORTH-ANDERSON, CHR. (1984), "The Concept of Quality and the Efficiency of Markets for Consumer Products," *Journal of Consumer Research,* 11 (2), 708–718.

———(1986), "More on Multidimensional Quality: A Reply," *Journal of Consumer Research,* 13 (June), 149–154.

HOFFMAN, GENE D. (1984), "Our Competitor Is Our Environment," *Progressive Grocer–Value,* Executive Report, 28–30.

HOLBROOK, MORRIS B. (1981), "Integrating Compositional and Decompositional Analyses to Represent the Intervening Role of Perceptions in Evaluative Judgments," *Journal of Marketing Research,* 18 (February), 13–28.

———, and KIM P. CORFMAN (1985), "Quality and Value in the Consumption Experience: Phaedrus Rides Again," in *Perceived Quality,* J. Jacoby and J. Olson, Eds. Lexington, MA: Lexington Books, 31–57.

HOWARD, J. A. (1977), *Consumer Behavior: Application of Theory.* New York: McGraw-Hill.

HUBER, JOEL, and JOHN MCCANN (1982), "The Impact of Inferential Beliefs on Product Evaluations," *Journal of Marketing Research,* 19 (August), 324–333.

JACOBY, J., R. W. CHESTNUT, W. D. HOYER, D. W. SHELUGA, and M. J. DONAHUE (1978), "Psychometric Characteristics of Behavioral Process Data: Preliminary Findings on Validity and Generalizability," in *Advances in Consumer Research,* Vol. 5, H. Keith Hunt, Ed. Ann Arbor, MI: Association for Consumer Research, 546–554.

———, and JERRY C. OLSON (1977), "Consumer Response to Price: An Attitudinal, Information Processing Perspective," in *Moving Ahead with Attitude Research,* Y. Wind and P. Greenberg, Eds. Chicago: American Marketing Association, 73–86.

———, and ———, Eds. (1985), *Perceived Quality.* Lexington, MA: Lexington Books.

———, ———, and RAFAEL A. HADDOCK (1973), "Price, Brand Name and Product Composition Characteristics as Determinants of Perceived Quality," *Journal of Applied Psychology,* 55 (6), 570–579.

———, G. J. SZYBILLO, and. J. BUSATO-SCHACH (1977), "Information Acquisition Behavior in Brand Choice Situations," *Journal of Consumer Research,* 3 (March), 209–215.

JOHNSON, MICHAEL D. (1983), "Decision Processing and Product Comparability: A Theory of Strategy Selection," unpublished doctoral dissertation, University of Chicago.

KIRMANI, AMNA and PETER WRIGHT (1987a), "Money Talks: Advertising Extravagance and Perceived Product Quality," working paper, Stanford University.

———, and ——— (1987b), "Schemer Schema: Consumers' Beliefs About Advertising and Marketing Strategies," working paper, Stanford University.

LAIRD, DONALD A. (1932), "How the Consumer Estimates Quality by Subconscious Sensory Impression," *Journal of Applied Psychology,* 16 (2), 241–246.

LAMBERT, ZARRYL (1972), "Price and Choice Behavior," *Journal of Marketing Research,* 9 (February), 35–40.

LANGER, ELLEN (1978), "Rethinking the Role of Thought in Social Interactions," in *New Directions in Attribution Research,* John Harvey, William Ickes, and Robert Kidd, Eds. Hillsdale, NJ: Erlbaum, 35–58.

LEIBOWITZ, ARLENE (1974), "Education and Home Production," *American Economic Review,* 64 (May), 243–250.

LEUTHOLD, JANE (1981), "Taxation and the Consumption of Household Time," *Journal of Consumer Research,* 7 (March), 388–394.

LEWIN, KURT (1936), *Principles of Topological Psychology,* New York: McGraw-Hill.

LINDER, S. B. (1970), *The Harried Leisure Class.* New York: Columbia University Press.

LUTZ, RICHARD (1986), "Quality is as Quality Does: An Attitudinal Perspective on Consumer Quality Judgments," presentation to the Marketing Science Institute Trustees' Meeting, Cambridge, MA.

MABRY, B. D. (1970, "An Analysis of Work and Other Constraints on Choices of Activities, *Western Economic Journal,* (8) 3, 213–225.

MAYNES, E. SCOTT (1976), "The Concept and Measurement of Product Quality," *Household Production and Consumption,* 40 (5), 529-559.

———, and TERJE ASSUM (1982), "Informationally Imperfect Consumer Markets: Empirical Findings and Policy Implications," *Journal of Consumer Affairs,* 16 (Summer), 62-87.

MAZUMDAR, TRIDIK (1986), "Experimental Investigation of the Psychological Determinants of Buyers' Price Awareness and a Comparative Assessment of Methodologies for Retrieving Price Information from Memory," working paper, Virginia Polytechnic Institute and State University.

MAZURSKY, DAVID, and JACOB JACOBY (1985), "Forming Impressions of Merchandise and Service Quality," in *Perceived Quality,* J. Jacoby and J. Olson, Eds. Lexington, MA: Lexington Books, 139-154.

MCCONNELL, J. D. (1968), "Effect of Pricing on Perception of Product Quality," *Journal of Applied Psychology,* 52 (August), 300-303.

MEHROTRA, SUNIL, and JOHN PALMER (1985), "Relating Product Features to Perceptions of Quality: Appliances," in *Perceived Quality,* J. Jacoby and J. Olson, Eds. Lexington, MA: Lexington Books, 81-96.

MILGROM, PAUL, and JOHN ROBERTS (1986), "Price and Advertising Signals of Product Quality," *Journal of Political Economy,* 94 (4), 796-821.

MINCER, J. (1963), "Market Prices, Opportunity Costs, and Income Effects," in *Measurements in Economics: Studies in Mathematical Economics and Econometrics in Memory of Yehuds Grunfeld.* Stanford, CA: Stanford University Press, 67-82.

MONROE, KENT B., and R. KRISHNAN (1985), "The Effect of Price on Subjective Product Evaluations," in *Perceived Quality,* J. Jacoby and J. Olson, Eds. Lexington, MA: Lexington Books, 209-232.

———, and WILLIAM B. DODDS (1988), "A Research Program for Establishing the Validity of the Price-Quality Relationship," *Journal of the Academy of Marketing Science,* forthcoming.

MORGAN, LEONARD A. (1985), "The Importance of Quality," in *Perceived Quality,* J. Jacoby and J. Olson, Eds. Lexington, MA: Lexington Books, 61-64.

MORRIS, BETSY (1985), "How Much Will People Pay to Save a Few Minutes of Cooking? Plenty," *Wall Street Journal* (July 25), 23.

MYERS, JAMES H., and ALLAN D. SHOCKER (1981), "The Nature of Product-Related Attributes," *Research in Marketing,* Vol. 5. Greenwich, CT: JAI Press, Inc., 211-236.

NELSON, PHILIP (1970), "Information and Consumer Behavior," *Journal of Political Economy,* 78 (20), 311-329.

———(1974), "Advertising as Information," *Journal of Political Economy,* 81 (4), 729-754.

NESLIN, SCOTT (1981), "Linking Product Features to Perceptions: Self-Stated Versus Statistically Revealed Importance Weights" *Journal of Marketing Research,* 18 (February), 80-93.

NICHOLS, D., E. SMOLENSKY, and T. N. TIDEMAN (1971), "Discrimination by Waiting Time in Merit Goods," *American Economic Review,* 61 (June), 312-323.

OLSHAVSKY, RICHARD W. (1985), "Perceived Quality in Consumer Decision Making: An Integrated Theoretical Perspective," in *Perceived Quality,* J. Jacoby and J. Olson, Eds. Lexington, MA: Lexington Books, 3-29.

OLSON, JERRY C. (1977), "Price as an Informational Cue: Effects in Product Evaluation," in *Consumer and Industrial Buying Behavior,* Arch G. Woodside, Jagdish N. Sheth, and Peter D. Bennett, Eds. New York: North Holland, 267-286.

———(1978), "Inferential Belief Formation in the Cue Utilization Process," Ann Arbor, MI: Association for Consumer Research, 706-713.

———, and JACOB JACOBY (1972), "Cue Utilization in the Quality Perception Process," in *Proceedings of the Third Annual Conference of the Association for Consumer Research,* M. Venkatesan, Ed. Iowa City: Association for Consumer Research, 167-179.

———, and THOMAS J. REYNOLDS (1983), "Understanding Consumers' Cognitive Structures: Implications for Advertising Strategy," *Advertising and Consumer Psychology,* L. Percy and A. Woodside, Eds. Lexington, MA: Lexington Books.

PARASURMAN, A., VALARIE A. ZEITHAML, and LEONARD BERRY (1985), "A Conceptual Model of Service Quality and Its Implications for Future Research," *Journal of Marketing,* 49 (Fall), 41-50.

———, ———, and ——— (1986), "SERVQUAL: A Scale for Measuring Service Quality," working paper, Marketing Science Institute.

PETERSON, ROBERT A. (1970), "The Price-Perceived Quality Relationship: Experimental Evidence," *Journal of Marketing Research,* 7 (November), 525-528.

———, and A. JOLIBERT (1976), "A Cross-National Investigation of Price Brand Determinants of Perceived Product Quality," *Journal of Applied Psychology,* 61 (July), 533-536.

———, and WILLIAM R. WILSON (1985), "Perceived Risk and Price-Reliance Schema and Price-Perceived-Quality Mediators," in *Perceived Quality,* J. Jacoby and J. Olson, Eds. Lexington, MA: Lexington Books, 247-268.

Progressive Grocer (1964), "How Much Do Customers Know About Retail Prices?" (February), 103-106.

RAO, AKSHAY R. (1987), "The Moderating Effect of Prior Knowledge on Cue Utilization in Product Evaluations," working paper, Department of Marketing and Business Law, University of Minnesota, Minneapolis.

———, and KENT B. MONROE (1987), "The Effects of Price, Brand Name and Store Name on Buyers' Subjective Product Assessments: An Integrative Review," working paper, Department of Marketing and Business Law, University of Minnesota, Minneapolis.

REYNOLDS, T. J., J. GUTMAN, and J. FIEDLER (1984), "Translating Knowledge of Consumers' Cognitive Structures into the Development of Advertising Strategic Operations: A Case History," in *Proceedings: Second Annual Advertising and Consumer Psychology Conference.* Toronto: American Psychological Association.

———, and LINDA F. JAMIESON (1985), "Image Representations: An Analytic Framework," in *Perceived Quality,* J. Jacoby and J. Olson, Eds. Lexington, MA: Lexington Books, 115-138.

RIESZ, P. (1978), "Price Versus Quality in the Marketplace, 1961-1975," *Journal of Retailing,* 54 (4), 15-28.

RIGAUZ-BRICMONT, BENNY (1982), "Influences of Brand Name and Packaging on Perceived Quality," in *Advances in Consumers Research,* Vol. 9, Andrew A. Mitchell, Ed. Ann Arbor, MI: Association for Consumer Research, 472-477.

ROEDDER-JOHN, DEBORAH, CAROL SCOTT, and JAMES BETTMAN (1986), "Sampling Data for Covariation Assessment: The Effect of Prior Beliefs on Search Patterns," *Journal of Consumer Research,* 13 (1), 38-47.

ROKEACH, M. J. (1973), *The Nature of Human Values.* New York: The Free Press.

RUSSELL, BERTRAND (1912), *The Problems of Philosophy.* London: Oxford University Press.

SAWYER, ALAN G. (1975), "Demand Artifacts in Laboratory Experiments in Consumer Research," *Journal of Consumer Research,* 1 (March), 20-30.

———, and PETER DICKSON (1984), "Psychological Perspectives on Consumer Response to Sales Promotion," in *Research on Sales Promotion: Collected Papers,* Katherine Jocz, Ed. Cambridge, MA: Marketing Science Institute.

———, PARKER M. WORTHING, and PAUL E. SENDAK (1979), "The Role of Laboratory Experiments to Test Marketing Strategies," *Journal of Marketing,* 43 (Summer), 60-67.

SCHECHTER, LEN (1984), "A Normative Conception of Value," *Progressive Grocer,* Executive Report, 12-14.

SCHMALENSEE, RICHARD (1978), "A Model of Advertising and Product Quality," *Journal of Political Economy,* 86 (3), 485-503.

——— and J. THISSE (1985), "Perceptual Maps and the Optimal Location of New Products," working paper, Massachusetts Institute of Technology.

SHAPIRO and ASSOCIATES (1985), "Value is a Complex Equation," *Chain Store Age* (May), 14-59.

SHAPIRO, B. P. (1968), "The Psychology of Pricing," *Harvard Business Review,* 46 (July-August), 14-25, 160.

——— (1973), "Price Reliance: Existence and Sources," *Journal of Marketing Research,* 10 (August), 286-294.

SMITH, E. M., and C. BROOME (1966), "Experimental Determination of the Effect of Price and Market-Standing Information on Consumers' Brand Preferences," in *Proceedings.* Chicago: American Marketing Association.

SPROLES, GEORGE B. (1977), "New Evidence on Price and Quality," *Journal of Consumer Affairs,* 11 (Summer), 63-77.

——— (1986), "The Concept of Quality and the Efficiency of Markets: Issues and Comments," *Journal of Marketing,* 13 (June), 146-147.

STAFFORD, J. E., and B. M. ENIS (1969), "The Price-Quality Relationship: An Extension," *Journal of Marketing Research,* 7 (November), 456-458.

STEVENSON, JIM (1984), "An Indifference Toward Value," *Progressive Grocer–Value,* Executive Report, 22-23.

STOKES, RAYMOND C. (1985), "The Effect of Price, Package Design, and Brand Familiarity on Perceived Quality," in *Perceived Quality,* J. Jacoby and J. Olson, Eds. Lexington, MA: Lexington Books, 233–246.

SWAN, JOHN (1974), "Price-Product Performance Competition Between Retailer and Manufacturer Brands," *Journal of Marketing,* 38 (July), 52–59.

SZYBILLO, G. J., and J. JACOBY (1974), "Intrinsic Versus Extrinsic Cues as Determinants of Perceived Product Quality," *Journal of Applied Psychology,* 59 (February), 74–78.

YOUNG, SHIRLEY, and BARBARA FEIGIN (1975), "Using the Benefit Chain for Improved Strategy Formulation," *Journal of Marketing,* 39 (July), 72–74.

ZEITHAML, VALARIE A. (1982), "Consumer Response to In-Store Price Information Environments," *Journal of Consumer Research,* 8 (March), 357–369.

——— (1983), "Conceptualizing and Measuring Consumer Response to Price," in *Advances in Consumer Research,* Vol. 10, R. P. Bagozzi and A. M. Tybout, Eds. Ann Arbor, MI: Association for Consumer Research, 612–616.

——— (1985), "The New Demographics and Market Fragmentation," *Journal of Marketing,* 49 (Summer), 64–75.

———, and LEONARD BERRY (1987), "The Time Consciousness of Supermarket Shoppers," working paper, Texas A&M University.

———, and WILLIAM L. FUERST (1983), "Age Differences in Response to Grocery Store Price Information," *Journal of Consumer Affairs,* 17 (2), 403–420.

3

THE EFFECTS OF PRODUCT CLASS KNOWLEDGE ON INFORMATION SEARCH BEHAVIOR*

Merrie Brucks

The effects of prior knowledge about a product class on various characteristics of prepurchase information search within that product class are examined. A new search task methodology is used that imposes only a limited amount of structure on the search task: subjects are not cued with a list of attributes, and the problem is not structured in a brand-by-attribute matrix. The results indicate that prior knowledge facilitates the acquisition of new information and increases search efficiency. The results also support the conceptual distinction between objective and subjective knowledge.

Many factors, including demographics and prior product class experience, have been studied in an attempt to account for individual differences in consumers' responses to a given set of information (e.g., Capon and Burke 1980; Jacoby, Chestnut, and Fischer 1978; Moore and Lehmann 1980). Drawing on the information processing paradigm, this paper examines the effect of prior knowledge on information search behavior.

The information processing paradigm fo-

*This article was the winning submission of the 1984 Robert Ferber Award for Consumer Research competition for the best interdisciplinary article based on a recent doctoral dissertation. The award is cosponsored by the Association for Consumer Research and the *Journal of Consumer Research*. Reprinted from the *Journal of Consumer Research*, 12 (June 1985), pp. 1–15.

cuses on the cognitive processes that occur after exposure to a stimulus and before the overt behavioral response to that stimulus. A crucial element in the information processing model of human behavior is information stored in memory—i.e., prior knowledge. Much empirical evidence supports the view that prior knowledge affects information processing activities (e.g., Chase and Simon 1973a, 1973b; Chi, Glaser, and Rees 1981; Chiesi, Spilich, and Voss 1979; Larkin et al. 1980).

In consumer behavior research, several studies have examined the effect of variables related to prior knowledge (e.g., familiarity, product experience) on various information processing activities (e.g., Alba 1983; Bettman and Park 1980; Johnson and Russo 1984; Park 1976; Srull 1983). Although each of these studies is theoretically measuring a concept similar to prior knowledge, the measures used differ considerably between studies, posing two problems for research in this area. First, each individual researcher, having no generally accepted measure to use, must develop his or her own measure (or borrow one). Second, it is difficult for researchers to build upon previous work when developing theories, since it is uncertain whether all these measures are measuring the same construct. Thus, one goal of this article is to clarify the meaning and measurement of consumer product class knowledge.

A second goal of this article is to analyze existing laboratory methodologies used to study information search behavior and to propose a new methodology that overcomes many of the limitations of these earlier methodologies. The article's third goal is to examine the effects of product class knowledge on information search behavior, using a new laboratory methodology.

BACKGROUND

Product Class Knowledge

The measures of consumer product class knowledge used in previous studies fall into three categories. The first measures an individual's perception of how much she or he knows (e.g., Gardner 1984; Park and Lessig 1981). The second category measures the amount, type, or organization of what an individual actually has stored in memory (e.g., Kanwar, Olson, and Sims 1981; Russo and Johnson 1980; Staelin 1978). The third category measures the amount of purchasing or usage experience with the product (e.g., Monroe 1976; Marks and Olson 1981).

The last of the three categories is somewhat inconsistent with the information processing approach, which holds that experience affects behavior only when experience results in differences in memory. If different individuals learn different things from similar experiences, then their behaviors are likely to be different. Thus, experience-based measures of knowledge are less directly linked to behavior than are the other types of knowledge measures, especially for product classes in which habit is not a major factor.

Differences between measures of subjective knowledge (i.e., what individuals perceive that they know) and measures of objective knowledge (i.e., what is actually stored in memory) occur when people do not accurately perceive how much or how little they actually know, assuming that the measures are equally sensitive. Of course, measures of objective knowledge can never be entirely objective in themselves. That is, such measures necessarily depend on some form of communication from the individual about his/her knowledge. Nevertheless, it is argued that measures of objective knowledge are conceptually and operationally distinct from measures of subjective knowledge.

Park and Lessig (1981) asserted that subjective knowledge provides a better understanding of decision makers' systematic biases and heuristics than does objective knowledge. Measures of subjective knowledge can indicate self-confidence levels as well as knowledge levels. Perceived self-confidence may affect decision strategies and tactics. For instance, a lack of confidence in one's knowledge might motivate increased search for information, independent of actual knowledge level. It has not been empirically demonstrated, however, that subjective knowledge is a better predictor of decision-making strategy.

Only one study (Rudell 1979) actually compared the effects of objective knowledge (quiz score) and subjective knowledge (self-rating) on information processing activities. Rudell concluded that objective knowledge facilitates deliberation and use of newly acquired information, while subjective knowledge increases the reliance on previously stored information. Neither objective nor subjective knowledge was significantly related to amount of information acquired.

In summary, there is a conceptual distinction between objective and subjective knowledge. Subjective knowledge can be thought of as including an individual's degree of confidence in his/her knowledge, while objective knowledge refers only to what an individual actually knows. It is likely that both of these types of knowledge are related to aspects of information search and decision-making behavior, although probably in different ways. In this article, the effects of objective and subjective measures of product class knowledge on information search behavior are compared.

Search Task Methodology

Most laboratory research has used information display boards (IDBs) to investigate consumer information search. This methodology, pioneered by Jacoby and several colleagues, employs a board that displays product information arranged in a brand-by-attribute matrix. The IDB methodology was an important advance in consumer research because it allowed researchers to trace the information search process and made possible new, more specific measures of search (Jacoby et al. 1976).

The IDB methodology, however, has some significant limitations. Most importantly, IDBs impose a well defined, comprehensive structure on what is often perceived to be an ill structured problem. Specifically, IDBs delimit the size of the brand choice problem by defining the number of available alternatives and attributes. IDBs identify the alternatives and attributes involved, and they structure the alternatives and attributes as a matrix. IDBs actually provide a partial solution to the original brand choice problem, since much of an expert's ability to solve problems lies in his/her ability to form a useful representation of a problem's structure (Chase and Simon 1973a, 1973b; Chi et al. 1981). Thus, the effects of knowledge or expertise on decision-making processes may be obscured by the use of IDBs, which impose a well defined structure.

Alternative Methodology

The methodology described in this section allows the experimental subject to structure the brand choice problem as well as to solve it. In this methodology, information about the attributes of several alternative brands or models is stored in a computer database. Subjects are able to access this database through a user interface that simulates a shopping situation. The alternatives and attributes are not presented in a matrix structure. In fact, the attributes are not presented at all. Rather, using their own words, subjects make inquiries about any attributes they please, and the computer responds to these questions.[1] Thus the contamination of prior knowledge by exposure to a list of product attributes is avoided.

Two methods are available for interpreting the subject's natural language queries: artificial intelligence and unobtrusive human intervention. Artificial intelligence—i.e., computer interpretation of natural language—is currently feasible only when the domain is quite limited and the user is restricted to simple syntactical forms (Barr and Feigenbaum 1981). Unobtrusive intervention uses a hidden experimenter to interpret a subject's query and signal to the computer the correct response. This second method was used in the present study and will be described in more detail later.

The task methodology used for this article

[1]Strictly speaking, the computer is not essential to the methodology. The same task structure could be implemented with human interaction, although this would be more obtrusive.

has greater external validity than IDBs in situations requiring active information search. In the present methodology, the presentation of the information encourages a realistic planning process: as is usually the case prior to making an actual purchase decision, people do not know what information will be available or how complete it will be. Furthermore, the individual determines for him/herself what information is relevant and how that information should be structured. On the other hand, the present methodology has some of the limitations that have been ascribed to IDBs. For example, subjects may modify their behavior when they know they are being observed (Bettman 1977). Other limitations of the present methodology relate to its lack of control on internal information search (i.e., retrieval of information from memory), its lack of direct measurement of internal processing of information, and its lack of accidental exposure to information (Arch, Bettman, and Kakkar 1978). These characteristics limit the applicability of both the IDBs and the methodology used in this study.

Prior Knowledge and Information Search

A number of studies have found a negative relationship between amount of product experience and amount of external search (Anderson, Engledow, and Becker 1979; Katona and Mueller 1955; Moore and Lehmann 1980; Newman and Staelin 1971, 1972; Swan 1969). One explanation for these results claims that experienced consumers have prior knowledge about the attributes of various alternatives, and consequently do not need to acquire such information from external sources. However, a second explanation for these results holds that experienced consumers perform more efficient (thus abbreviated) information searches because they know which attributes are the most useful for discriminating between brands and can more quickly determine which alternatives are inferior. Concurrently, a number of other studies have postulated that prior knowledge encourages information search by making it easier to process new information (Johnson and Russo 1984; Punj and Staelin 1983). For example, knowledge of product attributes may allow the individual to formulate more questions. Knowledge also helps the individual evaluate responses to questions, thus reducing the cognitive cost of using information and increasing the benefit of obtaining it, leading to greater search with increased knowledge. Such a hypothesis may explain the results of studies that have found a positive relationship between experience and amount of search (e.g., Jacoby et al. 1978).

Given such contradictory results and theories, it is not surprising that other studies have produced results that found an inverted-U shaped relationship between prior knowledge and information search (Bettman and Park 1980; Hempel 1969; Johnson and Russo 1984) or no relationship at all (Bennett and Mandell 1969; Claxton, Fry, and Portis 1974). The inverted-U relationship is particularly appealing because it provides an explanation for the inconsistent findings in the literature. The inverted U indicates a positive relationship between prior knowledge and information search at low-to-moderate levels of knowledge/experience and a negative relationship at moderate-to-high levels. A positive or negative relationship or no effects at all can result when a linear regression line is imposed on inverted-U shaped data. However, Punj and Staelin (1983) explicitly tested their data for an inverted-U shaped function and found only a negative, linear relationship between search and "usable prior knowledge"—i.e., knowledge directly associated with the available choice alternatives.

In sum, the findings regarding the relationship between experience and amount of information search have been inconsistent. Various theories have been proposed to account for these findings, but none has been directly tested. In this study, several explanations concerning the relationship between prior knowledge and amount of information search are directly tested. Only through an understanding of the mechanics of these explanations can this relationship be fully understood.

HYPOTHESES

Three explanations for the relationship between prior knowledge and amount of external information search were reviewed above. The first was that knowledgeable consumers substitute internal search for external search, thus reducing their amount of external search. By using unknown, hypothetical brands rather than actual brands we were able to rule out this explanation in the present study. If a negative relationship is found between knowledge and search, it can be more confidently attributed to the second explanation: knowledgeable consumers search more efficiently.

To test this explanation more directly, two dependent variables were examined: variability of search and appropriateness of search. Both of these variables indicate early elimination of unsatisfactory alternatives. High variability may result from using criteria stored in memory to eliminate inferior alternatives early in the search process. Variability of search is operationalized as the standard deviation of the amount of information acquired across alternatives (Payne 1976). Thus it is hypothesized that:

> **H1:** Product class knowledge is positively related to variability of search.

A high degree of appropriate search may result when the available alternatives are first judged on the basis of whether they are appropriate for the intended usage situation, reserving further search for those that are deemed appropriate. (Evidence that knowledgeable consumers recognize product alternatives as belonging to categories and subcategories is found in Sujan 1985.)

> **H2:** Product class knowledge is negatively related to the amount of search on inappropriate alternatives relative to the total amount of search.

Hypotheses 1 and 2 are related, since discriminating among alternatives on the basis of appropriateness results in high variability of search. However, high variability of search can also result from search strategies that discriminate among alternatives on other bases, such as attribute values.

Efficiency in information search may occur in attribute selection as well as in alternative selection. Specifically, highly knowledgeable consumers may search only those attributes that are useful for discriminating among alternatives. High knowledge predicts a negative relationship between knowledge and a number of attributes examined. On the other hand, a positive relationship between knowledge and number of attributes examined is predicted by the "knowledge facilitates information search" explanation. Specifically, knowledge allows one to ask more questions and increases the benefit/cost ratio of doing so. If both the efficiency and facilitating explanations are true, an inverted-U shaped relationship may result. Since there is no reason to predict the dominance of one explanation over another, the direction of this relationship is not hypothesized.

> **H3:** Product class knowledge is related to number of attributes examined. This relationship may be negative, positive, or inverted-U shaped.

If knowledge facilitates new learning, then consumers low in knowledge might be expected to seek summary information (e.g., wholistic dealer evaluations of the alternatives) to a greater degree than consumers high in knowledge, who are better able to acquire and integrate information about specific attributes. The relationship between product class knowledge and number of dealer evaluations sought only applies when summary information is believed to be less reliable than attribute information. Otherwise, knowledgeable people have little reason not to use summary information.

> **H4:** Product class knowledge is negatively related to the number of dealer evaluations acquired relative to the total amount of search.

Intended Usage Situation. The relationship between knowledge and amount of question asking (a type of information search behavior) appears to interact with the complexity of the situational context, according to Miyake and Norman (1979). They found that knowledge increases the number of questions asked when the context is relatively complex and requires specific domain knowledge in order to be understood, but the number of questions asked decreases when the context is relatively simple. In light of this issue, this study manipulated situational complexity through scenarios that described either a complex usage situation or a simple one. Subjects searched for information in order to choose a brand destined to be used by an expert for complex tasks or by a novice for simple tasks. Reasoning that differences between knowledgeable and less knowledgeable people should be stronger in situations where knowledge is important, it was hypothesized that the knowledge effects predicted in Hypothesis 1 through Hypothesis 4 would be greater in the complex usage situation than in the simple one.

H5: The relationships between the product class knowledge and search characteristics hypothesized in Hypothesis 1 through Hypothesis 4 are greater in a complex, expert usage situation than in a simple, novice usage situation.

Objective vs. Subjective Knowledge. Hypotheses 1–5 were derived with objective knowledge in mind As discussed earlier, subjective knowledge refers to how much people think they know. Subjective knowledge differs from objective knowledge when people are over- or under-confident about their actual knowledge level. To the extent that subjective knowledge is empirically separable from objective knowledge, different results may be expected when subjective knowledge is used as the independent variable.

For purposes of discussion, assume for a moment that subjective knowledge is independent of objective knowledge; i.e., that people's perceptions of what they know are unrelated to their actual knowledge level. If this were true, subjective knowledge would not affect the ability to formulate questions or the benefit/cost ratio of acquiring information. Furthermore, it would not affect the ability to classify brand alternatives into usage categories. On the other hand, subjective knowledge might affect choice of search strategy. Specifically, people high in subjective knowledge might be quick to rule out alternatives they believe to be inferior and might prefer to avoid relying on dealer opinions. In sum, it is predicted that only objective knowledge is related to aspects of search behavior requiring ability, and that both objective and subjective knowledge are related to aspects of search involving overall strategy. This discussion is consistent with that found in Park and Lessig (1981). Empirically, however, the degree to which objective and subjective knowledge differentially predict search behavior is a function of their correlation as well as a function of the above theory.

H6, H7: Subjective knowledge is positively related to variability of search and negatively related to search for dealer evaluations—two indicators of search strategy.

H8, H9: Compared to objective knowledge, subjective knowledge is less strongly related to number of attributes examined and amount of inappropriate search, two variables that are hypothesized to primarily depend on ability arising from actual memory content.

H10: Interactions between subjective knowledge and usage situation are weaker than those between objective knowledge and usage situation, since subjective knowledge is about equally useful in both situations.

METHOD

Overview

Three independent variables were used in this study: objective knowledge, subjective knowledge, and intended usage situation. Because experimentally induced knowledge may be stored and used differently than naturally occurring knowledge, only the intended usage situation was experimentally manipulated. Several measures were developed to assess objective and subjective knowledge.

Subjects

The subjects for the study were recruited from a consumer panel, whose members were demographically representative of the large, northeastern metropolitan area in which the panel was located. Because the study required subjects to come to the laboratory, only the 150 panel members who lived within an eight mile radius of the laboratory were contacted. Of these, 36 agreed to participate. The low participation rate was probably due to the perceived difficulty of negotiating city traffic and finding parking spaces near the laboratory. Four of these subjects had difficulties understanding the computerized search task and were dropped from analyses of search task variables. Three other subjects did not complete substantial portions of the objective knowledge measure and were dropped from analyses involving this measure. Twenty-nine subjects successfully completed all major aspects of the task.

All of the 32 subjects who successfully completed the task were female. Six subjects (19 percent) were black, the remainder white. The subjects varied widely in age, income, education, and product category knowledge. Although this sample was quite heterogeneous, the subjects tended to be older and better educated than the average United States resident. Only 9.4 percent did not graduate from high school, while 56.3 percent reported at least some college education. Fifty percent of the sample was over 45 years of age. Fifty percent of the women worked full time—close to the national average.

Product

Several different criteria were used in selecting the product category. First, the product category had to be one where buyers ordinarily conduct some prepurchase information search. Second, the subject population had to exhibit a high degree of variance in their prior knowledge about the product category, since prior knowledge was not manipulated. Third, the brand choice decision needed to be contingent on the intended usage situation—i.e., alternative brands should differ in their functionality. And last, the product category should be relatively impersonal (i.e., taste and style should be relatively unimportant) because subjects would not have an opportunity to see the product during the search task. Using a survey of 22 university staff members, five product categories were pretested: sewing machines, microwave ovens, food processors, steam irons, and electric typewriters. The product category of sewing machines best fit the above criteria and was chosen for use in the study.

Procedure

A laboratory session appointment was scheduled for each individual subject after she had completed and returned a mailed questionnaire that contained measures of the subject's objective and subjective knowledge.[2] Each subject completed another questionnaire when she arrived at the laboratory, typically spending about 30 minutes doing so. The subject then received instructions on how to use a video terminal and was given paper and a pen to allow note-taking during the search task.[3] The subjects gained experience in using the computer by first shopping for an unrelated product (irons). The subjects did not go on to the sewing machine task until they indicated that they understood how the computer task worked. The experimenter followed the subjects' progress during the task by using video and audio

[2]This questionnaire was mailed to 47 people who earlier had indicated a willingness to participate in the study. Thirty-nine were returned, and 36 people participated in the laboratory task.

[3]The note pad served as an external memory device; thus relatively few pieces of information were requested twice by the same subject. The decision process was not exclusively stimulus-based or memory-based; rather, there were elements of both.

monitoring devices in an adjoining room, unseen by the subject. Subjects' procedural questions were communicated to the experimenter by intercom; the answers were also relayed by intercom. The subjects took from 30 to 90 minutes to complete the computer search task; the average time was about 50 minutes. Another questionnaire, which took between 10 and 30 minutes to complete, was administered after the completion of the search task. Thus, the total time a subject spent in the laboratory ranged from 1 to 3 hours. These sessions took place over a two and one-half week period.

Four weeks after the last laboratory session, a final questionnaire was mailed to the participating subjects. Subjects were compensated for returning the mailed questionnaires using the panel's point system; points could later be used to buy items. Each subject also received fifteen dollars in cash for the laboratory participation. Previous experience with this methodology has indicated that extrinsic motivation is not necessary to ensure that the task is taken seriously; thus no monetary rewards were offered for "better" decisions.

Task Description

The task was designed to allow the subjects to use their prior knowledge about the product category (other than knowledge about specific brands) much as they would in an actual purchase situation. Realistic aspects of the shopping situation were included in the task to encourage the subjects to feel as though they were really shopping. Aspects of realism were not introduced, however, if they would interfere with the primary goal of measuring the impact of prior knowledge on search behavior. Thus, the task was structured to prevent subjects from acquiring new knowledge about the product category (as opposed to knowledge about specific brands) while executing the task. The objective of the task was to select the best sewing machine for a person whose needs were described to the subjects. Initially, the subjects did not know how many models were available and had no information about them. They were, however, given the opportunity to search for information using an interactive computer program, which simulated a shopping situation. A high speed terminal and a VAX computer were used for the experiment.

Stores. To learn what models were available and to obtain information about them the subjects had to contact one or more stores. In the initial instructions, subjects were told that there were four stores and that these stores differed in their price levels and distance from home. The subjects were not told the price levels of each of the stores, but they were informed of the travel times necessary to reach each store every time they made a decision to visit a store. Travel time was represented as a 20, 40, 60, or 80 second wait for information—important differences according to pretest subjects. Stores could be contacted in two ways: "phone calls" and "store visits." Phone calls did not involve transportation time and thus were significantly faster to make; however, the type and amount of information per phone call was limited. Specifically, only one question was allowed per phone call, and no requests for dealer evaluation were allowed.

Choice Alternatives. Six sewing machine models comprised the set of choice alternatives. Three of these models were designed to be appropriate for an expert sewer with complex needs and the other three for a novice sewer with only simple needs. For example, the expert-type machines were more complex, had more built-in features, and were more expensive than the novice-type machines. The differences between the two types of machines were based on distinctions made in sewing books (e.g., Hollis 1968; Schreiber and Houch 1972). To learn the total number of sewing machine models available for the task, the subjects needed to ask each store in the task which models it carried. Each of the six models was carried by three of the four stores.

Information. In addition to asking a store which models it carried, subjects could request information about an attribute of a particular model and/or request a salesperson's overall evaluation of a particular model. The subjects were informed that different salespeople often evaluate the same brand differently and were reminded of this every time they decided which type of information to request. Thus, using dealer evaluations could simplify the decision task for the subjects, but the information was perceived as somewhat unreliable.

To request information about an attribute of a particular model, the subjects were first asked to specify which model they were interested in and then asked to type their question on the terminal keyboard. Subjects were not prompted with a list of sewing machine attributes. Instead, they used their own knowledge about sewing machine attributes to acquire information about the hypothetical models. The hidden experimenter read the subject's questions on a video monitor. Responses to 100 possible questions about each of the six models were stored in the computer's database. The experimenter matched the subject's question to the set of 100 possible questions and typed a number associated with the appropriate response into a terminal (which was connected to the subject's computer). The subject's terminal then displayed the response to her question. To the subject, it appeared that the computer had understood and responded to her question. Forty-nine different attributes were examined by the pool of subjects; however, only 11 attributes were examined by five or more subjects, indicating a great deal of idiosyncrasy in the choice of attributes to be examined. Six percent of the subjects' questions did not match any of the predetermined questions. In these cases, the subjects were notified by computer that the requested information was not available.

Independent Variables

Usage Situation. Prior to starting the search task, subjects were randomly given one of two descriptions of a person and her sewing needs and were told to choose the best model for that person. Half of the subjects received the description of a frequent and expert sewer. The other half received the description of an infrequent sewer with simple needs. An open-ended question administered immediately after the search task revealed that all the subjects were able to recall accurately at least two facts about the intended usage situation. Since each choice alternative was constructed to be appropriate for only one usage situation, this manipulation allowed us to investigate the extent to which subjects search for and choose appropriate alternatives. A disadvantage of this manipulation was that subjects may not have been motivated to make an economical decision, since the scenarios did not emphasize cost considerations.

Objective Knowledge. Several different measures were used to operationalize objective knowledge. First, a set of free response questions was developed and pretested to measure several aspects of sewing machine knowledge including terminology, available attributes, criteria for evaluating attributes, perceived covariance between attributes, and factors of sewing usage situations that determine attribute importance. These aspects of product class knowledge were found to comprise 73 percent of all knowledge statements elicited in an earlier study (Brucks 1984).[4] Because answers to free response questions may be influenced by the subjects' degree of articulateness and verbosity, a second set of questions using a relatively structures response format was developed and pretested. Pretest data from the first set of questions were used to develop response choices for this second set of questions.

As noted previously, four questionnaires were used to administer the objective knowledge questions. With one exception, the free response questions were administered prior to the task. All of the structured response questions were administered after the task. A question was assigned to one of the questionnaires by estimating the likelihood the question had of being contaminated by, or contaminating, the task or other knowledge questions. (The questions used to measure objective knowledge are discussed in more detail in the Appendix.)

Scores for these questions were rescaled to a

[4]The other classifications of knowledge were facts about brands (6 percent), knowledge about purchasing procedures (9 percent), knowledge of personal experiences with the product (10 percent), and other (2 percent).

common range. However, to retain the information provided by measure variance, the variances were not rescaled. First, question scores were summed to produce scores for each of the five aspects of knowledge. The correlations between these scores were moderately high, ranging from 0.31 to 0.64 (all statistically significant at $p < 0.05$). These results support the utility of capturing these different aspects of knowledge, but discourage any attempt to examine the marginal effects of each of these types of knowledge. Table 3.1 displays the correlation matrix. It appears that we may have been overly cautious in using both free and structured response scales. The summation of the scores obtained with the free response method correlated 0.80 with that obtained with the structured response method. The measure of objective knowledge used in this article was obtained by collapsing all the scores into one scale. However, one of the items did not contribute to coefficient alpha and was subsequently dropped from the scale, resulting in a new coefficient alpha of 0.86.[5] The measure of objective knowledge ranged from 4.3 to 13.6 out of a possible 20. The scale mean was 8.9, and the standard deviation was 2.7.

Subjective Knowledge. Two measures of subjective knowledge were included in the first questionnaire. The first measure asked the subject to use a seven-point semantic differential scale to respond to the following statement: "Rate your knowledge of sewing machines, as compared to the average woman." The differential scale was anchored at the low end by "One of the LEAST knowledgeable" and at the high end by "One of the MOST knowledgeable." The second measure, included on a separate page, asked the subject to use a seven-point semantic differential scale to respond to the following: "Circle one of the numbers below to describe your familiarity with sewing machines." The anchors for this scale were "Not at all familiar" and "Extremely familiar." Responses to these questions were summed to form one scale with a coefficient alpha of 0.91. This measure of subjective knowledge correlates 0.54 ($p < 0.01$) with the measure of objective knowledge previously discussed.

Dependent Variables

The dependent variables were the number of different attributes examined, the percentage of inquiries that requested a dealer evaluation, the standard deviation of the number of inquiries made about each of the alternatives of which the subject was aware, and the proportion of search spent on alternatives that were inappropriate for the intended usage situation. Recall that three of the alternatives were designed for complex sewing needs and the other three for simple needs; thus, which alternatives were deemed inappropriate depended on which usage scenario a subject had read. This last measure controlled for the subject's propensity to

[5]The excluded item was the structured question on price attribute covariation. It reduced coefficient alpha by 0.04.

TABLE 3.1 Correlations Between Knowledge Types

	Terminology	*Available Attributes*	*Criteria for Evaluation*	*Attribute Covariation*
Terminology	–			
Available attributes	.64	–		
Criteria for evaluation	.47	.50	–	
Attribute covariation	.62	.61	.46	–
Usage situations	.60	.61	.31	.51

search and for the number of inappropriate alternatives examined by dividing the number of inquiries made about inappropriate alternatives by the number of inappropriate alternatives examined, and then dividing the result by the average number of pieces of information acquired for each appropriate alternative. Thus, a value of one means that the subject acquired an equal amount of information on appropriate and inappropriate alternatives. Values less than one indicate less search on inappropriate alternatives.

RESULTS AND DISCUSSION

General Search Task Behavior

The task employed in this study has not been used before; consequently, one would want to know (1) how easily the subjects learned to use this task, and (2) whether the subjects' task behavior differed markedly from search behaviors reported in other studies. Although the task is quite complex, it appears that it can be mastered by subjects with varying degrees of education and intelligence. Of the 36 subjects who attempted the task, 32 were able to complete it successfully. Immediately after the task, subjects were asked if "the way you chose the sewing machine in this experiment is similar to or different from the way you would choose a sewing machine for a friend in real life." The mean response was 1.9, measured on a 7-point scale where 1 was "very similar" and 7 was "very different," indicating that subjects not only understood the task but found it realistic as well.

Comparing search behavior in this task to aspects of search behavior described in field studies results in certain insights. Compared to field studies, subjects in this study visited fewer stores but considered more brands. Although the number of subjects visiting only one store (44 percent) is consistent with the literature (Newman (1977) generalizes that for major durables this percentage is usually between 40 and 60), only 3 percent (i.e., one subject) visited more than three stores (whereas Newman and Staelin (1972) found that 23 percent visited more than three stores). While this discrepancy may suggest that the subjects in this study were somewhat less concerned with price comparisons than were the shoppers in Newman and Staelin's study, it does not indicate that subjects were unconcerned with price. All but one subject requested information about price during the search task, and 47 percent of the subjects asked for two or more price quotations for their chosen brand. In this study, 69 percent of the subjects used the phone to contact stores, thus reducing the need for visitation. Subjects who used the phone made an average of 8.3 calls each.

The average subject in this study examined 3.9 models. Only one person considered just one model. In contrast, Dommermuth (1965) found that between 41 and 71 percent of household appliance purchasers examined only one brand. The difference between our results and Dommermuth's was expected, however, since the present study used hypothetical brands. Thus, the subject could not use prior brand knowledge to narrow down the set of available brands. Alternatively, demand artifacts may account for the larger number of brands examined in our study. However, this explanation is less appealing since the number of stores visited was not similarly increased.

Tests of Hypotheses

Plan of Analysis. First the data were analyzed for the presence of interaction effects (Hypothesis 5) by estimating ordinary least squares (OLS) regression equations, using objective knowledge, usage situation, and the interaction between knowledge and usage situation as the three independent variables. (Because usage situation is a dummy variable, testing for an interaction effect is equivalent to estimating a separate regression for each situation and then testing whether the slopes of these regressions are equal.) If the interaction were not statistically significant for a particular dependent variable, the data were pooled and estimated as one regression to test Hypotheses 1 through 4. An alpha level of 0.10 was used as the criterion in these tests, yielding a power level of 0.73 to detect a medium effect size (Cohen 1977).

To test Hypotheses 6 through 10, regression equations were estimated that were identical in form to those described above, substituting subjective knowledge for objective knowledge. Then for each dependent variable, the regression equations for objective knowledge and subjective knowledge were stacked to form a restricted model—i.e., the coefficients in the objective equation were constrained to be equal to the coefficients in the subjective knowledge equation. This model was then compared to the unrestricted model—i.e., separate estimations for objective and subjective knowledge—using an F-test. The presentation of the data analysis results is organized around the hypotheses. Tables 3.2 and 3.3 present the relevant regression coefficients. The figure displays the significant interaction effects.

TABLE 3.2 Regression Coefficients for Objective Knowledge*

	Complex Usage Situation		Simple Usage Situation			
Dependent Variable	*Intercept*	*Slope Coefficient*	*Intercept*	*Slope Coefficient*	*Overall F Statistic*	R^2
Number of attributes	−.035	.537[c]	4.140	.030	3.356[c]	.287
Variability of search[b]	.619	.201[c]	1.438	.047	3.983[c]	.323
Inappropriate search	1.224	−.067[c]	.751	.021	3.290[c]	.291

[a]The overall F statistic and R^2 were computed for the regression model: dependent = $\beta + \beta_1$ (usage situation) + β_2 (knowledge) + β_2 (interaction between knowledge and usage situation). The intercepts and slope coefficients shown in this table can be derived from this model because usage situation is a dummy variable. Degrees of freedom for the overall F tests were 3,25 except for amount of inappropriate search (3,24). Results of statistical tests are not reported for the intercepts.

[b]Two-tailed tests were performed for this variable.

[c]Significant at $p < 0.05$

TABLE 3.3 Regression Coefficients for Subjective Knowledge*

Dependent Variable	Intercept	Usage Situation Coefficient[b]	Slope Coefficient	Overall F Statistic[c]	R^2
Dealer evaluations	1.016	−.064	−.032[e]	1.774	.109
Number of attributes[d]	3.902	−.481	.161	.784	.051
Variability of search	1.737	−.440[f]	.098[e]	2.705[f]	.157
Inappropriate search	.925 (complex)		−.044 (complex)[f]	4.350[e]	.326
	.585 (simple)	N.A.[g]	.062 (simple)		

[a]Except for inappropriate search, the regression model was: dependent = $\beta_e + \beta_1$ (usage situation) + β_2 (knowledge.) Since usage situation is a dummy variahble, β_1 represents a mean shift. Since the knowledge × usage situation interaction was significant for inappropriate search, the model estimated for this dependent variable was identical in form to those in Table 2. Results of statistical tests are not reported for the intercepts.

[b]A negative sign indicates that the mean for the complex usage situation is higher than that for the simple usage situation.

[c]Data for this analysis were complete for 32 subjects; thus the degrees of freedom for the overall *F* test were 2,29—except for inappropriate search (3,27).

[d]Two-tailed tests were performed for this variable.

[e]Significant at $p < 0.05$.

[f]Significant at $p < 0.10$.

[g]Not applicable in this equation.

Variability and Appropriateness of Search. Hypothesis 1 states that search variability increases as objective knowledge increases. Hypothesis 2 states that the degree of inappropriate search—i.e., search for alternatives that are inappropriate for the usage situation—decreases as objective knowledge increases. Hypothesis 5 states that the relationships between search variability and objective knowledge and appropriate search and objective knowledge are stronger in a complex usage situation than in a simple usage situation. The regression analysis previously described supported all three hypotheses.

The interaction between knowledge and usage situation was significant ($p < 0.10$) for both search characteristics, indicating that the usage situations should be analyzed separately. In the complex usage situation, objective knowledge was positively related to variability of search ($p < 0.05$) and negatively related to degree of inappropriate search ($p < 0.05$), as hypothesized. These findings are not unrelated, since a search strategy that quickly eliminates inappropriate alternatives results in higher variability than no screening strategy at all. The results suggest that high knowledge subjects screen alternatives on the basis of appropriateness and perhaps other criteria as well. Low knowledge subjects, on the other hand, do not use appropriateness or any other criterion to screen alternatives. Thus, knowledge appears to increase search efficiency by allowing faster recognition of poor or inappropriate alternatives.[6] These findings apply only to the complex usage situation; none of the regression coefficients was significant in the simple usage situation.

Number of Attributes Examined. Hypothesis 3 states that the number of attributes examined is related to objective knowledge; it does not specify the direction or form of this relationship. Hypothesis 5 states that the relationship between knowledge and number of attributes examined is stronger in a complex usage situation than in a simple usage situation. Regression analysis found a statistically significant coefficient for the knowledge × usage situation interaction ($p < 0.10$), indicating that the usage situations should be analyzed separately.

In the complex usage situation, objective knowledge was linearly and positively related to number of attributes examined ($p < 0.05$, two-tailed). In the simple usage situation, objective knowledge did not have a statistically significant linear relationship with number of attributes examined. A visual examination of the data, as well as polynomial and piecemeal regression, failed to support an inverted-U shaped relationship between knowledge and number of attributes examined in either usage situation. Thus, the results confirm the hypothesis that knowledge facilitates the asking of questions about the attributes of alternatives in a complex usage situation. The competing hypothesis—that highly knowledgeable consumers may be more discriminating in their use of attributes—was not supported.

Requests for Dealer Evaluations. Hypothesis 4 states that the number of dealer evaluations acquired (expressed as a percentage of the total amount of information acquired) decreases as objective knowledge increases. Hypothesis 5 states that the dealer evaluation-objective knowledge relationship is stronger in a complex usage situation than in a simple usage situation. Neither hypothesis was supported by the data. The interaction coefficient was not significant ($p > 0.20$), so the data were pooled across usage situations, and a new regression was estimated. The coefficient for knowledge was not significant in this equation either (slope coefficient = -0.02; $p > 0.20$). Apparently, people chose to use dealer evaluations for reasons based on factors other than their level of objective knowledge.

Discussion of Objective Knowledge and Search. In only the complex usage situation did

[6] Although one might argue that less knowledgeable subjects were simply unaware of the distinction between appropriate and inappropriate alternatives, none of the subjects in the expert usage situation actually chose an inappropriate alternative. Thus it is likely that less knowledgeable subjects do make a distinction between appropriate and inappropriate alternatives, but take longer to distinguish which is which.

objective product class knowledge have a statistically significant effect on search characteristics. In this situation, knowledge was associated with seeking information about a larger number of attributes, indicating that knowledge facilitates the asking of attribute questions. Knowledge was also associated with seeking less information about inappropriate alternatives. Finally, subjects with objective product class knowledge used a pattern of search that exhibited a greater degree of variance in the number of questions asked about the known alternatives; this degree of variance, in conjunction with the result concerning inappropriate search, indicates greater search efficiency.

Explanations for the inverted-U shaped relationships between knowledge and total amount of search have hypothesized that the initial upward-sloping part of the curve is due to the facilitating effect of a moderate level of knowledge and that the downward-sloping part is due to increased efficiency and/or increased use of internal search (Bettman and Park 1980; Johnson and Russo 1984). The results reported here support the "facilitating" and "efficiency" explanations but do not address the "internal search" explanations since hypothetical brands were used.

The finding that knowledge increases both efficiency of search and ability to ask questions does not necessarily imply that the relationship between knowledge and total amount of search is always an inverted-U shape. The actual form of this relationship could be negative, flat, positive, or nonlinear, depending on which of the effects is the stronger and which occurs at the earlier stages of knowledge acquisition. In this study the attributes had to be recalled from memory rather than chosen from a display board, so we might expect that the facilitating effect would be particularly strong. In fact, in this study the relationship between knowledge and total amount of search was positive and linear (slope coefficient = 1.07; $p < 0.05$, two-tailed), and there was no evidence to support an inverted-U relationship. The interaction between knowledge and usage situation was not significant, so this relationship is based on data pooled across usage situations.

Subjective Knowledge. Hypotheses 6–10 state that subjective knowledge differs from objective knowledge in its effects on variability of search, inappropriateness of search, number of attributes examined, and dealer evaluations examined. However, tests to determine whether the estimated regression coefficients using subjective knowledge differed significantly from the estimated regression coefficients using objective knowledge did not produce any significant differences. Nevertheless, one might wonder whether analyzing the data for subjective knowledge effects would lead to the same conclusions that we drew for objective knowledge. In fact, such an analysis did lead to some different conclusions, as Table 3.3 indicates.

Hypotheses 6 and 7 state that subjective knowledge is positively related to search variability and negatively related to search for dealer evaluations, two indicators of search strategy. The regression analysis supported these two hypotheses ($p < 0.05$) for both usage situations. The interaction between subjective knowledge and usage situation was not significant ($p > 0.20$). These results contrast with those for objective knowledge, which did not have a significant effect on search for dealer evaluations in either usage situation and which affected search variability only in the complex usage condition. (See Figure 3.1 on page 68.)

Hypotheses 8 and 9 state that variables that are expected to depend primarily on actual memory content—i.e., number of attributes examined and inappropriateness of search—are less strongly related to subjective knowledge than to objective knowledge. As discussed previously, the regression coefficients for subjective knowledge did not differ significantly from regression coefficients for objective knowledge. However, analyzing subjective knowledge effects on these dependent variables did lead to an important conclusion that contrasts with the conclusions drawn for objective knowledge. Specifically, subjective knowledge was not significantly related to the number of attributes examined.[7] This finding is consistent with the

[7]Curvilinear analysis did not support an inverted-U relationship.

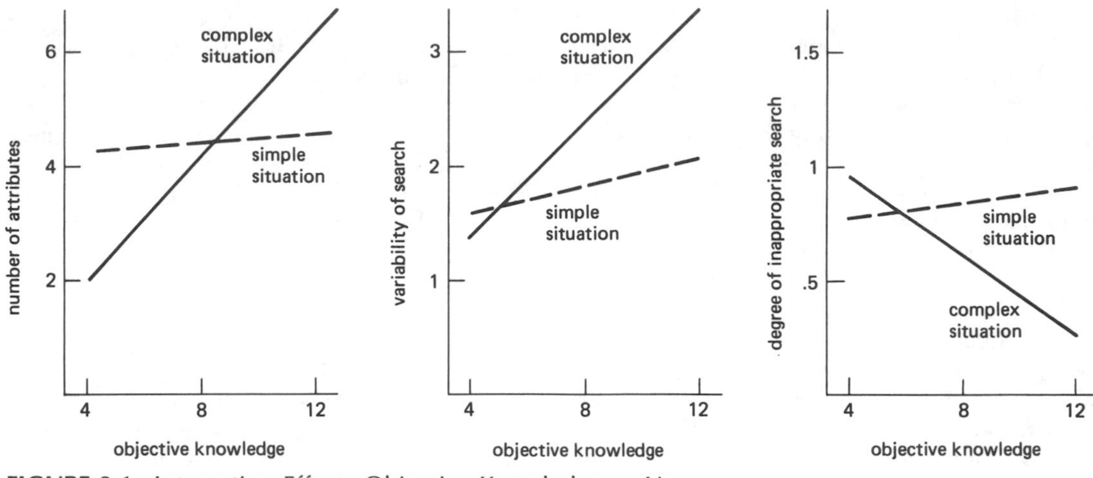

FIGURE 3.1 Interaction Effects Objective Knowledge × Usage Situation

theory that the number of attributes examined is determined primarily by actual memory content—i.e., objective knowledge. The finding for inappropriateness of search is analogous to the earlier finding. Knowledge was negatively related to inappropriateness of search ($p < 0.10$), but only in the complex usage situations (interaction significant at $p < 0.05$).

Discussion of Subjective Knowledge and Search. Individuals high in subjective knowledge appear to be efficient searchers. In both usage situations, these individuals appear to eliminate a subset of alternatives early in the process. In the complex usage situation, the alternatives that are quickly eliminated tend to be ones that are inappropriate for that usage situation. Other criteria are used to eliminate alternatives in the simple usage situation.

The facilitating effect of subjective knowledge is a greater reliance on one's own evaluation skills but not increased attribute search. Subjective knowledge appears to discourage reliance on dealer evaluations. This result indicates that the decision to use dealer evaluations is based more on an individual's perception of his/her ability to deal with attribute information than on actual information processing limitations arising from insufficient knowledge.[8] In situations where dealer evaluations are perceived to be highly credible, however, individuals high in subjective knowledge may be more willing to rely on dealer evaluations.

Subjective knowledge was unrelated to the number of attributes examined. Thus it appears that the number of attributes examined is determined more by actual memory content than by the individual's perception of his/her knowledge level.[9] As in the case for objective knowledge, the relationship between subjective knowledge and total amount of search

[8]One might also conjecture that this result was due to a demand artifact; namely, that high-knowledge subjects felt compelled to avoid dealer evaluations in order to appear consistent with their self-rating. This explanation is unlikely, however, since the self-rating scales were filled out weeks in advance and were only a small part of a long questionnaire.

[9]It should be noted that the significant effect for objective knowledge on variability of search may be due, in part, to the restricted number of attributes that less knowledgeable subjects examined. Similarly, range restrictions may have contributed to the lack of significant findings for variability of search in the simple usage situation. The results for the effect of subjective knowledge on variability of search are not subject to these alternative explanations, however, since this effect was significant in both usage situations and also because subjective knowledge was not significantly related to the number of attributes examined.

was not described by an inverted U. When modeled as a linear relationship, the coefficient for subjective knowledge was positive but statistically insignificant ($p > 0.10$).

SUMMARY AND CONCLUSIONS

Explanations for the inverted-U shaped relationship between knowledge and total amount of search have hypothesized that knowledge facilitates the learning of new information and that knowledge allows more efficient searching (Bettman and Park 1980; Johnson and Russo 1984). The results reported here support these hypotheses (at least in complex usage situations), but not the inverted-U shaped relationship itself.

In this study, objective knowledge was associated with seeking information about a greater number of attributes, indicating that knowledge facilitates the asking of attribute questions. Objective knowledge was also associated with seeking less information about inappropriate alternatives and with using a pattern of search that exhibits a greater degree of variance in the number of questions asked about the considered alternatives (indicating greater search efficiency). These results were significant only in the complex usage situation, which supports Miyake and Norman's (1979) proposition that "To ask a question, one must know enough to know what is not known." A simple usage situation does not necessarily require advanced product class knowledge.

Some evidence was generated for the conceptual distinction between objective and subjective knowledge. Specifically, it was found that only objective knowledge was significantly related to the number of attributes examined, and only subjective knowledge was significantly related to the tendency to request dealer opinions rather than attribute information. These findings are consistent with the view that subjective knowledge is closely related to confidence in one's decision-making abilities (with reference to the specific product category). While measures of subjective knowledge are undeniably easier to use, the result obtained may not be a valid measure of knowledge actually stored in memory. Furthermore, subjective knowledge appears to affect information processing activities differently than objective knowledge.

As is typical of studies involving knowledge or expertise (e.g., Johnson and Russo 1984; Sujan 1985), the knowledge level of the subjects in this study was not experimentally manipulated. Thus one could reason that variables related to knowledge might be driving the results. Specifically, motivational variables such as interest or involvement in the product class are likely to covary with knowledge and might be expected to influence search behavior. It is argued, however, that the constructs of objective and subjective knowledge provide a more convincing explanation of the whole set of results than do motivational constructs. Theoretically, one would expect that motivation always increases the amount of information search; yet the only increase observed in this study was the effect of objective knowledge on the number of attributes examined in the complex usage situation. A motivational viewpoint would predict increases in all usage situations and for both measures of knowledge. Furthermore, a motivational viewpoint would predict an increase in the number of product category alternatives examined, but this increase was not observed for either measure of knowledge ($p > 0.20$). Last, a motivational viewpoint cannot explain the increase in search efficiency that was observed. The results are clearly more consistent with a theory of knowledge than with a theory of motivation.

In an effort to provide a more detailed explanation for the results found in this study, hypotheses that focus on specific types of objective knowledge are presented next. Overall, it is hypothesized that different types of objective knowledge content have different effects on information search. Specifically, knowledge of which attributes may differentiate the alternatives allows the individual to formulate meaningful questions. Terminology knowledge makes it easier to ask questions and to interpret their answers. The other three types of knowledge measured here—criteria for evaluating attributes, perceived covariance of attributes, and usage situation knowledge—all contribute to search efficiency by allowing a quicker elimination of unsuitable alternatives. Knowledge of criteria for evaluating attributes permits the individual to decide whether an alternative is acceptable by allowing him/her to compare it to reference points stored in memory. Knowledge of attribute covariation allows inferences to be made about some attributes without external search. Usage situation knowledge leads to earlier—and possibly more accurate—categorization of alternatives, based on their appropriateness for the intended usage situation. And finally, in situations where known brands rather than hypothetical or unknown brands are used, knowledge of the attribute values of available brands is used as a substitute for more effortful external search (as evidenced by the decreasing amount of search among highly experienced subjects in Bettman and Park 1980). Unfortunately, these different types of knowledge were highly correlated in this study, prohibiting a meaningful empirical test of these hypotheses. Yet another direction for future research concerns the effects of various types of knowledge on the search styles proposed by Furse, Punj, and Stewart (1984).

In testing the effects of knowledge on search behavior, this paper introduced a new task methodology that uses a computer to simulate aspects of an actual shopping situation. Many of the limitations of the information display board are overcome by this methodology. First, this new methodology does not impose a matrix structure on the task as the information display boards do. Such a structure may influence acquisition strategy and is rarely found in real world environments. Second, the subject is not cued with a list of attributes from which to choose. Instead, the attributes are generated from memory. While it is acknowledged that people often learn about new attributes while making a purchase decision, they rarely possess a list of relevant attributes to guide their search. Such a list may be a possible bias when studying search strategies.

Third, in the present methodology the subjects do not know ahead of time how many brands and attributes are available from which to choose. It is probably more realistic to allow subjects to delimit the size of the problem for themselves rather than to define it for them. This seems particularly important since it has been demonstrated that the size of the perceived problem affects search behavior (e.g., Payne 1976). Finally, information boards do not usually vary the type of information available, the source of information, or the cost of acquiring information. All of these realistic features of search are captured in this new methodology.

Although good arguments can be made for the superiority of this task compared to the information display board task, such a comparison remains to be empirically tested. As new microcomputer technology becomes available, the computer task can be made more realistic, eventually including pictorial and auditory stimuli. In this way, consumer use of many informational sources (such as advertising and word of mouth) can be examined under the controlled circumstances of the laboratory.

[*Received May 1984. Revised January 1985.*]

APPENDIX

Measures of Objective Knowledge

1. Terminology. The free response question asked the subject to write a definition of ten terms (commonly found in sewing book glossaries) used to describe attributes of sewing machines. The structured response question included the same ten terms plus four others, three of which were "decoys" (i.e., not actual sewing terms). Written definitions of the eleven sewing terms were provided, and the subjects were asked to match the sewing terms with their correct definitions and to identify the nonsewing words.

2. Available Attributes. The first free response question asked the subject to list all the things a person might consider when choosing a new sewing machine, including things that she might not personally consider important. Since pretest indicated that people did not usually list specific features (such as zig-zag stitch) in response to this question, a second question was also used. This question asked the subject to list as many features of sewing machines as she could. To reduce measurement error caused by the variance in subjects' listing of standard of "obvious" attributes (e.g., sewing light), a third question explicitly asked the subjects to list features that are common to almost all modern sewing machines. Each mention of an attribute was scored as one point, and duplications between answers to the three questions were subtracted from the sum of these points. The structured response questions used to measure knowledge of attributes listed 27 different attributes of sewing machines along with six decoys and asked the subject to check all the words that she believed were attributes of sewing machines. The number of correct responses, minus a penalty point for each decoy checked, formed the score for this question.

3. Criteria for Evaluating Attributes. The free response question asked the subject to imagine that a friend of hers who knew nothing about sewing machines had offered to purchase a sewing machine for her. The subject was asked to write down everything that this friend should know about what she would want in a sewing machine, so that the friend could purchase the most appropriate model for her. The number of dichotomous attributes (i.e., the attribute is either present or absent) and the number of continuous attributes mentioned (i.e., multiple levels of the attribute are possible) were counted, as well as the number of criteria mentioned. In this way, both the breadth (number of important attributes mentioned) and the depth (number of criteria mentioned) of knowledge were measured. The distinction between dichotomous and continuous attributes has also been termed features vs. dimensions (e.g., Johnson and Kisielius 1985).

The first structured response question that measured knowledge of criteria provided ten continuous-type attributes and asked the subject to check the attributes that were important when making a purchase decision and also to write down any criteria she might have for that attribute. One point was assigned for each criterion mentioned as well as for each attribute checked. The second structured response question presented the subject with a list of 25 dichotomous attributes and asked subjects to choose a number between 1 and 5 to describe how important each of these features was to them, 1 being "definitely *do not* want this feature" and 5 being "definitely *do* want this feature." Two points were assigned for strong preferences (both positive and negative), and one point was assigned for weak preferences. Preferences were treated as knowledge because preferences indicate that a criterion has been stored in memory for a dichotomous attribute. Responses to questions in this category of knowledge, as well as to those in succeeding categories, were considered "wrong" only if they were not possible. For the most part, criteria for evaluation are subjective. It is the degree to which an individual has criteria for evaluation that will affect her search behavior, not whether a panel of experts agrees with these criteria. Thus, the most liberal standards for judging "correctness" were applied.

4. Attribute Covariation. The first free response question focused specifically on the relationship between price and other attributes. It asked the subject to explain how a $700 sewing machine typically differs from a $300 sewing machine. Each attribute listed was given one point. The second free response question asked the subject to list features of sewing machines that "always seem to occur together." Each pair of attributes mentioned was scored as one point.

The first structured response question asked the subject to think how a typical $700 sewing machine compares with a typical $300 machine and then to check phrases that describe this comparison from a list of 29 possible phrases that included four decoy phrases. The number of incorrect responses was subtracted from the number of valid (i.e., not incorrect) responses.

The second structured response question asked the subject to read nine statements, each of which described a possible relationship between two sewing machine attributes. For each statement, the subject was asked to circle one of four responses to indicate what she believed to be the relationship between these attributes. One point was given for every response that indicated belief in a relationship between the attributes.

Two questions measured knowledge of low variance attributes; i.e., attributes which vary very little between alternative models. The free response question asked the subject to list features common to almost all modern sewing machines. Previously, this question had been used to supplement other questions that measured knowledge of attributes. For the present purpose, however, it is used alone.[10] The structured response question provided a list of eighteen attributes that could be considered "standard" and five decoys, and asked the subject to check those attributes that are common to almost all modern sewing machines. The number of decoys checked was subtracted from the number of correct responses.

*5. **Usage Situations.*** The first free response question asked the subject to tell what she would want to know about a person in order to choose the best machine possible for that person. Each situational factor mentioned was given one point. The second free response question provided a list of situational factors and asked the subject to explain how each of these factors would affect her choice of sewing machines. The list of situational factors consisted of the individual's responses to the free response question described above. One point was given for every attribute mentioned for each of the situational factors.

The first structured question provided 29 situational factors (e.g., "number of family members") and asked subjects to choose a number from 1 to 3 to indicate the importance of that information for choosing the best possible sewing machine for someone. Two points were given for every factor rated as "very important" and one point was given for every factor rated as "somewhat important." The second structured response question presented eight sewing tasks and asked the subject to write down which features and characteristics of a sewing machine would be useful to make these sewing tasks easier or to improve the results. The responses were coded in two ways: the number of different features that a person listed for the entire question was counted, and the number of sewing tasks for which the subject had a response was counted. Each of these counts was used as a measure of knowledge.

[10]The question was only posed once to the subjects.

REFERENCES

ALBA, JOSEPH W. (1983), "The Effects of Product Knowledge on the Comprehension, Retention, and Evaluation of Product Information," in *Advances in Consumer Research,* Vol. 10, Eds. Richard P. Bagozzi and Alice M. Tybout. Ann Arbor, MI: Association for Consumer Research, 577-580.

ANDERSON, RONALD D., JACK L. ENGLEDOW, and HELMUT BECKER (1979), "Evaluating the Relationships Among Attitude Toward Business, Product Satisfaction, Experience, and Search Effort," *Journal of Marketing Research,* 16 (August), 394-400.

ARCH, DAVID C., JAMES R. BETTMAN, and PRADEEP KAKKAR (1978), "Subjects' Information Processing in Information Display Board Studies," in *Advances in Consumer Research,* Vol. 5, Ed. H. Keith Hunt. Ann Arbor, MI: Association for Consumer Research, 555-560.

BARR, EVRON, and EDWARD A. FEIGENBAUM, Eds. (1981), *The Handbook of Artificial Intelligence,* Vol. 1. Los Altos, CA: William Kaufman.

BENNETT, PETER D., and ROBERT M. MANDELL (1969), "Prepurchase Information Seeking Behavior of New Car Purchasers—The Learning Hypothesis," *Journal of Marketing Research,* 6 (November), 430-433.

BETTMAN, JAMES R. (1977), "Data Collection and Analysis Approaches for Studying Consumer Information Processing," in *Advances in Consumer Research,* Vol. 4, Ed. William D. Perreault, Jr. Atlanta, GA: Association for Consumer Research, 342-348.

———, and C. WHAN PARK (1980), "Effects of Prior Knowledge and Experience and Phase of the Choice Process on Consumer Decision Processes." *Journal of Consumer Research,* 7 (December), 234–248.

BRUCKS, MERRIE (1984), "The Effects of Product Class Knowledge on Information Search Behavior," unpublished dissertation, Graduate School of Industrial Administration, Carnegie-Mellon University, Pittsburgh, PA.

CAPON, NOEL, and MARIAN BURKE (1980), "Individual, Product Class, and Task-Related Factors in Consumer Information Processing," *Journal of Consumer Research,* 7 (December), 314–326.

CHASE, WILLIAM G., and HERBERT A. SIMON (1973a), "Perception in Chess," *Cognitive Psychology,* 4 (January), 55–81.

———, and HERBERT A. SIMON (1973b), "The Mind's Eye in Chess," in *Visual Information Processing,* Ed. William G. Chase. New York: Academic Press.

CHI, MICHELENE T. H., ROBERT GLASER, and ERNEST REES (1981), "Expertise in Problem Solving," in *Advances in the Psychology of Human Intelligence,* Ed. Sternberg, Hillsdale, NJ: Erlbaum.

CHIESI, HARRY L., GEORGE J. SPILICH, and JAMES T. VOSS (1979), "Acquisition of Domain-Related Information in Relation to High and Low Domain Knowledge," *Journal of Verbal Learning and Verbal Behavior,* 18 (June), 257–273.

CLAXTON, JOHN D., JOSEPH N. FRY, and BERNARD PORTIS (1974), "A Taxonomy of Prepurchase Information-Gathering Patterns," *Journal of Consumer Research,* 1 (December), 35–42.

COHEN, JACOB (1977), *Statistical Power Analysis for the Behavioral Sciences,* New York: Academic Press.

DOMMERMUTH, WILLIAM P. (1965), "The Shopping Matrix and Marketing Strategy," *Journal of Marketing Research,* 2 (May), 128–132.

FURSE, DAVID H., GIRISH PUNJ, and DAVID W. STEWART (1984), "A Typology of Individual Search Strategies Among Purchasers of New Automobiles," *Journal of Consumer Research,* 10 (March), 417–431.

GARDNER, MERYL P. (1984), "Advertising Effects on Attributes Recalled and Criteria Used for Brand Evaluations," *Journal of Consumer Research,* 10 (December), 310–318.

HEMPEL, D. J. (1969), "Search Behavior and Information Utilization in the Home Buying Process," in *Marketing Involvement in Society and the Economy,* Ed. P. R. McDonald. Chicago: American Marketing Association, 241–249.

HOLLIS, N. (1969), *"Successful Sewing, A Modern Guide,"* New York: Toplinger, 34–38.

JACOBY, JACOB, ROBERT W. CHESTNUT, and WILLIAM A. FISCHER (1978), "A Behavioral Approach in Non-Durable Purchasing," *Journal of Marketing Research,* 15 (November), 532–544.

———, ROBERT W. CHESTNUT, KARL C. WEIGL, and WILLIAM FISHER (1976), "Pre-Purchase Information Acquisition: Description of a Process Methodology, Research Paradigm, and Pilot Investigation," in *Advances in Consumer Research,* Vol. 3, Ed. Beverlee B. Anderson. Ann Arbor, MI: Association for Consumer Research, 306–314.

JOHNSON, ERIC, and J. EDWARD RUSSO (1984), "Product Familiarity and Learning New Information," *Journal of Consumer Research,* 11 (June), 542–550.

JOHNSON, MICHAEL D., and JOLITA KISIELIUS (1985), "Concreteness-Abstractness and the Feature-Dimension Distinction," in *Advances in Consumer Research,* Vol. 12, Eds. Elizabeth Hirshman and Morris Holbrook, in press.

KANWAR, RAJESH, JERRY C. OLSON, and LAURA S. SIMS (1981), "Toward Conceptualizing and Measuring Cognitive Structures, in *Advances in Consumer Research,* Vol. 7, Ed. Kent Monroe. Ann Arbor, MI: Association for Consumer Research, 122–127.

KATONA, GEORGE, and EVA MUELLER (1955), "A Study of Purchase Decisions," in *Consumer Behavior: The Dynamics of Consumer Reaction,* Ed. L. H. Clark. New York: New York University Press, 30–87.

LARKIN, JILL, JOHN MCDERMOTT, DOROTHEA P. SIMON, and HERBERT A. SIMON (1980), "Expert and Novice Performance in Solving Physics Problems," *Science,* 208 (June), 1335–1342.

MARKS, LARRY J., and JERRY C. OLSON (1981), "Toward a Cognitive Structure Conceptualization of Product Familiarity," in *Advances in Consumer Research,* Vol. 8, Ed. Kent Monroe. Ann Arbor, MI: Association for Consumer Research, 145–150.

MIYAKE, NAOMI, and DONALD A. NORMAN (1979), "To Ask a Question, One Must Know Enough to Know What is Not Known," *Journal of Verbal Learning and Verbal Behavior,* 18 (June), 357–364.

MONROE, KENT B. (1976), "The Influence of Price

Differences and Brand Familiarity on Brand Preferences," *Journal of Consumer Research,* 3 (June), 42–49.

MOORE, WILLIAM L., and DONALD R. LEHMANN (1980), "Individual Differences in Search Behavior for a Nondurable," *Journal of Consumer Research,* 7 (December), 296–307.

NEWMAN, JOSEPH W. (1977), "Consumer External Search: Amount and Determinants," in *Consumer and Industrial Buying Behavior,* Eds. Arch G. Woodside, Jagdish N. Sheth, and Peter D. Bennett. New York: Elsevier North-Holland, 79–94.

———, and RICHARD STAELIN (1971), "Multivariate Analysis of Differences in Buyer Decision Time," *Journal of Marketing Research,* 8 (May), 192–198.

———, and RICHARD STAELIN (1972), "Prepurchase Information Seeking for New Cars and Major Household Appliances," *Journal of Marketing Research,* 9 (August), 249–257.

PARK, C. WHAN (1976), "The Effect of Individual and Situation-Related Factors on Consumer Selection of Judgmental Models," *Journal of Marketing Research,* 8 (May), 144–151.

———, and V. PARKER LESSIG (1981), "Familiarity and its Impacts on Consumer Decision Biases and Heuristics," *Journal of Consumer Research,* 8 (September), 223–230.

PAYNE, JOHN W. (1976), "Task Complexity and Contingent Processing in Decision Making: An Information Search and Protocol Analysis," *Organizational Behavior and Human Performance,* 16 (August), 366–387.

PUNJ, GIRISH N., and RICHARD STAELIN (1983), "A Model of Consumer Information Search Behavior for New Automobiles," *Journal of Consumer Research,* 9 (March), 366–380.

RUDELL, FREDRICA (1979), *Consumer Food Selection and Nutrition Information.* New York: Praeger.

RUSSO, J. EDWARD, and ERIC J. JOHNSON (1980), "What Do Consumers Know About Familiar Products?" in *Advances in Consumer Research,* Vol. 7, Ed. Jerry C. Olson. Ann Arbor, MI: Association for Consumer Research, 417–423.

SCHREIBER, J., and C. MOUCK (1972). *Good and Easy Sewing Book, For You and Your Family.* New York: Universal Publishing.

SRULL, THOMAS K. (1983), "The Role of Prior Knowledge in the Acquisition, Retention, and Use of New Information," in *Advances in Consumer Research,* Vol. 10, Eds. Richard P. Bagozzi and Alice M. Tybout. Ann Arbor, MI: Association for Consumer Research, 572–576.

STAELIN, RICHARD (1978), "The Effects of Consumer Education on Consumer Product Safety Behavior," *Journal of Consumer Research,* 5 (June), 30–40.

———, and JOHN W. PAYNE (1976), "Studies of the Information Seeking Behavior of Consumers," in *Cognition and Social Behavior,* Eds. J. Carroll and John W. Payne. New York: Erlbaum, 185–202.

SUJAN, MITA (1985), "Consumer Knowledge: Effects on Evaluation Strategies Mediating Consumer Judgments," *Journal of Consumer Research,* 12 (June), 31–46.

SWAN, JOHN E. (1969), "Experimental Analysis of Predecision Information Seeking," *Journal of Marketing Research,* 6 (May), 192–197.

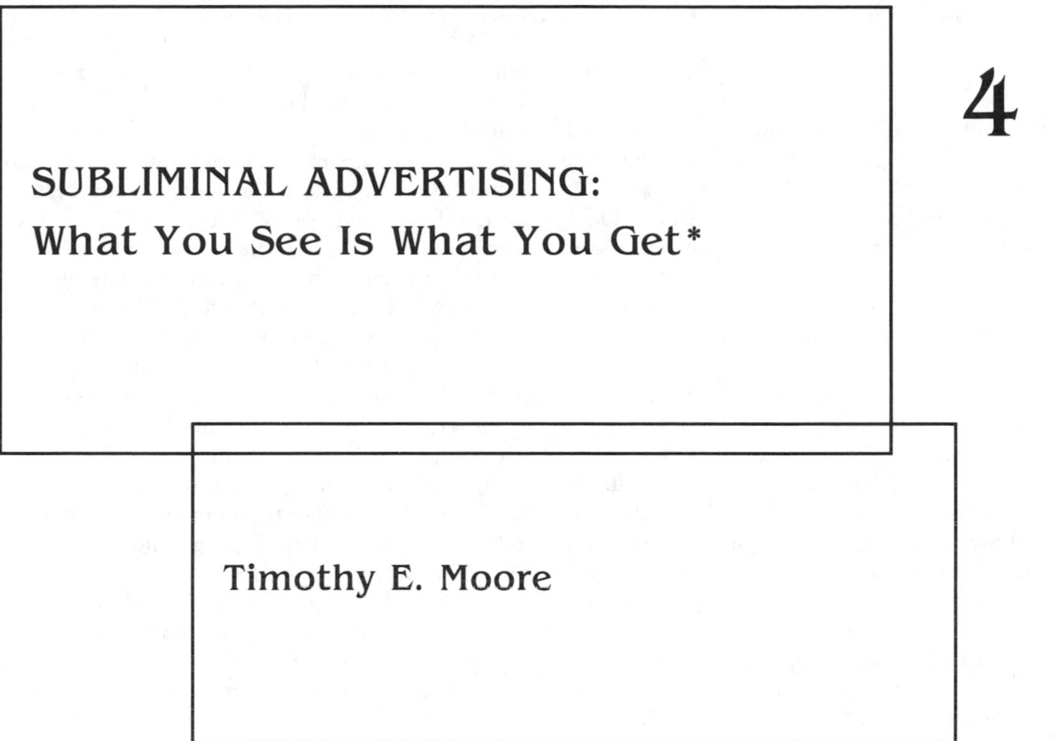

4

SUBLIMINAL ADVERTISING: What You See Is What You Get*

Timothy E. Moore

This paper provides an evaluation of the evidence and arguments advanced in support of the effectiveness of various subliminal advertising techniques. Such practices are purported to influence consumer behavior by subconsciously altering preferences or attitudes toward consumer products. While there is some marginal evidence that subliminal stimuli may influence affective reactions, the marketing relevance of this finding remains to be documented. The notion that subliminal directives can influence motives or actions is contradicted by a large body of research evidence and is incompatible with theoretical conceptions of perception and motivation.

In September 1957 some unwitting theatre audiences in New Jersey were invited to "drink Coca-Cola" and "eat popcorn" in briefly presented messages that were superimposed on the movie in progress. Exposure times were so short that viewers were unaware of any message. The marketing firm responsible reported a dramatic increase in coke and popcorn sales, although they provided no documentation of these alleged effects. Public reaction was, nevertheless, immediate and widespread:

". . . the most alarming and outrageous discovery since Mr. Gatling invented his gun." (*Nation,* 1957, p. 206)

". . . take this invention and everything connected with it and attach it to the center of the next nuclear explosive scheduled for testing." (Cousins, 1957, p. 20)

Opponents were indignant that unforgivable

*Reprinted from *Journal of Marketing,* 46 (Spring 1982), pp. 38-47. Published by the American Marketing Association, Chicago, IL 60606.

psychological manipulations would be visited upon innocent and unknowing consumers. Minds had been "broken and entered" according to the *New Yorker* (1957, p. 33). There was much talk of *Brave New World* and *1984*. But even while laws were being drafted prohibiting the use of subliminal advertising on television, Hollywood was incorporating the idea into two new movies, and a Seattle radio station started broadcasting 'subaudible' messages such as "TV's a bore."

In May 1978 police investigators in an unnamed midwestern city attempted to apprehend a murderer by interspersing subliminal messages among frames of TV news film describing the murder (*New York Times* 1978, p. c22). Later that year some department stores in Toronto began broadcasting subliminal auditory messages whose intent was to deter shoplifters. The "sinister implications" of such practices worried the *Globe and Mail.* Could unscrupulous prime ministers deliver political propaganda subliminally? (*Globe and Mail* 1978, p. 6). In British Columbia the following year, a Ministry of Human Resources policy manual on child abuse was denied inclusion in a government-commissioned publication because the manual's cover contained "sickening and obscene" sexual imagery imbedded in an apparently innocuous photograph of an adult's hand clasping a child's.

Reports of various forms of subliminal manipulation are fairly common. Evidently the practice is still with us, although a few twists have been added since 1957. Given its covert nature and the ethical considerations involved, the prevalence of subliminal advertising is very likely underestimated by reliance upon published reports. At any rate, such techniques are believed to be widespread by a great many people who can hardly be faulted for vigorously protesting against their use. John Q. Public has his hands full trying to cope with forms of exploitation of which he is fully aware. Should he also be worried that Madison Avenue is sneaking directives into his subconscious through the back door? Such a possibility has pervasive ramifications (Brown 1960). The potential importance of the topic has not escaped those in marketing (Hawkins 1970, Kelly 1979, Saegert 1979); however, all lament the dearth of empirical research.

There are at least three identifiable means of subliminal stimulation for which strong behavioral effects have been claimed. The first of these involves very briefly presented visual stimuli. Presentation is usually by means of a tachistoscope, a device for carefully controlling the exposure duration of a visual stimulus. Directives or instructions are flashed so quickly that the viewer is unaware of their presence. Such stimulation purportedly registers subconsciously and allegedly affects subsequent behavior. This method of stimulus presentation has been used frequently by investigators interested in subliminal perception, although their purposes have usually been quite different. As a result, a body of research literature exists that bears on the claims being made for some kinds of subliminal advertising. Some examples from this literature will be described and some studies analyzed in detail. It should be emphasized that stimulation below the level of conscious awareness *can* be shown to have measureable effects upon some aspects of behavior. The point at issue is whether these effects are sufficient to warrant the conclusion that goal-directed behavior can be manipulated by such stimulation.

Another means by which behavior control is attempted is through the use of accelerated speech in low volume auditory messages. Here too, the claim is that while the message may be unintelligible and unnoticed at a conscious level, it is nevertheless processed subconsciously and imparts direction to the receiver's behavior.

The third procedure consists of embedding or hiding sexual imagery (or sometimes words) in pictorial advertisements. These are concealed in such a way that they are not available to conscious perusal. They have, however, a subconscious effect or so it is argued.

The effects attributed to these procedures may consist of either (1) general, nonspecific, affective consequences that are assumed to have some positive but unspecified persuasive influence, or (2) a highly specific, direct impact upon some particular motive or behavior. In what follows, the evidence and arguments put forth in defense of the effectiveness of these procedures will be reviewed and critiqued.

SUBLIMINAL PERCEPTION

Measurable responses of one kind or another can sometimes be shown to be contingent upon stimulation that the perceiver is unaware of. Pierce and Jastrow (1884) demonstrated that subjects could make reliable discriminations among stimuli differing in weight, even though they reported that the stimuli were *not* discriminably different. In this classic study, subjects indicated the degree of confidence in their judgments concerning very slight differences in pressure applied to the subjects' fingers. In those instances where no confidence at all in perceived variation of pressure was reported, subjects were nevertheless obliged to say which of the two pressures was greater. Their judgments were correct 60 percent of the time.

The Threshold Concept

Today, the notion that people can respond to stimuli without being able to report on their existence is accepted and well documented (Bevan 1964a, 1964b; Dixon 1971; Erdelyi 1974). Taken literally, subliminal means "below threshold." However, there exists no absolute cut-off point for stimulus intensity below which stimulation is imperceptible and above which it is always detected. When stimuli of varying intensities are presented over several trials, the minimum signal strength that is always detected is much higher than the one that is almost never detected. If some absolute threshold existed, then there ought to be a determinable stimulus intensity above which the receiver always responds and below which there is no response. Instead, a particular stimulus is sometimes detected and sometimes goes unnoticed. As a result, an individual's perceptual threshold is usually defined as that stimulus value that is correctly detected 50 percent of the time. The threshold, or limen, is, therefore, a statistical abstraction.

For a given individual, this threshold may vary from day to day or from minute to minute. Moreover, thresholds differ rather widely between individuals. Many studies of subliminal perception are flawed because the investigators assumed that some specific exposure duration or stimulus intensity automatically guaranteed that the stimulus would be sufficiently below threshold that its presence would be undetected for all the experimental subjects on all the trials. Often this assumption is unwarranted. Stimuli below the statistical limen (which itself fluctuates) may be noticed as much as 49 percent of the time. As a result, studies that make little or no effort to determine a threshold for individual subjects are at risk because stimuli are presented that are effectively *supra*liminal for some subjects on some trials. The results may thus be due to the effects of weak (but not subliminal) stimulation.

Obviously the notion of a perceptual limen is of limited usefulness. For present purposes we may use the term subliminal perception to refer to the following situations (Dixon 1971, p. 12):

1. The subject responds to stimulation the energy or duration of which falls below that at which he *ever* reported awareness of the stimulus in some previous threshold determination.
2. He responds to a stimulus of which he pleads total unawareness.
3. He reports that he is being stimulated but denies any awareness of what the stimulus was.

In these instances the subject cannot recognize the stimulus. "These situations define subliminal perception, and are to be distinguished from those where the individual, though unaware of the stimulus response contingency, is either not necessarily unaware of the stimulus, or, alternatively, could be *made aware* of the stimulus if his attention were drawn to it" (Dixon 1971, p. 13). People are often unaware of stimulation or of the processes mediating the effects of a stimulus on a response (Nisbett and Wilson 1977). This is a separate issue from subliminal stimulation, wherein the subject *cannot* identify the stimulus.

Some Illustrations of Subliminal Perception

There is ample evidence that weak stimuli that are not reportable *can* be demonstrated to influence behavior. For example, a number of studies by Bevan and his associates (Bevan 1964b) have shown that subliminal stimuli can alter judgments of perceived intensity of supraliminal stimuli when the former are interpolated into the presentation series. In one of these studies subjects were asked to judge the intensity of weak electric shocks delivered to their wrists. Between trials subliminal levels of shock were also administered. Careful control procedures ensured that these stimuli were not detected. The effect of these interpolated stimuli was to elevate the judged intensities of the detectable shocks. A control group that received no subliminal stimulation routinely estimated their shocks to be less intense than the experimental group. A similar effect was found for judgments of the perceived loudness of tones. Apparently the subliminal stimuli trigger physiological activity that affects the perception of similar supraliminal stimuli.

Signal detection research provides another example. In a signal detection task, weak stimuli are presented; some are detectable, some are not. If subjects are asked to provide confidence ratings of their judgments about the presence or absence of a signal, their ratings are highly correlated with the stimulus intensity. This is true even for signals that were reportedly not detected (Green and Swets 1966, Swets 1961).

Perceptual defense literature provides yet another sort of illustration. Many studies have shown that taboo or emotionally loaded words have higher recognition thresholds than do neutral words. That is, it takes a longer exposure duration for *whore* to be identified than for *shore.* At first this may appear illogical. How can something taboo be defended against unless it is first recognized as being taboo? The paradox is resolved if it assumed that "perception" is by no means a discrete experiential event that is automatically determined by some particular stimulus pattern. Rather, perception is treated as a multiprocess chain of events that begins with stimulus input and terminates (subjectively) with conscious recognition of an object or event. However, not all input is subjected to the same sequence of mental processing. Stimuli are selectively filtered, transformed and attended to according to a variety of factors that are independent of the particular input. These include memory, expectations, attention, affect and other variables. Perception then, as we conventionally use the term, represents ". . . the conscious terminus of a sequence of nonconscious prior processes" (Erdelyi 1974). Conscious recognition need not be and often is not the end point for many sorts of input. Some stimuli may initiate mental activity of one sort or another without being available to conscious reflection or report. This is what is typically meant by the term subliminal perception. In the case of taboo items, some kind of defensive selectivity operates to bias the processing of emotionally charged input—such selectivity having its impact *prior* to a conscious recognition of the input.

Recently Zajonc (1980) has reviewed evidence from several studies showing that under some circumstances, unattended stimuli can be processed to a degree that is sufficient to elicit a subsequent affective reaction (i.e., like/dislike) *without* their being recognized as having been previously encountered. "Affective reactions can occur without extensive perceptual cognitive encoding. Reliable affective discriminations (like/dislike ratings) can be made in the total absence of recognition memory (old-new judgments)" (Zajonc 1980, p. 151). While unattended stimuli are not necessarily subliminal, one study purports to show that affect can be influenced by stimuli that *are* truly subliminal (Kunst-Wilson and Zajonc 1980). That some behavioral processes may be influenced by stimuli whose presence is not consciously noticeable by the receiver is not at issue here. The preceding examples testify to the validity of subliminal perception as a phenomenon. The important question is whether the subliminal effects obtained justify the claims made for subliminal advertising. This question is critical because what must be posited in order to support such a proposition is not merely *an* effect, but specific, (relatively) powerful and enduring effects on the buying preferences of the public.

SUBLIMINAL ADVERTISING

Could subliminally presented stimuli have a marketing application? Can advertising effectiveness be enhanced through subliminal stimulation? Before reviewing the few laboratory studies that have addressed this question directly, it will be useful to consider what sorts of subliminal influences would be necessary in order to obtain some marketing relevance. At a minimum, we might hypothesize that a subliminal stimulus produces (or increases) some positive affective reaction to that stimulus. Whether or not such an affective response, if obtained, could have any relevant motivating influence is another question. It is probably safe to assume that positive affect would not do any harm and could conceivably influence a product's attractiveness. A much stronger prediction for subliminal effects would be one that hypothesizes some direct behavioral consequence (i.e., purchasing). Since the former prediction does not *necessarily* entail any interesting marketing implications, and the latter prediction clearly does, these hypotheses will be referred to as weak and strong claims respectively.

Practical Difficulties

Regardless of which claim is under investigation, there are some profound if not insurmountable operational constraints associated with presenting subliminal stimuli in a typical marketing context. One problem has to do with individual differences in threshold. There is no particular stimulus intensity or duration that can guarantee subliminality for all viewers. In order to preclude detection by those with relatively low thresholds, the stimulus would have to be so weak that it would not reach viewers with higher thresholds at all. Lack of control over position and distance from the screen would further complicate matters. Finally, without elaborate precautions, supraliminal material (i.e., the film or commercial in progress) would almost certainly wash out any potential effects of a subliminal stimulus. In order to duplicate the results of laboratory studies that have shown subliminal effects, it is crucial to duplicate the conditions under which the effects were obtained. From a practical standpoint, this is virtually impossible. Nevertheless, it could be argued that if 1 percent of 10 million viewers are influenced by a subliminal ad that completely misses the other 99 percent, the subsequent behavior of that 1 percent might make the exercise cost effective.

Does the relevant research indicate that some positive affect could become associated with a particular product through the use of subliminally presented stimuli? The evidence is not strong. The Kunst-Wilson and Zajonc (1980) study referred to earlier used irregular, randomly constructed octagons as stimuli. The stimuli themselves were first presented at one-millisecond durations and filtered so that recognition was at chance level. Subjects were instructed to pay close attention to the screen, even if nothing was distinguishable. The same stimuli were subsequently presented for one-second intervals, paired with new stimuli. Subjects' recognition of old versus new stimuli was reported to be at chance; however, the old stimuli were judged to be preferable to the new ones 60 percent of the time. The effect was subtle but statistically reliable ($p < .01$, 2-tail).

It is tempting to speculate that repeated subliminal exposures could bring about an increasingly stronger affective reaction, with the stimuli themselves remaining unrecognized. A study by Shevrin and Fritzler (1968) does not support such a notion. These authors demonstrated a differential effect of two different subliminal stimuli upon evoked potentials (EEG) and free word associations in the absence of a conscious discrimination between the stimuli. The effect was a fleeting one, however: "the subliminal verbal effects appeared only in the first .001-second condition, suggesting that, beyond a certain point, multiple exposures of stimuli work against subliminal influences" (Shevrin and Fritzler 1968, p. 298). Two points about the Kunst-Wilson and Zajonc study are worth emphasizing.

First, the stimuli themselves, consisting of (relatively) meaningless geometric shapes, were subjected to subliminal exposure levels; this exposure seems to have had a subsequent effect upon preference. Second, the experimental subjects were actively attending to the stimuli throughout the subliminal viewing condition; during this time, no other stimulation was present that could distract attention or mask the subliminal stimuli.

Could this procedure be utilized in an advertising context? It is possible that a display's attractiveness could be subliminally enhanced by having that same display exposed for subliminal durations prior to its supraliminal presentation. Whether the magnitude of the resultant effect could have any practical importance is not known. Moreover, it is not obvious how the subliminal exposure could be accomplished. Superimposing the subliminal display on top of supraliminal material is not a good bet:

> ". . . Ongoing supraliminal stimulation to which attention may be directed almost certainly will swamp any effect by a simultaneous stimulus below the awareness threshold . . . at a peripheral level, lateral inhibition and contour suppressing mechanisms could well block any neural transmission from the weaker of two stimulus arrays . . . a similar effect of restricted channel capacity would almost certainly operate centrally as well. The potential effects of one stimulus may be completely negated by the presence of another" (Dixon 1971, p. 175–76).

Splicing or somehow integrating the subliminal stimulus into ongoing supraliminal material (even if technologically possible) is not too promising either, because unless a sufficient blank interval is included before and after the insert, supraliminal material will mask the subliminal stimulus (Kahneman 1968). If such intervals are provided, the viewer will most probably be aware of an interruption, even though the stimulus itself may not be detectable. At least 100 milliseconds of "clean" background on either side of the target stimulus would be necessary to preclude a masking effect. As a result, subjects could infer the presence of a stimulus. If complete unobtrusiveness is a priority, the stimulus and surrounding interval would have to be carefully located at naturally occurring breaks or cut points. Even then, completely disguising the fact of stimulation may not be possible.

Evidence Involving the Weak Claim

In addition to Kunst-Wilson and Zajonc (1980), two other studies report subliminal effects relevant to the weak claim. Byrne (1959) flashed the word "beef" for successive five millisecond intervals during a sixteen-minute movie. Experimental and control subjects did not differ in their verbal references to beef, as measured by word association tests. Nor did experimental subjects report a higher preference for beef sandwiches, when given a list of five alternatives. Experimental subjects did, however, rate themselves as hungrier than control subjects. This difference held up when ratings were co-varied with hours of food deprivation. Byrne offered no explanation for this finding. It is not obvious why the word "beef" should induce hunger particularly when it failed to influence semantic associates. Moreover, the method of presentation involved superimposing the stimulus on the movie. For reasons outlined earlier, such a procedure is likely to interfere with rather than enhance any potential subliminal affects.

In a similar study, Hawkins (1970) flashed the word "coke" for 2.7 millisecond-intervals during the presentation of other supraliminal material. Subjective thirst ratings were higher for the "coke" group than for a control group that received a subliminal nonsense syllable. Hawkins concludes that "a simple subliminal stimulus can serve to arouse a basic drive such as thirst." (p. 324). As Saegert (1979) has pointed out, "Hawkins's results may simply be a Type I error, especially in view of the fact that other tries have been made" (p. 55). The fact that Hawkins performed five independent 1-tail statistical tests where one analysis would have sufficed lends support to Saegert's position. There are methodological shortcomings in both of these studies. Even if the results are taken at face value, their relevance to advertising is minimal.

Evidence Involving the Strong Claim

The strong claim for subliminal advertising posits specific behavioral consequences as a result of a subliminal directive. A study by Zuckerman (1960) requiring student nurses to write stories describing the contents of a series of pictures that were projected onto a screen in front of them is pertinent to this issue. Unknown to the subjects, the instructions "write more" and "don't write" were tachistoscopically superimposed on the pictures at successive points during the presentations. A control group was treated in a similar fashion but received blank slides in place of those containing the subliminal directives.

The study was composed of three successive conditions: (1) baseline, during which no subliminal messages were presented, (2) "write more," during which subjects in the experimental group received a "write more" instruction for .02 seconds, concurrently with the picture they were asked to describe, and (3) "don't write," during which the experimental subjects received a "don't write" directive, again superimposed for .02 seconds on the picture being projected. During each condition, pictures were presented for 10 trials each. After each trial, subjects wrote a description of what they had seen. Zuckerman found that nurses in the experimental group wrote more during Condition 2 ("write more") than they had during baseline. Furthermore, he noted a slight drop in output between Condition 3 ("don't write") and Condition 2, and interpreted this as evidence that the subliminal instructions were effective.

Unfortunately, there is a strong possibility that these results were due to a methodological artifact which psychologists call a "ceiling effect." This occurs when performance reaches an asymptote and cannot be further improved upon. The slight drop that Zuckerman observed may not have been a real decrease in performance but rather, a levelling off. This interpretation is supported by a comparison of the performances of experimental and control subjects. For some reason the students in the experimental group were enthusiastic writers. They wrote much more during baseline than did the controls. They wrote still more during Condition 2 ("write more"), and the controls increased their output as well. By Condition 3 the experimental subjects may have reached asymptote. They were all "written out," and a slight drop was observed in the number of words written.

Because of time constraints (and possibly writer's cramp), experimental subjects may already have been writing as much as could reasonably be expected by the end of Condition 2. The slight drop during Condition 3 may be due to statistical artifact. When variability is possible in only one direction (in this case down), a slight decrease in performance is predictable. Controls were still increasing their output during Condition 3 and by the end, their output had barely surpassed that of the experimental subjects' performance during baseline. When differences between groups are large prior to any experimental manipulation, it is risky to attribute some subsequently observed differences to that manipulation. In this study, the preexisting difference between experimental and control subjects was as great or greater than any other subsequently observed difference between or within groups. Zuckerman has little to say by way of explaining the finding, but submits that "the subject's operant behavior is supposedly brought under control by suggestive cues of which he is not aware" (p. 404). This is not an explanation but rather a description of the outcome couched in operant terminology.

Dixon (1971), commenting on Zuckerman's results, speculates that "it may be impossible to resist instructions which are not consciously experienced" (p. 177). Again, this is more an assertion than an explanation, but it does reflect an apparently prevalent (although not articulated) notion that instructions, directives and/or slogans are intrinsically compelling.

When the instruction is delivered supraliminally the receiver can counter-argue or derogate the source, thereby diminishing the stimulus' influence. However, if the instruction is presented subliminally, the recipient is unaware of its presence and is consequently unable to counter-argue.

Several researchers have investigated and described some of the cognitive processes that may mediate acceptance of advertising claims (Harris et al. 1979, Wright 1973). Wright analyzed the responses of 160 women who were exposed to a target ad embedded in other surrounding material, and subsequently queried about their reactions to the arguments contained in the advertising message. Counter-arguing by the receiver was identified as an important processing strategy. Neither the reliability nor validity of this finding is being disputed. However, it would be a mistake to assume that "resistive cognitions" are an inevitable consequence of advertising. Such a position is reminiscent of a behavioristic view of people as passive receivers of inputs to which they respond in automatic and stereotyped ways.

Perhaps the single most important lesson to be learned from cognitive psychology in the last decade is that the meaning of a stimulus does not reside in the stimulus itself. Meaning is constructed by the receiver in active, complex and often specialized ways. With respect to advertising the selectivity of attention and the active control over subsequent processing of the input means that stimulation is not a sufficient condition for any response at all, let alone some particular response. We are constantly subjected to a barrage of external and internal stimuli, of which only a fraction acquire phenomenal representation. Some neural activity is no doubt provoked by stimuli that are not consciously processed. But to attribute to a subliminal stimulus a strong influence, which it cannot be shown to have when supraliminal, is not justified by any theoretical rationale. For this reason it is appropriate to insist on especially clear well-replicated empirical evidence before accepting such a proposition. To the author's knowledge, Zuckerman's (1960) finding has *not* been replicated, and the study itself is vulnerable to an important methodological criticism.

There is an additional problem with procedures that attempt subliminal persuasion through the use of written directives. In order for a subliminal message to exert a behavioral effect (the "strong" claim), the full and precise meaning of the message would have to be extracted from it. Dixon (1971) has reviewed many subliminal perception studies showing that when words are used as stimuli, "The stimulus tends to elicit responses from the same sphere of meaning" (p. 102). Since competitors' products may well be contained in this sphere, it would be essential that the full meaning of the stimulus words be identified. An effusion of mere semantic associates would be insufficient. There are no published studies that demonstrate that people educe the full meaning of a subliminal word stimulus, and there are at least two studies casting some doubt on the possibility (Heilbrun 1980, Severance and Dyer 1973). For this reason, it is difficult to construe a subliminal directive as an argument that cannot be consciously resisted.

Summary

Before turning to other methods that attempt subliminal persuasion, it will be useful to summarize the evidence reviewed. Research supporting the null hypothesis is much less likely to find its way into print than that which demonstrates some potential influence. The paucity of evidence may simply be a reflection of its lack of availability. On the basis of what little data are available, one could tentatively conclude that subliminal presentation of a stimulus may produce a positive affective response to that stimulus (Kunst-Wilson and Zajonc 1980). This positive affective response was obtained with subjects who were attending only to the subliminal stimuli. Whether this finding could be utilized successfully in a marketing context remains to be seen. Apart from the question of the magnitude of the effect, not to mention its validity (Birnbaum 1981, Mellers 1981), there are some practical difficulties associated with achieving a real-world application.

The evidence that subliminal directives can exert any control over behavior is much less compelling (Zuckerman 1960), although there has been ample opportunity for replication. Moreover, this strong claim for subliminal influence is not accompanied by a coherent explanatory rationale. Previous reviews of the strong claim have reached similar conclusions. One of the first rigorous scrutinies of this issue was described by McConnell et al. (1958), no doubt precipitated by the furor generated by the popcorn ad in New Jersey. These authors were skeptical that any but the simplest forms of behavior could be affected by stimulation below the level of conscious awareness. Bevan (1964a) concluded that the "influences of subliminal stimulation upon preference and choice, if they occur at all, are highly subtle, and the possibility that they could constitute an effective means of controlling consumer behavior or political opinion is highly unlikely" (p. 91). Equally strong misgivings were expressed by Goldiamond (1966) and Anastasi (1964). Empirical documentation has remained elusive: "all things considered . . . secret attempts to manipulate people's minds have yielded results as subliminal as the stimuli used" (McConnell 1977, p. 231).

SUBAUDIBLE MESSAGES

The eye is capable of receiving far more information in a short period of time than is the ear. Thus most studies of subliminal perception have involved visual stimulation because the investigator can attempt to determine what particular features of a display are responsible for various sorts of neural activity that may occur below the level of conscious awareness. In contrast, studies addressing auditory reception have been concerned primarily with signal detection—determining the presence versus absence of a weak signal. Because auditory information is, perforce, temporally extended, it is particularly vulnerable to loss through lack of attention or auditory masking.

This probably accounts for the total absence of published studies investigating possible effects of subaudible messages. While the eye is sensitive primarily to spatial information, the ear is basically a processor of temporal information, especially in the case of speech perception. The difference is an important one. A great deal of information can be presented simultaneously in a visual display. An auditory stimulus is more extended in time; information arrives in consecutive bits. A speech stimulus may be thought of as a sound pattern whose acoustic features fluctuate over time. Consequently, there is no procedure for creating tachistoscopic-like auditory stimuli. Controlling the exposure duration of a visual stimulus does not change the stimulus itself; it merely limits the time available for processing it.

If speech is compressed or telescoped in time, the signal itself is altered. While the speech stream can be subjected to a surprising amount of mutilation without intelligibility being affected (Licklider and Miller 1951), there is a limit to the amount of distortion that can be tolerated without a loss in comprehension. Information is transmitted at the rate of about 150 words per minute in normal speech. Studies have shown (Foulke and Sticht 1969) that comprehension declines fairly rapidly at rates beyond 300 words per minute. There are two reasons for this. The first involves signal degradation. When playback speed is increased, component frequencies and pitch are both altered. The intelligibility of the signal consequently suffers. Secondly, channel capacity is taxed when a critical word rate is reached. Speech comprehension requires the continuous registration, encoding and storage of information. These operations take time. When the word rate is too fast, not all the input can be processed as it is received. The result is that some speech information is lost. Reducing the volume of accelerated speech will only compound these difficulties. Mass media accounts of subaudible messages report presentation rates of greater than 2,300 words per minute

(*Toronto Star* 1978, p. c1; *Washington Post* 1979, p. c4; *Time* 1979, p. 63). The message is simply repeated 8- or 9,000 times an hour. Because of the fast rate, what may once have been a message is rendered an unintelligible scratching sound. That such stimuli could have any influence on behavior (except to annoy) is a claim totally lacking empirical support. Since the stimulus has no apparent meaning, presenting it at a supposedly subaudible level does not thereby confer any added significance.

The accelerated nature of subaudible messages is perhaps a tangential issue. Could such messages have an influence if the presentation rate were normal, but the volume at a subthreshold level? Relevant evidence mitigates against such a notion. Weak auditory stimuli are very susceptible to auditory masking. Moreover, there is some experimental evidence that attentional focus can effectively prevent weak auditory stimuli from receiving any processing at all (Broadbent 1958, Eriksen and Johnson 1964, Peterson and Kroener 1964). Studies in dichotic listening reveal that very little of the content of an unattended message is processed when attention is focussed on another concurrent message (Kahneman 1973, Moray 1969, Treisman and Geffen 1967). Moreover the unattended stimuli used in these investigations are by no means subliminal in strength.

Speech sounds are different in principle from other auditory inputs (Liberman et al. 1967). Because of speech's temporal dimension, a certain minimal amount of attention may be essential for comprehension. This would make subliminal presentation of auditory messages not just difficult but impossible. In fact, it is difficult to conceive of a means by which speech could be rendered subliminal according to the conventional definition outlined earlier (see Dixon 1971, 1981). Neither accelerating the message nor reducing its volume seems to provide appropriate analogs to the methods used in the visual modality. At any rate, the procedures tried to date do not appear promising.

Whether or not subliminal effects could be obtained from auditory messages under more carefully controlled conditions remains to be seen. At the present time there is no evidence that such influence is possible, let alone any practical application. It should also be emphasized that a change in modality does not provide a defense against some of the objections raised earlier regarding the subliminal effects of visual stimuli. The assumption that behavior can be automatically triggered by the presentation of some particular stimulus is as unwarranted for auditory messages as it is for visual ones.

EMBEDDED STIMULI

A different kind of procedure for achieving subliminal effects has been described by Key (1973, 1976, 1980). In these books the author alleges that various erotic images or words have been surreptitiously concealed in magazine, newspaper and television advertisements. High-speed photography and airbrushing are among the techniques whereby subtle appeals to subconscious sex drives are hidden. Their use is ubiquitous. Ritz crackers have the word *sex* baked into them; a Gilbey's Gin ad is full of microscopic erotica. None of these are visible to the naked eye. In fact, it apparently requires weeks of analysis for many of them to be discovered, and sometimes they are embedded upside down.

According to Key, ". . . humans can be assumed to have at least two sensory input systems, one encoding data at the conscious level and a second operating at a level below conscious awareness" (Key 1973). A concealed word or symbol, ". . . usually invisible to consciousness appears instantly perceivable at the unconscious level" (Key 1976). He goes on to claim that visual or auditory stimulation whose speed and/or intensity are beyond the range for normal sensory reception can nevertheless be transmitted directly into the unconscious, whence subsequent behavior is manipulated. Precisely how these implanted cues affect a given product's desirability is not too clear, but Key assures us that they are very effective. The Ritz crackers, in fact, are reported to taste better because they have the word *sex* stamped onto them. Key provides no documentation for the effects that he attributes to embedded stimuli. For this reason, his assertions should be regarded as hypotheses awaiting empirical investigation. Key also describes some psychological mechanisms through which embedded stimuli purportedly operate. These latter claims involving perception, memory, and the subconscious have probably rendered his speculations quite unpalatable to research psychologists. Man's sensory apparatus has been studied extensively for many years. There is no evidence for more than one class of sensory input systems, as Key claims, nor is there evidence of unconscious perception of stimuli that fall outside the functional range of our receptor organs. Key appears to invent whatever features of perception and memory would be necessary to achieve the results imputed to embedded stimuli. The notion of a separate super-powerful sensory system serving the subconscious (exclusively) cannot be accommodated by any theory of perception, past or present. It is not surprising that Key's books have not been favorably reviewed by the scientific community (Schulman 1981). They are mentioned here because while they contain the least scientific substance, these books are probably largely responsible for the promulgation of a belief in the power of subliminal manipulation.

Whether or not erotic imagery has been deliberately planted is not relevant to a consideration of the imagery's alleged effects. A diligent search for a phallic symbol will probably be successful. How its presence and relationship to an advertised product might be interpreted is another matter, but the consequence is by no means predictable. The amount of information available from a purposeful scrutiny of a display is limited only by the viewer's imagination. Holding advertisers responsible for one's erotic musing is analogous to accusing Rorschach of insinuating particular themes into the inkblots. A cursory glance yields far less information than a careful inspection. Under typical circumstances, the ad's most salient characteristics will receive the lion's share of perceptual activity (Hochberg 1978), if they receive any attention at all. Completely ignoring a stimulus is an option that people frequently exercise. If you do not actively search for hidden extras, what you see is what you get, and there is nothing subliminal about such perusal. The fine print near the bottom of an ad is likely to be far more important than any concealed genitalia could be.

While Key appears to have misjudged the efficacy of embedded stimuli, it would be a mistake to dismiss out of hand all of his remarks concerning the latent effects of advertising. Ads may influence us in some ways which have nothing to do with consumer behavior per se. For example, ads help to transmit various cultural stereotypes. If women are consistently portrayed in insignificant or demeaning roles, the viewer may develop an attitude towards them that is ultimately prejudicial and harmful to women as a group. Moreover, these attitudes are not consciously formed. The rich literature on observational learning investigates how such learning takes place (Comstock et al. 1978). While the acquisition of such attitudes may occur subconsciously, there is nothing subliminal about the presentation of the role models. On the contrary, they are distressingly conspicuous. This kind of implicit learning can have important and pervasive consequences (Poe 1976; Rush 1980; Walstedt, Geis and Brown 1980).

CONCLUSION

A century of psychological research substantiates the general principle that more intense stimuli have a greater influence on people's behavior than weaker ones. While subliminal perception is a bona fide phenomenon, the effects obtained are subtle and obtaining them typically requires a carefully structured context. Subliminal stimuli are usually so weak that the recipient is not just unaware of the stimulus but is also oblivious to the fact that he/she is being stimulated. As a result, the potential effects of subliminal stimuli are easily nullified by other ongoing stimulation in the same sensory channel or by attention being focused on another modality. These factors pose serious difficulties for any possible marketing application.

A second major problem pertains to the psychological mechanism through which a subliminal stimulus could in principle influence behavior. The proposition is appropriate only if one characterizes a person as a static organism who processes stimulus input passively and responds in automatic, predictable ways. In fact, psychological research has generated a large body of evidence that such a characterization would be false. There is substantial evidence for the importance of centralized control and mediating processes and good reason to believe that humans have highly mobile selective attention. The sheer volume of constant sensory stimulation implicates a constructive, synthetic model of focal attention and perception rather than a purely receptive one. As Broadbent (1973) said, ". . . the brain is made of unreliable components, so that it is very unlikely that any particular impulses in any particular nerve cells will occur predictably and consistently whenever a particular stimulus strikes our senses. In addition, we are being bombarded all the time by a very large quantity of information; and in relation to this large quantity of information we are all, like Winnie the Pooh, bears of very little brain" (p. 31).

Empirical support for subliminal influences of a pragmatic nature is neither plentiful nor compelling. On the basis of research evidence accumulated to date, the most one could hope for, in terms of marketing application, would be a potential positive affective response to a subliminal stimulus. Whether such an effect could actually be obtained in a realistic viewing situation, and whether the magnitude of the effect would make the exercise worthwhile is still an empirical question. There is no empirical documentation for stronger subliminal effects, such as inducing particular behaviors or changing motivation. Moreover, such a notion is contradicted by a substantial amount of research and is incompatible with experimentally based conceptions of information processing, learning and motivation.

None of this is to deny the existence of motives of which one may be unaware, nor to deny that subliminal stimulation can be used to investigate differences between unconscious and conscious processes (Carr and Bacharach 1976, McCauley et al. 1980, Shevrin and Dickman 1980). The point is simply that subliminal directives have not been shown to have the power ascribed to them by advocates of subliminal advertising. In general, the literature on subliminal perception shows that the most clearly documented effects are obtained only in highly contrived and artificial situations. These effects, when present, are brief and of small magnitude. The result is perhaps best construed as an epiphenomenon—a subtle and fleeting byproduct of the complexities of human cognitive activity. These processes have no apparent relevance to the goals of advertising.

REFERENCES

ANASTASI, A. (1964), "Subliminal Perception," in *Fields of Applied Psychology,* A. Anastasi. New York: McGraw-Hill.

BEVAN, W. (1964a), "Subliminal Stimulation: A Pervasive Problem for Psychology," *Psychological Bulletin,* 61 (2), 89–99.

——— (1964b), "Contemporary Problems in Adaptation Level Theory," *Psychological Bulletin,* 61 (3), 161–187.

BIRNBAUM, M. (1981), "Thinking and Feeling: A Skeptical Review," *American Psychologist,* 36 (1), 99–101.

BROADBENT, D. E. (1958), *Perception and Communication,* New York: Pergamon.

——— (1973), *In Defence of Empirical Psychology,* London: Camelot Press.

BROWN, K. C. (1960), "Hemlock For the Critic: A Problem in Evaluation," *Journal of Aesthetics and Art Criticism,* 18 (3), 316–319.

BYRNE, D. (1959), "The Effect of a Subliminal Food Stimulus on Verbal Responses," *Journal of Applied Psychology,* 43 (4), 249–251.

CARR, T., and V. BACHARACH (1976), "Perceptual Tuning and Conscious Attention," *Cognition,* 4 (3), 281–302.

COMSTOCK, G., S. CHAFFER, N. KATZMAN, M. MCCOMBE, and D. ROBERTS (1978), *Television and Human Behavior.* New York: Columbia University Press.

COUSINS, N. (1957), "Smudging the Subconscious," *Saturday Review,* 40 (October 5).

DIXON, N. F. (1971), *Subliminal Perception: The Nature of a Controversy,* London: McGraw-Hill.

——— (1981), *Preconscious Processing.* London: Wiley.

ERDELYI, M. H. (1974), "A New Look at the New Look: Perceptual Defense and Vigilance," *Psychological Review,* 81 (1), 1-25.

ERIKSEN, C. W., and H. J. JOHNSON (1964), "Storage and Decay Characteristics of Nonattended Auditory Stimuli," *Journal of Experimental Psychology,* 68 (1), 28-36.

FOULKE, E., and I. G. STICHT (1969), "Review of Research on the Intelligibility and Comprehension of Accelerated Speech," *Psychological Bulletin,* 72 (1), 50-62.

Globe & Mail (1978), October 13, 5.

GOLDIAMOND, I. (1966), "Statement on Subliminal Advertising," in *Control of Human Behavior,* Vol. 1, R. Ulrich, T. Stachnik and J. Mabry, Eds. Glenview, IL: Scott, Foresman.

GREEN, D. M., and J. A. SWETS (1966), *Signal Detection Theory and Psychophysics,* New York: Wiley.

HARRIS, R. J., T. M. DUBITSKY, and S. THOMPSON (1979), "Learning to Identify Deceptive Truth in Advertising," in *Current Issues and Research in Advertising,* J. H. Leigh and C. R. Martin, Eds. Ann Arbor, MI: U. of Michigan Graduate School of Business Administration, Division of Research.

HAWKINS, D. (1970), "The Effects of Subliminal Stimulation on Drive Level and Brand Preference," *Journal of Marketing Research,* 8 (August), 322-326.

HEILBRUN, K. S. (1980), "Silverman's Subliminal Psychodynamic Activation: A Failure to Replicate," *Journal of Abnormal Psychology,* 89 (4), 560-566.

HOCHBERG, J. (1978), *Perception* (2nd ed.). Englewood Cliffs, NJ: Prentice-Hall.

KAHNEMAN, D. (1968), "Method, Findings and Theory in Studies of Visual Masking," *Psychological Bulletin,* 70 (6), 404-425.

——— (1973), *Attention and Effort.* Englewood Cliffs, NJ: Prentice-Hall.

KELLY, J. S. (1979), "Subliminal Embeds in Print Advertising: A Challenge to Advertising Ethics," *Journal of Advertising,* 8 (3), 20-24.

KEY, W. B. (1973), *Subliminal Seduction.* Englewood Cliffs, NJ: Signet.

——— (1976), *Media Sexploitation.* Englewood Cliffs, NJ: Prentice-Hall.

——— (1980), *The Clamplate Orgy.* Englewood Cliffs, NJ: Prentice-Hall.

KUNST-WILSON, E., and R. ZAJONC (1980), "Affective Discrimination of Stimuli That Cannot Be Recognized," *Science,* 207 (1), 557-558.

LIBERMAN, A. M., F. S. COOPER, D. P. SHANKWEILER, and M. STUDDERT-KENNEDY (1967), "Perception of the Speech Code," *Psychological Review,* 74 (6), 431-461.

LICKLIDER, J., and G. MILLER (1951), "The Perception of Speech," in S. Stevens, Ed., *Handbook of Experimental Psychology.* New York: Wiley.

MCCAULEY, C., C. PARMELEE, R. SPERBER, and T. CARR (1980), "Early Extraction of Meaning From Pictures and Its Relation to Conscious Identification," *Journal of Experimental Psychology: Human Perception and Performance,* 6 (2), 265-276.

MCCONNELL, J. V. (1977), *Understanding Human Behavior,* (2nd ed.). New York: Holt, Rinehart & Winston.

———, R. CUTTER, and E. MCNEIL (1958), "Subliminal Stimulation: An Overview," *American Psychologist,* 13 (3), 229-242.

MELLERS, B. (1981), "Feeling More Than Thinking," *American Psychologist,* 36 (7), 802-803.

MORAY, N. (1969), *Attention: Selective Processes in Vision and Hearing.* London: Hutchinson.

Nation (1957), "Diddling the Subconscious: Subliminal Advertising," 185 (October 5), 206.

New York Times (1978), May 18, c22.

New Yorker (1957), 33 (September 21), 33.

NISBETT, R. E., and T. O. WILSON (1972), "Telling More Than We Can Know: Verbal Reports on Mental Processes," *Psychological Review,* 84 (3), 231-259.

PETERSON, L. R., and S. KROENER (1964), "Dichotic Stimulation and Retention," *Journal of Experimental Psychology,* 68 (2), 125-130.

PIERCE, C. S., and J. JASTROW (1884), "On Small Differences of Sensation," *Memoirs of the National Academy of Sciences,* 3, 73-84.

POE, A. (1976), "Active Women in Ads," *Journal of Communication,* 26 (4), 185-192.

RUSH, F. (1980), "Child Pornography," in *Take Back the Night: Women on Pornography,* L. Lederer, Ed. New York: Morrow.

SAEGERT, J. (1979), "Another Look at Subliminal

Perception," *Journal of Advertising Research,* 19 (1), 55–57.

SCHULMAN, M. (1981), "The Great Conspiracy," *Journal of Communications,* 31 (2), 209.

SEVERANCE, L. J., and F. N. DYER (1973), "Failure of Subliminal Word Presentations to Generate Interference to Colornaming," *Journal of Experimental Psychology,* 101 (1), 186–189.

SHEVRIN, H. and S. DICKMAN (1980), "The Psychological Unconscious: A Necessary Assumption for All Psychological Theory?" *American Psychologist,* 35, 421–434.

______, and D. FRITZLER (1968), "Visual Evoked Response Correlates of Unconscious Mental Processes," *Science,* 161 (19), 295–298.

SWETS, J. A. (1961), "Is There a Sensory Threshold?" *Science,* 134 (3473), 168–177.

Time (1979), 114 (September 10), 63.

Toronto Star (1978), October 23, c1.

TREISMAN, A. M., and G. GEFFEN (1967), "Selective Attention: Perception or Response?" *Quarterly Journal of Experimental Psychology,* 19 (1), 1–17.

WALSTEDT, J. J., F. GEIS, and V. BROWN (1980), "Influence of Television Commercials on Women's Self-Confidence and Independent Judgment," *Journal of Personality and Social Psychology,* 38 (2), 203–210.

Washington Post (1979), May 27, c4.

WRIGHT, P. L. (1973), "The Cognitive Processes Mediating Acceptance of Advertising," *Journal of Marketing Research,* 10 (February), 53–62.

ZAJONC, R. B. (1980), "Feeling and Thinking: Preferences Need No Inferences," *American Psychologist,* 35 (2), 151–175.

ZUCKERMAN, M. (1960), "The Effects of Subliminal and Supraliminal Suggestions on Verbal Productivity," *Journal of Abnormal and Social Personality,* 60 (3), 404–411.

5

CONSUMER DECISION MAKING—FACT OR FICTION?*

Richard W. Olshavsky
Donald H. Granbois

A synthesis of research on consumers' prepurchase behavior suggests that a substantial proportion of purchases does not involve decision making, not even on the first purchase. The heavy emphasis in current research on decision making may discourage investigation of other important kinds of consumer behavior.

The most pervasive and influential assumption in consumer behavior research is that purchases are preceded by a decision process. Writers who have suggested models of this process have used varying terminology, but all seem to agree that:

1. Two or more alternative actions exist and, therefore, *choice* must occur.
2. Evaluative criteria facilitate the forecasting of each alternative's consequences for the consumer's goals or objectives.
3. The chosen alternative is determined by a decision rule or evaluative procedure.
4. Information sought from external sources and/or retrieved from memory is processed in the application of the decision rule or evaluation procedure.

Virtually every text on consumer behavior includes a verbal or flow chart model of consumer decision processes. Engel, Blackwell, and Kollat (1978) base an elaborate stage model on five steps (problem recognition, search, alternative evaluation, choice, and outcomes) suggested 70 years ago by John Dewey. Howard's (1977) refinement of the concept of routinized response behavior, advanced in How-

*Reprinted from the *Journal of Consumer Research,* 6 (September 1979), pp. 93–100.

ard and Sheth (1969, p. 9), assumes that even simplified, habitual behavior reflects the earlier application of choice criteria to alternative brands. When situational constraints block the repetition of an earlier choice, a reduced-form evaluation process follows, in which dichotomized criteria are applied to a small evoked set of brands (Howard 1977, pp. 27-30).

Research on decision making currently takes several forms. Multidimensional scaling and conjoint measurement are widely applied measurement tools whose relevance grows out of the "multi-attribute nature of consumer decisions" (Green and Wind 1973, p. 5). Different processing rules, such as compensatory, disjunctive, conjunctive, lexicographic, and various hybrid procedures decision makers might use in multi-attribute problems are being tested in studies where subjects verbalize or report on their thought processes as they perform choice tasks (Bettman and Zins 1977; Lussier and Olshavsky 1974; Payne 1976; Russ 1971). Investigators in other studies observe or photograph the sequence and extent of information utilization by subjects provided with brochures, display boards, labeled packages, etc., containing attribute information for several brands from which a choice must be made (Bettman and Kakkar 1977; Jacoby, Szybillo, and Busato-Schach 1977; Russo and Rosen 1975; van Raaij 1977). Other approaches to the study of decision processes include correlational methods (Scott and Wright 1976) and information integration techniques (Bettman, Capon, and Lutz 1975).

In his presidential address to the Association for Consumer Research, Kassarjian (1978) raised the possibility that we may be attributing choice processes to consumers when no choice processes occur. Kassarjian was not simply saying that decision processes often are routinized or habitual rather than extended (as Howard and Sheth have already pointed out), but that in some cases no prepurchase process exists. This is a very bold charge, for it implies that much empirical research and theorizing on consumer decision making is less broadly applicable than has been assumed.

Assessing the Evidence

Kassarjian only raised the issue; he presented no supporting evidence. The validity of his position can be assessed in two ways. Applying an evaluation procedure to various alternatives on two or more evaluative criteria requires considerable information, sometimes more than is readily available in memory. Evidence of the circumstances of purchasing behavior occurring in the *absence* of external search, then, helps to establish the *maximum scope* of the nondecision behavior postulated by Kassarjian. Information processing of the sort assumed in alternative evaluation and choice can, of course, be performed with previously acquired and stored information alone. Therefore, the second condition leading to purchase without prior decision process is insufficiency of stored information suitable for alternative evaluation or nonuse of relevant stored information. While the nature of internal processing (or lack of processing) can be studied only indirectly, a convincing case can be made that internal information is frequently either not available, not relevant, or not consulted.[1]

There are several comprehensive reviews of research on consumer prepurchase behavior that provide considerable evidence of external prepurchase information search. These reviews have encompassed surveys in which consumers were asked to describe their prepurchase behavior retrospectively for a recent purchase, or their "usual" behavior, as well as studies of consumers in real-life purchasing situations during which some type of observational method was used to measure the decision process appearing to precede purchase.

It must be recognized that consumer researchers using observation and retrospective questionnaire techniques have probably been influenced by the assumption of decision process behavior, so that their results may reflect a

[1]Certain "process tracing" techniques, in particular protocol analysis, do permit direct monitoring of internal processing, although to a limited extent. However, when this technique is used, subjects are instructed, implicitly or explicitly, to engage in decision making.

subtle bias overstating the prevalence of decision-making behavior. To some extent, research instruments measure what their designers expect to find. Consumers, too, may overstate the extent of prepurchase deliberation and choice-making behavior, because this may appear desirable as well as expected behavior. What this means, then, is that the research to be cited probably *overstates* the extent of prepurchase behavior for which the decision model is appropriate.

Obejctives and Method

The primary purpose of this paper is to assess, through a synthesis of the review articles just mentioned, the apparent scope of consumer behavior not preceded by external search. Additional objectives, secondary only in that less substantial evidence is available for evaluation, include:

- identifying circumstances in which external environmental and situational constraints limit consumers to a single alternative; and
- identifying research in which purchase has been observed to occur without reference to relevant stored information.

Each of the four sections of the paper represents one element of the comprehensive classification of consumer behavior offered by Gredal (1966). These are renamed slightly here, and include: (1) budget allocation (savings/spending and allocation across broad expenditure categories); (2) generic allocation (expenditures for specific products and services); (3) store patronage (shopping and purchasing at specific shopping centers, stores, etc.); and (4) brand purchase.

In each section, conclusions from review articles on prepurchase behavior are cited. Discussion is then directed to why the behavior involved may be subject to influences and constraints precluding an internal evaluation of alternative actions. The principal review articles drawn upon include Ferber (1973) and Ölander and Seipel (1970) on budget allocation, Ferber (1973) on generic allocation, Granbois (1977) on store patronage, and Newman (1977) on brand purchases.

BUDGET ALLOCATION

Saving Versus Spending

How does the allocation of income between saving and spending come about? In his report of a wide ranging review of research on family economic behavior, Ferber (1973) concluded:

> Despite its basic importance for the understanding of consumer financial behavior, the role of financial planning within the family—in the sense of explicit consideration of the allocation of expected financial resources between saving and spending—seems to have received very little attention in empirical work, and would seem to be a prime area for future research (p. 34).

Since Ferber's review, there appears to have been no empirical studies of consumers' information-seeking relative to savings. There are, however, a few studies of consumers' information about alternative forms of savings and their self-assessment of the degree to which "planning" precedes savings. In his review, Ferber reported substantial proportions of households (up to 87 percent) without a "financial plan," although the meaning of "financial plan" was often not clearly defined (Ferber 1973, p. 35).

A review by Ölander and Seipel (1970) also evaluated consumers' knowledge of financial matters, e.g., interest rates, where stocks can be purchased, and tax regulations. One study reviewed reported: "The respondents' knowledge of tax regulations was good in many respects but often did not appear to influence behavior in the direction of using savings and investment forms which were more advantageous from the tax point of view" (p. 68). Further discussion by these reviewers suggests that individual characteristics, such as low achievement motivation, perceived inability to control one's own financial destiny, and very short future time orientation and planning horizon may inhibit planning. Other evidence on the extent of deliberation preceding savings behavior comes from four studies that found the proportion of self-identified systematic savers to be 15 percent, 27 percent, 28 percent, and 40 percent, respectively (p. 31). In another study, 36 percent of respondents predicted very accurately the extent of savings accumulated six months later (p. 33).

Thus, perhaps one-fourth to one-third of all consumers show evidence of some systematic planning and decision making regarding saving; the majority, however, may not be classified as deliberate choosers. An exception may be newlywed couples; Ferber and Nicosia found that half of the couples they interviewed three to six months after marriage reported a definite plan for saving (Ferber 1973, p. 51).

Allocation of Income Across Expenditure Categories

What, if any, type of decision process precedes the allocation of income across the various categories of goods and services, i.e., food/beverage, housing, household furnishings, etc.? We could find no studies of prepurchase behavior relative to household allocation behavior. Clearly, however, purchases within certain categories are nondiscretionary. Income must be allocated to the categories of food/beverage, housing, clothing, and medical care.

Products within certain other categories are not necessary for survival, yet they are essentially nondiscretionary. Certain items of personal care, recreation, and education are very strongly compelled by social pressure. Moreover, purchase of one product or service is often interlocked with other products or services. The purchase of an automobile, for instance, dictates the purchase of gasoline, repair services, and insurance.

Still other expenditures are compelled by consumers' strong preference for a culturally-mandated life style, usually acquired early in life. Most household furnishings, for example, are discretionary, yet 99.8 percent of the electrically wired homes in the United States have a refrigerator. Presumably this is because few American consumers will tolerate the type of life style implied by living without a refrigerator. Many products in the transportation, personal care, household furnishings, and household operations categories are nondiscretionary in this sense; they constitute what Riesman and Roseborough (1955) termed the "standard package," a set of products uniformly represented throughout American society.

Even allocations to categories that seem purely discretionary may not reflect true choice behavior. Tobacco expenditures, for example, are by no means universal; cigarette smoking, the dominant form of tobacco usage, occurs in only 35 percent of United States households [*Adult Use of Tobacco-1975* (1976)]. Studies reveal that smoking behavior is acquired largely in the preteen and teen-age years (*Teenage Smoking* 1976), primarily as a result of such "psychosocial factors" as curiosity, imitation, identification with adult roles, status striving, and rebellion (Lawton 1962). Striving for these goals is socially motivated and strongly influenced by the behavior of peers, siblings, and parents. Processes such as identification and imitation perhaps explain expenditures in this category better than does the notion of individual choice (Wohlford 1970).[2]

All this suggests that the manner in which income is allocated across categories is largely nondiscretionary. This is not to say, however, that consumers make no decisions regarding this type of allocation. Clearly, choices could be made concerning the priorities by which needs will be satisfied and the proportion of income spent within each category. One way to estimate the extent of such decision making in household budget allocation is to ask if a plan exists within the household for distributing income. A unique survey of 300 Minnesota families representing three generations found that only seven percent of grandparents, 21 percent

---

[2]Following experimental smoking during the "transition phase," those going on to become regular smokers (the "maintenance phase") apparently do so because they develop physiological and/or psychological dependence on cigarettes, and discontinuance becomes very difficult or impossible for most smokers.

of parents, and 24 percent of married children reported such plans, and similar proportions claimed to use procedures for estimating expenses and setting specific amounts aside (Hill 1963, pp. 127–137).

The relatively few empirical studies of household budget allocation have sought to discover the comparative roles of family members (Ferber 1973) rather than the nature, incidence, and extent of the process itself. If joint participation by husband and wife, rather than control over the allocation by one spouse, is more likely to indicate conscious deliberation over alternatives, then evidence presented by Ferber and Lee (1974) that the "family financial officer" role tends to shift from joint to individual performance with increasing length of marriage seems to support the hypothesis advanced earlier by Kyrk (1953) that deliberation over household budgets declines over the life cycle.

GENERIC ALLOCATION

What, if any, type of decision process precedes the allocation of income within expenditure categories? Ferber summarizes studies showing that from 20 to 25 percent of durable goods and clothing purchases appear to be "impulsive," in that urgency or a special purchase opportunity displaced deliberation and prepurchase planning, or that satisfaction with the product being replaced reduced family discussion and planning (Ferber 1973, pp. 44–45). Up to 50 percent of supermarket purchases and 33 percent of transactions in variety stores and drugstores are "impulsive purchases," in that shoppers do not state intentions to buy these items in store-entrance interviews (Engel, Blackwell, and Kollat 1978, p. 483). Evidence from other studies (e.g., Wells and LoSciuto 1966) suggests that for certain grocery products decision processes do not occur in the store either.

Additional evidence relating to the existence of prepurchase processes within expenditure category comes from studies of the adoption and diffusion of innovations. A general finding from this research is that substantial differences exist across consumers in the amount of prepurchase deliberation that occurs. Rogers and Shoemaker's (1971) review shows that 12 of 14 studies of information seeking found that early adopters sought more information about the innovation than did later adopters (p. 374). Their review also shows considerable evidence that early adopters have significantly greater exposure to change agents, mass media, and interpersonal communication channels (pp. 371–374). This declining intensity of decision making is explained, at least in part, by the "diffusion effect," the increasing social pressure on nonadopters to adopt the innovation as the percentage of adopters increases. Further, Rogers, and Shoemaker (1971, p. 122) and Robertson (1971, p. 61) acknowledge that evidence for the existence of "stages" in the adoption decision may be artifactual; both cite evidence that when unstructured questionnaires are used, certain stages are skipped or in some cases no decision process occurs.

Contemporary consumer researchers often overlook differences in the cognitive and motivational patterns associated with the many products and services involved in consumption. An early attempt to categorize these differences recognized products that are primarily hedonic (appealing to the senses), those with important symbolic meaning (ego-involving), and a third category valued primarily in terms of their functional performance (Woods 1961). While many generic products have two or even all three dimensions, prepurchase choice processes are most likely when functional performance dominates.

Sensory preferences are often well established in early childhood, although these may change somewhat with maturation, e.g., increasing preferences for salty and sharp flavors as children enter the teen years (Reynolds and Wells 1977, p. 83). Likes and dislikes for certain tastes, because of their early origins, may be reflected in consumption patterns without deliberation or even awareness by the consumer. Symbolic aspects of products are also often learned in childhood. Moore (1957) points out that eating, like other physiological activities, is especially prone to symbolic elaboration, perhaps because these activities "reach back into infancy, and are complexly patterned long before there is any autonomous intelligence or maturity with which to perceive the difference between the act itself and its accompanying feelings, social circumstances, contradictions, and coincidental motives" (Moore 1957, p. 77). One study of five-, seven-, and nine-year-olds found:

> Children apparently begin assigning social values to goods around age seven, particularly to elaborate toys. Nine-year-olds also are slightly fashion conscious in the sense that they may express a desire for certain articles of clothing being worn by other children, for example, tennis shoes and skirts . . . Children involve themselves considerably with some durable goods. In discussing automobiles with them, it was found that practically all of them have preferences for certain autos . . . (McNeal 1969, pp. 263, 265).

These examples suggest that better understanding of the processes leading to early childhood acquisition of taste preferences and symbolic interpretations of products may be more relevant for understanding preferences for "hedonic" and "symbolic" products than research structured on models of choice and decision.

Finally, in many instances consumers have no control over the specific products and services they purchase or consume. In the extreme case, consumers who are institutionalized (e.g., in hospitals, rest homes, or military institutions) typically have little or no control over the type of food, clothing, or furnishings they use. College students who live in dormitories and fraternities are similarly constrained. Apartment dwellers, and in many cases even home buyers, have little control over such items as fixtures, appliances, and floor coverings.

STORE PATRONAGE

Analysis of the spatial environment within which most consumers obtain goods and services reveals the potential relevance of choice models in portraying shopping and store patronage behavior. Consumers often find desired products and services to be available in two or more cities or towns within reasonable driving distance, or in numerous local shopping centers or areas, scattered retail outlets, and so forth. Catalogs, mail order, door-to-door sales organizations, telephone ordering services, etc., further expand the range of possible sources. A review of studies on shopping and patronage suggests, however, that extended search and evaluation typically does not precede store patronage (Granbois 1977).

Use of Nonstore Sources

While nonstore shopping sources are important in most product categories, studies of their use have revealed considerable city-to-city variation. One study found high users of mail order also to be high telephone order users; another found heavy in-home buyers also to be active store shoppers. Several studies have found distinctive socioeconomic characteristics associated with heavy use of these modes (Granbois 1977, p. 270). All the findings suggest that a significant subset of all consumers may not even consider sources other than the conventional retail outlets.

Patronage of Urban Areas/ Shopping Centers

Patronage of shopping areas tends to vary directly with assortment size and inversely with distance or effort involved in reaching them. Studies of patronage have firmly established the broad predictive usefulness of simple formal models establishing these relationships. Recent research, however, points to exceptions to, and constraints on, the patterns predicted by these models. For example, attention has been given to the impact of physical barriers, differential behavior of consumers with varying socioeconomic characteristics, and the impact of differing levels of promotion and price differences (Granbois 1977). The existence of limitations on the range of alternative shopping areas is further supported by the findings of "outshopping" studies, seeking determinants of shopping trips to nearby cities. Two studies found distinctive profiles of outshoppers with regard to variables such as income, age, race, sex, and beliefs, suggesting this pattern to be limited to certain market segments (Granbois 1977, p. 287).

Patronage Among and Within Store Types

Studies of shopping activity preceding major durable goods purchases have typically found a high incidence of purchases occurring after a single store visit, despite the fact that the high dollar value, physical complexity, relatively low purchase frequency, and the presence of a significant proportion of first-time purchasers in the samples would seem to indicate more extensive consideration of alternative outlets. The following data illustrate this finding (Granbois 1977, p. 264).

Type of Purchase	*Percent of Buyers Reporting a Single Store Visit*
Black and white television	39
Color television	50
Furniture	22
Carpet	27

Similar studies of soft goods purchases reveal that 75–80 percent of all purchases are made after visiting a single store (Granbois 1977, p. 266).

Deliberation and true choice might be expected to be at a maximum among residents new to an area. Nevertheless, such studies have consistently found that convenience and past loyalty to chains in the previous area are important criteria in making selections, and that new patterns are established quickly—supermarkets selected within three weeks, several other store types picked within five weeks (Granbois 1977, p. 272). These and other results indicate a less-than-full evaluation of alternatives. One study of supermarket shoppers using retrospective accounts of store selection found that nine percent of the sample reported to have made no choice; patronage occurred instead on bases such as personal recommendations or preferences acquired in early childhood (Olshavsky and MacKay 1978).

As in the case of generic product preferences, store preferences developed at an early age may serve as constraints on the range of choice alternatives considered by adults. Evidence of this pattern was also found by McNeal, who writes: "Starting as early as age five children show likes and dislikes for certain stores as well as specific types of stores" (McNeal 1969, p. 263).

BRAND PURCHASE

How does brand purchase occur? In his review of research on prepurchase information seeking, Newman (1977) found little evidence of extensive search and some evidence that no search or evaluation occurred in many instances. On sources of information, Newman reports that:

> One survey found that one-third of the buyers of major appliances received information from only one source . . . A more recent survey found that 15 percent of the buyers of major appliances and automobiles consulted no external source before buying . . . In both surveys source referred to a type or category such as friends and neighbors; books, pamphlets and articles; advertising; and retail outlets . . . A survey of small electrical appliance buyers found that 10 percent of them could not recall obtaining helpful information in any way other than by visiting a retail store (p. 80).

On number of alternatives considered, Newman writes:

> Several studies have shown that many consumers limit their attention to few alternatives. Forty-six percent of the buyers of major household appliances considered only one price range . . . appliance buyers who examined only one brand ranged from 41 percent for refrigerators to 71 percent for vacuum cleaners . . . of the buyers of household appliances and cars, 47 percent considered mainly a single brand at the outset of the decision process . . . These findings are consistent with other evidence that the buyer's "evoked set" of brands . . . is typically small (p. 81).

Finally, with respect to results based on studies that developed a comprehensive index of information seeking, Newman states:

> Using a scale ranging from one for no information seeking to six for very active search, Katona and Mueller reported that 40 percent of the buyers of major appliances had scale values of one or two while 10 percent had values of five or six . . . The results led Katona and Mueller to conclude that 'Any notion that careful planning and choosing, thorough consideration of alternatives, and information seeking accompanied every major purchase was contradicted by the data . . . Rather, it appeared . . . that many purchases were made in a state of ignorance or at least indifference.' In another study of major appliances and automobiles, on a 20-point scale representing out-of-store search (zero meaning none), 49 percent had scores of 5 or less; 38 percent scored from 6 to 11; and 13 percent had scores of 12 to 20 (p. 82).

There are only a few direct studies of the brand choice process, each with strong limitations. Wells and Lo Sciuto (1966) using an in-store, on-the-spot technique, observed 1,500 supermarket shoppers. Only representative data for cereals, candy, and detergent were presented. In 55 percent of the cases for cereals, 38 percent for candy, and 72 percent for detergent, there was no visible evidence of an in-store prepurchase choice process, such as inspecting two or more packages. In 15 percent of the cases for cereal, 44 percent candy, and 12 percent for detergent, no purchase occurred. Hence, according to these data, in only 30 percent of the cereal, 18 percent of the candy, and 12 percent of the detergent purchases was there even the possibility that an in-store prepurchase process occurred. Unfortunately, the technique used could not observe the mental processes; strong conclusions about the choice process, therefore, cannot be drawn from this study.

In another study of supermarket shoppers (Bettman 1970), a "process tracing" technique was used, which was more likely to reveal any choice processes that occurred. For a period of six to eight weeks, Bettman observed the shopping behavior of two homemakers and asked them to think aloud as they made their purchases. He analyzed these protocol data to obtain insights about the evaluative criteria and evaluation processes used. A similar study of women's ready-to-wear clothing was performed by Alexis, Haines, and Simon (1968).

While these and other studies using process tracing techniques generally find evidence for prepurchase process, the techniques are inherently biased; as Bettman and Zins (1977) point out:

> A second bias in the protocols occurs because the consumer is asked to give protocols for choices where in many cases a great deal of learning has already occurred . . . the consumer may have bought the same brand many times, and may not really think much about this type of choice while it is being made. The request from the experimenter to keep talking may then lead to retrospection about why the particular brand was bought in the first place, although such reasoning is not relevant now (p. 82).

In another study of in-store behavior, Olshavsky (1973) analyzed tape recorded conversations between customer and salesman for major appliance transactions, without the customer being aware of the recording. This study provided clear evidence of at least a limited amount of prepurchase processes. At the same time, however, in some cases customers relied entirely upon the salesman's recommendation.

Other studies provide more direct evidence concerning the way brand purchases occur without prior consideration of alternatives. Several studies document that consumers make purchases on the basis of recommendations from either personal or nonpersonal sources. Feldman and Spencer (1965) reported that 75 percent of newcomers to a community selected a physician solely on the basis of a recommendation. Some studies have indicated that brand purchase behavior represents conformity to group norms; this occurs particularly for highly conspicuous products. Venkatesan (1968) demonstrated in a laboratory study the influence of group pressure on selection of men's suits. Also, some evidence suggests that brand preferences are acquired early in life, as part of the general acculturation process (Ward 1974). It has even been found that brand purchases are influenced by such superficial factors as shelf height and shelf facings (Frank and Massy 1970).

Finally, there is some evidence that brand purchases are made on the basis of surrogates or indices of quality, rather than on the basis of a direct evaluation of the brands' attributes. Price, manufacturer's reputation, and packaging are but a few of the indices studied (Monroe 1973; Gardner 1971; McConnell 1968; Brown 1958).

CONCLUSIONS AND IMPLICATIONS

Our review of studies that provide some evidence, direct or indirect, for the existence of prepurchase processes and our analysis of the constraints and influences on purchasing behavior suggest that Kassarjian is right. A significant proportion of purchases may not be preceded by a decision process. This conclusion does not simply restate the familiar observation that purchase behavior rapidly becomes habitual, with little or no prepurchase processes occurring after the first few purchases. We conclude that for many purchases a decision process never occurs, not even on the first purchase.

How then does purchasing occur if not as a result of some type of decision process? This review identified a number of different ways: Purchases can occur out of necessity; they can be derived from culturally mandated lifestyles or from interlocked purchases; they can reflect preferences acquired in early childhood; they can result from simple conformity to group norms or from imitation of others; purchases can be made exclusively on recommendations from personal or nonpersonal sources; they can be made on the basis of surrogates of various types; or they can even occur on a random or superficial basis. Further research, free of the prepurchase decision assumption, may identify still other ways.

Another conclusion we draw from this review is that even when purchase behavior is preceded by a choice process, it is likely to be very limited. It typically involves the evaluation of few alternatives, little external search, few evaluative criteria, and simple evaluation process models. There is little evidence that consumers engage in the very extended type of search and evaluation a product testing organization like Consumers Union performs routinely.[3]

It would be an oversimplification, however, to characterize purchasing behavior as either involving predecision processes or not. While this may be an accurate characterization of some purchases, in general, we should allow for combination or "hybrid" strategies whereby choice and nonchoice are used; e.g., personal recommendations can be combined in various ways with limited search and evaluation. Indeed, future research may reveal that such hybrid strategies are the most common type of prepurchase behavior.

These conclusions have important implications for theories of consumer behavior. Certainly any theory whose central thesis is that purchases are preceded by a decision process (Engel, Blackwell, and Kollat 1978; Howard and Sheth 1969) can provide an adequate explanation of only certain types of consumer purchasing behaviors. Theory needs to be developed along at least two separate lines. Wright has argued that a process he calls "affect referral" often describes purchases. Global measures of affect, not attribute-specific information, provide the basis for choice, where either the "best" or the "first acceptable" option thought of is selected (Wright 1976). This first line of development will be particularly fruitful if it entails low involvement learning as part of an ongoing socialization process.

The second line of development is suggested by the work of Lussier and Olshavsky (1974), Payne (1976), and others who have argued for a contingent processing view of decision making. Payne, for example, points out that the various choice strategies (e.g., additive difference, con-

---

[3]This is not to imply that consumers who use *Consumer Reports* could not engage in extensive evaluation of the data presented, but that they do not gather such data themselves. Indeed, in most cases, this cannot be done by the typical consumer because of the time, effort, expense, or expertise involved.

junctive, and elimination-by-aspects) are not competing, but complementary.

In that regard, the four decision processes discussed in this paper might be conceptualized as different subroutines in a general choice program. The control conditions under which one of these sets of processes might be called would then seem to depend, at least in part, on the characteristics of the decision problem. In that respect, the less cognitively demanding decision procedures, conjunctive and elimination-by-aspects, might be called early in the decision process as a way of simplifying the decision task by quickly eliminating alternatives until only a few alternatives remained as choice possibilities. The subject might then employ one of the cognitively demanding choice procedures, e.g., additive difference model, to make the final evaluation and choice (Payne 1976, p. 385).

This contingent processing concept needs to be broadened to incorporate other purchasing heuristics of the type identified here, e.g., conformity, imitation, recommendations.

In view of the tremendous interest in consumer purchasing behavior it is surprising, to say the least, that there have been so few studies of prepurchase processes that involve actual consumers in actual settings using methodologies that permit observation of behaviors contrary to those predicted by models of choice and decision processes. Such research is fraught with difficulties that must be overcome if we are to have a secure empirical foundation for theory construction and testing.

These conclusions also have implications for private and public policy. Clearly, if some purchases are not preceded by any type of prior search and evaluation, then recommendations based on research that incorporates the assumption that they are may be inappropriate. The issue of "information overload," for instance, which has occupied so many pages in marketing journals recently, must be interpreted quite differently if a significant percentage of consumers of particular products or services do not engage in prepurchase activities.

REFERENCES

Adult Use of Tobacco-1975 (1976), U.S. Department of Health, Education, and Welfare, Public Health Service, Center for Disease Control, National Clearinghouse for Smoking and Health.

ALEXIS, MARCUS, HAINES, GEORGE H., and SIMON, LEONARD (1968), "Consumer Information Processing: The Case of Women's Clothing," in *Proceedings,* Chicago: American Marketing Association, pp. 197-205.

BETTMAN, JAMES R. (1970), "Information Processing Models of Consumer Behavior," *Journal of Marketing Research,* 7, 370-376.

______, CAPON, NOEL, and LUTZ, RICHARD (1975), "Cognitive Algebra in Multiattribute Attitude Models," *Journal of Marketing Research,* 12, 151-164.

______, and KAKKAR, PRADEEP (1977), "Effects of Information Presentation Format on Consumer Information Acquisition Strategy," *Journal of Consumer Research,* 3, 233-240.

______, and ZINS, MICHEL A. (1977), "Constructive Process in Consumer Choice," *Journal of Consumer Research,* 4, 75-85.

BROWN, ROBERT L. (1958), "Wrapper Influence on the Perception of Freshness in Bread," *Journal of Applied Psychology,* 42, 257-260.

ENGEL, JAMES F., BLACKWELL, ROGER D., and KOLLAT, DAVID T. (1978), *Consumer Behavior.* Hinsdale, IL: The Dryden Press.

FELDMAN, SIDNEY P., and SPENCER, MERLIN C. (1965), "The Effect of Personal Influence in the Selection of Consumer Services," in *Marketing and Economic Development,* Ed. Peter Bennett. Chicago: American Marketing Association, pp. 440-452.

FERBER, ROBERT (1973), "Family Decision Making and Economic Behavior: A Review," in *Family Economic Behavior: Problems and Prospects,* Ed. Eleanor B. Sheldon. Philadelphia: Lippincott, pp. 29-61.

______, and LEE, LUCY CHAO (1974), "Husband-Wife Influence in Family Purchasing Behavior," *Journal of Consumer Research,* 1, 43-50.

FRANK, RONALD E., and MASSY, WILLIAM F. (1970), "Shelf Position and Space Effects," *Journal of Marketing Research,* 7, 59-66.

GARDNER, DAVID M. (1971), "Is There a Generalized Price-Quality Relationship?" *Journal of Marketing Research,* 8, 241–243.

GRANBOIS, DONALD H. (1977), "Shopping Behavior and Preferences," in *Selected Aspects of Consumer Behavior—A Summary from the Perspective of Different Disciplines.* Washington, DC: U.S. Government Printing Office, pp. 259–298.

GREDAL, KAREN (1966), "Purchasing Behavior in Households," in *Readings in Danish Theory of Marketing,* Ed. Max Kjaer-Hansen. Copenhagen: Einar Harcks Forlag, pp. 84–100.

GREEN, PAUL E., and WIND, YORAM (1973), *Multiattribute Decisions in Marketing.* Hinsdale, IL: The Dryden Press.

HILL, REUBEN (1963), "Judgment and Consumership in the Management of Family Resources," *Sociology and Social Research,* 47, 460–466.

HOWARD, JOHN A. (1977), *Consumer Behavior: Application of Theory.* New York: McGraw-Hill.

———, and SHETH, JAGDISH N. (1969), *The Theory of Buyer Behavior.* New York: Wiley.

JACOBY, JACOB, SZYBILLO, GEORGE J., and BUSATO-SCHACH, JACQUELINE (1977), "Information Acquisition Behavior in Brand Choice Situations," *Journal of Consumer Research,* 3, 209–216.

KASSARJIAN, HAROLD H. (1978), "Presidential Address, 1977: Anthropomorphism and Parsimony," in *Advances in Consumer Research,* Vol. 5, Ed. H. Keith Hunt. Ann Arbor, MI: Association for Consumer Research, pp. xii–xiv.

KOLLAT, DAVID T., and WILLETT, RONALD P. (1967), "Customer Impulse Purchasing Behavior," *Journal of Marketing Research,* 21–31.

KYRK, HAZEL (1953), *The Family in the American Economy.* Chicago: University of Chicago Press.

LAWTON, M. P. (1962), "Psychosocial Aspects of Cigarette Smoking," *Journal of Health and Human Behavior,* 3, 163–170.

LUSSIER, DENIS A., and OLSHAVSKY, RICHARD W. (1974), "An Information Processing Approach to Individual Brand Choice Behavior," paper presented at the ORSA/TIMS Joint National Meeting, San Juan, Puerto Rico.

MCCONNELL, J. DOUGLAS (1968), "The Development of Brand Loyalty: An Experimental Study," *Journal of Marketing Research,* 5, 13–19.

MCNEAL, JAMES U. (1969), "An Exploratory Study of the Consumer Behavior of Children," in *Dimensions of Consumer Behavior,* Ed. James U. McNeal. New York: Appleton-Century-Crofts, 255–275.

MONROE, KENT B. (1973), "Buyers' Subjective Perceptions of Price," *Journal of Marketing Research,* 10, 70–80.

MOORE, HARRIET (1957), "The Meaning of Foods," *The American Journal of Clinical Nutrition,* 5, 77–82.

NEWMAN, JOSEPH W. (1977), "Consumer External Search: Amount and Determinants," in *Consumer and Industrial Buying Behavior,* Eds. Arch G. Woodside, Jagdish N. Sheth, and Peter D. Bennett. New York: North-Holland.

ÖLANDER, FOLKE, and SEIPEL, CARL-MAGNUS (1970), *Psychological Approaches to the Study of Saving.* Urbana, IL: Bureau of Economics and Business Research, University of Illinois.

OLSHAVSKY, RICHARD W. (1973), "Customer-Salesman Interaction in Appliance Retailing," *Journal of Marketing Research,* 10, 208–212.

———, and MACKAY, DAVID B. (1978), "An Empirical Test of Four Alternative Supermarket Choice Models," unpublished working paper, Indiana University, Department of Marketing.

PAYNE, JOHN W. (1976), "Task Complexity and Contingent Processing in Decision Making: An Information Search and Protocol Analysis," *Organizational Behavior and Human Performance,* 16, 366–387.

VAN RAAIJ, W. FRED (1977), "Consumer Information Processing for Different Information Structures and Formats," in *Advances in Consumer Research,* Vol. 4, Ed. William O. Perreault, pp. 176–184.

REYNOLDS, FRED D., and WELLS, WILLIAM D. (1977), *Consumer Behavior.* New York: McGraw-Hill.

RIESMAN, DAVID, and ROSEBOROUGH, HOWARD (1955), "Careers and Consumer Behavior," in *The Life Cycle and Consumer Behavior,* Vol. 2, Ed. Lincoln Clark. New York: New York University Press, pp. 1–18.

ROBERTSON, THOMAS S. (1971), *Innovative Behavior and Communication.* New York: Holt, Rinehart & Winston.

ROGERS, EVERETT M., and SHOEMAKER, F.

FLOYD (1971), *Communication of Innovations.* New York: The Free Press.

RUSS, FREDERICK A. (1971), "Evaluation Process Models and the Prediction of Preference," in *Proceedings,* Association for Consumer Research, Ed. David M. Gardner, pp. 256–261.

RUSSO, EDWARD J., and ROSEN, LARRY D. (1975), "An Eye Fixation Analysis of Multi-Attribute Choice," *Memory and Cognition,* 3, 267–276.

SCOTT, JEROME E., and PETER WRIGHT (1976), "Modeling an Organizational Buyer's Product Evaluation Strategy: Validity and Procedural Considerations," *Journal of Marketing Research,* 13, 211–224.

Teenage Smoking, National Patterns of Cigarette Smoking, Ages 12 through 18, in 1972 and 1974, (1976), U.S. Department of Health, Education and Welfare, Public Health Service, National Institute of Health.

VENKATESAN, M. (1966), "Experimental Study of Consumer Behavior Conformity and Independence," *Journal of Marketing Research,* 3, 384–387.

WARD, SCOTT (1974), "Consumer Socialization," *Journal of Consumer Research,* 1 (September), 1–14.

WELLS, WILLIAM, and LO SCIUTO, LEONARD A. (1966), "Direct Observation of Purchasing Behavior," *Journal of Marketing Research,* 3, 227–233.

WOHLFORD, PAUL (1970), "Initiation of Cigarette Smoking: Is It Related to Parental Smoking Behavior?" *Journal of Consulting and Clinical Psychology,* 34, 148–151.

WOODS, WALTER A. (1960), "Psychological Dimensions of Consumer Decision," *Journal of Marketing,* 24, 15–19.

WRIGHT, PETER (1976), "An Adaptive Consumer's View of Attitudes and Other Choice Mechanisms, as Viewed by an Equally Adaptive Advertiser," in *Attitude Research at Bay,* Eds. Deborah Johnson and William D. Wells. Chicago: American Marketing Association, pp. 113–131.

6

MEMORY AND ATTENTIONAL FACTORS IN CONSUMER CHOICE: Concepts and Research Methods*

John G. Lynch, Jr.
Thomas K. Srull

While consumer researchers have evinced considerable interest in cognitive processes in decision making, work has centered on the *conscious* mental manipulation of product information. This paper addresses memory and attentional processes that may occur below the level of consciousness. Methods developed within the field of cognitive psychology are presented to supplement the standard process tracing methods commonly used by consumer researchers.

Much of the current theoretical work in consumer behavior emphasizes the role of cognitive structure and process, and as a result of borrowing heavily from the field of cognitive psychology, new information processing concepts are continually being incorporated into consumer behavior theories. Although many people are convinced that these information processing concepts are useful and necessary for future theory development, skeptical and even critical comments have been voiced (e.g., Kassarjian 1978 1981). This skepticism is partially justified: The number of concepts and theoretical processes that have been hypothesized has grown enormously in recent years, but this increased sophistication in dealing with

*Reprinted from *Journal of Consumer Research,* 9 (June 1982), pp. 18–37.

cognitive processes has remained at the conceptual level. It has generally *not* been accompanied by methodologies that are capable of diagnosing such processes. Until such methodologies are systematically employed, there is a very real danger of being unable to discriminate between competing theoretical accounts.

Moreover, decision process researchers may be limiting their domain of inquiry by choosing problems for study that are suited to familiar methodologies, as Wright (1980) has suggested. The "process tracing" methodologies currently popular with scholars in the consumer decision making area (e.g., Bettman and Jacoby 1976; Ericsson and Simon 1980; Payne, Braunstein, and Carroll 1978) are most useful for studying aspects of information processing that are "molar" rather than "molecular," overt rather than covert, and voluntary rather than involuntary. They are markedly less informative in diagnosing mental states and events that do not fit this description (i.e., those that are molecular, covert, and/or involuntary). Thus the present paper has two goals:

- To suggest a broad range of issues pertaining to the roles of memory and attentional factors in decision making
- To outline research methodologies that adequately address those issues

Most of these methodologies have their roots in the field of cognitive psychology.

Before delving into this discussion, the history of decision researchers' interests in process issues will be briefly traced. This goal is not to provide an exhaustive review, but to illustrate how memory and attentional issues represent a natural outgrowth of the existing literature on consumer decision making.

During the 1960s and early 1970s, normative models of statistical inference served as a starting point for research that had the goal of describing actual choice behavior. Expected value, Bayes theorem, and multiple regression were proposed as approximations to the rules used to make day-to-day choices. It was assumed that manifest violations of these statistical models could be accounted for by making minor modifications to the parameters of the models. For example, violations of subjective expected utility theory (Savage 1954) were deemed explainable by a positive or negative utility for risk, or by the notion that subjective probabilities of complementary events may not sum to unity (Tversky 1967).

The era of descriptive decision theories based upon normative models was followed by one in which process concerns moved to the forefront (see Slovic, Fischhoff, and Lichtenstein 1977, and Einhorn and Hogarth 1981 for a thorough review of this generation of decision research). The stimulus for this shift was an accumulation of inconsistent results, in which tasks that were conceptually identical but different in surface structure yielded drastically different patterns of decisions (e.g., Lichtenstein and Slovic 1971). Kahneman and Tversky's rejection of Bayes' theorem as a descriptive model is typical of this era: ". . . man is apparently not a conservative Bayesian: he is not Bayesian at all" (1972, p. 450).

One of the basic thrusts of this generation of decision research involved a search for alternative composition models or heuristics that take into account the consumer's mental representation of the information upon which his decision is based (Tversky and Kahneman 1981); the consumer's limited ability to process more than a few pieces of information concurrently in order to arrive at a choice (Wallsten 1980); and the adaptive choice of a decision "strategy" as a function of task characteristics, such as the number and dimensionality of alternative brands (Einhorn 1971; Lussier and Olshavsky 1979; Olshavsky 1979; Payne 1976; Wright 1974).

While a complete review of this research is beyond the scope of this paper, it is important to make a few summary observations. There has been great enthusiasm for the idea of taking cognitive structure and process into account in attempting to explain decision behavior, but the theorizing that has attempted to accomplish this has been fairly rudimentary. It has focused almost exclusively on the *strategic,* conscious aspects of information processing in the Newell and Simon (1972) tradition. The picture that emerges is one of decision makers who understand their limitations and who know how to revise their information processing strategies to minimize any ill effects on decision quality.

One of the most important lessons of cognitive psychology is that most of the memory and attentional factors that affect our judgments are simply unavailable to consciousness. In a recent review of the literature, Lachman, Lachman, and Butterfield (1979) point out that "Most of what we do goes on unconsciously . . . *It is the exception, not the rule, when thinking is conscious*" (p. 207, italics added). This general theme has been echoed by Mandler (1975b), who notes that consciousness does not represent the *process* of cognition but the *result* of a long chain of prior, unconscious cognitive activity. He also notes that "The second problem to be faced is the fact that the contents of consciousness are not simply reproducible by some one-to-one mapping into verbal report. Even if these contents were always couched in language—which they surely are not—some theory of transmission would be required" (p. 52).[1] It would seem, then, that consumer research must not limit its focus to conscious decision strategies, but also explore the unconscious and/or involuntary aspects of information processing. This will necessitate a change in the methodologies used to study consumer information processing within the context of decision making.

MEMORY-BASED VS. STIMULUS-BASED JUDGMENTS

An active consideration of cognitive processes and the role they play in decision making raises a number of theoretical and practical issues that have been neglected thus far in the literature. For example, studies of consumer choice and decision making often begin by presenting subjects with a "brand X attribute matrix." Such a matrix might contain three different cars (e.g., Ford, Chevrolet, and Buick) and the corresponding values of three different attributes for each of the cars (e.g., price, mileage, and rate of repair). The subject might then be asked to choose the best car to buy. If all of the relevant information is directly present when a judgment is made, such a judgment may be called a "stimulus-based" judgment. However, consumers often make judgments on the basis of information that is not directly present at the time of judgment. Prior experience with a product, knowledge of the choices of other people, and other factors may also be relevant to a judgment. Since such information is stored in memory, it needs to be retrieved for use in making a choice at some later time.

Such considerations raise a number of issues concerning the way in which choice and decision processes operate, particularly in ecologically representative situations. At the one extreme, there are pure stimulus-based judgments. Buying from a mail-order catalogue may be an example of this sort. In examining this type of judgment, the theoretical and empirical emphasis is on the decision rules that people use. All of the past work on conjunctive, disjunctive, and lexicographic rules and on cognitive heuristics is relevant to stimulus-based judgments (for a review of this literature, see Svenson 1979). But many of the ecologically relevant decisions that people make are *not* stimulus-based: there are also pure "memory-based" judgments in which *none* of the relevant information is physically present, so that the consumer must rely exclusively on information stored in memory. Making up a grocery list while at work would be an example of such a judgment. Perhaps even more frequent are "mixed" judgments in which some information is physically present but other relevant information is stored in memory, such as a situation in which one visits J.C. Penney, Sears, and K-Mart in shopping for a kitchen appliance.

Pure memory-based and mixed judgments are extremely important because of their preva-

---

[1]Posner has discussed the role of unconscious processes in attentional phenomena, arguing that consciousness is essentially a "processing bottleneck" (Posner 1978; Posner and Klein 1973; Posner, Klein, Summers, and Buggie 1973; Posner and Snyder 1975). Blumenthal (1977) has discussed unconscious processes with respect to a wide range of cognitive tasks, and Pollio (1974) has discussed the role the unconscious plays in "higher-order" processes such as judgment and problem solving. Mandler (1975a, 1975b, 1979) has documented the extremely important role such processes play in emotion and affective reactions to various objects. Lachman, Lachman, and Butterfield (1979) present what is perhaps the best overall treatment of the subject.

lence; they also complicate a theoretical analysis of decision making considerably. A number of factors become important that affect one's ability to execute certain choice rules. For example, many choice rules discussed in the literature implicitly or explicitly assume that values on a common set of attribute dimensions characterize all alternatives in the choice set. Yet, any time a person must rely on memory for information, it is possible that the information s/he has available about certain attributes will be different for the various alternatives. This can eliminate entire classes of choice rules (such as Tversky's (1969) additive difference rule, conjunctive, disjunctive, and lexicographic rules) unless the person chooses to ignore some of the information available or infer some information that is not available. In either case, an explicit consideration of the underlying cognitive processes is imperative for any thorough theoretical analysis.

Retrieval Processes

Information that is stored in memory must be retrieved before it can be considered in making a particular judgment. In this regard, memory researchers typically make a fundamental distinction between "availability" and "accessibility" (see Tulving and Pearlstone 1966). Once information is fully comprehended and encoded into long-term memory, it is thought to be always available (e.g., Lewis 1979). That is, there are physiological mechanisms within the central nervous system that permanently retain such information in the absence of any profound injury to the brain. However, only a small portion of the vast quantities of information that we learn is "accessible" at any given time—i.e., we are only capable of retrieving a fraction of the total information we have available. Moreover, it is widely recognized that information that is accessible in one context will not necessarily be accessible in another, and that information that is accessible at one time will not necessarily be accessible at another time. The two most important determinants of whether information is accessible at any given time are: (1) the amount of competing information that has also been learned in the same "content domain," and (2) the self-generated and externally generated retrieval cues present at the time.

A simple example of how these processes operate may be helpful. Most people "know" the name of their first grade teacher and have that information "available." That is, once the information is learned it is probably never "forgotten." However, people learn thousands of names by the time they are adults. Thus adults may not be able to retrieve or spontaneously recall the name of their first grade teacher due to the large number of "competing responses." External retrieval cues will help. If shown old photographs or told the name of other old teachers or classmates, people are more likely to retrieve the name. Internal retrieval cues will also help. If people pause to reminisce about their old school and continue to think about their teacher and classmates, they are also more likely to retrieve the name. But even if they are successful in retrieving the name, it is likely that they will once again "forget" it or be unable to recall it at some later time. In general, any information that a person fully comprehends and encodes into long-term memory will be "available" from that point on, but it will be "accessible" only in a limited set of circumstances.

The fact that people can retrieve information in response to specific cues that they are unable to retrieve in the absence of such cues is exemplified in a classic study of "retroactive interference" by Tulving and Psotka (1971). Retroactive interference refers to the fact that later learning typically inhibits the recall of previously acquired information. Tulving and Psotka reasoned that material that is learned later can interfere with previously acquired information through at least two mechanisms. First, subsequent learning may result in a general decay or weakening of the memory traces associated with earlier items. Alternatively, subsequent learning may have no effect on earlier traces, but may make it more difficult for a person to independently access or retrieve previously learned information (perhaps by making it more difficult to independently produce relevant cues). To test these hypotheses, Tulving and Psotka presented subjects with various numbers of word lists. Each list contained 24 words, consisting of four words from each of six semantic categories (e.g., types of buildings). The category names themselves were not provided. Some subjects learned the target list and then recalled as many of the words as possible. Other subjects learned the target list and then learned from one to five additional, interpolated lists before attempting to recall words from the original list. The results of the study were quite clear: the number of words recalled from the target list declined consistently as the number of interpolated lists increased.

These results are consistent with those of many other studies showing the effects of retroactive interference. However, it was still not clear whether such results were due to a weakening of the original traces or to some retrieval failure. Tulving and Psotka addressed this question by administering a second (cued) recall test in which category cues for the six semantic categories were also presented. When the cued recall procedure was used, the number of words recalled from the target list was virtually unaffected by the number of interpolated lists. These results suggest that traces for the original items were still "available" and that the "forgetting" associated with the number of interpolated lists was really due to an inability to retrieve the original items. The results also indicated that information that can be retrieved in response to externally provided cues often cannot be retrieved when such cues are absent. Thus, information that is available is not always accessible. These general findings have been replicated many times in different contexts (e.g., Buschke 1973; Tulving and Pearlstone 1966). They have also led many contemporary theorists (e.g., Eysenck 1977; Raaijmakers and Shiffrin 1981) to propose that virtually all "forgetting" is due to retrieval failure. Information continues to be available but becomes less accessible without the aid of relevant retrieval cues.

In experiments like Tulving and Psotka's (1971), organizational strategies have a systematic effect on subsequent recall. Specifically, people tend to recall categories of information in what Cohen (1966) has termed a "some-or-none" fashion. This is true of both predefined categories and subjective attempts to categorize large amounts of information (Horowitz and Prytulak 1969; Mandler 1967, 1968; Mandler and Pearlstone 1966; Tulving and Pearlstone 1966; Tulving and Psotka 1971). People either fail to recall any instances from a category or recall six or seven instances from each category that is accessed. For example, Cohen (1963, 1966) found that the mean number of instances recalled from a category was virtually constant for lists ranging from 35 to 53 to 70 words. Graesser and Mandler (1978) observed a similar phenomenon in recall from natural categories. Moreover, variables that influence memory do so primarily by determining the number of categories that can be accessed rather than the number of items within a category that can be recalled (Cohen 1963, 1966; Patterson 1972; Tulving and Pearlstone 1966; Tulving and Psotka 1971; Wood 1972).

This implies that when people organize product information by brand, they are likely to "forget" entire brands rather than attributes within a brand. Alternatively, when the information is organized by attribute, they are likely to forget all of the values for a certain attribute rather than values associated with only a few brands. Once a person is able to "lock into" a given category, most—if not all—of the information within that category is likely to be recalled. Thus any variable that affects the way in which the information is initially organized will seriously limit the number of choice rules that can be plausibly executed. Presentation format (Biehal and Chakravarti 1982; Johnson and Russo 1978) is certainly one such variable; identifying others that have similar effects will be a major challenge to future investigators.

The Tulving and Psotka (1971) study demonstrates how information that is retrieved for use in making a particular decision will be largely determined by the retrieval cues in the environment. This implies that the same decision rule can produce *different* choices depending upon those retrieval cues present in the environment—i.e., as a function of the particular information that happens to be recalled at any given time.

An understanding of retrieval processes is crucial for any analysis of memory-based judgments. Any factor that affects the accessibility or retrievability of information will influence the input that is considered in making a decision; it may even partially determine the decision rule that is used. Standard marketing techniques, such as conjoint analysis, often show that expressed preferences are highly consistent: for example, additive part-worth models account for almost all of the variance in rank orders of multiattribute options. However, these models fare less well in predicting actual marketplace choice (Wright and Kriewall 1980). One plausible explanation is that the informational bases for conjoint analysis preferences and real life decisions differ. While this might be attributed to external factors of a social nature (such as salesperson influence, Olshavsky 1973), it seems likely that factors influencing what information is retrieved from memory play a major—and perhaps dominant—role. All of these considerations suggest that retrieval processes deserve much more careful scrutiny by consumer decision theorists. Fortunately, a number of general paradigms for studying retrieval processes have been developed in cognitive psychology, and several early experiments applying these techniques to decision making have been very promising.

METHODS FOR STUDYING RETRIEVAL PROCESSES

Comparison of Recall and Recognition

One very general technique for diagnosing when the retrievability of information is being affected entails a comparison of subjects' responses to free recall and recognition test items. Free recall involves a situation in which a subject must independently produce previously acquired information (e.g., list all the product attributes learned in a particular setting). In a recognition test, a subject is given possible choices and simply must indicate which one was previously presented (e.g., whether it was *Time, Newsweek,* or *Consumer Reports* that offered 10 free copies with each new subscription). One of the most simple and parsimonious theories of free recall is that it is a two-stage process in which a person must independently retrieve a particular item and then perform some recognition check on whether, in fact, the item was present in a particular context. For this reason, it is often referred to as the "generation-recognition" theory. In contrast to free recall, recognition tests are generally thought to bypass the retrieval stage and only to involve the single stage of a discrimination or recognition check, in which the familiarity strength of the item is compared to some criterion (cf. Mandler 1980). Thus, any independent variable that affects recall but *not* recognition performance is tapping a process that is localized in the retrieval stage of information processing (see, for example, Anderson and Bower 1972, 1974; Bahrick 1969, 1970; Eysenck 1977; Glass, Holyoak, and Santa 1979; Kintsch 1968, 1970, 1978; Watkins and Gardiner 1979).

Although this is a very simple conceptual approach, it easily accounts for numerous differences that are reliably found between recall and recognition performance. For example, recognition is almost always better than recall. The reason for this is that a breakdown can occur at either stage when a subject must recall an item, but only at one stage when recognition is required. Another standard finding in the verbal learning literature is that high frequency words (as determined by their use in the language) are easier to recall than low frequency words (Gregg 1976). Theoretically, this is because high frequency words are easier to retrieve. In contrast, low frequency words are easier to recognize than high frequency words (Gregg 1976). The reason for this is that it is harder to distinguish whether high frequency words are present in a particular experimental context, i.e., it is more difficult to tell whether these words have high item strength (familiarity) because they were experimentally presented or because of past exposure. In addition, although retroactive interference effects are sometimes quite large for recall, they are negligible in recognition tasks (for a review of this literature, see Postman 1976). Theoretically, successive presentation lists produce more interference in the retrieval stage than in the discrimination stage.

There are also several robust findings that are more closely related to the influence of memory on decision making. For example, organization is extremely important for recall but not for recognition (Kintsch 1970; McCormack 1972), presumably because it is important to have some organizational scheme available in order to retrieve various items. Thus, organizational strategies are extremely important for an understanding of memory-based judgments. Similarly, explicit instructions to learn a list typically produce greater levels of recall than do purely semantic orienting tasks (e.g., determining each word in a list is synonymous with some other), but they do not produce greater levels of recognition. This is what would be expected if one assumes that intentional learning conditions lead to greater levels of organization than do (some) incidental learning conditions. Finally, the presence of associative cues is very helpful in facilitation recall but does not affect recognition (Watkins and Gardiner 1979). Theoretically, such cues aid in the retrieval stage but not in the recognition stage. These points have some very practical implications, as Bettman (1979) points out. Advertising can be very effective, in that it evokes favorable reactions and beliefs from the consumer, but for these benefits to be manifested in purchase behavior, they must be salient at the time the consumer is making a brand selection. Advertisers can facilitate this by providing cues in the purchase environment that will aid the recall of critical information acquired through previous advertising. Life cereal, for example, attempted to cue recall of its successful "Mikey" television advertisements by displaying his picture on the cereal package, just as Kodak Instamatic cameras display the photo of Michael Landon.

Extensions of the Sternberg Paradigm

Another very general paradigm that can be used to study retrieval factors was introduced by Sternberg (1966, 1969), though it might be thought to be primarily relevant to the retrieval of information from short-term memory. A subject is given a particular set of items (e.g., a series of digits) to commit to memory. These items are then taken away, and the subject is given a probe with the task of indicating whether the probe item was or was not a member of the original set. The independent variable is "set size" or the number of items held in memory, and the dependent variable is the amount of time necessary to execute the response. A typical pattern of results obtained from such a study (see also Sternberg 1975) is represented in Figure 6.1.

The positive slope of the affirmative responses indicates that the retrieval process is serial or sequential in nature. That is, the subject must check the probe item against each member of the original set—the more items there are in the original set, the more comparisons need to be made and the greater the time required to make a response. The parallelism of

FIGURE 6.1 Typical Reaction Times as a Function of Set Size

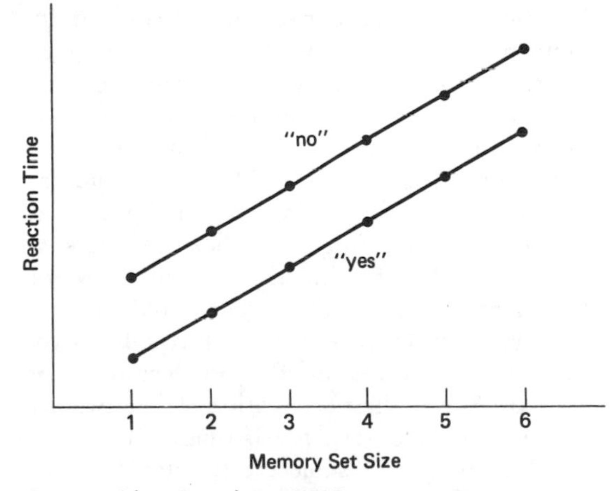

Source: After Sternberg (1969).

the "yes" and "no" curves indicates that this serial search is exhaustive and does not terminate as soon as the item is located in memory. If a serial self-terminating process were operative, negative responses would, on the average, require twice as many tests as positive responses. This would cause the slope of the "yes" curve to be exactly half of the slope of the "no" curve.

This very simple paradigm has been extended in several ways to examine some of the cognitive processes involved in decision making. For example, Lingle and Ostrom (1979) presented subjects with various numbers of personality traits and asked subjects to make occupational judgments (e.g., how good a doctor would a concientious, intelligent, and shy person make?). They found that the response time needed to make a particular judgment increased linearly with the set size (i.e., the number of personality traits presented). This suggests that subjects were sequentially retrieving each piece of information and that the more pieces of information there were, the longer it took.

Lingle and Ostrom also had subjects make a second occupational judgment based on the same information. Some of these occupations were similar to the first occupation (e.g., doctor-dentist), while others were dissimilar (e.g., doctor-fisherman). Two interesting findings emerged. First, when response time was plotted as a function of set size, there was zero slope. Specifically, subjects made the second judgment just as quickly when they were given seven traits as when they were given one trait. This was true of both similar and dissimilar judgments. Second, there was a significant main effect reflecting the fact that dissimilar judgments took longer in each of the set size conditions. Taken together, these results suggest that, unlike the initial judgment, subjects did *not* refer back to the original information. Rather, subjects appear to go through a two-stage process. First, the second occupation is compared to the first occupation. If the two are similar, a similar response is made. If the two are dissimilar, the subject estimates *how* dissimilar and makes a corresponding response. The insensitivity of reaction times to set size indicates that these similarity judgments were holistic. Supplementary data obtained by Lingle and Ostrom support this interpretation (Ostrom, Lingle, Pryor, and Geva 1980), and similar findings from quite different paradigms have also been reported (e.g., Carlston 1980).

A parallel in consumer decision making occurs when buying in a product class for the first time. The latency to reach a decision is initially a function of the complexity of the choice (number of attributes to be considered, etc.) Having gone through this once, the consumer may subsequently simply select the alternative that seems most similar to the product chosen on the first occasion. Svenson (1979, p. 93) has made a similar suggestion based upon independent considerations.

This type of research suggests that decision making may need to be examined in a much larger context than it traditionally has been. In particular, given the same type of information and the same type of goal, different decision rules may operate, depending on how recently or frequently a decision within the same domain has been made.

Retrieval and Cognitive Organization

Naus (1974) has reported one more way in which the Sternberg paradigm can be extended as well as some preliminary findings that have important implications for the study of consumer decision making. She used the original Sternberg task but included items from two separate categories in the acquisition set. Although the various items were presented in random order, Naus found that when the probe was from Category A, the reaction time was substantially affected by the number of other items from Category A in the acquisition set, but was completely unaffected by the number of items in the set from Category B. Conversely, when the probe was from Category B, reaction time was affected by the number of other items from Category B but not by the number of items in the acquisition set from Category A. These results suggest that subjects recognized that the target items fell into two different conceptual classes, and that they were able to mentally compartmentalize the two different classes of items. When a probe was given, they simply had to locate the appropriate set and serially search through the items in that set.

An extension of this type of research was then conducted by Johnson (1978), who used the standard Sternberg paradigm with two minor variations. First, in some conditions, the initial information could be organized into separate conceptual categories, while in others it could not. Second, rather than provide a single probe, Johnson provided a *pair* of probes; the task was to determine as quickly as possible whether *both* probes had been part of the original list. The results were quite interesting. When subjects were able to organize the information into separate categories, they were able to recognize two items from the same category much more quickly than two items from different categories.

Pryor and Ostrom (1981) used this phenomenon to examine the effects of prior familiarity with a particular content domain. Their research indicates that people will organize new information into distinct categories only if they are familiar with the particular content domain. In one study, the stimulus materials were people and personality traits. Subjects were given two personality traits and had to indicate whether both members of the pair had been previously presented. Traits pertaining to the same person were recognized much more quickly than traits pertaining to different people, but only when the stimulus persons were already well known. This indicates that subjects were using the stimulus persons as categories for the new information when they were well known, but were not doing so when they were unfamiliar.

This is a very general experimental technique that can be used to determine if and how subjects are organizing new information about various objects. For example, the method could easily be applied to the issue of whether product information is organized in memory around individual brands or around product-related attributes. Based on Pryor and Ostrom's findings, one might anticipate that mental representations of product information would tend to be brand based when the consumer has more familiarity with the brands than with the attributes of the brands. On the other hand, information about relatively unfamiliar brands might tend to be organized around attributes.[2]

EFFECTS OF TASK FACTORS AND PRIOR KNOWLEDGE ON ENCODING, COGNITIVE ORGANIZATION, AND RETRIEVAL

The Use of Verbal Protocols to Infer Memory Structure[3]

One theme of recent decision research is that the ease of executing a given choice rule depends upon its compatibility with the memory representation of information about the alternative brands. For example, "brand based" choice rules may be easier to execute when information in memory is organized around individual brands. Specifically, it has been argued that (1) the format of external information and task goals at the time of exposure to that information can affect certain voluntary aspects of processing, which in turn affect the nature of the encoding; (2) the encoded representation of the external information determines the form of the representation in long-term memory; and (3) the memory representation can then engender certain processing strategies in subsequent choice tasks making use of the information stored in memory (Bettman 1975, 1979; Bettman and Kakkar 1977; Biehal and Chakravarti 1982; Johnson and Russo 1978; Russo and Johnson 1980; Wallsten 1980).

For example, Biehal and Chakravarti (1982) presented product information to subjects, instructing one group to choose the best brand and the other to memorize the information. Both groups were given unaided free-recall tests. The group that had initially been asked to

[2]This idea was suggested by Joel Cohen.

[3]Thanks are extended to Joe Alba for several useful discussions pertaining to this section.

memorize the information was then asked to choose the best brand, based only on the information recalled. An analysis of transitions in the free-recall protocols of subjects who had initially memorized the information indicated that it tended to be organized around individual brands, although the original format of the information (brand, attribute, or brand X attribute matrix display) also had effects. In contrast, free-recall protocols of subjects who had initially chosen the best brand showed more tendency for memory to be organized around individual attributes. This was explained by the fact that these subjects had tended to use attribute-based choice strategies, and so had encoded the information in a manner that induced an attribute-organized representation in long-term memory.

Biehal and Chakravarti also demonstrated the effect of memory organization on choice processing by comparing concurrent verbal (choice) protocols of subjects who had initially been given the task of choosing the best brand with those of subjects who had first memorized the product information (in a primarily brand-organized manner) and had then been unexpectedly required to make a choice on the basis of remembered information. The latter group showed less tendency to choose by processing attributes.

This study is particularly important because it demonstrates both the indirect effects of task goals and information format on memory representation, and the effects of memory representation on overt aspects of information processing in choice. It is equally noteworthy for the methodology used to infer the nature and organization of memory representations, namely the analysis of transitions in free-recall (see also Bousfield 1953; Friendly 1977, 1979; Reitman and Rueter 1980; Srull 1981; Sternberg and Tulving 1977). For example, if the subject successively recalled two attributes of the same brand, this would be considered a "brand" transition, whereas if the values of two brands on the same attribute were successively recalled, this would be an "attribute" transition. (This is not the exact scheme used by Biehal and Chakravarti, but it is sufficiently close for purposes of discussion.)

Two assumptions seem to underlie this methodology:

- Information is organized in memory as a set of nodes representing concepts connected by arcs (relations), as assumed by various associative network models of memory (e.g., Anderson and Bower 1973, 1974; Collins and Loftus 1975).
- The generation of a free-recall protocol simply involves a traversal of these associative pathways; if there are two or more pathways leading from a particular node, that which is followed is assumed to be random.

Thus the recall protocol is assumed to be representative of the underlying structure with respect to both content and organization.

This approach shares a general problem with all methods that attempt to draw inferences about memory organization from behavioral data. For any set of data, it is possible to draw different inferences about the nature of the mental representation by changing one's assumptions about the processes operating on the stored knowledge base to produce the observed responses (e.g., a free-recall protocol). Anderson (1978) maintained that the indeterminacy is so great that one can *never* draw inferences about memory representations from behavioral (i.e., nonphysiological) data, because *any* hypothesized representation can be reconciled with an observed response by making appropriate assumptions about the processes that operated on the representation to produce the observed behavior. A less radical view (Hayes-Roth 1979; Kosslyn 1981; Pylyshn 1979, 1981) that we would endorse is that to draw inferences about memory structure from behavioral data, one must simultaneously consider both the memory representation and the processes that act upon it.

With respect to the specific method under discussion—the analysis of transitions in free-recall protocols—two related problems might arise:

- The assumption that retrieval simply involves a random traversal of associative pathways may be invalid: it is possible that memory for experimentally presented information is organized in a manner quite different from the one implied by the recall protocol, although some existing and related cognitive structure might function as a *retrieval plan* for searching the memory traces of the new material.

- The sequence and content of output in a free-recall protocol may be affected by voluntarily adopted *editing strategies,* and thus may be non-representative of the underlying structure with respect to both content and organization.

A study by Anderson and Pichert (1978) illustrates the first point. Subjects read a story that included a description of a home, either from the perspective of a burglar or from the perspective of a potential homebuyer. Some of the ideas in the story were more relevant to the burglar perspective than to the homebuyer perspective, and vice versa.

After subjects had read the story from one of the two perspectives, they were asked to recall it verbatim. Results showed that subjects recalled more information relevant to the perspective they had taken in reading the story. This result can be given in encoding interpretation, but a second set of results argues for a retrieval explanation. After completing the recall task for the first time, subjects were asked to generate a second free-recall protocol. Half of the subjects used the same perspective as they had initially; the others were given the other perspective as a retrieval cue. Results showed that the latter were able to retrieve information relevant to their *new* perspective that they had not been able to recall previously. They also recalled less of the information relevant to the perspective under which they had initially read the story. Anderson and Pichert interpreted these results as indicating that the adopted perspective activated a schema that served as a retrieval plan that automatically influenced recall.

A paper by Hasher and Griffin (1978) demonstrates that a voluntary editing strategy at the time of retrieval can influence the output of a free-recall protocol. Subjects read an ambiguous passage about a man walking through the woods, entitled either "Going Hunting" or "An Escaped Convict." Subjects were told that they would be asked to recall it completely. Some time later, they were asked to generate a free-recall protocol. Some subjects were given the same title they had originally seen as a cue ("same theme" condition). These subjects showed evidence of "reconstructive" recall (Bartlett 1932)—i.e., they falsely recalled information that had never been presented, although it was related to the assumed theme of the story. The other subjects were asked to recall the story, but were told by an ostensibly embarrassed experimenter that they had been given the wrong title for the story. They were told that the correct title was the one they were *not* given earlier ("An Escaped Convict" or "Going Hunting"). These subjects ("different theme" condition) showed superior recall to those who had not had their thematic code invalidated, and the advantage tended to increase with the amount of time between the reading of the story and the subsequent recall test. In particular, these subjects recalled more of the idea units that were actually included in the story and produced very few intrusions related either to the new or to the invalidated theme.

These differences appeared in spite of the fact that both groups of subjects (e.g., those who were told that the title was "Going Hunting" both at the time of learning and of recall, and those who learned the story as "Going Hunting" and recalled it as "An Escaped Convict") must have had *identical* stored representations of the information, since they were treated identically up to the point of recall. The authors interpreted their results as indicating that, although both thematic information and surface details are stored in memory, the former is normally more accessible. When the subject believes that the theme as encoded is invalid, she or he edits out information that pertains to the invalid theme if it makes no sense in relation to the correct theme. The retrieval plan then shifts to less accessible information pertaining to surface details.

One final set of studies is pertinent to the use of characteristics of free-recall protocols to infer cognitive structure. Several studies of the recall of text narratives show that when information is presented in an order that violates an expectancy, it tends to be recalled as having occurred in a more typical order (Bower, Black, and Turner 1979; Kintsch, Mandel, and Kazminsky 1977; Mandler 1978). This has been interpreted as indicating that the information is restructured as it is encoded, so that the stored representation tends to conform to the canonical order.

Research by Baker (1978) tends to affirm this interpretation, suggesting that the reordered output is a function of retrieval mechanisms. Subjects read short episodes either in a normal, chronological order, or in a "flashback" order (e.g., "Dan did X. Before that, he had done Y.") They were told that they would be tested on their recall of the underlying order of the sentences in the stories (i.e., the order in which the story implied they had actually occurred). Pairs of phrases from each story were flashed on a cathode ray tube, and subjects were asked to say whether their order corresponded to their underlying order in the story. Decisions were faster when the information had originally appeared in chronological order than when it had been presented in flashback order. Another experiment showed that when the stories were presented in flashback sequence, it was easier to make decisions about the order of inputs than about the underlying sequence of events. Taken together, these results indicate that the information is not stored in a reorganized form that reflects the underlying order of the events. Though recall protocols in experiments such as that of Bower, Black, and Turner (1979) suggest that such reorganization affects stored representations, Baker's (1978) results seem to indicate that this should be interpreted in terms of retrieval factors.

Let us return now to a discussion of how these results might bear upon the use of transitions in free elicitation (Russo and Johnson 1980) and free-recall (Biehal and Chakravarti 1982) protocols to infer the organization of consumers' knowledge about familiar products. Russo and Johnson asked subjects "to imagine that they had an English-speaking friend from a foreign country who needed to know about the products available in the United States." Subjects then generated all their knowledge that would be helpful to this friend. An analysis of transitions indicated a primarily brand-based organization of product knowledge in memory. Though this result is provocative, there are two potential ways in which retrieval strategies might have affected the nature of the output:

- The instruction to the subject to tell what she knows about *products* may have caused her to adopt a retrieval strategy that was object based. If the instruction had been to "tell what you know about the *attributes* of products," an attribute-based organization might have emerged.
- The brand-based organization may have been imposed at output so that what the subject said would "make sense" to the foreign friend.

One response to these sorts of objections is to try to provide a more neutral probe that does not suggest any particular retrieval strategy to the subject. The study by Biehal and Chakravarti (1982) described above used exactly this approach in prompting free-recall protocols. While this is quite reasonable, ideally one would like to more conclusively rule out the hypothesis that the ordering of output in a free-recall protocol is affected by voluntary retrieval strategies.

One way to accomplish this is to collect data not only on the order of output in free-recall, but on "interresponse latencies" as well (Pollio 1974; Pollio, Richards, and Lucas 1969; Reitman and Rueter 1980). Researchers have found that items grouped together in memory tend to be output with relatively short interresponse latencies, while items that are output adjacently in spite of the fact that they are not grouped together in memory tend to have longer interresponse latencies. For example, if subjects had stored information about cars in a brand-based manner, one might observe an output pattern such as "brand X gets 34 m.p.g., it costs $7,500, . . . (pause) . . . brand Y comes in a hatchback model, brand Y comes with standard radial tires . . ." The interesting aspect of this measure is that opposite results seem to be predicted by the hypothesis that adjacent items in the output tend to be stored together in memory and the hypothesis that the output order is produced by a voluntary editing strategy. That is, if subjects were editing their output to produce a brand-based organization, interresponse latencies would be longer between adjacent times in the output that pertain to the same brand than between adjacent items about different brands. Presumably, the latter transitions would reflect the "natural" cognitive organization, while the former would reflect the order imposed at output by a voluntary retrieval strategy. This possibility deserves to be empirically tested.

There is one final issue related to whether product information in memory is "brand based" or "attribute based." Johnson and Russo (1978) reported evidence suggesting that there is no natural order in which product information is always organized in memory. By analyzing recall times, they showed that the cognitive organization of experimentally presented information about products is strongly affected by the format in which this information is initially learned. A brand-based format seems to lead to a brand-based mental representation, while an attribute-based format leads to an attribute-based organization.

Biehal and Chakravarti (1982) replicated this effect using a different methodology and extended it by showing that the *task* in which product information is initially encountered also affects the form of the mental representation. They found that subjects who had initially memorized information about four brands of toothpaste stored it in a primarily brand based form, while those who had initially made a choice of one of the four brands had primarily attribute-based mental representations. This was consistent with their finding that the choice processing exhibited by the latter subjects consisted primarily of attribute-based operations.

It is possible, though, that the mental representations of consumers in Biehal and Chakravarti's (1982) study (and in Johnson and Russo's 1978 study) were not "brand-based" or "attribute-based" at all. Rather, the key organizational factor may have been "temporal contiguity"—i.e., the order in which consumers were initially exposed to the various items of product information.[4] According to this view, information format and task goals affect the order in which consumers voluntarily expose themselves to the items of information. Those items that reside together in short-term memory are likely to be stored contiguously in long-term memory. The key differences between this hypothesis and the hypothesis that product information is organized around brands are that:

- If information is organized around individual brands, information items about attributes of the same brand should be stored together even if these items were not initially encountered together.
- Information items that were initially encountered together should not be stored contiguously unless they pertain to the same brand.

Biehal and Chakravarti are currently testing for just such effects in their data. Future research might adapt Baker's (1978) methodology to investigate this very central theoretical issue.

Using the "Part-List Cuing Effect" to Study Cognitive Organization

There is one more general method that can be used to determine what the functional units are around which product information is organized in memory. This is related to a very robust phenomenon in the memory literature known as "the part-list cuing effect." Although associative cues generally facilitate recall, part-list cuing effects refer to the fact that intralist cues given at the time of recall often result in *poorer* recall of the items not presented, as compared to a control group that does not receive any intralist cues. For example, if one group of subjects was asked to recall the 50 states with no retrieval cues, and a second group was given the same task but provided with the names of 20 states as "cues," the latter group would exhibit inferior recall of the 30 unnamed states when compared with the former group (Brown 1968).

The size of such a decrement in recall has been found to increase as the number of cues increases. Moreover, when categorized lists are used, these "inhibition" effects are confined to a specific category from which the particular cue came, while recall of items from the remaining categories is unaffected (see Roediger 1974 for a brief review of this literature).

Srull has been conducting research in the domain of social cognition that has some interesting implications for studying how consumers organize product knowledge in memory. Subjects are given a list of 32 behavior statements, eight of which pertain to each of four target

---

[4] Landauer (1975) has made a similar suggestion.

persons (A, B, C, and D). They process this information under one of three sets: a memory set, an impression formation set, or an anticipated interaction set in which they will ostensibly meet each of four persons described by the information. All subjects are then asked to recall the information, given a subset of the previously presented statements as "cues." A virtually identical pattern of recall is manifested by subjects who receive the impression formation and the anticipated interaction sets. When these subjects were provided with intralist cues (behavior statements) pertaining to target person A, recall of the rest of the information about A was inhibited, but recall of information about B, C, and D was not. Moreover, the size of the decrement was directly related to the number of intralist cues that were provided. A similar "localized" inhibition of recall for information about target person B was observed when the intralist cues pertained to B.

These results suggest that, under impression set and anticipated interaction set conditions, subjects were organizing behavioral information around individual target persons. Quite different results were found when subjects had been instructed to memorize the behavior statements verbatim. Cues pertaining only to A or only to B inhibited recall of information pertaining to *all four* target persons, indicating that the information was not organized around individual persons. A variant of this general method could be quite useful for studying issues in consumer behavior, such as when product information is organized around brands versus attributes. If brands define the key conceptual categories, cues describing the attributes of a single brand would only inhibit recall of information about that brand and would not inhibit recall of information about other brands.

Parenthetically, the part-list cuing effect suggests some interesting advertising strategies geared toward inhibiting the entry of certain competitive brands into the consumer's "evoked set" (Howard and Sheth 1969). By designing comparative advertisements or point-of-purchase displays that mention only a subset of one's competitors, one may be able to inhibit recall of information about unmentioned brands with which one's own brand does not compare favorably. This very speculative remark assumes that product knowledge is organized hierarchically, with superordinate categories pertaining to product classes, middle level concepts pertaining to individual brands, and lower level categories pertaining to the attributes of each brand. If information were organized in terms of superordinate product class categories, middle level product attribute categories, and lower level information pertaining to the standing of individual brands on a given attribute, more traditional advertising strategies might inadvertently capitalize on the part-list cuing effect. By mentioning only those product attributes for which one has a competitive advantage, one may effectively inhibit retrieval of attributes that are not mentioned on which one's own product is at a competitive disadvantage.

Effects of Cognitive Structure on the Processing of New Information

The study by Pryor and Ostrom (1981) cited earlier is provocative in its implications for how familiarity with brands and product attributes might affect the cognitive organization of new information about products. Effects of familiarity on memory and cognitive processing have been found in a variety of other contexts, and only recently have their importance for decision making been considered. One classic example was reported by Chase and Simon (1973). These researchers showed chess board configurations to both chess masters and novices for relatively short durations. The chess masters showed an extremely large advantage in terms of their ability to remember the board configurations, but only when the board positions were realistic. When shown random patterns of board positions, there was no difference in the recall of masters and novices.

Although there are other studies indicating that prior familiarity enhances recall of new information, there are also studies indicating an inverted-U relationship between familiarity and amount of new information recalled. Johnson and Russo (1981) demonstrated that both types of relationships may result, depending upon the type of decision making task performed. They presented subjects with a realistic brand X attribute matrix, consisting of eight alternatives (small imported cars) and 10 attributes (estimated MPG, price, etc.). Half of the subjects were asked to *evaluate* each individual car on a seven point scale. The other subjects were asked to *choose* the single most desirable of the eight cars, rather than make individual judgments. Subjects in each of these two groups were divided into those who were very familiar with automobile products, those who were moderately familiar, and those who were relatively unfamiliar with automobiles. After completing their assigned tasks, all subjects were given a surprise recall task.

Johnson and Russo found that there was a significant linear relationship between product familiarity and amount of information recalled when subjects were judging the quality of each separate car. Consumers with high product familiarity recalled the most, and those with low product familiarity recalled the least. However, when subjects were given the *choice* task, an inverted-U relationship between product familiarity and recall was found. Why would consumers highly familiar with automobile products recall less of the information than those only moderately familiar with such products? One possibility is that, when given a choice task, highly familiar consumers attend only to what they know are the most discriminating attributes. Thus, their encoding and subsequent retrieval of the information are very selective. These issues will be considered below in the discussion of the role of attention, which presents some preliminary results indicating that such processing strategies have a profound impact on the amount and type of information that can be later recalled.

The issue of how prior knowledge about a brand or product class affects the encoding, storage, and utilization of new information about a brand is of growing importance in consumer information processing research. For example, evidence shows that even purchases of expensive durable goods are preceded by amazingly little search for information to guide brand choice and the selection of a retail outlet. Two hypotheses have been advanced to explain this perplexing lack of search: (1) that consumers perceive the benefits of search to be outweighed by the costs, and (2) that consumers' ignorance about product classes that are technologically complex makes them incapable of retaining and processing information that might be obtained via search. Johnson and Russo's study (1981) bears upon the second of these hypotheses, as does a recent paper by Bettman and Park (1980).

A careful examination of the interrelationships among encoding, cognitive organization, and retrieval processes is very important to the study of decision making, especially for those decisions that are "mixed" or "memory-based" choices. All the information relevant to a particular decision is not necessarily used. In some cases, people may use a prior judgment to make a subsequent, related one, without even considering the initial information. In addition, familiarity with a particular content domain may influence the way in which information is organized in memory. Depending upon the task, high familiarity may lead consumers to ignore prior information that experience tells them is not diagnostic. Since any factor that influences the accessibility or retrievability of information will have an indirect effect on decision making by altering the initial inputs, much more emphasis should be put on memory retrieval factors in future research.

INFERENCE MAKING

In the discussion of memory-based judgments, it was noted that only a subset of product information available in memory typically will be accessible, and that consumers appear simply to base their judgments on the subset retrieved. The information most likely to be recalled is often the information that seemed most important in terms of one's goals at the time the information was initially received (e.g., Ostrom et al. 1980). Consider a case in which an amateur cook reads an article about food processors in *Consumer Reports*. When reading the article, he considers slicing and chopping abilities to be the most important attributes. He concludes that if he were to buy a processor, the Moulinex "La Machine II" would be the best buy. Two years later, he believes that he really needs a food processor, so he goes to a department store to buy one. HIs circumstances have changed somewhat in the intervening years, in that he has begun to make his own bread and pasta. Thus, the ability of a food processor to knead bread and pasta dough has become an extremely important attribute. Unfortunately, the cook may have much poorer recall of the standing of the various brands on this attribute than on the slicing and chopping abilities that seemed most relevant when he initially read the article in *Consumer Reports*. He will not necessarily realize that his memory is poor and go back to the original article; rather, he may reconstructively *infer* the missing information from the information that is accessible—especially from thematic information, such as his memory that the Moulinex was the "best buy." He *might* go back to the original article, but factors such as time pressures and the perceived importance of the purchase are likely to render inference processes much more prevalent in consumer choice than researchers have realized.

The idea that people will infer attribute values when they are missing—either because they were never acquired in the first place or because they can no longer be recalled—is worthy of greater attention from decision researchers. Evidence from related areas suggests that such inferences are often made on the basis of evaluative consistency (D'Andrade 1965, Mulaik 1964, Passini and Norman 1966; Rosenberg and Sedlak 1972; Thorndike 1920; Zanna and Hamilton 1972). Much more research regarding such inference processes needs to be conducted *within the context of decision making*. In the consumer behavior area, for example, one might question whether evaluative consistency guides inferences along dimensions (such as price and quality) that are assumed to be evaluatively inconsistent on an *a priori* basis. In fact, social psychologists have reported cases in which people made a second judgment that was evaluatively consistent with an initial judgment even though it was semantically inconsistent with the implications of the original information (e.g., Carlston, 1980).

These types of inferences are relevant to both stimulus-based and memory-based judgments. In a recent paper, Yamagishi and Hill (1981) attempted to explain a robust phenomenon in the judgment literature—an ordinal violation of additive models called the "averaging crossover"—by appealing to inference processes (see also Cohen, Miniard, and Dickson 1980). Averaging crossover refers to the fact that variation in an attribute A has more effect on overall evaluations of a brand when information on A is presented alone than when information on A is also accompanied by information about other attributes (B, C, etc.). For example, Troutman and Shanteau (1976) found that because of this effect, a disposable diaper rated as "high on absorbency and above average on durability" was rated *lower* than a diaper described as merely "high on absorbency." Yamagishi and Hill argue that such results can be explained by inference processes, rather than by "averaging," e.g., subjects may infer that a disposable diaper that is described as "high on absorbency" is also fairly high on durability. Thus an additive information integration process may result in overall evaluations that appear to be consistent with an "averaging" process.

Yamagishi and Hill's model predicts that when attributes A and B are perceived to be negatively correlated, variation in A will have *less* effect when information on A is presented alone than when it is accompanied by information about attribute B. They tested this prediction by asking consumers to evaluate the attractiveness of hypothetical products, based either on price information alone, quality information alone, or information about both price and quality. Variation in price information had less effect when presented alone than when combined with quality information. According to Yamagishi and Hill, when subjects were given price information alone, they tended to infer the value of quality by a price-quality heuristic. Since explicitly stated price and inferred quality have directly opposite effects on perceived attractiveness, price information has relatively little effect on attractiveness when presented alone.

While the Yamagishi and Hill paper can be criticized on both methodological and conceptual grounds, its basic idea is quite intriguing. The inference processes it postulates, however, seem directly contrary to those that have been hypothesized to explain the effects of dimensional commensurability on cue utilization in choice and evaluation (Slovic and MacPhillamy 1974; Yates, Jagacinski, and Faber 1978). In Slovik and MacPhillamy's study, subjects were asked to make graded paired comparisons of hypothetical graduate students A and B. Each was described in terms of one common attribute and one unique attribute. For example, numerical scores of English skills were given for both A and B, but A was also described in terms of Quantitative Aptitude scores, while B was described in terms of Need to Achieve Success scores. Across a set of five experiments, it was consistently demonstrated that subjects gave greater weight to the common dimensions than to the noncommon ones. The authors related a suggestion by Castellan that this resulted because subjects inferred that the students were average on the dimensions for which no information was given. Yates, Jagacinski, and Faber (1978) set out to test this hypothesis directly, and concluded that their subjects inferred a negative attribute value whenever a multiattribute option was not described on a particular dimension.

Work on the effects of inferences about "missing" attribute values on evaluative judgments and decisions has been fairly inconclusive, primarily because it has focused exclusively on the decision *outcomes.* To date, no one has demonstrated that inferences of any type mediate evaluative judgments in these sorts of tasks. Indeed, Slovic (1972) has argued for a "principle of concreteness" that, among other things, implies that inferences about attributes not explicitly described should *not* be made in stimulus-based judgments.

There are many cases in which it is theoretically very important to determine whether values for particular attributes are being inferred. Since these inferences are entirely covert, they are quite difficult to investigate. In particular, the problem of demand characteristics makes it hazardous simply to ask people to report whether or not they made a particular inference. A method developed by Lynch and Shoben (Lynch 1981) could easily be brought to bear on this problem, although this has not been done to date.

Imagine a situation in which someone must choose between purchasing a Ford Mustang and a Chevrolet Citation. The person has information about price, gas mileage, and rate of repair for the Mustang, but only about price and mileage for the Citation. The theoretical question is whether the person will infer some rate of repair for the Citation before making a choice. One experimental paradigm that can be used to investigate this is to have some subjects first make a choice and then make an explicit inference about the missing rate of repair value. The response time needed to perform each of these two tasks is recorded. Other subjects, however, are asked to infer the missing rate of repair for the Citation and *then* choose between the partially described Citation and the fully described Mustang. Again, the response times are recorded. The most important comparison is between the time needed to make the choice in each of the two conditions. If there is a facilitating effect in the second condition relative to the first (i.e., if the time needed to make the choice is less when the missing value has been explicitly inferred beforehand than when it has not), one would conclude that an inference had been made before the choice was executed. On the other hand, if there is no facilitating effect, one would conclude that no inference was made prior to the choice. While the experiment described needs to be modified slightly to eliminate several alternative hypotheses (see Lynch 1981), this extremely general paradigm could be used to address a variety of theoretical questions concerning inference processes.

ATTENTIONAL PROCESSES IN DECISION MAKING

In addition to memory processes, researchers are beginning to recognize attention as another cognitive process that can often affect decision outcomes by modifying the inputs that are considered. The major aspect of the attentional system that decision theorists have examined to date is its limited capacity. Consumers are unable to consider more than a few items of information simultaneously, and this is true of externally available information as well as information retrieved from memory. Thus, it makes very little difference whether one speaks of the "span of short-term memory" or simply of "limited attentional capacity." In any case, it seems that the maximum number of information items that can be considered simultaneously is somewhere between four (Shiffrin 1976) and seven (Miller 1956). This has led decision researchers to reject hypothesized choice rules that require the consumer to consider large amounts of information simultaneously, and to regard as more plausible those heuristics that allow the consumer to *serially* integrate the information upon which a decision is based. For example, various sequential elimination rules (Bettman 1979; Svenson 1979; Tversky 1972), anchoring and adjustments heuristics (Tversky and Kahneman 1974), and "phased" decision strategies (Bettman and Park 1980; Lussier and Olshavsky 1979; Wright 1972) presumably allow the decision maker to simplify the choice task by considering product information sequentially rather than simultaneously.

Many of the general topics touched upon in the sections that follow have been addressed in the literature (e.g., Bettman 1979). The discussion therefore presents both unfamiliar methods for studying attention and new research issues pertaining to the role of attention in decision making.

Attentional Capacity[5]

Discussions of attention, such as Kahneman's (1973) classic treatise, typically discuss two aspects: its selective nature and its intensity. Attentional intensity pertains to changes in the total capacity of the system, as well as to the percentage of available capacity devoted to a particular task. It is believed that attentional capacity is finite but variable. Capacity seems to increase at a decreasing rate with task demands. The more difficult the mental task, the more capacity becomes available up to some limit. There are two related and rather unfortunate aspects of this growth in capacity. First, it is usually insufficient for adequately responding to increases in task demands; capacity rises, but so does the gap between the capacity demanded and that produced. Second, while there are voluntary aspects of attention, capacity cannot be voluntarily increased in the absence of increases in task demands. No matter how hard one tries, one cannot increase one's capacity in performing a very easy task to the level that would become possible in performing a difficult task.

Note that the concepts of task demands and capacity are closely related to the idea of "information load," which has been a major focus of interest among consumer researchers. Issues have already been raised concerning how much information to give consumers to facilitate wise decision making (Jacoby, Speller, and Kohn-Berning 1974; Wilkie 1974), what information formats are easiest to process (Bettman 1975; Scammon 1977), what choice heuristics best minimize cognitive strain (Bettman and Zins 1979; Wright 1975), and how to define information load (Scammon 1977; Wilkie 1974).

Concepts such as "information load" have usually been measured by one of three methods in consumer research. The first method simply asks for concurrent or retrospective ratings of the difficulty of performing a certain decision task (e.g., Bettman and Zins 1979; Wright 1975). The primary drawback of this method is its uncertain convergence with behavioral measures of information load (Kahneman 1973). Moreover, if between-subjects designs are used to compare the loads produced by various decision tasks, it is unclear whether the same mental context of tasks is used to compare and rate the different experimental decision tasks.

The second method is to examine various objective indications of the duration and extent of processing—e.g., the number of cards exam-

[5]This section has benefitted greatly from discussions with Dan Moore.

ined on an information display board or the total time required to produce a decision (Bettman and Zins 1979; Jacoby, Speller, and Kohn-Berning 1974; Payne 1976). While these measures do relate to task difficulty, they probably would not be taken as measures of the capacity required by a choice task at any given point in time. Rather, they are best thought of as indices of one *response* to increasing task demands—i.e., as simply stretching the required processing out over a longer period of time, so that the momentary load is minimized (Kerr 1973).

The third way consumer researchers have tapped information load is by measuring "decision quality." Choices actually made are sometimes compared to some objective standard (Scammon 1977). While this approach has merit from a public policy perspective, it is less satisfactory as a measure of "information load" as a psychological construct. Jacoby, Speller, and Kohn-Berning (1974) measured "decision quality" by comparing actual choices to those that would be optimal based upon measurements of the subjects' own utilities. The drawback of this approach is that is assumes that experienced overall utility (or "happiness") resulting from a choice obeys an additive part-worth model. But there is extensive evidence that the overall utility of a choice alternative is a *nonadditive* function of the part-utilities of the various outcomes of choice (Lynch and Cohen 1978; Lynch 1979; Shanteau 1974). This makes it almost impossible to designate a given choice alternative as "best," especially when the various outcomes of choice are experienced over time.

Alternative Measures of Attentional Capacity

Attention theorists have developed measures of "information load" or "task demands" that are quite different from those employed in consumer research but quite well suited to the problems with which consumer researchers are concerned.

One measure is pupilary dilation (Kahneman and Beatty 1967). This measure has the advantage that stable estimates of response to task demands can be developed on an individual subject basis, with only a few trials per subject. Also, this physiological measure converges well with behavioral measures of capacity (Kahneman 1970). Bettman (1979) voiced enthusiasm about the potential usefulness of this method in consumer research, though it does have several practical disadvantages that may limit its utility, such as the expense of the necessary equipment, the artificial laboratory conditions required to obtain reliable measurements, and so on.

A second method used by attention researchers is a primary task-secondary task paradigm, in which load produced by the primary task is tapped by behavioral measurements of performance on the secondary task (Kerr 1973; Posner and Boies 1971; Posner and Keele 1970; Posner and Klein 1973). For example, Kahneman (1970) assigned subjects a primary task of transforming a set of visually presented digits and a secondary task of monitoring an irregular string of letters for the appearance of the letter "K." The difficulty of various transformations assigned in the primary task was measured by the percentage of missed "K's" in the secondary task. Other approaches would be to measure the reaction time to respond to the "K's," or *d'* (McNicol 1972), a measure of accuracy in identifying "K's" that corrects for response biases.

Several assumptions underlie the use of secondary-task performance measures to examine load imposed by the primary task. First, it is assumed that total capacity required to perform the two tasks can be divided into two parts: capacity devoted to the primary task and "spare" capacity. This is shown in Figure 6.2. It is assumed that "spare" capacity is devoted to the secondary task, as well as to extra-experimental stimuli and various monitoring operations (i.e., performance of the secondary task does not affect capacity devoted to the primary task). Both total capacity and capacity devoted to the primary task are assumed to be monotonically increasing functions of the demands of the primary task. Also, the amount of spare capacity is assumed to be a monotonically decreasing function of the demands of the pri-

FIGURE 6.2 Attentional Capacity Available for Primary and Secondary Tasks

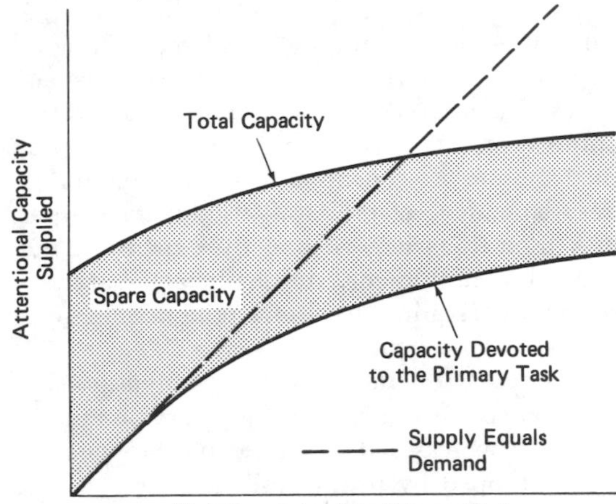

Source: After Kahneman (1973), p. 15.

mary task. Therefore, the more difficult the primary task, the more performance on the secondary task should suffer.

To our knowledge, Moore (1981) was the first person to realize the potential of this paradigm for the study of decision making. Moore has been concerned with assessing the information load placed upon consumers by various information environments and with assessing the effects of adaptive changes in the consumer's choice strategies on the cognitive load experienced. His paper reports evidence questioning the assumption that information load is a function of the number of brands considered times the number of attributes per brand (Jacoby, Speller, and Kohn-Berning 1974). For example, three brands with eight attributes per brand produce quite a different load than does information about eight brands, with three attributes per brand described.

Two general caveats should be considered in using the secondary task paradigm to compare the "difficulty" of different consumer decision tasks. First, it is risky to compare primary tasks that use different modalities (e.g., to compare audio and text versions of the same advertisement), because the secondary task may differentially interfere with the various primary tasks, clouding the interpretation of performance measures. This can occur when the primary and secondary tasks call for competing responses, or because the tasks utilize certain common structures that can process information only in a serial fashion (Kahneman 1973). Second, there may be cases in which the relationships diagrammed in Figure 6.2 are violated. Specifically, subjects may allocate low levels of capacity to primary tasks that place high demands on them. This can occur for at least two reasons:

- Under extremely high task demands, subjects may simply give up (Shulman and Greenberg 1971).
- Britton, Westbrook, and Holdredge (1978) have reported data from a secondary task paradigm that show that difficult text material requires less capacity to process than easy text material. This counterintuitive result was explained by arguing that easy text material keeps certain cognitive processors filled, whereas the reading of difficult text material is accompanied by frequent failures of comprehension that empty these processors, leaving more capacity available for secondary task performance.

Britton, Westbrook, and Holdredge distinguished between *momentary* capacity demanded (which is what is typically assessed by secondary task performance) and *total* capacity demanded. The latter is measured by multiplying a measure of momentary capacity by the total time taken to complete the primary task. While the difficult passages utilized less momentary capacity than did easy passages, the former took much longer to read. Hence, total capacity demanded was greater for the difficult passages.

This result poses an interesting parallel to work in decision making—e.g., consumers may deal with complex choice tasks by adopting choice heuristics that lessen momentary information load, but take longer to execute. The idea of total capacity demanded may be closer to what some consumer researchers mean when they refer to "information load" than is the measure of momentary capacity used by attention researchers. One final note of caution: the "Total Capacity = Momentary Capacity × Time

Spent Processing" measure of total capacity is valid only if both elements of the product are measured on ratio scales. While "Time Spent Processing" meets this criterion, most measures of "Momentary Capacity" can only be assumed to be monotonically related to the underlying construct.

Selective Aspects of Attention

Thus far, consumer researchers have been more interested in the effects of consumers' limited attentional capacity than in the selectivity of attention. A number of factors can be identified that direct attention more to some aspects of a stimulus array than to others. First, there are well-known "salience effects," in which physically salient events in the environment appear to capture a disproportionate amount of attention (for a review, see Taylor and Fiske 1978). These effects are most often discussed in the context of social judgment. If an observer watches a group discussion, the person directly across from the observer will be seen as more influential, important, and responsible than any other participant, presumably because more attention is paid to that participant than to any other. More information about that person will be remembered as well. These ideas are recognized implicitly by advertisers who try to make their ads physically salient (e.g., Brandt 1942).

A related issue is that one's attention is captured by information that is novel or inconsistent with a prior expectation. Information that is novel or unexpected seems to capture one's attention, is processed more extensively, and subsequently is much more likely to be recalled than information that is redundant or expected to appear in a given context. For example, von Restorff (1933) found that almost any technique that served to increase the novelty of particular items or led them to be unexpected enhanced the subsequent recall of those items. This has become known in the memory literature as the "von Restorff effect;" Hastie (1981), Srull (1980), and Wallace (1965) have reviewed literally hundreds of studies that have consistently replicated this same basic phenomenon. Enhanced recall for novel information has been found with bigrams (Smith 1973), nonsense syllables (von Restorff 1933), words (Jenkins and Postman 1948), complex action sequences in written prose (Bower, Black, and Turner 1979), courtroom trial evidence (Reyes, Thompson, and Bower 1980), written descriptions of personal behavior (Srull 1981), and filmed sequences of interpersonal behavior (Hastie 1980), indicating that it is an extremely robust phenomenon.

Interestingly, memory researchers have also known for some time that unexpected information not only captures more attention and is better recalled than expected information, but also that it does so at the expense of other information, whether it be displayed externally or stored in short-term memory. While the exact nature of the inhibition has varied from study to study (Brenner 1971, 1973; Detterman 1975; Detterman and Ellis 1972; Jenkins and Postman 1948; Jones and Jones 1942; Kimble and Dufort 1955; Newman and Saltz 1958; Smith and Stearns 1949) and has occasionally failed to attain statistical significance, the basic result seems quite robust. This suggests that one's attention is drawn to unexpected information. However, since one's attention and processing capacity are limited (Kahneman 1973; Norman 1976), this necessarily means that less attention can be allocated to the immediately surrounding information.

These results have some fascinating parallels with experiments on evaluative judgments that demonstrate "averaging" effects (Anderson 1971; Birnbaum 1974; Lynch 1979). A typical finding in studies in which people make evaluative judgments based upon two or more pieces of information is that information about one attribute (A) has more effect on overall evaluations if it is presented alone than it if is accompanied by information about other attributes (B, C, etc.). Furthermore, when information about attribute A is relatively extreme and/or negative, that piece of information receives additional weight, but only at the expense of the accompanying information about attributes B and C. In general, the more negative and extreme one piece of information is, the less the relative weight assigned to the accompanying information.

Several papers have appeared recently that have specifically attempted to relate the role of attention to judgment and decision making. Fiske (1980), for example, examined person-impression judgments using an information integration model. Pieces of information were presented sequentially and subjects could control their own looking times. Fiske assumed that the more time spent looking at a piece of information, the more attention it captured. She found that behaviors that were relatively extreme and those that were evaluatively negative were looked at longer and weighted more heavily in overall evaluations. She proposed that extremity and negativity both determine the "informativeness" of a given piece of information, and that informativeness in turn determines both the attention paid to the information and the weight given to it in overall judgments. A study by Lynch (1979) also demonstrated that extreme and negative information is given more weight in evaluations of combinations of outcomes. He has discussed in detail how these results can account for several well-known violations of additive utility models of evaluative judgment and decision making.

More recently, Lynch has been involved in a series of studies that also implicate the role of attention in choice. In a standard experiment, subjects are presented with pairings of cards and payoffs. Half of the subjects are told to remember the pairings as well as possible, while half are told that they will subsequently have to make a choice between certain bets. In addition, some subjects operate under relatively low, moderate, or high information-load conditions (e.g., when they get four, eight, or 12 pairings, respectively).

Although several of these studies are still in progress, it is clear that subjects simply cannot attend to all of the information under high information-load conditions—by trying to remember all of the pairings, they actually remember very few. However, subjects have certain adaptive responses that enable them to deal fairly effectively with the high information load. First, they tend to restrict attention to the pairings involving extreme payoffs. It is not clear at this point whether or not this is a voluntary strategy. The differential attention to extreme and moderate payoffs persists even when the task is structured so that there is no greater reward for remembering pairings involving extreme payoffs than for recalling those involving moderate ones. However, individual differences seem to be quite large. The subjects who are most successful in the high information-load conditions tend retrospectively to report focusing on only a subset of the pairings presented. The most typical strategy for accomplishing this seems to be to ignore pairings involving moderate payoffs. Whether this focusing of attention on evaluatively extreme information represents a voluntary or involuntary mechanism, it is quite successful in preventing overload of the attentional system and in remembering as much of the presented information as possible.

These preliminary results are reminiscent of those found by Johnson and Russo (1981) when they compared consumers with different levels of familiarity with automobiles. When given the task of choosing the best automobile on the basis of experimentally provided information, consumers highly familiar with the product class seemed to restrict attention to those attributes they had learned were important, while ignoring those they believed were trivial. The major difference between these results and Lynch's findings is that restricted focus of attention did not enhance overall levels of recall in Johnson and Russo's study.

At any rate, the evidence shows that regardless of prior familiarity, people are more likely to attend to those aspects of a choice alternative that are evaluatively extreme. When one is asked to make a memory-based judgment, these extreme aspects of the product are best recalled. This is important, because if consumers making memory-based choices recall only the evaluatively extreme aspects of choice alternatives, it is quite likely that the subset of attributes recalled will differ across brands. The idea that various memory and attentional factors will cause consumers to recall information about different subsets of attributes for the various choice alternatives has come up at several points in this paper. The decision process followed in this type of situation is an issue of considerable theoretical and practical significance, and deserves careful consideration in future research.

CONCLUSIONS

During the last 10 years, researchers in decision making have begun to show a strong interest in incorporating information processing concepts into their theories (e.g., Wallsten 1980). However, this interest has remained at a conceptual level; very few researchers have demonstrated a high level of sophistication in adapting the *methodologies* of cognitive psychology to test their theoretical propositions. Thus the present discussion of how various cognitive processes may affect decision making and of what methodologies would allow one to address these processes has been highly speculative. Very little empirical work, either in consumer choice or in behavioral decision making, has used such methodologies. This trend is a dangerous one. A more finely-tuned theoretical analysis of consumer behavior will require additional methodological tools if researchers' conceptualizations are to remain empirically grounded. An increasingly catholic approach will also allow consumer researchers to see many fascinating issues in decision making that methodological blinders have heretofore hidden from view. Consumer decision-making theories are becoming more and more sophisticated in their incorporation of information processing concepts. When researchers introduce an equal degree of methodological sophistication to their empirical investigations, a rapid increase in the scope and depth of our understanding should result.

REFERENCES

ANDERSON, JOHN R. (1978), "Arguments Concerning Representation for Mental Imagery," *Psychological Review,* 85: 249–277.

———, and BOWER, GORDON H. (1972), "Recognition and Retrieval Process in Free Recall," *Psychological Review,* 79: 97–123.

———, and BOWER, GORDON H. (1973), *Human Associative Memory,* Washington, DC: V. H. Winston.

———, and BOWER, GORDON H. (1974), "A Propositional Theory of Recognition Memory," *Memory and Cognition,* 2: 406–412.

ANDERSON, NORMAN H. (1971), "Integration Theory and Attitude Change," *Psychological Review,* 78: 177–206.

ANDERSON, RICHARD C., and PICHERT, JAMES W. (1978), "Recall of Previously Unrecallable Information Following a Shift in Perspective," *Journal of Verbal Learning and Verbal Behavior,* 17: 1–12.

BAHRICK, HENRY P. (1969), "Measurement of Memory by Prompted Recall," *Journal of Experimental Psychology,* 97: 213–219.

——— (1970), "Two-Phase Model for Prompted Recall," *Psychological Review,* 77: 215–222.

BAKER, LINDA (1978), "Processing Temporal Relationships in Simple Stories: Effects of Input Sequence," *Journal of Verbal Learning and Verbal Behavior,* 17: 559–572.

BARTLETT, FREDERICK C. (1932), *Remembering.* Cambridge, England: Cambridge University Press.

BETTMAN, JAMES R. (1975), "Issues in Designing Consumer Information Environments," *Journal of Consumer Research,* 2: 169–177.

——— (1979), *An Information Processing Theory of Consumer Choice,* Reading, MA: Addison-Wesley.

———, and JACOBY, JACOB (1976), "Patterns of Processing in Consumer Information Acquisition," in *Advances in Consumer Research,* Vol. 3, Ed. Beverlee B. Anderson. Chicago, Association for Consumer Research, pp. 315-320.

———, and KAKKAR, PRADEEP (1977), "Effects of Information Presentation Format on Consumer Information Acquisition Strategies," *Journal of Consumer Research,* 3: 233–240.

———, and PARK, C. WHAN (1980), "Effects of Prior Knowledge and Experience and Phase of the Choice Process on Consumer Decision Processes: A Protocol Analysis," *Journal of Consumer Research,* 7: 234–248.

———, and ZINS, MICHAEL (1979), "Information Format and Choice Task Effects in Decision Making," *Journal of Consumer Research,* 6: 141–153.

BIEHAL, GABRIEL, and CHAKRAVARTI, DIPANKAR

(1982), "Information Presentation Format and Task Goals as Determinants of Consumers' Memory-Retrieval and Choice Processes," *Journal of Consumer Research,* 8: 431–441.

BIRNBAUM, MICHAEL H. (1974), "The Nonadditivity of Personality Impressions," *Journal of Experimental Psychology Monograph* 102: 543–561.

BLUMENTHAL, ARTHUR L. (1977), *The Process of Cognition.* Englewood Cliffs, NJ: Prentice-Hall.

BOUSFIELD, W. A. (1953), "The Occurrence of Clustering in the Recall of Randomly Arranged Associates," *Journal of General Psychology,* 49: 229–240.

BOWER, GORDON H., BLACK, JOHN B., and TURNER, TERRENCE S. (1979), "Scripts in Memory for Text," *Cognitive Psychology,* 11: 177–220.

BRANDT, HERMAN (1942), "An Evaluation of the Attensity of Isolation by Means of Ocular Photography," *American Journal of Psychology,* 55: 230–239.

BRENNER, MALCOLM (1971), "Caring, Love, and Selective Memory," *Proceedings of the 7th Annual Convention of the American Psychological Association,* 6: 275–276.

——— (1973), "The Next-in-Line Effect," *Journal of Verbal Learning and Verbal Behavior,* 12: 320–323.

BRITTON, BRUCE L., WESTBROOK, ROBERT D., and HOLDREDGE, TIMOTHY S. (1978), "Reading and Cognitive Capacity Usage: Effects of Text Difficulty," *Journal of Experimental Psychology: Human Learning and Memory,* 4: 582–591.

BROWN, JOHN (1968), "Reciprocal Facilitation and Impairment of Free Recall," *Psychonomic Science,* 10: 41–42.

BUSCHKE, HENRY (1973), "Selective Reminding for Analysis of Memory and Learning," *Journal of Verbal Learning and Verbal Behavior,* 12: 543–550.

CARLSTON, DONAL E. (1980), "The Recall and Use of Traits and Events in Social Inference Processes," *Journal of Experimental Psychology,* 16: 303–328.

CHASE, WILLIAM G., and SIMON, HERBERT A. (1973), "Perception in Chess," *Cognitive Psychology,* 4: 55–81.

COHEN, BURTON H. (1963), "Recall of Categorized Word Lists," *Journal of Experimental Psychology,* 66: 227–234.

——— (1966), "Some-or-None Characteristics of Coding Behavior," *Journal of Verbal Learning and Verbal Behavior,* 5: 182–187.

COHEN, JOEL B., MINIARD, PAUL W., and DICKSON, PETER R. (1980), "Information Integration: An Information Processing Perspective," in *Advances in Consumer Research,* Vol. 7, Ed. Jerry Olson. Ann Arbor, MI: Association for Consumer Research.

COLLINS, ALAN M., and LOFTUS, ELIZABETH F. (1975), "A Spreading-Activation Theory of Semantic Processing," *Psychological Review,* 56: 54–59.

D'ANDRADE, ROY G. (1965), "Trait Psychology and Componential Analysis," *American Anthropologist,* 67: 215–228.

DETTERMAN, DOUGLAS K. (1975), "The Von Restorff Effect and Induced Amnesia: Production by Manipulation of Sound Intensity," *Journal of Experimental Psychology: Human Learning and Memory,* 1: 614–628.

———, and ELLIS, NORMAN R. (1972), "Determinants of Induced Amnesia in Short-Term Memory," *Journal of Experimental Psychology,* 95: 308–316.

EINHORN, HILLEL J. (1971), "The Use of Nonlinear, Noncompensatory Models as a Function Task and Amount of Information," *Organization Behavior and Human Performance,* 6: 1–27.

———, and HOGARTH, ROBIN M. (1981), "Behavioral Decision Theory: Processes of Judgment and Choice," *Annual Review of Psychology,* 32: 53–88.

ERICSSON, K. ANDERS, and SIMON, HERBERT A. (1980), "Verbal Reports as Data," *Psychological Review,* 87: 215–251.

EYSENCK, MICHAEL W. (1977), *Human Memory: Theory, Research, and Individual Differences.* Oxford: Pergamon Press.

FISKE, SUSAN T. (1980), "Attention and Weight in Person Perception: The Impact of Negative and Extreme Behavior," *Journal of Personality and Social Psychology,* 38: 889–906.

FRIENDLY, MICHAEL L. (1977), "In Search of the M-Gram: The Structure of Organization in Free Recall," *Cognitive Psychology,* 9: 188–249.

——— (1979), "Methods for Finding Graphic Representation of Associative Memory Structures," in *Memory Organization and Structure,* Ed. C. Richard Puff. New York: Academic Press.

GLASS, ARNOLD C., HOLYOAK, KEITH J., and SANTA, JOHN C. (1979), *Cognition.* Reading, MA: Addison-Wesley.

GRAESSER, ARTHUR, and MANDLER, GEORGE (1978), "Limited Processing Capacity Constrains the Storage of Unrelated Sets of Words and Retrieval from Natural Categories," *Journal of Experimental Psychology: Human Learning and Memory,* 4: 86–100.

GREGG, VERNON H. (1976), "Word Frequency, Recognition and Recall," in *Recall and Recognition,* Ed. John Brown. London: Wiley.

HASHER, LYNN, and GRIFFIN, MARY (1978), "Reconstructive and Reproductive Processes in Memory," *Journal of Experimental Psychology: Human Learning and Memory,* 4: 318–330.

HASTIE, REID (1980), "Memory for Behavioral Information that Confirms or Contradicts a Personality Impression," in *Person Memory: The Cognitive Basis of Social Perception,* Ed. Reid Hastie et al. Hillsdale, NJ: Erlbaum.

——— (1981) "Schematic Principles in Human Memory," in *Social Cognition: The Ontario Symposium on Personality and Social Psychology,* Ed. E. Tory Higgins, C. Peter Herman, and Mark P. Zanna. Hillsdale, NJ: Erlbaum.

HAYES-ROTH, FREDERICK (1979), "Distinguishing Theories of Representation: A Critique of Anderson's Arguments Concerning Mental Imagery," *Psychological Review,* 86: 376–392.

HOROWITZ, LEONARD M., and PRYTULAK, LUBY S. (1969), "Redintegrative Memory," *Psychological Review,* 76: 519–531.

HOWARD, JOHN A., and SHETH, JAGDISH N. (1969), *The Theory of Buyer Behavior,* New York: Wiley.

JACOBY, JACOB, SPELLER, DONALD, and KOHN-BERNING, CAROL (1974), "Brand Choice Behavior as a Function of Information Load: Replication and Extension," *Journal of Consumer Research,* 1: 33–42.

JENKINS, WILLIAM O., and POSTMAN, LEO (1948), "Isolation and Spread of Effect in Serial Learning," *American Journal of Psychology,* 61: 214–221.

JOHNSON, ERIC J., and RUSSO, J. EDWARD (1978), "The Organization of Product Information in Memory Identified Recall Times," in *Advances in Consumer Research,* Vol. 5, Ed. H. Keith Hunt. Chicago: Association for Consumer Research, pp. 79–86.

———, and RUSSO, J. EDWARD (1981), "Product Familiarity and Learning New Information," in *Advances in Consumer Research,* Vol. 8, Ed. Kent Monroe. Ann Arbor, MI: Association for Consumer Research, pp. 151–155.

JOHNSON, NEIL F. (1978), "The Memorial Structure of Organized Sequences," *Memory and Cognition,* 6: 233–269.

JONES, F. NOWELL, and JONES, MARGARET H. (1942), "Vividness as a Factor in Learning Lists of Nonsense Syllables," *American Journal of Psychology,* 55: 96–101.

KAHNEMAN, DANIEL (1970), "Remarks on Attention Control," *Acta Psychologica,* 33: 118–131. (*Attention and Performance III:* proceedings of a symposium, Ed. A. F. Sanders.)

——— (1973), *Attention and Effort.* Englewood Cliffs, NJ: Prentice-Hall.

———, and BEATTY, JACKSON (1967), "Pupillary Responses in a Pitch Discrimination Task," *Perception and Psychophysics,* 2: 101–105.

———, and TVERSKY, AMOS (1972), "Subjective Probability: A Judgment of Representativeness," *Cognitive Psychology,* 3: 430–454.

KASSARJIAN, HAROLD H. (1978), "Presidential Address," in *Advances in Consumer Research,* Vol. 5, Ed. H. Keith Hunt. Chicago: Association for Consumer Research, pp. xiii–xiv.

——— (1981), "Low Involvement: A Second Look," in *Advances in Consumer Research,* Vol. 8, Ed. Kent Monroe. Ann Arbor, MI: Association for Consumer Research, pp. 31–34.

KERR, BETH (1973), "Processing Demands During Mental Operations," *Memory and Cognition,* 1: 401–412.

KIMBLE, GREGORY A., and DUFORT, ROBERT H. (1955), "Meaningfulness and Isolation as Factors in Verbal Learning," *Journal of Experimental Psychology,* 50: 361–369.

KINTSCH, WALTER (1968), "Recognition and Free Recall of Organized Lists," *Journal of Experimental Psychology,* 78: 481–487.

——— (1970), "Models for Free Recall and Recognition," in *Models of Human Memory,* Ed. Donald A. Norman. New York: Academic Press.

——— (1978), "More on Recognition Failure of Recallable Words: Implications for Generation-Recognition Models," *Psychological Review,* 85: 470–473.

———, MANDEL, THEODORE S., and KAZMINSKY, ELY (1977), "Summarizing Scrambled Stories," *Memory and Cognition,* 5: 547–552.

KOSSLYN, STEPHEN M. (1981), "The Medium and the Message in Mental Imagery: A Theory," *Psychological Review,* 88: 46–66.

LACHMAN, ROY, LACHMAN, JANET L., and BUTTERFIELD, EARL C. (1979), *Cognitive Psychology and Information Processing: An Introduction.* Hillsdale, NJ: Erlbaum.

LANDAUER, THOMAS K. (1975), "Memory Without Organization: "Properties of a Model with Random Storage and Undirected Retrieval," *Cognitive Psychology,* 7: 495–531.

LEWIS, DONALD J. (1979), "Psychobiology of Active and Inactive Memory," *Psychological Bulletin,* 86: 1054–1083.

LICHTENSTEIN, SARAH, and SLOVIC, PAUL (1971), "Reversals of Preference between Bids and Choices in Gambling Decision," *Journal of Experimental Psychology,* 89: 46–55.

LINGLE, JOHN J., and OSTROM, THOMAS M. (1979), "Retrieval Selectivity in Memory-Based Impression Judgments," *Journal of Personality and Social Psychology,* 37: 180–194.

LUSSIER, DENIS A., and OLSHAVSKY, RICHARD W. (1979), "Task Complexity and Contingent Processing in Brand Choice," *Journal of Consumer Research* 6: 154–165.

LYNCH, JOHN G. (1979), "Why Additive Utility Models Fail as Descriptions of Choice Behavior," *Journal of Experimental Social Psychology,* 15: 397–417.

——— (1981), "A Method for Determining the Sequencing of Cognitive Processes in Judgment: Order Effects on Reaction Times," in *Advances in Consumer Research,* Vol. 8, Ed. Kent Monroe. Ann Arbor, MI: Association for Consumer Research, pp. 134–139.

———, and COHEN, JERRY L. (1978), "The Use of Subjective Expected Utility Theory as an Aid to Understanding Variables that Influence Helping Behavior," *Journal of Personality and Social Psychology,* 36: 1138–1151.

MANDLER, GEORGE (1967), "Organization and Memory," in *The Psychology of Learning and Motivation,* Vol. 1, Eds. Kenneth W. Spence and Janet T. Spence. New York: Academic Press.

——— (1968), "Organized Recall: Individual Functions," *Psychonomic Science,* 13: 235–236.

——— (1975a), "Consciousness: Respectable, Useful, and Probably Necessary," in *Information Processing and Cognition: The Loyola Symposium,* Ed. Robert Solso. Hillsdale, NJ: Erlbaum.

——— (1975b), *Mind and Emotion.* New York: Wiley.

——— (1979), "Emotion," in *The First Century of Experimental Psychology,* Ed. Elliot Hearst. Hillsdale, NJ: Erlbaum.

——— (1980), "Recognizing: The Judgment of Previous Occurrence," *Psychological Review,* 87: 252–271.

———, and PEARLSTONE, ZENA (1966), "Free and Constrained Concept Learning and Subsequent Recall," *Journal of Verbal Learning and Verbal Behavior,* 5: 126–131.

MANDLER, JEAN M. (1978), "A Code in the Node: The Use of a Story Schema in Retrieval," *Discourse Processes,* 1: 14–35.

MCCORMACK, P. D. (1972), "Recognition Memory: How Complex a Retrieval System?," *Canadian Journal of Psychology,* 26: 19–41.

MCNICOL, D. (1972), "A Primer of Signal Detection Theory, London: Allen & Unwin.

MILLER, GEORGE A. (1956), "The Magical Number Seven, Plus or Minus Two: Some Limits on Our Capacity for Processing Information," *Psychological Review,* 63: 81–97.

MOORE, DAN (1981), "The Behavioral Measurement of Information Load," Unpublished manuscript, University of Florida.

MULAIK, STANLEY A. (1964), "Are Personality Factors Raters' Conceptual Factors?," *Journal of Consulting Psychology,* 28: 506–511.

NAUS, MARY J. (1974), "Memory Search of Categorized Lists: A Consideration of Alternative Self-Terminating Search Strategies," *Journal of Experimental Psychology,* 102: 992–1000.

NEWELL, ALAN, and SIMON, HERBERT (1972), *Human Problem Solving.* Englewood Cliffs, NJ: Prentice-Hall.

NEWMAN, SLATER E., and SALTZ, ELI (1958), "Isolation Effects: Stimulus and Response Generalization as Explanatory Concepts," *Journal of Experimental Psychology,* 55: 467–472.

NORMAN, DONALD A. (1976), *Memory and Attention* (2nd ed.). New York: Wiley.

OLSHAVSKY, RICHARD W. (1973), "Customer-Salesman Interaction in Appliance Retailing," *Journal of Marketing Research,* 10: 208–212.

——— (1979), "Task Complexity and Contingent Processing in Decision-Making: A Replication and Extension," *Organizational Behavior and Human Performance,* 24: 300–316.

OSTROM, THOMAS M., LINGLE, JOHN J., PRYOR, JOHN B., and GEVA, NEHEMIA (1980), "Cognitive Organization of Person Impressions," in *Person Memory: The Cognitive Basis of Social Perception,* Ed. Reid Hastie et al. Hillsdale, NJ: Erlbaum.

PASSINI, FRANK T., and NORMAN, WARREN T. (1966), "A Universal Conception of Personality Structure?," *Journal of Personality and Social Psychology,* 4: 44–49.

PATTERSON, KATHLEEN E. (1972), "Some Characteristics of Retrieval Limitation in Long-term Memory," *Journal of Verbal Learning and Verbal Behavior,* 11: 685–691.

PAYNE, JOHN W. (1976), "Task Complexity and Contingent Processing in Decision Making: An Information Search and Protocol Analysis," *Organizational Behavior and Human Performance,* 16: 366–387.

———, BRAUNSTEIN, MYRON L., and CARROLL, JOHN S. (1978), "Exploring Predecisional Behavior: An Alternative Approach to Decision Research," *Organizational Behavior and Human Performance,* 22: 17–44.

POLLIO, HOWARD R. (1974), *The Psychology of Symbolic Activity.* Reading, MA: Addison-Wesley.

———, RICHARDS, STEVE, and LUCAS, RICHARD (1969), "Temporal Properties of Category Recall," *Journal of Verbal Learning and Verbal Behavior,* 8: 95–102.

POSNER, MICHAEL I. (1978), *Chronometric Explorations of Mind,* Hillsdale, NJ: Erlbaum.

———, and BOIES, STEPHEN J. (1971), "Components of Attention," *Psychological Review,* 78: 391–408.

———, and KEELE, STEVEN W. (1970), "Time and Space as Measures of Mental Operations," Invited Address, Division 3, American Psychological Association.

———, and KLEIN, RAYMOND M (1973), "On Functions of Consciousness," in *Attention and Performance IV* Ed. S. Kornblum. New York. Academic Press, Inc.

———, KLEIN, RAYMOND, M., SUMMERS, JEFFREY, and BUGGIE, STEPHEN (1973), "On the Selection of Signals," *Memory and Cognition,* 1: 2–12.

———, and SNYDER, CHARLES R. R. (1975), "Attention and Cognitive Control," in *Information Processing and Cognition: The Loyola Symposium,* Ed. Robert L. Solso. Hillsdale, NJ: Erlbaum.

POSTMAN, LEO (1976), "Interference Theory Revisited," in *Recall and Recognition,* Ed. John Brown. London: Wiley.

PRYOR, JOHN B., and OSTROM, THOMAS M. (1981), "The Cognitive Organization of Social Information: A Converging Operations Approach," *Journal of Personality and Social Psychology,* 41: 628–641.

PYLYSHYN, ZENON (1979), "Validating Computational Models: A Critique of Anderson's Indeterminacy of Representation Claim," *Psychological Review,* 86: 383–394.

——— (1981), "The Imagery Debate: Analogue Media Versus Tacit Knowledge," *Psychological Review,* 88: 16–45.

RAAIJMAKERS, JEROEN G., and SHIFFRIN, RICHARD M. (1981), "Search of Associative Memory," *Psychological Review,* 99: 92–134.

REITMAN, JUDITH S., and RUETER, HENRY H. (1980), "Organization Revealed by Recall Orders and Confirmed by Pauses," *Cognitive Psychology,* 12: 554–581.

REYES, ROBERT M., THOMPSON, WILLIAM C., and BOWER, GORDON H. (1980), "Judgmental Biases Resulting from Differing Availabilities of Arguments," *Journal of Personality and Social Psychology,* 39: 2–12.

ROEDIGER, HENRY L. (1974), "Inhibiting Effects of Recall," *Memory and Cognition,* 2: 261–269.

ROSENBERG, SEYMORE, and SEDLAK, ANDREA (1972), "Structural Representations of Implicit Personality Theory," in *Advances in Experimental Social Psychology,* Vol. 6, Ed. Leonard Berkowitz. New York: Academic Press

RUSSO, J. EDWARD, and JOHNSON, ERIC J. (1980), "What Do Consumers Know about Familiar Products?" in *Advances in Consumer Research,* Vol. 7, Ed. Jerry Olson. Ann Arbor, MI: Association for Consumer Research, pp. 417–422.

SAVAGE, LEONARD J. (1954), *The Foundation of Statistics,* New York: Wiley.

SCAMMON, DEBRA L. (1977), "Information Load and Consumers," *Journal of Consumer Research,* 4: 148–155.

SHANTEAU, JAMES C. (1974), "Component Processes in Risky Decision-Making," *Journal of Experimental Psychology,* 103: 680–691.

SHIFFRIN, RICHARD M. (1976), "Capacity Limitations in Information Processing, Attention and Memory," in *Handbook of Learning and Cognitive Processes,* Vol. 4, Ed. William K. Estes. Hillsdale, NJ: Erlbaum.

SHULMAN, HARVEY G. and GREENBERG, SETH N. (1971), "Perceptual Deficit Due to Division of Attention Between Memory and Perception," *Journal of Experimental Psychology,* 88: 171–176.

SLAMECKA, NORMAN J. (1968), "An Examination of Trace Storage in Free Recall," *Journal of Experimental Psychology,* 76: 504–513.

SLOVIC, PAUL (1972), "From Shakespeare to Simon: Speculations—and Some Evidence—About Man's Ability to Process Information," *Oregon Research Institute Research Monograph,* 12 (3).

______, FISCHHOFF, BARUCH, and LICHTENSTEIN, SARAH (1977), "Behavioral Decision Theory," *Annual Review of Psychology,* 28: 1–39.

______, and MACPHILLAMY, DOUGLAS (1974), "Dimensional Commensurability and Cue Utilization in Comparative Judgment," *Organizational Behavior and Human Performance,* 11: 172–194.

SMITH, KIRK H. (1973), "Effect of Exceptions on Verbal Reconstructive Memory," *Journal of Experimental Psychology,* 97: 119–139.

SMITH, MONCRIEF H. and STEARNS, ELLEN G. (1949), "The Influence of Isolation on the Learning of Surrounding Materials," *American Journal of Psychology,* 62: 369–381.

SRULL, THOMAS K. (1980), "Person Memory: The Role of Processing Strategy, Expectancy, and Level of Incongruity in the Processing of Interindividual and Intraindividual Behavior Variability," Unpublished Ph.D. dissertation, University of Illinois.

______ (1981), "Person Memory: Some Tests of Associative Storage and Retrieval Models," *Journal of Experimental Psychology: Human Learning and Memory,* 7: 440–463.

STERNBERG, ROBERT J. and TULVING, ENDEL (1977), "The Measurement of Subjective Organization in Free Recall," *Psychological Bulletin,* 84: 539–556.

STERNBERG, SAUL (1966), "High-Speed Scanning in Human Memory," *Science,* 153: 652–654.

______ (1969), "Memory Scanning: Mental Processes Revealed by Reaction-Time Experiments," *American Scientist,* 57: 421–457.

______ (1975), "Memory Scanning: New Findings and Current Controversies," *Quarterly Journal of Experimental Psychology,* 27: 1–32.

SVENSON, OLA (1979), "Process Descriptions of Decision-Making," *Organizational Behavior and Human Performance,* 23: 86–112.

TAYLOR, SHELLEY E., and FISKE, SUSAN T. (1978), "Salience, Attention, and Attribution: Top of the Head Phenomena," in *Advances in Experimental Social Psychology,* Vol. II, Ed. Leonard Berkowitz. New York: Academic Press.

THORNDIKE, EDWARD L. (1920), "A Constant Error in Psychological Ratings," *Journal of Applied Psychology,* 4: 25–29.

TROUTMAN, C. MICHAEL, and SHANTEAU, JAMES C. (1976), "Do Consumers Evaluate Products by Adding or Averaging Attribute Information?" *Journal of Consumer Research,* 3: 101–106.

TULVING, ENDEL, and PEARLSTONE, ZENA (1966), "Availability Versus Accessibility of Information in Memory for Words," *Journal of Verbal Learning and Verbal Behavior,* 5: 381–391.

______, and PSOTKA, JOSEPH (1971), "Retroactive Inhibition in Free Recall: Inaccessibility of Information Available in the Memory Store," *Journal of Experimental Psychology,* 87: 1–8.

TVERSKY, AMOS (1967), "Additivity, Utility, and Subjective Probability," *Journal of Mathematical Psychology,* 4: 175–201.

______ (1969), "Intransitivity of Preferences," *Psychological Review,* 76: 31–48.

______ (1972), "Elimination by Aspects: A Theory of Choice," *Psychological Review,* 79: 281–299.

______, and KAHNEMAN, DANIEL (1974), "Judgment Under Uncertainty: Heuristics and Biases," *Science,* 185: 1124–1131.

______, and KAHNEMAN, DANIEL (1981), "The Framing of Decisions and the Psychology of Choice," *Science,* 211: 453–458.

VON RESTORFF, HEDWIG (1933), "Uber die Wirkung Von Bereichsbildungen in Spurenfeld," *Psychologisch Forschung,* 18: 299–342.

WALLACE, WILLIAM P. (1965), "Review of the Historical, Empirical, and Theoretical Status of the Von Restorff Phenomenon," *Psychological Bulletin,* 63: 410–423.

WALLSTEN, THOMAS S., ED. (1980), *Cognitive Processes in Choice and Decision Behavior.* Hillsdale, NJ: Erlbaum.

WATKINS, MICHAEL J., and GARDINER, JOHN M. (1979), "An Application of Generate-Recognize Theory of Recall," *Journal of Verbal Learning and Verbal Behavior,* 18: 687–704.

WILKIE, WILLIAM L. (1974), "Analysis of Effects of Information Load," *Journal of Marketing Research,* 11: 462–466.

WOOD, GORDON (1972), "Organizational Processes and Free Recall," in *Organization of Memory,* Eds. Endel Tulving and Wayne Donaldson. New York: Academic Press.

WRIGHT, PETER L. (1972), "Consumer Judgment Strategies: Beyond the Compensatory Assumption," in *Proceedings of the Third Annual Conference,* Ed. M. Venkatesan. Chicago: Association for Consumer Research, pp. 316–424.

______ (1974), "The Harassed Decision Maker: Time Pressures, Distractions, and the Use of Evidence," *Journal of Applied Psychology,* 59: 555–561.

——— (1975), "Consumer Choice Strategies: Simplifying vs. Optimizing," *Journal of Marketing Research,* 11: 60–67.

——— (1980), "Message Evoked Thoughts: Persuasion Research Using Thought Verbalizations," *Journal of Consumer Research,* 7: 151–175.

———, and KRIEWALL, MAY ANN (1980), "State-of-Mind Effects on the Accuracy with Which Utility Functions Predict Marketplace Choice," *Journal of Marketing Research,* 17: 277–293.

YAMAGISHI, TOSHIO, and HILL, CHARLES T. (1981), "Adding versus Averaging Models Revisited: A Test of a Path-Analytic Integration Model," *Journal of Personality and Social Psychology,* 41: 13–25.

YATES, J. FRANK, JAGACINSKI, CAROLYN M., and FABER, MARK D. (1978), "Evaluation of Partially Described Multiattribute Options," *Organizational Behavior and Human Performance,* 21: 240–251.

ZANNA, MARK P., and HAMILTON, DAVID L. (1972), "Attribute Dimension and Patterns of Trait Inferences," *Psychonomic Science,* 27: 353–354.

7

A BEHAVIOR MODIFICATION PERSPECTIVE ON MARKETING*

Walter R. Nord
J. Paul Peter

This article presents an overview of behavior modification and investigates its applicability to marketing. It is suggested that this perspective provides a useful complement to the more cognitively-oriented approaches which currently dominate the marketing literature. Some of the approach's potential contributions and unresolved issues are also discussed.

Students of marketing have borrowed freely from many areas of psychology. For example, cognitive psychology, need satisfaction models, field theory, psychoanalytic theory, and stimulus-response theory have all provided useful insights for understanding and predicting consumer behavior. However, marketing scholars have given little consideration to one of the most influential perspectives developed in psychology in the last 40 years—the behavior modification approach stimulated by the work of B. F. Skinner[1] (e.g., 1953, 1969). The purpose of this paper is to provide an overview of the Behavior Modification Perspective (BMP) which has evolved from the work of Skinner and others and investigate its applicability to marketing.

*Reprinted from *Journal of Marketing,* 44 (Spring 1980), pp. 36–47. Published by The American Marketing Association, Chicago, IL 60606.

[1]Some psychologists consider Skinner and his followers to be S-R theorists. While there are important similarities, the differences are significant enough that leading psychologists consider Skinner's work separately from their treatment of S-R theory (see Hall and Lindzey 1970).

FUNDAMENTAL ELEMENTS OF BEHAVIOR MODIFICATION

There is an important basic difference between the BMP and the psychological perspectives which currently dominate the marketing literature: *the BMP focuses on environmental factors which influence behavior.* It takes the prediction and control of behavior as problematic and deliberately shuns speculation about processes which are assumed to occur within the individual such as needs, motives, attitudes, information processing, etc. In fact, the so-called radical behaviorists reject the value of considering these internal processes at all. Our approach is far less radical and more consistent with the social learning theories of Bandura (1978) and Staats (1975). We believe that it is useful and desirable to theorize about and investigate internal, psychological processes which affect behavior. However, we maintain that many marketing objectives can be (and in fact have been) accomplished without such theories by simply studying environmental conditions and manipulating them to influence consumer behavior. The BMP provides the stimulus and technology for systematizing this external focus.

Frequently, treatments of behavior modification are limited to two types of environmental manipulations—those which result in respondent (classical) conditioning and those which produce operant (instrumental) conditioning.[2] This treatment of behavior modification will include these manipulations as well as those which alter behavior through vicarious learning and ecological design.

A review of the literature revealed that these four ways of modifying behavior have been given little systematic attention in marketing. While respondent conditioning has been discussed at length in the marketing literature in an attempt to explain behavior, it has not been discussed as a method of modifying or controlling behavior. Operant conditioning has been discussed (e.g., Carey et al. 1976; Engel, Kollat, and Blackwell 1973; Kassarjian 1978; Ray 1973) but has not been integrated into the mainstream of marketing thinking. Treatment of vicarious learning and ecological design is almost totally absent.[3] As a result many students of marketing are apt to be unfamiliar with these processes. Therefore, all four will be described in some detail.

Respondent Conditioning

Respondents are a class of behaviors which are under the control of stimuli which precede them. Generally, these behaviors are assumed to be governed by the autonomic nervous system and, therefore, are not susceptible to conscious control by the individual. Pavlov's classical conditioning experiments provide the basic paradigm for this approach.

In general, respondent conditioning can be defined as a process through which a previously neutral stimulus, by being paired with an unconditioned stimulus, comes to elicit a response very similar to the response originally elicited by the unconditioned stimulus. It is well established that a variety of human behaviors including reflexes, glandular responses, and what are often called "emotions" can be modified through the process of respondent conditioning.[4] For example, when a new product for which people have neutral feelings is repeatedly advertised during exciting sports events, it is possible for the product to eventually generate excitement on its own solely through the repeated pairing with the exciting events. Similarly, an unknown political candidate may come to elicit patriotic feelings in voters simply by having patriotic music constantly played in the background of his/her political commercials.

---

[2]It has been argued that respondent and operant conditioning may not be as separable processes as previously thought. For a discussion of this point, see Miller (1969). However, for present purposes they will be treated as conceptually distinct.

[3]However, Kotler's (1976, p. 324) notion of atmospherics as well as several of Belk's (1974, 1975) situational influences, e.g., physical and social surroundings, are fully consistent with the principles of ecological design (and respondent conditioning).

[4]Miller (1969) has demonstrated that these behaviors can also be conditioned by stimuli which occur after them.

Since it is a process which can account for many of the responses which environmental stimuli elicit from individuals, respondent conditioning has a number of important implications for marketing. Through it, a particular stimulus can come to evoke positive, negative, or neutral feelings. Consequently, respondent conditioning influences whether a wide variety of objects or events are those which an individual will work to obtain, to avoid, or be indifferent to.

At this point, it should be clear that what the BMP views as respondent conditioning can account for many of the reactions to stimuli which have also been accounted for by cognitive or affective models. We are not saying that the BMP view is incompatible with these traditional concerns or that it is a perfect substitute for such models. However, these traditional concerns have led marketing scholars to accept models and to design research in which internal psychological processes are focal and assumed to be "causal." As a result, the role of external events has received insufficient attention. Respondent conditioning and other elements of the BMP focus on the manipulation of external factors and it is clear that consumer behavior can be influenced through this external emphasis without a complete psychology of internal processes.[5]

Consider a product or a product-related stimulus. External stimuli which elicit positive emotions can be paired with the product in ways which result in the product itself eliciting positive effect. Consequently, behavior may be triggered which brings the potential consumer into "closer contact" with the product.[6] Similarly, stimuli may be presented which produce certain general emotional responses such as relaxation, excitement, nostalgia, or some other emotion which is likely to increase the probability of some desired response such as product purchase. Note, while it may be useful to obtain verbal reports or physiological measures in deciding what stimuli to employ to elicit such emotions, the BMP bypasses these procedures and focuses directly on ways to modify behavior. While a number of psychological theories could be used to account for these processes, behavior can be modified without such theories. In fact, it seems clear that the actions of practitioners often follow this atheoretical approach.

Consider the following examples. Radio and television advertisements often use famous sportscasters whose voices have been paired for years with exciting sports events. These voices elicit excitement as a result of this frequent pairing. Repeated pairings of the voices with the advertised product can result, via higher-order respondent conditioning, in feelings of excitement associated with the product. Music, sexy voices and bodies, and other stimuli are used in similar ways. Often these stimuli may influence behavior without this "higher order conditioning" simply by drawing attention to the ad. Of course, the attention generating properties of the stimulus itself are apt to have developed through previous conditioning which occurs "naturally" in society. The use of telephones ringing or sirens in the background of radio and television ads, some legal version of the phrase "news bulletin," and the presence of famous celebrities, are common examples of how stimuli, which are irrelevant to the content of an ad or the function of the product, are used

[5]There are three basic ways by which researchers attempt to determine what properties certain stimuli have for people. One way is through verbal reports. A second method may be termed projection whereby the investigator infers the properties from his/her observations of another person's behavior. A third means can be termed empirical. This involves presentation of a stimulus and description of its consequences. Of course, these three are often used in combination. The BMP encourages marketers not to discount the advantages of the empirical approach.

[6]"Closer contact" refers to a general relationship between a person's behavior and a given stimulus (e.g., a product). For example, if a product elicits positive effect, an individual exposed to the product is more apt to move towards it than if negative emotions are elicited. Attending behavior is also apt to be a function of respondently conditioned effect. Stimuli which elicit stronger emotional responses (either positive or negative) are, at least over a considerable range, apt to receive more attention from an individual than are stimuli which are affectively neutral. To the degree that attending behavior is necessary for product purchase or other product-related behavior, respondent conditioning influences product contact.

to increase attention to the ad itself. In this sense, one of the major resources that organizations use to market their products is made available through previous respondent conditioning of members of society.

Stimuli at or near the point of purchase also serve the goals of marketers through their ability to elicit respondent behaviors. Christmas music in a toy department is a good example. Although no data area available to support the point, we suspect that Christmas carols are useful in eliciting the emotions labeled as the "Christmas spirit." Once these feelings have been elicited, we suspect (and retailers seem to share our expectations) that people are more apt to purchase a potential gift for a loved one. In other words, Christmas carols are useful in generating emotions which are incompatible with "sales resistance."

These examples can serve as a basis for several generalizations about the role of respondent conditioning as a marketing tool. First, the concept of respondent conditioning directs attention to the presentation of stimuli which, due to previous conditioning, elicit certain feelings in the potential consumer. Sometimes (as with Christmas music) these stimuli trigger certain emotions which are apt to increase the probability of certain desired behaviors or reduce the probability of undesired responses. Second, in many cases the marketer may find it useful to actually condition responses to stimuli. For example, as with the voices of famous sportscasters, it may be desirable to pair the stimuli with the product repeatedly in order to condition the feelings elicited by a particular stimulus to the product. Then, the product itself may stimulate similar reactions. Finally, some of the benefits which can be gained from employing the principles of respondent conditioning have already been used by marketing practitioners in an (apparently) ad hoc manner. While the systematic application of the respondent paradigm is unlikely to result in any new principles, by calling attention to the actual control process being employed, it is apt to yield a number of practical benefits both to advertising and to point of purchase promotion. In particular, stimuli are apt to be arranged in ways which are more effective in eliciting desired emotional responses. Thus, the primary benefit of respondent conditioning, as with other elements of the BMP, is that it encourages the systematic analysis of purchase and purchase-related behaviors and indicates specific techniques for modifying and controlling these behaviors.

Operant Conditioning

Operant conditioning differs from respondent conditioning in at least two important ways. First, whereas respondent conditioning is concerned with involuntary responses, operant conditioning deals with behaviors which are usually assumed to be under the conscious control of the individual. Second, respondent behaviors are elicited by stimuli which occur prior to the response; operants are conditioned by consequences which occur *after* the behavior.

In any given situation, at any given time, there is a certain probability that an individual will emit a particular behavior. If all of the possible behaviors are arranged in descending order of probability of occurrence, the result is a response hierarchy. Operant conditioning has occurred when the probability that an individual will emit one or more behaviors is altered by changing the events or consequences which follow the particular behavior. Some events or consequences increase the frequency that a given behavior is likely to be repeated. For example, a cash rebate given at the time of purchase increases the probability that a shopper will purchase in the same store in the future, other things being equal. In this case, since the cash rebate has the effect of increasing the probability of the preceding behavior, it is referred to as a positive reinforcer. In other cases, the frequency of a given behavior can be increased by removing an aversive stimulus. This is called negative reinforcement. Although there are few examples of negative reinforcement in marketing, one illustration is the situation where a consumer purchases a product primarily to avoid the high pressure tactics of an overzealous salesperson.

Sometimes operant techniques are used to

decrease the probability of a response. If the environment is arranged so that the particular response results in neutral consequences, over a period of time that response will diminish in frequency. This process is referred to as extinction. If the response is followed by a noxious or "undesired" result, the frequency of the response is likely to decrease. The term punishment is usually used to describe this process.[7]

In addition to these general procedures, there are a number of other principles of operant conditioning. (For a rather complete description of these possibilities, Honig 1966 and Staats 1975 are recommended.) However, there are three concepts which deserve specific mention: reinforcement schedules, shaping, and discriminative stimuli.

Reinforcement Schedules. A number of different schedules of reinforcement can be employed. For example, it is possible to arrange conditions where a positive reinforcer is administered after: (1) every desired behavior, (2) every second desired behavior, etc. When every occurrence of the behavior is reinforced, a continuous schedule of reinforcement is being employed. When every second, third, tenth, etc. response is reinforced, a fixed ratio schedule is being used. Similarly, it is possible to have a reinforcer follow a desired consequence on average one-half, one-third, one-fourth, etc. of the time, but not every second time or third time, etc. Such a schedule is called a variable ratio schedule.

The ratio schedules are of particular interest because they produce high rates of behavior which are reasonably resistant to extinction. Gambling devices are good examples. Slot machines are very effective in producing high rates of response, even under conditions which often result in substantial financial losses. This property of the ratio schedule is particularly important for marketers because it suggests how a great deal of desired behavior can be developed and maintained for relatively small, infrequent rewards. For example, Deslauriers and Everett (1977) found that by giving small rewards for riding a bus on a variable ratio schedule, the same amount of bus riding could be obtained as when rewards were given on a continuous schedule. Thus, for approximately one-third the cost of the continuous schedule, the same amounts of behavior were sustained.[8]

Numerous other examples of the use of the variable ratio schedule can be found in marketing practice. Lotteries, door prizes, and other tactics whereby individuals are asked to respond in a certain way to be eligible for a prize are common examples (when the prize is assigned by chance).

Shaping. Another concept from the operant tradition which has important implications for marketing is "shaping." Shaping is important because given an individual's existing response hierarchy, the probability that he/she will make a particular desired response may be very small. In general, shaping involves a process of arranging conditions which change the probabilities of certain behaviors not as ends in themselves, but to increase the probabilities of other behaviors. Usually, shaping involves the positive reinforcement of successive approximations of the desired behavior or of behaviors which must be performed before the desired response can be emitted.

Many firms already employ marketing activities which are roughly analogous to shaping. For example, loss leaders and other special deals are used as rewards for individuals coming to a store. Once customers are in the store, the probability that they will make some other response such as purchasing other full-priced items is much greater than when they are not in the store. Also, shopping centers or auto dealers who put carnivals in their parking lots may be

[7]In this paper, we will focus primarily on the use of positive reinforcement. We are making this choice for two reasons. First, we personally do not believe that aversive consequences should be used to sell products. Second, it is unlikely that the use of aversive consequences to sell products is generally practical in the current socioeconomic system even if organizations were predisposed to use them.

[8]There are a number of other possible reinforcement schedules. However, we will limit our attention to continuous and ratio schedules. Also we will not deal with the consequences that the different schedules have on the pattern, rate, and maintenance of behavior. For a detailed treatment of these effects, Honig (1966) is recommended.

viewed as attempting to shape behavior. Similarly, free trial periods may be employed to make it more likely that the user will have contact with the product so that he/she can experience the product's reinforcing properties.

Discriminative Stimuli. It is important to distinguish between the reinforcement and discriminative functions played by stimuli in the operant model. In our treatment of respondent conditioning, we noted that a stimulus can act as a reinforcer or can function to trigger certain emotions or other behaviors. So far in this section, the focus has been on the reinforcing function. However, the mere presence or absence of a stimulus can serve to change the probabilities of behavior; such stimuli are called discriminative stimuli.

Many marketing stimuli are of a discriminative nature. Store signs (e.g., "50 percent off sale") and store logos (e.g., K-Mart's big red "K") or distinctive brandmarks (e.g., the Levi tag) are good examples. Previous experiences have perhaps taught the customer that purchase behavior will be rewarded when the distinctive symbol is present and not rewarded when the symbol is absent. Here then is yet another parallel between the principles of behavior modification and common marketing practice.

Vicarious Learning

Vicarious learning (or modeling) refers to a process which attempts to change behavior by having an individual observe the actions of others (i.e., models) and the consequences of those behaviors.

According to Bandura (1969) there are three major types of vicarious learning or modeling influences. First, there are observational learning or modeling effects whereby an observer acquires one or more new response patterns that did not previously exist in his/her behavioral repertoire. Second, there are inhibitory and disinhibitory effects whereby an observer's inhibitory responses are either strengthened or weakened by observation of a model's behavior and its consequences. Third, there is response facilitation whereby the behavior of others ". . . serves merely as discriminative stimuli for the observer in facilitating the occurrence of previously learned responses . . ." (Bandura 1969, p. 120).

Developing New Responses. There are at least three types of new behaviors that marketers often wish to induce in consumers or potential consumers. First, it is often desirable to "educate" consumers in product usage. Second, it may be helpful to induce consumers to shop in certain ways. Finally, by developing certain types of "attending behavior," the sensitivity of a potential customer to advertising information can be increased. Vicarious learning can be very useful in achieving these three goals.

First, modeling can be used to develop behaviors which enable potential consumers to utilize particular products appropriately. The demonstration of ways of using a product may make purchase more probable, particularly if the model(s) appear to be experiencing positive consequences from using the product. Moreover, repurchase or purchase by one's friends may become more probable if the consumer has learned, by watching someone else, to use the product appropriately. This use of modeling is common to both industrial and consumer products salespeople who are attempting to sell technically complex products. Also, many self-service retail stores now use video cassette machines with taped demonstrations of proper product usage.

Second, models may be very helpful in developing the desired purchasing behaviors. For example, suppose a firm has a product which is currently technically superior to its competitors. It may be important to teach the potential consumer to ask questions about such technical advantages at the point of purchase. Advertisements showing individuals doing just this or behaving in other ways which appear to give a particular product a differential advantage may be useful.

Third, particularly at early stages in the purchase process, it is often necessary to find ways to increase the degree to which potential customers attend to information in advertisements and other messages about a product. Attaining this objective can be facilitated through the application of findings from recent research on factors which influence the attention observers pay to models. For example, attending behavior is influenced by such factors as: incentive conditions, the characteristics of the observers, the characteristics of the model, and the characteristics of the modeling cues themselves.

Advertising practitioners seem to be very sensitive to these factors. Many ads reflect their creators' acute awareness of salient characteristics of the target audience, the characteristics of the users of the product in the ad, and the behaviors exhibited by the model. Moreover, many ads show the models receiving positive social or other reinforcement from the purchase or use of the product.

Inhibiting Undesired Behaviors. Because of the obvious ethical and practical problems involved in attempting to use punishment in marketing, we have given little attention to ways of reducing the frequency of "undesired" responses. However, while these problems exist in the direct use of punishment, they are far less prevalent when aversive consequences are administered to models. Thus, vicarious learning may be one of the few approaches which can be used in marketing to reduce the frequency of unwanted elements in the behavioral repertoire of a potential or present consumer.

It is well known from the modeling literature that, under appropriate conditions, observers who see a model experience aversive outcomes following a particular act, will reduce their tendency to exhibit that behavior. Similarly, vicarious learning can employ an extinction situation to reduce the frequency of behavior.

While most marketing efforts are directed at increasing rather than decreasing behaviors, some ads are directed at reducing such behaviors as smoking, drinking, overeating, wasting energy, polluting and littering, as well as purchasing or using a competitor's product. The effectiveness of messages to achieve these goals may benefit from the use of vicarious negative conditioning.

Response Facilitation. In addition to its role in developing new behaviors and inhibiting "undesired" behaviors, modeling can be used to facilitate the occurrence of desired behaviors which are currently in the individual's repertoire. For example, modeling has been used extensively in advertising not only to illustrate the uses of a product but to show what "types" of people use it and in what settings. Since many of these uses involve behaviors already in the observer's response hierarchy, the function of the model is merely to facilitate these responses by depicting positive consequences for use of the product in a particular way. This technique appears frequently in advertising for high status products. Such ads do not demonstrate any new behaviors, but show the positive consequences of using a particular product. The recent series of Lowenbrau ads stressing the use of this beer for very special occasions is a clear example of this.

It is also possible to influence emotional behavior through a vicarious learning paradigm. Bandura (1969) noted that many emotional behaviors can be acquired through observations of others, as well as through direct respondent conditioning:

> . . . vicarious emotional conditioning results from observing others experience positive or negative emotional effects in conjunction with particular stimulus events. Both direct and vicarious conditioning processes are governed by the same basic principles of associative learning, but they differ in the force of the emotional arousal. In the direct prototype, the learner himself is the recipient of pain- or pleasure-producing stimulation, whereas in vicarious forms somebody else experiences the reinforcing stimulation and his affective expressions, in turn, serve as the arousal stimuli for the observer (p. 167).

To the degree that positive emotions toward a product are desired, vicarious emotional conditioning may be a useful concept for the design of effective advertisements.

In sum, vicarious learning or modeling has a number of current and potential uses in marketing. If a potential consumer has observed appropriate models, then he/she is more likely to know the appropriate behaviors; if the model has been rewarded appropriately, the potential consumer may be more likely to engage in these behaviors. Likewise, if the potential consumer has observed inappropriate models receiving aversive consequences, he/she may be less likely to emit them. Models may be used to develop, inhibit, or facilitate behavior. In short, as with the other components of the BMP, it is clear that this technique for modifying behavior is commonly employed in current television and other advertising messages. In fact, Markin and Narayana (1976, p. 225) suggest that many of today's most successful products are promoted and advertised on the basis of modeling approaches which show the model receiving positive functional or social benefits from the use of the product. Products they suggest have used this approach include "Coca-Cola," "Pepsi Cola," "McDonald's," "Kentucky Fried Chicken," "Nyquil," "Absorbine Jr.," "Alka Seltzer," Philip's "Milk of Magnesia," "Pepto Bismol," "Folgers," "Crest," and "Head and Shoulders." However, since the link of current marketing practice to the BMP has not been explicit, research exploring the application of the principles of vicarious learning to marketing settings is lacking. Such research is apt to have both practical importance for marketing and theoretical implications for students of modeling as previous findings are tested in more general, less artificial settings.

Ecological Design

Although knowledge about the role of physical space and other aspects of environmental design is meager, there is considerable evidence that the design of physical situations and the presence or absence of various stimuli have powerful effects on behavior (Barker 1968; Hall 1959, 1966; Sommers 1969). We will use the term ecological design to refer to the deliberate design of environments to modify human behavior.

Ecological design is widely used in marketing. For example, department stores place displays in high traffic areas (e.g., at the end of an escalator) to increase the likelihood that consumers will observe the product on display. Similarly, end aisle displays in supermarkets and the internal arrangements of stores involve efforts to place stimuli in positions which increase the likelihood of consumers making one or more desired responses. Direct mail is also a means of placing stimuli in the potential consumer's environment to increase the likelihood that the individual will at least be aware of the particular product. Other techniques include the use of sound, odors, lights, and other stimuli to increase attentive behaviors. In fact, store location and external arrangements (e.g., design of malls, arrangement of parking space) are all efforts to alter behavior through environmental design. In a behavioral sense, these are all ways to increase the probability that the individual will make certain responses which increase the likelihood that purchase or some other desired response will follow.

Like shaping, ecological manipulations are frequently employed to modify behavior early in the purchase process. Thus, their major impact is through their role in inducing the potential consumer to come into contact with the product and/or perform product-related behavior. As such, ecological design is best viewed as one part of a comprehensive marketing approach; ecological modifications can be conveniently sequenced with other techniques (e.g. modeling, respondent conditioning, operant conditioning).

As with other elements subsumed under the BMP, ecological designs to modify behavior have received far less attention in the academic literature than they deserve in view of how frequently they are used by marketing practitioners. A major advantage of the BMP is that it encourages the integration of these various techniques to lead to a coherent approach for modifying the entire sequence of behaviors desired of consumers and potential consumers.

SUMMARY OF SOME APPLICATIONS OF THE BMP IN MARKETING

Table 7.1 provides a framework for considering some applications of the BMP to marketing. Each of the four sections of the table outlines the general procedures which would be followed in applying one of the four basic elements of the BMP. The table lists a number of the specific behaviors which marketers may wish to develop

TABLE 7.1 Illustrative Applications of the BMP in Marketing

I. Some Applications of Respondent Conditioning Principles

A. Conditioning responses to new stimuli

Unconditioned or Previously Conditioned Stimulus	*Conditioned Stimulus*	*Examples*
Exciting event	A product or theme song	Gillette theme song followed by sports event
Patriotic events or music	A product or person	Patriotic music as background in political commercial

B. Use of familiar stimuli to elicit responses

Conditioned Stimulus	*Conditioned Response(s)*	*Examples*
Familiar music	Relaxation, excitement, "good will"	Christmas music in retail store
Familiar voices	Excitement, attention	Famous sportscaster narrating a commercial
Sexy voices, bodies	Excitement, attention, relaxation	Noxema television ads and many others
Familiar social cues	Excitement, attention, anxiety	Sirens sounding or telephones ringing in commercials

II. Some Applications of Operant Conditioning Principles

A. Rewards for desired behavior (continuous schedules)

Desired Behavior	*Reward Given Following Behavior*
Product purchase	Trading stamps, cash bonus or rebate, prizes, coupons

B. Rewards for desired behavior (partial schedules)

Desired Behavior	*Reward Given (sometimes)*
Product purchase	Prize for every second, or third, etc. purchase Prize to some fraction of people who purchase

C. Shaping

Approximation of Desired Response	*Consequence Following Approximation*	*Final Response Desired*
Opening a charge account	Prizes, etc., for opening account	Expenditure of funds
Trip to point-of-purchase location	Loss leaders, entertainment, or event at the shopping center	Purchase of products
Entry into store	Door prize	Purchase of products
Product trial	Free product and/or some bonus for using	Purchase of product

D. Discriminative Stimuli

Desired Behavior	*Reward Signal*	*Examples*
Entry into store	Store signs Store logos	50% off sale K-Mart's big red "K"
Brand purchase	Distinctive brandmarks	Levi tag

III. Some Applications of Modeling Principles

Modeling Employed	*Desired Response*
Instructor, expert, salesperson using product (in ads or at point-of-purchase)	Use of product in technically competent way
Models in ads asking questions at point-of-purchase	Ask questions at point-of-purchase which highlight product advantages
Models in ads receiving positive reinforcement for product purchase or use	Increase product purchase and use
Models in ads receiving no reinforcement or receiving punishment for performing undesired behaviors	Extinction or decrease undesired behaviors
Individual or group (similar to target) using product in novel, enjoyable way	Use of product in new ways

IV. Some Applications of Ecological Modification Principles

Environmental Design	*Specific Example*	*Intermediate Behavior*	*Final Desired Behavior*
Store layout	End of escalator, end-aisle, other displays	Bring customer into visual contact with product	Product purchase
Purchase locations	Purchase possible from home, store location	Product or store contact	Product purchase
In-store mobility	In-store product directories, information booths	Bring consumer into visual contact with product	Product purchase
Noises, odors, lights	Flashing lights in store window	Bring consumer into visual or other sensory contact with store or product	Product purchase

and organizes the examples presented in the previous sections of the paper. In reviewing this table, two qualifications should be kept in mind. First, there are many tactics for modifying behavior which are combinations of a number of techniques which do not fit neatly into the simple categories presented in the table. For example, Anheuser-Busch has a series of commercials which begin with a sports trivia question and then give the listener "time to think" while the virtues of a particular brand of beer are discussed. Then, the answer to the question is given. Determination of exactly which principles this approach uses and whether or not the approach can be reduced to principles of behavior modification at all requires a complex analysis of the acquisition and use of language. However, the approach is clearly one of picking a desired behavior (i.e., listening to the commercial) and organizing stimuli to increase the probability of this behavior.

Second, most, if not all of these tactics have already been used by practitioners. While the BMP may lead to some new tactics, its most important value to practitioners will be in systematizing and integrating marketing efforts by focusing attention on the *sequence of specific behaviors* which can be modified to change the probability of product purchase or of some other desired behavior.

POTENTIAL CONTRIBUTIONS OF THE BMP TO MARKETING

As the examples in the previous section illustrate, a number of tactics which are frequently used by marketing practitioners *can be* derived from the BMP. Of course, the fact that they can be derived does not mean that they were so derived or that they could not have been derived from other models. Nevertheless, the fact that such a varied array of tactics can be subsumed under a relatively simple model suggests that the perspective can be a valuable addition to the academic marketing literature. It is in this spirit that we speculate about the potential contributions of the BMP to marketing practice and to the study of consumer behavior.

Marketing Practice

The BMP can make at least two major contributions to marketing practice. First, it can facilitate the development of a comprehensive set of strategies and tactics which encompass those environmental and situational factors which *directly* influence behavior. If the behaviors desired from the potential buyer are specified, it will often be possible to be explicit about a set of actions which should occur in any given situation to move the potential buyer to behave in ways which are more likely to lead to purchase behavior. Marketing tactics developed with this degree of specificity force more careful planning and analysis of exactly what outcomes are sought and are more easily evaluated and refined. It should be noted here that in other systems where behavior modification has been introduced, it has often been found that there was considerable ambiguity about exactly what results previous methods of organization were really attempting to achieve (Nord 1969; Schneier 1974). We suspect that other than purchase behavior, many students of marketing have never delineated the basic sequence of behaviors that consumers must perform in order to purchase a product.

Second, the BMP can stimulate a closer interchange between academics and practitioners. In this connection it is important to emphasize that while marketing managers are rewarded for developing tactics which generate sales and profits, academics are more apt to be rewarded for attempting to provide theoretical explanations of consumer behavior. The BMP focuses academics on the investigation of behaviors and techniques which produce sales and profits. Moreover, its simplicity and pragmatic emphasis should help academics in their efforts to communicate with practitioners.

Study of Consumer Behavior

There are also two major contributions to the study of consumer behavior. First, the BMP forces explicit recognition that, to the degree that marketing efforts seek to increase sales, marketing is directly concerned with the influence, modification, and control of consumer behavior. Such recognition can have profound effects on consumer behavior research. While research on attitudes and decision processes will not be precluded, valuable empirical research may be conducted without attaching great significance to internal psychological processes. Instead, attention is apt to center on the manipulation of external factors which affect behavior in desired ways. Even in cases where internal psychological processes are the focus of research, the BMP forces explicit recognition that there are a variety of external influences which need to be accounted for in research designs. Several of Belk's (1974, 1975) situational influences as well as a variety of the stimuli discussed in this article could well be affecting both the internal validity (i.e., interpretability) and external validity (i.e., generalizability) of current consumer behavior research findings. The discussions by Snow (1974) and Petrinovich (1979) should be useful for developing research methods to incorporate these external influences.

Second, there is considerable evidence that the behavior of consumers is far more consistent with the principles of the BMP than with traditional explanations. For example Markin (1974) and Markin and Narayana (1976) note that empirical research on consumer decision processes documents that consumers: (1) do not seek extensive amounts of information in relation to purchase and consumption problems; (2) do not process large amounts of information in relation to purchase and consumption problems; and (3) do not appear to engage in extensive problem solving behavior even in relation to big ticket or capital intensive items such as automobiles, houses, and major appliances. Not only does the BMP account for the empirical data better than many other approaches, but it does so with fewer variables. In a word, it is more parsimonious. Further, it has long been recognized that purchase behavior often *precedes* attitudes about the product or brand purchased. Thus, the BMP may well provide insights into predicting and controlling the purchase-consumption process. It is important to emphasize here that the BMP does not nor is it intended to provide theoretical explanations of behavior. However, it is clear that any scientific explanation of the causes of consumer behavior will have to include not only internal psychological processes, but also the external influences embodied in the BMP.

SOME UNRESOLVED ISSUES

Based on our argument, we believe it is reasonable to conclude that a good deal of marketing, at least at the tactical or operational level, is as closely aligned with techniques of behavior modification as with those suggested by more complex, internally-oriented psychological models. To the degree this conclusion is valid, it raises a number of issues about the value of the BMP for marketing.

First, to what extent is the BMP a suitable replacement for more traditional approaches? We believe that it is a useful complement, not a replacement. The BMP focuses on external factors; it stops short of providing adequate explanation of internal processes. Although Skinner (1969) has argued persuasively that the skin is an arbitrary barrier, we do not find the attempts of many radical behaviorists to ignore the internal correlates of external stimuli intellectually satisfying. At the same time, we agree with Bindra (1959) that the efforts of motivational and cognitive psychologists to deal with these internal correlates often are merely classifications of acts, rather than adequate accounts for causes of behavior. Thus, we are driven to a psychological eclecticism which, unlike the current psychological eclecticism in marketing, incorporates an external perspective.

Second, there is the issue of the efficacy of behavior modification techniques. While existing research indicates that the technology exists to modify behavior very effectively, this technology can be used more effectively in controlled environments. While retail stores and shopping malls provide relatively closed environments, they do not permit the type of control which experimenters in hospitals, schools, prisons, and even work organizations may have. Moreover, the degree of control which is possible will vary at different stages in the purchasing process. Empirical research involving applications of behavior modification principles at different stages of the purchasing process would clearly be useful for investigating this issue. It is only at the latter stages that substantial control seems possible.

Third, there are major ethical/moral issues involved in the use of the BMP in marketing. In many areas, the ethical/moral challenges to the application of behavior modification are, at least in the minds of most behavior modifiers, relatively easy to refute. In most areas where behavior modification has been applied (e.g., psychotherapy, education, self-improvement), it is usually possible (although the possibility is often not translated into practice) for subjects of behavior modification to participate in defining the ends and also to what degree they will determine in the means. Thus human freedom and dignity are, to some degree, protected; in such situations, the BMP provides a useful technology for helping human beings achieve the ends they are seeking. However, even in these cases, behavior modification has been challenged on ethical grounds.

We maintain that behavior modification is not, in itself, immoral or unethical, but that valid ethical/moral concerns stem from (1) the ends to which the technology is used and (2) the process by which these ends are determined (see Nord 1976). The application of these techniques in marketing seems ethically vulnerable on both these counts. Efforts to market products rarely include the subject whose behavior is modified as a full participant in determining either the use of the technology or the ends to which it is put. There are, of course, examples of the use of behavior modification techniques in marketing to achieve purposes which many people believe are socially desirable. For example, certain outcomes such as reduction in littering, reduction in pollution, smoking, and other behaviors can be and are marketed through such techniques. Moreover, much of consumer education involves modifying the purchasing behavior of the uneducated poor to get better economic value for dollars spent. However, there appear to be many other applications which have few redeeming social benefits.

The BMP reveals that these concerns are relevant to the present—not just the future. It is clear that behavior modification techniques, even though they may be called something else, are being currently employed in marketing. Moreover, since it is clear that the type of emotions often labeled "needs" or motives can be developed through conditioning and modeling processes, the defense that marketing satisfies needs is not fully adequate. Thus, while explicit application of the BMP in marketing is apt to trigger ethical concerns, the BMP may be quite useful for viewing ethical problems involved in *current* marketing practice.

Fourth, there are a number of practical issues. In addition to the problem of developing sufficiently controlled environments, there are problems of selecting reinforcers, of designing and implementing effective schedules, and of designing effective ecological structures. Solutions to these problems can benefit from an eclectic research approach. The trial and error approach of the radical behaviorists derived from their research with animals can be useful, but is only one approach. In addition, analysis of historical data on the effectiveness of various marketing tactics in generating desired behaviors and laboratory or field experiments using different types of reinforcers is needed. Moreover, cognitively-oriented approaches which rely on verbal reports may offer insights into these questions. Of course, the most important practical issue requires cost-benefit analysis. While the bottom line will be the ultimate test, the BMP does lead to the analysis of the sequence of behaviors which is expected to lead to purchase or to other desired behavior. These outcomes can be defined and measured more precisely with current technology than can attitudes, needs, etc. Thus it is likely that research to test the BMP will have a clear action orientation as well as permit measurement of success at a number of intermediate steps.

CONCLUSIONS

This paper has attempted to provide an overview of behavior modification and investigate its applicability to marketing. While it appears that many marketing tactics currently employed are quite consistent with the BMP, these tactics appear to have been derived in an ad hoc manner. A more systematic application of the BMP to marketing may well provide insights for the development of improved tactics and overall strategies and for describing how the purchase-consumption process works. Although marketing academics and practitioners may be reluctant to view marketing as a technology for modifying and controlling consumer behavior, it is clear that marketing tactics which are fully consistent with this perspective will continue to be implemented. In terms of consumer behavior research, it will undoubtedly be some time before researchers actively catalog and sample elements of the external environment given the predilection toward the study of internal processes. In any case, the BMP may provide a clear understanding that one of the major de facto functions of marketing in our society is the modification of behavior.

REFERENCES

BANDURA, A. (1969), *Principles of Behavior Modification.* New York: Holt, Rinehart & Winston.

——— (1978), "The Self System in Reciprocal Determinism," *American Psychologist,* 33 (April), 344–358.

BARKER, R. G. (1968), *Ecological Psychology,* Stanford, CA: Stanford University Press.

BELK, RUSSELL W. (1974), "An Exploratory Assessment of Situational Effects in Buyer Behavior," *Journal of Marketing Research,* 11 (May), 156–163.

——— (1975), "Situational Variables and Consumer Behavior," *Journal of Consumer Research,* 2 (December), 157–164.

BINDRA, D. (1959), *Motivation: A Systematic Reinterpretation.* New York: Ronald Press.

CAREY, R. J., S. H. CLICQUE, B. A. LEIGHTON, and F. MILTON (1976), "A Test of Positive Reinforcement of Customers," *Journal of Marketing,* 40 (October), 98-100.

DESLAURIERS, B. C., and P. B. EVERETT (1977), "The Effects of Intermittent and Continuous Token Reinforcement on Bus Ridership," *Journal of Applied Psychology,* 62 (August), 369-375.

ENGEL, J. F., D. T. KOLLAT, and R. D. BLACKWELL (1973), *Consumer Behavior* (2nd ed.). New York: Holt, Rinehart & Winston.

HALL, C. S., and G. LINDZEY (1970), *Theories of Personality* (2nd ed.). New York: Wiley.

HALL, E. T. (1959), *The Silent Language.* New York: Doubleday.

——— (1966), *The Hidden Dimension.* New York: Doubleday.

HONIG, W. K. (1966), *Operant Behavior: Areas of Research and Application.* New York: Appleton-Century-Crofts.

KASSARJIAN, H. H. (1978), "Presidential Address, 1977: Anthropomorphism and Parsimony," in *Advances in Consumer Research,* Vol. 5, H. K. Hunt, Ed. Chicago: Association for Consumer Research, xiii-xiv.

KOTLER, PHILIP (1976), *Marketing Management* (3rd ed.). Englewood Cliffs, NJ: Prentice-Hall.

MARKIN, R. J. (1974), *Consumer Behavior: A Cognitive Approach.* New York: Macmillan, Chapter 17.

———, and C. L. NARAYANA (1976), "Behavior Control: Are Consumers Beyond Freedom and Dignity?" in *Advances in Consumer Research,* Vol. 3, B. B. Anderson, Ed. Chicago: Association for Consumer Research, 222-228.

MILLER, N. E. (1969), "Learning of Visceral and Glandular Responses," *Science,* 163 (January), 434-449.

NORD, W. R. (1969), "Beyond the Teaching Machine: The Neglected Area of Operant Conditioning in the Theory and Practice of Management," *Organizational Behavior and Human Performance,* 4 (November), 375-401.

——— (1976), "Behavior Modification Perspective for Humanizing Organizations," in *Humanizing Organizational Behavior,* H. Meltzer and F. D. Wickert, Eds. Springfield, IL: Charles E. Thomas, 250-272.

PETRINOVICH, L. (1979), "Probabilistic Functionalism: A Conception of Research Method," *American Psychologist,* 34 (May), 373-390.

RAY, M. L. (1973), "Psychological Theories and Interpretations of Learning," in *Consumer Behavior: Theoretical Sources,* S. Ward and T. S. Robertson, Eds. Englewood Cliffs, NJ: Prentice-Hall, 45-117.

SCHNEIER, C. E. (1974), "Behavior Modification in Management: A Review and Critique," *Academy of Management Journal,* 17 (September), 528-548.

SKINNER, B. F. (1953), *Science and Human Behavior.* New York: Macmillan.

——— (1969), *Contingencies of Reinforcement: A Theoretical Analysis.* New York: Appleton-Century-Crofts.

SNOW, R. (1974), "Representative and Quasi-Representative Designs for Research on Teaching," *Review of Educational Research,* 44 (Summer), 265-291.

SOMMERS, R. (1969), *Personal Space: The Behavioral Basis for Design.* Englewood Cliffs, NJ: Prentice-Hall.

STAATS, A. W. (1975), *Social Behaviorism.* Homewood, IL: The Dorsey Press.

8

THE EFFECTS OF MUSIC IN ADVERTISING ON CHOICE BEHAVIOR: A Classical Conditioning Approach*

Gerald J. Gorn

Do features like humor, sex, color, and music in a commercial merely increase our attention to product information in a message, or can they directly influence our attitudes? The results of an experiment using a classical conditioning approach suggest that hearing liked or disliked music while being exposed to a product can directly affect product preferences. A second experiment differentiated communication situations where a classical conditioning approach or an information processing approach might be appropriate in explaining product preference.

Commercials typically contain both product specific information and background features such as pleasant music, attractive colors, and humor. This paper examines the impact of the background features on product preferences. One experiment was conducted to determine whether background features of a commercial affected product preferences when only minimal product information was presented. A second experiment examined the relative importance of background features and product information in different situations.

The impact of product information in a commercial on beliefs and attitudes would typically be interpreted within an information processing framework. It is suggested here that a classical conditioning framework could account for the potential impact of background features on product attitudes. Classical conditioning suggests that positive attitudes towards an adver-

*Reprinted from the *Journal of Marketing,* 46 (Winter 1982), pp's 94–101. Published by the American Marketing Association, Chicago, IL 60606.

tised product (conditioned stimulus) might develop through its association in a commercial with other stimuli that are reacted to positively (unconditioned stimuli). Attractive colors, pleasant music, and humor are examples of potential unconditioned stimuli in a commercial. Potentially, classical conditioning could, in fact, explain the effect of many variables in communication-attitude change situations. For example, the communicator effect may to some extent be due to the association of the attitude object with positive affect attached to the communicator.

In marketing, classical conditioning is often mentioned and generally accepted as a process relevant to advertising (e.g., Engel, Blackwell, and Kollat 1978; Schiffman and Kanuk 1978). There is, however, little empirical research on whether preferences for objects can actually be classically conditioned. In psychology, where classical conditioning has been investigated more extensively, there is little evidence that attitudes can be classically conditioned (Brewer 1974; Fishbein and Ajzen 1975). The limited popularity of classical conditioning may be due to several difficulties associated with typical conditioning experiments.

DIFFICULTIES WITH CLASSICAL CONDITIONING

Demand Characteristics

Fishbein and Ajzen (1975) suggest that attitude change in conditioning experiments may be a function of the demand characteristics of the experimental situation. They believe that the subject must be consciously aware of the presence of the unconditioned stimulus when the conditioned stimulus is present in order for conditioning to take place. This awareness may lead subjects to believe that the experimenter wants them to respond positively to a conditioned stimulus if it is paired with a positive unconditioned stimulus. But awareness of the conditioned stimulus/unconditioned stimulus contingency should not automatically mean that attitude change is more likely the result of demand characteristics than conditioning. In fact, there is evidence of attitude conditioning even where demand type responses were minimized through elaborate cover stories later verified as believed by subjects (Zanna, Kiesler, and Pilkonis 1970).

Lack of Awareness

The consumer may not always be aware that the unconditioned stimuli in a commercial may affect his/her product attitudes. Even more generally, the consumer may not be aware of the real forces impacting on both attitudes and behavior. For example, many in-store features may influence consumers although they may not be easily evoked in postpurchase explanations of buying (amount of shelf space devoted to a product, color of the package, and so on).

Nisbett and Wilson (1977) reviewed empirical evidence casting doubt on people's ability to introspect accurately regarding their cognitive processes.[1] They suggest that people often speculate about the potential causes of their own behavior and select stimuli which they think are probable reasons for their behavior. They may conclude that what they think should be the cause of their behavior is in fact the cause of their behavior (Nisbett and Wilson 1977).

In a typical communication situation, people may not realize or accept the impact of unconditioned stimuli on their responses, since unconditioned stimuli should not logically be related to behavior. Possible classical conditioning effects might, therefore, be underestimated and underreported in self-reports. In analyzing their behavior, people may attempt to convince both themselves and the researcher that they are strictly rational. Cognitive bias can result from an attempt to think well of oneself (Greenwald 1980). A rational analysis of behavior in a communication situation might be biased in favor of information and, therefore, of an information processing model. For example, it may be more logical to say that you like the product

[1]The Nisbett and Wilson (1977) article is controversial; see both Ericson and Simon (1980) and Weitz and Wright (1979) for criticisms.

more after seeing a commercial, because you now believe it has X characteristic, rather than because you liked the music in the commercial. Thus evidence supporting classical conditioning is unlikely to emerge in self-reports.

Arousal

In testing for classical conditioning, product information in the commercial must be kept minimal, otherwise the unconditioned stimuli in the commercial might merely be arousing interest in product information. Background features such as sex, music, color, and humor have typically been treated as arousal stimuli or stimuli that reinforce the information in the commercial rather than unconditioned stimuli (see Engel, Blackwell, and Kollat 1978, for a discussion of this material). In the print medium, Kroeber-Riel (1979) found that ads that were arousing produced better recall of the information in the ad. A greater knowledge of the product information could presumably create more positive product attitudes. However, by minimizing product information in a commercial one can investigate the potential ability of unconditioned stimuli to change consumer attitudes directly.

Mere Exposure Versus Classical Conditioning

Mere exposure effects can be confounded with classical conditioning effects. While people may develop favorable attitudes towards products advertised in the context of unconditioned stimuli, these attitude shifts may be simply a function of mere exposure to the advertised product. Zajonc (1968) has emphasized that exposure leads to liking. Krugman (1965) suggested that in low involvement situations, people may purchase a product simply because they have been exposed to it before through a commercial. It is interesting to note that with the Krugman model, exposure leads to behavior, with attitude not conceptualized as an intervening variable. With classical conditioning, however, the person is not choosing an object simply because it's been seen before. His/her affect is also involved, so that if the product (conditioned stimulus) is paired with a negative unconditioned stimulus it would be avoided despite exposure.

The following experiment investigating the impact of the background features of a commercial on product preferences allowed for a test of mere exposure versus classical conditioning effects.

EXPERIMENT ONE

Basic Structure and Hypothesis

In the present study, subjects were exposed to a neutral product (conditioned stimulus) in the context of a background feature (unconditioned stimulus), often found in commercials. To minimize the difficulties mentioned earlier in employing a conditioning paradigm, a number of steps were taken. To lessen demand characteristics, an unobtrusive, behavioral measure of product preference was used instead of a paper and pencil measure. Information on the conditioned stimulus was kept as close to zero as possible to demonstrate that the unconditioned stimulus could directly affect product preference even where product information was minimal. A negative unconditioned stimulus condition was structured to test for mere exposure versus classical conditioning. Consistent with a conditioning interpretation, it was hypothesized that subjects would prefer an unexposed versus exposed product if the exposed product were paired with a negative unconditioned stimulus. In contrast, where the conditioned stimulus was paired with a positive unconditioned stimulus, subjects would choose the exposed rather than unexposed product.

Sample

Two-hundred forty-four undergraduates randomly assigned during registration to two sections of a first year management course at McGill University served as subjects.

Pilot

In a pilot, a group of 10 subjects evaluated 10 different pieces of music on a scale ranging from dislike very much (1) to like very much (5). The results of the pilot led to the choice of a one-minute extract of music from the movie "Grease" as the positive unconditioned stimulus ($\bar{x}$ = 4.3). One minute of classical Indian music ($\bar{x}$ = 1.5) served as the negative unconditioned stimulus.[2]

Two different colors of a pen were used as conditioned stimuli, light blue and beige, neutral enough so that associating them with liked or disliked music could change color preferences. A pilot on 23 subjects had revealed that 80 percent felt neutral about light blue and beige pens, whereas, for example, yellow pens were generally disliked, with black pens generally liked. A second sample (N = 41) of subjects were asked directly whether they preferred beige or light blue pens. It was expected that if subjects were neutral about the two colors, then half would choose each. The results supported this notion, as 22 out of 41 picked the beige pen, 19 the light blue pen.

Design and Procedure

The experiment was carried out during class time. The experimenter explained that an advertising agency was trying to select music (unconditioned stimulus) to use in a commercial for a pen (conditioned stimulus) produced by one of its clients. They would hear some music that was being considered while they watched the slide of the pen which the agency was planning to advertise. The pen was inexpensive looking and cost forty-nine cents. Very little information regarding the pen's attributes was visible in the slide.

The following conditions were structured: (1) condition L_1—*L*iked music, light blue pen; (2) condition L_2—*L*iked music, beige pen; (3) condition D_1—*D*isliked music, light blue pen; (4) condition D_2—*D*isliked music, beige pen.[3] While subjects had been randomly assigned to the two sections of the course, a counter-balancing procedure was used to control further for any differences that might have existed between the two sections. To counterbalance the music and the color of the pen within each class, one-half of the first class was randomly assigned to the liked music—light blue pen condition (L_1), while the other half was assigned to the disliked music—beige pen condition (D_2). In the second class, one-half of the students were randomly assigned to the liked music—beige pen condition (L_2), with the other half assigned to the disliked music—light blue pen condition (D_1). The two conditions in each class were run sequentially with one-half of the class taking a break while the other half participated in the project.

The subjects in each condition heard the music while they watched the slide. They then evaluated the music on a scale ranging from dislike very much (1) to like very much (5). They were told that they would receive either a light blue or beige pen for their help, donated by the company that manufactures the pen. The experimenter held up each pen briefly and commented that if they wanted a light blue one, to go over to the left side of the room to pick one up and drop off their question sheet in a box provided. If they wanted a beige one, they were told to go to the right side of the room to pick up the pen and drop off their question sheet. Using two different locations for the boxes (150 pens per box) of beige and blue pens, with question sheet drop-off boxes next to them, allowed for a relatively unobtrusive recording of choices and linking of these choices to the evaluation of the

[2]Although musical preferences are affected by prior learning, music was treated as the unconditioned stimulus since it was not being conditioned in the present experiment.

[3]No condition containing both positive and negative music was structured, since it was felt the demand characteristics would be too great under such circumstances; subjects would be more likely to think that we expected them to pick the color of the pen associated with the positive music if both positive and negative music were used in the same condition.

music.[4] As a result of the music evaluation ratings, approximately 10 subjects were eliminated from each of the four conditions. They were eliminated if in the liked music conditions, they did not evaluate the music from "Grease" as either like very much (5) or like somewhat (4), or in the disliked music conditions, if they did not evaluate the Indian music as either dislike very much (1) or dislike somewhat (2). For the remaining subjects, it was predicted that they would pick the color of the pen they saw when they heard the liked music and the alternative color when they heard the disliked music.

Once out of class, subjects were handed the following free response question: "Why did you pick the color of the pen you picked rather than the other color? If you have any reasons please list them below." There was room for three answers.

Finally, a discussion about the nature of the project was held with 10 students at the end of class one and 10 students at the end of class two. Not one mentioned that our real purpose was to influence their particular color preferences. When told that this was in fact the purpose, some wondered how we were able to detect their preferences, since they did not put the color of the pen they picked or their names down on the question sheet. They also did not see anyone recording their choices when they picked the pens from the boxes.

Results

Comparing the effect of liked versus disliked music (L_1 and L_2 collapsed versus D_1 and D_2 collapsed), there was a very clearcut impact of the music in the expected direction. As can be seen in Table 8.1, 74 out of 94 subjects (79 percent) picked the color of the pen associated with the liked music, while only 30 out of 101 subjects (30 percent) picked the color of the pen associated with the disliked music.[5]

TABLE 8.1 Liked Versus Disliked Music and Pen Choices

	Pen Choice		
	"Advertised" pen	*"Non-advertised" pen*	
Liked music	74	20	94
Disliked music	30	71	101
	104	91	195

$x^2 = 47.01$ ($p < .001$)
$\phi^2 = .24$

When asked for possible reasons for their choice, 126 out of 205 subjects (62 percent) indicated that they did have a particular reason. Of these 126 people, 114 (91 percent) mentioned color preference as their reason. Only five said the music had an influence on their choice and none mentioned that they were simply following a friend. When time permitted, subjects (n = 54) who gave color as a reason for choice were pressed further and asked if the music had any influence on them. They responded no, making comments such as "I have always liked light blue," or with beliefs such as "beige is stylish" (eight people).

Discussion

The major aim of the present study was to take a product relevant to the subject sample (students purchase and use pens) and to advertise it in a favorable or unfavorable context simply by associating it with liked or disliked music. The results supported the notion that the simple association between a product (con-

[4]A behavioral rather than verbal measure of preference was used, in part, because it could be recorded unobtrusively. In addition, behavioral measures of attitudes are generally preferred to verbal measures, although less prevalent in the literature (Carlsmith, Ellsworth, and Aronson 1976).

[5]The color of the pen did not seem to matter. 36 out of 43 people (84 percent) picked the light blue pen when it was associated with the liked music (L_1); 38 out of 51 (74 percent) picked the beige rather than the light blue pen when the beige pen was associated with the liked music (L_2). Similarly, 17 out of 52 (33 percent) chose the light blue pen when it was associated with disliked music (D_1) while 13 out of 49 (26 percent) picked the beige pen when it was associated with the disliked music (D_2). These differences were not statistically significant.

ditioned stimulus) and another stimulus such as music (unconditioned stimulus) can affect product preferences as measured by product choice.

While classical conditioning can parsimoniously explain the results, the data could also be interpreted within an information processing framework. While only minimal product information was presented, the music might have stimulated product-relevant thoughts. It might have suggested potential attributes of the pen or appropriate contexts in which it could be used. For example, liked music with an upbeat sound might stimulate the development of beliefs that a particular color of a pen is a fun color or that it is appropriate for an active lifestyle. These beliefs linking the pen to the music might then influence product choice. However, there were very few belief type comments that were elicited when subjects did in fact give reasons for their choice. Taken together with the fact that only minimal product information was presented, classical conditioning would seem to be at least as plausible an explanation of the results as information processing.

When a reason was given for choice, it was primarily that the pen of a particular color was preferred. Very few subjects pointed out that the music had an impact on their choice. Zajonc (1980) notes that even when questioned by others, people may have difficulty verbalizing reasons for feelings or describing them. Instead, they may utilize more rational and more easily verbalized cognitions (e.g., product specific information, or general statements of attitude like "beige is my favorite color") when justifying a product preference or purchase to themselves and especially to others. This would be particularly true if people are not aware of the forces that influence their behavior, which may be true in some cases (Nisbett and Wilson 1977).

The verbal reports were obtained with a free response format. This format was chosen and the questions presented in a matter of fact way, to elicit salient reasons for choice without encouraging the subject to engage in any justification of choice to both him/herself or to us. A more formal measure of beliefs regarding the colors of the pens chosen and not chosen could be incorporated in future research. However, even if beliefs consistent with choice are obtained, the causal relationship between beliefs and choice might remain unclear. Are the beliefs influencing choice, or to justify behavior, is the choice influencing the formation of beliefs?

Had time permitted in the present study, post hoc verbal reports of message evoked thoughts might have shed light on the extent and nature of cognitive activity during exposure. Message evoked thoughts related to the product would have favored an informational rather than conditioning interpretation. It is interesting to note that in the post project discussion with 20 subjects (10 per class), most said that they were thinking of very little when listening to the music. The six people that did recall something specific, recalled pleasant or unpleasant situations from their past.

Exposure

The results of the present study do not support an interpretation that mere exposure leads to liking. Those who heard disliked music avoided the color of the pen they were exposed to. Zajonc (1968) has pointed out that in many situations, exposure is confounded with a number of other variables (in the case of this experiment, liked or disliked music) that may be more crucial in attitude formation.

While there were no exposure effects in this study, feelings play as important a role in exposure theory as in a classical conditioning theory of communication effects. Zajonc (1980) notes that people tend to develop a positive feeling toward objects they have seen before even if they cannot recall prior exposure. While it may be true that there are reasons for these feelings, these reasons may come later and perhaps only when questioned by others. Zajonc (1980) stresses the primacy of affect and presents a viewpoint consistent with a perspective that people may not always be actively processing information and evaluating situations.

Kassarjian (1978, 1981) and Olshavsky and Granbois (1979) have suggested that there are situations where information search and evaluation are not relevant to purchase behavior. Probably there are also many communication situations where the individual is not really searching for or evaluating information. A second experiment was conducted to examine the importance of product information relative to the background features of a commercial, in two different communication situations.

EXPERIMENT TWO

Rationale and Hypothesis

We are often exposed to a commercial when we are not thinking of even potentially buying the advertised product. We are not in a decision making mode and are not likely to be seeking information from any source. In such situations, the commercial's impact may often be more related to stimuli that can arouse emotion, such as music and colors, than to product information. A recent study suggests that in fact, very little product information is contained in most American and Canadian commercials (Pollay, Zaichkowsky, and Fryer 1980).

An information processing explanation of postexposure attitudes and behavior might be more appropriate when the person at the time of exposure to the commercial is thinking about making a purchase in the relevant product category. For example, a buyer may see a commercial for car X while thinking of buying a new car. In such situations the buyer might be regarded as being in a decision making framework and, therefore, perhaps very interested in the information that commercial might contain about car X. The causal impact of such information on cognitive structure, and in turn, its effects on attitudes and behavioral intentions have been demonstrated in carefully controlled research (e.g., Lutz 1977).

Product information should be most important where the decision making context is salient at the time of exposure to a commercial. However, the unconditioned stimulus or background features could be more important than the product information where exposure is a nondecision making context. The present study was conducted to test this hypothesis.

Sample

The sample consisted of 122 students randomly assigned during registration to two sections of an upper level, undergraduate management course. Both classes were taught in the middle part of the day and by the same instructor. The experiment was conducted at the beginning of the term so that different class experiences were less likely to be a significant factor.

Design and Procedure

As a cover story, subjects in the decision making condition (n = 59) were told that an advertising agency would like their help in determining whether or not to purchase advertising time in an upcoming major network TV program. They were told that one of the advertising agency's specializations was producing commercials for companies that marketed pens. Two pens, each manufactured by a different company, were slated to be advertised on the program. For helping the agency evaluate the program they would later be given a three-pen packet of the company A or company B pen. Three pens were given rather than just one because it was thought that information relevant to a choice would be more influential if the decision were made somewhat more important.

Subjects were then told that they would be given an idea of the kinds of commercials planned for the program. They were shown a slide of company A's pen and told that the company was planning a musically-based ad to sell its pen. They then listened to one minute of "liked" music (the "Grease" music used in the first experiment) while they watched the slide of a beige pen. Afterwards they were shown a slide of a light blue pen and were told that company B was planning to emphasize in its commercial that the pen wrote very smoothly, that it never smudged, and could last a long time even with regular use.[6]

After seeing the pen slides and viewing the program (entitled "Drugs and Teenagers"), subjects circled yes or no on their answer sheets as to whether the ad agency should purchase time slots in the program. They were instructed that at the end of the class (one hour and 10 minutes later), they should drop the answer sheet in the box provided, and pick up their pens. The time delay between exposure and choice was included to try to mirror the real life situation where people usually do not make their actual purchases until some time after exposure to a commercial. At the end of the class, the experimenter pointed to two boxes in different locations where subjects could pick up the packets of beige or light blue pens. Subjects in the nondecision making condition (n = 63) followed exactly the same procedure but were not told until the end of the class that they would get a three-pen packet of the beige or light blue pens.

A significant difference in choices between the decision making context condition and the nondecision making context condition was hypothesized. It was predicted that subjects in the former condition would pick the light blue pen (the one advertised with information), and subjects in the latter condition, the beige pen (the one advertised with music).

Results

In the decision making condition, 42 out of the 59 (71 percent) subjects chose the light blue pen, advertised with information, with the remaining 17 (29 percent) choosing the beige pen, advertised with music. There was a strong crossover in the nondecision making condition with 40 out of 63 (63 percent) choosing the beige pen and the remaining 23 (37 percent) choosing the light blue pen. As expected, there was a significant difference in choices between the two conditions (decision vs. nondecision making conditions: $x^2(1) = 14.72, p < .001$).

Discussion

The results of this second experiment suggest that an individual in a decision making mode when exposed to a commercial is affected by the information it contains. In contrast, that information has less impact in nondecision making situations. In such situations, the classical conditioning of the advertised product through its pairing with the unconditioned stimuli in the commercial appears to account for subsequent choice behavior.

Possibilities for future research include varying the importance of the decision to be made and/or the time lag between exposure and actual choice. One could hypothesize that the importance of information to the process of selection is a function of the importance of the decision. This should be particularly true if the individual is in a decision making mode when exposed to that information. In addition, as the time lag between exposure and actual choice is increased, the relative impact of information should be reduced, particularly where the individual is not in a decision making mode when exposed to the information. In a nondecision making mode, one might not be interested in product information. Therefore, even if such information is acquired and remembered for a short while, with time it should be easily forgotten. Lengthening the time lag between exposure and choice could also help determine the longevity of classically conditioned preferences.

Future research might explore the tentative findings of this experiment in a context where real commercials are utilized. However, real commercials usually reflect the use of a number of techniques and may not always be appropriate for theory testing. For example, it might be very difficult to isolate an information based commercial totally devoid of such unconditioned stimuli as attractive colors or music.

---

[6]The results of experiment one suggested that beige and light blue were both neutral colors for a pen. Therefore, it did not seem necessary to incorporate color of pen as a variable in the second experiment.

IMPLICATIONS AND SPECULATIONS

Measures of the effectiveness of commercials typically stress recall of the basic selling points of the commercial. The impact of music and other background features is usually neglected (Honomichl 1981). A recent study by the Foote, Cone, and Belding ad agency found, however, that recall of good "feeling" commercials, created through the skillful use of music and visuals, was equal to that obtained with good "thinking" commercials, created through the rational presentation of product attributes (Honomichl 1981). This paper further suggests that the background features of commercials can influence product choice. It is argued that the positive emotions they generate become associated with the advertised product through classical conditioning.

The actual choices people made in the nondecision making conditions in these experiments would support a conditioning interpretation. To further test this interpretation physiological recording could be used in future research. The right hemisphere of the brain is the nonverbal, musical, and intuitive side; the left hemisphere is the analytical and verbal side (see Kassarjian 1981 for a summary of consumer research in this area). The results of this study suggest that recording of the activity in the two hemispheres during exposure to musically based versus product information based commercials would yield more activity in the right than left hemisphere with the former type of commercial, and the reverse with the latter. Furthermore, activity in the right hemisphere should also be higher in nondecision making contexts where people should not be seeking or analyzing product information from any source, with activity in the left hemisphere higher in decision making situations.

The situation in which many commercials are viewed may be characterized as nondecision making. In watching TV we make decisions about, and are interested in, programs, not commercials. The commercials we do see are often for brands in product categories we may not be interested in for one reason or another. We may have recently purchased in that category or we may not be interested in the whole product category in the first place. Even where purchase in a product category is contemplated we may not be attentive to product information in a relevant commercial because the product may be an unimportant one.

This suggests to the advertiser that an audience may be largely comprised of uninvolved potential consumers rather than cognitively active problem solvers. Reaching them through emotionally arousing background features may make the difference between their choosing and not choosing a brand.

REFERENCES

BREWER, W. F. (1974), "There is No Convincing Evidence for Operant and Classical Conditioning in Humans," in W. B. Weiner and D. S. Palermo, Eds., *Cognition and Symbolic Processes.* Hillsdale, NJ: Erlbaum.

CARLSMITH, J. J., P. C. ELLSWORTH, and E. ARONSON (1976), *Methods of Research in Social Psychology.* Reading, MA: Addison-Wesley.

ENGEL, J. F., R. D. BLACKWELL, and D. J. KOLLAT (1978), *Consumer Behavior.* Hinsdale, IL: The Dryden Press.

ERICSON, K. A., and H. A. SIMON (1980), "Verbal Reports as Data," *Psychological Review,* 87(3), 215–251.

FISHBEIN, M., and J. AJZEN (1975), *Belief, Attitude, Intention, and Behavior: An Introduction to Theory and Research.* Reading, MA: Addison-Wesley.

GREENWALD, A. G. (1980), "The Totalitarian Ego: Fabrication and Revision of Personal History," *American Psychologist,* 35(7), 603–618.

HONOMICHL, J. (1981), "FCB: Day-After Recall Cheats Emotion," *Advertising Age,* 52(20), 2.

KASSARJIAN, H. (1978), "Presidential Address, 1977: Anthropomorphism and Parsimony," in *Advances in Consumer Research,* H. Keith Hunt, Ed., Vol. 5. Ann Arbor, MI: Association for Consumer Research, 12–14.

——— (1981), "Consumer Psychology," Working Paper Series, Center for Marketing Studies, U.C.L.A., Paper No. 104.

KROEBER-RIEL, WERNER (1979), "Activation Research: Psychobiological Approaches in Consumer Research," *Journal of Consumer Research,* 5 (March), 240-250.

KRUGMAN, H. E. (1965), "The Impact of Television Advertising: Learning Without Involvement," *Public Opinion Quarterly,* 29 (Autumn), 349-356.

LUTZ, R. (1977), "An Experimental Investigation of Causal Relations Among Cognitions Affected and Behavioral Intention," *Journal of Consumer Research,* 3 (March), 197-208.

NISBETT, R. E., and J. D. WILSON (1977), "Telling More Than We Know: Verbal Reports on Mental Processes," *Psychological Review,* 84 (3), 231-259.

OLSHAVSKY, R. W., and D. H. GRANBOIS (1979), "Consumer Decision Making, Fact or Fiction?" *Journal of Consumer Research,* 6 (September), 93-100.

POLLAY, R. W., J. ZAICHKOWSKY, and C. FRYER (1980), "Regulation Hasn't Changed TV Ads Much!" *Journalism Quarterly,* 57 (3), 438-446.

SCHIFFMAN, L. G., and L. L. KANUK (1978), *Consumer Behavior.* Englewood Cliffs, NJ: Prentice-Hall.

WEITZ, B., and P. WRIGHT (1979), "Retrospective Self-Insight on Factors Considered in Product Evaluations," *Journal of Consumer Research,* 6 (December), 280-294.

ZAJONC, R. B. (1968), "Attitudinal Effects of Mere Exposure," *Journal of Personality and Social Psychology Monograph Supplement,* 9, Part 2, 1-27.

——— (1980), "Feeling and Thinking: Preferences Need to Inferences," *American Psychologist,* 35, 151-175.

ZANNA, M. P., C. A. KIESLER, and P. A. PILKONIS (1970), "Positive and Negative Attitudinal Affect Established by Classical Conditioning," *Journal of Personality and Social Psychology,* 14 (4), 321-326.

9

THE FRAMING OF DECISIONS AND THE PSYCHOLOGY OF CHOICE*

Amos Tversky
Daniel Kahneman

The psychological principles that govern the perception of decision problems and the evaluation of probabilities and outcomes produce predictable shifts of preference when the same problem is framed in different ways. Reversals of preference are demonstrated in choices regarding monetary outcomes, both hypothetical and real, and in questions pertaining to the loss of human lives. The effects of frames on preferences are compared to the effects of perspectives on perceptual appearance. The dependence of preferences on the formulation of decision problems is a significant concern for the theory of rational choice.

Explanations and predictions of people's choices, in everyday life as well as in the social sciences, are often founded on the assumption of human rationality. The definition of rationality has been much debated, but there is general agreement that rational choices should satisfy some elementary requirements of consistency and coherence. In this article we describe decision problems in which people systematically violate the requirements of consistency and coherence, and we trace these violations to the psychological principles that govern the perception of decision problems and the evaluation of options.

A decision problem is defined by the acts or options among which one must choose, the possible outcomes or consequences of these acts, and the contingencies or conditional probabilities that relate outcomes to acts. We use the

*Reprinted from *Science,* 211 (30 January, 1981), pp 453–458.

term "decision frame" to refer to the decision maker's conception of the acts, outcomes, and contingencies associated with a particular choice. The frame that a decision maker adopts is controlled partly by the formulation of the problem and partly by the norms, habits, and personal characteristics of the decision maker.

It is often possible to frame a given decision problem in more than one way. Alternative frames for a decision problem may be compared to alternative perspectives on a visual scene. Veridical perception requires that the perceived relative height of two neighboring mountains, say, should not reverse with changes of vantage point. Similarly, rational choice requires that the preference between options should not reverse with changes of frame. Because of imperfections of human perception and decision, however, changes of perspective often reverse the relative apparent size of objects and the relative desirability of options.

We have obtained systematic reversals of preference by variations in the framing of acts, contingencies, or outcomes. These effects have been observed in a variety of problems and in the choices of different groups of respondents. Here we present selected illustrations of preference reversals, with data obtained from students at Stanford University and at the University of British Columbia who answered brief questionnaires in a classroom setting. The total number of respondents for each problem is denoted by *N*, and the percentage who chose each option is indicated in brackets.

The effect of variations in framing is illustrated in Problems 9.1 and 9.2.

> Problem 9.1 [*N* = 152]: Imagine that the U.S. is preparing for the outbreak of an unusual Asian disease, which is expected to kill 600 people. Two alternative programs to combat the disease have been proposed. Assume that the exact scientific estimate of the consequences of the programs are as follows:
>
> If Program A is adopted, 200 people will be saved. [72 percent]
>
> If Program B is adopted, there is 1/3 probability that 600 people will be saved, and 2/3 probability that no people will be saved. [28 percent]
>
> Which of the two programs would you favor?

The majority choice in this problem is risk averse: the prospect of certainly saving 200 lives is more attractive than a risky prospect of equal expected value, that is, a one-in-three chance of saving 600 lives.

A second group of respondents was given the cover story of problem 9.1 with a different formulation of the alternative programs, as follows:

> Problem 9.2 [*N* = 155]:
>
> If Program C is adopted 400 people will die. [22 percent]
>
> If Program D is adopted there is 1/3 probability that nobody will die, and 2/3 probability that 600 people will die. [78 percent]
>
> Which of the two programs would you favor?

The majority choice in Problem 9.2 is risk taking: the certain death of 400 people is less acceptable than the two-in-three chance that 600 will die. The preferences in Problems 9.1 and 9.2 illustrate a common pattern: choices involving gains are often risk averse and choices involving losses are often risk taking. However, it is easy to see that the two problems are effectively identical. The only difference between them is that the outcomes are described in Problem 9.1 by the number of lives saved and in Problem 9.2 by the number of lives lost. The change is accompanied by a pronounced shift from risk aversion to risk taking. We have observed this reversal in several groups of respondents, including university faculty and physicians. Inconsistent responses to Problems 9.1 and 9.2 arise from the conjunction of a framing effect with contradictory attitudes toward risks involving gains and losses. We turn now to an analysis of these attitudes.

THE EVALUATION OF PROSPECTS

The major theory of decision making under risk is the expected utility model. This model is based on a set of axioms, for example, transitivity of preferences, which provide criteria for the rationality of choices. The choices of an individual who conforms to the axioms can be described in terms of the utilities of various outcomes for that individual. The utility of a risky prospect is equal to the expected utility of its outcomes, obtained by weighting the utility of each possible outcome by its probability. When faced with a choice, a rational decision maker will prefer the prospect that offers the highest expected utility (*1, 2*).

As will be illustrated below, people exhibit patterns of preference which appear incompatible with expected utility theory. We have presented elsewhere (*3*) a descriptive model, called prospect theory, which modifies expected utility theory so as to accommodate these observations. We distinguish two phases in the choice process: an initial phase in which acts, outcomes, and contingencies are framed, and a subsequent phase of evaluation (*4*). For simplicity, we restrict the formal treatment of the theory to choices involving stated numerical probabilities and quantitative outcomes, such as money, time, or number of lives.

Consider a prospect that yields outcome x with probability p, outcome y with probability q, and the status quo with probability $1 - p - q$. According to prospect theory, there are values $v(.)$ associated with outcomes, and decision weights $\pi(.)$ associated with probabilities, such that the overall value of the prospect equals $\pi(p)\, v(x) + \pi(q)\, v(y)$. A slightly different equation should be applied if all outcomes of a prospect are on the same side of the zero point (*5*).

In prospect theory, outcomes are expressed as positive or negative deviations (gains or losses) from a neutral reference outcome, which is assigned a value of zero. Although subjective values differ among individuals and attributes, we propose that the value function is commonly S-shaped, concave above the reference point and convex below it, as illustrated in Figure 9.1. For example, the difference in subjective value between gains of S10 and S20 is greater than the subjective difference between gains of S110 and S120. The same relation between value differences holds for the corresponding losses. Another property of the value function is that the response to losses is more extreme than the response to gains. The displeasure associated with losing a sum of money is generally greater than the pleasure associated with winning the same amount, as is reflected in people's reluctance to accept fair bets on a toss of a coin. Several studies of decision (*3, 6*) and judgment (*7*) have confirmed these properties of the value function (*8*).

The second major departure of prospect theory from the expected utility model involves the treatment of probabilities. In expected utility theory the utility of an uncertain outcome is weighted by its probability; in prospect theory the value of an uncertain outcome is multiplied by a decision weight $\pi(p)$, which is a monotonic function of p but is not a probability. The weighting function π has the following properties. First, impossible events are discarded, that is, $\pi(0) = 0$, and the scale is normalized so that $\pi(1) = 1$, but the function is not well behaved near the endpoints. Second, for low probabilities $\pi(p) > p$, but $\pi(p) + \pi(1 - p) \leq 1$. Thus low probabilities are overweighted, moderate and high probabilities are underweighted, and the latter effect is more pronounced than the former. Third, $\pi(pq)/\pi(p) < \pi(pqr)/\pi(pr)$ for all $0 < p,q,r \leq 1$. That is, for any fixed

FIGURE 9.1 A hypothetical value function

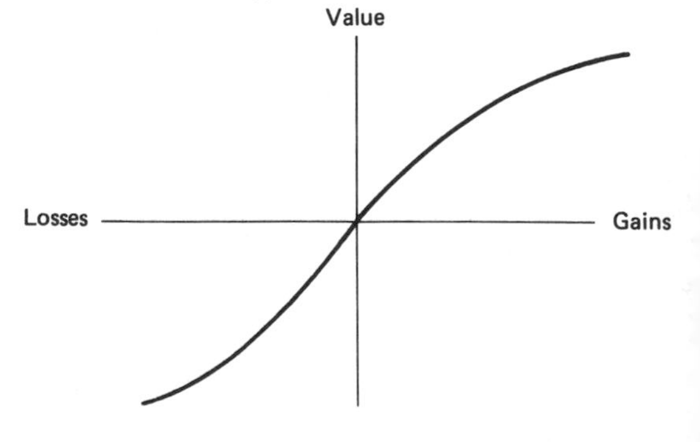

probability ratio q, the ratio of decision weights is closer to unity when the probabilities are low than when they are high, for example, $\pi(.1)/\pi(.2) > \pi(.4)/\pi(.8)$. A hypothetical weighting function which satisfies these properties is shown in Figure 9.2. The major qualitative properties of decision weights can be extended to cases in which the probabilities of outcomes are subjectively assessed rather than explicitly given. In these situations, however, decision weights may also be affected by other characteristics of an event, such as ambiguity or vagueness (*9*).

Prospect theory, and the scales illustrated in Figure 9.1 and 9.2, should be viewed as an approximate, incomplete, and simplified description of the evaluation of risky prospects. Although the properties of v and π summarize a common pattern of choice, they are not universal: the preferences of some individuals are not well described by an S-shaped value function and a consistent set of decision weights. The simultaneous measurement of values and decision weights involves serious experimental and statistical difficulties (*10*).

If π and v were linear throughout, the preference order between options would be independent of the framing of acts, outcomes, or contingencies. Because of the characteristic nonlinearities of π and v, however, different frames can lead to different choices. The following three sections describe reversals of preference caused by variations in the framing of acts, contingencies, and outcomes.

FIGURE 9.2 A hypothetical weighting function

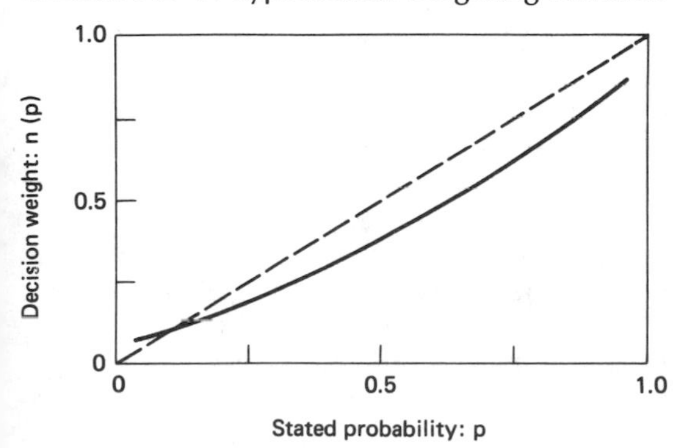

THE FRAMING OF ACTS

Problem 9.3 [$N = 150$]: Imagine that you face the following pair of concurrent decisions. First examine both decisions, then indicate the options you prefer.

Decision (i). Choose between:

A. a sure gain of $240 [84 percent]

B. 25% chance to gain $1000, and 75% chance to gain nothing [16 percent]

Decision (ii). Choose between:

C. a sure loss of $750 [13 percent]

D. 75% chance to lose $1000, and 25% chance to lose nothing [87 percent]

The majority choice in decision (i) is risk averse: a riskless prospect is preferred to a risky prospect of equal or greater expected value. In contrast, the majority choice in decision (ii) is risk taking: a risky prospect is preferred to a riskless prospect of equal expected value. This pattern of risk aversion in choices involving gains and risk seeking in choices involving losses is attributable to the properties of v and π. Because the value function is S-shaped, the value associated with a gain of $240 is greater than 24 percent of the value associated with a gain of $1000, and the (negative) value associated with a loss of $750 is smaller than 75 percent of the value associated with a loss of $1000. Thus the shape of the value function contributes to risk aversion in decision (i) and to risk seeking in decision (ii). Moreover, the underweighting of moderate and high probabilities contributes to the relative attractiveness of the sure gain in (i) and to the relative averseness of the sure loss in (ii). The same analysis applies to problems 9.1 and 9.2.

Because (i) and (ii) were presented together, the respondents had in effect to choose one prospect from the set: A and C, B and C, A and D, B and D. The most common pattern (A and D) was chosen by 73 percent of respondents, while the least popular pattern (B and C) was chosen by only 3 percent of respondents. However, the combination of B and C is definitely superior to the combination A and D, as is readily seen in Problem 9.4.

Problem 9.4 [*N* = 86]. Choose between:

A & D. 25% chance to win $240, and 75% chance to lose $760. [0 percent]

B & C. 25% chance to win $250, and 75% chance to lose $750. [100 percent]

When the prospects were combined and the dominance of the second option became obvious, all respondents chose the superior option. The popularity of the inferior option in Problem 9.3 implies that this problem was framed as a pair of separate choices. The respondents apparently failed to entertain the possibility that the conjunction of two seemingly reasonable choices could lead to an untenable result.

The violations of dominance observed in Problem 9.3 do not disappear in the presence of monetary incentives. A different group of respondents who answered a modified version of Problem 9.3, with real payoffs, produced a similar pattern of choices (*11*). Other authors have also reported that violations of the rules of rational choice, originally observed in hypothetical questions, were not eliminated by payoffs (*12*).

We suspect that many concurrent decisions in the real world are framed independently, and that the preference order would often be reversed if the decisions were combined. The respondents in Problem 9.3 failed to combine options, although the integration was relatively simple and was encouraged by instructions (*13*). The complexity of practical problems of concurrent decisions, such as portfolio selection, would prevent people from integrating options without computational aids, even if they were inclined to do so.

THE FRAMING OF CONTINGENCIES

The following triple of problems illustrates the framing of contingencies. Each problem was presented to a different group of respondents. Each group was told that one participant in ten, preselected at random, would actually be playing for money. Chance events were realized, in the respondents' presence, by drawing a single ball from a bag containing a known proportion of balls of the winning color, and the winners were paid immediately.

Problem 9.5 [*N* = 77]: Which of the following options do you prefer?

A. a sure win of $30 [78 percent]

B. 80% chance to win $45 [22 percent]

Problem 9.6 [*N* = 85]: Consider the following two-stage game. In the first stage, there is a 75% chance to end the game without winning anything, and a 25% chance to move into the second stage. If you reach the second stage you have a choice between:

C. a sure win of $30 [74 percent]

D. 80 % chance to win $45 [26 percent]

Your choice must be made before the game starts, i.e., before the outcome of the first stage is known. Please indicate the option you prefer.

Problem 9.7 [*N* = 81]: Which of the following options do you prefer?

E. 25% chance to win $30 [42 percent]

F. 20% chance to win $45 [58 percent]

Let us examine the structure of these problems. First, note that Problems 9.6 and 9.7 are identical in terms of probabilities and outcomes, because prospect C offers a .25 chance to win $30 and prospect D offers a probability of $.25 \times .80 = .20$ to win $45. Consistency therefore requires that the same choice be made in Problems 9.6 and 9.7. Second, note that Problem 9.6 differs from Problem 9.5 only by the introduction of a preliminary stage. If the second stage of the game is reached, then Problem 9.6 reduces to Problem 9.5; if the game ends at the first stage, the decision does not affect the outcome. Hence there seems to be no reason to make a different choice in Problems 9.5 and 9.6. By this logical analysis, Problem

9.6 is equivalent to Problem 9.7 on the one hand and Problem 9.5 on the other. The participants, however, responded similarly to Problems 9.5 and 9.6 but differently to Problem 9.7. This pattern of responses exhibits two phenomena of choice: the certainty effect and the pseudocertainty effect.

The contrast between Problems 9.5 and 9.7 illustrates a phenomenon discovered by Allais (*14*), which we have labeled the certainty effect: a reduction of the probability of an outcome by a constant factor has more impact when the outcome was initially certain than when it was merely probable. Prospect theory attributes this effect to the properties of π. It is easy to verify, by applying the equation of prospect theory to Problems 9.5 and 9.7, that people for whom the value ratio $v(30)/v(45)$ lies between the weight ratios $\pi(.20)/\pi(.25)$ and $\pi(.80)/\pi(1.0)$ will prefer A to B and F to E, contrary to expected utility theory. Prospect theory does not predict a reversal of preference for every individual in Problems 9.5 and 9.7. It only requires that an individual who has no preference between A and B prefer F to E. For group data, the theory predicts the observed directional shift of preference between the two problems.

The first stage of Problem 9.6 yields the same outcome (no gain) for both acts. Consequently, we propose, people evaluate the options conditionally, as if the second stage had been reached. In this framing, of course, Problem 9.6 reduces to Problem 9.5. More generally, we suggest that a decision problem is evaluated conditionally when (i) there is a state in which all acts yield the same outcome, such as failing to reach the second stage of the game in Problem 9.6, and (ii) the stated probabilities of other outcomes are conditional on the nonoccurrence of this state.

The striking discrepancy between the responses to Problems 9.6 and 9.7, which are identical in outcomes and probabilities, could be described as a pseudocertainty effect. The prospect yielding $30 is relatively more attractive in Problem 9.6 than in Problem 9.7, as if it had the advantage of certainty. The sense of certainty associated with option C is illusory, however, since the gain is in fact contingent on reaching the second stage of the game (*15*).

We have observed the certainty effect in several sets of problems, with outcomes ranging from vacation trips to the loss of human lives. In the negative domain, certainty exaggerates the aversiveness of losses that are certain relative to losses that are merely probable. In a question dealing with the response to an epidemic, for example, most respondents found "a sure loss of 75 lives" more aversive than "80 percent chance to lose 100 lives" but preferred "10 percent chance to lose 75 lives" over "8 percent chance to lose 100 lives," contrary to expected utility theory.

We also obtained the pseudocertainty effect in several studies where the description of the decision problems favored conditional evaluation. Pseudocertainty can be induced either by a sequential formulation, as in Problem 9.6, or by the introduction of causal contingencies. In another version of the epidemic problem, for instance, respondents were told that risk to life existed only in the event (probability .10) that the disease was carried by a particular virus. Two alternative programs were said to yield "a sure loss of 75 lives" or "80 percent chance to lose 100 lives" if the critical virus was involved, and no loss of life in the event (probability .90) that the disease was carried by another virus. In effect, the respondents were asked to choose between 10 percent chance of losing 75 lives and 8 percent chance of losing 100 lives, but their preferences were the same as when the choice was between a sure loss of 75 lives and 80 percent chance of losing 100 lives. A conditional framing was evidently adopted in which the contingency of the noncritical virus was eliminated, giving rise to a pseudocertainty effect. The certainty effect reveals attitudes toward risk that are inconsistent with the axioms of rational choice, whereas the pseudocertainty effect violates the more fundamental requirement that preferences should be independent of problem description.

Many significant decisions concern actions that reduce or eliminate the probability of a hazard, at some cost. The shape of π in the range of low probabilities suggests that a protective action which reduces the probability of a harm from 1 percent to zero, say, will be valued more highly than an action that reduces the probability of the same harm from 2 percent to 1 percent. Indeed, probabilistic insurance, which reduces the probability of loss by half, is judged to be worth less than half the price of regular insurance that eliminates the risk altogether (*3*).

It is often possible to frame protective action in either conditional or unconditional form. For example, an insurance policy that covers fire but not flood could be evaluated either as full protection against the specific risk of fire or as a reduction in the overall probability of property loss. The preceding analysis suggests that insurance should appear more attractive when it is presented as the elimination of risk than when it is described as a reduction of risk. P. Slovic, B. Fischhoff, and S. Lichtenstein, in an unpublished study, found that a hypothetical vaccine which reduces the probability of contracting a disease from .20 to .10 is less attractive if it is described as effective in half the cases than if it is presented as fully effective against one of two (exclusive and equiprobable) virus strains that produce identical symptoms. In accord with the present analysis of pseudocertainty, the respondents valued full protection against an identified virus more than probabilistic protection against the disease.

The preceding discussion highlights the sharp contrast between lay responses to the reduction and the elimination of risk. Because no form of protective action can cover all risks to human welfare, all insurance is essentially probabilistic: it reduces but does not eliminate risk. The probabilistic nature of insurance is commonly masked by formulations that emphasize the completeness of protection against identified harms, but the sense of security that such formulations provide is an illusion of conditional framing. It appears that insurance is bought as protection against worry, not only against risk, and that worry can be manipulated by the labeling of outcomes and by the framing of contingencies. It is not easy to determine whether people value the elimination of risk too much or the reduction of risk too little. The contrasting attitudes to the two forms of protective action, however, are difficult to justify on normative grounds (*16*).

THE FRAMING OF OUTCOMES

Outcomes are commonly perceived as positive or negative in relation to a reference outcome that is judged neutral. Variations of the reference point can therefore determine whether a given outcome is evaluated as a gain or as a loss. Because the value function is generally concave for gains, convex for losses, and steeper for losses than for gains, shifts of reference can change the value difference between outcomes and thereby reverse the preference order between options (*6*). Problems 9.1 and 9.2 illustrated a preference reversal induced by a shift of reference that transformed gains into losses.

For another example, consider a person who has spent an afternoon at the race track, has already lost $140, and is considering a $10 bet on a 15:1 long shot in the last race. This decision can be framed in two ways, which correspond to two natural reference points. If the status quo is the reference point, the outcomes of the bet are framed as a gain of $140 and a loss of $10. On the other hand, it may be more natural to view the present state as a loss of $140, for the betting day, and accordingly frame the last bet as a chance to return to the reference point or to increase the loss to $150. Prospect theory implies that the latter frame will produce more risk seeking than the former. Hence, people who do not adjust their reference point as they lose are expected to take bets that they would normally find unacceptable. This analysis is supported by the observation that bets on long shots are most popular on the last race of the day (*17*).

Because the value function is steeper for losses than for gains, a difference between options will loom larger when it is framed as a disadvantage of one option rather than as an advantage of the other option. An interesting example of such an effect in a riskless context has been noted by Thaler (*18*). In a debate on a proposal to pass to the consumer some of the costs associated with the processing of credit-card purchases, representatives of the credit-card industry requested that the price difference be labeled a cash discount rather than a credit-card surcharge. The two labels induce different reference points by implicitly designating as normal reference the higher or the lower of the two prices. Because losses loom larger than gains, consumers are less willing to accept a surcharge than to forego a discount. A similar effect has been observed in experimental studies of insurance: the proportion of respondents who preferred a sure loss to a larger probable loss was significantly greater when the former was called an insurance premium (*19, 20*).

These observations highlight the lability of reference outcomes, as well as their role in decision making. In the examples discussed so far, the neutral reference point was identified by the labeling of outcomes. A diversity of factors determine the reference outcome in everyday life. The reference outcome is usually a state to which one has adapted; it is sometimes set by social norms and expectations; it sometimes corresponds to a level of aspiration, which may or may not be realistic.

We have dealt so far with elementary outcomes, such as gains or losses in a single attribute. In many situations, however, an action gives rise to a compound outcome, which joins a series of changes in a single attribute, such as a sequence of monetary gains and losses, or a set of concurrent changes in several attributes. To describe the framing and evaluation of compound outcomes, we use the notion of a psychological account, defined as an outcome frame which specifies (1) the set of elementary outcomes that are evaluated jointly and the manner in which they are combined and (2) a reference outcome that is considered neutral or normal. In the account that is set up for the purchase of a car, for example, the cost of the purchase is not treated as a loss nor is the car viewed as a gift. Rather, the transaction as a whole is evaluated as positive, negative, or neutral, depending on such factors as the performance of the car and the price of similar cars in the market. A closely related treatment has been offered by Thaler (*18*).

We propose that people generally evaluate acts in terms of a minimal account, which includes only the direct consequences of the act. The minimal account associated with the decision to accept a gamble, for example, includes the money won or lost in that gamble and excludes other assets or the outcome of previous gambles. People commonly adopt minimal accounts because this mode of framing (1) simplifies evaluation and reduces cognitive strain, (2) reflects the intuition that consequences should be causally linked to acts, and (3) matches the properties of hedonic experience, which is more sensitive to desirable and undesirable changes than to steady states.

There are situations, however, in which the outcomes of an act affect the balance in an account that was previously set up by a related act. In these cases, the decision at hand may be evaluated in terms of a more inclusive account, as in the case of the bettor who views the last race in the context of earlier losses. More generally, a sunk-cost effect arises when a decision is referred to an existing account in which the current balance is negative. Because of the nonlinearities of the evaluation process, the minimal account and a more inclusive one often lead to different choices.

Problems 9.8 and 9.9 illustrate another class of situations in which an existing account affects a decision:

Problem 9.8 [N = 183]: Imagine that you have decided to see a play where admission is $10 per ticket. As you enter the theater you discover that you have lost a $10 bill.

Would you still pay $10 for a ticket for the play?
Yes [88 percent] No [12 percent]

Problem 9.9 [N = 200]: Imagine that you have decided to see a play and paid the admission price of $10 per ticket. As you enter the theater you discover that you have lost the ticket. The seat was not marked and the ticket cannot be recovered.

Would you pay $10 for another ticket?
Yes [46 percent] No [54 percent]

The marked difference between the responses to Problems 9.8 and 9.9 is an effect of psychological accounting. We propose that the purchase of a new ticket in Problem 9.9 is entered in the account that was set up by the purchase of the original ticket. In terms of this account, the expense required to see the show is $20, a cost which many of our respondents apparently found excessive. In Problem 9.8, on the other hand, the loss of $10 is not linked specifically to the ticket purchase and its effect on the decision is accordingly slight.

The following problem, based on examples by Savage (*2,* p. 103) and Thaler (*18*), further illustrates the effect of embedding an option in different accounts. Two versions of this problem were presented to different groups of subjects. One group (N = 93) was given the values that appear in parentheses, and the other group (N = 88) the values shown in brackets.

Problem 9.10: Imagine that you are about to purchase a jacket for ($125) [$15], and a calculator for ($15) [$125]. The calculator salesman informs you that the calculator you wish to buy is on sale for ($10) [$120] at the other branch of the store, located 20 minutes drive away. Would you make the trip to the other store?

The response to the two versions of Problem 9. 10 were markedly different: 68 percent of the respondents were willing to make an extra trip to save $5 on a $15 calculator; only 29 percent were willing to exert the same effort when the price of the calculator was $125. Evidently the respondents do not frame Problem 9.10 in the minimal account, which involves only a benefit of $5 and a cost of some inconvenience. Instead, they evaluate the potential saving in a more inclusive account, which includes the purchase of the calculator but not of the jacket. By the curvature of v, a discount of $5 has a greater impact when the price of the calculator is low than when it is high.

A closely related observation has been reported by Pratt, Wise, and Zeckhauser (*21*), who found that the variability of the prices at which a given product is sold by different stores is roughly proportional to the mean price of that product. The same pattern was observed for both frequently and infrequently purchased items. Overall, a ratio of 2:1 in the mean price of two products is associated with a ratio of 1.86:1 in the standard deviation of the respective quoted prices. If the effort that consumers exert to save each dollar on a purchase, for instance by a phone call, were independent of price, the dispersion of quoted prices should be about the same for all products. In contrast, the data of Pratt et al. (*21*) are consistent with the hypothesis that consumers hardly exert more effort to save $15 on a $150 purchase than to safe $5 on a $50 purchase (*18*). Many readers will recognize the temporary devaluation of money which facilitates extra spending and reduces the significance of small discounts in the context of a large expenditure, such as buying a house or a car. This paradoxical variation in the value of money is incompatible with the standard analysis of consumer behavior.

DISCUSSION

In this article we have presented a series of demonstrations in which seemingly inconsequential changes in the formulation of choice problems caused significant shifts of preference. The inconsistencies were traced to the interaction of two sets of factors: variations in the framing of acts, contingencies, and outcomes, and the characteristic nonlinearities of values and decision weights. The demonstrated effects are large and systematic, although by no means universal. They occur when the outcomes concern the loss of human lives as well as in choices about money: they are not restricted to hypothetical questions and are not eliminated by monetary incentives.

Earlier we compared the dependence of preferences on frames to the dependence of perceptual appearance on perspective. If while traveling in a mountain range you notice that the apparent relative height of mountain peaks varies with your vantage point, you will conclude that some impressions of relative height must be erroneous, even when you have no access to the correct answer. Similarly, one may discover that the relative attractiveness of options varies when the same decision problem is framed in different ways. Such a discovery will normally lead the decision maker to reconsider the original preferences, even when there is no simple way to resolve the inconsistency. The susceptibility to perspective effects is of special concern in the domain of decision making because of the absence of objective standards such as the true height of mountains.

The metaphor of changing perspective can be applied to other phenomena of choice, in addition to the framing effects with which we have been concerned here (*19*). The problem of self-control is naturally construed in these terms. The story of Ulysses' request to be bound to the mast of the ship in anticipation of the irresistible temptation of the Sirens' call is often used as a paradigm case (*22*). In this example of precommitment, an action taken in the present renders inoperative an anticipated future preference. An unusual feature of the problem of intertemporal conflict is that the agent who views a problem from a particular temporal perspective is also aware of the conflicting views that future perspectives will offer. In most other situations, decision makers are not normally aware of the potential effects of different decision frames on their preferences.

The perspective metaphor highlights the following aspects of the psychology of choice. Individuals who face a decision problem and have a definite preference (1) might have a different preference in a different framing of the same problem, (2) are normally unaware of alternative frames and of their potential effects on the relative attractiveness of options, (3) would wish their preferences to be independent of frame, but (4) are often uncertain how to resolve detected inconsistencies (*23*). In some cases (such as Problems 9.3 and 9.4 and perhaps Problems 9.8 and 9.9) the advantage of one frame becomes evident once the competing frames are compared, but in other cases (Problems 9.1 and 9.2 and Problems 9.6 and 9.7) it is not obvious which preferences should be abandoned.

These observations do not imply that preference reversals, or other errors of choice or judgment (*24*), are necessarily irrational. Like other intellectual limitations, discussed by Simon (*25*) under the heading of "bounded rationality," the practice of acting on the most readily available frame can sometimes be justified by reference to the mental effort required to explore alternative frames and avoid potential inconsistencies. However, we propose that the details of the phenomena described in this article are better explained by prospect theory and by an analysis of framing than by ad hoc appeals to the notion of cost of thinking.

The present work has been concerned primarily with the descriptive question of how decisions are made, but the psychology of choice is also relevant to the normative question of how decisions ought to be made. In order to avoid the difficult problem of justifying values, the modern theory of rational choice has adopted the coherence of specific preferences as the sole criterion of rationality. This approach enjoins the decision maker to resolve inconsistencies but offers no guidance on how to do so. It implicitly assumes that the decision maker who carefully answers the question "What do I really want?" will eventually achieve coherent preferences. However, the susceptibility of preferences to variations of framing raises doubt about the feasibility and adequacy of the coherence criterion.

Consistency is only one aspect of the lay notion of rational behavior. As noted by March (*26*), the common conception of rationality also requires that preferences or utilities for particular outcomes should be predictive of the experiences of satisfaction or displeasure associated with their occurrence. Thus, a man could be judged irrational either because his preferences are contradictory or because his desires and aversions do not reflect his pleasures and pains. The predictive criterion of rationality can be applied to resolve inconsistent preferences and to improve the quality of decisions. A predictive orientation encourages the decision maker to focus on future experience and to ask "What will I feel then?" rather than "What do I want now?" The former question, when answered with care, can be the more useful guide in difficult decisions. In particular, predictive considerations may be applied to select the decision frame that best represents the hedonic experience of outcomes.

Further complexities arise in the normative analysis because the framing of an action sometimes affects the actual experience of its outcomes. For example, framing outcomes in terms of overall wealth or welfare rather than in terms of specific gains and losses may attenuate one's emotional response to an occasional loss. Similarly, the experience of a change for the worse may vary if the change is framed as an uncompensated loss or as a cost incurred to achieve some benefit. The framing of acts and outcomes can also reflect the acceptance or rejection of responsibility for particular consequences, and the deliberate manipulation of framing is commonly used as an instrument of self-control (*22*). When framing influences the experience of consequences, the adoption of a decision frame is an ethically significant act.

REFERENCES AND NOTES

1. J. VON NEUMANN and O. MORGENSTERN, *Theory of Games and Economic Behavior* (Princeton Univ. Press, Princeton, N.J., 1947); H. Raiffa, *Decision Analysis: Lectures on Choices Under Uncertainty* (Addison-Wesley, Reading, Mass., 1968); P. Fishburn, *Utility Theory for Decision Making* (Wiley, New York, 1970).
2. L. J. SAVAGE. *The Foundations of Statistics* (Wiley, New York, 1954).
3. D. KAHNEMAN and A. TVERSKY. *Econometrica* 47, 263 (1979).
4. The framing phase includes various editing operations that are applied to simplify prospects, for example by combining events or outcomes or by discarding negligible components (*3*).
5. If $p + q = 1$ and either $x > y > 0$ or $x < y < 0$, the equation in the text is replaced by $v(y) + \pi(p)\ [v(x) - v(y)]$, so that decision weights are not applied to sure outcomes.
6. P. FISHBURN and G. KOCHENBERGER, *Decision Sci.* 10, 503 (1979); D. J. Laughhunn, J. W. Payne, R. Crum, *Manage. Sci.*, in press; J. W. Payne, D. J. Laughhunn, R. Crum, *ibid.*, in press; S. A. Eraker and H. C. Sox, *Med. Decision Making*, in press. In the last study several hundred clinic patients made hypothetical choices between drug therapies for severe headaches, hypertension, and chest pain. Most patients were risk averse when the outcomes were described as positive (for example, reduced pain or increased life expectancy) and risk taking when the outcomes were described as negative (increased pain or reduced life expectancy). No significant differences were found between patients who actually suffered from the ailments described and patients who did not.
7. E. GALANTER and P. PLINER, in *Sensation and Measurement*, H. R. Moskowitz *et al.*, Eds. (Reidel, Dordrecht, 1974), pp. 65–76.
8. The extension of the proposed value function to multiattribute options, with or without risk, deserves careful analysis. In particular, indifference curves between dimensions of loss may be concave upward, even when the value functions for the separate losses are both convex, because of marked subadditivity between dimensions.
9. D. ELLSBERG, *Q. J. Econ.* 75, 643 (1961); W. Fellner, *Probability and Profit—A Study of Economic Behavior Along Bayesian Lines* (Irwin, Homewood, Ill., 1965).
10. The scaling of v and π by pair comparisons requires a large number of observations. The procedure of pricing gambles is more convenient for scaling purposes, but it is subject to a severe anchoring bias: the ordering of gambles by their cash equivalents diverges systematically from the preference order observed in direct comparisons [S. Lichtenstein and P. Slovic, *J. Exp. Psychol.* 89, 46 (1971)].
11. A new group of respondents ($N = 126$) was presented with a modified version of problem 3, in which the outcomes were reduced by a factor of 50. The participants were informed that the gambles would actually be played by tossing a pair of fair coins, that one participant in ten would be selected at random to play the gambles of his or her choice. To ensure a positive return for the entire set, a third decision, yielding only positive outcomes, was added. These payoff conditions did not alter the pattern of prefer-

ences observed in the hypothetical problem: 67 percent of respondents chose prospect A and 86 percent chose prospect D. The dominated combination of A and D was chosen by 60 percent of respondents, and only 6 percent favored the dominant combination of B and C.

12. S. LICHTENSTEIN and P. SLOVIC, *J. Exp. Psychol.* 101, 16 (1973); D. M. Grether and C. R. Platt, *Am. Econ. Rev.* 69, 623 (1979); I. Lieblich and A. Lieblich, *Percept. Mot. Skills* 29, 467 (1969); D. M. Grether, *Social Science Working Paper No. 245* (California Institute of Technology, Pasadena, 1979).
13. Other demonstrations of a reluctance to integrate concurrent options have been reported; P. Slovic and S. Lichtenstein, *J. Exp. Psychol.* 78, 646 (1968); J. W. Payne and M. L. Braunstein, *ibid.* 87, 13 (1971).
14. M. ALLAIS, *Econometrica* 21, 503 (1953); K. McCrimmon and S. Larsson, in *Expected Utility Hypotheses and the Allais Paradox,* M. Allais and O. Hagan, Eds. (Reidel, Dordrecht, 1979).
15. Another group of respondents (N = 205) was presented with all three problems, in different orders, without monetary payoffs. The joint frequency distribution of choices in problems 5, 6, and 7 was as follows: ACE, 22; ACF, 65; ADE, 1; ADF, 20; BCE, 7; BCF, 18; BDE, 17; BDF, 52. These data confirm in a within-subject design the analysis of conditional evaluation proposed in the text. More than 75 percent of respondents made compatible choices (AC or BD) in problems 5 and 6, and less than half made compatible choices in problems 6 and 7 (CE or DF) and 5 and 7 (AE or BF). The elimination of payoffs in these questions reduced risk aversion but did not substantially alter the effects of certainty and pseudocertainty.
16. For further discussion of rationality in protective action see H. Kunreuther, *Disaster Insurance Protection: Public Policy Lessons* (Wiley, New York, 1978).
17. W. H. MCGLOTHLIN, *Am. J. Psychol.* 69, 604 (1956).
18. R. THALER, *J. Econ. Behav. Organ.* 1, 39 (1980).
19. B. FISCHHOFF, P. SLOVIC, S. LICHTENSTEIN, in *Cognitive Processes in Choice and Decision Behavior.* T. Wallsten, Ed. (Erlbaum, Hillsdale, N.J., 1980).
20. J. C. HERSHEY and P. J. H. SCHOEMAKER, *J. Risk Insur.*, in press.
21. J. PRATT, A. WISE, R. ZECKHAUSER, *Q. J. Econ.* 93, 189 (1979).
22. R. H. STROTZ, *Rev. Econ. Stud.* 23, 165 (1955); G. Ainslie, *Psychol. Bull.* 82, 463 (1975); J. Elster, *Ulysses and the Sirens: Studies in Rationality and Irrationality* (Cambridge Univ. Press, London, 1979); R. Thaler and H. M. Shifrin, *J. Polit. Econ.*, in press.
23. P. SLOVIC and A. TVERSKY, *Behav. Sci.* 19, 368 (1974).
24. A. TVERSKY and D. KAHNEMAN, *Science* 185, 1124 (1974); P. Slovic, B. Fischhoff, S. Lichtenstein, *Annu. Rev. Psychol.* 28, 1 (1977); R. Nisbett and L. Ross, *Human Inference: Strategies and Shortcomings of Social Judgment* (Prentice-Hall, Englewood Cliffs, N.J., 1980); H. Einhorn and R. Hogarth, *Annu. Rev. Psychol.* 32, 53 (1981).
25. H. A. SIMON, *Q. J. Econ.* 69, 99 (1955), *Psychol. Rev.* 63, 129 (1956).
26. J. MARCH, *Bell J. Econ.* 9, 587 (1978).
27. This work was supported by the Office of Naval Research under contract N00014-79-C-0077 to Stanford University.

10

CONSTRUCTIVE PROCESSES IN CONSUMER CHOICE*

James R. Bettman
Michel A. Zins

The degree to which consumers use rules or heuristics which have already been developed and stored in memory versus the degree to which consumers construct the rules they use on the spot, during the actual course of alternative selection, is examined, Detailed verbal protocol data from two consumers are analyzed. The results show substantial problems with such protocol data. Implications of the results for consumer choice theories are also considered.

Consumer choice heuristics have been the object of a great deal of study in recent years. This research has tended to have a narrow focus on the particular ways in which data is combined in comparing alternatives (e.g., studies of linear compensatory rules, conjunctive rules, or lexicographic rules). There is another dimension of choice, however, that has seen virtually no theorizing or empirical research. One can characterize not only the particular choice heuristics used, but also how those heuristics are implemented, or carried out. One distinction relating to how choice rules can be implemented is the focus of this study. That distinction concerns the degree to which consumers use rules or heuristics which have been already developed and stored in memory versus the degree to which consumers construct the rules they use on the spot, during the actual course of

*Reprinted from the *Journal of Consumer Research,* 4 (September 1977), pp. 75-85.

selecting an alternative. This paper has three major purposes in examining this distinction:

1. To introduce some new theoretical notions about how choice processes are carried out, namely the use of stored rules and the use of constructive processes, and to briefly review the relevant literature;
2. To consider what data collection methods might be used to examine these notions empirically;
3. To perform an exploratory study which might provide both some initial empirical and substantive insights into these notions and also some insights into the adequacy of the methodology used.

These three purposes provide an outline for the remainder of the paper. The stored rule and constructive notions are detailed next, followed by a review of the literature relevant to these areas. Then various methods for studying these notions are considered, and a particular method chosen. Finally, an exploratory study is described, and conclusions about both the phenomena and the methodology used are considered.

STORED RULE VS. CONSTRUCTIVE PROCESSES IN CARRYING OUT CHOICE

Characterization of Stored Rule and Constructive Processes

As just noted, consumers can carry out or implement choice processes in different ways. One distinction which seems relevant is the way in which specific choice heuristics are used. There are two basic characterizations which can be described. One characterization is that the consumer has a set of rules or heuristics which are already stored in memory, and these rules are called forth in their entirety when needed and directly applied. This might be called a *stored rule* mechanism for carrying out choice. The second characterization is that heuristics are developed at the time of choice, i.e., rules are constructed as the consumer goes along rather than being merely recalled and applied. This second notion can be called a *constructive* mechanism. Each of these two mechanisms is now considered in more detail.

The Stored Rule Mechanism. The assumptions underlying the stored rule concept imply that consumers have available a repertoire of strategies in memory, and control processes which in effect call these strategies when needed, much in the same manner as a computer program uses subroutines. Thus, the rule to be used is already built, exists in complete form in memory, and is directly implemented to choose the best alternative. Some calculation or processing may go on while actually implementing the preexisting rule, but this rule is not changed or built up. It is retrieved in its entirety and applied.

There are two main variations in this use of stored rules. In the first, the consumer has previously made a particular choice, and merely wishes to repeat that choice. Thus, brand, package, size, etc., have already been settled upon, and the only question is whether the chosen alternative is available or not. That is, the rule used is of the form, "buy Brand X." We call this use of stored rules *preprocessed choice.* In the second case, the consumer uses a heuristic which is already existing in memory, but which requires some further processing to apply, e.g., "buy the cheapest" or "choose the brand with the highest protein content." In this case the rule is known, but the alternative to be selected is not. This is called an *analytic implementation process.*

The Constructive Mechanism. The basic notion behind the constructive mechanism for carrying out choice is the notion that the heuristic used is developed at the actual time of choice. The consumer is seen as making up the rule as he or she goes along. The heuristics are constructed using fragments or elements of rules stored in memory. These fragments or elements may be beliefs about alternatives; evaluations; simple rules of thumb involving subsets of beliefs (e.g., "compare these products on Attribute A to see if they differ very much"); rules for integrating beliefs (e.g., "count how many attributes Alternative X is best on" or "average these ratings"); rules for assigning weights (e.g., "if performance is comparable across brands, weight price heavily"); or perhaps even computational rules. Using such component pieces, the consumer constructs a rule for selecting an alternative. Presumably, the specific elements or rule fragments used will be a function of what is available in the particular choice situation and how easy various pieces of information are to process. Thus, a "compare prices" element may not be used if unit prices are not given and different brands have different-sized packages.

The basic idea behind the distinction between the stored rule and constructive notions is that, in some cases, completed heuristics or rules are not already available in memory, but must be built up from subparts. Rather than retrieving in total some preexisting rule, the consumer constructs, or synthesizes, the heuristic used. In the constructive process, the consumer "constructs" the decision rule at the moment he or she has to use it. The consumer may have only a very general plan for constructing a heuristic in some particular situation. Thus, the heuristics constructed will, in general, vary from one situation to the next.

As examples of these methods for carrying out choice, consider possible types of processing for a decision about breakfast cereals. If an analytic implementation process were used a housewife might have a preexisting rule of "choose the brand of cereal with the highest protein level," and must determine which cereal in fact has the highest level. In the case of preprocessed choice, the consumer would already know Brand X had the highest protein, and would simply choose Brand X. With a constructive choice process, the consumer might develop the highest protein rule on the spot, developing a rationale for this rule after considering other possibilities.

The Use of Stored Rule and Constructive Mechanisms. In this section we consider under what conditions each type of mechanism is likely to be used. One is not "true" and the other "false;" rather, both the stored rule and constructive mechanisms are used in carrying out choices. The type of situations in which each is used will tend to differ, however. Constructive mechanisms will tend to be used when consumers have little experience with a particular choice, or when choice is difficult. Thus, when a choice is made for the first time, or when a changed situation is encountered, construction of heuristics will be seen most often. Under these conditions, the heuristic will be built up using information available in the specific choice environment.

If the consumer has had prior experience with a particular choice, elements of heuristics may exist in memory, and if used over time such elements may become organized into an overall rule. In effect, elements may be "chunked" into an overall rule. In this sense, use of stored rules is seen to be the result of habituation in the choice process. At any point in time, therefore, a particular consumer will be engaged in both construction for some choices and usage of stored rules for other choices, the extent of each being largely determined by the degree of experience with the various choices under consideration.

Significance of the Distinction. One might legitimately ask at this point why the distinction between use of stored rule and constructive processes matters; why should one care about these two methods? The answer is basically that different factors will influence the consumer depending upon which of these methods is used, and this has implications for how to provide information to consumers.

For example, if constructive methods are being used, the consumer is doing a good deal of processing in the store. This implies that information presented in the store may have more impact than that presented outside the store. Thus marketers or public policymakers who wish to present information to consumers may need to use package information or other in-store displays if constructive processes are being used, rather than relying on out-of-store methods like radio, television, or print advertising.

Thus, in-store methods might be used most where consumers have little prior experience with a choice. If stored rules are being used, out-of-store methods may be useful. In general, use of constructive processes means that situational factors will have a greater impact on the resulting choice.

A second reason for the importance of the distinction is that marketers or policymakers may wish to change the heuristics used by consumers. That is in addition to attempting to change the specific beliefs or evaluations held, there may be situations in which one wishes to change the actual heuristics used for comparing alternatives; to advocate use of a certain rule, for example. Wright and Barbour (1975) note that this strategy, although potentially effective, has not been applied to any extent in practice. Our discussion implies that attempts to advocate or change rules may be most effective when rules are being constructed or built up rather than when they are being simply recalled and applied. Thus, when constructive processes are used in situations where there is little prior experience, attempts to influence the heuristics used are likely to be most effective.

Previous Research

Now we consider previous research relevant to these notions, both in psychology and in consumer research.

Research in Psychology. A good deal of psychological research on these mechanisms has focused on memory phenomena. In particular, researchers have examined whether items are retrieved from memory as completed units, or whether remembering an item is in some sense constructive. Bartlett (1932) was among the first to argue that memory retrieval was in many cases a constructive process, particularly for unfamiliar material. Bartlett presented stories to his subjects, and had the subjects repeat these stories from memory. He argued, based on these studies, that humans reconstruct prior events based on their understanding of them, rather than directly arousing some already existing "memory" in its entirety. More recently, Neisser (1967) has argued in some detail that perception and memory processes are essentially constructive in nature.

Recent work in memory for stories and sentences has supported these conclusions. Subjects were presented with stories or sentences to read in these studies. Later, these subjects were given several sentences, some of which had been used in the earlier material and some of which had not, and were asked whether they had seen these sentences previously. The most interesting aspect of the results is that typically the subjects reported having previously seen sentences which were consistent with what was read earlier, but which had not actually been presented. Thus it appears that subjects remember meaning, but not necessarily exact wording. Humans remember the basic ideas presented to them, rather than the actual form of the information used to present those ideas, and they use these basic ideas to guide reconstruction of the information.[1]

These results imply, therefore, that individuals do have some basic elements, possibly quite general, in memory which are used to construct or build up recollections of previous events. Presumably, this type of construction process could also be used to develop heuristics for comparing alternatives. Note again that this research considers situations where unfamiliar material is being presented. For very familiar material, verbatim memory or simple recall of an existing "memory" might be expected.

Research in Consumer Behavior. There has been virtually no consideration in consumer choice on how choice rules are implemented. Rather, most research on choice seems to have implicitly assumed a stored rule approach. For example, a typical study of choice rules might examine the degree to which a linear rule, a

[1]For an overview of this literature, see Cofer (1973). For specific studies, see Gomulicki (1956), Sachs (1967), Jarvella (1971), Bransford and Franks (1971), Franks and Bransford (1971), Bransford, Barclay, and Franks (1972), Zangwill (1972), Loftus (1975), Prawat, Cancelli, and Cook (1976), Thorndyke (1977), and Mandler and Johnson (1977).

conjunctive rule, or a lexicographic rule might predict the choices made by a consumer. These rules are simply defined by the researcher and applied, perhaps using some beliefs and evaluations supplied by the consumer as inputs. The implicit assumption seems to be, therefore, that the consumer likewise simply recalls the entire rule and applies it.

Nakanishi was one of the first consumer researchers to attack this notion, particularly with regard to studies of decision nets. He noted the difficulties arising from "the conception of decision nets as fixed programs rigidly followed by the subject during a purchase decision" (1974, p. 77). In particular, he argued that the types of decision nets depicted in Bettman's work (1970) were far too complex for subjects to have memorized in their entirety and applied. Rather, he argued, subjects must construct such nets as they proceed. This theoretical argument is the only direct work using constructive notions in the consumer research literature.

The closest which previous work in consumer research has come to examining different modes of implementing choice are the works by several authors which note that consumers pass through stages in their choice processes (e.g., Robinson, Faris, and Wind 1967; Howard and Sheth 1969; Hansen 1972). For example, Howard and Sheth distinguish stages of routinized response behavior, limited problem solving, and extensive problem solving. These notions roughly correspond to the distinctions between preprocessed choice, analytic implementation processes, and constructive processes discussed here. However, note that the mechanisms proposed in this paper are more detailed and more narrowly focused than the Howard-Sheth notions. This paper deals with how heuristics are developed and carried out, and focuses on the extent to which rules are built up as the consumer goes along. This is a more detailed view than simply the extent of processing carried out, although the two are related, presumably. Thus the current notions consider the *type* of processing undertaken in more detail than past research, rather than focusing on the *amount* of processing.

Methods for Studying Stored Rule and Constructive Processes

The phenomena discussed here are fairly detailed, and will be observable only if the actual processes undertaken by the consumer in making a choice are examined. This argues for the use of some method for observing actual processes, as opposed to just observing outcomes. If observation of process is desired, certain methods are more applicable than others. Bettman (1977) discusses the major methods for actually observing choice processes. The most relevant process methods discussed are information monitoring, analysis of eye movements, and use of protocol collection. Correlational approaches are rejected because processing is typically not observed.[2]

Information monitoring and eye movement approaches are useful for examining the sequence of information examined by the consumer in making a choice. However, these methods provide little insight into how consumers are using what is stored in memory, and as noted before this is a crucial element for determining how consumers are carrying out choice heuristics—whether rules are recalled and applied, whether elements are used to build more complex heuristics, etc.

Protocol methods therefore seem to be the best available technique for studying the phenomenon. Protocols are obtained by having the consumer think out loud while in the process of actually making choices. Such data potentially allow a great deal of information to be collected on how consumers use memory, whether rules are built up on the spot, and so on. Also, the actual choice process is observed. Finally, protocol methods provide some of the most detailed data obtainable on choice.

The next section considers an exploratory study using the protocol method to examine the use of stored rule and constructive processes by consumers. The purposes of the exploratory study are two-fold:

---

[2]See Bettman (1977) for a more detailed discussion of each method.

- To obtain some initial empirical findings on the use of stored rule and constructive processes; and, equally important,
- To analyze the effectiveness of the protocol methodology for exploring these phenomena.

AN EXPLORATORY STUDY

Method

Data were obtained by gathering protocols from consumers while they shopped. Then judges were given these protocol data and attempted to categorize the data by the nature of the processing used.

The data utilized were the verbal protocol data described in Bettman (1970). Detailed think-aloud protocols were collected over a period of several months for the grocery shopping choices of two consumers, labeled C_1 and C_4 in the earlier study; they were collected in the store as the consumers made their choices.[3]

The protocol data were then broken down into individual "episodes;" each episode representing a particular choice. This process proved to be quite difficult, as many choices were often complexly intertwined in the protocols, and in some instances it was not clear whether a choice was really being made. The decision was made to use a broad definition of episode and to include as many episodes as possible in the sample. In total, 102 episodes were developed for C_1 and 70 for C_4.[4] The 172 episodes were then mixed, so that the episodes for each consumer did not all appear together. Since a pilot study had shown that the items required a good deal of time to judge, the total set of episodes was divided into two subsets of 86 items.

Fourteen judges, faculty members and doctoral candidates at UCLA (including the authors as two of the judges[5]), were used to judge the protocol episodes. Each judge received a total of 86 items, distributed so that each individual episode was categorized in total by seven judges. The judges received an instruction booklet describing the protocol data and defining the basic notions about types of processing to be used. The specific categories provided the judges are shown in Exhibit 10.1. This sheet was accompanied by lengthier descriptions roughly like those in the first section of this paper.

The judges were instructed to indicate for each episode the primary type of processing occurring in that episode. Also, if the judge felt there was more than one kind of processing being used, he could indicate a secondary processing type for that same episode. The distinction between the constructive consumer and constructive experimenter categories was made because some of the episodes seemed to involve a good deal of constructive processing that was not initiated by the consumer, but by leading questions from the experimenter gathering the protocols. The task took the judges an average of two hours.

Before examining the results of the study, a final comment about the episode categories is necessary. No specific rules for translating particular protocol episodes into categories were given, because making such rules involved premature narrowing of the definitions of the categories. Protocol data are simply verbal expressions which provide clues, often vague, to underlying processes. It was felt that to provide

[3]Since knowledge of characteristics of these consumers may aid in interpreting later results, brief descriptions are in order. Consumer C_1 had training in mathematics and her husband had recently finished medical school. Her decisions were for the most part based on price, although she let the family's five children have some of their favorites. Consumer C_4 was younger and newly married, with no children. She and her husband were both elementary school teachers. Neither had much prior shopping experience, and C_4 liked to use what others had tried and told her about. Her husband had very strong preferences, which also influenced her choices.

[4]In the original study, C_1 made 226 choices, of which 87 were able to be coded, and C_4 made 70 choices, of which 50 were coded. Thus essentially all of C_4's choices were translated into episodes but less than half of C_1's were. This may reflect the difficulty C_1 experienced in verbalizing as she shopped; many choices were made without accompanying verbal protocol data. Also, C_1's verbalizations were characterized by more intertwining of decisions than C_4's.

[5]This was considered acceptable because no specific hypotheses were being tested.

EXHIBIT 10.1 Episode categories used by judges

A. *Constructive consumer:* The consumer reports engaging in the construction of a decision rule. This can include reports elicited by the experimenter's request to verbalize what was going on.

B. *Constructive experimenter:* The consumer exhibits constructive behavior, but *mainly* in response to some specific question used by the experimenter. This does *not* include simple experimenter instructions to verbalize, but rather questions that are more clearly directive.

C. *Analytic implementation of a rule:* The consumer is just making calculations or doing some processing to *implement* a decision rule that was already determined.

D. *Preprocessed choice:* The consumer has already previously processed the choice and just executes the results of this previous processing.

E. *Can't tell—not clear cut:* The consumer may be constructing a decision rule, using analytic implementation, or using preprocessed choice; but given the protocol data, it is not clear and really impossible to tell which type of processing is involved.

F. *Other:* None of the above cases seems descriptive of the episode.

specific rules for relating such clues to presently ill-understood processing types was presumptuous, given current knowledge of the relation of protocol data to process and of these processing types. This decision is discussed more fully later.

Results

The total distribution of responses for all 14 judges is shown in Table 10.1. Indications of secondary processing types were used in roughly 25 percent of the episodes. Overall, analytic implementation, preprocessed choice, and constructive processing initiated by the consumer are the most common categories used by the judges. Secondary processing types are characterized more often as constructive activity in response to the experimenter, and less often as preprocessed choice.

TABLE 10.1 Percentage Distribution of Judges' Responses[a]

	Percent of responses		
Processing type	*Primary process*	*Secondary process*	*Total*
Constructive consumer	25.7	18.2	24.2
Constructive experimenter	8.6	32.2	13.3
Analytic implementation	28.6	32.2	29.3
Preprocessed choice	27.1	16.1	24.9
Can't tell	7.5	1.0	6.2
Other	2.5	.3	2.1

[a]There were 1,204 primary process and 298 secondary process responses.

Agreement Among the Judges. The criterion used for agreement among the judges for an episode was that at least five of the seven judges for that episode noted the *presence* of a particular process, either as primary or secondary. This was decided because the presence or absence of the process was the important factor, not whether a judge had labeled the process as primary or secondary. Using this criterion, Table 10.2 shows the number of episodes for which judges agreed, by processing type and by consumer. Using the stated criterion, 76 episodes, or 44.2 percent, were agreed upon by the judges.[6] This is a low proportion of agreements for a judging task. However, the protocol data proved quite difficult for the judges. Often an episode could be interpreted in several different ways, depending upon the meaning ascribed to a particular phrase or sentence. The decision, discussed previously, to not provide detailed judging rules also led to differences in inter-

[6]If only primary responses were used, 54 episodes were agreed upon. The relative proportions of the various processes were very similar to those reported in Table 10.1. There were 36 episodes where six or more judges agreed using both primary and secondary process responses (27 for primary process responses alone). In all cases these were significantly greater ($p < .001$) than the agreement expected under the appropriate random model.

TABLE 10.2 Summary of Episodes Where Judges Agreed[a]

Processing type	*Consumer* C_1	*Consumer* C_4	*Total*[b]	
Constructive consumer	8	8	16	(21.1)
Constructive experimenter	3	0	3	(3.9)
Analytic implementation	18	8	26	(34.2)
Preprocessed choice	11	19	30	(39.5)
Can't tell	0	1	1	(1.3)
Other	0	0	0	(.0)
Total	40[c]	36[c]	76[c]	

[a]At least five of seven judges, both primary and secondary process responses included.

[b]Numbers in parentheses are percentages of the total.

[c]There was agreement on 40 of 102 episodes (39.2%) for C_1; 36 of 70 episodes (51.4%) for C_4; and 76 of 172 episodes (44.2%) in total.

pretation among the judges, as discussed shortly.[7]

To better evaluate the degree of agreement obtained, a random model was constructed in which seven judges responded randomly, with probabilities equal to the actual empirical frequencies given in Table 10.1 for the total number of responses and gave a secondary process response with probabilities equal to those used by the judges.[8] This random model was simulated for 10,000 trials, and the estimated probability of five or more judges agreeing was .123. The obtained proportion is significantly greater ($p < .001$). Thus the agreement, although low, is well beyond chance levels.[9] Finally, Exhibit 10.2 displays examples of episodes where agreement was reached for constructive, analytic implementation, and preprocessed choice, and Exhibit 10.3 shows examples of episodes where no agreement was reached.

Examination of the Judgment Data. The data in Table 10.2 indicate that roughly 25 percent of the consumer choice processing in those episodes where judges agreed was constructive in nature, with roughly 75 percent nonconstructive. If only constructive consumer, analytic implementation, and preprocessed choice are considered, then the respective proportions are 22.2, 36.1, and 41.7 percent. Compared to Table 10.1 there are relatively fewer agreements on constructive processes, and relatively more on analytic implementation and preprocessed choice. This is to be expected, since these processing types are much easier to characterize than constructive processes. Finally, there was greater agreement on C_4's episodes. This is because C_1's episodes

[7]The low agreement levels could also be due to low reliability. Since the task was long, all of the judges were not asked to provide repeated judgments. However, one of the authors (JB) redid 17 episodes two weeks after the first judging. Of 28 responses, 22 matched those in the original judging if the primary and secondary process distinction is ignored. Of the 17 episodes, 10 were matched exactly, and 6 more erred only in one or the other of the primary or secondary processes or in the order of those processes (these 6 episodes all had both primary and secondary process responses).

[8]Since fourteen judges were used, the judges were ranked by the number of secondary process responses used, and then paired (i.e., the judges ranked 1 and 2 were paired, and so on). The average frequency of a secondary process response for each pair was then used as the secondary process response probability for one judge in the random model.

[9]One might argue that using the actual frequencies for the various responses understates the agreement achieved, since use of one category more than another by judges shows some agreement. A random model with equal probabilities for all responses yielded a probability of five or more judges agreeing of .031.

EXHIBIT 10.2 Examples of episodes where judges agreed[a]

A. CONSTRUCTIVE EPISODES

Episode 9A

C Alright, maybe you can help me. Kathy wants to have soup when she comes home from school, but she doesn't want it to be a fattening one. What should I get her?

B Oh, I'll tell you. I don't know. Well, chicken broth I think is your least fattening. You could get her bouillon, that's only about 6 calories per cube.

C Well, yeah, but she is also a growing girl.

B I'll tell you, in this stuff, this Hunter's soup is out of this world, and also, what was the one that we tried that was a very light and, it had meat and all kinds of stuff in it. It was this, yeah, chicken, beef, and vegetable soup. And you just open the can. It's expensive.

C Well, this is, I don't care if I can get her to lose weight. I'll pay anything.

B Yeah, well that's pretty thin. It's a thin broth and it has meat, and chicken and vegetables in it. Try it and see.

C Yeah, I'll try that, and see if it makes any difference. (looks for beef bouillon) No, I didn't, because they didn't have any beef Whoosie-whatsises. Well, I guess I'll just try the one, and then ask her. You can tell them I'd like them to put back plain cranberry juice sometime.

Judges' responses[b]

	A	B	C	D	E	F
Primary	6	0	0	0	1	0
Secondary	0	0	0	0	0	0

Episode 47B

C Pears is what I'm after.

J Everybody got that Dole pineapple in its own juice, so we finally had to try some, and it's great.

C Isn't it? It's very good, I like that . . . I'm after pineapple, but I like a larger can than that, because I don't think that will . . .

J Pears you mean?

C Pears, yes. You influenced me by the pineapple, see, but I'll, I'm really after pears. . . . This is the size I want. It's kind of six in one, half a dozen of the other. These look, some of them are bashed, I never get anything that has a bashed can. Well, this one is too. They're the same price, so I guess it doesn't matter. So I'll get the Richmond.

J What was running through your mind there, while you are sitting there debating?

C I was looking to see which of the cans, well, first I was looking for Bartlett pears, but they both said Bartlett, pears, so then I looked to see um, if one of the, if all of the cans were in good condition in one, and, I think I'll only get one of them, and if one of them, all of them were in good condition, then I'd get that one, over the ones that most of them were bashed in. The third thing I looked for was price, and they were the same price.

J What if the ones that had been some of them bashed in were lower in price? What would you have done then?

C I think it would depend on how many of them were bashed in. A lot of them are in this one. And only one of them over here, so I'd still probably get this one.

Judges' responses[b]

	A	B	C	D	E	F
Primary	5	1	1	0	0	0
Secondary	0	0	2	0	0	0

EXHIBIT 10.2 (Continued)

B. ANALYTIC IMPLEMENTATION EPISODES

Episode 14B

C The more weight you get, for the same number of pieces, in a chicken, usually, the more meat you get. . . . That's assuming that they're all the same size so that the bones are the same. . . . Well, I think they've bred them this way, sort of. It's a theory that I work under.

J If they're heavier it just means they're fatter and not bonier?

C No, well, they are bonier, but the relationship between the two. I, one hopes. After all, you've got to rely on something.

Judges' responses[b]	A	B	C	D	E	F
Primary	1	0	5	0	1	0
Secondary	0	0	0	0	0	0

Episode 24B

C Next are paper towels, but I don't know what kind I'm getting. He must be just doing them. There's not a price on anything. I wonder what the price is on that? Oh here. 2 for 69, Finast, how much are these? (unmarked, asks clerk).

CLERK: 37, I think.

C They're 37? Wow. That's a big difference. Well, could be. Oh, that's for napkins, I see. (the 2 for 69) 37, and these are 37. What about the other ones? Are there any other ones? What about the Scott? Those are 45. I'll get these. By price. We use them up fast, so I might as well get the cheapest thing. Cause I'll be getting more.

J So that's the case of a product where the brand doesn't really matter at all to you?

C No. . . . Paper products don't matter to me.

Judges' responses[b]	A	B	C	D	E	F
Primary	1	0	6	0	0	0
Secondary	1	0	0	0	0	0

C. PREPROCESSED CHOICE EPISODES

Episode 13A

C Mazola. The reason I get that instead of Wesson Oil, as a matter of fact, I used to get Wesson Oil, was that B wanted to try Mazola one time. We had a choice between the two, at one time, and we compared everything on them, what was in them, one was corn oil, and the other being vegetable oil that they were both vegetable oils, and he wanted this kind, and we cooked almost everything, we practically used up the bottle but we tried it on everything that I make, and it came out much better for some reason, so I keep on doing whatever works best. My theory, whatever works.

J How did you decide that it came out better?

C I liked the taste better, and he did too. We both agreed on it. Then we would have had to, if we didn't agree, then we'd have to keep trying one then the other. They've got a new bottle, I think, it did not use to be red in here.

Judges' responses[b]	A	B	C	D	E	F
Primary	1	0	2	4	0	0
Secondary	0	0	1	1	0	0

Episode 38A

C There's what he likes. Small pea beans, that looks like it. Yup, B&M, because that's the kind he likes, he doesn't like any other kind.

Judges' responses[b]	A	B	C	D	E	F
Primary	0	0	0	7	0	0
Secondary	0	0	2	0	0	0

[a]In the protocols, C is the consumer, J the experimenter, and B another consumer.

[b]The codes are A = constructive consumer; B = constructive experimenter: C = analytic implementation; D = preprocessed choice, E = can't tell; and F = other.

EXHIBIT 10.3 Examples of episodes where judges did not agree[a]

Episode 3A

C This part I really can't do without a child to tell me, which cereal is in favor this week.

J It sort of changes from week to week?

C Yes, it does.

Judges' responses[b]	A	B	C	D	E	F
Primary	1	0	2	1	2	1
Secondary	0	1	0	0	0	0

Episode 7A

C There happens to be only one kind of walnuts as far as I can see, but the recipe I'm using required California walnuts, and it says exactly what they want on the recipe. If there were another kind I'd probably still take these, because it's vacuum packed and sometimes you can get them in a kind of sealed plastic container, but I think that they're a lot fresher if they're vacuum packed in a can, so I think I'd probably still get these.

Judges' responses[b]	A	B	C	D	E	F
Primary	3	0	3	1	0	0
Secondary	0	0	1	0	0	0

Episode 19A

C And then I want, um, one stick of butter. So it'll be bound to, whichever kinds come in sticks first, and then Land O'Lake, if it comes in sticks, because I think I've gotten it before, and it's a name brand that I'm familiar with.

Judges' responses[b]	A	B	C	D	E	F
Primary	2	0	4	1	0	0
Secondary	0	0	0	3	0	0

Episode 50B

C Oh, that's dreadful stuff. At least this you can take it out of the bag and the smell is gone after a while, so when you get to use it, it doesn't stick to you. . . . Alright, now what color am I buying? Aqua. Dear me.

J Why did you decide on the Zest?

C Well, I like the, my daughter is starting to have facial difficulties, and she feels that a deodorant soap or hexachlorophene or whatever it is, is good for her face.

J So that, that isn't entirely by price?

C No, so I got the cheapest deodorant soap. And this stuff I use for the downstairs bathroom, where they usually wash their hands.

Judges' responses[b]	A	B	C	D	E	F
Primary	3	1	2	1	0	0
Secondary	0	0	1	1	0	0

[a] In the protocols, C is the consumer, J the experimenter.

[b] The codes are A = constructive consumer; B = constructive experimenter: C = analytic implementation; D = preprocessed choice, E = can't tell; and F = other.

tended to be much more complex than C_4's, often with several decisions inextricably intermixed. C_1 also tended to not verbalize as much as C_4, thus yielding sparser protocol data.

Splitting the 172 episodes into ten basic types of product choices, shows that preprocessed choice is low for meat and produce, as might be expected, since consumers cannot really rely on brand name for most choices of this type. More analytic implementation responses (application of rules) seem to be found, particularly for produce. Preprocessed choice was high for beverages and dairy, where either strong taste preferences may exist or only a limited number of brands are available. Judges tended to agree more for beverage and produce decisions, and less for snacks, desserts, and baking supplies.

Discussion

As noted previously, there were two major purposes in carrying out the study: determining how effective the protocol methodology is for studying constructive processes, and gaining some initial empirical insights into the use of stored rule and constructive processes. Each of these purposes is now considered.

Implications for the Protocol Judging Methodology Used. It was argued that collection of protocols during the actual process of making choices was the best method for studying the use of stored rule and constructive processes. The results of the exploratory study suggest several severe biases and limitations in this methodology.

Several types of biases in the protocols themselves could lead to over representation of both constructive and analytic implementation episodes. First, the protocols were collected in the store, while the consumer was shopping. Since constructive processes will usually be carried out in the store, this will make the protocols appear more constructive than might be the case if the protocols were taken when the shopper's list was being prepared outside the store, for example. Use of the in-store shelf display for making comparisons will lead to more constructive activity, as the consumer is confronted with various types of information on the packages.

A second bias in the protocols occurs because the consumer is asked to give protocols for choices where in many cases a great deal of learning has already occurred. In typical applications of protocol analysis in psychology, the subject is given a task, e.g., proving logic theorems, with which he is not familiar. Then the subject is doing a good deal of thinking in performing the task and can verbalize some portion of this thinking. In the shopping task, however, the consumer may have bought the same brand many times, and may not really think much about this type of choice while it is being made. The request from the experimenter to keep talking may then lead to *retrospection* about why the particular brand was bought in the first place, although such reasoning is not relevant now. This retrospection can appear like construction or analytic implementation, when in reality the choice was preprocessed, with the retrospection an artifact due to the demands to keep talking.

Another major problem with the protocol judging method was the low degree of agreement on episodes obtained. An analysis of those episodes where agreement was not reached suggests that four interrelated reasons seem to account for most of the problems. First, the problem of retrospection led to confusion. If a consumer bought what she always bought, but then gave a rationale for why she had originally started buying that brand, some judges would judge the episodes as preprocessed, while others judged the rationale itself, leading to constructive or analytic implementation responses. Episode 50B in Exhibit 10.2 shows this type of bias, where the consumer had always bought Zest, but gave her reasons in response to the experimenter.

Second, some episodes could be interpreted in several ways, with not enough detail in the protocol to allow an unambiguous interpretation. For example, in Episode 7A in Exhibit 10.3, the judge must decide whether the consumer had a rule in mind based on the recipe and applied that rule or whether she constructed that rationale in the store. Episode 19A poses the same kinds of problems. It can be interpreted as analytic implementation if the judge believes the consumer has a preexisting rule "choose, among kinds which come in sticks, a brand I have bought before," as preprocessed if the judge believes she is reciting a rationale and is merely buying her normal brand, or as constructive if the judge feels the rule did not exist *a priori.*

A third problem, related to the first two, is that the judge has *only the context of a single episode,* since episodes were not grouped by consumer and were judged one at a time. This means that the judge does not know "typical" rules for a consumer. For example, the consumer may always choose large sizes, but if the judge does not know this, the appearance of a statement about large sizes in the protocol may be judged as constructive rather than perhaps analytic implementation. It is very difficult for the judge to ascertain whether a rule preexists the specific episode he is judging or whether the rule was created on the spot. This problem occurred in Episodes 7A and 19A, as noted.

Finally, there were problems with the definition of episodes. Some episodes, such as 3A in Exhibit 10.3, gave virtually no information to the judge. Others had several decisions intermingled, making it difficult for the judge to determine how to respond.

This discussion of biases and limitations of the methodology suggests that to study constructive processes an iterative approach is needed, and that the adequacy of the protocol methodology used in the present study should be examined in some detail to allow improvements in future methods. Several of the choices made in this study regarding the judging task can now be examined in light of this discussion. First, judges were not given detailed judging rules. The major limitation which could be remedied by more detailed rules was the problem of retrospection. Judges could have been instructed to ignore any rationale in judging episodes where the consumer was buying what she always bought. This is not as easy to implement as might be imagined, since in many cases it was not clear from the protocols that the consumer was buying her normal brand. It would not have been possible to deal with the problems of context or interpretation by more detailed judging rules without making unwarranted assumptions, such as "assume that rules mentioned in the protocol exist before the consumer made the choice" (needed to clarify such episodes as 7A or 19A).

A second choice made was to define episodes broadly. As noted, some episodes, like 3A, were not informative enough, whereas others were too complex, containing several choices. A rule that each episode should refer to only one choice would be useful, but it is hard to determine when an episode has enough information to judge.

Finally, episodes were intermixed, so that each consumer's episodes did not appear together. This procedure limits the amount of context information that can be obtained. Episodes could be grouped by consumer, with judges instructed to read through all episodes before judging any. However, this might add its biases and would certainly make the judges' task even more burdensome.

Thus, one purpose of the exploratory study has been accomplished, in that much has been learned about the adequacy of the protocol judging methodology and how that methodology could be improved. First, consumers could be instructed at providing protocols, and told that to provide rationales where they were buying what they always bought. Second, judges could be told to ignore obvious retrospection. Third, multiple decision episodes could be eliminated, episodes could be grouped by consumer, and judges instructed to read each consumer's episodes before beginning judging. This would then necessitate reducing the number of episodes to be given to each judge.

Even with these changes, some ambiguity would remain. The shopping task, as noted, is characterized by a great deal of *prior* learning, which has not been observed. This makes interpretation of protocol data difficult and leads to potential problems of retrospection. In general, therefore, the protocol data, however detailed they may be, are still relatively ambiguous and in many cases uninformative as to the nature of internal processing.[10] Protocol data are perhaps the *most* detailed data collected by consumer researchers, so this poses the question of how one can study use of stored rule, constructive processing, or other similar complex information processing phenomena. Perhaps criteria can be devised which would allow other process

[10]As many researchers have noted and Haines (1974) has explicitly demonstrated, it is also very difficult to develop choice models from protocol data. Haines found that different modelers, given the same protocol data, developed quite different decision net depictions of the choice processes represented by the protocols.

methodologies to be useful;[11] but, as noted earlier, determining when a sequence of eye movements, say, represented a particular type of processing would be exceedingly difficult. The most promising approach seems to be to control experimentally the type of processing required, such as presenting choices for unfamiliar items to attempt to ensure constructive processing, and then trying to measure the nature of the resulting choice process, using process methods such as eye movements, protocols, and so on.

Some Initial Empirical Insights. The results of the exploratory study also have several interesting substantive implications. First, the specific results are congruent with the content of the decision nets for C_1 and C_4 as described in Bettman (1970). One of the major rules used by C_1 was to buy the cheapest, and C_4 used a rule of buying the same as the last time (Bettman 1971). These simple rules are found in the judges' responses: C_1 uses analytic implementation relatively more (calculation of price per unit, implementing her "buy the cheapest" rule) and C_4 is characterized more by preprocessed choice. The results do raise some questions about such past decision net research, however. As noted earlier, Nakanishi (1974) had questioned the depiction of decision nets as fixed programs invoked by the consumer for each choice as net research had treated these models.[12] The evidence for some degree of constructive processing found in the present study supports Nakanishi's contention. This then raises the issue of the meaning of past decision net models—are the nets depicted merely the results of particular construction processes, which may change from one choice occasion to the next; are they a kind of "average" depiction of these constructions; or are they some further alternative? This question cannot be answered given the present data, but this points out the need for research which can characterize constructive processes in terms of possible underlying regularities.

A second set of substantive implications concerns the specific proportions of each processing type found. If constructive, analytic implementation, and preprocessed choice are roughly related to Howard and Sheth's (1969) extensive problem solving, limited problem solving, and routinized response behavior, respectively, then this study represents the first empirical work on the extent of these stages. The surprising aspect of the percentages presented here, perhaps, is the relatively large number of constructive and analytic implementation episodes relative to preprocessed choice episodes. There is certainly evidence for a good deal of consumer learning of rules as units, but there is also much continuing information processing by the two consumers studied. As noted previously, the percentage of constructive and analytic implementation episodes may be biased upward. These figures are specific to the task and consumers used.

A final set of substantive implications relates to the notion of constructive processes as being synthesized during the process of choice rather than *a priori*. This view emphasizes the need for examining such factors as the form in which information is presented, the processability of such information, and other properties of the choice environment which might affect how information is acquired and integrated (Bettman 1975; Russo, Krieser, and Miyashita 1975). Also, this view points out the importance of influencing the consumer in the store, at the moment of decision, for decisions where there is little prior knowledge or experience; not necessarily relying on out-of-store information presentations or influence attempts. This is true both for the policymaker, who may wish to present information in the choice environment in addition to or in place of using media such as television advertising, and for the marketer.

Thus the present paper has introduced some new concepts about how consumers carry out choices, has considered how one might study these concepts, and has reported an exploratory study designed to provide insights into both

---

[11] For example, see studies of the eye movements (Russo and Rosen 1975) or of information acquisition (Bettman and Jacoby 1975).

[12] Thus Bettman (1970) applies the net in a fixed manner to data for each choice.

these concepts and the methodology proposed. The results suggest substantial changes in the kinds of methodologies required, and yield some interesting empirical findings. Further characterization of the ways in which consumers implement choices seems to be an intriguing area for future research, although studies of such details of consumer processing seem to be more difficult than might have been anticipated.

REFERENCES

BARTLETT, F. C. (1932), *Remembering.* Cambridge, England: Cambridge University Press.

BETTMAN, JAMES R. (1970), "Information Processing Models of Consumer Behavior," *Journal of Marketing Research,* 7, 370-376.

——— (1971), "The Structure of Consumer Choice Processes," *Journal of Marketing Research,* 8, 465-471.

——— (1975), "Issues in Designing Consumer Information Environments," *Journal of Consumer Research,* 2, 169-177.

——— (1977), "Data Collection and Analysis Approaches for Studying Consumer Information Processing," in *Advances in Consumer Research,* Vol. 4, Ed. William D. Perreault, Jr. Chicago: Association for Consumer Research, 342-348.

———, and JACOBY, JACOB (1976), "Patterns of Processing in Consumer Information Acquisition," in *Advances in Consumer Research,* Vol. 3, Ed. Beverlee B. Anderson. Chicago: Association for Consumer Research, 315-320.

BRANSFORD, JOHN D., BARCLAY, J. RICHARD, and FRANKS, JEFFREY J. (1972), "Sentence Memory: A Constructive Versus Interpretive Approach," *Cognitive Psychology,* 3, 193-209.

———, and FRANKS, JEFFREY J. (1971), "The Abstraction of Linguistic Ideas," *Cognitive Psychology,* 2, 331-350.

COFER, CHARLES N. (1973), "Constructive Processes in Memory," *American Scientist,* 61, 537-543.

FRANKS, JEFFREY J., and BRANSFORD, JOHN D. (1971), "Abstraction of Visual Patterns," *Journal of Experimental Psychology,* 90, 65-74.

GOMULICKI, B. R. (1956), "Recall as an Abstractive Process," *Acta Psychologica,* 12, 77-94.

HAINES, GEORGE H. (1974), "Process Models of Consumer Decision Making," in *Buyer/Consumer Information Processing,* Eds. G. David Hughes and Michael L. Ray. Chapel Hill, NC: University of North Carolina Press, 89-107.

HANSEN, FLEMMING, (1972), *Consumer Choice Behavior: A Cognitive Theory.* New York: Free Press.

HOWARD, JOHN A., and SHETH, JAGDISH N. (1969), *The Theory of Buyer Behavior.* New York: Wiley.

JARVELLA, ROBERT J. (1971), "Syntactic Processing of Connected Speech," *Journal of Verbal Learning and Verbal Behavior,* 10, 409-416.

LOFTUS, ELIZABETH F. (1975), "Leading Questions and the Eyewitness Report," *Cognitive Psychology,* 7, 560-572.

MANDLER, JEAN M., and JOHNSON, NANCY S. (1977), "Remembrance of Things Parsed: Story Structure and Recall," *Cognitive Psychology,* 9, 111-151.

NAKANISHI, MASAO (1974), "Decision Net Models and Human Information Processing," in *Buyer/Consumer Information Processing,* Eds. G. David Hughes and Michael L. Ray. Chapel Hill, NC: University of North Carolina Press, 75-88.

NEISSER, ULRIC (1967), *Cognitive Psychology.* New York: Appleton-Century-Crofts.

PRAWAT, RICHARD S., CANCELLI, ANTHONY, and COOK, BRUCE (1976), "A Developmental Study of Constructive Memory," *Journal of Psychology,* 92, 257-60.

ROBINSON, PATRICK J., FARIS, CHARLES W., and WIND, YORAM (1967), *Industrial Buying and Creative Marketing.* Boston: Allyn & Bacon.

RUSSO, J. EDWARD, KRIESER, GENE, and MIYASHITA, SALLY (1975), "An Effective Display of Unit Price Information," *Journal of Marketing,* 39, 11-9.

———, and ROSEN, LARRY D. (1975), "An Eye Fixation Analysis of Multi-Alternative Choice," *Memory and Cognition,* 3, 267-276.

SACHS, JACQUELINE (1967), "Recognition Memory for Syntactic and Semantic Aspects of Connected Discourse," *Perception and Psychophysics,* 2, 437-442.

THORNDYKE, PERRY W. (1977), "Cognitive Structures in Comprehension and Memory of Narrative Discourse," Cognitive Psychology, 9, 77-110.

WRIGHT, PETER L., and BARBOUR, FREDERIC (1975), "The Relevance of Decision Process Models in Structuring Persuasive Messages," *Communication Research,* 2, 246-259.

ZANGWILL, O. L. (1972), "Remembering Revisited," *Quarterly Journal of Experimental Psychology,* 24, 123-138.

EFFECTS OF PRIOR KNOWLEDGE AND EXPERIENCE AND PHASE OF THE CHOICE PROCESS ON CONSUMER DECISION PROCESSES: A Protocol Analysis*

11

James R. Bettman
C. Whan Park

Effects of prior knowledge and experience and phase of the choice on decision processes were investigated using a protocol coding scheme. Consumers with moderate knowledge and experience did more processing of available information than did the high or low groups. More knowledgeable consumers tended to process by brand. Consumers tended to use attribute-based evaluations in early and brand-based evaluations in later phases of choice.

Two primary aspects of the consumer choice environment are: (1) there is usually a great deal of product information available and (2) consumers often have prior experience with products. Despite this observation, the effect of prior knowledge and experience on consumer choice processes has been a relatively neglected area of research. There have been several conceptual analyses, ranging from early theorizing on the effects of varying levels of prior experience (Hansen 1972; Howard 1977; Howard and Sheth 1969) to recent treatments of consumer memory processes (Bettman 1979; Olson 1978). In addition, there has been research on how prior choices affect present choices (e.g., the linear learning model). However, there has been relatively little empirical work on the effects of knowledge and experience on choice *processes* (Edell and Mitchell 1978; Olson and Muderrisoglu 1979; Park 1976; Russo and Johnson 1980).

*Reprinted from the *Journal of Consumer Research,* 7, (December, 1980), pp. 234–248.

Additional research on how prior knowledge and experience affect choice processes seems potentially quite valuable. The presence or absence of knowledge structures of various sorts should affect the types of information processed and the processing heuristics used by consumers. For example, inexperienced consumers may spend more time evaluating levels of attributes as they try to develop criteria for choice than consumers with more knowledge and experience.

In addition to prior knowledge and experience, other factors can influence the form of choice processes. The phase of the process is a factor that has been shown to have such effects. That is, consumers may use different types of information and heuristics at different stages of a choice. For example, comparisons of attribute levels to standards may be used early in a choice process to eliminate brands (Lussier and Olshavsky 1979). Simultaneous study of both phase and knowledge and experience effects may be particularly useful, as prior knowledge and experience and phase may interact in some cases. That is, choice processes may unfold in different ways, depending on the knowledge structures present. For example, when using comparisons to standards, consumers with prior knowledge and experience may tend to use such standards earlier in the choice process than consumers without such existing knowledge. The inexperienced consumers may need to spend some time developing such standards.

Research concerning these effects on choice processes is important for two reasons. First, both marketers and policymakers provide information at various points during the choice process to consumers with varying levels of experience. Insights into how phase and knowledge and experience effect choice processing are needed to determine what types of information might be most effective for various types of consumers during each phase. Second, research on the effects of phase and prior knowledge and experience on choice processes is important for theory. As just noted, consumer choice theories postulate such effects, but little empirical research has been done. In addition, the research so far (e.g., Bettman 1979, pp. 215–216) has not considered both phase and prior knowledge and experience simultaneously.

Much of this prior theorizing on the effects of phase and prior knowledge and experience concerns processing details (e.g., differing use of attribute evaluations in different phases of choice, use of brand versus attribute processing in various phases, and so on). In order to investigate these processes proposed by theory, this study developed a procedure that allows examination of the details of choice processing, utilizing verbal protocol data (obtained from having consumers think aloud). There are many ways that such protocol data can be analyzed. However, consideration of the implications of a constructive view of choice for analysis of protocol data led to the development of a particular analytic approach. That approach and its rationale are now considered (Bettman and Park 1980).

The basic concept underlying a constructive view of choice (Bettman 1979; Bettman and Zins 1979) is that consumers may not have complete rules or heuristics stored in memory, which they use to make a choice. Rather, consumers may have only fragments or elements of heuristics in memory, which are put together during the actual choice process to "construct" a heuristic. Such elements may be beliefs about alternatives, evaluations, simple rules of thumb (e.g., "compare these brands on attribute A to see if they differ very much"), rules for integrating data (e.g., "count how many attributes alternative X is best on"), and so on.

To the extent that such elements are put together at the time of choice, the elements used for a particular choice and the sequence in which they are used will be a function of such factors as: what externally present information is available; the format in which that information is presented; the degree to which various pieces of information "stand out" in the environment; intermediate processing results; and other task-specific factors. Thus, the choice heuristics that result from the construction process may vary from one situation to the next. Constructive processes will not always be used, of course. Where there is a great deal of prior experience with a choice, consumers may have more complete heuristics available in memory.

This notion of constructive processes has important implications for the analysis of protocol data on choice processes. If consumers build up heuristics as they go along, and the elements used are sensitive to many task-specific factors (salience, format, and so on), the resulting choice "heuristic" may consist of a sequence of elements with no necessarily coherent overall structure. The following sequence illustrates this point:

1. A consumer considers several attributes to see if their levels are acceptable for several brands (a component of a conjunctive rule).
2. The consumer then notes a good value for a particular brand on some attribute, and eliminates all brands still being considered that are not "close" to that value.
3. Next, the consumer compares two brands to see which is better on more attributes, and so on.

Thus, each element or short sequence of elements may be used *to process only a few brands.* Different sequences of elements are used for different brands. Lest this appear farfetched, examples of this fragmented overall structure appeared in many of the individual protocols used in this study. One does not often find systematic use of well-structured "rules" such as lexicographic, conjunctive, or linear compensatory in these protocol data. Thus, looking for an overall strategy or rule applied to all brands may be unsuccessful.

These arguments lead to an extension of the notion that the choice heuristic used is contingent on the choice task. Prior research guided by this contingency perspective has examined relatively stable properties of the task—time pressure (Wright 1974), format (Bettman and Zins 1979), incomplete information (Slovic and MacPhillamy 1974), type of response required (Slovic 1972), and so on. However, the constructive view implies a more complex notion of contingency, where many properties of the "choice task" itself change as the consumer progresses. Thus, the elements of choice heuristics used may not even be the same for all brands during a given choice. The task is *not* the same for all brands. The constructive view implies a more detailed contingency notion: the *elements* of choice heuristics used at any given time are contingent on the properties of the choice task at that particular time.[1]

In this view, the detailed elements of choice heuristics are the most appropriate unit of analysis for research on choice processes. Hence, a detailed scheme for coding protocol data for such elements was developed (Bettman and Park 1979; 1980) and is used here. In summary, the purpose of the present study is twofold: to gain insights into the ways in which phase of the process and prior knowledge and experience affect choice processes, and to present a methodology for studying choice processes that is sufficiently detailed to capture such insights.

HYPOTHESES

Two main types of effects of phase and prior knowledge and experience on choice processes were investigated in this study: effects on the *types of information used,* and effects on the kinds of *processing* used. In considering these effects, three levels of prior knowledge and experience are distinguished: low, moderate, and high. Operationalization of these levels, of the phases of the choice process, and of the other concepts considered in the hypothesis is deferred until a later section.

---

[1]This detailed contingency notion is similar to the production system concept of Newell and Simon (1972). A production system consists of a set of individual productions, each consisting of a condition and an action. When the condition is met, the corresponding action is executed. A production system operates by having control start at the top of the list of productions, with the condition portion of each production tested until a condition is met. Then the corresponding action is taken and control once again reverts to the top of the set of productions (pp. 44–46). An example of a production for a consumer choice might be: "If the number of brands to be compared is two, and the number of attributes for each is greater than three, then count the number of desirable features for each brand."

Effects on Types of Information Used

Consumers engaged in a choice process can focus on information they bring with them from prior search or experience, or information available in the choice situation itself (e.g., on packages). One seemingly obvious hypothesis might be that the relative degree of usage of "prior" information would increase directly with the level of prior knowledge and experience. However, although this straightforward hypothesis may be true for simple choice tasks, consumers engaged in complex choice tasks and low in prior knowledge and experience ("low" consumers) may find it overwhelming to attempt to process the available information. Hence, they may rely more on what prior information they have, even though they may have very little. For a complex and difficult choice task, low and high consumers may, then, rely relatively more on prior information than moderate consumers. As the choice task used in the current study (a hypothetical choice among microwave ovens) seems fairly complex, this latter reasoning is used. Other studies provide indirect support for this notion. For example, more effort may be devoted to tasks of moderate difficulty than to tasks of high or low difficulty (Weiner, Heckhausen, Meyer, and Cook 1972).

Use of prior knowledge might also vary over the time phase of the choice process. Prior information could be very useful in narrowing the scope of the choice task early in the process by allowing the consumer to focus on certain brands and attributes. More reliance on information available in the choice task itself may be found in later phases.

H1: The reliance on information from prior search and experience is:

- highest for consumers low or high in prior knowledge and experience, and lowest for consumers with moderate experience and prior knowledge;
- negatively related to the phase of the choice process, i.e., highest for the earliest phase of the choice process, and lowest for the final phase.

A second hypothesis concerns the degree to which consumers engage in various types of evaluations regarding attribute levels or weights. These evaluations might be either statements of preference for particular attribute levels, or statements of attribute weight or importance. Several theorists have argued that consumers with varying degrees of prior knowledge and experience engage in qualitatively different types of choice processes (Hansen 1972; Howard 1977; Howard and Sheth 1969). In perhaps the best known of these theories, Howard and Sheth (1969) and Howard (1977) postulate that consumers with little experience and knowledge engage in extensive problem solving. In particular, the consumer must "form criteria by which to identify and judge all things in the class" (Howard 1977, p. 87). Thus, one would hypothesize that consumers lower in prior knowledge and experience attempt to use relatively more evaluations of attribute levels and weights, whereas more knowledgeable consumers use fewer such evaluations. If consumers with little knowledge and experience prove unable to perform such evaluations, however, then this hypothesized pattern of results might not occur.

The pattern of use of evaluations should also change over the course of the choice process. As consumers eventually have to *choose* some alternative, they should rely less on such evaluations of attributes and more on actual processing and comparison of alternatives as the choice process unfolds (Russo and Johnson 1980). Thus, one should find lower usage of attribute evaluations in the later phases of the choice process. One might then postulate the following based on the above arguments:

H2: The usage of evaluations of attribute levels and weights is:

- negatively related to degree of prior knowledge and experience;
- negatively related to phase of the choice process (highest for the earliest phase; lowest for the final phase).

Effects on Types of Processing

One area in which a reasonable amount of research has been done concerns the degree to which consumers process by attribute or by brand. In attribute processing, a consumer first examines values for several brands on a particular attribute, then selects another attribute and compares several brands on it, and so on. In brand processing, a consumer might select one brand, examine several of its attributes, then select another brand and consider its attributes, and so on. Previous research has considered both experience and choice phase effects on the degree of attribute versus brand processing. Jacoby, Chestnut, Weigl, and Fisher (1976), Bettman and Kakkar (1977), and van Raaij (1976, p. 170) all find that greater knowledge and experience is associated with increased brand processing, perhaps because this greater experience takes place in a brand-based environment. However, the evidence for the effects of choice phase is more ambiguous. Johnson and Russo (1978), Russo and Johnson (1980), and van Raaij (1976, pp. 75 and 157) provide support for highest attribute processing early in the choice process, and highest brand processing late in the choice process. However, Bettman (1979, pp. 219–221) summarizes work that suggests that brand processing may be used in early phases to eliminate alternatives, with more attribute processing used in later phases. The latter hypothesis will be used, although the mixed results above do not allow a confident choice.

H3: The degree of attribute processing is:

- negatively related to degree of prior knowledge and experience;
- positively related to phase in the choice process.

The degree of brand processing follows the reverse pattern.

A second area for hypotheses about processing details concerns the use of comparison of attribute levels to standards. When using comparisons to standards, consumers relate a brand's level on a single attribute to some cutoff, without making tradeoffs across attributes. Consumers can use comparisons to standards in either attribute (e.g., elimination by aspects) or brand (e.g., conjunctive) processing. One might hypothesize the use of such comparisons in early phases of the choice process to eliminate alternatives.

It is not clear what hypothesis might be made about the main effects of prior knowledge and experience on usage of comparison to standards. However, there may be an interaction with choice phase: consumers with little knowledge or experience may need time to develop standards, and, hence, use standards more in the middle phases of choice, whereas experienced consumers may use standards more in the earliest phases.

H4: The use of comparisons to standards:

- is negatively related to phase in the choice process;
- displays an interaction between phase in the choice process and degree of prior knowledge and experience.

One final area in which processing details can be examined concerns elements compatible with various choice "rules." For example, the element "compare an attribute level to a standard," when used in a brand-processing fashion, may be a component of a conjunctive rule. In a similar fashion, elements that are compatible with each of several such "standard" choice rules can be enumerated. Hypotheses can then be made about these elements based on prior research on choice rule usage (Bettman 1979, pp. 214–215; Park 1976).[2] In general, this re-

[2]The choice rules to be considered are conjunctive, lexicographic, elimination by aspects, heuristic additive difference, weighted compensatory, and a counting rule. Descriptions of all of those except heuristic additive difference and a counting rule can be found in Bettman (1979, pp. 179–182). Versions of the heuristic additive difference rule have been found by Russo and Dosher (1975), Wright and Barbour (1977), and Lussier and Olshavsky (1979). In applying this rule, the consumer considers attribute differences across two or more brands, and then trades off these differences in some fashion. A typical tradeoff procedure may be to count which brand is better on more attributes. For more details on this rule, see Bettman and Zins (1979).

search supports the notions that "simple" rules (i.e., rules that require only simple calculations to be performed in comparing alternatives, such as comparing values on one attribute or counting features—lexicographic, heuristic additive difference, and counting rules) tend to be used more by consumers with little prior knowledge and experience. Use of more complex rules appears to be associated with greater experience, e.g., conjunctive elimination by aspects, and weighted compensatory.[3] It is, of course, possible that the reasoning underlying Hypothesis 1 could be used to argue that use of all of these rules should be highest for consumers with moderate levels of knowledge and experience; prior research provides some support for this motion, e.g., Park 1976 for the conjunctive rule. However, there is so little knowledge about the effects of experience on specific choice heuristics that it was considered more appropriate to postulate the simpler monotonic relationships for the present.

With regard to usage during the course of the choice process, prior research has shown that some rules tend to be used in early phases to eliminate alternatives, e.g., conjunctive and elimination by aspects, whereas others are used in later phases. The following hypotheses stem from this kind of reasoning (specific studies are cited for each hypothesis where appropriate). Note that these hypotheses refer to *elements* of these rules, not the rules themselves.

H5: Degree of prior knowledge and experience is:

- positively related to the usage of elements compatible with the conjunctive, elimination by aspects, and weighted compensatory (Park 1976) rules;
- negatively related to the usage of elements compatible with the lexicographic, heuristic additive difference, and counting rules.

H6: Phase in the choice process is:

- positively related to the usage of elements compatible with the lexicographic (Wright and Barbour 1977), heuristic additive difference, weighted compensatory, and counting rules;
- negatively related to the usage of elements compatible with the conjunctive (Lussier and Olshavsky 1979; Pras and Summers 1975) and elimination by aspects (Payne 1976) rules.

METHOD

Subjects

The subjects were 99 housewives in a midwestern college community. Roughly 80 percent of these subjects were obtained by random selection from the telephone directory. Each individual was called, informed about the study, and asked to participate. The refusal rate was very low, less than 10 percent. Each participant was then scheduled for a personal interview, for which she received a five-dollar payment. In addition, potential participants were screened during the phone call on their prior knowledge and experience with microwave ovens, the product used in the study. A consumer durable with fairly low levels of usage in the population was chosen so that more separation on the degree of prior knowledge and experience could be achieved.

Subjects were asked specifically whether they had ever searched for information on,

---

The counting rule found in the protocols of this study was a very simple one. Subjects appeared to count the numbers of desirable and undesirable features possessed by each alternative, and use these counts to make brand comparisons.

[3]This reasoning becomes more complex if the notions of attribute and brand processing are also considered. As noted in Hypothesis 3, attribute processing may be used more by consumers with little prior knowledge and experience, with the reverse true for brand processing. This would imply that rules based on attribute processing (lexicographic, elimination by aspects, heuristic additive difference) would be used more by consumers without much experience, with rules based on brand processing (conjunctive, weighted compensatory, and counting) used more by experienced consumers. Thus, the rationale based on the complexity of the rule and that based on brand versus attribute processing agree for the elements of conjunctive, lexicographic, heuristic additive difference, and weighted compensatory rules, and disagree for elements of elimination by aspects and counting rules. The hypotheses for these latter rules are, therefore, less clear.

used, or owned a microwave oven. Subjects who responded negatively to all three of these questions were assigned to the Low Prior Knowledge and Experience group. Subjects who had searched for information or used, but not owned, a microwave oven were assigned to the Moderate group. Subjects who owned a microwave oven were assigned to the High Prior Knowledge and Experience group. In an attempt to balance roughly the number of subjects in these three groups, the remaining 20 percent of the subjects were selected from the wives of faculty and friends, and screened in a similar fashion until enough subjects were available for each group. The resulting group sizes were Low 37, Moderate 29, and High 33.

In addition to the screening questions, a further manipulation of knowledge was carried out. Subjects in the Moderate and High groups were mailed information on microwave ovens and on various attributes of microwave ovens. These subjects were instructed to read this material before the personal interview and once again during the interview before the actual choice task. The screening questions and the reading material were designed to obtain some separation across groups in the degree of prior knowledge and experience. The Low group clearly appears to differ from the Moderate and High groups. The procedure for the Moderate and High groups was intended to equate these groups to some degree on certain aspects of product knowledge, but to leave these two groups clearly differing in product ownership and degree of usage experience.

Procedure and Tasks

Subjects were personally interviewed by graduate students who were unaware of the research hypotheses. Subjects were given a questionnaire to complete, which first asked them to rate their familiarity with microwave ovens as a manipulation check. Subjects were then given a matrix table of data on microwave ovens, as shown in Table 11.1 This table provides information on nine attributes for 15 brands of microwave ovens. This task mirrors the information individuals might obtain from a publication such as *Consumer Reports*. However, it does not reflect the information structure present in a store, in advertising, or in other situations.

Subjects were then asked to perform two choice tasks. First, they were asked to select all those brands that would be acceptable to them from the matrix. The time taken for selection was recorded and perceived task difficulty and choice confidence were measured. Subjects were then asked to choose the brand they most preferred from the set of acceptable brands. Time taken was again recorded, and perceived task difficulty and several other variables were measured (for analysis of these and other more aggregate variables, see Park and Lessig 1979). During both choice tasks, the subjects were asked to think aloud, and their verbalizations were tape recorded. Thus, the consumer's choice process was split into an "elimination stage," where acceptable brands were chosen, and a "choice stage," where a final choice was made.[4]

Analysis of the Protocols

The protocols were first transcribed from the tapes. Usable elimination stage protocol data obtained from 68 subjects and complete protocol data from 62 subjects were available for analysis.[5] Of these 62 subjects, 23 were in the Low, 16 in the Moderate, and 23 in the High groups, respectively.

The protocols were then edited and divided by the authors into short phrases; each phrase consisted of a single task-related statement

[4]Several studies support the existence of such stages (Bettman 1979, pp. 215–216). Therefore, structuring the task so that subjects must use such stages does not seem inappropriate. In future studies, however, researchers should also examine the present hypotheses without imposing such a structure. That is, one might simply ask subjects to choose a brand, in order to determine if structuring the study into stages biases the results in some way.

[5]The loss of subjects was due largely to technical problems: protocols for 14 subjects were understandable only in part or totally unintelligible due to background noise; a tape containing protocols for 17 subjects was inadvertently destroyed; and the choice stage was mistakenly not recorded for six subjects.

TABLE 11.1 Data on Microwave Ovens

Brand	*Price*	*Microwave distribution*	*Number of cooking levels*	*Temperature scale timer*	*Temperature setting*	*Browner*	*Microwave leakage*[a] *(mW/cm²)*	*Safety start*	*Capacity (cubic feet)*
Montgomery Ward	$500	F	7	Y	Y	Y	2.0	Y	1.21
Litton	500	F	6	Y	Y	N	3.0	N	1.17
Amana	500	F	6	Y	N	N	0.7	Y	1.03
Magic Chef	370	F	5	Y	N	N	>20	N	.71
Montgomery Ward	380	F	7	Y	Y	N	2.5	Y	.79
Sears	370	F	10	Y	N	N	3.0	Y	1.25
Montgomery Ward	350	F	2	Y	N	N	2.3	Y	1.41
Amana	418	F	2	N	N	N	0.9	Y	1.03
Litton	400	F	6	Y	N	N	2.9	N	1.17
Sharp	500	RT	4	Y	N	N	0.5	Y	1.41
Sharp	540	RT	4	Y	N	Y	0.6	Y	1.17
Frigidaire	560	F	3	Y	N	N	1.2	Y	1.03
Sears	300	F	4	N	N	N	2.2	Y	0.79
Hotpoint (GE)	300	F	1	N	N	N	6.5	N	1.32
Sears	420	F	10	Y	Y	N	3.1	Y	1.25

[a]Measured under severe conditions of use that are contrary to manufacturer's instructions. (When radiation leakage was checked under conditions specified by the manufacturer, none of the models leaked in excess of 0.5 mW/cm^2.)

Note: F means a stirring fan is used; RT means a rotating turntable is used; Y means yes; N means no.

(Newell and Simon 1972; Payne and Ragsdale 1978).[6] The length of these phrases depends to some extent on the focus of the research. The coding scheme presented here focuses on processing details to a large extent. Thus, phrases related to such details tended to be short. However, phrases recounting prior knowledge and experience in some detail could be rather lengthy. On the average, there were roughly 34 phrases per protocol.

Each protocol was then coded using the protocol coding scheme described in more detail by Bettman and Park (1979; 1980). The final categories used and their frequencies of occurrence in all 68 available protocols are shown in the Appendix. After pilot testing and revising the codes on six of the protocols, the authors served as independent judges in coding the remaining 62. For these 62 protocols, 1,977 phrases were coded. The two coders agreed on 1,547 phrases, or 78.3 percent. The phrases upon which the coders disagreed were discussed by them until a code was agreed upon. The percentage of agreement ranged from 49 percent to 100 percent across the 62 individuals examined.[7]

Operationalization of the Hypotheses

In considering how the concepts utilized in the hypotheses were operationalized, the division of the protocols into phases is examined first, and then the usage of the various codes is discussed.

The protocols were naturally divided into two stages, elimination and choice, by the structure of the tasks outlined earlier. The average number of phrases in these two stages was 29.0 and 5.8, respectively. Hence, it was felt that the most appropriate way to divide the total choice task into phases of reasonable length, and to preserve the nature of each phase, was to have three phases: (1) the first half (in number of phrases) of the elimination stage; (2) the second half of the elimination stage; and (3) the choice stage. These three phases were used in the later analyses. It is possible that the division of the process into phases in this manner may not have the same meaning for subjects with differing degrees of prior knowledge and experience. For example, the highly experienced subject may have already gone through an elimination stage prior to the experiment. However, dividing the protocol into the three phases described above seems to preserve the relative lengths of the stages in the current experiment, as well as possible.

It is obvious from examination of the frequencies in the Appendix that some individual codes may occur rather infrequently. Thus, in many cases one must use combinations of codes for meaningful analysis. To operationalize many of the dependent variables for the hypotheses, several codes were aggregated. In all cases, the attempt was made to choose the most reasonable combinations, as discussed later. However, many combinations are often plausible, so these aggregations represent only one interpretation of the meaning of the hypotheses.

The operationalization of the three phases resulted in phases with different numbers of coded phrases, i.e., phases one and two are either equal or differ in length by one phrase if the elimination phase had an odd number of phrases; these two phases are typically longer than phase three, the choice stage, as noted earlier. Therefore, the measures for the combinations of codes used below are standardized. That is, these measures are computed as the number of coded phrases for each combination occurring in each phase, divided by the total

---

[6]The editing consisted of removing any portions containing interviewer interaction with the subject, other than simple reminders to keep verbalizing. Such interactions were typically attempts by the interviewer to obtain a summary of the process to that point in time. These interactions were always easy to discern and remove as a single "unit." The incidence of such interactions was spread roughly evenly across the three experimental groups.

[7]Only one subject had less than 50 percent agreement, and for 56 of the 62 subjects the percentage was 60 percent or greater.

See Bettman and Park (1980) for further details on the coding scheme and its implementation. The analyses reported in this study use only the 62 individuals with complete protocol data.

number of phrases for that phase, e.g., if the combination of codes occurred two times in a phase that had 18 phrases in total, the measure used for that combination of codes for that phase was 2/18, or 0.111. Now the operationalizations for each hypothesis are considered.

Hypothesis 1. Hypothesis 1 does not distinguish among types of information based on prior search and experience. Hence, all such types of information are included in testing the hypothesis. In the formulation of the coding scheme, information based on prior search and experience was grouped together as Codes E1 to E20.[8] Hence, the amount of information based on prior search and experience is operationalized by summing these codes. One shortcoming of the verbal protocol data is that subjects do not always verbalize enough to allow one to determine whether information is based on prior knowledge. The judges simply coded the phrases as well as they could, given the verbal data available.

Hypothesis 2. An index was formed summarizing use of evaluations of attribute levels and weights. It was composed of codes specifically mentioning attribute evaluations, weights, and their rationales (A10–A13 for continuous attributes and A14–A15 for binary or discrete attributes); the code for comparisons of attribute weights, A19; and two other codes, A4 and A8. These latter codes were included because they refer to operations (finding the range on an attribute and finding the number of brands with a particular level on an attribute) used by the subjects to infer attribute weight or importance. Codes such as A16 and A17 were not included because they involved trading off attribute *differences,* which was felt to be more closely related to comparison of alternatives than to formation of criteria.

Hypothesis 3. The phrases in the protocols were coded by the authors as to whether brand or attribute processing was occurring, e.g., phrases 1–6 might show brand processing, phrases 7–10 attribute processing, and so on. All phrases were coded into two categories of processing, brand or attribute. Then the number of phrases showing each type of processing in each phase was counted and divided by the total number of phrases in that phase. This relatively rough approach was taken, rather than using more detailed categories (e.g., brand, attribute, or other) because, in most cases, the protocols are not complete enough to determine detailed transitions with the accuracy required.[9]

Hypothesis 4. The usage of comparison to standards was examined by combining codes A7, A9, A18, and B4. Codes A9 and B4 refer to explicit comparison to a standard. Codes A7 and A18 were also included because it was felt that searching for alternatives with particular attribute levels involved an implicit comparison to a standard.

Hypotheses 5 and 6. The following combinations of codes were used to measure elements related to the various heuristics: conjunctive (B4); lexicographic (A5, A6); elimination by aspects (A7, A9, A18); heuristic additive difference (A1, A2, A3, A16, A17, A20); compensatory (B9, B10, B11); and counting (B5, B6). Brief rationales are now presented for these combinations of codes. For the conjunctive rule, the major feature is comparison of attribute levels to a standard in a brand processing fashion. Hence, Code B4 was used. Finding the best or worst brand on an attribute is the major feature of a lexicographic rule, hence A5 and A6 were used. Attribute importance ratings are also a part of the lexicographic rule (finding the most important attribute). However, none of the attribute codes developed refer specifically

[8]See the Appendix. Codes E21 to E24 were not included because they refer mainly to statements of lack of knowledge rather than to reliance on specific knowledge.

[9]This assessment of brand versus attribute processing was used rather than simply summing B1–B11 or A1–A21, because it was felt the judgmental procedure was a more reasonable measure. For example, a subject might, in the middle of processing all the attributes of a given brand, say: "It has a browner. I prefer to have a browner." This would have been divided into two phrases, one for each sentence, and the second would have been coded as A14. Thus, adding the A or B codes could provide a misleading picture.

to finding the most important attribute, so this aspect was not included.

For the elimination by aspects heuristic, the major feature is comparison of attribute levels to standards in an attribute processing manner. The codes that refer to either explicit (A9) or implicit (A7, A18) comparisons to standards were used. In the heuristic additive difference rule, consumers take attribute differences or compare brands on an attribute to see which is better (A1, A2, A3). Then they either trade off those differences (A16, A17) or compare counts of the number of features on which each brand is most desirable (A20).

Developing combinations for the compensatory and counting rules was the most difficult. For the compensatory heuristic, a wide range of codes could be included, ranging from all the attribute weight and evaluation codes to simple statements of brand-attribute features (e.g., B1). However, inclusion of such a range was felt to be too broad to interpret the results meaningfully. A narrow approach was taken, therefore, where only codes specifically referring to within-brand compensatory processes (B9) or overall evaluations (B10, B11) were used. Finally, delineation of the counting rule elements was also not obvious. In particular, it was very difficult to determine the most appropriate placement for A20, with the heuristic additive difference rule or the counting rule. It was decided to place it with heuristic additive difference, as the main feature of the observed counting rule was by far the prevalence of counts of positive and negative features (B5, B6).[10]

[10]The percentage of initial agreement between coders was also computed for the various code combinations noted above. These percentages were H1 (E1–E20, 79 percent), H2 (A4, A8, A10–A15, A19, 82 percent), H4 (A7, A9, A18, B4, 49 percent), H5 and H6 (B4, 60 percent; A5, A6, 65 percent; A7, A9, A18, 33 percent; A1, A2, A3, A16, A17, A20, 71 percent; B9, B10, B11, 75 percent; and B5, B6, 94 percent). These percentages are for the most part reasonably high. However, those codes for comparison to standards in an attribute fashion were subject to a great deal of initial disagreement between coders. Although these initial disagreements were resolved upon discussion, results involving these codes might best be regarded with more caution.

The hypotheses were each tested using the measures for the various combinations of codes as the dependent measures, with a one-between, one-within mixed factor analysis of variance design. The three phases of the choice process provided the levels for the within-subjects factor phase. The degree of prior knowledge and experience, a between-subjects factor, also had three levels, Low, Medium, and High, as previously discussed.

RESULTS

Manipulation Check

The manipulation of prior knowledge and experience was examined by performing a one-way analysis of variance on subjects' responses to the question: "How familiar are you with microwave ovens?" (5 = very familiar, 1 = unfamiliar). Familiarity was defined in the questionnaire for the subjects in terms of their knowledge about which features are important in choosing among microwave ovens. The groups differed significantly on the familiarity responses in the expected direction ($p < 0.0001$). It was also determined that the Low group (mean = 1.74) was less familiar than the Moderate group (mean = 3.19) ($p < 0.001$), and that the Moderate group was less familiar than the High group (mean = 4.17) ($p < 0.001$).[11]

Hypothesis 1

Hypothesis 1 proposed that use of information based on prior search and experience is highest for the Low and High groups, and is highest for the earliest phase of the choice process. The mean values for the measures based on the sum of codes E1 to E20 are shown in Table 11.2. The analysis of variance results show a main effect for prior knowledge and experience ($p < 0.04$), no main effect for

[11]Here and in the rest of the paper, all planned comparisons are made with one-tailed *t*-tests using the between-subjects error term from the overall analysis of variance.

TABLE 11.2 Treatment Means for Hypotheses 1–4

Degree of prior knowledge and experience/phase of choice process	*Sum of E1–E20 (H1)*	*Attribute evaluation index (H2)*	*Attribute processing (H3)*	*Comparison to standards (H4)*
Low (23)[a]	**.180**	**.166**	**.555**	**.043**
Phase 1	.186	.212	.648	.047
Phase 2	.142	.211	.509	.060
Phase 3	.212	.075	.509	.021
Moderate (16)	**.067**	**.201**	**.504**	**.071**
Phase 1	.068	.347	.630	.054
Phase 2	.084	.213	.485	.142
Phase 3	.049	.044	.398	.016
High (23)	**.232**	**.186**	**.364**	**.040**
Phase 1	.226	.273	.451	.048
Phase 2	.252	.236	.388	.036
Phase 3	.220	.049	.253	.034
Combined (62)	**.170**	**.182**	**.471**	**.049**
Phase 1	.170	.269	.570	.049
Phase 2	.168	.221	.458	.072
Phase 3	.173	.057	.385	.025

[a]Sample sizes for each cell.

phase, and no significant interaction. The results for prior knowledge and experience provide some support for the first part of the first hypothesis, in that usage of prior information is highest for the Low and High groups. The Moderate group uses less. The Low group and High group differ marginally from the Moderate group ($p < 0.154$ and $p < 0.068$, respectively), but not from each other. There is no support for the hypothesized phase effects.

The results for the prior knowledge and experience part of the first hypothesis are intriguing, and can be examined more carefully. Although both the High and Low groups (particularly the High group) appear to use phrases coded as prior knowledge to a somewhat larger extent than the Moderate group, the composition of the usage by the High and Low groups differs. Codes E6–E20 represent prior knowledge of brand features and attribute evaluations. The three groups show significant differences in usage of this type of prior knowledge (High 0.095, Moderate 0.016, Low 0.012, $p < 0.0001$), with the High group showing more usage than the Low and Moderate groups ($p < 0.01$). The three groups also show differences in usage of E23 (generally statements of lack of knowledge of an attribute): High 0.011, Moderate 0.015, and Low 0.068 ($p < 0.0001$). Finally, although there is a tendency for the High and Low groups to use prior attitudes or evaluations (E1–E5) more than the Moderate group (High 0.137, Moderate 0.051, Low 0.167), the results are not statistically significant.

Thus, the detailed analysis shows that the High group appears to use prior task-relevant information (E6–E20) or attitudes (E1–E5) (many of the High group chose their present oven), whereas, the Low group relies mainly on prior attitudes or evaluations (E1–E5), apparently backed by little firm knowledge. That is, although the three groups were not significantly different in usage of prior attitudes and evaluations, a large proportion of the prior knowledge statements made by the Low group were statements of usage of prior attitudes or evaluations. In many cases, the protocols revealed the Low group to be simply overwhelmed by the task and thus they chose a brand they "had heard of." This view of the Low group is supported by the means for perceived task difficulty (5 = extremely difficult, 1 = extremely easy) and time taken to reach a choice (in minutes). For the elimination stage, the mean perceptions of task difficulty were: High 3.09, Moderate 3.50, Low 4.35 ($p < 0.06$ in a one-way analysis of variance). For the choice stage, the means are: High 2.52, Moderate 2.94, Low 3.04, not significantly different. The means for the time taken in the elimination stage are: High 7.74, Moderate 10.31, Low 6.35 ($p < 0.01$). For the choice stage they are: High 1.00, Moderate 2.56, Low 2.87, $F(2,59) = 4.72$ ($p < 0.01$). Thus, in the elimination stage, those in the Low group see the task as extremely difficult and take little time at it, perhaps because they feel they do not have the ability to handle the task. The choice stage, however, does not show this pattern. When the task seems manageable, the Low group takes the most time and does not see the task as particularly hard. The Moderate group appears to rely more on processing the available information. They take the most time in the elimination stage and the most time overall.

Hypothesis 2

Hypothesis 2 states that usage of evaluation of attribute levels and weights is negatively related to both degree of prior knowledge and experience and phase of the choice process. The results (Table 11.2) show a main effect for phase ($p < 0.0001$), no effect for prior knowledge and experience, and no interaction. Thus, the proposed effects of prior knowledge and experience are not supported, but the hypothesized phase effects receive strong support, as the usage of attribute evaluations declines over the phases of the choice process. In examining more detailed breakdowns, one combination of codes with a significant difference across the knowledge and experience groups is A14 and A15 (means are High 0.138, Moderate 0.094, Low 0.063, $p < 0.009$). However, this result is opposite to that predicted. Apparently the rationale used for this hypothesis, based on the notions of extensive problem solving, requires some minimal level of knowledge to be operable. The Low group may know so little that they experience great difficulty in performing attribute evaluations (recall the findings for E23).

Hypothesis 3

The hypothesized pattern of results was that the degree of attribute processing is negatively related to degree of prior knowledge and experience, and positively related to phase in the choice process. The mean values for the use of attribute processing are shown in Table 11.2. The operationalization of brand versus attribute processing required the proportions of brand and attribute processing to sum to unity, so the brand processing findings are the reverse of the attribute processing results, and are, hence, not presented. The results show a main effect for prior knowledge and experience ($p < 0.05$), a main effect for phase ($p < 0.01$), and no interaction.

The means show that the first part of Hypothesis 3 is supported, as more experienced subjects use less attribute and more brand processing. However, the results are opposite to those predicted for the phase effects: the early phases have more attribute processing, with later phases dominated more by brand processing. These results agree with the findings of Johnson and Russo (1978), van Raaij (1976), and Russo and Johnson (1980). Perhaps this is due to the matrix format used to provide data to the subjects in the present study. The data cited by Bettman (1979) in support of early brand-based phases were all from studies in which the information was arranged by brand. This format may encourage processing by brand, particularly in early phases where there are many alternatives (Bettman and Kakkar 1977). However, the proposition in Bettman (1979, p. 211) appears to be wrong as currently stated. Rather, subjects appear to begin the choice process by making comparisons using attribute processing, when the format allows such comparisons to be made easily. Eventually, however, subjects must switch to a brand-based process, because they must make a brand choice. Hence, brand processing is found in later phases. The analysis in Russo and Johnson (1980) comes to the same conclusion.

Hypothesis 4

Hypothesis 4 proposes that use of comparisons to standards is negatively related to phase of the choice process, and that there will be an interaction between phase and degree of prior knowledge and experience. The index for comparison to standards is shown in Table 11.2. The use of standards shows a main effect for phase ($p < 0.01$), no main effect for prior knowledge and experience, and an interaction that approaches significance ($p < 0.08$). The interaction is as hypothesized: the Low and Moderate groups require some time to develop standards, whereas the High group uses standards most in the first phase. The results for phase cannot be interpreted clearly due to this qualifying interaction, but they do not support the negative relationship hypothesized. Note that for comparison to standards, the Moderate group has the highest means, even though the main effect of prior knowledge and experience is not significant. Once again there is a hint that the Moderate group is engaging in more processing.

Hypotheses 5 and 6

Hypotheses 5 and 6 proposed various patterns of results for elements compatible with several choice heuristics. The mean values for the indices needed to test these hypotheses are presented in Table 11.3. The analysis of variance results (Table 11.4) show a consistent pattern; the hypothesized effects for prior knowledge and experience are not supported, whereas several of the hypothesized phase effects are supported. In particular, the effects for elimination by aspects, heuristic additive difference, and counting elements are as predicted, with elimination by aspects elements used early in the choice process and elements of the latter two heuristics used in later phases. The results for the lexicographic and weighted compensatory rules are nonsignificant. Finally, for the conjunctive rule element (B4), the interaction approaches significance. It appears that the pattern in the High group differs from that of the Low and Moderate groups across phases. In

TABLE 11.3 Treatment Means for Hypotheses 5 and 6

Degree of prior knowledge and experience/phase of choice process	Elements					
	Conjunctive	*Lexicographic*	*Elimination by aspects*	*Heuristic additive difference*	*Weighted compensatory*	*Counting rule*
Low (23)[a]	**.025**	**.029**	**.017**	**.084**	**.019**	**.094**
Phase 1	.016	.023	.031	.021	.012	.056
Phase 2	.052	.009	.009	.078	.010	.064
Phase 3	.009	.054	.013	.153	.037	.163
Moderate (16)	**.047**	**.004**	**.023**	**.106**	**.020**	**.153**
Phase 1	.021	.006	.033	.022	.024	.054
Phase 2	.112	.002	.029	.072	.016	.122
Phase 3	.008	.004	.009	.225	.020	.283
High (23)	**.029**	**.023**	**.010**	**.053**	**.012**	**.101**
Phase 1	.029	.014	.019	.026	.008	.061
Phase 2	.025	.004	.011	.017	.028	.075
Phase 3	.034	.051	.000	.116	.000	.166
Combined (62)	**.033**	**.020**	**.016**	**.078**	**.017**	**.112**
Phase 1	.022	.016	.027	.023	.014	.057
Phase 2	.057	.005	.015	.054	.018	.083
Phase 3	.018	.040	.007	.158	.019	.195

[a]Sample sizes for each cell.

TABLE 11.4 Anova Results for Hypotheses 5 and 6

Rule	*Degree of Prior Knowledge and Experience (H5)*	*Phase (H6)*	*Interaction*
Conjunctive	.82[a]	5.04	2.34
	(n.s.)[b]	($p<0.008$)	($p<0.059$)
Lexicographic	.61	1.57	.34
	(n.s.)	(n.s.)	(n.s.)
Elimination by aspects	1.03	3.34	.47
	(n.s.)	($p<0.039$)	(n.s.)
Heuristic additive difference	1.46	17.95	1.07
	(n.s.)	($p<0.0001$)	(n.s.)
Weighted compensatory	.28	.07	1.06
	(n.s.)	(n.s.)	(n.s.)
Counting	1.39	14.47	.91
	(n.s.)	($p<0.0001$)	(n.s.)

[a]F-values.

[b]Significance level.

general, as found in the analysis for Hypothesis 4, the use of a comparison to standard appears to require time to develop the standard. Hence, the hypothesis that conjunctive rule elements will be used most in the earliest phase is not supported.

Thus, consumers appear to use elements that eliminate alternatives by comparisons to standards in the middle phase of choice, turning to alternative comparisons in the later phase.[12] Note that the results presented refer to *elements* of choice rules; one cannot claim that these results show that consumers are using some complete rules more than others. Finally, note that although the effects for prior knowledge and experience are not significant, in five of six cases the Moderate Group has the highest means, again hinting that this group is engaging in more processing.

[12]This finding may appear to be tautological, as subjects were given the task of eliminating alternatives in the first two phases. However, although the subjects were asked to eliminate alternatives, there are many ways this elimination could be accomplished, such as by interalternative comparison and elimination. Comparison to standards is only one of many possible elimination strategies. As noted earlier, these findings should also be examined in a study where the phases are not structured for the subjects.

DISCUSSION AND IMPLICATIONS

Implications for Research and Theory

In summary, the results show some interesting overall patterns. The effects of prior knowledge and experience give a fairly consistent picture. The Moderate group appears to do more processing of the currently available information and relies on prior knowledge to a lesser extent than the High and Low groups. This pattern of results, although not significant in all cases, is consistent. The observed pattern is readily understandable if one considers two potential determinants of amount of processing: one must have the ability to process the information, and one must possess the motivation to perform the processing. The Low group may not possess the ability to process the information in the current choice task. They lack the prior knowledge structures that allow them to make sense of the data. Thus, the Low group does not have the requisite ability, which may also in this case lead to lack of motivation. The task is too difficult, so they give up and seek a simple solution. The High group, on the other hand, has enough ability, but is not necessarily motivated to process much current information, as they do not need to. They can rely on information in memory and their prior experiences. The Moderate group, however, may possess enough ability and have enough motivation to devote substantial processing effort to the task. They have enough prior knowledge to be able to process the information presented, but not so much that they do not need to process it.[13]

The second major finding related to prior knowledge and experience is that consumers with more knowledge tend to use brand processing to a greater extent. This may be explainable in terms of the structure of their prior knowledge and experience. As Russo and Johnson (1980) point out, much experience is brand based—advertising, point-of-purchase displays, usage experience, and so on. This may lead to a memory structure that tends to be more and more organized around brands as one accumulates experience. Hence, brand processing may be more likely for consumers with the most experience. Consumers with less experience use attribute processing to a greater extent, perhaps reflecting the ease of attribute-based comparisons.[14]

Finally, there are some consistent findings with respect to the phases of choice processes. Consumers tend to start with attribute-based evaluations and comparisons, turning to brand processing as the choice process unfolds. They also tend to use comparisons to standards as elements to eliminate alternatives in the middle phases of the choice process, with tradeoffs and comparisons of alternatives being made in the later phase.

These results both clarify some earlier work and provide some new findings. The methodology used, a detailed protocol coding analysis of elements of choice processes, deserves some comment. This approach allows one to examine details of choice processes not otherwise possible. In the present case, the approach appears to have worked quite well. Future research using such an approach might examine the extent to which the Moderate group processes more, particularly as this might be affected by task difficulty, i.e., the processing effort-degree of prior knowledge relationship may be different for simple tasks than for complex tasks. In addition, research on the phased nature of choice processes appears promising.

Research on the methodology itself would also be valuable. The coding scheme used relies on a very detailed unit of analysis, i.e., the phrase. This assumes that such phrases are accurate mirrors of aspects of processing, and that such phrases can be meaningfully interpreted. In the present study these assumptions appear to have been supported, but more research on the nature of verbal reports about processing is essential (Ericsson and Simon 1980; Nisbett and Wilson 1977). The focus on the phrase as the unit of analysis appears to be very useful for studying detailed contingencies in choice processes. However, such a focus may be too detailed for attempting to examine subjects' plans, or what subjects are attempting to do in a more global sense when they use the elements of heuristics. Attempts to determine whether larger sets of elements can be analyzed meaningfully should also be a high research priority.

Finally, one important consideration for future research not addressed by the present study is the conceptualization and measurement of degree of prior knowledge and experience. Prior knowledge and experience presumably is manifested by the availability in memory of knowledge structures of various sorts. Such knowledge structures might refer to product features and their interrelationships, specific brands, useful heuristics or comparison strategies, and so on. The amount and mix of various types of knowledge structures are probably crucial factors that underlie the observed

---

[13]An alternative explanation is that the Moderate group was selected based partially on prior search for information on microwave ovens. Hence, this group may contain individuals who have more interest in microwave ovens than the Low group. The present data do not allow one to distinguish between ability-based and motivational explanations.

[14]However, uninformed consumers may become motivated to undertake attribute processing by first hearing about one or two brands. That is, some brand may be the starting point for information search.

effects of prior knowledge and experience. However, measurement of such knowledge structures is at a very rudimentary stage. Conceptualization and measurement of knowledge structures of various types are crucial next steps in research on the effects of knowledge and experience on choice. Such advances would allow more detailed examination of the effects of particular aspects of prior knowledge and experience than the broad manipulation used in the current study.

Implications for Policy

One implication of the present study is that one may be able to help consumers, to some extent, by providing information processable by attribute, as there was high usage of attribute processing by consumers with low to moderate degrees of prior knowledge and experience and in the early phases of the choice process. For durables of the sort used in this study, one might provide tabular information in the store. However, provision of such aids to attribute processing may not be enough. As pointed out by Russo and Johnson (1980), consumers ultimately need to make the transition to a brand-based process, as the focus eventually is brand choice. Thus, there may be some need to assist consumers with making tradeoffs involving the information gathered using attribute comparisons.

In addition, the results show that consumers with little prior knowledge did not appear to search, as the task may have been too overwhelming. One way of interpreting this result is that provision of tabular, label-type information alone may not be sufficient to aid consumers with little prior knowledge and experience. These consumers may not have enough knowledge about attributes and their weights to be able to effectively utilize the detailed information presented to them in the table. This has serious implications, as consumer education in determining standards and making tradeoffs may be needed to ensure that consumers without experience do not simply give up. Making information easier to process by format and other means may well allow some improvements in choice processing, but consumer education, either from the marketer or public policymaker, may be needed for the least knowledgeable and experienced groups.

Appendix A Protocol Coding Scheme for Elements of Choice Processes

Code	*Frequency*		*Description*
Attribute comparison process			
A1	21	(0.9%)	Single attribute, compare difference between two brands
A2	42	(1.8)	Single attribute, compare two brands without taking actual difference
A3	42	(1.8)	Single attribute, compare more than two brands without taking actual difference
A4	24	(1.0)	Single attribute, more than two brands, find range or comment on range
A5	26	(1.1)	Single attribute, more than two brands, find best brand
A6	5	(0.2)	Single attribute, more than two brands, find worst brand
A7	18	(0.7)	Single attribute, more than two brands, find set with particular level or levels
A8	71	(3.0)	Single attribute, more than two brands, refer to count/number with particular level of that attribute
A9	27	(1.2)	Single attribute, more than two brands, comparison of brands to standard on that attribute
A10	38	(1.6)	Single attribute, nonbrand based, statement of evaluation of particular attribute level or continuous attribute
A11	8	(0.3)	Single attribute, nonbrand based, statement of reasoning behind evaluation of particular attribute level for continuous attribute
A12	108	(4.6)	Single attribute, nonbrand based, statement of attribute weight or importance for continuous attribute

Appendix *(Continued)*

Code	*Frequency*		*Description*
A13	17	(0.7)	Single attribute, nonbrand based, statement of reasoning behind attribute weight or importance for continuous attribute
A14	202	(8.7)	Single attribute, nonbrand based, statement of preferred level of binary or discrete attribute
A15	30	(1.3)	Single attribute, nonbrand based, reasoning behind preferred level of binary or discrete attribute
A16	24	(1.0)	More than one attribute, two brands or more, tradeoff differences between brands
A17	16	(0.7)	More than one attribute, nonbrand based, tradeoff differences
A18	4	(0.2)	More than one attribute, two brands or more, find set with particular levels
A19	10	(0.4)	More than one attribute, nonbrand based, ranking of relative attribute weight or importance
A20	21	(0.9)	More than one attribute, two brands or more, compare counts of desirable features possessed by each brand
A21	9	(0.4)	More than one attribute, two brands or more, compare overall evaluations
Total	763	(32.8)	
Within-brand processes			
B1	60	(2.9)	One brand, one attribute, statement of level of attribute
B2	30	(1.3)	One brand, one attribute, evaluation of level of attribute
B3	51	(2.2)	One brand, one attribute, position of attribute level within range
B4	80	(3.4)	One brand, one attribute, compare to standard for that attribute
B5	148	(6.4)	One brand, one or more attributes, count or statement of desirable features(s)
B6	121	(5.2)	One brand, one or more attributes, count or statment of undesirable feature(s)
B7	0	(0.0)	One brand, more than one attribute, search for worst feature
B8	0	(0.0)	One brand, more than one attribute, search for best feature
B9	16	(0.7)	One brand, more than one attribute, compensatory combination or tradeoff of attributes
B10	25	(1.1)	One brand, intermediate or preliminary evaluation
B11	13	(0.6)	One brand, statement of overall evaluation, not based on prior knowledge
Total	552	(23.7)	
Use of prior knowledge			
E1	27	(1.2)	Brand evaluation: based on prior choice process, ownership or usage
E2	35	(1.5)	Brand evaluation: based on word-of-mouth
E3	27	(1.2)	Brand evaluation: generalization from other products
E4	15	(0.6)	Brand evaluation: based on advertising
E5	45	(1.9)	Brand evaluation: other
E6	12	(0.5)	Prior knowledge of attributes of a specific brand: based on prior choice process, ownership or usage
E7	2	(0.1)	Prior knowledge of attributes of a specific brand: based on word-of-mouth
E8	0	(0.0)	Prior knowledge of attributes of a specific brand: generalization from other products
E9	1	(0.0)	Prior knowledge of attributes of a specific brand: based on advertising
E10	2	(0.1)	Prior knowledge of attributes of a specific brand: other
E11	39	(1.7)	Prior knowledge of evaluation of particular levels of an attribute (discrete or continuous): based on prior choice process, ownership, or usage
E12	12	(0.5)	Prior knowledge of evaluation of particular levels of an attribute (discrete or continuous): based on word-of-mouth
E13	3	(0.1)	Prior knowledge of evaluation of particular levels of an attribute (discrete or continuous): generalization from other products

Appendix *(Continued)*

Code	*Frequency*		*Description*
E14	3	(0.1)	Prior knowledge of evaluation of particular levels of an attribute (discrete or continuous): based on advertising
E15	5	(0.2)	Prior knowledge of evaluation of particular levels of an attribute (discrete or continuous): other
E16	11	(0.5)	Prior knowledge of attribute weighting or importance (continuous attributes): based on prior choice process, ownership or usage
E17	3	(0.1)	Prior knowledge of attribute weighting or importance (continuous attributes): based on word-of-mouth
E18	0	(0.0)	Prior knowledge of attribute weighting or importance (continuous attributes): generalization from other products
E19	0	(0.0)	Prior knowledge of attribute weighting or importance (continuous attributes): based on advertising
E20	1	(0.0)	Prior knowledge of attribute weighting or importance (continuous attributes): other
E21	8	(0.3)	Statement about level of product class knowledge
E22	45	(1.9)	Statement about level of knowledge of a particular brand
E23	70	(3.0)	Statement about level of knowledge of an attribute
E24	15	(0.6)	Statement of brand ownership
Total	380	(16.3)	
Statements of plans or needs			
P1	0	(0.0)	Plan or need to do external search about the general product class
P2	15	(0.6)	Plan or need to search about a specific attribute
P3	6	(0.3)	Plan or need to search about specific brand information
P4	12	(0.5)	Plan or need to physically examine a brand
P5	46	(2.0)	Choice strategy statement
Total	79	(3.4)	
General			
G1	65	(2.8)	Statement of selection of a brand for processing
G2	178	(7.6)	Statement of acceptance of a brand
G3	78	(3.4)	Statement of elimination of a brand
G4	79	(3.4)	Statement of selection of an attribute for processing
G5	4	(0.2)	Statement of elimination of an attribute
G6	17	(0.7)	Statement of conflict, difficulty, etc.
G7	6	(0.3)	Product class statements
G8	109	(4.7)	Statements about the task
G9	18	(0.8)	Don't know, ambiguous
Total	554	(23.8)	

REFERENCES

BETTMAN, JAMES R. (1979), *An Information Processing Theory of Consumer Choice.* Reading, MA: Addison-Wesley.

———, and KAKKAR, PRADEEP (1977), "Effects of Information Presentation Format on Consumer Information Acquisition Strategies," *Journal of Consumer Research,* 3, 233–240.

———, and PARK, C. WHAN (1979), "Description and Examples of a Protocol Coding Scheme for Elements of Choice Processes," working paper no. 76, Center for Marketing Studies, University of California, Los Angeles.

———, and Park, C. Whan (1980), "Implications of a Constructive View of Choice for Analysis of Protocol Data: A Coding Scheme for Elements of Choice Processes," in *Advances in Consumer Research,* Vol. 7, Ed. Jerry C. Olson. San Francisco: Association for Consumer Research, pp. 148–153.

———, and Zins, Michel A. (1977), "Constructive Processes in Consumer Choice," *Journal of Consumer Research,* 4, 75–85.

———, and Zins, Michel A. (1979), "Information Format and Choice Task Effects in Decision Making," *Journal of Consumer Research,* 6, 141–153.

Edell, Julie A., and Mitchell, Andrew A. (1978), "An Information Processing Approach to Cognitive Response," in *Research Frontiers in Marketing: Dialogues and Directions,* Ed. S. C. Jain. Chicago: American Marketing Association, pp. 178–183.

Ericsson, K. Anders, and Simon, Herbert A. (1980), "Verbal Reports as Data," *Psychological Review,* 87, 215–251.

Hansen, Flemming (1972), *Consumer Choice Behavior.* New York: The Free Press.

Howard, John A. (1977), *Consumer Behavior: Application of Theory.* New York: McGraw-Hill.

———, and Sheth, Jagdish N. (1969), *The Theory of Buyer Behavior.* New York: Wiley.

Jacoby, Jacob, Chestnut, Robert W., Weigl, Karl C., and Fisher, William (1976), "Prepurchase Information Acquisition: Description of a Process Methodology, Research Paradigm, and Pilot Investigation," in *Advances in Consumer Research,* Vol. 4, Ed. William D. Perreault. Atlanta, GA: Association for Consumer Research, pp. 306–314.

Johnson, Eric J., and Russo, J. Edward (1978), "What Is Remembered After a Purchase Decision?" working paper, Graduate School of Business, University of Chicago.

Lussier, Denis A., and Olshavsky, Richard W. (1979), "Task Complexity and Contingent Processing in Brand Choice," *Journal of Consumer Research,* 6, 154–165.

Newell, Allan, and Simon, Herbert A. (1972), *Human Problem Solving.* Englewood Cliffs, NJ: Prentice-Hall.

Nisbett, Richard E., and Wilson, Timothy De Camp (1977), "Telling More Than We Can Know: Verbal Reports on Mental Processes," *Psychological Review,* 84, 231–259.

Olson, Jerry C. (1978), "Theories of Information Encoding and Storage: Implications for Consumer Research," in *The Effect of Information on Consumer and Market Behavior,* Ed. Andrew A. Mitchell. Chicago: American Marketing Association, pp. 49–60.

———, and Muderrisoglu, Aydin (1979), "The Stability of Responses Obtained by Free Elicitation: Implications for Measuring Attribute Salience and Memory Structure," in *Advances in Consumer Research,* Vol. 6, Ed. William L. Wilkie. Miami, FL: Association for Consumer Research, pp. 269–275.

Park, C. Whan 91976), "The Effect of Individual and Situation-Related Factors on Consumer Selection of Judgmental Models," *Journal of Marketing Research,* 13, 144–151.

———, and Lessig, Parker V. (1979), "The Construct of Familiarity and Its Impact on Consumer Choice Decisions: Cognitive Biases and Heuristics," working paper, Graduate School of Business, University of Pittsburgh.

Payne, John W. (1976), "Task Complexity and Contingent Processing in Decision Making: An Information Search and Protocol Analysis," *Organizational Behavior and Human Performance,* 16, 366–387.

———, and Ragsdale, E. K. Easton (1978), "Verbal Protocols and Direct Observation of Supermarket Shopping Behavior: Some Findings and a Discussion of Methods," in *Advances in Consumer Research,* Vol. 5, Ed. H. Keith Hunt. Chicago: Association for Consumer Research, pp. 571–577.

Pras, Bernard, and Summers, John O. (1975), "A Comparison of Linear and Nonlinear Evaluation Process Models," *Journal of Marketing Research,* 12, 276–281.

van Raaij, W. F. (1976), *Consumer Choice Behavior: An Information-Processing Approach.* Voorschoten, Netherlands: VAM.

Russo, J. Edward, and Dosher, Barbara A. (1975), "Dimensional Evaluation: A Heuristic for Binary Choice," working paper, Department of Psychology, University of California, San Diego.

———, and Johnson, Eric J. (1980), "What Do Consumers Know About Familiar Products?" in *Advances in Consumer Research,* Vol. 7, Ed. Jerry C. Olson. San Francisco: Association for Consumer Research, pp. 417–423.

Slovic, Paul (1972), "Information Processing, Situation Specificity, and the Generality of Risk-Taking Behavior," *Journal of Personality and Social Psychology,* 22, 128–134.

———, and MacPhillamy, Douglas (1974), "Dimensional Commensurability and Cue Utilization in Comparative Judgment," *Organizational Behavior and Human Performance,* 11, 172–194.

Weiner, Bernard, Heckhausen, H., Meyer, W. U., and Cook, R. E. (1972), "Causal Ascription and Achievement Motivation: A Conceptual Analysis of Effort and Reanalysis of Locus of Control," *Journal of Personality and Social Psychology,* 21, 239–248.

Wright, Peter L. (1974), "The Harrassed Decision Maker: Time Pressures, Distractions, and the Use of Evidence," *Journal of Applied Psychology,* 59, 555–561.

———, and Barbour, Frederic (1977), "Phased Decision Strategies: Sequels to an Initial Screening," in *North Holland/TIMS Studies in the Management Sciences,* Vol. 6: *Multiple Criteria Decision Making,* Eds. Martin K. Starr and Milan Zeleny. Amsterdam: North Holland, pp. 91–109.

12

CONSUMER KNOWLEDGE: Effects on Evaluation Strategies Mediating Consumer Judgments*

Mita Sujan

This study suggests that category-based evaluative responses supplement the piecemeal-based evaluation processes more often studied in Consumer Research. The alternative modes of processing were found to be contingent upon the match/mismatch of information to category expectations. Compared to piecemeal (mismatch) processing, category-based (match) processing resulted in faster impression formation times, more verbalizations related to the product category, fewer verbalizations related to the product's attributes, and fewer references to subtypes. Expertise exaggerated these effects.

The relevance of understanding consumer information processing strategies has been well established (Bettman 1979; Wright 1975). One important question involving processing strategies is whether product attributes are reviewed, evaluated, and combined to yield an overall evaluation, or whether some simpler processes mediate final judgments and choices. Categorization research (Cohen 1982; Fiske 1982; Medin and Smith 1984; Mervis and Rosch 1981; Rosch 1975; Smith and Medin 1981) provides a theoretical basis for approaching this issue, suggesting that consumers' prior knowledge plays an important role in determining the types of

*Reprinted from the *Journal of Consumer Research,* 12 (June 1985), pp. 31–46.

evaluation processes mediating final judgments.

Piecemeal Versus Category-Based Processes

Algebraic multiattribute models of attitude and product evaluation provide a rough approximation of the type of processing consumers might do when they engage in effortful processing (Fishbein and Ajzen 1975; Green and Wind 1973; Shocker and Srinivasan 1979; Wilkie and Pessemier 1973). In this type of processing, consumers can be characterized as reviewing the information available from an advertisement, package, or some other source, evaluating each piece of information separately, and through some kind of attribute integration process, arriving at a final judgment. One of the principles underlying this process is that products are evaluated on an attribute-by-attribute—or piecemeal—basis (Anderson 1974; Fiske 1982): products are perceived to be made up of discrete attributes, with each attribute having a distinct subjective value. The assumption is that the decision maker combines (often by adding or averaging) the pieces of attribute information to determine the overall value of the product under consideration.

An alternative to the piecemeal approach is the categorization approach (Mervis and Rosch 1981; Rosch 1975; Rosch and Mervis 1975; Smith and Medin 1981). Its basic premise is that people naturally divide the world of objects around them into categories, enabling an efficient understanding and processing of the environment. According to the categorization approach, if a new stimulus can be categorized as an example of a previously defined category, then the affect associated with the category can be quickly retrieved and applied to the stimulus (Cohen 1982; Fiske 1982; Fiske and Pavelchak in press). The belief is that affect is cued by the categorization of stimuli rather than through a constructive attribute review process. This process of retrieving evaluations is termed "schema-driven affect" because one's prior experiences with the category or the category "schema"[1] serve as a guide to evaluations (Fiske 1982).

The purpose of this research was to determine when consumers would engage in piecemeal processes versus simple category-based affective processes to arrive at final judgments. In this attempt the study investigated the effects of consumers' product knowledge bases upon evaluation processes. In particular, it explored the effects upon evaluation processes of the match of communicated information to consumer knowledge and of the level of consumer knowledge.

A CATEGORIZATION APPROACH TO CONSUMER KNOWLEDGE

Over time, consumers are likely to develop a set of expectations about a product category; these expectations will be organized around the most typical category members. Categories can be best represented either by typical category "exemplars" or by "prototypes." Exemplars are known good examples of the category. Prototypes are abstract images embodying features or attributes most commonly associated with members of the category. The prototype need not be identical to any particular exemplar.

While recent research has debated whether individuals perceive categories in terms of exemplars or prototypes (Medin and Smith 1984), no strong distinction is made between the two views in this paper. In fact, "mixed prototype" models have been proposed in which both specific examples and abstract features representing the category are assumed to be stored (Elio and Anderson 1981). According to this view, either a product prototype or a typical exemplar can represent a consumer's best guess at what a category has to offer, providing consumers with a pattern of expectations about

[1] A schema is "an internal structure developed through experience which organizes incoming information relative to previous experience" (Mandler and Parker 1976, p. 39). Thus, a schema is an organized pattern of expectations about the environment (Bettman 1979; Olson 1978).

the product category—a set of hypotheses about what attributes go together, what constitutes typical configurations of attributes, and what performance levels can be expected. The presence of such expectations is the only prerequisite for the arguments presented in this paper; the basis for the expectations—prototype or exemplar—is not crucial. The term *category knowledge* will be used throughout the paper to refer to this organized set of expectations.

The Importance of Category Knowledge

Recognition of standard categories of patterns has been shown to be useful in a variety of domains. In the classical chess studies, it has been demonstrated that the master's "intuition" for the game came from his/her rapid recognition of standard patterns of chess positions (Chase and Simon 1973). In problem solving studies, several researchers have demonstrated that the process of categorizing a problem cues heuristics useful for the problem's solution and that the link between categorization and heuristics is especially strong for experts (e.g., Chi, Feltovich, and Glaser 1981; Larkin et al. 1980). For example, in physics, "expertise" was shown to result from the ability to categorize a problem based on the underlying principle and then apply the solution associated with that category of physics problems (Larkin et al. 1980).

In the area of person perception, Fiske (1982) has extended the notion of categories to include affective reactions. According to Fiske, affective reactions towards an individual result through a process of matching up the individual to a person category. If the match is good, the affect stored with the category is immediately triggered, and a strong spontaneous affective reaction toward the individual is felt.

The category-based model has been developed further in a paper by Fiske and Pavelchak (in press). People's reactions to an individual were hypothesized to consist of an initial categorization stage and a second evaluation stage. If categorization were successful the individual could be evaluated in a category-based mode—that is, the perceiver could respond at the category level rather than on the basis of all the individual attributes. Alternatively, the categorization attempt could fail, either because no category was cued, or because the most available category implied some attributes that were inconsistent with those the target individual actually possessed. Given unsuccessful categorization, the perceiver was forced to evaluate the individual in a piecemeal mode—attribute-by-attribute. Thus, two modes of affective response were hypothesized—category-based affective processing and piecemeal processing—given successful and unsuccessful categorization, respectively.

The notion of category-based affect resembles closely—but is not identical to—the affect-referral processes discussed by Wright (1976a, 1976b): it involves no review of individual attributes. In category-based affect an already formed global, affective reaction is retrieved from memory and applied to the instance on hand. It differs from affect referral, and is more general, in that no previous experience with the specific instance is necessarily assumed. Category-based affect most closely resembles Kahneman and Tversky's (1972) representativeness heuristic, as judgments are hypothesized to be based on similarity to a prototype or exemplar in memory.

To summarize, research findings across various domains allow one to make two generalizations about the effects of category knowledge on information processing. First, a match to a category can serve to trigger relevant "actions"—either affective reactions or heuristics—that cue a problem's solutions. If the match between incoming information and category knowledge is low, however, then slower, more analytical processes would need to be used to arrive at judgments or problem solutions.

Second, expertise seems to be linked to the knowledge of categories. The basis of expertise appears to be the ability to solve problems through the rapid recognition of standard categories of patterns that otherwise would need to be examined more slowly and analytically. Based on these generalizations, the following propositions about when consumers would engage in simple category-based processes versus piecemeal processes are put forward:

P1: When incoming product information matches product category knowledge in memory, category-based affective processes will mediate consumer judgments.

P2: When incoming product information is discrepant from product category knowledge in memory, piecemeal processes will mediate consumer judgments.

P3: The link between match-mismatch to product category knowledge in memory and the type of evaluation processes used will be stronger for expert consumers than for novice consumers.

RESEARCH HYPOTHESES

Distinguishing Category-Based Processing from Piecemeal Processing

The theoretical model from which the research hypotheses in this paper are derived proposes a two-step process for reaching evaluative judgments: (1) the assessment of match-to-category knowledge, and (2) the use of either category-based affective processes or piecemeal processes, given successful and unsuccessful categorization, respectively (Fiske and Pavelchak in press). This study distinguished between these two processing methods that occur after the initial phase of assessing matches or mismatches to category knowledge through the use of multiple indicators. The cognitive response approach to persuasive communication provided one set of indicators of the mediating processes—the number of responses and the type of responses (Greenwald 1968). In the field of marketing, the coding scheme that has been generally adopted is that used by Wright (1973, 1980), wherein responses are separated into counter arguments, support arguments, and source derogations. Given the purpose of this research, two modifications to this coding scheme were made.

First, if consumers are indeed using piecemeal processes in evaluation, then their responses should reflect statements of the specific operations performed on the information provided. In addition to support arguments and counter arguments, then, this study focused on consumers' descriptions of how attribute information was combined, evaluations of attribute levels, comparisons of attributes to an acceptable standard, references to a likely attribute trade-off, or any other attribute-oriented thoughts that would indicate construction of an evaluation from the pieces of attribute information provided (Bettman and Park 1980).

Second, Wright (1973, 1980) has excluded statements of simple affect—i.e., global liking or dislike—because they are purported to spoil the causal relationship between "cognitive" mediators and final attitude. However, it seems reasonable to consider such statements as potential mediators, especially when they occur during, or right after, message reception and before evaluation (Ericsson and Simon 1978). In particular, the relative importance of simple statements of acceptance and rejection is probably greater when simple category-based affective processes mediate judgments. Therefore, attribute-oriented responses versus simple evaluative responses are likely to be indicators of very different processes underlying evaluations—piecemeal attribute review processes and category-based affective processes, respectively.

Further, since consumers can generate other types of responses to communication (e.g., source derogations, statements of familiarity, etc.), attribute-oriented responses and simple evaluative responses do not necessarily sum to total responses. Predictions can therefore be made separately for these two types of thoughts. More attribute-oriented responses and/or fewer simple evaluative responses would be indicators of piecemeal processes. Conversely, fewer attribute-oriented responses and/or more simple evaluative responses would be indicators of category-based affective processes. Another measure of piecemeal processes versus category-based processes is based on Fiske's (1982) argument that schematic processing spontaneously evokes strong and extreme affect. Thus, extreme evaluations would be an indicator of category-based affective processes and moderate evaluations would be an indicator of piecemeal processing.

Cognitive response and evaluation measures assume that piecemeal processes and category-based affective processes are conscious processes that can be verbalized. However, more rapid, covert processes may be involved. In this study verbalization measures were thus supplemented by response-time analysis, offsetting (presumably) inherent limitations of any one measure by nonoverlapping limitations of alternative measures. Response-time measures of the time taken to reach evaluations may also help to distinguish the two types of processing. Since category-based affective processes should be faster than piecemeal processes, a response-time measure would provide support for whether category-based affective processes or piecemeal processes mediate evaluations, independent of the number and type of responses.

Effects of Match/Mismatch-to-Category Knowledge

Central to the notion of category-based affect is that information is consistent with consumers' knowledge base (Bettman 1982; Fiske and Beattie 1982; Sherman et al. 1983). It is hypothesized that matches to product category knowledge would evoke category-based affective processes, and that mismatches would evoke piecemeal processes. Thus,

H1: When information is discrepant from category knowledge, compared to when information is consistent with category knowledge,

1. more product-related thoughts are generated
2. more attribute-oriented thoughts are generated
3. fewer simple evaluative thoughts are generated
4. overall evaluations are reached more slowly
5. overall evaluations are less extreme

Effects of Expertise

Expertise is likely to have an independent effect on evaluation processes. Cognitive response studies have found that certain types of cognitive responses are accessible only to subjects who have a well developed knowledge base (Edell and Mitchell 1978; Wright 1975; Wright and Rip 1980). These studies indicate that attribute-oriented thoughts may be more difficult for less knowledgeable subjects. Given the extended knowledge structures upon which experts can draw, it also seems likely that compared to novice consumers, knowledgeable consumers would produce more total responses to communication (Edell and Mitchell 1978).

The difference between expert and novice consumers in the number and type of thoughts does not necessarily imply a difference in response times. Since experts may have stronger associations between concepts in memory (e.g., Anderson 1982), it is likely that they can generate more total thoughts and more attribute-oriented thoughts compared to novices without necessarily spending more time. Evidence also suggests that experts can take longer or shorter times than novices to process information, depending on the judgment (Fiske and Taylor 1984). Therefore, no predictions are made for response time.

Experts and novices may also differ in the number of simple evaluative statements generated to a communication. Simple evaluative statements might be easier to produce for novice subjects. Given that novices have at least a rudimentary knowledge structure, they may prefer to use prior evaluations based on simplistic criteria than to process available information in making judgments and choices (Bettman and Park 1980). Thus, it is argued that novice consumers will tend to use category-based affective processes more often, and generate small numbers of simple evaluative responses to all communications.

Consistent with the notion that novices rely on their prior evaluations and use category-based affective processing more often, it is also argued that novices are likely to be more extreme in their evaluations than are experts.

Some empirical support for this hypothesis is available: Linville (1982) found that the less complex a person's representation of a given domain, the more extreme a person's evaluation of stimuli from that domain. Thus, the following effects of expertise are hypothesized:

H2: Knowledgeable consumers, compared to novice consumers:

1. generate more product-related thoughts
2. generate more attribute-oriented thoughts
3. generate fewer simple evaluative thoughts
4. are less extreme in their evaluations

Expertise and Match/Mismatch-to-Category Knowledge

Category knowledge is likely to be more developed for expert consumers, and the category-affect link is likely to be more clearly defined. Using schemas understood by both experts and novices, it has been demonstrated that only relative experts were sensitive to the discrepancy of information from the schema (Fiske, Kinder, and Larter 1983; Taylor and Winkler 1980). Anderson (1982) suggests that the link between knowledge structures and processing strategies is tenuous for novices, and that procedural knowledge—appropriate rules and heuristics for processing—is acquired last. Hence, it is hypothesized that compared to experts, novice consumers' evaluation strategies are less likely to be influenced by the match or mismatch of information to category knowledge. Thus, for experts, significant differences between the match and mismatch conditions are predicted for all of the process measures. For novices, no differences between the match and mismatch conditions on the process measures are proposed. The separate hypotheses for experts and novices imply that the overall effects due to match/mismatch-to-category knowledge (Hypothesis 1) are due solely to experts.

H3: When information is discrepant from category knowledge, compared to when information is consistent with category knowledge, expert (knowledgeable) consumers:

1. generate more product-related thoughts
2. generate more attribute-oriented thoughts
3. generate fewer simple evaluative thoughts
4. reach overall evaluations more slowly
5. are less extreme in their overall evaluations

H4: Novice consumers are not influenced by the match or mismatch of information to category knowledge in:

1. total product-related thoughts
2. attribute-oriented thoughts
3. simple evaluative thoughts
4. time taken to reach overall evaluations
5. extremity of their overall evaluations

METHOD

An experiment was designed to examine how expert and novice consumers process information that is either consistent with or discrepant from their expectations for the product class. Subjects were classified as either experts or novices for a particular product category. Half of the subjects received descriptions that were consistent with and half of the subjects received descriptions that were discrepant from category knowledge. Two different descriptions were used in simulated print ads. Subjects were asked to read one ad and to form an impression of the advertised product. After viewing the ad, subjects verbalized their responses to it, and then evaluated the product. The time taken to make the evaluative judgment was recorded. Thus, a 2 (expert/novice) × 2 (match/mismatch to category) × 2 (description) between-subjects design with several process measures was used.

Experimental Design

Two descriptions were given in simulated print ads and were used in both match and mismatch conditions to eliminate the confound between the manipulation of information match/mismatch and the actual content of the information. To do this, two product types within a product class—35mm Single Lens Reflex (SLR) and 110 cameras—were chosen. Information typical of 35mm SLR cameras (interchangeable lenses, sturdy, versatile) is atypical of 110 cameras and vice versa. Thus, the 2 (expert/novice) × 2 (match/mismatch to category) × 2 (description) between-subjects design allowed match-to-category knowledge to be manipulated while it held the actual information constant.[2]

Pretest: Measuring Product Category Knowledge

Thirty-two MBA students at the UCLA Graduate School of Management participated in a preliminary study to measure product category knowledge. Half of the subjects were asked to describe 35mm SLR cameras and the other half were asked to describe 110 cameras. Subjects were instructed to "list attributes characteristic of and common to" the product category and were given two and one-half minutes to describe the category (Rosch et al. 1976). To arrive at the typical attributes for each product category, idiosyncratic attributes (that is, attributes listed by only one subject) were eliminated, leaving for each product category attributes generated by two or more subjects as descriptive of the category. The attributes that were finally used to construct the stimuli were listed by at least 25 percent of the subjects.

No distinction was made between the category knowledge of subjects at different levels of expertise, though one might expect the categories of experts and novices to vary in the number and type of attributes. The reliance on consensual categories—categories understood by both experts and novices—to construct the experimental stimuli may dampen the processing differences between expert and novice groups. However, it would demonstrate that any differences obtained could be attributed, at least in part, to differential use of categories by experts and novices in information processing (Fiske and Kinder 1980; Fiske, Kinder, and Larter 1983). Though it is possible to reach expert and novice groups separately, much of the product information in the shopping environment is aimed at, and is available to, all consumers (e.g., information on packages, in-store displays, instruction manuals, and so on). Thus it is important to understand how the same information is processed differently by consumers with differing levels of knowledge and familiarity with the product class.

THE EXPERIMENT

Stimuli

The stimuli were simulated print ads. By combining type of camera (35 mm SLR and 110) with the two different descriptions, four ads were generated. Two ads described cameras which were typical and two described cameras which were atypical of the category. Each ad provided information on five attributes of the camera, each of which was followed by one or two short sentences restating the attribute in greater detail. The category was evoked by using bold category labels intended to focus attention on the label and thus to maximize the probability that the relevant category was available in memory. The camera descriptions used are given in Exhibits 12.1 and 12.2.

Expertise

One of the factors in the design—expertise—is a measured variable. It was felt that it would be difficult to manipulate in a laboratory the complex patterns of expectations or knowledge structures that develop over time with increasing familiarity and expertise in a domain. Further, it was felt that measuring, rather than manipulating, expertise would add ecological realism to the study of the effects of consumer knowledge on processing. The risk, of course, is that other unmeasured factors associated with

---

[2]This match/mismatch manipulation is potentially confounded with factors such as novelty and interest. However, the verbalization measures collected in this study do allow a check on whether the results obtained are due to perceptions of match/mismatch-to-category knowledge. Fiske and Pavelchak (in press) provide other operationalizations of match/mismatch to control for this potential confound.

EXHIBIT 12.1 Camera description

A 110 CAMERA

This particular 110 camera has the following features:

- easy to operate

All you do is frame the picture, focus for maximum sharpness, and shoot. The camera automatically controls exposure.

- small and pocketable

The camera is engineered to easily fit a jacket pocket or small purse. It has a lighweight plastic casing and compact design.

- very easy to load and unload

The film is loaded into a cartridge which has only to be dropped into the camera thus eliminating any chance of misloading.

- has a normal lens plus a close-up feature

The close-up lens can be easily switched into position and it has a magnification of 2.0 times that of the normal image.

- is a self-contained camera

The camera body and lenses form an "all-in-one" camera package which is convenient to use.

Note: In the mismatch conditions, the label was switched to "A 35 mm Single Lens Reflex."

EXHIBIT 12.2 Camera description

A 35MM SINGLE LENS REFLEX

This particular 35 mm SLR has the following features:

- many fine interchangeable lenses

The fine lenses permit high quality enlargements. The choice of lenses include normal, wide angle and telephoto.

- great versatility

The range of shutter speeds and aperture settings allows for perfectly exposed pictures in very low light or bright sunlight.

- a full system of accessories

This includes a motor drive which can advance the film one frame at a time or in sequences as fast as three frames per second.

- is solidly constructed

The special metal alloy body casing prevents the passage of dust and moisture. The textured exterior provides a firm grip.

- accepts a wide variety of film speeds

The camera's light meter allows the use of a wide range of film speeds, including the new "fast" films.

Note: In the mismatch conditions, the label was switched to "A 110 camera."

different levels of expertise may provide alternative explanations for the results.

A 15-question, multiple choice scale to measure objective knowledge about cameras was developed and administered to known groups of experts (photography students) and novices (students who knew very little about cameras). Experts scored an average of 11.33 correct answers (standard deviation = 2.5; n = 15 subjects) and novices scored an average of 5.86 correct answers (standard deviation = 2.3; n = 15 subjects). Based on these results, an absolute cutoff of nine or more correct answers was set as the criterion measure for expertise. The score of nine was approximately one standard deviation away from the means of both the expert and the novice groups. Based on assumptions of normality for the expert and novice population groups, this would correctly classify 83 percent of the expert group and 91 percent of the novice group. The cell sizes across conditions, given the split into expert and novice groups, varied between 14 and 18. Cell sizes for each condition are reported at the bottom of Table 12.1.

TABLE 12.1 Cell Means for Various Dependent Measures

	Expert				Novice			
	Description of 35 mm SLR		*Description of 110*		*Description of 35 mm SLR*		*Description of 110*	
Dependent measures	*Match*	*Mismatch*	*Match*	*Mismatch*	*Match*	*Mismatch*	*Match*	*Mismatch*
Thoughts								
Total	2.33	4.40	2.80	5.25	2.71	2.81	3.00	3.39
Attribute-oriented	0.60	1.87	0.93	3.06	0.86	0.75	0.88	1.72
Simple evaluative	0.13	0.87	0.67	0.69	0.64	0.56	0.59	0.78
Categorization	1.07	0.13	0.87	0.06	0.29	0.31	0.76	0.17
Subtyping	0.07	0.33	0.07	0.75	0.14	0.06	0.06	0.22
Discrepancy	0.00	0.73	0.07	0.38	0.00	0.25	0.18	0.22
Impression time (seconds)	32.61	35.49	30.94	37.24	38.13	37.30	28.87	33.24
Final affect/(1 = very good; 7 = very bad)	2.67	2.67	4.13	3.56	2.43	3.31	2.94	2.72
Cell sizes	15	15	15	16	14	16	17	18

Subjects

Graduate students at the UCLA School of Management were recruited for the study. Announcements were made in classes asking for volunteers for a study on photography and cameras. This procedure ensured that even the novices would have a rudimentary knowledge structure about cameras. As an incentive, a lottery of $150 was offered. Ninety-three percent of those who volunteered kept their appointment. A total of 126 subjects participated in the experiment.

Procedure

Two rooms were set up for the experiment. Each room was equipped with a response-time button and a tape recorder. The response-time buttons were connected to an event recorder placed outside the rooms and not visible to subjects. Upon entering the lab, individual subjects were randomly assigned to one of the four manipulated conditions (match/mismatch to category, 110/35 mm SLR camera). They were told that the study was on cameras and that the questionnaire was divided into three parts.

In the first part of the study, subjects read a nonevaluative passage on photography. The purpose of this was to obtain a reading speed measure for subjects. The instructions were to push the button, read the passage at their normal speed, and push the button again when they were done reading. An instruction statement on the page prompted subjects to push the response-time button.

In the second part of the study, subjects received one of the four experimental stimuli. Subjects were instructed to read the camera description to form an impression of the camera. They were asked to push the response-time button when they started reading the description and again when they had formed an impression of the camera. After reading the description, they were asked to verbalize aloud all of the thoughts and ideas that they experienced while reading the camera description. They were asked to report all thoughts no matter how simple, complex, relevant, or irrelevant they might seem. Next, subjects were given the instruction "Based on your impression, on the scale below, please indicate your overall evaluation of the camera." They then pushed the response-time button, responded on a 7-point bipolar attitude scale, and pushed the button again.

The interviewer then left the room, and subjects completed the rest of the questionnaire. Part three of the questionnaire related to measurement of knowledge. Subjects filled in the

15-question objective expertise scale. The knowledge measures were collected at the end of the questionnaire rather than at the beginning because it was felt that subjects' perceptions of how they performed on the knowledge scale might influence their responses to the experimental stimuli. Also, the objective knowledge scale was constructed so that exposure to the experimental stimuli would not influence answers to the knowledge questions. Thus it was felt that the knowledge scale was sufficiently protected from any contamination from responses to the earlier parts of the questionnaire.

To test for possible confounds of knowledge with interest or involvement in the category, subjects were also asked to rate their interest and involvement in the product class in general, and in 35mm SLR and 110 cameras in particular. These measures corresponded more closely to Petty and Cacioppo's (1979) operationalization of long-term issue or product involvement rather than to task involvement or to involvement in the specific experiment (Wright 1973). Subjects were debriefed and thanked. They then signed their names for the lottery and left.

Dependent Measures

Cognitive Responses. Verbal responses were collected on a tape recorder immediately after subjects read the descriptions and before the evaluation measures. The coding scheme was developed after examining the protocols of the first few subjects. Besides simple evaluative responses and attribute-oriented thoughts, three important categories of thoughts were evident from the protocol data. Thoughts that noted how the camera was similar to the overall category of 35mm SLR or 110 cameras were coded as categorization thoughts. Thoughts that noted how the camera was different from the overall category of 35mm SLR or 110 cameras were coded as discrepancy thoughts. Thoughts that related the camera to more specific subcategories of cameras or specific models were coded as subtyping thoughts. Thus, five main groups of thoughts were established for analysis and are presented in Exhibit 12.3. These five types of thoughts accounted for 85 percent of subjects' total responses to the communication.

Subjects' responses were separated into individual thoughts and coded by three judges. Two of the judges each coded half of the cognitive responses and the third judge coded all of them. The judges were blind to the hypotheses and the treatment condition. The interjudge agreement was on average 86 percent. (The agreement between Judge One and Judge Two was 87.2 percent. The agreement between Judge Two and Judge Three was 84.5 percent.) Disagreements were resolved through discussion, so that all responses were coded. The total of product-related thoughts was computed for each subject by adding together the five main groups and other product cognitions. The proportion of each of the five types of analyzed thoughts to total product-related thoughts was also computed.

Response Times. Three sets of response-time measures were collected: reading speed, time taken to read the product description and form an impression of the product, and time taken to evaluate the product. The reading speed time was used as a covariate in the analysis of impression time to control for individual differences in reading speed. Response times were measured to one-fourth of a second.

Evaluations. Subjects provided an overall evaluation of the product on a 7-point bipolar scale from "very good" to "very bad." Absolute deviations of their evaluative ratings from the scale mid-point were used as the extremity ratings.

Manipulation Checks

To ensure that they had the relevant category available in memory, subjects were asked to recall the type of camera about which they had received information. Ninety-eight percent correctly identified the category. Data from all subjects were used in the analysis. Subjects responded on a 7-point agree-disagree scale to "the product is different from the standard 35 mm SLR (110) camera," where 7 was maxi-

EXHIBIT 12.3 Coding scheme for responses

CODE AND DESCRIPTION	EXAMPLE
A. Simple evaluative thoughts	
1. Overall evaluation of the product	"I like it"
2. Qualified evaluation of the product	"It would be good for trips"
3. Overall impression of the product	"Seems high priced, premium quality"
B. Attribute-oriented thoughts	
1. Attribute evaluation	"Cartridge loading is useless"
2. Attribute tradeoff	"Small would make it less versatile"
3. Attribute comparison to standard	"In size it is towards the smaller ones"
4. Attribute clarification	"Is it a fixed focus lens or not?"
5. Request for information on additional attributes	"I wondered about the flash"
C. Categorization thoughts	"It sounds like a typical 35mm SLR"
D. Subtyping thoughts	"It sounds like the Olympus AX-7"
E. Discrepancy thoughts	"This 110 is different from the usual instamatic"
F. Other thoughts	
1. Attribute recall	"Its features were: compact, easy to load, pocketable"
2. Product imagery	"A picture of the lens came to mind"
3. Prior knowledge/familiarity	"I'm not familiar with 35's"
4. Disbelief thoughts	"I find it hard to believe"
5. Ad-related thoughts	"It was technical"
6. Task-related thoughts	"I decided to read only the bold print"
7. Irrelevant	

mally different, to check the success of the match and mismatch to category knowledge manipulation.

RESULTS

The hypotheses were examined in a 2 (expertise) × 2 (match/mismatch to category) × 2 (description) between-subjects analysis of variance design.[3]

Manipulation Check

The main effect of match/mismatch to category was significant at the $p < 0.001$ level ($F[1,117] = 100.7$). The described camera was rated to be more different from the category's typical camera in the mismatch conditions (Mean = 5.4, where 7 is maximally different) than in the match conditions (Mean = 2.8). In addition, there was an expertise by match/mismatch interaction ($F[1,117] = 29.4$, $p < 0.001$). This interaction was caused by experts'

[3]When data were missing, rather than delete the entire case, the analysis for the individual measures was carried out with the number of observations available for that measure. Most of the missing data occurred for the response time measures ($n = 121$ for the time taken to form an impression, $n = 115$ for time taken to reach an evaluation), and resulted because subjects failed to press the response-time button. The missing data were spread equally across all cells.

greater sensitivity to the match or mismatch of information to the category (Means = 6.1 versus 2.0) than novices' (Means = 4.8 versus 3.6). However, it was determined that even for novices the difference between match and mismatch was significant ($t[117] = 3.20$, $p < 0.01$). Thus the categories were indeed consensual—i.e., the match/mismatch distinction was understood by both expert and novice consumers.

Finally there was a match/mismatch by description interaction ($F[1,117] = 9.8$, $p < 0.001$). The description that matched the 35 mm SLR camera was judged to be more typical in the match condition and more atypical in the mismatch condition (Means = 2.2 versus 5.7) than the description that matched the 110 camera (Means = 3.4 versus 5.2). However, the difference between match and mismatch conditions was significant for both descriptions (description of 35 mm SLR = $t[117] = 9.13$, $p < 0.001$; description of 110 = $t[117] = 4.85$, $p < 0.001$). Thus it was established that the manipulation of the difference of the product description from the typical product in the category was successful for both descriptions used and for both expert and novice subjects.

Overall Test of Hypotheses

A multivariate analysis of variance was conducted to examine the effects of match/mismatch to category and expertise on all of the process measures taken together. The process measures used were: (a) number of product-related thoughts, (b) number of attribute-oriented thoughts, (c) number of simple evaluative thoughts, (d) impression time, and (e) extremity of affect. The mean values for each condition are shown in Table 12.1.

The results support a main effect of match/mismatch to category on evaluation processes. Information that matched categories was processed differently from information that was discrepant from category knowledge ($F[5,103] = 3.1$, $p < 0.01$). A main effect for expertise on processing was not supported ($F[5,103] = 1.9$, $p < 0.12$). However, the expertise by category interaction was significant ($F[5,103] = 2.5$, $p < 0.04$), which suggests that expert and novice groups do indeed respond differently to the match or mismatch of information to categories. To explore the results further, separate analyses of variance were conducted for each of the dependent measures.

Number of Thoughts

Hypothesis 1a proposed that more total thoughts related to the product would be generated in the mismatch conditions than in the match conditions. The analysis of variance results using the number of product-related thoughts as the dependent measure showed a main effect for match/mismatch to category ($F[1,118] = 10.3$, $p < 0.001$). More thoughts were generated in the mismatch conditions (Mean = 3.9) than in the match conditions (Mean = 2.7). Thus, Hypothesis 1a was supported.

Hypothesis 2a proposed that experts would generate more product cognitions than would novices. There was a main effect for expertise that approached significance ($F[1,118] = 3.4$, $p < 0.07$). More thoughts were generated by experts (Mean = 3.7) than by novices (Mean = 3.0), marginally supporting Hypothesis 2a.

Finally, a significant interaction between match/mismatch and expertise was proposed. Experts were hypothesized to generate more thoughts in the mismatch conditions than in the match conditions (Hypothesis 3a). Novices were hypothesized to not be influenced by the match or mismatch of information to categories in the number of product-related thoughts generated (Hypothesis 4a). The analysis of variance results supported a match/mismatch by expertise interaction ($F[1,118] = 31.8$, $p < 0.01$). This was examined by conducting planned comparisons between the cell means. Experts, as hypothesized, produced more thoughts when information was discrepant from category knowledge (Mean = 4.8) than when information matched category knowledge (Mean = 2.6), supporting Hypothesis 3a ($t[118] = 4.07$, $p < 0.001$). Novices did not produce more (or less) thoughts depending upon the mismatch or match of information, supporting Hypothesis 4a (Means = 3.1 versus 2.9; $t[118] < 1$, n.s.). This interaction is graphed in Part A of the figure, and the cell means are reported in the table. Thus all the hypotheses relating to number of product-related thoughts were at least marginally supported.

An analysis of the means also confirmed that the expertise by match/mismatch interaction was caused by experts producing more thoughts in the mismatch conditions compared to novices ($t[118] = 3.18$, $p < 0.01$). There were no differences due to expertise in the match conditions ($t[118] < 1$, n.s.). Thus the results indicate that, relative to novices, experts generate more thoughts to communication only when information is discrepant from their expectations of the category. When information matches their expectations, experts do not engage in more thoughts.

Types of Thoughts

The analysis for types of thoughts was conducted using both the number and proportion of thoughts to total thoughts. The pattern of results was essentially similar. Therefore only the number of thoughts will be reported.

Attribute-Oriented Thoughts. Attribute-oriented thoughts relate to evaluation of attributes, evaluation of the product tied to the evaluation of an attribute or set of attributes, recognition of attribute tradeoffs, comparison of attributes to a standard, and requests for information on additional attributes (see the coding scheme in Exhibit 12.1). Thoughts generally coded as support arguments and counter arguments (Wright 1973, 1980) fall into this category of thoughts.

Hypothesis 1b stated that more attribute-oriented responses would be generated in the mismatch conditions compared to the match conditions. This hypothesis was supported ($F[1,118] = 12.0$, $p < 0.001$). More attribute-oriented thoughts were produced in the mismatch conditions (Mean = 1.9) than in the match conditions (Mean = 0.8).

Hypothesis 2b predicted that experts would generate more attribute-oriented thoughts than would novices. The effect for expertise approached significance for the number of attribute-oriented thoughts ($F[1,118] = 3.6$, $p < 0.06$). More attribute-oriented thoughts were produced by experts (Mean = 1.6) than by novices (Mean = 1.1), marginally supporting Hypothesis 2b.

A significant expertise × match/mismatch interaction was also predicted. This interaction was significant for the number of attribute-oriented thoughts ($F[1,118] = 5.0$, $p < 0.03$) and is graphed in Part B of Figure 12.1. Experts produced a greater number of attribute-oriented thoughts in the mismatch conditions than in the match conditions (Means = 2.5 versus 0.7; $t[118] = 4.03$, $p < 0.001$). For novices, there were no significant differences between the mismatch and match conditions for number of attribute-oriented thoughts (Means = 1.3 versus 0.9). Thus, as shown in Part B of the figure, the match or mismatch of information to product category knowledge was significant for experts but not for novices, supporting Hypotheses 3b and 4b. The pattern of results for total product-related thoughts is mirrored by the results for attribute-oriented thoughts.

Simple Evaluative Thoughts. Simple evaluative thoughts were statements referring to overall impressions of the product and overall evaluations of the product that were not supported by attribute information. There were no differences in the number and proportion of simple evaluative thoughts across conditions. On average, 19 percent of the product-related cognitions were simple evaluative thoughts. Thus Hypotheses 1c, 2c, 3c, and 4c were not supported.

Categorization Thoughts. Categorization thoughts were a post hoc addition to the analysis. These thoughts were defined as statements noting similarity between the product and the overall category. Thus, statements indicating how the advertised product was similar to the category prototype, the category exemplar, or the consumer's own camera were coded as categorization thoughts. Though no hypotheses

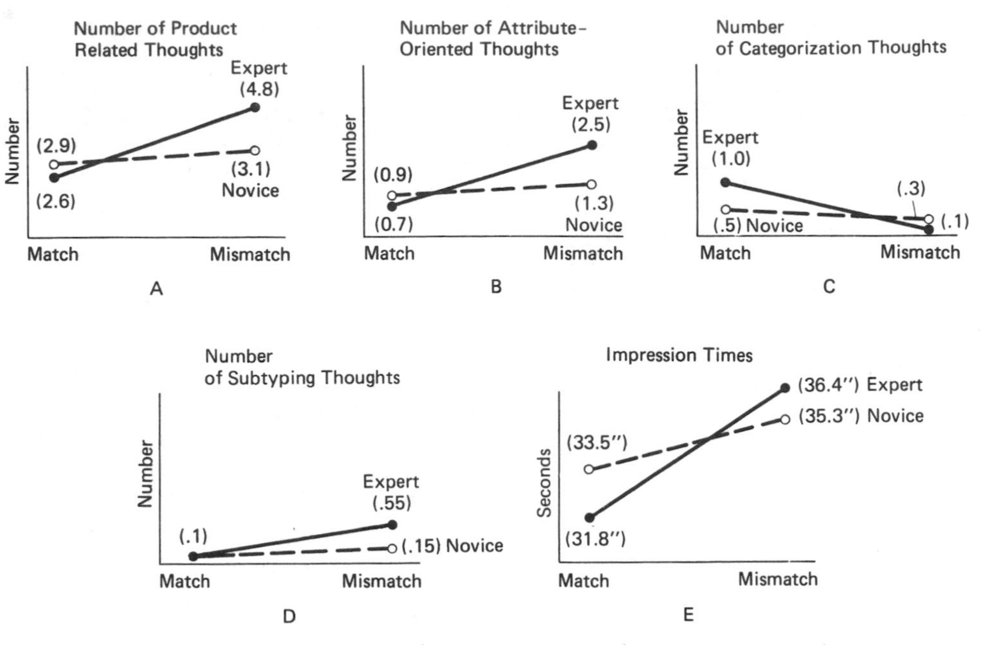

FIGURE 12.1 Dependent Measures for Category-Based versus Piecemeal Processing

were proposed a priori, the likely pattern of results would be a main effect for match/mismatch-to-category knowledge and a significant expertise × match/mismatch interaction. When the product description matches category expectations, experts should be more likely than novices to type it as typical of the category.

For categorization thoughts there was a significant main effect for match/mismatch ($F[1,118] = 48.9$, $p < 0.001$). There were more categorization thoughts in the match conditions (Mean = 0.75) than in the mismatch conditions (Mean = 0.17). The expertise × match/mismatch interaction was significant ($F[1,118] = 12.5$, $p < 0.001$), but there was also a significant three-way expertise × match/mismatch × description interaction for categorization thoughts ($F[1,118] = 5.2$, $p < 0.02$). To explore the higher level interaction, comparisons between the cell means were examined separately for the expert and novice groups.

For expert consumers, there was a significant difference due to match/mismatch-to-category knowledge ($t[118] = 7.35$, $p < 0.001$). The mean number of categorization thoughts in the match conditions was approximately 1.0 (Mean = 0.97). In the mismatch conditions there were virtually no categorization thoughts (Mean = 0.10). The results held for both product descriptions. Thus, when asked to form an impression of the product, expert subjects in the match conditions related the product to the typical product in the category.

The results for novice consumers differed for each of the two product descriptions. The description that matched the 110 camera—a simple, instamatic camera with which novices are likely to be familiar—showed a significant difference in the number of categorization thoughts between the match (Mean = 0.76) and mismatch (Mean = 0.17) conditions ($t[118] = 3.83$, $p < 0.001$). However, for the 35mm SLR camera description, there were no differences in the number of categorization thoughts between the match (Mean = 0.28) and mismatch (Mean = 0.31) conditions ($t[118] < 1$, n.s.). Thus, given a familiar camera type, novices also tended to characterize the product as typical of the category, but they were unable to do this for the more sophisticated 35 mm SLR camera, with which they were less familiar. The analysis is consistent with the notion that when product information matches consumers' knowledge bases, they tend to form an impression of the specific product by recognizing it as an example of a previously defined category in memory. These findings are graphed in Part C of Figure 12.1.

Subtyping Thoughts. Again, no hypotheses were made a priori, but subjects' protocols revealed a number of statements attempting to relate the stimulus product to specific subcategories or models—e.g., modern 35mm SLRs, the Olympus AX-7, and the recent Polaroid cameras. There was a significant main effect on the number of subtyping thoughts for match/mismatch to category ($F[1,118] = 9.2$, $p < 0.01$). There was a significantly greater number of subtyping thoughts in the mismatch conditions (0.34) than in the match conditions (0.09). Thus discrepant products appear to be subtyped. There was also a main effect for expertise ($F[1,118] = 4.6$, $p < 0.03$). More subtyping thoughts were produced by experts (0.30) than by novices (0.12), indicating that subtyping is a strategy followed more by experts than by novices.

There was a significant expertise × match/mismatch interaction for number of subtyping thoughts ($F[1,118] = 6.4$, $p < 0.01$). The interaction is graphed in Part D of Figure 12.1. Experts produced a greater number of subtyping thoughts ($t[118] = 3.94$, $p < 0.001$) in the mismatch conditions (Mean = 0.55) than in the match conditions (Mean = 0.07). Novices were not influenced in the number of subtyping thoughts ($t[118] < 1$, n.s.) by the manipulation of match (Mean = 0.10) or mismatch-to-category knowledge (Mean = 0.15). Experts also produced significantly more subtyping thoughts in the mismatch condition than did novices ($t[118] = 3.38$, $p < 0.001$).

The data revealed that when product information was discrepant from the category, experts attempted to subtype the discrepant product. Thus, when information is discrepant from expectations, expert subjects still attempt to reach impressions by categorizing the product; categorization simply now occurs at a more specific level. Rosch et al. (1976) has suggested that experts share consensual categories with novices but are also capable of categorizing at a more specific level. Though this proposition has never been empirically tested, the data here provide initial support that experts can employ more specific subcategories in information processing when consensual categories become inappropriate.

Discrepancy Thoughts. Discrepancy thoughts—statements of how the product described is different from other products in the category—were also a post hoc addition to the analysis. There was a main effect for match/mismatch for the number of discrepancy thoughts ($F[1,118] = 12.8$, $p < 0.001$), but this was modified by an expertise × match/mismatch interaction ($F[1,118] = 4.0$, $p < 0.05$). Experts produced more discrepancy thoughts in the mismatch conditions compared to the match conditions ($t[118] = 3.9$, $p < 0.001$; Means = 0.55 versus 0.03). Novices were not influenced by match/mismatch in the number of such thoughts ($t[118] = 1.06$, $p < 0.25$; Means = 0.23 versus 0.10). This result is consistent with other research hypothesizing that experts, relative to novices, focus on incongruent information (Fiske, Kinder, and Larter 1983; Taylor and Winkler 1980).

Response Times

Two separate response-time measures were collected: (1) the time taken to read and assimilate the information into an overall impression of the product (impression time), and based on this impression, (2) the time taken to make an overall good-bad evaluation of the product (evaluation time). However, subjects' protocols suggested that subjects had already formed an evaluation during the impression formation stage. (Simple evaluative responses did not vary by condition and averaged a frequency of 0.62 per subject.) Therefore, impression-time data were used to test the hypotheses.

Subjects' reading speed was found to be significantly related to the time taken to form an impression and was used as a covariate in the analysis for impression time. (The analysis of covariance assumptions were verified.) Hypothesis 1d stated that overall evaluations will be made faster when information matches categories than when information is discrepant from categories. For impression time, there was a main effect for match/mismatch of information ($F[1,112] = 10.3, p < 0.01$). On average, subjects reached impressions faster when information matched category knowledge than when it was discrepant from category knowledge (Adjusted Means = 23.6 seconds versus 35.8 seconds). Thus there was support for Hypothesis 1d.

Further, an expertise × match/mismatch interaction was hypothesized: experts would reach overall evaluations faster when information matches category knowledge than when information is discrepant from category knowledge (Hypothesis 3d). It was further hypothesized that the match/mismatch of information would not influence the time taken for novices to reach evaluations (Hypothesis 4d). For impression time, the expertise × match/mismatch interaction was not significant ($F[1,112] < 1.0$, n.s.). However, since differences between the expert and novice groups had been hypothesized, planned comparisons were conducted. The difference in impression time between the match and mismatch conditions was significant for experts (Adjusted Means = 36.4 seconds versus 31.8 seconds $t[112] = 3.31, p < 0.01$) but not for novices (Adjusted Means = 35.3 seconds versus 33.5 seconds, $t[112] = 1.26, p < 0.2$) and are shown in Part E of Figure 12.1. Thus, this measure indicates that category-based judgments are more efficient—i.e., faster—than piecemeal judgments. There is partial support for the notion that expertise exaggerates this effect.[4]

Extremity of Affect

A final measure of the differences in processing was extremity of affect. The basic hypothesis was that evaluations would be more extreme when information is perceived as consistent with category knowledge than when information is perceived as discrepant from category knowledge. Hypotheses relating to extremity of affect were not supported. However, it is important to note that the evaluative extremity prediction (Fiske 1982) depends on one particular stimulus configuration. The prediction only holds under those special conditions when the category is more affectively extreme than the individual attributes. This study does not meet these conditions. To meet them, one has to obtain isolated evaluations of the category and each of its attributes, as was done in the original Fiske (1982) study.

The affect measures were significant in that there was an expertise × description interaction ($F[1,118] = 8.8, p < 0.01$). Experts preferred the description of the 35mm SLR camera to the description of the 110 camera ($t[118] = 4.02, p < 0.01$). Thus, experts were not concerned with the label of the camera (i.e., whether it was labeled 35mm SLR or 110 as in the match and mismatch conditions), but preferred the description that listed the features of the 35 mm SLR to the description that listed the features of the 110 camera (Means = 2.6 versus 3.8). Novices, on the other hand, rated the camera that was labeled 35mm SLR more positively than the camera labeled 110 whether or not the features listed were actually those of the 35mm SLR camera or the 110 camera (Means = 2.5 versus 3.1; $t[118] = 1.96, p < 0.05$). The results suggest that experts are concerned with product descriptions in making evaluations, and novices are more influenced by product category labels.

[4]Although subjects had been responding affectively during the initial impression formation stage, the expertise × match/mismatch interaction for time taken to make an overall good-bad evaluation of the product was still significant ($F[1,107] = 5.65, p < 0.05$). Experts took significantly less time to evaluate the typical product than the atypical product (8.2 seconds versus 11.8 seconds; $t[107] = 2.82, p < 0.01$). For novices there were no differences between the match and mismatch conditions (11.0 seconds versus 10.1 seconds; $t[107] = 0.65, p < 0.25$). A comparison between the experts and novices in the match conditions indicated that experts were significantly faster than novices ($t[107] = 2.03, p < 0.05$). This result further supports the notion that for experts, matches to category knowledge cue affective judgments.

DISCUSSION

The results are summarized in Exhibit 12.4. Since the results were different for the expert and novice groups, the results are discussed separately for these two groups of subjects.

Expert Consumers

The results provide substantial evidence that evaluation processes are contingent upon consumers' prior knowledge and the match of information to this knowledge base. The effects of expertise are rather clear. When information matches category-based knowledge, knowledgeable consumers rapidly reach final impressions and evaluations and generate more thoughts related to the product category and fewer thoughts related to the product's attributes. When information is discrepant from category knowledge, knowledgeable consumers engage in more analytical processing and take longer to form an impression of the product. Their final evaluation also appears to be based on a more constructive or piecemeal review of attributes. Thus it seems that for expert con-

EXHIBIT 12.4 Summary of results for category-based versus piecemeal processing[a]

MISMATCH VERSUS MATCH TO CATEGORY

(H1a) More product-related thoughts[b]
(H1b) More attribute-oriented thoughts[b]
(H1c) Fewer simple evaluative thoughts
(H1d) Longer response times[b]
(H1e) Less extreme evaluations
- Fewer categorization thoughts[b]
- More subtyping thoughts[b]
- More discrepancy thoughts[b]

EXPERT VERSUS NOVICE CONSUMERS

(H2a) More product-related thoughts[c]
(H2b) More attribute-oriented thoughts[c]
(H2c) Fewer simple evaluative thoughts
(H2d) Less extreme evaluations
- More subtyping thoughts[b]

EXPERT CONSUMERS—MISMATCH VERSUS MATCH TO CATEGORY

(H3a) More product-related thoughts[b]
(H3b) More attribute-oriented thoughts[b]
(H3c) Fewer simple evaluative thoughts
(H3d) Longer response times[b]
(H3e) Less extreme evaluations
- Fewer categorization thoughts[b]
- More subtyping thoughts[b]
- More discrepancy thoughts[c]

NOVICE CONSUMERS-MISMATCH VERSUS MATCH TO CATEGORY

(H4a) More product-related thoughts (n.s., as predicted)
(H4b) More attribute-oriented thoughts (n.s., as predicted)
(H4c) Fewer simple evaluative thoughts
(H4d) Longer response times (n.s., as predicted)
(H4e) Less extreme evaluations
- Categorization thoughts (n.s., for SLR; see text)
- Subtyping thoughts (n.s., as fits analysis)
- Discrepancy thoughts (n.s., as fits analysis)

• = no hypotheses made, but results support general analyses.
[b]$p < 0.05$.
[c]$p < 0.10$.

sumers, when information matches product knowledge in memory, the category-based affect model best describes their evaluation processes; when information is discrepant from product knowledge, the piecemeal model better approximates their evaluation processes.

However, support for these alternative models needs to be qualified. The distinction between the evaluation processes engaged in when information is consistent with expectations and when it departs from them is not as strong as these models might portray. When product information was discrepant from category knowledge, expert consumers still attempted to categorize the product to form an impression of it, but they used more subordinate level categories; i.e., they related the product to more specific types of cameras or specific models. The subtyping of discrepant stimuli is evidence that the processing of new information draws heavily upon consumers' prior knowledge about the category. Thus, at least for the discrepant stimuli used here, the piecemeal and categorization approaches to evaluation seem inextricably mixed.

Further, it is important to note that while category-based processing and piecemeal processing are different processes for eliciting affect, their outcomes need not necessarily differ. Both processes resulted in an equal number of simple evaluative statements and equally extreme (or moderate) affective judgments. Thus the mediating processes (as measured by the number and type of thoughts as well as response times) distinguish the two processes, but both processes produce affect—sometimes even the same amount or extremity of affect.

Novice Consumers

The data for novices indicate that they can recognize when information is consistent with or discrepant from their expectations about the category, but that they differ from experts in their use of category knowledge in processing product information. As hypothesized, novice consumers use category-based processing more than experts—both when information is consistent with and discrepant from category expectations. Novices rated the camera labeled 35mm SLR more positively than the camera labeled 110, whether or not the product description matched the product label. It appears that novices know that 35mm SLRs are good cameras and that they use this category-based knowledge rather than attribute information to evaluate products. Thus, novices have global affect associated with general aspects of products—for example, with product category labels rather than with detailed product descriptions. One implication of this might be that product labeling strategies might have a greater influence on novice than on expert consumers.

Alternative Theoretical Models

Although the category-based affect model (Fiske 1982; Fiske and Pavelchak in press) was used to generate many of the predictions examined in this paper, the findings are consistent with alternative models. In particular, the findings are consistent with the impression formation literature (e.g., Hastie 1980). This literature provides considerable evidence that discrepant information, because it is unexpected and is perceived to be more novel and interesting, is elaborated more, and that this elaboration accounts for its advantages in recall (e.g., Srull 1981). The findings are also consistent with a general schema perspective that suggests that schema-consistent information can be chunked into large perceptual units (Chase and Simon 1973) and processed more easily (Sherman et al. 1983).

Despite the availability of competing models, the category-based affect model does make an important contribution to understanding the data in this study. Specifically, there are three pieces of data that support the category-based model over alternative models. First, there is evidence that subjects were forming affective judgments rather than merely arriving at cognitive impressions. Simple evaluative thoughts averaged a frequency of 0.62 per subject or 19 percent of total thoughts. Since cognitive models (e.g., Hastie 1980) do not include evaluations or affect as a consequence of information processing, the results are best interpreted within the category-based affect model.

Second, as predicted by the category-based model, when information was consistent with category knowledge, evaluations were formed by categorizing the product; when information was discrepant from category knowledge, attribute-oriented piecemeal processing was used. Again, though the effects of consistent and inconsistent information have been studied from other perspectives (e.g., the influence on recall), the effects of consistent and inconsistent information on evaluation strategies have been addressed only by the category-based affect model. In addition, no other model specifically predicts that impressions and evaluations are formed by relating the target object to the overall category. The categorization thoughts provide nice support for the proposed model.

Finally, the data for novices provide support for category-based processing. Novices liked the SLR camera better than the 110 camera, and they used this category-based knowledge rather than attribute information to evaluate the product. In sum, the category-based affect model provides a cogent framework for examining the effects of match/mismatch of information to consumers' knowledge base on evaluation strategies mediating product judgments.

Effects of Involvement and Interest

In this study, knowledge is a measured rather than a manipulated variable. Therefore, other variables might be related to the knowledge construct. In particular, one could argue that motivation might be confounded with knowledge. Subjects in the experiment rated their involvement and interest in cameras. Scores on the knowledge scale and self-rated measures of interest ($r = 0.52$, $p < 0.001$) and involvement ($r = 0.51$; $p < 0.001$) showed a moderate but significant correlation. Thus it appears that knowledge is correlated with involvement in the category: one could attempt to explain the results in terms of differences in involvement rather than differences in knowledge between the "expert" and "novice" groups.

It is argued here that knowledge has an independent effect on processing, and that involvement or interest cannot explain the pattern of results obtained. It can be assumed that involvement increases the amount of processing (Petty and Cacioppo 1979). Therefore, the involvement construct would predict that the expert group (more knowledgeable, more involved) would always process more than the novices. It could not predict the interaction hypothesized between expertise and the extent of match of information to consumers' knowledge base.

To test this notion, the analyses for number and types of thoughts and response times were repeated in this study, using involvement and interest in cameras as covariates. (Separate analyses were done for involvement and interest.) The effects of involvement and interest were consistently insignificant and did not change the effect of expertise, the effect of match/mismatch-to-category knowledge, or the effects of the interaction between expertise and match/mismatch-to-category knowledge on the process measures. Thus, at least in this study, consumer knowledge had an effect on evaluation processes independent of interest or involvement in the category.

IMPLICATIONS FOR FUTURE RESEARCH

The categorization approach is potentially a useful way of examining how consumers perceive and react to marketing stimuli. It suggests that consumers have well defined product categories in memory and that expectations about these categories guide evaluation and decision processes. This approach might be particularly relevant for obtaining customer-oriented product market definitions that complement some of the more quantitative approaches for identifying product market boundaries (Day, Shocker, and Srivastava 1979). In addition, the finding that experts perceive subtypes might serve as the focus for possible positioning strategies in which a product is positioned within an overall category but yet perceived to be distinctly different.

Finally, it appear that examining the process of subtyping in some detail would be one avenue for future research. Several of the subtypes referred to in this experiment were specific brand exemplars (e.g., the Pentax 110, the Olympus AX-7). Thus, specifying the parameters that lead to the use of subtypes might help elucidate the relative roles of the product category's general principles and knowledge of specific brand exemplars in consumer decision processes (Brooks 1978; Read 1983). This might be particularly helpful in determining the efficacy of comparative advertising strategies, which explicitly reference either the overall product class or knowledge of prominent brands within the product class.

REFERENCES

ANDERSON, JOHN R. (1982), "Acquisition of Cognitive Skill," *Psychological Review,* 89 (July), 369–406.

ANDERSON, NORMAN H. (1974), "Information Integration Theory: A Brief Survey," in *Contemporary Developments in Mathematical Psychology,* Vol. 2, Eds. David H. Krantz, R. Duncan Luce, Richard C. Atkinson, and Patrick Suppes. San Francisco: W. H. Freeman, 236–305.

BETTMAN, JAMES R. (1979), *An Information Processing Theory of Consumer Choice.* Reading, MA: Addison-Wesley.

——— (1982), " Functional Analysis of the Role of Overall Evaluation of Alternatives in Choice Processes," in *Advances in Consumer Research,* Vol. 9, Ed. Andrew A. Mitchell. Ann Arbor, MI: Association for Consumer Research, 87–93.

———, and C. WHAN PARK (1980), "Effects of Prior Knowledge and Experience and Phase of the Choice Process on Consumer Decision Processes: A Protocol Analysis," *Journal of Consumer Research,* 7 (December), 234–248.

BROOKS, LEE (1978), "Non-Analytical Concept Formation and Memory for Instances," in *Cognition and Categorization,* Eds. Eleanor Rosch and Barbara B. Lloyd. Hillsdale, NJ: Erlbaum, 169–210.

CHASE, WILLIAM G., and HERBERT A. SIMON (1973), "Perceptions in Chess," *Cognitive Psychology,* 4 (January), 55–81.

CHI, MICHELENE T. H., PAUL J. FELTOVICH, and ROBERT GLASER (1981), "Categorization and Representation of Physics Problems by Experts and Novices," *Cognitive Science,* 5 (April), 121–152.

COHEN, JOEL B. (1982), "The Role of Affect in Categorization: Towards a Reconsideration of the Concept of Attitude, in *Advances in Consumer Research,* Vol. 9, Ed. Andrew A. Mitchell. Ann Arbor, MI: Association for Consumer Research, 94–100.

DAY, GEORGE S., ALLAN D. SHOCKER, and RAJENDRA K. SRIVASTAVA (1979), "Customer-Oriented Approaches to Identifying Product Markets," *Journal of Marketing,* 43 (Fall), 8–19.

EDELL, JULIE, and ANDREW MITCHELL (1978), "An Informational Processing Approach to Cognitive Responses," in *Research Frontiers in Marketing,* Ed. Subhash C. Jain. Chicago: American Marketing Association, 178–183.

ELIO, RENEE, and JOHN R. ANDERSON (1981), "The Effects of Category Generalizations and Instance Similarity on Schema Abstraction," *Journal of Experimental Psychology: Human Learning and Memory,* 7 (November), 397–417.

ERICSSON, K. ANDERS, and HERBERT A. SIMON (1978), "Thinking Aloud Protocols and Data," CIP Working Paper, Department of Psychology, Carnegie-Mellon University, Pittsburgh, PA.

FISHBEIN, MARTIN, and ICEK AJZEN (1975), *Belief, Attitude, Intention and Behavior: An Introduction to Theory and Research.* Reading, MA: Addison-Wesley.

FISKE, SUSAN T. (1982), "Schema-Triggered Affect: Applications to Social Perception," in *Affect and Cognition: The 17th Annual Carnegie Symposium on Cognition,* Eds. Margaret S. Clark and Susan T. Fiske. Hillsdale, NJ: Erlbaum, 55–78.

———, and ANN E. BEATTIE (1982), "Two Modes of Processing Affect in Social Cognition," paper presented at American Psychological Association, Washington, DC.

———, and DONALD R. KINDER (1980), "Involvement, Expertise and Schema Use: Evidence from Political Cognition," in *Personality Cognition and*

Social Interaction, Eds. Nancy Cantor and John F. Kihlstrom. Hillsdale, NJ: Erlbaum, 171–190.

———, DONALD R. KINDER, and MICHAEL W. LARTER (1983), "The Novice and the Expert: Knowledge-Based Strategies in Political Cognition," *Journal of Experimental Social Psychology,* 19, 381–400.

———, and MARK A. PAVELCHAK (in press), "Category-Based Versus Piecemeal-Based Affective Responses: Developments in Schema-Triggered Affect," in *The Handbook of Motivation and Cognition: Foundations of Social Behavior,* Eds. Richard M. Sorrentiono and E. Tory Higgins. New York: Guilford Press.

———, and SHELLEY E. TAYLOR (1984), *Social Cognition.* Reading, MA: Addison-Wesley.

GREEN, PAUL, and YORAM WIND (1973), *Multiattribute Decisions in Marketing: A Measurement Approach.* Hinsdale, IL: Dryden.

GREENWALD, ANTHONY G. (1968), "Cognitive Learning, Cognitive Response to Persuasion and Attitude Change," in *Psychological Foundation of Attitudes,* Eds. Anthony G. Greenwald, Timothy C. Brock, and Thomas M. Ostrom. New York: Academic Press, 147–170.

HASTIE, REID (1980), "Memory for Behavioral Information that Confirms or Contradicts a Personality Impression," in *Person Memory: The Cognitive Basis of Social Perception,* Eds. Reid Hastie et al. Hillsdale, NJ: Erlbaum.

KAHNEMAN, DANIEL, and AMOS TVERSKY (1972), "Subjective Probability: A Judgment of Representativeness," *Cognitive Psychology,* 3 (July), 430–454.

LARKIN, JILL H., JOHN MCDERMOTT, P. DOROTHEA SIMON, and HERBERT A. SIMON (1980), "Expert and Novice Performance in Solving Physics Problems," *Science,* 208 (June), 1335–1342.

LINVILLE, PATRICIA W. (1982), "The Complexity Extremity Effect and Age-Based Stereotyping," *Journal of Personality and Social Psychology,* 42 (February), 193–211.

MANDLER, JEAN M., and RICHARD E. PARKER (1976), "Memory for Descriptive and Spatial Information in Complex Pictures," *Journal of Experimental Psychology: Human Learning and Memory,* 2 (January), 38–48.

MEDIN, DOUGLAS L., and EDWARD E. SMITH (1984), "Concepts and Concept Formation," *Annual Review of Psychology,* 35, 113–138.

MERVIS, CAROLYN B., and ELEANOR ROSCH (1981), "Categorization of Natural Objects," *Annual Review of Psychology,* 32, 89–115.

OLSON, JERRY C. (1978), "Inferential Belief Formation in the Cue Utilization Process," in *Advances in Consumer Research,* Vol. 5, Ed. H. Keith Hunt. Ann Arbor, MI: Association for Consumer Research, 703–713.

PETTY, RICHARD E., and JOHN T. CACIOPPO (1979), "Issue Involvement Can Increase or Decrease Persuasion by Enhancing Message-Relevant Cognitive Responses," *Journal of Personality and Social Psychology,* 37 (October), 1915–1926.

READ, STEPHEN J. (1983), "Once Is Enough: Causal Reasoning from a Single Instance," *Journal of Personality and Social Psychology,* 45 (August), 323–334.

ROSCH, ELEANOR (1975), "Cognitive Representation of Semantic Categories," *Journal of Experimental Psychology: General,* 104 (September), 192–233.

———, and CAROLYN B. MERVIS (1975), "Family Resemblance: Studies in the Internal Structure of Categories," *Cognitive Psychology,* 7 (October), 573–605.

———, CAROLYN B. MERVIS, WAYNE D. GRAY, DAVID M. JOHNSON, and PENNY BOYES-BRAEM (1976), "Basic Objects in Natural Categories," *Cognitive Psychology,* 8 (July), 382–439.

SHERMAN, STEVEN J., KIM S. ZEHNER, JAMES JOHNSON, and EDWARD R. HIRT (1983), "Social Explanation: The Role of Timing, Set and Recall on Subjective Likelihood Estimates," *Journal of Personality and Social Psychology,* 44 (June), 1127–1143.

SHOCKER, ALAN D., and V. SRINIVASAN (1979), "Multiattribute Approaches for Product Concept Evaluation and Generation: A Critical Review," *Journal of Marketing Research,* 16 (May), 159–180.

SMITH, EDWARD E., and DOUGLAS L. MEDIN (1981), *Categories and Concepts.* Cambridge, MA: Harvard University Press.

SRULL, THOMAS K. (1981), "Some Tests of Associative Storage and Retrieval Models," *Journal of Experimental Psychology: Human Learning and Memory,* 7 (November), 440–463.

TAYLOR, SHELLEY E., and JOHN D. WINKLER (1980), "The Development of Schemas," paper presented at the American Psychological Association Meetings, Montreal, Canada.

WILKIE, WILLIAM L., and EDGAR A. PESSEMIER (1973), "Issues in Marketing's Use of Multiple-

Attribute Attitude Models," *Journal of Marketing Research,* 10 (November), 428–441.

WRIGHT, PETER L. (1973), "The Cognitive Processes Mediating the Acceptance of Advertising," *Journal of Marketing Research,* 4 (February), 53–62.

——— (1975), "Factors Affecting Cognitive Resistance to Advertising," *Journal of Consumer Research,* 2 (June), 1–9.

——— (1976a), "An Adaptive Consumers' View of Attitudes and Choice Mechanisms as Viewed by an Equally Adaptive Advertiser," in *Attitude Research at Bay,* Ed. William D. Wells. Chicago: American Marketing Association, 113–311.

——— (1976b), "Conditional Consumer Choice Processes and Advertising Strategy: An Introduction to the Principle of Control Via Advocacy and the 'Mod Squad' for Advertising Strategists," in *Attitude Research Moves Ahead,* Ed. Yoram Wind. Chicago: American Marketing Association, 101–106.

——— (1980), "Message-Evoked Thoughts: Persuasion Research Using Thought Verbalizations," *Journal of Consumer Research,* 7 (September), 151–175.

——— and PETER D. RIP (1980), "Product Class Advertising Effects on First-Time Buyers' Decision Strategies," *Journal of Consumer Research,* 8 (September), 176–188.

13

ACTIVATION RESEARCH: Psychobiological Approaches in Consumer Research*

Werner Kroeber-Riel

Activation is a psychobiological concept that plays an important role in explaining consumer behavior. Following an introduction to the theory and measurement of activation, results of experimental research in advertising effectiveness are presented. The stronger the activation elicited by a stimulus, the better was the level of cognitive performance—a relationship that poses new questions for consumer research.

Psychobiology is an interdisciplinary branch of research incorporating the findings of biology, physiology (neurophysiology, in particular), and psychology. It has also been termed neuropsychology and psychophysiology. In simplified terms, psychobiology can be described as a science concerned with the relationship between behavior and the physiological processes of the nervous system—in particular, those taking place in the brain.

Psychobiological explanations are generally based on the findings of experiments in which brain activity is taken as the independent variable and behavior as the dependent variable; sometimes this is reversed. Brain activity is manipulated by physical intervention (brain lesions) or by external stimulation. Usually the following processes are taken as dependent variables: learning, activation and attention, emotion and motivation, sleeping and dreaming, as well as the interacting effects between these processes. Both the independent variables (brain activity) and the dependent variables (behavior) are usually measured by physiological indices.

*Reprinted from the *Journal of Consumer Research,* 5 (March 1979), pp. 240-250.

Typical questions posed by researchers in psychobiology include:

- How are stimuli aimed at a person's receptors converted into inner signals, transported along nerve pathways, and processed in the central nervous system?
- Why do these stimuli create emotions?
- How are physiological processes, conscious experiencing, and behavior linked together during emotional processes?

In answering questions of this kind, psychobiology has made it clear that psychological processes originate from physiological ones, and that behavior evolves according to biological laws. This is what Thompson (1975, p. 7) is alluding to when he tersely states, "Man is an animal. This simple fact is all too often ignored in psychology." Yet, "Man is a unique animal—an obvious fact all too often ignored in biology."

This also implies certain fundamental insights for consumer research. For example, to a large extent the consumer responds automatically, according to biologically determined patterns of behavior.[1] Almost like an animal, s/he can be manipulated by classical conditioning. In short, there are biological limits imposed on "consumer sovereignty"—on the person's deliberate and conscious control of his/her behavior. In consumer research there is a tendency to overlook this fact, for the following reasons:

1. The "cognitive revolution" in psychology (McGuire 1976, p. 314) has given priority to investigations into cognitive processes; that is, into the processing of information. Yet in the field of consumer research, psychobiological knowledge has not advanced as far as it has in the study of human drives (emotions, motivations).
2. Ideological barriers stand in the way. Considering the enthusiasm with which proponents of consumerism are trying to make consumer sovereignty a reality, mention of natural (biological) limits to this sovereignty can only be embarrassing. [Who wants to have the (easily acquired) reputation of denying the consumer's sovereignty?]
3. Psychobiological research demands many years of experience, entailing considerable expenditure for laboratory equipment.
4. In consumer research there are preconceived notions against the application of psychobiological methods, because in market research psychobiological measurements are often interpreted incorrectly, as discussed in a later section.

In this paper we outline the significance and applicability of psychobiological findings and methodology for consumer research, drawing upon activation research carried out at the Institut für Konsum- und Verhaltensforschung (Institute for Consumer and Behavioral Research) at the University of the Saarland, Germany.

ACTIVATION RESEARCH: A PSYCHOBIOLOGICAL APPROACH

Theoretical Basis

Activation, like cognition, is a basic variable of human behavior. It can also be described as arousal, inner tension, or alertness. Activation provides the organism with energy and is responsible for the psychological and motor activity of the organism. In neurophysiological theories, the way in which activation comes about and its effects are described as the result of physiological processes in the central nervous system. These theories are based on Lindsley's (1951) earlier work, on Routtenberg's (1968) further elaborations, and on numerous more recent studies (Birbaumer 1975 offers a critical summary).

Activation is provoked by stimulating a subcortical unit known as the reticular activation system (RAS). The RAS consists of the *formatio reticularis,* and is located, roughly speaking, in

[1] In this connection, one should think above all of automatic responses in the affective and cognitive domain. See, for example, the remarks of Staats and Staats (1957) and Staats (1968) on the classical conditioning of emotional dispositions, or those by Shiffrin and Schneider (1977) on automatic information processing. Reference to activation by means of "manipulative" stimuli and the influence of activation on cognitive performance can also be classified among the responses that occur automatically.

the brain stem. The limbic system, closely interrelated to the reticular system, also takes part in this activation process.

Excitement is triggered in the RAS by impulses directly evoked from external stimuli (arriving at the *formatio reticularis* via collateral connections) or from other areas of the central nervous system. For example, the sight of a product can activate the RAS in the same way as might a thought process. The arousal, first released in the RAS, travels to other functional units of the brain, alerting them to take a stand-by position. Figuratively speaking, the RAS awakens the other cortical units, spurring them to activity. By this chain of reactions, the RAS becomes a chief regulator of central nervous system activities.

In addition, the RAS is linked to the cerebral cortex in a variety of ways, and can therefore alert the upper areas of the brain.[2] It is in these upper cerebral areas that the processing of information takes place (perception, thought, memory). Physiological investigations have proven that processes of arousal in the RAS have the effect of increasing the overall cortical processing of information.[3]

As a result of directly provoking arousal processes in the RAS, there is an increase in the processing of information. The relationships between arousal processes in the RAS and information processing in the cortex are expressed by the ∩-hypothesis (the inverted ∪-hypothesis): moving from low activation to an optimum activation level, an individual's performance increases. Beyond the optimum level, however, increasing activation leads to lower performance scores. (By performance we are referring to any psychological or motor performance of the individual.)

This ∩-hypothesis, however, is little more than a highly obvious assumption. Transferring the ∩-hypothesis to the realm of consumer behavior in communication and decision making leads to a host of important questions that have received little attention in previous research. It is still, for example, an open question whether there are situations in which the strength of arousal is so great that cognitive performance is substantially impeded. For example this might be the case for the consumer who is suffering under the burden of very strong conflicts or is under stress, such as severe time pressure.

Hansen borrowed the concept of "optimal arousal" from Berlyne (1960) for use in consumer research. He proceeds on the assumption that individuals strive to attain an "optimal level of arousal," and he formulates hypotheses dealing with the effects on choice behavior of a level of arousal that deviates from the optimum (Hansen 1972). However, it is still unclear whether the optimal level of arousal can be equated with the optimum according to the ∩-hypothesis. The individual strives to attain optimal arousal because s/he perceives this as pleasant. Strengths of arousal that exceed the optimum are perceived as unpleasant. There is, however, no basis for assuming that this strength of arousal, which is perceived by the individual as unpleasant, has a negative influence on cognitive performance. There are very few examples of the negative effect of a very strong arousal (Hebb 1972, p. 199). Experiments that attempted to produce such strong arousal under laboratory conditions were largely unsuccessful.[4]

In operationalizing the ∩-hypothesis, it is important to distinguish between two forms of activation:

1. long-lasting, tonic level of activation,
2. briefer, phasic activation.

[2]Actually, it would be more accurate to call it the ARAS (ascending reticular activation system). This is the term used for that part of the RAS that works in cooperation with the cortex.

[3]The physiologically present and measurable strength of activation (arousal) directly influences cortical activity. The interconnection between activation and cognitive performance (efficiency), described in a later section, takes place independent of the subjective (qualitative) interpretation of activation, in Schachter's sense (1975).

[4]"It seems that if an inverted U-relationship exists, the peak of the curve may not be reached in the rather narrow range of activation normally encountered in the laboratory" (Duffy 1972, p. 607).

In the course of daily rhythm, tonic activation fluctuates between mild arousal (e.g., during sleep or boredom) and very intense arousal (e.g., during a fit of rage). The level rises and falls slowly, and is governed primarily by the individual's emotional and motivational state. When, for example, Hebb (1972, p. 199) talks of the ∩-hypothesis as the "relation of the effectiveness with which stimuli guide behavior to the level of arousal," or when Krech and Crutchfield (1974) describe the ∩-hypothesis as the relationship between "degree of motivation and problem-solving efficiency," they are referring to tonic activation.[5]

The individual's level of activation stimulates his/her entire performance: a rise in tonic activation encourages the processing of information in general, affecting the processing of any stimulus. We leave open the question of the validity of the ∩-hypothesis for tonic activation, because in the following remarks we intend to limit our observations to phasic activation.

At a given level of activation there are also brief periods (usually a matter of seconds) when activation again fluctuates. These short-term variations have been called phasic activation—changes in excitement that determine an individual's performance in processing single stimuli. Phasic activation is thus a short-term fluctuation in activation. It appears in attention responses and in orienting responses, and serves to sensitize the organism to the pick-up and processing of stimuli.[6] It remains unclear to what extent the ∩-hypothesis also holds true for phasic activation, because a distinction between tonic and phasic activation is seldom made in presentations that deal with the ∩-hypothesis. Schönpflug (1968) explicitly relates the ∩-hypothesis to tonic and phasic activation, but is skeptical regarding the ∩-hypothesis as it relates to the interconnections between phasic activation and information retention.

In light of the lack of empirical findings on the destructive effects of very strong phasic activation on performance, and in view of the fact that an extremely strong phasic activation is unlikely in consumer behavior, we formulate the following basic hypothesis:

BH: The higher the phasic activation triggered by a specific stimulus, the more efficient will be the processing of the information mediated by this stimulus.

Operational Bases

Apart from examining the human brain through surgery for brain injuries, etc., direct (micro-) observation of brain activity (cellular activity) is not feasible. We are, therefore, dependent on indices obtainable without injury to the brain, which shed light on brain activity and on related psychological processes. The indices can be measured on three levels:

- physiological-organic,
- reported subjective experiences,
- observed behavior.

Physiological methods seem to be the most valid in determining activation, because physiological responses are universal; that is, they always occur when the organism is aroused or when there is a change in the level of activation. This is not true for directly observable motor activities. For example, a person reading a

---

[5]The strength of an emotion or motivation can be seen as equivalent to the extent of tonic activation.

[6]The close interconnection between attention and activation has been stressed by many authors (e.g., see Posner 1975). It is hardly possible to clearly differentiate and distinguish between short-term fluctuations in activation and attention. It is in this context that the meta-linguistic character of such definitions should be seen. For example, Kahneman (1973) uses the concepts "attention," "effort," and "arousal" to designate essentially the same thing (he understands "attention" as "mental effort"). Among other authors, Pribram and McGuinness criticize this equating of terms (1975), p. 135. They view "effort" only as a special ancillary phenomenon associated with many processes of attention. Pribram and McGuinness equate the attention that appears during the processing of sensory inputs with phasic activation (which they term "arousal"), following the usage of Berlyne (1960). A special problem in the area of attention and activation, not further discussed here, is habituation effects (see Sharpless and Jasper 1956; Birbaumer 1975).

book shows no external signs of his constantly changing activation responses to particularly exciting passages. Neither do subjective experiences verbally expressed by the individual sufficiently reflect variations in activation. We do know, though, that physiological methods are the most accurate in detecting slight (yet still influential for behavior) changes in activation that are not subjectively perceived at all.[7]

If we use verbal methods to measure activation or processes of arousal in the brain, we are only making a needless detour. We will be measuring the perception of responses in the nervous system, when the responses themselves can be measured directly. Besides, verbal statements are tremendously influenced by cognitive processes. Often the subject being interviewed is neither able nor willing to divulge his/her excitement when, for example, his/her self-esteem is at stake. A psychophysiological investigation carried out by Kroeber-Riel, Barg, and Bernhard (1975) into the stimulating effect of political slogans demonstrated that although the subjects claimed to be highly moved by noble political ideals (such as justice and equal opportunity), physiological measurements and data yielded by experiments suggested that in reality they were stirred only to a slight extent by such ideals. Summarizing these and other arguments discussed in the literature on measuring activation, Schönpflug (1969) maintains that physiological indices are a sensitive and valid measurement of activation levels and changes.

The physiological indices can be divided into the following areas: (1) electrophysiological, (2) blood circulation, respiration, and energy expenditure, and (3) biochemical.[8] Electrophysiological indices are the most revealing; they reflect bioelectric processes. Sensors (electrodes) are attached to a person's skin, which receive bioelectric body impulses. These signals are then converted, usually after being amplified, into digital values. An instrument called a polygraph records analogous values in the form of curves. Figure 13.1 shows part of one of these curves with the parameters used for the analysis.

The electrophysiological indices reflect either responses of the central nervous system (central indices) or those of the peripheral nervous system (peripheral indices). Responses in the central and peripheral nervous systems constitute an integrated system, so that peripheral responses, too, are able to shed light on the processes in the central nervous system.

The electroencephalogram (EEG) is a central index, which measures rhythmic fluctuations of the electric potential in the brain. It is probably the most versatile and sensitive procedure for detecting arousal, but involves expensive laboratory apparatus, as activation research (in contrast to the medical use of the

FIGURE 13.1 Polygraph Curve with Parameters of Computation

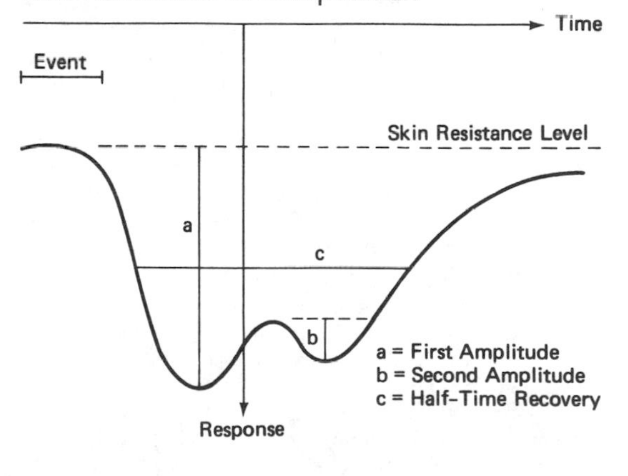

[7]For a comparison of physiological methods with verbal methods, see Schönpflug (1969). Thayer developed a verbal method (AD-ACL), which can be regarded as a "measure of total orgasmic energy release" (Thayer 1970, p. 87). It is thus related to tonic activation. Clements, Hafer, and Vermillion (1976, p. 393) designate this method as a "simple phenomenological self-report measure." As we have chosen to restrict ourselves to a measurement of phasic activation, we will not examine this method in greater detail. There are also verbal methods that can be used to evaluate the activating ability of stimuli and thus the associated phasic activation. On the basis of cognitively filtered findings, however, these verbal measures appear suitable for determining subjective experiences, but not for dealing with our questions.

[8]Of the extensive literature on physiological indices, the handbooks of Brown (1967) and Greenfield and Sternbach (1972) are worthy of particular mention.

EEG) requires complex data analysis by means of computer.[9]

An example of a peripheral index is the electrodermal response (EDR), most commonly termed galvanic skin response (GSR) or skin resistance reaction (SRR). This index reflects changes in the electric resistance of the skin associated with activation processes. Extensive tests of the validity and reliability of the EDR have yielded satisfactory results.[10] At the present time, the EDR is the most frequently applied activation index.[11]

The activation rates cited in this paper were detected by measuring the EDR. A small electric current of constant intensity is sent into the skin through electrodes attached to the palmar side of the fingers. The changes in voltage observed between the electrodes indicate the amplitude of skin resistance, and are plotted in the Figure. Each curve shows, first, the level of activation (the level prior to a phasic fluctuation) and second, the phasic fluctuation itself. The latter is termed the "response segment" of the curve and is rated by means of various parameters (e.g., amplitude, half-time recovery). We use amplitudes as the basis for digital ratings—either the amplitude of the first response or the sum of all the amplitudes released by one stimulus.[12] The measurement of EDR is based on:

1. amplitude of an EDR to a corresponding stimulus,
2. skin resistance level before stimulus presentation.

These two scores are related to each other to eliminate individual differences due to different initial resistance levels that influence the range of the EDR. We call this relation RELAMP (RELative AMPlitude). The logarithm of RELAMP tends to produce a normal distribution, necessary for a parametric statistical test (Craig and Wood 1971; Fletcher 1971).

EMPIRICAL WORK

The experimental research at our Institute served primarily to test the preceding hypothesis. Activation is taken as the independent variable, the consumer's performance (that is, his/her processing of information) as the dependent variable.

Variables

Independent variable. A person can be aroused by exposure to certain stimuli in the same way that s/he is stimulated by "drugs" (such as coffee, adrenalin, etc.). The stimuli most likely to have an impact are those that evoke innate reactions. These function to a large extent automatically. Color and erotic appeal are examples of this type of stimulus (Berlyne 1960). By exposing a subject to them, the

[9]In using the EEG, a distinction should be made between the spontaneous EEG and the evoked potential. The spontaneous EEG records the rhythmic potential fluctuations of the brain in the form of curves that primarily indicate tonic activation, that is, the level of response and state of awareness. This spontaneous EEG, however, does not react to brief, phasic activation that occurs when single stimuli are picked up. Fluctuations of this kind are indicated by the evoked potential; these latter EEG fluctuations cannot be obtained until the spontaneous EEG has undergone a complex statistical analysis.

[10]On the validity of EDR measurements of activation, see the summary of Barg (1977) with comments on the contributions of Lykken and Venables (1971), Burstein et al. (1965), McCurdy (1950), and others.

[11]Pupillary dilation is less suitable for purposes of measurement. According to Kahneman (1973) and Janisse (1977, p. 105), pupillary dilation measures the arousal responses that appear during mental effort, and is much less valid as a measure of the phasic activation appearing in the processing of sensory input. Eysenck (1977, p. 184) states that "pupillary dilation appears to measure some combination of arousal, mental effort, processing load, and anxiety." Phasic activation responses (arousal) alone are better measured by means of EDR (e.g., see Berlyne 1960).

[12]The EDR amplitudes are regarded as a measure of the strength of activation. See also Roessler, Burch, and Childers (1966, p. 120), who note: "There was a greater amplitude of GSR's associated with greater intensities of stimulation." Half-time recovery and other parameters are less valid for our purposes. For computation of EDR parameters see Venables and Christie (1973) and a new survey by Walschburger (1976).

independent variable, activation, can be manipulated systematically.[13]

In the investigations reported here, advertisements were used as arousing stimuli. By planning the advertising copy and illustration accordingly, activation was evoked in exact dosages. In preliminary experiments, stimulating material was selected so that the variance between individuals would be relatively low.[14] The success of manipulating the independent variable was determined by measuring the evoked changes in activation by means of the EDR (represented by RELAMP scores).

Dependent variable. A consumer's overall processing of information may be seen as his total performance. We can divide this performance into parts. Thus, partial performances would be his pick-up, processing, and storing of the information (as well as even smaller partial performances, such as short- and long-term storage). Each of these separate, partial performances is, in its own way, determined by activation. Activation influences the *level* of the performance, not its *content*. The dependent variable, performance, has thus also been termed "behavioral efficiency."

When we say that, based on our hypotheses, activation will result in "better" perception, this means that perception will be quicker, or more accurate, always regardless of *what* is perceived. This is an important stipulation for application purposes: increased activation does not necessarily imply more effective manipulation of the consumer. As an example, suppose that the message projected by an advertisement evokes cognitive processes that work counter to the advertising aim. Activation will still promote the processing of a message, even though it counteracts the original intention of the advertiser.

In the experiments reported here, two elements of information processing were singled out as dependent variables:

- pick-up of information,
- storage of information.

The theoretical background for our conception of these information processes is provided by the so-called multi-store memory system, described by Lindsay and Norman (1977, with more references to literature). The pick-up of information is defined as the transfer of a sensory input into the short-term memory (STM) for further processing. Information acquisition can be operationalized by measuring eye movement: recording the eye-movement patterns during exposure to advertisements shows which elements of the advertisement the eyes are fixed upon. Only these elements are picked up and transferred to the STM for further processing. "The transfer of information into the short-term memory is presumed to take place in discrete units, with each unit of information the result of one fixation" (Bernhard 1978, p. 50; Gaarder 1975, p. 98; in the latter study, saccades, not fixations, are mentioned). Fixations can thus be used as indices for the pick-up of information. In our projects the BIOMETRICS Eye-Movement Monitor was used, which functions according to the cornea reflex method.

Long-term storage of information can be determined in various ways by recall and recognition tests. For our purposes, we administered recall tests approximately 20 minutes and 24 hours after the information had been received. As no significant differences were noticed between the relative scores obtained in these two recall tests (recall scores at a certain degree of arousal in comparison to the scores of another

---

[13]Because of this automatic mechanism the consumer is often not aware of his activation.

[14]The preliminary experiments and copy tests indicated that both the EDR values of erotic pictures and the responses to colors showed a relatively minor intersubjective dispersion around the mean statistical values. This is in agreement with the findings of Traxel (1960): the erotic stimuli had the smallest interquartile deviation (0.4, median 1.7) of all tested stimuli. For this reason, erotic pictorial motifs and color designs were used in the experiments carried out by both Barg (1977) and Witt (1977). It is always amazing to see the constancy and uniformity with which pictorial or verbal stimuli can provoke activation in the laboratory. The fact that activation, to a large extent, is an automatic response—particularly to physical or emotional stimuli—is also an argument for applying laboratory findings in real field studies.

degree), we shall refer here to the 20-minute recall data.[15]

Experimental research into activation demands particularly accurate control of the artifacts that, in addition to being independent variables, can also influence activation. These factors may be related to the particular person being tested (his/her introversion/extraversion), the stimulus material (subject's interest in the advertised product, the sequence in which the stimuli are exposed), or the situation (time of day, temperature of the room). A large number of possible artifacts (also affecting the dependent variable, the consumer's performance) must be eliminated or controlled.

Experimental Findings

In an investigation by Witt (1977), the 60 students who served as subjects were shown advertisements on a projection screen for a standardized duration of six seconds. Each advertisement was of similar design, with the same slogan, brand names, copy, and kind of illustration. By modifying the illustration (illustrated person wearing less, thus achieving more erotic stimulus), mild and intense arousal was created. Four advertisements, each in one mild and one intense version, were projected—totalling eight advertisements. The subject's eye movement was recorded during each exposure.

A manipulation check demonstrated that three of the more intense versions (with the erotic illustration) had stimulated considerably higher activation than their milder counterparts ($p \leq 0.01$). Only Advertisement 2 did not produce significant differences between the two versions. The reason for this was a technical defect in Advertisement 2 (poor quality of the picture).

The frequency of eye fixation serves as a dependent variable. This frequency was determined separately for the pictorial elements that evoked the activation, and for the textual elements. The figures in Table 13.1 refer to frequency of fixations on the arousing pictorial elements of the advertisement, and indicate the subject's pick-up of information. Even if we include Advertisement 2 in our computations, we still conclude that higher activation increases the frequency of fixations, from an average of 3.9 to 5.5.

These findings substantiate the preceding hypothesis (BH): stronger activation will promote the pick-up of information. Here the question arises whether activation really is the independent variable in the relationship between activation and the frequency of fixations. This is presumed to be true because according to psychobiological findings the activation potential of a stimulus determines the viewer's orientation reaction and consequently eye behavior. The activation called forth by the pictorial elements of the advertisement had no influence on the fixation of the textual elements.

TABLE 13.1 Activation and Acquisition of Information from an Advertisement Illustration

Advertisement	Frequency of fixation *A-version*	*B-version*	*Level of significance (t-test)*	df[a]
1 A/B	3.0	6.0	.01	58
2 A/B	4.6	4.3	—	58
3 A/B	3.4	6.0	.01	58
4 A/B	4.7	5.7	.05	58
Average 1–4	3.9	5.5	.01	238

Source: Witt (1977, p. 85).

[a]*df* = discriminant function.

Note: The figures indicate the frequency of fixations for illustrations with low activation potential (A-version) and with high activation potential (B-version). Each version was presented to 30 subjects.

[15]The small deviations in the values for 20-minute and 24-hour recall scored—insignificant in terms of our study—can be accounted for consistently within the framework of memory research; the formation of a lasting memory trace takes from a few minutes to a half hour. However, one can assume in this case that the stimuli employed here (meaningful and familiar pictorial motifs and words, with the exception of the brand name) are retained relatively quickly (Craik and Lockhart 1972, p. 676) and do not require longer than 10 to 15 minutes for stabilization of the long-term memory. Most of the experiments that deal with the interconnection between activation and retention proceed on the basis of this assumption. The short-retention interval ends "15 to 20 minutes after presentation of the material" (Eysenck 1977, p. 165).

There was approximately the same fixation frequency on the text in all of the ads. Thus, the activation effect was not transferred to the entire ad. This finding will be examined in greater detail later in a comparison with the results of the next experiment.

Another finding yielded by Witt's testing of recall corroborates the empirically supported hypothesis (Loftus 1972; Tversky 1974; Bernhard 1978): the more frequently a person fixes his/her eyes upon a stimulus, the better s/he will recall it.[16] Elements of the advertisement upon which a person fixes his/her eyes more frequently are thus recalled better. The correlations between these two variables, however, are not particularly high, ranging from 0.3 to 0.4. These correlations were also supported by Bernhard (1978). A closer relationship exists between the duration of fixation and recall of the advertisement elements.

Barg (1977) concerned himself exclusively with the relationship between activation and recall, using advertisements similar to those just described. He examined the impact of an advertisement, modifying its illustration so that he could distinguish between these different degrees of activation. The activation was ascertained in the preliminary experiment by means of verbal judgments. The ads were classified in terms of "weak," "average," and "strong" activation. The EDR measurements showed that the differences between the activating ability of Ads 1 and 2 were substantially less than the differences between Ads 2 and 3 (Table 13.2).

A total of 84 male students participated in the study. After exposure to the advertisements, there was a measurement of the short retention, followed by a change of room and a subsequent interview. After the interview, and at least 20 minutes after the presentation of the material, the long retention was measured by means of a structured recall. This recall measurement was checked once again after an interval of 24 hours, and no significant deviations were found. For purposes of recall, the subjects were presented with sheets that indicated the schematic structure of the ads, and were asked to fill in the elements they recalled. A point score was then tabulated for these elements, and is presented in Table 13.2 both for the activating pictorial elements and the ad as a whole.

Among the controlled variables were age (no significant correlation, corresponding to the findings of Mundy-Castle and McKiever 1953), extraversion (no significant correlation, corresponding to the findings of Perry 1971; for diverse results, see Eysenck 1977), and the influence of the time of day (no significant correlation; but note that the relativized phasic activation, not the tonic activation, was measured). A large number of additional interfer-

[16]It should be borne in mind that fixations and looking time are not identical. Looking time is a macro-variable that provides no information about its distribution in terms of fixations and saccades. For this reason, there are also varying interconnections between looking time and recall, as indicated by Morrison and Dainoff (1972), and between eye-fixation and recall as described here.

TABLE 13.2 Activation and Recall for Three Illustrated Advertisements

Item	*1 (Weak Activation)*	*2*	*3 (Strong Activation)*	*Significance Level (F test)*
Activation score	0.95	1.05	1.38	.01
Recall score A pictorial elements	1.22	1.39	2.48	.01
Recall score B all elements	4.28	4.49	6.77	.01

Source: Barg (1977).

ing variables were eliminated by keeping them constant (Barg 1977).

The findings conform with the hypothesis: higher activation leads to higher recall values. A smaller increase in recall values also corresponds to the smaller difference in activation between Ads 1 and 2. The increase in the recall values is related to the activating pictorial elements and to the text, and thus to the entire ad. The findings also lend support to a number of psychological studies in which, however, much simpler stimuli were used (See Eysenck 1976).

There is a discrepancy between the findings of Barg and Witt. In both instances, the activating advertisement elements (Element A–illustration of the ads) were processed better. The processing of the remaining ad elements (Element B–slogan, brand name) was, on the other hand, not promoted by higher activation in the experiment by Witt. This is in keeping with our basic hypothesis, which states that the activation elicited by a stimulus only benefits the processing of *this* stimulus.

Nonetheless, under certain conditions the activation provoked by Element A may promote the processing of the information contained in Element B. Witt (1977, p. 116) was the first to formulate this condition in a more precise manner: if the content of one activating element is coordinated or integrated into another (nonactivating) element, the activating effect of the first element will enhance the processing of information contained in the second. In other words, when the elements are integrated and one element has the potential to stimulate more activation, the entire advertisement will be better retained. This condition was not present in Witt's experiment, but was fulfilled in Barg's experiment (Barg 1977, p. 139). As a result, the higher activation there, which was evoked by the pictorial elements, also stimulated recall of the textual elements, and thus benefited the entire ad.

Practical Implications

These experimental findings have important implications for advertising. Advertisements that fail to arouse will have no effect, as the information conveyed by the advertisement will not be processed efficiently. The more advertising arouses, the more prepared the target audience is to respond, i.e., to pick up, process, and store the information presented.

Strong activation stimulates processing of information transmitted independent of whether this information is effective or not in terms of the advertising goal. In other words, activation is a necessary condition for advertising impact, but it is by no means a sufficient condition. Activation contributes only if the advertising message is processed in such a manner as to guide the decision process of the consumer in the desired direction. It is not sufficient to evaluate simply the activating effectiveness to determine the impact of an advertisement. In addition, the cognitive effects must always be examined and rated. The arousal potential of an advertisement, however, should be seen in terms of both tonic and phasic activation.

If the advertisement succeeds in provoking a lasting increase in the consumer's level of activation, that is, a rise in his tonic activation, this will affect overall performance in processing information. An increase in tonic activation level then promotes the processing of all stimuli, regardless of which elements created the increase. This type of tonic change in activation level will be brought about most successfully if long-lasting emotional or motivational tensions are evoked by strong stimuli.

If the advertisement arouses only short-term, phasic activation, the effect will usually be limited to stimuli that provoked the phasic activation. Because it is difficult to predict with any certainty the influence of an advertisement on the consumer's activation *level,* the easiest way to increase its impact is to expose the most important information (key informative elements) in an arousing form. In this way, the key elements will evoke phasic activation. Berlyne (1960) deals with the properties that a stimulus must possess to evoke phasic activation and to spur on the processing of information. In this connection, it should be noted that extremely pronounced and striking stimuli can have cognitive side-effects that reduce the acceptance of the advertising (Peterson and Kerin 1977).[17]

Illustrations are particularly useful in arousing the consumer. For this reason, it is advantageous to communicate the message as much as possible through pictures. If this is not possible, and if pictures are used only to stir an initial arousal, the less arousing areas of the copy will only be processed more efficiently if the activating (pictorial) and nonactivating (copy) elements are integrated with each other, by either content or some other association. Deliberately aimed arousal and stimulation can be dispensed with if the consumers are already aroused and thus more receptive toward what is being solicited. This would apply when the consumers are actively seeking information.

BENEFITS OF ACTIVATION RESEARCH FOR CONSUMER RESEARCH

First, we inquire about the value of the findings presented here for psychobiological activation research. Our hypotheses distinguish between tonic and phasic activation. Such a distinction has important consequences: tonic activation reflects a general disposition, while phasic activation reflects a disposition that is specifically stimulus-related. Nevertheless, this distinction is not made consistently enough in the literature. Investigations into the influence of activation on cognitive performance are sometimes related to both tonic activation (e.g., stimulated by white noise) and phasic activation (e.g., stimulated by emotional words) without further differentiation.[18] Moreover, our investigations deviate from lines of basic psychophysiological research in so far as we make use of more complex stimulus material (printed advertisements). Our findings should be viewed as a further contribution to the study of the still controversial interconnections between activation and information processing (in its broadest sense).

Next, we consider the value of activation research for consumer research. Activation research can be regarded as a veritable paradigm of psychobiological research, which is concerned with gaining insight into intervening variables of consumer behavior by using biological responses, such as the EDR or eye movement. The systematic transference of this area of research to the field of consumer research satisfies the desideratum expressed by Ferber that there must be "interdisciplinary research in consumer behavior" (Ferber 1977, p. 189).

It is precisely the field of activation research that must not be excluded from consumer research, because activation is a basic variable "that would have to be assigned a value if the psychological condition of a human being . . . were to be adequately described" (Berlyne 1960, p. 48). This holds true for the theoretical frame of reference created by activation theory. Activation is a variable that indicates the strength of energetic processes taking place in the consumer. As our hypotheses show, cognitive performance depends on activation. The activation of the consumer is determined over the short term by the influence of definite stimuli, and over the long term by the affective state in which the consumer finds himself. The available studies on the "problem of arousal" in communication and consumer research reveal just how important a clear activation-theoretical conception is. Fletcher (1971) deals with the influence of activating radio commercials on retention. His finding, namely, that more strongly activating commercials produce less retention, conflicts with the great bulk of other research findings.

---

[17]As Barg (1977) and Witt (1977) demonstrate, cognitive side effects of this type, such as lowered credibility, do not change the stimulating effect of the activation evoked in the processing of information. Such side-effects occur relatively seldom in professional advertising and can, in any case, be taken into account in the copy-test by using the corresponding measurements.

[18]For similar investigations, in which both phasic and tonic activation are related to retention processes, see Kahneman (1973, p. 43) and Eysenck (1977). Possible differential effects of phasic and tonic activation (above all in connection with the ∩-hypothesis) result from the neuronal and functional differences between phasic and tonic activation, according to Pribram and McGuinness (1975), as well as from the possible dependence of phasic activation on tonic activation.

This apparent contradiction can be explained, however, if we take a look at the inadequate classification of variables used by Fletcher. On the one hand, he measures the phasic activation triggered by commercials by electrodermal means, without, however, classifying this activation in terms of its causative elements (words, music). On the other hand, he measures retention using individual elements of the commercial. For this reason, it remains unclear whether the activating elements are those for which retention was tested. It is therefore not possible simply to compare the activation aroused by Element A with the recall of Element B.

Psychophysiological methods have fallen into disrepute as a result of such inadequately designed and poorly interpreted studies. Further examples worth mentioning in this connection are several investigations that attempt to measure the effect of advertising by using physiological methods (Kohan 1968; Krugman 1971; King 1972; Blackwell, Hensel, and Sternthal 1970).[19] The results of these investigations, which do not take psychological literature on arousal or activation into consideration, allow the authors no more than conjecture as to what is being measured. None of these studies examines what interconnections exist between the values measured and the processing of the advertising message. As a result, the significance of the psychobiological variables remains unclear.[20]

With the aid of the concept of activation, it is possible to reduce a number of very different problems in consumer research to a common denominator. The fact that more strongly aroused and alert consumers react "better" involves a broad range of different situations and circumstances: for example, the stimulating effect exerted by store windows on the consumer's search for information and information pick-up, the influence of the activating potential of packaging or product design on perception, the effects of conflicts or other arousal states on decision behavior, etc.

Since activation expresses the intensity of affective processes, psychobiological activation measurements can be used to measure the strength of emotions, motives, and attitudes. These can replace other less valid methods. The measuring and explanation of emotional and motivational behavior according to psychobiological guidelines, e.g., as Buck (1976) advocates, is a modern alternative to classical motivation research. This might help to overcome the stagnation in which motivation research now finds itself due to the psychoanalytical approach of Dichter (1964) and to its present, one-sided cognitive way of looking at problems.

It should be borne in mind that the advertising studies reported here encompass only one area of the practical application for activation research. We are interested in other applications as well: thus, Trommsdorff (1978) was able to conclude that arousing labels tempt the consumer to reach for the product more often. In each instance, it is a matter of arousing the consumer by deliberately stimulating him in doses, thus increasing the chances for information to be communicated more efficiently.[21]

The insights of activation research are also noteworthy from the point of view of consumer policy. The consumer often reacts to activating stimuli automatically, without being able to control his behavior. Activation, then, is a means of manipulation from which the consumer is not able to escape. Kroeber-Riel (1977 a,b) discusses the consequent implications for consumer policy.

Nevertheless the question arises whether psychobiological research is nothing but an "exotic orchid" of research—whether its appli-

[19]One exception is the article by Blackwell, Hensel, and Sternthal (1970), which cites, among others, the work of Kahneman. But here too there is a lack of clarity as to what pupil dilation measures. The significance these psychobiological measurements have for behavior remains an open question (Pribram and McGuinness 1975, p. 18).

[20]See also Barg's (1977, p. 84) criticism of the experiments of Caffyn (1964), which amount solely to "a demonstration of the sensitivity of the measuring instruments."

[21]In addition to activation theory, the psychobiological research program at our Institute deals with the classical conditioning of consumers (borrowing from attempts by Staats and Staats 1957), as well as with determining the consumer's emotions and motives for market research.

cability and significance are severely limited. In answering this question, a distinction should be made between the use of psychobiological measuring methods and the theoretical knowledge gained by these methods.

It is indeed true that psychobiological measurements are costly and awkward, requiring expensive equipment and expertise. For the most part the researcher is dependent on a laboratory as well as on people's willingness to come to the laboratory—limitations that prevent wide use of these measuring methods. The fact remains, however, that psychobiological measurements are in many cases considerably more valid than other methods, and are thus indispensable for scientific research. This is particularly so when measuring psychological processes that the subject is not conscious of or cannot easily verbalize. (These processes cannot be ignored just because they are difficult to measure.) Moreover, psychobiological methods of measurement have practical implications: they can help validate simplified and more economic methods, such as verbal measurements of attention, which would create a basis for the use of more simplified measurements.

On the theoretical aspect—the limited applicability of psychobiological methods does not mean that the knowledge gained thereby must be put to only limited use. Thus, the most direct and valid measure of pick-up (acquisition) of information is to record eye movements. Undoubtedly, this is a costly psychobiological method and hardly suitable for wide use. By recording eye movements, relationships between activation and information acquisition, or relationships between acquisition and recall of information, can be determined, as shown earlier. These relationships are highly significant for explaining and influencing consumer behavior. The same holds true for the theoretical findings gained by EDR measurements on the relationship between activation (arousal, strength of emotion) and human information processing. Apart from these considerations, psychobiological research can contribute greatly to broadening and substantiating psychological research.

To look into the future, we are beginning a series of experiments using a thermo-vision-system: we assume that the thermographs of a human face, which are obtained by using infrared detectors, can be used to record changes in the level of activation. As it is possible to make thermographs by thermo-vision at a distance—unobserved by the subjects—the possibility exists for a new *nonreactive* method of measuring activation. Using this technique, we hope to be able to measure the strength of affect in field situations, i.e., during collective decision processes or during conflict behavior at the cash register.

REFERENCES

BARG, CLAUS-DIETER (1977), "Measurement and Effects of Psychological Activation Through Advertising," Ph.D. dissertation, University of the Saarland, Germany (in German).

BERHARD, ULRICH (1978), "Exposure to Advertising: Eye Movement and Memory," Ph.D. dissertation, University of the Saarland, Germany (in German).

BERLYNE, DANIEL E. (1960), *Conflict, Arousal and Curiosity*. New York: McGraw-Hill.

BIRBAUMER, NIELS (1975), *Physiological Psychology An Introduction*. Berlin: Springer-Verlag, (in German).

BLACKWELL, ROBERT D., HENSEL, JAMES S., and STERNTHAL, BRIAN (1970), "Pupil Dilation: What Does It Measure?" *Journal of Advertising Research,* 10, 15–19.

BROWN, CLINTON C. (1967), *Methods in Psychophysiology,* Baltimore, MD: Williams and Wilkins.

BUCK, ROSS (1976), *Human Motivation and Emotion.* New York: Wiley.

BURSTEIN, KENNETH R., FRENZ, WALTER D., BERGERON, JAMES, and EPSTEIN, SEYMOUR (1965), "A Comparison of Skin Potential and Skin Resistance Responses as Measures of Emotional Responsivity," *Psychophysiology,* 2, 14–25.

CAFFYN, J. M. (1964), "Psychological Laboratory Techniques in Copy Research," *Journal of Advertising Research,* 4, 45–50.

CLEMENTS, PAUL R., HAFER, MARILYN D., and

VERMILLION, MARY E. (1976), "Psychometric, Diurnal, and Electrophysiological Correlates of Activation," *Journal of Personality and Social Psychology,* 33, 387–395.

CRAIG, KENNETH D., and WOOD, KEITH (1971), "Autonomic Components of Observers' Responses to Pictures of Homicide Victims and Nude Females," *Journal of Experimental Research in Personality,* 5, 304–309.

CRAIK, FERGUS I. M., and LOCKHART, ROBERT S. (1972), "Levels of Processing: A Framework for Memory Research," *Journal of Verbal Learning and Verbal Behavior,* 11, 671–680.

DICHTER, ERNEST (1964), *Handbook of Consumer Motivations.* New York: McGraw-Hill.

DUFFY, ELIZABETH (1972), "Activation," in *Handbook of Psychophysiology,* Eds. Norman S. Greenfield and Richard A. Sternbach. New York: Holt, Rinehart & Winston.

EYSENCK, MICHAEL W. (1976), "Arousal, Learning, and Memory," *Psychological Bulletin,* 83, 389–404.

——— (1977), *Human Memory: Theory, Research and Individual Differences.* Elmsford, NY: Pergamon Press.

FERBER, ROBERT (1977), "Can Consumer Research Be Interdisciplinary?" *Journal of Consumer Research,* 4, 189–192.

FLETCHER, JAMES E. (1971), "The Orienting Response as an Index of Mass Communication Effect," *Psychophysiology,* 8, 699–703.

GAARDER, KENNETH R. (1975), *Eye Movements, Vision, and Behavior.* Washington, DC: Halsted Press.

GREENFIELD, NORMAN S., and STERNBACH, RICHARD A., EDS. (1972), *Handbook of Psychophysiology.* New York: Holt, Rinehart & Winston.

HANSEN, FLEMMING (1972), *Consumer Choice Behavior—A Cognitive Theory.* New York: The Free Press.

HEBB, DONALD O. (1972), *Textbook of Psychology* (3rd ed.). Philadelphia: Saunders.

JANISSE, MICHAEL P. (1977), *Pupillometry—the Psychology of the Pupillary Response.* New York: Wiley.

KAHNEMANN, DANIEL (1973), *Attention and Effort.* Englewood Cliffs, NJ: Prentice-Hall.

KING, ALBERT S. (1972), "Pupil Size, Eye Direction, and Message Appeal: Some Preliminary Findings," *Journal of Marketing,* July, 55–58.

KOHAN, XAVIER (1968), "A Physiological Measure of Commercial Effectiveness," *Journal of Advertising,* 8, 46–48.

KRECH, DAVID, and CRUTCHFIELD, RICHARD S. (1974), *Elements of Psychology.* New York: Knopf.

KROEBER-RIEL, WERNER (1977a), "Goals of Consumer Policy," *Der Arbeitnehmer,* 5, 221–229 (in German).

——— (1977b), "Criticism and New Conceptions of Consumer Policy—a Behavioral Approach," *Die Betriebswirtschaft,* 37, 89–103 (in German).

——— (1975), *Konsumentenverhalten* (Consumer Behavior) (2nd ed.). München: Vahlen Verlag.

———, BARG, CLAUS-DIETER, and BERNHARD, ULRICH (1975), "The Stimulus Intensity of Political Slogans," paper of the Institute of Consumer and Behavioral Research, University of the Saarland, Germany, Vol. 29 (in German).

KRUGMAN, HERBERT E. (1971), "Brainwave Measures of Media Involvement," *Journal of Advertising Research,* 11, 3–9.

LINDSAY, PETER H., and NORMAN, DONALD A. (1977), *Human Information Processing* (2nd ed.). New York: Academic Press.

LINDSLEY, DONALD B. (1951), "Emotion," in *Handbook of Experimental Psychology,* Ed. S. S. Stevens. New York: Wiley.

LOFTUS, GEOFFREY R. (1972), "Eye Fixations and Recognition Memory for Pictures," *Cognitive Psychology,* 3, 525–551.

LYKKEN, DAVID T., and VENABLES, PETER H. (1971), "Direct Measurement of Skin Conductance: a Proposal for Standardization," *Psychophysiology,* 8, 656–672.

MCCURDY, HAROLD GRIER (1950), "Consciousness and the Galvanometer," *Psychological Review,* 57, 322–327.

MCGUIRE, WILLIAM J. (1976), "Some Internal Psychological Factors Influencing Consumer Choice," *Journal of Consumer Research,* 2, 302–319.

MORRISON, BRUCE JOHN, and DAINOFF, MARVIN J. (1972), "Advertisement Complexity and Looking Time," *Journal of Marketing Research,* 9, 396–400.

MUNDY-CASTLE, A. C., and MCKIEVER, B. L. (1953), "The Psycho-physiological Significance of the Galvanic Skin Response," *Journal of Experimental Psychology,* 46, 15–24.

PERRY, JOHN W., JR. (1971), "Arousal and Memory: Psychophysiological and Personality Factors," Ph.D. dissertation, University of Texas.

PETERSON, ROBERT A., and KERIN, ROGER A. (1977), "The Female Role in Advertisements: Some Experimental Evidence," *Journal of Marketing* (October) 59-64.

POSNER, MICHAEL J. (1975), "Psychobiology of Attention," in *Handbook of Psychobiology,* Eds. Michael S. Gazzaniga and Colin Blakemore. New York: Academic Press.

PRIBRAM, KARL H., and MCGUINNESS, DIANE (1975), "Arousal Activation, and Effort in the Control of Attention," *Psychological Review,* 82, 116-149.

ROESSLER, ROBERT, BURCH, NEIL R., and CHILDERS, HAROLD E. (1966), "Personality and Arousal Correlates of Specific Galvanic Skin Responses," *Psychophysiology,* 3, 115-131.

ROUTTENBERG, ARYEH (1968), "The Two-Arousal Hypothesis: Reticular Formation and Limbic System," *Psychological Review,* 75, 51-80.

SCHACHTER, STANLEY (1975), "Cognition and Peripheralist-Centralist Controversies in Motivation and Emotion," in *Handbook of Psychobiology,* Eds. Michael S. Gazzaniga and Colin Blakemore. New York: Academic Press.

SCHÖNPFLUG, WOLFGANG (1968), "Memory and Generalized Psychophysiological Activation," *Zeitschrift für erziehungswissenschaftliche Forschung,* 2, 195-221 (in German).

______ (1969), *Methodology of Research into Activation,* Bern: Huber-Verlag (in German).

SHARPLESS, SETH, and JASPER, HERBERT (1956), "Habituation of the Arousal Reaction," *Brain,* 79, 655-681.

SHIFFRIN, RICHARD M., and SCHNEIDER, WALTER (1977), "Controlled and Automatic Human Information Processing: II. Perceptual Learning, Automatic Attending, and a General Theory," *Psychological Review,* 84, 127-191.

STAATS, ARTHUR W. (1968), *Learning, Language and Cognition,* New York: Holt, Rinehart and Winston, Inc.

STAATS, CAROLYN K., and STAATS, ARTHUR W. (1957), "Meaning Established by Classical Conditioning," *Journal of Experimental Psychology,* 54, 74-80.

THAYER, ROBERT E. (1970), "Activation States as Assessed by Verbal Report and Four Psychophysiological Variables," *Psychophysiology,* 7, 86-94.

THOMPSON, RICHARD F. (1975), *Introduction to Physiological Psychology,* New York: Harper & Row.

TRAXEL, WERNER (1960), "The Possibility of an Objective Measurement of the Strength of Feelings," *Psychologische Forschung,* 26, 75-90 (in German).

TROMMSDORFF, VOLKER, "Attitudes Towards New Brands—Study on Validity of Experimental Methods for the Pretest of New Products," Saarbrücken (in preparation).

TVERSKY, BARBARA (1974), "Eye Fixations in Prediction of Recognition and Recall," *Memory and Cognition,* 2, 275-278.

VENABLES, P. H., and CHRISTIE, M. J. (1973), "Mechanisms, Instrumentation, Recording Techniques and Quantification of Responses," in *Electrodermal Activity in Psychological Research,* Eds. William F. Prokasy and David C. Raskin. New York: Academic Press.

WALSCHBURGER, PETER (1976), "Description of Activation Processes," Ph.D. dissertation, University of Freiburg/Br., Germany (in German).

WITT, DIETER (1977), "Emotional Advertising: The Relationship Between Eye-Movement Patterns and Memory—Empirical Study With the Eye-Movement Monitor," Ph.D. dissertation, University of Saarland, Germany (in German).

14

AFFECTIVE AND COGNITIVE FACTORS IN PREFERENCES*

Robert B. Zajonc
Hazel Markus

Affective factors play an important role in the development and maintenance of preferences. The representation of affect can take a variety of forms, including motor responses and somatic reactions. This explains why cognitive methods of preference change that are directed at only one form of representation have seldom been effective.

One of the clearest manifestations of the puzzling interplay of cognitive and affective influences is found in food preferences. All collectivities—be they ethnic groups, tribes, or nations—have a favorite food, which often carries a symbolic and ceremonial significance. This food is an important element of ethnic identity, and there are rigid standards about its proper taste and preparation. Any group member who dislikes it or rejects it on grounds other than health is treated as a deviant whose ethnic loyalty—and perhaps mental health—should be seriously questioned. Yet for each of these collectivities, there is another one somewhere in the world who finds this food entirely inedible, if not repulsive. Dog meat is a delicacy in some parts of East Asia, but few Americans would find it appetizing. The same can be said of snakes, birds' nests, chocolate-covered cockroaches, fish eyes, veal pancreas, and rams' testicles. Most Americans like corn, but in various countries corn has been thought suitable only for pigs. Consider martinis, for example:

*Reprinted from the *Journal of Consumer Research 9* (September 1982), pp. 123–131.

the first martini we taste as children is an abominable experience and we wonder what on earth could prompt adults to ingest such a vile substance.

Some foods are so pungent that a considerable period of habituation is required to neutralize the fiery effects and severe irritation of the oral mucosa. Chili pepper, which is an indispensable food ingredient in Mexico, is a case in point. Chili pepper is the major flavoring of food in a Zapotec village extensively studied by Rozin and Schiller (1980). The inhabitants of that village have chili pepper with every meal—at least three times a day—and they start eating chili at age five. All nonsweet food receives chili flavoring. When forced to do without chili, the villagers miss it and complain. There is other research indicating this remarkable tenacity of food habits. Rozin and Rozin (1981) report that Vietnamese refugees in an American resettlement camp were so desperate for *nuoc mam*, a spicy sauce which is made of salty fermented fish and which they habitually use, that when they were supplied with soy and hot pepper sauce as substitutes, these spices disappeared from the dinner tables as rapidly as they were served. In all instances, the fanciers of these pungent foods must have started with a strong aversion that gradually became transformed into a strong preference, sometimes verging on addiction.

PREFERENCES: TRADITIONAL AND ALTERNATIVE VIEWS

These examples dramatize two questions that are basic in social psychology and of some importance in consumer research as well: how preferences are acquired and how they are modified. Mexican children are not born with a craving for chili pepper; it is clearly an acquired taste. But to say that it is an acquired taste is a serious understatement, because one acquires a taste for chili pepper only after overcoming a powerful innate aversion. The initial reaction is far from neutrality or indifference. It if is possible to change an innate aversion to something like chili pepper, then it should be possible to change almost any attitude and any preference. How is this accomplished? Clearly, people do not acquire a craving for chili pepper by being told about its nutritive properties. One cannot tell people that chili pepper contains vitamins A and C and expect an instant, insatiable craving for chili pepper. Because the aversive reaction that invariably occurs on initial encounters with pungent food represents powerful negative affect, Mexican mothers in the Zapotec village studied by Rozin and Schiller (1980) start feeding children unseasoned versions of various foods and add chili pepper very gradually. At the same time, a great deal of social support comes from the surroundings—all the neighbors and relatives eat seasoned food—and eating seasoned food seems to be a mark of growing up. Thus, becoming fond of the pungent flavoring involves overcoming strong negative affect by other significant affective factors, such as parental reinforcement, social conformity pressures, identification with the group, machismo, and so on.

Of course, many attitudes can be formed without these affective supports, by means of cognitive factors alone—for example, when a person is given some persuasive communication. If some authority such as *Consumer Reports* prints a very favorable evaluation of an otherwise unknown and unused product—say a newly patented corkscrew—some segment of the population will become favorably disposed to it. Thus, the antecedents of preferences may involve cognitive *and* affective components in a variety of combinations. In some cases the cognitive component may be dominant, in some the cognitive and affective factors may interact with each other, and in other cases the affective factors may be dominant and primary. This point is clearly recognized by Bettman (1981), who attempted to isolate and specify the conditions associated with these different cases.

Preferences are themselves primarily *affectively based behavioral phenomena.* A preference for X over Y is a tendency of the organism to approach X more often and more vigorously than Y. Approach, in turn, which is manifested in the attainment and maintenance of proximity, is a tendency controlled mainly by affective processes. The prototype of such an approach tendency is seen in imprinting in animals. Thus, a precocial bird that is repeatedly presented with a conspicuous object soon after hatching shows a strong preference for that object by remaining close to it over extended periods of time (Bateson 1966). Approach tendency among humans may be evidenced in a variety of other ways, such as making favorable comments, buying a product, proselytizing, contributing money, giving blood, or giving life.

Most of the literature on development and change of preferences has a cognitive emphasis. In this paper, however, we shall stress affective factors. In doing so, we mean neither to negate cognitive influences in preferences, nor to minimize their importance. Cognitive influences are quite important. We shall only argue that, in themselves, they do not always tell the whole story.

Preferences as Combined Utilities

Preferences occupy a very important position in social psychology. They must be considered and examined in attitude research, in impression formation, in decision making, in experimental aesthetics, and in many other fields. All these fields share a theoretical paradigm in which preferences are conceptualized as the subjective counterparts of object utilities and values. In the confines of the preference paradigm, if X is preferred to Y, it is because X has greater utility or value than Y. In turn, preferences and utilities are understood by decomposing the overall utilities and values into their more elementary components, each of which has utility of its own. According to this traditional view, if we wish to know why a given individual prefers one brand of cigarettes to another, we need only know how much he likes each of its features and how important these features are in contributing to the overall evaluation. We may examine such features as tar content, length, taste, smell, price, and so forth.

The contemporary analysis of preferences begins with this formulation and takes it as a given. The only questions that remain are how the elementary attributes can be isolated, how their utilities can be discovered, and how these utilities combine. Thus one major school of thought in this area takes it for granted that the preference of X over Y can be fully explicated by the weighted preferences for the components and features of X and Y.

The second, equally important assumption of this research is that these component utilities attach themselves to the very same features that allow the subject to detect X and Y, to discriminate between X and Y, to recognize X and Y, and to categorize X and Y. In other words, the analysis of preferences is simply the analysis of cognitive representations of the features of objects, with the addition that these descriptive representations now have some affect attached to them in the form of utilities. In fact, in some cases, utility is conceived of as a property of an object—a property that is not essentially different from other properties, such as hue, shape, age, or function. There are no *a priori* grounds for distinguishing between utilities and other features of objects in analyzing preferences; as such, the strictly cognitive analysis of preferences represents a parsimonious approach to the problem. It follows that, in attempts to change a given preference, it is first necessary to identify the features of the object and, once these features have been identified, to try to influence the person's evaluation of these features.

Preferences as Cognitive Constructs

It should be quite obvious that in the study of preferences, we cannot hope to write models that focus on object attributes alone. Could we explain, on the basis of even the most exacting and painstaking analysis of the attributes of chili pepper and of its component utilities, why millions of people crave this spice?

A preference for an object can be radically changed with experience while its properties remain constant. This means that object properties do not contain the complete information on object utilities. Hence a complete analysis of preference dynamics and antecedents must involve an *interaction* between object properties and the history of the individual's experience with the alternatives among which the choice is made.

The approach to the study of preferences and decision making that relies exclusively on object properties has been prevalent for almost a century—since Fechner—and progress has been shamefully slow. We are quite far from a successful prediction of object utilities on the basis of their features. As Cohen (1981) suggested, even in the case of successful choice models, it is not clear that an accurate fit of a decision model describing choice as a function of weighted attribute utilities can always be taken as evidence of its validity. For example, the fit need not show that the subject made his choice by "computing" (consciously or unconsciously) the component utilities as specified by the model. In many cases, the information offered by the subject about the attributes of the object and about their utilities may well represent his justification for rather than the basis of his choice. Assuming that individuals strive to supply consistent justifications for their choice behavior, weighted linear models in themselves might not be able to distinguish between the ratings of attributes that *justify* the choice and the ratings that *determine* the choice. Only experimental manipulations of attributes could reveal their contributions to the choice. Models that are successful in describing these types of experimental situations are quite rare and, for the most part, deal with choices among trivial alternatives (e.g., Yntema and Torgerson 1961).

It is, therefore, not a folly to question these basic assumptions about preferences. In a recent paper, the reasons these assumptions cannot be accepted unconditionally were extensively examined (Zajonc 1980). The assumption questioned here is that affect, such as that contained in preferences, is necessarily *postcognitive,* which implies that a feeling of a preference is generated *upon* the encoding of the specific properties of the object, *after* the evaluation of their utilities, and *after* the computation of the individual component utilities into a joint product that represents the overall preference.

In contrast to this traditional view, it has been suggested (Zajonc 1978) that under some circumstances, affective responses, including preference judgments, may be fairly independent of cognition. The argument was developed on a number of grounds that we shall not review here, with the exception of some empirical evidence.

Role of Cognitive Factors in Preferences

According to the traditional approach, affect in preferences attaches itself to cognitive representations of the properties and attributes of the object: before you can like something, you must know what it is. If you say that you like John because John is intelligent, rich, and generous, you must have discovered—*before* making up your mind about liking John—that he is indeed intelligent, rich, and generous. It follows that the judgments of John's attractiveness should be predictable from the judgments of John's intelligence, wealth, and generosity. They should also be more reliable, more consistent, they should be made more rapidly, and the individual should have more confidence in these judgments.

In contrast, consider the possibility that the judgment and choice process can be quite the opposite. Under some circumstances, affect or preference comes as the first experience. The cognitions that have generally been taken to be the very basis of this preference can actually occur afterwards—perhaps as justification. Note that, like Bettman (1981) and Wright (1981), we are not suggesting that affect contained in preferences always comes first, although some affect always does come first (Zajonc 1980, pp. 170–172). For purposes of this discussion, however, we are stating that there are many circumstances in which the affective reaction *precedes* the very cognitive appraisal on which the affective reaction is presumed to be based.

Acquiring Preferences Through Exposures

We have carried out a number of studies in our laboratory to investigate the relationship between some primitive affective and cognitive factors. The paradigm studied was that of the so-called exposure effect. This effect, in the form of the enhancement of positive affect toward a given object, arises merely as a result of repeated stimulus exposure. When objects are presented to the individual on repeated occasions, the mere exposure is capable of making the individual's attitude toward these objects more positive. A great deal of research has confirmed these results—both in humans as well as in animals—and there is little doubt today about its validity (Harrison 1977; Hill 1978; Matlin and Stang 1978). However, we have never been sure why exposure has these positive effects. The traditional theories, based mainly on the ideas of Titchener (1910), explained liking for familiar objects as depending on subjective factors and, in particular, on the subjective feelings of recognition. When confronted with a familiar object, the individual was said to experience a "glow of warmth, a sense of ownership, a feeling of intimacy" (p. 411).

The exposure effect is indeed a remarkable psychological phenomenon. It is a basic process in preference and attitude formation and change. It ranges from very trivial to very serious manifestations. On the one hand, a mild preference for nonsense syllables can be established in just a few exposures. On the other hand, similar exposures can produce a powerful attachment such as we find in imprinting, where the removal of an object (as innocuous as a rotating cube) to which the animal has become attached by virtue of previous exposures causes an enormous distress (Zajonc, Markus, and Wilson 1974).

The phenomenon of exposure is very easy to demonstrate. It occurs in a variety of contexts and can be produced by a number of *sufficient* conditions that are quite well known and understood. But no one has discovered whether there are *necessary* conditions for its occurrence or what they are. It is possible that there are no necessary conditions for the exposure effect, but only sufficient ones. Because the exposure effect represents a very basic process that has considerable adaptive significance, it may well be that nature has provided several different but substitutable conditions assuring that, in one way or another, the organism will develop preferences for objects with which it has repeated experience.

The results of our experiments on the exposure effect revealed that recognition—which, according to the traditional view, was thought to be the basic necessary condition for its occurrence—was in fact not necessary. Recognition was found to be a factor that *could* influence affective ratings of the stimuli, but it was not at all a necessary factor. Stimuli that had been presented previously but that the person did not recognize as having seen before were liked more than objectively new stimuli that the person also thought were new. Several experiments using a variety of stimulus materials were performed; all show the same pattern of results. These experiments generally consist of two sessions. During the first session, stimuli such as nonsense paralogs, photographs of faces, or Chinese ideographs are presented, usually in varied frequencies. During the second session, the subjects judge the stimuli either for familiarity or for liking, or in some experiments, for both. Thus, for example, Matlin (1971) found that objectively old stimuli were liked more than objectively new stimuli, regardless of the subject's impression of their familiarity.

The same results were obtained by Moreland and Zajonc (1977, 1979). This latter study went even further: Out of the array of stimuli, only those were selected that the subject thought she/he had never previously seen. All these stimuli, however, had in fact been previously shown—some once, others three or nine times. The subject simply had no recognition memory for them at all. For these stimuli, which the subject had actually confronted before but which she/he thought she/he had never seen, there was a substantial correlation between the *actual* frequency of exposure and liking (0.43 in one experiment and 0.50 in another). Thus, if recognition memory represents one of the basic cognitive processes that the traditional theory hypothesizes to be responsible for an affective influence—in this case, a change in preference—then it follows that affective change may take place *without* the participation of these cognitive processes. Under other circumstances, cognitive participation or mediation may well be necessary; we are considering only those instances where it is not, and we wish only to demonstrate that affective consequences are possible without much cognitive support.

The most convincing results come from studies of exposure effects in which the stimulus exposure during the first session takes place under suboptimal conditions. In these studies, either by means of interference or by presenting the stimuli at very low energy levels, the person is prevented from acquiring any sort of recognition memory of the stimuli: when these stimuli are shown subsequently and the person is asked to say which is which for pairs of stimuli (one of which is, in fact, new and one old) she/he is unable to do so better than chance. In one such experiment, Wilson (1979) used tonal patterns in a dichotic listening situation. The subject was given a series of tonal patterns in one ear and a story to track in another ear. When presented for a subsequent recognition test, the exposed tonal patterns could not be distinguished from similar ones that had not been presented at all. Yet subjects liked the tonal patterns that had been played previously more than those that were played for the first time, even though they had no idea which was which.

In another study, Kunst-Wilson and Zajonc (1980) presented visual stimuli—high contrast polygons—at viewing conditions that resulted in chance recognition. Exposure parameters, such as duration and level of illumination, were established to bring the subjects to no better than chance recognition. The polygons were exposed a number of times each, under the conditions observing the established parameter values. During the second session, the subject was shown pairs of stimuli, now under perfectly optimal viewing conditions. In each pair, one item was an old stimulus, shown during the exposure series, and the other was a similar, new stimulus, never previously exposed. Subjects were asked which of the two polygons was new and which was old, and which of the two they preferred. These results showed no recognition above chance. However, this was not the case with liking judgments. Subjects liked the old stimuli more than the new ones, even though they were unable to recognize them.

Inadvertently, this study repeated one carried out a quarter of a century ago and published under the suggestive title, "A Methodological Study of Cigarette Brand Discrimination" (Littman and Manning 1954). These authors asked smokers of *Camels, Chesterfields,* and *Lucky Strikes* to taste camouflaged *Camels, Chesterfields,* and *Lucky Strikes* and to answer two questions: (1) which cigarette they were tasting, and (2) how much they liked each sample cigarette. In Littman and Manning's study, as in Kunst-Wilson and Zajonc's, the subjects given the blind cigarette test were unable to discriminate the cigarettes reliably: they did not know whether they were smoking their own brand or another one. However, when asked about preference among the three camouflaged sample cigarettes, they thought that their own brand tasted best, even though they could not at the time tell which of the three samples *was* their own brand.

These experiments tell us something about preferences and about their relative independence of cognitive factors—even of quite primitive cognitive factors, such as recognition memory. There are many other considerations that would lead us to believe that, in general, affect is partially independent of cognition and that preferences are as well. Even when a preference has been developed out of cognitive material (say you learned to like something because of some favorable information), the preference may eventually become functionally autonomous and lose its original cognitive justification.

In part, the dissociation of a preference from its origins is suggested by the fact that, when asked about the reasons for preferring one stimulus to another, participants in exposure studies never mention familiarity, subjective recognition, or frequency of exposure. Instead, they point to stimulus features. In experiments with Chinese ideographs, the subjects often mentioned the form of a particular ideograph that seemed quite pleasing to them. In experiments with photographs of faces, it was generally a particular feature (nice eyes, fine hair) or the overall appearance ("he looks kind") that was given as the reason for liking. In experiments with nonsense paralogs, the subjects often said that they liked the frequently presented paralog because it "reminded them of something good" or because "it sounded nice."

According to our theoretical argument, cognitive participation is not necessary for the occurrence of an affective reaction. Mandler (1982) holds to the view that a cognitive process *always* precedes evaluative judgments. Lazarus (1981), too, sees affect as requiring cognitive participation. Certainly, evaluative judgments necessarily involve cognition, especially when they are communicated to the experimenter. The subject must somehow "look inside" for the affective reaction that has arisen in him/her and report this reaction to the experimenter. Clearly, the subject processes a good deal of information in the course of this event. The crucial question is whether the original affective reactions themselves, on which overt evaluative judgments are presumably based, must also contain cognitive components. Given the current state of knowledge and research technology, no empirical test can be made that would rule out such participation entirely and categorically. To date, we have no empirical means to decide in favor of one view or the other, so they must be considered primarily on theoretical and heuristic grounds. Some affective reactions may *appear* not to have been preceded by cognitive input, when in fact some form of covert cognitive processes may have accompanied them. For example, when the routines become highly automated (e.g., Broadbent 1977; Langer, Blank, and Chanowitz 1978; Shiffrin and Schneider 1977), the resulting information processing becomes covert, rapid, and contracted. The possibility cannot be ruled out that this automated, covert form of cognition—a form, however, that cannot be demonstrated as having occurred—is essentially implicated in affective reactions.

Note that the primacy of affective reactions and their independence of prior cognitive process require only one demonstration. We need to find only one experimental situation where affect can be shown to have occurred without an antecedent cognitive process and the matter will be settled. In part, of course, the question of the participation of cognitive functions in affective reactions is a matter of definition. There may not have been cognitive processes involved in the experiment by Kunst-Wilson and Zajonc (1980) or in the one by Littman and Manning (1954), but we cannot be sure. If by "cognition" we mean a nonsensory process that transforms sensory input and produces or recruits representations, then the question of cognitive participation in affect is reduced to the presence of representational processes. A sensory process must have taken place in the experiment by Kunst-Wilson and Zajonc; was there also a transformation of the sensory input into a representational form, or was the sensory process itself, in unadulterated form, sufficient for an affective discrimination? The possibility of direct sensory-motor links has been demonstrated in animals for various, even complex affect-triggered behavior, such as escape (Ingle 1973, 1977). Such links also exist in human beings (Goodale 1982). Were the stimuli in Kunst-Wilson and Zajonc's experiment represented by the subjects as cognitions? Even if they were, were these representations *necessary* for the generation of differential affective reactions to familiar and unfamiliar stimuli?

Affective and Cognitive Factors in Attitudes

It is entirely plausible that there are significant differences in attitudes and preferences depending on their basis of origin. Preferences acquired in infancy and childhood are formed primarily on affective basis. A taste for chili pepper is acquired through habituation, familiarization, and positive reinforcement from the social surroundings, not by means of persuasive information. On the other hand, some later preferences—say for certain makes of cars or food processors—have as their basis a rich cognitive structure. To change an attitude that has evolved primarily from affective sources and so has considerable extracognitive supports, may require methods different from those needed to change an attitude based on cognition: it may require an attack on the affective basis of the preference.

Of course, psychotherapy is one such method, in that it seeks to attack an affective predisposition that has pathological consequences. We are not suggesting psychotherapeutic methods in the advertising and marketing of commercial products (although there is a great deal to be learned from these methods, since many product preferences and loyalties have a near-pathological character). If preferences are to be changed, both the affective and the cognitive elements must be carefully examined, because in the end, it is the affective element that must be altered. This appears to be quite well understood in psychotherapy and in advertising, although it is not always understood at a systematic level. For example, it is very clear that affect is recruited to help out in various forms of advertising: you are shown a soft drink *and* a smile, a brand of whisky *and* sex, a new automobile model *and* excitement. It is the same in psychotherapy when transference is exploited for gaining an affective support in dealing with an affective disturbance.

Preference and Attitude Development and Change

What is the interplay between affective and cognitive factors in the course of preference development? By the time the child develops an extensive knowledge structure about chili peppers—i.e., before he learns to discriminate among them, identify various subtle features, and discover all their uses—his preference for them may well be completely established. In this case, it is unlikely that affect would become attached to the *specific* features of chili peppers that the child discovers after his preference is formed, although he may nevertheless learn to describe and express his preference in terms of these features. Appeals to the features of chili peppers in describing one's preferences may be simply justifications that overlay the affective aspects of the preference but do not reflect the affective *representation* of the object. Efforts to change attitudes in which the affective components have been fully developed before the cognitive elements became articulated are likely to meet with failure. An effective method would have to take direct aim at the affective component and bring in affective consequences—an idea that appears to be implicitly understood in brainwashing (Lifton 1956). It may be that attitudes that have a firm emotional basis, developed prior to cognitive elaboration, can be changed only by methods that have a direct emotional influence on the one hand, and that bypass cognitive components on the other.

Other attitudes may have quite a different natural history of acquisition and development. In the example of the new corkscrew mentioned previously, the affective component and the cognitive component of the attitude may develop very much in tandem; in fact, most of the cognitive elements may have become consolidated before one's preference is fully developed. In this case, these cognitions may form an important basis for the preference and thus figure significantly in its formation. The process of preference acquisition may start with an initial overall affective reaction to the corkscrew arising out of a previously developed knowledge structure—i.e., after the person has learned a great deal about the infallibility of the corkscrew's performance, its durability, its low cost, and all its other advantages over other corkscrew designs. It is this knowledge structure that is the original source of positive feelings and the major basis of preference formation (which, as previously noted, is not the case in the acquisition of preference for chili pepper). Thus it is likely that, in the case of the corkscrew, particular preferences will attach themselves to particular features of the corkscrew, so that the affective and the cognitive components will be more closely intertwined than in the case of chili pepper. Hence an attempt to change preferences by cognitive methods would be more effective than in the case of chili pepper, because in the case of the corkscrew, it is the cognitions that "carry" the affect.

It is possible to change preference by cognitive means alone only in the early stages of preference formation, because even when a preference has been built up from cognitions, its affect may become partly or fully autonomous and independent of the cognitive elements that were originally its basis. With the passage of time and due to habitual contact with and use of the corkscrew, one tends to forget its particular advantages because contact and comparison with other designs is precluded. One tends to pay little attention to the fact that the corkscrew works well, how little it cost, and that it has lasted all these years. One begins to like it simply by virtue of repeated exposure. The impact of this type of separation of affective basis of preference from its original cognitive support can be easily appreciated when one is asked why he likes an old friend. Such a question is often followed by a long pause, as one tries to retrieve the original cognitive supports for the attitude. The current attachment and affection are held in place by reciprocal "good feeling" (surely a diffuse and nondescript state) and by habitual patterns of positive interaction. As friendship grows, relatively little attention is paid to the particular features of the friend. The original bases no longer provide support for the affection and do not form a part of the attitude complex.

REPRESENTATION OF AFFECT

Once we acknowledge the possibility of a separation of affect from cognition, it becomes necessary to establish, conceptually and empirically, how affect is represented and, for the purposes of this paper, how preferences are represented. Traditionally, preferences and decisions have been analyzed in a heavily cognitive context, so psychologists are used to thinking that preferences "sit" somewhere in the mental space—as representations—and that they are, therefore, like any other representations. Is this always the case, and is it the case for all forms of preference? In the final analysis, preferences are *behavioral* phenomena. A preference is a behavioral tendency that exhibits itself not so much in what the individual thinks or says about the object, but how she/he acts toward it. Does she/he take it, does she/he approach it, does she/he buy it, does she/he marry it? The study of attitudes, aesthetics, decision making, and consumer preference must take as its basic aim the prediction of what is taken, approached, bought, and married.

Somatic Representations of Preferences

We wish to consider quite literally the proposition that preferences are, above all, behavioral tendencies. In the early days of attitude research, attitude was perceived as a motor disposition. One spoke of an approach attitude as "leaning toward" an object, and of an avoidance attitude as "moving away" from an object. Sir Francis Galton wrote about attitudes as *inclinations* in the physical sense of the word and suggested that interpersonal attitudes could be measured by physical methods: it was simply a matter of placing a pressure gauge under each leg of a chair at a dinner table! The pressure gauges would indicate how the guests felt about each other by showing how they were leaning during the course of the dinner (cited in Fleming 1967).

Not only preferences but all affect has a significant motor component. The expression of emotion occurs above all at the motor level, although, of course, the visceral, glandular, cardiovascular, and autonomic systems are very much involved as well.

Thus far, the study of preferences and of the ways whereby they are established and modified has relied primarily on cognitive methods. For the most part, social psychologists have tried to see what information could be given to a person so that she/he would become fond of some item. They asked how should this information be imparted and, for best results, who should do it. Needless to say, the method of attitude change by means of persuasion has not met with a great deal of success.

The study of preferences involves knowledge about the interaction between affect and cognition. This interaction has been studied in a number of other areas of psychology as well, such as perceptual defense, cognitive dissonance, and social comparison. Typically, it has been studied at the subjective level—i.e., at the level of higher mental processes. For example, in the analysis of the effects of mood on learning and remembering word lists, mood is conceptualized in terms of associative structures (Bower 1981). Mood has nodes in memory, just like any other cognitive representation. These nodes, which are parts of the associative structures that represent the mood state, are said to make contact with the nodes of the associative structure that represent the word lists. The effect of mood on the retention of the words in the list takes place by virtue of the contact between the two associative structures.

Another very reasonable possibility exists (Zajonc and Markus in press): The motor component of affect, which is primarily the expressive aspect of emotion, can also serve *representational* and *mnestic* functions—i.e., behavioral correlates of affect can be considered as much a representation of the affective state as the higher mental structures. After all, what is a representation? What is recalled when we recall affect? A representation is nothing more than some event within the organism that *stands for* some other event, whether outside of the organism in the environment, or inside the organism itself. There need not be a one-to-one correspondence between the two events: such a correspondence does not exist in language, for example. Nor need there be an isomorphism between the two events, because there is hardly any isomorphism assumed for *any* form of representation. It suffices that the correspondence be repeatable, that on some occasion the same internal event arises in representing its referent, that it is possible to combine it with some other events that are representations, and that structures of representations could be formed. If this is the case, then any class of events—subjective, muscular, visceral, cardiovascular, glandular, hormonal, or neural—could very well serve representational functions.

Thus, it is quite reasonable to say that when a person "stores" affect, what he "stores" (among other things) are motor tendencies and other somatic manifestations. He also stores subjective and cognitive features in affect, which neither substitute for nor preclude the presence of other forms of representation. Note that we do not mean to involve the subjective representations of the attitudinal motor correlates. We assume that the motor output itself can serve significant representational and mnestic functions, without the participation of the subjective processes and without kinesthetic feedback or the proprioceptive cues that constitute a basis for the subjective process.

The motor features of affect that serve representational functions and the motor features that may be recalled when the person recalls an affective experience need not occur with the same intensity as they did on the original occasion. When a person recalls an incident that enraged him, his fists may not be quite as clenched and he may not need to scream as loudly as he did at the time. But the same muscles may well be involved at lower amplitudes. If electromyographic measures were taken, low amplitude impulses would be revealed in the same muscles that were involved in the original expression of the person's rage. The growing sophistication in electromyography today allows us to do many complicated procedures that were previously not possible. Subtle levels of impulses coming from multiple sites can be recorded, integrated, and compared with previous ones obtained under similar or different conditions (Cacioppo and Petty 1981).

Attitudes and preferences have a significant motor component that can be a postural tendency or some other somatic form. The behavioral correlates that are involved intaking and ingesting a chili pepper are quite numerous and involve a variety of components, glandular organs, and the alimentary and gastrointestinal systems, for example. These somatic components of preference may become quite independent of the original cognitions that were at one time responsible for establishing these preferences. The behavior pattern is not easy to change. The behavioral correlates involved in eating chili peppers have a stability of their own and are hard to overcome by persuasion. It follows that while preferences have cognitive correlates, they may become functionally autonomous of these cognitive correlates and persist merely by virtue of the behavioral tendencies that have become their expressions. Once they are autonomous, behavioral tendencies that represent attitudes and preferences are hard to change, particularly if only cognitive means are to be employed. A simple communication is seldom sufficient to change a well-established behavioral habit. Methods are needed that can reach habitual behavior and motor output. What these specific methods are may well be a question for skill learning, behavior modification, and human factors theory—areas that have not heretofore been thought of as parts of attitude theory. We know little about these processes as methods of attitude change, but we will have to consider them in the future.

There are a few good examples of what may be done, such as Wells and Petty's (1981) attempt to change attitudes by a simple and ingenious behavioral method. The ostensible purpose of the experiment was to evaluate the quality of headphones. Subjects were told that since headphones are now used by joggers, runners, and bikers, it was important to study how well they work when the listener is moving. They were given a set of headphones to put on and listened to a variety of auditory samples. Some were pieces of music; others were bits of verbal material including an editorial about tuition. One group of subjects was instructed to listen to these auditory samples while shaking their heads from left to right. Another group listened to the same pieces while nodding their heads up and down. These movements were ostensibly presented to the subjects as motions that simulate the motions people make while jogging and biking.

Afterwards, all subjects judged the quality of the headphones and were asked questions about the material they heard. They were asked how much they liked the music and whether the music came through the headphones without distortion. Attitude questions relating to the editorial presented over the headphones were also asked: the subjects were asked what they thought about the editorial and whether they agreed or disagreed with it.

The results were quite clear. The attitudes were more positive among the subjects who nodded their heads than among those who shook their heads from left to right. The very act of appropriately engaging the motor system apparently was sufficient to influence the subjects' attitudes. The effects were quite strong—stronger, in fact, than they would have been had Wells and Petty tried to change these attitudes by simple persuasion.

In general, we should not be terribly surprised that it is so difficult to change attitudes and preferences by cognitive methods. These methods do not reach the motor system and other somatic representational systems of the organism. They only deal with one representational system—the one that exists in the form of associative structures, images, and other subjective states. Since attitudes contain such a substantial affective component, they are likely to have multiple representations—and somatic representations are probably among the more significant ones. We should—and can—take a closer look at them—a much closer look, at any rate, than we can take at associative structures, cognitive organizations, nodes, or scripts, which are hard to see. Muscles are out there in the open to be seen, measured, and manipulated.

Motor Basis of Preferences and Attitude Change

In general—as was the case with affect and cognition—the somatic representations of a person's affect toward a given object can gain autonomy from his knowledge structures about that object. For example, a rich and stable pattern of habitual sensorimotor correlates emerges in relation to chili pepper. There are powerful sensory inputs: gustatory, olfactory, gastrointestinal, and visual. Particular motor responses of the lips, tongue, and esophagus are acquired and attached to the sensory input. A fixed sequence of eating the various courses of meals develops as a strong habit. The reactions of others—especially of the uninitiated—to the chili pepper are quickly recognized and readily interpreted. This rich configuration of sensorisomatic reactions, organized around the chili pepper, forms an integral part of the preference. It can be much more significant than its cognitive counterpart because it participates quite intimately in the *expression of the preference,* i.e., in the consumption of the substance.

With respect to the new corkscrew design, the motor representations of the affect and of the preference are more diffuse and emerge later in the course of preference development. These representational motor correlates are probably associated with actions such as reaching into the drawer to take out the corkscrew (a motion representing a positive *inclination* toward it); they may also occur in association with a particular twist of the wrist when inserting the corkscrew into a cork, or they may be parts of the pulling motion. All these muscular responses may have parameters that *represent* the person's affective predisposition to the corkscrew. Reaching for the corkscrew, taking it out, and screwing it in may all have a "good feeling." Therefore, a change of preference for a corkscrew would have to be accomplished by attention to these motor correlates, since they are so firmly fixed within the structure of the preference.

CONCLUSIONS

An open field for research emerges from the view of affect and cognition presented here. A number of research problems can be readily formulated and explored. In our laboratory, we are now engaged in the study of the interaction of affect and cognition at a more general level. We are looking at the motor system more closely and trying to see what it can tell us about information processing and about how information processing is influenced by emotion (Pietromonaco, Zajonc, and Bargh 1981; Zajonc and Markus in press). It is not unlikely that this approach may have a number of useful consequences for basic consumer research.

REFERENCES

BATESON, PATRICK P. G. (1966), "The Characteristics and Context of Imprinting," *Biological Review,* 41, 183–220.

BETTMAN, JAMES R. (1981), "A Functional Analysis of the Role of Overall Evaluation of Alternatives in the Choice Process," in *Advances in Consumer Research,* Vol. 9, Ed. Andrew A. Mitchell. Ann Arbor, MI: Association for Consumer Research, 87–93.

BOWER, GORDON H. (1981), "Mood and Memory," *American Psychologist,* 36: 129–148.

BROADBENT, DONALD E. (1977), "The Hidden Preattentive Process," *American Psychologist,* 32, 109–118.

CACIOPPO, JOHN T., and RICHARD E. PETTY (1981), "Electromyograms as Measures of Extent and Affectivity of Information Processing," *American Psychologist,* 36, 441–456.

COHEN, JOEL (1981), "The Role of Affect in Categorization: Toward a Reconsideration of the Concept of Attitude," in *Advances in Consumer Research,* Vol. 9, Ed. Andrew A. Mitchell. Ann Arbor, MI: Association for Consumer Research, 94–100.

FLEMING, DONALD (1967), "Attitude: The History of a Concept," in *Perspectives in American History,* Vol. 1, Eds. D. Fleming and B. Bailyn. Cambridge, MA: Charles Warren Center in American History, Harvard University.

GOODALE, M. A. (1982), "Vision as a Sensorimotor System," in *A Behavioral Approach to Brain Research,* Ed. T. E. Robinson. New York: Oxford University Press.

HARRISON, ALBERT A. (1977), "Mere Exposure," in *Advances in Experimental Social Psychology,* Vol. 10, Ed. L. Berkowitz. New York: Academic Press.

HILL, WINFRED F. (1978), "Effects of Mere Exposure on Preference in Nonhuman Mammals," *Psychological Bulletin,* 85, 1177–1198.

INGLE, D. (1973), "Two Visual Systems in the Frog," *Science,* 181, 1053-1055.

——— (1977), "Detection of Stationary Objects by Frogs (*Rana pipiens*) after Ablation of Optic Tectum," *Journal of Comparative and Physiological Psychology,* 91, 1359-1364.

KUNST-WILSON, WILLIAM R., and ROBERT B. ZAJONC (1980), "Affective Discrimination of Stimuli That Cannot Be Recognized," *Science,* 207, 557-558.

LANGER, ELLEN, ARTHUR BLANK, and BENZION CHANOWITZ (1978), "The Mindlessness of Ostensibly Thoughtful Action: The Role of 'Placebic' Information in Interpersonal Interaction," *Journal of Personality and Social Psychology,* 36, 635-642.

LAZARUS, RICHARD S. (1981), "A Cognitivist's Reply to Zajonc on Emotion and Cognition," *American Psychologist,* 36, 222-223.

LIFTON, ROBERT J. (1956), " 'Thought Reform' of Western Civilians in Chinese Communist Prisons," *Psychiatry,* 19, 173-195.

LITTMAN, RICHARD A., and HORACE M. MANNING (1954), "A Methodological Study of Cigarette Brand Discrimination," *Journal of Applied Psychology,* 38, 185-190.

MANDLER, GEORGE (1982), "The Structure of Value: Accounting for Taste," in *Cognition and Affect,* Eds. S. Fiske and M. Clarke. New York: Academic Press.

MATLIN, MARGARET W. (1971), "Response Competition, Recognition, and Affect," *Journal of Personality and Social Psychology,* 19, 295-300.

MATLIN, MARGARET W., and DAVID J. STANG (1978), *The Pollyanna Principle.* Cambridge: Schenkman.

MORELAND, RICHARD L., and ROBERT B. ZAJONC (1977), "Is Stimulus Recognition a Necessary Condition for the Occurrence of Exposure Effects?" *Journal of Personality and Social Psychology,* 35, 191-199.

———, and ROBERT B. ZAJONC (1979), "Exposure Effects May Not Depend on Stimulus Recognition," *Journal of Personality and Social Psychology,* 37, 1085-1089.

PIETROMONACO, PAULA, ROBERT B. ZAJONC, and JOHN BARGH (1981), "The Role of Motor Cues in Recognition Memory for Faces," paper presented at the Annual Convention of The American Psychological Convention, Los Angeles, CA.

ROZIN, ELISABETH, and PAUL ROZIN (1981), "Culinary Themes and Variations," *Natural History,* 90, 6-14.

ROZIN, PAUL, and DEBORAH SCHILLER (1980), "The Nature and Acquisition of a Preference for Chili Pepper by Humans," *Motivation and Emotion,* 4, 77-101.

SHIFFRIN, RICHARD M., and WALTER SCHNEIDER (1977), "Controlled and Automatic Human Information Processing: II. Perceptual Learning, Automatic Attending, and a General Theory," *Psychological Review,* 84, 127-190.

TITCHENER, EDWARD B. (1910), *A Textbook of Psychology.* New York: Macmillan.

WELLS, GARY L., and RICHARD E. PETTY (1980), "The Effects of Overt Head Movement on Persuasion: Compatibility and Incompatibility of Responses," *Basic and Applied Social Psychology,* 1, 219-230.

WILSON, WILLIAM R. (1979), "Feeling More Than We Can Know: Exposure Effects Without Learning," *Journal of Personality and Social Psychology,* 37, 811-821.

WRIGHT, PETER (1981), "Attitudes as Decision Relevant Evidence," paper presented at the 1981 Convention of the Association for Consumer Research, October 22-25, St. Louis, MO.

YNTEMA, D. B., and W. S. TORGERSON (1961), "Man-Computer Cooperation in Decisions Requiring Common Sense," *IRE Transactions of the Professional Group on Human Factors in Electronics,* Vol. HRE-2(1), 20-26.

ZAJONC, ROBERT B. (1978), "Preferenda and Discriminanda: Processing of Affect," paper read as part of the Symposium on New Directions in Experimental Aesthetics, 86th Annual Convention of the American Psychological Association, Toronto, ONT.

——— (1980), "Feeling and Thinking: Preferences Need No Inferences," *American Psychologist,* 35, 151-175.

———, and HAZEL MARKUS (in press), "Affect and Cognition: The Hard Interface," forthcoming in *Emotions, Cognition, and Behavior,* Eds. Carroll E. Izard, Jerome Kagan, and Robert B. Zajonc. New York: Cambridge University Press.

———, HAZEL MARKUS, and WILLIAM R. WILSON (1974), "Exposure, Object Preference, and Distress in the Domestic Chick," *Journal of Comparative and Physiological Psychology,* 86, 581-585.

15

MOOD STATES AND CONSUMER BEHAVIOR: A Critical Review*

Meryl Paula Gardner

A conceptual framework is presented that depicts both the mediating role of mood states and their potential importance in consumer behavior. Reviewing findings from the psychological literature indicates that mood states have direct and indirect effects on behavior, evaluation, and recall. The scope and limitations of these effects are addressed, and the implications for consumer behavior in three areas—service encounters, point-of-purchase stimuli, and communications (context and content)—are examined. Finally, the potential feasibility and viability of mood-related approaches to marketing research and practice are discussed.

Individuals often try to anticipate each other's moods prior to interactions and to read each other's moods during encounters. In these ways, mood information is acquired and used informally to facilitate social and professional interactions. For example, knowledge of the boss's mood on a particular day may help an employee anticipate the boss's reactions to a request for a raise. Analogously, knowledge of consumers' mood states in marketing situations may provide marketers with a more complete understanding of consumers and their reactions to marketing strategies and tactics. This mood-state knowledge may be particularly relevant for understanding consumer behavior as it is affected by service encounters, point-of-purchase stimuli, the content of marketing communications, and the context in which these communications appear.

*Reprinted from the *Journal of Consumer Research,* 12 (December 1985), pp. 281–300.

More generally, insights into consumer behavior may be gleaned by examining consumers' thoughts and feelings. Considerable research using a traditional information processing paradigm has enriched our understanding of the cognitive mediators of consumer behavior. Significant insights into consumer behavior have also come from research that has examined noncognitive (nonbelief) factors such as subjective familiarity (Park, Gardner, and Thukral 1984), fun and fantasy (Hirschman and Holbrook 1982; Holbrook and Hirschman 1982), motor and somatic representation of affect (Zajonc and Markus 1982), emotion (Fennell 1981; Weinberg and Gottwald 1982), and attitude toward the advertisement (Gardner 1985; Lutz, MacKenzie, and Belch 1983; Mitchell and Olson 1981; Moore and Hutchinson 1983; Rossiter and Percy 1980; Shimp 1981). Findings indicate that these feelings-oriented factors may play a major role in consumer-attitude formation and brand selection.

Since mood states are a particularly important set of affective factors (Gardner and Vandersteel 1984; Westbrook 1980), they form a part of all marketing situations (Belk 1975; Lutz and Kakkar 1975) and may influence consumer behavior in many contexts, e.g., advertisement exposure and brand selection. Mood states may be quite transient and easily influenced by little things (Isen et al. 1982). Small changes in physical surroundings may influence consumers' moods at the point of purchase, and slight deviations in communications strategies may significantly affect moods upon exposure to advertising. In fact, although consumers' moods are often affected by factors beyond a marketer's control, moods can be greatly influenced by seemingly small aspects of marketer behavior, e.g., a salesperson's smile or a long wait for a doctor's appointment.

Because mood states are omnipresent and readily influenced by marketer action, they may have important effects on consumer behavior. This article provides a preliminary exploration of this potentially important, but inadequately charted territory. Specifically, we propose to examine the effects of consumers' moods on behavior, evaluation, and recall in marketing contexts. Informal analysis has suggested three areas where mood effects appear to be significant and where mood states can be influenced by marketing tactics: service encounters, point-of-purchase stimuli, and communications (context and content). The present article will focus on these domains, although they are not the only areas where mood states may have important effects on consumer behavior.

First, I will define terms to help clarify the distinctions between moods and other feeling states. Second, I will present a conceptual framework and discuss findings about the nature and limitations of the direct and indirect effects of mood on behavior, evaluation, and recall. Third, I will examine the potential implications of these findings for consumer behavior with respect to service encounters, point-of-purchase stimuli, and communications. In each of these areas I will address three questions:

1. What inferences can be drawn for consumer behavior from our knowledge of the effects of mood states on behavior, evaluation, and recall?
2. Can marketers take advantage of the opportunities suggested by the effects of mood states on consumer behavior, or do logistical limitations prohibit implementation of mood-oriented marketing approaches?
3. What is the current status and future potential of research to assess the impact of mood on consumer behavior?

Fourth, I will discuss the implications of mood effects on consumer behavior as they relate to the design of marketing-research studies, and the development of marketing actions. Finally, I will make suggestions for future research.

Definition of Terms

The word "mood" has a wide range of usages and meaning. One might use the term to describe a phenomenological property of an individual's subjectively perceived affective state; e.g., someone may be in a cheerful mood or a hostile mood. One might also use mood to describe a property of an inanimate object; e.g., a point-of-purchase display may have a "sophisticated mood" or a "fun mood." For the purposes of this article, we will adopt the former, phenomenological, approach and view moods as feeling states that are subjectively perceived by individuals. As such, moods are a subcategory of feeling states.

The phrase "feeling state" will be used to refer to an affective state that is general and pervasive. Such states "suffuse all one's experiences, even though directed at none in particular" (Fiske 1981, p. 231). These states can be contrasted with feelings directed toward specific objects, e.g., the affective component of brand attitude.

Mood will refer to feeling states that are transient; such states are particularized to specific times and situations (Peterson and Sauber 1983) and may be contrasted with those that are relatively stable and permanent (Westbrook 1980). Examples of invariant feeling states include personality dispositions such as optimism/pessimism (Goldman-Eisler 1960; Tiger 1979), and enduring global attitude structures such as satisfaction (Andrews and Withey 1976).

Moods may be distinguished from emotions, which, in contrast, are usually more intense, attention-getting, and tied to a specifiable behavior (Clark and Isen 1982). One is almost always aware of one's emotions and their effects, which may redirect attention to the source of the emotion and interrupt ongoing behavior (Simon 1967). One may or may not be aware of one's mood and its effects, which may color attentional processes and influence, but rarely interrupt ongoing behavior (Clark and Isen 1982).

Different types of positive moods (e.g., cheeriness, peacefulness, and sexual warmth) and negative moods (e.g., anxiety, guilt, and depression) can be readily identified. Although categorizing moods as positive or negative may be an oversimplification (Belk 1984), existing research does not provide much insight into the effects of specific moods. In fact, most studies have involved broad manipulations designed to induce positive and/or negative moods and have not attempted to affect or assess specific moods. It is often difficult to infer the induced mood or its strength; e.g., subjects told that they have failed a test of perceptual motor skills may not respond emotionally or they may feel depressed, frustrated, or anxious. In addition, many common manipulations may fail to induce discrete moods, and naturally occurring feeling states may appear in clusters (Polivy 1981). Only two studies have investigated the effects of more than one positive or negative mood (Fried and Berkowitz 1979; Laird et al. 1982). To enable readers to form their own inferences about specific positive and negative mood states induced in the relevant studies, Table 15.1 provides information about the induction procedures used.

Although it is difficult to compare findings for specific positive and negative moods across studies since the induction procedures and dependent variables are confounded, the effects of different negative mood states seem to be more heterogeneous than the effects of positive mood states (Isen 1984). For example, Baumann, Cialdini, and Kenrick (1981) note that helping may be enhanced by some negative mood states (e.g., sadness) but not by others (e.g., frustration). Research is needed to investigate the effects of specific positive and negative moods on behavior, evaluation, and recall.

CONCEPTUAL FRAMEWORK

Common models of consumer behavior do not explicitly recognize the role of mood states. At best, the term "antecedent state" is used to encompass all of the momentary financial, psychological, and physiological baggage with which a consumer arrives at a marketing interaction (Belk 1975). In order to examine the role of mood states in consumer behavior and suggest their marketing implications, a framework is needed that interconnects strategic areas, marketing tactics, and consumer-behavior processes. The framework adopted for this article attempts to meet this need and appears in Figure 15.1. It is not all-inclusive, but facilitates the examination of:

1. Relationships between some key strategic marketing areas (indicated by rectangles in Figure 15.1) and mood induction tactics (indicated by ovals).
2. Effects of induced mood states on some important psychological processes underlying consumer behavior (indicated by triangles).

The depicted relationships are discussed in the next two sections.

Strategic Areas and Mood Induction Tactics

Although it may seem obvious that some marketing actions affect consumers' mood states, the relationship between strategic areas and mood-related tactics requires systematic investigation. Examining three strategic areas—service encounters, point-of-purchase stimuli, and communications (context and content)—serves two purposes. First, it facilitates the discussion of tactics that are useful in more than one area. Second, it facilitates the evaluation of the importance and feasibility of mood-related approaches in each area.

In the service sector, mood induction can be contiguous to an encounter, thus increasing the likelihood that its effects will have an impact on a transaction. Mood induction may be affected by aspects of the transaction procedure, interactions with service providers, and physical settings (see Figure 15.1). At the point of purchase, a mood may be induced by aspects of the retail environment and by interactions with sales personnel. Because these mood inducers are contiguous with much in-store information acquisition and decision making, they may have a substantial impact on such processes. Communications effects on consumers' mood states include those effects due to media context and advertisement content. Media-context ef-

FIGURE 15.1 A Conceptual Model of the Role of Mood States in Consumer Behavior

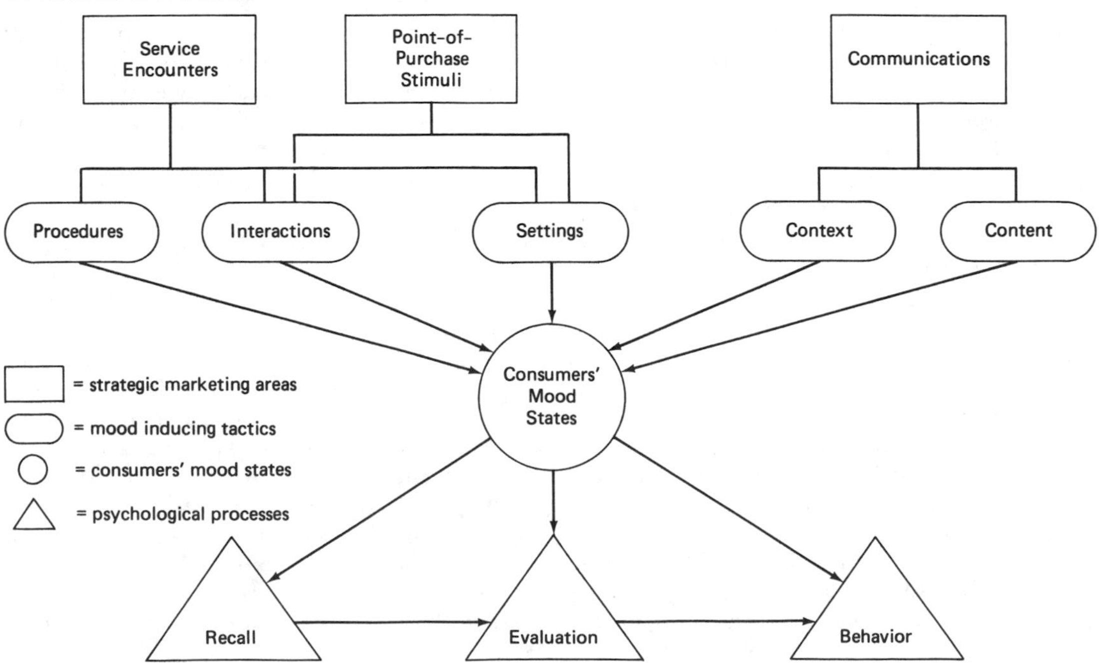

fects relate to material that precedes or surrounds the advertiser's message in a communications vehicle. Advertisement content may affect consumers' mood states through the use of emotional music, graphics, or copy.

EFFECTS OF MOOD STATES ON PSYCHOLOGICAL PROCESSES

Research in psychology indicates that mood states exert an important influence on behavior, judgment, and recall (see Figure 15.1). As a result of this, several conclusions about the effects of mood states emerge. Many of these findings are based upon laboratory studies and require replication under more realistic conditions.

Effects of Mood States on Behavior

Positive moods appear to enhance the likelihood that a host of behaviors may be performed (see Table 15.1). It appears that a positive mood makes one kinder both to oneself and to others (Underwood, Moore, and Rosenhan 1973). Some positive moods appear to increase the likelihood of performance of behaviors with expected positive associations and to decrease the likelihood of performance of behaviors that lead to negative outcomes (perhaps by enhancing one's sense of personal power and self-perceived freedom to do as one wishes—Forest et al. 1979; Isen and Simmonds 1978). Research is needed to predict *a priori* which activities are believed to have positive outcomes and which are thought to have negative outcomes.

Studies reviewed in Table 15.1 suggest that the behavioral effects of negative moods may be more complex than the effects of positive moods. Two factors may contribute to the diversity of effects of negative mood states. First, there are some indications that negative mood states are themselves more heterogeneous than positive mood states (Isen 1984). Second, controlled processes that terminate unpleasant negative mood states may compete with automatic tendencies to engage in mood-congruent behavior (Clark and Isen 1982).

The link between mood states and behavior may be seen as both direct and indirect (see Figure 15.1). A direct linkage may involve associations in memory between mood states and behaviors. In this context, a behavior may be viewed as a conditioned response. (For a review of theoretical issues in conditioning, see Bugelski 1982; for a discussion of the consumer behavior implications of conditioning, see McSweeney and Bierley 1984; Peter and Nord 1982). In some cases, automatic behavioral responses may be largely inborn or instinctive. Zajonc (1980) discusses the universality of affective responses among animal species, citing the example of the frightened rabbit running from a snake. Plutchik (1980) has postulated that feelings mediate situation perceptions and instinctive responses. Although Plutchik (1980) and Zajonc (1980) provide phyllogenetic and ontogenic support for an innate link between emotions and behavior, research is needed to investigate the possibility of such a link between mood states and behavior.

It may be more likely that associations between mood states and behaviors may be learned from repeated experience, socialization, or acculturation. For example, Cialdini and Kenrick (1976) found that an experimentally induced depressed condition increased helpfulness among older children, but not among younger ones. The data were taken as support for the notion that socialization forms the basis for the effects of negative mood on altruistic behavior.

One may also view the link between mood states and behavior as indirect, in the sense that the behavioral effects of mood states may be somewhat mediated by their effects on expectations, evaluations, and judgments. This view suggests that positive moods may increase the likelihood that a behavior will be performed by increasing the accessibility of positive associations to the behavior, thus leading to more positive evaluations of the behavior (Clark and Isen 1982).

TABLE 15.1 Studies Investigating the Effects of Mood States on Psychological Processes: Inductions and Findings

Study	Induction	Finding
Behavioral Effects		
Berkowitz and Connor (1966)	(a) Success (b) Failure (c) No experience on a preliminary irrelevant task	Success subjects were more willing to work for a dependent peer than control subjects. Failure subjects expressed stronger dislike for their peer the greater their peer's dependency on them.
Mischel, Coates, and Raskoff (1968)	(a) Success (b) Failure	Relative to children in condition (b), those in condition (a) were more noncontingently generous to themselves under some conditions.
Isen (1970)	Receiving feedback that is: (a) Above the norm—success (b) Below the norm—failure	Subjects in the success condition (a) were more generous and helpful than those in the failure condition (b).
Aderman (1972)	Reading Velten statements designed to induce: (a) Elation (b) Depression	Subjects who read the elation statements (a) outperformed those who read the depression statements (b) on a helping task. In addition, subjects in condition (a) were more likely than those in condition (b) to volunteer for a future unpleasant experiment, perhaps because the latter groups resented their induced depression. This finding can be *contrasted* with those of other investigations of the effects of positive mood on the likelihood of performance of unpleasant tasks. Research indicates that performance is less likely for subjects in positive mood conditions than for those in control conditions (Forest et al. 1979; Isen and Simmonds 1978).
Isen and Levin (1972)	Study 1: (a) Receiving cookies while studying in a library (b) No manipulation Study 2: (a) Finding a dime planted in a phone booth (b) No manipulation	In each study, subjects in condition (a) were more willing to help others than those in condition (b).
Regan, Williams, and Sparling (1972)	Camera would not work. Experimenter implies: (a) The subject broke the camera (b) The misfunction was not the subject's fault	Subjects in condition (a) were more likely than those in condition (b) to perform an unrelated helping task.
Moore, Underwood, and Rosenhan (1973)	Self-generated thoughts: (a) Happy (b) Sad (c) Neutral	Children in condition (a) contributed the most and those in condition (b) contributed the least to a charity in the experimenter's absence.
Isen, Horn, and Rosenhan (1973)	(a) Success (b) Failure (c) Control	Success was associated with increased charitability in children subjects. The effect of failure *depended* on the circumstances of the failure.
Underwood et al. (1973)	Self-generated thoughts: (a) Happy (b) Sad (c) Neutral	Relative to children in condition (b), those in condition (a) reward themselves more generously in the experimenters' absence.

TABLE 15.1 (Continued)

Study	Induction	Finding
Effects of Recall		
Seeman and Schwarz (1974)	(a) Success (b) Failure	Relative to children in the failure condition, those in the success condition chose a large delayed reward rather than a small immediate reward.
Blevins and Murphy (1974)	(a) Finding a dime planted in a phone booth (b) No manipulation	*No relationship* was observed between finding a dime and helping.
Fry (1975)	Self-generated thoughts: (a) Happy (b) Unhappy (c) Neutral	Children in condition (a) resisted temptation longer than those in condition (c), who in turn resisted longer than those in condition (b).
Donnerstein, Donnerstein, and Munger (1975)	(a) Viewing slides showing flowers, animals, and sunsets (b) Viewing slides showing old people and migrant workers (c) Writing pro/con arguments	Condition (a) *did not* appear to influence helping, but condition (b) was associated with enhanced willingness to help. The authors explain this finding in terms of expiation of guilt.
Moore, Clyburn, and Underwood (1976)	Self-generated thoughts: (a) Happy (b) Sad (c) Neutral	Relative to children in condition (c) those in condition (a) were more likely to choose a large delayed reward than a small immediate reward and those in condition (b) were more likely to choose a small immediate reward than a large delayed reward.
Cialdini and Kenrick (1976)	Self-generated thoughts: (a) Sad (b) Neutral	Older children, but not younger ones, were more generous when in condition (a) then when in condition (b)
Isen and Simmonds (1978)	(a) Finding a dime planted in a phone booth (b) No manipulation	Relative to subjects in condition (b), those in condition (a) were more willing to read statements allegedly designed to induce good moods and less willing to read statements designed to induce bad moods.
Weyant (1978)	Feedback on test: (a) Positive (b) Negative No Test taken; (c) Control	Helping was enhanced in condition (a) and dependent upon the costs and benefits associated with the helping task in condition (b).
Batson et al. (1979)	(a) Finding a dime planted in a phone booth (b) No manipulation	Subjects who found the dime were more likely to help another person and to acquire information than those who did not.
Forest et al. (1979)	False meter feedback regarding feelings: (a) Positive (b) Negative (c) Neutral	Condition (a) was associated with enhanced helping on an agreeable task, but not a disagreeable one.
Cunningham (1970)	No induction, but sunshine, temperature, humidity, wind velocity, and lunar phase assessed	Sunshine related to enhanced self-reports of mood, greater willingness to assist an interviewer, and larger tips for restaurant waitresses.
Fried and Berkowitz (1979)	Subjects heard music: (a) Mendelssohn's "Songs Without Words"	Condition (a) was associated with peaceful feelings, condition (b) with joyful feelings, and condition (c) with irritated feelings on self-

TABLE 15.1 (Continued)

Study	Induction	Finding
Behavioral Effects		
	(b) Duke Ellington's "One O'Clock Jump" (c) John Coltrane's "Meditations" No music heard: (d) Control condition	report measures. In addition, subjects in condition (a) were most apt to be helpful immediately afterwards, significantly more so than those in conditions (c) or (d).
Effects on Affective Reactions and Judgments		
Mood states bias evaluations of novel stimuli in mood-congruent directions		
Griffitt (1970)	Effective temperature	High effective temperature associated with negative mood and negative evaluations of anonymous others.
Laird (1974)	Instructions to: (a) Smile (b) Frown without awareness of the nature of their expressions	Subjects appeared to feel more happy in condition (a) and more angry in condition (b). In addition, cartoons viewed in condition (a) were rated funnier than those viewed in condition (b).
Veitch and Griffitt (1976)	Heard broadcasts conveying: (a) Good news (b) Bad news	Subjects in condition (a) reported greater positive affect and evaluated anonymous others more favorably than those in condition (b).
Isen and Shalker (1982)	(a) Finding a dime planted in a phone booth (b) Receiving success test feedback (c) Receiving failure test feedback (d) No manipulation	Relative to subjects in condition (d), those in condition (a) rated slides more favorably and those in condition (c) rated slides less favorably. The ratings of subjects in condition (b) *did not* differ from those of subjects in condition (d).
Mood states bias evaluations of familiar stimuli in mood-congruent directions		
Isen et al. (1978)	(a) Receiving a free gift (b) No manipulation	Subjects in condition (a) rated products they owned more favorable than those in condition (b).
Carson and Adams (1980)	Reading Velten statements designed to induce: (a) Elation (b) Depression (c) Neutral mood	Expected enjoyableness of activities was enhanced in condition (a) and diminished in condition (c).
Schwarz and Clore (1983)	Study 1 (a) Self-generated happy life events (b) Self-generated sad life events Study 2 (a) Sunny weather (b) Rainy weather	In both studies, relative to subjects in condition (b), those in condition (a) indicated more satisfaction with their lives.
Mood states bias judgments of the likelihood of mood-congruent events		
Masters and Furman (1976)	Self-generated: (a) Happy thoughts (b) Neutral thoughts	Relative to children in condition (b) those in condition (a) had a greater expectancy for positive unrelated serendipitous outcomes.
Johnson and Tversky (1983)	(a) Reading an account of a tragic event (b) Control	Condition (a) was associated with increased estimates of the frequency of many risks and unrelated, undesirable events.

TABLE 15.1 (Continued)

Study	Induction	Finding
Effects on recall		
Exposure mood enhances recall of mood-congruent items		
Bower (1981)	Post hyponotic suggestion—i.e., hypnotizing subjects and asking them to relive (a) happy or (b) sad experiences from their own lives.	Subjects read stories with happy and sad characters. Subjects in condition (b) attended more to sad material, identified with the sad character from the story, and recalled more about that character.
Bower, Gilligan, and Monteiro Experiment 5 (1981)	Post hypnotic suggestion—i.e., hypnotizing subjects and asking them to recall (a) happy or (b) sad experiences from their own lives.	Subjects read stories with happy and sad characters associated with both happy and sad events. Subjects in condition (a) remembered happy events better than sad events and those in condition (b) remembered sad events, regardless of the character with which the events were associated.
Retrieval mood enhances recall of mood-congruent items		
Isen et al. (1978)	(a) Receiving a small gift (b) No manipulation	Condition (a) was associated with the ability to recall positive material in memory about products subjects own.
Teasdale and Fogarty (1979)	Reading Velten statements designed to induce: (a) Elation (b) Depression	Time to retrieve pleasant memories of life experiences relative to time to retrieve unpleasant memories was significantly longer in condition (b) than in condition (a).
Natale and Hantas (1982)	Post-hypnotic suggestion: (a) Elation (b) Depression	Condition (a) was associated with decreased recall for negative life events and increased recall for positive events. Condition (b) was associated with decreased recall of positive life experiences and weaker memory strength for positive information about oneself.
Laird et al. (1982)	Instructions to manipulate facial expressions without awareness of the nature of the expressions. Mood response to manipulated expressions was first assessed in a separate procedure. Subjects whose moods were affected were designated the self-produced cue group.	
	Study 1: (a) Frowning (b) Smiling	Study 1—In the self-produced cue group, recall for anger-provoking editorials was significantly better in condition (a) and for humorous selections in condition (b). In the non-self cue group, expressions did not affect recall.
	Study 2: (a) Angry expression (b) Sad expression (c) Fearful expression	Study 2—In the self-produced cue group, recall was better for sentences consistent with expression, In the non-self cue group, recall was not affected.
Clark and Waddell (1983)	Receiving feedback about test performance: (a) Positive (b) Negative (c) No feedback	Subjects were asked to respond to descriptions of 3 situations with whatever thoughts came to mind first. Subjects in condition (a) had significantly more positive first affective reactions to *2 out of 3* situations. Subjects in

TABLE 15.1 (Continued)

Study	Induction	Finding
Effects of Recall		
		condition (b) had more negative first affective reactions to all 3 situations, but these differences were *not statistically significant.*
Srull (1983a)	Self-generated thoughts: (a) Happy experiences (b) Sad experiences from own life	Subjects recalled more attribute information that was *incongruent* with their retrieval conditions than material that was congruent, perhaps due to cue overload.
Match between exposure and retrieval mood enhances recall		
Bower et al. (1978)	Post-hypnotic suggestion-hypnotized and asked to recall thoughts: (a) Positive (b) Negative	Match between learning and retrieval conditions facilitated recall only where confusion and interference may have otherwise occurred.
Bartlett and Santrock (1979)	Telling children stories with appropriate pictures and experimenter behavior: (a) Happy (b) Sad	Same condition upon exposure and retrieval facilitated the generation of cues needed to perform free recall task, but did not affect recognition or cued recall.

Note: Findings that indicate somewhat limited or atypical effects of mood states are italicized.

Effects of Mood States on Affective Reactions and Judgments

In general, mood states seem to bias evaluations and judgments in mood congruent directions.[1] Folk wisdom and experimental evidence agree: a good mood may be associated with looking at one's world through rose-colored glasses, while a bad mood may analogously color evaluations (Clark and Isen 1982). And mood states appear to bias several types of judgments in mood-congruent directions (see Table 15.1). These directions include evaluations of novel stimuli (Griffitt 1970; Isen and Shalker 1982; Laird 1974; Veitch and Griffitt 1976), evaluations of familiar stimuli (Carson and Adams 1980; Isen et al. 1978; Schwarz and Clore 1983), and evaluations of the likelihood of mood congruent events (Johnson and Tversky 1983; Masters and Furman 1976).[2]

The link between mood states and affective responses and judgments may be viewed as both direct and indirect (see Figure 15.1 on page 256). A direct linkage may involve associations in memory between mood states and affective reactions; in this context, an affective reaction may be viewed as a conditioned response. Griffitt and Guay have postulated (1969, pp. 1–2):

> evaluation of any given stimulus object is a positive linear function of the proportion of stimuli with positive reinforcement properties associated with it.

[1]This general conclusion may not hold in all cases; products strongly associated with reducing negative mood states may be evaluated more favorably by consumers when in such negative states.

[2]Positive mood may be associated with increased yielding to persuasive messages (Dabbs and Janis 1965; Dribben and Brabender 1979; Galizio and Hendrick 1972; Janis, Kaye, and Kirschner 1965). Additional research is needed to investigate the limitations of this finding and the psychological processes involved.

Stimuli with positive and negative reinforcement properties are hypothesized to act as unconditioned stimuli which evoke implicit affective responses. Any discriminable stimulus, including a person, associated with such unconditioned stimuli becomes a conditioned stimulus capable of eliciting the implicit affective responses. The affective responses, in turn, mediate overt evaluative responses such as verbal assessments, preferences, and approach-avoidance behaviors.

Note that stimuli with positive reinforcement properties may be viewed as inducers of positive mood states. Conditioning may involve a wide range of mood inducers—including music (e.g., Gorn 1982; Milliman 1982)—and may sometimes involve extensive acculturation and socialization (Zajonc and Markus 1982).

One may also view the association between positive mood inducers and favorable evaluations as indirect, and influenced by information processing. This approach posits that the effects of positive mood may be mediated by such cognitive activity as information retrieval; i.e., mood may affect evaluations by making mood congruent items more accessible in memory, and thus, more likely to affect evaluations (Isen et al. 1978). The information-processing approach is compatible with a situational perspective that views attitudes as a function of readily accessible information.

Effects of Mood States on Recall

One way to understand the effects of mood on recall involves the use of network models of memory (Collins and Loftus 1975). In such models, constructs may be conceptualized as nodes, and relationships between constructs as links. From this perspective, mood may be viewed as stored with, or linked to, a set of constructs or experiences in memory. As indicated in Table 15.1, recall may be affected by the consumer's mood at the time of exposure or retrieval, or by a match between exposure and retrieval moods. (For an extensive review of the effects of mood on cognition, see Isen 1984).

Mood at the time of exposure may affect what information is recalled by facilitating the retrieval of mood-congruent items. This effect may be due to greater encoding-elaboration of mood-congruent material at the time of exposure. The facilitating effect seems to appear only when retrieval cues are needed (Bower 1981; Bower, Gilligan, and Monteiro 1981).

Retrieval mood may facilitate overall retrieval of mood-congruent material from memory (Clark and Waddell 1983; Isen et al. 1978; Natale and Hantas 1982; Teasdale and Fogarty 1979) and may enhance recall of specific mood-congruent information, if sufficient cues are available for the identification of such items (Laird et al. 1982). Retrieval mood may not enhance recall for specific mood-congruent material if cues to identify such items are inadequate. In the absence of sufficient cues, recall for mood-congruent items may suffer, and recall of mood-incongruent items may be enhanced (Srull 1983a).

Several researchers (e.g., Bartlett and Santrock 1979; Bower, Monteiro, and Gilligan 1978) have found indications that unaided recall is enhanced when mood at the time of retrieval matches mood at the time of encoding and when the encoding mood can serve as a retrieval cue. If such a cue is unnecessary because of the properties of the task or of the stimulus, recall does not appear to be enhanced by a match between encoding and retrieval moods. Analogous findings have been reported for other variables that affect an individual's psychological or physical state such as alcohol, drugs, or underwater submersion. (For a review of state dependent effects on recall, see Eich 1980; cf., Isen 1984).

Scope of the Effects of Mood States

The preceding discussion examined the effects of mood states on behavior, evaluation, and recall and noted the specific limitations of these effects. I now turn to more general issues, including the prevalence of the impact of mood states and the factors that may attenuate mood-related effects.

It is difficult to assess the prevalence of mood-related effects because published studies may be biased toward research that reports statistically significant findings. (N.B., research that failed to produce significant results may have been performed, but not published.) Some of the difficulties involved in empirical mood studies may have encouraged those investigators who failed to produce significant results to modify their procedures continually until they obtained significant findings. For example, given the difficulties involved in evaluating experimental mood-induction procedures, failure to observe postulated effects may be viewed as a failure of the induction manipulation, not of the hypothesis under scrutiny. Such studies may be rejected by journals as inadequately supported by manipulation checks, or discarded by experimenters as pretest results. Given enough attempts, statistically significant results may be obtained—if only by chance. I do not mean to imply that all observed results are due to chance, but the replication of existing studies should be encouraged and careful attention paid to nonsignificant results. Findings that indicate somewhat limited or atypical effects of mood states are in italics in Table 15.1.

In addition, it is difficult to assess the scope of mood effects because induction procedures are almost completely confounded with the types of effects investigated. The studies reviewed in Table 15.1 suggest that, in general, memory effects have been investigated with relatively strong or direct induction procedures, while behavioral effects have involved milder, less direct manipulations. Additional research is needed to replicate the findings of prior studies using new and varied procedures.

Mood states are not expected to significantly affect behavior, evaluation, or recall under all conditions. Mood-state effects may be diminished or enhanced by circumstances related to situational ambiguity, degree of arousal, time between mood induction and assessment of effects, situational factors that encourage precision, and the specific moods involved.

The effects of mood states may be greater for situations that are somewhat ambiguous than for clear-cut situations. Mood states may have the greatest impact when differences are marginal and no alternative dominates the choice set (Clark and Isen 1982). This view is supported by Isen and Shalker's (1982) study that found that:

1. Subjects in experimentally induced positive/negative mood conditions rated slides more/less favorably than those in a control mood condition, but that the rank order of slide types (pleasant, neutral, and unpleasant) remained constant across mood conditions.
2. Mood conditions appeared to influence evaluations of neutral slides more than assessments of pleasant or unpleasant slides.

These findings suggest that mood effects do not dominate the mood-incongruent aspects of stimuli and that mood effects have a greater impact when evaluations are ambiguous than when they are clear-cut.

In addition, a moderate level of arousal may facilitate mood effects, perhaps because naturally occurring feeling states are often associated with arousal. Bartlett, Burleson, and Santrock (1982) found that the state dependent effects of mood on recall were absent when relaxation exercises preceded an experimental task. Clark, Milberg, and Ross (1983) found that arousal in combination with positive mood enhanced the effect of the positive mood on subsequent judgments.

It should be noted that the effect of any given mood is not long-lasting (Schellenberg and Blevins 1973). The effect of a positive mood induction on the performance of a helping task has been found to last approximately twenty minutes (Isen, Clark, and Schwartz 1976).

In addition, mood effects may be minimized by factors that encourage objectivity or precision. Under such circumstances, controlled processes may be used to retrieve all relevant information from memory, and the effect of mood on accessibility may be unimportant. For example, when assessment encourages subjects to respond with stored evaluations, responses do not appear to be biased by mood (Srull 1983b, 1984; Westbrook 1980). Factors that encourage the use of controlled processes may involve experimental settings and the perceived consequences of responses.

Research is needed to investigate the limitations of the effects associated with specific mood states. In general, the effects of negative moods may be more limited than those of positive moods. Support is provided by Schwarz and Clore (1983). Findings indicate that:

1. Subjects in positive mood conditions indicated more satisfaction with their lives than those in negative mood conditions
2. The negative impact of bad mood on assessments of life satisfaction disappeared when subjects were directed to attribute negative feelings to transient external circumstances
3. The positive impact of good mood was not similarly affected.

These findings suggest that people in some negative mood states may try to resist negative thinking and do so whenever possible.

The preceding discussion suggests that the effects of mood states may be greatest in those consumer-behavior situations where stimuli are ambiguous, consumers are somewhat aroused, induction and action are temporally contiguous, perceived benefits of being precise are low, and moods are positive. Opportunities for consumer-behavior situations which meet these criteria arise during service encounters, at the point-of-purchase, and with respect to advertising, i.e., communications content and context. The potential for mood effects to have a significant impact in each of these areas is explored in the next three sections.

SERVICE ENCOUNTERS

The literature reviewed for this article suggests that mood states may at least marginally influence behavior, affective responses, and recall. In order to evaluate the importance of these influences on consumer behavior, marketing-related settings and potential mood inducers under the control of a manager must be examined. Key findings from the preceding section are summarized in Table 15.2, and areas in which each finding may be important for service encounters, point-of-purchase stimuli, and communications are indicated. The present section examines the possible consumer-behavior implications of the effects of consumers' mood states during service encounters.

In the service sector, both consumers' and service providers' mood states may be important. The study of service-provider or seller behavior has been neglected by marketing research (Lutz 1979), but this behavior is particularly important to the service sector, given the dyadic nature of many service encounters. Ser-

TABLE 15.2 Summary of Mood-State Effects for Three Consumer Behavior Situations

	Situation			
			Communications	
Effects of Mood States	*Service Encounters*	*Point-of-Purchase Stimuli*	*Context*	*Content*
Positive moods may enhance the likelihood of performance of behaviors with positive expected outcomes and decrease the liklihood of performance of behaviors with negative expected outcomes.	X	X	X	X
Mood may bias evaluations and likelihood assessments in mood congruent directions.	X	X	X	
Exposure mood may enhance recall of mood-congruent items.	X	X	X	X
Retrieval mood may enhance recall of mood-congruent items.	X	X		
Match between exposure and retrieval moods may enhance recall.		X		X

Note: X = presence of effect.

vice providers' mood states may affect their job performance, whereas consumers' moods may affect consumer behavior during a service encounter, the evaluation of the encounter and its result, and the subsequent recall of the service encounter.

Mood Effects in Service Encounters

Mood may affect behavior during service encounters; consumers in good moods may be more likely to be helpful and easy to please than consumers in neutral moods. For example, consumers in good moods may be willing to postpone gratification, follow doctors' orders, or bag their own groceries. On the other hand, service recipients in good moods may be less likely to perform acts with expected negative consequences such as painful rehabilitation exercises or undergo medical tests that may indicate illness. But when the need for the behavior is unambiguous, mood effects on performance may be minimal or nonexistent. However, the effects of negative mood on behavior in the service sector may depend on the nature of the negative mood (e.g., guilt versus anger), the reasons consumers give for the mood, and the costs/benefits of the behavior to be performed.

Mood may affect consumer evaluation of service encounters or the encounters' results by biasing the evaluations in mood-congruent directions. If consumers form global impressions of a service encounter, they may later recall the impressions rather than the specific facts on which the impressions were based. Consumers in good/bad moods may evaluate novel and familiar encounters more positively/negatively than consumers in neutral moods.

Exposure mood may affect a consumer's subsequent recall of a service encounter or its results by enhancing the consumer's recall of mood-congruent items. For example, customers who are in a good mood when they open bank accounts may be more likely to recall positive information about their accounts later. Mood may affect the recall/retrieval of past service encounters by enhancing recall of mood-congruent items, which, in turn, may be associated with biased assessments of the likelihood of mood-congruent events. For example, patients admitted to hospitals in bad moods may retrieve more negative information about past hospital experiences than those in good moods and may be more likely to presume the worst about an impending hospital stay.

Mood Induction in Service Encounters

Service encounters offer marketers many opportunities for mood inductions that are temporally contiguous to a transaction and so are of potential strategic importance. The service setting, the procedure, and the interaction with the service provider present opportunities for marketers to influence or respond to mood states.

Physical Surroundings. Aspects of ambient environments have been found to correlate with assessments of mood and postulated mood effects. For example, nice weather has been found to correlate positively with self-assessments of mood and with tips left in restaurants (Cunningham 1979). Effective temperature has been found to correlate negatively with several measures of mood and with evaluations of anonymous others (Griffitt 1970). Kotler (1974) has postulated that the effects of ambient environments should be more important in situations where products are purchased or where the seller has design options. Such conditions are frequently met in the service sector.

The many aspects of an environment's physical surroundings that are under marketer control encourage optimism about the potential for inducing moods that will serve specific marketing ends. There is evidence to indicate that design-related factors can have powerful effects on human behavior. For example, in order to reduce the number of suicides attempted from Blackfriar Bridge in England, the black bridge was repainted bright green (Hatwick 1950, p. 188). In addition, Wener (1984) has noted that confusing or disorienting service settings may induce feelings of frustration and anxiety in service providers and recipients. These negative effects may be ameliorated by using simple linear layouts with orientation aids and maximum visibility. Aids may be overt (such as signs and guides) or covert (such as artwork or plants that serve as landmarks).

Designing a mood-inducing service setting involves a consideration of the interaction of the setting with consumers' perceptions of other facets of the setting's sponsor. Kotler and Rath (1983) have deemphasized the role of individual components and have stressed the importance of the overall design of a sponsor's settings, image, and products. Recent efforts in environmental psychology have developed research techniques to facilitate the investigation of environments as contextual settings rather than as sets of components (Stokols 1982). Research is needed to explore both the effects of various marketing settings on consumer behavior and the mediating role of mood states. Studies are also needed that compare the impact of marketer-controlled factors to the impact of factors that marketers do not control.

Procedures and Interactions. For monadic interactions (e.g., customer/machine transactions), procedures may be designed to move customers from an entry mood toward a desired mood. Frequently, these procedures may involve such positive mood inducers as clear instructions, user-friendly systems, and positive feedback throughout a task.

For dyadic interactions (e.g., customer/service-provider transactions), the moods of both parties may affect interactions. Service companies must develop interaction strategies and tactics appropriate to customers with different moods. If consumers vary widely in mood, it may sometimes be efficient to segment on the mood variable and train service providers to specialize in serving consumers in specific mood states.

Because both monadic and dyadic interactions involve the use of limited mechanical or human resources, consumers must often wait to engage in a transaction. Waiting is generally considered to be a disagreeable experience, and it may be so distasteful to some consumers that they will hire others to wait in their place (Geist 1984). The negative moods induced by waiting for service may persist through contiguous service encounters. Suggested tactics for improving waiting consumers' mood states have been proposed by Maister (1984). In addition, consumers may look for ways to pull themselves out of the bad moods associated with waiting for service. Marketers may find it advantageous to investigate and encourage such consumer-originated mechanisms.

Service companies may also benefit by examining the moods of their employees and understanding the role of these feelings during interactions with consumers. Hochschild (1983) provides evidence to show that at least some service providers (stewardesses and bill collectors) do a great deal of emotional work, e.g., mood management. Companies may find it profitable to institute programs to help service providers handle their own feelings and the interaction of their moods with the customer's mood.

Current Status and Future Potential

Many service encounters involve at least minimal levels of ambiguity and arousal and they do not encourage service recipients to be particularly objective or precise. Mood induction can be contiguous to the service encounter, increasing the likelihood that its effects will have an impact on transactions. However, the magnitude of the induced effects is an empirical question that requires further research.

Additionally, because service providers have personal contact with consumers, they can adjust their tactics to suit consumers' mood states. Training procedures might be used to help service providers interpret consumers' moods, perhaps by interpreting facial cues. (For a discussion of one interpretation technique, see Weinberg and Gottwald 1982.)

POINT-OF-PURCHASE STIMULI

Store atmospherics and interactions with salespeople may affect the consumer's mood at the point-of-purchase in a retail setting. In turn, mood states may influence purchase behavior, brand evaluation, and information acquisition.

Mood Effects at Point-of-Purchase

Positive mood states at the point-of-purchase may both increase shoppers' willingness to perform tasks with positive expected outcomes, and decrease their willingness to perform behaviors with negative expected outcomes. In order to anticipate the effects of positive moods on target activities, we must be able to categorize consumers' own assessments of whether their behavior will lead to positive or negative outcomes and we must be able to understand the effects of consumers' mood states on their assessments. For some activities, valences of expected outcomes may vary widely across consumers. For example, trying on clothing may be associated with positive outcomes for some shoppers and with negative outcomes for others. Expected outcomes may be related to media exposure (e.g., reading fashion magazines) or responsiveness to marketing-mix variables (e.g., being greatly influenced by advertising).

In-store mood may also affect the evaluation of familiar and novel stimuli. Research is needed to compare the effects of mood on the evaluation of new and familiar brands. Also, the potential implications for understanding trial and repeat purchasing should be investigated.

Information acquisition at the point-of-purchase may have important effects on subsequent brand evaluation. The consumer's mood at the time of initial exposure to a product may affect the valence of product features readily accessible to subsequent recall. This effect may be particularly important in family buying; i.e., exposure effects may influence the valence of stored information brought home by information gatherers and used to make purchase decisions.

In-store mood may affect the retrieval of information from memory related to brands, personal usage experience, or advertisements. Compared to shoppers in neutral moods, shoppers in good moods may be more likely to retrieve positive stored information.

If the mood created by a brand's advertising matches the mood induced at the point-of-purchase, message recall may be enhanced as the result of state-dependent memory effects. To induce such effects, manufacturers may select appropriate retail outlets or influence in-store settings near their merchandise by using special personnel, events, colors, and lighting.

Mood Induction at Point-of-Purchase

Consumers' mood states at the point-of-purchase may be influenced by physical settings and interactions with sales personnel. Belk's work on situational effects in buyer behavior emphasized the importance of consumer subjective reactions to environmental stimuli and called for a taxonomy of environmental variables (Belk 1974, 1975). Kotler (1974) has suggested that store atmospherics may be especially important when stores carry similar product lines and are equally convenient (which is often the case in retailing today).

There are indications that environmental factors can significantly influence evaluations. Maslow and Mintz (1956) found that evaluations made in a "beautiful" room were significantly higher than those made in either an "average" room or an "ugly" room. Griffitt (1970) found that high ambient temperature was associated with negative assessments of mood and with less favorable ratings of anonymous others. If these findings can be generalized to product evaluations, they might suggest that comfortable settings may enhance merchandise evaluation. Obermiller and Bitner (1984), however, found that under some conditions favorable environments may be associated with unfavorable product evaluations; i.e., the environments can distract consumers and detract from merchandise. Obermiller and Bitner found indications that atmosphere had a marginally greater ($p = 0.14$) effect on evaluations when subjects were instructed to browse in a simulated shopping environment than when they were instructed to evaluate products. This suggests that in-store environments may be even more important for understanding shopping behavior than for investigating choice behavior.

Donovan and Rossiter (1982) provide indications that mood states induced by retail environments may affect purchase intentions. In a study, measures of mood (arousal and pleasantness) and purchase intentions were assessed by students who were randomly assigned to visit 66 stores and fill out questionnaires in each. The relationship of mood measures to assessments of behavioral intentions in each environment were explored. Findings indicated that (1) for stores rated as pleasant, shopping intentions increased with increased levels of arousal, and (2) for stores rated neutral or unpleasant, intentions were unrelated to arousal. Note that biases may exist due to students assessing their own in-store moods and purchase intentions. In addition, whenever possible consumers may subjectively self-select stores that induce positive moods and avoid those which induce negative moods. Thus, some settings may induce negative moods in some individuals, but stores which induce negative moods in all consumers may not be able to survive. This suggests that it is inappropriate to label stores as pleasant or unpleasant without specifying the group for which such subjective assessments apply. A conservative interpretation of the reported findings appears to be warranted; the links among atmospherics, mood, and purchase intentions require further research.

A second way in which in-store mood may be induced involves interactions with sales personnel. On an aggregate level, the tone set by salespeople may induce appropriate moods, e.g., an upbeat mood in a disco boutique. On a more personal level, salespeople may develop relationships with specific customers and adjust their selling tactics to an individual's moods. Research is needed to explore the relationship between mood-related sales techniques and success on the selling floor.

Current Status and Future Potential

The effects of mood states on consumer behavior at the point-of-purchase may be substantial and potentially important for marketing. Physical settings and interactions with store personnel may be powerful mood inducers, contiguous with much decision making. Findings from empirical studies of mood effects conducted in shopping malls (e.g., Isen et al. 1978) indicate that the level of arousal associated with walking around a mall is great enough to make mood effects observable. Point-of-purchase environments are often ambiguous and rarely encourage precise processing. However, research is needed to investigate the magnitude of mood effects and the feasibility of evoking desired moods from different consumers.

In many cases, designing point-of-purchase displays and retailing environments to induce particular moods involves the selection of sets of mood-related symbols (see Kotler and Rath 1983). To select appropriate symbols, marketers must be aware of the current trends and fads of their target market. This suggests that marketers who attempt to use mood-related strategies—especially at the point-of-purchase—must maintain intense, informal contact with their consumers.

In addition, research is needed to examine the effects of mood states on such basic decisions as whether or not to shop, what to shop for, and whether to shop alone or with others. Note that the behavioral effects of mood states at the point-of-purchase may be mediated by whether the consumer anticipates that the shopping trip will be a positive or negative experience. To fully understand the effects of point-of-purchase moods, marketers must gain insight into the role of shopping in the consumer's life.

COMMUNICATIONS STIMULI: CONTEXT

Service encounters and point-of-purchase stimuli may induce moods that affect on-site consumer behavior. Analogously, marketing communications, e.g., advertising, may affect at-home consumer responses by inducing mood states from the context in which the communication appears. The moods created by the context in which ads appear may be quite strong—e.g., the negative moods induced by "The Day After"—and may affect the mood states induced by exposure to advertising messages (Gardner and Raj 1979). In turn, these mood states may affect behavior, evaluation, and recall with respect to advertised brands.

Effects of Context-Induced Moods

Positive moods induced by media contexts may affect behavioral responses to advertising strategies. Insights into this thesis may be gleaned from two studies reported by Cunningham, Steinberg, and Grev (1980). The findings of Study 1 indicated that either a positive mood induction (in this case, finding a dime in a phone booth) or a negative mood induction such as guilt (in this case, making subjects feel that they had broken the experimenter's camera) increased helping (in this case, picking up dropped papers). The findings of Study 2 indicated that the positive mood manipulation increased helping (in this case, donating money to a charity) only when a request stressing the desirability of helping was made, while the guilt manipulation produced increases only when a request stressing an obligation to help was made. The Cunningham et al. findings for the positive mood condition are consistent with findings (Forest et al. 1979; Isen and Simmonds 1978) that suggest that subjects in a good mood may readily generate positive associations toward donating money when presented with a request that stresses the desirability of helping, but feel that they have enough personal power to resist the coercive appeal of a request stressing an obligation to help. Cunningham et al. (1980) discuss a variety of mechanisms that are consistent with the performance of subjects in the guilty mood condition and suggest the need for research to explore the proposed mechanisms. Research is also needed to extend these findings to moods of different types and to the product marketing domain.

Media exposure may also induce mood states that may, in turn, affect beliefs about products. Axelrod (1963) found that the mood states induced by viewing emotional films appeared to enhance subjects' assessments that use of a product would lead to the induced mood state.

Finally, moods induced by exposure to commercials may enhance the learning of mood-congruent message arguments. Yuspeh (1979) found that the individual's recall of commercials was greatly affected by the programs in which they were viewed, but she did not investigate the specific mood states induced. Research is needed to explore qualitative media effects in general and the mediating role of mood states in particular.

Mood Induction Via Communications Context

The material preceding an advertisement may include such cognitive mood inducers as positive or negative statements and such non-cognitive mood inducers as scary or happy music. Although a full discussion of the techniques involved in the induction of feelings in media contexts is beyond the scope of this article, it should be noted that laboratory studies involving simple verbal messages have found that statements in radio or newspaper reports can influence mood under forced exposure conditions. Veitch and Griffitt (1976) have manipulated the affective content of presented information and found that hearing good/bad news was associated with measures of positive/negative moods. Johnson and Tversky (1983), using newspaper reports of negative events, found that self-report mood scales yielded significant differences. The effects of such induction procedures should be investigated to gain insight into the importance of mood states relative to that of other mediators of context effects (Hornstein et al. 1975).

Current Status and Future Potential

Evidence for the mediating role of context-induced mood on consumer response to advertising is extremely limited. Research is needed to explore the range of moods induced under normal exposure conditions. If consumers self-select programs, newspapers, and magazines that make them feel good, the range may be narrow, and the impact of context-induced moods may be small.

In some cases, target-market consumers may have extremely selective media habits, leaving marketers little latitude in which to select vehicles with specific mood inducing properties. In such cases, understanding the effects of the moods commonly induced by the media selected by members of a target audience may help advertisers develop appropriate strategies and tactics.

For some products, contexts which induce negative moods may be more effective than those which induce positive moods. Although consumers may avoid contexts which are extremely unpleasant or threatening, those contexts that induce mildly negative moods may increase consumers' assessments that a negatively valenced event is likely to occur. This, in turn, may increase the consumer's self-perceived need for the products (e.g., insurance) associated with such an event, in spite of the limited effects associated with negative moods.

At times, marketers may have little control over the story line or advertisement immediately preceding their messages, so they may have little control over the moods induced by media context. In such cases, media managers cannot effectively implement mood-oriented approaches, but the effects of context-induced mood may be important for copytesting. Since advertisements are frequently tested in a single context, the mood induced by that context may bias the results of the test. Research is needed to assess the magnitude of such biases and to determine the types of advertisements whose ratings are most strongly affected.

Some insights are provided by Isen and Shalker's (1982) work with slides of landscapes. As discussed earlier, results indicate that the assessments of stimuli that were neutrally rated were more strongly influenced by induced moods than the assessments of stimuli that were rated favorably or unfavorably. Research is needed to explore these effects for exposure to advertisements under natural viewing conditions and to investigate the possibility that the resulting attitude toward the advertisement is strong enough, and sufficiently associated with a brand, to affect brand attitude. If the mood → attitude toward advertising → attitude toward brand chain is supported by future evidence, this suggests that there may be a general advantage to placing advertisements in contexts which induce positive moods. Additionally, the effect may be more critical for neutrally rated advertisements than for those advertisements that produce more extreme evaluations. The relationship between neutral advertisement ratings and aspects of copy execution—e.g., pictures versus words—is unclear. Research is now underway that examines the effects of mood-inducing media contexts on the effectiveness of emotional and informational copy strategies. Finally, media contexts may sometimes encourage very low arousal levels; research is needed to investigate the mediating role of arousal on mood effects associated with media contexts.

COMMUNICATIONS STIMULI: CONTENT

Media contexts may provide background moods for advertising exposures, but for many product classes, moods induced by brand advertisements play a critical role in brand identification and evaluation. Such moods may affect purchase behavior, brand evaluation, and information acquisition.

Effects of Content-Induced Mood States

Feelings induced by direct-marketing commercials may affect consumer behavior with respect to advertised brands when mood induction is contiguous to required action—mail-in or phone-in orders. The positive feelings induced by commercials may enhance the likelihood that consumers will engage in purchase activities associated with positive outcomes. If so, commercials that induce positive moods may be effective for the direct marketing of products associated with improving one's home or one's life.

The effects of advertisement-induced negative moods may be more complex. Extremely depressing commercials may attract attention because of their relative rarity, or they may be ignored due to a perceptual defense (as documented by the fear-appeal literature, see Sternthal and Craig 1974). However, the negative moods induced by commercials may increase consumers' perceptions that a negative outcome is likely. If this is so, then commercials that induce mildly negative moods may be effective direct marketing tools for disaster-related products, e.g., life insurance and burglar alarms, in spite of the somewhat limited impact of negative moods. Research is needed to investigate these possibilities.

Advertisements that induce positive exposure moods may facilitate the learning, integration, and acquisition of favorable material and may enhance the evaluation of advertised brands. Such ads are also likely to be favorably evaluated; at times, a positive relationship between attitude toward the advertisement and attitude toward the brand may be observed (see Gardner 1984; Mitchell and Olson 1981; Shimp and Yokum 1982).

Advertisements may be designed to elicit the mood states associated with particular life situations or experiences. When such experiences occur, the elicited moods may key the retrieval of advertisements associated with these moods, because of state-dependent memory effects. For example, thinking about loved ones in distant places may elicit warm, sentimental feelings. These feelings may, in turn, elicit the retrieval of similarly toned advertisements for Hallmark cards. However, such tactics are not expected to be equally effective for all brands and product classes. A Hallmark campaign may be able to take advantage of state-dependent memory effects, because the company has a favorable image, and product use is associated with feeling states that, in turn, are linked to particular life experiences.

Mood Induction Via Communications Content

Advertisements, like media contexts, may include such cognitive mood inducers as positive or negative statements, and such noncognitive mood inducers as scary or happy music. Some advertisers (e.g., Ralph Lauren) buy blocks of consecutive pages in a periodical, in part to accentuate the mood-inducing properties of their ads. In addition, Moore (1982) has presented evidence that subliminal stimuli may influence mood states without conscious awareness.

The importance of advertising-induced feelings is underscored by efforts to assess noncognitive reactions to advertisements. Schlinger (1979) and Wells et al. (1971) have developed measurement instruments to assess individuals' emotional reactions to advertisements. Batra and Ray (1984) have proposed a coding scheme to classify consumer affective responses to advertisements.

Current Status and Future Potential

Research is needed to evaluate the effects of mood-related advertising strategies on consumer behavior. Wells (1983) has suggested that mood should play a more central role in the advertising for products associated with pleasurable usage experiences, i.e., approach products. This guideline requires *a priori* knowledge of consumers' feelings toward product use and is consistent with previously cited findings indicating that positive moods may be associated with the performance of behaviors that have positive expected outcomes.

Researchers in consumer behavior are currently exploring the role of affect-inducing commercials from many perspectives. Shimp (1981) has noted that moods induced by advertisement content are not contiguous to in-store decision making and that research is needed to investigate possible reinduction at the point-of-purchase. Shimp has also postulated that an attitude toward an advertisement has an emotional aspect which may be related to feeling states, and Allen and Madden (1983) have empirically examined this component. In addition, researchers have investigated the relationship of emotional stimuli in advertising to advertiser goals (e.g., Mizerski and White 1985), low involvement exposure situations (e.g., Batra and Ray 1983; Ray and Batra 1983), the assessment of advertising effects (e.g., Leckenby and Stout 1985), physiological measures (e.g., Kroeber-Riel 1979, 1984), and advertisement sequence (e.g., Aaker, Stayman, and Hagerty 1985). Although much research is being done to gain insight into the effects of mood-inducing advertisements, their prevalence and importance encourages even greater efforts.

DISCUSSION

Implications for Marketing Research

The preceding sections of this article have examined areas where it may be wise to consider the effects of mood on consumer behavior. Such mood effects may also have important implications for developing marketing research techniques to assess consumers' attitudes and predict behavior.

In some contexts, the effects of respondents' moods on their evaluations may be viewed as a biasing nuisance factor. Peterson and Sauber (1983) present evidence for such biases and provide a measurement instrument to take them into account. If respondents' moods upon completion of a questionnaire are distributed in the same way as their moods during relevant activities (e.g., shopping), the biases would not be critical for aggregate-level analysis. However, if moods are systematically related to filling out questionnaires or going shopping, biases due to the effects of mood states may be problematical. If participation in a survey is viewed as an experience that has a favorable expected outcome, consumers in positive moods may be more inclined to complete questionnaires than those in neutral or negative moods. This would suggest that mood states in the respondent sample may be skewed in a positive direction.

Mood in the population of shoppers may be bimodally distributed. People in good moods may choose to perform or avoid consumption-related behavior, depending on their assessments of the likelihood of the activities being associated with positive or negative outcomes. Consumers in bad moods may also choose to shop, perhaps to cheer themselves up. Langer (1983) has suggested that difficult economic conditions may increase consumers' needs for products to serve as treats and emotional charges.

To gain insight into the magnitude of biases resulting from the effects of mood states, the distribution of moods of individuals engaged in activities of interest must be examined. Activities related to participation in research should be investigated as well as shopping, buying, and consuming activities. If the distribution of moods during the completion of a questionnaire differs from the distribution during an activity of interest, biases resulting from this difference may require closer examination.

Implications for Marketing Actions

I have used the term "mood states" to refer to the general, pervasive, affective states that are transient and particularized to specific times and situations. A conceptual framework has been presented to depict the effects of consumers' mood states and their potential relevance to marketing strategy and tactics. Findings from the psychological literature were reviewed, and they indicated that mood states affect behavior, evaluation, and recall. I have examined the implications of these effects for consumer behavior in three areas: service encounters, point-of-purchase stimuli, and communications (context and content). In addition, I have assessed the feasibility of mood induction in each area. Several conclusions and unanswered questions emerge for each area.

1. Mood states may have important effects on consumer behavior with respect to services, but research is needed to assess the magnitude of such effects. There appear to be many opportunities for mood induction in the service sector, e.g., settings, procedures, and interactions with service providers. Mood induction can be contiguous to the service encounter, increasing the likelihood that its effects will have an impact on transactions. In addition, because service providers have personal contact with consumers, they can adjust their tactics to suit consumers' mood states.
2. The effects of mood states at the point-of-purchase may be substantial and potentially important for marketing action, but research is needed to investigate the strength of mood effects. Although physical settings and interactions with store personnel may be powerful mood inducers contiguous with much decision making, research is needed that examines the effects of mood states on such basic decisions as whether or not to shop, what to shop for, and whether to shop alone or with others. In addition, the behavioral effects of mood states at a point of purchase may be mediated by whether the consumer anticipates that the shopping trip will be a positive or negative experience. To fully understand the effects of point-of-purchase moods, marketers must gain insight into the role of shopping in the consumer's life.
3. Although context-induced moods may significantly affect consumer response to advertising, there is a dearth of evidence supporting this claim. Research is needed to explore the range and impact of moods induced under normal exposure conditions. Additionally, the following questions must be addressed: (1) for which types of advertisements are the effects of context-induced mood states most significant, and (2) when should contexts be sought that induce specific positive or negative moods? Note that the role of context-induced moods may be more important for copy-testing procedures than it is for media selection if institutional factors limit the control media managers have over the immediate context in which advertising is placed.
4. The role of mood states induced by advertising has recently received some well-deserved attention, but many important issues remain unresolved. It is clear that advertisements can affect consumer moods, but the impact of these effects may depend on the advertiser's purpose, product, and target audience. Although much research is being done to address these issues, the prevalence and importance of mood-inducing advertising encourages even greater efforts.

Directions for Future Research

The nature of the preceding discussion has necessarily been very tentative, but it should help guide thinking and should serve as a basis for research in this area. In addition to the specific issues discussed above, more general questions must be addressed:

1. Does social responsibility suggest limitations for the appropriate use of mood-induction strategies and tactics? This issue is particularly problematical with respect to the induction of negative moods and the use of mood inductions in advertising directed at children.
2. Can marketer-induced moods significantly affect consumer behavior? Research is needed that compares the impact of marketer-induced moods to moods induced by other aspects of the consumer's life. Research is also needed to explore the interaction of marketer-controlled inductions and pre-existing mood states. Guidelines are needed to help marketers assess the potential value of mood-oriented approaches under alternative sets of circumstances.
3. How can marketers design strategies and implement tactics to influence consumers' moods? Psychometric measurement instruments that assess the effects of mood induction procedures must be developed and evaluative criteria established. Also, the implications for interdepartmental relations must be considered. For example, lawyers must be consulted before individual-specific mood induction procedures that may appear discriminatory are implemented. Personnel departments and labor unions must be involved in the

development of mood-management training programs for employees.

In spite of the need for further empirical work, there are indications that consumer-mood states may influence behavior, evaluation, and recall. Although many unanswered questions must be addressed, the effects of mood states on consumer behavior with respect to service encounters, point-of-purchase stimuli, and communications seem to merit further exploration.

REFERENCES

AAKER, DAVID A., DOUGLAS M. STAYMAN, and MICHAEL R. HAGERTY (1986), "Warmth in Advertising: Measurement, Impact, and Sequence Effects," *Journal of Consumer Research,* 12 (March), in press.

ADERMAN, DAVID (1972), "Elation, Depression, and Helping Behavior," *Journal of Personality and Social Psychology,* 24 (1), 91-101.

ALLEN, CHRIS, and THOMAS MADDEN (1983), "Examining the Link Between Attitude Towards an Ad and Brand Attitude: A Classical Conditioning Approach," Working Paper No. 83-30, Management Research Center, School of Business Administration, University of Massachusetts, Amherst, MA.

ANDREWS, FRANK, and STEPHEN WITHEY (1976), *Social Indicators of Well Being.* New York: Plenum Press.

AXELROD, JOEL (1963), "Induced Moods and Attitudes Towards Products," *Journal of Advertising Research,* 3 (June), 19-24.

BARTLETT, JAMES, and JOHN SANTROCK (1979), "Affect-Dependent Episodic Memory in Young Children," *Child Development,* 50 (2), 513-518.

———, GEORGIA BURLESON, and JOHN SANTROCK (1982), "Emotional Mood and Memory in Young Children," *Journal of Experimental Child Psychology,* 34 (August/December), 59-76.

BATRA, RAJEEV, and MICHAEL L. RAY (1983), "Advertising Situations: The Implications of Differential Involvement and Accompanying Affect Responses," in *Information Processing Research in Advertising,* Ed. Richard J. Harris. Hillsdale, NJ: Erlbaum, 127-151.

———, and MICHAEL L. RAY (1984), "Affective Responses Mediating Acceptance of Advertising," working paper, Columbia University. New York, NY.

BATSON, C. DANIEL, JAY COKE, FRED CHARD, DEBRA SMITH, and ANTONIA TALIAFERRO (1979), "Generality of the 'Glow of Goodwill': Effects of Mood on Helping and Information Acquisition," *Social Psychology Quarterly,* 42 (2), 176-179.

BAUMANN, DONALD J., ROBERT B. CIALDINI, and DOUGLAS T. KENRICK (1981), "Altruism as Hedonism: Helping and Self-Gratification as Equivalent Responses," *Journal of Personality and Social Psychology,* 40 (6), 1039-1046.

BELK, RUSSELL (1974), "An Exploratory Assessment of Situational Effects in Buyer Behavior," *Journal of Marketing Research,* 11 (May), 156-163.

——— (1975), "Situational Variables and Consumer Behavior," *Journal of Consumer Research,* 2 (December), 157-164.

——— (1984), "Applications of Mood Inducement in Buyer Behavior," in *Advances in Consumer Research,* Vol. 11, Ed. Thomas Kinnear. Provo, UT: Association for Consumer Research, 544-547.

BERKOWITZ, LEONARD, and WILLIAM CONNOR (1966), "Success, Failure, and Social Responsibility," *Journal of Personality and Social Psychology,* 4 (6), 664-669.

BLEVINS, GREGORY, and TERRANCE MURPHY (1974), "Feeling Good and Helping: Further Phonebooth Findings," *Psychological Reports,* Vol. 34 (February), p. 326.

BOWER, GORDON (1981), "Mood and Memory," *American Psychologist,* 36 (2), 129-148.

———, STEPHEN GILLIGAN, and KENNETH MONTEIRO (1981), "Selectivity of Learning Caused by Affective States," *Journal of Experimental Psychology: General,* 110 (December), 451-473.

———, KENNETH MONTEIRO, and STEPHEN GILLIGAN (1978), "Emotional Mood as a Context for Learning and Recall," *Journal of Verbal Learning and Verbal Behavior,* 17, 573-585.

BUGELSKI, B. R. (1982), "Learning and Imagery," *Journal of Mental Imagery,* 6 (2), 1-92.

CARSON, TRACEY, and HENRY ADAMS (1980), "Activity Valence as a Function of Mood Change," *Journal of Abnormal Psychology,* 89 (3), 368-377.

CIALDINI, ROBERT, and DOUGLAS KENRICK (1976), "Altruism as Hedonism: A Social Development Perspective on the Relationship of Negative Mood State and Helping," *Journal of Personality and Social Psychology,* 34 (5), 907-914.

CLARK, MARGARET, and ALICE ISEN (1982), "Toward Understanding the Relationship Between Feeling States and Social Behavior," in *Cognitive Social Psychology,* Eds. Albert Hastorf and Alice Isen. New York: Elsevier/North-Holland, 73-108.

———, SANDRA MILBERG, and JOHN ROSS (1983), "Arousal Cues Arousal-Related Material in Memory: Implications for Understanding Effects of Mood on Memory," *Journal of Verbal Learning and Verbal Behavior,* 22 (December) 633-649.

———, and BARBARA WADDELL (1983), "Effects of Moods on Thoughts About Helping, Attraction and Information Acquisition," *Social Psychology Quarterly,* 46 (1), 31-35.

COLLINS, ALLAN M., and ELIZABETH A. LOFTUS (1975), "A Spreading-Activation Theory of Semantic Processing," *Psychological Review,* 82 (November), 407-428.

CUNNINGHAM, MICHAEL (1979), "Weather, Mood, and Helping Behavior: Quasi Experiments With the Sunshine Samaritan," *Journal of Personality and Social Psychology,* 37 (11), 1947-1956.

———, JEFF STEINBERG, and RITA GREV (1980), "Wanting to and Having to Help: Separate Motivations for Positive Mood and Guilt-Induced Helping," *Journal of Personality and Social Psychology,* 38 (2), 181-192.

DABBS, JAMES M., and IRVING L. JANIS (1965), "Why Does Eating While Reading Facilitate Opinion Change?," *Journal of Experimental Social Psychology,* 1 (May), 133-144.

DONNERSTEIN, EDWARD, MARCIA DONNERSTEIN, and GERRY MUNGER (1975), "Helping Behavior as a Function of Pictorially Induced Moods," *The Journal of Social Psychology,* 97 (December), 221-225.

DONOVAN, ROBERT, and JOHN ROSSITER (1982), "Store Atmosphere: An Environmental Psychology Approach," *Journal of Retailing,* 58 (Spring), 34-57.

DRIBBEN, ELLEN, and VIRGINIA BRABENDER (1979), "The Effect of Mood Inducement Upon Audience Receptiveness," *The Journal of Social Psychology,* 107 (February), 135-136.

EICH, JAMES (1980), The Cue-Dependent Nature of State-Dependent Retrieval," *Memory and Cognition,* 8 (2), 157-173.

FENNELL, GERALDINE (1981), "Emotion: A Neglected Aspect of Consumer Behavior," in *Proceedings of Division 23 Program,* 89th Annual Convention of the American Psychological Association, Ed. Richard Lutz. Nashville, TN: Owen Graduate School of Management, Vanderbilt University.

FISKE, SUSAN (1981), "Social Cognition and Affect," in *Cognition, Social Behavior, and the Environment,* Ed. John Harvey. Hillsdale, NJ: Erlbaum, 227-264.

FOREST, DUNCAN, MARGARET CLARK, JUDSON MILLS, and ALICE ISEN (1979), "Helping as a Function of Feeling State and Nature of the Helping Behavior," *Motivation and Emotion,* 3 (2), 161-169.

FRIED, RONA, and LEONARD BERKOWITZ (1979), "Music Hath Charms . . . And Can Influence Helpfulness," *Journal of Applied Social Psychology,* 9 (2), 199-208.

FRY, P. S. (1975), "Affect and Resistance to Temptation," *Developmental Psychology,* 11 (4), 466-472.

GALIZIO, MARK and CLYDE HENDRICK (1972), "Effect of Musical Accompaniment on Attitude: The Guitar as a Prop for Persuasion," *Journal of Applied Social Psychology,* 2 (4), 350-359.

GARDNER, MERYL P. (1985), "Does Attitude Toward the Ad Affect Brand Attitude Under a Brand Evaluation 'Set'?," *Journal of Marketing Research,* 22 (May), 192-198.

———, and S. P. RAJ (1983), "Responses to Commercials in Laboratory Versus Natural Settings: A Conceptual Framework," in *Advances in Consumer Research,* Vol. 10, Eds. Richard Bagozzi and Alice Tybout. Ann Arbor, MI: Association for Consumer Research, 142-146.

———, and MARION VANDERSTEEL (1984), "The Consumer's Mood: An Important Situational Variable," in *Advances in Consumer Research,* Vol. 11, Ed. Thomas Kinnear. Provo, UT: Association for Consumer Research, 525-529.

GEIST, WILLIAM (1984), "They're Hiring Others to Stand in Line," *New York Times,* June 6.

GOLDMAN-EISLER, FRIEDA (1960), "Breastfeeding and Character Formation," in *Personality in Nature, Society, and Culture,* Eds. C. Kluckholn and H. Murray. New York: Knopf.

GORN, GERALD (1982), "The Effects of Music in Advertising on Choice Behavior: A Classical

Conditioning Approach," *Journal of Marketing,* 46 (Winter), 94–101.

GRIFFITT, WILLIAM (1970), "Environmental Effects on Interpersonal Affective Behavior: Ambient Temperature and Attraction," *Journal of Personality and Social Psychology,* 15 (3), 240–244.

———, and PETER GUAY (1969), " 'Object' Evaluation and Conditioned Affect," *Journal of Experimental Research in Personality,* 4 (July), 1–8.

HATWICK, MELVIN (1950), *How to Use Psychology for Better Advertising.* Englewood Cliffs, NJ: Prentice-Hall, 188.

HIRSCHMAN, ELIZABETH, and MORRIS HOLBROOK (1982), "Hedonic Consumption: Emerging Concepts, Methods and Propositions," *Journal of Marketing,* 46 (Summer), 92–101.

HOCHSCHILD, ARLIE (1983), *The Managed Heart: The Commercialization of Human Feeling.* Berkeley, CA: University of California Press.

HOLBROOK, MORRIS, and ELIZABETH HIRSCHMAN (1982), "The Experiential Aspects of Consumption: Consumer Fantasies, Feelings, and Fun," *Journal of Consumer Research,* 9 (September), 132–140.

HORNSTEIN, HARVEY, ELIZABETH LAKIND, GLADYS FRANKEL, and STELLA MANNE (1975), "Effects of Knowledge About Remote Social Events on Prosocial Behavior, Social Conception, and Mood," *Journal of Personality and Social Psychology,* 32 (6), 1038–1046.

ISEN, ALICE (1970), "Success, Failure, Attention, and Reaction to Others: The Warm Glow of Success," *Journal of Personality and Social Psychology,* 15 (4), 294–301.

——— (1984), "Toward Understanding the Role of Affect in Cognition," in *Handbook of Social Cognition,* Eds. Robert Wyer, Jr. and Thomas Srull. Hillsdale, NJ: Erlbaum, 179–236.

———, MARGARET CLARK, and MARK F. SCHWARTZ (1976), "Duration of the Effect of Good Mood on Helping: Footprints on the Sands of Time," *Journal of Personality and Social Psychology,* 34 (3), 385–393.

———, NANCY HORN, and D. L. ROSENHAN (1973), "Effects of Success and Failure on Children's Generosity," *Journal of Personality and Social Psychology,* 27 (2), 239–247.

———, and PAULA LEVIN (1972), "Effect of Feeling Good on Helping: Cookies and Kindness," *Journal of Personality and Social Psychology,* 21 (3), 384–388.

———, BARBARA MEANS, ROBERT PATRICK, and GARY NOWICKI (1982), "Some Factors Influencing Decision-Making Strategy and Risk Taking," in *Cognition and Affect,* Eds. Margaret Clark and Susan Fiske. Hillsdale, NJ: Erlbaum, 243–261.

———, and THOMAS SHALKER (1982), "The Effect of Feeling State on Evaluation of Positive, Neutral, and Negative Stimuli: When you 'Accentuate the Positive,' Do You 'Eliminate the Negative'?," *Social Psychology Quarterly,* 45 (1), 58–63.

———, THOMAS SHALKER, MARGARET CLARK, and LYNN KARP (1978), "Affect, Accessibility of Material in Memory, and Behavior: A Cognitive Loop?," *Journal of Personality and Social Psychology,* 36 (January), 1–12.

———, and STANLEY SIMMONDS (1978), "The Effect of Feeling Good on a Helping Task That Is Incompatible with Good Mood," *Social Psychology,* 41 (4), 346–349.

JANIS, IRVING, DONALD KAYE, and PAUL KIRSCHNER (1965), "Facilitating Effects of 'Eating-While-Reading' on Responsiveness to Persuasive Communications," *Journal of Personality and Social Psychology,* 1 (2), 181–186.

JOHNSON, ERIC, and AMOS TVERSKY (1983), "Affect Generalization, and the Perception of Risk," *Journal of Personality and Social Psychology,* 45 (1), 20–31.

KOTLER, PHILIP (1974), "Atmospherics as a Marketing Tool," *The Journal of Retailing,* 49 (Winter), 48–64.

———, and G. ALEXANDER RATH (1983), "Design: A Powerful But Neglected Marketing Tool," paper presented at the Fourteenth Annual Conference of the Association for Consumer Research, Chicago, IL.

KROEBER-RIEL, WERNER (1979), "Activation Research: Psychobiological Approaches in Consumer Research," *Journal of Consumer Research,* 5 (March), 240–250.

——— (1984), "Emotional Product Differentiation by Classical Conditioning," in *Advances in Consumer Research,* Vol. 11, Ed. Thomas Kinnear. Provo, UT: Association for Consumer Research, 538–543.

LAIRD, JAMES (1974), Self-Attribution of Emotion: The Effects of Expressive Behavior on the Quality of Emotional Experience," *Journal of Personality and Social Psychology,* 29 (4), 475–486.

———, JOHN WAGENER, MARK HALAL, and MARTHA SZEGDA (1982), "Remembering What You

Feel: Effects of Emotion on Memory," *Journal of Personality and Social Psychology,* 42 (4), 646-657.

LANGER, JUDITH (1983), "Treats and Luxuries: Marketing in Hard Times," *Marketing Review,* 38 (December/January), 31-37.

LECKENBY, JOHN D., and PATRICIA A. STOUT (1985), "Conceptual and Methodological Issues in Persuasion Measurement," Winter Marketing Educators' Conference, American Marketing Association, Phoenix, AZ.

LUTZ, RICHARD J. (1979), "Opening Statement," in *Conceptual and Theoretical Developments in Marketing,* Eds. O. C. Ferrell, S. W. Brown, and Charles W. Lamb. Chicago: American Marketing Association, 3-6.

———, and PRADEEP KAKKAR (1975), "The Psychological Situation as a Determinant of Consumer Behavior," in *Advances in Consumer Research,* Vol. 1, Eds. Scott Ward and Peter Wright, 439-453.

———, SCOTT MACKENZIE, and GEORGE BELCH (1983), "Attitude Toward the Ad as a Mediator of Advertising Effectiveness: Determinants and Consequences," in *Advances in Consumer Research,* Vol. 10, Eds. Richard Bagozzi and Alice Tybout. Ann Arbor, MI: Association for Consumer Research, 532-539.

MCSWEENEY, FRANCES K., and CALVIN BIERLEY (1984), "Recent Developments in Classical Conditioning," *Journal of Consumer Research,* 11 (September), 619-631.

MAISTER, DAVID (1985), "The Psychology of Waiting Lines," in *The Service Encounter,* Eds. John Czepiel, Michael Solomon, and Carol Suprenant. Lexington, MA: Lexington Books, 113-123.

MASLOW, A. H., and N. L. MINTZ (1956), "Effects of Esthetic Surroundings: I. Initial Effects of Three Esthetic Conditions Upon Perceived 'Energy' and 'Well-being' in Faces," *The Journal of Psychology,* 41 (January), 247-254.

MASTERS, JOHN, and WYNDOL FURMAN (1976), "Effects of Affective States on Noncontingent Outcome Expectancies and Beliefs in Internal or External Control," *Developmental Psychology,* (5), 481-482.

MILLIMAN, RONALD (1982), "Using Background Music to Affect the Behavior of Supermarket Shoppers," *Journal of Marketing,* 46 (Summer), 86-91.

MISCHEL, WALTER, BRIAN COATES, and ANTONETTE RASKOFF (1968), "Effects of Success and Failure on Self-Gratification," *Journal of Personality and Social Psychology,* 10 (4), 381-390.

MITCHELL, ANDREW, and JERRY OLSON (1981), "Are Product Attribute Beliefs the Only Mediator of Advertising Effects on Brand Attitude?" *Journal of Marketing Research,* 18 (August), 318-332.

MIZERSKI, RICHARD W., and J. DENNIS WHITE (1985), "Understanding and Using Emotions in Advertising," working paper, Florida State University, Tallahassee, FL.

MOORE, BERT, ANDREA CLYBURN, and BILL UNDERWOOD (1976), "The Role of Affect in Delay of Gratification," *Child Development,* 47, 273-276.

———, BILL UNDERWOOD, and D. L. ROSENHAN (1973), "Affect and Altruism," *Developmental Psychology,* 8 (1), 99-104.

MOORE, DANNY, and J. WESLEY HUTCHINSON (1983), "The Effects of Ad Affect on Advertising Effectiveness," in *Advances in Consumer Research,* Vol. 10, Eds. Richard Bagozzi and Alice Tybout. Ann Arbor, MI: Association for Consumer Research, 526-531.

MOORE, TIMOTHY (1982), "Subliminal Advertising: What You See Is What You Get," *Journal of Marketing,* 46 (Spring), 38-47.

NATALE, MICHAEL, and MICHAEL HANTAS (1982), "Effect of Temporary Mood States on Selective Memory About the Self," *Journal of Personality and Social Psychology,* 42 (5), 927-934.

OBERMILLER, CARL, and MARY BITNER (1984), "Store Atmosphere: Peripheral Cue for Product Evaluation," Proceedings of Annual Conference, American Psychological Association, Consumer Psychology Division.

PARK, C. WHAN, MERYL P. GARDNER, and VINOD THUKRAL (1984), "Effects of Actual and Perceived Knowledge on Selected Aspects of Consumer Information Processing," working paper, School of Business Administration, New York University, New York, NY.

PETER, J. PAUL, and WALTER R. NORD (1982), "A Clarification and Extension of Operant Conditioning Principles in Marketing," *Journal of Marketing,* 46 (Summer), 102-107.

PETERSON, ROBERT, and MATTHEW SAUBER (1983), "A Mood Scale for Survey Research," in *1983 AMA Educators' Proceedings,* Eds. Patrick

Murphy et al. Chicago, IL: American Marketing Association, 409–414.

PLUTCHIK, ROBERT (1980), *Emotion: A Psychoevolutionary Synthesis.* New York: Harper & Row.

POLIVY, JANET (1981), "On the Induction of Emotion in the Laboratory: Discrete Moods or Multiple Affective States?" *Journal of Personality and Social Psychology,* 41 (October), 803–817.

RAY, MICHAEL, and RAJEEV BATRA (1983), "Emotion and Persuasion in Advertising: What We Do and Don't Know About Affect," in *Advances in Consumer Research,* Vol. 10, Eds. Richard Bagozzi and Alice Tybout. Ann Arbor, MI: Association for Consumer Research, 543–548.

REGAN, DENNIS, MARGO WILLIAMS, and SONDRA SPARLING (1972), "Voluntary Expiation of Guilt: A Field Experiment," *Journal of Personality and Social Psychology,* 24 (1), 42–45.

ROSSITER, JOHN, and LARRY PERCY (1980), "Attitude Change through Visual Imagery in Advertising," *Journal of Advertising,* 9 (Winter), 10–16.

SCHELLENBERG, JAMES, and GREGORY BLEVINS (1973), "Feeling Good and Helping: How Quickly Does the Smile of Dame Fortune Fade?," *Psychological Reports,* 33, 72–74.

SCHLINGER, MARY JANE (1979), "A Profile of Responses to Commercials," *Journal of Advertising Research,* 19 (April), 37–46.

SCHWARZ, NORBERT, and GERALD CLORE (1983), "Mood, Misattribution, and Judgments of Well-Being: Informative and Directive Functions of Affective States," *Journal of Personality and Social Psychology,* 45 (3), 513–523.

SEEMAN, GLORIA, and J. CONRAD SCHWARZ (1974), "Affective State and Preference for Immediate Versus Delayed Reward," *Journal of Research in Personality,* 7, 384–394.

SHIMP, TERENCE (1981), "Attitude Toward the Ad as a Mediator of Consumer Brand Choice," *Journal of Advertising,* 10 (2), 9–15.

———, and J. THOMAS YOKUM (1982), "Advertising Inputs and Psychophysical Judgments in Vending-Machine Retailing," *Journal of Retailing,* 58 (Spring), 95–113.

SIMON, HERBERT (1967), "Motivational and Emotional Controls of Cognition," *Psychological Review,* 74 (1), 29–39.

SRULL, THOMAS (1983a), "Affect and Memory: The Impact of Affective Reactions in Advertising on the Representation of Product Information in Memory," in *Advances in Consumer Research,* Vol. 10, Eds. Richard Bagozzi and Alice Tybout. Ann Arbor, MI: Association for Consumer Research, 520–525.

——— (1983b), "The Role of Prior Knowledge in the Acquisition, Retention, and Use of New Information," in *Advances in Consumer Research,* Vol. 10, Eds. Richard Bagozzi and Alice Tybout. Ann Arbor, MI: Association for Consumer Research, 572–576.

——— (1984), "The Effects of Subjective Affective States on Memory and Judgment," in *Advances in Consumer Research,* Vol. 11, Ed. Thomas Kinnear. Provo, UT: Association for Consumer Research, 530–533.

STERNTHAL, BRIAN, and C. SAMUEL CRAIG (1974), "Fear Appeals: Revisited and Revised," *Journal of Consumer Research,* 1 (December), 22–34.

STOKOLS, DANIEL (1982), "Environmental Psychology: A Coming of Age," *G. Stanley Hall Lecture Series,* Vol. 2, 155–205.

TEASDALE, JOHN and SARAH FOGARTY (1979), "Differential Effects of Induced Mood on Retrieval of Pleasant and Unpleasant Events From Episodic Memory," *Journal of Abnormal Psychology,* 88, 248–257.

TIGER, LIONEL (1979), *Optimism, The Biology of Hope.* New York: Simon & Schuster.

UNDERWOOD, BILL, BERT MOORE, and D. L. ROSENHAN (1973), "Affect and Self-Gratification," *Developmental Psychology,* 8 (2), 209–214.

VEITCH, RUSSELL, and WILLIAM GRIFFITT (1976), "Good News—Bad News: Affective and Interpersonal Effects," *Journal of Applied Social Psychology,* 6 (1), 69–75.

WEINBERG, PETER, and WOLFGANG GOTTWALD (1982), "Impulsive Consumer Buying as a Result of Emotions," *Journal of Business Research,* 10 (March), 43–57.

WELLS, WILLIAM (1986), "Three Useful Ideas," in *Advances in Consumer Research,* Vol. 13, Ed. Richard Lutz. Provo, UT: Association for Consumer Research, in press.

———, CLARK LEAVITT, and MAUREEN MCCONVILLE (1971), "A Reaction Profile for TV Commercials," *Journal of Advertising Research,* 11 (6), 11–17.

WENER, RICHARD (1985), "The Environmental Psychology of The Service Encounter," in *The Service Encounter,* Eds. John Czepiel, Michael Solomon, and Carl Suprenant. Lexington, MA: Lexington Books, 101–112.

WESTBROOK, ROBERT (1980), "Intrapersonal Affective Influences on Consumer Satisfaction with Products," *Journal of Consumer Research,* 7 (June), 49–54.

WEYANT, JAMES (1978), "Effects of Mood States, Costs, and Benefits on Helping," *Journal of Personality and Social Psychology,* 36 (10), 1169–1176.

YUSPEH, SONIA (1979), "The Medium Versus the Message," in *A Look Back, A Look Ahead,* Proceedings of the 10th National Attitude Research Conference, Ed. George Hafer. Chicago: American Marketing Association, 109–138.

ZAJONC, ROBERT (1980), "Feeling and Thinking: Preferences Need No Inferences," *American Psychologist,* 35 (February), 151–175.

——, and HAZEL MARKUS (1982), "Affective and Cognitive Factors in Preferences," *Journal of Consumer Research,* 9 (September), 123–131.

16

PERSONALITY AND CONSUMER BEHAVIOR: An Update*

Harold H. Kassarjian
Mary Jane Sheffet

INTRODUCTION

One of the most enduring topics in the field of consumer research has been the study of the relationship of personality to consumer behavior. For some four decades it has engrossed students and researchers. From automobile purchase to cigarette smoking, attempts have been made to study the influence of personality on the behavior of the consumer in the market place. Purchasing behavior, media choice, innovation, segmentation, fear, social influence, product choice, opinion leadership, risk taking, attitude change and almost anything else one can think of have been linked to personality. And several overviews of that work have already been published (e.g., 94, 103, 198).

The purpose of this paper is to update our previous articles (103, 106), and again organize the contributions of personality research around the theoretical stems from which it grew. Although in recent years the number of such studies has decelerated, by 1990 over 300 studies were available to us. An overview of the studies on personality effects can be summarized by the single word "equivocal."

Unfortunately, analysts do not agree on any general definition of the term personality, except to somehow tie it to the concept of consistent responses to the world of stimuli surround-

*Prepared especially for this volume. Portions of this chapter are reprinted.

ing the individual.[1] People tend to be consistent in coping with their environment. This consistency of response allows us to type politicians as charismatic or obnoxious, students as aggressive or submissive, and colleagues as charming or "blah." Since individuals do react fairly consistently in a variety of environmental situations, these generalized patterns of response or modes of coping with the world can be called personality.

Personality—or better yet, the inferred hypothetical constructs relating to certain persistent qualities in human behavior—have fascinated both laymen and scholars for many centuries. The study of the relationship between behavior and personality has a most impressive history, ranging back to the earliest writings of the Chinese and Egyptians, Hippocrates, and some of the great European philosophers. In the fields of marketing and consumer behavior, the work in personality dates from Sigmund Freud and his popularizers in the commercial world—the motivation researchers of the post-World War II era (for example, see 53, 128).

PSYCHOANALYTIC THEORY

The psychoanalytic theories and philosophies of Freud have influenced not only psychology but also literature, social science, and medicine, as well as marketing. Freud emphasized the unconscious nature of personality and motivation and said that much, if not all, behavior is related to the stresses within the personality system. The personality's three sets of forces—id, ego, and superego—interact to produce behavior.

According to Freudian theory, the id is the source of all driving psychic energy, but its unrestrained impulses cannot be expressed without running afoul of society's values. The superego is the internal representative of traditional values and can be conceptualized as the moral arm of personality. The manner in which the ego guides the libidinal energies of the id and the moralistic demands of the superego accounts for the rich variety of personalities, interests, motives, attitudes, and behavior patterns of people. It supposedly accounts for the purchase of a four-door sedan rather than a racy sports car and the use of Ultra-Brite toothpaste with its promise of sex appeal. The tools of the ego are defenses such as rationalization, projection, identification, and repression; its goals are integrated action.

Freud further believed that children pass through various stages of development—the oral, anal, phallic, and genital periods—that determine the dynamics of their personalities. The degrees of tension, frustration, and love experienced at these stages are responsible for adult personality and behavior.

The influence of Freud and psychoanalytic theory cannot be overestimated. Most of the greatest names in psychiatry and psychology have been followers, disciples, or critics of Freud, much as many good marketing research studies have been criticisms of motivation researchers or experiments applying scientific procedures to motivation research. The work of Sidney Levy, and the proprietary studies of Social Research, Inc., are in the latter tradition as is the more recent work by Dennis Rook.

However, we no longer find much research from a psychoanalytic point of view in the literature. One interesting attempt to use a projective technique is a replication of the classic Mason Haire Shopping List study by Webster and Von Pechmann [193] which, interestingly, yielded results significantly different from those of the original study—instant coffee users are no longer perceived as psychologically different from drip grind users. Other attempts and the use of projective techniques are studies by David Gardner [70] and Hughes, Juhasz, and Contino [92] in which McClelland's TAT-type

[1] Hall and Lindzey, in attempting to deal with the dozens of approaches that exist in the literature, submit that personality is defined by the particular concepts which are part of the theory of personality employed by the observer. Because this article reviews marketing literature rather than psychological literature, the various theories are not described in detail. For a very brief description of several theories and a bibliographic listing of primary sources and references, as well as examples of about a dozen well-known volumes on the general topic, see [84].

pictures were used to measure need for achievement. Landon [118] measured the same variable but by using Merabian's paper-and-pencil test avoided the interpretation problems of a projective tool.

Although today the critics of psychoanalytic applications to consumer behavior far outweigh the adherents, Freud and his critics have contributed much to advances in marketing theory.

SOCIAL THEORISTS

In his lifetime, several members of Freud's inner circle became disillusioned with his insistence on the biological basis of personality and began to develop their own views and their own followers. Alfred Adler, for example, believed that the basic human drive is not the channelization of the libido but rather the striving for superiority. The basic aim of life, he reasoned, is to overcome feelings of inferiority imposed during childhood. Occupations and spouses are selected, homes purchased, and automobiles owned in the effort to perfect the self and feel less inferior to others.

Eric Fromm stressed people's loneliness in society and their seeking of love, companionship, and security. The search for satisfying human relationships is of central importance to behavior and motivations.

Karen Horney, also one of the neo-Freudian social theorists, reacted against theories of the biological libido, as did Adler, but thought that childhood insecurities stemming from parent-child relationships create basic anxieties and that the personality is developed as the individual learns to cope with these anxieties.

Although these and other neo-Freudians have influenced the work of motivation researchers, they have had minimal impact on research in consumer behavior. However, much of their theorizing can be seen in advertising today, which exploits the striving for superiority and the needs for love, security, and escape from loneliness to sell toothpaste, deodorants, cigarettes, and even detergents.

The only research in consumer behavior based directly on a neo-Freudian approach is Cohen's psychological test that purports to measure Horney's three basic orientations toward coping with anxiety—the compliant, aggressive, and detached types [44]. Cohen found that compliant types prefer brand names and use more mouthwash and toilet soaps; aggressive types tend to use a razor rather than an electric shaver, use more cologne and after-shave lotion, and buy Old Spice deodorant and Van Heusen shirts; and detached types seem to be least aware of brands. Cohen, however, admitted to picking and choosing from his data. Although the published results are by no means conclusive, his work does indicate that the Horney typology may have some relevance to marketing.

Cohen's CAD test of Horney's classification scheme has been used by others in their research. Kernan's paper [111] concerning message advocacy, group influence, fashion, brand loyalty, and new product information produced significant results, suggesting that the instrument "works." Cohen and Golden [45] again produced positive results, and Nicely [145] found correlations between CAD, Eyesenck's introversion-extroversion variable, and Riesman's inner-and-other-direction variables. Noerager [146], in a study assessing the reliability and validity of CAD as a marketing measurement instrument, concluded that further development and refinement were necessary.

Slama, Williams and Tashchian [172] used Cohen's CAD scale and Slama and Tashcian's involvement scale and found the detached personality type to be less involved in purchasing than the compliant or aggressive types.

STIMULUS-RESPONSE THEORIES

The stimulus-response, or learning theory, approach to personality presents perhaps the most elegant view, with a respected history of research and laboratory experimentation supporting it. Its origins are in the work of Pavlov, Thorndike, Skinner, Spence, Hull, and the Institute of Human Relations at Yale University.

Although the various theorists differ among themselves, there is agreement that the link between stimulus and response is persistent and relatively stable. Personality is seen as a conglomerate of habitual responses acquired over time to specific and generalized cues. The bulk of theorizing and empirical research has been concerned with specifying conditions under which habits are formed, changed, replaced, or broken.

A drive leads to a response to a particular stimulus, and if the response is reinforced or rewarded, a particular habit is learned. Unrewarded and inappropriate responses are extinguished or eliminated. Complex behaviors such as consumer decision processes are learned in a similar manner. According to Dollard and Miller, a drive is a stimulus strong enough to impel activity; it energizes behavior but, by itself, does not direct it. Any stimulus may become a drive if it reaches sufficient intensity. Some stimuli are linked to the physiological processes necessary for the survival of the individual; others are secondary or acquired. With the concepts of cues, drives, responses, and reinforcement, the learning of complex motives such as the need for achievement or self-esteem is explained in the same manner as the learning of brand preference, racism, attitudes towards big business, purchasing habits, or dislike of canned spinach.

Marketing is replete with examples of the influence of learning theory, ranging from Krugman's work to the Yale studies on attitudes and attitude change, from lightweight discussions on the influence of repetition and reinforcement in advertising texts to Howard and Sheth's buyer behavior theory and the work in mathematical models. However, very few personality studies have used this theoretical orientation.

The reason for its lack of impact is probably that there are no personality tests and measuring instruments using this theoretical base. Until such instruments are developed, there will be little use of these theories in relating consumer behavior to personality, irrespective of their completeness and their relevance.

TRAIT AND FACTOR THEORIES

As learning theory approaches to personality have evolved from the tough-minded empirical experimentation of the animal laboratories, factor theories have evolved from the quantitative sophistication of statistical techniques and computer technology. The core of these theories is that personality is composed of a set of traits or factors, some general and others specific to a particular situation or test. In constructing a personality instrument, the psychometrician typically begins with a wide array of behavioral measures, mostly responses to test items, and with statistical techniques distills factors which are then defined as the personality variables.

For one large group of personality instruments, the researcher begins with the intent to measure certain variables, for example, need for achievement or aggressiveness. Large samples of subjects predetermined as aggressive or not aggressive (say, by ratings from teachers and employers) are given the instrument. Each item is statistically analyzed to see if it discriminates aggressive from nonaggressive subjects. By a series of such distilling measures and additional validation and reliability studies, an instrument is produced which measures the traits the researcher originally was attempting to gauge. Several of these variables are often embodied in, for example, a single 200-item instrument.

A second type of personality instrument is created not with theoretically predetermined variables in mind, but rather to identify a few items (by factor analysis) which account for a significant portion of the variance. Subjects are given questionnaires, ratings, or tests on a wide variety of topics, and test items are grouped in the factor analysis by how well they measure the same statistical factor. The meaning of a particular factor is thus empirically determined and a label arbitrarily attached to it that hopefully best describes what the researcher presumes the particular subset of items measures. Further reliability and validation measures lead to creation of a test instrument with several variables that supposedly account for the diversity and complexity of behavior. The theoretical structure is statistical, and the variables are empirically determined and creatively named or labeled.

The concept of traits, factors, or variables that can be quantitatively measured has led to virtually hundreds of personality scales and dozens of studies in consumer behavior.

Gordon Personal Profile

This instrument purports to measure ascendancy, responsibility, emotional stability, and sociability. Tucker and Painter [183] found significant correlations between use of headache remedies, vitamins, mouthwash, alcoholic drinks, automobiles, chewing gum, and the acceptance of new fashions and one or more of these four personality variables. The correlations ranged from .27 to .46, accounting for perhaps 10 percent of the variance.

Kernan [110] used decision theory in an empirical test of the relationship between decision behavior and personality. He added the Gordon Personal Inventory to measure cautiousness, original thinking, personal relations, and vigor. Pearsonian and multiple correlations indicated few significant relationships, but canonical correlation between sets of personality variables and decision behavior gave a coefficient of association of .77, significant at the .10 level. Cluster analysis then showed that behavior is consistent with personality profiles within clusters. Kernan's results, like those of Tucker and Painter [183] and four more recent studies [76, 89, 169, 175], show interesting relationships but are by no means startling.

Edwards Personal Preference Schedule

The EPPS has been used in about two dozen studies or rebuttals in consumer behavior from a trait and factor theory approach. The purpose of the instrument was to develop a factor-analyzed, paper-and-pencil, objective instrument to measure the psychoanalytically oriented needs or themes developed by Henry Murray. Its popularity in consumer behavior can be traced to Evans' landmark study [60], in which he could find no differences between Ford and Chevrolet owners to an extent that would allow for prediction. He was, however, able to account for about 10 percent of the variance. Criticism of Evans' study and conclusions came from many fronts and on many grounds (for example, [94, 204]). Rejoinders were written [61, 62], and finally Evans replicated the study [63]. The controversy over Evans' study is in the finest tradition of the physical and social sciences, with argument and counterargument, rejoinder and replication, until the facts begin to emerge—something very seldom seen in marketing and consumer behavior research. The final conclusion that seems to trickle through is that personality does account for some variance but not enough to give much solace to personality researchers in marketing.

Along other lines, Koponen used the EPPS scale with data collected on 9,000 persons in the J. Walter Thompson panel [117]. His results indicate that cigarette smoking is positively related to sex dominance, aggression, and achievement needs among males and negatively related to order and compliance needs. Further, he found differences between filter and nonfilter smokers and found that these differences were made more pronounced by heavy smoking. In addition, there seemed to be a relationship between personality variables and readership of three unnamed magazines.

Massy, Frank, and Lodahl used the same data in a study of the purchase of coffee, tea, and beer [131]. Their conclusion was that personality accounted for a very small percentage of the variance. In fact, personality plus socioeconomic variables accounted for only 5 percent to 10 percent of the variance in purchases.

In a sophisticated study, Claycamp presented the EPPS to 174 subjects who held savings accounts in banks or savings and loan associations [43]. His results indicate that personality variables predict better than demographic variables whether an individual is a customer of a bank or a savings and loan association. These results contradict those of Evans, who concluded that socioeconomic variables are more effective predictors than personality as measured by the same instrument. Using personality variables alone, Claycamp correctly classified 72 percent of the subjects.

Brody and Cunningham reanalyzed Koponen's data employing techniques like those of Claycamp and Massy, Frank, and Lodahl with similar results [32], accounting for about 3 percent of the variance. Further, these results are similar to those from the Advertising Research Foundation's study on toilet paper [1] in which 5 percent to 10 percent of the variance was accounted for by personality and other variables. Brody and Cunningham argued that the weak relationships may have been caused by an inadequate theoretical framework. Theirs consisted of three categories: perceived performance risk—the extent to which different brands perform differently in important ways; specific self-confidence—how certain consumers are that a brand performs as they expect; and perceived social risk—the extent to which they think they will be judged on the basis of their brand decision. The authors concluded that, "when trying to discriminate the brand choice of people most likely to have perceived high performance risk and to have high specific self-confidence, personality variables were very useful" [32, p. 56]. For people who were 100 percent brand loyal, eight personality variables explained 32 percent of the variance. As the minimum purchase of the favorite brand dropped from 100 percent to 40 percent, the explained variance fell to 13 percent. The EPPS scale was also used in studies by Alpert [4, 5], Bither and Dolich [27] and Peterson [157]. Horton [88], in a penetrating article, attacked the use of this and similar paper-and-pencil tools on procedural grounds.

Thurstone Temperament Schedule

This is another factor-analyzed instrument. Westfall, in a well-known study that is often interpreted as a replication of Evans' study, compared personalities of automobile owners and could find no differences between brands [200]. He further found no differences between owners of compact and standard cars on the Thurstone variables. However, personality characteristics did differ between owners of convertibles and standard models.

Using the same instrument, Kamen showed a relationship between the number of people who had no opinion on foods to be rated and the number of items they left unanswered on the Thurstone scale. Using a specially created questionnaire, he concluded that the dimension of "no opinion" is not related to food preference [101]. Proneness to have an opinion does not seem to be a general trait, but rather is dependent on the content area (see also [206]).

California Personality Inventory

The CPI is still another paper-and-pencil test used extensively. Robertson and Myers [165] (see also [166] and Bruce and Witt [34]) developed measures for innovativeness and opinion leadership in the areas of food, clothing, and appliances. A multiple stepwise regression with eighteen traits on the CPI indicated poor R^2s; the portion of variance accounted for was 4 percent for clothing, 5 percent for food, and 23 percent for appliances. The study tends to support the several dozen previous studies on innovation and opinion leadership that show a minimal relationship between personality variables and behavior toward new products. Several studies indicate that gregariousness and venturesomeness are relevant to opinion leadership. Two studies using personality inventories have found a relationship between innovation and personality, while three others could find none. Other traits, such as informal and formal social participation, cosmopolitanism and perceived risk are related to innovative behavior in about half a dozen studies, while an additional half a dozen studies show no differences. These studies are reviewed in [164].

A study by Boone attempted to relate the variables on the California Personality Inventory to the consumer innovator on the topic of a community antenna television system [31]. His results indicate significant differences between innovators and followers on ten of eighteen scales. Unfortunately, the statistical techniques were quite different from those employed by Robertson and Myers, so it is not possible to determine whether or not the two studies are in basic agreement.

Vitz and Johnston, using the masculinity scale of both the CPI and the Minnesota Multiphasic Personality Inventory, hypothesized that the more masculine a smoker's personality, the more masculine the image of his regular brand of cigarettes [190]. The correlations were low but statistically significant, and the authors concluded that the results moderately support product preference as a predictable interaction between the consumer's personality and the product's image. Similar conclusions are reported by Gentry, Doering, and O'Brien [71]. Later studies include those by Peters and Ford [156], who could find no personality difference between women who buy and do not buy from door-to-door salesmen; Hughes, Juhasz, and Contino [92], who compared the CPI and Rotter's Locus of Control to bargaining behavior; and Webster [192], who aimed the CPI at social responsibility, concluding that the better socially and psychologically integrated consumer displays greater social consciousness.

Dogmatism

Jacoby has demonstrated that Rokeach's concepts of open- and closed-mindedness are relevant to consumer behavior and found that low dogmatics tend to be more prone to innovation [95, 96]. The correlation between innovation and dogmatism was −.32, the explained variance about 10 percent. Rokeach's dogmatism as a variable has continued to appear in studies [7, 28, 46, 51, 99, 135, 156] which correlate the variable to risk, innovation and adoption, and gift giving generally with weak but significant results. In summary, it seems that open-mindedness is positively related to risk taking and willingness to innovate.

In addition, personal values a la Rokeach have remained of interest to marketing researchers despite their poor explanatory power [140, 141, 188, 189]. See also Mizerski and Settle's study [136].

Recently values have become a more important research topic with the studies done on List of Values (LOV) and Values and Life Styles (VALS) [19, 100, 181].

THEORIES OF SELF AND SELF-CONCEPT

Relationships of product image and self image have been studied quite thoroughly by the motivation researchers, particularly Levy [125] and Gardner [69]. The theoretical base for this work presumably rests in the writings and philosophies of Carl Rogers, William James, and Abraham Maslow and the symbolic interactionism proposed by Susan Langer and others.

The core of these views is that the individual has a real and an ideal self. The combined *self* is "the same total of all that a man can call his—his body, traits, and abilities; his material possessions; his family, friends, and enemies; his vocations and avocations and much else" [84, first edition, p. 467]. It includes a person's evaluations and definitions of the self and may be reflected in much of the person's actions, including evaluations and purchases of products and services. The belief is that individuals perceive products that they own, would like to own, or do not want to own in terms of the products' symbolic meaning to themselves and to others. Congruence between the symbolic image of a product (for example, a .38 caliber pistol is aggressive and masculine, a Jaguar automobile is extravagant and wealthy) and a consumer's self-image implies greater probability of positive evaluation, preference, or ownership of that product or brand. For example, Jacobson and Kossoff studied self-perception and attitudes toward small cars [93]. Individuals who perceived themselves as "cautious conservatives" were more likely to favor small cars as a practical and economic convenience. Another self-classified group of "confident explorers" preferred large cars, which they saw as a means of expressing their ability to control the environment.

Birdwell, using the semantic differential, tested the hypotheses that: (1) automobile owners' perceptions of their cars are essentially congruent with their perceptions of themselves; and (2) the average perception of a specific car type and brand is different for owners of different sorts of cars [25, 26; see also 64]. The hypotheses were confirmed with varying degrees of strength. However, this does not prove that products have personalities and that consumers purchase those brands whose images are congruent with their self-concepts; Birdwell's study did not test causality. It could be that only after a product is purchased does the owner begin to perceive it as an extension of his own personality.

Grubb [78] and Grubb and Grathwohl [79] found that consumers' different self-perceptions are associated with varying patterns of consumer behavior. They claimed that self-concept is a meaningful mode of market segmentation. Grubb found that beer drinkers perceived themselves as more confident, social, extroverted, forward, sophisticated, impulsive, and temperamental than their non-beer-drinking brethren. However, the comparison of self-concept and beer brand profiles revealed inconclusive results: drinkers and nondrinkers perceived brands similarly.

In a follow-up study of Pontiac and Volkswagen owners, Grubb and Hupp indicated that owners of one brand of automobile perceived themselves as similar to others who owned the same brand and significantly different from owners of the other brand [80]. Sommers indicated by the use of a Q-sort of products that subjects are reliably able to describe themselves and others by products rather than adjectives, say on a semantic differential or adjective checklist [173, 174]. That is, individuals are able to answer the questions, "What kind of a person am I? and "What kind of people are they?" by Q-sorting products.

Dolich further tested the congruence relationship between self-images and product brands and concluded that there is a greater similarity between people's self-concepts and images of their most preferred brands than images of their least preferred brands [54]. Dolich claimed that favored brands are consistent with and reinforce self-concept.

Hamm [85] and Hamm and Cundiff [86] related product perception to what they call self-actualization—that is, the discrepancy between the real self and ideal self. Those with a small discrepancy were called low self-actualizers, a definition which does not seem consistent with Maslow's work on the hierarchy of needs. High self-actualizers describe themselves in terms of products differently than low self-actualizers, and in turn perceive products differently. For both groups, some products tend to represent an ideal self, while others do not.

As is evident from the number of studies discussed above, self-confidence was heavily examined prior to 1969, and its fascination for researchers has not diminished. Studies by Bither and Wright [28], Barach [13], and Ostlund [147, 148, 149] have since appeared. Work in self-concept continues to appear, for example, in some dozen studies cited here [20, 21, 55, 67, 77, 81, 91, 99, 119, 129, 130, 167]—and to attempt to explain purchase behavior by measuring the concepts of ideal self and actual self.

PSYCHOGRAPHICS

An integration of the richness of motivation research studies and the thorough-mindedness and statistical sophistication of computer technology has led to another type of research involving personality, variously called psychographic, AIO, or lifestyle research. The lifestyle concept is based on distinctive or characteristic modes of living of segments of society [122]. The technique divides the total market into segments based on interests, values, opinions, personality characteristics, attitudes, and demographic variables using techniques of cluster analysis, factor analysis, and canonical correlation. Wells dubbed the methodology "backward segmentation" because it groups people by behavioral characteristics before seeking correlates [195]. Pessemier and Tigert reported that some preliminary relationships were found between the factor-analyzed clusters of people and market behavior [154]. Similar results were reported in other studies [124, 199, 202]. These factor-analyzed scales have been applied to media exposure [112, 134], credit card usage [160], advertising [159], creativity [205], opinion leadership and innovation [180], food shopping behavior [163], and market segmentation [38, 50, 74, 162, 211], the adoption of alternative long distance services [191], attendance at performing arts events [9], brand loyalty in the beer market [75], complaining behavior [137], and young male drinking and driving [121]. Articles discussing the methodology [161, 212] as well as reliability and validity studies [36, 37, 178, 179] are now available. These articles, however, merely scratch the surface. Books by King and Tigert [113] and William Wells [196], the AMA Attitude Research Proceedings [6], and Wells' splendid review article [197] contribute still more to this field. Generally, the relationship of the attitude-interest-personality clusters, when correlated with actual buyer behavior, accounts once again for 10 percent or less of the variance.

MISCELLANEOUS OTHER APPROACHES

The overall results of other studies with other points of view are quite similar. Some researchers interpret their results as insignificant while others interpret similarly minimal relationships as significant, depending on the degree of statistical sophistication and the statistical tools used. A hodgepodge of other studies indicates that heavy and light users of several product classes do not differ on the McClosky Personality Inventory or Dunnette Adjective Checklist [168]. Axelrod found a predictable relationship between the mood produced by viewing a movie—The Nuremburg Trial—and attitudes towards consumer products such as savings bonds, sewing machines, typewriters, and daiquiris [12]. Summers found a minimal relationship between characteristics of opinion leaders and the Borgatta personality variables [176]. Pennington and Peterson have shown that product preferences are related to vocational interests as measured on the Strong Vocational Interest Blank [151, 158]. Myers, in a study of attitudes toward private brands, found that Cattell's Sixteen Personality Factor Inventory explained about 5 percent of the variance [142, 143]. Several other instruments have appeared in consumer type studies. Morris and Cundiff [138] and Vavra and Winn [184] turned their attention to anxiety and the Taylor Manifest Anxiety Scale, and Hawkins [87] used the State-Trait Anxiety Inventory. The mixed results generally indicate that low anxiety is related to acceptance of more threatening material, such as males' acceptance of products considered feminine. Fornell and Westbrook [66] examined the relationship between aggressiveness, assertiveness, and consumer complaining behavior.

Another widely used instrument in consumer behavior research is the Jackson Personality Research Form. Wilson, Mathews, and Sweeney [203] correlated these scores with segmentation variables; Fry [68] and Ahmed [2] with cigarette smoking; Kinnear, Taylor, and Ahmed [114, 115] with ecological products; Worthing, Venkatesan, and Smith [209, 210] with a variety of consumer products; and Mathews, Slocum, and Woodside [132] with perceived risk.

Studies using intolerance of ambiguity [30, 127] and Rotter's internal and external control [92, 140] have appeared using available instruments. Additional new instruments appeared in the literature as Paul and Enis [150], Goldberg [75], Kirchner [116], Kegerreis and Engel [109], Baumgarten [18], and Feldman and Armstrong [65] developed their own tools to measure venturesomeness, Murray's needs, ordinal birth position, personal competence, and so on.

Social Character

Several researchers have turned their attention to Riesman's theories, which group human beings into three types of social character: tradition-directed, inner-directed, and other-directed. A society manifests one type predominantly, according to its particular phase of development.

Riesman by no means intended his typology

to be interpreted as a personality schema, yet in the consumer behavior literature social character has been grouped with personality, and hence the material is included in this review.

A society of tradition-directed people, seldom encountered in the United States today, is characterized by general slowness of change, a dependence on kin, low social mobility, and a tight web of values. Inner-directed people are most often found in a rapidly changing, industrialized society with division of labor, high social mobility, and less security; these persons must turn to inner values for guidance. In contrast, other-directed society is industrialized to the point that its orientation shifts from production to consumption. Thus, success in the other-directed society is not achieved through production and hard work but rather through ability to be liked by others, develop charm or "personality," and manipulate other people. The contemporary United States is considered by Riesman to be almost exclusively populated by the latter two social character types and to be rapidly moving toward an other-directed orientation.

Dornbusch and Hickman content-analyzed consumer goods advertising over the past decades and noted a clear trend from inner- to other-direction [58]. Zinkham and Shermohamad's [213] content analysis of 30 years of advertising in *Good Housekeeping* and *Popular Science* found additional support. W. M. Kassarjian [107] and Centers [41] have shown that youth is significantly more other-directed and that people born in foreign countries or reared in small towns tend to be inner-directed.

Gruen found no relationship between preference for new or old products and inner-other-direction [82]. Arndt [10, 11] and Barban, Sandage, Kassarjian, and Kassarjian [15] could find little relationship between innovation and social character; Donnelly, however, has shown a relationship between housewives' acceptance of innovations and their social character, with the inner-directed being slightly more innovative [56]. Linton and Graham indicated that inner-directed persons are less easily persuaded than other-directed persons [127]. Centers and Horowitz found that other-directed individuals were more susceptible to social influence in an experimental setting than were inner-directed subjects [42]. Kassarjian found that subjects expressed a preference for appeals based on their particular social character type. There was minimal evidence for differential exposure to various mass media between the two Riesman types [102].

In a similar study, Woodside found no relationship between consumer products and social character, although he did find a minimal relationship between advertising appeals and inner-other-direction [207]. Donnelly and Ivancevich [57] found a weak but positive relationship between inner-other-direction and innovator characteristics. Perry [152] tied in anxiety, the Eysenck variables, and heredity to product choice, concluding that consumption was genetically influenced. He claimed that this genetic relationship has application to primary demand but not product choice.

Kassarjian and Kassarjian found a relationship between social character and Allport's scale of values, as well as vocational interests, but could find no relationship between inner-other-direction and personality variables as measured by the MMPI [105, 108]. Once again, the results follow the same pattern: a few studies find and a few do not find meaningful relationships between consumer behavior and other measures.

Personality and Persuasibility

To complete a review on the relationship between personality and consumer behavior, the wide body of research findings relating personality to persuasibility and attitude change must be included. In addition to the dozens of studies carried out under Carl Hovland, for example [90], there are many relating personality characteristics to conformity, attitude change, fear appeals, and opinions on various topics (see [123]). The consumer behavior literature studies by Cox and Bauer [48], Bell [23, 24], Carey [39], and Barach [13, 14] tied self-confidence to persuasibility in the purchase of goods. These studies indicated a curvilinear relationship between generalized self-confidence and persuasibility and between specific self-confidence and persuasibility. Venkatesan's results, however, throw some doubt on these findings [185]. In recent reanalysis and review of much of this literature, Shuchman and Perry found contradictory data; they claim that neither generalized nor specific self-confidence appears to be an important determinant of persuasibility in marketing [170]. Bauer, in turn, has found fault with the Shuchman and Perry reanalysis [17].

SUMMARY AND CONCLUSIONS

A review of these dozens of studies and papers can be summarized in a single word—equivocal. A few studies indicate a strong relationship between personality and aspects of consumer behavior, a few indicate no relationship, and the great majority indicate that if correlations do exist they are so weak as to be questionable or perhaps meaningless. Several reasons can be postulated to account for these discrepancies. Perhaps the major one is based on the validity of the particular personality-measuring instruments used. A typically "good" instrument has a test-retest reliability of about .80 and a split-half reliability of about .90. Validity coefficients range at most from .40 to about .70, that is, when correlated against a criterion variable, the instrument typically accounts for about 20 percent to 40 percent of the variance. Tests validated for specific uses on specific populations—such as for college students or as part of mental hospital intake batteries—have been applied to available subjects in the general population. The results may indicate that 10 percent of the variance is accounted for; this is then interpreted as a weak relationship, and personality is rejected as a determinant of purchase. The consumer researcher too often expects more from an instrument than it was originally intended to furnish.

An additional problem for the marketing researcher is the conditions under which the test instrument is given. The instrument is often presented in the classroom or on the doorstep rather than in the office of a psychometrician, psychotherapist, or vocational counselor. As Wells has pointed out [194, p.188]:

> The measurements we take may come from some housewife sitting in a bathrobe at her kitchen table, trying to figure to what it is she is supposed to say in answering a questionnaire. Too often, she is not telling us about herself as she really is, but instead is telling us about herself as she thinks she is or wants us to think she is.

To compound the error, consumer researchers often forget that the strength of a correlation is limited by the reliability of the measures being correlated. Not only the personality test but also the criterion itself may be unreliable under these conditions. Often the criterion used in these studies is the consumer's own account of his or her purchasing behavior. More often than not, these data are far less reliable than we may wish to admit.

Adaptation of Instruments

Much too often, in order to adjust test items to fit specific demands, researchers make changes in the instrument being used. Items are taken out of context of the total instrument, words are changed, items are arbitrarily discarded, and the test is often shortened drastically [33, 187]. This adjustment would undoubtedly horrify the original developer of the instrument, and the disregard for the validity of the modified instrument should horrify the rest of us. Just how much damage is done when a measure of self-confidence or extroversion is adapted, revised, and restructured is simply not known, but it would not be a serious exaggeration to claim that it is considerable. And, most unfortunately, from time to time even the name of the variable is changed to fit the needs of the researchers. For example, Cohen has pointed out that in the Koponen study [117] male smokers scored higher than average on self-depreciation and association, variables not included in the Edwards instrument, which the study purported to use. The researcher was apparently using the abasement and affiliation scales [44]. Such changes may or may not be proper; but although they may not necessarily violate scientific canons, they certainly do not help reduce the confusion in attempting to sort out what little we know about the relationship of personality to consumer behavior.

Psychological Instruments in Marketing Research

A second reason for discrepancies in the literature is that instruments originally intended to measure gross personality characteristics such as sociability, emotional stability, introversion, or neuroticism have been used to make predictions of the chosen brand of toothpaste or cigarettes. The variables that can characterize people who would assassinate a president, be confined in a mental hospital, or commit suicide may not be identical to those that are relevant in the purchase of a washing machine, a pair of shoes, or chewing gum. Clearly, if unequivocal results are to emerge, consumer behavior researchers must develop their own definitions and design their own instruments to measure the personality variables that go into the purchase decision rather than using tools designed as part of a medical model to measure schizophrenia or mental stability.

Development of definitions and instruments can perhaps be handled in two ways. One will require some brilliant theorizing as to what variables do relate to the consumer decision process. If neuroticism and sociability are not the relevant personality variables, then perhaps such terms as risk aversion, status seeking, and conspicuous consumption can be used. Personality variables that in fact are relevant to the consumer model need to be theorized and tests developed and validated.

Only with marketing-oriented instruments will we be able to determine just what part personality variables play in consumer decision process and, further, whether they can be generalized across product and service classes or must be product-specific instruments. At that stage, questions of the relevancy of these criteria for segmenting markets, shifting demand curves, or creating and sustaining promotional and advertising campaigns can be asked.

Hypotheses

A third reason for the lackluster results in the personality and consumer behavior literature is that many studies have been conducted by a shotgun approach with no specific hypotheses or theoretical justification. Typically, a convenient, available, easily scored, and easy-to-administer personality inventory is selected and administered along with questionnaires on purchase data and preferences. The lack of proper scientific method and hypothesis generation is supposedly justified by the often-used disclaimer that the study is exploratory. As Jacoby has pointed out [96, p.244]:

> Careful examination reveals that, in most cases, no *a priori* thought is directed to how, or especially why, personality should or should not be related to that aspect of consumer behavior being studied. Moreover, the few studies which do report statistically significant finding usually do so on the basis of post-hoc "picking and choosing" out of large data arrays.

Statistical techniques are applied and anything that turns up looking halfway interesting furnishes the basis for the discussion section [94].

An excellent example of the shotgun approach to science, albeit a more sophisticated one than most, is Evans' original study examining personality differences between Ford and Chevrolet owners. Jacoby noted that Evans began his study with specific hypotheses culled from the literature and folklore pertaining to personality differences to be expected between Ford and Chevrolet owners [94]. He then presented the EPPS to subjects, measuring eleven variables, five of which seemed to be measuring the variables in question; the remaining six were irrelevant to the hypotheses, with no *a priori* basis for expecting differences. If predictions were to have been made on these six scales, Jacoby says, they should have been ones of "no difference." Using one-tailed tests of significance, since the directions also should have been hypothesized, three of the five key variables were significant at the .05 level and none of the remaining six were significant. In short, Evans' data could have been interpreted such that nine of the eleven scales were "significant" according to prediction. Jacoby's interpretation leads to a conclusion quite different from Evans' inference that there are no personality differences between Ford and Chevrolet owners. Also, with *a priori* predictions, Jacoby did not have to pick and choose from his data, as others have done.

Nakanishi, in a most insightful paper [144] presented at the 1972 meetings of the Association for Consumer Research, has suggested that the low explanatory power of personality characteristics may have stemmed, in part, from the naive conceptualizations of the relationship between personality and consumer behavior often held by researchers in the field. A more recent discussion of that point can be found in Crosby and Grossbart [49]. It may be that simple statistics such as variance analysis, chi square, and t-tests are insufficient. For example, canonical correlations have been used by Sparks and Tucker [175], Bither and Dolich [27], Alpert [4], and Darden and Reynolds [51] with more complex results and somewhat more variance statistically explained. Unfortunately, this adding of additional variables still involves a static view of the consumer. Personality may perhaps be better conceived of as a dynamic concept which is not constant over a variety of situations. Rather, personality is a consistency in the manner in which the individual adjusts to change over time and over situations. Nakanishi writes that it is perhaps "more correct to conceive of personality as a moderator variable whose function is to moderate the effects of environmental change in the individual's behavior. This dynamic concept of personality has not been taken seriously in personality research."

Nakanishi seems to be suggesting that what we need is data somewhat analogous to a combination of cross-sectional and time series analyses. The studies conducted to date are of the cross-section variety, correlating test inventory variables with consumption variables over subjects. And yet, as Wells and Beard [198] point out, a single personality trait may lead to a variety of behaviors. For instance, compulsiveness can lead to extremely orderly behavior or explusive, disorderly behavior, depending on the situation. Correlating a single trait with a single behavior is bound to be frustrating.

Hence, according to Nakanishi, the relevant variables include personality traits, response and behavior patterns, moderator variables, situations, and individuals. Furthermore, for some of these variables it is essential that measurements be taken over time. That is, as we sample individuals, traits, and responses, we should also take samplings of situations over time.

If one turns to other concepts in consumer research, an overview of the results again at times appears to be frustrating. For example, static research and linear statistics on the relationship between attitudes, values, or beliefs and the behavior of the individual appear to be weak. Research on repetition and learning, perceived risk, motivation, level of involvement, group influence, reference groups, and class and cultural influences have produced similar conclusions. The data indicate relationships between the concept and behavior sufficient to be enticing and to encourage further research but insufficient to satisfy a statistician attempting to validate a simple mathematical model or a marketer seeking explanations of the variances in consumer behavior that are not so small as to be meaningless.

If one can generalize from Nakanishi, the low explanatory power of each of these variables stems from naive conceptualizations of the relationships between the variable and the actions of the consumer in the marketplace. Hence, if the Edwards schedule does not account for the variance, perhaps the Jackson Inventory will; if not, there are still Fishbein attitude models, reference groups, and measures of the level of involvement to be tried.

We have yet to internalize the conception that the individual must be perceived as a dynamic whole. We ought not be concerned with rigid connections but rather with temporally extended whole individuals. In short, further traditional research attempting to connect the purchase of canned peas with a personality variable using cross-section data is bound to fail; it does not take into account the effects of the interaction of that personality variable with other personality characteristics, the interaction effects accounted for by needs, motives, moods, memories, attitudes, beliefs, opinions, perceptions, values, and so on, or the effects of the situation or field. As Tucker [182] has already suggested, our theories must begin with the study of the whole individual in a purchase act at a point in time. In short, Tucker seems to be saying that every specific instance of behavior must be viewed as the result of the interaction and integration of a variety of influences or forces impinging upon the person. The description of behavior cannot concentrate exclusively on one or another of the variables involved. Only after the analysis examines the situation as a whole is it possible to turn to the specific elements and the interactions among the elements [104]. Unfortunately, no simple methodology for research of this sort has yet emerged. We do not necessarily advocate a return to the extensive study of a single individual such as the psychoanalytic methodology employed by Freud or to the environmental probability of Egon Brunswick. Perhaps the post-positivism movement now emerging in consumer behavior will help point out the location of the light at the end of the tunnel.

Only when we can explain the behavior of a single individual in a variety of situations over time can we grasp the idea that there are, in fact, interactions among personality, attitudes, perceived risk, and the psychological field, or situation. Once the concept of an interaction effect has been internalized, we can turn from an examination of the whole to analyses of the parts. The proper question then will be, "All other things being equal, what is the relationship between a specific personality variable and a specific act?" The present problem with the literature is that "all other things" are not equal; and yet we continue to express dismay, surprise, or pleasure that personality measures, or attitude measures, or what have you, account for only 5 percent of the variance. As has already been expressed [103], "what is amazing is not that there are many studies that show no correlation between consumer behavior and personality, but rather that there are any studies at all with positive results. That 5 percent or 10 percent or any portion of the variance can be accounted for by personality variables (taken out of context and studied independently of other cognitive or physical variables) . . . is most remarkable indeed!"

REFERENCES AND NOTES

1. ADVERTISING RESEARCH FOUNDATION (1964), *Are There Consumer Types?* New York: Advertising Research Foundation.
2. AHMED, S. A. (1972), "Prediction of Cigarette Consumption Level with Personality and Socioeconomic Variables." *Journal of Applied Psychology,* 56(October): 437–438.
3. ALPERT, LEWIS, and RONALD GATTY (1969), "Product Positioning by Behavioral Life Style." *Journal of Marketing,* 33(April): 65–69.
4. ALPERT, MARK I. (1971), "A Canonical Analysis of Personality and the Determinants of Automobile Choice." In *Combined Proceedings.* Chicago: American Marketing Association, pp. 312–316.
5. ______ (1972), "Personality and the Determinants of Product Choice." *Journal of Marketing Research,* 5(February): 89–92.
6. AMERICAN MARKETING ASSOCIATION (1971), "Attitude Research Reaches New Heights." Chicago: American Marketing Association.
7. ANDERSON, W. T., and WILLIAM H. CUNNINGHAM (1967), "Gauging Foreign Product Promotion." *Journal of Advertising Research,* 4(August): 291–295.
8. ANDERSON, W. THOMAS JR., and LINDA L. GOLDEN (1983), "Lifestyle and Psychographics: A Critical Review and Recommendation." In *Proceedings 11th Conference,* Ed. Thomas Kinnear. Association for Consumer Research, pp. 405–411.
9. ANDREASEN, ALAN R., and RUSSELL W. BELK (1980), "Predictors of Attendance at the Performing Arts." *Journal of Consumer Research,* 7(September): 112–120.
10. ARNDT, JOHAN (1967), "Role of Product-Related Conversations in the Diffusion of a New Product." *Journal of Marketing Research,* 4(August): 291–295.
11. ______ (1968), "Profiling Consumer Innovators." In *Insights into Consumer Behavior,* Ed.

Johan Arndt. Boston: Allyn & Bacon, pp. 71–83.

12. AXELROD, JOEL N. (1963), "Induced Moods and Attitudes Towards Products." *Journal of Advertising Research,* 3(June): 19–24.

13. BARACH, JEFFREY A. (1967), "Self-Confidence and Reactions to Television Commercials." In *Risk Taking and Information Handling in Consumer Behavior,* Ed. Donald F. Cox. Boston: Division of Research, Graduate School of Business, Harvard University, pp. 428–441.

14. ——— (1969), "Advertising Effectiveness and Risk in the Consumer Decision Process." *Journal of Marketing Research,* 6(August): 314–320.

15. BARBAN, ARNOLD N., C. H. SANDAGE, WALTRAUD M. KASSARJIAN, and HAROLD H. KASSARJIAN (1970), "A Study of Riesman's Inner-Other-Directedness Among Farmers." *Rural Sociology,* 35(June): 232–243.

16. BASS, FRANK M., DOUGLAS J. TIGERT, and RONALD T. LONSDALE (1968), "Marketing Segmentation: Group Versus Individual Behavior." *Journal of Marketing Research,* 5(August): 264–270.

17. BAUER, RAYMOND (1970), "Self-Confidence and Persuasibility: One More Time." *Journal of Marketing Research,* 7(May): 256–268.

18. BAUMGARTEN, STEVEN A. (1975), "The Innovative Communicator in the Diffusion Process." *Journal of Marketing Research,* 12(February): 12–18.

19. BEATTY, SHARON E., PAMELA M. HOMER, and LYNN R. KAHLE (1988), "Problems with VALS in International Marketing Research: An Example From An Application Of The Empirical Mirror Technique." In *Proceedings 15th Conference,* Ed. Michael J. Houston. Association for Consumer Research, pp. 375–380.

20. BELCH, GEORGE E. (1978), "Belief Systems and the Differential Role of the Self-Concept." In *Advances in Consumer Research,* Vol. 5. Ann Arbor, MI: Association for Consumer Research, pp. 320–325.

21. BELCH, GEORGE E., and E. LAIRD LANDON, JR. (1977), "Discriminant Validity of a Product-Anchored Self-Concept Measure." *Journal of Marketing Research,* 14(May): 252–256.

22. BELK, RUSSELL W. (1988), "Possessions and the Extended Self." *Journal of Consumer Research,* 15(September): 139–168.

23. BELL, GERALD D. (1967), "Self-Confidence and Persuasion in Car Buying." *Journal of Marketing Research,* 4(February): 46–52.

24. ——— (1968), "Persuasibility and Buyer Remorse Among Automobile Purchasers." In *Consumer Behavior,* Eds. Montrose S. Sommers and Jerome B. Kernan. Austin, TX: Bureau of Business Research, University of Texas, pp. 77–102.

25. BIRDWELL, AL E. (1968), "A Study of the Influence of Image Congruence on Consumer Choice." *Journal of Business,* 41(January): 76–88.

26. ——— (1968), "Automobiles and Self Imagery: Reply." *Journal of Business,* 41(October): 486–487.

27. BITHER, STEWART W., and IRA J. DOLICH (1972), "Personality as a Determinant Factor in Store Choice." In *Proceedings 3rd Conference,* Ed. M. Venkatesen. College Park, MD: Association for Consumer Research, pp. 9–19.

28. BITHER, STEWART W., and PETER L. WRIGHT (1973), "The Self Confidence-Advertising Response Relationship: A Function of Situational Distraction." *Journal of Marketing Research,* 10(May): 146–152.

29. BLAKE, BRIAN, ROBERT PERLOFF, and RICHARD HESLIN (1970), "Dogmatism and Acceptance of New Products." *Journal of Marketing Research,* 7(November): 483–486.

30. BLAKE, BRIAN, ROBERT PERLOFF, ROBERT ZENHAUSEN, and RICHARD HESLIN (1973), "The Effect of Intolerance of Ambiguity upon Product Perceptions." *Journal of Applied Psychology,* 58(October): 239–243.

31. BOONE, LOUISE E. (1970), "The Search for the Consumer Innovator." *Journal of Business,* 43(April): 135–140.

32. BRODY, ROBERT P., and SCOTT M. CUNNINGHAM (1968), "Personality Variables and the Consumer Decision Process." *Journal of Marketing Research,* 5(February): 50–57.

33. BROOKER, GEORGE (1978), "Representativeness of Shortened Personality Measures." *Journal of Consumer Research,* 5(September): 143–145.

34. BRUCE, GRADY D., and ROBERT E. WITT (1970), "Personality Correlates of Innovative Buying Behavior." *Journal of Marketing Research,* 7(May): 259–260.

35. BURNETT, JOHN J. (1981), "Psychographic and Demographic Characteristics of Blood Do-

nors." *Journal of Consumer Research,* 8(June): 62–67.

36. BRUNO, ALBERT V., and EDGAR A. PESSEMIER (1972), "An Empirical Investigation of the Validity of Selected Attitude and Activity Measures." In *Proceedings 3rd Conference,* Ed. M. Venkatesan. College Park, MD: Association for Consumer Research, pp. 456–473.
37. BURNS, ALVIN C., and MARY CAROLYN HARRISON (1979), "A Test of the Reliability of Psychographics." *Journal of Marketing Research,* 16(February): 32–38.
38. BUSHMAN, F. ANTHONY (1971), "Market Segmentation via Attitudes and Life Style." In *Combined Proceedings.* Chicago: American Marketing Association, pp. 594–599.
39. CAREY, JAMES W. (1963), "Personality Correlates of Persuasibility." In *Proceedings of Winter Conference.* Chicago: American Marketing Association, pp. 30–43.
40. CARMAN, JAMES M. (1970), "Correlates of Brand Loyalty: Some Positive Results." *Journal of Marketing Research,* 7(February): 67–76.
41. CENTERS, RICHARD (1962), "An Examination of the Riesman Social Character Typology: A Metropolitan Survey." *Sociometry,* 25(September): 231–240.
42. CENTERS, RICHARD, and MIRIAN HOROWITZ (1963), "Social Character and Conformity." *Journal of Social Psychology,* 60(August): 343–349.
43. CLAYCAMP, HENRY J. (1965), "Characteristics of Owners of Thrift Deposits in Commercial Banks and Savings and Loan Associations." *Journal of Marketing Research,* 2(May): 163–170.
44. COHEN, JOEL B. (1967), "An Interpersonal Orientation to the Study of Consumer Behavior." *Journal of Marketing Research,* 4(August): 270–278.
45. COHEN, JOEL B., and ELLEN GOLDEN (1972), "Informational Social Influence and Product Evaluation." *Journal of Applied Psychology,* 50(February): 54–59.
46. CONEY, KENNETH A. (1972), "Dogmatism and Innovation: A Replication." *Journal of Marketing Research,* 9(November): 453–455.
47. CONEY, KENNETH A., and ROBERT R. HARMON (1979), "Dogmatism and Innovation: A Situational Perspective." *Advances in Consumer Research,* Vol. 6, Ed. William L. Wilke. Ann Arbor, MI: Association for Consumer Research, pp. 118–121.
48. COX, DONALD F., and RAYMOND A. BAUER (1984), "Self-Confidence and Persuasibility in Women." *Public Opinion Quarterly,* 28(Fall): 453–466.
49. CROSBY, LAWRENCE A., and SANFORD L. GROSSBART (1983), "A Blueprint for Consumer Behavior Research on Personality." *Proceedings 11th Conference,* Ed. Thomas Kinnear. Association for Consumer Research, pp. 447–452.
50. DARDEN, WILLIAM R., and WILLIAM D. PERREAULT, JR. (1976), "Identifying Interurban Shoppers: Multiproduct Purchase Patterns and Segmentation Profiles." *Journal of Marketing Research,* 13(February): 51–60.
51. DARDEN, WILLIAM R., and FRED D. REYNOLDS (1972), "Predicting Opinion Leadership for Men's Apparel Fashions." *Journal of Marketing Research,* 9(August): 324–328.
52. ——— (1974), "Backward Profiling of Male Innovators." *Journal of Marketing Research,* 11(February): 79–85.
53. DICHTER, ERNEST (1960), *The Strategy of Desire.* New York: Doubleday.
54. DOLICH, IRA J. (1969), "Congruence Relationships Between Self Images and Product Brands." *Journal of Marketing Research,* 6(February): 80–84.
55. DOLICH, IRA J., and NEB SHILLING. (1971), "A Critical Evaluation of 'The Problem of Self-Concept in Store Image Studies.' " *Journal of Marketing,* 35(January): 71–73.
56. DONNELLY, JAMES H., JR. (1970), "Social Character and Acceptance of New Products." *Journal of Marketing Research,* 7(February): 111–113.
57. DONNELLY, JAMES H., JR., and JOHN M. IVANCEVICH (1974), "A Methodology for Identifying Innovator Characteristics of New Brand Purchasers." *Journal of Marketing Research,* 11(August): 331–334.
58. DORNBUSCH, SANFORD M., and LAUREN C. HICKMAN (1959), "Other-Directedness in Consumer Goods Advertising: A Test of Riesman's Historical Theory." *Social Forces,* 38(December): 99–102.
59. ENGEL, JAMES F., DAVID T. KOLLAT, and ROGER D. BLACKWELL (1969), "Personality

Measures and Market Segmentation." *Business Horizons,* 12(June): 61–70.

60. EVANS, FRANKLIN B. (1959), "Psychological and Objective Factors in the Prediction of Brand Choice." *Journal of Business,* 32(October): 340–369.

61. ______ (1961), "Reply: You Still Can't Tell a Ford Owner from a Chevrolet Owner." *Journal of Business,* 34(January): 67–73.

62. ______ (1964), "True Correlates of Automobile Shopping Behavior." *Journal of Marketing,* 28(January): 65–66.

63. ______ (1968), "Ford Versus Chevrolet: Park Forest Revisited." *Journal of Business,* 41(October): 445–459.

64. ______ (1968), "Automobiles and Self-Imagery: Comment." *Journal of Business,* 41(October): 484–485.

65. FELDMAN, LAURENCE P., and GARY M. ARMSTRONG (1975), "Identifying Buyers of a Major Automobile Innovation." *Journal of Marketing,* 38(January): 47–53.

66. FORNELL, CLAES, and ROBERT A. WESTBROOK (1979), "An Exploratory Study of Assertiveness, Aggressiveness and Consumer Complaining Behavior." *Advances in Consumer Research,* Vol. 6, Ed. William L. Wilkie. Ann Arbor, MI: Association for Consumer Research, pp. 105–110.

67. FRENCH, WARREN A., and ALAN B. FLASCHNER (1971), "Levels of Actualization as Matched Against Life Style Evaluation of Products." In *Combined Proceedings.* Chicago: American Marketing Association, pp. 358–362.

68. FRY, JOSEPH N. (1971), "Personality Variables and Cigarette Brand Choice." *Journal of Marketing Research,* 8(August): 298–304.

69. GARDNER, BURLEIGH B., and SIDNEY J. LEVY (1955), "The Product and the Brand." *Harvard Business Review* 33(March/April): 33–39.

70. GARDNER, DAVID M. (1972), "An Exploratory Investigation of Achievement Motivation Effects on Consumer Behavior." In *Proceedings 3rd Conference,* Ed. M. Venkatesan. College Park, MD: Association for Consumer Research, pp. 20–33.

71. GENTRY, JAMES W., MILDRED DOERING, and TERRENCE V. O'BRIEN (1978), "Masculinity and Femininity Factors in Product Perception and Self Image." *Advances in Consumer Research,* Vol. 5, Ed. H. Keith Hunt. Ann Arbor, MI: Association for Consumer Research, pp. 326–332.

72. GOBLE, ROSS LAWRENCE (1969), "New Psychometric Measurements for Consumer Credit Behavior." In *Proceedings of Fall Conference.* Chicago: American Marketing Association, pp. 368–376.

73. GOLDBERG, MARVIN E. (1971), "A Cognitive Model of Innovative Behavior: The Interaction of Product and Self-Attitudes." In *Proceedings 2nd Conference,* Ed. David M. Gardner. College Park, MD: Association for Consumer Research, pp. 313–330.

74. ______ (1976), "Identifying Relevant Psychographic Segments: How Specifying Product Functions Can Help." *Journal of Consumer Research,* 3(December): 163–169.

75. GOLDBERG, STEPHEN M. (1981), "An Empirical Study of Lifestyle Correlates to Brand Loyal Behavior." *Proceedings 9th Conference,* Ed. Andrew Mitchell. Association for Consumer Research, pp. 456–460.

76. GREENO, DANIEL W., MONTROSE S. SOMMERS, and JEROME B. KERNAN (1973), "Personality and Implicit Behavior Patterns." *Journal of Marketing Research,* 10(February): 63–69.

77. GREEN, PAUL E., ARUN MAHESHWARI, and V. R. RAO (1969), "Self Concept and Brand Preference: An Empirical Application of Multidimensional Scaling." *Journal of the Marketing Research Society,* 11(1969): 343–360.

78. GRUBB, EDWARD L. (1965), "Consumer Perception of 'Self Concept' and Its Relationship to Brand Choice of Selected Product Types." In *Proceedings of Winter Conference.* Chicago: American Marketing Association, pp. 419–422.

79. GRUBB, EDWARD L., and HARRISON L. GRATHWOHL (1967), "Consumer Self-Concept, Symbolism and Marketing Behavior: A Theoretical Approach." *Journal of Marketing,* 31(October): 22–27.

80. GRUBB, EDWARD L., and GREGG HUPP (1968), "Perception of Self, Generalized Stereotypes, and Brand Selection." *Journal of Marketing Research,* 5(February): 58–63.

81. GRUBB, EDWARD L., and BRUCE L. STERN (1971), "Self-Concept and Significant Others."

Journal of Marketing Research, 8(August): 382-385.

82. GRUEN, WALTER (1960), "Preference for New Products and Its Relationship to Different Measures of Conformity." *Journal of Applied Psychology,* 44(December): 361-366.

83. GUTMAN, JONATHAN, and DONALD E. VINSON (1978), "Value Structure and Consumer Behavior." *Advances in Consumer Research,* Vol. 5, Ed. H. Keith Hunt. Ann Arbor, MI: Association for Consumer Research, pp. 335-339.

84. HALL, CALVIN S., and GARDNER LINDZEY (1969), *Theories of Personality* (2nd ed.). New York: Wiley.

85. HAMM, B. CURTIS (1967), "A Study of the Differences Between Self-Actualizing Scores and Product Perceptions Among Female Consumers." In *Proceedings of Winter Conference.* Chicago: American Marketing Association, pp. 275-276.

86. HAMM, B. CURTIS, and EDWARD W. CUNDIFF (1969), "Self-Actualization and Product Perception." *Journal of Marketing Research,* 6(November): 470-472.

87. HAWKINS, DEL I. (1972), "Reported Cognitive Dissonance and Anxiety: Some Additional Findings." *Journal of Marketing,* 36(July): 63-66.

88. HORTON, RAYMOND L. (1974), "The Edwards Personal Preference Schedule and Consumer Personality Research." *Journal of Marketing Research,* 11(August): 333-337.

89. ______ (1979), "Some Relationships Between Personality and Consumer Decision Making." *Journal of Marketing Research,* 16(May): 233-246.

90. HOVLAND, CARL I., and IRVING L. JANIS, EDS. (1950), *Personality and Persuasibility.* New Haven, CT: Yale University Press.

91. HUGHES, G. DAVID, and JOSE L. GUERRERO (1971), "Automobile Self-Congruity Models Reexamined." *Journal of Marketing Research,* 8(February): 125-127.

92. HUGHES, G. DAVID, JOSEPH B. JUHASZ, and BRUNO CONTINO (1973), "The Influence of Personality on the Bargaining Process." *Journal of Business,* 46(October): 593-603.

93. JACOBSON, EUGENE, and JEROME KOSSOFF (1963), "Self-Percept and Consumer Attitudes Toward Small Cars." *Journal of Applied Psychology,* 47(August): 242-245.

94. JACOBY, JACOB (1969), "Personality and Consumer Behavior: How Not to Find Relationships." Purdue Papers in Consumer Psychology, No. 102. Lafayette, IN: Purdue University.

95. ______ (1970), "A Multiple Indicant Approach for Studying Innovators." Purdue Papers in Consumer Psychology, No. 108. Lafayette, IN: Purdue University.

96. ______ (1971), "Personality and Innovation Proneness." *Journal of Marketing Research,* 8(May): 244-247.

97. ______ (1971), "Multiple-Indicant Approach for Studying New Product Adopters." *Journal of Applied Psychology,* 55: 384-388.

98. JACOBY, JACOB, and LEON B. KAPLAN (1972), "The Components of Perceived Risk." In *Proceedings 3rd Conference,* Ed. M. Venkatesan. College Park, MD: Association for Consumer Research, pp. 382-393.

99. JOYCE, TIMOTHY (1972), "Personality Classification of Consumers." Paper read at Annual Meeting, American Psychological Association.

100. KAHLE, LYNN R., SHARON E. BEATTY, and PAMELA HOMER (1986), "Alternative Measurement Approaches to Consumer Values: The List of Values (LOV) and Values of Life Style (VALS)." *Journal of Consumer Research,* 13(December): 405-409.

101. KAMEN, JOSEPH M. (1964), "Personality and Food Preferences." *Journal of Advertising Research,* 4(September): 29-32.

102. KASSARJIAN, HAROLD H. (1965), "Social Character and Differential Preference for Mass Communication." *Journal of Marketing Research,* 2(May): 146-153.

103. ______ (1971), "Personality and Consumer Behavior: A Review." *Journal of Marketing Research,* 8(November): 409-418.

104. ______ (1973), "Field Theory in Consumer Behavior." In *Consumer Behavior: Theoretical Sources,* Ed. Scott Ward and Thomas S. Robertson. Englewood Cliffs, NJ: Prentice-Hall, pp. 118-140.

105. KASSARJIAN, HAROLD H., and WALTRAUD M. KASSARJIAN (1966), "Personality Correlates of Inner- and Other-Direction." *Journal of Social Psychology,* 70(June): 281-285.

106. KASSARJIAN, HAROLD H., and MARY JANE SHEFFET (1975), "Personality and Consumer Behavior: One More Time." In *Combined Proceedings.* Chicago: American Marketing Association, pp. 197-201.

107. Kassarjian, Waltraud M. (1962), "A Study of Riesman's Theory of Social Character." *Sociometry,* 25(September): 213–230.

108. Kassarjian, Waltraud M., and Harold H. Kassarjian (1966), "Occupational Interests, Social Values and Social Character." *Journal of Counseling Psychology,* 12(January): 48–54.

109. Kegerreis, Robert J., and James F. Engle (1969), "The Innovative Consumer Characteristics of the Earliest Adopters of a New Automotive Service." In *Proceedings.* Chicago: American Marketing Association, pp. 357–361.

110. Kernan, Jerome (1968), "Choice Criteria, Decision Behavior, and Personality." *Journal of Marketing Research,* 5(May): 155–164.

111. ______ (1971), "The CAD Instrument in Behavioral Diagnosis." In *Proceedings 2nd Conference,* Ed. David M. Gardner. College Park, MD: Association for Consumer Research, 1971, pp. 301–312.

112. King, Charles W., and John O. Summers (1971), "Attitudes and Media Exposure." *Journal of Advertising Research,* 11(February): 26–32.

113. King, Charles W., and Douglas J. Tigert, Eds. (1971), *Attitude Research Reaches New Heights.* Chicago: American Marketing Association.

114. Kinnear, Thomas C., James R. Taylor, and Sadrudin A. Ahmed (1972), "Socioeconomic and Personality Characteristics as They Related to Ecologically Constructive Purchasing Behavior." In *Proceedings 3rd Conference,* Ed. M. Venketesan. College Park, MD: Association for Consumer Research, pp. 34–60.

115. ______ (1974), "Ecologically Concerned Consumers: Who Are They?" *Journal of Marketing,* 38(April): 20–24.

116. Kirchner, Donald F. (1971), "Personal Influence, Ordinal Position and Purchasing Behavior." In *Proceedings 2nd Conference,* Ed. David M. Gardner. College Park, MD: Association for Consumer Research, pp. 82–98.

117. Koponen, Arthur (1960), "Personality Characteristics of Purchasers." *Journal of Advertising Research,* 1(September): 6–12.

118. Landon, E. Laird, Jr. (1972), "A Sex-Role Explanation of Purchase Intention Differences of Consumers Who are High and Low in Need Achievement." In *Proceedings 3rd Conference,* Ed. M. Venkatesan. College Park, MD: Association for Consumer Research, pp. 1–8.

119. ______ (1974), "Self Concept, Ideal Self Concept, and Consumer Purchase Intentions." *Journal of Consumer Research,* 1(September): 44–51.

120. Lastovicka, John L., and Erich A. Joachimsthaler (1988), "Improving the Detection of Personality-Behavior Relationships in Consumer Research." *Journal of Consumer Research,* 14(March): 583–587.

121. Lastovicka, John L., John P. Murray, Jr., Erich A. Joachimsthaler, Gauray Bhalla, and Jim Scheurich (1987), "A Lifestyle Typology to Model Young Male Drinking and Driving." *Journal of Consumer Research,* 14(September): 257–263.

122. Lazer, William (1963), "Life Style Concepts and Marketing." In *Proceedings of Winter Conference.* Chicago: American Marketing Association, pp. 130–139.

123. Lehmann, Stanley (1970), "Personality and Compliance: A Study of Anxiety and Self-Esteem in Opinion and Behavior Change." *Journal of Personality and Social Psychology,* 15(May): 76–86.

124. Lessig, V. Parker, and John O. Tollefson (1971), "Marketing Segmentation Through Numerical Taxonomy." *Journal of Marketing Research,* 8(November): 480–487.

125. Levy, Sidney J. (1959), "Symbols for Sales." *Harvard Business Review,* 37(July/August): 117–124.

126. Lewin, Kurt (1935), *A Dynamic Theory of Personality.* New York: McGraw-Hill, pp. 43–65.

127. Linton, Harriet, and Elaine Graham (1959), "Personality Correlates of Persuasibility." In *Personality and Persuasibility,* Ed. Carl I. Hoviland and Irving L. Janis. New Haven, CT: Yale University Press, pp. 69–101.

128. Martineau, Pierre (1957), *Motivation in Advertising.* New York: McGraw-Hill.

129. Martin, Warren S. (1973), *Personality and Product Symbolism.* Austin, TX: Bureau of Business Research, Graduate School of Business, University of Texas.

130. Mason, Joseph Barry, and Morris L. Mayer (1970), "The Problem of the Self-Concept in Store Image Studies." *Journal of Marketing,* 34(April): 67–69.

131. Massy, William F., Ronald E. Frank, and

Thomas M. Lodahl (1968), *Purchasing Behavior and Personal Attributes.* Philadelphia: University of Pennsylvania Press.

132. Mathews, H. Lee, John W. Slocum, Jr., and Arch G. Woodside (1971), "Perceived Risk, Individual Differences, and Shopping Orientation." In *Proceedings 2nd Conference,* Ed. David M. Gardner. College Park, MD: Association for Consumer Research, pp. 299–306.
133. Mazis, Michael B., and Timothy W. Sweeney (1972), "Novelty and Personality with Risk as a Moderating Variable." In *Combined Proceedings.* Chicago: American Marketing Association, pp. 406–411.
134. Michaels, Peter W. (1972), "Life Style and Magazine Exposure." In *Combined Proceedings.* Chicago: American Marketing Association, pp. 324–331.
135. Michman, Ronald D. (1971), "Market Segmentation Strategies: Pitfalls and Potentials." In *Combined Proceedings.* Chicago: American Marketing Association, pp. 322–326.
136. Mizerski, Richard W., and Robert B. Settle (1979), "The Influence of Social Character on Preference for Social Versus Objective Information in Advertising." *Journal of Marketing Research,* 16(November): 552–558.
137. Morganosky, Michelle Ann, and Hilda Mayer Buckley (1987), "Complaint Behavior: Analysis by Demographics, Lifestyle, and Consumer Values." *Proceedings 14th Conference,* Ed. Melanie Wallendorf and Paul Anderson. Association for Consumer Research, pp. 223–226.
138. Morris, George P., and Edward W. Cundiff (1971), "Acceptance by Males of Feminine Products." *Journal of Marketing Research,* 8(August): 372–374.
139. Morrison, Bruce John, and Richard C. Sherman (1972), "Who Responds to Sex in Advertising." *Journal of Advertising Research,* 12(April): 15–19.
140. Munson, J. Michael, and Shelby H. McIntyre (1979), "Developing Practical Procedures for the Measurement of Personal Values in Cross-Cultural Marketing." *Journal of Marketing Research,* 16(February): 48–52.
141. Munson, J. Michael, and Edward F. McQuarrie (1988), "Shortening the Rokeach Value Survey for Use in Consumer Research." *Proceedings 15th Conference,* Ed. Michael J. Houston. Association for Consumer Research, pp. 381–386.
142. Myers, John G. (1967), "Determination of Private Brand Attitudes." *Journal of Marketing Research,* 4(February): 73–81.
143. ______ (1968), *Consumer Image and Attitude.* Berkeley, CA: Institute of Business and Economic Research, University of California.
144. Nakanishi, Masao (1972), "Personality and Consumer Behavior: Extensions." In *Proceedings 3rd Conference,* Ed. M. Venkatesan. College Park, MD: Association for Consumer Research, pp. 61–65.
145. Nicely, Roy E. (1972), "E, I-O, and CAD Correlations." Unpublished working paper, Virginia Polytechnic Institute and State University.
146. Noerager, Jon P. (1979), "An Assessment of CAD-A Personality Instrument Developed Specifically for Marketing Research." *Journal of Marketing Research,* 16(February): 53–59.
147. Ostlund, Lyman E. (1969), "The Role of Product Perceptions in Innovative Behavior." In *Proceedings of Fall Conference.* Chicago: American Marketing Association, pp. 259–266.
148. ______ (1971), "The Interaction of Self Confidence Variables in the Context of Innovative Behavior." In *Proceedings, 2nd Conference,* Ed. David M. Gardner. College Park, MD: Association for Consumer Research, pp. 351–357.
149. ______ (1972), "Identifying Early Buyers." *Journal of Advertising Research,* 12(April): 25–30.
150. Paul, Gordon W., and Ben M. Enis (1969), "Psychological and Socioeconomic A Typicality of Consumer Panel Members." In *Proceedings of Fall Conference.* Chicago: American Marketing Association, pp. 387–391.
151. Pennington, Allan A., and Robert A. Peterson (1969), "Interest Patterns and Product Preferences: An Exploratory Analysis." *Journal of Marketing Research,* 6(August): 284–290.
152. Perry, Arnon (1973), "Heredity, Personality Traits, Product Attitude and Product Consumption—An Exploratory Study." *Journal of Marketing Research,* 10(November): 376–379.
153. Pessemier, Edgar A., and T. P. Hustad (1971), "Segmenting Consumer Markets with Activity and Attitude Measures." Unpublished paper, Marketing Science Institute, 1971.
154. Pessemier, Edgar A., and Douglas J. Tigert (1967), "Socio-Economic Status of the

Family and Housewife Personality, Life Style and Opinion Factors." Paper No. 197. Lafayette, IN: Institute for Research on the Behavioral, Economic and Management Sciences, Purdue University.

155. PETERS, MICHAEL P., and M. VENKATESAN (1973), "Exploration of Variables Inherent in Adopting an Industrial Product." *Journal of Marketing Research,* 19(August): 312-315.

156. PETERS, WILLIAM H., and NEIL M. FORD (1972), "A Profile of Urban Inhome Shoppers: The Other Half." *Journal of Marketing,* 36 (January): 62-64.

157. PETERSON, ROBERT A. (1972), "Psychographics and Media Exposure." *Journal of Advertising Research,* 12(June): 17-20.

158. PETERSON, ROBERT A., and ALLAN L. PENNINGTON (1969), "SVIB Interests and Product Preference." *Journal of Applied Psychology,* 53(August): 304-308.

159. PLUMMER, JOSEPH T. (1971), "Life Style and Advertising: Case Studies." In *Combined Proceedings.* Chicago: American Marketing Association, pp. 290-295.

160. ______ (1971), "Life Style Patterns and Commercial Bank Credit Card Usage." *Journal of Marketing,* 35(April): 35-41.

161. REYNOLDS, FRED D., and WILLIAM R. DARDEN (1972), "An Operational Construction of Life Style." In *Proceedings 3rd Conference,* Ed. M. Venkatesan. College Park, MD: Association for Consumer Research, pp. 475-489.

162. RICHARDS, ELIZABETH A., and STEPHEN S. STURMAN (1977), "Life-Style Segmentation in Apparel Marketing." *Journal of Marketing,* 41(October): 89-91.

163. ROBERTS, MARY LOU, and LAWRENCE H. WORTZEL (1979), "New Life-Style Determinants of Women's Food Shopping Behavior." *Journal of Marketing,* 43(Summer): 28-39.

164. ROBERTSON, THOMAS S. (1971), *Innovation and the Consumer.* New York: Holt, Rinehart & Winston.

165. ROBERTSON, THOMAS S., and JAMES H. MYERS (1969), "Personality Correlates of Opinion Leadership and Innovative Buying Behavior." *Journal of Marketing Research,* 7(May): 164-168.

166. ______ (1970), "Personality Correlates of Innovative Buying Behavior: A Reply." *Journal of Marketing Research,* 7(May): 260-261.

167. ROSS, IVAN (1971), "Self Concept and Brand Preference." *Journal of Business,* 44(January): 38-50.

168. RUSH, DUDLEY M. (1966), "Limitations of Current Approaches to Understanding Brand Buying Behavior." In *On Knowing the Consumer,* Ed. Joseph W. Newman. New York: Wiley, pp. 174-186.

169. SCHANINGER, CHARLES, and V. PARKER LESSIG (1978), "Sparks and Tucker Revisited: A Reanalysis and Replication." *Advances in Consumer Research,* Vol. 5, Ed. H. Keith Hunt. Ann Arbor, MI: Association for Consumer Research, pp. 295-299.

170. SCHUCHMAN, ABE, and MICHAEL PERRY (1969), "Self-Confidence and Persuasibility in Marketing: A Reappraisal." *Journal of Marketing Research,* 6(May): 146-154.

171. SIRGY, M. JOSEPH (1982), "Self-Concept in Consumer Behavior: A Critical Review." *Journal of Consumer Research,* 9(December): 298-300.

172. SLAMA, MARK E., TERRELL G. WILLIAMS, ARMEN TASHCHIAN (1988), "Compliant, Aggressive and Detached Types Differ in Generalized Purchasing Involvement." *Proceedings 15th Conference,* Ed. Michael J. Houston. Association for Consumer Research, pp. 158-162.

173. SOMMERS, MONTROSE S. (1963), "Product Symbolism and the Perception of Social Strata." In *Proceedings of Winter Conference.* Chicago: American Marketing Association, pp. 200-216.

174. ______ (1964), "The Use of Product Symbolism to Differentiate Social Strategy." *University of Houston Business Review,* 11(Fall): 1-102.

175. SPARKS, DAVID L., and TUCKER, W. T. (1971), "A Multivariate Analysis of Personality and Product Use." *Journal of Marketing Research,* 9(February): 67-70.

176. SUMMERS, JOHN O. (1970), "The Identity of Women's Clothing Fashion Opinion Leaders." *Journal of Marketing Research,* (May): 178-185.

177. SWAN, JOHN E., and FREDERICK E. MAY (1970), "Comments on Personality and Persuasibility in Consumer Decision Making." *Journal of Advertising Research,* 10(June): 1-27.

178. SZYBILLO, GEORGE J., SHARON BINSTOK, and LAURANNE BUCHANAN (1979), "Measure Validation of Leisure Time Activities: Time Bud-

gets and Psychographics." *Journal of Marketing Research,* 16(February): 74–79.

179. ______ (1969), "Psychographics: A Test-Retest Reliability Analysis." In *Proceedings of Fall Conference.* Chicago: American Marketing Association, pp. 310–315.

180. TIGERT, DOUGLAS J., and STEPHEN J. ARNOLD. (1971), "Profiling Self-Designated Opinion Leaders and Self-Designated Innovators Through Life Style Research." In *Proceedings 2nd Conference,* Ed. David M. Gardner. Ann Arbor, MI: Association for Consumer Research, 425–445.

181. TSE, DAVID K., JOHN K. WONG, and CHIN TIONG TAN (1988), "Towards Some Standardized Cross-Cultural Consumption Values." *Proceedings 15th Conference,* Ed. Michael J. Houston, pp. 387–395.

182. TUCKER, WILLIAM T. (1967), *Foundations for a Theory of Consumer Behavior.* New York: Holt, Rinehart & Winston.

183. TUCKER, WILLIAM T., and JOHN PAINTER (1961), "Personality and Product Use." *Journal of Applied Psychology,* 45(October): 325–329.

184. VAVRA, TERRY G., and PAUL R. WINN (1971), "Fear Appeals in Advertising: An Investigation of the Influence of Order, Anxiety and Involvement." In *Combined Proceedings.* Chicago: American Marketing Association, pp. 444–449.

185. VENKATESAN, M. (1968), "Personality and Persuasibility in Consumer Decision Making." *Journal of Advertising Research,* 8(March): 39–45.

186. ______ (1970), "Personality and Persuasibility in Consumer Decision Making: A Reply." *Journal of Advertising Research,* 10(June): 1–12.

187. VILLANI, KATHRYN E. A., and YORAM WIND (1975), "On the Usage of 'Modified' Personality Trait Measures in Consumer Research." *Journal of Consumer Research,* 2(December): 223–228.

188. VINSON, DONALD E., J. MICHAEL MUNSON, and MASAO NAKANISHI (1977), "An Investigation of the Rokeach Survey for Consumer Behavior Applications." *Advances in Consumer Research,* Vol. 4, Ed. William D. Perreault, Jr. Atlanta, GA: Association for Consumer Behavior, pp. 247–252.

189. VINSON, DONALD E., JEROME E. SCOTT, and LAWRENCE M. LAMONT (1977), "The Role of Personal Values in Marketing and Consumer Behavior." *Journal of Marketing,* 41(April): 44–50.

190. VITZ, PAUL C., and DONALD JOHNSTON (1965), "Masculinity of Smokers and the Masculinity of Cigarette Images." *Journal of Applied Psychology,* 49(June): 155–159.

191. WARREN, WILLIAM E., C. L. ABERCROMBIE, and ROBERT L. BERL (1988), "Characteristics of Adopters and Nonadopters of Alternative Residential Long-Distance Telephone Services." *Proceedings 15th Conference, Ed. Michael J. Houston. Association for Consumer Research,* pp. 292–298.

192. WEBSTER, FREDERICK E., JR. (1975), "Determining the Characteristics of the Socially Conscious Consumer." Unpublished paper.

193. WEBSTER, FREDERICK E., JR., and FREDRICK VON PECHMANN (1970), "A Replication of the 'Shopping List' Study." *Journal of Marketing,* 34(April): 61–63.

194. WELLS, WILLIAM D. (1966), "General Personality Tests and Consumer Behavior." In *On Knowing the Consumer,* Ed. Joseph Newman. New York: Wiley, pp. 187–189.

195. ______ (1968), "Backward Segmentation." In *Insights into Consumer Behavior,* Ed. Johan Arndt. Boston: Allyn & Bacon, pp. 85–100.

196. ______ (1974), *Life Style and Psychographics.* Chicago: American Marketing Association.

197. ______ (1975), "Psychographics: A Critical Review." *Journal of Marketing Research,* 12(May): 196–213.

198. WELLS, WILLIAM D., and ARTHUR D. BEARD (1973), "Personality and Consumer Behavior." In *Consumer Behavior: Theoretical Sources,* Eds. Scott Ward and Thomas S. Robertson. Englewood Cliffs, NJ: Prentice-Hall, pp. 141–199.

199. WELLS, WILLIAM D., and DOUGLAS J. TIGERT (1971), "Activities, Interests and Opinions." *Journal of Advertising Research,* 11(August): 27–35.

200. WESTFALL, RALPH (1962), "Psychological Factors in Predicting Product Choice." *Journal of Marketing,* 26(April): 34–40.

201. WHEATLEY, J. J., and S. OSHIKAWA (1970), "The Relationship Between Anxiety and Positive and Negative Advertising Appeals." *Journal of Marketing Research,* 7: 85–89.

202. WILSON, CLARK L. (1966), "Homemaker Living Patterns and Market-place Behavior—A

Psychometric Approach." In *Proceedings of World Congress.* Chicago: American Marketing Association, pp. 305–331.

203. WILSON, DAVID T., H. LEE MATHEWS, and TIMOTHY W. SWEENEY (1971), "Industrial Buyer Segmentation: A Psychographic Approach." In *Combined Proceedings.* Chicago: American Marketing Association, pp. 327–331.

204. WINICK, CHARLES (1961), "The Relationship Among Personality Needs, Objective Factors, and Brand Choice: A Re-examination." *Journal of Business,* 34(January): 61–66.

205. WINTER, EDWARD, and JOHN T. RUSSELL (1973), "Psychographics and Creativity." *Journal of Advertising,* 2: 32–35.

206. WISEMAN, FREDERICK (1971), "A Segmentation Analysis on Automobile Buyers During the New Model Year Transition Period." *Journal of Marketing,* 35(April): 42–49.

207. WOODSIDE, ARCH G. (1969), "Social Character, Product Use and Advertising Appeal." *Journal of Advertising Research,* 8(December): 31–35.

208. ——— (1974), "Effects of Prior Decision Making, Demographics and Psychographics on Marital Roles for Purchasing Durables." In *Proceedings.* Association for Consumer Research, pp. 81–91.

209. WORTHING, PARKER M., M. VENKATESAN, and STEVE SMITH (1971), "A Modified Approach to the Exploration of Personality and Product Use." In *Combined Proceedings.* Chicago: American Marketing Association, pp. 363–367.

210. ——— (1973), "Personality and Product Use Revisited: An Exploration with the Personality Research Form." *Journal of Applied Psychology,* 57(April): 179–183.

211. ZIFF, RUTH (1971), "Psychographics for Market Segmentation." *Journal of Advertising Research,* 11(April): 3–9.

212. ——— (1972), "Closing the Consumer-Advertising Gap Through Psychographics." *Combined Proceedings.* Chicago: American Marketing Association, pp. 457–461.

213. ZINKHAN, GEORGE M., and ALI SHERMOHAMAD (1986), "Is Other-Directedness on the Increase? An Empirical Test of Riesman's Theory of Social Character." *Journal of Consumer Research,* 13(June): 127–130.

17

THE EXPERIENTIAL ASPECTS OF CONSUMPTION: Consumer Fantasies, Feelings, and Fun*

Morris B. Holbrook
Elizabeth C. Hirschman

This paper argues for the recognition of important experiential aspects of consumption. Specifically, a general framework is constructed to represent typical consumer behavior variables. Based on this paradigm, the prevailing information processing model is contrasted with an experiential view that focuses on the symbolic, hedonic, and esthetic nature of consumption. This view regards the consumption experience as a phenomenon directed toward the pursuit of fantasies, feelings, and fun.

In its brief history, the study of consumer behavior has evolved from an early emphasis on rational choice (microeconomics and classical decision theory) to a focus on apparently irrational buying needs (some motivation research) to the use of logical flow models of bounded rationality (e.g., Howard and Sheth 1969). The latter approach has deepened into what is often called the "information processing model" (Bettman 1979). The information processing model regards the consumer as a logical thinker who solves problems to make purchasing decisions. The information processing perspective has become so ubiquitous in consumer research that, like fish in water, many researchers may be relatively unaware of its pervasiveness.

Recently, however, researchers have begun to question the hegemony of the information

*Reprinted from the *Journal of Consumer Research,* 9 (September 1982), pp. 132–140.

processing perspective on the grounds that it may neglect important consumption phenomena (e.g., Olshavsky and Granbois 1979; Sheth 1979). Ignored phenomena include various playful leisure activities, sensory pleasures, daydreams, esthetic enjoyment, and emotional responses. Consumption has begun to be seen as involving a steady flow of fantasies, feelings, and fun encompassed by what we call the "experiential view." This experiential perspective is phenomenological in spirit and regards consumption as a primarily subjective state of consciousness with a variety of symbolic meanings, hedonic responses, and esthetic criteria. Recognition of these important aspects of consumption is strengthened by contrasting the information processing and experiential views.[1]

CONTRASTING VIEWS OF CONSUMER BEHAVIOR

Our bases for contrasting the information processing and experiential views appear in Figure 17.1. This diagram is not all-inclusive. It simply represents some key variables typically considered in logical flow models of consumer behavior. In brief, various environmental and consumer inputs (products, resources) are processed by an intervening response system (cognition-affect-behavior) that generates output consequences which, when appraised against criteria, result in learning feedback loop. Individual differences, search activity, type of involvement, and task definition affect the criteria by which output consequences are evaluated.

Though Figure 17.1 neglects some variables that have interested consumer researchers,[2] it reflects the general viewpoint embodied by most popular consumer behavior models. Moreover, the diagram facilitates the intended comparison between approaches by distinguishing between the phenomena of primary interest to the information processing perspective (left side of slash marks) and those of central concern to the experiential view (right side of slash marks). In the following sections, we discuss these distinctions as they pertain to (1) environmental inputs, (2) consumer inputs, (3) intervening responses, and (4) output consequences, criteria, and learning effects.

ENVIRONMENTAL INPUTS

Products

Much consumer research has focused on the tangible benefits of conventional goods and services (soft drinks, toothpaste, automobiles) that perform utilitarian functions based on relatively objective features (calories, fluoride, miles per gallon). By contrast, the experiential perspective explores the symbolic meanings of more subjective characteristics (cheerfulness, sociability, elegance).

All products—no matter how mundane—may carry a symbolic meaning (Levy 1959, 1980). In some cases, the symbolic role is especially rich and salient: for example, entertainment, the arts, and leisure activities encompass symbolic aspects of consumption behavior that make them particularly fertile ground for research. These areas have recently received increased attention from consumer researchers concerned with products like musical recordings, singers, fashion designs, architectural styles, paintings, museum exhibitions, novels, concerts, performing arts series, and associated patterns of leisure activity (Hirschman and Holbrook 1981). The growth of research on leisure, entertainment, and the arts reflects a shift of attention toward the experiential side of the distinctions shown in Figure 17.1

Methodologically, this shift promotes certain advantages. One benefit stems from the tendency for leisure, entertainment, and arts prod-

[1]Throughout the discussion, most arguments are supported by one or two key references. Much more extensive documentation appears in earlier versions of the paper that may be obtained from the authors.

[2]For example, Figure 17.1 omits the effects of general economic conditions and related expectations, some elements of the marketing mix (e.g., channels of distribution), social influence through reference groups, perceived risk and other conflict-related phenomena, joint decision making in households, and considerations of economic externalities or social welfare.

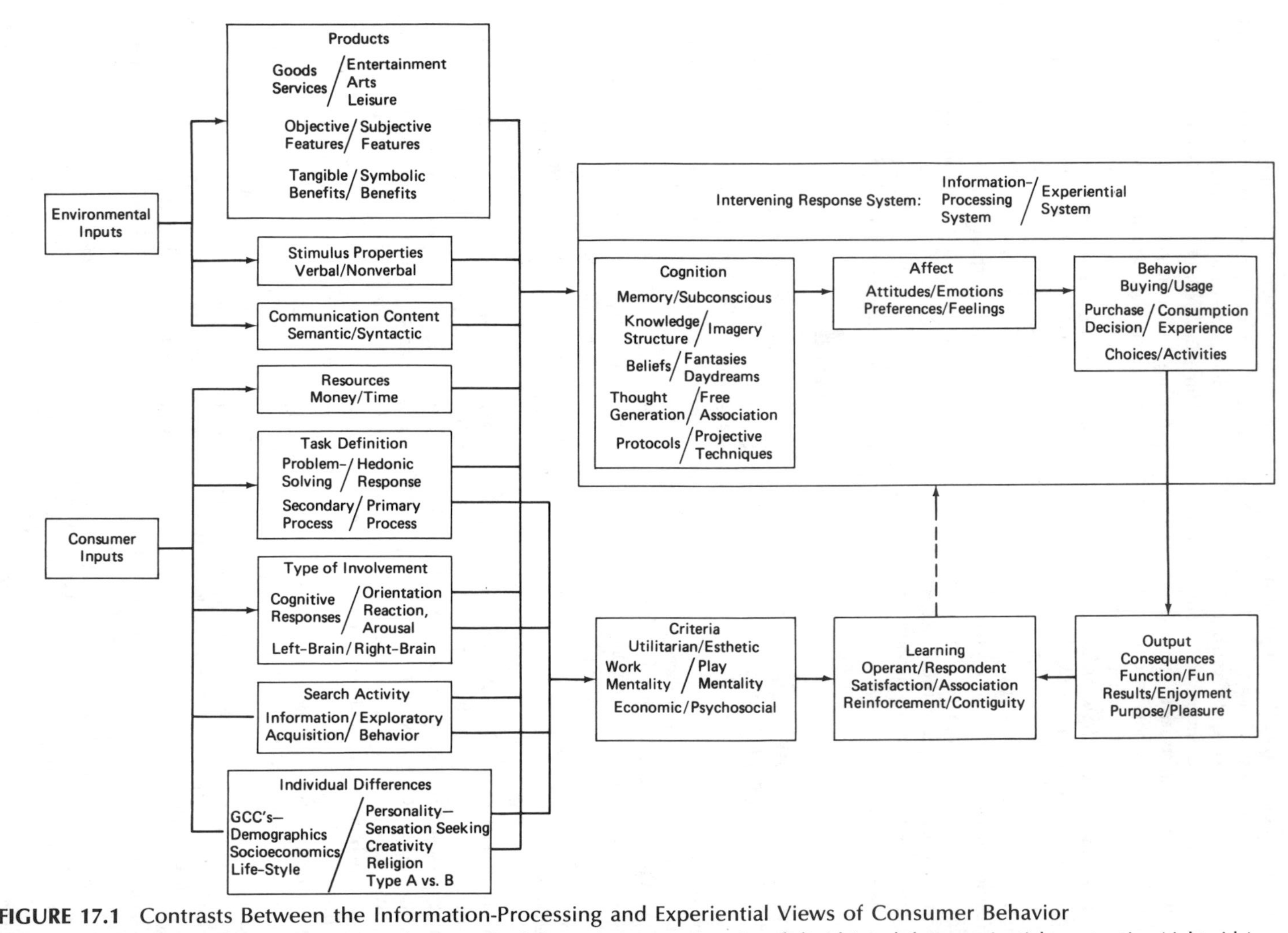

FIGURE 17.1 Contrasts Between the Information-Processing and Experiential Views of Consumer Behavior

Note: The slash marks indicate a comparison between the information-processing view (left side) and the experiential perspective (right side).

ucts to prompt high levels of interest and involvement among their target markets. The growing body of work in these areas suggests that respondents can typically provide meaningful data on perceptions and preferences across a broad array of relevant objects or activities. Hence, applications of multivariate methods may be more valid with this type of product than with some low-involvement consumer nondurables, such as detergents or canned peas, for which consumers may be unable to make valid perceptual or affective distinctions among more than a few different brands. For this reason, many of our available statistical procedures—especially those directed toward intraindividual analysis across brands—may actually be more appropriate within the context of experiential consumption than for the frequently purchased nondurables to which they have typically been applied.

Stimulus Properties

Traditional consumer research paradigms have concentrated on product attributes that lend themselves to verbal descriptions. Both conjoint analysis and multiattribute models, for example, have relied heavily on designs that make use of verbal stimuli. However, many products project important nonverbal cues that must be seen, heard, tasted, felt, or smelled to be appreciated properly. Indeed, in many consumption situations (viewing a movie, eating at a restaurant, playing tennis), several sensory channels operate simultaneously. Yet scant research on nonverbal multisensory properties has been reported in the literature. Accordingly, the experiential perspective supports a more energetic investigation of multisensory psychophysical relationships in consumer behavior.

Turning one's attention from primary verbal to nonverbal sensory cues requires a very different mode of presenting experimental stimulus objects. While verbal descriptions have often sufficed in conventional research on consumer preferences, an experiential outlook must involve subjects in consumption-like experiences based on real—or at least realistic—product samples.

Communication Content

Content analyses of communication in consumer research have more often focused on drawing inferences about the source of a message than on explaining its effects (Kassarjian 1977). When the latter perspective has been considered, it has generally involved an information processing orientation toward the study of consumer responses to the semantic aspects of communication content (Shimp and Preston 1981). Focusing on effects attributable to the syntactic aspects of message content—that is, their structure and style—is more germane to the experiential perspective.

In other disciplines, message syntax has often been found to exert a directed effect on hedonic response. This concept is central, for example, to the so-called Wundt curve and its relationship to collative stimulus properties such as uncertainty or complexity (Berlyne 1971). This information theoretic perspective has been applied at length in analyses of emotional responses to music and other art forms by researchers exploring its relevance to the esthetic process (Platt 1970).

Work on syntactic structure in consumer research is less well developed. However, Taylor's (1953) "Cloze" technique has been used to measure subjective verbal uncertainty in English prose (Wallendorf, Zinkhan, and Zinkhan 1981) and advertising copy (Zinkhan and Martin 1981).

CONSUMER INPUTS

Resources

In examining the resources that a consumer brings to the exchange transaction, conventional research has generally focused on monetary income constraints and the effects of prices. In more recent economic analysis, this money-oriented focus has been expanded to acknowledge the fundamental role played by the consumer's allocation of time resources to the "household production function" (Becker 1976). In this view, households both produce and consume "commodities" that combine inputs of goods and time to maximize overall utility, subject to resource constraints.

The investigation of subjective time resources may help to unravel the mysteries of the psychotemporal expenditures involved in experiential consumption. Studying the nature and allocation of discretionary time deserves high priority. Movement in this direction has appeared in several review articles, in special conference sessions, and in a recent issue of the *Journal of Consumer Research* devoted to the subject of time in consumer behavior (March 1981).

Task Definition

In making assumptions concerning the consumer's task definition, the information processing and experiential perspectives envision different kinds of consumption behavior. The information processing view conjures up an image of the consumer as a problem solver engaged in the goal-directed activities of searching for information, retrieving memory cues, weighing evidence, and arriving at carefully considered judgmental evaluations. Freud called such mental activities "secondary process" thinking. It is "secondary" in the sense that it reflects the way our mental processes function as a result of socialization (Hilgard 1962).

By contrast, the experiential view emphasizes the importance of primary process thinking in accord with the pleasure principle. Primary process thinking involves a task definition oriented toward hedonic response and is "primary" in the sense that it hearkens back to the way a baby pursues immediate pleasure or gratification (Hilgard 1962). This type of consumption seeks fun, amusement, fantasy, arousal, sensory stimulation, and enjoyment. Indeed, the evidence suggests that consumers typically spend the majority of their lives eating, sleeping, chatting with friends, making love, and watching television (Robinson 1977, p. 35). Surely, any meaningful attempt to model such relatively pleasure-oriented consumption must pay attention to its hedonic components.

Regarding consumption as a primary process directed toward the hedonic pursuit of pleasure raises certain methodological issues. These include (1) the need to develop better measures of hedonic response—especially valid and operational definitions of what constitutes "pleasure"; (2) the fact that hedonic responses are likely to be unusually susceptible to fluctuations across situations, thereby posing problems of reliability and validity; and (3) the difficulty of using available indices of chronic hedonic energy, such as sensation seeking, in the context of explaining acute, volatile, sensory-emotive phenomena. The experiential view performs a useful role by insistently calling attention to these conceptual and methodological problems.

Type of Involvement

We focus here not on the degree of involvement (low versus high), but rather on its type (engagement of cognitive responses versus orientation reaction involving arousal). Krugman's (1965) early definition of involvement emphasized the tendency to make personal connections between one's own life and the stimulus, explicitly excluding components such as attention, interest, or excitement. This early view has proven most congenial to information processing proponents, who define involvement in terms of personal relevance or multiplicity of cognitive responses (Leavitt, Greenwald, and Obermiller 1981). Attention, interest, excitement, and so forth bear more directly on the experiential view by emphasizing degree of activation or arousal, with consequent implications for the availability of psychobiological indices (Kroeber-Riel 1979). Krugman's (1971) later work on brain-wave patterns has moved in this direction and thus appears to represent a shift toward the experiential model.

Further, any argument that involvement is primarily a left-brain phenomenon refers implicitly to cognitive responses associated with analytic, logical, problem-oriented cerebration

(Hansen 1981). If one referred instead to "involvement" in the sense of the orientation reflex, its arousal component might be more closely associated with right-brain phenomena related to emotion.

The use of psychobiological indices of arousal and the interest in right-brain hemispheric specialization have prompted increased attention from consumer researchers. Numerous problems arise when interpreting the results of these physiological approaches. Ryan (1980) has challenged the construct validity of psychobiological measures. In this light, Olson, Reynolds, and Ray's (1982) findings on psychophysiological advertising effects raise almost as many questions as they answer. Similarly, Hansen and Lundsgaard (1981) have reported rather discouraging convergent validities among various indices of brain lateralization. Taken together, these difficulties point out that work on the physiological components of consumption remains in its infancy and needs further conceptual and methodological development in measures of arousal and hemispheric involvement.

Search Activity

The nature of the associated search activity is closely tied to involvement issues. Here, proponents of the information processing perspective adopt various strategies for the study of information acquisition. Those inclined toward laboratory methods have developed ingenious techniques to study how cues are acquired (Russo 1978). Meanwhile, survey researchers have investigated the general characteristics of information seekers at the cross-cultural level (Thorelli, Becker, and Engledow 1975).

By contrast, an experiential view of search activity might draw more heavily from the work by psychologists on exploratory behavior (Berlyne 1960). For example, Howard and Sheth (1969) consider stimulus ambiguity, working through arousal, as a determinant of specific exploration via what they call "overt search." More diversive exploration—such as that involved in exposure to entertainment media—has sometimes been explained as a form of play, as in the "ludic" theory of mass communication (Huizinga 1970; Stephenson 1967).

Diversive exploration via the entertainment and arts media appears to be a context well suited to the extension of Berlyne's (1960) work on exploratory behavior. Indeed, toward the end of his career, Berlyne (1971) devoted increased attention to the experimental study of esthetics, focusing particularly on a proposed nonmonotonic relationship between stimulus complexity and hedonic value. Aspects of his approach may be usefully applied to an investigation of the consumption experience. However, in making such extensions, three methodological refinements appear critical: (1) esthetic stimuli should be designed to vary in complexity over a range broad enough to permit the full nonmonotonic relationship to appear; (2) the success of this experimental manipulation should be checked by obtaining a measure of subjective uncertainty analogous to the Cloze-based index described earlier; and (3) the subjective uncertainty measure should be treated as an intervening variable that mediates the effect of stimulus complexity on hedonic response.

Individual Differences

For some time, consumer researchers' interest in individual differences has focused on general customer characteristics such as demographics, socioeconomic status, and psychographics. The relatively poor performance of personality measures in predicting consumer behavior has encouraged their gradual abandonment in favor of the subcategory of psychographics known as life style variables. Recently, in a move toward the experiential view, the concept of lifestyle has been generalized to include more explicit consideration of the use of time (Lee and Ferber 1977).

The investigation of experiential consumption appears to offer considerable scope for the revival of personality and allied variables, such as subculture, though the specific dimensions investigated will almost certainly differ from those of interest to the information processing view. Some experientially relevant personality constructs include:

- *Sensation seeking* (Zuckerman 1979), a variable likely to affect a consumer's tendency to enjoy more complex entertainment, to be fashion conscious, to prefer spicy and crunchy foods, to play games, and to use drugs
- *Creativity* and related variables tied to variety-, novelty-, or arousal-seeking (Raju 1980)
- *Religious world view* (Hirschman 1982), a dimension that affects daydreaming as well as other forms of sensation and pleasure seeking
- *Type A versus Type B personality* (Friedman and Rosenman 1974), a dimension closely linked with perceived time pressure and therefore likely to affect the way one allocates psychotemporal expenditures among work and leisure activities

Research on individual differences in experiential consumption has already found contrasts among religions and nationalities in the types of entertainment preferred, hedonic motives for engaging in leisure activities, and resulting levels of enthusiasm expressed. These ethnic differences appear to depend on intervening variables such as use of imagery, sensation seeking, and the desire to escape reality.

INTERVENING RESPONSE SYSTEM

Cognition

Due to its cognitively oriented perspective, the information processing approach has focused on memory and related phenomena: the consumer's cognitive apparatus is viewed as a complex knowledge structure embodying intricately interwoven subsystems of beliefs referred to as "memory schemas" or "semantic networks" (Olson 1980). Such knowledge structures include what Freudians call "manifest" content—those ideas that are accessible to introspection and therefore form the substances of conscious thought patterns.

By contrast, the experiential perspective focuses on cognitive processes that are more subconscious and private in nature. Interest centers on consumption-related flights of fancy involving pictorial imagery (Richardson 1969), fantasies (Klinger 1971), and daydreams (Singer 1966). Such material often masks embarrassing or socially sensitive ideas and perceptions. This "latent" content does not appear in overt verbal reports, either because it has been repressed or because its anxiety-provoking nature encourages disguise at a subconscious level.

In its treatment of cognitive phenomena, particularly material of a subconscious nature, the experiential view borders somewhat on motivation research (e.g., Dichter 1960). However, there are two methodological differences. First, we believe that much relevant fantasy life and many key symbolic meanings lie just below the threshold of consciousness—that is, that they are subconscious or preconscious as opposed to unconscious—and that they can be retrieved and reported if sufficiently indirect methods are used to overcome sensitivity barriers. Second, we advocate the use of structured projective techniques that employ quantifiable questionnaire items applicable to samples large enough to permit statistical hypothesis testing.

Affect

It might be argued that, in the area of affect, the conventional information processing approach has been studying experiential consumption all along. After all, the traditional expectancy value models (Σ E • V) conform in spirit to Bentham's felicific calculus. Fundamentally, however, the information processing perspective emphasizes only one aspect of hedonic response—namely, like or dislike of a particular brand (attitude) or its rank relative to other brands (preference). This attitudinal component represents only a tiny subset of the emotions and feelings of interest to the experiential view.

The full gamut of relevant emotions includes such diverse feelings as love, hate, fear, joy, boredom, anxiety, pride, anger, disgust, sadness, sympathy, lust, ecstasy, greed, guilt, elation, shame, and awe. This sphere of human experience has long been neglected by psychologists, who are just beginning to expand early work on arousal in order to develop systematic and coherent models of emotion (Plutchik 1980).

Such psychological conceptualizations of emotion are still in their seminal stages and, understandably, have not yet cross-pollinated the work of consumer researchers. Yet, it is clear that emotions form an important substrate of consumption and that their systematic investigation is a key requirement for the successful application of the experiential perspective.

Behavior

At the behavioral level, traditional consumer research has focused almost exclusively on the choice process that generates purchase decisions culminating in actual buying behavior. Thus, brand purchase is typically viewed as the most important behavioral outcome of the information processing model.

A quarter of a century ago, however, Alderson (1957) drew a sharp distinction between buying and consuming. This contrast was further elaborated in Boyd and Levy's (1963) discussion of the consumption system with its emphasis on brand-usage behavior. By focusing on the configuration of activities involved in consumption, this viewpoint calls attention to the experiences with a product that one gains by actually consuming it.

Few consumer researchers have followed this lead, although the study of product usage and related activities is clearly a requisite cornerstone to the development of the experiential model. The importance of such study is reinforced by the emphasis on entertainment-, arts-, and leisure-related offerings, which often depend more on the allocation of time than of money. Given the operation of the pleasure principle in multisensory gratification, exciting fantasies, and cathected emotions, one's purchase decision is obviously only a small component in the constellation of events involved in the overall consumption experience.

In exploring the nature of that overall experience, the approach envisioned here departs from the traditional positivist focus on directly observable buying behavior and devotes increased attention to the mental events surrounding the act of consumption. The investigation of these mental events requires a willingness to deal with the purely subjective aspects of consciousness. This exploration of consumption as conscious experience must be rigorous and scientific, but the methodology should include introspective reports, rather than relying exclusively on overt behavioral measures. The necessary methodological shift thus leads toward a more phenomenological approach—i.e., "a free commentary on whatever cognitive material the subject is aware of" (Hilgard 1980).[3]

A recent state-of-the-art review of theory, method, and application in the study of conscious experience has been provided by Singer (1981/1982). Comparable approaches in conventional consumer research would include problem-solving protocols, thought-generation techniques, and similar ideation-reporting procedures. It remains for the experiential perspective to extend this cognitively oriented work toward the investigation of *all* aspects of the consumption experience. In such a phenomenological approach, experience is "acknowledged as a part of the psychological universe and addressed as an object of study" (Koch 1964, p. 34):

> The phenomenologist . . . accepts, as the subject-matter of his inquiry, all data of experience. . . . Colors and sounds are data; so are impressions of distance and duration; so are feelings of attraction and repulsion; so are yearnings and fears, ecstasies and disillusionments; . . . .These are data, given in experience, to be accepted as such and wondered about (MacLeod 1964, p. 51).

MacLeod's statement comes close to encapsulating our central theme—namely, that the

[3]The recently accumulating studies on the stream of consciousness serve also to introduce the new introspectionism. In this light, consider the avowed objective of the new journal entitled *Imagination, Cognition and Personality:* "An important purpose of this journal is to provide an interdisciplinary forum for those interested in the scientific study of the stream of consciousness, directly relevant to theory, research, and application" (Pope and Singer 1981/1982, p. 2).

conventional approach to consumer research addresses only a small fraction of the phenomenological data that compose the entire experience of consumption. Investigation of the remaining components of the consumption experience should serve as one key target of future methodological developments in consumer research.

One qualitative approach, advocated by Levy, "accepts introspection as data" and involves the use of personal narratives: "A protocol in which a consumer tells the story of how the product is consumed can be examined for how the consumer interprets the consumption experience" (1981, p. 50). Such relatively unstructured procedures may be usefully complemented by more structured quantitative methods.[4] Toward this end, Pekala and Levine argue for a "phenomenological or introspective approach" to investigate the "structure of conscious experience" (1981/1982, pp. 30–31) and present a Phenomenology of Consciousness Questionnaire (PCQ) consisting of 60 Likert-type items drawn from 15 different content areas. Factor analysis of the PCQ suggests the existence of nine important dimensions: altered experience, awareness, imagery, attention/memory, negative affect, alertness, positive affect, volition, and internal dialogue. This instrument has not (to our knowledge) been applied in consumer research, but future applications may help elucidate the experiential aspects of consumption.

OUTPUT CONSEQUENCES, CRITERIA, AND LEARNING

Output Consequences and Criteria

From the information processing perspective, the consequences of consumer choice typically are viewed in terms of the product's useful function. The criteria for evaluating the success of a purchasing decision are therefore primarily utilitarian in nature—as, when judging a "craft," one asks how well it serves its intended purpose or performs its proper function (Becker 1978). The operative logic behind this criterion reflects a work mentality in which objects attain value primarily by virtue of the economic benefits they provide.

By contrast, in the experiential view, the consequences of consumption appear in the fun that a consumer derives from a product—the enjoyment that it offers and the resulting feeling of pleasure that it evokes (Klinger 1971, p. 18). In this generally neglected perspective, the criteria for successful consumption are essentially esthetic in nature and hinge on an appreciation of the product for its own sake, apart from any utilitarian function that it may or may not perform (McGregor 1974). This is analogous to the appreciation of a work of "art" (versus a "craft") as a thing in itself, without regard to its functional utility (Becker 1978). In making such appraisals, one conforms to a play mentality (Huizinga 1970) wherein perceived benefits are primarily psychosocial and "episodes designated as playful are assumed to be free from any immediate purpose" (Lancy 1980, p. 474): "Play is disinterested, self-sufficient, an interlude from work. It brings no material gain" (Stephenson 1967, pp. 192–193).[5]

As indicated in Figure 17.1, the relative salience of evaluative criteria is assumed to depend in part on the individual's task definition, type of involvement, search activity, and personality. For example, where the consumption task is defined as the pursuit of hedonic response, esthetic criteria would be likely to apply. A similar play mentality should prevail

[4]Levy (1981) views his analysis as "structural." The distinction between "structured" and "unstructured" methods pursued here refers to the type of data-collection procedure.

[5]Note that, in no sense, do we imply that the esthetic criteria involved in the play mentality are irrational or maladaptive. Indeed, as Becker's (1976) work has made clear, rational economic models can be built to account for playful activities—not to mention child bearing, marriage, and other forms of behavior generally viewed as psychosocial or nonpurposive in origin. We merely wish to indicate that, in our current state of knowledge, the psychodynamics of enjoyment and fun are perhaps less well understood than are the more technological and physiological relationships that underlie the conventional utilitarian approach to customer value (cf. Becker 1976, pp. 13–14).

when involvement is primarily right cerebral hemisphere oriented, when diversive exploration is directed toward the alleviation of boredom, and when a sensation-seeking, creative, non-Protestant, or Type B personality is involved.

Consumer researchers have devoted little attention to the underlying determinants of fun and playful activities even though it appears that consumers spend many of their waking hours engaged in events that can be explained on no other grounds. It would be difficult, for example, to account for the popularity of a television program like *Dallas* on the basis of its functional utility in providing solutions to life's many problems. Clearly, its success depends instead on conformity to some set of esthetic standards associated with the play mentality. Better understanding of such standards is a vital link in the further development of the experiential view.

Learning

Ever since Howard and others included a feedback loop via brand satisfaction in the early models of buyer behavior (Howard and Sheth 1969), it has been clear that learning effects exert a strong impact on future components of the intervening response system (shown by a dotted feedback line in Figure 17.1). The traditional view of learning in consumer behavior has been based on operant conditioning or instrumental learning, where satisfaction with the purchase serves to reinforce future behavioral responses in the form of repeat purchases.

But Howard and Sheth (1969) also recognized a second learning principle, contiguity, which depends on the frequency with which neural events have been paired in experience. The resulting patterns of association, which Osgood (1957) called "associative hierarchies," exhibit a form of respondent conditioning. When extended to the experiential perspective, this contiguity principle suggests that sensations, imagery, feelings, pleasures, and other symbolic or hedonic components which are frequently paired together in experience tend to become mutually evocative, so that "fantasy, dreams, and certain forms of play can similarly be construed as respondent sequences" (Klinger 1971, p. 35). This argument implies that—though satisfaction certainly constitutes one important experiential component—the stream of associations that occur during consumption (imagery, daydreams, emotions) may be equally important experiential aspects of consumer behavior.

CONCLUSION

Much buyer behavior can be explained usefully by the prevailing information processing perspective. Conventional research, however, has neglected an important portion of the consumption experience. Thus our understanding of leisure activities, consumer esthetics, symbolic meanings, variety seeking, hedonic response, psychotemporal resources, daydreaming, creativity, emotions, play, and artistic endeavors may benefit from a broadened view.

Abandoning the information processing approach is undesirable, but supplementing and enriching it with an admixture of the experiential perspective could be extremely fruitful. Such an expansion of consumer research will raise vital but previously neglected issues concerning (1) the role of esthetic products, (2) multisensory aspects of product enjoyment, (3) the syntactic dimensions of communication, (4) time budgeting in the pursuit of pleasure, (5) product-related fantasies and imagery, (6) feelings arising from consumption, and (7) the role of play in providing enjoyment and fun. This is the point of asking questions concerning the nature of experiential consumption—questions such as:

- "Which painting is the most beautiful?"
- "Which tastes better, chocolate or strawberry?"
- "What makes Beethoven great?"
- "How much do you watch television?"
- "What do you see when you turn out the lights?"
- "What makes you happy?"
- "How did you spend your vacation?"

In sum, the purpose of this paper has been neither to advocate a "new theory of consumer behavior nor to reject the "old" approach, but rather to argue for an enlarged view that avoids any adherence to the "-isms" or "-ologies" that so often constrict scientific inquiry. One cannot reduce the explanation of human behavior to any narrowly circumscribed and simplistic model, whether that model be behavioristic or psychoanalytic, ethological or anthropomorphic, cognitive or motivational: the behavior of people in general and of consumers in particular is the fascinating and endlessly complex result of a multifaceted interaction between organism and environment. In this dynamic process, neither problem-directed nor experiential components can safely be ignored. By focusing single mindedly on the consumer as information processor, recent consumer research has tended to neglect the equally important experiential aspects of consumption, thereby limiting our understanding of consumer behavior. Future research should work toward redressing this imbalance by broadening our area of study to include some consideration of consumer fantasies, feelings, and fun.

REFERENCES

ALDERSON, WROE (1957), *Marketing Behavior and Executive Action.* Homewood, IL: Irwin.

BECKER, GARY S. (1976), *The Economic Approach to Human Behavior.* Chicago: University of Chicago Press.

BECKER, HOWARD S. (1978), "Arts and Crafts," *American Journal of Sociology,* 83(4), 862–889.

BERLYNE, DANIEL E. (1960), *Conflict, Arousal, and Curiosity.* New York: McGraw-Hill.

——— (1971), *Aesthetics and Psychobiology.* New York: Appleton-Century-Crofts.

BETTMAN, JAMES R. (1979), *An Information Processing Theory of Consumer Choice.* Reading, MA: Addison-Wesley.

BOYD, HARPER W., JR., and SIDNEY J. LEVY (1963), "New Dimensions in Consumer Analysis," *Harvard Business Review,* 41(November/December), 129–140.

DICHTER, ERNEST (1960), *The Strategy of Desire.* Garden City, NY: Doubleday.

FRIEDMAN, MEYER, and RAY H. ROSENMAN (1974), *Type A: Your Behavior and Your Heart.* New York: Knopf.

HANSEN, FLEMMING (1981), "Hemispherical Lateralization: Implications for Understanding Consumer Behavior," *Journal of Consumer Research,* 8(June), 23–36.

———, and NIELS ERIK LUNDSGAARD (1981), "Brain Lateralization and Individual Differences in People's Reaction to Mass Communication," working paper, Copenhagen School of Economics and Business Administration.

HILGARD, ERNEST R. (1962), "Impulsive Versus Realistic Thinking: An Examination of the Distinction Between Primary and Secondary Processes in Thought," *Psychological Bulletin,* 59(6), 477–488.

——— (1980), "Consciousness in Contemporary Psychology," *Annual Review of Psychology,* 31, 1–26.

HIRSCHMAN, ELIZABETH C. (1982), "Religious Affiliation and Consumption Processes: An Initial Paradigm," *Research in Marketing.*

———, and MORRIS B. HOLBROOK, EDS. (1981), *Symbolic Consumer Behavior.* Ann Arbor, MI: Association for Consumer Research.

HOWARD, JOHN A., and JAGDISH N. SHETH (1969), *The Theory of Buyer Behavior.* New York: Wiley.

HUIZINGA, JOHAN (1970), *Homo Ludens: A Study of the Play Element in Culture.* New York: Harper & Row.

KASSARJIAN, HAROLD H. (1977), "Content Analysis in Consumer Research," *Journal of Consumer Research,* 4(June), 8–18.

KLINGER, ERIC (1971), *Structure and Functions of Fantasy.* New York: Wiley-Interscience.

KOCH, SIGMUND (1964), "Psychology and Emerging Conceptions of Knowledge as Unitary," in *Behaviorism and Phenomenology,* Ed. T. W. Wann. Chicago: University of Chicago Press, 1–45.

KROEBER-RIEL, WERNER (1979), "Activation Research: Psychobiological Approaches in Consumer Research," *Journal of Consumer Research,* 5(March), 240–250.

KRUGMAN, HERBERT E. (1965), "The Impact of

Television Advertising: Learning Without Involvement," *Public Opinion Quarterly,* 29(Fall), 349–356.

——— (1971), "Brain Wave Measures of Media Involvement," *Journal of Advertising Research,* 11(February), 3–10.

LANCY, DAVID F. (1980), "Play in Species Adaptation," *Annual Review of Anthropology,* 9, 471–495.

LEAVITT, CLARK, ANTHONY G. GREENWALD, and CARL OBERMILLER (1981), "What is Low Involvement Low In?" in *Advances in Consumer Research,* Vol. 8, Ed. Kent B. Monroe. Ann Arbor, MI: Association for Consumer Research, 15–19.

LEE, LUCY CHAO, and ROBERT FERBER (1977), "Use of Time as a Determinant of Family Market Behavior," *Journal of Business Research,* 5(March), 75–91.

LEVY, SIDNEY J. (1959), "Symbols for Sale," *Harvard Business Review,* 37(July/August), 117–124.

——— (1980), "The Symbolic Analysis of Companies, Brands, and Customers," Albert Wesley Frey Lecture, Graduate School of Business, University of Pittsburgh, PA.

——— (1981), "Interpreting Consumer Mythology: A Structural Approach to Consumer Behavior," *Journal of Marketing,* 45(Summer), 49–61.

MACLEOD, R. B. (1964), "Phenomenology: A Challenge to Experimental Psychology," in *Behaviorism and Phenomenology,* Ed. T. W. Wann. Chicago: University of Chicago Press, 47–78.

MACGREGOR, ROBERT (1974), "Art and the Aesthetic," *Journal of Aesthetics and Art Criticism,* 32(Summer), 549–559.

OLSHAVSKY, RICHARD W., and DONALD H. GRANBOIS (1979), "Consumer Decision Making—Fact or Fiction?" *Journal of Consumer Research,* 6(September), 93–100.

OLSON, JERRY C. (1980), "Encoding Processes: Levels of Processing and Existing Knowledge Structures," in *Advances in Consumer Research,* Vol. 7, Ed. Jerry Olson. Ann Arbor, MI: Association for Consumer Research, 154–160.

———, THOMAS REYNOLDS, and WILLIAM J. RAY (1982), "Using Psychophysiological Measures in Advertising Effects Research," paper presented at the 1981 Convention of the Association for Consumer Research, October 22–25, St. Louis, MO.

OSGOOD, CHARLES E. (1957), "Motivational Dynamics of Language Behavior," in *Nebraska Symposium on Motivation,* Ed. Marshall R. Jones. Lincoln, NE: University of Nebraska Press, 348–424.

PEKALA, RONALD, J., and RALPH L. LEVINE (1981/1982), "Mapping Consciousness: Development of an Empirical-Phenomenological Approach," *Imagination, Cognition and Personality,* 1(1), 29–47.

PLATT, JOHN (1970), *Perception and Change.* Ann Arbor, MI: University of Michigan Press.

PLUTCHIK, ROBERT (1980), *Emotion: A Psychoevolutionary Synthesis.* New York: Harper & Row.

POPE, KENNETH S., and JEROME L. SINGER (1981/1982), "Imagination, Cognition, and Personality: Personal Experience, Scientific Research, and Clinical Application," *Imagination, Cognition and Personality,* 1(1), 1–4.

RAJU, P. S. (1980), "Optimum Stimulation Level: Its Relationship to Personality, Demographics, and Exploratory Behavior," *Journal of Consumer Research,* 7(December), 272–282.

RICHARDSON, ALAN (1969), *Mental Imagery.* New York: Springer.

ROBINSON, JOHN P. (1977), *A Social-Psychological Analysis of Everyday Behavior.* New York: Praeger.

RUSSO, J. EDWARD (1978), "Eye Fixations Can Save the World: A Critical Evaluation and a Comparison Between Eye Fixations and Other Information Processing Methodologies," in *Advances in Consumer Research,* Vol. 5, Ed. H. Keith Hunt. Ann Arbor, MI: Association for Consumer Research, 561–570.

RYAN, MICHAEL J. (1980), "Psychobiology and Consumer Research: A Problem of Construct Validity," *Journal of Consumer Research,* 7(June), 92–96.

SHETH, JAGDISH N. (1979), "The Surpluses and Shortages in Consumer Behavior Theory and Research," *Journal of the Academy of Marketing Science,* 7(4), 414–427.

SHIMP, TERENCE A., and IVAN L. PRESTON (1981), "Deceptive and Nondeceptive Consequences of Evaluative Advertising," *Journal of Marketing,* 45(Winter), 22–32.

SINGER, JEROME L. (1966), *Daydreaming: An Introduction to the Experimental Study of Inner Experience.* New York: Random House.

——— (1981/1982), "Towards the Scientific Study of Imagination," *Imagination, Cognition and Personality,* 1(1), 5–28.

STEPHENSON, WILLIAM (1967), *The Play Theory of Mass Communication.* Chicago: University of Chicago Press.

TAYLOR, WILSON L. (1953), "'Cloze Procedure:' A New Tool for Measuring Readability," *Journalism Quarterly,* 30(Fall), 415–433.

THORELLI, HANS B., HELMUT BECKER, and JACK ENGLEDOW (1975), *The Information Seekers.* Cambridge, MA: Ballinger.

WALLENDORF, MELANIE, GEORGE ZINKHAN, and LYDIA ZINKHAN (1981), "Cognitive Complexity and Aesthetic Preference," in *Symbolic Consumer Behavior,* Ed. Elizabeth C. Hirschman and Morris B. Holbrook. Ann Arbor, MI: Association for Consumer Research, 52–59.

ZINKHAN, GEORGE M., and CLAUDE R. MARTIN, JR. (1981), "Two Copy Testing Techniques: The Cloze Procedure and the Cognitive Complexity Test," working paper, Graduate School of Business, University of Michigan.

ZUCKERMAN, MARVIN (1979), *Sensation Seeking: Beyond the Optimal Level of Arousal.* Hillsdale, NJ: Erlbaum.

18

THE ROLE OF ATTITUDE THEORY IN MARKETING*

Richard J. Lutz

The term *attitude,* like so many concepts in the behavioral sciences, is also a word used in everyday conversation (for example, there is always a basketball player somewhere who has been benched by the coach because of the player's "bad attitude"). Yet, while the everyday use of the term *attitude* is relatively common, the term has a more precise meaning within the context of psychology. As we shall see, the more precise usage of the term *attitude* refers to positive or negative feelings directed at some object, issue, or behavior. Thus, to say that someone "has a bad attitude" is not a meaningful use of the term in a scientific or managerial sense. The purposes of this chapter are (1) to clarify the nature of the attitude concept as it is used in consumer research, (2) to present a brief review of some of the more important theories of attitude formation and change, and (3) to specify the applicability of the attitude concept in a variety of marketing decision-making contexts.

DEFINITION

An *attitude* can be defined as "a learned predisposition to respond in a consistently favorable or unfavorable manner with respect to a given object" (Fishbein and Ajzen 1975, p. 6). Several aspects of this definition bear further discussion.

Attitudes Are Learned

We are not born with the attitudes that we hold toward various objects in our environment. Rather, we learn our feelings of favorability or unfavorability through *information* about the attitude object (for example, from advertising), or through direct *experience* with the attitude object (for example, from tasting a

*This paper was written especially for this volume by Richard J. Lutz.

new brand of beer), or some combination of the two. Because attitudes are learned, and not innate, marketers can attempt to create or modify attitudes toward their brands through the use of marketing communications tools such as advertising, personal selling, product sampling, and the like. Unfortunately, from the marketer's perspective, brand attitudes can also be learned on the basis of information provided by sources unfavorable to the firm's products. For instance, many people developed negative attitudes toward smoking cigarettes based on information provided by the federal government regarding smoking's potentially harmful health effects.

Attitudes Are Predispositions to Respond

Attitudes are not something that can be directly observed by some third party (say, a market researcher). They are not *overt* behaviors; rather they are *covert,* or unobservable, internal reactions. No one has ever seen an attitude, and no one ever will. In fact, we do not even know for sure that attitudes really exist. An attitude is a *hypothetical construct,* which is to say that it is something that can never be directly verified. The existence of attitudes is postulated by theorists seeking to explain behavior. To the extent that people behave as if they truly hold attitudes, then *attitude,* as a construct, is a useful theoretical tool. As we shall see in a later section of this paper, attitude is perhaps the most widely used theoretical construct in marketing decision making.

Thus, while attitudes cannot be directly observed because of their covert nature, they are nevertheless useful because they are assumed to be precursors of behavior. In other words, attitude theorists believe that an attitude is a predisposition to respond overtly and that this predisposition leads to actual overt behavior. So, if a person is favorably predisposed toward a brand, that favorable predisposition should lead to favorable behaviors with respect to the brand (as seen through purchasing, making recommendations to friends, and so on).

Consistently Favorable or Unfavorable Responses

Attitudes serve as organizing mechanisms for the individual. As residues of either positive or negative feelings, attitudes govern a wide array of overt behaviors that the individual may express toward the attitude object. Thus, if one were to observe an individual's behaviors with respect to a particular brand, there would be evidence of a basic consistency in those responses, whether favorable or unfavorable. For instance, think of your best friend, someone you like very much (that is, someone you hold a favorable attitude toward). Now think of your actions toward your friend. You may go to sporting events together, share class notes, or engage in long discussions about the meaning of life; and you would almost certainly do him or her a favor if asked. Now think of someone you dislike. Would you engage in any of the above behaviors with that person? While not every behavior you engage in with respect to your friend will necessarily be favorable (sometimes even friends make each other angry), and while not every behavior with respect to your nonfriend will be unfavorable, the *pattern* of your behaviors will be consistently favorable in the former case and consistently unfavorable in the latter. Marketers stand to benefit from favorable consumer attitudes, as reflected in the consistency of consumer behaviors with respect to their brand—as seen, for example, through brand loyalty, more frequent consumption of the product, positive word-of-mouth recommendations to others, and the like.

Attitude Objects

As noted previously, attitudes are directed toward some object. In this case, *object* is rather broadly construed, so that an *object* can be not only a true *object* (such as a product class, a specific brand, or a retail store) but also a *person, issue,* or *behavior.* For instance, presidential candidates are concerned about the attitudes that voters hold toward them. Similarly, we hold attitudes toward issues, such as legalized abortion or the Equal Rights Amendment. Specific behaviors can also be the targets of attitudes, such as your attitude toward voting in the next election or going out to a movie next Friday night.

To summarize, attitudes represent our covert feelings of favorability or unfavorability toward an object, person, issue, or behavior. We learn these attitudes over time by being exposed to the object through direct experience or through receiving information about the object. Our learned attitudes serve as general guides to our overt behavior with respect to the attitude object, giving rise to a consistently favorable or unfavorable pattern of responses.

TWO THEORETICAL ORIENTATIONS

Historically, two major orientations have emerged in the study of attitudes. The first is often referred to as the *tripartite* view of attitude, because it specifies three underlying components of attitude. The second, the *unidimensionalist* position, treats attitude as a single affective construct. While these two orientations are regarded as competing viewpoints, they are really not that inconsistent with one another. Each will be described in more detail subsequently.

The Tripartite View of Attitude

Under the tripartite view, attitude is seen as being made up of three underlying components: *cognition, affect,* and *conation* (see Figure 18.1). Briefly, *cognition* refers to all beliefs that an individual holds with respect to the attitude object ("Crest prevents tooth decay"; "K-Mart has the lowest prices in town"). *Affect* pertains to positive or negative emotional reactions to the object ("I like Crest"; "I like shopping at K-Mart"). *Conation* encompasses intended and actual behaviors with respect to the attitude object ("I am brand loyal to Crest"; "I intend to shop at K-Mart"). According to proponents of the tripartite conceptualization, all three components are integral parts of any attitude; that is, every attitude consists of greater or lesser degrees of each component.

Furthermore, the three components are expected to exhibit a basic consistency in terms of favorability or unfavorability toward the attitude object. In other words, if a consumer believes that a brand will deliver positive benefits (cognition), then the consumer will also be expected to like the brand (affect) and engage in favorable behaviors toward it (conation).

The tripartite view of attitude, while well established conceptually, has seen very little empirical investigation. In fact, a major criticism of many attitude measurement approaches is that they fail to measure all three components of attitude. Most measurement procedures rely on a series of belief-type statements that are combined to yield an overall measure of attitudinal affect. With a few limited exceptions, the cognitive and conative components of attitude have not been measures in empirical investigations of attitude. Thus, the tripartite view is not currently a major force in the study of attitude, nor does it provide direct impetus to the application of attitude in marketing research.

The Unidimensionalist View of Attitude

The unidimensionalist conception of attitude can perhaps best be regarded as an evolution of the tripartite view. The same basic components of the tripartite attitude appear in the unidimensionalist view, but their conceptual status is altered significantly.

Under the unidimensionalist approach, the cognitive and conative components are "pulled out" of attitude; cognition is relabeled *beliefs* and conation is relabeled *intentions* and *behaviors.*

FIGURE 18.1 The Tripartite View of Attitude

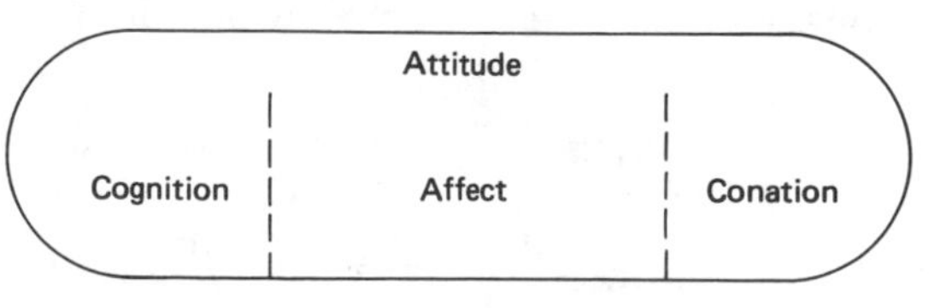

Thus, the unidimensionalist position is that attitude consists of affect only (see Figure 18.2). That is, attitude is unidimensional, consisting of only one component, *affect,* which represents the degree of favorability or unfavorability with respect to the attitude object. Other belief and behavioral dimensions are not seen as being components of attitude per se, but rather are viewed as antecedents or consequences of attitude (Fishbein and Ajzen 1975).

The specification of the relationships among the various concepts is an important contribution of the unidimensionalist view. While the tripartite view incorporated the notion of consistency among the components, the unidimensionalist view posits a *causal flow* through the components to account for this consistency. As shown in Figure 18.2 beliefs are seen as the immediate causal antecedents of attitude, while intentions are the immediate causal consequences, with actual behavioral consequences being one step removed from attitude. What this means is that if a consumer learns something about a new brand (say, from an advertisement), this learning, in the form of a belief, gives rise to an attitude, which in turn leads to the formation of an intention to purchase or not to purchase the brand.

The causal flow depicted in Figure 18.2 is not the only possible flow of effects, but it is the dominant one, at least from a theoretical perspective. The cognition-affect-conation flow is consistent with the various *hierarchy-of-effects* models, which form the basis for much current advertising decision making (see, for example, Lavidge and Steiner 1961).

The unidimensionalist perspective, then, goes beyond the tripartite view in specifying causal linkages among various theoretical constructs related to attitude. The resultant theoretical network contains a series of relationships that have both theoretical and practical merit. Thus, the unidimensionalist view of attitude is the underpinning of much current attitude research. For the remainder of this chapter, then, the unidimensionalist perspective will be adhered to. That is, attitude will be considered to consist solely of affect, and it will be treated as conceptually and operationally distinct from beliefs, intentions, and behaviors.

THEORIES OF ATTITUDE FORMATION AND CHANGE

In this section, we will examine theories of attitude formation and change; that is, we will examine explanations for the origins of attitudes and for ways of modifying already-existing attitudes. Both formation and change are important to marketers. Firms introducing new products are concerned with creating marketing programs designed to engender favorable attitudes toward their new brands, whereas marketing programs for existing products focus on strategies designed to modify brand attitudes in a favorable direction.

Over the years, many theories of attitude have been offered. In this chapter, attention will be limited to three theories: consistency theory, learning theory, and functional theory. Each has been selected because of its particular relevance to the marketing application of attitude research. Also, many theories of attitude deal with either attitude formation or attitude change; the above three theories deal with both processes and are thus more comprehensive.

Consistency Theory

Consistency theory is perhaps better regarded as a class of theories, rather than a single theory, in that a number of theories of attitude fall under this general rubric. Heider's (1946) Balance Theory, Festinger's (1957) Theory of Cognitive Dissonance, and Rosenberg's

FIGURE 18.2 The Unidimensionalist View of Attitude

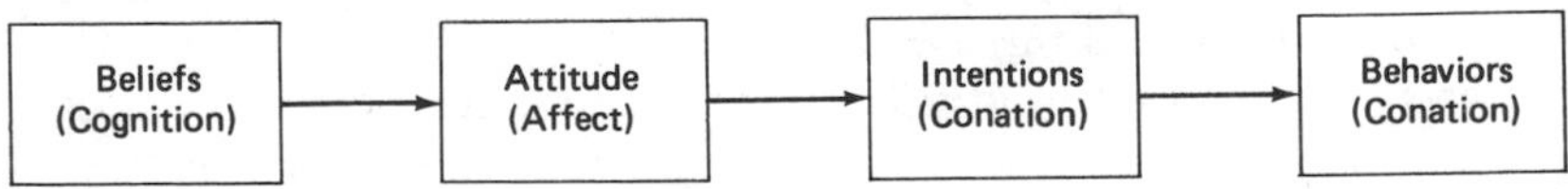

(1960) Affective-Cognitive Consistency Theory are all examples of this general class called consistency theory.

Balance Theory. Balance Theory derives its name from the basic hypothesis that forms its foundation—that an individual seeks to achieve a "balanced configuration" among cognitive and affective elements. The meaning of this assertion can best be understood by examining Figure 18.3. In the figure, the link between the person (*P*) and the attitude object (*O*) is the attitude in question. In Heider's system, the attitude is represented solely by its valence, either positive (+) or negative (−). There is no degree of positivity or negativity, a frequently noted shortcoming of the model. The link between *O* and *X* represents an association (+) or dissociation (−) between the attitude object and some related object, broadly construed to include people, attributes, consequences, and so on. For example, Michael Jordan's (*X*) endorsement of Nike basketball shoes (*O*) is intended to build a positive association between the two in the mind of the consumer.

The final link in the system, that between *P* and *X*, represents the person's feelings, positive or negative, toward the related object. These feelings presumably exist prior to the formation of the attitude in question. Continuing the previous example, most basketball fans would have had initially positive feelings toward Michael Jordan before learning that he was endorsing Nike.

According to Heider, the valence of the attitude (*P–O*) can be predicted on the basis of the valences attached to the *P–X* and *O–X* links. Because the individual is motivated to achieve a balanced state, the *P–O* valence will be determined by the algebraic multiplication of the other two valences. That is, we can think of all valences as being either +1 or −1. So, for instance, when a positively evaluated (+1) Michael Jordan endorses (+1) Nike, the predicted attitude toward Nike is positive ($+1 \times +1 = +1$).

FIGURE 18.3 Schematic Representation of Heider's (1946) Balance Theory

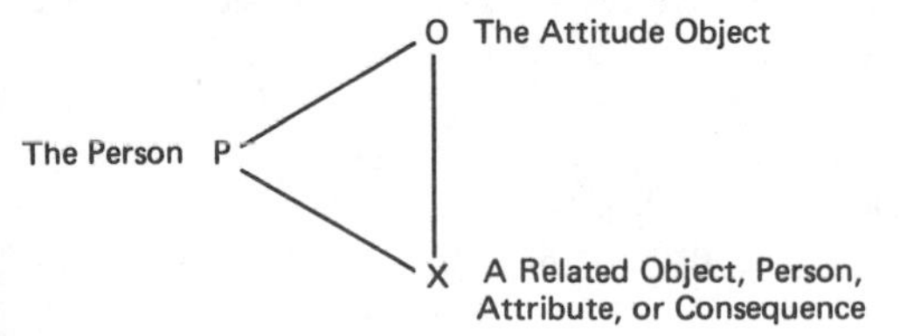

Balance theory also predicts that a negative *P–X* link and a negative *O–X* link will yield a positive attitude. For example, widely disliked former sportscaster Howard Cosell once endorsed Slim Jim's Meat Snacks by saying, "And now I'd like to tell you about a snack you may not like. Slim Jim's Meat Snacks—you either love them or you don't. Me? I can't stand 'em." The reasoning behind this commercial was consistent with balance theory. All those people who disliked Howard Cosell (*P–X* = −1), upon hearing that he disliked Slim Jim's (*O–X* = −1), should have immediately formed positive attitudes toward the product.

As shown in Figure 18.4, four different balanced configurations are possible under balance theory. Two of these yield positive attitudes, and two of them support negative attitudes. A marketer faced with one of the latter two situations could use balance theory in order to change consumer brand attitudes. For example, if consumers perceive a brand as not possessing (*O–X* = −1) a desirable attribute (*P–X* = +1), then the job of the marketer is to communicate either that the attribute is in fact undesirable or that the brand actually does possess the desired attribute. While the latter strategy is much more frequently employed, either of these changes would create an imbalance in the system, which should lead the consumer to reevaluate the brand.

Balance theory has two major weaknesses that prevent it from being widely used in applied settings. First, as noted previously, it does not allow for quantitative variation of the valences—all links are either +1 or −1. Second, the theory as specified incorporates only one related object (*X*) for each attitude object. There is no mechanism for combining the effects of multiple related objects to arrive at a prediction of brand attitude. Yet, most brands have more than one attribute of importance to

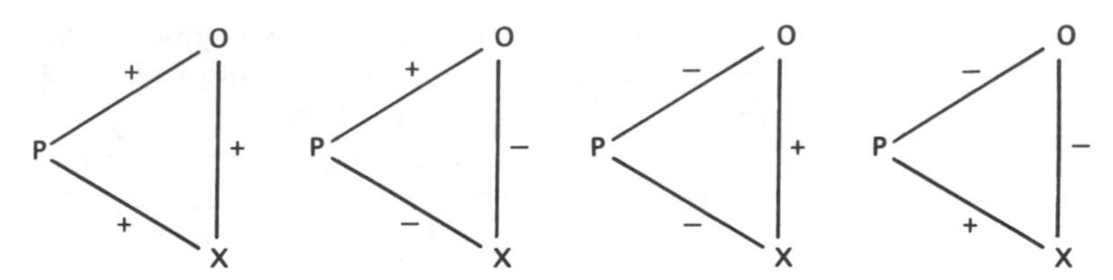

FIGURE 18.4 Four Possible Balanced Configurations

consumers. Therefore, the balance theory model is not sufficient for most applications.

Nevertheless, the basic notions incorporated in balance theory provided an impetus for much subsequent work on attitude theory. As we shall see later, most current attitude research in marketing can be viewed as an extension of Heider's ideas. Thus, balance theory has served as a powerful orientation to the study of attitude, even though it is not widely used in its original form.

Theory of Cognitive Dissonance. One of the best known consistency theories, the theory of cognitive dissonance, or more simply *dissonance theory,* was proposed in 1957 by psychologist Leon Festinger. Of all the consistency theories, dissonance theory has attracted the most attention in consumer research, although it has fallen into disuse over the past decade. The term *dissonance* was used by Festinger to denote cognitive *in*consistency, that is, a circumstance in which two cognitions (i.e., thoughts) are inconsistent with one another. Cognitions can be with respect to beliefs one holds about an object, one's attitude toward the object, or one's behavior in relation to the object. Dissonance can be present between two beliefs or between a belief and an attitude. The most frequently studied form of dissonance, however, involves that occurring between an attitude and a behavior.

One type situation that is analyzed from this theoretical perspective is that in which an individual engages in some *counterattitudinal* behavior, thereby creating dissonance. For instance, a consumer may be induced to purchase a brand other than his or her preferred brand through a special sales promotion such as a coupon or sweepstakes. Dissonance would be aroused between the two cognitions: "I prefer Brand A" and "I purchased Brand B." Because dissonance is thought to be a motivational state, it is assumed that the consumer will undertake steps to reduce the dissonance created by the purchase of the nonpreferred brand. Since the behavior (i.e., the purchase) is generally nonreversible, the behavior cognition cannot be altered. Therefore, the only dissonance reduction route available to the consumer is to modify the cognition about his or her preference. Dissonance theory predicts that the individual's attitude (i.e., preference for) Brand B will become more favorable, thereby making the two cognitions more consonant. Thus, the purchase behavior induced by an extrinsic factor (the sales promotion) leads to a change in brand attitude as the consumer seeks to alleviate the dissonance aroused by the purchase of the initially nonpreferred brand.

An even more common application of dissonance theory has been the study of *postchoice* cognitive dynamics. In a typical consumer purchase scenario, multiple brands are available; the consumer must make a choice from a set of competing alternatives. Each brand has some positive features, and each has some negatives (e.g., a high price). When the consumer makes a choice, he or she automatically receives the negative features associated with the chosen brand and forgoes the positive features associated with the rejected brands. This is thought to be dissonance-arousing for the consumer. In order to reduce the dissonance associated with the choice, the consumer may utilize one or more of the following strategies: (1) minimize the importance of the choice; (2) actively search for and/or recall positive attributes of the chosen brand; and (3) avoid positive information and/or seek negative information about the nonchosen brands. It is interesting to note that many manufacturers attempt to encourage the consumer to employ strategy Number 2 by including additional promotional materials *inside* the package, where the consumer cannot see it until after the purchase has been made. Similarly, automobile companies routinely mail "congratulatory" materials to new car buyers, and real estate agents send house-warming gifts to their clients who have purchased a home.

Because of its emphasis on postdecision and postchoice processes, dissonance theory has a narrower domain of application than the other attitude theories considered in this chapter. Although it has been applied to the study of consumer satisfaction and complaining behavior, it is of very limited value in predicting behavior in advance, which is one of the traditional uses of the attitude construct in marketing research. Consequently, interest in dissonance theory has waned in recent years, as new theories with broader scopes of application have been advanced.

Affective-Cognitive Consistency Theory. The final consistency theory to be considered here was conceived by Rosenberg (1960) in an attempt to more specifically delineate the structural relationships between attitude and certain cognitive variables. Rosenberg was particularly concerned with the underlying *values* of the individual and with how these values related to overall attitude. By values he meant certain basic desires that individuals may hold to a greater or lesser degree. Table 18.1 shows a partial list of values that Rosenberg used in his research.

TABLE 18.1 A Partial List of Individual Values

1. Being looked up to by others
2. Making one's own decisions
3. Having change and variety; having new experiences
4. Having power and authority
5. Being good looking
6. Being liked or loved by the opposite sex
7. Being like others in general
8. Being well educated
9. Having strict moral standards
10. Being allowed the privacy of one's own thoughts and feelings

Because of its emphasis on values, Rosenberg's theory is often identified not only as a consistency theory but also as an expectancy-value theory. Expectancy-value theories posit that an individual's attitude toward an object is a function of the individual's expectation that the object can help or hinder the attainment of some desired values. For example, in Rosenberg's formulation, each value is measured with respect to its *value importance* (V) to the individual, and with respect to its *perceived instrumentality* (P), that is, the extent to which the value would be blocked or attained by the attitude object in question. Thus, the perceived instrumentality term is a reflection of the expectancy on the part of the individual about the attitude object's relationship to the value in question.

Table 18.2 shows the exact measurement procedures employed by Rosenberg to measure both perceived instrumentality and value importance. In this case, the attitude in question is that toward studying for three hours each evening. As can be seen from the table, the term value importance is somewhat a misnomer in that importance is not what is being measured; rather, the degree of satisfaction or dissatisfaction provided by the value is being assessed.[1] Thus, the value importance term is quite similar to the P–X link in Heider's balance theory, but the scale used by Rosenberg allows for degrees of quantification of the valence attached to the value.

Similarly, the perceived instrumentality term is analogous to the O–X link in the balance theory configuration. Both values and instrumentalities are measured on bipolar scales, meaning that a negative value combined with a negative instrumentality would yield a positive contribution to attitude, just as would a positive value and positive instrumentality. Note the use in the preceding sentence, of the phrase

[1] This rather unfortunate labeling of the value construct led to much confusion in the attitude research literature in marketing. Many researchers claiming to be using the Rosenberg model mistakenly measured "importance" of values rather than satisfaction or dissatisfaction.

TABLE 18.2 Measures of Rosenberg's (1960) Perceived Instrumentality and Value Importance

Value Importance

Being well educated . . .

gives me maximum satisfaction	+3:___:___:_0_:___:___:−3	gives me maximum dissatisfaction[a]

Perceived Instrumentality

The condition of "being well educated" . . .

is completely attained	+3:___:___:___:___:___:−3	is completely blocked[a]

by studying for three hours each evening.

[a]In Rosenberg's original work, both measures were twenty-one point scales, ranging from +10 to −10. The seven-point scales shown here are much easier for respondents to use than are the longer scales.

"contribution to attitude" rather than simply "attitude." While Heider's model analyzed the impact of only one related object on attitude, Rosenberg's explicitly includes multiple "related objects"—that is, values. Hence, no one value is seen as the sole determinant of attitude; rather, all relevant values and their instrumentalities must be combined in order to yield a predictor of attitude.

Rosenberg postulated the following formula as the mechanism for combining multiple values and instrumentalities:

$$\text{Attitude} = f\left(\sum_{i=1}^{n} V_i P_i\right) \qquad (18.1)$$

where:

Attitude is an independent measure of overall favorability or unfavorability toward the attitude object[2];

f stands for "is a function of," meaning that attitude is somehow related to the formula inside the parentheses;

V_i is the measured value importance of the *i*th value (for example, the value importance of being good looking);

P_i is the perceived instrumentality of the attitude object with respect to the *i*th value (for example, the degree to which using Ultra-brite toothpaste blocks or attains being good looking);

n is the number of values that were measured; and

Σ represents the summation of all n V_i and P_i combinations.

Rosenberg considered the term inside the parentheses to be an index of the *cognitive structure* supporting the observed attitude. As indicated in Equation 18.1, attitude and cognitive structure are thought to be directly related; furthermore, a change in cognitive structure should lead to a change in attitude, and vice versa (hence, the name affective-cognitive consistency theory). A change in either attitude or cognitive structure would lead to *inconsistency* between the two constructs, an inconsistency that would be psychologically uncomfortable for the individual. Therefore, the individual would seek to reduce this inconsistency by

[2]Perhaps the most popular summary attitude measure in attitude research is the evaluative scale of the Semantic Differential (Osgood, Suci, and Tannenbaum 1957). Other acceptable measures include the Likert, Thurstone, and Guttman scales, although they are much more difficult to construct than is a Semantic Differential measure.

bringing attitude more into line with the new cognitive structure, or vice versa.

Affective-cognitive consistency theory, with its incorporation of underlying values into cognitive structure, provides an attractive explanation for the origins of attitude. It is also quite congenial with personality theory and with the lifestyle, or psychographic, view of consumer behavior in that attitudes and behavior are seen as being grounded in basic values of some centrality to the individual.[3] That these basic values can be used to predict attitudes toward any number of objects is at once the major strength and the major weakness of Rosenberg's theory. General values, while useful to some degree in a large number of settings, are almost never as strong predictively as are more situation-specific determinants, as we shall see in the next section.

One possibility is that the Rosenberg approach is useful for explaining attitudes toward highly involving topics (which, unfortunately, are relatively uncommon in consumer choice), or that it is more applicable at the level of product class selection ("Am I favorable or unfavorable toward cold cereals in general?") than it is at the level of brand selection ("Am I more favorable toward Cheerios than I am toward Wheaties?") Whether that assertion is true awaits further empirical testing in consumer research.

Learning Theory

The major theory to be discussed here is one proposed by Fishbein (1963). His theory has, perhaps, had the greatest influence on consumer attitude research over the past two decades. Structurally, Fishbein's theory is identical to Rosenberg's, as shown by the following equation:

$$\text{Attitude} = f\left(\sum_{i=1}^{n} b_i e_i\right) \qquad (18.2)$$

[3]The interested reader should consult Rokeach (1973) for an excellent treatment of values and their centrality in human behavior. Of particular interest is his distinction between terminal and instrumental values.

where:

Attitude is an independent measure of affect for or against the attitude object;

b_i is the strength of the belief (expressed as a subjective likelihood) that the attitude object possesses the *i*th attribute (for example, the likelihood that Listerine mouthwash tastes "mediciny");

e_i is the evaluative aspect associated with the *i*th attribute (for example, how good or bad is a "mediciny" taste);

n is the number of salient attributes of the attitude object; and

f and Σ have the same interpretation as in Equation 18.1.

As should be readily apparent, Fishbein's formulation is also quite compatible with the basic consistency model originally proposed by Heider; in this case, b_i represents the O–X link and e_i corresponds to the P–X link. Similar to Rosenberg, Fishbein measures b_i and e_i on bipolar scales of the type shown in Table 18.3

The basic similarity of the Rosenberg and Fishbein formulations is clear in that they both posit a consistency between cognitions and attitudes, and they both fall into the general class of expectancy-value models. However, two fundamental differences can be found in the two theories regarding the following two issues: (1) the proposed underlying theoretical mechanisms and (2) the level of centrality of the cognitive structure supporting the attitude.

Underlying Theoretical Mechanism. Whereas Rosenberg relied on a consistency theory explanation for the relationship between attitudes and cognitions, Fishbein drew his support for this proposition from behavioral learning theory. Simply stated, his contention was that an attitude toward an object is more or less automatically learned as one learns about a new product, and that learning occurs in the form of beliefs about product attributes. For example, consider a new brand of toilet tissue:

Brand X is strong.
Brand X is soft.

TABLE 18.3 Measures of Fishbein's (1963) Belief Strengths and Evaluative Aspects

Belief Strength		
Sure aerosol deodorant contains hydrocarbons		
very likely	+3:__:__:__:__:__:−3	very unlikely
Evaluative Aspect		
Hydrocarbons are		
very good	+3:__:__:__:__:__:−3	very bad

Brand X is inexpensive.
Brand X has a pleasant scent.
Brand X is pastel colored.

As the consumer learns these attributes of Brand X, through advertising, word-of-mouth, or experience with the product, each attribute becomes "connected" to Brand X to a greater or lesser degree; this is the belief strength (b_i) component of Fishbein's theory (see Figure 18.5).

Associated with each attribute is an evaluative aspect (e_i), which can be thought of as a "mini-attitude," an attitude that already exists toward that attribute. That is, you knew how you felt about softness in a toilet tissue before you ever heard of Brand X. Through the psychological processes of mediated generalization and classical conditioning, the affect associated with softness becomes associated with Brand X,

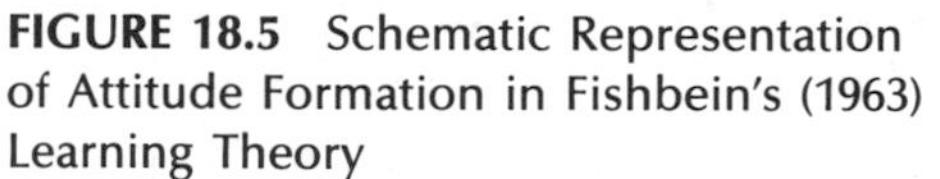

FIGURE 18.5 Schematic Representation of Attitude Formation in Fishbein's (1963) Learning Theory

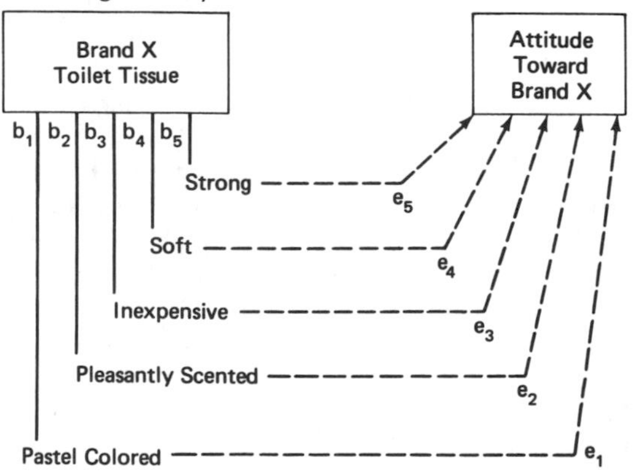

as shown in the figure. Thus, the overall attitude toward Brand X is derived from the original, underlying attitudes toward the attributes of Brand X. The "amount" of affect transferred from each e_i to attitude is a function of the belief strength (b_i) associated with the attribute; the stronger the belief, the greater the amount of the attribute's evaluative aspect that will generalize to the attitude object. Hence, the multiplicative, summative formula shown in Equation 18.2 captures the essence of how beliefs about brand attributes lead to brand attitudes.

Level of Centrality of Cognitive Structure. It was previously noted that Rosenberg's theory dealt with fairly central individual values that could be related to a wide variety of attitude objects. In contrast, Fishbein's theory is quite situation-specific and deals with more stimulus-bound attributes; therefore, his theory operates at a level not nearly so central to the individual's self-concept. This lesser degree of centrality probably makes sense for a wide range of consumer products (for instance, can you imagine trying to predict toilet tissue brand choice from measures of values such as "being looked up to by others" or "having strict moral standards"?), which do not represent important purchases as far as the consumer is concerned.

While the values employed by Rosenberg could be used as predictors for virtually any attitude, the attributes present in cognitive structure under the Fishbein approach are more specific to the attitude object in question. These attributes are determined by asking respondents in a free-response format, "What comes to mind when you think of (the attitude object in question)?" The things an individual mentions in response to this question are taken to be the salient attributes of the attitude object—that is, those aspects of the object of which the individual is aware without prompting. Most theorists believe that, for most attitude objects, there are somewhere between five and nine salient attributes, for the typical person. Thus, in most applications of the Fishbein model, free responses from a small number of people (say, twenty to thirty) are combined to discover the *modal salient attributes,* that is, those five to nine attributes that are mentioned most often. These attributes are then used in constructing questionnaires to measure the b_i and e_i elements associated with each attribute (refer back to Table 18.3).

Managerial Utility of the Learning Theory Approach

The notion of attribute salience has important implications for attitude change within the Fishbein theory. Since attitudes are viewed as being causally determined by cognitive structure, the Fishbein theory implies three basic strategies for attitude change based on modification of cognitive structure:

1. Change the belief strength (b_i) associated with an attribute.
2. Change the evaluative aspect (e_i) associated with an attribute.
3. Introduce a previously nonsalient attribute into cognitive structure.

Consider the hypothetical case shown in Table 18.4. The data contained therein represent a hypothetical consumer's responses to questions about local radio stations. As shown in the table, the consumer has one set of e_i measures, but three sets of b_i measures, one for each station in the market. Ignoring for a moment the row in parentheses, we can compute the consumer's attitude toward each station using the formula in Equation 18.2. The results are displayed in the next to the last row in the table and show Station WHEE to be this consumer's preferred station, with WHOA least preferred.

Let us suppose that you are the station manager for WHOA and wish to improve your market position. What strategies are available to you? A belief change strategy might focus on playing more music. If you could convince the consumer that it is very likely that WHOA plays lots of music (b_i = +3), then the new overall attitude toward WHOA would be increased by six points [(+3 − +1) × +3 = +6] to +7. Or, you could air fewer commercials, so that the consumer would not expect to hear lots of commercials on WHOA (b_i = −3). This would lead to a gain of ten points in over-

TABLE 18.4 Hypothetical Responses of a Consumer to Questionnaire on Radio Stations[a]

		Station (b_i)		
Attribute	e_i	*WHEE*	*WHOA*	*WYLD*
Plays lots of music	+ 3	+ 2	+ 1	− 2
Plays lots of commercials	− 2	+ 2	+ 2	− 2
Gives news updates	+ 1	+ 1	+ 2	+ 3
Has interesting Djs	+ 2	+ 2	0	+ 1
(interviews rock stars)[b]	(+2)	(−3)	(+1)	(−3)
Overall attitude (before)[c]		+ 7	+ 1	+ 3
Overall attitude (after)[d]		+ 1	+ 3	− 3

[a]Note all b_i and e_i elements measured in seven-point bipolar scales as shown in Table 3.

[b]Parentheses in this row indicate that this attribute was initially nonsalient. The values shown for b_i and e_i reflect the result of a salience change strategy undertaken by station WHOA.

[c]Computed before salience change.

[d]Computed after salience change.

all attitude [(−3 − +2) × −2] = +10, or a new attitude score of +11.

Alternatively, you could attempt evaluation change by trying to convince consumers that interesting DJs are not as positive as they thought and that, in fact, DJs really don't matter too much (e_i = 0). This change, if carried off successfully, would not increase the consumer's attitude toward WHOA, but would decrease his or her attitudes toward WHEE and WYLD to +3 and +1, respectively. However, it is generally thought that evaluation change of this type is difficult to achieve. Therefore, a salience change strategy might be employed instead. In this instance, WHOA could introduce interviews with rock stars and promote that as being exclusive to WHOA. If the consumer likes to hear such interviews (e_i = +2) and realizes that neither WHEE nor WYLD is likely to air similar ones, attitudes toward these two stations will drop and the attitude toward WHOA increase. The final row in the table shows the impact of the salience change strategy; WHOA is now the preferred station. To successfully undertake a salience change strategy, two conditions must be met:

1. The brand undertaking the strategy should be superior to other brands on the market for the attribute being made salient.
2. The attribute being made salient should be one that is positively evaluated by members of the target market.[4]

The Fishbein theory thus serves as a useful *diagnostic* device for suggesting attitude change strategies. Aiming informational or persuasive campaigns at selected cognitive structure elements should result in cognitive change, which in turn should be reflected in attitude change. This causal pattern, from belief (b_i) or evaluation (e_i) change to attitude change, has been successfully undertaken in a marketing context (for example, in Lutz 1985; Mazis and Adkinson 1976), which gives us confidence in both the validity of the underlying theory and its utility for marketing decision making.

The Fishbein and Rosenberg theories have spawned a great deal of marketing research on what have come to be known as *multiattribute models of attitude.* The basic thrust of all these models is that attitudes can be predicted on the basis of brand attribute perceptions, typically weighted by some evaluation or importance term. For reviews of these variants to the basic Fishbein and Rosenberg theories, see Wilkie and Pessemier (1973) and Lutz and Bettman (1977).

Functional Theory

The functional theory of attitude derives its name from the idea that an individual develops and holds attitudes that are designed to "function" in a certain fashion for that individual. We might say that attitudes exist in order to assist the individual in meeting certain goals or fulfilling underlying needs. A general term which we can use is that attitudes reflect basic *motives* of the individual; hence, functional theory, which was conceived by Smith, Bruner, and White (1956) and Katz (1960), is often referred to as a "motivational" approach to attitude formation and change.

Again recalling that attitude is a single affective dimension, we can see that a functional theory is needed when we consider that two people may exhibit identical degrees of affect for a brand, but for entirely different reasons. For instance, one person may like Marlboro cigarettes because they taste good, while another person may like Marlboros because smoking them makes him feel more masculine. In other words, the former consumer's attitude is based on the physical properties of the attitude object, while the latter's attitude is based on the image projected by advertising for the brand.

According to the functional theorists, it is of utmost importance to understand the motivational underpinnings of attitude before attempting to undertake attitude change. For example, trying to influence the consumer with

[4]Theoretically, an alternative strategy would be to point out (make salient) a negatively evaluated attribute that is more likely to be present in competing brands. This, however, could lead to a decrease in primary demand for the entire product class.

the image-based attitude by stressing Marlboro's good taste would be as fruitless as trying to persuade the taste-oriented consumer by showing the Marlboro man on horseback. Thus, an identification of the function or functions being served by an attitude is a prerequisite for successful attitude modification. The phrase "function or functions" is important because it points out that any given attitude may be serving more than one function simultaneously. Thus, the functions are not seen as mutually exclusive but rather as complementary and, in some instances, overlapping. Let us now turn to an examination of the various functions attitudes can serve. Katz (1960) specified four functions of attitude, as well as the conditions conducive to the formation and change of attitudes serving each function.

The Utilitarian, Instrumental, or Adjustive Function. The essential component of the utilitarian function is that people act in such a way as to maximize their rewards and minimize their punishments from the external environment. Thus, utilitarian attitudes are favorable toward those objects in the environment that provide more pleasure than pain, more positive benefits than negative costs, and so on.

It seems likely that many brand attitudes are serving the utilitarian function. Katz (1960) stated that the utilitarian function was closely aligned with behavioristic learning theory, which, it will be recalled, was the basis of Fishbein's (1963) learning theory. Fishbein's theory posits brand perceptions (beliefs) as the determinants of attitude, which suggests that the perceptions of brand benefits (attributes) form the building blocks of the utilitarian function. Thus, in most instances, the utilitarian function can be regarded as being virtually identical to the Fishbein theory in its reliance on situation-specific brand benefits as the precursors of brand attitude.

The Value-Expressive Function. The value-expressive function is served by attitudes that allow individuals to *express their self-concepts* or centrally held values. Thus, this function is very similar to Rosenberg's (1960) affective-cognitive consistency theory, as it also relies on central values as the origins of attitude.

Value-expressive attitudes are seen as a means of enhancing one's image in the eyes of the world and hence are of great relevance to marketers. Many products are sold not so much on the basis of their physical *product attributes,* but rather on the basis of the attributes of the supposed typical user of the product (*people attributes*): For example, "superstars" like Bo Jackson train in Nikes, Jaclyn Smith lends her sophisticated image to K-Mart, Michael J. Fox epitomizes the youthful Pepsi drinker, and James Garner embues Mazda with his casual ruggedness. The image associated with the celebrity endorser is thought to be transferred through the brand to the individual who purchases the product (McCracken 1989), thus forming the basis of the value-expressive function.

It would appear that most attitudes of concern to marketers fall under either the utilitarian or the value-expressive function or some combination of the two. Perhaps in part because of the widespread use of both product attribute and user attribute appeals by marketers, it seems that many consumers evaluate potential purchases along these two general dimensions. In contrast, the remaining two functions of attitude identified by Katz appear to be less critical to most marketing applications.

The Ego-Defensive Function. Freudian psychology forms the basis for the description of ego-defensive function, which refers to attitudes that serve to protect the individual from internal insecurities or external threats. It can thus be seen as the functional opposite of the value-expressive function, which allows individuals to express their inner selves to others. The ego-defensive function, in contrast, protects the individual from others in the environment by *concealing* the individual's most basic feelings and desires, many of which may be regarded as socially undesirable.

A brief historical note may help to explicate the workings of the ego-defensive function. Katz and his colleagues at Michigan were concerned with the foundations of prejudicial attitudes toward blacks, Jews, and other minority groups. Similarly, Smith and his associates at Harvard were investigating attitudes toward Russia during the time when the Cold War was of major concern to many Americans. Thus, the attitudes being studied by the early functionalists were very "involving" attitudes with their roots in the deepest, darkest aspects of the individual's personalities.

As mentioned previously, few brand attitudes would appear to be operating at a very deep or involving level. The one major exception may lie in the area of sex appeal, which is used by marketers in promoting a variety of products. To the extent that a person is insecure about his or her attractiveness to the opposite sex, then ego-defensive (negative) attitudes may develop toward products that make that insecurity salient, and positive attitudes may be formed toward products that alleviate the insecurity by implicitly or explicitly promising increased attractiveness as a result of using them. For instance, wearers of English Leather may feel more masculine, and users of Chanel No. 5 more feminine, as a result of wearing those brands.

Fear appeals are another area where ego-defensive attitudes may be evoked. Fear of having bad breath, foot odor, or dandruff may not operate at an extremely deep level, but the fear of death sometimes aroused by life insurance ads may be powerful enough to give rise to an ego-defensive attitudinal response.

The Knowledge Function. The final function of attitude is based upon an individual's general desire to understand and given order to his or her environment. The knowledge function is consistent with Gestalt theory in its emphasis on organizing diverse perceptions into a meaningful overall picture. An attitude serving the knowledge function thus supplies a "frame of reference" for interpreting an otherwise chaotic set of stimuli.

Knowledge function attitudes can be seen as general affective dimensions that, in part, govern *selective perception* by the individual. If an attitude object is generally positively evaluated, the knowledge function would cause the individual to discount negative information encountered about the object; the opposite would be the case for a generally disliked object—that is, positive information would be ignored. Work by psychologist Russell Fazio on the nature of attitude-behavior relationships has invoked the knowledge function; his model will be discussed in a subsequent section of this paper. Knowledge function attitudes may help to explain brand loyalty. Once consumers use a brand and find it satisfactory, they resists persuasive attempts by competing manufacturers; by doing so, they maintain order and stability in their consumption pattern. The knowledge function may also underlie people's resistance to product innovations. To the extent that a new product is poorly understood by the consumer or is perceived as disrupting "the way things have always been," then a negative attitude toward the product may develop, dooming the product to failure.

Conditions for Attitude Arousal and Change

Table 18.5, adapted from Katz (1960), summarizes the conditions under which the various functions of attitudes are likely to be aroused and modified. As was stated earlier, and as is apparent from inspection of the table, the utilitarian function is likely the dominant one in most brand attitudes, followed by the value-expressive function. Ego-defensive attitudes are probably the least common in situations of concern to marketers because of the low-involvement nature of most consumer products. Knowledge function attitudes would also not appear to be nearly as prevalent as utilitarian and value-expressive ones, although the knowledge function may be present to a lesser degree in many marketing situations and dominant in a few selected instances. Due to measurement difficulties, until recently the functional approach has not undergone the rigorous empirical testing necessary to document its utility as a theory of attitude formation and change.

Nevertheless, the functional approach has been generally regarded as a very powerful orientation to the study of attitudes. And, as indicated previously, there is reason to believe that

TABLE 18.5 Determinants of Attitude Formation, Arousal, and Change in Relation to Type of Function[a]

Function	*Origin and Dynamics*	*Arousal Conditions*	*Change Conditions*
Utilitarian	Utility of attitudinal object in need satisfaction. Maximizing external rewards and minimizing punishments	1. Activation of needs 2. Salience of cues associated with need satisfaction	1. Need deprivation 2. Creation of new needs and new levels of aspiration 3. Shifting rewards and punishments 4. Emphasis on new and better paths for need satisfaction
Ego-defensive	Protecting against internal conflicts and external dangers	1. Posing of threats 2. Appeals to hatred and repressed impulses 3. Rise in frustrations 4. Use of authoritarian suggestion	1. Removal of threats 2. Catharsis 3. Development of self-insight
Value-expressive	Maintaining self identity; enhancing favorable self-image; self-expression and self-determination	1. Salience of cues associated with values 2. Appeals to individual to reassert self-image 3. Ambiguities which threaten self-concept	1. Some degree of dissatisfaction with self 2. Greater appropriateness of new attitude for the self 3. Control of all environmental supports to undermine old values
Knowledge	Need for understanding for meaningful cognitive organization, for consistency and clarity	1. Reinstatement of cues associated with old problem or of old problem itself	1. Ambiguity created by new information or change in environment 2. More meaningful information about problems

[a]Modified from Katz (1960, p. 192).

the Fishbein and Rosenberg theories actually capture quite well the essence of the utilitarian and value-expressive functions, respectively. Since these two functions are almost certainly the key ones from a marketing perspective, a systematic combination of the Fishbein and Rosenberg models may yield at least a partial application of functional theory in marketing. Conceptual (Lutz 1981) and empirical work (Locander and Spivey 1978; Snyder and DeBono 1985; Shavitt 1989) on functional theory in marketing has yielded some promising results, so it appears to be finding its way into the mainstream of consumer attitude research.

ATTITUDE-BEHAVIOR RELATIONSHIPS

Thus far we have dealt with theories of attitude formation and change, which have tended to focus on underlying perceptual variables (that is, cognition) as the determinants of attitude. However, it is of little consequence to understand attitude and its determinants if attitude bears no relationship to overt behavior, as some critics have claimed (e.g., Wicker 1969). Marketing managers and other applied researchers rely on the attitude construct because of its supposed causal influence on behavior. The presumed "attitude-leads-to-behavior" relationship allows the use of attitude measurements as predictors of behaviors toward the brand in the marketplace. To the extent that this relationship does not hold, then attitude measurements are not only useless but also misleading to the marketing-decision maker. Numerous researchers in both psychology and marketing have failed to document the attitude-behavior relationship, leading some to question the utility of attitude in understanding behavior. However, research has begun to more systematically investigate the attitude-behavior relationship; the major current approaches to this problem are summarized subsequently.

Theory of Reasoned Action (TRA)

In an extension of his earlier learning theory (discussed previously), Fishbein (1967, 1975) and his colleague Icek Ajzen (1980) have developed a theory of the relationship between attitude and behavior. The basic proposition underlying this *theory of reasoned action* is that in order to predict a specific behavior (such as the purchase of a particular brand during some specified time period) it is necessary to measure the person's attitude toward performing that behavior, not just the general attitude toward the object at which the behavior is directed.

For example, a person's attitude toward a Cadillac automobile may be quite favorable; yet the person may never purchase a Cadillac because of its relatively high price. According to the TRA, this person should show an unfavorable attitude toward purchasing a Cadillac, even though the general attitude toward Cadillac is favorable. The latter attitude is an *attitude-toward-the-object* (A_O), while the former attitude is an *attitude-toward-the-behavior* (A_B). According to the TRA, A_B should predict a specific overt behavior better than A_O, because A_B is more specific to the behavior in question.

In addition to a more situation-specific attitudinal predictor, the TRA includes a second determinant of overt behavior: the *subjective norm* (*SN*). *SN* is intended to measure the social influences on a person's behavior (for example, friends' or family members' expectations). This recognizes that there are some situations where behavior is simply not under the *attitudinal control* of the individual; rather, the expectations of relevant others are major factors in the ultimate behavioral performance. In this case, the behavior is said to be under *normative control.*

Figure 18.6 depicts the entire TRA; thus far, we have focused attention on the links between attitude and intention (which mediates behavior) and between norms and intention. The relative strengths of these two links, as indicated by w_1 and w_2, determine whether the formation of intention is primarily attitudinal or normative. If w_1 is greater than w_2, then intention and behavior are under attitudinal control; if w_2 is greater than w_1, then normative

FIGURE 18.6 Schematic Diagram of Ajzen and Fishbein's (1980) Theory of Reasoned Action

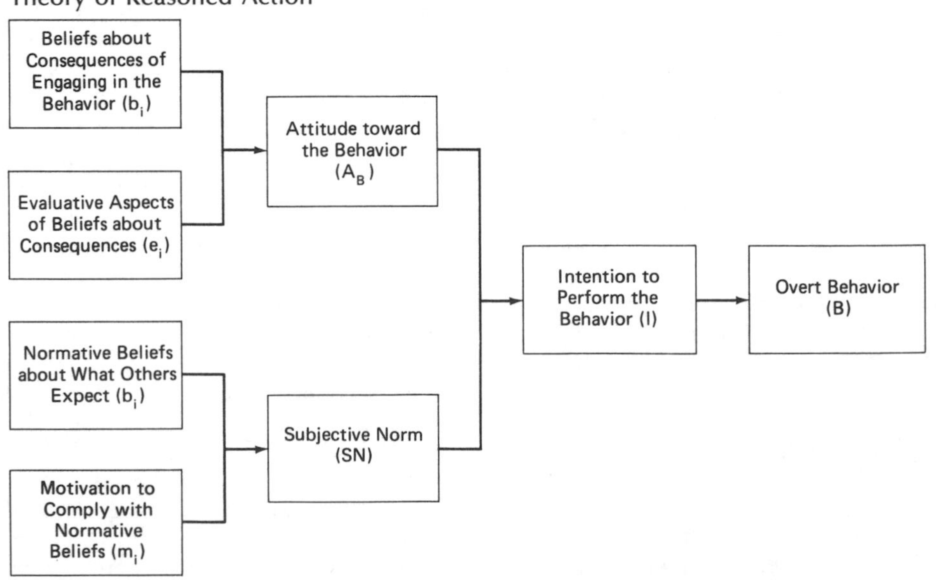

control is operative. This distinction is an important one, because it dictates the proper approach to designing behavioral change strategies. Unless a behavior is under attitudinal control, attitude change strategies will have no impact on behavior. Instead, some form of normative change strategy is needed.

As shown in the figure, the TRA also specified the cognitive antecedents of both A_B and *SN*. These antecedent variables in both instances combine via a multiplicative summation such as those shown in Equations 18.1 and 18.2. The attitudinal antecedents are quite similar to those in Fishbein's earlier theory but differ in that they deal with the *perceived consequences* of engaging in a behavior rather than the perceived attributes of an object. For example, the consequences relevant to brushing one's teeth with Crest may be that:

It whitens teeth.
It prevents tooth decay.
It has a pleasant taste.
It freshens breath.

Associated with each consequence are a belief strength (b_i) and an evaluative aspect (e_i). These terms are measured on seven-point bipolar scales ("likely" "unlikely" for b_i, "good"–"bad" for e_i) identical to the ones shown earlier in Table 18.3

Measures of the normative antecedents of *SN* are shown in Table 18.6. Identification of modal salient referents is accomplished through the use of the focus group procedure described earlier for the determination of salient attributes. Typically, two to four referents are used to construct a model of the cognitive index underlying *SN*.

Similar to the attitude change strategies described earlier for Fishbein's learning theory, three possible attitude change strategies and three possible normative change strategies can be derived from his attitude-behavior model. The attitude change strategies include:

1. Changing the belief strength (b_i) associated with a perceived consequence (for example, convincing consumers that brushing with Ultra-Brite gives their mouths sex appeal).
2. Changing the evaluation aspect (e_i) associated with a consequence (for example, convincing consumers that the "mediciny" taste they experience when they gargle with Listerine is actually a good thing).
3. Making salient a previously nonsalient consequence (for example, telling consumers that

TABLE 18.6 Measures of Normative Belief, Motivation to Comply, and Subjective Norm

Normative Belief (b_j)

My spouse thinks that I should purchase Brand X.

Very likely +3:___:___:___:___:___:−3 Very unlikely

Motivation to Comply (m_j)

With respect to purchasing Brand X,

I want very much to do +3:___:___:___:___:___:−3 I want very much to do the opposite of

what my spouse thinks I should do.

Subjective Norm (SN)

Most people who are important to me think that

I should +3:___:___:___:___:___:−3 I should not

purchase Brand X.

dying their hair with Preference hair coloring will leave it soft).

The three normative change strategies are identified as the following:

1. Changing the normative believe strength (b_i) associated with a referent (for example, letting people know that doctors think that people should drink only decaffeinated coffee).
2. Changing the motivation to comply (m_j) with a referent (for example, stressing the importance of paying attention to doctors' advice).
3. Introducing a previously nonsalient referent (for example, convincing consumers that all the people of the free world are counting on them to use less oil).

Research on the theory of reasoned action has revealed that purchasing behaviors are by and large under attitudinal rather than normative control (Ryan and Bonfield 1975; Sheppard, Hartwick, and Warshaw 1988). Thus, attitude change strategies will typically be more appropriate than normative change strategies in most marketing settings. Nevertheless, the model provides a more complete framework for marketing decision making by incorporating social (that is, normative) as well as intraindividual (that is, attitudinal) factors in explaining consumer behavior.

Returning to Figure 18.6, it can be seen that intervening between attitudes (and norms) and behavior is *intention,* which is simply the person's subjective estimate of the likelihood that he or she will engage in the behavior under study. Researchers in a variety of marketing settings have found intentions to be very good predictors of subsequent behavior; however, there are instances in which intentions do not accurately forecast behavior, as we shall see later. For now, it is important to note that Figure 18.6 portrays a causal flow of effects that is consistent with the unidimensionalist view of attitude (see Figure 18.2). The process begins with beliefs, moves through attitude and intention, and ends in behavior. The theory of reasoned action deviates from "classical" attitude theory only in that it explicitly incorporates normative influences into the overall model. Support for the model has generally been strong in marketing applications (Ryan and Bonfield 1975; Sheppard, et al. 1988), which is a good sign for its eventual use on a more widespread basis by marketing decision makers.

The "Other Variables" Approach

Another general approach to the resolution of apparent attitude-behavior discrepancies is the use of situational variables, or what Wicker (1971) termed *other variables.* The basic notion of the other variables approach is much the same as underlies the subjective norm in the theory of reasoned action: there are many instances where attitude alone is not sufficient for explaining behavior. Wicker (1971) summarizes the other variables approach as consisting of two main classes of variables—personal factors and situational factors.

Personal Factors. Personal factors include such things as attitudes other than the one in question (for example, your attitude toward frugality may prevent you from splurging on a new compact disk that you like). Also of importance is the ability to perform the behavior under investigation (for example, you may have a positive attitude toward a new CD player but be unable to purchase it because of an acute shortage of funds). Previous patterns, or habits, may be quite difficult to break, with the result that attitudes may change more quickly than behavior.

Situational Factors. There is a wide variety of possible situational factors that may impinge on the attitude-behavior relationship. The real or implied presence of other people is of major importance in many purchase decisions. Anticipated or unanticipated extraneous events (say, your favorite brand of potato chips is out of stock) can alter behavioral performance. The availability of alternative behaviors is also of some importance (for example, you may like *Time* magazine but find yourself in a situation that makes it very easy for you to subscribe to *Newsweek,* and you don't need subscriptions to both).

Situational variables have recently become an important area for investigation within marketing. Figure 18.7 portrays two ways in which situational factors are relevant to attitude-behavior relationships (Engel, Blackwell, and Kollat 1978). As shown in the figure, anticipated situational factors (such as the TRA's subjective norm) can influence the intention to behave; in this case, the attitude-intention relationship may be weakened. Further, unanticipated events or circumstances may prevent consumers from carrying out their intentions, precipitating a breakdown in the intention-behavior link. Thus, the attitude-behavior relationship may be attenuated in two separate places. The strength of the "other variables" approach is that it attempts to specify and account for the influences that cause the attitude-behavior attenuation. The approach is actually quite consistent with the theory of reasoned action, but the former incorporates a broader range of possible influences, while the latter focuses on only normative influences.

Fazio's Process Model of Attitude-Behavior Relations

The final approach to the study of attitude-behavior relations to be considered here is psychologist Russell Fazio's *process model.* Over the past decade Fazio and his associates (e.g., Fazio 1986; Fazio, Powell, and Williams 1989) have amassed an impressive amount of evidence in support of his model, which is based on principles of *information processing.* Fazio defines attitude as a learned association between an object and an evaluation; this definition is quite consistent with the unidimensionalist view of attitude in that it excludes beliefs, intentions, and other cognitive elements.

FIGURE 18.7 Two Sources of Situational Impact on the Attitude-Behavior Relationship

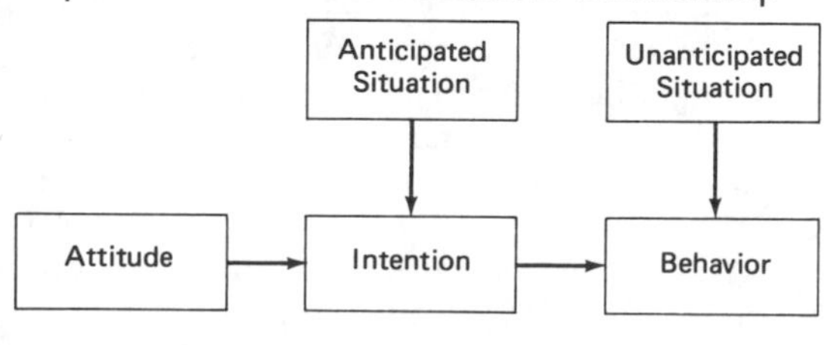

Fazio goes on to argue that, like any learned association, attitudes vary in the *strength* of learning; that is, some attitudes are more strongly learned than others. One of the factors identified by Fazio that leads to more strongly learned attitudes is the *mode of attitude formation;* attitudes that are formed on the basis of *direct personal experience* with the object tend to be more strongly held than those that are formed only on the basis of *information* about the object. For example, Berger and Mitchell (1989) found that consumers' attitudes toward five new candy bars were more predictive of their subsequent choice behavior when they had been given a free sample of each to taste, as compared with a group who had seen an ad for each of the brands but had no opportunity to sample them.

Central to Fazio's model is the notion that a strongly held attitude is more likely than a weakly held attitude to be *spontaneously retrieved* when the individual encounters the object in a behavioral setting. Only if the attitude is retrieved will it play an important role in guiding the individual's behavior. The likelihood that an attitude will be retrieved is referred to as its *accessibility.* Hence, just as a student will cram for an exam in order to memorize key facts (i.e., make them more accessible), a consumer in a sense "memorizes" attitudes toward brands and products, making them more accessible and thereby useful in guiding purchase behavior.

Fazio's process model is depicted in Figure 18.8. As shown, the attitude-to-behavior process is initiated when the attitude is activated (i.e., retrieved from memory). This attitude, whether favorable or unfavorable, serves to guide the processing of information about the attitude object. As noted in the earlier discussion of functional theory, attitudes that serve the knowledge function are thought to operate by giving rise to selective perception; that is, attending to information in the environment (or in memory) that is consistent with the acti-

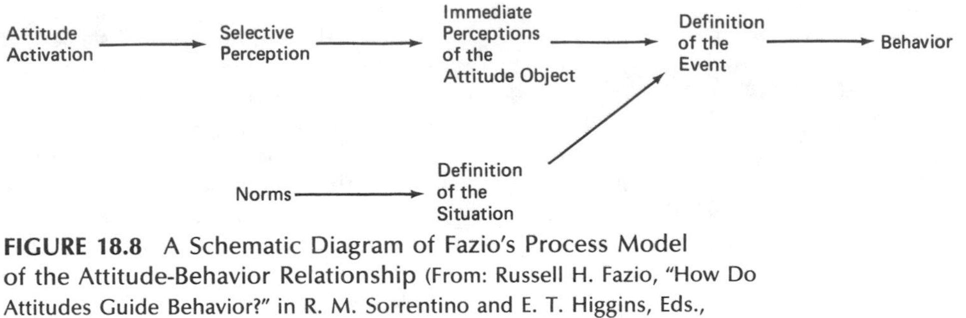

FIGURE 18.8 A Schematic Diagram of Fazio's Process Model of the Attitude-Behavior Relationship (From: Russell H. Fazio, "How Do Attitudes Guide Behavior?" in R. M. Sorrentino and E. T. Higgins, Eds., *Motivation and Cognition: Foundations of Social Behavior,* New York: Guilford Press, 1986, p. 212.)

vated attitude. Thus, Fazio's model is very much aligned with the functional perspective.[5]

Continuing Fazio's analysis, the immediate perceptions of the attitude object in any given situation will be governed by the attitude toward the object through the selective perception process. Similar to the theory of reasoned action, the perceptions of the object itself are combined with perceptions of norms operating in the situation to yield a definition of the event. Thus, the individual's behavior with respect to the attitude object will be a function of all the information, both properties of the object and properties of the normative environment, that is pertinent to the behavior in question. To the extent that the attitude is strong and provides a potent selective "filter" through which the object is perceived, it will carry a substantial amount of weight in the ultimate determination of behavior, yielding a strong correlation between attitude and behavior.

It should be noted that attitude accessibility is only one of several indicants of attitude strength. Raden (1985) provides a thorough review of recent research on a number of strength-related dimensions of attitude, for example, the *confidence* or *certainty* with which the attitude is held, its *centrality* to the individual, and its *importance, relevance,* and *extremity*. In the Berger and Mitchell (1989) study described earlier, attitude confidence displayed a different pattern of results than did attitude accessibility. Thus, although the various strength-related dimensions of attitude are generally correlated with one another, there nevertheless may be important insights revealed by consideration of their independent effects on the functioning of attitudes. In a sense, this line of research can be viewed as analogous to the "other variables" approach described earlier. Wicker's (1971) other variables were classified as personal factors and situational factors that can have an effect on the attitude-behavior relationship. To these factors, then, one can add a third class consisting of properties of the attitude itself (beyond the simple evaluative dimension). As discussed briefly here, research has already demonstrated that attitude strength dimensions can influence attitude-behavior relations. Future research on consumer attitudes will probably attempt to account for all three classes of factors in moving toward a deeper understanding of how attitudes influence behavior.

ATTITUDE'S ROLE IN MARKETING DECISION MAKING

Throughout this chapter, examples have been given of how the various approaches to attitude might be used to facilitate marketing decision making. This section will summarize some of the more important uses of attitude, particularly the general multiattribute model spawned by the original Fishbein theory of attitude.

[5]Fazio has identified his model as representing Smith, et al.'s (1956) *object-appraisal* function, which is very similar to Katz's (1960) knowledge function.

Market Segmentation

One of the most powerful approaches to market segmentation goes by the term *benefit segmentation.* Generally, benefit segmentation rests on the proposition that different groups, or segments, of consumers place different emphasis on various product benefits, or attributes. Within the context of attitude theory as developed in this chapter, benefit segments can be defined in terms of different patterns of evaluation aspects (e_i) attached to attribute dimensions.

Thus, one consumer in the market for a new automobile may place a high value ($e_i = +3$) on fuel economy and a low value ($e_i = -2$) on acceleration, whereas a second consumer may value acceleration highly ($e_i = +3$) but not care too much about fuel economy ($e_i = 0$). These two consumers would thus fall into different benefit segments and would most likely not end up purchasing the same make of automobile. Many marketers and advertising agencies conduct nationwide market surveys designed to determine and allow for benefit segmentation of the markets for their products. Because of its situation specificity, benefit segmentation is more useful than most other segmentation approaches, but it is also more costly to undertake.

New Product Concept Testing

Based on the premise that consumers form attitudes on the basis of perceived brand attributes, many marketers attempt to apply the marketing concept by building new products with attribute profiles matched to consumer attribute evaluations. This product design effort often follows a benefit segmentation study wherein key target segments are identified. In the concept test, consumers are given descriptions of various new products that vary along previously determined important attribute dimensions. The consumers are asked to indicate which new product, or combination of attributes, they prefer and the likelihood of their purchasing it. Thus, the theoretical notion of beliefs leading to attitude that then leads to behavior is used to determine which new product would be most likely to succeed in the marketplace. The insights afforded by Fazio's research point to the desirability of incorporating some form of direct product trial into new product testing, since consumers' attitudes would be more confidently held after direct experience.

Promotional Strategy

Much of the utility of attitude models lies in their ability to prescribe appropriate attitude change strategies. As shown earlier (see Table 18.4), a diagnosis of attitude based on beliefs and their associated evaluative aspects is an invaluable aid to deriving advertising and promotional strategy. Once again, marketers conduct thorough market surveys in order to determine where they stand initially and how best to achieve a favorable change (i.e., which attribute dimensions to attack).

In the pretesting phase of an advertising campaign, multiattribute measures are used to ascertain if the intended message is getting through to target consumers. During and after the actual campaign, further market surveys are conducted to see if the campaign achieved a measurable and persistent effect on attribute perceptions, attitudes, and purchasing behaviors. Again, Fazio's work provides a basis for researching the relative merits of advertising and product sampling in the promotion of a new product.

CONCLUSION

In conclusion, the attitude construct is an exceedingly valuable tool that is used in many phases of marketing decision making. Its utility supports the old adage that "there is nothing as practical as a good theory." The various theories discussed here tend to converge on a master approach to attitude, which is most clearly depicted by the unidimensionalist position (see Figure 18.2): Attitude is a key link in the causal chain between attribute perceptions on the one hand and intentions and behaviors on the other. Marketers who understand that causal sequence, and who use it in decision making, have a powerful ally in their battle for superiority in the marketplace.

REFERENCES

AJZEN, I., and M. FISHBEIN (1980), *Understanding Attitudes and Predicting Social Behavior,* Englewood Cliffs, NJ: Prentice-Hall.

BERGER, I. E., and A. A. MITCHELL (1989), "The Effect of Advertising on Attitude Accessibility, Attitude Confidence, and the Attitude-Behavior Relationship," *Journal of Consumer Research,* 16: 269–279.

ENGEL, J. F., R. D. BLACKWELL, and D. T. KOLLAT (1978), Consumer Behavior (3rd ed.). Hinsdale, IL: Dryden Press.

FAZIO, R. H. (1986), "How Do Attitudes Guide Behavior?" In *Handbook of Motivation and Cognition: Foundations of Social Behavior,* Eds. R. M. Sorrentino and E. T. Higgins. New York: Guilford, pp. 204–243.

———, M. C. POWELL, and C. J. WILLIAMS (1989), "The Role of Attitude Accessibility in the Attitude-to-Behavior Process." *Journal of Consumer Research* 16: 280–288.

FESTINGER, L. A. (1957), *Theory of Cognitive Dissonance.* Evanston, IL: Row, Peterson.

FISHBEIN, M. (1963), "An Investigation of the Relationship Between Beliefs About an Object and the Attitude Toward That Object." *Human Relations,* 233–240.

——— (1967), "Attitude and the Prediction of Behavior." In *Readings in Attitude Theory and Measurement,* Ed. M. Fishbein. New York: Wiley, pp. 477–492.

———, and I. AJZEN (1975), *Beliefs, Attitude, Intention, and Behavior: An Introduction to Theory and Research.* Reading, MA: Addison-Wesley.

HEIDER, F. (1946), "Attitudes and Cognitive Organization." *Journal of Psychology,* 107–112.

KATZ, D. (1960), "The Functional Approach to the Study of Attitudes." *Public Opinion Quarterly* 24: 163–204.

LAVIDGE, R. J., and G. A. STEINER (1961), "A Model for Predictive Measurement of Advertising Effectiveness." *Journal of Marketing* 25: 59–62.

LOCANDER, W. B., and W. A. SPIVEY (1978), "A Functional Approach to Attitude Measurement." *Journal of Marketing Research* 15: 576–587.

LUTZ, R. J. (1975), "Changing Brand Attitudes Through Modification of Cognitive Structure." *Journal of Consumer Research* 1: 49–59.

——— (1981), "A Reconceptualization of the Functional Approach to Attitude." In *Research in Marketing,* Vol. 5. Ed. J. N. Sheth. Greenwich, CT: JAI Press, pp. 165–210.

LUTZ, R. J., and J. R. BETTMAN (1977), "Multiattribute Models in Marketing: A Bicentennial Review." In *Consumer and Industrial Buying Behavior,* Eds. A. G. Woodside, J. N. Sheth, and P. D. Bennett. New York: North-Holland, pp. 137–150.

MAZIS, M. B., and J. E. ADKINSON (1976), "An Experimental Evaluation of a Proposed Corrective Advertising Remedy." *Journal of Marketing Research* 13: 178–183.

MCCRACKEN, G. (1989), "Who Is the Celebrity Endorser? Cultural Foundations of the Endorsement Process." *Journal of Consumer Research* 16: 310–321.

OSGOOD, C. E., G. J. SUCI, and P. H. TANNENBAUM (1957), *The Measurement of Meaning.* Urbana, IL: University of Illinois Press.

RADEN, D. (1985), "Strength-Related Attitude Dimensions." *Social Psychology Quarterly* 48: 312–330.

ROKEACH, M. (1973), *The Nature of Human Values.* New York: Free Press.

ROSENBERG, M. J. (1960), "An Analysis of Affective-Cognitive Consistency." In *Attitude Organization and Change,* Eds. C. I. Hovland and M. J. Rosenberg. New Haven, CT: Yale University Press, pp. 15–64.

RYAN, M. J., and BONFIELD, E. H. (1975), "The Fishbein Extended Model and Consumer Behavior." *Journal of Consumer Research* 2: 118–136.

SHAVITT, S. (1989), "Operationalizing Functional Theories of Attitude." In *Attitude Structure and Function,* Eds. A. R. Pratkanis, S. J. Breckler, and A. G. Greenwald. Hillsdale, NJ: Erlbaum, pp. 311–337.

SMITH, M. B., J. S. BRUNER, and R. W. WHITE (1956), *Opinions and Personality.* New York: Wiley.

SNYDER, M., and DEBONO, K. G. (1985), "Appeals to Image and Claims about Quality: Understanding the Psychology of Advertising." *Journal of Personality and Social Psychology* 49: 586–597.

WICKER, A. W. (1969), "Attitudes vs. Actions: The Relationship of Verbal and Overt Behavioral Responses to Attitude Objects." *Journal of Social Issues* 25: 41–78.

——— (1971), "An Examination of the 'Other Variables' Explanation of Attitude-Behavior Inconsistency." *Journal of Personality and Social Psychology* 19: 18–30.

WILKIE, W. L., and E. A. PESSEMIER. (1973), "Issues in Marketing's Use of Multiattribute Attitude Models." *Journal of Marketing Research* 10: 428–441.

19

CENTRAL AND PERIPHERAL ROUTES TO ADVERTISING EFFECTIVENESS: The Moderating Role of Involvement*

Richard E. Petty
John T. Cacioppo
David Schumann

Undergraduates expressed their attitudes about a product after being exposed to a magazine ad under conditions of either high or low product involvement. The ad contained either strong or weak arguments for the product and featured either prominent sports celebrities or average citizens as endorsers. The manipulation of argument quality had a greater impact on attitudes under high than low involvement, but the manipulation of product endorser had a greater impact under low than high involvement. These results are consistent with the view that there are two relatively distinct routes to persuasion.

Over the past three decades, a large number of studies have examined how consumers' evaluations of issues, candidates, and products are affected by media advertisements. Research on the methods by which consumers' attitudes are formed and changed has accelerated at a pace such that Kassarjian and Kassarjian were led to the conclusion that "attitudes clearly have become the central focus of consumer behavior research" (1979, p. 3). Not only are there a large number of empirical studies on consumer attitude formation and change, but there are also a large number of different theories of persuasion vying for the attention of the discipline (see Engel and Blackwell 1982; Kassarjian 1982).

*Reprinted from the *Journal of Consumer Research,* 10 (September 1983), pp. 135–146.

In our recent reviews of the many approaches to attitude change employed in social and consumer psychology, we have suggested that—even though the different theories of persuasion possess different terminologies, postulates, underlying motives, and particular "effects" that they specialize in explaining—these theories emphasize one of two distinct routes to attitude change (Petty and Cacioppo 1981, 1983). One, called the *central route,* views attitude change as resulting from a person's diligent consideration of information that she/he feels is central to the true merits of a particular attitudinal position. The theoretical approaches following this route emphasize factors such as (1) the cognitive justification of attitude discrepant behavior (Cummings and Venkatesan 1976; Festinger 1957); (2) the comprehension, learning, and retention of issue- or product-relevant information (Bettman 1979; Hovland, Janis, and Kelley 1953; McGuire 1976); (3) the nature of a person's idiosyncratic cognitive responses to external communications (Cacioppo and Petty 1980a; Greenwald 1968; Petty, Ostrom, and Brock 1981; Wright 1980); and (4) the manner in which a person combines and integrates issue- or product-relevant beliefs into an overall evaluative reaction (Ajzen and Fishbein 1980; Lutz and Bettman 1977; Troutman and Shanteau 1976). Attitude changes induced via the central route are postulated to be relatively enduring and predictive of behavior (Cialdini, Petty, and Cacioppo 1981; Petty and Cacioppo 1980).

A second group of theoretical approaches to persuasion emphasizes a more *peripheral route* to attitude change. Attitude changes that occur via the peripheral route do not occur because an individual has personally considered the pros and cons of the issue, but because the attitude issue or object is associated with positive or negative cues—or because the person makes a simple inference about the merits of the advocated position based on various simple cues in the persuasion context. For example, rather than diligently considering the issue-relevant arguments, a person may accept an advocacy simply because it was presented during a pleasant lunch or because the source is an expert. Similarly, a person may reject an advocacy simply because the position presented appears to be too extreme. These cues (e.g., good food, expert sources, extreme positions) and inferences (e.g., "If an expert says it, it must be true") may shape attitudes or allow a person to decide what attitudinal position to adopt without the need for engaging in any extensive thought about issue- or product-relevant arguments. The theoretical approaches following the peripheral route emphasize factors such as (1) whether a simple attitudinal inference can be made based on observing one's own behavior (Bem 1972; Scott 1978); (2) whether the advocacy falls within one's latitude of acceptance or rejection (Newman and Dolich 1979; Sherif, Sherif, and Nebergall 1965); (3) whether some transient situational utility is associated with adopting a particular attitude (Schlenker 1978, 1980); and (4) whether an advocated position or product is classically conditioned to basic but issue-irrelevant cues, such as food and pain (Janis, Kaye, and Kirschner 1965; Sternthal and Craig 1974), or is associated with secondary cues, such as pleasant pictures and attractive endorsers (Kelman 1961; Mitchell and Olson 1981; Mowen 1980). Attitude changes induced under the peripheral route are postulated to be relatively temporary and unpredictive of behavior.[1]

---

[1]Our categorization of the traditional theoretical approaches under one or the other route to persuasion is meant to be suggestive rather than absolute. For example, the theoretical process of self-perception (Bem 1972) might generally lead to attitude change because of a simple inference (peripheral route), but might also be capable of initiating extended issue-relevant thinking in other circumstances (e.g., when personal relevance is high; see Liebhart 1979). Additionally, we note that the view that there are different "kinds" of persuasion can be traced back to Aristotle's *Rhetoric,* and that the distinction we have made between the central and peripheral routes to attitude change has much in common with Kelman's (1961) earlier view of "internalization" vs. "identification" and with the recent psychological distinctions between "deep" vs. "shallow" processing (Craik and Lockhart 1972), "controlled" vs. "automatic" processing (Schneider and Shiffrin 1977), "systematic" vs. "heuristic" processing (Chaiken 1980), "thoughtful" vs. "scripted" or "mindless" processing (Abelson 1976; Langer et al. 1978), and others. For more details on similarities and differences among the approaches, see Petty and Cacioppo (forthcoming a).

Unfortunately, none of the unique theories of persuasion has yet provided a comprehensive view of attitude change. For example, cognitive response theory—an approach that falls under the central route—assumes that people are usually interested in thinking about and elaborating incoming information, or in self-generating issue- or product-relevant thoughts (Brock and Shavitt 1983). Yet, as Miller and his colleagues have noted, "It may be irrational to scrutinize the plethora of counterattitudinal messages received daily. To the extent that one possesses only a limited amount of information processing time and capacity, such scrutiny would disengage the thought process from the exigencies of daily life." (Miller, Maruyama, Beaber, and Valone 1976, p. 623). Haines (1974), in fact, has proposed a principle of information-processing parsimony according to which consumers seek to process as little data as necessary in order to make decisions.

The accumulated research on persuasion clearly indicates that neither the central not the peripheral approach alone can account for the diversity of attitude-change results observed. Thus, a general framework for understanding attitude change must consider that in some situations people are avid seekers and manipulators of information, and in others they are best described as "cognitive misers" who eschew any difficult intellectual activity (Burnkrant 1976; McGuire 1969). An important question for consumer researchers then is: when will consumers actively seek and process product-relevant information, and when will they be more cursory in their analysis of ads? Recent research in consumer behavior and social psychology has focused on the concept of "involvement" as an important moderator of the amount and type of information processing elicited by a persuasive communication (see Burnkrant and Sawyer 1983; Petty and Cacioppo 1981, 1983). One major goal of the experiment reported in this paper was to test the hypothesis that under "high involvement," attitudes in response to an advertisement would be affected via the central route, but that under "low involvement," attitudes would be affected via the peripheral route.

INVOLVEMENT AND ATTITUDE CHANGE

Methods of Studying Involvement

Although there are many specific definitions of involvement within both social and consumer psychology, there is considerable agreement that high involvement messages have greater personal relevance and consequences or elicit more personal connections than low involvement messages (Engel and Blackwell 1982; Krugman 1965; Petty and Cacioppo 1979; Sherif and Hovland 1961).[2] Various strategies have been employed in studying involvement. For example, both social (Hovland et al. 1957) and consumer (Newman and Dolich 1979) researchers have investigated existing groups that differed in the extent to which an issue or product was personally important, or have employed designs allowing subjects to assign themselves to high and low involvement groups. These correctional methods may be high in external validity, but they confound involvement with all other existing differences between the high and low involvement groups (attitude extremity, amount of prior information, and so on), and thus compromise internal validity (Kiesler, Collins, and Miller 1969). Other social (Rhine and Severance 1970) and consumer (Lastovicka and Gardner 1979) researchers have defined involvement in terms of the specific issue or product under consideration. This procedure, of course, confounds involvement with aspects of the issue or product that may be irrelevant to its personal importance. Finally, some researchers have studied involvement by varying the medium of message presentation. Interestingly, some investigators

[2]In the present paper, we use the term involvement to refer to "issue" or "product" involvement rather than "response" involvement. In the former, the attitude issue or the product itself has some direct personal relevance or consequence, and people are concerned with forming a reasoned opinion (Petty and Cacioppo 1979). In the latter, the attitude response is important, and people are more concerned with expressing an attitude that will produce immediate situational rewards (such as gaining favor with others) than with forming a veridical opinion (Zimbardo 1960).

have argued that television is a more involving medium than print (Worchel, Andreoli, and Eason 1975), whereas others have argued just the opposite (Krugman 1967).

A preferred procedure for studying involvement would be to hold recipient, message, and medium characteristics constant and randomly assign participants to high and low involvement groups. Apsler and Sears (1968) employed an ingenious method to manipulate involvement: some participants were led to believe that a persuasive proposal had personal implications for them (an advocated change in university regulations would take effect while the student participants were still in school), while others were led to believe that it did not (i.e., the change would not take effect until after the students had graduated). A variation of this procedure was developed by Wright (1973, 1974) to manipulate involvement in an advertising study. Participants in the high involvement group were told that they would subsequently be asked to evaluate the product in an advertisement they were about to see, and were given some additional background information. Participants in the low involvement group did not expect to evaluate the product and were given no background information. The background information provided to the high involvement subjects explained the relevance of their product decisions to "their families, their own time and effort, and their personal finances" (Wright 1973, p. 56). However, it is somewhat unclear to what extent this background information made certain product-relevant arguments salient or suggested appropriate dimensions of product evaluation for high but not low involvement subjects.

In the present experiment, participants in both the high and low involvement groups were told that they would be evaluating advertisements for products, but subjects in the high involvement group were led to believe that the experimental advertised product would soon be available in their local area, and that after viewing a variety of advertisements they would be allowed to choose one brand from the experimental product category to take home as a gift. Low involvement participants were led to believe that the experimental advertised product would not be available in their local area in the near future, and that after viewing the ads they would be allowed to take home one brand from a category of products other than the experimental category.

Theories of Involvement

In addition to the methodological differences that have plagued the involvement concept, another area of disagreement concerns the effects on persuasion that involvement is expected to have. Perhaps the dominant notion in social psychology stems from the Sherifs' social judgment theory (Sherif et al. 1965). Their notion is that on any given issue, highly involved persons exhibit more negative evaluations of a communication because high involvement is associated with an extended "latitude of rejection." Thus, incoming messages on involving topics are thought to have an enhanced probability of being rejected because they are more likely to fall within the unacceptable range of a person's implicit attitude continuum. Krugman (1965) has proposed an alternative view that has achieved considerable recognition among consumer researchers. According to this view, increasing involvement does not increase resistance to persuasion, but instead shifts the sequence of communication impact. Krugman argues that under high involvement, a communication is likely to affect cognitions, then attitudes, and then behaviors, whereas under low involvement, a communication is more likely to affect cognitions, then behaviors, then attitudes (see also Ray et al. 1973).

As noted earlier, a focal goal of this study is to assess the viability of a third view of the effects of involvement on consumer response to advertisements. This view stems from our Elaboration Likelihood Model (ELM) of attitude change (Petty and Cacioppo 1981). The basic tenet of the ELM is that different methods of inducing persuasion may work best depending on whether the elaboration likelihood of the communication situation (i.e., the probability of message- or issue-relevant thought occurring) is high or low. When the elaboration likelihood is high, the central route to persuasion should be particularly effective, but when the elaboration likelihood is low, the peripheral route should be better. The ELM contends that as an issue or product increases in personal relevance or consequences, it becomes more important and adaptive to forming a reasoned and veridical opinion. Thus, people are more motivated to devote the cognitive effort required to evaluate the true merits of an issue or product when involvement is high rather than low. If increased involvement increases one's propensity to think about the true merits of an issue or product, then manipulations that require extensive issue- or product-relevant thought in order to be effective should have a greater impact under high rather than low involvement conditions. On the other hand, manipulations that allow a person to evaluate an issue or product without engaging in extensive issue- or product-relevant thinking should have a greater impact under low rather than high involvement.

Research in social psychology has supported the view that different variables affect persuasion under high and low involvement conditions. For example, the quality of the arguments contained in a message has had a greater impact on persuasion under conditions of high rather than low involvement (Petty and Cacioppo 1979; Petty, Cacioppo, and Heesacker 1981). On the other hand, peripheral cues such as the expertise or attractiveness of a message source (Chaiken 1980; Petty, Cacioppo, and Goldman 1981; Rhine and Severance 1970) have had a greater impact on persuasion under conditions of low rather than high involvement. In sum, under high involvement conditions people appear to exert the cognitive effort required to evaluate the issue-relevant arguments presented, and their attitudes are a function of this information-processing activity (central route). Under low involvement conditions, attitudes appear to be affected by simple acceptance and rejection cues in the persuasion context and are less affected by argument quality (peripheral route). Although the accumulated research in social psychology is quite consistent with the ELM, it is not yet clear whether or not the ELM predictions would hold when involvement concerns a product (such as toothpaste) rather than an issue (such as capital punishment), and when the persuasive message is an advertisement rather than a speech or editorial.

Central and Peripheral Routes to Advertising Effectiveness

One important implication of the ELM for advertising messages is that different kinds of appeals may be most effective for different audiences. For example, a person who is about to purchase a new refrigerator (high involvement) may scrutinize the product-relevant information presented in an advertisement. If this information is perceived to be cogent and persuasive, favorable attitudes will result, but if this information is weak and specious, unfavorable attitudes will result (central route). On the other hand, a person who is not considering purchasing a new refrigerator at the moment (low involvement) will not expend the effort required to think about the product-relevant arguments in the ad, but may instead focus on the attractiveness, credibility, or prestige of the product's endorser (peripheral route). Some evidence in consumer psychology is consistent with this reasoning. For example, Wright (1973, 1974) exposed people to an advertisement for a soybean product under high and low involvement conditions (see earlier description) and measured the number of source comments (derogations) and message comments (counterarguments) generated after exposure. Although Wright (1974) predicted that involvement would increase both kinds of comments, he found that more message comments were made under high rather than low involvement, but that more source comments were made under low involvement conditions. This finding, of course, is consistent with the ELM.

In an initial attempt to provide a specific test of the utility of the ELM for understanding the effectiveness of advertising messages (Petty and Cacioppo 1980), we conducted a study in which three variables were manipulated: (1) the personal relevance of a shampoo ad (high involvement subjects were led to believe that the product would be available in their local area, whereas low involvement subjects were not); (2) the quality of the arguments contained in the ad; and (3) the physical attractiveness of the endorsers of the shampoo. Consistent with the ELM predictions, the quality of the arguments contained in the advertisement had a greater impact on attitudes when the product was of high rather than low relevance. Contrary to expectations, however, the attractiveness of the endorsers was equally important under both the high and low involvement conditions. In retrospect, in addition to serving as a peripheral cue under low involvement, the physical appearance of the product endorsers (especially their hair) may have served as persuasive visual testimony for the product's effectiveness. Thus, under high involvement conditions, the physical attractiveness of the endorsers may have served as a cogent product-relevant argument.

The present study was a conceptual replication of previous work (Petty and Cacioppo 1980), except that we employed a peripheral cue that could not be construed as a product-relevant argument. In the current study, participants were randomly assigned to high and low involvement conditions and viewed one of four different ads for a fictitious new product, "Edge disposable razors." The ad was presented in magazine format and was embedded in an advertising booklet along with 11 other ads. Two features of the Edge ad were manipulated: the quality of the arguments in support of Edge (strong or weak), and the celebrity status of the featured endorsers of Edge (celebrity or average citizen). It is important to note that preliminary testing revealed that for most people, the celebrity status of the endorsers was irrelevant to an evaluation of the true merits of a disposable razor, but that because the celebrity endorsers were liked more than the average citizens, they could still serve as a positive peripheral cue.

We had two major hypotheses. First, we expected the quality of the arguments presented in the ad to have a greater impact on product attitudes under high rather than low involvement conditions. Second, we expected the celebrity status of the product endorsers to have a greater impact on product attitudes under low rather than high involvement conditions. If these hypotheses were supported, it would provide the first evidence that the Elaboration Likelihood Model can contribute to understanding the effects of involvement on attitudinal responses to advertisements.

METHOD

Subjects and Design

A total of 160 male and female undergraduates at the University of Missouri–Columbia participated in the experiment to earn credit in an introductory psychology course; 20 subjects were randomly assigned to each of the cells in a 2 (involvement: high or low) × 2 (argument quality: strong or weak) × 2 (cue: celebrity or noncelebrity status) factorial design. Subjects participated in groups of three to 15 in a very large classroom. The subjects were isolated from each other so that they could complete the experiment independently, and subjects in a single session participated in different experimental conditions. In fact, if enough subjects were present it was possible to conduct all eight experimental conditions simultaneously. This procedure avoided confounding session with experimental condition.

Procedure

Two booklets were prepared for the study. The first contained the advertising stimuli and the second contained the dependent measures. The first page of the advertising booklet explained that the study concerned the evaluation of magazine and newspaper ads and that the psychology department was cooperating with the journalism school in this endeavor. The first page also contained part of the involvement manipulation (see below). It was explained that each ad in the booklet was preceded by an introductory statement that told a little about the advertisement that followed (e.g., "The ______ company of Paris, France has just opened an American office in New York City. This élite men's clothing company originally sold clothing only in Europe, but is now in the process of attempting to enter the American market. The ad on the next page is one that they will be testing soon in Tampa, Florida, before running the ads in other major cities that will eventually carry their products"). The instructions told subjects to continue through the booklet at their own pace and to raise their hands when finished. The ad booklet contained 10 real magazine ads for both relatively familiar (e.g., Aquafresh toothpaste) and unfamiliar (e.g., Riopan antacid) products, and two bogus ads. The sixth ad in each booklet was the crucial fictitious ad for Edge razors (the nature of the other bogus ad was varied but is irrelevant to the present study). When subjects had completed perusing their ad booklets, they were given a questionnaire booklet to complete. Upon completion of the questionnaire, the subjects were thoroughly debriefed, thanked for their participation, and dismissed.

Independent Variables

Involvement. Involvement was embedded in two places in the ad booklet. First, the cover page offered subjects a free gift for participation in the experiment. Subjects were either informed that they would be allowed to choose a particular brand of disposable razor (high involvement with the fictitious Edge ad) or that they would be allowed to choose a brand of toothpaste (low involvement with Edge). A toothpaste ad did appear in the ad booklet, but it was the same ad for all subjects. To bolster the involvement manipulation, the page that introduced the Edge ad also differed in the high and low involvement conditions. High involvement subjects were told that the advertisement and product would soon be test-marketed in medium-sized cities throughout the Midwest, including their own city (Columbia, Missouri); low involvement subjects were told that the advertisement and product were being test-marketed only on the East Coast. Thus high involvement subjects were not only led to believe that they would soon have to make a decision about the product class, they were also led to believe that the product would be available in their area in the near future. Low involvement subjects, on the other hand, did not expect to make a decision about razors (but did expect to make one about toothpaste), and were led to believe that Edge razors would not be available for purchase in their area in the foreseeable future.

Argument Quality. A variety of arguments for disposable razors were pretested for potency on a sample of undergraduates. In the strong arguments ad, the razor was characterized as "scientifically designed," and the following five statements were made about the product:

- New advanced honing method creates unsurpassed sharpness
- Special chemically formulated coating eliminates nicks and cuts and prevents rusting
- Handle is tapered and ribbed to prevent slipping
- In direct comparison tests, the Edge blade gave twice as many close shaves as its nearest competitor
- Unique angle placement of the blade provides the smoothest shave possible

In the weak arguments version of the ad, the razor was characterized as "designed for beauty," and the following five statements were made about the product:

- Floats in water with a minimum of rust
- Comes in various sizes, shapes, and colors
- Designed with the bathroom in mind
- In direct comparison tests, the Edge blade gave no more nicks and cuts than its competition
- Can only be used once but will be memorable

Peripheral Cue. In the "famous endorser" conditions, the headline accompanying the advertisement read "Professional Athletes Agree: Until you try new Edge disposable razors you'll never know what a really close shave is." In addition, the ad featured the pictures of two well-known, well-liked golf (male) and tennis (female) celebrities. In the "nonfamous endorser" conditions, the headline read "Bakersfield, California Agrees: ______," and the ad featured pictures of average looking people who were unfamiliar to the subjects. The average citizens in the ad were middle-aged and characterized as coming from California to minimize perceptions of similarity to the subjects (Missouri college students). Figure 19.1 depicts two of the four Edge ads used in the present study.

Dependent Measures

On the first page of the dependent variable booklet, subjects were asked to try to list all of the product categories for which they saw advertisements, and to try to recall the brand name of the product in that category. On the next page, subjects were given descriptions of the 12 product categories and were asked to select the correct brand name from among seven choices provided. Although we had no specific hypotheses about brand recall and recognition, these measures were included because of their practical importance and for purposes of comparison with the attitude data.

Next, subjects responded to some questions about one of the legitimate ads in the booklet; this was followed by the crucial questions about Edge razors. The questions about Edge were placed relatively early in the booklet to avoid subject fatigue and boredom and to maximize the effectiveness of the manipulations. Subjects were first asked to rate, on a four-point scale, how likely it would be that they would purchase Edge disposable razors "the next time you needed a product of this nature." The descriptions for each scale value were: 1 = "I definitely would not buy it," 2 = "I might or might not buy it," 3 = "I would probably buy it," and 4 = "I would definitely buy it." Following this measure of purchase intentions, subjects were asked to rate their overall impression of the product on three nine-point semantic differential scales anchored at −4 and +4 (bad–good, unsatisfactory–satisfactory, and unfavorable–favorable). Since the intercorrelations among these mea-

FIGURE 19.1 Example Mock Ads

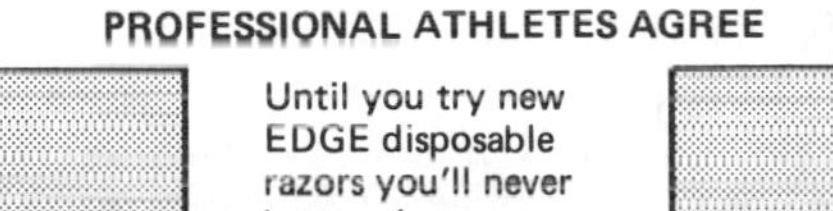
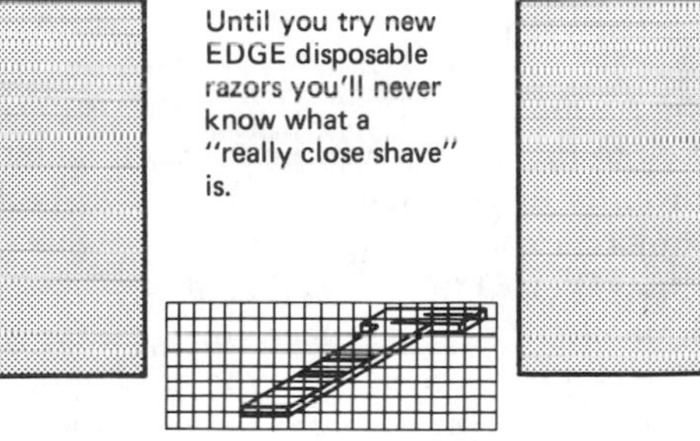

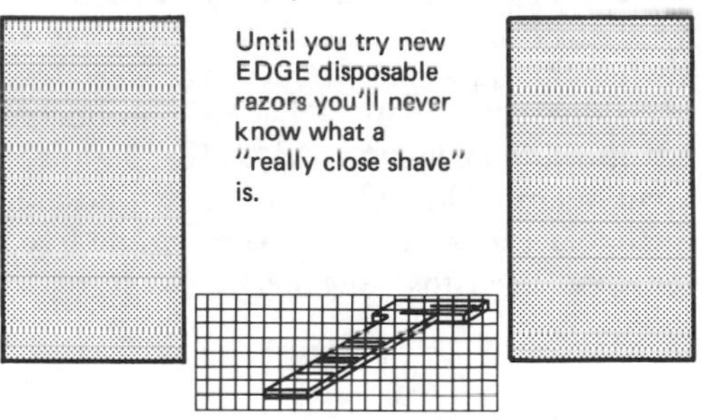

(Note: Left panel shows celebrity endorser ad for Edge razors employing the strong arguments. Right panel shows average citizen endorser ad for Edge razors employing the weak arguments. Pictures of celebrities and citizens have been blacked out to preserve propriety and anonymity.)

sures were very high (average $r = 0.86$), responses were averaged to assess a general positive or negative attitude toward the product.

Following some additional questions that were consistent with the cover story, subjects were instructed to list the thoughts that crossed their minds as they examined the ad for Edge disposable razors. These thoughts were subsequently scored on several dimensions by trained judges. Since subjects listed very few thoughts about the product ($M = 1.18$) and since the manipulations failed to affect this measure, it will not be discussed further. This "cognitive response" measure would probably have been more sensitive if it had been administered immediately after exposure to the Edge ad rather than after exposure to all 12 ads, but in the present study this would have compromised the cover story (for an extended discussion of the reliability, validity, and sensitivity of the thought-listing measure in persuasion research, see Cacioppo and Petty 1981).

After listing their thoughts, several questions were asked to check on the experimental manipulations, and subjects were asked to try to list as many of the attributes mentioned in the ad about Edge razors as they could recall. Following the questions about Edge were several questions about some of the other products and ads in the booklet. As a check on the involvement manipulation, the very last question in the booklet asked subjects to recall the free gift they had been told to expect.

RESULTS

Manipulation Checks

In response to the last question in the dependent variable booklet asking subjects what gift they had been told to expect, 92.5 percent of the subjects in the high involvement conditions correctly recalled that they were to select a brand of disposable razor. In the low involvement conditions, none of the subjects indicated a razor and 78 percent correctly recalled that they were to select a brand of toothpaste. Thus, subjects presumably realized what product they were soon to make a decision about as they examined the ad booklet.

To assess the effectiveness of the endorser manipulation, two questions were asked. First, subjects were asked if they recognized the people in the ad for the disposable razor. When the famous athletes were employed, 94 percent indicated "yes," whereas when the average citizens were employed, 96 percent indicated "no." In addition, subjects were asked to rate the extent to which they liked the people depicted in the ad on an 11-point scale, where 1 indicated "liked very little" and 11 indicated "liked very much." An analysis of this measure revealed that the famous endorsers were liked more ($= 6.06$) than the average citizens ($M = 3.64$; $F(1, 143) = 40.81$, $p < 0.0001$); on average, women reported liking the endorsers more ($M = 5.32$) than did men ($M = 4.44$; $F(1, 143) = 5.25$, $p < 0.03$).

As a check on the argument-persuasiveness manipulation, two questions were asked. The first required respondents to "rate the reasons as described in the advertisement for using EDGE" on an 11-point scale anchored by "unpersuasive" and "persuasive"; the second question asked them to rate the reasons on an 11-point scale anchored by "weak reasons" and "strong reasons." On the first measure, subjects exposed to the strong arguments rated them as significantly more persuasive ($M = 5.46$) than did subjects exposed to the weak arguments ($M = 4.03$; $F(1, 139) = 12.97$, $p < 0.0004$). Additionally, a main effect for gender was found such that women rated the arguments as more persuasive ($M = 5.26$) than did men ($M = 4.28$; $F(1, 139) = 5.25$, $p < 0.02$). Finally, an Arguments × Gender interaction emerged ($F(1, 139) = 5.43$, $p < 0.02$), indicating that the tendency for females to find the arguments more persuasive than males was greater for the strong than for the weak arguments. On the second manipulation check measure, subjects rated the strong arguments as "stronger" ($M = 5.58$) than the weak ones ($M = 4.13$; $F(1, 138) = 14.31$, $p < 0.0002$). Again, an Arguments × Gender interaction occurred, indicating that females especially tended to rate the strong arguments more highly than did males. In short, all of the variables were manipulated successfully. The tendency for females to be more positive in their ratings of both endorsers and the arguments in the ads is generally consistent with previous psychological research portraying women as more concerned with social harmony than men (Eagly 1978). Importantly, these sex differences did not lead to any significant gender effects on the crucial measures of attitude and purchase intention.

Attitudes and Purchase Intentions

Table 19.1 presents the means and standard deviations for each cell on the attitude index. A number of interesting main effects emerged. First, involved subjects were somewhat more skeptical of the product ($M = 0.31$) than were less involved subjects ($M = 0.99$; $F(1, 148) = 6.64$, $p < 0.01$). Second, subjects liked the product significantly more when the ad contained cogent arguments ($M = 1.65$) than when the arguments were specious ($M = -0.35$; $F(1, 148) = 57.81$, $p < 0.0001$). Third, subjects tended to like the product more when it was endorsed by the famous athletes ($M = 0.86$) than by the average citizens of Bakersfield, California ($M = 0.41$; $F(1, 148) = 2.91$, $p < 0.09$).

Each of these main effects must be qualified and interpreted in light of two important two-way interactions. First, an Involvement × Endorser interaction ($F(1, 148) = 5.94$, $p < 0.02$) revealed that the nature of the product endorser had a significant impact on product attitudes only under low involvement ($F(1, 148) = 5.96$, $p < 0.02$), but not under high involvement ($F < 1$; see top panel of Figure 19.2). On the other hand, an Involvement × Arguments interaction ($F(1, 148) = 18.47$, $p < 0.0001$) revealed that although argument quality had an impact on product attitudes under both low involvement ($F(1, 148) = 5.40$, $p < 0.02$) and high involvement ($F(1, 148) = 71.36$, $p < 0.0001$), the impact of argument quality on attitudes was significantly greater under high rather than low involvement (see bottom panel of Figure 19.2). Neither the Endorser × Arguments nor the three-way interaction approached significance ($F = 0.14$ and 0.54, respectively).

Two significant effects emerged from the question asking subjects to rate their likelihood of purchasing Edge disposable razors the next time they needed a product of this nature. Subjects said that they would be more likely to buy the product when the arguments presented were strong ($M = 2.23$) rather than weak ($M = 1.68$; $F(1, 152) = 25.37$, $p < 0.0001$). Additionally, an Involvement × Arguments interaction emerged ($F(1,152) = 4.25$, $p < 0.04$). This interaction paralleled that obtained on the attitude measure and indicated that argument quality was a more important determinant of purchase intentions under high rather than low involvement.

The correlation between attitudes and purchase intentions for low involvement subjects

TABLE 19.1 Means and Standard Deviations for Each Experimental Cell on the Attitude Index

	Low Involvement		High Involvement	
	Weak Arguments	*Strong Arguments*	*Weak Arguments*	*Strong Arguments*
Citizen endorser	−.12 (1.81)	.98 (1.52)	−1.10 (1.66)	1.98 (1.25)
Celebrity endorser	1.21 (2.28)	1.85 (1.59)	−1.36 (1.65)	1.80 (1.07)

Note: Attitude scores represent the average rating of the product on three nine-point semantic differential scales anchored at −4 and +4 (bad–good, unsatisfactory–satisfactory, and unfavorable–favorable). Standard deviations are in parentheses.

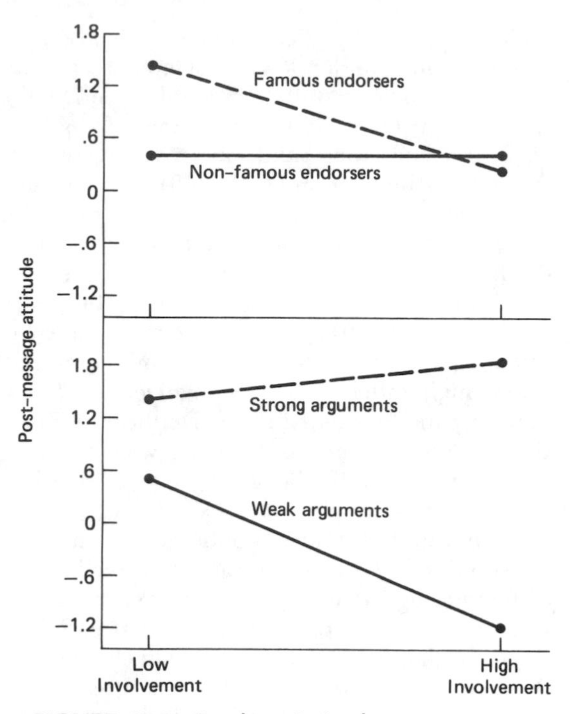

FIGURE 19.2 Product Attitudes

Note: Top panel shows interactive effect of involvement and endorser status on attitudes toward Edge razors. Bottom panel shows interactive effect of involvement and argument quality on attitudes toward Edge razors.

was 0.36; and for high involvement subjects it was 0.59. Although both correlations are significantly different from zero ($ps < 0.001$), it is interesting to note that the low involvement correlation is considerably smaller than the high involvement correlation ($p < 0.07$). The fact that the argument quality manipulation affected behavioral intentions while the endorser manipulation did not (although it did affect attitudes)—and the fact that attitudes were better predictors of behavioral intentions under high rather than low involvement—provide some support for the ELM view that attitudes formed via the central route will be more predictive of behavior than attitudes formed via the peripheral route.

Recall and Recognition Measures

Subjects were asked to list all of the products for which they saw ads and all of the brand names they encountered. Following this, all subjects were told that they had seen an advertisement for a disposable razor and were asked to select the correct brand name from a list of seven (Gillette, Wilkinson, Schick, Edge, Bic, Schaffer, and Remington). The proportion of subjects showing correct recall or recognition was calculated for each cell. These proportions were then subjected to an arcsin transformation (Winer 1971) and analyzed by the procedure recommended by Langer and Abelson (1972).

The involvement manipulation had a significant impact on free recall of the product category, with more high involvement subjects (81 percent) recalling the product category than low involvement subjects (64 percent; $Z = 2.4$, $p < 0.02$). Additionally, exposure to the famous endorser increased recall of the product category under low involvement conditions (from 52 percent to 75 percent; $Z = 2.14$, $p < 0.03$), but had no effect on product category recall under high involvement 80 versus 82 percent).

Involvement affected free recall of the brand name of the product, increasing it from 42 percent in the low involvement conditions to 60 percent in the high involvement conditions ($Z = 2.28$, $p < 0.01$). There was also an effect for gender on this measure, with males showing greater brand name recall (61 percent) than females (39 percent; $Z = 2.78$, $p < 0.007$). The endorser manipulation had a marginally significant effect on brand name recall, with the famous endorsers tending to enhance recall over average citizens from 43 to 58 percent ($Z = 1.89$, $p < 0.06$).

On the measure of brand name recognition, an interaction pattern emerged. Under low involvement, the use of famous endorsers reduced brand name recognition from 85 to 70 percent, but under high involvement, the use of famous endorsers improved brand name recognition from 77 to 87 percent ($Z = 1.96$, $p < 0.05$).[3]

To summarize the recall and recognition data thus far, it appears that increasing involvement with the product enhanced recall not only of the product category, but also of the brand name of the specific product advertised. The effects of the endorser manipulation were more complex and depended on the level of involvement. In general, under low involvement a positive endorser led to increased recall of the product category but reduced brand name recognition. Thus, people may be more likely to notice the products in low involvement ads when they feature prominent personalities, but because of the enhanced attention accorded the people in the ads and the general lack of interest in assessing the merits of the product (due to low involvement), reductions in brand recognition may occur. This finding is similar to the results of studies on the use of sexually oriented material in ads for low involvement products—the sexual material enhances recognition of the ad, but not the brand name of the product (e.g., Chestnut, LaChance, and Lubitz 1977; Steadman 1969). Under high involvement, however, the use of prominent personalities enhanced brand name recognition. When people are more interested in the product category, they may be more motivated to assess what brand the liked personalities are endorsing. The manipulation of argument quality had no effect on recall of the product category, brand name recall, or brand name recognition.

A final recall measure assessed how many of the specific arguments for Edge razors the subjects could spontaneously recall after they had examined the entire ad booklet. Overall, subjects were able to correctly reproduce only 1.75 of the five arguments presented. This was not affected by any of the experimental manipulations.

Clearly, the manipulations produced a very different pattern of effects on the recall and recognition measures than on the attitude and purchase intention measures. In addition, the recall and recognition measures were uncorrelated with attitudes or intentions toward Edge razors. This finding is consistent with a growing body of research indicating that simple recall or recognition of information presented about an attitude object is not predictive of attitude formation and change (e.g., Cacioppo and Petty 1979; Greenwald 1968; Insko, Lind, and LaTour 1976).

The present data also argue against using measures of brand name recall or recognition as the sole indicants of advertising effectiveness. For example, in the present study, enhancing involvement led to a significant improvement in brand name recall, but increasing involvement led to a decrement in attitude toward the brand when the arguments presented were weak.

DISCUSSION

As we noted earlier, previous research on attitude formation and change has tended to characterize the persuasion process as resulting either from a thoughtful (though not necessarily rational) consideration of issue-relevant arguments and product-relevant attributes (central route), or from associating the attitude object with various positive and negative cues and operating with simple decision rules (peripheral route). Over the past decade, investigators in both social psychology and consumer behavior

[3]Some authors have suggested that it may be appropriate to analyze dichotomous data using analysis of variance without biasing the results greatly (e.g., Winer 1971). We subjected our recall and recognition data (scored 0 or 1) to ANOVA, and the following significant effects were obtained. On the measure of recall of the product category, a main effect of involvement ($F(1, 152) = 6.42$ $p < 0.01$) and an involvement × endorser interaction ($F(1, 152) = 3.28$, $p < 0.07$) were obtained. On the measure of brand name recall, main effects for involvement ($F(1, 145) = 6.34$, $p < 0.01$), gender ($F 1, 145) = 7.20$, $p < 0.008$), and endorser ($F(1, 145) = 3.49$, $p < 0.06$) were obtained. On the measure of brand name recognition, an involvement × endorser interaction was obtained ($F(1, 152) = 4.04$, $p < 0.05$). This pattern of significant effects is identical to the significant pattern of effects reported in the text.

have tended to emphasize the former process over the latter. Consider the recent comments of Fishbein and Ajzen (1981, p. 359):

The general neglect of the information contained in a message . . . is probably the most serious problem in communication and persuasion research. We are convinced that the persuasiveness of a communication can be increased much more easily and dramatically by paying careful attention to its content . . . than by manipulation of credibility, attractiveness . . . or any of the other myriad factors that have caught the fancy of investigators in the area of communication and persuasion.

The present study suggests that, although the informational content of an advertisement may be the most important determinant of product attitudes under some circumstances, in other circumstances such noncontent manipulations as the celebrity status (likeability) or credibility of the product endorsers may be even more important. Specifically, we have shown that when an advertisement concerned a product of low involvement, the celebrity status of the product endorsers was a very potent determinant of attitudes about the project. When the advertisement concerned a product of high involvement, however, the celebrity status of the product endorsers had no effect on attitudes, but the cogency of the information about the product contained in the ad was a powerful determinant of product evaluations.[4] These data clearly suggest that it would be inappropriate for social and consumer researchers to overemphasize the influence of issue-relevant arguments or product-relevant attributes and ignore the role of peripheral cues. Each type of attitudinal influence occurs in some instances, and the level of personal involvement with an issue or product appears to be one determinant of which type of persuasion occurs.

According to the Elaboration Likelihood Model, personal relevance is thought to be only one determinant of the route to persuasion. Personal relevance is thought to increase a person's motivation for engaging in a diligent consideration of the issue- or product-relevant information presented in order to form a veridical opinion. Just as different situations may induce different motivations to think, different people may typically employ different styles of information processing, and some people will enjoy thinking more than others (Cacioppo and Petty 1982). However, a diligent consideration of issue- or product-relevant information requires not only the motivation to think, but also the ability to process the information. This situational variables (e.g., distraction; Petty, Wells, and Brock 1976) and individual difference variables (e.g., prior knowledge; Cacioppo and Petty 1980b) may also be important moderators of the route to persuasion. In the present study, subjects' ability to think about the product was held at a high level across experimental conditions—that is, the messages were easy to understand, the presentation was self-paced, and so on. Thus the primary determinant of the route to persuasion was motivational in nature.[5]

It is important to note that although our "peripheral" manipulation was a source variable presented visually and our "central" manipulation was a message variable presented verbally, neither the source/message nor the visual/verbal dichotomy is isomorphic with the central/peripheral one. Thus a source variable may induce persuasion via the central route, and a message variable may serve as a peripheral cue.

[4]Although not tested in the present study, the ELM predicts that under moderate involvement conditions, source information serves neither as a simple cue (as under low involvement) nor is it ignored (as under high involvement). Instead, source information helps a person determine how much thinking to do about the message (Petty and Cacioppo 1981a, forthcoming).

[5]An anonymous reviewer of this article took issue with our motivational interpretation of the effects of involvement and suggested that perhaps our effects resulted because our experimental task overtaxed our subjects' cognitive abilities. This suggestion assumes that subjects lacked the ability to evaluate both the source *and* the message, and therefore had to choose one over the other. We find this explanation implausible for several reasons. First, since the subjects paced themselves through the ad booklet, they could spend as much time as they wished evaluating each ad; the "overtaxed" explanation may thus be more plausible for research in which the message is externally paced. Second, our experiment included several checks on whether or not subjects attended to the source and message information. For example, all subjects were asked if they recognized and liked the endorsers appearing in the ad. If the reviewer's

For example, in one study described previously (Petty and Cacioppo 1980), we observed that a physically attractive message endorser might serve as a cogent product-relevant argument for a beauty product. In another study (Petty and Cacioppo, forthcoming b), we found that the mere number of message arguments presented may activate a simple decision rule (the more the better) under low involvement, but not under high involvement, where argument quality is more important than number. Similarly, a "central" manipulation may be presented visually—e.g., depicting a kitten in an advertisement for facial tissue to convey the product-relevant attribute "softness" (Mitchell and Olson 1981)—and a "peripheral" manipulation may be presented verbally—e.g., providing a verbal description of a message source as an expert or as likable (Chaiken 1980; Petty, Cacioppo, and Goldman 1981). The critical feature of the central route to persuasion is that an attitude change in based on a diligent consideration of information that a person feels is central to the true merits of an issue or product. This information may be conveyed visually, verbally, or in source or message characteristics. In the peripheral route, attitudes change because of the presence of simple positive or negative cues, or because of the invocation of simple decision rules which obviate the need for thinking about issue-relevant arguments. Stimuli that serve as peripheral cues or that invoke simple decision rules may be presented visually or verbally, or may be part of source or message characteristics.

In the present study, the overall pattern of results on the attitude and purchase intention measures is more consistent with the Elaboration Likelihood Model formulation than with the Sherif, Sherif, and Nebergall (1965) social judgment model or with Krugman's (1965, 1967) sequence model of involvement. Although increasing involvement did produce a main effect on the attitude measure (more resistance to the product under high rather than low involvement), as anticipated by social judgment theory, the more complicated interactions of endorser and argument quality with involvement cannot be accounted for by the theory. Thus the social judgment theory view that it is more difficult to change attitudes under high involvement is, at best, only partially correct, and is unable to account for the complete pattern of attitude data. The attitude and behavioral data are generally inconsistent with Krugman's sequence formulation. Krugman suggested that under high involvement, attitude change preceded behavior change, but that under low involvement, behavior change preceded attitude change. This reasoning would suggest that on immediate measures, attitudinal effects should be easier to detect than behavioral effects under high involvement, while behavioral effects should be easier to detect than attitudinal effects under low involvement. In the present study, both attitudinal and behavioral (intention) effects were observed under high involvement, which is consistent with both models. Under low involvement, however, effects were obtained on the measure of attitude but not on the measure of behavioral intentions. This finding is inconsistent with Krugman's formulation, which expects stronger behavioral effects under low involvement than under high involvement, but it is consistent with the ELM, which postulates a greater correspondence between attitudes and behaviors under high involvement (central route) than under low involvement (peripheral route).

In sum, the present study has provided support for the view that different features of an advertisement may be more or less effective, depending upon a person's involvement with it. Under conditions of low involvement, periph-

suggestion is correct, we would expect subjects in the high involvement group (who diligently processed the message content) to be less likely to report recognizing the endorsers in the ad, and hence to show less liking for the ad endorsers. However, the involvement manipulation failed to affect either the recognition or the liking measure. In fact, subjects in the high involvement group reported slightly (though not significantly) greater recognition and liking of the famous endorsers than did the low involvement subjects. Thus high involvement subjects were not overtaxed. They recognized and liked the famous endorsers to the same extent as did low involvement subjects. It is just that the product attitudes of the high involvement subjects were not affected by this liking, while the product attitudes of the low involvement subjects were.

eral cues are more important than issue-relevant argumentation, but under high involvement, the opposite is true. The realization that independent variables may have different effects, depending on the level of personal relevance of a message may provide some insight into the conflicting pattern of results that is said to characterize much attitude research. It may well be that attitude effects can be arranged on a continuum, depending on the elaboration likelihood of a particular persuasion situation. This continuum would be anchored at one end by the peripheral route and at the other end by the central route to persuasion. Furthermore, these two routes may be characterized by quite different antecedents and consequents. If so, future work could be aimed at uncovering the various moderators of the route to persuasion and at tracking the various consequents of the two different routes.

REFERENCES

ABELSON, ROBERT P. (1976), "Script Processing in Attitude Formation and Decision Making," in *Cognition and Social Behavior,* Eds. John S. Carroll and John W. Payne. Hillsdale, NJ: Erlbaum.

AJZEN, ICEK, and MARTIN FISHBEIN (1980), *Understanding Attitudes and Predicting Social Behavior.* Englewood Cliffs, NJ: Prentice-Hall.

APSLER, ROBERT, and DAVID O. SEARS (1968), "Warning, Personal Involvement, and Attitude Change," *Journal of Personality and Social Psychology,* 9 (June), 162-166.

BEM, DARYL J. (1972), "Self-Perception Theory," in *Advances in Experimental Social Psychology,* Vol. 6, Ed. Leonard Berkowitz. New York: Academic Press, 2-57.

BETTMAN, JAMES R. (1979), "Memory Factors in Consumer Choice: A Review," *Journal of Marketing,* 43 (Spring), 37-53.

BROCK, TIMOTHY C., and SHARON SHAVITT (1983), "Cognitive Response Analysis in Advertising," in *Advertising and Consumer Psychology,* Eds. Larry Percy and Arch Woodside. Lexington, MA: Lexington Books, 91-116.

BURNKRANT, ROBERT E. (1976), "A Motivational Model of Information Processing Intensity," *Journal of Consumer Research,* 3 (June), 21-30.

———, and ALAN G. SAWYER (1983), "Effects of Involvement and Message Content on Information Processing Intensity," in *Information Processing Research in Advertising,* Ed. Richard Harris. Hillsdale, NJ: Erlbaum.

CACIOPPO, JOHN T., and RICHARD E. PETTY (1979), "Effects of Message Repetition and Position on Cognitive Responses, Recall, and Persuasion," *Journal of Personality and Social Psychology,* 37 (January), 97-109.

———, and RICHARD E. PETTY (1980a), "Persuasiveness of Communications is Affected by Exposure Frequency and Message Quality: A Theoretical and Empirical Analysis of Persisting Attitude Change," in *Current Issues and Research in Advertising,* Eds. James H. Leigh and Claude R. Martin. Ann Arbor, MI: University of Michigan, 97-122.

———, and RICHARD E. PETTY (1980b), "Sex Differences in Influenceability: Toward Specifying the Underlying Processes," *Personality and Social Psychology Bulletin,* 6 (December), 651-656.

———, and RICHARD E. PETTY (1981), "Social Psychological Procedures for Cognitive Response Assessment: The Thought Listing Technique," in *Cognitive Assessment,* Eds. Thomas V. Merluzzi, Carol R. Glass, and Myles Genest. New York: Guilford Press, 309-342.

———, and RICHARD E. PETTY (1982), "The Need for Cognition," *Journal of Personality and Social Psychology,* 42 (January), 116-131.

———, and RICHARD E. PETTY (forthcoming), "The Need for Cognition: Relationships to Social Influence and Self Influence," in *Social Perception in Clinical and Counseling Psychology,* Eds. Richard P. McGlynn, James E. Maddux, Cal D. Stoltenberg, and John H. Harvey. Lubbock, TX: Texas Tech Press.

CHAIKEN, SHELLY (1980), "Heuristic Versus Systematic Information Processing and the Use of Source Versus Message Cues in Persuasion," *Journal of Personality and Social Psychology,* 39 (November), 752-766.

CHESTNUT, ROBERT W., CHARLES C. LACHANCE, and AMY LUBITZ (1977), "The Decorative Female Model: Sexual Stimuli and the Recognition of Advertisements," *Journal of Advertising Research,* 6, 11-14.

CIALDINI, ROBERT B., RICHARD E. PETTY, and

JOHN T. CACIOPPO (1981), "Attitude and Attitude Change," *Annual Review of Psychology,* 32, 357-404.

CRAIK, FERGUS M., and ROBERT S. LOCKHART (1972), "Levels of Processing: A Framework for Memory Research," *Journal of Verbal Learning and Verbal Behavior,* 11 (October), 671-684.

CUMMINGS, WILLIAM H., and M. VENKATESAN (1976), "Cognitive Dissonance and Consumer Behavior: A Review of the Evidence," *Journal of Marketing Research,* 13 (August), 303-308.

EAGLY, ALICE H. (1978), "Sex Differences in Influenceability," *Psychological Bulletin,* 85 (January), 86-116.

ENGEL, JAMES F., and ROGER D. BLACKWELL (1982), *Consumer Behavior.* Hinsdale, IL: Dryden Press.

FESTINGER, LEON (1957). *A Theory of Cognitive Dissonance.* Stanford, CA: Stanford University Press.

FISHBEIN, MARTIN, and ICEK AJZEN (1981), "Acceptance, Yielding, and Impact: Cognitive Processes in Persuasion," in *Cognitive Responses in Persuasion,* Eds. Richard E. Petty, Thomas Ostrom, and Timothy C. Brock. Hillsdale, NJ: Erlbaum, 339-359.

GREENWALD, ANTHONY G. (1968), "Cognitive Learning, Cognitive Response to Persuasion, and Attitude Change," in *Psychological Foundations of Attitudes,* Eds. Anthony G. Greenwald, Timothy C. Brock, and Thomas Ostrom. New York: Academic Press, 147-170.

HAINES, GEORGE H. (1974), "Process Models of Consumer Decision Making," in *Buyer/Consumer Information Processing,* Eds. G. David Hughes and Michael L. Ray. Chapel Hill, NC: University of North Carolina Press. 89-107.

HOVLAND, CARL I., O.J. HARVEY, and MUZIFER SHERIF (1957), "Assimilation and Contrast Effects in Reactions to Communication and Attitude Change," *Journal of Abnormal and Social Psychology,* 55 (September), 244-252.

———, IRVING JANIS, and HAROLD KELLEY (1953), *Communication and Persuasion.* New Haven, CT: Yale University Press.

INSKO, CHESTER A., E. ALLEN LIND, and STEPHEN LATOUR (1976), "Persuasion, Recall, and Thoughts," *Representative Research in Social Psychology,* 7, 66-78.

JANIS, IRVING L., D. KAYE, and P. KIRSCHNER (1965), "Facilitating Effects of 'Eating while Reading' on Responsiveness to Persuasive Communication," *Journal of Personality and Social Psychology,* 1 (February), 181-186.

KASSARJIAN, HAROLD H. 1982), "Consumer Psychology," *Annual Review of Psychology,* 33, 619-649.

———, and WALTRAUD M. KASSARJIAN (1979), "Attitudes under Low Commitment Conditions," in *Attitude Research Plays for High Stakes,* Eds. John C. Maloney and Bernard Silverman. Chicago: American Marketing Association. 3-15.

KELMAN, HERBERT C. (1961), "Processes of Opinion Change," *Public Opinion Quarterly,* 25 (Spring), 57-78.

KIESLER, CHARLES A., BARRY E. COLLINS, and NORMAN MILLER (1969), *Attitude Change: A Critical Analysis of Theoretical Approaches.* New York: Wiley.

KRUGMAN, HERBERT E. (1965). "The Impact of Television Advertising: Learning without Involvement," *Public Opinion Quarterly,* 29 (Fall), 349-356.

———, (1967), "The Measurement of Advertising Involvement," *Public Opinion Quarterly,* 30 (Winter), 583-596.

LANGER, ELLEN J., and ROBERT P. ABELSON (1972), "The Semantics of Asking a Favor: How to Succeed in Getting Help without Really Dying," *Journal of Personality and Social Psychology,* 24 (October), 26-32.

———, ARTHUR BLANK, and BENZION CHANOWITZ (1970), "The Mindlessness of Ostensibly Thoughtful Action: The Role of 'Placebic' Information in Interpersonal Interaction," *Journal of Personality and Social Psychology,* 36 (June), 635-642.

LASTOVICKA, JOHN L., and DAVID M. GARDNER (1979), "Components of Involvement," in *Attitude Research Plays for High Stakes,* Eds. John C. Maloney and Bernard Silverman. Chicago: American Marketing Association, 53-73.

LIEBHART, ERNST H. (1979), "Information Search and Attribution: Cognitive Processes Mediating the Effect of False Autonomic Feedback," *European Journal of Social Psychology,* 9 (January/March), 19-37.

LUTZ, RICHARD J., and JAMES R. BETTMAN (1977), "Multiattribute Models in Marketing: A Bicentennial Review," in *Consumer and Industrial Buying Behavior,* Eds. Arch Woodside, Jagdish Sheth, and Peter D. Bennett. New York: Elsevier North-Holland, 137-150.

McGuire, William J. (1969), "The Nature of Attitudes and Attitude Change," in *The Handbook of Social Psychology,* Vol. 3, Eds. Gardner Lindzey and Elliot Aronson. Reading, MA: Addison-Wesley, 136–314.

———, (1976), "Some Internal Psychological Factors Influencing Consumer Choice," *Journal of Consumer Research,* 2 (March), 302–319.

Miller, Norman, Geoffrey Maruyama, Rex Julian Beaber, and Keith Valone (1976), "Speed of Speech and Persuasion," *Journal of Personality and Social Psychology,* 34 (October), 615–624.

Mitchell, Andrew A., and Jerry C. Olson (1981), "Are Product Attribute Beliefs the Only Mediator of Advertising Effects on Brand Attitude?" *Journal of Marketing Research,* 18 (August), 318–332.

Mowen, John C. (1980), "On Product Endorser Effectiveness: A Balance Model Approach," in *Current Issues and Research in Advertising,* Eds. James H. Leigh and Claude R. Martin. Ann Arbor, MI: University of Michigan, 41–57.

Newman, Larry M., and Ira J. Dolich (1979), "An Examination of Ego-Involvement as a Modifier of Attitude Changes Caused from Product Testing," *Advances in Consumer Research,* Vol. 6, Ed. William L. Wilkie. Ann Arbor, MI: Association for Consumer Research, 180–183.

Petty, Richard E., and John T. Cacioppo (1979), "Issue Involvement Can Increase or Decrease Persuasion by Enhancing Message-Relevant Cognitive Responses," *Journal of Personality and Social Psychology,* 37 (October), 1915–1926.

———, and John T. Cacioppo (1980), "Effects of Issue Involvement on Attitudes in an Advertising Context," in *Proceedings of the Division 23 Program,* Eds. Gerald G. Gorn and Marvin E. Goldberg. Montreal, Canada: American Psychological Association, 75–79.

———, and John T. Cacioppo (1981), *Attitudes and Persuasion: Classic and Contemporary Approaches.* Dubuque, IA: William C. Brown.

———, and John T. Cacioppo (1983), "Central and Peripheral Routes to Persuasion: Application to Advertising," in *Advertising and Consumer Psychology,* Eds. Larry Percy and Arch Woodside. Lexington, MA: Lexington Books, 3–23.

———, and John T. Cacioppo (forthcoming a), *Attitude Change: Central and Peripheral Routes to Persuasion.* New York: Springer/Verlag.

———, and John T. Cacioppo (forthcoming b), "The Effects of Involvement on Responses to Argument Quantity and Quality: Central and Peripheral Routes to Persuasion," *Journal of Personality and Social Psychology.*

———, John T. Cacioppo, and Rachel Goldman (1981), "Personal Involvement as a Determinant of Argument-Based Persuasion," *Journal of Personality and Social Psychology,* 41 (November), 847–855.

———, John T. Cacioppo, and Martin Heesacker (1981), "The Use of Rhetorical Questions in Persuasion: A Cognitive Response Analysis," *Journal of Personality and Social Psychology,* 40 (March), 432–440.

———, Thomas Ostrom, and Timothy C. Brock (1981), "Historical Foundations of the Cognitive Response Approach to Attitudes and Persuasion," in *Cognitive Responses in Persuasion,* Eds. Richard E. Petty, Thomas Ostrom, and Timothy C. Brock. Hillsdale, NJ: Erlbaum, 5–29.

———, Gary L. Wells, and Timothy C. Brock (1976), "Distraction Can Enhance or Reduce Yielding to Propaganda: Thought Disruption Versus Effort Justification," *Journal of Personality and Social Psychology,* 34 (November), 874–884.

Ray, Michael L., Alan G. Sawyer, Michael L. Rothschild, Roger M. Heeler, Edward C. Strong and Jerome B. Reed (1973), "Marketing Communication and the Hierarchy of Effects," in *New Models for Mass Communication Research,* Vol. 2, Ed. Peter Clarke. Beverly Hills, CA: Sage Publications, 147–176.

Rhine, Ramon, and Laurence J. Severance (1970), "Ego-Involvement, Discrepancy, Source Credibility, and Attitude Change," *Journal of Personality and Social Psychology,* 16 (October), 175–190.

Schlenker, Barry R. (1978), "Attitudes as Actions: Social Identity Theory and Consumer Research," *Advances in Consumer Research,* Vol. 5, Ed. H. Keith Hunt. Ann Arbor, MI: Association for Consumer Research, 352–359.

———, (1980), *Impression Management: The Self-Concept, Social Identity, and Interpersonal Relations.* Monterey, CA: Brooks/Cole.

Schneider, Walter, and Richard M. Shiffrin (1977), "Controlled and Automatic Human Information Processing: I. Detection, Search, and Attention," *Psychological Review,* 84 (January), 1–66.

SCOTT, CAROL A. (1978), "Self-Perception Processes in Consumer Behavior: Interpreting One's Own Experiences," *Advances in Consumer Research*, Vol. 5, Ed. H. Keith Hunt. Ann Arbor, MI: Association for Consumer Research, 714-720.

SHERIF, MUZIFER, and CARL I. HOVLAND (1961), *Social Judgment*. New Haven: Yale University Press.

SHERIF, CAROLYN W., MUZIFER SHERIF, and ROGER E. NEBERGALL (1965), *Attitude and Attitude Change*, Philadelphia: Saunders.

STEADMAN, MAJOR (1969), "How Sexy Illustrations Affect Brand Recall," *Journal of Advertising Research*, 9 (1), 15-19.

STERNTHAL, BRIAN, and C. SAMUEL CRAIG (1974), "Fear Appeals: Revisited and Revised," *Journal of Consumer Research*, 1 (December), 22-34.

TROUTMAN, C. MICHAEL, and JAMES SHANTEAU (1976), "Do Consumers Evaluate Products by Adding or Averaging Attribute Information," *Journal of Consumer Research*, 3 (December), 101-106.

WINER, B. J. (1971), *Statistical Principles in Experimental Design*. New York: McGraw-Hill.

WORCHEL, STEPHEN, VIRGINIA ANDREOLI, and JOE EASON (1975), "Is the Medium the Message? A Study of the Effects of Media, Communicator, and Message Characteristics on Attitude Change," *Journal of Applied Social Psychology*, 5 (April/June), 157-172.

WRIGHT, PETER L. (1973), "The Cognitive Processes Mediating Acceptance of Advertising," *Journal of Marketing Research*, 10 (February), 53-62.

———, (1974), "Analyzing Media Effects on Advertising Responses," *Public Opinion Quarterly*, 38 (Summer), 192-205.

———, (1980), "Message-evoked Thoughts: Persuasion Research Using Thought Verbalizations, *Journal of Consumer Research*, 7 (September), 151-175.

ZIMBARDO, PHILLIP (1960), "Involvement and Communication Discrepancy as Determinants of Opinion Conformity," *Journal of Abnormal and Social Psychology*, 60 (January), 86-94.

20

RECENT ATTRIBUTION RESEARCH IN CONSUMER BEHAVIOR: A Review and New Directions*

Valerie S. Folkes

Recent consumer behavior research testing attribution theory principles is summarized and critiqued. Most studies on antecedents of causal inferences focus on how information about a product influences attributions, how the discounting effect influences liking for products, and how self-perception processes influence willingness to participate in marketing research. Research examining consequences of causal inferences focuses on product satisfaction. Major trends in attribution theory and future research directions are indicated.

Attribution research is concerned with all aspects of causal inferences: how people arrive at causal inferences, what sort of inferences they make, and what the consequences of these inferences are. Nine years ago, Mizerski, Golden, and Kernan (1979) provided an overview of four major attribution theories and reviewed the relevant consumer behavior research from 1971 to 1978. Since that time attribution theory has remained a popular approach in social psychology (e.g., see recent reviews by Harvey and Weary 1984; Ross and Fletcher 1985); however, most of us probably agree that despite a promising beginning, attribution theory has had little impact on the field of consumer behavior.

This apparent neglect is surprising. Understanding consumers' perceptions of cause-and-effect relationships would seem to be central to consumer behavior. It is this author's opinion

*Reprinted from the *Journal of Consumer Research,* 14 (March 1988), pp. 548–565.

that many, if not most, products and services are purchased because consumers infer a causal relationship: they believe that analgesics reduce pain, deodorants improve one's social life, athletic shoes enhance performance, and so on. As the present review will substantiate, attribution theory is a rich and well-developed approach that has a great deal to say about a wide range of consumer behavior issues. For example, attribution research indicates when consumers recommend products to other consumers and when they complain about problems. It sheds light on such questions in persuasion as source credibility and two-sided messages. Attribution research illuminates the relationship between consumers' attitudes and behaviors.

The purpose of this article is to increase the awareness of attribution theory's contributions to consumer behavior, as well as to review research since the Mizerski et al. article. Many recent studies address issues not raised in the Mizerski et al. review, which focused on theories forming the foundation of attribution research (Bem 1972; Heider 1958; Jones and Davis 1965; Kelley 1967, 1973). Besides summarizing studies in consumer behavior journals, the present review includes consumer behavior experiments published in psychology journals. When studies on a topic are published in a variety of outlets, as is true of attribution research in consumer behavior, its impact may be diffused. By consolidating the research, this review aims to more clearly identify issues that have attracted the interest of investigators. A secondary aim is to identify up-to-date reviews of specific topics in attribution research to aid those who wish to explore an issue in depth.

The review is organized into four sections. The first section provides a brief summary of attribution theory development and key concepts. The second section identifies causal ascriptions of interest to those in consumer behavior, thus specifying the domains in which attribution theory is and might be useful. The article next reviews theory and recent research examining antecedents and consequences of these causal ascriptions. The final section provides an overview of central issues in attribution theory since the Mizerski et al. (1979) article and indicates additional directions for future research.

THE ORIGINS OF ATTRIBUTION THEORY

Attribution theory is actually several theories that share core assumptions. The seminal concepts underlying attributional approaches are found in Heider's (1958) book, *The Psychology of Interpersonal Relations*. First, Heider believed it was valuable to understand an individual's "naive" or common sense explanations of the world. This phenomenological approach contrasted with behaviorist theories popular at the time. Heider even used layman's terms, such as "can" and "try," to analyze how people make causal inferences. Second, Heider distinguished among types or categories of causes. A basic distinction was between actions due to personal causes and those related to the environment or situation. For example, a canoeist might reach the other side of the lake because of personal causes (e.g., the canoeist's effort) or because of environmental causes (e.g., currents).

Another core concept involves the nature of this inferential process. The layman's explanations are naive in that they are not scientifically conceptualized, analyzed, and tested. Yet the process by which people arrive at explanations is similar to the way scientists arrive at explanations—in a fairly logical and analytical fashion. This is not to say that people are error-free when making causal inferences. Heider pointed out a number of biases or distortions, such as overestimating the impact of features salient in the perceiver's environment. Regardless of accuracy, perceived causality influences the perceiver's subsequent actions.

Heider's book contains many fascinating ideas, but Harold Kelley drew attention to those dealing with attributions in an early book review. Additionally, Kelley (1967, 1972) wrote several theoretical papers that elaborated on how individuals infer causes. These models of attributional antecedents are more complex than Heider's. Both Heider and Kelley (1967) identified covariation of cause and effect as an important determinant of causal inferences. For example, because turning a light switch is closely followed by a room's lights being turned on or off, people infer that one causes the other. Kelley identified types of causal inferences arising from fairly complex configurations of events covarying over time, across situations, and across individuals. But each occasion does not give rise to the extensive assembling of information required by covariation analysis. People learn cause and effect patterns that enable them to make inferences quickly. These schemata facilitate the attribution process.

Another early theory about causal inferences, correspondent inference theory, was developed by Jones and Davis (1965) and later modified by Jones and McGillis (1976). Correspondent inference theory is more narrow than Kelley's approach. It emphasizes inferences made about another's intentions and dispositions from the other's actions. Although correspondent inference theory has not had much influence on attribution research, a related phenomenon, the actor-observer bias, has (Jones and Nisbett 1972). While the observer is inclined to attribute the actor's behavior to the actor's personal dispositions, the actor is more likely to attribute the same action to situational factors. Consistent with Heider's orientation, explanations for this bias draw on cognitive or perceptual factors as well as on motivational or egocentric factors.

Whereas the actor-observer bias examined how attributions for one's own behavior differ from those of an observer, Bem (1972) focused on similarities between actors' and observers' causal inferences. He argued that one forms attributions about one's own behavior the same way one arrives at attributions for others' behaviors. One observes the behavior and the context in which it occurs and then makes inferences about what caused it. This approach contrasts with Heider's theory. Bem maintains that actions precede cognition; people act, then arrive at explanations for the action that may in fact have had no influence on that action.

Heider's analysis of types of causes has been most extensively developed by Weiner (1985a, 1986). Heider identified general properties of causes (such as the personal versus the situational), but Weiner elaborated on and more precisely identified causal dimensions or underlying causal structure. These causal dimensions (e.g., locus of control), as well as specified causes (e.g., effort, ability), influence a variety of behavioral consequences (e.g., expectancies, affect). Although Weiner's theory was originally grounded in achievement behavior, Weiner has extended the model into a more general theory of human motivation.

These theoretical developments attracted consumer researchers' attention in the early seventies (e.g., Settle 1972; Settle and Golden 1974). During this time, consumer research using an attributional approach typically drew on either Kelley's or Bem's theory, primarily contributing to the attitude and persuasion literature. Studies examined a variety of topics, including source credibility (e.g., Dholakia and Sternthal 1977), the effects of coupons and other promotional incentives on consumers' attitudes (e.g., Scott 1977), and children's inferences about advertisers' motives (e.g., Robertson and Rossiter 1974). Research prior to 1978 has been reviewed by Mizerski et al. (1979) and will not be detailed in this article.

CAUSAL ASCRIPTIONS EXAMINED BY CONSUMER RESEARCH

Recent attribution research has examined consumers' causal inferences for a variety of outcomes—inferences about the consumer's own behavior, about a product's success or failure, and about a communicator's endorsement of a product (cf. Zaltman and Wallendorf 1983). A commonly studied paradigm examines attributions for product purchase or selection; consumers infer why they have purchased or selected a product. These studies typically manipulate consumers' beliefs so that they attribute selection either to liking for the product or to situational constraints or incentives, such as the consumer selected it to please someone else or because a coupon could be redeemed (e.g., Scott and Yalch 1980; Tybout and Scott 1983).

A related body of research concentrates less on the consumer as a causal agent than on the myriad causal inferences a consumer makes for product performance. These studies examine one's own and others' attributions for why a product or service failed, although a few have also examined product success (e.g., Curren and Folkes 1987; Richins 1983). Attributions for product failure range from product defects and service delivery flaws to environmental interference and even to consumers' misuse of the product (Folkes 1984b). Mazursky, La Barbera, and Aiello (1987) examined reasons for switching brands of grocery products. Over 75 percent of the reasons related to price, coupon redemption, and desire to try a new brand.

Consumers also infer reasons for a product endorser's recommendation, i.e., Why did the celebrity agree to appear in the advertisement? (e.g., Sparkman 1982; Wiener and Mowen 1986). Investigators have typically manipulated consumers' perceptions of intrinsic incentives (the endorser's liking for the product) versus extrinsic (monetary) incentives for endorsement. A similar line of research assumes that consumers make causal inferences for others' positive and negative evaluations of products (e.g., Hunt, Domzal, and Kernan 1981; Kamins and Assael 1987).

Consumers also provide information about preferences and usage to marketers, so several studies examine effects of attributions on responses to market research mail surveys, i.e., Why should I take the time to complete this questionnaire? (e.g., Allen, Schewe, and Wijk 1980; Furse, Stewart, and Rados 1981; Hansen and Robinson 1980). Consumers' attributions for the firm's actions that are unrelated to product performance are relevant to the field but have yet to be explored (e.g., Why did the firm bribe the government? Why are the firm's employees on strike?), as well as attributions for consumer group, legislative, and regulatory actions (e.g., Why does Ralph Nader support this position? Why are gun control regulations lax?).

These slightly different attributional questions arise partly because different theories guide the research. For example, self-perception studies derive from Bem's (1972) work and focus on conditions facilitating the consumer's inference that purchase was intrinsically motivated by the product's qualities, whereas product performance studies derive from Weiner's (1986) taxonomy of causes and focus on attributional consequences.

ANTECEDENTS OF CONSUMERS' ATTRIBUTIONS

Most attribution research deals with how people go about forming causal inferences. There are three types of antecedents for causal inferences: motivations, information, and prior beliefs (Kelley and Michela 1980). Consumers may be motivated to arrive at certain causal inferences from hedonic or esteem needs. On the other hand, information about an action, such as how frequently it occurs and with what other actions it covaries, forms the basis for many attributions. Finally, people may have prior beliefs about the relationships among causes, such as beliefs about the strength of a cause when alternative possible causes are present, that lead to certain causal inferences. Whereas all three factors—motivations, information, and beliefs—often influence the kinds of attributions made in a single study, most research frames a problem in terms of just one type of antecedent.

Motivation

Protecting one's esteem forms the basis for motivational biases in most attributional research. A few consumer behavior studies have also found attributional patterns that may reflect motivational or esteem-related biases, that is, the tendency to attribute good outcomes to one's self (an internal or dispositional cause) and bad outcomes to external or situational causes. For example, consumers appear to blame others for bad experiences with products. In a survey of Netherlands' households, 90 percent of the respondents placed at least some blame for their dissatisfaction with clothing and appliance purchases on marketing institutions (Richins 1985).

But finding such a striking pattern of blaming firms does not necessarily mean that esteem needs bias consumer attributions. Patterns that observers interpret as ego protective may in fact arise because individuals have more complete access to their own intentions and expectations than do observers (but see Nisbett and Wilson 1977 for a different perspective). Most consumers use a product intending and even devoting effort toward its success, so attributing failure to others could be due to rational rather than to self-serving reasons. Consistent with this view is the finding that when making attributions for product failure, buyers (and sellers) display a pattern of self-serving biases even when they are in the "observer" role (i.e., reading about another's experiences) and self-esteem needs are minimized (Folkes and Kotsos 1986).

Some have suggested that research trying to identify the superiority of motivational or cognitive explanations for attributional biases is fruitless; both influence causal influences but under different circumstances (e.g., Tetlock and Levi 1982). Thus, research should try to identify situations eliciting types of biases. Of course, there may be other reasons for these attributional patterns that relate to self-presentational goals or the public nature of communications about privately held beliefs (Harvey and Weary 1984). Researchers must depend on what consumers are willing to reveal about themselves.

Consumers may sometimes be in a similar predicament as the attributional researcher when evaluating the source and nature of causal inferences; buyers may have to evaluate whether sellers reveal reasons for their behaviors that are biased in self-serving ways. For example, shareholders in a company may be concerned with whether the information given to them by the firm's employees is systematically biased and want to determine the source of the bias. Bettman and Weitz (1983) found that employees show a pattern of self-serving attributions in their letters to shareholders in annual reports. External (environmental), unstable (temporary), and firm-uncontrollable reasons were given for poor performance (e.g., lower profits were attributed to unusual economic conditions), but internal (firm-related), stable (permanent), and firm-controllable reasons were more frequent for good earnings (e.g., high profits due to the firm's research and development efforts). The data could support neither a purely motivational nor a purely informational explanation for the firms' explanations.

The False Consensus Effect. Some studies published in psychology journals examine a special type of motivational bias, the tendency to assume a false consensus for one's behavior. Consumers prefer to believe that others share the same preferences and consumption habits; common behaviors seem more appropriate and reasonable than unusual behaviors and so bolster one's self-esteem. As an example, consider smoking, an activity a minority of people engage in. Compared to nonsmoking adolescents, adolescent smokers overestimate the percent of others who smoke, partially as a means of self-validation (Sherman et al. 1983). Midwestern adolescent smokers show greater errors in estimating smoking rates than do Southwestern adolescent smokers because Midwesterners are more motivated to justify their behavior; smoking is a more deviant behavior in the Midwest. On the other hand, adult smokers and nonsmokers give similar estimates of the adult men in their city who smoke; adult smoking is a less deviant behavior than adolescent smoking and so requires less perceived commonality.

Similarly, nonconservationists justify their irresponsible behavior by believing that most others waste energy (Van der Pligt 1984, 1985). Engaging in a negative behavior (e.g., using phosphate detergents) led to extreme but favorable trait ratings of those who refrained from that negative behavior (e.g., phosphate users rated nonusers as more responsible, clean, and environment-conscious than did nonusers). Apparently consumers engaging in disapproved of behaviors are motivated to believe those who refrain from these same behaviors do so because of unusual dispositional tendencies.

Motivational distortion of perceived consensus has also been demonstrated even when consumers' actions are not negative. When undergraduates estimated their peers' attitudes toward a possible tuition surcharge, hedonic relevance increased the students' tendency to assume that others shared the same belief (Crano 1983). The greater the vested interest in the tuition surcharge, the more extreme were the estimates of agreement.

Whereas the false consensus studies reviewed here are limited to consumers' attributions and these studies have found evidence for motivational influences, a meta-analysis of 115 false consensus studies found more evidence for information-based sources than for motivationally driven processes (Mullen et al. 1985). A recent review of the false consensus literature suggests that threat to self or highly evaluative situations motivate the individual to distort perceived similarity, but in other situations cognitive factors can lead to distortion (Marks and Miller 1987). Consider a cognitively based explanation of Sherman et al.'s (1983) study of smokers' false consensus. Because people associate with similar others and because adolescent peer groups form exceptionally strong associative bonds, overestimating the number of fellow smokers may be a rational assumption for young people. (However, information based explanations seem unable to account for the greater false consensus effect among Midwestern adolescents compared to those in the Southwest.)

At least one study of consumers supports an informational basis for the false consensus effect (Gilovich, Jennings, and Jennings 1983). Undergraduates rated their own preferences and consensus estimates for behaviors, including several consumption behaviors (e.g., eating white bread or brown bread, heating with wood or oil, purchasing IBM or Exxon stock). The false consensus effect was reduced or eliminated when students received information that their own preferences were idiosyncratic, but not when the information suggested their preference arose from situational characteristics. This malleability suggests that the false consensus effect for consumers can arise from incomplete information. As noted earlier, both hedonic needs and cognitive processes seem able to give rise to attributional biases.

Other Motivational Biases. In sum, motivational needs can lead to self-serving and false consensus attributions. Having documented these biases, future research should determine which situations give rise to motivational and cognitive biases. Other research might examine implications of these biases. For example, the false consensus effect may aggravate buying panics over scarce products. Because consumers assume others are competing against them for the same merchandise, delaying the purchase may appear especially risky.

Other possible consumer biases have yet to be fully explored. For example, although defensive attributions (the tendency to blame victims for events) have been explored peripherally in one study (Folkes and Kotsos 1986), it is clearly quite important to explore more deeply when these occur and more generally how consumers attribute blame. Numerous conflicts center on whether consumers or firms are to blame for consumers' problems. For example, banks and consumer groups are in conflict over banks' responsibility for robberies committed at automated teller machines (Schmitt 1987). Motivational and cognitive factors may bias attributions of blame in such instances (e.g., tendencies to blame the victim). Another attributional bias unexplored in consumer behavior is the false uniqueness effect—the tendency to see one's own actions as more atypical or unique (see Ross and Fletcher 1985 for a review). The snob appeal of some products may arise from consumers' desires to believe that they are more highly discriminating than others.

Information

The typical theoretical approach to understanding how consumers use information to make causal inferences is based on Kelley's (1967) covariation theory. Consensus, consistency over time and modality, and distinctiveness influence whether people attribute an effect to the person, the stimulus, or the situation. Applied to consumers, the corresponding causal agents could be the consumer, the product, and the situation (Bettman 1979). Thus, attributions to the individual purchaser, the product, or the particular occasion on which the consumer purchased or used the product depend on consensus with other consumers' responses toward the product, consistency of the individual consumer's response over time and situations, and distinctiveness of the consumer's response to this particular product as opposed to other products. For example, when few consumers like a certain brand (low consensus) but one particular consumer always likes that brand (high consistency), as well as many other brands (low distinctiveness), brand preference can be attributed to that particular consumer's personal idiosyncrasies rather than to the brand's inherent properties.

In the social psychological literature, Kelley's predictions receive general support, although some controversy has arisen over the use of consensus information (see Kassin 1979 for a review) and the kinds of information essential to make an attribution (e.g., Orvis, Cunningham, and Kelley 1975). Most supportive studies follow a methodology first employed by McArthur (1972), in which subjects read scenarios about hypothetical persons and indicate the likely source of causality for the person's behavior. Consensus, consistency, and distinctiveness information is presented as high or low in a within-subjects design. Rholes and Pryor (1982) used a similar methodology to examine how information about consensus, consistency, and distinctiveness influences attributions for a consumer's behavior. Students read sentences following the format "the person likes the product," varying type of occupation (e.g., minister, teacher, writer) and product (e.g., cafe, movie, jacket), as well as consensus, consistency, and distinctiveness. Subjects made attributions consistent with Kelley's hypotheses.

In a study examining only consensus information (Folkes and Kotsos 1986), high consensus (product failure is experienced by most consumers) was associated with attributions to the product (e.g., the product is poorly made) and low consensus (product failure experienced by only a few consumers) with attributions to the consumer (e.g., the consumer is careless) in a manner predicted by Kelley. Specifically, given an automobile breakdown shortly after being repaired, beliefs that cars commonly break down were related to identifying an inept mechanic as the source of the current problem; beliefs that the problem is uncommon for most drivers were related to identifying the individual driver as causing the present breakdown.

Recent studies examining consistency and distinctiveness as well as consensus find only mixed support for Kelley's theory. Sparkman and Locander (1980) found consensus influenced product attributions, but consistency over time and modality, and distinctiveness did not. Yalch and Yoshida (1983) varied covariation information about a new food co-op and then asked students to evaluate the store and indicate their confidence in their judgments. They found nonsignificant results for most attributions, but some results consistent with Kelley's conception.

Lichtenstein and Bearden (1986) suggest that mixed results in these studies arise from the dependent measure's level of abstraction, rather than from problems with Kelley's person, stimulus, and circumstance typology. Their research followed a similar methodology but used both general and specific causes as dependent measures. General attributions could be made to the person (an auto dealership), the stimulus (the model of car), and to circumstances; dependent measures in the study also included specific aspects of the person (e.g., the dealer's desire to enhance customer goodwill), the specifics of the stimulus (e.g., the car has poor styling), or the specific circumstances (e.g., to reduce inventory). The results suggest specific dependent measures better captured subjects' phenomenology than did more general categories of causes.

Another possible explanation for the weak results in the Sparkman and Locander (1980) and Yalch and Yoshida (1983) studies is that prior beliefs influenced subjects' attributions. Both studies involved more realism than the traditional McArthur paradigm. Sparkman and Locander asked mall shoppers to make attributions about an advertising spokesman's endorsement while Yalch and Yoshida asked undergraduates to evaluate a new food co-op actually being proposed for the campus. Whereas increased realism is an advantage of their methodologies in terms of external validity, beliefs about why people appear in advertisements and why people shop in co-ops may have more strongly influenced subjects' attributions than the manipulation. Thus, subjects' prior beliefs may have been given more weight than information provided by the experimenter.

Beliefs

Most recent research into antecedents of consumers' causal ascriptions investigates consumers' preexisting hypotheses, suppositions, and expectations. Of particular interest has been Kelley's (1973) discounting principle, often explored in conjunction with Bem's self-perception notions. Studies published since the Mizerski et al. review that examine the effect of discounting on communicator credibility will be reviewed, then studies focusing on Bem's work.

The Discounting Principle and Communicator Credibility. The discounting principle represents one type of believe about how causes are related (Kelley 1973). People are hypothesized to discount or minimize the effect of an attribution for an action when an alternative attribution could account for the behavior. Although discounting and overjustification have been examined within a variety of contexts in the social psychology literature, consumer research on the discounting effect has emphasized its relevance for communicator credibility and market research response rates. When a product endorser has external reasons to account for favorable comments about a product, recipients of the communication often believe the product less worthy than when endorsement involves minimal or no external incentives. Thus, internal reasons for liking the product are discounted when an alternative reason for endorsement is presented. For example, when Frank Sinatra's endorsement of Chrysler autos was identified as being compensated at the rate of $1.00 per year, consumers evaluated Chryslers more positively than when no rate of pay was specified (Sparkman 1982). Similarly, secondhand autos were evaluated less positively when the mechanic endorsing the product had incentives for endorsing the auto's purchase compared to when no incentives were present (Wiener and Mowen 1986).

Because consumers often expect spokespersons to show bias in their product descriptions, Hunt et al. (1981) suggested that communicators gain credibility by disconfirming expectancies. Students reading ads in which the product's spokesperson admitted one attribute was "less than superior" evaluated the product more positively than when the spokesperson maintained all product attributes were superior. Surprisingly, ratings of the spokesperson's honesty and sincerity showed no effect. Thus, there was no evidence that perceived spokesperson trustworthiness mediated liking for the product.

In a field experiment also examining the impact of negative information in an ad (Swinyard 1981), some households received fliers describing both positive and negative store attributes (two-sided appeal), while other households received a flier giving only positive information (one-sided appeal). Consistent with the Hunt et al. study, two-sided ads were perceived as more credible than one-sided ads. Swinyard hypothesized that less counterargumentation in the two-sided condition mediated the effect, but the results did not support this interpretation.

Kamins and Assael (1987) found similar results in two experiments. One-sided appeals led to more source derogation than two-sided appeals. Further, subjects given one-sided appeals lowered their product evaluations when experience disconfirmed the source's promise. In contrast to Swinyard's (1981) study, one-sided appeals elicited less support and more counterargumentation than two-sided appeals.

Whereas the latter studies examined consumer's discounting as a result of spokesperson and employee endorsements, Mizerski (1982) compared evaluations of products when endorsed by another consumer as opposed to being disparaged. Students read purportedly real consumers' ratings of an automobile or a film, and then stated their own attitude toward the product. Reading disparaging or negative information led to stronger, more extreme evaluations of the film than did reading positive information, although findings were weaker for the auto. Apparently, students reading others' positive comments about films and autos tended to discount the evaluations, believing that praise is more socially acceptable and so less likely to reveal one's true feelings than are negative comments. These results are also consistent with research finding that negative evaluators (in this case, book reviewers) are seen as more intelligent, competent, and expert than are positive evaluators (Amabile 1983), and research finding a negativity bias in evaluations (Kanouse and Hansen 1972).

In sum, incentives for product endorsements influence the message recipient's liking for the product. Consumers appear to discount a communicator's recommendation if incentives or constraints are presented or are inferred. The result can be differential effects for negative information. On the one hand, consumers weigh negative product information from another consumer more heavily than positive information. On the other hand, including some negative information in an ad may enhance the credibility of positive information in the ad. Although the mediating role of attributions in this process is not as clear as one would hope, the social psychological persuasion literature lends confidence to an attributional interpretation (see reviews by Cooper and Croyle 1984; Eagly and Chaiken 1984).

This line of research might benefit by taking into account Eagly and Chaiken's (1984) distinction between reporting biases and knowledge biases. Endorsers may mislead targets because of reluctance to report their true beliefs (e.g., the mechanic in the Wiener and Mowen study had incentives for lying about the car) or because they possess nonveridical knowledge (e.g., Sinatra might sincerely recommend Chryslers but lack expertise about cars or Chryslers, in particular). Yet message involvement may limit the conditions under which inferences about communicators' motives influence persuasion (e.g., see Chaiken and Stangor 1987; Petty and Cacioppo 1986). On the one hand, credibility cues might be used more in low-involvement situations because they require less effort than evaluating the quality of the argument; on the other hand, low-message involvement might reduce the consumer's motivation to make complex inferences about incentives or constraints on the communicator.

Self-Perception Theory. The discounting principle has also been examined within the framework of Bem's self-perception theory. Although not originally conceived within an attribution framework, Bem (1972) argued that people arrive at attributions for their own behavior similar to the way an observer would; they observe their behavior and the external constraints on it and then form inferences. If so, then just as consumers discount internal reasons for another's behavior if external constraints are present, so should the individual apply the discounting principle to a causal analysis of his or her own behavior. Mizerski et al. (1979) reviewed numerous consumer behavior studies using this approach (e.g., Scott 1976, 1977).

Interest in Bem's predictions has continued. Offering an intrinsic reward (a coupon) for subjects to taste test a soft drink led to fewer internal attributions by these subjects for their own behavior (e.g., reports that they tried the product because of taste or curiosity) than for subjects not offered rewards (Scott and Yalch 1980). Similarly, respondents to a mail survey provided poorer quality data (e.g., shorter open-ended responses to questions) when given an incentive to respond (a quarter or a 25-cent pen) than when not given any incentive (Hansen 1980). Presumably, the extrinsic reward reduced intrinsic interest in answering the questionnaire, consistent with the discounting principle. It is somewhat surprising that these effects occur considering the trivial incentives.

Whereas the self-perception research reviewed by Mizerski et al. (1979) was generally content to demonstrate the effect, more recent studies examine the underlying processes and have found a number of limitations. According to Bem's theory, an extrinsic reward for product trial leads a consumer to infer external attributions for his or her behavior, and consequently to less liking for the product. But Scott and Yalch's (1980) self-perception experiment suggests that the opportunity to test hypotheses about one's behavior is essential to changing one's attitudes about a product. When evaluating new soft drinks, subjects sought information about the product to confirm their attributions. External rewards (coupons for tasting the drink) undermined liking for the product only after consumers were able to validate their hypotheses about their actions. Thus, consumers seek information to confirms their attributions before changing their attitudes.

The "taste-test" methodology has been used in other studies to explore the limits of self-perception theory. Tybout and Scott (1983) found that availability of well-defined internal knowledge mediates attitude formation. Subjects who had tasted a soft drink formed attitudes toward the drink by retrieving and evaluating stored information about the product. An extrinsic reward for choosing the product did not undermine liking for the product. However, liking for the product was undermined by the extrinsic reward when well-defined, internal data (a taste of the product) was unavailable. Then individuals observed their own behavior and judged their attitudes from it, consistent with Bem's predictions.

Other studies have explored self-labelling effects as a self-perception phenomenon. Labelling oneself as a certain type of person should lead consumers to behave consistently with that label. For example, a consumer embracing the conservationist label should behave in an energy-conserving manner. Allen (1982) compared the labelling effect to other persuasive appeals by presenting subjects with a variety of advertisements exhorting energy saving. An appeal labelling "the American consumer a willing participant in solving the energy problem" was more effective in influencing consumers' energy consumption cognitions than were other appeals, e.g., stressing personal and monetary gains from conservation (Allen 1982; Allen and Dillon 1983). Support for the labelling effect has also been found in a field experiment examining agreement to participate in a market research survey (Reingen and Bearden 1982). Respondents to a telephone survey told that "you are a very helpful person and I wish more of the people we call were as helpful as you are" were more likely to agree to participate in a subsequent mail survey than those not so labelled.

However, Tybout, and Yalch (1980) maintain that self-perception theory by itself cannot explain how future behavior is influenced by past experience; it must be augmented by an understanding of how salience affects labelling. In an experiment in the political realm, salience of a label for one's behavior influenced voting. Registered voters told that their questionnaire responses indicated a high likelihood of voting were more likely to actually vote one week later than those told their responses indicated more "average" voting behavior. When subjects were distinguished on the basis of initial self-perceptions of being voters or nonvoters, the effect occurred only when the feedback was consistent with their self-schema (i.e., being a voter). Furthermore, the effect was short term, lasting only as long as the cue was salient. Thus, self-perception theory could not fully explain the results.

Whereas the previous research identifies a number of limitations of self-perception theory, the theory has suffered most damage in regard to the foot-in-the-door paradigm. The foot-in-the-door technique specifies that a small request is more likely to elicit compliance to a large request than if only the large request is made. According to self-perception theory predictions, the small favor should elicit greater compliance only when the target of the request perceives the self as the sort of person who complies to this sort of request. Typically, the foot-in-the-door effect has been tested in recent consumer research by examining compliance to requests to participate in market research surveys. Respondents given a brief telephone interview were asked to complete a mail questionnaire (Hansen and Robinson 1980). Subjects contacted by telephone were more likely to respond and to respond more quickly to the subsequent mail questionnaire (small request followed by large) than those not contacted by telephone first (large request only). When the requester in a small request condition also explicitly encouraged the subject to engage in causal search, the large request elicited even greater compliance.

A similar study also found increased compliance with large requests when preceded by small requests (Allen et al. 1980). One small request condition asked for commitment to complete the second questionnaire (the large request), while another small request condition manipulated self-perception as well as gaining commitment. Allen et al. argued that the self-perception manipulation should have increased compliance over and above commitment, but both small favor conditions elicited similar levels of compliance.

More problematic than these results are null effects often found for the foot-in-the-door effect. Furse et al. (1981) found weak effects on compliance using the survey response paradigm. A meta-analysis of 120 tests of the foot-in-the-door effect also concluded that the effect on compliance is weak (Beaman et al. 1983), and an older review of this literature noted a surprising number of nonsignificant effects (DeJong 1979). Beaman et al. concluded that self-perception theory was, at best, only a partial explanation for the foot-in-the-door effect.

The most prominent explanation for the weak results is based on availability of issue relevant information in memory (Tybout, Sternthal, and Calder 1983). Basically, this explanation states that easy retrieval of information favorable to compliance facilitates compliance, whereas easy retrieval of information unfavorable to compliance hinders actual compliance. Prior notification of a subsequent mail survey increases response rates because acceptance of the initial request is more available and memorable than the more unfavorable information about the request. However, if escalation from a small request to a large request is more available than information about acceptance, then the small request can actually undermine compliance to the subsequent larger request. In the large-favor-only condition, lack of notification leads to availability of unfavorable information about complying to the request. A recent review examines this explanation in some detail (Fern, Monroe, and Avila 1986), so the availability approach is only briefly mentioned here.

In sum, recent research suggests that self-perception theory has more limited usefulness for understanding consumer behavior than was originally thought. This conclusion is somewhat ironic considering that this is the single body of research most closely identified with attribution theory in consumer behavior.

Changing Attributions by Changing Antecedents

Research on how people arrive at attributions indicates that consumers' attributions can be modified in three general ways: by influencing the consumer's motivations, by controlling the information available, and by creating certain beliefs. Nevertheless, consumers' causal inferences may not be as malleable as the research reviewed here suggests. Studies typically provide information or manipulate beliefs to create attributions rather than change already-formed attributions. There are two literatures dealing with attribution change, each suggesting differing difficulty of intervention.

On the one hand, the attribution change literature suggests ease in changing attributions. Attribution change programs typically use subjects experiencing some deficit in functioning—the lonely, the depressed, the failing student (see Forsterling 1986 for a review). Change agents provide these subjects with information facilitating external and unstable or temporary attributions for the undesirable behavior, often finding improved behavior over considerable time periods. The success of these change attempts may be partially due to subjects' motivation to escape negative consequences of their previous behavior patterns.

In contrast, consumers often have incentives for maintaining unrealistic or inaccurate attributions. For example, the consumer can benefit from believing that a product is defective rather than accepting responsibility for product failure. Perhaps even more problematic for the consumer, the seller may have equally strong incentives for arguing the reverse. Studies conducted by Ross and his colleagues (Ross and Anderson 1982; Ross, Lepper, and Hubbard 1975) find considerable difficulty in changing attributions, even when information upon which the attribution is based is shown to be false. It appears that once an attribution has become integral to an established belief structure, much greater evidence is required to falsify the inference than was required to create it. The malleability of consumers' attributions is an issue that warrants further research.

CONSEQUENCES OF CAUSAL ASCRIPTIONS

Whereas a distinction has been drawn between studies examining antecedents of causal inferences and those examining consequences of causal inferences, many studies examine both (Kelley and Michela 1980). For example, numerous studies manipulate beliefs about causes and examine attitudes, assuming attributions mediate the effects. Studies focusing on attributional consequences also manipulate antecedents, in the sense that research only manipulates information given to subjects and cannot directly influence or measure cognitions. However, studies of attributional consequences emphasize distinctions among various behaviors, intentions, and affects as a function of causal inferences (Weiner 1985a, 1986). Compared to the field when reviewed by Mizerski et al. (1979), the eighties have brought much more interest and progress in understanding consequences.

Consequences of Consumers' Attributions

Typically, linkages between causes and consequences are made in terms of broad categories of causes, with the single most common distinction being between internal and external locations (see Weiner 1985a, 1986). For example, suppose a bottle of wine tastes bad. The location of the cause of the problem may reside with the consumer (e.g., the consumer stored the bottle in a hot place), or with the vintner (e.g., the vintner stored the bottle in a hot place). Conventionally, the former cause would be described as internal to the consumer while the latter would be external to the consumer.

When multiple causal agents play a role (e.g., a buyer and a seller), possible confusion over the internality of the cause has sometimes led the researcher to substitute such terms as buyer-related and seller-related (e.g., Folkes 1984b). The simple buyer/seller distinction may often capture consumers' phenomenology; however, the consumer behavior expert more typically perceives multiple causal agents in the distribution chain. Increased complexity arises when distinguishing among more than two sources of causality, such as buyer-related, retailer-related, and wholesaler-related. Thus, the researcher is sometimes torn between capturing perceived causality and parsimony when determining whether to use a simple internal/external locus categorization or more complex categories.

The locus distinction is not always clear-cut either, such that disagreement arises over categorization of causes (e.g., is a broker's or agent's action a seller-related cause or a buyer-related cause?). Similarly, in the persuasion literature, it is not always clear whether consumers perceive product endorsers and spokespersons rather than a firm or an advertising agency as the message source. Further, the central role of the internal-external distinction in attribution research has been criticized (e.g., Kruglanski 1975, 1982).

Some problems in classifying causes can be seen in a study aiming to manipulate consumers' perceptions of locus of causality. Hunt, Kernan, and Mizerski (1983) suggested that competitive pressures from being a new, small firm with many rivals is an external factor compelling the company to use misleading advertising. But they found that consumers were equally distressed by deceptive advertising that led to a bad purchase decision when the firm advertised falsely due to these competitive pressures as when no pressures were present. Perhaps subjects believed that the appropriate response to competition is to provide a better product rather than to cheat consumers. Thus, they made internal rather than external attribution for the firm's deceptive advertising. Clearly, care is necessary in classifying and manipulating causes.

Related to the locus dimension is the distinction between intrinsic and extrinsic motivation for purchasing a product. A consumer may purchase a product because the purchase yields inherent satisfaction or to achieve some extrinsic goal (e.g., to use a coupon or to please the experimenter). The intrinsic/extrinsic distinction frequently occurs in studies of discounting and attitudes toward products. The self-perception studies described earlier suggest that providing extrinsic incentives for using a product decreases liking for the product.

Two other causal dimensions have been used in consumer research. Causes can be classified by the degree to which they are under volitional control (Weiner 1986). Consumers can perceive themselves and be perceived as controlling many aspects of consumption, but some events are due to uncontrollable causes (e.g., weather). Causes also differ in temporal stability. An event's cause may be temporary and fluctuating or permanent and stable. Because locus, controllability, and stability are perceived as independent dimensions (Weiner 1986), they are often manipulated orthogonally in experimental designs.

Consequences Linked to Locus. Locus influences beliefs about who should solve problems; problems arising from consumers' actions should be solved by consumers, whereas problems arising from firms' actions should be solved by firms. Such beliefs may be related to the representativeness heuristic—the tendency to match reasons that are similar to or representative of the action to the action itself (Kahneman and Tversky 1982). In a survey of Salt Lake City households, those attributing the energy crisis to the general public favored the public's solving the problem by such actions as voluntary conservation, whereas those attributing the energy crisis to the oil companies more strongly favored government pressure on oil companies as a solution (Belk, Painter, and Semenik 1981). Another survey found that respondents who blamed individuals for polluting the air and littering the environment identified these individuals as responsible for solving the problems (Belk and Painter 1983). When other sources of the problems were identified, they were generally held responsible for solutions. Similarly, locus of causality influences whether consumers believe a firm should provide a refund and an apology for product failure (Folkes 1984b). When product failure is seller-related, firms owe consumers refunds and apologies; when product failure is consumer-related, firms are not obligated to provide redress.

A number of studies relate locus to product satisfaction. Oliver and DeSarbo (1988) manipulated locus of causality in an experiment. Investors' successful stock purchases resulting from external causes (the broker's research and recommendation) led to more satisfaction with the broker compared to internal causes (the investor's research and decision). Netherlands' consumers who felt seller-related causes played some role in their problem experienced more product dissatisfaction than those not detecting seller-related causes (Richins 1985). A survey of 261 U.S. consumers reporting a recent product dissatisfaction collected information about their attributions for the problem, how extensively they engaged in negative word-of-mouth with other consumers about the product, and whether they complained to the firm. External attributions led to more criticism than did internal attributions (Richins 1983).

Except for Folkes (1984b), the empirical research cited above and earlier research (e.g., Valle and Koeske 1977; Valle and Wallendorf 1977) distinguish causes only in terms of locus. Yet causes have additional properties or dimensions that could influence these same behaviors. Unless these dimensions are explicitly included in the research, misleading conclusions about the influence of locus may result. For example, the product satisfaction literature shows that controllability and locus influence consumers' desires to engage in word-of-mouth communications with other consumers and to communicate to firms about products (Curren and Folkes 1987).

Consequences Linked to Controllability. Causes also differ in controllability over outcomes; for some actions a consumer "could have done otherwise" and so had volitional control over an outcome, while at other times the situation forces or constrains the consumer to follow a certain course of action (Weiner 1985a). Evaluation of product hazard may be related to consumers' control over problems. Risks people voluntarily assume (e.g., snow skiing) are perceived as more acceptable than those perceived as imposed by firms (Rethans and Albaum 1980).

Firms can also be perceived as having varying amounts of control over their actions. For example, passengers perceive airline personnel problems such as slow baggage handling to be more firm-controllable reasons for flight delays than mechanical problems (Folkes, Koletsky, and Graham 1987). Research has primarily examined how consumers' perceptions of firms' control (external locus) influence consumers' evaluations. Controllability influences willingness to communicate with others about product success (Curren and Folkes 1987). When consumers perceive product success to be controlled by the firm (e.g., a dry cleaning service removes stains because of the firm's efforts to diagnose the problem), they are more willing to compliment the firm and to recommend the product to others than when situational constraints dictate the firm's actions (e.g., the dry cleaning service's standard formula happens to remove this stain). Conversely, product failure controlled by the firm increases the desire to complain to the firm and warn others against product purchase than if product failure is not controlled by the firm.

Controllability also influences consumer anger over product failure (Folkes 1984b). Consumers express more anger over product failure when the firm had volitional control over a problem (e.g., a repair was not ready on time due to the shop's carelessness) than when the firm lacked control over the problem (e.g., a repair was not ready on time due to a power failure in the area). Firm controlled attributions increase the consumer's desire to hurt the firm's business. Affective reactions appear to mediate the relationship between attributions and some consumer responses (cf. Weiner 1985a, 1986). Delayed airline passengers who believed that flight delay was controllable by the airline felt angrier at the airline than those who believed the delay was uncontrollable (Folkes et al. 1987). Anger, in turn, influenced passengers' desires to complain about a problem to the airline and willingness to fly the same airline again.

Consequences Linked to Stability. Another causal dimension investigated in consumer behavior studies is temporal stability (stable and permanent causes versus unstable and temporary causes). Stability influences expectancies such that stable causes for an outcome lead to more confidence that the same outcome will recur than do unstable outcomes (Weiner 1986). In research manipulating causal locus, controllability, and stability, unstable causes led consumers to change expectancies for product failure. Thus, when products fail for stable reasons, e.g., the dishwasher stops because the product is defective or because the consumer never scrapes food off before filling the dishwasher, the consumer is more certain the product will fail again than when due to unstable reasons, e.g., the refrigerator stops because of a power failure or because the consumer forgot to plug it in after cleaning (Folkes 1984b).

Stability influences the type of redress preferred when a product fails; compared to unstable reasons, stable attributions lead consumers to more strongly prefer refunds rather than exchanges. However, locus also affects redress. Preference for refunds increases when products fail for firm-related reasons as opposed to consumer-related reasons.

Causal Dimensions and Product Performance. In sum, causes for service and product performance can be classified by locus, stability, and controllability. Sometimes consequences of attributions are linked to a single causal dimension, e.g., consumers believe refunds are owed when problems arise due to firm-related reasons but not for consumer-related reasons (Folkes 1984b). For other consequences, more dimensions are involved. For example, locus, controllability, and stability influence how consumers communicate about products, with successful performance due to firm-controlled and stable causes leading to the greatest desire to recommend the product to friends and to compliment the firm (Curren and Folkes 1987). In contrast to the research reviewed by Mizerski et al. (1979), research classifying causes by several causal dimensions identifies distinct responses (e.g., expectancies for product performance, anger at the firm), as opposed to merely valence of the response (e.g., a more positive response toward the product).

Although progress has been made in elucidating consequences of attributions for product performance, these relationships require further elaboration. Other affects, such as pity, surprise, and regret, may mediate relationships between attributions and behavioral responses. For example, greater pity for victims of birth defects, famine, and crime than for those of seemingly more controllable outcomes (e.g., alcoholism) may lead consumers to contribute less money to charities helping the latter (Weiner 1986).

It is particularly important to clarify the relationship between attribution and decision making. Attributions have often been studied as a postpurchase phenomenon. Complex inferences about product attributes are initiated after products are selected. Attributions probably also play an important role at the beginning of the decision-making process. Problem recognition must often entail causal inferences, inferences which then limit the kinds of solutions considered by consumers. For example, many advertisements for personal care products try to portray personal rejection as due to some offensive property of the consumer (e.g., the consumer's need for an effective deodorant). The consumer who accepts this definition of his or her problem will search for different solutions more so than someone who attributes romantic rejection to being unlucky in love. Thus, consumers' attributions can guide and define decision making.

Consequences of Attributions for Sales Performance

A relatively new stream of research that should be briefly mentioned examines salespersons' causal inferences for sales. Because most of these studies also use Weiner's (1986) framework they address some issues described earlier. However, they link specific causes to evaluations of and expectancies for sales.

Consistent with previous research, the stability dimension influences expectancies for salespersons' success (Anderson 1983). Despite this support for Weiner's theory, some research has been interpreted as contradicting the theory. In two studies (Anand and Stern 1985; Mowen et al. 1985), marketers seemed to perceive effort as a stable cause, in contrast to early theorizing by Weiner et al. (1972) that suggested it is an unstable cause. Indeed, Weiner (1985a, 1986) changed his categorization system to include stable and unstable effort, pointing out the importance of assessing the subject's phenomenology when classifying causes. Controllability is another recent development in Weiner's classification system not taken into account in many salesperson motivation studies.

Whereas most of the previously described studies manipulate causal perceptions, a few studies examine how attributional styles influence salespersons' motivation and behavior. Predispositions to make certain attributions lead some salespersons to work harder after failure experiences; others perform worse or change selling strategies (Anderson 1983; Sujan 1986). Sujan's work emphasizes an important distinction in changeable causes (effort and strategy) and their behavioral consequences (intensity and change in direction). Salespersons who attributed poor sales to a bad strategy adopted new techniques (changed direction), whereas attributions to low effort led to intentions to work longer hours (increased intensity).

Attributional styles have also been examined from a learned helplessness framework. A person who habitually makes internal, stable, and global attributions in the face of repeated failure will display lowered self-esteem and fewer response initiatives (Abramson, Seligman, and Teasdale 1978). Globality refers to the extent to which a cause generalizes beyond the present situation or is specific to the immediate situation. Noting that life insurance salespersons face repeated rejections, Seligman and Schulman (1986) found that those who had "pessimistic" explanatory styles (internal, stable, and global attributions for negative life events) were more likely to sell less insurance and then to quit their jobs than those with more "optimistic" styles (external, unstable, and specific). Whereas consumer behavior researchers may be tempted to apply these concepts to consumers, they should also be aware of articles critical of this line of research (e.g., Cutrona, Russell, and Jones 1984; Weisz, Rothbaum, and Blackburn 1984).

In sum, an attributional approach to understanding sellers' behaviors is quite promising. Attributional concepts have been incorporated into theories of salesperson motivation (Teas and McElroy 1986; Weitz, Sujan, and Sujan 1986) and, more generally, organizational behavior (e.g., Green and Linden 1980; Mitchell, Green, and Wood 1981; Porac, Nottenburg, and Eggert 1981). But future research needs to clarify implications of causal inferences for such issues as sales projections, sales training, personnel compensation, and employee turnover—marketing decisions that impinge on consumers.

OVERVIEW OF RECENT DEVELOPMENTS AND FUTURE DIRECTIONS

With the review of research since the Mizerski et al. (1979) article complete, we should now step back and get a better sense of the scope and direction of the field. Many of the issues discussed in the present article have been debated since the mid-seventies. Yet, some new research streams have emerged.

Current Issues in Attribution Research

Mizerski et al. (1979) placed emphasis on four major attribution theories: Heider (1958), Kelley (1967, 1973), Bem (1972), and Jones and Davis (1965). Heider provided the seminal concepts for theories about causal inferences; more recently published writings also display the wealth of his insights (Benesh and Weiner 1982). However, Kelley's theories have provided the starting point for much more of the empirical work. Kelley's covariation theory and discounting principle, in particular, stimulated research reviewed by Mizerski et al., as well as recent work in marketing (e.g., Lichtenstein and Bearden 1986; Yalch and Yoshida 1983).

In the seventies, predictions from Bem's self-perception theory were often pitted against those of cognitive dissonance theory, but interest in this controversy has greatly declined without being clearly resolved in favor of either theory. Because many major issues in self-perception theory have been addressed, future research is likely to be concerned with refinements (e.g., Tybout and Scott 1983; Tybout et al. 1983). Although Bem's self-perception theory has attracted decreased interest, a related position articulated by Nisbett and Wilson (1977) has generated considerable controversy (e.g., Kellogg 1982; Wegner and Vallacher 1986). Nisbett and Wilson's initial position—that individuals lack access to the cognitive processes influencing their behavior—seems to have been too extreme. Finally, Jones and Davis's correspondent inference theory has stimulated relatively little research both within and outside of consumer behavior (but see Kamins and Assael 1987; Mizerski 1982).

These four major attribution theories and most attribution research view people as naive scientists, carefully gathering data upon which to make a causal inference. Recent investigators have sometimes conceived of a much less industrious information processor, a cognitive economizer (e.g., Hansen 1985). Also in contrast to the early research, which emphasized data-driven or bottom-up information-processing strategies when arriving at causal inferences, more recent approaches have emphasized conceptually driven or top-down strategies (e.g., Hastie 1983). For example, Leddo, Abelson, and Gross (1984) have been highly critical of Kelley's models, suggesting that a "knowledge structure" approach better describes how people explain events. People arrive at causes by first finding an appropriate schema for the event, then comparing the event to the information contained in the schema. For example, consumers may hold the belief that large firms care little about individual consumers. When encountering a large firm's poor service, the consumer fits the firm's actions to this belief rather than compare experiences with large and small firms. If Leddo et al. are correct, changing consumers' attributions will entail changing "knowledge structures" or modifying the fit between schema and incident, rather than providing information. Along this line, some consumer behavior research has examined when people form hypotheses about the cause of an event, which they then test against data (e.g., Scott and Yalch 1980).

During the seventies and eighties, a common research approach has been to compare normative models of attributional inferences against actual causal inferences. Departures from the ideal are generally described as biases, such as the fundamental attribution error—the tendency to make person attributions rather than situational attributions for another's behavior (e.g., Ross 1977, but see also Funder 1987), underuse of consensus information (e.g., Borgida and Brekke 1981; Kassin 1979) and the self-serving bias (e.g., Bradley 1978; Miller 1978). Interest in attributional biases is also evident in recent consumer behavior research (e.g., Folkes and Kotsos 1986; Sherman et al. 1983).

Researchers remain interested in identifying biases, some of which are clearly relevant for consumer behavior. Consider the group attribution error—the tendency to infer the attitude of group members from the decision made by the group, regardless of how the decision was arrived at (Allison and Messick 1985). Consumers may infer that employees implementing a policy mandated by top management also agree with those policies. Thus, a disgruntled consumer may assume that a customer service representative denying a refund personally shares the firm's attitude toward redress. Consequently, the complainer might fruitlessly try to persuade the complaint handler to change policies and might hold the complaint handler personally responsible for lack of redress.

Even in the case of self-serving attributions, the source of attributional biases has often been identified using concepts from cognitive psychology, such as memory, ease of processing, and perceptual salience. Cognitive psychology has increasingly provided the impetus for theory development. For example, Einhorn and Hogarth (1986) have approached attributions from a decision-making framework, noting that people often make judgments about the probable or likely cause of an event. Their analysis suggests yet another way to understand the often studied discounting effect in consumer behavior. Research in text comprehension and scripts suggests hypotheses about how people make causal inferences in complex scenarios (Read 1987). Because many commercials require viewers to make inferences about characters' intentions and goals, this sort of analysis should provide guidelines for understanding advertising effects.

Although attribution theory focuses on cognitive processes, interest in consequences of causal inferences has always been strong. Recently most progress has been made in identifying attributions' effects on consumers' responses to product problems (e.g., Richins 1983). A trend emerging since the Mizerski et al. (1979) review, but with roots in early attributional investigations (e.g., Schachter 1964), is research on how causal inferences for an outcome influence the type of affective reaction to that outcome (e.g., Weiner 1986). This approach has received relatively little attention in consumer behavior, with the exception of some research on attributions for product failure and consumers' anger (Folkes 1984b; Folkes et al. 1987).

Yet, emotions play an important role in consumption behavior. For example, receiving a gift may give rise not only to knowledge that one is obligated to reciprocate but also feelings of gratitude (Weiner 1986). These feelings may motivate subsequent actions, as well as enhance or even change the nature of the relationship between giver and recipient. A woman who attributes a gift of flowers to romantic attraction will have a different relationship with the giver than if she believes the gift is a sympathy gesture for illness.

Consider the emotions of pride and embarrassment in consumption situations. A consumer may feel great pride in a purchase when attributing the price paid to skilled negotiating, while another consumer might attribute the same price to negotiating ineptitude and so feel embarrassed (cf. Weiner 1986). These feelings may, in turn, influence subsequent behavior. Pride would logically lead to boasting about the purchase while embarrassment might generate reticence to discuss the purchase. Thus attributions might, through their effects on pride and shame, influence the diffusion of product information.

Although attribution theory cannot provide a comprehensive understanding of affective life, causal inferences do have an important role in what Smith and Ellsworth (1987) have termed appraisal theories of emotions. Further, many consumption activities may be motivated by a naive analysis of the effects of emotions. For example, an individual may believe that an ice cream cone or a glass of wine will cheer him or her up (Weiner et al. 1987). An interesting line of research would explore the nature and source of such beliefs.

As noted in this review, most attribution research examines antecedents and consequences of causal inferences. Other fundamental issues receive less attention. One important line of research has examined factors instigating causal search (e.g., Hastie 1984; Weiner 1985b). Unexpected and negative events are more likely to generate attributional activity. Uncertainty about one's feelings toward a product seems to motivate consumers to engage in causal analysis (Scott 1981). Other research has examined how causal inferences differ from other kinds of inferences, e.g., Locksley and Stangor's (1984) work on "how" versus "why" questions. Consumer researchers will probably want to follow up on Wilson and Dunn's (1986) finding that attitudes toward usage of products differ depending on whether users introspect about reasons for their attitudes toward products or their feelings about products.

An Assessment of the Theory

This overview merely highlights recent trends in this vast field, necessarily omitting some research streams (for more extensive reviews, see Harvey and Weary 1984, 1985; Kelley and Michela 1980; Ross and Fletcher 1985; Weiner 1986). Even this brief summary shows that attribution theory has not remained stagnant but has expanded its scope while refining basic issues. Oftentimes attributional concepts have spurred the researcher to examine more general processes. For example, Nisbett and Ross's (1980) interest in attributional biases evolved into a larger concern with human judgment processes.

In contrast to the past explosive growth of research in the field, the theory has now settled down to a respectable middle age. Most of the basic theoretical issues have been delineated. Most of the original theories are in the refinement stage. Many controversies have been resolved or declared unresolvable. Past research is so extensive that a contribution to the field typically requires the investigator to acquire considerable sophistication in the field. Nevertheless, as indicated by the present review, attribution theory is certainly not on its death bed as a paradigm. Attributional concepts will have a long lasting impact. People do make causal attributions; these causal inferences have important consequences.

Directions for Attribution Research in Consumer Behavior

Turning more specifically to the development of attribution theory in consumer behavior, one sees uneven growth. Many areas, such as research examining self-perception theory, have considerable maturity and suggest limited horizons in terms of future research. Some earlier work has not received the follow-up it deserves. For example, Robertson and Rossiter (1974) found important differences in children's ability to infer the intent of advertisers behind commercials, but consumer researchers have not pursued these sorts of developmental differences.

Other issues of interest to consumer researchers have received surprisingly little attention. For example, the absence of extrinsic incentives influences a person's defining an activity as leisure or recreation (e.g., Lepper and Green 1978), yet this distinction receives little attention in the consumer behavior literature. Causal inferences influence the extent to which people tolerate crowded and noisy environments (e.g., Darley and Gilbert 1985), but little research has examined shopping and consumption environments from this perspective.

Attributional concepts are relevant to a variety of other issues important to consumer researchers. Causal inferences may influence consumers' perceptions of prices. Consumers may perceive price increases due to reasons uncontrollable by the firm (e.g., higher costs of raw materials) as more legitimate than price increases due to controllable reasons (e.g., the firm's desire for higher profits). Citizens' demands for governmental price controls may arise from such perceptions. Additionally, consumers' willingness to purchase generic or "plain wrap" products may depend on causal inferences for lower prices charged for these products. Evaluations of warranties may depend partly on causal inferences for why the warranty is offered. On the one hand, people may infer that a firm offers a warranty because of confidence the product will not fail. The warranty will cost the firm nothing. On the other hand, people may infer the firm anticipates problems with the product that they will be obligated to remedy anyway.

Causal inferences may play an important role in buyer-seller interactions. Negotiation tactics may depend on inferences for why the other is making an offer. A buyer makes a different counteroffer when attributing the seller's initial high-priced offer to confidence in demand for the seller's product as opposed to a desperate need for funds. Meta-attributions may also be important here; negotiators may try to infer what the other will infer about offers. An interesting avenue for research would determine how people arrive at these sorts of inferences.

Considering the multiple consequences of attributions for product failure, it is easy to see how buyer-seller conflict may focus on causal inferences for an outcome (Folkes 1984a; Folkes and Kotsos 1986). If buyers and sellers disagree about causes of product failure, they may consequently disagree about whether refunds are owed, what product performance should be expected, and whether the consumer should be angry about the problem. On the other hand, when buyers and sellers are in conflict over an outcome, excuses, justifications, and explanations for events are ways of maintaining, protecting, and building relationships between buyers and sellers (e.g., Snyder, Higgins, and Stucky 1980; Weiner et al. 1987).

Attributional concepts can be used to understand nutrition, health, and safety issues. For example, consumers probably have naive models of how food intake promotes health. A simple, "graded effects" causal schema (Kelley 1972) that assumes causes that have beneficial consequences in small quantities will have even larger beneficial consequences in large quantities may be responsible for the common vitamin overdose problem. Beliefs about what causes and what cures illness probably influence when consumers decide they should see a physician and patient compliance with physicians' recommendations. In sum, attributional approaches can shed light on a variety of consumer behavior issues.

CONCLUSION

The introduction to this review noted that attribution theory has had relatively little impact on the field of consumer behavior. Moreover, some have expressed doubt over the value of this approach to our discipline. As recently as 1980, a newly elected fellow in the Association for Consumer Research reported he was "glad . . . to see the advocates of attribution theory challenged to show what, if anything, it has contributed to existing knowledge" (Engel 1980). The research reviewed here clearly shows causal inferences influence a variety of important consumer responses, as well as those whose actions impinge on consumers, such as salespersons.

Yet, attributional concepts have been underutilized. One reason may be that the relevance of some issues central to the theory has not been obvious. For example, causal inferences to personal dispositions have been a central topic in attribution research but have less importance for consumer behavior. Another reason may be that some studies examining consumer behavior present themselves as testing attributional principles and do not explicitly recognize their relevance to the field of consumer behavior. For example, this article reviewed studies investigating consumers' tendency to assume a false consensus for their preferences, a controversial issue in attribution theory. The issue has not been addressed in consumer behavior publications, but has been examined in psychology journals. These studies rarely mention the word "consumer." Although one is tempted to speculate on other causes for attribution theory's relative lack of influence, one reason that can be ruled out is that attribution theory has little to offer.

REFERENCES

ABRAMSON, LYN T., MARTIN E. P. SELIGMAN, and JOHN TEASDALE (1978), "Learned Helplessness in Humans: Critique and Reformulation," *Journal of Abnormal Psychology,* 87 (February), 49–74.

ALLEN, CHRIS T. (1982), "Self-Perception Based Strategies for Stimulating Energy Conservation," *Journal of Consumer Research,* 8 (March), 381–390.

———, and WILLIAM R. DILLON (1983), "Self-Perception Development and Consumer Choice Criteria: Is There a Linkage?" in *Advances in Consumer Research,* Vol. 10, Eds. Richard P. Bagozzi and Alice M. Tybout, Ann Arbor, MI: Association for Consumer Research, 45–50.

———, CHARLES D. SCHEWE, and GOSTA WIJK (1980), "More on Self-Perception Theory's Foot Technique in the Pre-Call/Mail Survey Setting," *Journal of Marketing Research,* 17 (November), 498–502.

ALLISON, SCOTT T., and DAVID M. MESSICK (1985), "The Group Attribution Error," *Journal of Experimental Social Psychology,* 21 (November), 563–579.

AMABILE, TERESA M. (1983), "Brilliant But Cruel: Perceptions of Negative Evaluators," *Journal of Experimental Social Psychology,* 19 (March), 146–156.

ANAND, PUNAM, and LOUIS STERN (1985), "A Sociopsychological Explanation for Why Marketing Channel Members Relinquish Control," *Journal of Marketing Research,* 22 (November), 365–376.

ANDERSON, CRAIG A. (1983), "Motivational and Performance Deficits in Interpersonal Settings: The Effect of Attributional Style," *Journal of Personality and Social Psychology,* 45 (November), 1136–1147.

BEAMAN, ARTHUR L., C. MAUREEN COLE, MARILYN PRESTON, BONNEL KLENTZ, and NANCY MEHRKENS STEBLAY (1983), "Fifteen Years of Foot-in-the-Door Research: A Meta Analysis," *Personality and Social Psychology Bulletin,* 9 (June), 181–196.

BELK, RUSSELL, and JOHN PAINTER (1983), "Effects of Causal Attributions on Pollution and Litter Control Attitudes," in *Non-Profit Marketing: Conceptual and Empirical Research,* Eds. F. Kelly Shuptrine and Peter Reingen. Bureau of Business and Economics Research, Arizona State University, Tempe, AZ, 22–25.

———, JOHN PAINTER, and RICHARD SEMENIK (1981), "Preferred Solutions to the Energy Crisis as a Function of Causal Attributions," *Journal of Consumer Research,* 8 (December), 306–312.

BEM, DARYL (1972), "Self Perception Theory," in *Advances in Experimental Social Psychology,* Vol. 6, Ed. Leonard Berkowitz. New York: Academic Press.

BENESH, MARIJANA, and BERNARD WEINER (1982), "On Emotion and Motivation: From the Notebooks of Fritz Heider," *American Psychologist,* 37 (August), 887–895.

BETTMAN, JAMES R. (1979), *An Information Processing Theory of Consumer Choice.* Reading, MA: Addison-Wesley.

———, and BARTON A. WEITZ (1983), "Attributions in the Board Room: Causal Reasoning in Corporate Annual Reports," *Administrative Science Quarterly,* 28 (June), 165-183.

BORGIDA, EUGENE, and N. BREKKE (1981), "The Base-Rate Fallacy in Attribution and Prediction," in *New Directions in Attribution Research,* Vol. 3, Eds. John H. Harvey, William J. Ickes, and Robert F. Kidd. Hillsdale, NJ: Erlbaum, 63-95.

BRADLEY, GIFFORD WEARY (1978), "Self-Serving Biases in the Attribution Process: A Re-Examination of the Fact or Fiction Question," *Journal of Personality and Social Psychology,* 36 (January), 56-71.

CHAIKEN, SHELLY, and CHARLES STANGOR (1987), "Attitudes and Attitude Change," *Annual Review of Psychology,* 38, 575-630.

COOPER, JOEL, and ROBERT T. CROYLE (1984), "Attitudes and Attitude Change," *Annual Review of Psychology,* 35, 395-426.

CRANO, WILLIAM D. (1983), "Assumed Consensus of Attitudes: The Effect of Vested Interest," *Personality and Social Psychology Bulletin,* 9 (December), 597-608.

CURREN, MARY T., and VALERIE S. FOLKES (1987), "Attributional Influences on Consumers' Desires to Communicate About Products," *Psychology and Marketing,* 4 (Spring), 31-45.

CUTRONA, CAROLYN E., DAN RUSSELL, and R. DALLAS JONES (1984), "Cross-Situational Consistency in Causal Attributions: Does Attributional Style Exist?" *Journal of Personality and Social Psychology,* 47 (November), 1043-1058.

DARLEY, JOHN M., and DANIEL T. GILBERT (1985), "Social Psychological Aspects of Environmental Psychology," in *Handbook of Social Psychology,* Vol. 2, Eds. Gardner Lindzey and Elliot Aronson. New York: Random House, 949-992.

DEJONG, WILLIAM (1979), "An Examination of Self Perception Mediation of the Foot-in-the-Door Effect," *Journal of Personality and Social Psychology,* 37 (December), 2221-2239.

DHOLAKIA, RUBY R., and BRIAN STERNTHAL (1977), "Highly Credible Sources: Persuasive Facilitators or Persuasive Liabilities?" *Journal of Consumer Research,* 3 (March), 223-232.

EAGLY, ALICE H., and SHELLY CHAIKEN (1984), "Cognitive Theories of Persuasion," in *Advances in Experimental Social Psychology,* Vol. 17, Ed. Leonard Berkowitz. New York: Academic Press, 267-359.

EINHORN, HILLEL J., and ROBIN M. HOGARTH (1986), "Judging Probable Cause," *Psychological Bulletin,* 99 (January), 3-19.

ENGEL, JAMES F. (1981), "The Discipline of Consumer Research: Permanent Adolescence or Maturity?" in *Advances in Consumer Research,* Vol. 8, Ed. Kent B. Monroe. Ann Arbor, MI: Association for Consumer Research, 12-14.

FERN, EDWARD F., KENT B. MONROE, and RAMON A. AVILA (1986), "Effectiveness of Multiple Request Strategies: A Synthesis of Research Results," *Journal of Marketing Research,* 23 (May), 144-152.

FOLKES, VALERIE S. (1984a), "An Attributional Approach to Postpurchase Conflict Between Buyers and Sellers," in *Advances in Consumer Research,* Vol. 11, Ed. Thomas C. Kinnear. Provo, UT: Association for Consumer Research, 500-503.

______ (1984b), "Consumer Reactions to Product Failure: An Attributional Approach," *Journal of Consumer Research,* 10 (March), 398-409.

______, SUSAN KOLETSKY, and JOHN GRAHAM (1987), "A Field Study of Causal Inferences and Consumer Reaction: The View from the Airport," *Journal of Consumer Research,* 13 (March), 534-539.

______, and BARBARA KOTSOS (1986), "Buyers' and Sellers' Explanations for Product Failure: Who Done It," *Journal of Marketing,* 50 (April), 74-80.

FORSTERLING, FRIEDRICH (1986), "Attributional Conceptions in Clinical Psychology," *American Psychologist,* 41 (March), 275-285.

FUNDER, DAVID C. (1987), "Errors and Mistakes: Evaluating the Accuracy of Social Judgment," *Psychological Bulletin,* 101 (January), 75-90.

FURSE, DAVID H., DAVID W. STEWART, and DAVID L. RADOS (1981), "Effects of Foot-in-the-Door, Cash Incentives, and Follow-ups on Survey Response," *Journal of Marketing Research,* 18 (November), 473-478.

GILOVICH, THOMAS, DENNIS JENNINGS, and SUSAN JENNINGS (1983), "Causal Focus and Estimates of Consensus: An Examination of the False Consensus Effect," *Journal of Personality and Social Psychology,* 45 (September), 550-559.

GREEN, STEPHEN G., and ROBERT C. LINDEN (1980), "Contextual and Attributional Influences on Control Decisions," *Journal of Applied Psychology,* 65 (August), 453-458.

HANSEN, RANALD D. (1985), "Cognitive Economy and Commonsense Attribution Processing," in *Attribution: Basic Issues and Applications,* Eds. John

H. Harvey and Gifford Weary. Orlando, FL: Academic Press, 65–85.

Hansen, Robert A. (1980), "A Self-Perception Interpretation of the Effect of Monetary and Nonmonetary Incentives on Mail Survey Respondent Behavior," *Journal of Marketing Research,* 17 (February), 77–83.

———, and Larry M. Robinson (1980), "Testing the Effectiveness of Alternative Foot-in-the-Door Manipulations," *Journal of Marketing Research,* 17 (August), 359–364.

Harvey, John H., and Gifford Weary (1984), "Current Issues in Attribution Theory and Research," *Annual Review of Psychology,* 35, 427–459.

———, and Gifford Weary (1985), *Attribution: Basic Issues and Applications.* Orlando, FL: Academic Press.

Hastie, Reid (1983), "Social Inference," *Annual Review of Psychology,* 34, 511–542.

——— (1984), "Causes and Effects of Causal Attribution," *Journal of Personality and Social Psychology,* 46 (January), 44–56.

Heider, Fritz (1958), *The Psychology of Interpersonal Relations.* New York: Wiley.

Hunt, James M., Teresa J. Domzal, and Jerome B. Kernan (1982), "Causal Attributions and Persuasion: The Case of Disconfirmed Expectancies," in *Advances in Consumer Research,* Vol. 9, Ed. Andrew Mitchell. Ann Arbor, MI: Association for Consumer Research, 287–290.

———, Jerome B. Kernan, and Richard W. Mizerski (1983), "Causal Inference in Consumer Response to Inequitable Exchange: A Case of Deceptive Advertising," in *Advances in Consumer Research,* Eds. Richard P. Bagozzi and Alice M. Tybout. Ann Arbor, MI: Association for Consumer Research, 136–141.

Jones, Edward E., and Keith Davis (1965), "From Acts to Dispositions: The Attribution Process in Person Perception," in *Advances in Experimental Social Psychology,* Vol. 2, Ed. Leonard Berkowitz. New York: Academic Press, 219–266.

———, and Daniel McGillis (1976), "Correspondent Inferences and the Attribution Cube: A Comparative Reappraisal," in *New Directions in Attribution Research,* Vol. 1, Eds. John Harvey, William Ickes, and Robert Kidd. Hillsdale, NJ: Erlbaum, 389–420.

———, and Richard E. Nisbett (1972), "The Actor and the Observer: Divergent Perceptions of the Causes of Behavior," in *Attribution: Perceiving the Causes of Behavior,* Eds. Edward E. Jones et al. Morristown, NJ: General Learning Press, 79–84.

Kahneman, Daniel, Paul Slovic, and Amos Tversky (1982), *Judgment Under Uncertainty: Heuristics and Biases.* Cambridge: Cambridge University Press.

Kamins, Michael A., and Henry Assael (1987), "Two-Sided Versus One-Sided Appeals: A Cognitive Perspective on Argumentation, Source Derogation, and the Effect of Disconfirming Trial on Belief Change," *Journal of Marketing Research,* 24 (February), 29–39.

Kanouse, David, and L. Reid Hanson (1972), "Negativity in Evaluations," in *Attribution: Perceiving the Causes of Behavior,* Eds. Edward E. Jones et al. Morristown, NJ: General Learning Press, 47–62.

Kassin, Saul M. (1979), "Consensus Information, Prediction, and Causal Attribution: A Review of the Literature and Issues," *Journal of Personality and Social Psychology,* 37 (November), 1966–1981.

Kelley, Harold H. (1967), "Attribution Theory in Social Psychology," in *Nebraska Symposium on Motivation,* Ed. David Levine. Lincoln, NE: University of Nebraska Press, 192–238.

——— (1972), "Causal Schemata and the Attribution Process," in *Attribution: Perceiving the Causes of Behavior,* Eds. Edward E. Jones et al. Morristown, NJ: General Learning Press, 151–174.

——— (1973), "The Process of Causal Attribution," *American Psychologist,* 28 (February), 107–128.

———, and John L. Michela (1980), "Attribution Theory and Research," *Annual Review of Psychology,* 31, 457–501.

Kellogg, Ronald T. (1982), "When Can We Introspect Accurately About Mental Processes?" *Memory and Cognition,* 10 (March), 141–144.

Kruglanski, Arie (1975), "The Endogenous-Exogenous Partition in Attribution Theory," *Psychological Review,* 82 (November), 387–428.

——— (1980), "Lay Epistemo-Logic-Process and Contents: Another Look at Attribution Theory," *Psychological Review,* 87 (January), 70–87.

Leddo, John, Robert P. Abelson, and Paget H. Gross (1984), "Conjunctive Explanations: When Two Reasons are Better Than One," *Journal of Personality and Social Psychology,"* 47 (November), 933–943.

Lepper, Mark R., and D. Greene (1978), *The Hidden Costs of Reward: New Perspectives on the Psychology of Human Behavior.* Hillsdale, NJ: Erlbaum.

LICHTENSTEIN, DONALD R., and WILLIAM O. BEARDEN (1986), "Measurement and Structure of Kelley's Covariance Theory," *Journal of Consumer Research,* 13 (September), 290–296.

LOCKSLEY, ANNE, and CHARLES STANGOR (1984), "Why Versus How Often: Causal Reasoning and the Incidence of Judgmental Bias," *Journal of Experimental Social Psychology,* 20 (September), 470–483.

MARKS, GARY, and NORMAN MILLER (1987), "Ten Years of Research on the False-Consensus Effect: An Empirical and Theoretical Review," *Psychological Bulletin,* 102 (July), 72–90.

MAZURSKY, DAVID, PRISCELLA LABARBERA, and AL AIELLO (1987), "When Consumers Switch Brands," *Psychology and Marketing,* 4 (Spring), 17–30.

MCARTHUR, LESLIE Z. (1972), "The How and What of Why: Some Determinants and Consequences of Causal Attribution," *Journal of Personality and Social Psychology,* 22 (May), 171–193.

MILLER, DALE T. (1978), "What Constitutes a Self-Serving Attributional Bias?" *Journal of Personality and Social Psychology,* 36 (November), 1221–1223.

MITCHELL, TERENCE R., STEPHEN G. GREEN, and ROBERT E. WOOD (1981), "An Attributional Model of Leadership and the Poor Performing Subordinate: Development and Validation," in *Research in Organization Behavior,* Vol. 3, Eds. L. L. Cummings and Barry M. Staw. Greenwich, CT: JAI Press, 197–234.

MIZERSKI, RICHARD W. (1982), "An Attribution Explanation of the Disproportionate Influence of Unfavorable Information," *Journal of Consumer Research,* 9 (December), 301–310.

———, LINDA L. GOLDEN, and JEROME B. KERNAN (1979), "The Attribution Process in Consumer Decision Making," *Journal of Consumer Research,* 6 (September), 123–140.

MOWEN, JOHN C., JANET E. KEITH, STEPHEN W. BROWN, and DONALD W. JACKSON, JR. (1985), "Utilizing Effort and Task Difficulty Information in Evaluating Salespeople," *Journal of Marketing Research,* 22 (May), 185–191.

MULLEN, BRIAN, JENNIFER L. ATKINS, DEBBIE S. CHAMPION, CECELIA EDWARDS, DANA HARDY, JOHN E. STORY, and MARY VANDERKLOK (1985), "The False Consensus Effect: A Meta-Analysis of 115 Hypothesis Tests," *Journal of Experimental Social Psychology,* 21 (May), 262–283.

NISBETT, RICHARD, and LEE ROSS (1980), *Human Inference: Strategies and Shortcomings of Social Judgment.* Englewood Cliffs, NJ: Prentice-Hall.

———, and TIMOTHY DECAMP WILSON (1977), "Telling More Than We Can Know: Verbal Reports on Mental Processes," *Psychological Review,* 84 (May), 231–259.

OLIVER, RICHARD L., and WAYNE S. DESARBO (1988), "Response Determinants in Satisfaction Judgments," *Journal of Consumer Research,* 14 (March), 495–507.

ORVIS, BRUCE, JOHN CUNNINGHAM, and HAROLD H. KELLEY (1975), "A Closer Examination of Causal Inferences: The Roles of Consensus, Distinctiveness and Consistency Information," *Journal of Personality and Social Psychology,* 32 (October), 605–616.

PETTY, RICHARD E., and JOHN T. CACIOPPO (1986), "The Elaboration Likelihood Model of Persuasion," in *Advances in Experimental Social Psychology,* Vol. 19, Ed. Leonard Berkowitz. New York: Academic Press, 123–205.

PORAC, JOSEPH F., GAIL NOTTENBURG, and JONES EGGERT (1981), "On Extending Weiner's Attributional Model to Organizational Contexts," *Journal of Applied Psychology,* 66 (February), 124–126.

READ, STEPHEN J. (1987), "Constructing Causal Scenarios: A Knowledge Structure Approach to Causal Reasoning," *Journal of Personality and Social Psychology,* 52 (February), 288–302.

REINGEN, PETER H., and WILLIAM O. BEARDEN (1983), "Salience of Behavior and the Effects of Labeling," in *Advances in Consumer Research,* Vol. 10, Eds. Richard P. Bagozzi and Alice M. Tybout. Ann Arbor, MI: Association for Consumer Research, 51–55.

RETHANS, ARNO J., and GERALD S. ALBAUM (1980), "Towards Determinants of Acceptable Risk: The Case of Product Risks," in *Advances in Consumer Research,* Vol. 8, Ed. Kent B. Monroe. Ann Arbor, MI: Association for Consumer Research, 506–510.

RHOLES, WILLIAM S., and JOHN B. PRYOR (1982), "Cognitive Accessibility and Causal Attributions," *Personality and Social Psychology Bulletin,* 8 (December), 719–727.

RICHINS, MARSHA L. (1983), "Negative Word-of-Mouth by Dissatisfied Consumers: A Pilot Study," *Journal of Marketing,* 47 (Winter), 68–78.

——— (1985),The Role of Product Importance in Complaint Initiation," in *Consumer Satisfaction/Dis-*

satisfaction and Complaining Behavior, Eds. H. Keith Hunt and Ralph L. Day. Bloomington, IN: Indiana University School of Business, 50–53.

ROBERTSON, THOMAS S., and JOHN R. ROSSITER (1974), "Children and Commercial Persuasion: An Attribution Theory Analysis," *Journal of Consumer Research,* 1 (June), 13–20.

ROSS, LEE (1977), "The Intuitive Psychologist and His Shortcomings: Distortions in the Attribution Process," in *Advances in Experimental Social Psychology,* Vol. 10, Ed. Leonard Berkowitz. New York: Academic Press.

———, and CRAIG A. ANDERSON (1982), "Shortcomings in the Attribution Process: On the Origins and Maintenance of Erroneous Social Assessments," in *Judgment Under Uncertainty: Heuristics and Biases,* Eds. Daniel Kahneman, Paul Slovic, and Amos Tversky. Cambridge: Cambridge University Press.

———, MARK R. LEPPER, and M. HUBBARD (1975), "Perseverance in Self Perception and Social Perception: Biased Attributional Processes in the Debriefing Paradigm," *Journal of Personality and Social Psychology,* 32 (November), 880–892.

ROSS, MICHAEL, and GARTH J. O. FLETCHER (1985), "Attribution and Social Perception," in *Handbook of Social Psychology,* Vol. II, Eds. Gardner Lindzey and Elliot Aronson. New York: Random House, 73–122.

SCHACHTER, STANLEY (1964), "The Interaction of Cognitive and Physiological Determinants of Emotional State," in *Advances in Experimental Social Psychology,* Vol. 1, Ed. Leonard Berkowitz. New York: Academic Press, 49–80.

SCHMITT, RICHARD B. (1987), "Rising Crime Against Cash-Machine Users Has More Banks Facing Victims in Court," *The Wall Street Journal,* May 5, Section 2, 39.

SCOTT, CAROL (1976), "The Effects of Trial Incentives on Repeat Purchase Behavior," *Journal of Marketing Research,* 13 (August), 263–269.

——— (1977), "Modifying Socially Conscious Behavior: The Foot-in-the-Door Technique," *Journal of Consumer Research,* 4 (December), 156–164.

——— (1981), "Forming Beliefs about Experience," in *Perspectives in Consumer Behavior,* Eds. Harold H. Kassarjian and Thomas S. Robertson. Glenview, IL: Scott, Foresman.

———, and RICHARD F. YALCH (1980), "Consumer Response to Initial Product Trial: A Bayesian Analysis," *Journal of Consumer Research,* 7 (June), 32–41.

SELIGMAN, MARTIN E. P., and PETER SCHULMAN (1986), "Explanatory Style as a Predictor of Productivity and Quitting Among Life Insurance Sales Agents," *Journal of Personality and Social Psychology,* 50 (April), 832–838.

SETTLE, ROBERT B. (1972), "Attribution Theory and Acceptance of Information," *Journal of Marketing Research,* 9 (February), 85–88.

———, and LINDA GOLDEN (1974), "Attribution Theory and Advertiser Credibility," *Journal of Marketing Research,* 11 (May), 181–185.

SHERMAN, STEVEN J., CLARK C. PRESSON, LAURIE CHASSIN, ERIC CORTY, and RICHARD OLSHAVSKY (1983), "The False Consensus Effect in Estimates of Smoking Prevalence: Underlying Mechanisms," *Personality and Social Psychology Bulletin,* 9 (June), 197–207.

SMITH, CRAIG A., and PHOEBE C. ELLSWORTH (1987), "Patterns of Appraisal and Emotion Related to Taking an Exam," *Journal of Personality and Social Psychology,* 52 (March), 475–488.

SNYDER, C. R., RAYMOND L. HIGGINS, and RITA J. STUCKY (1983), *Excuses: Masquerades in Search of Grace.* New York: Wiley.

SPARKMAN, RICHARD M., JR. (1982), "The Discounting Principle in the Perception of Advertising," in *Advances in Consumer Research,* Vol. 9, Ed. Andrew Mitchell. Ann Arbor, MI: Association for Consumer Research, 277–280.

———, and WILLIAM B. LOCANDER (1980), "Attribution Theory and Advertising Effectiveness," *Journal of Consumer Research,* 7 (December), 219–224.

SUJAN, HARISH (1986), "Smarter Versus Harder: An Exploratory Attributional Analysis of Salespeople's Motivation," *Journal of Marketing Research,* 23 (February), 41–49.

SWINYARD, WILLIAM (1981), "The Interaction Between Comparative Advertising and Copy Claim Variation," *Journal of Marketing Research,* 18 (May), 175–186.

TEAS, R. KENNETH, and JAMES C. MCELROY (1986), "Causal Attributions and Expectancy Estimates: A Framework for Understanding the Dynamics of Sales Force Motivation," *Journal of Marketing,* 50 (January), 75–86.

TETLOCK, PHILLIP E., and ARIEL LEVI (1982), "Attribution Bias: On the Inconclusiveness of the

Cognition-Motivation Debate," *Journal of Experimental Social Psychology,* 18 (January), 68–88.

TYBOUT, ALICE M., and CAROL A. SCOTT (1983), "Availability of Well-Defined Internal Knowledge and the Attitude Formation Process: Information Aggregation Versus Self-Perception," *Journal of Personality and Social Psychology,* 44 (March), 474–491.

______, BRIAN STERNTHAL, and BOBBY J. CALDER (1983), "Information Availability as a Determinant of Multiple Request Effectiveness," *Journal of Marketing Research,* 20 (August), 280–290.

______, and RICHARD F. YALCH (1980), "The Effect of Experience: A Matter of Salience?" *Journal of Consumer Research,* 6 (March), 406–413.

VALLE, VALERIE A., and RANDI KOESKE (1977), "Elderly Consumer Problems: Actions, Sources of Information and Attributions of Blame," in *Proceedings of Division 23,* 85th Annual Convention of Psychology Association, Ed. Clark Leavitt, 7–8.

______, and MELANIE WALLENDORF (1977), "Consumer Attributions of the Cause of Their Product Satisfaction and Dissatisfaction," in *Consumer Satisfaction, Dissatisfaction, and Complaining Behavior,* Ed. Ralph L. Day, Bloomington, IN: Indiana University, 26–30.

VAN DER PLIGT, JOOP (1984), "Attributions, False Consensus and Valence: Two Field Studies," *Journal of Personality and Social Psychology,* 46 (January), 57–68.

______ (1985), "Energy Conservation: Two Easy Ways Out," *Journal of Applied Social Psychology,* 15 (1), 3–15.

WEGNER, DANIEL M., and ROBIN R. VALLACHER (1986), "Action Identification," in *Handbook of Motivation and Cognition,* Eds. Richard M. Sorrentino and E. Tory Higgins. New York: Guilford Press.

WEINER, BERNARD (1985a), "An Attributional Theory of Achievement Motivation and Emotion," *Psychological Review,* 92 (October), 548–573.

______ (1985b), "Spontaneous Causal Thinking," *Psychological Bulletin,* 97 (January), 74–84.

______ (1986), *An Attributional Theory of Motivation and Emotion.* New York: Springer-Verlag.

______, JAMES AMIRKHAN, VALERIE S. FOLKES, and JULIE A. VERETTE (1987), "An Attributional Analysis of Excuse Giving: Studies of a Naive Theory of Emotion," *Journal of Personality and Social Psychology,* 52 (February), 316–324.

______, IRENE FRIEZE, ANDY KUKLA, LINDA REED, STANLEY REST, and ROBERT M. ROSENBAUM (1972), "Perceiving the Causes of Success and Failure," in *Attribution: Perceiving the Causes of Behavior,* Eds. Edward E. Jones et al. Morristown, NJ: General Learning Press, 95–119.

WEISZ, JOHN R., FRED M. ROTHBAUM, and THOMAS C. BLACKBURN (1984), "Standing Out and Standing In: The Psychology of Control in America and Japan," *American Psychologist,* 39 (September), 955–969.

WEITZ, BARTON, HARISH SUJAN, and MITA SUJAN (1986), "Knowledge, Motivation and Adaptive Behavior: A Framework for Improving Selling Effectiveness," *Journal of Marketing,* 50 (October), 174–191.

WIENER, JOSHUA L., and JOHN C. MOWEN (1986), "Source Credibility: On the Independent Effects of Trust and Expertise," in *Advances in Consumer Research,* Vol. 13, Ed. Richard J. Lutz. Provo, UT: Association for Consumer Research, 306–310.

WILSON, TIMOTHY D., and DANA S. DUNN (1986), "Effects of Introspection on Attitude-Behavior Consistency: Analyzing Reasons Versus Focusing on Feelings," *Journal of Experimental Social Psychology,* 22 (May), 249–263.

YALCH, RICHARD F., and SUZANNE YOSHIDA (1983), "Consumer Use of Information and Confidence in Making Judgments About a New Food Store: An Attribution Theory Experiment," in *Advances in Consumer Research,* Vol. 10, Eds. Richard P. Bagozzi and Alice M. Tybout. Ann Arbor, MI: Association for Consumer Research, 40–44.

ZALTMAN, GERALD, and MELANIE WALLENDORF (1983), *Consumer Behavior: Basic Findings and Management Implications.* New York: Wiley.

21

ECONOMIC PSYCHOLOGY*

W. Fred van Raaij

Economic psychology studies the economic behavior of consumers and entrepreneurs. Economic behavior involves decisions on money, time, and efforts. The models of Katona and Strümpel are discussed and a new model is proposed. This new model stresses the cyclical character of economic behavior on a micro and a macro level. Economic psychology is related to organizational psychology, marketing research, mass communication research, economic sociology, and the household production approach.

INTRODUCTION

Economic psychology is concerned with the study of economic behavior.

Economic behavior is the behavior of consumers/citizens that involves economic decisions, and the determinants and consequences of economic decisions.

Economic decisions involve money, time, and effort to obtain products, services, work, leisure, the choice between product alternatives, spending *vs.* saving decisions. In fact, all decisions that involve a choice or trade-off of some alternatives or an investment that will bring future profits or benefits may be called an economic decision. Economic decisions are characterized by sacrifices to be made by the actor, an evaluation of present or future benefits of one's expenditure (spending *vs.* saving), an evalua-

*Reprinted from the *Journal of Economic Psychology,* 1 (1981), pp. 1–24.

tion of the expected benefits of some alternatives, and a relatively concrete variable of behavior. A customary criterion for an economic decision is the monetary, temporal, or effort sacrifice, for expected present or future well-being of oneself and/or one's household.

The determinants of economic decisions include personal, cultural, situational, and general-economic factors that stimulate or inhibit economic decisions.

Personal factors are personality characteristics of the consumer (e.g., venturesomeness, cognitive style, internal control of reinforcement), life-style characteristics of the household (e.g., traditional *vs.* modern), and the norms and values of a society or a subculture that stimulate or inhibit certain behaviors.

Cultural and religious *values* forbid certain types of consumption, for instance alcohol consumption with Moslems or birth control devices with Roman Catholics. Norms and values may differ for subcultures, regions, and age groups.

Situational factors are the conditions and circumstances that normally constrain economic decisions within certain boundaries. Disposable income, family size, type of home, market situation determine consumption decisions; the style and color of one's furniture determine new additions to the home interior. Anticipated or unanticipated situations may change one's consumption intentions.

General-economic factors include the perceived fairness of the income distribution, the rates of inflation and interest, the degree of unemployment, the economic policy of the government. These general-economic factors generate optimistic or pessimistic attitudes and expectations with consumers, which influence the desire to spend or to save household income.

The consequences of economic decisions are the satisfactions and the well-being consumers derive from consumption. Dissatisfaction may lead to complaints with the responsible producer or institution. For many purposes, the consequences of economic decisions are employed as criterion measures of economic or consumption policy. We may distinguish the evaluative and behavioral consequences of satisfaction and well-being, and complaints and problems consumers have with products and services. The consequences of economic decisions provide some kind of learning experience for people that may influence further economic decisions.

This article will discuss the relationships between economics and psychology, a number of relevant areas within economic psychology, and areas related to economic psychology. Three models of economic behavior will be discussed. Research on economic behavior can very well be placed in the framework of the third model.

SOCIETAL PROBLEMS

At the beginning of this article we want to stress the relevance of economic psychology for the solution of societal problems. At the present time of rising unemployment in many countries, rising energy prices and energy shortages, air, water, and soil pollution, food problems and poverty in the third world, the behavior of consumers and citizens is of vital importance. Due to the economic circumstances we have to change our consumption habits and aspirations. We want people to save energy and other resources. The welfare state has become too expensive to maintain the extensive present welfare benefits. And we want to develop the third world economies.

The human factor in all these programs of economic and social change cannot be ignored. All programs involve behavioral change. Economic policy measures may change behavior but not always in the desired directions. Information extension as such may change no behavior at all. Research on how people react to altered economic conditions and to policy measures may improve the impact of economic policy. Comparative studies of the relative impacts and efficiencies to change behavior by various methods (information, prompting, feedback, reward or punishment) have already been conducted to promote energy saving among consumers.

Thus, economic measures do not always have the intended effects of the policy maker. Second, policy makers often do not know the relative efficiencies of policy measures to generate behavioral change. Third, satisfaction and well-being of citizens is of great concern, even a criterion measure for economic policy. Fourth, consumer reactions to changed economic conditions, e.g. inflation, have impacts on the continuation or discontinuation of these conditions. The proposed (third) model in this article will serve as a framework for studying the effects of economic policy and marketing policy, the perception and evaluation of economic well-being and satisfaction.

ECONOMICS AND PSYCHOLOGY

Katona (1963) and Simon (1963) discussed the relationship between economics and psychology. Katona (1963) argues that psychological variables contribute to a better understanding of the behavior of economic agents. In pure economic research, only the effects of economic behavior are studied, e.g. supply-demand relationships, without considering the intervening psychological processes of evaluation, decision, and choice. Economic "laws" assume one-to-one relationships between economic variables without systematic behavioral "disturbances." When economists deal with behavior they either assume that individual tastes and preferences "cancel out" against each other, or they assume a rational behavior of utility maximization, complete knowledge, and control over means. Recent approaches in behavioral economics make more realistic assumptions about economic behavior. Not utility maximization but utility optimalization (Simon 1963) and bounded rationality have become the basic concepts.

Katona (1963) further argues that not the objective economic conditions but the economic conditions as perceived by the consumer/citizen/household determine economic behavior. The perceptions and evaluations of the economic reality and the optimistic or pessimistic expectations regarding personal finances and economic developments in a country determine spending or saving of a household. Psychological variables complement the economic variables for a better description or prediction of economic behavior. For instance, the Index of Consumer Sentiment (Katona 1975), a comsite score based on five survey questions about the perception and evaluation of personal finances, inflation, and general economic conditions, adds to a better prediction of consumer expenditure on automobiles and other durable goods than economic variables, such as absolute or relative income, or the price increases of durable goods, alone will do.

Simon (1963) provides a more comprehensive approach. Economics is the science that describes and predicts the behavior of "economic man." Economic people (men and women) are consumers, producers, entrepreneurs, retailers, workers, and investors. All these people make economic decisions about expenditure, expected benefits or profits, expected turnover, income, and career, and expected return on investment. Within the boundaries of their knowledge, aspirations, capacities, and abilities they try to make optimal decisions. In micro-economics, the behavior of an individual consumer or household, or a firm is studied. In normative micro-economics, advice and recommendation is provided to consumers, households, businessmen, and firms. Related to normative micro-economics are management science and operations research. Descriptive micro-economics constitutes the foundation for macro-economics. Two economic principles, rational behavior of "economic man" and perfect competition in markets, in fact eliminate, once accepted and verified, the necessity of studying individual or business behavior. Thus, these principles eliminate the necessity of studying behavior within economics. This might explain why there has been so little interaction between economists and psychologists. Traditional economics is not concerned with the behavior of people but with the "behavior" of commodities (Boulding 1956), stressing that the economist is not really interested in human behavior. Interrelations between objective economic variables are expressed in "laws" of the "behavior" of prices, interest rates, unemployment, perceived as impersonal phenomena of the economic environment (Katona 1975). Behavioral economics or economic psychology, instead, studies the behavior of people who set the prices and whose actions bring about the higher or lower interest rates, inflation rates, or unemployment.

Economic psychology comprises the motivation, perception, evaluation, and cognitive processes of consumers, entrepreneurs, citizens in their economic decisions. Psychology is not the study of the soul (psyche) but the study of human and animal behavior, and the determinants and consequences of behavior. Although many general principles of behavior are established in psychology, it is not true that all behavior can be predicted from these general principles. In economic psychology, human behavior is studied within the conditions and constraints of the perceived economic environment. Economic behavior is the function of human motives, perceptions, attitudes, expectations, and bounded by the economic conditions.

This paradigm fits very well in the Lewinian function $B = f(P,E)$, that behavior B is a function of personality variables P and environmental (economic) variables E. See Hall and Lindzey (1978; ch. 11).

Economic psychology is both part of psychology and part of economics, It is part of *psychology* in the sense that it employs psychological principles of behavior and psychological methods of measurement in survey, interview, and laboratory research. Economic psychology is not applied psychology, although it applies psychological theories and techniques. Economic psychology is developed by studying economic behavior. Through the interaction of empirical findings and theoretical developments new insights are obtained. New theories of human behavior may be developed within the area of economic psychology, e.g. the study of expectations and aspirations. The same is true in the areas of child psychology, psychiatric behavior, and social behavior. Related areas of psychology that are of importance for the development of economic psychology, are cognitive psychology, social psychology, and experimental psychology. Even the study of animal behavior is relevant for economic psychology (Lea 1978).

Economic psychology is also part of *economics* in the sense that new (behavioral) variables contribute to a better explanation and prediction of economic phenomena. Additional psychological variables may increase the explained variance in a multiple regression equation. Economic psychology, then, plays a servant's role in an economic model. A better integration of psychological variables in economic science will be reached, when both economic and psychological variables are entered into a model, into hypotheses, and theories. Behavioral economics becomes economics as a social science. The sequence of hypothesis-observation-measurement-test is then applied to economic behavior. Behavioral economics is largely inductive, starting from guided observations and leading to empirically determined relationships between concepts, while traditional economics tends to be largely deductive, starting from assumptions about (bounded) rationality and complete knowledge, and leading to testable deductions from the basic assumptions.

KATONA'S MODEL

Katona (1951, 1960, 1964, 1975) may be considered the founding father of psychological economics in the U.S.A. In his writings he states that psychological variables intervene between the economic stimuli and the behavioral responses. See Fig. 21.1. E are the economic conditions and situations, such as a recession, the degree of unemployment, the rates of inflation and interest, contractual obligations of the household, discretionary income, standard of living, tax rates, public transportation modes and frequencies. E stands for the objective economic conditions and opportunities for the individual of the small group (household, management team). P are the personal charac-

FIGURE 21.1 Katona's Model.

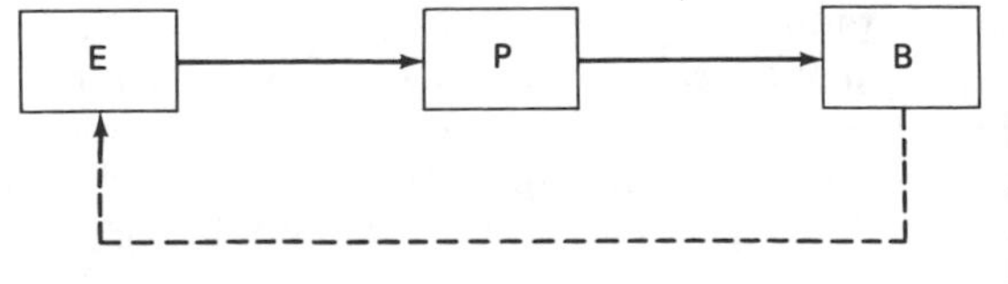

teristics, such as aspirations, expectations, internal *vs.* external control of reinforcement, life style. The economic conditions *E* and the personal characteristics *P* influence *B,* the economic behavior of the individual consumer or entrepreneur. *B* includes the purchase, use, and disposition of goods and services, investment and savings decisions. On the aggregate level, the behavior of consumers and entrepreneurs influences the fluctuations in and the success of an economic system. Hence, the feedback loop from *B* to *E.* For instance, consumers contribute to economic fluctuations through their spending and saving behavior. A tax increase or a tax cut may have "perverse" consequences of consumers spending more or less, depending upon people's understanding of the situation and expectations elicited by the changed fiscal policy. The virtue of Katona's model is its basic simplicity. The economic stimuli *E,* in fact, do not influence the personal characteristics, but *E* and *P* do influence economic behavior *B.* Katona's contribution is that psychological variables obtained a place in the thinking of some economists. Katona's Index of Consumer Sentiment (Katona 1975: 92–97) contributes to the prediction of durable good expenditures in predictive time series regressions. Turning points of the index predict economic fluctuations with a time lag of 4 through 6 months.

STRÜMPEL'S MODEL

Strümpel (1972) developed a more elaborate model, as shown in Fig. 21.2. In his model, the determinants of *SW,* subjective well-being, are the economic environment *E* and the personal characteristics *P,* similar to Katona's model. Subjective well-being *SW* comprises satisfaction with consumption, work, income, marriage, standard of living, sense of opportunities. According to this model, two divergent outcomes, societal discontent *SD* and economic behavior *B* are the consequences. Societal discontent includes dissatisfaction with employment, prices, government policy, and the political system. Economic behavior includes spending, saving,

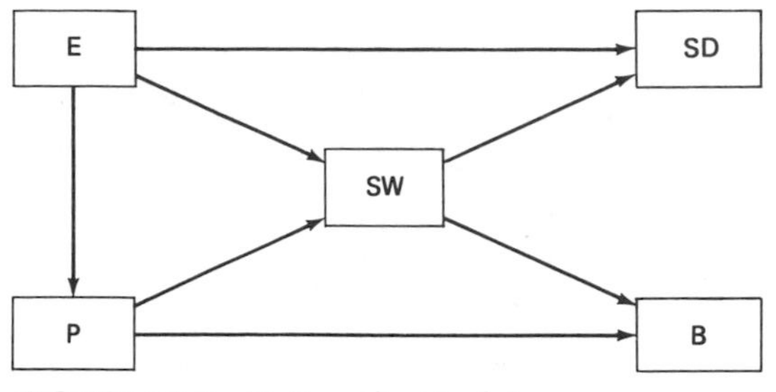

FIGURE 21.2 Strümpel's Model.

consumer demand, occupational choice, work-leisure trade-offs, investment in education. *E, P,* and *SW* not only determine economic behavior *B* but also create satisfaction and dissatisfaction, and attitudes toward societal issues and problems.

Although Strümpel's model is richer than Katona's, some critical problems remain. Societal discontent *SD* is not only dependent upon subjective well-being *SW* but also upon economic behavior *B.* Consumers develop satisfactions, dissatisfactions, and even complaints as a consequence of their consumption activities. Another problem is that no or only a very artificial relationship can be thought of between *E* and *SD.* Which economic conditions cause societal discontent without *P* and/or *SW* as intervening variables? A third criticism is the absence of a feedback loop from *SD* and *B* to *E* and *P.* Societal discontent and economic behavior, on the aggregate level, tend to have a strong influence on people's aspirations and expectations and on their perception of the economic reality. Thus, *SD* and *B* influence the performance of the economic system. Strümpel (1974) provides an interesting application of his model in empirical research.

A NEW MODEL

A basic model for economic psychology should include economic and psychological variables; should contain feedback loops from economic behavior to economic conditions and personal aspirations; and should be as simple as possible, grouping variables with a similar function in one category. Fig. 21.3 gives the basic new

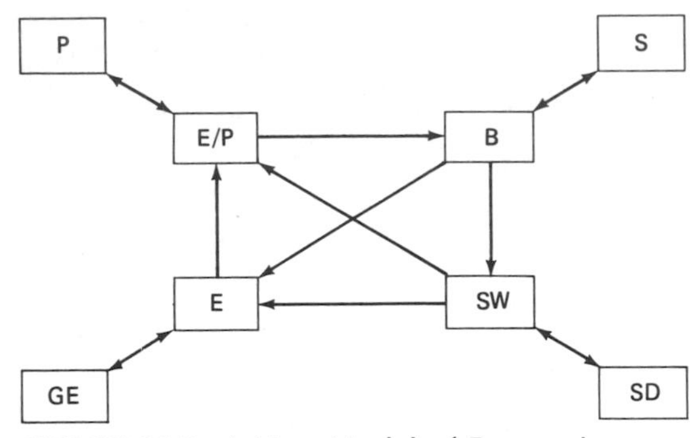

FIGURE 21.3 A New Model of Economic-Psychological Relationships.

model, comparable with the model in Van Raaij (1979).

The economic environment *E* of personal finances, market conditions, type of employment, source of income, is influenced by the general environment *GE* of recession or upswing, economic policy of the government, ecological conditions of pollution, war and peace, structural violence. *E/P* is the economic environment as perceived by consumers and entrepreneurs. *E/P* includes business climate, market conditions, expected price developments, perceived opportunity structure, perception of fair income distribution, perceived position of reference groups. Not so much *E* but *E/P* tends to influence economic behavior *B*. The relationship between *E* and *E/P* is a relationship of personal experience, social and mass communication. The objective economic environment is only partly experienced by consumers and entrepreneurs themselves. Consumers experience retail price increases as a sign of inflation. Businesspeople find interest rates acceptable or not for investment credit. Social communication among consumers or among entrepreneurs may influence one's perception of the economic environment. Persons influence each other in determining what are acceptable rates of inflation, interest, unemployment, pollution, and what are acceptable energy prices. From mass communication, as a third factor, people learn facts and evaluations of the economic environment. Newspapers, magazines, radio, and television may even "create" the issues, according to the agenda-setting theory of McCombs and Shaw (1972). Most people only get information about economic events through the mass media. The mass media tend to ignore some and to give disproportionate attention to other economic events thereby "creating" the economic and political issues.

E/P is influenced by the personal factors *P:* goals, values, aspirations, expectations, internal *vs.* external control of reinforcement, cognitive style, information processing abilities, interest in political and economic affairs. Sociodemographic correlates such as family composition, education, age, occupation may have impact on *E/P*.

The perceived economic environment *E/P* influences economic behavior *B*. The relationship between *E/P* and *B* resembles the "effect hierarchies" (Palda 1966). Effect hierarchies postulate a sequence perception-evaluation-behavior, or belief-attitude-attention, or attention-interest-desire-action (AIDA). Engel *et al.* (1978) give the sequence exposure-attention-comprehension-retention-behavior in their model of consumer behavior. Howard and Sheth (1969) use the sequence attention-comprehension-attitude-intention-purchase. In all of these hierarchies, perceived information from the environment is evaluated (attitude); comprehended and evaluated information leads to behavior intentions to purchase or to save. In low involvement situations, the sequence may seem to be the reverse. Attitude change comes after the behavior. However, some knowledge and evaluation of the environment is always present before the behavior, while also after the behavior further attitude change and acquisition of knowledge (experience) may take place.

Behavioral intentions lead to behavior, if no anticipated or unanticipated situations *S* arise and prevent the realization of the behavioral intentions. These situations may be emergencies, accidents, illness, a bank refusing credit, sudden unemployment, marriage, birth of a child. The longer the time lag between behavioral intention and actual behavior, the higher the probability of situational interventions. Economic behavior is also influenced by anticipated situations: a party, a weekend trip, being with your partner. Consumers tend to differentiate their product selection according to anticipated usage situations (Belk 1975).

Subjective well-being *SW* is the consequence of economic behavior *B*. Subjective well-being includes the satisfactions and dissatisfactions with the purchase, consumer complaints to the retailer or the producer, and consumer problems with the product or service. After-purchase processes such as learning and reduction of cognitive dissonance contribute to the degree of subjective well-being. External effects of consumption (pollution, noise, other persons' envy) may decrease the subjective well-being of non-consumers. Recreational activities may increase the subjective well-being of the participants, while at the same time they decrease the subjective well-being of the neighboring non-participants.

Subjective well-being *SW* may be defined as the discrepancy between expected and actual performance of a product or a service, or the discrepancy between the expected and actual benefits of an economic decision. The subjective well-being will be lower, if prior expectations were too high or actual performance proved to be too low. Advertising may create too high and irrealistic expectations about product performance, and this may cause dissatisfaction with consumers. Subjective well-being *SW* is related to societal discontent *SD*. Consumer satisfaction, along with work and marriage satisfaction, good health, will influence one's general happiness or satisfaction with societal structures and the economic system (capitalism, socialism, communism). Societal discontent, on the other hand, may influence subjective well-being. Persons with a basic discontent or mistrust will probably derive less satisfaction from consumption and other economic decisions.

Subjective well-being *SW* has impacts on the economic environment *E*. This closes the cycle of Fig. 21.3. Marketeers study consumer satisfactions and complaints in order to provide better and more competitive products and services. Government policy makers study the well-being of the citizens in order to provide better public programs. Subjective well-being also has impacts on the perceived economic conditions *E/P*. After experiencing the performance of a product or the quality of a service, consumers may change their perceptions. Learning effects are the changes in the belief structure of *E/P* and the revisions of opinion and attitude.

Note that economic behavior *B* may have a direct influence on the economic environment *E*. Spending or saving behavior of consumers or entrepreneurs directly influences economic fluctuations. Consumer preferences and purchases of certain brands directly influence the market share of these brands. However, *B* and *SW* together influence repeat purchase of a brand or repeat visits of a store, thus brand or store loyalty.

The main advantage of the new model is its dynamic and cyclical character. The four groups of variables, *E*, *E/P*, *B*, and *SW*, are independent variables in one research design and dependent variables in another research design. Most studies in economic psychology involve at least two groups of variables, one group of variables explaining one or more variables of the "following" group. A number of possible research designs emerge:

(1)	$E \rightarrow E/P$	studies how people perceive economic realities; mass communication and agenda-setting studies; the money illusion.
(2)	$E/P \rightarrow B$	studies about perceptions, attitudes, as related to behavior; hierarchy of effect studies.
(3)	$B \rightarrow SW$	studies on consumer satisfaction and complaints, well-being and welfare.
(4)	$B \rightarrow E$	economic research on demand and supply of goods and services.
(5)	$SW \rightarrow E$	studies on the design and development of products, services, and programs based on consumer/participant's satisfactions and experiences; program evaluation studies.
(6)	$SW \rightarrow E/P$	studies how confirmed and disconfirmed expectations change consumer perceptions of the market and products.

(7) $GE \rightarrow E$ economic studies of the correspondence of general economic conditions and personal finances and opportunities of the household.

(8) $P \rightarrow E/P$ studies on the effects of personality, cognitive style, and life style on the perception and categorization of economic reality.

(9) $S \rightarrow B$ studies on situational influences on economic behavior.

(10) $SD \rightarrow SW$ studies on the correspondence of consumption, economic satisfaction with life, work, and marriage satisfaction.

ORGANIZATIONAL ECONOMIC BEHAVIOR

Compared with consumer economic behavior, organizational economic behavior is a relatively unknown area of economic psychology, although there is a vast amount of research and knowledge. Simon (1963) was one of the first to include "producer behavior" in economic psychology. Managers, entrepreneurs, and business executives control the decision variables in the firm. They decide on make-buy-or-lease, investments, and set goals for short-term and long-term profits. Both economic (financial) and non-economic (power, prestige) motivations direct their behavior. The traditional assumption of profit maximization is now replaced by a satisficing criterion. The firm will take a viable course of action to satisfy the various stakeholder groups: workers, consumers, suppliers, competitors, neighbors, government. Contributions from psychology provide essential clarification of business decision making and entrepreneurial motivation.

Sheth (1977) provides an overview of organizational buyer behavior. He mentions the following reasons why organizational buyer behavior is less well-known than consumer buyer behavior. (1) Most research in organizational buyer behavior has been practice-oriented, and (2) has been scattered across several disciplines such as management science, organizational psychology, political science, and business areas such as production, finance, marketing, personnel management. (3) It is easier for researchers to experience the role of a consumer than a manager's role within an organization. (4) More new approaches and techniques are applied in the study of consumer behavior because consumer behavior is considered to be more complex and irrational than entrepreneur behavior. The latter is not true, especially not for the independent owner-manager of a small firm.

The model of Fig. 21.3 is also applicable to organizational economic behavior. The economic environment *E* is the environment of the firm or the environment of the department, division, or profit center within the firm, including the type and size of the organization. Organizational climate and style, the role of purchasing within the firm, lateral and vertical involvement, perceptions of one's own role and position within the organization belong to the group of *E/P* variables. The *P* correlates pertain to the factors already mentioned and choice criteria, learning, loyalty, and risk perception. The situational correlates *S* are failures of delivery, strikes, legal-political considerations, and governmental protection measures. Organizational economic behavior *B* includes the decisions to make, buy, or lease products or components, the choice of facilities, suppliers, distribution channels, the commercialization of new product types, and entering a new market.

Aspects of subjective well-being *SW* in an organizational context are sometimes called the non-economic motivations of the manager or entrepreneur: power, prestige, and status. Business executives tend to identify themselves very much with their organization, and, consequently, derive subjective well-being from the successes of their company.

RELATED DISCIPLINES

1. Relationship to Organizational Psychology

Organizational psychology is in fact part of economic psychology, as far as workers and managers in an organization make economic decisions about career, work load, promotions, overtime work. However, the separate research tradition of organizational psychology is much older than economic psychology. Research interests and publication outlets of organizational psychology center around worker motivation and satisfaction, the impact of the organizational structure, equity of pay distributions. The model of Fig. 21.3 also applies to organizational psychology, where *E* represents the formal organization, *P* represents employee motivations, personality, goals, and aspirations, *B* represents employee behavior, while *S* represents situational constraints and opportunities. *SW* stands for job satisfaction and employee well-being.

While economic psychology is generally not concerned with research on employee motivation and satisfaction, interesting relationships and parallels exist between organizational and economic psychology. Economic psychology is concerned with the expenditure or saving of income and only partly with the earning of income. Economic psychology is concerned with economic behavior outside the organizational and labor conditions. However, when persons have discretion over the number of hours they work and, hence, their income, and when consumption aspirations and obligations determine one's income, instead of income determining one's consumption, interesting perspectives for economic psychologists emerge. Similarly, when pay increases are seen in relation to inflation rates and other economic conditions, the study of income and inflation becomes part of economic psychology.

In the next years, a growing interaction between consumption and work may be expected. First, the number of working hours depends on the income aspirations of the household. The number of jobs for working wives and part-time jobs seems to increase. More households will have a variable number of wage-earners and a variable number of working hours. In a developed social security system, one may choose to be employed or to remain unemployed with a lower benefit income. Second, the younger generation entertains less materialistic values and is less focussed on material products, and, hence, may be satisfied with a lower-paid but more rewarding job. Third, a number of consumption items may become part of the fringe benefits of a job, such as a free lunch and a free car, creating (tax-free) income in natura.

Jacoby (1976) discusses the theoretical relationships between organizational and economic psychology. Interesting parallel models of worker and consumer motivation and satisfaction lead to the conclusion that cooperation and interaction of organizational and economic psychologists (and economists) will lead to fruitful synergies of theory corroboration and mutual contribution. Organizational and economic psychology are both interested in influencing behavior and the factors that determine behavioral change. Word-of-mouth processes and informal communication occur among consumers and among employees. Opinion leadership and informal leadership are phenomena within the consumption and work context. Innovations are diffused among consumers, while similar processes take place in organizations under the heading of "planned change." Cooperation of organizational and economic psychologists will certainly bring new perspectives for both disciplines.

2. Relationship with Marketing Research

Marketing research studies consumer reactions to marketing mix variables from the producer's viewpoint. The producer's goal is an increase in market share and the fulfillment of consumer needs and wants at a profit. Marketing research is mainly directed toward the specific (brand or type) choice, while economic psychologists are more interested in spending *vs.* saving, immediate or delayed consumption, and the effects of economic environment on economic decisions. Van Raaij (1978) presents some differences between marketing research and economic psychology:

1. Marketing research derives its meaning and objectives from marketing. Economic psychology is an autonomous science, directed toward the antecedents and consequences of economic behavior, and the processes and mechanisms underlying economic decisions.

2. Marketing research has a limited interest in consumer behavior, only as far as the relevant product or service is concerned, and often only the purchase stage of it. Economic psychologists have a broader scope: the total consumption cycle of prepurchase-purchase-use-disposition, and the satisfactions and self-actualization people derive from consuming goods and services.
3. Marketing information and knowledge about the consumer is used to influence that behavior by advertising and promotion. Economic psychology studies consumer behavior as a part of economic behavior from the objective of scientific knowledge and consumer policy (governmental agencies, consumer organizations).
4. Economic psychologists are more interested in the total expenditure in a market than in specific choice of brands and types. Typically for economic psychology is the development of consumer indexes to describe and to predict economic fluctuations in the sales of consumer durable goods.

Marketing research and economic psychology have a number of common interests and research techniques, and may very well contribute to each other's development. The wider scope of economic psychology may provide better insights into the dynamics of consumer demand. Marketing research with a broader scope on consumer behavior (see Arndt 1976) is compatible with the interests of economic psychologists.

3. Research on the Adoption of Innovations

The study of the adoption of innovations is related to economic psychology. The model of Rogers and Shoemaker (1971) can be transformed into the model of Fig. 21.3. The economic environment *E* includes the norms and values of the community regarding change, innovation, and modernization; the tolerance of deviancy; and the communication network among people and between people and mass communication sources. *E/P* is not only the perception of *E* by the prospective innovator or non-innovator but also the perceived characteristics of the innovation (relative advantage, compatibility, complexity, trialability, observability, availability). Both the *E/P* factors and person factors *P* determine the adoption of an innovation. The person factors *P* are the personality characteristics (venturesomeness, dogmatism, cosmopolitanism), the position in the social network of communication, the perceived need for and the perceived risk of the innovation. The adoption or non-adoption of the innovation is the criterion variable in adoption of innovation research (*B*). Situational influences *S* may inhibit the adoption of an innovation, such as lack of money or unavailability of the innovation. Subjective well-being *SW* of the innovator depends on the relative advantage of the innovation over existing products or procedures, the approval by relevant others of the innovation, and the confirmed expectation with regard to the innovation. The approval of relevant others provides a legitimation of the adoption. Even mass communication sources may provide legitimation of one's adoption. Users of a product tend to read more advertising of that product than of other products. *SW* factors determine the continued adoption of an innovation.

What are the roles of mass communication in the innovation-adoption process? Mass communication performs three functions in the process: (1) to increase awareness of the innovation, (2) to inform people of the advantages/disadvantages of the innovation, and (3) legitimize the adoption or nonadoption decision. The first and second function operate in the *E/P* block; the third function in the *SW* block of variables. Persuasion, in the Rogers and Shoemaker model, refers to the formation of favorable attitudes toward the innovation. In the model of Fig. 21.3 this occurs between *E/P* and *B,* although advertising may create biased perceptions of the innovation in *E/P*.

Adoption of an innovation by an individual consumer or household is only part of the diffusion of an innovation in a social structure. Diffusion theory stresses the social network and the influence of (outside) mass communication sources. Essential are the connections in the social network, through which the diffusion process trickles over time.

4. Sociological Concepts

Many research studies and theories incorporate sociological concepts, e.g. the adoption of innovation studies incorporate the concept of a social network with cliques and liaisons. It is not very effective to create sharp boundaries between economic sociology and economic psychology. Nicosia and Mayer (1976) have written one of the few contributions of sociology to the study of consumer behavior. They note an overemphasis on individual choice processes, and, consequently, less emphasis on the structural and societal context in which consumers operate. Cultural values are of crucial importance. The traditional values of freedom of choice and success through individual achievement tend to inhibit solidarity between persons, groups, and countries. These values also tend to oppose programs to inform consumers about impending depletion of resources and energy. Do younger generations adhere to less materialistic values? And can we rechannel young people's aspirations and expectations into a non-materialistic direction, instead of frustrating legitimate aspirations of a new generation? (Katona 1975: ch. 25.)

Culture, sub-culture, and social class are also sociological concepts in economic behavior. While the importance of social class for consumption behavior may decrease, subcultures increase in importance. A growing awareness of ethnic background ("roots"), regional, racial, and sexual differences ("liberation") create a rising number of minorities with their own life-style, consumption habits, work and leisure preferences. The most likely future of the advanced industrial societies will be one of *fragmentation.* In the recent OECD report "Facing the Future" (1979), a double fragmentation of values has been marked. "The first fragmentation is represented by the continuation of past tendencies and the cleavages of the post-war period, the search for equality by some and the defense of relative positions by others, generating constant conflicts over the distribution of national income. The second fragmentation would be caused by an evolution of values which produces the emergence of numerous minorities each with its own set of different and to some extent volatile demands" (OECD 1979: 109–110).

This double fragmentation has consequences for the allocation of time (life style is characterized by time budgets), job applications (search for meaningful work), smaller production units (decentralization, "human scale"), and protection of the environment.

The changes in values and life style may create even a third system of production, next to the market (commercial) and planning (collective) system (Galbraith 1973): the household production system. The household of community production system is a non-market form of self-organization to produce vegetables, groceries, children's toys, books, energy, and to trade secondhand furniture, clothing, and household utensils.

5. The Household Production Function

Becker advocates a reformulation of the economic theory of consumer behavior, based on the household production function (Becker 1965; Michael and Becker 1973). In this approach, the household, consisting of one individual to many members, is a production unit, combining purchased market goods and services with inputs from household members in the form of added value or transformations. A familiar example is the preparation of a dinner, combining purchased meat, vegetables, potatoes, and spices with preparation efforts, time, and energy. Homegrown potatoes and vegetables may be used instead, even increasing the contribution of household production. The household, in this perspective, becomes a small production unit employing capital (household income), raw or prepared materials (food, clothing, detergents), production means (house, household appliances), labor (time and effort of household members and servants) in order to create commodities and benefits for the household members. Or, to say it in another way, to create subjective well-being *SW* for the household members and their guests. A bed, bedroom, time, absence from noise, and (sometimes) sleeping-pills produce the benefits of a sound sleep. A concert ticket, travel time and money, and an evening dress produce the benefits of a fine musical experience.

Household production are the unpaid activities carried on by and for household members but which could be replaced by market goods and services. The home-cooked dinner can be replaced by the restaurant dinner. Garden work can be replaced by hiring a gardener. A household may clean its home or may hire a servant to do the cleaning work. Interesting hypotheses emerge on the trade-offs between time and money. High-income households with high opportunity costs of time are more likely to hire servants. Low-income households with low opportunity costs of time may stretch their income by performing many household tasks themselves, e.g. home improvement and car repair. High-income households will economize on time but may be lavish on consumption goods, especially when these consumption goods save time (dishwasher, TV dinner, second car). Transportation studies show that high-income people economize on time and prefer air travel over car or train travel. However, high-income families spend more time on commuting (with high opportunity costs) because they prefer to live in more spacious suburbs and not in densely populated city centers.

The growing proportion of unemployed and the stagnation of income growth will probably lead to more household production in order to have meaningful daily pursuits and to stretch one's income. The outputs of household production can even be sold or traded for other household products. The automobile mechanic maintains his neighbor's car, while the neighbor who is a painter, paints the mechanic's home. As indicated, the household production system may create a third system of production.

Traditionally, women tend to do most of the unpaid household production of feeding children, cooking dinners, cleaning the home, and washing the clothes. Modern values and the feminist movement are increasingly opposed to this sexist division of labor. While men will get a larger share, the household production will increase in importance.

Similar to the firm in standard production theory, the household invests in capital assets (savings), capital equipment (durable goods), and human capital (skills and education of the household members). The household decides on family labor supply, time, expenditures on raw materials and services, on family size, marriage, and labor force attachment. Time is a scarce resource in the households. Time-saving equipment is bought to reduce the time spent on household chores (at least for high-income households). On the other hand, the satisfaction of many goods and services depends on the amount of time with which they are consumed, e.g. sports, a fancy dinner, making love).

SUMMARY AND CONCLUSIONS

Economic psychology is concerned with the study of economic behavior, its antecedents and consequences. Economic behavior comprises consumer behavior, employment behavior, fiscal behavior, and the reactions of consumers/citizens to economic conditions. Economic psychology has a micro and a macro aspect. The micro aspects pertain to individual economic behavior including consumer behavior; the macro aspects include aggregate indexes of consumer sentiment, attitudes, and expectations.

A new model is proposed to describe economic behavior. The (perceived) economic environment determines the individual's economic behavior with subjective well-being as its consequence. The results of economic behavior and subjective well-being feed back to the objective and perceived economic environment (Fig. 21.3).

The new model can very well be applied to organizational economic behavior, marketing research with a broader scope, the adoption of innovations, and the theory of the household production function.

Economic psychology or behavioral economics emphasizes the human factor in economic research. Economics, then, becomes a social science richer in its explanation of economic phenomena than the study of the "behavior of commodities." Hopefully, economic psychology contributes to elucidate much of the unpredictability of the human "disturbances" in economic predictions.

REFERENCES

ARNDT, J., 1976. 'Reflections on research in consumer behavior,' In: B. B. Anderson (ed.), Advances in consumer research, Vol. 3. Atlanta: Association for Consumer Research.

BECKER, G. S., 1965. A theory of the allocation of time. Economic Journal 75, 493-517.

BELK, R. W., 1975. Situation variables and consumer behavior. Journal of Consumer Research 2, 157-164.

BOULDING, K. E., 1956. The image. Ann Arbor, MI: University of Michigan Press.

ENGEL, J. F., R. D. BLACKWELL and D. T. KOLLAT, 1978. Consumer behavior. (3rd ed.) Hinsdale, IL: The Dryden Press.

GALBRAITH, J. K., 1973. Economics and the public purpose. Boston, MA: Houghton Mifflin.

HALL, C. S. and G. LINDZEY, 1978. Theories of personality. (3rd ed.) New York: Wiley.

HOWARD, J. and J. N. SHETH, 1969. The theory of buyer behavior. New York: Wiley.

JACOBY, J., 1976. 'Consumer and industrial psychology: prospects for theory corroboration and mutual contribution.' In: M. D. Dunnette (ed.), Handbook of industrial and organizational psychology, Chicago, IL: Rand McNally.

KATONA, G., 1951. Psychological analysis of economic behavior. New York: McGraw-Hill.

KATONA, G., 1960. The powerful consumer. New York: McGraw-Hill.

KATONA, G., 1963. 'The relationship between psychology and economics.' In: S. Koch (ed.), Psychology: a study of a science. New York: McGraw-Hill.

KATONA, G., 1964. The mass consumption society. New York: McGraw-Hill.

KATONA, G., 1975. Psychological economics. New York: Elsevier.

LEA, S. E. G., 1978. The psychology and economics of demand. Psychological Bulletin 85, 441-466.

MCCOMBS, M. E., and D. L. SHAW, 1972. The agenda-setting function of mass media. Public Opinion Quarterly 36, 176-187.

MICHAEL, R. T. and G. S. BECKER, 1973. On the new theory of consumer behavior. Swedish Journal of Economics 75, 378-396.

NICOSIA, F. M. and R. N. MAYER, 1976. Toward a sociology of consumption. Journal of Consumer Research 3, 65-75.

OECD, 1979. Facing the future. Paris: Organization for Economic Co-operation and Development.

PALDA, K. S., 1966. The hypothesis of a hierarchy of effects: a partial evaluation. Journal of Marketing Research 3, 13-24.

ROGERS, E. M. and F. F. SHOEMAKER, 1971. Communication of innovations. A cross-cultural approach. New York: The Free Press.

SHETH, J. N., 1977. 'Recent developments in organizational buying behavior.' In: A. G. Woodside, J. N. Sheth and P. D. Bennett (eds.), Consumer and industrial buying behavior. New York: North-Holland.

SIMON, H. A., 1963. 'Economics and psychology.' In: S. Koch (ed.). Psychology: a study of a science. New York: McGraw-Hill.

STRÜMPEL, B., 1972. 'Economic behavior and economic welfare. Models and interdisciplinary approaches.' In: B. Strumpel, J. N. Morgan and E. Zahn (eds.), Human behavior in economic affairs. Amsterdam: Elsevier.

STRÜMPEL, B., 1974. 'Economic well-being as an object of social measurement.' In: B. Strümpel (ed.), Subjective elements of well-being. Paris: OECD.

VAN RAAIJ, W. F., 1978. 'Economic psychology and marketing.' In: G. Fisk, J. Arndt and K. Gronhaug (eds.), Future directions for marketing. Cambridge, MA: Marketing Science Institute.

VAN RAAIJ, W. F., 1979. 'European consumer research: frontier issues.' In: W. L. Wilkie (ed.), Advances in consumer research, Vol. 6. Atlanta, GA: Association for Consumer Research.

22

THE ROLE OF FAMILY COMMUNICATION IN CONSUMER SOCIALIZATION OF CHILDREN AND ADOLESCENTS*

George P. Moschis

While studies of communication effects on consumer behavior of the young have focused mainly on the effects of mass media (advertising in particular), little research has examined the effects of interpersonal communication. One finds relatively little theoretical and empirical work regarding the role of interpersonal communication in the development of consumer behavior of young people. This article deals with one important type of interpersonal communication—family communication. It conceptualizes the family communication processes and effects, reviews literature regarding the role of family communication in consumer learning of children and adolescents, develops a set of propositions on the basis of theory research, and suggests directions for future research.

Research on consumer learning has focused primarily on the effects of mass media advertising on select groups of people. For example socialization research has examined the effects of television commercials on children's consumer learning (Adler 1977). Similarly, research has investigated the effects of television commercials on the learning of consumer orientations during the later stages in the life cycle (e.g., Smith and Moschis forthcoming). Furthermore, models of communication deal al-

*Reprinted from the *Journal of Consumer Research,* 11, (March 1985), pp. 898–913.

most exclusively with the impact of persuasive mass communication on consumer behavior, and much effort has been devoted to understanding the factors that contribute to communication effectiveness (e.g., factors related to source, message, channel, and audience). Considerably less effort has been devoted to understanding the role of informal communications in consumer learning, including processes leading to effective consumer socialization and criteria for measuring interpersonal communication effects. For example, the effects of informal communications are often examined in the context of diffusion of innovations rather than in terms of processes leading to effective consumer socialization.

Although informal interpersonal communication processes occur in several types of social settings (e.g., with peers, siblings, parents), it is the family context of interpersonal communication that is believed to have the greatest influence in consumer socialization. In spite of the commonly held belief regarding the significant role of family in consumer socialization, research on the skills, values, attitudes, and behaviors that young people acquire from their parents and the role family communication processes play in the development of such orientation is lacking.

This article presents a research update on family communication processes and their effects on consumer learning of children and adolescents. Specifically, family communication is conceptualized and its role in consumer learning is examined. Next, research on the effects of parent–child interaction on consumer learning is presented and, based on theoretical and research perspectives, a set of propositions is developed. Finally, the article summarizes existing knowledge in the area and suggests directions for future research.

CONCEPTUAL FRAMEWORK

While there is a tendency to look within the individual for explanations of human behavior, individual-level concepts seem out of place in the study of interpersonal communications. Definitions of interpersonal communication all agree that at least two people must be involved and that an object of communication must be present. As a result, much of the recent human communication research has adopted an interpersonal (rather than intrapersonal) perspective, seeking explanations for one's communication behavior on the level of one's social relations and using co-orientational variables in line with Newcomb's (1953) A–B–X paradigm.

The Newcomb co-orientation model assumes that two persons, A and B, who are attracted to one another positively or negatively, are co-oriented to an object of communication, X. This model is only one among many consistency or balance theories that have generated a vast amount of attitude change research during the past 30 years. However, Newcomb's co-orientation model has been particularly useful in the study of interpersonal communications because it is applicable to groups and to the actual interpersonal relations among people and their cognitions and perception. In addition, the model provides a useful framework for conceptualizing the differences in orientation between two general approaches to social communication research.

Social communication theorists can be divided roughly between those who are concerned with the interactants' cognitive orientations to events and issues in the world outside their immediate context (A–X and B–X relationships) and those who stress elements of interpersonal relationships (A–B relationships). The first group of theorists is typically interested in several aspects of public opinion (e.g., Chaffee and McLeod 1968; McLeod and Chaffee 1972), but the approach is also amenable to the study of such institutionalized relationships as parent–child and husband–wife (O'Keefe 1973; Pasdirtz 1969). The second group of theorists is typically interested in person perception research, psychiatrist–patient interaction, marital discord, and the communication of relationship information (cf. Chaffee and Tims 1976).

Family Communication Patterns

Following Newcomb's model, McLeod and Chaffee (1972) developed a typology of parent-child communication structures and patterns. While parent-child relations are usually described as an undimensional portrayal of the power situation within the family—such as "autocratic-democratic," "controlling-permissive," and "traditional-modern"—studies of parent-child communication processes have consistently found two relatively uncorrelated dimensions of communication structure (McLeod and Chaffee 1972). The first (which is analogous to the types of social power), called *socio-oriented,* is the type of communication that is designed to produce deference and to foster harmonious and pleasant social relationships at home. In terms of Newcomb's paradigm, this type of communication stresses A–B relationships. The child in homes characterized by such a communication structure may be taught to avoid controversy and repress his/her feelings on extrapersonal topics, for example, by not arguing with adults and giving in on arguments rather than risking offending others.

The second type of communication structure, called *concept-oriented,* is a pattern that focuses on positive constraints that help the child to develop his/her own views about the world, stressing A–X relationships. The parents may, for example, encourage the child to weigh all alternatives before making a decision, or they may expose him/her to controversy, either by differing openly on an issue or by discussing it with guests at home (McLeod and Chaffee 1972). The two general dimensions of parent-to-child communication produce a four-fold typology of family communication patterns expressed in co-orientational terms using Newcomb's (1953) A–B–X paradigm (see Figure 22.1)—namely, laissez-faire, protective, pluralistic, and consensual (McLeod and Chaffee 1972.

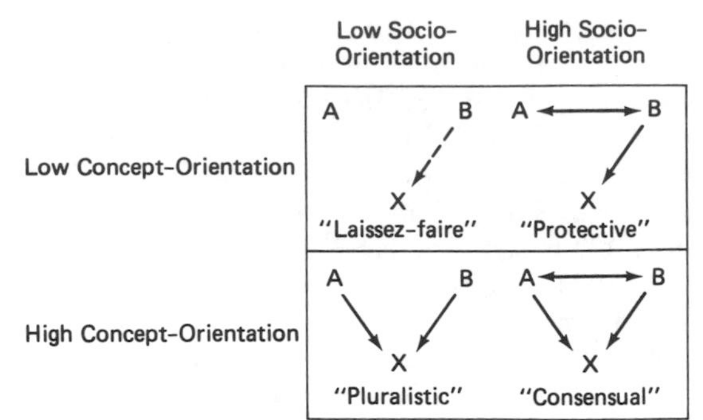

FIGURE 22.1 Family Communication Pattern Typology Interpreted by Relations from Newcomb's ABX Paradigm (*Source:* McLeod and O'Keefe (1972).)

Laissez-faire families lack emphasis on both kinds of communication; there is little parent-child communication in these families. *Protective* families stress obedience and social harmony in their communication with their child; there is little concern over conceptual matters. *Pluralistic* families encourage open communication and discussion of ideas without insisting on obedience to authority; the child is encouraged to explore new ideas and express them without fear of retaliation. The emphasis in this communication structure appears to be on mutual respect and interests. *Consensual* families stress both types of communication; the child is encouraged to take an interest in the world of ideas, yet to do so without disturbing the family's hierarchy of opinion and internal harmony.

Extensive research evidence has led researchers to assume that family communication patterns help guide the individual in coping with various situations she/he encounters outside the immediate family context—for instance, situations in relation to public affairs issues and mass media use (e.g., Chaffee, McLeod, and Atkin 1971; Chaffee, McLeod, and Wackman 1966; McLeod and Chaffee 1972). In addition, the evidence suggests that "the influence of family communication, as generalized to other situations, persists well into adulthood; it appears to become part of the developing individual's personality that he carries outside the home" (Chaffee et al. 1971, p. 331).

Units of Analysis

Although the family communication patterns (FCP) typology was initially conceptualized in a parent–child dyadic context, it was later extended to other interpersonal settings at home, including husband–wife dyads (e.g., O'Keefe 1973), and to settings outside the home, such as informal communication with peers (Chaffee and Tims 1976).

With respect to parent–child communication in a dyadic setting, communication and influence relations can be of four dyadic types: mother–daughter, mother–son, father–daughter, and father–son. The majority of studies of family communication processes and effects have examined parent–child interactions in a broad context, without addressing specific parent–child dyadic relations. Although some studies have addressed more specific units of analysis, these were not addressed in the context of family communication processes. For example, Saunders, Salmi, and Tozier (1973) investigated the degree of agreement or disagreement between mother and daughter in selecting the daughter's school clothing. They found a higher percentage of consensus of mother–daughter opinion for expressive items (e.g., coats) than for nonexpressive items, and less conflict when the money used for purchases was provided by the parent than when the money was earned by the daughter. Another study of high school students found greater parental influence on the clothing behavior of boys than on the clothing behavior of girls (Hamilton and Warden 1966).

DEFINITION AND MEASUREMENT

Because previous research in the area has dealt neither with specific dyadic (A–B) relationships nor with specific objects (Xs) of communication, the term "family communication" is broadly defined. It is used here to refer both to parent–child overt and cognitive (nonverbal) communication processes and to patterns of interaction, without specific reference to content. The content of communication reported in various studies varies from very broad issues/topics to very specific situations (e.g., Chaffee et al. 1971; Moore and Moschis 1981). Research on family communication usually focuses on two different but often confounded dimensions. The first pertains to interpersonal communication processes, and the second to its effects.

Communication Processes

Family members may communicate certain information to other members through various mechanisms. First, by performing certain acts, a family member may consciously or unconsciously communicate certain norms and expectations to others. The communication in this case is likely to take place at a cognitive level, and consumer learning is likely to be the result of observation or imitation of these behaviors. For example, a child may make a conscious effort to emulate the behavior of his/her parents because the parents' behavior is the most salient alternative open to him/her—i.e., she/he does the same thing his/her parents do in an effort to be like them. Common operational definitions of such modeling processes include source-learner similarity of behaviors and attitudes (McLeod and O'Keefe 1972). It should be noted, however, that while a high level of similarity may be a necessary condition for such cognitive communication effects, it is hardly a sufficient one, since the learner may develop similar orientations through other processes, such as overt communication. Furthermore, the learner's interpretation of the source's behavior or intent may differ, as could the source's actual or usual behavior outside the family context. Awareness of the source's behavior is also necessary for such communication to take place.

Second, a member in the family may influence the consumer behavior of others by using various reinforcement mechanisms, both positive and negative. For example, in attempting to communicate certain desires to others, a person may reward certain behaviors which are consistent with such desires and punish others that are inconsistent. Reinforcement may involve overt communication, such as praise for (positive) and complaining about (negative) using a product; it may also involve cognitive communication, where a person may dictate his/her desires to others by, say, showing affection (positive reinforcement) or psychologically punishing them (negative reinforcement). In fact, affection and psychological punishment are very common examples of operational definitions of positive and negative reinforcement, respectively (McLeod and O'Keefe 1972).

Finally, family members may affect the consumer behavior of other members through overt communication processes, often referred to as the "social interaction" mechanism. The social interaction mechanism is less specific, and it may involve a combination of modeling and reinforcement (McLeod and O'Keefe 1972). During the course of the person's interaction with other family members, she/he may acquire certain attitudes, values, and behaviors, which are often communicated explicitly.

Social interaction processes can have content and structure. Content includes expectations (norms) held by the communicator about what the desirable or prescribed behaviors should be; it can also be information about consumption. Structure usually refers to family relations concerning power and communication relations. For example, with respect to parent–child relations, one finds power structures such as "controlling–permissive" and "traditional–modern." In a consumer behavior context, such power relations are applied only to adult family member relations (e.g., "husband dominant," "wife dominant"); they are not relevant to parent–child relations, perhaps due to the relatively low power the child exerts upon his/her parents. For example, Davis' (1976) "consensual" and "accommodative" concepts apply to problem solving in household decisions, and they may include bargaining, coercion, and compromise; hence communication is viewed as a facilitator in decision making. Parent–child communication relations, in contrast, include "socio-oriented" and "concept-oriented" family communication structures (Chaffee et al. 1971) and parental encouragement (Haller and Portes 1973). In the field of consumer behavior, for example, consumer learning has been associated with family communication patterns and structures (e.g., Moore and Moschis 1981; Moschis and Moore 1979b). These communication processes accounted for significant differences in consumer socialization which are beyond differences already accounted for by other types of family communication processes—i.e., overt communication, modeling, positive reinforcement, and negative reinforcement (Moschis, Moore, and Smith 1983).

Measurement of family communication processes often focuses on overt family-member interaction, with emphasis on the frequency, content, and structure of communication. Most of the studies of consumer socialization, for example, have used frequency measures of overt parent–child interaction about consumption (e.g., Moschis 1981). Considerably less attention has been devoted to the measure of the content of family communication, which is usually inferred from correlational data. Thus, if one finds a relationship between parent–child interaction about consumption and the child's ability to price products accurately, the assumption is made that such communication focuses on prices. However, the child's ability to price products accurately may not necessarily develop as a result of family communications but may be due to a third variable (e.g., development of product desires), which can result both in greater awareness of product attributes and in child-initiated communication with family members. Finally, the structure of interaction has been investigated in relatively few studies, such as those examining the effects of family communication patterns (e.g., Moore and Moschis 1981; Moschis and Moore 1978, 1979b).

Communication Effects

Measures of family communication effects (content of learning) present a rather different picture than do studies of processes, in that both absolute and relative measures can be used. Absolute measures of family communication effects on consumer learning often consist of cognitive, affective, and behavioral outcomes measured in relation to some norm or expected direction in much the same way that one measures advertising effects. For example, learning about products (awareness) and developing skills at budgeting (behaviors) are used as unidirectional measures of the effects of parent–child communications about consumption. When such measures are used, the assumption is often made that the family member's intention is to communicate socially desirable or expected norms and behaviors.

Yet measures of relative effects are assessed in terms of the communicator's intent, attitudes, and cognitions, by pitting the source's orientations against the audience's orientations toward the object of communication. Thus, the emphasis shifts from the individual's orientation toward the object of communication (absolute measures) to co-orientation (relational measures), and from sampling individuals as units of analysis to sampling dyads (e.g., McLeod and Chaffee 1973). In the context of Newcomb's A–B–X paradigm, the single best criterion for assessing communication effectiveness is considered to be the degree of similarity between (1) one person's (A) estimate of the other person's (B) cognitions about the object of communication (X), and (2) the other person's (B) actual cognitions (McLeod and Chaffee 1973).

Foci of Measurement

At times, interpersonal communication effects on consumer learning assessed using co-orientational variables are difficult to evaluate in terms of exactly the same elements of X (object of communication). Although it is very rare that both A and B would perceive exactly the same elements of X, some degree of similarity in their orientation toward the object of communication is necessary to apply the model sensibly at the co-orientational level. At times, the availability of symbols of X (often referred to as "codability") may hamper communication—as would "connotation," a term that describes variance between A and B in their respective usages of words to denote Xs (McLeod and Chaffee 1973). Finally, communication effects on consumer learning may be not only in terms of "overlaps," in line with the co-orientational model, but also in terms of changes in or development of cognitive and behavioral patterns. For example, much of consumer socialization literature suggests that parent–child communications about consumption are related to the child's development of several cognitive and behavioral orientations about consumption (Moschis 1981). There may also be other messages or cues that can often be unintentionally communicated from one person to the other during the course of interaction. Thus, it is often the effect—rather than the perceived intent—of the communication that should be measured.

Because of the several ways family members can influence one another, several types of indices of communication effectiveness are often recommended in assessing interpersonal communication and influence. Tannenbaum and McLeod (1967) suggested several indices, in concept judgments using the D statistic. In the area of consumer socialization, Rossiter and Robertson (1979) used confirmatory factor analysis to assess the similarity of factor structures between mothers and their children.

To summarize, family communication appears to involve several dyadic dimensions, including processes, structures, patterns, frequency, and content of communication. In the context of the present conceptualization of family communication processes and effects, the following section presents the results of studies useful in developing a number of propositions.

FAMILY COMMUNICATION IN CONSUMER LEARNING

Communication with family members, both overt and cognitive, plays an important role in shaping consumer learning. The effects of these communications can be direct or indirect, and they can mediate the effects of other nonfamily sources of consumer information. Direct influences of family communications on a person's consumer behavior involve the acquisition of consumption-related information and subsequent formation of patterns of beliefs, norms, and behaviors from other members. Indirect influences involve the learning of patterns of interaction with other sources of consumer information, which may in turn affect consumer learning. Finally, family communications may affect consumer learning by mediating the effects of other sources of consumer learning outside the family, such as mass media and peers.

Direct Influences

For discussion purposes, the direct effects of family are grouped into three categories: (1) the content of learning—i.e., what young people learn from their parents without reference to specific communication processes, cognitive or overt; (2) the effects of various types of family communication processes—i.e., how types of family influences consumer learning; and (3) the effects of specific structures and patterns of overt family communication processes.

Content of Learning. Riesman and Roseborough (1955) as well as others (Parsons, Bales, and Shils 1953) speculated that the family is instrumental in teaching young people basic rational aspects of consumption, including basic consumer needs. Support for this speculation is provided by several studies. Ward and Wackman (1973) found that parents' general consumer goals for their children include learning price-quality relationships. In addition, Ward, Wackman, and Wartella (1977) found that such goals included experiences with use of money and learning to shop for quality products. Similarly, parent-adolescent communication about consumption predicted fairly well the child's knowledge of prices of selected products (Moore and Stephens 1975) and "rational" consumer behaviors, such as managing money and comparative shopping (Moschis 1976). In another study, the frequency of parent-child communication about consumption was positively associated with the adolescent's tendency to use price reduction ("sales") as a criterion for choosing among brands (Moschis and Moore 1980).

In an earlier study of expenditure patterns and money management practices among approximately 52,000 teenaged girls, Hurt (1961) found that 47 percent of the seventh graders reported parental assistance in deciding how to spend their money. This proportion declined with age, with only 27 percent of the twelfth graders reporting parents' help. Similar findings were reported by Remmers and Radler (1957) in a study of teenagers (ninth through twelfth graders) over a 15-year period.

Parental influence on offspring consumer learning appears to extend beyond the basic elements of consumer decision making. Data reported in one study (Moore and Moschis 1978b) suggest that parents may encourage their children to work to save money for anticipatory consumption, especially for large ticket items. Another study found parental influence on both economic and social motivations for consumption (Churchill and Moschis 1979).

A study by Moschis and Moore (forthcoming) reveals a significant relationship between family communication about consumption matters and the adolescent's career decision, suggesting that intrafamily interactions may provide opportunities for occupational socialization, a finding consistent with data reported by Levine (1976) and Kahl (1953). In addition, such interaction was associated with the adolescent's development of role perceptions regarding effective consumer behavior. These findings suggest that parents may be instrumental in teaching general as well as specific rational orientations regarding consumption, and that they may emphasize normative consumer skills while interacting with their children.

Finally, parental influence may be an important factor in the development of several other dimensions of consumer behavior. For example, the study by Moschis and Moore (forthcoming) finds that overt parent-child interactions are associated with the development of desires for major types of products that teenagers do not normally buy (e.g., a house). Similarly, two other studies suggested that the family may affect the development of materialistic orientations (Moore and Moschis 1981; Moschis and Moore 1979b). Furthermore, a longitudinal study investigating the effects of the family on adolescent consumer learning, both in the short run and in the long run, found that parent–child interaction about consumption has some long-run influence on the development of brand preferences as well as on the adolescent's ability to distinguish facts from exaggerations in advertising messages (Moschis 1984).

Parental influence on adolescent brand preferences is also reported by Fauman (1966), Arndt (1971), and Yankelovich, Skelly, and White (*Advertising Age* 1980), although the latter speculated about mother–daughter similarity in brand preference development. Unfortunately, it is not clear from these studies how family communications affect brand preference development, nor whether such influence is the result of purposive parental training or whether it is simply due to the availability of brands at home (i.e., convenience). For example, a study of brand preferences among 1,346 college students indicated considerable influence of parents on bank patronage, with 93 percent of the freshmen patronizing the same bank their parents did. Yet such "loyalty" may be due not to the child's preferences but to the father's preference for convenience (Fry et al. 1973).

To summarize, there appears to be reasonably good supportive evidence that the family is instrumental in teaching young people basic rational aspects of consumption. It influences the development of rational consumption orientations related to a hierarchy of consumer decisions delineated by previous writers (e.g., Arndt 1975; Olshavsky and Granbois 1979); spending/savings, expenditure allocation, and product decisions, including some evaluative criteria. Considerably less is known about how parents influence children's development of decision patterns regarding variant decisions—such as brand and store preferences—as well as motives and information processing skills. This leads to our first proposition:

P1: Parents are likely to influence the development of their offspring's selective preferences in the marketplace and processes leading to such preferences. They are likely to influence the development of:

a. Preferences for brands
b. Preferences for stores
c. Motivations for consumption
d. Skills relating to evaluation of information in advertising

The effects of family communication on the development of decision-making patterns appear to vary across stages of the decision-making process and type of product. For example, a cross-sectional study of the development of adolescents' decision-making patterns suggested that parental influence may vary by stage of the decision-making process, with greater likelihood of influence at the information-seeking stage than at the product-evaluation stage (Moschis and Moore 1979a). In a longitudinal analysis, family communication effects were found to be stronger on the development of information-seeking patterns than product-evaluation criteria (Moschis and Moore 1983):

P2: Parental influence on the consumer learning of their offspring is present, although not similar, across main stages of the decision-making process. It is likely to affect the:

a. Need-recognition stage
b. Information-seeking stage
c. Product-evaluation stage
d. Purchasing stage
e. Post-purchase stage

Findings of a study of 608 adolescents also suggested that the effects of the family on adolescent consumer behavior may vary by type of product (Moschis, Moore, and Stephens 1977). The data indicated that purchasing role structures vary significantly across selected items that are likely to be consumed by adolescents. Specifically, the data suggested that adolescent shopping goods (clothing) tend to be purchased jointly by the adolescent consumer and family members, whereas adolescent specialty goods (records or tapes, sporting equipment, and movie tickets) tend to be purchased in the absence of family members. Within the shopping goods category, the extent of adolescent–family-member involvement in purchasing appears to be related to the social visibility and price of the product. These findings suggest that the degree of adolescent–family-member involvement in purchasing may be a function of the socioeconomic risk in a purchasing situation.

In another study of the development of decision-making patterns, it was found that the extent to which adolescents take parental preferences/suggestions into account in choosing among brands may be a function of perceived risk associated with the specific decision, with higher parental influence more likely to be present in purchases of high-risk products (Moschis and Moore 1979a). Other studies have also shown that family influence in the adolescent decision-making process is a function of product type. For example, research on child and adolescent decision making by Hamilton and Warden (1966), Mehrotra and Torges (1976), Saunders et al. (1973), Vener (1957), and Ward and Wackman (1972) suggested variation in parental influence by type of product:

P3: Parental influence on consumer learning of their offspring varies by product characteristic:

a. It is greater for decisions concerning shopping goods than convenience or specialty goods.

b. It is greater for decisions concerning products of high perceived risk.

Finally, family influence on the development of the youth's consumer decision-making patterns appears to be based upon certain parent–child characteristics such as age, social class, and sex. Generally, youths attain greater family independence in decision making with age (e.g., Moschis and Moore 1979b; Moschis et al. 1977; Vener 1957), although the degree of independence varies by product type. However, the extent to which young people attain family independence in decision making may be conditioned by specific characteristics such as social class and sex. For example, middle-class adolescents appear to attain less independence in purchasing as they grow older than do adolescent consumers in lower and upper social classes. This finding has been attributed to middle-class families' greater consciousness of the normative standards of their class, and their subsequent greater desire to closely supervise their children's activities in an effort to socialize them into the class norms (Moschis et al. 1977; Psathas 1957).

Similar findings may apply to other stages in the decision making process (need recognition, information seeking, product evaluation, and post-purchase stage). Furthermore, parental influence on the development of the consumer behavior of their offspring appears to be affected by the sex of the child. For example, the higher need for conformity to peer group norms found among female adolescents (e.g., Cannon, Staples, and Carlson 1952; Saunders et al. 1973; Vener 1957) was reflected in their purchasing patterns through greater family independence (and thus less influence) in purchasing products relevant to physical appearance, such as health care products and clothing (shirts and jeans; Moschis et al. 1977):

P4: Parental influence on the learning of consumer decision patterns of their offspring is affected by the child's socio-demographic characteristics:

a. Parental influence on consumer decision patterns declines with age to a significantly greater extent among the lower and upper classes than among middle-class youths.

b. Parental influence on consumer decision patterns is greater among middle-class than among lower- and upper-class youths.

c. For products of high social risk, parental influence on the decision-making patterns of their offspring is stronger for boys than for girls.

Communication Processes. While the family is believed to be an important source of consumer information, the ways in which it influences the child's consumer learning are not clearly known. After reviewing related literature, Engel, Blackwell, and Kollat concluded that "the family plays an important role in interpersonal communication in the socialization of children," but that the specific ways it may influence consumer learning are not clear (1978, p. 280). Similarly, Ward summarized much of the consumer socialization literature and concluded that (1974b, pp. 31–32):

> The studies show that there is a great deal of parental activity, both purposive and non-purposive, which is related to children's experience with money, attitudes toward consumption, purchase influence attempts and the success of those attempts, and so forth. These studies were far from explicit, however, concerning how family members influence children in ways which affect their present, if limited, behavior as consumers or the patterns of consumer behavior they will adopt in the future.

Ward et al. (1977) identified five methods mothers use to teach children consumer skills: (1) prohibiting certain acts; (2) giving lectures on consumer activities; (3) holding discussions with the child about consumer decisions; (4) acting as an example; and (5) allowing the child to learn from his/her own experiences. Their research showed that most mothers use relatively few teaching methods, and that there is considerable variation among them in how they teach their children consumer skills.

Most consumer socialization research examining family influences has focused upon overt interaction in particular (e.g., Moschis et al. 1983; Ward and Wackman 1971). These studies have investigated how such interactions affect consumption-related properties. Overt interaction processes could be classified as social interaction mechanisms that lack a specific structure or pattern, according to McLeod and O'Keefe (1972), although a few studies (e.g., Moore and Moschis 1981; Moschis and Moore 1978) have examined family communication structures and patterns in line with McLeod and Chaffee's (1972) typology. Consumer learning has been found to be related not only to frequency but also to the patterns or quality of communication that takes place within the home (Moore and Moschis 1981; Moschis and Moore 1978, 1979b; Moschis et al. 1983). This is in line with family communication patterns (FCP) research in political socialization, in which patterns were found to have a more significant influence than frequency or amount of parent–child interaction (McLeod and Chaffee 1972).

Although the family plays an important role in consumer socialization of the young, parental influence is often incidental—and hence far from purposive consumer training. In fact, the study by Ward et al. (1977) suggests that parents often expect their children to learn through observation. Parent-child discussions about consumption are most likely to be initiated as a result of the child's request for a product that she/he sees advertised.

In the study by Moschis et al. (1983), the effects of several communication processes were examined simultaneously. The results suggest that different processes may be used in the transmission of consumer cognitions and behaviors from parent to child. In general, parents make limited attempts to teach their children consumer skills. Such limited efforts seem to focus upon the desirability of performing certain acts (behaviors), but they provide little education or understanding (cognitions). Cognitions (especially consumer behavior norms) appear to be acquired from parents through observation, suggesting that parents may try to act as role models to their children and then expect them to learn such roles through observation.

In an earlier study, Marshall and Magruder (1960) found that children are more knowledgeable about the use of money when they are given wide experience and opportunity in saving and spending and when their parents handle the family income wisely. Knowledge of the use of money was not increased either by giving an allowance or by the opportunity to earn money at home. Fairly similar findings were reported by Phelan and Schvaneveldt (1969). These findings suggest that money management skills may develop as a result of both purposive consumer training and observation of parental consumer behaviors.

Studies examining reinforcement mechanisms are almost nonexistent. A recent study of adolescent consumer socialization suggests that positive reinforcement may encourage the development of effective consumer behaviors, whereas negative reinforcement may constrain the development of consumer knowledge (Moschis et al. 1983).

These findings suggest that two types of communication processes may be of primary importance in transmitting cognitive and behavioral orientations from parent to child. Overt communication processes may be important in teaching behavioral dimensions, while modeling influences may be important in transmitting cognitive and affective norms:

P5: Different communication processes, both overt and cognitive, operate in the transmission of consumer behaviors from parent to child:

a. Purposive consumer training by parents of their offspring focuses upon performing socially desirable consumer behaviors.
b. Observation of parental behavior by the offspring is likely to lead to the development of socially desirable consumer values and norms.
c. Positive reinforcement will encourage the development of socially desirable consumer behaviors.

Theory and research suggest that socialization processes vary by socio-demographic characteristics, including age, sex, social class, and race. Specifically, the adolescent's frequency of interaction with his/her family regarding consumption matters has been shown to decline with age (e.g., Moschis and Churchill 1978; Moschis et al. 1983), but this does not necessarily imply that the family's influence over the youth's consumer behavior declines. The study reported by Moore and Moschis (1983) found that although overt communication about consumption declines with age, the adolescent's tendency to observe parental behaviors is not related to age. This observational measure was a strong predictor of some aspects of his/her consumer behavior, especially consumer role perceptions. Reinforcement mechanisms (e.g., giving the child an allowance) are likely to be frequent during early childhood (Ward et al. 1977). With increasing age, the child may find other sources of income, thus reducing his/her economic dependence on his/her parents. This, in turn, may diminish the importance of the reinforcement mechanism and, consequently, parent–child interaction about consumption.

Another study examined the effects of sex and other characteristics on various family communication processes, including overt parent–child communication about consumption, modeling process, reinforcement (positive and negative), and family communication patterns (Moschis et al. 1983). Males were found to be less likely than females to communicate overtly with their parents about consumption, and less likely to receive positive reinforcement; they were more likely to receive negative reinforcement. These findings suggest that parents may treat their offspring differently (on the basis of their sex) while interacting with them about consumption matters. The results of another study seem to support this line of reasoning. Specifically, the study investigated relationships between several adolescent–parent interactions and selected dependent variables by sex. Frequency of adolescents' communication with their parents was correlated with their ability to retain information in advertisements and their level of knowledge about consumer matters only among females, suggesting that purposive consumer training may focus upon teaching the female child more than the male child (Moschis and Moore 1979c).

Furthermore, previous theory and research suggest that communication processes vary by the social class and race of the child. For example, socialization theory suggests that socialization practices tend to vary among families of different socioeconomic (SES) characteristics (Hess 1970). This also appears to be the case in the specific area of consumer socialization. Previous research has suggested that purposive parental training of youths is more likely to occur among upper SES families than among families from lower SES backgrounds (Ward and Wackman 1973). Similarly, another study of adolescents examined relationships between measures of adolescent–parent interactions and several dependent variables among lower-, middle-, and upper-class adolescents (Moschis and Moore 1979c). The data showed that parent–child communication about consumption is associated with the youth's consumer role perceptions only among children from upper social classes, suggesting that purposive consumer training may occur only in the upper social strata. In lower social classes, family communication appears to focus upon product brand names. Discussions about consumer matters with parents among middle-class adolescents appears to focus upon product attributes (e.g., prices).

In the Moschis et al. (1983) study, the effects of adolescents' observation of parental behaviors were also assessed by socioeconomic and racial factors. Observation of parental behaviors were associated with increasing brand preferences among lower-class and black adolescents, but with decreasing preferences for brands and increasing consumer knowledge among middle-class adolescents. These findings suggest that such learning may be due to the middle-class family's inclination to "shop around"—i.e., consider a larger number of alternatives (e.g., Engel et al. 1978)—a behavior which can be imitated by the youngster and expressed in terms of weak brand "loyalties." In contrast, lower-class and black youths may develop preferences for brands as a means of avoiding mistakes in decision making (Bauer, Cunningham, and Wortzel 1965). In another study, observation of parental behaviors was found to be more frequent among white than among black adolescents (Moschis and Moore 1984). This appeared to be the cause even after controlling for socioeconomic status:

P6: Parental communication processes and their effects on children's consumer learning vary by socio-demographic characteristics:

a. Overt parent–child communication about consumption declines with age.
b. Overt parent–child communication about consumption is more frequent between parents and their male children than between parents and their female children.
c. Purposive consumer training is more likely to be directed at the female child than at the male child.
d. Purposive consumer training is more likely to be present in upper class than in lower social class families.
e. White youths are more likely than their black counterparts to learn consumer behavior through observation.

Structures and Patterns of Communication. Socialization studies also have examined the effects of family communication structures on consumer learning. Ward speculated that families stressing conformity to others may implicitly encourage children to "learn to purchase and to derive satisfaction from their purchases, on the basis of the perceived effects on others" (1974b, p. 40). Thus, it can be speculated that a socio-oriented communication structure that encourages the child to develop respect for others and other social orientations may lead to the development of materialistic orientations and learning of "expressive" aspects of consumption.

The data presented in two studies support this line of reasoning. The correlations between socio-oriented family communication structure and materialism were statistically significant, while the relationship between concept-oriented communication structure and materialism was insignificant (Moore and Moschis 1981; Moschis and Moore 1979b). The findings further suggested that parents who emphasize the importance of pleasant social relationships in the family (socio-oriented structure) in their communications with their children may implicitly encourage their children to evaluate their actions (including consumption behaviors) on the basis of their perceived effects on others. This may result in the development of materialistic orientations in the child's consumer behavior.

With respect to the adolescent's preference for kinds of information, previous researchers had speculated that the socio-oriented person would be sensitive to "social" kinds of information, while the concept-oriented person would be sensitive to information regarding "functional" aspects of the situation (McLeod and Chaffee 1972). The data presented in one study appear to support this line of reasoning. Emphasis on socio-oriented communication at home correlated positively with the adolescent's preferences for social kinds of information and negatively with preferences for functional or rational types of information (Moore and Moschis 1978a).

The importance of socio-orientation was also illustrated in a study by Stone and Chaffee (1970). Subjects were presented with a list of 20 topics and asked to indicate for each whether "who says it" or "what is said" is more important. It was found that socio-subjects (protective and consensual) were more source-oriented ("who says it"), while the low socio-groups (pluralistic and laissez-faire) were more message-oriented. When the subjects were given messages in which the expertise of the source was manipulated, the high socio-oriented subjects showed higher overall levels of attitude change.

If family communication structures influence consumer learning, one would expect those youths from homes stressing the socio-oriented family communication dimension (A–B relationships in line with Newcomb's A–B–X model) to behave according to a nonrational or social influence model, while those from concept-oriented families (stressing A–X and B–X relationships) would be expected to behave according to a rational or economic model (cf. Bauer 1964, 1967):

P7: Consumer behavior is influenced by the person's family communication structure:

a. Socio-oriented family communication structure fosters the development of consumer needs and behaviors geared to emulating others and conforming to generally accepted norms.

b. Concept-oriented family communication structure fosters the development of consumer needs and behaviors geared to evaluating alternatives according to their objective (nonsocial) attributes.

With respect to the influence of the specific family communication patterns on consumer learning, the results of recent research are fairly similar to those found in the area of political socialization. Specifically, children from families characterized by insistence on conceptual matters and absence of social constraints in their communications ("pluralistics") were found to have more knowledge about consumer-related matters: they were better able to filter puffery in advertising and to manage a typical family budget, and they had more information about products and their characteristics and were more likely to perform socially desirable consumer behaviors (Moore and Moschis 1978a; Moschis and Moore, 1978, 1979b). In addition, pluralistic children had significantly greater preferences for functional kinds of information than did children from the other three groups. Thus, it would seem that preferences for functional types of information may develop when the family communication structure is characterized by positive impetus for self-expression and lacks social constraint.

The study by Moore and Moschis (1978a) also examined the extent to which adolescent preferences for type of information sources vary by family communication pattern. Previous research suggested that laissez-faire children, in the absence of any parent–child communication at home, may tend to rely less on parents and more on external sources of consumer information such as peer groups (McLeod and Chaffee 1972). Pluralistic children, who seem to show relatively higher regard for their parents' opinions, were expected to prefer this source of consumer information more than their counterparts in the other groups, and since they are trained to evaluate several alternatives prior to decision making, they were expected to show relatively higher preferences for sources of consumer information containing a large number of alternative solutions, such as *Consumer Reports* (Chaffee et al. 1966; McLeod and Chaffee 1972). Protective children were expected to be more susceptible to—and therefore have greater preferences for—consumer information both from peer groups and from persuasive messages in the mass media (Eswara 1968; Stone and Chaffee 1970).

As expected, it was found that laissez-faire children tend to rely relatively less on their parents as a source of consumer information. However, they do not necessarily tend to rely more on peers; rather, they are less likely to rely on peer groups. Pluralistic children tend to prefer parental advice to a greater extent than do children from the other three groups, and they show relatively greater preferences for information contained in *Consumer Reports,* as posited. Children from pluralistic homes also are more likely to note consumer news in the mass media than are their counterparts, and they tend to prefer information from a variety of communication sources, in line with the researchers' expectations. The data also seem to support the reasoning that children from protective homes are highly receptive to (and thus susceptible to) consumer information from external sources such as peers and, to a lesser extent, television advertisements. This susceptibility to outside influences has been attributed to parental efforts to protect the child from controversy within the home (McLeod and Chaffee 1972).

The influence of family communication patterns as they affect similar consumer learning properties was also investigated among 734 adolescents in rural and urban Georgia (Moore and Moschis 1981). As expected, adolescents from pluralistic homes know more about consumer matters and are more likely to perform consumer activities portrayed as socially desirable. In addition, these children tend to score lower on materialism than do their counterparts.

In another study of the development of consumer skills among children, it was found that children learn consumer skills when they are given opportunities to participate in consumer decision making and share family responsibilities (Turner and Brandt 1978). Although the study did not directly examine the effects of family communication patterns, those practices found to foster the development of consumer skills are more likely to be present among "pluralistic" families than any other type of family (Moschis and Moore 1978):

P8: The family communication patterns to which a young person is exposed early in life directly influence the development of his/her consumer behavior:

a. A pluralistic FCP pattern fosters the development of consumer competencies.
b. A protective FCP pattern contributes to the person's susceptibility to outside-the-home influences, both commercial and noncommercial.

Indirect Influences

In addition to the direct effects that family communications appear to have on consumer learning, such processes may affect consumer behavior indirectly. Indirect influence can take place when family communication processes influence the offspring's interaction with other sources of consumer information which, in turn, directly (or indirectly) affect the development of consumer behavior. The findings of several studies have established the presence of relationships between family communication processes—including family communication patterns—and the individual's interaction with other socialization agents (e.g., Lull 1980; McLeod et al. 1982) that subsequently affect behavior. This indirect pattern of family influence has also been found in studies of consumer socialization. In fact, path analysis suggested that different communication processes that take place within the home may lead to differential exposure to and use of the mass media (newspapers and television) which, in turn, could lead to the development of various consumer orientations (Moore and Moschis 1981). Thus family communication may indirectly influence the child's interaction with other socialization agents, which may then influence consumer learning.

Previous researchers have reported that purposive consumer training is a rare occurrence at home (Ward 1974a; Ward et al. 1977), suggesting that the effect of family communication on consumer learning may be indirect. Studies have found that consumer and political skill acquisition is strongly related to the child's frequency of reading and viewing consumer/political news (Chaffee et al. 1971; Moschis 1976), which is influenced by the family communication structures at home (Chaffee et al. 1971). Similarly, the results of a longitudinal study

(Moschis and Moore 1982) suggest that learning from television may be a second-order consequence of interpersonal processes, including family communications. These results appear to be consistent with longitudinal findings in political socialization (Atkin and Gantz 1978), and they are in line with speculations about learning from television based on cross-sectional data (Moschis and Churchill 1978).

With respect to the influence of specific parent–child communication processes on mass media use, one study examined whether motivations for TV viewing could be the result of family communication structure at home (Moore and Moschis 1981). It was speculated that a socio-oriented communication structure may implicitly encourage the child to pay attention to the mass media as a means of learning how to behave in various social settings. The results were in line with this expectation, suggesting that families characterized by a socio-oriented communication structure may be encouraging their children to turn to the media to learn social orientations or consumption behaviors appropriate to certain roles. This may then lead to the learning of materialistic orientations, since people are believed to learn the "expressive" aspects of consumption from mass media (e.g., Moschis and Moore 1982; Riesman and Roseborough 1955). Similar findings are reported by Lull (1980), whose research has shown that socio-oriented individuals use television for social purposes.

Additional support for these speculations comes from previous research (Moschis 1976; Ward and Wackman 1971), which also found materialistic attitudes to be related to social motivations for watching television commercials and programs (e.g., watching commercials and programs to learn what products to buy to make a good impression on others), and such motivations to be the result of family communication structure at home (Moore and Moschis 1981; Moschis and Moore 1979b).

On the other hand, these studies show that concept-oriented family communication structure is positively associated with exposure to public affairs information in the mass media (e.g., Chaffee et al. 1971), which may in turn have a positive impact upon consumer knowledge and other consumer competencies (Moschis and Moore 1978, 1979b; Moschis et al. 1983). For example, the results of path analysis of 301 Wisconsin adolescents suggest that a concept-oriented family communication structure leads to exposure to public affairs information in the mass media, which may subsequently lead to the learning of consumer skills. The influence does not appear to be direct, nor to be totally explained by the antecedent variables. Specifically, age and concept-oriented family communication structure were the best predictors of the adolescent's frequency of interacting with the media regarding public affairs content—i.e., frequency of reading news about the economy, government, and advertisements, and of viewing national and local news on television (Moschis and Moore 1978, 1979b). Similar findings emerged from data collected in Georgia (Moore and Moschis 1981).

Family influences may also operate indirectly by affecting the child's social relations with peer groups. Social comparison theory (Festinger 1954) suggests that adolescents need to evaluate some of their perceived knowledge about consumption acquired from their parents by comparing it with the knowledge of other persons who are likely to have similar value perspectives about consumption. Such persons are likely to be peers (Sebald 1968), and empirical findings are in line with this type of reasoning. For example, a study of adolescent females by Brittain (1963) showed that in areas such as taste in clothes, in which girls perceived their ideas to be like those of their peers, the girls tended to favor peer-suggested alternatives. Similarly, several other studies suggest that the typical teenager is responsive to peer opinions on topics about which they have similar interests, opinions, and attitudes, such as clothes choice and hair style (Moschis and Moore 1979a; Remmers and Radler 1957; Saunders et al. 1973; Vener 1957). Another study demonstrated a positive relationship between the frequency of communication about consumption from parent to adolescent and frequency of adolescent communication with peers (Moore and Moschis 1978b). While these findings do not explicitly show how family communication processes affect peer relations, they do suggest that the youth is likely to discuss with his/her peers topics that are discussed at home.

It is also possible that peer communications initiated outside the home are likely to be discussed with parents. One study which attempted to determine the flow of influence of interpersonal communication was not successful in isolating the effects of family communication about consumption on peer communication about consumption, and vice versa. However, the data showed that family communication about consumption may lead to communication with peers about such matters, a finding that can be interpreted in line with Festinger's theory of social comparison (Churchill and Moschis 1979). Thus, the child's need to evaluate some consumption-related cognitions learned at home may cause him/her to seek out others who are similar and to initiate discussions with them.

In sum, the findings suggest that family communication processes lead to rather different interaction patterns with other agents of consumer socialization, which in turn affect consumer learning. Considerably less is known about the specific family communication processes leading to specific interactions and how these subsequently affect consumer learning.

The preceding discussion can be summarized as:

P9: Family communication about consumption, including frequency and structure of family communication that takes place within the home, indirectly affects the consumer learning by affecting interaction with other socialization agents:

a. Concept-oriented family communication structure leads to higher use of public affairs information in the mass media by the youth.

b. Socio-oriented family communication structure leads to higher use of mass media for social purposes by the youth.

c. The frequency of the youth's interaction about consumption with his/her parents leads to communication with peers about such matters.

Mediating Effects

There is considerable evidence to suggest that family communication processes modify the effects of other socialization agents, particularly television (Comstock et al. 1978; McLeod et al. 1982). The mediating role of family communications has also been investigated in the context of consumer socialization. After reviewing studies on the effects of television advertising, Robertson (1979) concluded that parents mediate such affects. Additional studies (Churchill and Moschis 1979; Moschis and Moore 1982) found that the effects of television advertising on consumer learning were contingent upon the adolescent's frequency of communication with his/her parents about consumption matters, with television advertising effects having a stronger impact for families in which discussions about consumption are less frequent.

Parental mediation is often the result of a child's requests for advertised products. For example, Atkin (1982) found that parents and children often discuss and argue over consumer purchase decisions that are stimulated by television advertising. Such discussions and opportunities for mediation can be attributed to high adult-child co-viewing behavior, which has been estimated to be as high as 70 percent for prime-time programming (Nielsen 1975).

While the family's mediating role is well documented, the nature and consequences of parental mediation are not very clear. Reviews outside the field of consumer behavior suggest that parental mediation of television effects are either strengthened or weakened in the interpersonal context (McLeod et al. 1982). There is some evidence to suggest that the impact of outside-the-family influences such as television advertising is greater under conditions of parental restrictiveness (Atkin et al. 1979). Similarly, Hawkins and Pingree (1982) found reduced effects of television for youngsters in families that are low in conflict and parental control. These findings may be attributed to family communication patterns. For example, it has been found that protective families stress obedience and social harmony and make a conscious effort to protect the child from controversy within the home. Since parental control using restrictiveness is likely to be present in these families, parental efforts to protect the child within the home may leave the youngster unprotected from outside influences (McLeod and Chaffee 1972). Thus, it is not surprising that studies find children from protective homes to be susceptible to the influence of external sources, such as peers and television advertising (Moore and Moschis 1978b).

To summarize, the evidence indicates that family mediates the effects of socialization agents on consumer learning. Such mediation is the result of opportunity for mediation, such as parent–child television co-viewing behavior. The specific effects of parental mediation on consumer socialization are not very clear and have been examined mainly in the context of television advertising. These appear to be a function of parent–child relations, including family communication processes:

P10: Family communication processes modify and channel the influence of information from non-family sources:

a. Television advertising viewing by the youth stimulates parent–child communication about consumption.
b. Parent–child communication about consumption weakens the effects of television advertising.
c. A "protective" family communication pattern contributes to the youth's susceptibility to television advertising more than any other family communication pattern.
d. A "protective" family communication pattern contributes to the youth's susceptibility to peer groups more than any other family communication pattern.

CONCLUSIONS AND DIRECTIONS FOR FUTURE RESEARCH

The information presented in this article suggests some generalizations supported by reasonably adequate evidence and others which are more speculative and require additional research. Parents appear to play an important role in the consumer socialization of their offspring, and they are instrumental in teaching them the rational aspects of consumption. In addition, youngsters appear to acquire a variety of other consumption-related orientations and skills from their parents. Parental influence on the consumer behavior of their offspring is situation-specific; it varies across products, stages in the decision making process, and consumer characteristics.

Parents can influence the development of consumer behavior in their children both directly and indirectly. Parents influence their children's consumer learning directly through several communication processes (both overt and cognitive), including overt interaction about consumption matters (e.g., purposive training), using reinforcement mechanisms (both positive and negative), and providing opportunities for the child to observe their own consumer behaviors. Apparently, different communication processes are involved in the direct transmission of specific values and behaviors from parent to child, and these processes vary by socio-demographic characteristics.

The family can affect consumer learning indirectly by influencing the youngster's interaction with other sources of consumer influence. Family communication processes lead to rather different interaction patterns with other sources of consumer learning. Finally, the evidence indicates that family mediates the effects of other socialization agents, and that family communication processes play an important role in this mediation process.

Several avenues for future research are possible. Clearly, there is a need for better understanding of the nature of family influence—namely, of additional aspects of consumer behavior that are acquired from parents and parental influence across situations. We also need to understand the communication processes involved in the transmission and acquisition of certain values and behaviors from parent to child and how these vary by socio-demographic characteristics.

Another pressing need is evidenced by the

findings which show that a great deal of the family influence in consumer socialization operates indirectly, by affecting other sources of consumer learning. It would be useful to understand and separate the direct from the indirect effects of family communication processes. The mediating effects of family also deserve some attention. It would be useful to know how out-of-home influences are modified and channeled in the context of specific family communication processes.

Research in the area could be facilitated by developing better conceptualizations and applying more rigorous methodologies. For example, one pressing need for research appears to be the need for studying the influence of family in the context of specific dyads, focusing upon specific pairs. The research reviewed here suggests that family communications have been examined only in the broad context of how parents affect the development of consumer behavior of their children. Research should also address specific dyads and directions of influence, such as mother–son, mother–daughter, father–son, and father–daughter. It would also be useful to examine communication effects when one parent's style of communication with the child (FCP) is quite different from that of the other parent. The study of family communications in the context of specific parent–child dyads may be useful in understanding the effects of specific communication processes on the development of various types of consumer behaviors.

In addition, there appear to be methodological issues that need to be addressed in measuring family communication processes and effects. Specifically, research is needed that would address the area of family communication processes in a somewhat similar vein to the one that communication researchers have used to examine mass communication processes. For example, communication processes conceptualized according to mass communication models have recently departed from the traditional assumption of "exposure equals effect," and they have included additional processes of interaction with mass media, such as "gratifications sought" and "gratifications received" from the source (e.g., McLeod et al. 1982). And in evaluating family communication effects, research could focus on methods for measuring such effects and developing meaningful criteria of consumer learning, both relational and absolute.

Much of the research needed in this area can only be addressed using certain research designs. Because communication involves exchange of information and subsequent "effects," cross-sectional designs may not be adequate for studying certain types of family communication processes. Rather, experimental and longitudinal designs could enable the researcher to better study such processes and their effects.

In summary, this article has attempted to present an update on the present knowledge and research on the role of family communications in the consumer learning of children and adolescents. It has also attempted to integrate much of the information in the area and has presented propositions to guide future research and theory development.

REFERENCES

ADLER, RICHARD P. (1977), *Research on the Effects of Television Advertising on Children.* Washington, DC: U.S. Government Printing Office.

Advertising Age (1980), "Youth Marketing," (April 28), S1–S24.

ARNDT, JOHAN (1971), "A Research Note on Intergenerational Overlap of Selected Consumer Variables," *Markeds Kommunikasjon,* 3, 1–8.

——— (1975), "Reflections on Research in Consumer Behavior," in *Advances in Consumer Research,* Vol. 3, Ed. Beverlee B. Anderson. Cincinnati, OH: Association for Consumer Research, 213–221.

ATKIN, CHARLES K. (1982), "Television Advertising and Socialization to Consumer Roles," in *Television and Behavior,* Vol. 2, Eds. David Pearl, Lorraine Bouthilet, and Joyce Lazar. Rockville, MD: National Institute of Mental Health, U.S. Department of Health and Human Services, 191–200.

_____, and WALTER GANTZ (1978), "Television News and Political Socialization," *Public Opinion Quarterly,* 42 (Summer), 183–198.

_____, BYRON REEVES, and WENDY GIBSON (1979), "Effects of Television Food Advertising on Children," paper presented to Advertising Division of Association for Education in Journalism, Annual Convention, Houston, TX.

BAUER, RAYMOND A. (1964), "The Obstinate Audience: The Influence Process from the Point of View of Social Communications," *American Psychologist,* 19 (May), 319–328.

_____ (1967), "Games People and Audience Play," paper presented to Seminar on Communication in Contemporary Society, University of Texas.

_____, SCOTT CUNNINGHAM, and LAWRENCE WORTZEL (1965), "The Marketing Dilemma of Negroes," *Journal of Marketing,* 29 (July), 1–6.

BRITTAIN, CLAY V. (1963), "Adolescent Choices and Parent-Peer Cross Pressures," *American Sociological Review,* 28 (June), 385–391.

CANNON, KENNETH C., RUTH STAPLES, and IRENE CARLSON (1952), "Personal Appearance as a Factor in Personal Acceptance," *Journal of Home Economics,* 44 (November), 710–713.

CHAFFEE, STEVEN H., and JACK M. MCLEOD (1968), "Sensitization in Panel Design: A Coorientational Experiment," *Journalism Quarterly,* 45 (Winter), 661–669.

_____, JACK M. MCLEOD, and CHARLES K. ATKIN (1971), "Parental Influences on Adolescent Media Use," *American Behavioral Scientist,* 14 (January/February), 323–340.

_____, JACK M. MCLEOD, and DANIEL B. WACKMAN (1966), "Family Communication and Political Socialization," paper presented to the Association for Education in Journalism, Iowa City, IA.

_____, and ALBERT R. TIMS (1976), "Interpersonal Factors in Adolescent Television Use," *Journal of Social Issues,* 32 (4), 98–105.

CHURCHILL, GILBERT A., JR., and GEORGE P. MOSCHIS (1979), "Television and Interpersonal Influences on Adolescent Consumer Learning," *Journal of Consumer Research,* 6 (June), 23–35.

COMSTOCK, G., S. CHAFFEE, N. KATZMAN, M. MCCOMBS, and D. RIOVERT (1978), *Television and Human Behavior.* New York: Columbia University Press.

DAVIS, HARRY L. (1976), "Decision Making Within the Household," *Journal of Consumer Research,* 2 (March), 241–260.

ENGEL, JAMES, ROGER BLACKWELL, and DAVID KOLLAT (1978), *Consumer Behavior* (3rd ed.). New York: Holt, Rinehart & Winston.

ESWARA, H. S. (1968), "An Interpersonal Approach to the Study of Social Influences: Family Communication Patterns and Attitude Change," unpublished doctoral dissertation, University of Wisconsin, Madison, WI.

FAUMAN, B. C. (1966), "Determinants of Adolescents' Brand Preferences," unpublished dissertation, Sloan School of Management, MIT, Cambridge, MA.

FESTINGER, L. (1954), "A Theory of Social Comparison Processes," *Human Relations,* 7 (May), 117–140.

FRY, JOSEPH N., DAVID C. SHAW, C. HAELING VON LANZENAUER, and CECIL R. DIPCHAUD (1973), "Customer Loyalty to Banks: A Longitudinal Study," *Journal of Business,* 46 (October), 517–525.

HALLER, ARCHIBALD O., and ALEJANDRO PORTES (1973), "Status Attainment Process," *Sociology of Education,* 46 (Winter), 51–91.

HAMILTON, JANICE, and JESSIE WARDEN (1966), "Student's Role in a High School Community and His Clothing Behavior," *Journal of Home Economics,* 58 (December), 789–791.

HAWKINS, ROBERT P., and SUZANNE PINGREE (1982), "Television's Influence on Social Reality," in *Television and Behavior,* Vol. 2, Eds. David Pearl, Lorraine Bouthilet, and Joyce Lazar. Rockville, MD: National Institute of Mental Health, U.S. Department of Health and Human Services, 224–247.

HESS, ROBERT D. (1970), "Social Class and Ethnic Influences on Socialization," in *Manual of Child Psychology,* Vol. 2 (3rd ed.), Ed. Paul H. Mussen. New York: Wiley, 457–559.

HURT, MARY LEE (1961). *Teenagers and Their Money.* Washington, DC: National Education Association.

KAHL, JOSEPH A. (1953), "Educational and Occupational Aspirations of 'Common Man' Boys," *Harvard Educational Review,* 23 (Summer), 186.

LEVINE, ADELINE (1976), "Educational and Occupational Choice: A Synthesis of Literature from Sociology and Psychology," in *Selected Aspects of Consumer Behavior,* Ed. R. Ferber. Washington, DC: U.S. Government Printing Office, 131–143.

LULL, JAMES (1980), "Family Communication Patterns and the Social Uses of Television," paper presented at the International Communication Association Meeting, Acapulco, Mexico.

MARSHALL, HELEN R., and LUCILLE MAGRUDER (1960), "Relations Between Parent Money Education Practices and Children's Knowledge and Use of Money," *Child Development,* 31 (June), 253-284.

McLEOD, JACK M., CARL R. BYBEE, and JEAN A. DUVALL (1982), "Evaluating Media Performance by Gratifications Sought and Received," *Journalism Quarterly,* 59 (Spring), 3-12.

———, and STEVEN H. CHAFFEE (1972), "The Construction of Social Reality," in *The Social Influence Process,* Ed. J. T. Tiedeschi. Chicago: Aldine-Atherton, 50-99.

———, and STEVEN H. CHAFFEE (1973), "Interpersonal Approaches to Communication Research," *American Behavioral Scientist,* 16 (April), 469-499.

———, MARY ANN FITZPATRICK, CARROLL J. GLYNN, and SUSAN F. FALLIS (1982), "Television and Social Relations: Family Influences and Consequences for Interpersonal Behavior," in *Television and Behavior,* Vol. 2, Eds. David Pearl, Lorraine Bouthilet, and Joyce Lazar. Rockville, MD: National Institute of Mental Health, U.S. Department of Health and Human Services, 272-286.

———, and GARRETT J. O'KEEFE (1972), "The Socialization Perspective and Communication Behavior," in *Current Perspectives in Mass Communication Research,* Eds. F. G. Kline and P. J. Tichenor. Beverly Hills, CA. Sage.

MEHROTRA, TUNIL, and SANDRA TORGES (1976), "Determinants of Children's Influence on Mothers' Buying Behavior," in *Advances in Consumer Research,* Vol. 4, Ed. William D. Perreault, Jr. Atlanta, GA: Association for Consumer Research, 56-60.

MOORE, ROY L., and GEORGE P. MOSCHIS (1978a), "Family Communication Patterns and Consumer Socialization," paper presented to the Mass Communication and Society Division, Association for Education in Journalism Annual Convention, Seattle, WA.

———, and GEORGE P. MOSCHIS (1978b), "Teenagers' Reactions to Advertising," *Journal of Advertising,* 7 (Fall), 24-30.

———, and GEORGE P. MOSCHIS (1981), "The Effects of Family Communication and Mass Media Use on Adolescent Consumer Learning," *Journal of Communication,* 31 (Fall), 42-51.

———, and GEORGE P. MOSCHIS (1983), "Role of Mass Media and the Family in Development of Consumption Norms," *Journalism Quarterly,* 60 (Spring), 67-73.

———, and LOWNDES F. STEPHENS (1975), "Some Communication and Determinants of Adolescent Consumer Learning," *Journal of Consumer Research,* 2 (September), 80-92.

MOSCHIS, GEORGE P. (1976), "Acquisition of the Consumer Role by Adolescents," unpublished doctoral dissertation, Graduate School of Business, University of Wisconsin, Madison, WI.

——— (1981), "Socialization Perspectives and Consumer Behavior," in *Marketing Review 1981,* Eds. Ben Enis and Kenneth Roering. Chicago: American Marketing Association, 43-56.

——— (1984), "A Longitudinal Study of Consumer Socialization," in *Proceedings of the American Marketing Association Theory Conference,* Ed. Michael Ryan. Chicago: American Marketing Association, in press.

———, and GILBERT A. CHURCHILL, JR. (1978), "Consumer Socialization: A Theoretical and Empirical Analysis," *Journal of Marketing Research,* 15 (November), 599-609.

———, and ROY L. MOORE (1978), "Family Communication and Consumer Socialization," in *Advances in Consumer Research,* Vol. 6, Ed. William L. Wilkie. Ann Arbor, MI: Association for Consumer Research, 359-363.

———, and ROY L. MOORE (1979a), "Decision Making Among the Young: A Socialization Perspective," *Journal of Consumer Research,* 6 (September), 101-112.

———, and ROY L. MOORE (1979b), "Family Communication Patterns and Consumer Socialization," in *1979 AMA Educators' Conference Proceedings,* Eds. Neil Beckwith, Michael Houston, Robert Mittelstaedt, Kent B. Monroe, and Scott Ward. Chicago: American Marketing Association, 226-230.

———, and ROY L. MOORE (1979c), "Mass Media and Personal Influences on Adolescent Consumer Learning," *Development in Marketing Science,* Vol. 2.

———, and ROY L. MOORE (1980), "Purchasing Behavior of Adolescent Consumers," in *1980 AMA Educators' Conference Proceedings,* Eds. Richard P. Bagozzi, Kenneth L. Bernhardt, Paul S. Busch, David W. Cravens, Joseph F. Hair, Jr., and Carol A. Scott. Chicago: American Marketing Association, 89-92.

______, and ROY L. MOORE (1982), "A Longitudinal Study of Television Advertising Effects," *Journal of Consumer Research,* 9 (December), 279-286.

______, and ROY L. MOORE (1983), "A Longitudinal Study of the Development of Purchasing Patterns," in *Proceedings of the American Marketing Association Conference,* Eds. Patrick E. Murphy, Gene R. Laczniak, Paul F. Anderson, Russell W. Belk, O. C. Ferrell, Robert F. Lusch, Terence A. Shimp, and Charles B. Weinberg. Chicago: American Marketing Association, 114-117.

______, and ROY L. MOORE (1984), "Racial and Socioeconomic Influences on the Development of Consumer Behavior," in *Advances in Consumer Research,* Vol. 12, Eds. Elizabeth Hirschman and Morris Holbrook. Ann Arbor, MI: Association for Consumer Research, in press.

______, and ROY L. MOORE (forthcoming), "Anticipatory Consumer Socialization," *Journal of the Academy of Marketing Science,* in press.

______, ROY L. MOORE, and RUTH B. SMITH (1983), "The Impact of Family Communication on Adolescent Consumer Socialization," in *Advances in Consumer Research,* Vol. 11, Ed. Thomas C. Kinnear, Chicago: Association for Consumer Research, 314-319.

______, ROY L. MOORE, and LOWNDES F. STEPHENS (1977), "Purchasing Patterns of Adolescent Consumers," *Journal of Retailing,* 53 (Spring), 17-26, 92.

NEWCOMB, THEODORE M. (1953), "An Approach to the Study of Communicative Acts," *Psychological Review,* 60 (November), 393-404.

NIELSEN, A. C. (1975), *The Television Audience: 1975.* Chicago: A. C. Nielsen Company.

O'KEEFE, GARRETT J., JR. (1973), "Co-orientation Variables in Family Studies," *American Behavioral Scientist,* 16 (April), 513-536.

OLSHAVSKY, RICHARD W., and DONALD H. GRANBOIS (1979), "Consumer Decision Making—Fact or Fiction," *Journal of Consumer Research,* 6 (September), 93-100.

PARSONS, TALCOTT, ROBERT F. BALES, and E. A. SHILS (1953), *Working Papers in the Theory of Action.* Glencoe, IL: The Free Press.

PASDIRTZ, G. W. (1969), "An Approach to the Study of Interaction Processes," paper presented to the Association for Education in Journalism, Berkeley, CA.

PHELAN, GLADYS K., and JAY D. SCHVANEVELDT (1969), "Spending and Saving Patterns of Adolescent Siblings," *Journal of Home Economics,* 61 (February), 104-109.

PSATHAS, GEORGE (1957), "Ethnicity, Social Class and Adolescent Independence from Parental Control," *American Sociological Review,* 22 (August), 415-423.

REMMERS, H. H., and D. H. RADLER (1957), "The Basis of Teenage Behavior," *The American Teenager.* New York: Boules-Mezri, 229-237.

RIESMAN, DAVID, and HOWARD ROSEBOROUGH (1955), "Careers and Consumer Behavior," in *Consumer Behavior, Vol. II: The Life Cycle and Consumer Behavior,* Ed. Lincoln H. Clark. New York: New York University Press, 1-18.

ROSSITER, JOHN R., and THOMAS S. ROBERTSON (1979), "Children's Independence from Parental Mediation in Learning about OTC Drugs," *1979 Educators' Conference Proceedings.* Chicago: American Marketing Association, 653-657.

ROBERTSON, THOMAS S. (1979). "Parental Mediation of Television Advertising Effects," *Journal of Communication,* 29 (Winter), 12-25.

SAUNDERS, JOSEPHINE R., A. COSKUM SALMI, and ENID F. TOZIER (1973), "Congruence and Conflict in Buying Decisions of Mothers and Daughters," *Journal of Retailing,* 49 (Fall), 3-18.

SEBALD, HANS (1968), *Adolescence: A Socio-Psychological Analysis.* New York: Appleton-Century-Crofts.

SMITH, RUTH BELK, and GEORGE P. MOSCHIS (forthcoming), "A Socialization Perspective on Selected Consumer Characteristics of the Elderly," *Journal of Consumer Affairs,* in press.

STONE, VERNON A., and STEVEN H. CHAFFEE (1970), "Family Communication Patterns and Source-Message Orientation," *Journalism Quarterly,* 47 (Summer), 239-246.

TANNENBAUM, PERCY H., and JACK M. MCLEOD (1967), "On the Measurement of Socialization," *Public Opinion Quarterly,* 31 (Spring), 27-37.

TURNER, JOSEPHINE, and JEANETTE BRANDT (1978), "Development and Validation of a Simulated Market to Test Children for Selected Consumer Skills," *Journal of Consumer Affairs,* 12 (Winter), 266-276.

VENER, ARTHUR M. (1957), "Adolescent Orientation to Clothing: A Social Psychological Interpretation," unpublished doctoral dissertation, Michigan State University, East Lansing, MI.

WARD, SCOTT (1974a), "Consumer Socialization," *Journal of Consumer Research,* 1 (September), 1-16.

——— (1974b), "Consumer Socialization," Marketing Science Institute working paper.

———, and DANIEL B. WACKMAN (1971), "Family and Media Influence on Adolescent Consumer Learning," *American Behavioral Scientist,* 14 (January/February), 415–427.

———, and DANIEL B. WACKMAN (1972), "Children's Purchase Influence Attempts and Parental Yielding," *Journal of Marketing Research,* 9 (August), 316–319.

———, and DANIEL B. WACKMAN (1973), *Effects of Television Advertising on Consumer Socialization.* Cambridge, MA: Marketing Science Institute.

———, DANIEL B. WACKMAN, and ELLEN WARTELLA (1977), *How Children Learn to Buy: The Development of Consumer Information Processing Skills.* Beverly Hills, CA: Sage.

23

JOINT DECISIONS IN HOME PURCHASING: A Muddling-Through Process*

C. Whan Park

This study characterizes joint decision-making as being reached by a muddling-through process rather than by a synoptic strategy. In spite of this muddling-through, joint decision-making is conceptualized as being effectively based on three conflict-avoiding heuristics.

Researchers have long stressed the need for a significant research effort in family decision-making (e.g., Davis 1970; Ferber 1971), but it is only recently that considerable research interest has been generated. Several important issues remain to be investigated. Two of them are:

- A conceptual characterization of joint decision-making in terms of the decision process and the heuristics employed in making a joint decision
- Development of methodologies for examining joint decision-making, particularly with respect to the similarities and dissimilarities of decision strategies

The purpose of the present study is to examine the joint decision-making process using a method called the "decision plan net" in the context of a husband and wife's joint decision in home purchasing. Theoretical characterizations of joint decision-making as a muddling-through process are discussed, and a decision plan net is introduced as a method that opera-

*Reprinted from the *Journal of Consumer Research,* 9 (September 1982), pp. 151–162.

tionalizes the decision maker's strategies for future decision situations. This method is designed to examine (1) the joint decision makers' similarities in terms of their decision strategies and (2) changes in their strategies over time. Finally, hypotheses based upon the muddling-through process are specified and tested with the decision plan net.

THEORY

Joint Decision Process

It is often stated that joint decision-making is different from individual decision-making not only in terms of the unit of analysis, but also in terms of the process itself (Davis 1971). These process differences have not been spelled out clearly in previous studies, however.

There have been consistent research findings regarding joint or group decision makers' inability to recognize the part each played in the decision (Davis 1970, 1971; Grandbois and Willett 1970; Haberman and Elinson 1967; Kenkel and Hoffman 1956; Patchen 1974; Scanzoni 1965; Silk and Kalwani 1980; Spekman 1978). For instance, Kenkel and Hoffman (1956) found that after reaching a decision, most couples were able neither to predict nor to report correctly their respective roles with regard to the amount of talking, the amount of ideas and suggestions contributed, or their respective contributions to smoothing out differences.

Two major factors appear to explain the dyad's (husband and wife's) inability to recognize the mutual interaction process. First, individuals normally face complex decision tasks with limited information processing capabilities (short-term memories). Such tasks would require a considerable effort on the part of the individual in terms of learning and identifying salient dimensions as well as choice alternatives. This would not be an easy task to execute. It would be an added cognitive burden to individuals if they had to identify their spouses' preference function. Second, individuals are normally not used to measuring their spouses' preference function and decision strategy—e.g., a husband may be able to identify his wife's preferences on some dimensions, but is not likely to know his wife's choice strategy in terms of (1) the dimensional weight and utility associated with each level on each salient dimension (Curry and Menasco 1979), (2) their changes over time (Park and Lutz 1982), and (3) which heuristic choice strategy would be employed in a particular situation.

In view of these two limitations, theories of group problem solving such as the "synoptic ideal" type—which assumes that the dyad is rational, analytical, and plans comprehensively to maximize joint utility—are simply not convincing. According to synoptic thinking, the dyad identifies opportunities and constraints in the market and assesses their preferences and utilities. Strategic decision plans are then devised to achieve maximum joint utility through optimization rules. It should also be noted that researchers who examined corporate decision-making pointed out several problems with this rational synoptic thinking attributed to strategy makers (Mintzberg, Raisinghani, and Theoret 1976; Murray 1978).

In contrast to the synoptic process, the present study characterizes joint decisions as a muddling-through process that assumes little understanding of the method necessary to achieve the most desirable joint decision. Specifically, each spouse may wish to maximize the joint utility from their decision. However, the decision maker (DM), who is informationally impoverished (MacKenzie 1976), is expected neither to be able to process detailed information about the spouse's utility function nor to possess effective tools by which to identify that function.

Thus each spouse follows his or her own decision strategy (enhancing one's own utility) while attempting to minimize conflict, which often involves groping through a recursive, discontinuous process. This seemingly frustrating joint decision is achieved more easily than it appears through use of a set of conflict-avoiding heuristics. By following conflict-avoiding heuristics, the dyad believes that it "makes" a decision jointly, when in fact it more or less "reaches" a decision through a disjointed, unstructured, and incremental strategy. Thus it is not surprising that the members of the dyad believe they are more similar to each other than they actually are and think they know each other's decision strategy more than they actually do.[1]

Heuristics for Reaching a Joint Decision

A joint decision can be conceptualized as being reached through conflict-avoiding heuristics. Three major heuristics can be identified.

Common Preference Levels on Salient Objective Dimensions. There are a set of dimensions on which one's preference can be easily identified by another. To illustrate, identification of each spouse's preference on salient objective dimensions—such as the number of bedrooms, price, or home style (bi-level, ranch, two-story, and so on)—does not require as much cognitive processing effort and ability as that required for identification of preferences on salient subjective dimensions—such as interior design, neighborhood, appearance of home, and insulation (Park 1978). This is to be expected, since both spouses may find it less difficult to articulate the preferred levels of objective dimensions than those of subjective dimensions, and may have a more clearly defined frame of reference toward the former (e.g., a ranch style, three-bedroom home) than toward the latter (e.g., a well-insulated home). There is related cognitive research that supports this distinction. Words, sentences, and paragraphs of "connected discourse" are recalled and recognized more accurately if the words are concrete rather than abstract (Begg and Paivio 1969; Holmes and Langford 1976; Paivio 1971).

The presence or absence of a preference difference between the spouses on these salient objective dimensions can be identified with relative ease. Presence of preference differences on these dimensions may make the joint decision more difficult than it would be if there are differences on salient subjective dimensions, since there may be rigid standards of reference on the former (e.g., three or four bedrooms), as opposed to some degree of flexibility on the latter (e.g., insulation).

Due to the ease of identifying the spouse's preference level and the critical importance of preference differences on the subsequent purchasing decision, agreement on these dimensions is sought at an early stage of the joint decision process.

Task Specialization. Each spouse may differentiate his or her evaluation task by the dimensions to be examined, based on each one's degree of expertise. Several previous studies have reported this type of complementary task differentiation in joint decision-making (Davis 1970; Ferber and Lee 1974; Kenkel 1961; Kenkel and Hoffman 1956; Munsinger, Weber, and Hansen 1975; Strodtbeck 1951). Such task specialization is assumed to be based on the mutual recognition of the role of each member of the dyad.

Concessions Based on Preference Differences. Spouses may differ in their desired levels on each salient dimension and in their degree of intensity about obtaining these levels. Those differences (disagreements) are often resolved through concessions, the concession being made by the one with a lower intensity. For example, if the wife feels that four bedrooms is a "must," while the husband prefers three bedrooms but considers four also acceptable, a four-bedroom home would enhance the dyad's joint utility; the husband makes a concession to his wife.

[1]Earlier research evidence of this muddling-through process comes from the organizational decision-making literature. Studies include Lindblom's work on the science of muddling through (1959, 1979); Braybrooke and Lindblom's notion of disjoint incrementalism (1963); Mintzberg et al.'s work on the structure of "unstructured" strategic decision processes (1976); Murray's work on strategic choice as a negotiated outcome (1978); Simon's behavioral theory of the firm (1945), which assumes satisfying the constraints rather than maximizing the objectives; and Arrow's impossibility theorem (1963).

The concession heuristic assumes that the spouses recognize their preference conflict, if present, and the subsequent conflict resolution. Research evidence exists for this heuristic. Specifically, Siegel and Fouraker (1960) found that bargainers were able to agree on contracts yielding maximum total profit even under conditions when both information and communication were quite limited. Each bargainer knew only the profits he derived from the various possible contracts, and even though the two could not communicate anything about their respective profits (they could only make offers and counter offers), the pairs were often able to make deals yielding the largest possible combined profits.

According to Kelley (1964), this was possible through a succession of bids by which concessions could be made to the opponent without making offers below the minimum aspiration level. Thus it may not be unusual that, in pursuing their individual interests, joint decision makers often maximize their joint outcome through concessions.

Examining a Dyad's Choice Decision Strategy

A method of examining each spouse's choice decision strategy or plan is needed to understand the dynamic decision process resulting from a dyad's interaction, including changes in choice decision strategies. In the present study, a method termed a "decision plan net" is employed to examine the structural similarity of a dyad's choice decision plan and the convergence of the planned strategies over time.

The Decision Plan. The concept of a decision plan has been proposed previously as a useful construct for understanding the individual's goal-oriented behavior (Bettman 1979; Miller, Galanter, and Pribram 1960).[2] Another concept of decision plan and ideas for its operationalization that differ somewhat from Bettman's were proposed elsewhere (Park et al. 1981). Specifically, Park et al. described a decision plan as the DM's intended decision strategies in future decision situations, operationalized at both the attribute level ("what home features do I want in buying a home and what do I do with them?") and the alternative level ("which home would I choose among several potential alternatives?").

In this study, the decision plan is operationalized at an attribute level, which refers to the DM's intended strategies about choice criteria. This type of decision plan is regularly found in conversations between customers and realtors. To illustrate, a customer may describe his or her plan to the realtor as follows: "I am looking for a home priced under $50,000. If above $50,000, I cannot afford to buy it. I also want four bedrooms, although three are acceptable if a home is satisfactory on other important features. A basement is also needed. If a home does not have a basement, it should have at least a single-car garage. I prefer a home with a fenced yard, but this is not a necessary condition."

At an attribute level, the decision plan is presumed to have been developed by the DM internally at an earlier stage. This is consistent with what Bettman (1979) has postulated. The decision plan at an attribute level is identified in a decision plan net, developed as a tool to aid the DM in either clarifying or establishing his/her decision strategy toward a future decision task (Park, Hughes, Thukral, and Friedmann 1981). A hypothetical example of a decision plan net is shown in Figure 23.1 in the form of a net structure.[3]

In constructing a net, the DM is asked to name a list of the attributes she/he would consider sequentially in evaluating a home (Step 1). Once the DM completes this task, she/he is further asked what she/he would do with an alternative if each attribute listed were not satis-

[2]Bettman (1979), for example, postulated that a decision plan refers to a blueprint of an intended course of action that the DM has developed internally in a goal hierarchical structure.

[3]It should be noted that this net structure is used for illustrative purposes rather than for describing the decision plan in a goal hierarchical structure. Since a step-by-step guide to decision plan net construction has been discussed elsewhere (Park et al. 1981), only a brief summary of the net construction method is reported here (see also Figure 23.1 for its interpretation).

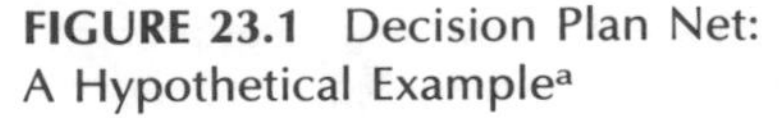

FIGURE 23.1 Decision Plan Net: A Hypothetical Example[a]

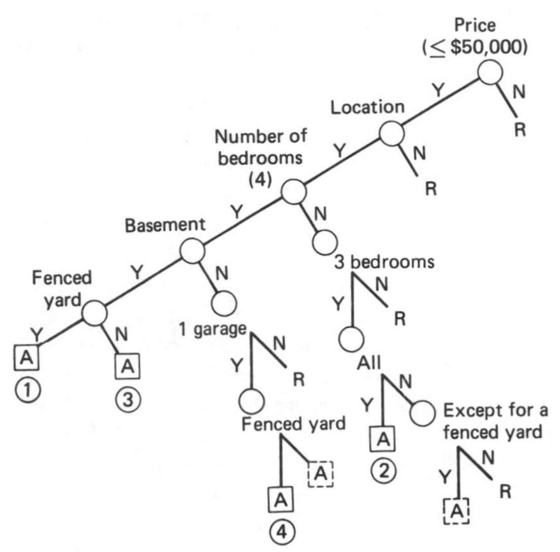

[a]The five home features (choice criteria) listed down the left side, if present ("Y"), render a home acceptable ("A") for consideration. A right branch indicates a home without a satisfactory level on the feature ("N"). For example, the right branch from the price node indicates a home costing more than $50,000. The "R" means that such a home will be rejected from further consideration. The right branch from the third node indicates a home with only three bedrooms (asuming satisfactory features on the first two nodes). It is aceptable if satisfactory on *all of the remaining features* ("all"). A three-bedroom home without a fenced yard is also acceptable if it has a basement ("except a fenced yard"). Numbers under some "As" refer to preference rankings among acceptable alternatives.

factory (Step 2). Possible responses are either "reject" or "still consider the alternative." If the latter, DM is then asked to identify under what conditions the alternative will be accepted (Step 3). One of three possibilities will occur in this situation:

- The alternative is acceptable when all of the remaining attributes are satisfactory.
- The alternative is acceptable even if some of the remaining attributes are not satisfactory.
- The alternative is acceptable if there are other redeeming features to compensate for the unsatisfactory level of the current attribute.

After completing this task, the DM is asked to assign preference rankings among the acceptable alternatives.

Identification of Decision Plan. The present study distinguishes three ways of using product dimensions for choice on the basis of previous research (Goldberg 1968; Park 1978). They are rejection inducing dimensions (RIDs), relative preference dimensions (RPDs), and trade-off dimensions (TDs). This distinction serves to determine the dyad's similarity in their decision strategies. The conceptual distinction among these three types and their identification in a decision plan net are as follows:

- A dimension is defined as a *rejection inducing dimension* (RID) when a DM establishes a minimum acceptable threshold on the product dimension. When the alternative does not satisfy such a requirement, the DM would reject that alternative, regardless of the other features.
- A dimension is defined as a *relative preference dimension* (RPD) when a DM specifies only a differential threshold of acceptance on the product dimension. To illustrate, if a home has a fenced yard (Figure 23.1), the DM views it as highly desirable, with a preference ranking of 1 (assuming all other dimensions are satisfactory). Even if a home does not possess a fenced yard, the DM would still consider it acceptable, with a preference ranking of 3. Thus, the presence or absence of this dimension influences only the degree of preference for an alternative that is acceptable to the DM.
- *Trade-off dimensions* (TD) differ from RPDs because the absence of a satisfactory level on a TD requires an off-setting improvement on another feature for the alternative to be acceptable.

In the present study, a rejection inducing dimension (RID) is operationalized as a dimension which leads to immediate rejection of any alternative failing to reach a satisfactory level on that dimension. Price and location dimensions are RIDs in Figure 23.1. A dimension is operationally defined as a RPD when the absence of the desired level on the dimension leads to:

- The first node on the right-hand branch is either an "all" node (all of the remaining dimensions) or a different level of the same dimension (i.e., three bedrooms) that leads to an "all" node; and
- An "all" node with a "Y" leads to an acceptable path with a specific preference ranking.

In Figure 23.1, the number of bedrooms and fenced yard dimensions are RPDs. The basement dimension is a TD, because an absence of the desired level on this dimension requires the presence of a one-car garage.

These three types of dimensions differ in the DM's degree of intensity about obtaining the desired levels. According to the definitions, the DM would desire satisfactory levels of RIDs more strongly than those of TDs, which are, in turn, preferred to those of RPDs.

An important issue concerning a decision plan net constructed in the manner described previously is whether such a plan existed at a prior time, or is created only through the DM's interaction with the researcher. Although the confounding of both sources is likely, the decision plan used in the present study is assumed to have existed prior to the researcher's intervention. This does not seem to be a strong assumption, because the DM is normally expected to have engaged in preplanning a highly involved decision such as a home purchase. It should also be noted that a decision plan was defined as the DM's intended decision strategies in future decision situations. As long as these strategies possess descriptive validity (rather than being instant improvisations without any validity), the source of decision plan formation (whether internally generated or newly acquired) would not affect the decision plan concept as it is employed in the present study. It is interesting to note that, in a study by Aschenbrenner, Jaus, and Villani (1980), subjects who developed planned strategies through decision aids similar to the decision plan net demonstrated not only superior information processing ability, but also the lasting effect of this processing capability.

HYPOTHESES

If one believes that each spouse normally follows his or her own decision strategy while relying upon a set of heuristics to minimize conflict, this suggests that a dyad does not share a high degree of similarity in its members' decision strategies. Due to processing limitations and the lack of effective measurement tools for identifying each other's preference or utility functions, a dyad is also expected to reveal biases in similarity perception. The dyad members' perceptions of similarity in their decision strategies would be heavily influenced by their agreement on a limited number of important dimensions, such as RIDs. To be more specific, each member of the dyad is preoccupied with "ills to be remedied rather than positive goals to be sought" (Lindblom 1979), thus revealing greater concern about home features the other can not accept (RIDs) than about those the other would like to have.

It was also noted earlier than each member of a dyad would recognize each other's influence for *some* dimensions on which task specialization and/or concession heuristics were activated during their decision. On these dimensions, the spouse who influenced the other more is expected to perceive more satisfaction. If this holds true, it would be additional indirect support of an individual's own utility enhancing decision strategy.

Finally, two of the three major conflict-avoiding heuristics are empirically examined in the present study. The dyad is expected to establish common preference levels on the salient objective dimensions (e.g., the number of bedrooms) more than on salient subjective dimensions (e.g., insulation). Ease of identification of the spouse's preference level and a rigid standard on objective dimensions have already been pointed out as reasons for this expectation. Based upon a task specialization heuristic, dyad members are also hypothesized to be aware of their mutual relative influence, primarily on the role-differentiated dimensions only.

From this rationale, the following hypotheses are derived:

H1: Dyads do not reveal a high degree of similarity in their decision plans over several decision stages.

H2: A dyad's self-perception of similarity in its members' decision plans is heavily determined by agreement on rejection inducing dimensions (RIDs).

H3: Members of a dyad perceive more satisfaction with those dimensions of the chosen home for which they influenced the other more.

H4: Dyad members agree with each other more on the salient objective dimensions than on salient subjective dimensions.

H5: Dyad members' awareness of their mutual relative influence on salient dimensions is limited mostly to role-differentiated dimensions.

METHOD

Overview

The study was conducted in a moderate-sized midwestern university town in January 1977. The daily newspaper in the university community publicized the author's real estate research, its purpose, and its potential benefits for home buyers, students, and realtors. The publicity prompted six real estate agencies to provide financial support and staff cooperation.

When prospective customers (joint buyers) contacted the real estate agency, the salesperson showed them a letter soliciting their cooperation in the present study. The letter explained the study's purpose, the amount of time required, and the conditions for qualifying as a participant. These conditions were that (1) they needed to either make an offer for a home they would like to buy or purchase a home, and (2) the offer or purchase must be made within a six-month period after initial contact with the researcher. These conditions were imposed to ensure that the subjects were serious buyers. A further condition was that both spouses be actively involved in the search process. Finally, $20 was promised as a token of appreciation for their help. The salesperson also solicited customer cooperation by explaining the potential benefits from participating in the study, such as gaining greater insights into their choice decision.

Once the customers agreed to participate in the study, the salesperson informed the author of the customers' names and telephone numbers. In most cases, personal contact was made with both spouses within two or three days after notification by the salesperson.

The subjects were informed that there were three occasions when personal contact with the research team would be required: (1) before the customer engaged in home search with a salesperson; (2) after the customer had examined 12 homes, or three weeks after the initial contact, whichever came first; and (3) after the customer either made an offer on a home of purchased a home.

Subjects

Sixty dyads agreed to participate in the present study. Twelve did not make an offer by the end of the data collection period; thus 48 met the requirements of the study. The responses of two of these subjects contained missing information, so for some of the analyses reported later, they were not included. Of the total of 48 dyads, 41 purchased their homes, while the remaining seven made offers on homes that were not accepted.[4] Only 15 dyads were questioned at the after-search stage, before the offer or purchase stage, since the remaining dyads had already made an offer to buy a home they liked before the after-search stage measures could be taken.[5]

[4]The respondents were all ages 30 to 49, and highly educated (73 percent of household heads had a bachelor's degree or beyond); the median household income was $18,800.

[5]A time period of three weeks after the before-search stage contact was the minimum time required for the after-search stage contact. In most cases the actual contact at the after-search stage took place 4 to 6 weeks after the before-search stage, due to the problem of identifying a mutually convenient time.

Measurement

Each subject's decision plan net was constructed by one of the two different interviewers (the author and a graduate student).[6] Interviews took place in the subjects' homes. Each subject was asked separately to perform two tasks: construct a decision plan net and respond to a questionnaire. Due to the time required, the actual administration of the questionnaire and the net construction were performed sequentially by both spouses, so that they would be completed within the same period of time—i.e., while the interviewer was constructing one spouse's decision plan net, the other filled out the before-search stage questionnaire, and vice versa. The sequence of who first filled out the questionnaire was alternated at the after-search and post-choice stages.[7] The entire interview took 40 to 90 minutes.

In constructing the net, subjects were asked to familiarize themselves with a list of 24 basic dimensions that had been identified as a representative set of home features, according to American Home Builder's Association. This list of dimensions (along with some descriptions) was provided because it was necessary that a common vocabulary (dimensions) be used in describing decision strategies; it was also desirable to minimize the possible failure to retrieve salient dimensions from memory.[8] The net construction procedure was carried out at the three different stages (before-search, after-search, and post-choice) in the same way. At the post-choice stage, the subjects were asked to reconstruct their choice as accurately as possible.

The before-search questionnaire information consisted of:

- Self-reported similarity perceptions: the question was "how similar do you feel your spouse's preference is to yours for various features of a home in a home selection decision?" A seven-point scale was employed ranging from "same" (7) to "very different" (1).
- Upper limit of planned purchase price and tax amount for the home to be chosen.

The after-search stage questionnaire included a question on how confident the spouse felt about the other's ability to properly evaluate each of the 24 home features, on a seven-point scale ranging from "very confident" (7) to "neutral" (4) to "not confident at all" (1). Each subject was then asked to evaluate his or her own ability.

The post-choice stage questionnaire sought information about the actual price and tax amount paid for a home; the subject's perceived relative importance, from "very important" (7) to "not important at all" (1) on each of the 24 dimensions for his or her home selection decision; and perceived satisfaction on each of the 24 dimensions. (In the case of the 11 objective features, the satisfaction question was asked for each of the identifiable levels.) A seven-point scale ranging from "very satisfactory" (7) to "average" (4) to "not satisfactory at all" (1) was used to measure satisfaction. The question of "who influenced more" on each of the 24 dimensions in making a home selection decision was measured using three discrete categories: "I influenced more," "my spouse influenced more," and "don't know." Finally, several subjects were asked to construct their own decision plan nets (based on the interviewer's instruction) 20 to 30

---

[6]The two interviewers practiced the same procedure in constructing a net using two prospective home buyers (a couple not included in the present sample) to ensure that the procedure would work. Finally, two additional prospective homebuyers' (a couple's) decision plan nets were constructed independently by the two interviewers to assess interviewer consistency. The two nets were identical.

[7]Prior to actual data collection, this alternation of sequence was compared with no such alternation using four prospective buyers. This comparison did not reveal any apparent bias. A further test of possible bias was performed using data from seven couples for whom the net construction and questionnaire responses were administered sequentially without alternating their sequence. The results were very similar to those reported in the present study for the total sample.

[8]During net construction, the subjects were allowed to use features other than those on the list that they viewed as influential in their choice decision. In specifying a decision plan, each subject was told to provide carefully considered responses that would reflect his/her future decisions. Each subject was also asked not to be concerned about the time taken to complete the task.

minutes after completing their responses at the post-choice stage.

RESULTS

> Hypothesis 1: *Dyads do not reveal a high degree of similarity in their decision plans over several decision stages.*

To test the first hypothesis, the degree of the dyad members' similarity in their decision plans and their convergence during several decision stages were examined. Consider a husband who specified insulation, number of bedrooms, and price as a choice criteria in his decision plan net at the before-search stage, defining all three dimensions as RIDs. Suppose further that his wife selected price, interior design, and number of bedrooms as her choice criteria, defining the first two dimensions as RIDs and the third as a RPD at the before-search stage. Decision plans nets of both spouses are shown in Figure 23.2

Given both spouses' decision plans, the extent of similarity (agreement) can be examined using two different bases: choice criteria and intended strategies (RIDs, RPDs, or TDs). To illustrate the similarity measure based on choice criteria, consider the decision plan nets in Figure 23.2. A total of four dimensions appear either in the husband's or in the wife's nets. Of these four, two dimensions—price and number of bedrooms—appear in both spouses' nets. Agreement by both spouses on choice criteria is thus calculated to be 0.5 (2/4). Agreement by both spouses on choice criteria is referred to as "partial agreement."

A similarity measure based on both spouses' intended strategies for these choice criteria is somewhat different from that of partial agreement. An examination of both spouses' intended strategies on price and number of bedrooms shows that they have the same strategy for the price dimension (a RID), while revealing a difference for the number-of-bedrooms dimension. In terms of their intended strategies, both spouses agreed with each other on only one of four dimensions (price) that appeared in one or both of the two nets. The similarity measure is therefore calculated to be 2.5 (1/4). This measure of similarity (agreement) is referred to as "perfect agreement." Unlike the perfect agreement case, no consideration was given in the partial agreement case to the difference in spouses' intended strategies on choice criteria.

Following the procedure outlined above, a similarity analysis was performed, with the results shown in Table 23.1.[9] Only 15 of the 48 couples' decision plans were obtained at the after-search stage. Values without parentheses in Table 23.1 are based on these 15 couples' responses, while those in the parentheses are based on all 48 couples' responses. These results

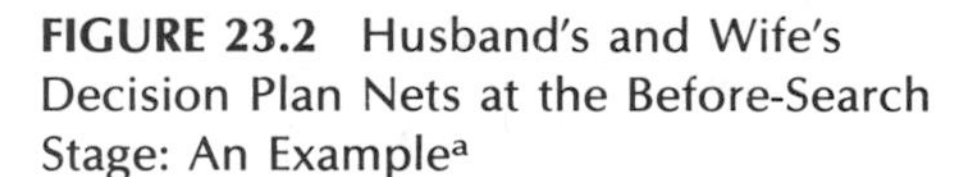

FIGURE 23.2 Husband's and Wife's Decision Plan Nets at the Before-Search Stage: An Example[a]

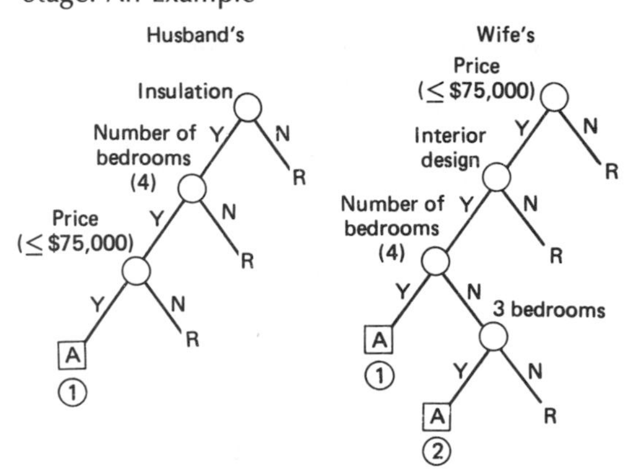

[a]A similarity measure based upon choice criteria only (partial agreement) = 0.5 (2/4); a similarity measure based upon intended strategies on the choice criteria (perfect agreement) = 0.25 (1/4).

[9]It should be noted that in identifying the subject's decision strategies on price and other objective dimensions, differences in the dyad members' threshold levels were explicitly considered. To illustrate, both the husband and wife may have defined price as a rejection inducing dimension (RID) at the before-search stage. However, suppose the husband's threshold level was $60,000, while his wife's threshold level was $80,000. The present study treated the dyad as "different" in its intended strategies if the difference between the two threshold values exceeded 10 percent of the lower of the two. For the subjective dimensions, threshold levels were not included because it was not feasible to identify them.

TABLE 23.1 Dyadic Decision Plan Similarity by Choice Stages

Wife	*Husband* Before-search Stage	After-search Stage	Post-choice Stage
	A. Partial Agreement		
Before-search stage	0.41[a] (0.41)[b]	0.39	0.41 (0.35)
After-search stage	0.45	0.47	0.42
Post-choice stage	0.35 (0.32)	0.44	0.47 (0.38)
	B. Perfect agreement		
Before-search stage	0.25 (0.22)	0.20	0.23 (0.20)
After-search stage	0.17	0.30	0.22
Post-choice stage	0.14 (0.14)	0.24	0.30 (0.23)

[a]Based on the 15 couples who were measured at the before-search, after-search, and post-choice stages.

[b]Based on the 48 couples who were measured at the before-search and post-choice stages.

reveal relatively low similarity between the members of a dyad in their decision plans at any given choice stage.

The proportions under "partial agreement" in Table 23.1 are relatively low. On average, less than half of the dimensions considered by both spouses were common ones. The extent of this agreement can hardly be stated to be high, considering that it is a relatively loose agreement criterion, and that a list of the dimensions was available to couples during net construction at each of the three stages, thus making temporary failure in retrieving the salient dimensions from their long-term memory unlikely. The level of agreement is further reduced under "perfect agreement," which is a more rigid requirement for the similarity measure.

More significantly, there appears to be no convergence between dyad members over the two or three different choice stages. Of all the dimensions appearing in one or both of a dyad members' nets, only 25 percent reveal perfect agreement at the before-search stage. At neither the after-search stage nor the post-choice stage does this proportion reveal any significant increase. The increases from the before-search stage to either the after-search or the post-choice stages are not significant ($t = 1.09$, $df = 14$, $p < 0.29$, and $t = -1.52$, $df = 14$, $p < 0.15$, respectively). Similar results are found for partial agreement. Approximately 41 percent of all dimensions that appeared in one or both of the spouses' nets at the before-search stage are common ones (i.e., the dimension appeared in both spouses' nets), and this proportion remains virtually the same at the post-choice stage.

These results suggest that each spouse follows his or her own choice strategy, without any significant convergence in later choice stages. Furthermore, comparison of proportions in the off-diagonal cells with those in the diagonal cells in Table 23.1 reveals interesting results. Compare the proportion in the cell with both spouses at the before-search stage (0.25) to that in the cell with a husband's after-search net and a wife's before-search net (0.20) in the perfect agreement section of Table 23.1. The small change in proportions between these two cells suggests that, given a difference in both spouses' decision strategies at the before-search stage, husbands at the after-search stage did not incorporate their wives' decision strategies. The small change in proportions between the wife before-search, husband before-search cell (0.25) and the husband before-search, wife after-search cell (0.17) also suggests that, given a rather low similarity between both spouses at the before-search stage, wives did not incorporate their husbands' decision strategies at the after-search stage. This comparison reveals that there appeared to be no systematic pattern of influence by husbands over their wives or vice versa over the several decision stages.

Finally, dyad members' low similarity in their choice criteria (partial agreement) at the post-choice stage (as well as at the early decision stage) suggests that they reached the decision mostly for different reasons.

> Hypothesis 2: *A dyad's self-perception of similarity in its members' decision plans is heavily determined by agreement on rejection inducing dimensions (RIDs).*

To test the second hypothesis, each spouse's

self-report of the perceived similarity in their home choice decisions was examined. The average self-reported similarity responses from husbands and wives were 5.57 and 5.56, respectively, which are relatively high in terms of the absolute level of the similarity response. However, the correlation between the similarity responses of husbands and wives is not high ($r = 0.25$, $p < 0.05$). This suggests differences in each couples similarity perceptions. To identify what factors affect the degree of their perceived similarity or dissimilarity (H2), a two-group discriminant analysis was performed. Two groups were established, based upon whether or not the two spouses' responses fell simultaneously in the "similarity zone." That is, couples whose similarity responses were both equal to or greater than 5 (7 = "the same" and 1 = "very different") were assigned to the first group (30 couples), and the remaining couples were assigned to the second group (16 couples). Four independent variables were used:

- The first variable (RIDC) refers to the total number of dimensions that both the husband and wife defined in the same way as RIDs (rejection inducing dimensions).
- The second variable (PTC) refers to the total number of dimensions that both the husband and wife defined in the same way as RPDs (relative preference dimensions) or as TDs (trade-off dimensions).
- The third variable (RPTC) is the total number of dimensions that both spouses defined differently. To illustrate, suppose a husband defined a dimension as a RID and his wife defined the same dimension as a RPD or a TD. This would count as a dimension the spouses defined differently.
- The fourth variable (RPTAC) refers to the total number of dimensions that a husband (wife) defined as either a RID, a RPD, or a TD and that a wife (husband) did not mention in her (his) decision plan net.

These four variables are examined in terms of their contribution to the distinction between the two groups in a step-wise discriminant analysis. The discriminating power of the variable sets is represented by Rao's V, and the significance of changes is determined by a chi-square test.

Three variables (RIDC, PTC, and RPTC) were selected sequentially before the addition to Rao's V became nonsignificant. They produced a significant separation, as indicated by a final Wilk's lambda value of 0.81 and a significant Rao's V (at the 0.02 level). However, the first variable (RIDC) alone provides significant discriminating power (at the 0.04 level, Wilks $\Lambda = 0.91$) similar to that obtained with all three variables (Wilks $\Lambda = 0.81$). Standardized discriminant function coefficients (-0.99 for RIDC, in contrast to -0.45 and -0.58 for PTC and RPTC, respectively) further support the importance of the first variable (RIDC). It is interesting that RPTC (the number of dimensions defined differently by both spouses) contributed to similarity perception, while in fact it should have contributed to dissimilarity perception.

This latter result suggests that each spouse perceives similarity on the basis of the presence or absence of the dimensions themselves, and is less concerned with the judgment within that dimension (how the dimension is defined). Once presence/absence has been determined and the focus shifts to within a dimension, the rejection inducing dimension (RIPD) appears to be the most significant in influencing the similarity perception. This renders partial support for Hypothesis 2.

It was pointed out earlier that the average self-reported similarities were relatively high (5.57 and 5.56). These high self-reported similarities are an interesting contrast to the relatively low similarity in the dyad members' decision plans (H1). This contrast suggests that the dyad members think they are more similar to each other than they actually are.

> Hypothesis 3: *Members of a dyad perceive more satisfaction with those dimensions of the chosen home for which they influenced the other more.*

If Hypothesis 3 is supported, it is additional indirect evidence of a couple's disjoint decision strategy. The 40 couples who reported agreement on their relative influence on at least one dimension were included in this analysis. The result reveals only partial support for the hypothesis. For the husbands, the result is not the anticipated direction. Specifically, when a wife felt that she played a more influential role than her husband on certain dimensions (confirmed by the husband), her satisfaction with those dimensions for their chosen home was significantly higher than the husband's satisfaction ($p < 0.07$) with the same dimensions. However, husbands did not feel more satisfaction on the dimensions on which they were more influential ($p < 0.83$).

In addition, a wife's mean satisfaction toward the dimensions on which she was more influential is significantly higher (6.20) than her satisfaction (5.70) toward the dimensions on which her husband was more influential ($p < 0.03$). On the other hand, a husband's mean satisfaction toward the dimensions on which he had more influence (5.75) is not significantly different from his satisfaction (5.80) toward the dimensions for which his wife was more influential ($p < 0.82$).

Regardless of who influenced more, the satisfaction revealed by each spouse was far greater than "average" (a scale value of 4). The lowest average satisfaction rating is 5.70, for wives on dimensions on which husbands influenced more. This suggests that agreement by one spouse with another's decision is reached most often when the latter's decision (or preference) is also above the minimum level of aspiration for the former.

Hypothesis 4: *Dyad members agree with each other more on salient objective dimensions than on salient subjective dimensions.*

To test this hypothesis, the salient dimensions that appeared in either one or both of the spouses' nets were divided into two types: objective and subjective dimensions. Any dimension for which levels can be objectively articulated was classified as an objective dimension: age of home, central air conditioning, basement, fireplace, fenced yard, humidifier, number of bedrooms, number of bathrooms, garage, patio, price, size of home, tax amount, and wet bar. The remaining were assigned to the subjective dimension category: appearance (attractiveness), builder's reputation, insulation, interior design, landscaping, location, neighborhood, recreational facilities, and resale value.

Two proportions were then derived for each couple for objective and subjective dimensions by dividing the number of dimensions showing perfect agreement by the total frequency of the perfect, partial, and no agreement categories. Note that the no agreement category refers to dimensions that appeared in either the husband's or the wife's decision plan nets, but not in both. The mean values across couples were then compared. The result reveals higher agreement (mean = 0.28) for the objective dimension type than for the subjective dimension type (mean = 0.18). This difference is statistically significant at the 0.004 level ($t = 3.01$, $df = 45$).

Hypothesis 5: *Dyad members' awareness of their mutual relative influence on salient dimensions is limited mostly to role-differentiated dimensions.*

The role-differentiated dimension is identified based on agreement between both spouses on their perceived confidence of self and spouse's ability to properly evaluate each dimension that appeared in one or both of their decision plan nets at the before-search stage. This confidence measure was obtained from 15 couples.[10] For example, if the husband feels more confident than his wife on the proper evaluation of insulation, and his wife agrees that he is more knowledgeable on that dimension, insulation is defined as a role-differentiated dimension.

There were 30 dimensions in total that were role differentiated. On 22 of these 30 dimensions, there was agreement on their mutual relative influence. On the other hand, there were 126 dimensions without role differentia-

[10]This confidence measure was administered at the after-search stage, when only 15 couples were measured. Thus a test of this hypothesis is based on the data from these 15 couples alone.

tion. The 15 couples agreed on relative influence for only 44 of these 126 dimensions. The difference between the two proportions is statistically significant at the 0.01 level ($z = 3.8$).

This suggests that for dimensions with role differentiation, dyad members are aware of their mutual relative influence in making a choice decision, and maintain a complementary relationship that facilitates their joint decision. This result may appear circular, in the sense that if both spouses agree that one member is able to evaluate a dimension better, it may be just another way of asking who had more influence. However, the present result is intended to reveal that it is only in such role-differentiated cases that both spouses are able to recognize their mutual relative influence.

Further analysis of the dyad members' mutual relative influence was performed for each dimension. As noted in the methods section, each member of the dyad was asked to indicate "who influenced more" on each of the 24 dimensions in making a home selection decision. Three discrete categories were provided: "I influenced more," "my spouse influenced more," and "don't know." An examination of the response distributions reveals interesting results (Table 23.2):[11] husbands were predominantly responsible for financial dimensions such as price, resale value, and insulation, while wives were very influential for dimensions such as attractiveness, interior design, location, and home style. These results are similar to those of Davis (1970) on the roles played by husbands and wives.

An earlier analysis (H3) revealed that husbands did not feel higher satisfaction for the dimensions they influenced more than their wives. This may have been due to the specific dimensions the husbands influenced. Very often a couple cannot purchase a satisfactory home within the price range and tax amount originally planned (Park et al. 1981). In the present study, 15 of the 46 couples bought homes at prices exceeding their (husband's) planned upper-limit price. Further, 13 other couples paid prices which were within 10 percent of their upper limit. Recognition of such discrepancies between the intended and the actual prices paid might have negatively affected the husband's felt satisfaction for financial dimensions such as price (tax amount) and resale value. This could explain why the husbands did not feel higher satisfaction with dimensions they influenced more than their wives.

Comparison of the dyad's decision plans over several decision stages did not reveal either high initial similarity or evidence of convergence over time. This finding was interpreted as evidence of a muddling-through process. However, it may be argued that the decision plan net methodology may have encouraged each spouse to report his or her own decision strategy rather than any joint strategy that may have emerged. Therefore, the earlier result (low similarity and lack of convergence) may not be used to support the muddling-through process.

This argument cannot be supported, however, in view of the results associated with Hypothesis 5. The dyad members were not aware of their mutual influence on a majority of the salient dimensions indicated at the before-search stage. Additional evidence is also available for supporting the muddling-through process. The subjects (15 couples) providing data for testing Hypothesis 5 gave "don't know" responses for 49 percent of the dimensions in the decision plan nets at the before-search stage. The result, based on all of the 46 couples, also revealed similar results at the before-search stage ("don't know" responses for 51 percent of the dimensions). When a dyad's relative influence responses are examined using dimensions that appeared in the post-choice stage net, a similar result is obtained ("don't know" responses for 48 percent of the dimensions). Even after they had made a home choice decision, there was no significant decrease in "don't know" responses. If, as the synoptic ideal suggests, the couples were aware of each other's

[11] Both spouses were defined as in agreement when one member of the dyad indicated that s/he influenced the other more, with the latter's agreement. Both spouses were defined as in disagreement when they indicated that each influenced the other more. When one or both spouses gave a "don't know" response, both spouses were classified "don't know."

TABLE 23.2 Couple's Relative Influence Responses on Dimensions Appearing in the Before-Search Net

	Agreement[a]				
Dimension	*Husband Influence*	*Wife Influence*	*Subtotal*	*Disagreement[b]*	*Don't Know Response[c]*
Age of home	2	7	(9)	3	16
Attractiveness	1	11	(12)	4	10
Central air conditioning	4	3	(7)	0	18
Basement	9	5	(14)	3	13
Builder's reputation	1	0	(1)	1	4
Fireplace	4	4	(8)	1	18
Fenced yard	3	4	(7)	2	10
Humidifier	0	0	(0)	0	1
Insulation	11	3	(14)	1	10
Interior design	0	13	(13)	6	8
Landscaping	3	1	(4)	1	13
Location	3	13	(16)	7	19
Neighborhood	2	6	(8)	4	18
Bedroom	3	9	(12)	7	26
Bathroom	3	5	(8)	2	17
Garage	10	1	(11)	0	20
Patio	0	0	(0)	0	7
Price	17	3	(20)	8	16
Recreation facilities	1	1	(2)	0	3
Resale value	13	2	(15)	2	7
Size of home	1	8	(9)	7	9
Style of home	2	11	(13)	1	10
Tax amount	7	0	(7)	3	10
Wet bar	0	0	(0)	0	0

[a]A dyad's response reveals an agreement about who influenced more on the dimension.

[b]A dyad's response reveals a disagreement about who influenced more on the dimension (i.e., each spouse indicated that s/he influenced the other more).

[c]Either one or both of a dyad revealed a "don't know" response about who influenced more on the dimension.

decision strategies, then the above finding is difficult to explain.

Further support for a muddling-through process can be found in examining the frequency of couples' agreements in relative influence on the dimensions in the RPTAC category, which refers to a situation where a dimension such as a basement is salient in a husband's decision plan net but not in the wife's net. If both spouses were aware of each other's choice decision strategy, a wife would be aware of her husband's preference for this dimension, thus either finding a home with a basement or overruling her husband's preference. Under this situation, a high frequency of "agreement" responses (either "husband influenced more" or "wife influenced more" responses by both spouses) should be expected compared with "don't know" responses.

The results of this category (RPTAC), based on the before-search stage nets, revealed that "don't know" responses (48 percent) were higher than either "agreement" (41 percent) or "disagreement" (11 percent) responses. The results based on the post-choice stage net revealed a similar pattern (51 percent, 39 percent, and 10 percent for "don't know," "agreement," and "disagreement" responses, respectively). These results support the argument that a husband and wife are relatively poor in understanding each other's decision strategies and identifying their mutual relative influence. The dyad members could certainly have discussed their preferences and decision strategies with each other during the decision process. However, they seemed neither to provide information about their decision strategies nor to process information about the other member's decision strategies.

DISCUSSION

The present study conceptualized a joint decision as a muddling-through process, characterized by limited knowledge and awareness of each spouse's decision strategies. However, by relying on conflict-avoiding heuristics, the dyad was hypothesized to reach a choice effectively. The results of the present study appear to support this conceptualization.

The concession heuristic proposed as facilitating joint decision-making was not tested directly because preference conflict, a necessary condition for this heuristic, was either difficult to identify or not commonly present. It could not be identified for subjective dimensions, since there were no objectively identifiable levels (e.g., interior design). For objective dimensions, most dyad members did not reveal preference conflicts. Perhaps a controlled experimental setting would be a better way to test this heuristic.

Some discussion concerning the reliability and validity of a decision plan net is called for. Reliability may be assessed from the comparison of two constructions of the decision plan net, one by the interviewer and the other by the subject. Specifically, as noted in the methods section, 24 subjects were asked to construct their own decision plan nets after the net had been constructed by the interviewer. Comparison of the two nets revealed that, for the 19 respondents who were able to complete the construction of their own nets, there was a perfect match on 125 of the total of 179 dimensions (70 percent). The mismatches on the remaining dimensions (30 percent) were as follows:

- 24 dimensions appeared in the nets constructed by the interviewer, but not in the subjects' own nets
- 17 dimensions appearing in the two nets were defined in different ways
- 13 dimensions appeared in the subjects' nets but not in the nets constructed by the interviewer

This result appears to support the reliability of the decision plan net. Note also that Park and Lutz (1982) found that subjects maintained their decision plans over three or more weeks of an actual decision period with a relatively low degree of variation.

Earlier studies (Park et al. 1981; Park and Lutz 1982) employed the decision plan net for the purpose of predicting a DM's choice and for examining the dynamic changes of the DM's decision plan. The results of these studies provide several findings that support the predictive as well as the descriptive validity of the instrument. First, when used to predict the DM's choice among alternatives at a later time, the decision plan net was found to be a useful and effective predictor. Second, an examination of the importance ratings of attributes contained in the DM's decision plan supports the descriptive validity of the decision plan net. Specifically, the rejection inducing, trade-off, and relative preference dimensions should be assigned monotonically decreasing importance ratings by subjects, and these ratings should be higher than those assigned to dimensions that do not appear in the decision plan net (absent dimensions).

Examination of importance ratings for these four dimensions types at the post-choice stage, for example, appears to support this expectation.[12] Importance ratings of 6.29, 5.71, 5.56 and 4.04 (on the seven-point scale) were revealed by the subjects for the rejection inducing, trade-off, relative preference, and absent dimensions, respectively. The same result was also obtained in a previous study (Park and Lutz 1982), which used individual home buyers as subjects instead of couples.

Finally, as Park and Lutz (1982) also pointed out, changes in the subjects' decision plans were accompanied by corresponding

[12]The subjects were not asked to provide importance ratings on some of the 24 dimensions at the before-search stage. Thus importance rating on the four dimension types at the before-search stage were not examined.

changes in importance ratings. For example, when a particular dimension did not appear in the net at the before-search stage but did appear at the post-choice stage, the subject's importance rating on the dimension tended to increase between the two time periods. This result is an added support for the descriptive validity of the decision plan net. Hence there is a reasonable amount of support for the validity of the decision plan net technique as a method of investigating decision strategies.

Caution is called for in generalizing the results of this study to all home buyers. As pointed out previously, the subjects were essentially self-selected and their educational distribution was not representative of the larger population. Finally, the value of a decision plan net in aiding joint decision makers in reaching a decision is yet to be determined, since in the present study, each member of the dyad was not allowed to examine the other's decision strategies as revealed in the net. However, given the results showing dyad members' limited knowledge about each other's decision plans, comparing each other's decision plan nets may be useful for identifying differences on salient dimensions, for developing a jointly acceptable set of alternatives, and for developing contingent decision strategies when the most preferred alternative is not available. Improvement in the quality of joint decisions may be expected with respect to the required amount of decision time, both spouses' appreciation of each other's role in their joint decision, and their satisfaction with a chosen alternative. These are important topics for further applied research in the marketing setting.

REFERENCES

ARROW, KENNETH J. (1963), *Social Choice and Individual Values,* New York: Wiley.

ASCHENBRENNER, MICHAEL K., DOROTHEE JAUS, and CIPRIANO VILLANI (1980), "Hierarchical Goal Structuring and Pupil's Job Choices: Testing a Decision AID in the Field," *Acta Psychologica,* 45, 35–79.

BEGG, IAN, and ALLAN PAIVIO (1969), "Concreteness and Imagery in Sentence Meaning," *Journal of Verbal Learning and Verbal Behavior,* 8, 831–837.

BETTMAN, JAMES R. (1979), *An Information Processing Theory of Consumer Choice.* Reading, MA: Addison-Wesley.

BRAYBROOKE, D., and CHARLES E. LINDBLOM (1963), *A Strategy of Decision: Policy Evolution as a Social Process.* New York: The Free Press.

CHOFFRAY, JEAN-MARIE (1977), "A Methodology for Investigating the Nature of the Industrial Adoption Process and the Differences in Perceptions and Evaluation Criteria Among Decision Participants," Ph.D. thesis, Massachusetts Institute of Technology, Cambridge, MA.

CURRY, DAVID J., and MICHAEL B. MENASCO (1979), "Some Effects of Differing Information Processing Strategies on Husband-Wife Joint Decisions," *Journal of Consumer Research,* 6, 192–203.

DAVIS, L. HARRY (1970), "Dimensions of Marital Roles in Consumer Decision Making," *Journal of Marketing Research,* 7, 168–177.

——— (1971), "Measurement of Husband-Wife Influence in Consumer Purchase Decisions," *Journal of Marketing Research,* 8, 305–312.

———, and PENNY RIGAUX (1974), "Perception of Marital Roles in Decision Processes, *Journal of Consumer Research,* 1, 51–62.

FERBER, ROBERT (1955), "On the Reliability of Purchase Influence Studies," *Journal of Marketing,* 19, 225–232.

——— (1971), "Family Decision-Making and Economic Behavior," Faculty Working Paper No. 35, College of Commerce and Business Administration, University of Illinois at Urbana-Champaign.

———, and LUCY CHAO LEE (1974), "Husband-Wife Influence in Family Purchasing Behavior," *Journal of Consumer Research,* 1, 43–50.

GOLDBERG, LEWIS (1968), "Simple Models or Simple Processes," *American Psychologist,* 23, 483–496.

GRANBOIS, DONALD H., and RONALD P. WILLETT (1970), "Equivalence of Family Role Measures Based on Husband and Wife Data," *Journal of Marriage and the Family,* 32, 68–72.

HABERMAN, PAUL W., and JACK ELINSON (1967), "Family Income Reported in Surveys: Husbands and Wives," *Journal of Marketing Research,* 4, 191–197.

HOLMES, V. M., and J. LANGFORD (1976), "Comprehension and Recall of Abstract and Concrete Sentences," *Journal of Verbal Learning and Verbal Behavior,* 15, 559-566.

KELLEY, HAROLD H. (1964), "Interaction Process and the Attainment of Maximum Joint Profit," in *Decision and Choice: Contributions of Sidney Siegel,* Eds. Samuel Messick and Arthur H. Brayfield. New York: McGraw-Hill.

KENKEL, WILLIAM F. (1961), "Husband-Wife Interaction in Decision Making and Decision Choices," *the Journal of Social Psychology,* 54, 255-262.

______, and D. K. HOFFMAN (1956), "Real and Conceived Roles in Family Decision Making," *Marriage and Family Living,* 18, 311-316.

LINDBLOM, CHARLES E. (1959), "The Science of Muddling Through," *Public Administration Review,* 19, 79-88.

______ (1979), "Still Muddling, Not Yet Through," *Public Administration Review,* 39, 517-526.

MACKENZIE, KENNETH D. (1976), "Group Problem Solving and Informational Impoverishment," paper presented at the Symposium on Consumer and Industrial Buying Behavior, University of South Carolina, March 25-26.

MILLER, GEORGE A., EUGENE GALANTER, and KARL H. PRIBRAM (1960), *Plants and the Structure of Behavior.* New York: Holt, Rinehart & Winston.

MINTZBERG, HENRY, DURU RAISINGHANI, and ANDRE THEORET (1976), "The Structure of Unstructured Decision Process," *Administrative Science Quarterly,* 21, 246-275.

MUNSINGER, GARY M., JEAN E. WEBER, and RICHARD W. HANSEN (1975), "Joint Home Purchasing Decisions by Husbands and Wives," *Journal of Consumer Research,* 1, 60-66.

MURRAY, EDWIN A., JR. (1978), "Strategic Choice as a Negotiated Outcome," *Management Science,* 24, 960-972.

OLSON, DAVID H. (1969), "The Measurement of Family Power by Self-Report and Behavioral Methods," *Journal of Marriage and the Family,* 31, 545-550.

PAIVIO, ALLAN (1971), *Imagery and Verbal Process.* New York: Holt, Rinehart & Winston.

PARK, C. WHAN (1978), "A Conflict Resolution Choice Model," *Journal of Consumer Research,* 5, 124-137.

______, ROBERT W. HUGHES, VINOD THUKRAL, and ROBERTO FRIEDMANN (1981), "Consumers' Decision Plans and Subsequent Choice Behavior," *Journal of Marketing,* 45, 33-47.

______, and RICHARD J. LUTZ (1982), "Decision Plans and Consumer Choice Dynamics," *Journal of Marketing Research,* 19, 108-119.

PATCHEN, MARTIN (1974), "The Locus and Basis of Influence in Organizational Decision," *Organizational Behavior and Human Performance,* 11, 195-221.

SCANZONI, JOHN (1965), "A Note on the Sufficiency of Wife Responses in Family Research," *Pacific Sociological Reviews,* 8, 109-115.

SHETH, JAGDISH N. (1974), "A Theory of Family Buying Decisions," in *Models of Buyer Behavior,* Ed. Jagdish N. Sheth. New York: Harper & Row.

______, and STEPHEN COSMAS (1975), "Tactics of Conflict Resolution in Family Buying Behavior," Faculty Working Paper No. 291, College of Commerce and Business Administration, University of Illinois at Urbana-Champaign.

SIEGEL, SIDNEY, and LAWRENCE E. FOURAKER (1960), *Bargaining and Group Decision Making.* New York: McGraw-Hill.

SILK, ALVIN J., and MANHAR U. KALWANI (1980), "Measuring Influence in Organizational Purchase Decisions," working paper, Sloan School of Management, Massachusetts Institute of Technology, Cambridge, MA.

SIMON, HERBERT A. (1945), *Administrative Behavior.* New York: The Free Press.

SPEKMAN, ROBERT E. (1978), "A Macro-Sociological Examination of the Industrial Buying Center: Promise or Problem?" *Proceedings, 1978 Educator's Conference,* Series No. 43. Chicago: American Marketing Association, 111-115.

STRODTBECK, FRED L. (1951), "Husband-Wife Interaction Over Revealed Differences," *American Sociological Review,* 16, 468-473.

SWINTH, ROBERT L. (1976), "A Decision Process Model for Predicting Job Preferences," *Journal of Applied Psychology,* 61, 242-245.

______, JACK E. GAUMNITZ, and CAROLOS RODRIGUEZ (1975), "Decision Making Processes: Using Discrimination Nets for Security Selection," *Decision Sciences,* 6, 439-448.

24

REFERENCE GROUP INFLUENCE ON PRODUCT AND BRAND PURCHASE DECISIONS*

William O. Bearden
Michael J. Etzel

Consumer perceptions of reference group influence on product and brand decisions were examined using 645 members of a consumer panel and 151 respondents in a followup study. Differences for 16 products in informational, value expressive, and utilitarian influence were investigated in a nested repeated measures design. The results support hypothesized differences in reference group influence between publicly and privately consumed products and luxuries and necessities.

For some time, social scientists have recognized group membership as a determinant of behavior. The fact that people act in accordance with a frame of reference produced by the groups to which they belong is a long-accepted and sound premise (Merton and Rossi 1949). However, even casual observation revealed perplexing contradictions between group membership and behavior. Many individuals simply did not behave like the majority of people in their recognized groups (e.g., social class or educational level). Though much of this uncharacteristic behavior was explainable by constructs other than group membership, the apparent instability of group influence created confusion. A partial solution was found in the concept of "reference groups," which recognizes that people frequently orient themselves to other than membership groups in shaping their behavior and evaluations and that reference groups can perform a diversity of functions (Merton and

*Reprinted from the *Journal of Consumer Research,* 9 (September 1982), pp. 183–194.

Rossi 1949). Marketers have generally accepted the reference group construct as important in at least some types of consumer decision making. The present study investigated reference group influence on product and brand purchase decisions by examining the interrelationships among two forms of product use conspicuousness (Bourne 1957) and three types of reference group influence (Park and Lessig 1977).

REFERENCE GROUP CONSTRUCT

The operationalization of reference groups is actually relatively recent. Hyman (1942) coined the term in a study of social status when he asked respondents with which individuals or groups they compared themselves. This initial characterization was followed by additional research (Newcomb 1943; Sherif 1948) and numerous refinements (Campbell et al. 1960; French and Raven 1959; Merton 1957; Sherif and Sherif 1964; Shibutani 1955; Smith, Bruner, and White 1956; Turner 1955) that clarified and expanded the meaning of the concept. For example, Kelly (1947) distinguished between reference groups used as standards of comparison for self-appraisal (comparative) and those used as a source of personal norms, attitudes, and values (normative).

This developing body of literature provided a basis for a series of applications undertaken in a number of fields. For example, Hyman and Singer (1968, p. 7) note that the concept has been applied in studies of farmers, scientists, alcoholics, newspaper people, the mentally ill, consumers, voters, juvenile delinquents, and opinion leaders. To that list could be added steel distributors (Kreisberg 1955), physicians (Coleman, Katz, and Menzel 1966), auto owners (Grubb and Stern 1971), cosmetic users (Moschis 1976), and students and housewives (Park and Lessig 1977).

In addition to investigating the presence of reference group influence within identifiable groups, there have been a series of consumer research studies into specific aspects of reference group influence. Venkatesan (1966) attempted to test the differential effects of compliance (Kelman 1961) and reactance (Brehm 1966) in an experiment involving subjects selecting the "best" from among identical suits under different forms of group pressure. He was able to establish the influence of voiced group sentiment on a subject (compliance); however, the method used in operationalizing reactance has been questioned (Clee and Wicklund 1980). Burnkrant and Cousineau (1975) demonstrated that people use others' product evaluations as a source of information about products.

In a study of consumer brand choice, Witt (1969) confirmed earlier nonmarketing studies which indicated that group cohesiveness influences behavior. The far-reaching influence of groups was suggested by Cocanongher and Bruce (1971), who found that socially distant reference groups can influence consumers if consumers hold favorable attitudes toward the members or activities of that group. Taking a somewhat different approach, Witt and Bruce (1970) found the operation of group influence related to the extent of social involvement associated with the product being investigated. Stafford (1966) found individual brand choice was affected by group influence.

The concept of group influence in consumer research has been further refined through studies of various aspects of the social influence process. Witt and Bruce (1972) suggested the existence of at least seven different determinants of influence including perceived risk, expertise of the referent, and the individual's need for social approval. Moschis (1976) found that consumers use both reflective and comparative appraisal (Jones and Gerard 1967) in product choices. That is, they engage in direct, verbal interaction to determine the reference group's evaluation as well as observing the behavior of reference group members in regard to the decision under consideration. Park and Lessig (1977) investigated reference group influence and found students more susceptible than housewives to group influence for a variety of products.

The construct is commonly used by marketing practitioners. Reference group concepts have been used by advertisers in their efforts to persuade consumers to purchase products and brands. Portraying products being consumed in socially pleasant situations, the use of prominent/attractive people endorsing products, and the use of obvious group members as spokespersons in advertisements (Kotler 1980) are all evidence that marketers and advertisers make substantial use of potential reference group influence on consumer behavior in the development of their communications. Alluding to reference groups in persuasive attempts to market products and brands demonstrates the belief that reference groups expose people to behavior and lifestyles, influence self-concept development, contribute to the formation of values and attitudes, and generate pressure for conformity to group norms.

RESEARCH HYPOTHESES

A reference group is a person or group of people that significantly influences an individual's behavior. Within this general framework, several types of influence have been identified. Based on the work of Deutsch and Gerard (1955) and Kelman (1961), information, utilitarian, and value-expressive influences have been identified (Park and Lessig 1977). Informational influence is based on the desire to make informed decisions. Faced with uncertainty, an individual will seek information. From the many sources available, the most likely to be accepted are those viewed as credible. Referents with high credibility include those with presumed expertise or significant others.

Utilitarian reference group influence is reflected in attempts to comply with the wishes of others to achieve rewards or avoid punishments. In an individual feels that certain types of behavior will result in rewards or punishments from others and these outcomes are viewed as important, he or she will find it useful to meet the expectations of these significant others.

A third type of influence, value-expressive, is characterized by the need for psychological association with a person or group and is reflected in the acceptance of positions expressed by others. This association can take two forms. One form is an attempt to resemble or be like the reference group. The second type of value-expressive influence flows from an attachment or liking for the group. The individual is responsive to the reference group out of a feeling for it, not because of a desire to be associated with it.

The occurrence of all of these forms of influence requires the opportunity for social interaction or public scrutiny of behavior. Seeking information, complying with the preference of others, and adopting values of others all involve some form of communication or observation of decisions, opinions, or behavior. In a purchase context, this implies products that will be seen by others. Besides the opportunity for observation, it is important to consider what elements of an item will be noticeable. Certainly one is the product itself, and another is the brand of the product. This approach is presented in what is probably the most recognized marketing discussion of reference group influence (Bourne 1957), in which the distinction between product and brand decisions is stressed.

Bourne (1957), p. 218) originally proposed that reference group influence on product and brand decisions is a function of two forms of "conspicuousness." The first condition, affecting product decisions, is that the item must be "exclusive" in some way. No matter how visible a product is, if virtually everyone *owns* it, it is not conspicuous in this sense. This is operationalized here as the distinction between luxuries and necessities. By definition, necessities are possessed by virtually everyone, while luxuries have a degree of exclusivity. Second, for reference group influence to affect brand decisions, the item must be "seen or identified by others." This can be operationalized in terms of *where* an item is consumed. Publicly consumed products are seen by others, while privately consumed products are not. That is, those brand decisions involving products which can be noticed and identified are more susceptible to reference group influence.

Combining the concepts of public—private consumption and luxury—necessity items produces the following four conditions: (1) publicly consumed luxuries, (2) publicly consumed necessities, (3) privately consumed luxuries, and (4) privately consumed necessities. When applied to product and brand decisions, these conditions create a total of eight relationships that are the basis underlying this study:

1. *Publicly consumed luxury (PUL)*—a product consumed in public view and not commonly owned or used (e.g., golf clubs). In this case, whether or not the product is owned and also what brand is purchased is likely to be influenced by others (Bourne 1957, p. 219).

Relationships with reference group influence:

   a. Because it is a luxury, influence for the *product* should be *strong*.
   b. Because it will be seen by others, influence for the *brand* of the product should be *strong*.

2. *Privately consumed luxury (PRL)*—a product consumed out of public view and not commonly owned or used (e.g., trash compactor). In many cases, the brand is not conspicuous or socially important and is a matter of individual choice, but ownership of the product does convey a message about the owner (Bourne 1957, p. 220).

Relationships with reference group influence:

   a. Because it is a luxury, influence for the *product* should be *strong*.
   b. Because it will not be seen by others, influence for the *brand* of the product should be *weak*.

3. *Publicly consumed necessity (PUN)*—a product consumed in public view that virtually everyone owns (e.g., wristwatch). This group is made up of products that essentially all people or a high proportion of people use, although differing as to the type of brand (Bourne 1957, p. 220).

Relationships with reference group influence:

   a. Because it is a necessity, influence for the *product* should be *weak*.
   b. Because it will be seen by others, influence for the *brand* of the product should be *strong*.

4. *Privately consumed necessity (PRN)*—a product consumed out of public view that virtually everyone owns (e.g., mattress). Purchasing behavior is largely governed by product attributes rather than by the influences of others. In this group, neither products nor brands tend to be socially conspicuous and are owned by nearly all consumers (Bourne 1957, p. 221).

Relationships to reference group influence:

   a. Because it is a necessity, influence for the *product* should be *weak*.
   b. Because it will not be seen by others, influence for the *brand* of the product should be *weak*.

These relationships are summarized in a modification of the Bourne framework in Exhibit 24.1 and presented in the form of the following 12 hypotheses for testing. The six product decision hypotheses (H_{1p} – H_{6p}) reflect the proposition that a luxury–necessity main effects exists, while no such effect is postulated for public–private influences. Consequently, for product decision comparisons, reference group influence is hypothesized to adhere to the following pattern:

$\mathbf{H_{1p}}$: PUL > PUN
$\mathbf{H_{2p}}$: PUL = PRL
$\mathbf{H_{3p}}$: PUL > PRN
$\mathbf{H_{4p}}$: PUN < PRL
$\mathbf{H_{5p}}$: PUN = PRN
$\mathbf{H_{6p}}$: PRL > PRN

In contrast, for the six brand decision hypotheses, a significant public–private main effect is hypothesized, while no such effect is postulated for the luxury–necessity factor. Reference group influence is expected then to follow the pattern embodied in these remaining six hypotheses:

$\mathbf{H_{1b}}$: PUL = PUN
$\mathbf{H_{2b}}$: PUL > PRL
$\mathbf{H_{3b}}$: PUL > PRN
$\mathbf{H_{4b}}$: PUN > PRL
$\mathbf{H_{5b}}$: PUN > PRN
$\mathbf{H_{6b}}$: PRL = PRN

METHOD

Preliminary Procedures

To select products for testing, a preliminary list of 81 products was developed. This list consisted of approximately 20 items that the au-

EXHIBIT 24.1 Combining Public–Private and Luxury–Necessity Dimension with Product and Brand Purchase Decisions

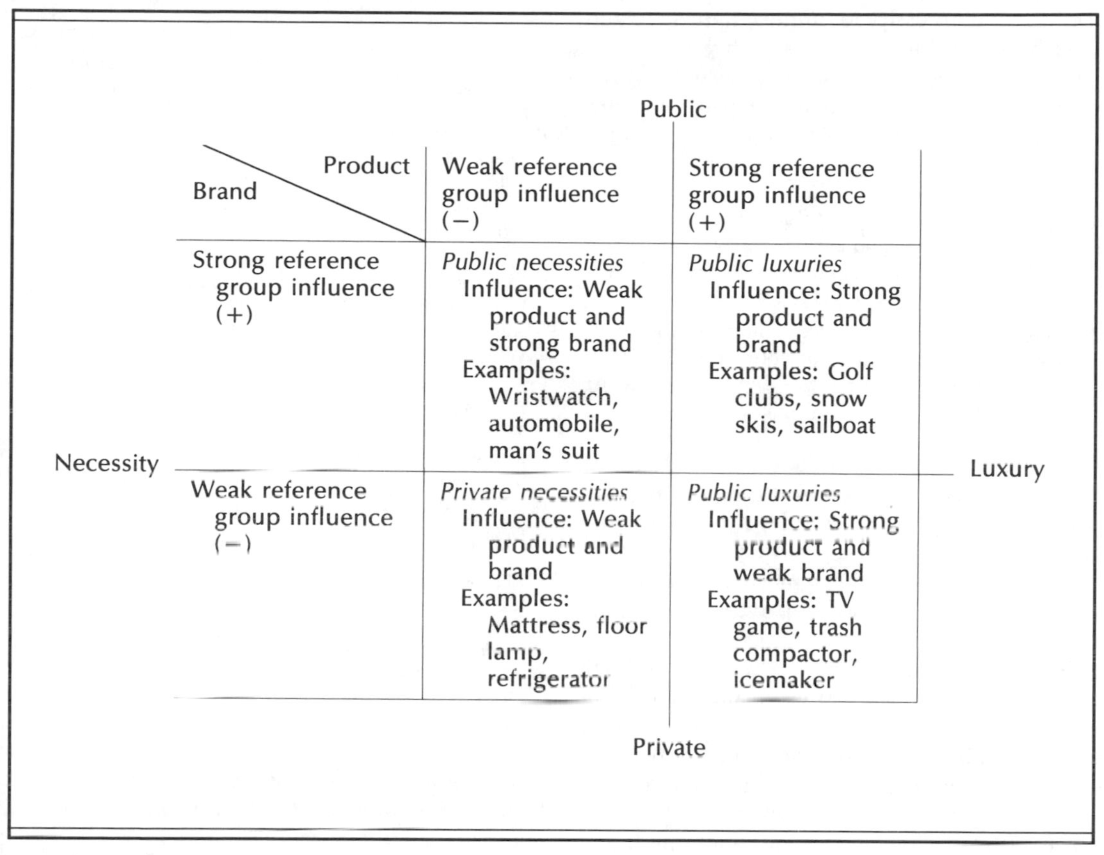

thors felt fell into each of the four conditions described previously. A questionnaire was constructed to assess perceptions of the individual products as publicly or privately consumed and as luxuries or necessities.

A convenience sample of nonstudent adults participated in this preliminary phase. The questionnaire was administered door-to-door in a middle-class residential area of Columbia, South Carolina in the spring of 1979. Adults agreeing to cooperate were given a copy of the survey, and completed responses were picked up the following day. One hundred households were initially contacted and a total of 57 usable responses were collected. Nonrespondents included those who did not complete the questionnaires and people not at home when the return visit was made. Demographic characteristics of the sample were: median education, 15 years; median age category, 31 to 35 years; and median family income category, $25,000 to $30,000.

Respondents were requested to indicate their perceptions about whether the 81 products were, first, luxury or necessity items, and then, publicly or privately used, on a series of six-point scales. The instructions to the instrument described luxuries as not needed for ordinary, day-to-day living. Necessities were described as being necessary for ordinary, day-to-day living. Response categories were labeled and scored as follows: (1) a luxury for everyone, (2) a luxury for almost all people, (3) a luxury for the majority of people, (4) a necessity for the majority of people, (5) a necessity for almost all people, and (6) a necessity for everyone.

The same 81 items were assessed by the respondents as being publicly or privately consumed. The following definitions were provided:

- A *public* product is one that other people are aware you possess and use. If they want to, others can identify the brand of the product with little or no difficulty.
- A *private* product is one used at home or in private at some location. Except for your immediate family, people would be unaware that you own or use the product.

The six-item scales were labeled: (1) a public product for everyone, (2) a public product for almost all people, (3) a public product for the majority of people, (4) a private product for the majority of people, (5) a private product for almost all people, and (6) a private product for everyone.

These two dimensions, i.e., public-private and luxury-necessity, represent the underlying determinants of conspicuousness, which Bourne assumed to be "the most general attribute bearing on a product's susceptibility to reference group influence" (1957, p. 218). First, the product must be conspicuous in the sense that it can be seen and identified (it is, consequently, presumed to be subject to disapproval). Second, the product must be conspicuous in the sense of exclusivity because it is not owned by everyone (Bourne 1957).

Based on the distribution of the resulting mean scores, four products were selected as representing each of the product categories: public-luxury (PUL), public-necessity (PUN), private-luxury (PRL), and private-necessity (PRN). The 16 products selected and their mean scores are presented in Table 24.1

TABLE 24.1 Pretest Mean Scores for Sixteen Products Examined[a]

	Scale comparison (value)	
Product category	*Public (1)–Private (6)*	*Luxury (1)–Necessity (6)*
Public luxury (PUL)		
Golf clubs	2.74	1.86
Sailboat	2.61	1.46
Snow skis	2.66	1.77
Tennis racket	2.66	2.28
Public necessity (PUN)		
Man's suit	2.85	4.39
Woman's dress	2.63	4.86
Automobile	1.64	4.66
Wristwatch	2.65	3.96
Private luxury (PRL)		
Pool table	4.12	1.57
Trash compactor	4.29	1.74
Automatic icemaker	4.28	1.73
Videogame	4.21	1.51
Private necessity (PRN)		
Refrigerator	4.02	5.35
Blanket	4.58	5.51
Mattress	4.33	5.19
Lamp	4.05	5.19

[a]Pretest results based on convenience sample of 57 nonstudent adults. Scales were bipolar items labeled public-private and luxury-necessity; scores ranged from 1 to 6.

Survey Design

The research design called for separate reference group influence evaluations of product and brand decisions for 16 products, for a total of 32 evaluations. To have a management questionnaire, it was decided that an individual respondent should be required to deal with a total of four evaluations. Thus, eight different versions of the survey instrument were constructed. Four versions contained only product decisions, and four contained brand decisions. One product was selected from each of the four categories—PUL, PUN, PRL, and PRN—to make up each of the versions. Thus an individual respondent received a packet containing a series of reference group influence questions regarding either product or brand decisions for four different products representing each of the four categories (i.e., public luxury through private necessity). Order of the product categories was randomized across the eight questionnaire versions to avoid order bias. The questionnaire and sample configurations are illustrated in Exhibit 24.2. This design results in decisions (product versus brand) and the product config-

EXHIBIT 24.2 Research Design Layout

			LUXURY	NECESSITY
Product Decisions	Group 1 (n = 88)	Public	PUL (golf clubs)	PUN (man's suit)
		Private	PRL (pool table)	PRN (refrigerator)
	Group 2 (n = 85)	Public	PUL (tennis racket)	PUN (wristwatch)
		Private	PRL (TV game)	PRN (floor lamp)
	Group 3 (n = 71)	Public	PUL (snow skis)	PUN (automobile)
		Private	PRL (icemaker)	PRN (mattress)
	Group 4 (n = 78)	Public	PUL (sailboat)	PUN (woman's dress)
		Private	PRL (trash compactor)	PRN (blanket)
Brand Decisions	Group 5 (n = 82)	Public	PUL (golf clubs)	PUN (man's suit)
		Private	PRL (pool table)	PRN (refrigerator)
	Group 6 (n = 75)	Public	PUL (tennis racket)	PUN (wristwatch)
		Private	PRL (TV game)	PRN (floor lamp)
	Group 7 (n = 80)	Public	PUL (snow skis)	PUN (automobile)
		Private	PRL (icemaker)	PRN (mattress)
	Group 8 (n = 86)	Public	PUL (sailboat)	PUN (woman's dress)
		Private	PRL (trash compactor)	PRN (blanket)

urations (e.g., mattress, automobile, golf clubs) serving as between-subjects factors. The luxury versus necessity and public versus private dimensions represent within-subject factors.

Reference group influence was assessed using 13 of the 14 individual items developed by Park and Lessig (1977, p. 105).[1] These items were designed to reflect informational, value-expressive, and utilitarian reference group influences. Informational reference group influence occurs when a person actively seeks information from people viewed as knowledgeable or observes the behavior of acknowledged experts. It is based on the concept of comparative influence suggested by Deutsch and Gerard (1955). Value-expressive reference group influence is characterized by a person behaving in a manner that will improve his or her self-image or create the impression of attachment to the group (Kelman 1961). Utilitarian reference group influence is reflected in compliance to group norms or standards to gain rewards or avoid punishments that may be forthcoming from the group (Asch 1952).

The individual items were operationalized as six-point bipolar agree(6)–disagree(1) statements. Scales were scored so that higher values represented greater influence perception. This is in contrast to the four-place "not relevant" to "highly relevant" scales that provided the option of three positive and one negative position used by Park and Lessig (1977). A balanced six-point scale offered respondents a more complete range of alternatives. The sampling procedure used by Park and Lessig (1977) in studying housewives and students involved telephone and mail surveys. This is somewhat different from the panel mailing used here, but is similar to the followup study described later.

Respondents were instructed to indicate their degree of agreement with each item as it applied to product or brand selection decisions. Example items regarding product decisions for each of the three reference group subscales follow:

- *Informational:* An individual would seek information about pool tables from fellow workers who are familiar with them.
- *Value-expressive:* An individual would probably feel that purchasing a pool table would enhance his or her image among other people.
- *Utilitarian:* An individual's decision about whether or not to buy a pool table would be influenced by the expectations of family members.

The three variations of group influence were represented as a summed composite of four informational, five value-expressive, and four utilitarian items. Since the items were designed to reflect three types of reference group influence, the individual items were combined to form measures of informational, value-expressive, and utilitarian reference group influence. Combining items into separate measures of three constructs was supported across brand and product decisions by coefficient alpha internal consistency estimates.[2] An informational influence item referring to independent testing agencies was omitted because it appeared awkward for some products included in the study.[3]

Data were collected from a mailing to 800 members of a statewide consumer panel during

---

[1]One of the eight versions was pretested on a convenience sample of 20 nonstudent adults for ease of understanding and completion. Based on the results of this pretest, several items in the reference group scale were slightly modified to improve clarity.

[2]Average internal consistency estimates (coefficient alpha) for the product decisions were 0.63, 0.88, and 0.71 for the informational, value-expressive, and utilitarian subscales, respectively. For the brand decisions, the respective internal consistency estimates averaged 0.70, 0.80, and 0.77. Test-retest reliability was assessed using two convenience samples of 78 and 40 students for one version of the product questionnaire and one version of the brand questionnaire in a three-week test-retest administration. All the test-retest correlations were significant ($p < 0.01$); the average values ranged from 0.53 to 0.68.

[3]Using the reference group subscales (e.g., informational) as methods and the product categories (e.g., PUL) as traits in an analysis similar to that reported by Park and Lessig (1977), the reference group subscales were further examined using the multitrait-multimethod procedure suggested by Campbell and Fiske (1959). The resulting correlations between measures of the same trait as evidence of convergence suggest that the informational measures are distinct from the value-expressive and utilitarian scales. Evidence of discrimination as demonstrated when correlations between a measure and another measure on the same

the summer of 1979. Panel households are selected to be representative of urban and rural residents with annual incomes above $5,000. However, the panel is somewhat upscale as a whole in terms of education and income when compared to Bureau of Census averages for the area.

The total sample of 800 was divided into eight subsamples of 100. Each subsample was sent one of the eight versions of the questionnaire (see Exhibit 24.2). Followup mailings resulted in 645 completed responses (80 percent usable response rate). The remaining 20 percent were equally divided between nonrespondents and incomplete or unusable replies. Cell sizes ranged from 71 to 88 for the four product decisions survey, and from 75 to 86 for the four brand decision evaluations. Comparisons of the demographic characteristics of the original 800 with the 645 respondents did not suggest significant differences between respondents and nonrespondents or unusable responses. The median family income category and average education for the respondents were $18,000 to $24,000 and 14.4 years, respectively. This is slightly lower than the profile for respondents to the pretest questionnaire.

The instructions introducing the questionnaire carefully distinguished between product and brand decisions. This was followed by an example in which product decisions were described as those involving a decision whether or not to buy, for example, a color television set. Choosing a color TV from among Magnavox, RCA, Zenith, and others was used to exemplify a brand decision. Instructions were then provided for responding to a six-point agree–disagree scale. Depending on whether it was a product or brand decision questionnaire, a sample product or brand question about 10-speed bicycles was presented, along with a scale to reinforce the type of decision the respondent was to make. At the beginning of each section of the questionnaire, the words "product decisions" or "brand decisions" were printed and underlined.

RESULTS

The overall results of the nested design were first examined using repeated measures multivariate analysis of variance. These results—along with the results of a followup study described later—are presented in Table 24.2. The type of decision (product versus brand) approached significance only for the informational reference group influence. Variations in the product configurations (the products included in each questionnaire) were significant for the value-expressive and utilitarian influence evaluations.

The within-subjects factors (i.e., luxury versus necessity, public versus private) and the interactions were all significant across the three reference group subscales, but there were differences in the pattern of results. The luxury–necessity dimension of conspicuousness appeared particularly sensitive regarding respondents' perceptions of informational reference group influence ($F = 550.98$, $p < 0.01$). In contrast, these overall results suggest that the public–private dimension affected value-expressive ($F = 761.22$, $p < 0.01$) and utilitarian ($F = 214.30$, $p < 0.01$) perceptions to a greater degree.

Product Category Comparisons

Differences in responses to the reference group influence scales across the four product categories (e.g., PUL, PUN, PRL, PRN) were examined separately for the product and brand decisions. The results of the repeated measures analysis of variance are presented in Table 24.3. In 23 of the 24 cases (8 product configurations × 3 influence dimensions), the individual analysis of variance F-values were significant ($p < 0.001$). These results suggest substantial differences in consumer perceptions of reference group influence across the four product categories represented by the specific products used in this study.

[3](Continued from page 442) trait are greater than correlations between measures having neither trait nor method in common was provided for the product and brand analyses 66 of 72 and 65 of 72 times, respectively.

TABLE 24.2 Overall Results of Manova Analyses

	Informational			Value-expressive			Utilitarian		
	F-value	*df*	*Probability*	*F-value*	*df*	*Probability*	*F-value*	*df*	*Probability*
Primary study (n = 645)									
Between-subjects factors									
Decision: Product vs. brand (PB)	5.18	1	.02	.58	1	.45	.57	1	.02
Grouping: Product configuration (PC)	1.41	3	.24	9.79	3	.00	5.41	3	.00
Interaction: PB × PC	1.75	3	.16	.96	3	.41	.98	3	.40
Within-subjects factors									
Luxury vs. necessity (LN)	550.98	1	.00	14.86	1	.00	16.22	1	.00
Public vs.private (PP)	5.85	1	.02	761.22	1	.00	214.30	1	.00
Interaction: LN × PP	14.96	1	.01	67.39	1	.00	70.91	1	.00
Followup study (n = 151)									
Between-subjects factors									
Grouping: Product configuration (PC)[a]	.01	1	.91	7.44	1	.01	4.01	1	.05
Within-subjects factors									
Decision: Product vs. brand (PB)	3.47	1	.06	28.31	1	.00	28.43	1	.00
Luxury vs. necessity (LN)	60.91	1	.00	5.98	1	.02	1.82	1	.18
Public vs. private (PP)	70.58	1	.00	124.23	1	.00	31.36	1	.00
PB × LN	18.38	1	.00	70.92	1	.00	25.15	1	.00
PB × PP	8.03	1	.00	.81	1	.37	.12	1	.72
LN × PP	16.84	1	.00	.02	1	.89	2.56	1	.11
PB × LN × PP	5.52	1	.02	1.25	1	.27	1.69	1	.20

[a]Difference in degrees of freedom (df) for product configuration factor are attributable to use of only two product combinations in the followup study.

TABLE 24.3 Mean Scores and Subgroup Anova Results[a]

		Product decisions				
Group/Influence	***N***	***PUL***	***PUN***	***PRL***	***PRN***	***F-value***
Group 1	88	Clubs	Suit	Pool table	Refrigerator	
Informational		19.88	14.68	19.02	18.39	55.20
Value-expressive		15.94	18.60	13.51	8.49	65.05
Utilitarian		11.96	14.62	12.77	9.53	31.16
Group 2	85	Racket	Watch	TV game	Lamp	
Informational		20.01	17.01	19.82	16.52	37.93
Value-expressive		14.29	11.34	10.40	8.61	30.63
Utilitarian		10.75	9.06	10.46	9.25	7.30
Group 3	71	Skis	Automobile	Icemaker	Mattress	
Informational		19.20	18.77	18.24	14.73	38.78
Value-expressive		13.44	14.69	9.19	8.10	45.49
Utilitarian		10.49	12.13	9.57	9.34	13.96
Group 4	78	Sailboat	Dress	Trash compactor	Blanket	
Informational		21.22	15.13	20.33	15.50	67.97
Value-expressive		18.29	18.95	9.32	8.21	123.13
Utilitarian		12.68	14.01	9.78	8.43	42.78

		Brand decisions				
Group/Influence	***N***	***PUL***	***PUN***	***PRL***	***PRN***	***F-value***
Group 5	82	Clubs	Suit	Pool table	Refrigerator	
Informational		19.98	14.35	19.04	18.00	58.02
Value-expressive		16.44	16.31	14.20	10.35	34.79
Utilitarian		12.15	12.78	11.99	9.53	13.65
Group 6	75	Racket	Watch	TV game	Lamp	
Informational		20.61	17.09	19.97	17.28	26.91
Value-expressive		14.96	13.43	10.88	11.72	16.36
Utilitarian		11.29	10.93	11.01	9.96	2.65
Group 7	80	Skis	Automobile	Icemaker	Mattress	
Informational		20.37	20.27	19.29	17.66	24.77
Value-expressive		12.62	13.49	9.67	8.51	28.53
Utilitarian		11.03	11.41	10.67	8.82	39.78
Group 8	86	Sailboat	Dress	Trash compactor	Blanket	
Informational		20.88	16.76	20.77	16.75	47.50
Value-expressive		15.28	18.72	10.66	9.74	81.62
Utilitarian		13.12	14.26	9.77	9.29	14.29

[a]All F-values except one (i.e., Group 6—Utilitarian) were significant ($p < 0.001$).

Given these overall differences, individual paired-comparison tests were run for each of the possible pairs of product categories by each type of reference group influence to test the research hypotheses.[4] These results, which are analyzed separately for the product and brand decisions, are provided in Table 24.4, along with the directional hypotheses. One-tailed tests were used when direction of influence was hypothesized. A conservative significance level ($p < 0.001$) was used to account for the increased probability of finding differences with the large number of individual comparisons.

For the nonequal hypotheses, 21 of 24 comparisons were significantly different. Eighteen of these differences were in the hypothesized

[4]In an effort to simplify presentation of the results, the paired-comparison hypothesis tests are based on averages across the product configurations for the brand and product decisions. Paired t-tests were also run on a product by product basis. These results were consistent with the average score results summarized in Table 24.4.

TABLE 24.4 Paired-Comparison Hypotheses and Results[a]

		Influence					
Comparison	***Hypotheses***	***Informational***		***Value-expressive***		***Utilitarian***	
Products (n = 322)							
PUL-PUN	>	20.02	16.21[b,e]	15.52	15.85	11.51	12.41
PUL-PRL	=[c]	20.02	19.33[b]	15.52	10.70[b]	11.51	10.71[a]
PUL-PRN	>	20.02	16.29[b,e]	15.52	8.38[b,e]	11.51	9.16[b,e]
PUN-PRL	<	16.21	19.33[b,e]	*15.85*	*10.79*[b]	*12.42*	*10.70*[b]
PUN-PRN	=[d]	16.21	16.29[e]	15.85	8.38[b]	12.42	9.16[b]
PRL-PRN	>	19.33	16.29[b,e]	10.79	8.38[b,e]	10.70	9.16[b,e]
Brands (n = 323)							
PUL-PUN	=[c]	20.17	16.99[b]	14.72	15.42[e]	11.83	12.27[e]
PUL-PRL	>	20.17	19.57[b,e]	14.72	11.26[b,e]	11.83	10.73[b,e]
PUL-PRN	>	20.17	17.19[b,e]	14.72	10.00[b,e]	11.83	9.31[b,e]
PUL-PRL	>	*16.99*	*19.57*[b]	15.42	11.26[b,e]	12.27	10.74[b,e]
PUN-PRN	>	16.99	17.19	15.42	10.00[b,e]	12.27	9.31[b,e]
PRL-PRN	=[d]	19.57	17.19[b]	11.26	10.00[b]	10.74	9.31[b]

[a]Figures represent scale mean scores combined across subgroups. Italics indicate pairs represent nonequal hypotheses significantly different but counter to expected direction.

[b]Paired *t*-tests were significantly different ($p < 0.001$); one-tailed tests were used when direction hypothesized. Informational and utilitarian values had possible ranges of 4 to 24; value-expressive values had a possible range of 5 to 30.

[c]Equivalent but strong reference group influence hypothesized.

[d]Equivalent but weak reference group influence hypothesized.

[e]Consistent with hypothesized influence.

direction. The three italicized pairs of values in Table 24.4 represent nonequal hypotheses that were found to be significantly different but counter to the expected direction. These three significant differences reflected public necessity-private luxury comparisons.

Eight of the 12 equal hypothesis comparisons were found to be significantly different. This is not particularly discouraging because hypothesizing that two measures are equal for different product categories is a fairly stringent assumption.

In sum, 22 of the 36 comparisons were consistent with the hypotheses. For the product analyses, these consistent findings were clustered (5 of 6) in the informational reference group influences; in the brand analyses, they were concentrated in the value-expressive (5 of 6) and utilitarian (5 of 6) reference group influences.

The fact that three types of reference group influences were measured does not imply that all three should be present or absent in an individual case. In fact, it would seem reasonable to find one type of influence operating and the others absent in a particular situation. For example, in the purchase of a man's suit, value-expressive influence might play a much larger role than either informational or utilitarian influence. Thus it is reasonable to consider the hypotheses from the point of view of the presence or absence of any type of reference group influence. From that perspective, all six relationships for product decisions and five out of six relationships for brand decisions are supported by the result of the panel study.

Additional Findings

A followup study was conducted in an attempt to partially replicate and extend the findings. The respondents in the previously described panel study were exposed to questions dealing with either product or brand decisions (i.e., the type of decision was a between-subjects factor). By means of the instructions and examples described earlier, care was taken to stress the distinction between brand and product decisions. The question is raised, however, whether the responses reflected differences in the two types of decisions. In this followup study, each respondent was asked first about reference group influence on product decisions, then about brand decisions. To verify the earlier product selection procedures, manipulation checks were included at the end of each survey regarding the luxury–necessity and public–private dimensions.

Respondents. Three hundred households selected randomly from the telephone directory of a medium-sized SMSA were contacted by telephone and asked to participate in a study of consumer purchase decisions; 270 agreed to respond to a mail questionnaire. The original phone respondents who were willing to participate were randomly assigned to one of two questionnaire versions. Larger subsamples than those used in the panel study were felt to be justified, given the nature of the two samples (i.e., random phone selection versus a panel survey) and the lower anticipated response rate in the followup study. This followup was based on 151 completed responses (50 percent response rate based on the original telephone sample of 300). Data were collected from the adult in each household agreeing to participate.

Survey Design. Two of the four product combinations used in the panel study were selected for this analysis. Two questionnaires were constructed, each containing the reference group influence questions regarding product *and* brand decisions for four different products representing the four categories (e.g., PUL). In both questionnaires, product design questions preceded brand decision items. Again, the order of the product categories was randomized between the two survey versions.

The reference group influence statements were identical to those used in the panel study. Each version was mailed to half of the adults agreeing to participate as a result of the telephone interview. The completed responses were almost equally divided (75 and 76) between the two survey versions.

Reliability and Manipulation Check Estimates. Internal consistency was again estimated using coefficient alpha. The estimates averaged 0.64, 0.84, and 0.70 for the informational, value-expressive, and utilitarian subscales, respectively. Scaled statements similar to those used in the product selection procedure for public–private and luxury–necessity dimensions were included at the end of each questionnaire as manipulation checks. These tests for significance regarding the public–private and luxury–necessity dimensions were, for each possible comparison, consistent with the preliminary product selection procedures. The average t-values were 4.62 for the public–private comparisons and 18.53 for luxury–necessity comparisons. Specifically, those products selected as representing privately consumed goods different significantly from the products perceived as being publicly consumed, and the products selected as luxuries were perceived differently from those selected as necessities.

Results. The followup study data were also examined in an overall analysis using repeated measures multivariate analysis of variance. These results are presented in the lower half of Table 24.2. As in the panel study, differences in the product configurations used to form the questionnaires apparently did affect respondents' perceptions of value-expressive (F = 7.44, $p < 0.01$) and utilitarian (F = 4.01, $p < 0.05$) influence. However, unlike the panel study, the decision factor (product versus brand) was marginally significant for the informational (F = 3.47, $p < 0.06$) and significant for the value-expressive (F = 28.31, $p < 0.01$) and utilitarian (F = 28.43, $p < 0.01$) dimensions. It appears that when subjects responded to reference group influence questions for both product and brand decisions, the distinction affected responses. With the exception of the luxury–necessity factor for utilitarian influence, the two conspicuousness dimensions hypothesized to affect reference group influence perceptions were again significant.

Differences in responses to the reference group influence scales across the four product categories (e.g., PUL, PUN, PRL, PRN) were again examined separately for the two decisions. In 10 of the 12 analyses, the *F*-values were significant ($p < 0.001$), again suggesting substantial differences in consumer perceptions of reference group influence across the four product categories.

The results of the paired-comparison tests for the 12 hypotheses are shown in Table 24.5 for both the product and brand decisions. Based on the followup data, 25 of the 36 comparisons were consistent with the hypotheses. For the nonequal hypotheses, only one significant comparison was counter to the hypothesized direction. Fifteen of the 25 paired-comparison tests that were consistent with the reference group influence hypotheses involved the brand decision analyses.

DISCUSSION

Summary

The present effort investigated three types of reference group influence on product and brand decisions across four product categories delineated by variations in product conspicuousness. The interaction of public–private consumption and luxury–necessity dimensions resulted in four different product/brand combinations. Bourne's (1957) original framework hypothesized strong reference group influence for public–luxury product and brand decisions and negligible influence on private–necessity product and brand decisions. Differential influence was hypothesized for public–necessity and private–luxury items.

This study is limited by the normal problems associated with a mail survey design and the use of projective responses. A caveat is also appropriate regarding the implications of omitted variables, such as perceived risk and product familiarity, as well as other confounding effects. For example, without a more complex design it is impossible to tell whether the significant effects for the decision factor (product versus brand) in the followup study are due to demand effects or whether the inclusion of both decisions for each respondent resulted in the presence of meaningful differences. Regarding the possibility of confounding effects due to omitted variables, similar efforts in the future should consider covariance analysis in attempting to control for other influences. This is particularly noteworthy because the distinction between luxuries and necessities implies varying costs, and hence risk.

Given these limitations, what was learned about reference group influence? When respondents were faced with a single decision type (e.g., product versus brand), the decision factor was only significant for informational group influence. However, in both studies the absolute values were consistently greater for brand choices as opposed to product choice decisions. This suggests a greater role for appeals based on reference groups in stimulating selective demand. Variations in the sets of products selected affected perceptions of value-expressive and utilitarian reference group influence. The absence of significant informational reference group effects suggests consistent information seeking by individuals across similar types of products.

Consistent with Bourne's (1957) framework, the luxury–necessity and public–private dimensions were consistently significant as within-subject factors in both studies. This finding was reflected in substantial differences across the four categories—public luxuries, public necessities, private luxuries, and private necessities. Nineteen of 36 paired-comparison hypotheses were supported in both the panel and followup study.[5] Further, if these results are tempered by the fact that all three types of reference group influence would not be expected to be operative in all purchase situations, the results provide fairly strong evidence for the need to consider differential effects of reference group influence across purchase situations.

Reexamination on a product-by-product basis of both the hypotheses tests and the reliability estimates did not reveal any noticeable patterns regarding products with confirmed hypotheses versus products with disconfirmed hy-

[5]In total, 24 of the mean pairs in terms of direction and significance were replicated by the followup study.

TABLE 24.5 Paired-Comparison Hypotheses and Results: Follow-up Study[a]

		Influence					
Comparison	*Hypotheses*	*Informational*		*Value-expressive*		*Utilitarian*	
Products							
PUL-PUN	>	20.16	18.85[b,e]	15.37	13.21[b,e]	11.08	10.49
PUL-PRL	=[c]	20.16	19.32[e]	15.37	11.21[b]	11.08	10.26[e]
PUL-PRN	>	20.16	16.19[b,e]	15.37	8.74[b,e]	11.08	8.73[b,e]
PUN-PRL	<	18.85	10.32	*13.21*	*11.21*[b]	10.49	10.26
PUN-PRN	=[d]	18.85	*16.19*[b]	13.21	8.74[b]	10.49	8.73[b]
PRL-PRN	>	19.32	16.19[b,e]	11.21	8.74[b,e]	10.26	8.73[b,e]
Brands							
PUL-PUN	=[c]	19.91	19.28[e]	15.19	15.95[e]	11.63	12.31[e]
PUL-PRL	>	19.91	19.24	15.19	11.08[b,e]	11.63	10.47[b,e]
PUL-PRN	>	19.91	17.85[b,e]	15.19	12.07[b,e]	11.63	10.75[b,e]
PUN-PRL	>	19.28	19.24	15.95	11.08[b,e]	12.31	10.47[b,e]
PUN-PRN	>	19.28	17.85[b,e]	15.95	12.07[b,e]	12.31	10.75[b,e]
PRL-PRN	=[d]	19.24	17.85[b]	11.08	12.07[e]	10.47	10.75[e]

[a]Figures represent scale mean scores combined across subgroups. Italics indicate pairs represent nonequal hypotheses significantly different but counter to expected direction.

[b]Paired t-tests were significantly different ($p < 0.001$); one tailed tests were used when direction hypothesized. Informational and utilitarian values had possible ranges of 4 to 24; value-expressive values had a possible range of 5 to 30.

[c]Equivalent but strong reference group influence hypothesized.

[d]Equivalent but weak reference group influence hypothesized.

[e]Consistent with hypothesized influence.

potheses. However, three observations are noteworthy. When considered individually, the two clothing items included as public necessities were involved in slightly more of the disconfirmed hypotheses for product decisions. In general, the hypotheses were more often supported for the brand decisions. Based on the results presented in Tables 24.4 and 24.5, four of the directional hypotheses were disconfirmed in both studies. Three of these four were significant and dealt with the public necessity and private luxury comparisons. For product decisions, public necessities were perceived as involving more value-expressive and utilitarian influence than private luxuries. This may reflect fear of embarrassment from not owning products which many feel are required for normal living. Also unexpected from the hypotheses, brand decisions for public necessities involved less informational influences than private luxuries. This may be attributable to the fact that because ownership is so common, less information seeking is necessary.

Unresolved Issues

The processes through which reference group influences operate and affect information processing, evaluation of alternatives, and eventual decision making are in need of study. The extended behavioral intention model (Fishbein and Ajzen 1975) provides a logical framework for examining many of these interactions. The model is capable of handling various types of decisions (e.g., brands versus products), incorporating different levels of specificity (e.g., situational factors and product differences), and is amenable to the use of experimental manipulations. Further, through examining salient reference groups at the individual level, the differential role that varying groups may have on an individual's product and brand decisions can be explored.

Situational variations and their impact on the complexity of studying reference group influences on purchase decisions also need to be addressed. For example, the purchase of a product such as beer may be viewed by others, but consumption may occur in private. Or visitors to the home may well have the opportunity to identify the brands of private luxuries, hypothesized here to involve weak reference group reference.

As alluded to earlier, future efforts should consider including other socioeconomic and attitudinal variables, either in covariance designs or as moderator variables. This premise is substantiated by the differential effects of reference group influence between housewives and students found by Park and Lessig (1977). Similarly, perceived risk should increase susceptibility to reference group influence in many instances. Prior experience and knowledge have been found to affect product attribute versus brand processing (Bettman and Park 1980). Likewise, product class familiarity may be hypothesized to affect reference group influences. Generalized self-confidence and product-specific self-confidence found relevant in previous studies on information seeking may also inhibit or encourage communication about products and brands among reference group members (Locander and Hermann 1979).

Finally, the potential for changes in the perceptions of products among consumers and the pervasiveness of product ownership on reference group influence need to be acknowledged. Through promotion, it is possible to associate certain images with products that might bring reference group influence into play (Bourne 1957; Lessig and Park 1978) under conditions (e.g., private necessities) that might not otherwise be expected. In contrast, product diffusion may shift products over time from exclusive to common ownership, and hence reduce the significance of reference group influence.

REFERENCES

ASCH, S. (1952), *Social Psychology.* Englewood Cliffs, NJ: Prentice-Hall.

BETTMAN, JAMES R., and C. WHAN PARK (1980), "Effects of Prior Knowledge and Experience and Phase of the Choice Process on Consumer Decision Processes: A Protocol Analysis," *Journal of Consumer Research,* 7 (December), 243–248.

BOURNE, FRANCIS S. (1957), "Group Influence in Marketing and Public Relations," in *Some Applications of Behavioral Research,* Eds. R. Likert and S. P. Hayes. Basil, Switzerland: UNESCO.

BREHM, JACK W. (1966). *A Theory of Psychological Reactance.* New York: Academic Press.

BURNKRANT, ROBERT E., and ALAIN COUSINEAU (1975), "Informational and Normative Social Influence and Buyer Behavior," *Journal of Consumer Research,* 2 (December), 206–215.

CAMPBELL, ANGUS, PHILIP E. CONVERSE, WARREN E. MILLER, and DONALD STOKES (1960), *The American Voter.* New York: Wiley.

CAMPBELL, DONALD T., and DONALD W. FISKE (1959), "Convergent and Discriminant Validation by the Multitrait-Multimethod Matrix," *Psychological Bulletin,* 56, 81–105.

CLEE, MONA, and ROBERT A. WICKLUND (1980), Consumer Behavior and Psychological Reactance," *Journal of Consumer Research,* 4, 389–405.

COCANONGHER, A. BENTON, and GRADY D. BRUCE (1971), "Socially Distant Reference Groups and Consumer Aspirations," *Journal of Marketing Research,* 8, 379–381.

COLEMAN, JAMES S., ELIHU KATZ, and HERBERT MENZEL (1966), *Medical Innovation: A Diffusion Study.* Indianapolis, IN: Bobbs-Merrill.

DEUTSCH, M., and HAROLD B. GERARD (1955), "A Study of Normative and Informational Social Influences Upon Individual Judgment," *Journal of Abnormal and Social Psychology,* 51, 624–636.

FORD, JEFFRY D., and ELWOOD A. ELLIS (1980), "A Reexamination of Group Influence on Member Brand Preference," *Journal of Marketing Research," 17, 125–132.*

FISHBEIN, MARTIN, and ICEK AJZEN (1975), *Belief, Attitude, Intention and Behavior.* Reading, MA: Addison-Wesley.

FRENCH, JOHN R. P., JR., and BERTRAM RAVEN (1959), "The Bases of Social Power," in *Studies in Social Power,* Ed. Dorwin Cartwright. Ann Arbor, MI: University of Michigan Press. 150–167.

GRUBB, EDWARD L., and BRUCE L. STERN (1971), "Self-Concept and Significant Others," *Journal of Marketing Research,* 8, 382–385.

HAWKINS, DEL I., KENNETH A. CONEY, and

ROGER J. BEST (1980), *Consumer Behavior.* New York: Wiley.

HYMAN, HERBERT H. (1942), "The Psychology of Status," *Archives of Psychology,* 269, 94-102.

———, and ELEANOR SINGER (1968), *Readings in Reference Group Theory and Research.* New York: The Free Press.

JONES, EDWARD E., and HAROLD B. GERARD (1967), *Social Psychology.* New York: Wiley.

KELLEY, HAROLD H. (1947), "Two Functions of Reference Groups," in *Readings in Social Psychology,* Eds. Guy E. Swanson, Theodore M. Newcomb, and E. L. Hartley. New York: Holt, Rinehart & Winston, 410-414.

KELMAN, HERBERT C. (1961), "Processes of Opinion Change," *Public Opinion Quarterly,* 25, 57-78.

KOTLER, PHILIP (1980), *Marketing Management: Analysis, Planning, and Control.* Englewood Cliffs, NJ: Prentice-Hall.

KREISBERG, LOUIS (1955), "Occupational Controls Among Steel Distributors," *American Journal of Sociology,* 56, 203-212.

LESSIG, V. PARKER, and C. WHAN PARK (1978), "Promotional Perspectives of Reference Group Influence: Advertising Implications," *Journal of Advertising,* 7, 41-47.

LOCANDER, WILLIAM B., and PETER W. HERMANN (1979), "The Effect of Self-Confidence and Anxiety on Information Seeking in Consumer Risk Reduction," *Journal of Marketing Research,* 16 (May), 268-274.

MCNEAL, JAMES U. (1973), *An Introduction to Consumer Behavior.* New York: Wiley.

MERTON, ROBERT K. (1957), "Continuities in the Theory of Reference Groups and Social Structure," in *Social Theory and Social Structure,* Ed. Robert K. Merton. New York: The Free Press, 281-368.

———, and ALICE KITT ROSSI (1949), "Contributions to the Theory of Reference Group Behavior," in *Social Theory and Social Structure,* Ed. Robert K. Merton. New York: The Free Press, 225-275.

MOSCHIS, GEORGE P. (1976), "Social Comparison and Informal Group Influence," *Journal of Marketing Research,* 13, 237-244.

NEWCOMB, THEODORE M. (1943), *Personality and Social Change.* New York: The Dryden Press, 374-386.

NEWCOMB, THEODORE M. (1950), *Social Psychology.* New York: Holt, Rinehart & Winston, 225.

PARK, C. WHAN, and V. PARKER LESSIG (1977), "Students and Housewives: Differences in Susceptibility to Reference Group Influences," *Journal of Consumer Research,* 4, 102-110.

SHERIF, MUZAFER (1948), "An Outline of Social Psychology. New York: Harper & Row.

——— (1953), "The Concept of Reference Groups in Human Relations," in *Group Relations at the Crossroads,* Eds. Muzafer Sherif and M. O. Wilson. New York: Harper & Row.

———, and CAROLYN SHERIF (1964), *Reference Groups.* New York: Harper & Row.

SHIBUTANI, TAMOTSU (1955), "Reference Groups as Perspectives," *American Journal of Sociology,* 60, 562-569.

SMITH, M. BREWSTER, JEROME BRUNER, and ROBERT W. WHITE (1956), *Opinions and Personality.* New York: Wiley.

STAFFORD, JAMES E. (1966), "Effects of Group Influence on Consumer Brand Choice Preference," *Journal of Marketing Research,* 3, 68-75.

TURNER, RALPH H. (1955), "Reference Groups and Future-Oriented Men," *Social Forces,* 34, 130-136.

VENKATESAN, M. (1966), "Experimental Study of Consumer Behavior Conformity and Independence," *Journal of Marketing Research,* 3, 384-387.

WITT, ROBERT E. (1969), "Informal Social Group Influence on Consumer Brand Choice," *Journal of Marketing Research,* 6, 473-477.

———, and GRADY D. BRUCE (1970), "Purchase Decisions and Group Influence," *Journal of Marketing Research,* 7, 533-535.

———, and GRADY D. BRUCE (1972), "Group Influence and Brand Choice Congruence," *Journal of Marketing Research,* 9, 440-443.

25

EFFECTS OF GROUP PRESSURE UPON THE MODIFICATION AND DISTORTION OF JUDGMENTS*

Solomon E. Asch

We shall here describe in summary form the conception and first findings of a program of investigation into the conditions of independence and submission to group pressure.

Our immediate object was to study the social and personal conditions that induce individuals to resist or to yield to group pressures when the latter are perceived to be *contrary to fact.* The issues which this problem raises are of obvious consequence for society; it can be of decisive importance whether or not a group will, under certain conditions, submit to existing pressures. Equally direct are the consequences for individuals and our understanding of them, since it is a decisive fact about a person whether he possesses the freedom to act independently, or whether he characteristically submits to group pressures.

The problem under investigation requires the direct observation of certain basic processes in the interaction between individuals, and between individuals and groups. To clarify these seems necessary if we are to make fundamental advances in the understanding of the formation and reorganization of attitudes, of the functioning of public opinion, and of the operation of propaganda. Today we do not possess an adequate theory of these central psycho-social processes. Empirical investigation has been predominantly controlled by general propositions concerning group influence which have as a rule been assumed but not tested. With few exceptions investigation has relied upon descriptive formulations concerning the operation

*"Effects of Group Pressure upon the Modification and Distortion of Judgments," by Solomon E. Asch, is reprinted from *Readings in Social Psychology,* 3d ed., edited by Eleanor E. Maccoby, Theodore M. Newcomb, and Eugene L. Hartley. Prepared by the author from data previously reported in *Groups, Leadership and Men,* edited by H. Guetzkow (Carnegie Press 1951; Russell & Russell 1963). Reprinted by permission of Carnegie-Mellon University. Copyright 1951 by Carnegie Press; copyright renewed 1979 by Harold Guetzkow.

of suggestion and prestige, the inadequacy of which is becoming increasingly obvious, and upon schematic applications of stimulus-response theory.

Basic to the current approach has been the axiom that group pressures characteristically induce psychological changes *arbitrarily,* in far-reaching disregard of the material properties of the given conditions. This mode of thinking has almost exclusively stressed the slavish submission of individuals to group forces, has neglected to inquire into their possibilities for independence and for productive relations with the human environment, and has virtually denied the capacity of men under certain conditions to rise above group passion and prejudice. It was our aim to contribute to a clarification of these questions, important both for theory and for their human implications, by means of direct observation of the effects of groups upon the decisions and evaluations of individuals.

THE EXPERIMENT AND FIRST RESULTS

To this end we developed an experimental technique which has served as the basis for the present series of studies. We employed the procedure of placing an individual in a relation of radical conflict with all the other members of a group, of measuring its effect upon him in quantitative terms, and of describing its psychological consequences. A group of eight individuals was instructed to judge a series of simple, clearly structured perceptual relations—to match the length of a given line with one of three unequal lines. Each member of the group announced his judgments publicly. In the midst of this monotonous "test" one individual found himself suddenly contradicted by the entire group, and this contradiction was repeated again and again in the course of the experiment. The group in question had, with the exception of one member, previously met with the experimenter and received instructions to respond at certain points with wrong—and unanimous—judgments. The errors of the majority were large (ranging between 1/2 in. and 1 3/4 in.) and of an order not encountered under control conditions. The outstanding person—the critical subject—whom we had placed in the position of a *minority of one* in the midst of a *unanimous majority*—was the object of investigation. He faced, possibly for the first time in his life, a situation in which a group unanimously contradicted the evidence of his senses.

This procedure was the starting point of the investigation and the point of departure for the study of further problems. Its main features were the following: (1) The critical subject was submitted to two contradictory and irreconcilable forces—the evidence of his own experience of a clearly perceived relation, and the unanimous evidence of a group of equals. (2) Both forces were part of the immediate situation; the majority was concretely present, surrounding the subject physically. (3) The critical subject, who was requested together with all others to state his judgments publicly, was obliged to declare himself and to take a definite stand vis-à-vis the group. (4) The situation possessed a self-contained character. The critical subject could not avoid or evade the dilemma by reference to conditions external to the experimental situation. (It may be mentioned at this point that the forces generated by the given conditions acted so quickly upon the critical subjects that instances of suspicion were infrequent.)

The technique employed permitted a simple quantitative measure of the "majority effect" in terms of the frequency of errors in the direction of the distorted estimates of the majority. At the same time we were concerned to obtain evidence of the ways in which the subjects perceived the group, to establish whether they became doubtful, whether they were tempted to join the majority. Most important, it was our object to establish the grounds of the subject's independence or yielding—whether, for example, the yielding subject was aware of the effect of the majority upon him, whether he abandoned his judgment deliberately or compulsively. To this end we constructed a comprehensive set of questions which served as the basis of an individual interview immediately following the experimental period. Toward the conclusion of the interview each subject was informed fully of the purpose of the experiment, of his role and of that of the majority. The reactions to the disclosure of the purpose of the experiment became in fact an integral part of the procedure. The information derived from the interview became an indispensable source of evidence and insight into the psychological structure of the experimental situation, and in particular, of the nature of the individual differences. It should be added that it is not justified or advisable to allow the subject to leave without giving him a full explanation of the experimental conditions. The experimenter has a responsibility to the subject to clarify his doubts and to state the reasons for placing him in the experimental situation. When this is done most subjects react with interest, and some express gratification at having lived through a striking situation which has some bearing on them personally and on wider human issues.

Both the members of the majority and the critical subjects were male college students. We shall report the results for a total of 50 critical subjects in this experiment. In Table 25.1 we summarize the successive comparison trials and the majority estimates. The reader will note that on certain trials the majority responded correctly; these were the "neutral" trials. There were 12 critical trials on which the majority responded incorrectly.

The quantitative results are clear and unambiguous.

1. There was a marked movement toward the majority. One third of all the estimates in the critical group were errors identical with or in the direction of the distorted estimates of the majority. The significance of this finding becomes clear in the light of the virtual absence of errors in the control group, the members of which recorded their estimates in writing. The relevant data of the critical and control groups are summarized in Table 25.2.
2. At the same time the effect of the majority was far from complete. The preponderance of estimates in the critical group (68 percent) was correct despite the pressure of the majority.
3. We found evidence of extreme individual differences. There were in the critical group subjects who remained independent without exception, and there were those who went nearly all the time with the majority. (The maximum possible number of errors was 12, while the actual range of errors was 0–11.) One fourth of the critical subjects was completely independent; at the other

TABLE 25.1 Lengths of Standard and Comparison Lines

Trial	*Length of Standard Line (in Inches)*	Comparison Lines (in Inches)			*Correct Response*	*Group Response*	*Majority Error (in Inches)*
		1	*2*	*3*			
1	10	8 3/4	10	8	2	2	–
2	2	2	1	1 1/2	1	1	–
3	3	3 3/4	4 1/4	3	3	1*	+3/4
4	5	5	4	6 1/2	1	2*	−1.0
5	4	3	5	4	3	3	–
6	3	3 3/4	4 1/4	3	3	2*	+1 1/4
7	8	6 1/4	8	6 3/4	2	3*	−1 1/4
8	5	5	4	6 1/2	1	3*	+1 1/2
9	8	6 1/4	8	6 3/4	2	1*	−1 3/4
10	10	8 3/4	10	8	2	2	–
11	2	2	1	1 1/2	1	1	–
12	3	3 3/4	4 1/4	3	3	1*	+3/4
13	5	5	4	6 1/2	1	2*	−1.0
14	4	3	5	4	3	3	–
15	3	3 3/4	4 1/4	3	3	2*	+1 1/4
16	8	6 1/4	8	6 3/4	2	3*	−1 1/4
17	5	5	4	6 1/2	1	3*	+1 1/2
18	8	6 1/4	8	6 3/4	2	1*	−1 3/4

*Note: Starred figures designate the erroneous estimates by the majority.

TABLE 25.2 Distribution of Errors in Experimental and Control Groups

Number of Critical Errors	*Critical Group*[a] *(N = 50)* F	*Control Group (N = 37)* F
0	13	35
1	4	1
2	5	1
3	6	
4	3	
5	4	
6	1	
7	2	
8	5	
9	3	
10	3	
11	1	
12	0	
Total	50	37
Mean	3.84	0.08

[a]All errors in the critical group were in the direction of the majority estimates.

extreme, one third of the group displaced the estimates toward the majority in one half or more of the trials.

The differences between the critical subjects in their reactions to the given conditions were equally striking. There were subjects who remained completely confident throughout. At the other extreme were those who became disoriented, doubt-ridden, and experienced a powerful impulse not to appear different from the majority.

For purposes of illustration we include a brief description of one independent and one yielding subject.

Independent

After a few trials he appeared puzzled, hesitant. He announced all disagreeing answers in the form of "Three, sir; two, sir"; not so with the unanimous answers on the neutral trials. At Trial 4 he answered immediately after the first member of the group, shook his head, blinked, and whispered to his neighbor: "Can't help it, that's one." His later answers came in a whispered voice, accompanied by a deprecating smile. At one point he grinned embarrassedly, and whispered explosively to his neighbor: "I always disagree—darn it!" During the questioning, this subject's constant refrain was: "I called them as I saw them, sir." He insisted that his estimates were right without, however, committing himself as to whether the others were wrong, remarking that "that's the way I see them and that's the way they see them." If he had to make a practical decision under similar circumstances, he declared, "I would follow my own view, though part of my reason would tell me that I might be wrong." Immediately following the experiment the majority engaged this subject in a brief discussion. When they pressed him to say whether the entire group was wrong and he alone right, he turned upon them defiantly, exclaiming: "You're *probably* right, but you *may* be wrong!" To the disclosure of the experiment this subject reacted with the statement that he felt "exultant and relieved," adding, "I do not deny that at times I had the feeling: 'to heck with it, I'll go along with the rest.'"

Yielding

This subject went with the majority in 11 out of 12 trials. He appeared nervous and somewhat confused, but he did not attempt to evade discussion; on the contrary, he was helpful and tried to answer to the best of his ability. He opened the discussion with the statement: "If I'd been first I probably would have responded differently"; this was his way of stating that he had adopted the majority estimates. The primary factor in his case was loss of confidence. He perceived the majority as a decided group, acting without hesitation: "If they had been doubtful I probably would have changed, but they answered with such confidence." Certain of his errors, he explained, was due to the doubtful nature of the comparisons; in such instances he went with the majority. When the object of the experiment was explained, the subject volunteered: "I suspected about the middle—but tried to push it out of my mind." It is of interest that his suspicion did not restore his confidence or diminish the power of the majority. Equally striking is his report that he assumed the experiment to involve an "illusion" to which the others, but not he, were subject. This assumption too did not help to free him; on the contrary, he acted as if his divergence from the majority was a sign of defect. The principal impression this subject produced was of one so caught up by immediate difficulties that he lost clear reasons for his actions, and could make no reasonable decisions.

A FIRST ANALYSIS OF INDIVIDUALS' DIFFERENCES

On the basis of the interview data described earlier, we undertook to differentiate and describe the major forms of reaction to the experimental situation, which we shall now briefly summarize.

Among the *independent* subjects we distinguished the following main categories:

1. Independence based on *confidence* in one's perception and experience. The most striking characteristics of these subjects is the vigor with which they withstand the group opposition. Though they are sensitive to the group, and experience the conflict, they show a resilience in coping with it, which is expressed in their continuing reliance on their perception and the effectiveness with which they shake off the oppressive group opposition.
2. Quite different are those subjects who are independent and *withdrawn*. These do not react in a spontaneously emotional way, but rather on the basis of explicit principles concerning the necessity of being an individual.
3. A third group of independent subjects manifests considerable tension and doubt, but adhere to their judgment on the basis of a felt necessity to deal adequately with the task.

The following were the main categories of reaction among the *yielding* subjects, or those who went with the majority during one half or more of the trials.

1. *Distortion of perception* under the stress of group pressure. In this category belong a very few subjects who yield completely, but are not aware that their estimates have been displaced or distorted by the majority. These subjects report that they came to perceive the majority estimates as correct.
2. *Distortion of judgment.* Most submitting subjects belong to this category. The factor of greatest importance in this group is a decision the subjects reach that their perceptions are inaccurate, and that those of the majority are correct. These subjects suffer from primary doubt and lack of confidence; on this basis they feel a strong tendency to join the majority.
3. *Distortion of action.* The subjects in this group do not suffer a modification of perception nor do they conclude that they are wrong. They yield because of an overmastering need not to appear different from or inferior to others, because of an inability to tolerate the appearance of defectiveness in the eyes of the group. These subjects suppress their observations and voice the majority position with awareness of what they are doing.

The results are sufficient to establish that independence and yielding are not psychologically homogeneous, that submission to group pressure and freedom from pressure can be the result of different psychological conditions. It should also be noted that the categories described above, being based exclusively on the subjects' reactions to the experimental conditions, are descriptive, not presuming to explain why a given individual responded in one way rather than another. The further exploration of the basis for the individual differences is a separate task.

EXPERIMENTAL VARIATIONS

The results described are clearly a joint function of two broadly different sets of conditions. They are determined first by the specific external conditions, by the particular character of the relations between social evidence and one's own experience. Second, the presence of pronounced individual differences points to the important role of personal factors, or factors connected with the individual's character structure.

We reasoned that there are group conditions, which would induce produce independence in all subjects, and that there probably are group conditions that would induce intensified yielding in many, though not in all. Secondly, we deemed it reasonable to assume that behavior under the experimental social pressure is significantly related to certain characteristics of the individual. The present account will be limited to the effect of the surrounding conditions upon independence and submission. To this end we followed the procedure of experimental variation, systematically altering the quality of social evidence by means of systematic variation of the group conditions and of the task.

The Effect of Nonunanimous Majorities

Evidence obtained from the basic experiment suggested that the condition of being exposed *alone* to the opposition of a "compact majority" may have played a decisive role in determining the course and strength of the effects observed. Accordingly we undertook to investigate in a series of successive variations the effects of *nonunanimous* majorities. The technical problem of altering the uniformity of a majority is, in terms of our procedure, relatively simple. In most instances we merely directed one or more members of the instructed group to deviate from the majority in prescribed ways. It is obvious that we cannot hope to compare the performance of the same individual in two situations on the assumption that they remain independent of one another; at best we can investigate the effect of an earlier upon a later experimental condition. The comparison of different experimental situations therefore requires the use of different but comparable groups of critical subjects. This is the procedure we have followed. In the variations to be described we have maintained the conditions of the basic experiment (e.g., the sex of the subjects, the size of the majority, the content of the task, and so on) save for the specific factor that was varied. The following were some of the variations studied:

1. The Presence of a "True Partner." (a) In the midst of the majority were two naive, critical subjects. The subjects were separated spatially, being seated in the fourth and eight positions, respectively. Each therefore heard his judgments confirmed by one other person (provided the other person remained independent), or prior to, the other after announcing his own judgment. In addition, each experienced a break in the unanimity of the majority. There were six pairs of critical subjects. (b) In a further variation the "partner" to the critical subject was a member of the group who had been instructed to respond correctly throughout. This procedure permits the exact control of the partner's responses. The partner was always seated in the fourth position; he therefore announced his estimates with each case before the critical subject.

The results clearly demonstrate that a disturbance of the unanimity of the majority markedly increased the independence of the critical subjects. The frequency of promajority errors dropped to 10.4 percent of the total number of estimates in variation (a), and to 5.5 percent in variation (b). These results are to be compared with the frequency of yielding to the unanimous majorities in the basic experiment, which was 32 percent of the total number of estimates. It is clear that the presence in the field of one other individual who responded correctly was sufficient to deplete the power of the majority, and in some cases to destroy it. This finding is all the more striking in the light of other variations which demonstrate the effect of even small minorities provided they are unanimous. Indeed, we have been able to show that a unanimous majority of three is, under the given conditions, far more effective than a majority of eight containing one dissenter. That critical subjects will under these conditions free themselves of a majority of seven and join forces with one other person in the minority is, we believe, a result significant for theory. It points to a fundamental psychological difference between the condition of being alone and having a minimum of human support. It further demonstrates that the effects obtained are not the result of a summation of influences proceeding from each member of the group; it is necessary to conceive [of] the results as being relationally determined.

*2. **Withdrawal of a "True Partner."*** What will be the effect of providing the critical subject with a partner who responds correctly and then withdrawing him? The critical subject started with a partner who responded correctly. The partner was a member of the majority who had been instructed to respond correctly and to "desert" to the majority in the middle of the experiment. This procedure permits the observation of the same subject in the course of the transition from one condition to another. The withdrawal of the partner produced a powerful and unexpected result. We had assumed that the critical subject, having gone through the experience of opposing the majority with a minimum of support, would maintain his independence when alone. Contrary to this expectation, we found that the experience of having had then lost a partner restored the majority effect to its full force, the proportion of errors rising to 28.5 percent of all judgments, in contrast to the preceding level of 5.5 percent. Further experimentation is needed to establish whether the critical subjects were responding to the sheer fact of being alone, or to the fact that the partner abandoned them.

*3. **Late Arrival of a "True Partner."*** The critical subject started as a minority of one in the midst of a unanimous majority. Toward the conclusion of the experiment one member of the majority "broke" away and began announcing correct estimates. This procedure, which reverses the order of conditions of the preceding experiment, permits the observation of the transition from being alone to being a member of a pair against a majority. It is obvious that those critical subjects who were independent when alone would continue to be so when joined by a partner. The variation is therefore of significance primarily for those subjects who yielded during the first phase of the experiment. The appearance of the late partner exerts a freeing effect, reducing the level of yielding to 8.7 percent. Those who had previously yielded also became markedly more independent, but not completely so, continuing to yield more than previously independent subjects. The reports of the subjects do not cast much light on the factors responsible for the result. It is our impression that some subjects, having once committed themselves to yielding, find it difficult to change their direction completely. To do so is tantamount to a public admission that they had not acted rightly. They therefore follow to an extent the precarious course they had chosen in order to maintain an outward semblance of consistency and conviction.

*4. **The Presence of a "Compromise Partner."*** The majority was consistently extremist, always matching the standard with the most unequal line. One instructed subject (who, as in the other variations, preceded the critical subject) also responded incorrectly, but his estimates were always intermediate between the truth and the majority position. The critical subject therefore faced an extremist majority whose unanimity was broken by one more moderately erring person. Under these conditions the frequency of errors was reduced but not significantly. However, the lack of unanimity determined in a strikingly consistent way the *direction* of the errors. The preponderance of the errors, 75.7 percent of the total, was moderate, whereas in a parallel experiment in which the majority was unanimously extremist (i.e., with the "compromise" partner excluded), the incidence of moderate errors was 42 percent of the total. As might be expected, in a unanimously moderate majority, the errors of the critical subjects were without exception moderate.

The Role of Majority Size

To gain further understanding of the majority effect, we varied the size of the majority in several different variations. The majorities, which were in each case unanimous, consisted of 2, 3, 4, 8 and 10–15 persons, respectively. In addition, we studied the limiting case in which the critical subject was opposed by one instructed subject. Table 25.3 contains the mean and the range of errors under each condition.

With the opposition reduced to one, the majority effect all but disappeared. When the opposition proceeded from a group of two, it pro-

TABLE 25.3 Errors of Critical Subjects with Unanimous Majorities of Different Size

Size of Majority	*Control*	*1*	*2*	*3*	*4*	*8*	*10–15*
N	37	10	15	10	10	50	12
Mean number of errors	0.08	0.33	1.53	4.0	4.20	3.84	3.75
Range of errors	0–2	0–1	0–5	1–12	0–11	0–11	0–10

duced a measurable though small distortion, the errors being 12.8 percent of the total number of estimates. The effect appeared in full force with a majority of three. Larger majorities did not product effects greater than a majority of three.

The effect of a majority is often silent, revealing little of its operation to the subject, and often hiding it from the experimenter. To examine the range of effects it is capable of inducing, decisive variations of conditions are necessary. An indication of one effect is furnished by the following variation in which the conditions of the basic experiment were simply reversed. Here the majority, consisting of a group of 16, was naive; in the midst of it we placed a single individual who responded wrongly according to instructions. Under these conditions the members of the naive majority reacted to the lone dissenter with amusement. Contagious laughter spread through the group at the droll minority of one. Of significance is the fact that the members lacked awareness that they drew their strength from the majority, and that their reactions would change radically if they faced the dissenter individually. These observations demonstrate the role of social support as a source of power and stability, in contrast to the preceding investigations which stressed the effects of social opposition. Both aspects must be explicitly considered in a unified formulation of the effects of group conditions on the formation and change of judgments.

The Role of the Stimulus Situation

It is obviously not possible to divorce the quality and course of the group forces which act upon the individual from the specific stimulus conditions. Of necessity the structure of the situation molds the group forces and determines their direction as well as their strength. Indeed, this was the reason that we took pains in the investigations described above to center the issue between the individual and the group around an elementary matter of fact. And there can be no doubt that the resulting reactions were directly a function of the contradiction between the observed relations and the majority position. These general considerations are sufficient to establish the need to vary the stimulus conditions and to observe their effect on the resulting group forces.

Accordingly we have studied the effect of increasing and decreasing the discrepancy between the correct relation and the position of the majority, going beyond the basic experiment which contained discrepancies of a relatively moderate order. Our technique permits the easy variation of this factor, since we can vary at will the deviation of the majority from the correct relation. At this point we can only summarize the trend of the results which is entirely clear. The degree of independence increases with the distance of the majority from correctness. However, even glaring discrepancies (of the order of 3 to 6 in.) did not produce independence in all. While independence increases with the magnitude of contradiction, a certain proportion of individuals continues to yield under extreme conditions.

We have also varied systematically the structural clarity of the task, employing judgments based on mental standards. In agreement with other investigators, we find that the majority effect grows stronger as the situation diminishes in clarity. Concurrently, however, the disturbance of the subjects and the conflict quality of the situation decrease markedly. We consider it of significance that the majority achieves its most pronounced effect when it acts most painlessly.

SUMMARY

We have investigated the effects upon individuals of majority opinions when the latter were seen to be in a direction contrary to fact. By means of a simple technique we produced a radical divergence between a majority and a minority, and observed the ways in which individuals coped with the resulting difficulty. Despite the stress of the given conditions, a substantial proportion of individuals retained their independence throughout. At the same time a substantial minority yielded, modifying their judgments in accordance with the majority. Independence and yielding are a joint function of the following major factors:

1. *The character of the stimulus situation.* Variations in structural clarity have a decisive effect: with diminishing clarity of the stimulus conditions the majority effect increases.
2. *The character of the group forces.* Individuals are highly sensitive to the structural qualities of group opposition. In particular, we demonstrate the great importance of the factor of unanimity. Also, the majority effect is a function of the size of group opposition.
3. *The character of the individual.* There were wide and, indeed, striking differences among individuals within the same experimental situation.

26

A PROPOSITIONAL INVENTORY FOR NEW DIFFUSION RESEARCH*

Hubert Gatignon
Thomas S. Robertson

The diffusion theory literature offers a fairly well-developed conceptual framework for the study of communications. As developed across a number of disciplines, diffusion applies to the flow of information, ideas, and products; its uniqueness is its focus on interpersonal communication transfer. This paper offers new theoretical propositions to advance consumer diffusion research and to provide a foundation for diffusion modeling.

One of the more widely used theories of communication is diffusion theory. The diffusion literature has developed across a number of disciplines and has been of value in explaining the flow of information, ideas, practices, products, and services within and across cultures and subcultures, or markets and market segments. Diffusion's theoretical roots can be found in rural sociology (Rogers 1983), geography (Brown 1981), medical sociology (Coleman, Katz, and Menzel 1957), cultural anthropology (Barnett 1953), and industrial economics (Mansfield 1961).

As a theory of communications, diffusion theory's special focus is on interpersonal communications within social systems. The process of personal influence is seen to mediate mass media effects, and individuals are shown to have different propensities for relying on mass media or personal channels. This is particularly true by adoption category, from innovators to laggards. Personal influence is also a key factor accounting for the speed and shape of the diffusion process.

*Reprinted from the *Journal of Consumer Research,* 11 (March 1985), pp. 849-867.

The diffusion perspective was introduced to the emerging consumer behavior literature in the mid-1960s (Arndt 1967; Frank, Massy, and Morrison 1964; King 1963; Robertson 1967; Silk 1966). In the ensuing years, consumer behavior scholars have contributed to the cumulative development of diffusion theory, but the conceptual impact has been somewhat limited. The consumer diffusion literature reflects the same concepts as the general diffusion literature; for the most part, researchers have merely demonstrated how diffusion theory can be used in consumer research. This is a valuable first step, but it is insufficient.

The current malaise in consumer diffusion research reflects a lack of new insights and methods on the part of consumer behavior scholars. Indeed, the very directions for future research on consumer diffusion have been identified by Rogers, rather than by consumer researchers. Rogers (1976), posited three "biases" in diffusion research: (1) a lack of process orientation such that research has not tracked the individual's decision process over time; (2) a pro-innovation bias which assumes that all innovation is desirable; and (3) a lack of sociometric analysis. These observations have validity but have not advanced consumer research on diffusion in the intervening years.

Considerable potential exists for enriched conceptualizations and new research directions in consumer diffusion. Such research should be encouraged in order to expand the theoretical domain of the consumer behavior field. At the same time, further research and conceptualization is likely to be quite useful to marketing managers and social policy makers, since diffusion theory is frequently looked to for guidance on the dissemination of new technologies, new products, new services, and new regulatory initiatives.

Diffusion modelers, represented by our colleagues in management and marketing science, are particularly interested in an advanced theory of consumer diffusion. A number of interesting propositions have been developed by diffusion modelers explaining how diffusion occurs in the consumer domain, but they remain largely untested by consumer researchers (Bass 1969; Mahajan and Muller 1979). An integration of the behavioral and modeling literatures on diffusion could be beneficial to both constituencies.

Our objective here is to provide an enhanced and updated view of diffusion theory that is of direct relevance to consumer behavior. To do so, we integrate recent evidence concerning diffusion processes based on research in a number of fields, as well as new perspectives from the modeling of diffusion processes (Gatignon and Robertson 1984).

THE CONSUMER DIFFUSION PARADIGM

The conceptual foundations of diffusion theory are quite familiar (Rogers 1983):

- The concept of the *innovation*
- Its *diffusion* over time
- The *personal influence* and *opinion leadership* processes
- The *adoption* process
- The roles of the *innovator* and other *adopter categories*
- The *social system* or market segment within which diffusion occurs

To these we would add:

- The role of *marketing* (change agent) actions
- The role of *competitive* actions

The relationships among these elements in the diffusion process are shown in Figure 26.1. Diffusion occurs within the boundaries of the social system or market segment. The diffusion pattern at the social system level is an outcome of the distribution of individual adoption decisions. These individual adoption decisions are influenced by personal characteristics, perceived innovation characteristics, personal influence, and marketing and competitive actions. The latter also have an influence in defining the perceived innovation characteristics and affecting the personal influence process.

Figure 26.1 represents not only a model of

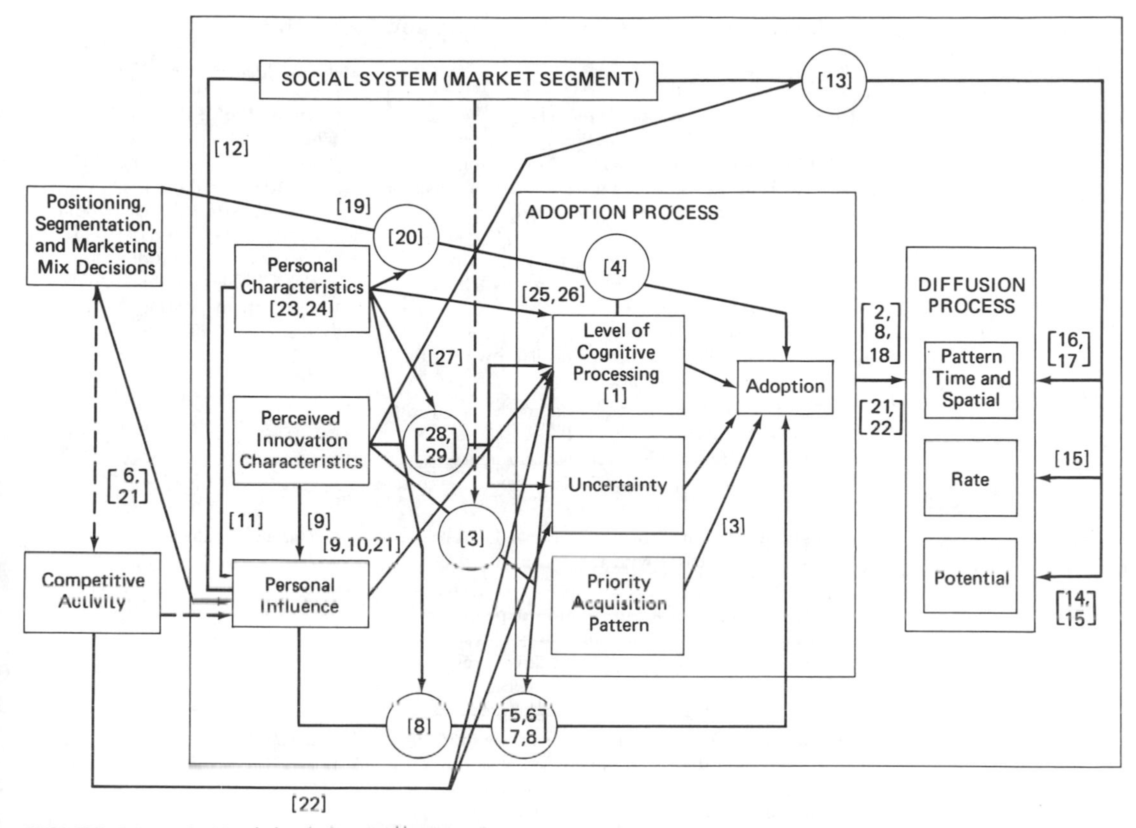

FIGURE 26.1 A Model of the Diffusion Process

the diffusion process but also a vehicle for specifying propositions to guide future theory construction and empirical research. These propositions are developed throughout the text and are summarized in Table 26.1. The numbers shown in Figure 26.1 coincide with the numbers of the propositions as elaborated in Table 26.1.

There are three types of propositions represented in Figure 26.1:

1. *Construct descriptions.* An example of this is Proposition 1, which describes the adoption process in terms of high versus low cognitive processing. The number 1 is shown in the box "Level of Cognitive Processing." The proposition does not involve a causal relationship between two concepts, but rather an elaboration and definition of what is meant by adoption.
2. *Direct causal relationships.* An example of this is Proposition 15, which specifies a direct causal relationship between the homogeneity of the social system and the rate of diffusion. The number 15 appears in Figure 26.1 on the line connecting the two constructs.
3. *Interactions.* This third type of proposition is concerned with causal links with interactions. An example is Proposition 5, which states that personal influence is operative in affecting adoption primarily under the hierarchy of effects model of cognitive processing. In this case, the effect of personal influence on adoption is moderated by the level of cognitive processing. This is represented in Figure 26.1 by the number 5 in a circle at the junction where the line from the level of cognitive processing meets the line from personal influence to adoption.

This model, although reasonably comprehensive, is not exhaustive, and further interactions are possible. The model could also be

TABLE 26.1 Propositional Inventory for New Consumer Diffusion Research

Diffusion concept	*Propositions*	*Relevant literature*
The adoption process	1. The two basic adoption models are the high cognitive processing "hierarchy of effects" model and the low cognitive processing "low involvement" model. The hierarchy of effects adoption model is to be expected under conditions of: • High consumer learning requirements • High innovation costs or high switching costs • High social imitation • A multiperson adoption decision within the family or organization The low involvement adoption model is to be expected under conditions of: • Low consumer learning requirements • Low innovation costs or low switching costs • Low social imitation	Krugman (1965); Ozanne and Churchill (1971); O'Neal; Thorelli, and Utterback (1973); Ray (1973); Zaltman, Duncan, and Holbek (1973); Davis and Rigaux (1974); Davis (1976); Robertson (1976); Adler et al. (1980); Robertson and Wind (1980); Sheth (1981); Hirschman (1981)
	2. The maximum diffusion potential for the product increases with the width and depth of adoption.	No references identified.
	3. The adoption of an innovation depends on its fit within the existing consumption system and its ability to compete for scarce resources in order to achieve a position in the consumer's priority acquisition pattern.	Hill (1970)
	4. The less the level of cognitive processing, the greater the impact of advertising and other impersonal marketing sources throughout the adoption process.	Robertson (1971); Swinyard and Coney (1978); Bettman (1979)
Personal influence and Opinion leadership	5. Personal influence is operative mainly under a hierarchy-of-effects adoption process.	Katz and Lazarsfeld (1955); Weimann (1982)
	6. When personal influence is operative, it is interdependent with mass media and its effect is most pronounced at later stages of the adoption process. • When personal influence and mass media are in conflict, personal influence has greater impact.	Robertson (1971); Bettman (1979); Rogers (1983)
	7. The impact of personal influence is greater under information-seeking conditions and least under information-giving conditions.	No references identified
	8. Consumers who are highly dependent on normative influence (conformity intention) will be slower to adopt.	Burt (1973)
	9. Personal influence may be of a verbal or visual form. • The impact of visual influence increases with the information content that can be visually communicated for a particular product category. • Visual influence is likely to have greatest impact at awareness, whereas verbal influence is likely to have greatest influence at evaluation.	Kisielius (1982); Edell and Staelin (1983)

TABLE 26.1 (*Continued*)

Diffusion concept	*Propositions*	*Relevant literature*
Personal influence and Opinion leadership	10. Negative personal influence has greater persuasive impact than positive personal influence, assuming a credible source and consistent information content.	Arndt (1967); Kanouse and Hanson (1972); Oliver (1977); Sternthal, Phillips, and Dholakia (1978); Mizerski (1982); Mahajan, Muller, and Kerin (1984); Richins (1983).
	11. Opinion leader traits vary by product category. • Exposure to personal influence is positively related to in-person information source preference and social integration.	Silk (1966); King and Summers (1970); Summers (1970); Robertson (1971); Myers and Robertson (1972); Baumgarten (1975); Langeard, Crousillat, and Weisz (1977); Bettman (1979); Westbrook and Fornell (1979)
	12. Homophilous influence is more common, but heterophilous influence beyond the boundaries of the social system is common among innovators. • There is a point of optimal heterophily that maximizes the effectiveness of personal influence.	Barnett (1953); Granovetter (1973); Kaigler-Evans, Leavitt and Dickey (1978); Rogers (1983)
The social system	13. The diffusion rate and the maximum penetration level are positively related to the innovation's compatibility with social system values.	Rogers (1983)
	14. The maximum level of penetration of the innovation in the social system is affected by normative change.	Mahajan and Peterson (1978); Peterson and Mahajan (1978); Mahajan, Peterson, Jain, and Malhotra (1979); Heeler and Hustad (1980)
	15. The more homogenous the social system, the faster the diffusion rate and the higher the maximum penetration level.	Jeuland (1981); Eliashberg, Tapiero, and Wind (1983)
	16. The spatial pattern of diffusion is determined by a hierarchy effect when market and infrastructure factors controlling the availability of the new product are dominant and a neighborhood effect when terrestrial or social factors are dominant.	Hagerstrand (1965); Brown, Malecki, and Spector (1976)
	17. The sequence of countries adopting an innovation is dominated by a hierarchical pattern. The physical distance between countries and the social similarity between countries are negatively related to the diffusion sequence across countries.	Hagerstrand (1965); Brown, Malecki, and Spector (1976)
The diffusion process	18. The diffusion process tends to follow one of two ideal type patterns—sigmoid or exponential. A sigmoid pattern is expected under conditions of: • The operation of personal influence • A learning hierarchy process of adoption • High innovation costs or high switching costs	Ryan and Gross (1943); Coleman, Katz, and Menzel (1957); Fourt and Woodlock (1960); Mansfield (1961); Cox (1967); Bass (1969); Polli and Cook (1969); Robertson (1971); Nevers (1972); Dodds (1973); Rink and Swan (1979); Heeler

TABLE 26.1 *(Continued)*

Diffusion concept	*Propositions*	*Relevant literature*
The diffusion process (continued)	• Unimodal distribution of initial beliefs toward the innovation within the social system • High uncertainty An exponential curve is expected under conditions of: • A relative lack of personal influence • A low-involvement process of adoption • Low uncertainty • Low innovation and switching costs • A uniform pattern of initial beliefs within the social system	and Hustad (1980); Teece (1980); Stoneman (1981); Tigert and Farivar (1981); Feder and O'Mara (1982); Jensen (1982); Wind, Robertson, and Fraser (1982)
	19. Marketing expenditures affect the rate of diffusion and the maximum penetration level but not the pattern of diffusion. • Marketing variables have long-term, cumulative effects on diffusion. • The effectiveness of marketing variables on the diffusion curve shows decreasing returns to scale.	Dhalla and Yuseph (1976); Bass (1980); Lilien, Rao, and Kalish (1981); Simon and Sebastian (1982); Horsky and Simon (1983)
	20. The greater the sensitivity of the marketing program to the changing characteristics of segments at different stages of the diffusion process, the faster the rate of diffusion and the greater the penetration level.	Robertson and Wind (1980)
	21. The expected speed of diffusion increases with the average time of active information dissemination within the social system, which is heightened by the level of mass media communication expenditures.	Midgley (1976); Bartholomew (1976); Karmeshu and Pathria (1980); Zielske and Henry (1980)
	22. The greater the level of competitive activity, the faster the rate of diffusion and the higher the maximum penetration level, if the products are similar. • However, the larger the number of competing technologies, the slower the rate of diffusion.	Young (1964); Hirschman (1980); Olshavsky (1980)
Personal characteristics: Innovators	23. Variables most likely to characterize innovators are: • Higher income • Higher education • Younger • Greater social mobility • Favorable attitude toward risk (venturesome) • Greater social participation • Higher opinion leadership	Midgley and Dowling (1978); Rogers (1983); Robertson, Zielinski, and Ward (1984)
	24. New product innovators will be drawn from the heavy users of other products within the product category.	Frank, Massy, and Morrison (1964); Robertson (1971); Peters and Venkatesan (1973); Taylor (1977); Danko and MacLachlan (1983); Dickerson and Gentry (1983)

TABLE 26.1 *(Continued)*

Diffusion concept	*Propositions*	*Relevant literature*
Personal characteristics: Innovators	25. Consumers with better-developed schemas need less cognitive effort for innovation comprehension and evaluation, and so are more likely to adopt early.	Hirschman (1981)
	26. The greater the individual propensity to use information from mass media or from sources external to the immediate social system (relative to interpersonal contacts within the social system), the earlier the adoption.	Bass (1969); Summers (1972); Lekvall and Wahlbin (1973); Green, Langeard, and Favell (1974); Midgley and Dowling (1978); Yapa and Mayfield (1978); Jeuland (1981)
Perceived innovation characteristics	27. Innovation characteristics affect speed of diffusion. Relative advantage, compatibility, trialability, and observability are positively related and complexity and perceived risk are negatively related.	Fliegel and Kivlin (1966); Zaltman, Duncan, and Holbek (1973); Ostlund (1974); Cooper (1979); Hopkins (1980); Booz-Allen & Hamilton (1981); Calantone and Cooper (1981); Hirschman (1981); Labay and Kinnear (1981); Feder (1982); Heany (1983); Rogers (1983)
	28. The speed of diffusion of technological innovations depends on the consumer's ability to develop new knowledge and new patterns of experience.	Robertson (1971); Hirschman (1980); Booz-Allen & Hamilton (1981); Day (1981); Wilton and Pessemier (1981); Dickerson and Gentry (1983); Heany (1983); Houston (1983)
	29. Related knowledge and experience of an innovation are associated with a faster rate of adoption. • Alternatively, the greater the disparity between an innovation and the consumer's existing knowledge and experience base, the slower the rate of adoption.	Brandner and Kearl (1964); Dickerson and Gentry (1983)

more fully elaborated for each construct. The dotted line relationships in Figure 26.1 concerning competitive activity are, in fact, not supported by propositions in this paper due to a lack of conceptualization and empirical results.

Our intent now is to discuss the various constructs, causal relationships, and interactions. The propositions specified are based on a comprehensive review of the diffusion literature across a number of fields. Our focus, however, is on the development of propositions which are directly relevant to consumer diffusion and which will contribute toward a theory of consumer diffusion.

THE ADOPTION PROCESS

Diffusion research has been content to rely on the traditional learning-oriented "hierarchy of effects" model and has ignored low involvement adoption process models, such as those proposed by Krugman (1965), Ray (1973), and Robertson (1976).

The hierarchy of effects is a useful schematic but its appropriateness seems to vary with the amount of cognitive processing that characterizes the adoption decision. Under conditions of high cognitive processing, the hierarchy of effects model seems to be a reasonable presentation of the adoption process: awareness, knowledge, attitude formation, trial, and adoption. However, under conditions of low cognitive processing, the low involvement model appears to represent the adoption process more accurately: awareness, trial, attitude formation, and adoption.

The variables that determine the amount of cognitive processing expended in the adoption of innovations are fourfold:

1. *Consumer learning requirements.* For products requiring high consumer learning, a hierarchy of effects model should be expected. This is likely for technology-based products or products that are toward the discontinuous end of the innovation continuum.
2. *Innovation or switching costs.* The costs involved in adoption include the transaction cost of the product as well as the "switching cost." This concept is more common in the adoption of production system innovations, but is also relevant for consumer innovations that have consequences or costs for the consumption system in which they are placed (Sheth 1981). For instance, the adoption of an innovation might require other changes in the consumption system or the adoption of ancillary services, which would raise the total cost of innovating (e.g., the purchase of software and peripherals to accompany a personal computer).
3. *Social relevance.* Some products are highly dependent on social acceptance and may even by symbolically defined by social referents (Hirschman 1981). It would be expected that the greater the social relevance, the more likely a hierarchy of effects adoption process.
4. *Multiperson adoption unit.* To the extent that the adoption decision involves other household members, the adoption process is more likely to follow a hierarchy of effects adoption pattern. The same thesis holds for organizational adoption (Ozanne and Churchill 1971; O'Neal, Thorelli, and Utterback 1973; Robertson and Wind 1980; Zaltman, Duncan, and Holbek 1973). The level of household involvement in adoption varies considerably by product category and by household characteristics (Davis and Rigaux 1974). The existing research base within consumer behavior has been limited primarily to husband–wife (Davis 1976) or parent–child decision processes (Adler et al. 1980); it has neither focused on total household decision processes nor recognized the multiple forms of households in today's society (with the weakening first of the extended family and now of the nuclear family). Research is needed which examines the roles played in adoption decisions within households and the variables that affect role enactment.

P1: The hierarchy of effects model is to be expected under conditions of:

- High consumer learning requirements
- High innovation costs or high switching costs
- High social imitation
- A multiperson adoption decision within the family or organization

The low involvement model is to be expected under conditions of:

- Low consumer learning requirements
- Low innovation costs or low switching costs
- Low social imitation

The concept of adoption has been used in a rather limited way to refer to a *single decision.* Yet for consumer product diffusion, adoption should be conceptualized more multidimensionally. For many consumer products, repeat purchase is the key to adoption; for others, it is important to assess adoption as to both width and depth. By *width* we mean the number of people within the adoption unit who use the product, or the number of different uses for the product, while *depth* indicates the amount of usage or the purchase of related products (such as accompanying software or peripherals).

The maximum long-run diffusion potential appears to be a function of both width and depth of adoption. For many product categories, multiple units of adoption are possible (color televisions, videotext applications), migration to higher performance units is possible (personal computers, calculators), or purchase of ancillary products or software is possible (personal computers, VCR systems, and so on). For applied purposes and for the sake of theoretical integrity, diffusion research should reorient beyond single adoption decisions to an examination of adoption width and depth.

Only in so doing will it be possible to assess maximum diffusion potential within the social system.

> **P2:** The maximum diffusion potential for the product increases with the width and depth of adoption.

Research on diffusion has generally focused on the adoption of a specific innovation. No attention has been directed to the relationship of that decision to the consumer's consumption system objectives. Yet the purchase of any innovation is dependent on the consumer's priority acquisition pattern and on the existing inventory of goods and services in the home.

Future research could contribute by focusing on how an innovation fits into existing consumption system and inventory patterns. A major barrier to diffusion occurs if consumers already have a similar product in inventory, such as a camera. Should the innovation then be positioned as more extreme in order to maximize the disparity with existing inventory? A further barrier to diffusion occurs when the innovation does not fit within the existing consumption system—for example, when a new product requires the consumer to change the way in which the entire consumption event is conducted. Also, since all consumption decisions involve an allocation of resources, how can an innovation break the priority acquisition pattern? Research by Hill (1970) has shown the similarity of product acquisitions within generations of consumers; yet significant innovations, such as microwaves, must change this acquisition pattern.

> **P3:** The adoption of an innovation depends on its fit within the existing consumption system and its ability to compete for scarce resources in order to achieve a position in the consumer's priority acquisition pattern.

Marketing actions directed to the consumer may have a considerable bearing on the speed of adoption. In general, the source from which information is sought is subject to change by stage of the decision process (Bettman 1979). There is a preference for more personal sources, and particularly personal influence, at later stages of the adoption process (Robertson 1971). However, the role and relative influence of marketing actions depend on the level of cognitive processing expended by product category. Advertising and other impersonal sources may be effective throughout the entire adoption process in low cognitive processing situations (Swinyard and Coney 1978).

> **P4:** The less the level of cognitive processing, the greater the impact of advertising and other impersonal marketing sources throughout the adoption process.

PERSONAL INFLUENCE AND OPINION LEADERSHIP

Personal influence is a basic underlying component of diffusion theory and diffusion models. As conceptualized in the Bass model, for example, *imitation* is a key parameter in determining the speed of diffusion (Bass 1969). Interestingly, however, personal influence and opinion leadership have received only limited research attention (Czepiel 1975)—perhaps consistent with the general lack of sociologically based research in consumer behavior.

The diffusion literature still relies heavily on the primitive two-step model of Katz and Lazarsfeld (1955) and the notion of a dominant opinion leader in touch with the mass media who exerts homophilous influence on a set of passive followers. A number of weaknesses exist in the two-step model, including the following (Weimann 1982):

- *Relevance.* Personal influence may or may not be relevant.
- *Role.* Personal influence and mass media may be complementary and play different roles.
- *Direction.* "Opinion sharing" may occur as well as "opinion seeking" and "opinion giving."
- *Intent.* Personal influence may be for conformity or for informational purposes.

- *Form.* Visual influence may be as important as verbal influence ("word of mouth").
- *Sign.* Positive and negative personal influence may have different levels of impacts.
- *Personal Factors.* Characteristics of opinion leaders vary by product category, but preference for personal influence as an information source may extend across product categories.
- *Network Analysis.* Although it is assumed that influence is transmitted among similar individuals in a social system, there may be conditions where heterophilous (dissimilar) influence occurs.

Relevance

The incidence of personal influence which occurs for an innovation depends on the consumer's involvement in the purchase decision. As a generalization, personal influence will be operative mainly under a hierarchy-of-effects adoption process and not under a low-involvement adoption process. As discussed earlier, a hierarchy-of-effects adoption process is expected under conditions of high consumer learning requirements, high innovation or switching costs, high social relevance, and a multiperson adoption decision.

> **P5:** Personal influence is operative mainly under a hierarchy-of-effects adoption process.

Role

Given the operation of personal influence, what is its role in the adoption process? Personal influence is generally interdependent with mass media. The effect of personal influence is most pronounced at later stages of the adoption process, whereas mass media's effect is most pronounced at earlier stages of the adoption process (Bettman 1979; Robertson 1971; Rogers 1983). As such, personal influence and mass media are generally complementary rather than competing. When conflict does occur, personal influence has greater impact. Obviously, when personal influence is nonoperative (in a low-involvement adoption sequence), then mass media may have direct effects.

> **P6:** When personal influence is operative, it is interdependent with mass media and its effect is most pronounced at later stages of the adoption process. When personal influence and mass media are in conflict, personal influence has greater impact.

Direction

The extant two-step model depicts mass media reaching opinion leaders who, in turn, influence a set of followers. This information-giving flow may, in fact, be valid for some percentage of personal influence transactions. However, other flows are possible, including information seeking and information sharing. Explicit research evidence is lacking, but we would expect the impact of personal influence to be greatest for information seeking and least for information giving. It seems logical to suggest that persuasibility would be enhanced when the individual seeks out the influential.

Research is needed which more definitively distinguishes the direction of personal influence when it is operative. This has particular implications for marketing and change agent strategies that seek to affect the personal influence process. To do so, it is necessary to know whether to focus on the source or the recipient as the influence instigator.

> **P7:** The impact of personal influence is greatest under information-seeking conditions and least under information-giving conditions.

Intent

There is a bias in the diffusion literature that the acceptance of personal influence is tied to conformity behavior. This is also true in the modeling of diffusion (Bass 1969; Mahajan and Muller 1979), where the imitation coefficient is essentially a conformity coefficient. Yet the acceptance of personal influence may emanate from conformity or from information-seeking intentions (Bauer 1967; Deutsch and Gerard 1955). To understand or to affect the process of personal influence, it is necessary to know the motivations behind the acceptance of personal influence.

It has also be suggested, although not explicitly pursued, that there are two distinct networks operating in the transfer of personal influence. In research on diffusion within a less developed country, Burt (1973) concluded that the network for the transfer of information (information-seeking intention) can be distinguished from the network for the transfer of social influence (conformity intention). He found that the length of time to make an adoption decision was most protracted for respondents who were well integrated into the social influence network, probably because of the high amount of norms-related communication which had to transpire before it was clear that a majority of friends supported the innovation. It would be interesting to extent this research into the consumer behavior arena and to test the following proposition.

> **P8:** Consumers who are highly dependent on normative influence (conformity intention) will be slower to adopt.

Form

The study of personal influence has focused almost exclusively on verbal influence—i.e., "word of mouth." Some significant proportion of personal influence may, however, be of a visual form—as in fashion, cars, and other goods on public display. Indeed, visual influence could even be more persuasive for some products (such as symbolic innovations), due to its potentially higher information content. In the case of fashion, for example, viewing the fashion on display may communicate more information than countless advertisements or personal discussions. For nonsymbolic innovations, however, visual influence may have limited information content.

It may also be that visual and verbal influence play different roles in the decision process. Visual influence may have its greatest impact at awareness, whereas verbal influence may have its greatest impact at evaluation due to the need for interpersonal confirmation and the need to ask questions.

Recent research in consumer behavior has begun to focus on visual imagery in advertising (Edell and Staelin 1983; Kisielius 1982), but personal influence of a visual form and its functioning remains an untapped research area.

> **P9:** The impact of visual influence increases with the information content that can be visually communicated for a particular product category.
>
> Visual influence is likely to have greatest impact at awareness, whereas verbal influence is likely to have greatest influence at evaluation.

Sign

Until recently, it was generally the case that only positive personal influence was examined in consumer behavior research or diffusion models. Very little distinction is made in the literature between the processes operating for the positive or negative transfer of information. What evidence we do have suggests that negative personal influence will have considerably greater persuasive impact than positive personal influence (Arndt 1967; Mizerski 1982; Richins 1983). This is consistent with the "negativity bias" in impression information and cognitive processing (Kanouse and Hanson 1972). Recent modeling of negative personal influence has been undertaken by Mahajan, Muller, and Kerin, (1984).

The particular impact of personal influence, whether positive or negative, also seems to depend on the credibility of the source (Sternthal, Phillips, and Dholakia 1978) and the discrepancy of the influence attempt from the recipient's initial opinion (Oliver 1977). The consistency of information received also affects the acceptance of influence. In general, adoption will be faster given positive influence from a credible source and given a lack of conflicting opinions.

> **P10:** Negative personal influence has greater persuasive impact than positive personal

influence, assuming a credible source and consistent information content.

Personal Factors

Based on extant diffusion theory, we can conclude that opinion leader characteristics vary by product category and that there is no generalized opinion leader (King and Summers 1970; Langeard, Crousillat, and Weisz 1977; Myers and Robertson 1972; Silk 1966).

We have not, however, studied information acceptance characteristics. For example, consumers may have different information source preferences (Bettman 1979; Westbrook and Fornell 1979), and these preferences may be consistent across product categories. Perhaps some consumers have a general preference for either impersonal or personal sources. It has also been suggested that social integration or gregariousness is related to the probability of personal influence exposure (Baumgarten 1975; Robertson 1971; Summers 1970).

P11: Opinion leader traits vary by product category.

Exposure to personal influence is positively related to information source preference and social integration.

Network Analysis

Most personal influence is transmitted within a network of peers who possess similar demographic characteristics; thus it is referred to as homophilous influence. The probability of such influence is high, simply because people are most likely to interact with similar others. Some significant level of influence may be heterophilous, however—that is, transmitted among people who are dissimilar. This may be particularly true for innovators, who have no knowledgeable internal social system sources of influence for that innovation and hence must look to external sources. As Rogers notes, heterophilous communication has a special informational potential, even though it may be realized only rarely" (1983, p. 275).

The value of heterophilous influence has been documented by Granovetter (1973), who discovered that "weak ties" are important in job searches, mainly because people with homophilous ties are unlikely to know anything more than the information recipients (because their contacts are similar). To some extent, this may parallel the concept of the "marginal" in the anthropology literature—a marginal being a person who transcends cultures and who is, therefore, critical to the dissemination of innovations (Barnett 1953).

In the consumer behavior literature Kaigler-Evans, Leavitt, and Dickey (1977) have used the notion of a "point of optimal heterophily." This is the balance point between personal contact that is so similar as to provide minimum new information, and personal contact that is so dissimilar that communication breaks off. Kaigler-Evans et al. provide preliminary evidence for the effectiveness of sources who are in this middle range of optimal heterophily.

P12: Homophilous influence is more common, but heterophilous influence beyond the boundaries of the social system is common among innovators.

There is a point of optimal heterophily that maximizes the effectiveness of personal influence.

THE SOCIAL SYSTEM

The diffusion theory literature assumes that diffusion occurs within the boundaries of a social system. As such, the identification of the social system is assumed to be known and to remain constant. These may be reasonable premises within some fields of study, such as rural or medial sociology, but they are questionable in consumer diffusion, where mass-media marketing programs cross social system boundaries. Consequently, any study of a social system should consider the characteristics of the immediate social system and its interactions with other social systems.

The social system can be characterized along three dimensions: values and norms, system evolution, and homogeneity of population characteristics.

Values and Norms

Diffusion occurs within a social system that possesses a set of values and norms. The innovation's degree of compatibility with these values and norms determines the speed of diffusion (Rogers 1983). Whereas Rogers assumes that this occurs within a system of fixed size, when dealing with consumer diffusion there is a difficulty in identifying the social system. The size of the potential market is frequently quite problematic for consumer innovations. The entire population of the social system cannot be considered as potential adopters. Instead, the social system size is variable, and only certain members can potentially adopt the innovation under specified conditions. The values and norms of the system are basic characteristics which determine the size of the group of potential adopters. For example, a cross-country comparison of the status of women (as represented, say, by the percentage of women in the labor force) shows that the sales potential of products such as dishwashers varies according to women's percentage in the labor force.

P13: The diffusion rate and the maximum penetration level are positively related to the innovation's compatibility with social system values.

System Evolution

Values and norms are not constant over the diffusion time horizon. This normative evolution affects market potential over time. For example, over the last 20 years, women in Europe have come to value time more highly. Accordingly, new markets for time-saving products have developed. Other variables characterizing the consumer environment, such as economic and legal considerations, also affect the size of the market over time.

Some recent diffusion models have incorporated environmental variables as determinants affecting the potential size of the market (Mahajan and Peterson 1978; Mahajan et al. 1979; Peterson and Mahajan 1978). However, the environmental variables included are limited in scope—new housing starts, for example. More general environmental variables, such as communication patterns or economic conditions, are factors that would be particularly relevant in explaining differences in diffusion patterns across social systems (Heeler and Hustad 1980).

P14: The maximum level of penetration of the innovation in the social system is affected by normative change.

System Homogeneity

Market segments have different diffusion patterns, represented by different speed and sales potentials. However, segments do not form distinct social systems. The degree of interaction between segments violates the condition of relative independence in defining a social system; the degree of fragmentation of a market into segments represents a measure of social system heterogeneity. Such heterogeneity, for example, can be due to differences in the consumer's propensity to purchase, which depends on the consumer's underlying utility function (Eliashberg, Tapiero, and Wind 1983; Jeuland 1981). The prediction is that the speed of diffusion decreases as the degree of heterogeneity increases because of the resulting reduction in interpersonal contact.

P15: The more homogeneous the social system, the faster the diffusion rate and the higher the maximum penetration level.

Social system heterogeneity has been studied in spatial diffusion research. Two general theories have been identified that lead to different patterns of diffusion across the landscape (market). The first approach focuses on the flow of information between potential adopting units. Whereas original work emphasized terrestrial barriers to communication, such as the geographical distance between potential adopting units, more recent research has generalized this notion of barriers to include social and economic barriers as well. The pattern of diffusion which occurs when the time of adoption is a function of the distance between communicators has been called the "neighborhood effect" (Hagerstrand 1965).

The second approach "stresses the importance of market and infrastructure factors that control the availability of the innovation to potential adopters" (Brown, Malecki, and Spector 1976, p. 100). This conceptual model seems particularly appropriate in the consumer context when distribution is not immediately national, but follows a specific pattern, such as giving priority to large distributors. A "hierarchical pattern" would thus occur, since the time of availability of the innovation in a given distributor's area is related to the size of the market.

The diffusion pattern across countries is also expected to be influenced by marketing decisions regarding country entry. Given the importance of these decisions, the hierarchical pattern should dominate the countries' order of adoption. However, these foreign entry decisions are based on factors that are related to the perceived risks of the venture. Physical and social barriers are examples of such factors because of the difficulty of communication that they create. Consequently, these barriers, which are typical of the "neighborhood effect," also influence the pattern of diffusion across countries. Within a country, the neighborhood effect is most often observed, so the two effects can be combined. Thus both factors—the terrestrial or social distance and the market infrastructure factors—determine the spatial pattern of diffusion of the innovation.

P16: The spatial pattern of diffusion shows a hierarchy effect when market and infrastructure factors controlling the availability of the new product are dominant, and a neighborhood effect when terrestrial or social factors are dominant.

P17: The sequence of countries adopting an innovation is dominated by a hierarchical pattern. The physical distance between countries and the social similarity between the countries are negatively related to the diffusion sequence across countries.

THE DIFFUSION PROCESS

The diffusion process can be characterized in terms of three dimensions: the rate of diffusion, the pattern of diffusion, and the potential penetration level. The *rate* of diffusion reflects the speed at which sales occur over time. The diffusion *pattern* concerns the shape of the diffusion curve. Typically, the curve showing only decreasing returns and the S-shaped or sigmoid curve have been represented by exponential and logistic function forms, respectively. The *potential penetration level* is a separate dimension indicating the size of the potential market—i.e., the maximum cumulative sales (or adoption) over time.

The diffusion process generally has been assumed to follow an S-shaped (sigmoid) pattern. This pattern dominates the classic research on diffusion, including the hybrid corn study (Ryan and Gross 1943) and the physician study (Coleman et al. 1957). The consumer diffusion theory literature has invariably conceptualized the diffusion process as sigmoid. However, other diffusion patterns have been documented, particularly exponential patterns (Cox 1967; Polli and Cook 1969; Rink and Swan 1979; Robertson 1971). The behavioral assumptions underlying the diffusion process determine the diffusion pattern.

It has been proposed that the pure logistic pattern is due to the concept of social imitation or personal influence (Mansfield 1961; Teece 1980). When these sources of information are minimal compared to direct marketing effects or to the level of interactions with contacts outside the immediate social system an exponential curve of diffusion is predicted (Fourt and Woodlock 1960). The S-shaped pattern has been observed in a number of marketing studies of consumer durables diffusion (Bass 1969; Dodds 1973; Heeler and Hustad 1980; Nevers 1972; Tigert and Farivar 1981).

Both processes of personal influence internal

to the social system and social interactions external to the system are hypothesized to occur in these studies. Yet social imitation is not the only factor that may determine the shape of the diffusion curve. Individuals in the social system have different initial opinions or beliefs about the attributes of the innovation. Feder and O'Mara (1982) and Jensen (1982) suggest that the shape of the distribution of these beliefs across individuals determines whether the shape of the diffusion curve is sigmoid or exponential.

There are two such cases that affect the shape of the diffusion curve. In the first case there is a range of initial beliefs with equal probabilities. In the second case there is a unimodal distribution of initial beliefs around a mean value. The first predicts an exponential diffusion curve. The reasoning follows the fact that, in the case of a uniform distribution of initial beliefs across individuals in the social system, the adoption potential is depleted at a constant rate. The second case produces a sigmoid curve. This occurs because the manufacturer begins by convincing the few consumers in one tail of the distribution. Eventually, the many individuals in the mid-range of the distribution become convinced, producing sharp sales increases. Thus, the pattern of convincing few, then many, leads to the sigmoid curve.

The amount of learning required before adopting the innovation also influences the shape of the diffusion process. In decisions that involve a learning hierarchy process with a substantial amount of information processing, the diffusion process starts slowly. Conversely, under low learning requirements and limited cognitive processing, which is typical of a low-involvement decision process, the speed of diffusion is not impeded by slow learning process and diffusion tends to be exponential.

The uncertainty attached to the innovation (or its attributes) is related to the notion discussed above of learning requirements. The greater the uncertainty, the greater the need for additional information before the consumer can make a decision. A Bayesian model of learning under uncertainty is consistent with the expectation of an exponential curve under low learning requirements (Stoneman 1981). The costs of the innovation, including costs of switching from one product or technology to another, contribute to the risks of the decision and hence have the same effect as uncertainty on the shape of diffusion.

P18: The diffusion process tends to follow one of two ideal type patterns—sigmoid or exponential. A sigmoid pattern is expected under conditions of:

- The operation of personal influence
- A learning hierarchy process of adoption
- High innovation costs or high switching costs
- Unimodal distribution of initial beliefs toward the innovation within the social system
- High uncertainty

An exponential curve is expected under conditions of:

- A relative lack of personal influence
- A low-involvement process of adoption
- Low uncertainty
- Low innovation and switching costs
- A uniform pattern of initial beliefs within the social system

Marketing actions are also important in influencing the speed of diffusion, as well as the diffusion process by market segment. Indeed, in most cases marketing actions are designed to achieve faster penetration to secure a quicker return on investment, to block competition, and to establish a market franchise. Commitment of sizeable marketing expenditures in advertising, sampling programs, and distribution programs is likely to result in a diffusion function that is more similar to an exponential curve than to a sigmoid curve—provided consumer learning needs are low and the product is not high on social visibility.

Thus marketing expenditures have their greatest potential impact for which might be termed low-involvement innovations—i.e., innovations for which the learning requirements and the level of cognitive processing are low. Although important for other products, marketing impact is longer term and less dramatic. In neither case, however, do marketing expenditures fundamentally alter the shape of the diffusion curve from a sigmoid to an exponential pattern, since this would require a change in the adoption decision process. This is unlikely to occur for most consumer innovations; instead, marketing expenditures operate to affect the rate of diffusion, given either a sigmoid or an exponential pattern. Marketing expenditures are also used to expand demand or to increase the market potential. Consequently, the level of potential penetration is positively related to marketing expenditures.

The marketing impact on diffusion has been almost completely ignored in diffusion theory. That diffusion theory has not encompassed marketing-mix variables is probably due to the fields in which the theory is developed—e.g., rural sociology and geography. Yet it is surprising that consumer behavior researchers, who have applied diffusion theory, have not extended the theory by incorporating marketing policies. The diffusion pattern has been viewed from a passive perspective. The product life cycle concept, which has its roots in diffusion theory, suffers from the same passivity (Dhalla and Yuspeh 1976).

However, modelers of the diffusion process have included marketing-mix variables—namely, advertising, price, and personal selling (Bass 1980; Horsky and Simon 1983; Lilien, Rao, and Kalish 1981; Simon and Sebastian 1982)—thus demonstrating the impact of these variables on new product diffusion. The larger the marketing effort—i.e., greater advertising, lower price, greater personal communication, greater sampling or demonstration level, or the more widespread distribution level—the faster the rate of adoption.

In addition, these diffusion modeling studies show that marketing efforts accumulate in effectiveness over time. There is also some evidence for decreasing returns to scale in the effectiveness of marketing-mix variables.

P19: Marketing expenditures affect the rate of diffusion and the maximum penetration level but not the pattern of diffusion.

- Marketing variables have long-term, cumulative effects on diffusion.
- The effectiveness of marketing variables on the diffusion curve shows decreasing returns to scale.

At a more strategic level, the greater the degree of compatibility between the market segment targeted and the innovation's characteristics, the faster the rate of adoption. Actually, the rate of diffusion varies by market segment (Robertson and Wind 1980). The strategy of the firm marketing the innovation has a major impact on the speed of diffusion. As the number of segments targeted and the degree of fit between the segments' needs and the marketing policies increase, the diffusion rate increases and the product life cycle is shortened.

P20: The greater the sensitivity of the marketing program to the changing characteristics of segments at different stages of the diffusion process, the faster the rate of diffusion and the greater the penetration level.

Most of the literature on personal influence in diffusion theory assumes a two-step flow of communication (as discussed earlier), whereby opinion leaders undertake the task of transmitting information. Midgley (1976) identifies different types of information flow based on a decomposition of the social system into four groups: potential adopters, active adopters, active rejectors, and passives. Depending on the group, a different type of information is communicated to the other groups. A concept developed in mathematical sociology refines this idea in the sense that the influencer—most often an early adopter—will have a limited time span during which she/he will be interested in the innovation.

The flow of communication and the influence from an early adopter will thus stop after a certain time. The result of including the duration of interest in the personal influence process is reflected in the pattern of diffusion. The expected speed of adoption increases with the average time of active information dissemination in the system (Bartholomew 1976; Karmeshu and Pathria 1980). Since one of the effects of mass media communication is to prevent consumers from forgetting the brand name or attributes (Zielske and Henry 1980), mass communication expenditures should be positively related to the average time of active personal influence dissemination.

P21: The expected speed of diffusion increases with the average time of active information dissemination within the social system, which is heightened by the level of mass media communication expenditures.

Competition has a major impact on the diffusion process, although research has neglected this area. In general, under conditions resembling pure competition—i.e., where there is little differentiation among brands—a positive effect of competition on primary demand can be expected. Consequently, the more similar the brands in a market, the faster the rate of product category diffusion due to the intensity of competition expected in such a market.

However, when new competing technologies are involved, diffusion may be slowed. In this case, consumers face uncertainty about which technology will eventually become the standard. Because of such uncertainty and the increased risk of making an early decision, purchase is postponed and the diffusion process slows.

There is considerable implicit belief that diffusion cycles have shortened over time in high technology product categories. Young (1964) documented that this was indeed the case for household appliance innovations. Olshavsky (1980) subsequently confirmed this finding based on an analysis of sales data for the same product category. We might suppose that the phenomenon holds for technological innovations in general. Whether the same phenomenon holds for symbolic innovations (Hirschman 1980)—that is, innovations which communicate a new social meaning—remains to be researched.

P22: The greater the level of competitive activity, the faster the rate of diffusion and the higher the maximum penetration level, if the products are similar.

However, the larger the number of competing technologies, the slower the rate of diffusion.

PERSONAL CHARACTERISTICS: INNOVATORS

The diffusion theory literature has focused considerable attention on the characteristics of innovators and other adopter categories, defined in terms of the number of standard deviations from the mean time of adoption for the population. Innovators are "venturesome," early adopters "respectable," the early majority "deliberate," the late majority "skeptical," and laggards "traditional" (Rogers 1983). The validity of these traits in consumer research is questionable due to the lack of consistent findings in empirical studies. This is especially true to low-involvement products, since the predictor variables are typically based on research on major innovations (Midgley and Dowling 1978; Rogers 1983).

Perhaps the most prevalent research topic within consumer diffusion theory has been to derive profiles of innovators for particular product categories. A review of research across product categories by Robertson, Zielinski, and Ward (1984) shows some tendencies for innovators to bear the following characteristics: higher income, higher education, younger, more socially mobile, more favorable attitudes toward risk, greater social participation, and higher opinion leadership.

P23: Variables most likely to characterize innovators are higher income, higher education, younger, greater social mobility, favorable attitude toward risk (venturesome), greater social participation, and higher opinion leadership.

These personal characteristics apply more to some product categories than others. The overriding conclusion is that innovators must be identified and characterized on a product category basis and that there is not a generalized innovator across product category or interest domains.

One finding which has been replicated across many product categories is that innovators are drawn from the heavy users within the product category or from those with significant experience in similar product categories. This finding extends from food and personal care products (Frank, Massy, and Morrison 1964; Taylor 1977) to consumer appliances (Robertson 1971) to computers and computer services (Danko and MacLachlan 1983; Dickerson and Gentry 1983; Peters and Venkatesan 1973).

> **P24:** New product innovators will be drawn from the heavy users of other products within the product category.

Perhaps a reason for the correlation between product category usage rate and innovativeness is the greater knowledge and ability that heavy users have to evaluate new information. Heavy users have different knowledge structures—or ways to relate components of knowledge—such that improved predictions of outcomes can be made. The completeness and complexity of these information structures or schema determine the ability to mentally represent a problem, to isolate solution criteria, to identify decision strategies, and to evoke the products with the relevant attributes (Hirschman 1980). Consumers with better-developed schemas need less cognitive effort to comprehend and evaluate innovations. These individuals acquire knowledge more efficiently and are more likely to adopt early.

> **P25:** Consumers with better-developed schemas need less cognitive effort for innovation comprehension and evaluation, and so are more likely to adopt early.

A possible explanation for the lack of a generalized innovator profile might come from the definition of adopter categories. Typically, a normal distribution of adopter categories is assumed and arbitrary cutoff points are chosen to separate consumers into groups. Consumer diffusion research generally uses different cutoff points than does sociological research, and variation occurs even among studies in the same field (Midgley and Dowling 1978). Therefore, this categorization is only a heuristic that might be useful; it is not based on theoretical grounds with a clear-cut assignment of individuals to categories.

Modelers of the diffusion processes have identified two categories of adopters. In Bass's model (1969), "innovators" are described as those consumers who are not influenced by previous adopters in the social system. Such consumers are influenced only by sources outside the set of prospective adopters (Jeuland 1981; Lekvall and Wahlbin 1973). Indeed, there is some empirical support for the contention that innovators are exposed more to mass media (Green, Langeard, and Favell 1974; Summers 1972) and are more cosmopolitan—i.e., have a higher degree of orientation to the world beyond their immediate social system (Yapa and Mayfield 1978).

Bass' distinction is such that "innovators" may adopt at any point throughout the diffusion process—early or late. The terminology is confusing, but it does separate consumers who are influenced purely by external sources. They constitute the seed of the contagion (personal influence) process.

We therefore propose that the type of information sources accessed may be used to characterize innovators or noninnovators. The usage of sources of information can be defined by the ratio to which the consumer relies on mass media—or sources of information external to the immediate social system—versus relying on interpersonal contacts within the social system.

This characterization of consumers based on information sources could be more fruitful than the traditional categorization of adopters according to time of adoption (as evaluated ex post facto). In fact, the lack of a theoretical basis for the traditional categorization of consumers could explain the inconsistent research results in terms of personal trait characteristics. In addition, by defining innovators in terms of communication variables, diffusion research would be more relevant to consumer marketing. This point of view corresponds to Midgley and Dowling's definition of innovativeness as "the degree to which an individual is receptive to new ideas and makes innovation decisions independently of the communicated experience of others" (1978, p. 236).

> **P26:** The greater the individual's propensity to use information from mass media or from sources external to the immediate social system (relative to interpersonal contacts within the social system), the earlier the adoption.

PERCEIVED INNOVATION CHARACTERISTICS

The characteristics of an innovation obviously affect the likelihood and speed of its diffusion within a social system. Nevertheless, this topic has received limited attention in the consumer diffusion literature (Zaltman and Stiff 1973). Most research on innovation characteristics has been conducted in rural sociology (Feder 1982; Fliegel and Kivlin 1966) and in organizational behavior (Zaltman et al. 1973).

Much of the conceptualization and research which has been reported recently concerning innovation characteristics within the marketing literature is for industrial innovations (Booz-Allen & Hamilton 1981; Calantone and Cooper 1981; Cooper 1979; Heany 1983; Hopkins 1980). The focus of this thinking is both on the innovation's relationship to the market and on the innovation's relationship and compatibility to the firm. For example, the Booz-Allen & Hamilton report suggests that the firm's diffusion objectives should vary with the new product's "strategic role." Much of this literature suggests that new product success is a function of the "product/company fit." Despite the value of this literature to marketing strategy, it does not provide us with much insight into the behavior of the consumer, so we shall not review it in depth.

Readers are undoubtedly familiar with Rogers' (1983) scheme evaluating innovations as to their relative advantage, compatibility, trialability, observability, and complexity. The first four characteristics are positively related to speed of diffusion and the last is negatively related.

Only a few consumer behavior researchers—such as Ostlund (1974), Labay and Kinnear (1981), and Hirschman (1981)—have seriously studied innovation characteristics within the consumer behavior literature. Ostlund's results for consumer-packaged goods' innovations confirm Rogers' expectations, and find that perceived risk is also negatively related to speed of adoption. Ostlund also concludes that for the product category studied, "the perceptions of innovations by potential adopters can be very effective predictors of innovativeness, more so than personal characteristic variables" (1974, p. 28). In a somewhat similar vein, in a study of solar energy systems Labay and Kinnear (1981) found that innovation perceptions were better predictors of innovativeness than were demographics. Their variables included Rogers' variables, together with financial and social risk.

Hirschman has proposed that innovations can be classified on two dimensions—symbolic and technological. A symbolic innovation communicates a new social meaning, whereas a technological innovation provides new tangible features. These types of innovations may have quite different diffusion patterns.

> **P27:** Innovation characteristics affect speed of diffusion. Relative advantage, compatibility, trialability, and observability are positively related, and complexity and perceived risk are negatively related.

The existing concept of an innovation in the consumer diffusion literature is limited. Little effort has been directed to the development of a broader conceptualization for understanding and classifying innovations. A modest step in this direction was Robertson's (1971) innovation continuum, which suggests that innovations be arrayed in terms of their effects on established consumption patterns from continuous (minor) to discontinuous (major) innovations. From the vantage point of the firm,

Booz-Allen & Hamilton (1981) has suggested a continuum as follows: brand proliferations or repositionings, flankers and brand extensions, line extensions, new to the company, and new to the world. Similarly, Heany (1983) has proposed a product-innovation spectrum: style changes, product line extensions, product improvements, new products for the current market served, and new products for new (to the firm) markets.

Unfortunately, research has not been conducted relating innovation *characteristics* (such as those specified by Rogers) to innovation *types* (from continuous to discontinuous). An initial contribution would be to specify an elaborated set of assessor variables and the types of innovations for which they are appropriate. For example, Day (1981, p. 61) has elaborated the problems of diffusion analysis under conditions of multiple definitions of innovation types by level of aggregation characterizing "hierarchical product structures, ranging from the generic product class and industry, to the product type or form, and down to variants and brands."

In particular need of development is a conceptualization for the diffusion of consumer technology innovations. *The Journal of Consumer Research* recently tried to produce a special issue on this topic, but there were not enough scholars actively researching the topic to warrant an entire issue. The outcome of this endeavor was the publication of two interesting articles (Dickerson and Gentry 1983; Houston 1983).

The key to the diffusion of technological innovations may be in building the consumer knowledge and experience base for this type of technology. Existing research on consumer innovations tends to make the assumption that consumers have knowledge of and experience with the product category. Indeed, much of the marketing methodology for new product assessment—such as multidimensional scaling and conjoint analysis—assumes consumer understanding of the product category and focuses on new product opportunities within the existing benefit profile. Wilton and Pessemier (1981) have recognized this limitation and suggest that it may be necessary to educate consumers about new technologies before testing reactions and assessing diffusion potential. Their research on electric vehicles provides a method for the early forecast of diffusion based on artificially advancing knowledge to the state normally encountered prior to adoption.

As Hirschman notes (1980), technological innovations are likely to be discontinuous in their effects on established consumption patterns, as opposed to symbolic innovations. Of course, this is not always the case, since an advanced technology could simply replace an existing technology without much consumer impact. But as a generalization, we find Hirschman's conclusion meaningful. For most technological innovations, diffusion will depend on consumers developing new knowledge and new patterns of experience.

P28: The speed of diffusion of technological innovations depends on the consumer's ability to develop new knowledge and new patterns of experience.

The speed of diffusion of a technological innovation will be fastest among those consumers who already have some related knowledge or experience. This thesis is supported by Dickerson and Gentry's (1983) research on home computers, which found that experience with computer-related products (in this case, video games and programmable calculators) was the major variable in explaining innovative behavior. Similarly, Brandner and Kearl (1964) have found that perceived congruency with past favorable experiences is related to innovative behavior among farmers.

P29: Related knowledge and experience of an innovation are associated with a faster rate of adoption.

Alternatively, the greater the disparity between an innovation and the consumer's existing knowledge and experience base, the slower the rate of adoption.

There is a compelling need to research the diffusion of new consumer technologies. We must go beyond the assumption that new products represent only an extension of the existing consumer experience base. For many new products—such as personal computers, videotext, or electronic banking—consumers may have to develop new consumption patterns. Yet most consumer diffusion research has focused on innovations which are relatively continuous ones.

CONCLUSION

Diffusion theory represents an important perspective on communication effects. It is robust in scope and has been useful in explaining the spread of new ideas, new practices, and new products. The basic constructs of diffusion—the innovation, adopter categories, the adoption process, personal influence, and the pattern of diffusion—have been of value in conceptualizing the information dissemination process and in suggesting the value of particular change agent interventions.

One of the most intriguing aspects of diffusion theory is its interdisciplinary nature. The diffusion paradigm has been found to be meaningful in a number of disciplines; its research base encompasses rural sociology, agricultural economics, industrial economics, geography, marketing science, and consumer behavior. Based on a research foundation of thousands of publications, a considerable amount is known about diffusion.

The applied value of diffusion theory has also been demonstrated. Diffusion concepts have proven useful to managers and change agents. Diffusion is a major focus of thinking regarding new product marketing (Urban and Hauser 1980; Wind 1982) as well as advertising (Aaker and Myers 1982; Ray 1982). The diffusion focus is useful product life cycle planning: it suggests differential communications programs to reach innovators versus later adopters and suggests strategies for affecting the personal influence process. Diffusion theory may also be of value at the product design stage—i.e., in assessing consumer perceptions of innovations and the product attributes most likely to be associated with adoption.

Nevertheless, it is our thesis that consumer diffusion theory has considerable further potential as a theory of communications and as an important framework for new product marketing. Indeed, diffusion theory has been utilized in the development of a number of normative diffusion models in recent years. Yet the assumptions underlying these models have not been adequately tested by consumer behavior researchers. Furthermore, although diffusion theory is well accepted within the consumer behavior literature, only limited intellectual endeavor has been expended on conceptualization and empirical research in the past decade. The consumer diffusion paradigm is essentially similar to that developed in rural sociology; consumer behavior scholars have made little progress in advancing diffusion theory. Consumer diffusion research also accounts for only a small percentage of total diffusion research.

A common characteristic of past diffusion research is its emphasis on the antecedents of early adoption, in terms of either individual (innovator) characteristics or innovation characteristics. The literature has been largely concerned with direct relationships of main effects. Analysis of direct effects provides insufficient explanation for the diffusion of most consumer innovations. New research must consider interactions among diffusion constructs as well as marketing (change agent) and competitive initiatives. The framework proposed in this paper develops a set of interrelated concepts with cause-effect relationships. Because of the complex nature of the diffusion of consumer innovations, the entire framework should be considered in order to produce predictions that are robust. The Table demonstrates the range of propositions suggested, and the Figure specifies their relationships and interactions. Our goal has been to posit new research directions and to develop an enriched theory of consumer diffusion. The propositions attempt to specify the factors on which adoption and diffusion depend.

The proposed framework can be extended to a causal model specification which could be estimated through an analysis of covariance structure. Although beyond the scope of the present paper, this extension would imply (1) operational definitions of the constructs presented in this paper, and (2) multiple measures of these constructs. These two steps are required in order to advance consumer diffusion theory to the level of a tested, comprehensive set of interrelated propositions.

Empirical research is now needed to advance a theory of consumer diffusion. The propositional inventory offered here might serve to guide this research in the most fruitful directions. New research should view the diffusion process as contingent in nature, rather than as a set of direct effects. New research might also consider the marketing (change agent) actions of the innovating firms and the actions of competitors as important effects on the process of diffusion.

REFERENCES

AAKER, DAVID and JOHN MYERS (1982), *Advertising Management.* Englewood Cliffs, NJ: Prentice-Hall.

ADLER, RICHARD P., GERALD S. LESSER, LAURENE KRASNY MANINGOFF, THOMAS S. ROBERTSON, JOHN R. ROSSITER, and SCOTT WARD (1980), *The Effects of Television Advertising on Children.* Lexington, MA: Lexington Books, Chap. 11.

ARNDT, JOHAN (1967), "Role of Product-Related Conversations in the Diffusion of a New Product," *Journal of Marketing Research,* 4 (August), 291-295.

BARNETT, HOMER G. (1953), *Innovation: The Basis of Culture Change.* New York: McGraw-Hill.

BARTHOLOMEW, D. J. (1976), "Continuous Time Diffusion Models with Random Duration of Interest," *Journal of Mathematical Sociology,* 4 (2), 187-199.

BASS, FRANK M. (1969), "A New Product Growth Model for Consumer Durables," *Management Science,* 15 (5), 215-227.

______ (1980), "The Relationship Between Diffusion Curves, Experience Curves, and Demand Elasticities for Consumer Durable Technological Innovations," *Journal of Business,* 53 (July), S51-S57.

BAUER, RAYMOND A. (1967), "Source Effect and Persuasibility: A New Look," in *Risk Taking and Information Handling in Consumer Behavior,* Ed. Donald F. Cox. Boston, MA: Harvard Business School, 559-578.

BAUMGARTEN, STEPHEN A. (1975), "The Innovative Communicator in the Diffusion Process," *Journal of Marketing Research,* 12 (February), 12-18.

BETTMAN, JAMES R. (1979), *An Information Processing Theory of Consumer Choice.* Reading, MA: Addison-Wesley.

BOOZ-ALLEN & HAMILTON INC. (1981), *New Product Management of the 1980's.* Chicago: Booz-Allen & Hamilton, Inc.

BRANDNER, LOWELL, and BRYANT KEARL (1964), "Evaluation for Congruence as a Factor in Adoption Rate of Innovations," *Rural Sociology,* 29 (3), 288-303.

BROWN, LAWRENCE A. (1981), "Innovation Diffusion: A New Perspective. New York: Methuen.

BROWN, LAWRENCE A., EDWARD J. MALECKI, and ARON N. SPECTOR (1976), "Adopter Categories in a Spatial Context: Alternative Explanations for an Empirical Regularity," *Rural Sociology,* 41 (Spring), 99-118.

BURT, RONALD S. (1973), "The Differential Impact of Social Integration on Participation in the Diffusion of Innovations," *Social Science Research,* 2 (2), 125-144.

CALANTONE, ROGER, and ROBERT G. COOPER (1981), "New Product Scenarios: Prospects for Success," *Journal of Marketing,* 45 (Spring), 48-60.

COLEMAN, JAMES, ELIHU KATZ, and HERBERT MENZEL (1957), "The Diffusion of an Innovation Among Physicians," *Sociometry,* 20 (December), 253-270.

COOPER, ROBERT G. (1979), "The Dimensions of Industrial New Product Success and Failure," *Journal of Marketing,* 43 (Summer), 93-103.

COX, WILLIAM E., JR. (1967), "Product Life Cycles as Marketing Models," *Journal of Business,* 40 (October), 375-384.

CZEPIEL, JOHN A. (1975). "Patterns of Interorganizational Communications and the Diffusion of a Major Technological Innovation in a Competitive Industrial Community," *Academy of Management Journal,* 18 (March), 6-24.

DANKO, WILLIAM D., and JAMES M. MACLACHLAN (1983), "Research to Accelerate the Diffusion of a New Invention," *Journal of Advertising Research,* 23 (June/July), 39-43.

DAVIS, HARRY L. (1976), "Decision Making Within the Household," *Journal of Consumer Research,* 2 (March), 241-260.

———, and BENNY P. RIGAUX (1974), "Perception of Marital Roles in Decision Processes," *Journal of Consumer Research,* 1 (June), 51-62.

DAY, GEORGE S. (1981), "the Product Life Cycle: Analysis and Applications Issues," *Journal of Marketing,* 45 (Fall), 60-67.

DEUTSCH, MORTON,and H. B. GERARD (1955), "A Study of Normative and Informational Social Influences upon Individual Judgment," *Journal of Abnormal and Social Psychology,* 51, 629-636.

DHALLA, NARIMAN K., and SONIA YUSPEH (1976), "Forget the Product Life Cycle Concept," *Harvard Business Review,* 54 (January/February), 102-112.

DICKERSON, MARY DEE, and JAMES W. GENTRY (1983), "Characteristics of Adopters and Non-Adopters of Home Computers," *Journal of Consumer Research,* 10 (September), 225-235.

DODDS, WELLESLEY (1973), "An Application of the Bass Model in Long-Term New Product Forecasting," *Journal of Marketing Research,* 10 (August), 308-311.

EDELL, JULIE A., and RICHARD STAELIN (1983), "The Information Processing of Pictures in Print Advertisements," *Journal of Consumer Research,* 10 (June), 45-61.

ELIASHBERG, JEHOSHUA, CHARLES S. TAPIERO, and YORAM WIND (1983), "Diffusion of New Products in Heterogeneous Populations: Incorporating Stochastic Coefficients," working paper, University of Pennsylvania.

FEDER, GERSHON (1982), "Adoption of Interrelated Agricultural Innovations: Complementarity and the Impacts of Risk, Scale, and Credit," *American Journal of Agricultural Economics,* 64 (February), 94-101.

———, and GERALD T. O'MARA (1982), "On Information and Innovation Diffusion: A Bayesian Approach," *American Journal of Agricultural Economics,* 64 (February), 145-147.

FLIEGEL, FREDERICK C., and JOSEPH E. KIVLIN (1966), "Attributes of Innovations as Factors in Diffusion," *American Journal of Sociology,* 72 (November), 235-248.

FOURT, LOUIS A., and JOSEPH W. WOODLOCK (1960), "Early Prediction of Market Success for New Grocery Products," *Journal of Marketing,* 25 (October), 31-38.

FRANK, RONALD E., WILLIAM F. MASSY, and DONALD G. MORRISON (1964), "The Determinants of Innovative Behavior with Respect to a Branded, Frequently Purchased Food Product," in *Proceedings of the American Marketing Association,* Ed. L. George Smith. Chicago: American Marketing Association, 312-323.

GATIGNON, HUBERT A., and THOMAS S. ROBERTSON (1985), "Integration of Consumer Diffusion Theory and Diffusion Models: New Research Directions," *Innovation Diffusion Models of New Product Acceptance,* Vijay Mahajan and Yoram Wind. Cambridge: MA: Ballinger, 37-60.

GRANOVETTER, MARK S. (1973), "The Strength of Weak Ties," *American Journal of Sociology,* 78 (6), 1360-1380.

GREEN, ROBERT T., ERIC LANGEARD, and ALICE C. FAVELL (1974), "Innovation in the Service Sector: Some Empirical Findings," *Journal of Marketing Research,* 11 (August), 323-326.

HAGERSTRAND, T. (1965), "A Monte Carlo Approach to Diffusion," *Archives Europeennes de Sociologie,* 6 (1), 43-67.

HEANY, DONALD F. (1983), "Degrees of Product Innovation," *Journal of Business Strategy,* 3 (Spring), 3-14.

HEELER, ROGER M., and THOMAS P. HUSTAD (1980), "Problems in Predicting New Product Growth for Consumer Durables," *Management Science,* 10 (October), 1007-1020.

HILL, REUBEN (1970), *Family Development in Three Generations.* Cambridge, MA: Schenkman.

HIRSCHMAN, ELIZABETH C. (1980), "Innovativeness, Novelty Seeking, and Consumer Creativity," *Journal of Consumer Research,* 7 (December), 289-295.

——— (1981), "Technology and Symbolism as Sources for the Generation of Innovations," in *Advances in Consumer Research,* Vol. 9, Ed. Andrew Mitchell. St. Louis, MO: Association for Consumer Research, 537-541.

HOPKINS, DAVID S. (1980), *New-Product Winners and Losers.* New York: The Conference Board.

HORSKY, DAN, and LEONARD S. SIMON (1983), "Advertising and the Diffusion of New Products," *Marketing Science,* 2 (Winter), 1-17.

HOUSTON, DOUGLAS A. (1983), "Implicit Discount Rates and the Purchase of Untried, Energy-Saving Durable Goods," *Journal of Consumer Research,* 10 (September), 236-246.

JENSEN, RICHARD (1982), "Adoption and Diffusion

of an Innovation of Uncertain Profitability," *Journal of Economic Theory,* 27 (1), 182-193.

JEULAND, ABEL P. (1981), "Parsimonious Models of Diffusion of Innovation Parts A and B: Derivations and Comparisons," working paper, University of Chicago.

KAIGLER-EVANS, KAREN, CLARK LEAVITT, and LOIS DICKEY (1978), "Source Similarity and Fashion Newness as Determinants of Consumer Innovation," in *Advances in Consumer Research,* Vol. 5, Ed. H. Keith Hunt. Ann Arbor, MI: Association for Consumer Research, 738-742.

KANOUSE, DAVID E., and L. REID HANSON, JR. (1972), "Negativity in Evaluations," in *Attribution: Perceiving the Causes of Behavior,* Eds. E. E. Jones et al. Morristown, NJ: General Learning Press.

KARMESHU, and R. K. PATHRIA (1980), "Stochastic Evolution of a Nonlinear Model of Diffusion of Information," *Journal of Mathematical Sociology,* 7, 59-71.

KATZ, ELIHU, and PAUL F. LAZARSFELD (1955), "Personal Influence, New York: The Free Press.

KING, CHARLES W., JR. (1963), "Fashion Adoption: A Rebuttal to the 'Trickle Down' Theory," in *Proceedings of the American Marketing Association,* Ed. Stephen A. Greyser. Chicago: American Marketing Association, 108-125.

KING, CHARLES W., JR., and JOHN O. SUMMERS (1970), "Overlap of Opinion Leadership Across Consumer Product Categories," *Journal of Marketing Research,* 7 (February), 43-50.

KISIELIUS, JOLITA (1982), "Detecting and Explaining Vividness Effects in Attitudinal Judgment," unpublished doctoral dissertation, Northwestern University, Evanston, IL.

KRUGMAN, HERBERT E. (1965), "The Impact of Television Advertising: Learning Without Involvement," *Public Opinion Quarterly,* 29, 349-356.

LABAY, DUNCAN G., and THOMAS C. KINNEAR (1981), "Exploring the Consumer Decision Process in the Adoption of Solar Energy Systems," *Journal of Consumer Research,* 8 (December), 271-278.

LANGEARD, E., M. CROUSILLAT, and R. WEISZ (1977), "Exposure to Cultural Activities and Opinion Leadership," in *Advances in Consumer Research,* Vol. 5, Ed. H. Keith Hunt. Ann Arbor, MI: Association for Consumer Research, 606-610.

LEKVALL, PER, and CLAS WAHLBIN (1973), "A Study of Some Assumptions Underlying Innovation Diffusion Functions," *Swedish Journal of Economics,* 75, 362-377.

LILIEN, GARY L., AMBAR G. RAO, and SHLOMO KALISH (1981), "Bayesian Estimation and Control of Detailing Effort in a Repeat Purchase Diffusion Environment," *Management Science,* 27 (May), 493-506.

MAHAJAN, VIJAY, and EITAN MULLER (1979), "Innovation Diffusion and New Product Growth Models in Marketing," *Journal of Marketing,* 43 (Fall), 55-68.

———, EITAN MULLER, and ROGER A. KERIN (1984), "Introduction Strategies for New Products with Positive and Negative Word-of-Mouth," *Management Science,* 30 (December), 1340-1389.

———, and ROBERT A. PETERSON (1978), "Innovation Diffusion in a Dynamic Potential Adopter Population," *Management Science,* 24 (15), 1589-1597.

———, ROBERT A. PETERSON, ARUN K. JAIN, and NARESH MALHOTRA (1979), "A New Product Growth Model with a Dynamic Market Potential," *Long Range Planning,* 12 (4), 62-69.

MANSFIELD, EDWIN (1961), "Technical Change and the Rate of Imitation," *Econometrica,* 29 (October), 741-766.

MIDGLEY, DAVID F. (1976), "A Simple Mathematical Theory of Innovative Behavior," *Journal of Consumer Research,* 3 (June), 31-41.

———, and GRAHAME R. DOWLING (1978), "Innovativeness: The Concept and Its Measurement," *Journal of Consumer Research,* 4 (March), 229-242.

MIZERSKI, RICHARD W. (1982), "An Attribution Explanation of the Disproportionate Influence of Unfavorable Information," *Journal of Consumer Research,* 9 (December), 301-310.

MYERS, JAMES H., and THOMAS S. ROBERTSON (1972), "Dimensions of Opinion Leadership," *Journal of Marketing Research,* 9 (February), 41-46.

NEVERS, JOHN V. (1972), "Extensions of a New Product Growth Model," *Sloan Management Review,* (Winter), 77-91.

OLIVER, RICHARD L. (1977), "Effects of Expectation and Disconfirmation on Postexposure Product Evaluations: An Alternative Interpretation," *Journal of Applied Psychology,* 62 (4), 480-486.

OLSHAVSKY, RICHARD W. (1980), "Time and the Rate of Adoption of Innovations," *Journal of Consumer Research,* 6 (March), 425-428.

O'NEAL, CHARLES R., HANS B. THORELLI, and

JAMES M. UTTERBACK (1973), "Adoption of Innovation by Industrial Organizations," *Industrial Marketing Management,* 2 (3), 235–250.

OSTLUND, LYMAN E. (1974), "Perceived Innovation Attributes as Predictors of Innovativeness," *Journal of Consumer Research,* 1 (June), 23–29.

OZANNE, URBAN G., and GILBERT A. CHURCHILL, JR. (1971), "Five Dimensions of the Industrial Adoption Process, *Journal of Marketing Research,* 8 (August), 322–328.

PETERS, MICHAEL P., and M. VENKATESAN (1973), "Exploration of Variables Inherent in Adopting an Industrial Product," *Journal of Marketing Research,* 10 (August), 312–315.

PETERSON, R. A., and V. MAHAJAN (1978), "Multi-Product Growth Models," in *Research in Marketing,* Ed. Jagdish N. Sheth. Greenwich, CT: JAI Press.

POLLI, ROLANDO and VICTOR COOK (1969), "Validity of the Product Life Cycle," *Journal of Business,* 42 (October), 305–400.

RAY, MICHAEL L. (1973), "Marketing Communication and the Hierarchy of Effects," in *New Models for Mass Communication Research,* Vol. 2, Ed. Peter Clarke. Beverly Hills, CA. Sage, 147–176.

——— (1982), *Advertising and Communications Management.* Englewood Cliffs, NJ: Prentice-Hall.

RICHINS, MARSHA L. (1983), "Negative Word-of-Mouth by Dissatisfied Consumers: A Pilot Study," *Journal of Marketing,* 47 (Winter), 68–78.

RINK, D. R., and J. E. SWAN (1979), "Product Life Cycle Research: A Literature Review," *Journal of Business Research,* 7 (September), 219–242.

ROBERTSON, THOMAS S. (1967), "Determinants of Innovative Behavior," in *Proceedings of the American Marketing Association,* Ed. Reed Moyer. Chicago: American Marketing Association, 328–332.

——— (1971), *Innovative Behavior and Communication.* New York: Holt, Rinehart & Winston.

——— (1976), "Low-Commitment Consumer Behavior," *Journal of Advertising Research,* 16 (April), 19–24.

———, and YORAM WIND (1980), Organizational Psychographics and Innovativeness," *Journal of Consumer Research,* 7 (June), 24–31.

———, JOAN ZIELINSKI, and SCOTT WARD (1984), *Consumer Behavior.* Glenview, IL: Scott, Foresman.

ROGERS, EVERETT M. (1976), "New Product Adoption and Diffusion," *Journal of Consumer Research,* 2 (March), 290–301.

——— (1983), *Diffusion of Innovations.* New York: The Free Press.

RYAN, BRYCE, and NEAL GROSS (1943), "The Diffusion of Hybrid Seed Corn in Two Iowa Communities," *Rural Sociology,* 8 (March), 15–24.

SHETH, JAGDISH N. (1981), "Psychology of Innovation Resistance," *Research in Marketing,* 4, 273–282.

SILK, ALVIN J. (1966), "Overlap Among Self-Designated Opinion Leaders: A Study of Selected Dental Products and Services," *Journal of Marketing Research,* 3 (August), 255–259.

SIMON, HERMANN, and KARL-HEINZ SEBASTIAN (1982), "Diffusion and Advertising: The German Telephone Campaign," working paper, The Marketing Science Group of Germany, WP 0.9

STERNTHAL, BRIAN, LYNN W. PHILLIPS, and RUBY DHOLAKIA (1978), "The Persuasive Effect of Source Credibility: A Situational Analysis," *Public Opinion Quarterly,* 42 (Fall), 285–314.

STONEMAN, P. (1981), "Intra-Firm Diffusion, Bayesian Learning and Profitability," *The Economic Journal,* 91 (June), 375–388.

SUMMERS, JOHN O. (1970), "The Identity of Women's Clothing Fashion Opinion Leaders," *Journal of Marketing Research,* 7 (May), 178–185.

———, (1972), "Media Exposure Patterns of Consumer Innovators," *Journal of Marketing,* 36 (January), 43–49.

SWINYARD, WILLIAM R., and KENNETH A. CONEY (1978), "Promotional Effects on a High- Versus Low-Involvement Electorate," *Journal of Consumer Research,* 5 (June), 41–48.

TAYLOR, JAMES W. (1977), "A Striking Characteristic of Innovators," *Journal of Marketing Research,* 14 (February), 104–107.

TEECE, DAVID J. (1980), "The Diffusion of an Administrative Innovation," *Management Science,* 26 (5), 464–470.

TIGERT, DOUGLAS, and BEHROOZ FARIVAR (1981), "The Bass New Product Growth Model: A Sensitivity Analysis for a High Technology Product," *Journal of Marketing,* 45 (Fall), 81–90.

URBAN, GLEN L., and JOHN R. HAUSER (1980), *Design and Marketing of New Products.* Englewood Cliffs: NJ: Prentice-Hall.

WEIMANN, GABRIEL (1982), "On the Importance of Marginality: One More Step in the Two-Step

Flow of Communication," *American Sociological Review,* 47 (December), 764–773.

WESTBROOK, ROBERT A., and CLAES FORNELL (1979), "Patterns of Information Source Usage Among Durable Goods Buyers," *Journal of Marketing Research,* 16 (August), 303–312.

WILTON, PETER C., and EDGAR A. PESSEMIER (1981), "Forecasting the Ultimate Acceptance of an Innovation: the Effects of Information," *Journal of Consumer Research,* 8 (September), 162–171.

WIND, YORAM J. (1982), *Product Policy: Concepts, Methods and Strategy.* Reading, MA: Addison-Wesley.

______, THOMAS S. ROBERTSON, and CYNTHIA FRASER (1982), "Industrial Product Diffusion by Market Segment," *Industrial Marketing Management,* 11, 1–8.

YAPA, LAKSHMAN S., and ROBERT C. MAYFIELD (1978), "Non-Adoption of Innovations: Evidence From Discriminant Analysis," *Economic Geography,* 54 (2), 145–156.

YOUNG, ROBERT B. (1964), "Product Growth Cycles—A Key to Growth Planning," unpublished results, Stanford Research Institute, Menlo Park, CA.

ZALTMAN, GERALD, and RONALD STIFF (1973), "Theories of Diffusion," in *Consumer Behavior: Technical Sources.* Eds. Scott Ward and Thomas S. Robertson. Englewood Cliffs: NJ: Prentice-Hall, 416–468.

______, ROBERT DUNCAN, and JONNY HOLBEK (1973), *Innovations and Organizations.* New York: Wiley.

ZIELSKE, HUBERT A., and WALKER A. HENRY (1980), "Remembering and Forgetting Television Ads," *Journal of Advertising Research,* 20 (April), 7–13.

27

THE CONTINUING SIGNIFICANCE OF SOCIAL CLASS TO MARKETING*

Richard P. Coleman

Social class is conceptually complicated, philosophically upsetting, and methodologically challenging, yet it continues to offer provocative insights into consumption choices. The latest thinking from sociologists points to a basic continuity in the American status structure: fundamental differences among the classes in self-image, social horizons, and consumption goals continue despite changes in income distribution, the demographics of family composition, and life styles. The question of whether class or income is the better predictor of marketplace behavior should be rephrased: How does class affect use of income?

There are no two ways about it: social class is a difficult idea. Sociologists, in whose discipline the concept emerged, are not of one mind about its value and validity. Consumer researchers, to whose field its use has spread, display confusion about when and how to apply it. The American public is noticeably uncomfortable with the realities about life that it reflects. All who try to measure it have trouble. Studying it rigorously and imaginatively can be monstrously expensive. Yet, all these difficulties notwithstanding, the proposition still holds: social class is worth troubling over for the insights it offers on the marketplace behavior of the nation's consumers. "Hot" and "new" in the 1950s, social class fell from favor and use in the 1970s—it turned "cold" and "old," as it were, hurt by mistakes in employment and by controversy over its merits vis-à-vis income. A fresh view of

*Reprinted from the *Journal of Consumer Research,* 10 (December 1983), pp. 265–280.

class is needed, a reassertion of its value and such is the present purpose.

This paper represents a much-abbreviated, highlighting stab at updating the social class concept and practice. The purpose here is to present some ideas that hopefully will suggest the continuing importance of the social class concept to practitioners and educators in the field. I have drawn heavily on privately financed research, the detailed results of which are not yet in the public domain.

THE SOCIAL CLASSES AT LATEST LOOK

The storyline on the American status structure with which the marketing profession is most familiar was introduced into sociology by W. Lloyd Warner with the first volume of his Yankee City series (1941). Six social classes were identified in this work: upper-upper, lower-upper, upper-middle, lower-middle, upper-lower, and lower-lower. This view of the status system crossed over into marketing in the 1950s, and has been forwarded almost intact ever since, although in recent years its currency has been questioned. The social classes that Warner "discovered" offered a new perspective on community life. His were not the economic classes, power clusters, or political interest groups postulated by other social scientists as the meaningful divisions of American society: they were—as defined by Warner—classes of people who were approximately equal in community esteem, and were made up of men and women who regularly socialized among themselves, in both formal and informal ways, and shared behavioral expectations. It was Warner's conviction that these classes represented the most basic ordering of Americans in terms of the self-feelings involved and of shared community respect. Researchers and marketers took note of this concept when Warner and his colleagues at the University of Chicago and Social Research, Inc., began demonstrating that members of different social classes displayed different purchase goals and shopping behaviors. The classes were thus motivational groupings as well as status categories—cause, thereby, not merely correlate, of consumption choice.

To ask how applicable this social class view is today, given the decades that have passed since its initial formulation and subsequent adoption by the marketing profession, is, of course, a reasonable question. The critical issues are:

- Do we really have the same classes now as then, and if not, what are they?
- How do the status groupings that characterize today's America affect consumer behavior?
- How do we now tell who ranks where when we study status phenomena?

Marketing literature was singularly lacking in attention to these issues throughout the 1970s—and not without cause, since sociology, from whence social class had sprung, paid similarly little attention for almost two decades.

An Updated Classification

For sociologists, the 1960s and early 1970s were years of cultural ferment and research excitement: the civil rights movement, the feminist struggle for increased equality, the gay liberation drive, and student uprisings in the colleges dominated the sociological agenda. Research in social stratification moved away from contemplative studies of the community hierarchy toward programmatic investigations into all forms of discrimination—between the sexes, the races, ethnic groups, and age cohorts, for example—plus inquiry into any inequities in income, political power, and educational opportunity which might suggest (or "prove") exploitation of one group in America by another, and/or that life chances varied "unfairly" by social origin. Implicit in all this was a conviction among sociologists that what should matter most to individual Americans is the situations in which they find themselves—not something so ephemeral as a point they might occupy on some social status hierarchy by virtue of personal reputation and that of their network of friends. In this, "situations" meant occupational role, income level, living conditions, and identification with a possibly disadvantaged ethnic/racial group. It is the thrust of this sociological view that Dennis Gilbert and Joseph Kahl have brought into combination with theories from political economy to frame their story in *The American Class Structure: A New Synthesis* (1982). This most recent sociological contribution to status analysis is a dramatic updating of Kahl's previous, synthesizing study, *The American Class Structure* (1957), in which, reviewing the literature of community studies from the 1950s and before, Kahl treated class in the United States as essentially a matter of style, social networks, and personal prestige reputation. In the new work, a change of mind has taken place—and this is how Gilbert and Kahl put it (1982, p. 354):

> We have reversed the direction of emphasis . . . We pay more attention to capitalist ownership and to the occupational division of labor as the defining variables . . . then treat prestige, association, and values as derivative. This difference in viewpoint reflects shifts in the general orientation of the discipline of sociology.

A thumbnail characterization of the class structure which Gilbert and Kahl offer as their new synthesis of political theory and sociological analysis appears in the left column of Exhibit 27.1. In the right column, for comparison, is a similarly abbreviated characterization of the class structure set forth in *Social Standing in America* (Coleman and Rainwater 1978), which can be thought of as "the latest look" at social class taken from a Warnerian social-psychological perspective. This work is the product of a study sponsored in the 1970s by the Joint Center for Urban Studies of MIT and Harvard, in which a cross-section of 900 residents from the Boston and Kansas City metropolitan areas were interviewed intensively on status matters, focusing on their individual perceptions of the social hierarchy and felt participation in it.

What first strikes the eye in Exhibit 27.1 is how much these two "latest looks" at the status structure have in common. To a certain extent, however, this is deceiving, since the two views proceed on different classificatory principles. Gilbert and Kahl take a functionalist, "situations" stance, drawn in major part from economic as well as social-political theory. Coleman and Rainwater's view is reputational and behavioral, borrowing heavily from "man in the street" imagery. Nevertheless, there are two important similarities: they both acknowledge three principal groupings of Americans, and to each they assign almost identical portions of the population.

The roots for a threefold status division are very deep right now. This is the way the middle mass of citizens most readily talk about the hierarchy: there are "people (like us) in the middle," "people above," and "people below," with economic status the major differentiating factor, followed by educational credentials and behavioral standards as secondary influences. And this is the way some of the wisest political analysts are looking at the electorate. In *The Real American Majority,* for example, Scammon and Wattenberg (1970) proposed that on social issues—in people's ideas about crime and justice, morality and law—the white-collar middle class became allied with the blue-collar working class in the late 1960s to form a great American center wherein is found the "real majority" that swings elections.[1] What we see in these tripartite divisions of American society is truly a dramatic shift away from the bipartite view common to earlier interpretations. Before World War II, social scientists commonly pictured American society as split into opposing halves—a higher-half business class versus a lower-half working class, white-collars on the one side and blue on the other—or, put even more harshly, "have" superiors versus "have-not" inferiors. Now, in both models shown in Exhibit 27.1, that split has diminished to a

[1]The label "Middle Americans" for these people who form the political and social-philosophical center is commonly attributed to columnist Joseph Kraft, who began using it toward the end of 1967 in reference to that part of the public generally given to hardline anti-communism and conservative views on domestic social issues. In Kraft's initial usage and perception, Middle Americans tended to live more in the heartland than on the coasts, in small towns or in middle-income suburbia. In status, they tended to be either lower white-collar or upper blue-collar; it is this occupation image that sociologists have adopted in applying the phrase to the social status hierarchy.

EXHIBIT 27.1 Two Recent Views of the American Status Structure

THE GILBERT–KAHL NEW SYNTHESIS CLASS STRUCTURE:[a]
A situations model from political theory and sociological analysis

Upper Americans

The Capitalist Class (1%)–Their investment decisions shape the national economy; income mostly from assets, earned/inherited; prestige university connections

Upper Middle Class (14%)–Upper managers, professionals, medium businessmen; college educated; family income ideally runs nearly twice the national average

Middle Americans

Middle Class (33%)–Middle level white-collar, top level blue-collar; education past high school typical; income somewhat above the national average

Working Class (32%)–Middle level blue-collar; lower level white collar; income runs slightly below the national average; education is also slightly below

Marginal and Lower Americans

The Working Poor (11–12%)–Below mainstream America in living standard, but above the poverty line; low-paid service workers, operatives; some high school education

The Underclass (8–9%)–Depend primarily on welfare system for sustenance; living standard below poverty line; not regularly employed; lack schooling

THE COLEMAN–RAINWATER SOCIAL STANDING CLASS HIERARCHY:[b]
A reputational, behavioral view in the community study tradition

Upper Americans

Upper-Upper (0.3%)–The "capital S society" world of inherited wealth, aristocratic names

Lower-Upper (1.2%)–The newer social elite, drawn from current professional, corporate leadership

Upper-Middle (12.5%)–The rest of college graduate managers and professionals; life style centers on private clubs, causes, and the arts

Middle Americans

Middle Class (32%)–Average pay white-collar workers and their blue-collar friends; live on the "the better side of town," try to "do the proper things"

Working Class (38%)–Average pay blue-collar workers; lead "working class life style" whatever the income, school background, and job

Lower Americans

"A lower group of people but not the lowest" (9%)–Working, not on welfare; living standard is just above poverty; behavior judged "crude," "trashy"

"Real Lower-Lower" (7%)–On welfare, visibly poverty-stricken, usually out of work (or have "the dirtiest jobs"); "bums," "common criminals"

[a]Abstracted by Coleman from Gilbert, Dennis and Joseph A. Kahl (1982), "The American Class Structure: A Synthesis," Chapter 11 in *The American Class Structure: A New Synthesis.* Homewood, IL: The Dorsey Press.

[b]This condensation of the Coleman-Rainwater view is drawn from Chapters 8, 9, and 10 of Coleman, Richard P. and Lee P. Rainwater, with Kent A. McClelland (1978), *Social Standing in America: New Dimensions of Class.* New York: Basic Books.

mere dividing factor within Middle America, while two formerly secondary division lines—one between Warner's upper-middle and lower-middle, the other between his upper-lower and lower-lower—have risen to primary status (leading, indeed, to class name changes).

The Gilbert–Kahl model is likely to prove of less interest in the long run to marketing people than is the Coleman–Rainwater model, but the rationales for its six subdivisions illustrate contemporary academic thinking about class in the United States. Gilbert and Kahl have organized their New Synthesis model around a "series of qualitative economic distinctions and their symbolization," and explain it this way:

1. The capitalist class, containing just 1 percent of the population, yet "controlling some 51–52 percent of the nation's wealth," is distinguished from the upper middle class most noticeably by its *impressive ownership of income-producing assets.*
2. The upper middle class is distinguished from the middle class by *possession of sophisticated educational credentials* which have given its members their entrée to the valued managerial and professional posts they occupy.
3. The middle class is distinguished from the working class by a *combination of job security and freedom from routinization at work;* members of the class, wearing white or blue collars (but mostly the former), frequently "give orders to those below" in the workplace hierarchy, and they "usually feel secure" in their situations.
4. The working class is distinguished from the working poor by having *escaped entrapment in the marginal sector of the labor market,* and because their living standard tends to place them "in the mainstream" (albeit in "the lower half").
5. The working poor are distinguished from the underclass because, while not sure of steady employment, they are more often at work than not—and are *not nearly so severely limited in labor force participation.*
6. The underclass is distinguished from all the other classes because in this class alone do people *"receive a majority of their income* either from illegal activities or *from government transfers."*

The Coleman–Rainwater approach to construction of a national status hierarchy is very different: it is designed to reflect popular imagery and observation of how people interact with one another—as equals, superiors, or inferiors. Personal and group prestige is at its heart. In this hierarchy, social standing is a multi-factored, richly textured phenomenon. Identification with each class is influenced most heavily by educational credentials and occupation (including income as a measure of work success), but it is also affected to varying degrees by social skills, status aspirations, community participation, family history, cultural level, recreational habits, and physical appearance; ultimately, the proper index to status is a person's social circle of acceptance. No simple statements of qualitative distinction define each stratum with such theoretical precision as in the Gilbert–Kahl model. Nevertheless, three or four words can be used to communicate each stratum's thematic core—successively, from top down in Exhibit 27.1, these might be "old family names," "accepted new money," "collegiate credentials expected," "white-collar associations," "blue-collar life style," "definitely below the mainstream," and "the welfare world." If these phrases remind readers of the conventional portraits of the status hierarchy, this is because the social ranking Americans apply to one another in reputation and interaction is demonstrating impressive thematic continuity from one generation and era to the next.

Applying the New Classification

What, then, should the marketing world do with these "latest looks" at social class? Drawing from my own research experience with the social class variable during the past two decades, I would suggest two ways this concept might be used in research and strategy planning. One is to divide the consuming public into four main status groups—Upper Americans, Middle Class, Working Class, and Lower Americans. The second suggestion is more a reminder than a new idea—namely, that it must always be kept in mind that a diversity of family situations and a nearly unbelievable range in income totals are contained within each class. The thumbnail sketches and three-word thematic summaries so commonly used to characterize status groups oversimplify in ways that cause people to forget the great variety of life circumstances found in every status group, whether it is the narrow world of upper-upper Upper Americans or the extremely large world of the working class. To illustrate:

A "prototype" household of middle-class Middle American status has as its head a man employed in some lower management office job, earning between $24,000 and $29,999 a year (1983 urban-average dollars), whose wife isn't working, so that is all the family income. Almost as likely to be middle class is a divorcee with two years of college as an educational credential, who is trying to support two children on a legal secretary's salary of as little as $13,500—and who may be best friend and frequent bridge-playing chum to the wife in the first case. Another middle-class home will contain a working couple, both in office jobs, earning in combined total $42,000 or even $45,000 a year. A fourth might have as its head the owner of a bowling alley and restaurant whose wife may or may not be helping to run it—or the owner could be a widow, divorcee, or never-married woman; in any case, the living standard projected by house, car(s), and clothes suggests an income of $60,000 or $70,000 a year, yet the social status is still middle class because, through lack of mobility aspirations and/or social skills, no Upper American connections and acceptance have been established.

A picture of equally great income and situational differences could be painted for every social level. When marketers and researchers use social class conceptually, they must remember the variations in age of household heads, the broken families, the single people, and the working couples found in each class, and must realize that all these people are trying to maintain similar social class identities and that in so doing, the motives and goals they bring to the marketplace may be functionally the same, although their means differ greatly.

A single class category of Upper Americans, formed by the bracketing together of upper-uppers with lower-uppers and upper-middles, is recommended on several counts. One is that in a representative sample there would be too few respondents from the two upper-class layers for separate study and statistical treatment unless the total survey size were to exceed 2,000 persons. A second is that diagnosis of social rank—as between these three levels—is not reliably accomplished via the kinds of class-measuring instruments used in the typical mass survey study; the data required for precise placement at these levels are not ordinarily collected, and machine scoring cannot easily be made sensitive to all the nuances involved.[2] A third reason is that the motives and goals in consumption of most mass-marketed products do not necessarily differ significantly between these three substrata of Upper Americans: only regarding luxury goods and services or specialty items are differences commonly critical.

The two social levels counted as Middle Americans—middle class and working class—are most assuredly worth separate attention from the marketing profession, even though they may not be so sharply differentiated in public image or political views as they were a generation ago, when Warner names them lower-middle and upper-lower, respectively. That they still represent distinct social worlds with different behavioral norms and life styles, despite marked overlap in income, was one of the crucial findings in the Coleman-Rainwater research for *Social Standing in America* (1978). Educational background, class of origin, and a wife's social aspirations often override a husband's white-collar/blue-collar job definition in determining family identification with one class or the other. Consumption priorities and marketplace choices vary accordingly.

Lower Americans are separated into two subclasses in the Gilbert-Kahl as well as in the

[2]Club memberships, specific colleges attended, religious affiliations, and ethnic identifications are all, on occasion, critical evidence of the exact step occupied on the Upper American social ladder—these are among "the nuances involved." Possibly one out of 15 or 20 families who rank upper-upper in social acceptance may not indeed be "old-money"; a portion of families never achieve upper-upper status even through three generations of wealth; and "nouveau riche" families are not always lower-upper—in a goodly share of instances, they fall somewhere below that, in a category best described as Non-Upper Rich. For further detail on the "nuances" of Upper American rank in metropolitan areas, see Coleman and Neugarten (1971) and Coleman and Rainwater (1978). Still another kind of "nuance" is how to equate the high-status worlds of people living in smaller communities with those in metropolitan areas, this has not yet been solved to anyone's satisfaction.

Coleman–Rainwater model. Both models thus reflect how, in the past 30 years, the public has come to differentiate between people who survive on government transfer payments and those who are poor but who do not usually depend on such assistance. In the 1970s, welfare workers and social scientists began referring to the former as "the underclass," while applying "disadvantaged" to the class as a whole (Auletta 1982). The two levels combined account for no more than one-fifth of the adult population and less than one-tenth of the disposable income (8 or 9 percent by the Gilbert–Kahl definition, and only 6 or 7 percent by the Coleman–Rainwater classification).[3]

CONTINUITY AND CHANGE IN CLASS CONSUMPTION CHOICES

The class concept won entry into the marketing discipline when the proposition that consumer motivations varied consistently by social class was set forth in the 1950s by "the Chicago group" (the *Tribune*'s Pierre Martineau and the Social Research Incorporated's Lloyd Warner, Burleigh Gardner, Lee Rainwater, and Sidney Levy). Pierre Martineau, director of research at the *Chicago Tribune,* is usually credited with taking the lead in advocating that marketers and advertisers pay attention to the social class variable, by writing *Motivations in Advertising* (1957), speaking at conventions, and submitting journal articles (e.g., Martineau 1958). This effort was abetted by SRI's issuance of *Women and Department Store Advertising,* edited by Charles McCann (1958). Appearance in 1959 of *Workingman's Wife,* co-authored by SRI's Rainwater, Coleman, and Handel, won further interest from the marketing profession for class as a consumption factor, as well as attracting the eye of sociologists through its detailing of blue-collar couples' life styles.

The research the Chicago group blazed trails with in the very late 1940s showed upper-middle Americans pursuing different goals in home furnishing, appliances, clothing, food, and leisure time use than lower-middles, who in turn displayed consumption objectives (and aesthetic preferences) markedly different from upper-lowers. Certain "catch" phrases encapsulated these inter-class variations: upper-middles were identified with consumption choices reflecting "quality" and "taste," lower-middles with "respectability" and "conformity," upper-lowers with "modernity" and "quantity," and lower-lowers with "instant gratification." This became the accepted wisdom in marketing's theory and textbooks, holding sway through the 1960s.

During the 1970s, involvement with social class declined as alternatives emerged—most notably life styles, but also age cohorts, ethnic and racial subgroups, and even geographically related population breakdowns. One source for the distance marketers put between themselves and social class was the rise in the late 1960s of a counterculture that grew out of opposition to the Vietnam war, initially created divisions inside each class, and ultimately affected all classes, bringing new habits of grooming, sexual attitudes, language usage, and musical preference into the mainstream.

Another source for disaffection from class was the differentiation by age cohorts in public

---

[3]The share of population percentages assigned to the status groups in this paper (see Exhibit 27.1) should be treated as suggestive, not conclusive because these classes should be regarded as conceptual categories—not as precisely defined, measured-and-closed entities. The estimates for the Coleman–Rainwater model were reached after study of several community social-class samplings, contact with a few national cross-section panels, and examination of census data. The findings from these sources were pooled and filtered into a single "best guess" statement. These estimates of social class distribution vary from those printed in various textbooks and in early works on class because (1) the times have changed, (2) the class definitions have changed, and (3) these are projections to the nation rather than findings from one particular community.

Any estimates on income share by class are even more speculative. No documented study is available, the best that can be done is to project from sample data and census reports on distribution of each income level within the national total. Estimates the author would make on income share for other Coleman–Rainwater status groups are: 7–8 percent for the two upper-class levels of Upper Americans, 26–27 percent for the upper-middle sector, 33–34 percent for the middle class, and 26–27 percent for the working class. If this is correct, the two smaller upper-class strata exceed the entire class of Lower Americans in income.

behavior that became so extreme in the late 1960s, and remained strong—though in modified ways—through the middle 1970s; generations appeared united across class lines in philosophy, marketplace priorities, and consumption choices. A third source—in some ways a product of the other two—was an increasing visual confusion in the public signs of high status and low status. John Brooks gave partial explanation for this in *Showing Off in America* (1981):

> The most effective status seeking style is mockery of status seeking . . . thus the well-to-do wear blue jeans, even worn and threadbare, to proclaim that one is socially secure enough to dress like an underpaid ranch hand.

Brooks' phrase for this was "parody display." Confronted with such ambiguous consumption choices and status messages, marketers have asked: If people of different social standing no longer seek to present themselves differently in public, are the classes still distinguished from each other in the self-image motives of their members and in their responses to advertising appeals?

Life-style segmentation was, in its origin, part and parcel with class, which was the very rationale for its importance to marketers—as in Levy (1966, 1971) and Myers and Gutman (1974), who proclaimed life style "the essence of social class." In the last eight or 10 years, however, life style has become an independent concept, a catch-all of psychographic categories and recreational interest groupings that sometimes brings together people from several classes into one group and at other times divides a single class into subsegments. Some life-style typologies are broad, signifying the basic thrust of a family's expenditure choices in time and money; others are narrow, referring to a single small piece of the total behavior by dividing Americans into runners, watersports enthusiasts, opera buffs, jazz fans. As such, life-style categories are of direct and obvious concern to merchandisers of products and services. Clearly, life-style research has a place in any proper sociology of consumption; ideally, though, life style should not replace social class, but exist in combination with it.

It is not surprising that social class sometimes seems forgotten in the 1980s, since there was a noticeable lack of fresh evidence on its marketplace impact in the literature of the latter 1970s. Indeed, almost as far back as 1960, little was published about class that was truly new; most of what appeared in print merely repeated findings from the 1950s (and some suggested new, contradicting developments). A very large problem is that much of what has been learned about the social class role in consumption choices has remained the private property of research houses and their clients. Another part of the problem is that not all that much research on the class variable was done in those years, both because it is not easy and because new variables emerged and captured contemporary interest. I would like to propose that diminished interest in social class is not so justified as has been assumed in recent years. In illustrating this proposition, I will draw heavily from studies not previously reported, which suggest that social class is continuing to serve as a significant behavioral segmenter in most—though not all—consumer markets, and that it is doing so in surprising and occasionally dramatic ways.[4]

One such study—an inquiry into neighborhood change processes conducted by a research team at the Joint Center for Urban Studies of MIT and Harvard—demonstrated with aston-

[4]The research referred to in this and in the next two sections was almost invariably a team effort, involving the author and his associates at either Social Research, Inc., in Chicago or the Joint Center for Urban Studies of the Massachusetts Institute of Technology and Harvard University. Nearly 200 different projects figure in this experience, featuring depth interviews with over 70,000 persons. For all practical purposes, these sample-survey respondents represent a cross-section of the American public—except for a bent toward residents of metropolitan areas rather than small towns and rural counties. The behaviors studied cover the gamut: television response, newspaper readership, attitudes toward cars, neighborhood preferences, cigarette choice, brand favoritism among beers, and sparetime usage, to name but a few. Findings not referenced to the bibliography have been drawn from research documents which remain the private property of clients who chartered the studies.

ishing clarity how the social-geographic horizons of working-class Americans differ from those of the middle class (Coleman 1977b). A cross-section of 1,000 men and women residing in the metropolitan areas of Houston, Dayton, and Rochester were asked to specify where the physically closest of their relatives then lived and to suggest how this might have influenced their own residential location. The finding was this: whereas more than half (55 percent) of the lower-class and nearly half (45 percent) of the working-class respondents occupied a house or apartment within a linear mile of where a parent, sibling, in-law, aunt, uncle, cousin, grandparent, or grown child resided, less than one-fifth (19 percent) of the middle-class sample and barely one-eighth (12 percent) from Upper American status categories lived in such proximity to any kin whatsoever. In future locational intentions, working-class people usually considered the whereabouts of their extended family, while in the classes above, such concern was almost never reported. Here we see a reflection of the Gilbert and Kahl (1982) proposition that "social classes generate their own subcultures . . . distinctive in life styles, consumption . . . [and] relationships in marriage."

Working-Class Pride in Family, Place, and Country

That working-class Americans are "family folk," depending heavily on relatives for economic and emotional support, was a story first forwarded in detail in *Workingman's Wife* (Rainwater et al. 1959). Further studies throughout the 1960s and 1970s found this class continuing to depend on relatives—relying on kin for tips on job opportunities, soliciting advice from them on purchases, and counting on them in times of "trouble." This emphasis on family ties is only one sign of how much more limited—and how different—working-class horizons are socially, psychologically, and geographically, compared with those of the middle class. In almost every respect, a parochial view characterizes this blue-collar world.

This locational narrowness has been exhibited in such diverse matters as sports heroes, TV news interest, vacation patterns, and automotive choices. When working-class men are asked which sports figure they most eagerly follow in newspaper sports pages, three-fourths name a player on some local amateur or professional team, whereas less than half of middle-class men and a mere quarter of men from the Upper-American strata are so geographically confined in their preferences. When it comes to television news, much the same principle applies: working-class people like the local segments far more than do middle-class audiences, who show more enthusiasm for national and world coverage. Working-class vacation patterns also illustrate the point: staying in town is not uncommon, and "going away" quite frequently means to a lake or resort area no more than two hours distant; if the trip is a longer one, it's likely that "relations" are the destination.

A 1976 study of car ownership by social status offers yet another perspective on working-class loyalties—in this instance to their own country, accompanied by great pride in its industrial accomplishments. By the mid-1970s, ownership of an imported car (whether an economy or a luxury model) had penetrated 40 percent of families in upper-status groups and 25 percent in the middle class, but had not reached even one-tenth in the working class. This was three years after the first gas price shock! Yet working-class car owners were still showing a marked preference for the standard sizes and larger cars, rejecting both domestic and foreign compacts; they were choosing used standards over any kind of new compact; and gas-guzzling pickups and recreational vehicles were still in great favor. Thus was the working class remaining the xenophobic heart of resistance to the foreign car invasion and dragging its heels in accepting the idea that America should reduce the size of its automotive equipment; the men of this class were not yet ready to given up this macho symbol of roadway conquest.

It is often speculated that the affluence which came to so much of blue-collar America in the 1950s, 1960s, and 1970s must surely have produced a change of attitudes and values; the phrase for this hypothesized change is "embourgeoisment." Yet research has usually demonstrated the contrary: the studies by Berger (1960), Glenn and Alston (1968), Hamilton (1972), and LeMasters (1975) are examples. Their observations on the life styles of economically successful blue-collar workers hold that essentially no value change has occurred. For example, the traditional family structure marked by sharp sex-role division and stereotyping has been maintained: for women, the world continues to center on immediate kin, the extended clan, and perhaps a few longtime friends from neighborhood and growing-up days; for men, a rich peer-group life is continuing at work and in such gathering places as the corner tavern or Moose Lodge, plus outings of masculine camaraderie (fishing trips, stock car races). Indeed, what sociologists and motivation researchers have been finding throughout the past 20 years is that working-class life styles have been almost impervious to change in their basic characteristics—i.e., the limited horizons, the centrality of family and clan, the chauvinistic devotion to nation and neighborhood have been little altered by the automobile, telephone, or television. The modernity—and change—that these people seek is in possessions, not in human relationships or "new ideas." For them, "keeping up with the times" focuses on the mechanical and recreational, and thus ease of labor and leisure is what they continue to pursue.

The men and women of Lower America are no exception to the rule that diversities and uniformities in values and consumption goals are to be found at each social level. Some members of this world, as has been publicized, are prone to every form of instant gratification known to humankind when the money is available. But others are dedicated to resisting worldly temptations as they struggle toward what some imagine will be a "heavenly reward" for their earthly sacrifices.

Value Variations in Upper America

Through the 1960s and 1970s, the life styles and self-conceptions of people identified with the upper sixth of the nation appear to have changed more than those of people in the classes below. The life-style variations that have emerged exist vertically within Upper America, crossing the substrata and combining people from several status layers into one consumer group with common goals that are differentiated internally mainly by income. There are, of course, continuities from the past: there are still some upper-uppers pursuing a traditionally aristocratic life style, lower-uppers showing off their accession to wealth in flamboyant fashion, and upper-middles leading a country- and service-club existence little different in essence from that described half a century ago by novelists (*Babbitt* by Sinclair Lewis, 1922) and social scientists (the Lynds' *Middletown,* 1929). At the same time, significant numbers of upper-uppers are following less circumscribed patterns of consumption in goods and leisure, while many more lower-uppers and upper-middles are volunteering their time to causes (both left-wing and right) and/or centering their spare time on current cultural and athletic activities. The result is that Upper America is now a vibrant mix of many life styles, which might be labeled post-preppy, sybaritic, counter-cultural, conventional, intellectual, political, and so on. Such subdivisions are usually of more importance for targeting messages and goods than are the horizontal, status-flavored, class-names strata.

One subdivision of Upper Americans that sociologists and demographers have singled out in recent years is a combination of media influentials (men and women with roles in TV, newspapers, and magazines) and nonprofit professionals (whose expertise is in the employ of government, schools, and foundations). Irving Kristol (1978) has referred to this group as "The New Class," differentiating them from older-type Upper Americans to the extent that they tend to be "anti-capitalists . . . (who) often take life and energy from an adversary culture whose anti-bourgeois themes infuse our educational system, our media, our arts, and our literature." Eric Goldman, speaking of approximately the same people in "The Emergence of the Upper Americans" (1980), characterizes them as "essentially a mind-set group" whose basic thrust in ideology and consumption style has been to establish themselves as different from, and above, the Middle American classes—as he puts it, they want to "shake off the tacky in everything." This Kristol–Goldman type of Upper American probably does not yet account for more than a fourth or a fifth of the total, but its growing presence has produced an indisputable change in the flavor of this status level from that of just two decades ago: liberalism is far more common in social philosophy; the Republican Party is much less firmly entrenched; and "socially conscious consumers" (Webster 1975) are a very noticeable presence.

There are still large reservoirs of subscription to bourgeois values among Upper Americans, and clearly the class as a whole remains that segment of our society in which quality merchandise is most prized, special attention is paid to prestige brands, and the self-image ideal is "spending with good taste" (and being so judged). Self-expression is more prized than in previous generations, and neighborhood—always important—is still so, but with this twist: "interesting neighborhoods," such as gentrified inner-city areas, are appealing as well as the conventional suburbs, and living in a "charming place" in the country—in "exurbia"—also has cachet (Coleman 1977b). Meanwhile, all the longstanding Upper American dreams of more theatre going when income increases, more purchase of books, investment in art, and more European travel endure (and possibly in greater strength), along with aspiration for "more help in the house," more "nights out on the town," more club memberships for golf, swimming, and tennis, and prestige schooling for the children. For most Upper Americans, income is not sufficient to afford all these dreams simultaneously, so priorities are a must—only a lucky few don't have to make sacrifices and choices.

The Middle Class: More Pleasure Mixed into the Propriety

This status level ("lower-middle," to stick with Warner's terminology) has been recognized from the beginning as the home of people who most definitely want to "do the right thing" and buy "what's popular." They have been very concerned with fashion all along, following—with affordable modifications—the recommendations of "experts" in the print media. When families of this class have increased their earnings to manage it, better living has meant—and still seems to mean—a "nicer home" in a "nicer neighborhood," "on the better side of town," with "good schools." It also means spending more money on "worthwhile experiences" for the children, and aiming them toward a college education; shopping at more expensive stores for clothing with "one of the better brand names"; and constant concern over the appearance of public areas in one's home—i.e., wherever guests may visit and pass judgment.

Interviews in the 1970s with men and women of this class suggest that a spirit of "individualism" has been entering into their life styles far more than before. This has happened in part because "doing your own thing" was that decade's fashion, and in part because emulating the self-expressiveness of Upper Americans, in qualified ways, became a conscious goal. This upward gaze of middle-class people continues to distinguish them from the working class; they are among the big supporters of dinner theater and all the other cultural trickle-down from Upper America. The ongoing middle class struggle to uplift oneself has led significant numbers to enroll sporadically at local universities and community colleges. Imaged as a mental challenge and storehouse for knowledge, the home computer will do particularly well here when it reaches mass-market pricing.

There is not so much "stuffiness" in middle-class self-presentation these days as there was in the 1950s. Public dress codes have relaxed, and these people have taken their cue from Upper Americans. They eat out more, talk more comfortably about having cocktails, and enjoy trips to Las Vegas (if it's no more than a two- or three-hour flight away). "Doing things for the children" commonly includes enjoyment for the parents too, as in winter ski trips for the whole family in which the children acquire a socially valued skill and the parents maintain one. Indeed, such themes as physical activity form a new image of middle-class life in which possessions–pride has yielded a bit to activities–pleasure. Life seems more fun, not quite so serious at this status level in the 1980s. Deferred gratification may still be an ideal, but it is not so often practiced; self-denial and self-indulgence are in closer balance.

As in the world of Upper America, so too in the Middle American middle class, varieties of life style are found. Some reflect a split within the class between traditional outlooks and the more liberated, contemporary view; others are related to which kinds of possessions are most treasured, which pleasures most eagerly pursued.

CLASS VS. INCOME

In the late 1960s and early 1970s, a number of studies reported conflicting conclusions as to whether social class or income better predicts buyer behavior. The end result was that the role assigned to social class by marketing professionals went into decline. Little further attention was paid to social class versus income until 1981, when two noteworthy reexaminations of the question were published almost simultaneously by Schaninger (1981) and Dominquez and Page (1981). These two articles constitute so thorough and thoughtful a review of the several technical and substantive issues involved that yet another examination here would serve no useful purpose.[5]

Among the conclusions reached by Dominquez and Page were (1) that "new stratification scales" should be developed to accord with the new status realities of the 1980s, and (2) that future research should look closely into how the value and communication systems associated with each class underlie consumption patterns.

Schaninger proposed the "tentative generalizations" that:

1. "Social class is superior . . . for areas of consumer behavior that do not involve high dollar expenditures, but do reflect underlying life-style value";
2. "Income is superior for products which require substantial expenditure . . . and reflect ability to pay" yet are not perceived to be class-linked status symbols; and
3. Both must be used in combination for "product classes that are highly visible, serve as symbols of . . . status within class, and require either moderate or substantial expenditure."

Schaninger thus pronounced himself in agreement with Wind (1978), whose contention was that the entire controversy as to whether income or social class is the more basic segmentation variable is spurious, since it is better to accept both as valuable, then determine product by product what contribution each makes. Reynolds (1965) took the same view when he argued that the forecasting powers of class and income should be expected to differ from one market arena to the next, so that neither should be ignored or assigned automatic dominance.

There are many reasons for considering both class and income when trying to understand the consumer, but the truly critical one is this: *class and income are not really very well correlated.* They index two quite different aspects of life circumstances, although it is common for Americans to assume that class is really a product of income. Had Warner (1941) found class and income to be as closely related as he anticipated when he began his Yankee City studies in the early 1930s (correlated, for example, at or above 0.75), he would have stayed with his original hypothesis that income standing is the crucial organizing principle in American society. Instead, his findings indicated how little of social position in a community is explained by income variation, so he postulated class as the critical organizing factor. In the United States of the 1980s, each social class contains such a mix of family types that the class–income cor-

---

[5]Examples of class versus income studies reviewed by Schaninger (1981) and Dominquez and Page (1981) include: Coleman (1960), Carman (1965), Rich and Jain (1968), Wasson (1969), Matthews and Slocum (1969), Peters (1970), Slocum and Matthews (1970), Myers, Stanton, and Haug (1971), Myers and Mount (1973), Hisrich and Peters (1974), and Prasad (1975).

relation may well have dipped to little more than 0.40—and perhaps lower.[6]

It must not be forgotten that social status derives, in its root, more from occupational differentiation than from income. This is an ancient observation, dating to pre-Christian societies. There has never been a perfect correlation between the social honor paid different occupations and the income derived from their pursuit. Twentieth century America may illustrate this proposition to an extreme degree: blue-collar workers can outearn both white-collar workers and salaried professionals, yet they still do not rise above either in social status. To put this in the vernacular, the blue-collar workers "have more money than class," the white-collar workers "more class than money."

A second explanation for the unextraordinary correlation between class and income is that income varies markedly according to its earner's location in the age cycle. Young people—who are first apprentices, then in the junior stages of their careers—typically receive paychecks far below average for members of the social class with which they are identified by virtue of family origin, education, and occupational type. Class "norms" in earning power—i.e., what is publicly assumed to be average earnings for members of the class—are typically realized after age 35. Beyond 55, earnings tend to either exceed the norm or fall below it, depending on whether the benefits of seniority or the hazards of ill health and/or occupational obsolescence prevail.

A third source of income overlap between the social classes is family variation in the number and sex of earners. This can almost certainly be considered in the class-income correlation over the last 20 years. As more families at all social levels have experienced divorce, leading to households headed by a female earner, household incomes far below class averages have been added to the picture in larger portions. Meanwhile, as more wives have become part- or full-time members of the nation's paid workforce, household incomes far above the class average have also been added to each status group's continuum in far greater proportions than before. The result of these and other changes—such as more households in all classes headed by young singles, retirees, and the elderly widowed—is that the picture of income distribution in each class resembles an elongated oblong more than a compact, bell-shaped curve.

Clarification of Income and Class

In considering family variation in number and sex of earners as a contributor to the reduced class-income correlation, two points must be kept in mind:

1. Total household income is an illusory index to family living standards—much less to social class—wherever it includes money earned by household members that is not pooled toward the common good.
2. Increases in family income resulting from more of the individual members becoming earners almost never produce a change in the family's social class.

What, then, is the best income figure—household total, individual earnings, or some factored partial product—for use in predicting the marketplace behavior of the individual members (and combinations thereof) in a multi-income household? An inquiry into this problem, using detailed data from the University of Michigan Survey Research Center's Panel Study of Income Dynamics, produced more questions than answers (Coleman 1977a). For example, it was found that when young adults work full time and live at home, their

[6]In the mid-1950s study of Kansas City by the University of Chicago's Committee on Human Development, a 0.55 correlation between social class and income was produced in a sample limited to households with heads in the middle-age range of 40–69 years (Coleman and Neugarten 1971). With households of all types drawn from the total age range, the correlation would not have been higher than 0.45, which leads to the assumption that today's is even lower. Studies where social class is indexed by a relatively uncomplicated socio-economic status scale may show higher correlations with income, but depth studies of class versus income will consistently report lower ones.

contribution to parental well-being ranges from 10¢ on the dollar to 50 or 60¢. Wives' earnings contribute more than children's to the household's public projection of well-being, but vary markedly in whether the money goes toward life-style extras or living-standard basics. Clearly, the most widely used measure—total income earned by all a household's members, as reported by the survey respondent (inaccuracies in which abound!)—has its drawbacks; when income has turned out to be a poor predictor of consumer choice behavior, this definitional approach may well have been part of the fault.

Also, why does an increase in household income rarely result in class change when members of a family beyond its head join the workforce? A major reason is that these other earners usually work at jobs of no higher status than the primary earner's; more commonly, their jobs are of less stature. This applies especially when adult children go to work; usually, it also applies when a wife finds employment. Take a lower-class, trash-collecting husband, for example: when his wife enters the labor force, she is apt to become some sort of cleanup helper. Although the couple's income is thereby increased, community judgments of its social class are likely to remain the same, especially if no change is made in friendship circles and the major observable alteration in living standard is ownership of more "junk" cars and consumption of more beer. By the same token, when the wife of a factory worker husband goes to work in a factory too, the couple's total income may rise far beyond the middle-class average, but the pair will remain working class in social identity because middle-class America does not readily accept women with blue-collar employment—and such a woman probably isn't even trying for it.

The truth is that the classes we are talking about have mostly to do with social networks and peer judgments of "people quality," and have little to do with income levels except as these latter can be construed as proof of that quality. Thus it is that social class changes ordinarily come to a family only when the major earner—who may well be a woman—manages a shift in the public's definition of relationship to the occupational hierarchy. This change in occupational definition is accompanied by a change in friendship circles, and new consumption goals replace the old; hence the family value system and its public behavior are deemed appropriate for acceptance by a higher status circle.

That changes in economic status do not more often lead to changes in social class is yet one more explanation for the very modest class-income correlation. The sum impact of all these contemporary sources for difference between income status and social class is a lower correlation between the two than was the case in the 1950s, when social scientists first called the marketing world's attention to the class concept. As an allied development we have this: substantially greater percentages of each class's families are either "overprivileged" or "underprivileged"—and thus not "average"—than was the case two decades ago, when this way of parceling off the income continuum was first proposed (Coleman 1960). All these changes mean that it is still useful to look at social classes as divided into three economic subclasses—perhaps even more so.

The definitions offered for these economic substrata are as before. The "overprivileged" families in each social class are those with money left over (after the class-standard package of shelter, clothing, and transportation has been acquired) for the forms of "better living" that families of their class prefer; their incomes are usually 25 or 30 percent above the class median. The "class-average" families are those in the middle of the class income range who can therefore afford the kind of house, car, apparel, food, furniture, and appliances expected at their status level. The "underprivileged" are those who, while not truly poor (except, of course, in the lower class), can consider themselves in difficult straits, given what is expected from people of their status in the way of social participation and projected standard of living. Many of their consumer choices amount to scrimping, saving, and sacrificing in order to make proper appearances where these really count; their incomes fall at least 15 percent or more below the class midpoint.

Taking these definitions as guides, we might think of income minimums for "class-average" status in 1983 dollars this way: $100,000 (or a little more) if upper-upper or lower-upper, and $45,000 for upper-middles in the Upper American world; $24,000 for middle-class Middle Americans and $16,000 for working class; and $9,900 for Lower Americans, that figure being the most recent government-declared "poverty line." Just below those minimums is where the "underprivileged" state begins, class by class. The opposite "overprivileged" condition starts at $15–16,000 for Lower Americans, $24–26,000 in the working class, $36–39,000 in the middle class, $70–80,000 in upper-middle, and $200–250,000 for the upper class. These figures are of course no more than approximations, the loosest of guidelines for looking at the significance of income in the social class context. They relate to urban areas where the cost of living is presently at average for the nation, and most properly only to the Bureau of Labor Statistics' hypothetical four-person family (father 43 years of age, mother 38, and two children, ages 13 and 8). For families of other situation and size, appropriately varied standards should be applied when examining buyer behavior for impact of income status within class. Indeed, this is more a conceptual tool than a tidy research device.

Research Support

The continuing vitality of this income-in-class concept has been affirmed during the last 10 years by a series of depth studies of life-style and consumption choices in which special emphasis has been given to families of above-average income. Observe, for illustration, how different is the marketplace behavior among Upper American families with annual incomes of $30,000 to $75,000 (in 1983 dollars) from that of families with the same income who would be judged to be Middle Americans (either middle class or working class). The former are, of course, either "class-average" or "underprivileged" within their Upper American status world, while the latter are "overprivileged" in Middle America. The "overprivileged" Middle Americans can be distinguished from the "underprivileged" Upper Americans by the much greater frequency with which they own motorboats, RVs, campers, pickup trucks for sport as well as work, tractor lawnmowers, snowblowers, remote control TV, swimming pools in the backyard and/or a lakeside home, late-model sports cars for their teen-aged collegiate offspring, and expensive, largish cars for themselves. Upper Americans of the same income spend relatively greater amounts—of both time and money—on private club memberships, special educational experiences for their children, high-culture objects and events, and civic affairs participation ("causes," boards, and so on); their houses are not particularly more expensive than Middle Americans' but are much more "properly" addressed, and their cars are not so often domestic and pretentious as small and/or foreign. Equally noteworthy differences in consumption choices appear up and down the scale when people of the same income but of different social class are compared.

This illustration of how class and income are continuing to interact points to a resolution for the class-income debate. The question of whether class or income is the better segmentation variable should be put aside. What researchers should ask instead is how social class affects use of income in the marketplace—and also, when, why, and to what extent.

Income is the obvious first-order segmenting variable whenever expenditure decisions are studied; income and outflow both involve dollars, so a correlation of sorts is inevitable. It makes perfect sense to assume that in a major number of marketplace transactions, income will govern how much can be spent (and hence will be). Yet we always have to use other variables—age, perhaps, or sex, family composition, life style, self-image, and social class—to understand why income has sometimes operated quite well as a predictor and other times rather poorly. As often as not, the reason will be found in social class, which may be acting all by itself or possibly in concert with one or more other social-psychological or demographic variables.

Researchers can expect to find every conceivable mix of class impact on income use, from almost nil in some product or service areas to nearly conclusive in others. An instance of the latter might be spending money to watch stock car races: very few people outside the working class or lower class are interested, so this is almost entirely a matter of class-related entertainment preferences, rather than cost considerations. The purchase of squash racquets is equally a matter of class experience, and only coincidentally an income consideration, since very few men outside Upper America play squash. Extremes like this are not, however, the rule.

Far more common a market areas in which the effect of class follows the privilege-level model. The car market used to be an example (see Coleman 1960), which choice behavior best explained when each class was broken down into its "privilege" segments. By the early 1970s, however, the whole business of car buying had become so heavily infused with lifestyle goals and self-imagery expressions that income position within social class was not a ready predictor. By that point in auto market history, class was having its maximum impact (income almost totally aside) in determining who was most likely to buy foreign and who domestic, or who would opt to intermediates (and/or compacts) versus who would stick with standards.

It is still necessary to look at social class and income simultaneously when trying to understand how people house themselves and where they choose to do so in a metropolitan area. Class identification and status aspirations govern neighborhood choice (Coleman 1977b), then pocketbook power dictates which house or apartment. This has not changed through the years. Yet Schaninger (1981) has suggested change in the income–class relationships in kitchen appliance choice. Indeed, change may be more the rule that constancy; nothing can be taken for granted.

Finally, there are product areas in which the impact of social class is at best unclear and slight, although probably not absent entirely. Examples might be cigarettes and perhaps beer. Among cigarette smokers and beer drinkers, there is usually a heavy investment in feelings of maturity and toughness, perhaps a bit of rebellion against prudish morality, a willingness (even eagerness) to identify with all of "sinning" humanity. Social status statements are not so commonly the goal as are psychosexual ones. Brand choices may still correlate with class, but at a low level, so they are hardly predictable.

Too much may have been expected of social class by too many, so that disappointment has been the result. Were class treated as proposed here, this should not happen.

PROPOSITIONS FOR THE MEASUREMENT OF CLASS

Stratification of consumer study populations by social class is not a simple process because so many variables are involved. Yet it is not hopelessly difficult, if less than perfect placement of cases is acceptable. It is proper for standards to vary, depending on the research purposes; thus new, alternative approaches are needed that are of varying complexity.

Dominquez and Page (1981) concluded their survey of the stratification literature with a cataloguing of deficiencies in status-measuring instruments used in the 1960s and 1970s. A major problem, they found, is that the two most widely employed instruments are badly showing their age: one, the Index of Status Characteristics, dates back to the 1940s (Warner, Meeker, and Eells 1949b) and the other, the Index of Social Position, to the 1950s (Hollingshead and Redlich 1958). Most critical in this regard is that scaling of the variables—occupation, education, neighborhood, and/or house type—seems "out of date . . . [predicated on] a society that no longer exists." Alternate scaling devices are faulted as typically "oversimplified," not truly indexing social class (as defined here); more properly, they should be designated measures of "socio-economic status."

One more problem is that all class measuring sticks do a poor job of indexing the status of households that fall outside the marital-couple mold (i.e., male head in the middle of his career with wife who is a homemaker/mother). This flaw becomes more serious with the yearly rise in two-income families, female-headed households, independent young singles, retired people, and so on, all of whom are easily misidentified for social class when different score criteria are not applied to their particular circumstances.

In the earliest studies of social class, status identification was determined by extensive interviewing in a community about reputations of individuals and groups; this was coupled with elaborate charting of formal and informal interaction patterns, and the combination of these procedures was labeled Evaluated Participation (Warner et al. 1949b). Such an approach is possible only in small communities and with virtually unlimited funds. Yet its end product—personal placement according to identification with ranked status networks—is the goal researchers seek when looking at the impact social class has on choice behaviors in the consumption arena. This is what must be aimed for in less time-consuming, less expensive ways.

In an "ideal world" (just one step down in methodological complexity from Evaluated Participation), survey respondents would be interviewed for about 90 minutes, with all manner of socio-economic facts elicited—i.e., a full accounting of present life style, plus biographical data back to childhood. The interviewer would then attach two or three pages of detailed observation on the respondent's speech, appearance, and manner (and likewise for the spouse and other family members), household furnishings and upkeep, the home's exterior appearance, and characteristics of the neighborhood. This kind of data base would provide the researcher with almost as much evidence for placement of sample members as Americans at large use in their daily lives when they rate one another and decide whom to consider status equals, inferiors, and superiors. In a real world of limited budgets, researchers must settle for less, of course: how much less—and what kind of "less"—will vary depending on their funds and objectives.

It would also be ideal if the social class placements for a researched population could be rendered by an "expert," a sensitive interpreter of the data who would subjectively analyze how all the bits and pieces of fact and impression about a given individual go together to produce a ranking in the status hierarchy. But there are only a few such experts around, so less talented placers or mechanized devices must suffice in almost all research situations. Whether some level of human skill must be brought to bear or whether a machine-graded scale is sufficient depends on whether social class is at center focus in the research or merely one of many variables contemplated.

I would now like to offer four propositions about what combinations (and kinds) of skill and scale should be called on by researchers in different circumstances, with this caveat: these propositions are guidelines, not final solutions. They are first steps, as it were, toward updated, improved techniques in the research indexing of the social class variable.

Proposition 1: *For the consumer researcher who is seeking nothing more than suggestive evidence of class's impact in a product area, it is recommended that a simplified, proxy measure be accepted.*

An example of such a measure, the Computerized Status Index (CSI), is presented in Exhibit 27.2, which shows the latest version in a series of such computerized indexes originally developed for Social Research, Inc. in the late 1960s. Researchers are encouraged to treat this version as illustrative and to experiment with similar measuring sticks more appropriate for the field approach they employ and data they will generate.

Exhibit 27.2 is the page in an interview protocol given over to field collection of data, ratings, and coding for a CSI. In this particular version, occupation is weighted double when computing the total score; other versions include an occupation scaling specifically for em-

EXHIBIT 27.2 Example of a computerized status index (CSI)

Interviewer circles code numbers (for the computer) which in his/her judgment best fit the respondent and family. Interviewer asks for detail on occupation, then makes rating. Interviewer often asks the respondent to describe neighborhood in own words. Interviewer asks respondent to specify income—a card is presented the respondent showing the eight brackets—and records R's response. If interviewer feels this is over-statement or under, a "better-judgment" estimate should be given, along with explanation.

EDUCATION	Respondent		Respondent's Spouse	
Grammar school (8 yrs or less)	–1	R's age: ____	–1	Spouse's age: ____
Some high school (9 to 11 yrs)	–2		–2	
Graduated high school (12 yrs)	–3		–3	
Some post high school (business, nursing, technical, 1 yr college)	–4		–4	
Two, three years of college—possibly Associate of Arts degree	–5		–5	
Graduated four-year college (B.A./B.S.)	–7		–7	
Master's or five-year professional degree	–8		–8	
Ph.D. or six/seven-year professional degree	–9		–9	

OCCUPATION PRESTIGE LEVEL OF HOUSEHOLD HEAD: Interviewer's judgment of how head-of-household rates in occupational status.

(Respondent's description—ask for previous occupation if retired, or if R. is widow, ask husband's: ______________________________)

Chronically unemployed—"day" laborers, unskilled; on welfare	–0
Steadily employed but in marginal semi-skilled jobs; custodians, minimum-pay factory help, service workers (gas attendants, etc.)	–1
Average-skill assembly-line workers, bus and truck drivers, police and firefighters, route deliverymen, carpenters, brickmasons	–2
Skilled craftsmen (electricians), small contractors, factory foremen, low-pay salesclerks, office workers, postal employees	–3

EXHIBIT 27.2 *(Continued)*

Owners of very small firms (2–4 employees), technicians, salespeople, office workers, civil servants with average level salaries	–4
Middle management, teachers, social workers, lesser professionals	–5
Lesser corporate officials, owners of middle-sized businesses (10–20 employees), moderate-success professionals (dentists, engineers, etc.)	–7
Top corporate executives, "big successes" in the professional world (leading doctors and lawyers), "rich" business owners	–9

AREA OF RESIDENCE: Interviewer's impressions of the immediate neighborhood in terms of its reputation in the eyes of the community.

Slum area: people on relief, common laborers	–1
Strictly working class: not slummy but some very poor housing	–2
Predominantly blue-collar with some office workers	–3
Predominantly white-collar with some well-paid blue-collar	–4
Better white collar area: not many executives, but hardly any blue-collar either	–5
Excellent area: professionals and well-paid managers	–7
"Wealthy" or "society"-type neighborhood	–9

TOTAL FAMILY INCOME PER YEAR:

TOTAL SCORE ____

Under $5,000	–1	$20,000 to $24,999	–5
$5,000 to $9,999	–2	$25,000 to $34,999	–6
$10,000 to $14,999	–3	$35,000 to $49,999	–7
$15,000 to $19,999	–4	$50,000 and over	–8

Estimated Status ____

(Interviewer's estimate: ________ **and explanation:** ________________ **)**

R's MARITAL STATUS: Married ___ Divorced/Separated ___ Widowed ___ Single ___ (CODE: ___)

ployed women, to be used whether they are the spouse or the household head, and a somewhat different weighting scheme. When a respondent is not married, education is given a double weight along with occupation. Status interpretation of the total score for conventional marital-couple cases, with male household head between 35 and 64 years of age, would run this way:

Upper American	37 to 53
Middle Class	24 to 36
Working Class	13 to 23
Lower American	4 to 12

Variations in score interpretation sometimes must be employed if, for instance, some levels where the study is conducted are markedly below or above the national average, or if the interviewers appear to have been unusually generous in their ratings of occupation and/or neighborhood status. When sensitivity by age, marital status, and household situation is introduced into the score-interpretation programming, the minimum totals required for any given social class assignment are dropped by one, two, or three points, depending on the circumstances.[7]

Proposition 2: *When the research objective is an in-depth study of the relationship between social class and consumption choice, assignment of sample cases to class groupings should be rendered in qualitative fashion by "expert" judgment.*

This should be the case whether the data available for the judgment cover only three or four variables or extend to an extensive battery of 20 or 30 class-related behavioral and demographic factors. Such qualitative and "expert" judgment is required for proper balancing of the variables and weighing of their differential status impact, depending on the ages involved, the household composition, and locale. This in-depth approach to classification is recommended to all research institutes and advertising agencies that have established consumer panels for regular collection of consumption data and intensive analysis of marketplace choice correlates.

Proposition 3: *Research in social class will benefit from the development of fresh scales for measurement of the component variables.*

These scales should be constructed so that, when combined in a multi-factored index, they produce a visual profile of status assets and liabilities in each case under study; to do this, scores on each variable should relate to social class in the same way. How this principle works is exemplified by the eight scales that form the Index of Urban Status (Coleman and Neugarten 1971; Coleman 1973). Another promising approach for the updated scaling of variables lies in application of magnitude-estimation techniques as reported in Coleman and Rainwater (1978).

Proposition 4: *Status measurement in the future must do a better job of accounting for the woman's contribution to family social standing than the typical class index has done in the past.*

[7]Total scores on the illustrated Computerized Status Index (CSI) produce a "correct" social class placement for at least 75 percent of cases in a sampled population, when no special coding or score interpretation is applied for households at the age extremes or to unmarried respondents. When instructions for these special circumstances are programmed in, the class identification accuracy rises toward 90 percent.

The reader may ask, with complete justification: "What is the standard of proof for a 'correct' status placement?" The answer is this: if all data on a person's social network were available, and intensive community study had placed that network in the status hierarchy—and if, in addition, extensive reputational data had been assembled on the person to be classified—a "correct" status call could be made by the research team involved. Such occurred in the early days of class research, but it will never happen again. Anything we can today call a "correct placement" is one based on 30 or 40 pieces of evidence, rather than only three, four, or five. The basis for the assertion above that the CSI gives a "correct placement" just 75 (or maybe 80) percent of the time is comparisons made between placements rendered by a three- or four-factor CSI and those rendered by an "expert" using 10 times that many strands of status-relevant data on the same cases. Again, the reader must be cautioned: social class is a conceptual tool and, lacking precise definition, is ultimately not susceptible to perfect measurement, nor to absolute standards of validity in case placements.

Shimp and Yokum (1981) called attention to this deficiency, stating that "measurement of social class has always . . . [wrongfully] assumed the husband's (characteristics) are the sole determinants of a household's class standing." They had a name for this defect—"the husband only fallacy"—and they are only too right! The role of women in the class equation has never been properly measured. This indictment applies whether the woman is the household head, married and an earner along with the husband, or a nonearning wife who is nonetheless a potent contributor to family social status through her choice of friends, clubs, church, and neighborhood. That women's differing educational credentials, cultural interests, and ancestry frequently produce a one-class difference in the status of families where husbands are equal in occupational status, income, and education has been detailed in Coleman and Neugarten (1971).

What is needed in light of "the husband only fallacy"? For one, the neighborhood variable should be included as often as possible in status-measuring devices. Neighborhood is almost always a measure—albeit indirect—of a woman's social horizons and aspirations. A scale for female educational background is even more necessary, and should be weighted as heavily in any family total score as the male scale for schooling. Ideally, it should measure the "which school" factor of collegiate education, what personal associations were formed while there (such as membership in a sorority), and number of years completed, since these associational factors have historically been the most socially consequential part of a woman's post-high-school educational credentials (Coleman and Neugarten 1971; Coleman 1973). A scale for women's occupations, as distinguished from men's, is also recommended because different principles of status consequence have applied in the past—and probably still do. Whatever the job, the work setting (factory vs. office or school, high-status retail store vs. low) and the clientele served can be critical indicators of a woman's class identification. Introducing scales such as these into status-measuring instruments would greatly increase their relevance for households headed by women; it would also improve their predictive accuracy for marital couples especially those at the age extremes.

CONCLUSION

The four propositions just described are offered in the hope that they will lead to the regeneration of social class as a research variable. They are a start only, and do not begin to solve new problems that will emerge.[8] There is much to be done if social class is to be reinvigorated as a variable in the analysis of marketplace behavior. Class placement of research samples should be attempted as often as possible, employing modernized status measuring sticks. How Americans of each status level vary from one another in self-concept, values, and consumption goals must be examined repeatedly, and the findings must be applied to specific product and service areas.

As we survey the past 30 years, what is perhaps most astonishing is how much continuity there has been in class value systems, which have remained relatively intact through economic cycles of inflation and recession and through pronounced changes in apparel customs, car purchases, and food habits. The many life-style variations that have appeared within each class—and that have crossed class lines to unite members of different status groups in common spare-time pursuits—have tended to obscure the fundamental continuity of the class structure; so too have changing educational standards and occupational shifts

[8]One problem not touched upon here is the class identification of farm families and the measurement thereof. The relationship of rural Americans and residents of the smaller country towns to the urban status structure has remained unexamined since World War II as Americans have flocked to the metropolitan areas and their burgeoning suburbs. If, as witnessed in the 1970s, our population continues its contrary move away from metropolis and out to exurbia, small towns, and smaller cities, this nonmetropolitan sector will become more important in the future. In any event, we should extend our social class investigations and concepts to include those millions of Americans who live outside the Standard Metropolitan Statistical Areas (SMSAs).

in income reward, not to mention declining family stability.

The social class concept is not so much outdated as it is underutilized. Sophisticated application has not been easy, and never will be. Marketers, however, must not let this difficulty turn them away from keeping constant track of how (and whether) social class is continuing to be significant—as shaper of consumer goals, as influence on marketplace choice.

REFERENCES

AULETTA, KEN (1982), *The Underclass.* New York: Random House.

BERGER, BENNETT M. (1960), *Working Class Suburb.* Berkeley, University of California Press.

BROOKS, JOHN (1981), *Showing Off in America.* Boston: Little, Brown.

CAPLOW, THEODORE (1980), "Middletown Fifty Years After," *Contemporary Sociology,* 9 (January), 46-50.

———, HOWARD M. BARR, ET AL. (1982), *Middletown Families: A Half-Century of Continuity and Change.* Minneapolis, MN: University of Minnesota Press.

CARMAN, JAMES M. (1965), *The Application of Social Class in Market Segmentation.* Berkeley, CA: Institute of Business and Economic Research, University of California.

COLEMAN, RICHARD P. (1960), "The Significance of Social Stratification in Selling," in *Marketing: A Maturing Discipline, Proceedings of the American Marketing Association 43rd National Conference,* Ed. Martin L. Bell. Chicago: American Marketing Association, 171-184.

——— (1973), "The Index of Urban Status: A Manual for Assessing Family Class Standing." Cambridge, MA: Joint Center for Urban Studies of Massachusetts Institute of Technology and Harvard University, Monograph Series.

——— (1977a), "Husbands, Wives, and Other Earners: Notes from the Family Income Assembly Line." Cambridge, MA: Joint Center for Urban Studies of Massachusetts Institute of Technology and Harvard University, Working Paper No. 48.

——— (1977b), "Attitudes Toward Neighborhoods: How Americans Want to Live." Cambridge, MA: Joint Center for Urban Studies of Massachusetts Institute of Technology and Harvard University, Working Paper No. 49.

———, and BERNICE L. NEUGARTEN (1971), *Social Status in the City.* San Francisco: Jossey-Bass.

———, and LEE P. RAINWATER, with KENT A. MCCLELLAND (1978), *Social Standing in America: New Dimension of Class.* New York: Basic Books.

CURTIS, WILLIAM H. (1972), "Social Class or Income?" *Journal of Marketing,* 36 (January), 67-68.

DAVIS, ALLISON, BURLEIGH B. GARDNER, and MARY GARDNER (1941), *Deep South: A Social-Anthropological Study of Caste and Class.* Chicago: University of Chicago Press.

DOMINQUEZ, LOUIS V., and ALBERT L. PAGE (1981), "Stratification in Consumer Behavior Research: A Re-Examination," *Journal of the Academy of Marketing Science,* 9 (Summer), 250-271.

FOXALL, GORDON R. (1975), "Social Factors in Consumer Choice: Replication and Extension," *Journal of Consumer Behavior,* 2 (June), 60-74.

GILBERT, DENNIS, and JOSEPH A KAHL (1982), *The American Class Structure: A New Synthesis.* Homewood, IL: The Dorsey Press.

GLENN, NORVAL D., and JOHN P. ALSTON (1968), "Cultural Distances Among Occupational Categories," *American Sociological Review,* 33 (June), 365-382.

GOLDMAN, ERIC F. (1980), "The Emergence of the Upper American," in *Reflections of America: Commemorating the Statistical Abstract Centennial,* Ed. Norman Cousins. Washington, DC: United States Bureau of the Census.

HAMILTON, RICHARD F. (1972), *Class and Politics in the United States.* New York: Wiley.

HAUG, MARIE R. (1973), "Social Class Measurement and Women's Occupational Roles," *Social Forces,* 52 (September), 86-98.

——— (1977), "Measurement in Social Stratification," *Annual Review of Sociology,* 3, 51-77.

———, and MARVIN B. SUSSMAN (1971), "The Indiscriminate State of Social Class Measurement," *Social Forces,* 48 (June), 549-563.

HISRICH, ROBERT D., and MICHAEL P. PETERS (1974), "Selecting the Superior Segmentation Correlate," *Journal of Marketing,* 38 (July), 60-63.

HOLLINGSHEAD, AUGUST B. (1949), *Elmtown's Youth: The Impact of Social Class on Adolescents.* New York: Wiley.

———, and FREDRICK C. REDLICH (1958), *Social Class and Mental Illness: A Community Study*. New York: Wiley.

HUGSTAD, PAUL S. (1981), "A Reexamination of the Concept of Privilege Groups," *Journal of the Academy of Marketing Science,* 9 (Fall), 399–408.

HYMAN, HERBERT H. (1966), "The Value Systems of Different Classes," in *Class, Status, and Power,* Eds. Reinhard Bendix and Seymour M. Lipset. New York: The Free Press, 488–499.

KAHL, JOSEPH A. (1957), *The American Class Structure.* New York: Rinehart.

KRISTOL, IRVING (1978), "The New Class" in *Two Cheers for Capitalism: A Collection of Essays.* New York: Harper & Row.

LEMASTERS, E. E. (1975), *Blue Collar Aristocrats: Life Styles at a Working-Class Tavern.* Madison, WI: University of Wisconsin Press.

LEVISON, ANDREW (1974), *The Working Class Majority.* New York: Coward McCann and Geoghegan.

LEVY, SIDNEY J. (1966), "Social Class and Consumer Behavior," in *Knowing the Consumer,* Ed. J. W. Newman. New York: Wiley, 146–160.

——— (1971), "Symbolism and Life Style," in *Perspectives in Marketing Management,* Ed. F. D. Sturdivant. Glenview, IL: Scott, Foresman, 112–118.

——— (1978), *Marketplace Behavior—Its Meaning for Management.* New York: American Management Associations.

LEWIS, SINCLAIR (1922), *Babbitt.* New York: Harcourt Brace Jovanovich.

LYND, ROBERT S., and HELEN MERRELL LYND (1929), *Middletown.* New York: Harcourt Brace Jovanovich.

———, and HELEN MERRELL LYND (1937), *Middletown in Transition.* New York: Harcourt Brace Jovanovich.

MARTINEAU, PIERRE (1957), *Motivations in Advertising.* New York: McGraw-Hill.

——— (1958), "Social Classes and Spending Behavior," *Journal of Marketing,* 23 (October), 121–130.

MATTHEWS, HERBERT LEE, and JOHN W. SLOCUM, JR. (1969), "Social Class and Commercial Bank Credit Card Usage," *Journal of Marketing,* 33 (January), 71–78.

———, and JOHN W. SLOCUM, JR. (1972), "A Rejoinder to 'Social Class or Income?' " *Journal of Marketing,* 36 (January), 69–70.

MCCANN, CHARLES B. (1958), *Women and Department Store Advertising.* Chicago: Social Research.

MYERS, JAMES H., and JONATHAN GUTTMAN (1974), "Life Style: The Essence of Social Class," Chapter 10 in *Life Style and Psychographics,* Ed. William D. Wells. Chicago: American Marketing Association, 235–256.

———, and JOHN F. MOUNT (1973), "More on Social Class vs. Income as Correlates of Buying Behavior," *Journal of Marketing,* 37 (April), 71–73.

———, ROGER R. STANTON, and ARNE F. HAUG (1971), "Correlates of Buying Behavior: Social Class vs. Income, *Journal of Marketing,* 35 (October), 8–15.

PETERS, WILLIAM H. (1970), "Relative Occupational Class Income: A Significant Variable in the Marketing of Automobiles," *Journal of Marketing,* 34 (April), 74–77.

PRASAD, V. KANTI (1975), "Socio-Economic Product Risk and Patronage Preferences of Retail Shoppers," *Journal of Marketing,* 39 (July), 42–47.

RAINWATER, LEE P., RICHARD P. COLEMAN, and GERALD HANDEL (1959), *Workingman's Wife: Her Personality, World, and Life Style.* New York. Oceana Press; reprinted in 1979 by Arno Press Inc., New York, in "Perennial Works in Sociology" series.

REYNOLDS, W. H. (1965), "More Sense About Segmentation," *Harvard Business Review,* 43, 107–114.

RICH, STUART U., and SUBHASH C. JAIN (1960), "Social Class and Life Cycles as Predictors of Shopping Behavior," *Journal of Marketing Research,* 5 (February), 41–49.

RITTER, KATHLEEN, and LOWELL HARGENS (1975), "Occupational Positions and Class Identifications of Married Women," *American Journal of Sociology,* 80 (January), 934–948.

SCAMMON, RICHARD M., and BEN T. WATTENBERG (1970), *The Real Majority.* New York: Coward McCann.

SCHANINGER, CHARLES M. (1981), "Social Class Versus Income Revisited: An Empirical Investigation," *Journal of Marketing Research,* 18 (May), 192–208.

SHIMP, TERENCE A., and J. THOMAS YOKUM (1981), "Extensions of the Basic Social Class Model Employed in Consumer Research," in *Advances in Consumer Research,* Vol. 8, Ed. Kent Monroe. Ann Arbor, MI: Association for Consumer Research.

SLOCUM, JOHN W., and H. LEE MATTHEWS (1970), "Social Class and Income as Indicators of Consumer Credit Behavior," *Journal of Marketing,* 34 (April), 69–74.

WARNER, W. LLOYD, with PAUL S. LUNT (1941), *The Social Life of a Modern Community.* New Haven, CT: Yale University Press.

______, and ASSOCIATES (1949a), *Democracy in Jonesville.* New York: Harper & Row.

______, MARCHIA MEEKER, and KENNETH EELLS (1949b), *Social Class in America.* Chicago: Science Research Associates; reprinted in Harper Torchbook Series by Harper & Row, New York.

WASSON, CHESTER, R. (1969), "Is It Time to Quit Thinking of Income Classes?" *Journal of Marketing,* 33 (April), 54–57.

WEBSTER, FREDERICK E. JR. (1975), "Determining the Characteristics of the Socially Conscious Consumer," *Journal of Consumer Research,* 2 (December), 188–196.

WELLS, WILLIAM D., and GEORGE GUBAR (1966), "Life Cycle Concept in Marketing Research," *Journal of Marketing Research,* 3 (November), 353–363.

WIND, YORAM (1978), "Issues and Advances in Segmentation Research," *Journal of Marketing Research,* 15 (August), 317–337.

28

THE SACRED AND THE PROFANE IN CONSUMER BEHAVIOR: Theodicy on the Odyssey*

Russell W. Belk
Melanie Wallendorf
John F. Sherry, Jr.

Two processes at work in contemporary society are the secularization of religion and the sacralization of the secular. Consumer behavior shapes and reflects these processes. For many, consumption has become a vehicle for experiencing the sacred. This article explores the ritual substratum of consumption and describes properties and manifestations of the sacred inherent in consumer behavior. Similarly, the processes by which consumers sacralize and desacralize dimensions of their experience are described. The naturalistic inquiry approach driving the insights in this article is advanced as a corrective to a premature narrowing of focus in consumer research.

It has been argued that revelatory incidents are the primary source of insight in ethnographic fieldwork (Fernandez 1986; Sherry 1988). These are highly charged encounters suffused with meaning. Because these incidents are directly experienced by the researcher, the significance of the phenomenon under study is more fully appreciated than might otherwise be possible. A number of such revelatory incidents have caused us to reevaluate some of the field's fundamental constructs for understanding mar-

*Reprinted from the *Journal of Consumer Research,* 16 (June 1989), pp. 1–38.

ketplace and consumer behavior. Consider the following abbreviated examples:

Among the wares for sale at the edge of the midway of a bustling Southwestern swap meet are decorative brooms and handcrafted dolls which closely resemble Cabbage Patch Kids. The vendor, a vibrant middle-aged woman named Sarah, fashions the dolls with loving detail born of remarkable social circumstance. After the birth of her first child—a son now embarking upon a trying preadolescence—an automobile accident prevented Sarah from conceiving other children, most notably the daughter she always wanted. During her recovery, Sarah began doing handicrafts, and eventually began "making the babies." In joining the dolls' fabric bodies and faces, Sarah sees the babies "come to life." She views her skill as a special gift, just as babies are a gift from God. As she talks about her dolls, she adopts a different linguistic register, shifting into baby-talk, and caresses their foreheads as she speaks. Prior to closing the sale of each doll, Sarah performs a deliberate transaction. She kisses the doll before releasing it to a customer, wishing it well and knowing all the while how happy the doll will make other children.

Describing his arrangement of sculpted ceramic figures alternately as a "surrealistic fantasy" and a "dream," Garth Warren watches viewers strolling past his exhibit at the open air art festival. The young Southern California artist has created a series of figures ("Eygot," "Wewants," "Sleep Drive," "Swollen Pride") complete with framed misspelled proem cautionary tales, which represent aspects of his own personality (notably "consumerism") which he purports to dislike greatly. He is building a portfolio suitable to entering galleries, and is using this show to gain some exposure. Significantly, he is little concerned with business matters, and finds pricing his artwork troublesome. He gives many of his pieces away for nothing, and is as content with a talkative looker as a paying customer. His younger sister, however, is sales-oriented, and has undertaken to protect Garth from his own philanthropy. Using a pricing policy that is at turns intuitive and strategic, she is not above reviling critical lookers or altering her brother's work to suit a prospective buyer. Garth's philosophy of "If people smile, it's enough; they don't have to buy" contrasts strikingly with the sister's philosophy of "I make sure he gets what's coming to him." Theirs is a symbiotic relationship in which commerce assumes a custodial role with respect to art.

The middle-aged proprietor of Mr. Ed's Elephant Museum and Gift Shop speaks with considerable pride of opening his present business. Operating on intuition he likens to predestination, Mr. Ed risked starting a venture sustained through the display and sale of elephant replicas and peanuts. His museum houses a collection of hundreds of elephant replicas he has amassed for the enjoyment of others and for posterity. His gift shop is similarly laden with elephantiana. Despite the apparent similarity of contents, Mr. Ed regards the two areas as sublimely distinct. The museum items will never be offered for sale at any price, regardless of their similarity (or even apparent inferiority) to items in the gift shop. Mr. Ed can conceive of no compelling argument (including his own hypothetically imminent destitution) for moving a piece from the museum to the gift shop. Mr. Ed maintains with axiomatic, heartfelt certainty that to attempt such a move would be "wrong."

Each of these vignettes reflects a dimension of buyer and seller world views previously undescribed in consumer research. Each is an example of the ritual substratum of consumer behavior. These observations make it apparent that consumption involves more than the means by which people meet their everyday needs. Consumption can become a vehicle of transcendent experience; that is, consumer behavior exhibits certain aspects of the sacred. It is the premise of this article that this sacred dimension can be clinically described and interpreted, thereby enhancing our understanding of consumer behavior. In the following pages, we explore the qualities of sacredness and the underlying processes of transformation manifest in consumer behavior.

Theory and research in the sociology of religion suggest that a fundamental distinction structuring social life is between what is set apart and regarded as sacred and what is regarded as profane or ordinary. In some societies, the sacred involves magic, shamanism, animism, and totemism. Such societies often accord sacred status to components of the natural environment that are revered, feared, worshiped, and treated with the utmost respect. In contemporary Western religion, the sacred/profane distinction is also important, although the elements of experience considered sacred differ. Contemporary Western religions define as sacred certain gods, shrines, clothing, days, relics, and songs. While less a part of nature, these objects are regarded by the faithful of contemporary Western religions as sacred, and there are parallels with the regard for certain natural objects by participants in non-Western religions. Both sets of objects fulfill a need to believe in something significantly more powerful and extraordinary than the self—a need to transcend existence as a mere biological being coping with the everyday world.

For many contemporary consumers, there are also elements of life with no connection to formal religion that are nonetheless revered, feared, and treated with the utmost respect. Examples include flags, sports stars, national parks, art, automobiles, museums, and collections. Whether we call the reverence for these things religious, contemporary consumers treat them as set apart, extraordinary, or sacred, just as elements of nature are sacred in naturistic religions and certain icons are sacred to followers of contemporary, organized religions. Although the specific focal objects differ, the same deeply moving, self-transcending feelings may attend each, and the same revulsion may occur when these objects are not treated with respect. Religion is one, but not the only, context in which the concept of the sacred is operant.

Explicit recognition of the sacred status accorded to many consumption objects illuminates aspects of contemporary North American consumer behavior that, while basic and pervasive, have not been explained by prior theory and research. The substantial body of social science theory on the role of the sacred in religion is used here in developing an understanding of sacred aspects of consumption. This body of related theory is used in analyzing and interpreting the Consumer Behavior Odyssey data (Belk 1987c; Wallendorf and Belk 1987; Holbrook 1987; Kassarjian 1987; Sherry 1987a; Wallendorf 1987b) and in building a theory of the sacred aspects of consumption.

The conditions and characteristics of consumption interpretable through the constructs of sacred and profane are detectable through introspection and a close reading of a diverse literature set. However, the processes of meaning investment and divestment—the sacralization rituals we treat at length in this article—are resistant to such distanced exposition. To reflect the insights immanent in armchair and field, we employ a compromise strategy of presentation. That is, *conditions* for and *foci* of sacredness are explored principally through literature evaluation tempered by fieldwork. *Processes* are examined principally through analysis of field data tempered by literature. This work is intended as a conceptual contribution to parallel disciplines and as an empirical contribution to consumer research.

After explaining the naturalistic methodology through which the insights in this article were derived, we review the sacred and profane in scholarly theories of religion. To understand what these theories can contribute to our understanding of consumer behavior, we next explore shifts in contemporary boundaries between the sacred and the profane. In so doing, we illuminate what is considered sacred in the secular world of consumption. Going beyond merely categorizing objects or experiences as either sacred or profane, we then develop a theory of the central processes by which transcendence is achieved through consumption, using data from participant-observation and depth interviews from the Consumer Behavior Odyssey. Finally, we outline areas of consumer research that can benefit most from this theoretical perspective.

METHOD

The importance of the distinction between sacred and profane aspects of consumption emerged in interpreting our data from a pilot project (Belk, Sherry, and Wallendorf 1988). Subsequently, the Consumer Behavior Odyssey collected data primarily through naturalistic, qualitative fieldwork as detailed by Lincoln and Guba (1985). Data analysis and interpretation with corroboration from the religious and social science literatures were guided by the constant comparative method of Glaser and Strauss (1967) and techniques specified by Miles and Huberman (1984) and Becker (1986). We used natural settings, emergent design, multiple sites, purposive sampling, cross-context testing for transferability, depth and intimacy in interviewing, triangulation of data across researchers and data collection media, and triangulation of interpretation across researchers. Despite a long history of usage in anthropology and sociology, these approaches have been employed less commonly in the study of consumer behavior and, thus, are explained briefly here.

Before and during fieldwork, and throughout postfield coding and further analysis, we immersed ourselves in the literatures that address the sacred/profane distinction. Our reading of these literatures was both close and emergent, and has shaped and reflected the interpretation presented here. Unlike positivistic research, which supposedly evaluates extant literature to discover gaps to address through additional research, the Odyssey did not begin with a literature-based problematique. Rather, fieldwork prompted library research, which in turn led to additional fieldwork. What was at one moment a need to interpret consumer behavior in context, became at the next moment a desire to deconstruct and reconstruct scholarly theories. We employ a presentation style that reflects this balance between library and field.

Emergent Design

Data collection and analysis were guided by emergent design. This approach differs from surveys or experiments, which assume that the researcher understands the phenomenon prior to doing the research, so that hypotheses and fully specified data collection and analysis plans are possible.

In naturalistic inquiry, no such assumption is made. Instead, researchers build an understanding of the phenomenon as it occurs *in situ,* later testing the veracity of that understanding, also *in situ.* The first step is to observe and record the phenomenon in detail. Researchers then specify their understanding and construct guidelines for further data collection to test the emerging understanding. This iterative process continues in what Glaser and Strauss (1967) call the constant comparative method. Rather than data collection followed by analysis, data collected previously form the basis for an interpretation, which then defines what data still are required to test the interpretation. The process continues until conceptual categories are saturated and reach a point of redundancy, making further data collection unnecessary. For example, by the time we interviewed the collector of elephant replicas mentioned earlier, we had explicit hypotheses concerning the separation of sacred possessions from profane, usable commodities available for sale. This collector echoed the views of prior informants that collections are sacred and thereby differentiated from salable commodities.

Neither the number nor type of interviews needed to reach this point of saturation can be specified a priori. This results in a substantial amount of time spent by the researchers themselves gathering data and developing "thick description" (Geertz 1973). Initial interviews are largely nondirective (Briggs 1986), but later blend into more directed, semistructured ones.

Sites and Purposive Sampling

This article is based on data from a pilot study conducted in the fall of 1985, as well as data collected by the Consumer Behavior Odyssey in the summer of 1986 (see Kassarjian 1987 for the project's history). The Odyssey's goal was to develop a deep understanding of consumption, broadly defined. To accomplish this goal, a rotating team of academics employed naturalistic methods while traveling across the United States. Themes from the pilot study were pursued, but other themes and concepts also emerged as the project advanced.

Data for the pilot project were collected at a swap meet (Belk, Sherry, Wallendorf 1988). A major theme detected was that consumers made sacred and profane distinctions in their behaviors and uses of space, time, and objects. At the completion of the pilot study, this theme was not fully developed into theoretical propositions and was understood only with regard to the phenomena present at this site, but it appeared to be powerful enough to warrant broader investigation.

During the Odyssey, we first checked whether the sacred/profane distinction noted in the pilot study was apparent at other swap meets. This approach differs from that of single-site ethnographies and was stimulated by our sense that these were broadly applicable theoretical concepts. Finding that the concept generalized well to four other swap meets, other outdoor periodic sales events were sampled, including two antique flea markets, a farmers' market, and a yard sale. Other outdoor events that combined the sales interactions already observed with entertainment or celebrations were added, including a Fourth of July festival, three county fairs, two community festivals, three art festivals, one historical festival, and two ethnic festivals. To generalize beyond outdoor events, we included fieldwork at two indoor antique fairs or auctions. We also did fieldwork at indoor sites housing more permanent sellers, including three museums, a gas station, a bookstore, an ethnic grocery store, several restaurants, and a fast food restaurant. To generalize to sites that are more permanent to consumers, we also went to informants' homes.

Homes were sampled purposively to represent sacred space, in contrast with commercial sites, which are generally more profane. In sampling for sacredness, we spoke with people about their collections and other objects given special status, such as cars in a car show. These data were contrasted with data gathered at temporary homes such as recreational vehicle parks, a summer trailer park, six resorts and hotels, a national park campground, a weight loss resort, a nursing home, and two homeless shelters. People in the midst of a long-distance move were interviewed, as were people encountered on the street or highway rest stops. Other sacred sites purposively sampled included a temple, a chapel, and two evangelical services. No interviews were conducted utilizing CB radios, although this approach was tried. Although differences in the specific focus of the sacred varied, we saw no indication that the sacred and profane processes discussed here applied only to certain sites or geographic areas in the United States.

Depth Interviewing

Data were collected through depth interviews and observations requiring unstructured responsiveness to consumers (Briggs 1986) as well as the development of intimacy between researcher and informant (Wallendorf 1987a). Informants were told that the interaction was part of a project attempting to understand American consumers. Possibly the field of consumer research has not explored sacred aspects of consumption previously because the sacred aspects of consumption are less likely to emerge in experimental and survey research interactions.

Data Record

Although fieldnotes were written for all interactions with informants, many interactions were also recorded on videotape. Although not problem-free, our experience with videorecordings leads us to challenge the speculative claim of Hirschman (1986) that videorecording should be avoided due to its intrusiveness. Videotaping captures the rich detail of an interview, while simultaneously leading researchers to examine their membership roles in the field (Adler and Adler 1987). Video and still photography are data collection techniques finding increasing support among experienced ethnographers in sociology and anthropology (Briggs 1986; Collier and Collier 1986; Ives 1974; Werner and Schoepfle 1987).

Since informed consent necessitates some level of intrusiveness (Punch 1986), video photography is not the problem it would be if covert participant-observation were being attempted. The extensive literatures on deviance indicate the wide range of behaviors accessible to research using undisguised, naturalistic methods and speak to the possibility and importance of acknowledging informants' rights to informed consent. Video captures informants' explanations constructed in response to researchers' inquiries, called "perspectives of action," as well as informants' actions in their social setting, called "perspectives in action" (Snow and Anderson 1987, after Gould et al. 1974). It provides rich temporal and nonverbal detail reminiscent of Bateson and Mead's (1942) early work with film and still photos and Leahy's photo ethnographies in the 1930s (Connolly and Anderson 1987).

Still photography was used to document sites and participants. These visual records were combined with written research records in the form of fieldnotes, journals, and photo and video logs. Fieldnotes consist of detailed notes about each interaction written on a daily basis by each researcher. Fieldnotes are the primary data record and the only material in those cases when video or still photo records were not made. Supplementing the fieldnotes are the more introspective journals of each researcher, which contain reflections, emerging interpretations, and memos to other researchers.

The pilot study data consist of 121 single-spaced pages of fieldnotes and journals, 130 still photographs and slides, two hours of videotaped interviews, and an artifact file. The Odyssey data include approximately 800 pages of fieldnotes and journals, 4,000 still photographs and slides, 137 videotapes lasting 15–18 minutes each, about a dozen audio tapes, and the artifact file. Odyssey data are archived at the Marketing Science Institute in Cambridge, Massachusetts. Pilot project data materials were audited by three scholars, whose reports on the trustworthiness of interpretations are available. The point of listing the quantity of data is not to imply that it is related to the quality of data, but rather to indicate the extensiveness of the documentation from which this work draws. As is typical in ethnographic research, the depth and richness of the data is indicated by including verbatim excerpts from fieldnotes within the article.

Triangulation

Two forms of triangulation employed enhanced the thickness of description and sharpened the accuracy of researchers' observations. These two forms are triangulation across researchers and across media. Since Odyssey data collection was conducted by a team, several researchers often wrote fieldnotes on the same interview. These were written separately and without discussion prior to writing, permitting the assessment of completeness and convergence. Differences in emotions experienced may be expected to occur in journals, given the subjective nature of human interaction. However, triangulation across researchers minimizes discrepancies in the recording of factual information and improves the recall of the research team. As the team gained experience as a research instrument, the observational skills and perceptual biases of individual members allowed a division of labor to emerge that reduced redundancy in description and increased effectiveness and comprehensiveness in recording interactions; for example, we divided the labor required to simultaneously interview an informant, attend to the video camera, and shoot photographs. Triangulation across media involved examination and comparison of video interviews, photographs, and fieldnotes.

Triangulation is also useful in assessing the mutuality or uniqueness of the interpretation. We blended the perspectives of a bi-gender team (as recommended by Levinson 1987) of three consumer behavior researchers with theoretical and methodological training in psychology, sociology, and anthropology. These differences led to few disagreements regarding the appropriateness of the sacred/profane interpretation, although there were minor differences in the highlights given to this theme. For example, a psychological orientation leads the interpretation toward a definition of sacred experience as individually motivated, while the sociological focus is on consequences for societal integration and cohesion. Generally, we found our differing theoretical perspectives mutually compatible rather than mutually exclusive. Where such differences exist, they are noted in the text.

Interpretive Contexts

In building the interpretation, the data were obtained and structured by context. We use the term *site* for a particular type of physical location where data were collected (e.g., a swap meet), and the term *context* for categories of consumption phenomena, a distinction comparable to the "focal settings" and "cultural domains" identified by Snow and Anderson (1987). Contexts that emerged were gifts, collections, heirlooms, pets, time, souvenirs, art, mentions of "special" items, photographs, physical space, holidays, and pilgrimages. In building and testing interpretations, contexts were examined sequentially, with each succeeding context acting as a check on the interpretations supported by preceding ones (as in Lincoln and Guba's suggestion that researchers use referential adequacy materials to check the credibility and confirmability of an interpretation). Just as saturation was used to guide the emergent sampling design, redundant support over different contexts was used to assess generalizability of findings. We do not present propositions that were disconfirmed as we moved across contexts.

Analysis

During fieldwork, we circulated memos on our emerging understandings. As data collection progressed, these memos specified propositions to be challenged through purposive sampling. Contrary to the conception of interpretive methods described by Calder and Tybout (1987), naturalistic inquiry uses purposive sampling and constant comparative method to test by developing, challenging, and reformulating the emergent conceptualization.

Fieldnotes, journals, and photo and video indices were computerized for use in systematic data analysis. This data analysis was completed using ZyIndex, a computerized program for qualitative data management and analysis (see Belk 1988a). Analysis of each context also included examination of photographs and videotapes. Triangulation between researchers occurred with separate examinations of computer analyses and visual records.

Based on understandings developed in the pilot project and memos concerning emerging interpretations, two focal processes were identified: the transformation of profane commodities into sacred objects, and the maintenance and loss of sacredness (desacralization). Data for each context were coded using margin notations concerning each process. The transferability of these propositions was tested by sequentially analyzing contexts. Consistent with the constant comparative method (Glaser and Strauss 1967), propositions were revised in successive comparisons with new data until saturation and redundancy were achieved. What we refer to here as testing is in fact a large series of tests continued until the theory fully captured the phenomenon. Limitations and modifications are noted as the results are presented. The discussion is organized by process and draws from each context.

THE SACRED AND THE PROFANE IN RELIGION

What Is Religion?

William James's (1961, pp. 42, 45/orig. 1902) behavioral definition of religion still serves well:

> (Religion) shall mean for us *the feelings, acts, and experiences of individual men in their solitude, so far as they apprehend themselves to stand in relation to whatever they may consider the divine.* . . . We must interpret the term "divine" very broadly, as denoting any object that is god*like,* whether it be a concrete deity or not.

In its avoidance of a particular theological perspective, this definition is hardly singular among social scientists. For example, Roberts (1984, p. 90) states:

Religion has to do with a unique and extra-ordinary experience—an experience that has a sacred dimension and is unlike everyday life . . . the experience of the holy. Such an experience is often called nonrational, for it is neither rational nor irrational.

Such definitions stress the special quality of sacredness that makes something religious. Marcel Mauss (quoted in Ferrarotti 1979, p. 674) contrasted this observation with the more common assumption that religion involves particular deities:

It is not the idea of god, the idea of a sacred person, that one finds over again in any religion, it is the idea of the sacred in general.

To understand how this perspective on religious experience applies to contemporary consumer behavior, we must specify the properties of sacredness.

Properties of Sacredness

The sacred can best be understood by contrasting it with the profane, as in the extensive theoretical treatments by Emile Durkheim and Mircea Eliade. Their perspectives are similar, although Durkheim's notion of religion is more sociological, focusing on societal consequences, while Eliade's is more psychological (Stirrat 1984). We present 12 properties of sacredness synthesized from the writings of Durkheim, Eliade, and subsequent theorists. Of these, hierophany, kratophany, opposition to the profane, contamination, sacrifice, commitment, objectification, ritual, and mystery all apply in both individual and social treatments of the sacred. Communitas and myth are primarily social concepts, and ecstasy and flow are primarily psychological.

Hierophany. Hierophany is "The *act of manifestation* of the sacred . . . i.e., that *something sacred shows itself to us*" (Eliade 1958, p. 7), conveying the idea that, phenomenologically, people do not create sacred things. Instead, sacredness manifests itself experientially as "something of a wholly different order, a reality that does not belong to our world" (Beane and Doty 1975, p. 141). In Eliade's psychological view, hierophany involves the notion that the sacred does not manifest itself to everyone. A sacred stone continues to appear like other stones except to those who believe it has revealed itself to them as unique, supernatural, or *ganz andere* (totally other).

Durkheim (1915) also sees the sacred as being beyond individual creation; however, in his sociological view, the sacred emerges collectively when society removes certain things from ordinary human use. Something is defined as being sacred through a social process that brings a system of meaning to individuals (hierophany), resulting in societal cohesion.

Kratophany. The sacred elicits both strong approach and strong avoidance tendencies (Durkheim 1975/orig. 1896). This ambivalence creates an overwhelming power, the manifestation of which is called kratophany (Eliade 1958). Although the vernacular usage of the term sacred implies only that which is good and desirable, Durkheim distinguishes between beneficent sacred powers, such as those associated with gods, protectors, and holy places, and evil sacred powers, such as those associated with corpses, sickness, and impure objects (Pickering 1984). Both are imbued with sacred power through strong ambivalent reactions (kratophany) that combine fascination and devotion with repulsion and fear. Because people simultaneously seek the beneficence of the sacred and fear the evil it can unleash, they approach it with a care appropriate to its kratophanous power.

Opposition to the Profane. The extraordinary sacred is defined partly by its opposition to the ordinary profane. Profane refers to that which is ordinary and part of everyday life, not to that which is vulgar or offensive, as in vernacular usage. Although Durkheim recognized various degrees of sacredness, the extremely sacred was held to be inviolably distinct from the profane. "The sacred . . . cannot, without losing its nature, be mixed with the profane. Any mixture or even contact, *profanes* it, . . . destroys its essential attributes" (Durkheim 1953, p. 70). Such sacrilege includes trespass on the sacred by profane persons; only a priest or shaman can cross from the profane to the sacred realm, and only after appropriate purification. A primary societal function is the exercise of social control to maintain the separateness of the two spheres, protecting the inviolate status of the sacred and maintaining its position as set apart.

Contamination. Both beneficent and evil sacred things have the power to contaminate through contact. However, in contradistinction to medical usage of the term, contamination in this context generally indicates the spread of positive sacredness rather than evil (negative sacredness). Objects blessed through sacred ritual are thus said to be contaminated with sacredness. A religious example of contamination is the Christian ritual sacrament of communion, in which a congregation eats symbols of the body and blood of Christ (in some traditions, transubstantiation is said to occur). Similarly, possessions of sacred persons become venerated icons because they are contaminated with sacredness; places where sacred activities occurred are contaminated with sacredness that the faithful seek to attain through pilgrimages (O'Guinn 1987; O'Guinn and Belk 1989; Turner and Turner 1978).

Sacrifice. As an act of abnegation and submission, sacrifice establishes communication with the sacred by purifying and preparing the sacrificer (Hubert and Mauss 1964). Sacrifice usually involves a "gift to the gods" of otherwise profane material goods, such as domestic animals in pastoral societies (James 1962). But sacrifice can also involve asceticism, fasting, sexual abstinence, self-mutilation, and martyrdom (Mol 1976). Sacrifices prepare one to commune with the sacred, bring about a strong degree of commitment to sacred experience, and indicate appropriate deference to reinforce the extraordinary character of the sacred.

Commitment. Individuals feel a "focused emotion or emotional attachment" to that which is considered sacred (Mol 1976, p. 216). Psychologically, such commitment directs attention to the sacred, which becomes a strong part of one's identity. This aspect of sacredness shares some features with what has been called involvement in the consumer research literature. However, sacredness goes beyond the concept of involvement, as will be explained more fully later.

Sociologically, collective formation of shared commitment to a definition of the sacred is the integrative basis for society (Durkheim 1915, 1960/orig. 1902; Weber 1962/orig. 1920). Regardless of what is chosen to signify the sacred in society, shared commitment results in what Durkheim terms mechanical solidarity, in which religious participants replicate the social order by maintaining commitment to the collective definitions of sacred and profane. Individual commitment to the sacred is so strong that initial experience with the sacred may result in conversion—an identity change resulting in an unshakable conviction.

Objectification. Objectification is "the tendency to sum up the variegated elements of mundane existence in a transcendental frame of reference where they can appear in a more orderly, more consistent, and more timeless way" (Mol 1976, p. 206). Through representation in an object, the sacred is concretized. This allows things of this world to take on greater meaning than is evident in their everyday appearance and function. A stone may continue to appear as a stone, but it is a sacred object when its origin is understood through a creation myth to be the tear of an animal. We find this aspect of the sacred to be particularly important in understanding the sacredness of some contemporary consumption.

Ritual. Rituals are "rules of conduct which prescribe how a man should comport himself in the presence of . . . sacred objects" (Durkheim 1915, p. 56). Rituals are often performed without deliberate thought to the rationale that guides them. They are functional through their performance, apart from their content (Bossard and Boll 1950). Like sacrifice, ritual prepares one to approach the sacred and may be enacted as an individual or, more commonly, as a group. Ritual surrounds the contact of profane persons with the sacred to ensure that the evil powers feared in kratophany will not be unleashed. Ritual also protects the sacred from contact with mere mortals and alleviates human anxiety about this contact (Malinowski 1954).

Myth. Myths often surround the sacred and are used historically to document its status through narratives, iterative tales, or speculations about existence (Kirk 1970). Such accounts define our place within the world and maintain sacred status through repetition (Eliade 1964; Mol 1976). They socialize participants' understanding of the collective definitions of the sacred and instruct new participants such as children and recent converts.

Mystery. The sacred "has conferred upon it a dignity that raises it above the ordinary or 'empirical' " (Pickering 1984, p. 159). It cannot be understood cognitively, for the sacred commands love, devotion, fear, and related spiritual or emotional responses rather than rational thought. This mystery is characteristic of phenomena that do not fit human behavior models based on presumptions of self-interest or competition, but rather derive from a desire for more profound experiences and meanings (Nisbet 1966). When something loses this mystery, it loses its sacredness and becomes ordinary and profane.

Communitas. Communitas is a social antistructure that frees participants from their normal social roles and statuses and instead engages them in a transcending camaraderie of status equality (Turner 1969). It is most likely to occur when the individual is in a "liminal" or threshold state betwixt and between two statuses, such as may occur on religious pilgrimages (Turner and Turner 1978) and in initiation ceremonies, fraternal organizations, countercultural groups, and occasionally among research teams (Sherry 1987a). This spirit of communitas emerges from shared ritual experiences "which transcend those of status-striving, money-grubbing, and self-serving" and act as "proofs that man does not live by bread alone" (Turner 1972, pp. 391–392).

Ecstasy and Flow. The sacred is capable of producing ecstatic experience, in which one stands outside one's self (Colpe 1987). Durkheim (see Pickering 1984) describes a joy that arises from the transcendent reality of sacred things. According to James (1961, p. 55/orig. 1902),

> Like love, like wrath, like hope, ambition, jealousy . . . it (religion) adds to life an enchantment which is not rationally or logically deducible from anything else.

The sacred can take a person outside of self, matter, and mortality, but such ecstatic experiences are momentary rather than constant (Greeley 1985). Ecstasy marks the extraordinary character of sacred experience and distinguishes it from the common pleasures of everyday life.

A psychological interpretation refers to the effect of participation in the sacred as flow (Csikszentmihalyi 1975) or peak experience (Maslow 1964). Flow experiences include a centering of attention, a loss of self, a feeling of being in control of self and environment, and an autotelic aspect such that the activity is its own reward (Csikszentmihalyi 1975).

Victor Turner (1977) has subsequently distinguished communitas as involving a "shared flow." Like the differences between Durkheim and Eliade regarding sacred experiences, the differences between flow or peak experience and communitas are not so much in the nature of the experience as in whether it is a group or an individual phenomenon. Although group ritual does not appear necessary for ecstatic experiences (Hardy 1979; Laski 1962), such rituals can and do bring about sacred experiences. To begin to explore the applicability of the concept of the sacred to contemporary consumption, we must consider the contemporary boundaries between the sacred and the profane.

SHIFTING BOUNDARIES BETWEEN THE SACRED AND THE PROFANE

The sociology of religion has noted changes in contemporary society that make interpretations of the sacred and the profane somewhat different than Durkheim's—in which the sacred resided in the sphere of religion and the profane resided in the secular world. Changes in contemporary life indicate that the sacred/profane distinction is no longer isomorphic with the religious/secular distinction (Becker 1957). Two trends work together to support the applicability of the concept of the sacred to the secular context of consumption. The first trend involves the gradual secularization of contemporary institutional religion, while the second involves the gradual sacralization of the secular. Both processes reflect shifting boundaries between the sacred and the profane.

Secularization of Religion

The secularization of religion is a widely noted pattern. For example, Ducey (1977) found growth in nontraditional church services in the United States during the 1970s. Nontraditional services substituted the profane for the sacred, such as lay for clerical dress, contemporary guitar for classical organ music, and oral participation by parishioners in addition to sermons by the pastor. These changes reflect culture's dynamic definitions of the sacred and the profane.

Others have found a gradually more secular celebration of traditional religious events, such as Christmas (Belk 1987a; Bock 1972; Luschen et al. 1972), and a marked decline in family religious rituals, such as prayers at meals and bedtime, and collective readings from sacred literature (Bossard and Boll 1950). The discontinuance of Latin in the Catholic Mass exemplifies a secularization of religion involving demystification, lesser separation of sacred and profane times, and lesser preservation of ritual and myth.

The use by contemporary religions of radio and television media also demonstrates secularization through the broadcast of sacred rituals into what may be profane spaces or times (O'Guinn and Belk 1989). "Televangelism" secularizes religion also by its association with the secular medium of television (Frankl 1987). By becoming more linked to the secular, religion may have undermined its own sacredness, opening the way for other foci of sacredness. That is, as religion provides less of an extraordinary experience, people look elsewhere for experiences that transcend everyday life.

Sacralization of the Secular

The emergence of sacred in secular contexts has coincided with the secularization of institutional religion. As the Catholic church lost control of politics, knowledge, art, and music, each of these spheres developed sacred status of its own. To characterize this trend, Rousseau formulated the term "civil religion," which refers to finding the essence of religion in what is traditionally regarded as secular. The notion has been treated in greatest depth by Bellah (1967, 1985), whose theory of civil religion attempts to resolve the ambiguous role of religious symbols in secular society (Fenn 1986). Contemporary sacralization of the secular is seen as occurring in the cultural arenas of politics, science, art, and consumption. Evidences from each of these areas will be briefly reviewed.

Nationalistic celebrations reflect the sacralization of the secular within politics (Demerath 1974; Shiner 1972). National holidays are celebrated more widely than many religious holy days; national anthems are sung with all the reverence of hymns; national flags are icons; and contemporary national heroes and monuments have supplanted the widespread worship of religious saints and shrines (Geist 1978; Roberts 1984; Rook 1984; Warner 1959). Market forces accelerate and focus this sacralization of nationalism, creating invented traditions, such as Scottish clan tartans (Hobsbawm and Ranger 1983), and replacements for evil eye and hex symbols in official-looking commercial security system and security patrol signs on the doors and windows of many American homes (Rook 1987). Europeans venerate royalty (e.g., Williamson 1986) with a mystique imparted by longstanding rituals and symbols (Hayden 1987; Shils and Young 1953). The crown jewels are regarded as icons that are as unthinkable to sell as it would be to turn the Statue of Liberty into condominiums.

A second area where the secular is sacralized is science. Rather than religion, science is considered the ultimate arbiter of truth in societies that venerate rational thought and causal explanations (Capra 1975), much to the dismay of fundamentalists. Weber called the substitution of scientific for religious belief "the disenchantment of the world," while Schiller called it "the disgodding of nature" (quoted in Berman 1984, p. 57). The miracles of god and nature have gradually been replaced by scientific explanations (Inkeles 1983). Now it is science rather than religion that is viewed as imparting knowledge, although a number of authors see this as an unfortunate divorce of eros from logos (Bateson and Bateson 1987; Berman 1984; Highwater 1981; Hyde 1983; Keller 1985; Pirsig 1974; Plato 1955/orig. 400 B.C.) that leaves us with an incomplete understanding of the world.

A third arena that provides evidence of the sacralization of the secular is art and music. Since the Reformation, religious content in music and art has declined and secular themes have increased (Berger 1967). Yet, both are sacred to many consumers. Art, like science, is not only sacred, it sacralizes. Placement in a gallery, museum, university, or other scientific or artistic institution can sacralize objects (Clifford 1985). Museum curators are among the priests of the art world. Prominent collectors are also accorded expert status to authenticate artwork and act as "missionaries" in promoting art to the uninitiated (Lynes 1980).

In a definition reminiscent of the sacred/profane distinction, Becker (1978) differentiates between art and craft, noting that both may be aesthetically appealing, but a craft object has a use. This accords with the idea that the sacred is set apart and beyond mundane utility and also accords with the noble portrait of the starving artist, which Becker (1982) finds accurate given the difficulty of having one's work defined as art.

The presence of the sacred is as evident in popular music as it is in the so-called high arts, but there are clearer deities—charismatic rock stars. The sacralization of rock music is accomplished by each generation of youth, which draws its collective identity from the songs of these rock stars (Martin 1979) via a process that Goodman (1960) calls "the sacramental use of noise." The ecstasy here derives from the liminal experiences of sex, violence, and mysticism (e.g., drugs) associated with this music (Martin 1979), as well as deriving from the music experience itself (Holbrook and Hirschman 1982).

This leads us to consider evidence of the sacralization of the secular from the realm of consumption. Although consumption historically has often been opposed by institutional religious teaching (Belk 1983), it has gained sacred status in our consumption-oriented and hedonistic society (Campbell 1987; Mol 1983). Mol illustrates the "cosmic straddling, deep commitment, solemn rites, and expressive symbolism" that may attach to art, sports, music, and even secular objects such as some clothing and automobiles. That consumption has become a secular ritual through which transcendent experience is sought has been noted, but not empirically explored, in the consumer behavior literature (Hirschman and Holbrook 1982; Holbrook and Hirschman 1982; Leiss, Kline, and Jhally 1986; Rook 1985; Sherry 1987b, 1987c; Wallendorf and Arnould 1988; Williamson 1986). Just as Protestantism helped secularize religion in Weber's (1958/orig. 1904) view, the rise of individualism has made it possible to define the sacred as that which brings secular ecstasy to the individual. According to Campbell (1983, p. 293):

> Although nominally "secular" in character (this principle) . . . derived from the idea of a "covenant" or compact between each individual and his own "self," in which in return for acknowledging one's duty to serve the spirit of self, that spirit would in turn bring happiness to the individual. Heaven in such a doctrine is the fulfillment of self.

It is the sacralizing of certain aspects of consumption that will serve as the focus for the remainder of this article.

What Is Sacred?—The Domains of Sacred Consumption

As a result of the secularization of religion and the sacralization of the secular, the sacred/profane distinction has become applicable to the secular context of consumption. While anything can potentially become sacred (Acquaviva 1979), sacred status is not distributed randomly across the elements of a culture. Instead, consumers enact the sacred/profane distinction within common domains of experience. Potentially sacred consumer domains, like potentially sacred religious domains, fall into six major categories: places, times, tangible things, intangibles, persons, and experiences. We will discuss the meaning of the sacred/profane distinction for contemporary consumers in each of these as a means of building a definition of sacredness.

Places. In agricultural societies, one's homeland is the sacred center of the world. Even contemporary displaced cultural groups such as the Navajos experience a fractured social fabric as a result of losing their land (Scudder 1982). Some sacred places, especially those in nature, have the beauty, majesty, and power to evoke ecstasy and flow without help from myth, ritual, or contamination (Brereton 1987; Lipsey 1984). In other cases, these means may be needed to sacralize a place.

Places may reveal their sacredness through hierophanous signs, as with the Aztec city of Tenochtitlan, founded where an eagle landed on a blooming cactus (Brereton 1987). A place may also become sacred by contamination through events that occurred there (e.g., Jerusalem). Places where sacred persons were born, performed miracles, received mystic revelations, and are buried become sacred through contamination. Rituals may also sacralize a place, as with groundbreaking ceremonies, burials, and housewarming parties.

Once a place is regarded as sacred, it may command reverential behaviors such as pilgrimages, removal or wiping of shoes, silence, purification prior to entry, or sacrificial offerings. If they do not already exist, boundaries may be marked and shrines erected. The sacredness of some spaces is defined by the activities that occur there. In religion, churches, temples, and shrines are viewed as sacred. But distinctions are also made between sacred and profane areas in the secular world. A secular place commonly designated as sacred is the geographic area of a person's childhood. Pilgrimages are often made to these areas on vacations, especially when accompanied by other family members. Going back can be either a positive or negative sacred experience, depending upon how much the place has been changed and how much of one's former identity, familiarity, and mastery is retained (Belk 1988b).

The primary locus of the sacred in the secular world of consumption is the dwelling (Eliade 1959; Jackson 1953; Tuan 1978). It is sacred because it houses the family, because it is a home (Kron 1983). The most sacred and secret family activities occur there, including eating, sleeping, cooking, having sex, caring for children and the sick, and dressing (Saegert 1985). It is separated from the profane world "outside" (Altman and Chemers 1984; Rapoport 1982) through the careful attention given to entry thresholds (Deffontaines 1953; Rapoport 1981). In societies organized around nuclear families rather than collective groups, the dwelling imposes order by centering the world for its inhabitants (Duncan 1985). Within the home, private spaces serve as inner sanctums in a society favoring individualism (Tuan 1978). The hearth is often a communal family altar where family photos are enshrined and greeting cards connecting the family to others are displayed (Collier and Collier 1986; Jackson 1953; Levi-Strauss 1965).

Consumption also has its public cathedrals that enhance the mystery and sense of otherworldliness of the sacred. Such places have been instrumental in the development of consumer culture. Perhaps the most influential of these has been the department store. Rather than following the wheel of retailing pattern of entering the market as low-price institutions, turn-of-the-century department stores entered the market as extravagant show places where functional and financial considerations paled in the magnificence of their grandiose architecture, theatrical lighting, and sumptuous display (Bowlby 1985; Williams 1981). Today, the simple department store is eclipsed in grandeur by the shopping mall (Kowinski 1985; Mann 1980; Zepp 1986), where shopping has become a ritual in a consumption-oriented society.

Other cathedrals of consumption in the past two centuries have included the grand opera house (Naylor 1981), the theatre (May 1980; Sharp 1969), the museum (Rochberg-Halton 1986), world's fairs (Benedict 1983; Rydell 1984), and the grand hotel (d'Ormesson 1984). Such places gave consumers a taste of opulent luxury, often even being named "palaces" in the early 1900s. Although consumers could not aspire to live in such grand places, attending events there enlarged desires and created a sense of reverent awe for luxury and consumption.

Times. Just as sacred and profane places are separated, time is separated into sacred and profane periods. Sacred time is not merely an interval that is otherwise profane. Once sacred time begins, it seems infinite and without meaning. For example, creation myths form a history within a different time plane than that of the profane world. The sacred past is recoverable through rituals such as New Year celebrations that reenact a creation myth (Eliade 1958, 1959) or festivals such as Christian Easter, which reenacts the resurrection of Christ and renewal of nature. During initiations, graduations, weddings, funerals, and birthdays, we participate in the sacred.

Sacred times occur cyclically during the day (e.g., Islamic prayers, the morning coffee break), week (e.g., the sabbath, a leisurely reading of the Sunday newspaper), month (e.g., new moon ceremonies), and year (e.g., the harvest feast, birthday celebrations). As with entry into sacred places, purification rituals may accompany entry into sacred time to separate it from profane time. Special clothing, fragrances, prayers, utensils, and foods may accompany sacred time (Farb and Armelagos 1980; Leach 1961; Wolowelsky 1977). Sacred time may even serve in lieu of sacred place, as with the Jewish calendar, which has been suggested to be replete with sacred times due to the long exile of the Jews from their sacred homeland (Zerubavel 1981).

Sacred time also occurs episodically in secular consumption contexts; e.g., for the fan attending a sporting event or concert or for a gourmet sitting down to a fine meal. Irreverent behaviors, such as interruptions, inappropriate noise, or too casual an attitude toward the focus of attention at these times, are considered not only rude but sacrilegious. Such actions profane events that devotees think should be regarded with awe and appreciation. Ritual garb, behaviors, foods, and vocabularies or silence may also be expected during these sacred intervals. As Rheims (1961, p. 29) notes:

> Museums are the churches of collectors. Speaking in whispers, groups of visitors wander as an act of faith from one museum gallery to another. Until the end of the nineteenth century it was customary to visit the Hermitage Museum at Leningrad in a white tie. The almost ritual habits practiced in the sales-rooms in London and Paris have been the same for two hundred years. The Hotel Dourot (an art auction site) is a sort of temple. It has fixed ceremonies, and its daily hour from ten to eleven has a completely religious atmosphere.

During a rock concert the behaviors considered appropriately reverential differ, but are still defined as sacred to participants. These behaviors include use of marijuana, lighting matches to indicate reverence at the end of a concert, ecstatic dance, and purchase of tour t-shirt relics. Here it is the quiet, seemingly uninvolved concert-goer who is considered inappropriate.

Tangible Things. Sacred tangible things include icons, clothing, furnishing, artifacts, and possessions that are symbolically linked with and objectify the sacred. Shrines honor sacred relics and separate them from the profane world (Geary 1986). In naturalistic religions, animals may be totemic and sacred (Houghton 1955;

Levi-Strauss 1962), whereas in vegetation cults, trees and plants are regarded as sacred symbols of life, creation, renewal, youth, and immortality (Eliade 1959). Sacred religious objects are sometimes fine pieces of art, but are sometimes quite simple things like the bone, top, ball, tambourine, apples, mirror, fan, and fleece shown to novices in the Lesser Eleusinian Mysteries of Athens (Turner 1972). Ordinary as these things may appear to be, they are made sacred by myths, rituals, and signs. They are the media by which a society's "deep knowledge" is passed on to succeeding generations. Objects may also be defined as sacred because of their rarity and beauty, marking them as inherently non-ordinary (Clark 1986), as with precious metals and gems (Eliade 1958).

Sacred objects are not treated as ordinary objects, but rather seem to require special handling. They are revered with a "bow, a prostration, a pious touch of the hand" (Eliade 1959, p. 25). They are consecrated, used in prayer, sung about, and used to trigger inspiration and ecstasy. Further, they may be believed to have magical powers, both beneficent and evil. As Eliade (1958) notes, rare stones and metals are often believed to have aphrodisiac, fertilizing, and talismanic qualities. They may be considered poisonous, able to cure diseases, preserve dead bodies, protect from harm, or bring prosperity.

Sacred objects are imbued with kratophanous power. Some possessions within the home are also sacred, even though they may be as humble-appearing as odds and ends on a bureau, a pincushion lid, a cigar box, faded American Legion poppies, and assorted pills and patent medicines (Morris 1948). Particularly favored possessions represent aspects of the person's life that are regarded as sacred (Wallendorf and Arnould 1988).

A sacred possession for many in the United States is the automobile (Levy 1978; Marsh and Collett 1986; Neal 1985; Sherry 1986a). As satirized by Mol (1976, p. 152):

> Once upon a time there was a country that was ruled by a god named Car. In the beginning it did not amount to much. Then it came to pass that out of Dearborn, Michigan, there came a man who took Car and said, "Let there be mass production," and slowly Car took over the country. Car temples were built, car stables were put up and special stores sprang up where people could go and buy gifts for Car. Weekends became ritualistic: On Saturday the people would wash Car gently with soap and on Sunday they would pet it with a soft rag to remove any stray dust and ride around the countryside. Car ruled the country for many years, demanding annual sacrifices of several thousand people and keeping most of the people in a downtrodden state as the people tried to meet financial pledges they had made to Car.

Thus, ordinary consumption items can serve as sacred icons.

Intangible Things. Immaterial things considered sacred include magic formulae, dances, crests, names, and songs (Beaglehole 1932). More contemporary examples include fraternity and sorority rituals, secrets between friends or lovers, and family recipes for stuffing the Thanksgiving turkey. Like tangible sacred things, intangibles exhibit kratophany and are approached with both attraction and fear (Clodd 1920).

Persons and Other Beings. While Durkheim held that individuals in general are sacred in modern Western society (Pickering 1984) due to values of possessive individualism, what is meant here is that certain persons are sacred and set apart from others. Gods, prophets, and saints are religious examples. The lives of saints take on a sacred character through good deeds, self-abnegation, sacrifice, martyrdom, and piety. At a slightly less sacred level are the leaders and officials of the church. They are not thought of as choosing their positions, but rather are "chosen" or "called," most often by a non-rational, hierophanous vision. In many religions, they too live a life of sacrifice, self-abnegation, poverty, chastity, and good deeds.

Some sacred persons have prophetic charisma that gives them magical power over followers (Weber 1968/orig. early 1900s). This power can be greater than that residing in impersonal things, so that the charismatic leader can redefine ideas of what is sacred. Over time, the power of the charismatic leader is routinized in a bureaucracy, which then confers sacred status on particular positions, and subsequently to those who occupy these positions. The sacredness of a charismatic leader, then, shifts over time from the person to a structure, to positions, and then to role occupants.

As an immediate manifestation of the self, the body may be regarded as sacred. It is ritually bathed, anointed with oils, groomed, arrayed in sacred clothing, and decorated, as with tattoos (Hope 1980; Rook 1984, 1985; Sanders 1985; T. Turner 1977; Wallendorf and Nelson 1986). Clothing adorns the body to symbolize group membership, as in the clothing signs that devotees of long distance running use to distinguish themselves from joggers (Nash 1977). Miner (1956) has deftly pointed out that contemporary body care rituals regard the bathroom as a shrine, the medicine cabinet as a treasure chest of magical potions and charms, and doctors and pharmacists as priests.

Pets are a type of sacralized animal (Sussman 1985; Tuan 1984). Apart from the way pets structure family interactions, their sacralization shapes human food preferences. Just as cannibalism is taboo, eating a pet or any animal considered suitable as a pet is unthinkable (Harris 1985). In ancient Polynesia, pigs were family pets (Titcomb 1969), but in modern agribusiness, the pig "has been reduced to the status of a strictly utilitarian object, a thing for producing meat and bacon" (Serpell 1986, p. 6).

Experiences. The experiences of prepared individuals at sacred times and places are themselves sacred, as with the travels of pilgrims. The distinction between sacred and profane travel can be made according to purpose and destination; travel to a shrine is sacred, while a journey away from home for business is profane (Fabien 1983). While the religious pilgrimage is a traditional form of sacred travel (Turner and Turner 1978), a part of any touring involves a seeking of the sacred. Worship of the pure, uncrowded natural site recalls naturistic religion. There are also new sacred sites, including such playful centers as Disneyland and Walt Disney World. The nostalgic motifs of these centers are designed to convey the visitor into a sacred time (Moore 1980) by evoking what Durkheim calls a nostalgia for paradise (Cohen 1979; Culler 1981; Giesz 1969; Tuan 1978). Sightseeing has become a modern ritual (MacCannell 1976) within the sacred, non-ordinary time of a vacation (Graburn 1977). It is a festive, liminal time when behavior is different from ordinary work time. An important part of the tourist's quest is to bring back a part of the sacred experience, place, and time. The objectified result is frequently a photograph or souvenir (Gordon 1986; Stewart 1984). An outsider may regard these as kitsch, but they are sacred for the pilgrim (Giesz 1969; Whetmore and Hibbard 1978).

Eating is a sacred experience in many contexts (Farb and Armelagos 1980), primarily when food has meaning beyond mere physical energy replenishment. Meals are eaten ritually at certain times, in certain places, with certain implements and procedures (Jones 1982). Eating is a ritual connecting the nuclear family, and there are a number of holiday occasions in which extended family and friends are bonded by sharing food that symbolizes life. For North Americans, these include Thanksgiving, Easter, Passover, Christmas, and birthdays (Wolowsky 1977). Contamination through food is a strong symbolic perception, as evidenced by the rumors embodied in consumer oral tradition that deal with profanation and taboo (Koenig 1985; Sherry 1984). Certain foods, such as Big Macs and Kentucky Fried Chicken, can become sacred icons that nostalgically represent culture (Curry and Jiobu 1980; Kottak 1975).

Additional sacralization of experiences and of persons, places, and times attend the ritual consumption of spectator sports. Guttman (1978) reviews the original religious basis of spectator sports and argues that, while no longer religious, sports are still sacred. In spectator sports, the fan participates in an experience in which teams and heroes are revered, stadiums are temples that may be the site of pilgrimages, and artifacts may serve as sacred relics. Fans participate in various pre-, post-, and during-game rituals (Birrell 1981; Mac-

Aloon 1984; Stein 1977; Voigt 1980), and sports seasons are sacred times for them. Myths involving players, teams, and the principles they are thought to exemplify help sacralize sports, with the Super Bowl being the largest mythic spectacle in the United States (Birrell 1981; Cummings 1972; Real 1975).

Although not comprehensive in listing everything that is regarded as sacred, this discussion points out areas of secular consumption in which the sacred is experienced. This discussion highlights parallels between religious experience and the broad range of places, times, tangible things, intangibles, persons, and experiences that contemporary consumers may regard as sacred. What is of interest is not a mere listing of what is regarded as sacred, since almost anything can become such a focus, but rather the processes supporting individual and collective definitions of sacred consumption and the distinctions separating sacred from profane consumption. Rather than listing everything that may be labeled sacred consumption, we will outline the processes by which consumers understand and preserve particular aspects of consumption as set apart, extraordinary, and sacred.

Interpretive Summary of What Is Sacred

We have detailed a number of properties of the sacred, and have shown how conventional scholarly interpretations of religion enhance our understanding of consumer behavior. Our discussion of shifts in the boundary between the sacred and the profane demonstrates the selectively permeable nature of these domains of experience. Religion has become secularized, and the secular sacralized in contemporary Western society. In this context, consumption may become a primary means of transcendent experience. Rather than experiencing the kind of extraordinary meaning previously attained primarily through religion, contemporary consumers define certain objects or consumption experiences as representing something more than the ordinary objects they appear to be. In this, they participate in what the sociology of religion calls the sacred. The focal interest here is not on *what* is regarded as sacred, as almost anything can be imbued with this meaning. Rather, our primary interest is in the *processes* by which particular consumption becomes and remains sacralized.

Before examining the processes by which consumption is sacralized and preserved as sacred, it may be helpful to recapitulate our understanding of the sacred. We take the sacred in the realm of consumption to refer to that which is regarded as more significant, powerful, and extraordinary than the self. Sacred occurrences may be ecstatic; they are self-transcending. Such self-transcending experiences may, but need not, be aided by a social context involving fellow believers who also revere the object or experience. The profane, by contrast, is ordinary and lacks the ability to induce ecstatic, self-transcending, extraordinary experiences. Profane objects are treated casually rather than reverently and are not a focus of devotion.

Perhaps the closest existing analog in consumer research to our concept of the sacred is the involvement construct. Conceptually, high enduring product involvement (Houston and Rothschild 1978) is related to, but is not the same as, sacred consumption. It is likely that many of the high enduring involvement automobile owners identified by Bloch (1981) and Richins and Bloch (1986) regard their automobiles as sacred. However, high enduring product involvement and sacred consumption are distinctly separate concepts. The notion of sacredness in consumption is not restricted to products; it may also attach to people, places, times, and experiences. More importantly, high enduring product involvement is not a sufficient indicant of sacredness. A consumer who watches television frequently and who regards it as an important source of life satisfaction need not regard television or television programming as sacred. For television to be sacred to a consumer, it would also need reliably to provide self-transcending, extraordinary experiences, and be capable of being profaned. High enduring product involvement is often characteristic of those for whom a particular type of consumption is sacred, but not all who exhibit high enduring product involvement will regard the consumption as sacred. Involvement is a component of sacred experience, but is insufficient to fully capture the experience of sacred consumption. The involvement construct does not explain the processes of movement between sacred and profane that are explained in the theory of sacred consumption explicated in the remainder of this article.

Nor is recent work on self-concept and fluid body boundaries sufficient to encompass the sacred in consumer behavior. Whether objects are viewed in Western, masculine perspective as extensions of self (Belk 1988b) or in more feminine, Eastern terms as incorporated into self, no sacralization need occur in either event. Ultimately, the meaning of the sacred may lie in the discovery or creation of connectedness, but without a confluence of the properties we have described, sacredness will go undetected.

We know of no extant quantitative measures of consumption sacredness, which is why we have described the properties of the sacred in such detail, emphasizing the variety of the experience rather than relative degrees of intensity. We have not called for the development of quantitative measures because the nature and experience of the sacred may be antithetical to such measurement. The ontological and epistemological assumptions of positivist methods are not sympathetic to the mystical and experiential nature of sacredness, but instead are oriented to a different universe of discourse. Qualitative assessment becomes important in developing an understanding of sacred consumption processes and in discovering the dimensions along which their properties might be measured eventually. We will now examine the processes characteristic of sacred consumption.

RESULTS: PROCESSES OF SACRED CONSUMPTION

Anything may become sacred. Sacredness is in large part an investment process. Consumers construe meaning in various fashions and in different degrees of ontological intensity. Objects (broadly construed) potentiate and catalyze experience of the sacred. This experience may be ritualized at the level of ceremony or even of habit; it may be subject to much exegesis, or so deeply subconscious as to resist everyday inspection. The sacred adheres in that which is designed or discovered to be supremely significant; in this regard, industrialized society is no different from any other society, hegemonic and ethnocentric Western values notwithstanding. However, groups and individuals satisfy the universal need to experience the sacred quite differently. A comprehensive analysis must describe not just what is considered sacred, but also the *ways* objects and people move between the sacred and profane realms. Our analysis will focus on two processes that occur regarding sacred and profane aspects of consumption: sacralization processes and maintenance processes that perpetuate sacredness.

Sacralization Processes

How do certain possessions attain sacred status? Is sacredness something that is acquired with the object, as power steering is acquired with an automobile, or is it something that happens after the object is acquired? Our data indicate that there are at least seven ways through which an object can become sacralized in contemporary consumer culture: ritual, pilgrimage, quintessence, gift-giving, collecting, inheritance, and external sanction.

Sacralization through Ritual. An ordinary commodity may become sacred by rituals designed to transform the object symbolically. Much ritual behavior in contemporary consumer culture has been secularized—in effect reduced to ceremony or habit—but some ritual may be reclaimed, or singularized, and consciously returned to the realm of the sacred. These rituals may be public or private, collective or individual.

Sacralization through ritual is evident in informants' descriptions of the process of moving into a new house and turning it into a home. (For additional material on the architectural dimensions of sacralization, see Oliver 1987 and Slesin, Clift, and Rozensztroch 1987). A man in a homeless shelter who was moving into his own room in a boarding house estimated that turning this space into a home would happen quickly; he expected that his new room would feel like home the first night that he slept there. For him, merely sleeping in the room for one night, combined with the knowledge that it was his, was sufficient ritual for transforming it into a home.

However, for lower middle-class people spending the summer in a trailer campground, making the place feel like home involved extensive work to the exterior of the trailer and the rented space, as indicated by the following excerpt from field notes:

There is an amazing amount of work which has gone into outdoor settling and decorating. The sites have wood piles, awnings, colored gravel to be raked around the yard, white painted rocks to line the driveway, American flags, lawn statuary of all types including animals which are in fact native here such as squirrels, hanging lantern lights in abundant variety, and plastic chain strung around the space like a fence. There are lawn chairs of heavy metal, twirling daisies and other whirligigs, woodburned signs with the residents' names on them, planters with flowers, and even some annual flowers planted in the ground.

Kopytoff's (1986) call for a "cultural biography of things" provides the concept of singularization for interpreting this behavior. Singularization is the process by which a commodity becomes decommoditized (see also Appadurai 1986). A relatively undifferentiated object is individuated by the consumer through this process, which is paramorphic to management's intent in the practice of branding (Gardner and Levy 1955). Singularization can be tracked in the successive investments and divestitures of meaning associated with a consumer's relationship with an object. Since excessive commoditization homogenizes value, and in this sense is "anticultural," decommoditizing rituals ensure that some things remain unambiguously singular (Kopytoff 1986). Thus, in a Durkheimian sense, culture (through its bearers, i.e., consumers) sacralizes portions of itself; consumers transform a house into a home. Sacralized objects embody the power inherent in cultural integration. Although singularization does not guarantee sacralization at the level of culture, it does allow consumers to bring order to their own world of goods and make sacralization a possibility.

In the trailer campground, artificial nature was brought in to singularize the home. This was not unique to camper parks where people spent the entire summer; similar rituals for settling and designating as sacred were observed at a recreational vehicle park where most people spent only one or two days.

Some campers have a great many plants about their sites, as if trying to cultivate the illusion of being at home in their yard, or of somehow having tamed nature while living in its midst.

Rather than finding this a waste of time, the owner of the first camper park mentioned was proud of the work many of the residents had done to decorate their sites. They were proudly demonstrating the lower middle class orientation toward home ownership and care of possessions (Coleman 1983; Levy 1966) by working diligently on their space—even while on vacation. One woman who lived in this park was getting a new trailer. She said that it would take a while before the new place would seem like home, and outlined the ritual transformations she and her husband would use to make it a home. They planned to build a deck around the new trailer, and she was making craft objects to decorate the interior. In addition to the desire to make the trailer more aesthetically pleasing, these rituals serve to singularize and transmute the trailer into a home.

Sacralization may be accomplished in part by imposing one's own identity on possessions through transformations. The urge to change, customize, or just symbolically appropriate, as with photographs (e.g., Sontag 1973), appears to be strong, as illustrated in this comment by a woman who was renovating the house she shares with her husband and children:

"The first day that we were able to be here, which was two minutes after settlement I guess, we ran in.

My husband's stepfather came and photographed inside and outside; and (then we also took pictures of) stages of change as we redid last summer. It's just fun to get those out and remember how, oh, it was awful." (wf, 35)[1]

The photographs are a reminder of the time when this was a profane house. The celebration of such sacralizing transformations is common. A teen-aged male described his months-long work altering his first automobile to make it just the way he wanted it. He ritually cares for the finished car with twice-a-week baptismal washings and once-a-week anointing with wax.

An elderly informant explained that she and her husband had spent much of their adult lifetimes fixing their home just the way they wanted it. They then purchased a second farm home that they renovated extensively, including putting in a lake. Furniture pieces made from walnut trees removed from the lake site were given to each of their three children as symbols of the transformation of the farm into a singularized home.

"It was such fun to do. Even though you didn't make them yourself, you felt like you were responsible for them." (wf, 65)

Her description unconsciously echoes a mythic theme in *The Odyssey* (Homer, Book 23:190–204) in which the bed of Odysseus and Penelope is hewn from Zeus's sacred olive tree. Although this informant hired a cabinetmaker, she feels responsible for the pieces because the ideas carried out were hers, as was the case in the restoration of the farm house. The transformation of the trees into furniture provides a tangible object to represent self and family heritage. This was supported by her 35-year-old daughter who observed in a separate interview:

"It's very lovely furniture. But it makes it more than personal; it's like a piece of me." (wf, 35)

The furniture is a ritual symbol of the daughter's connection to her family.

[1]Parenthetical notations with fieldnote material indicate race, gender, and age.

Sacralization through Pilgrimage. A second means by which an aspect of consumption may be sacralized is through a secular pilgrimage. By secular pilgrimage, we refer to a journey away from home to a consumption site where an experience of intense sacredness occurs. The most extraordinary pilgrimage we encountered among informants was being made by a middle-aged couple and their son traveling by horse-drawn, covered wagons. They had sold their house, truck, and possessions, and had given up jobs and school-based education to roam freely through the American and Canadian West. What was being sacralized through this pilgrimage was the self via self-sufficiency wrung from hardship, and through contamination by the natural sites they visited.

Other secular pilgrimages encountered were being undertaken by people in motor vehicles or on bicycles and were to last either months or weeks. These often involved historic destinations such as Gettysburg, Washington, D.C., and the mansions of Newport, RI. Whereas the first two destinations celebrate nation, the third celebrates the American ethos of wealth and worldly success. Through such pilgrimages, the sacredness of the site is maintained.

Such places are seen as shrines and are often visited on mass pilgrimages by tourists to attain a sacred state of being through contamination. This includes shrines with positive power, such as the Statue of Liberty, as well as those exhibiting kratophanous power, such as the Vietnam Memorial (Lopes 1987; Spencer and Wolf 1986). Secular pilgrimages typically occur during the liminal time of vacation when one is temporally away from the everyday, ordinary world.

In some cases, we encountered groups of pilgrims who had banded together much as the religious pilgrims chronicled by Chaucer (1948/orig. circa 1400). Three males and one female in their early twenties were camping near each other in a national park, although they had only encountered each other that evening. Two were doing long tours by bicycle and the other two had done so previously. A shared sense of values as well as a shared liminal state (Turner and Turner 1978) prompted their camaraderie, as was also true of those participating in the Consumer Behavior Odyssey (Belk 1987c; Sherry 1987a).

Not all persons we encountered traveling were involved in secular pilgrimages. Those moving to a new home were invariably rushing to their next destination, and the interim travel was an annoyance rather than an experience to be enjoyed as a favored state of grace. They were anxious to get to what was sacred to them: a place they could call home.

Sacralization through Quintessence. Not all sacralized objects are as unique as handcrafted walnut furniture or a cross-country bicycle trip. Some sacred objects seem ordinary, yet are regarded and treated as extraordinary. Initially this puzzled us, particularly for objects that are sacralized and cherished precisely for their similarity to other objects. We observed the sale of jewelry "As seen on Dynasty and Dallas," complete with photographic murals of Linda Evans. We observed the use of Don Johnson cardboard mannequins to sell jackets similar in appearance to those worn on his television show "Miami Vice." While the concept of contamination is at work here, there appears to be something more operating to sacralize commodity objects. It was even more apparent in one automobile enthusiast's explanation that he was a believer in Chevrolets and came from a family of "Chevy people," while another was a "Ford man." Simply put, how can mass-produced, anonymous, commodity-like objects acquire sacred status?

One enlightening concept is quintessence. Quintessential objects possess a "rare and mysterious capacity to be just exactly what they ought to be . . . unequivocally right," according to Cornfeld and Edwards (1983). Objects cited by both Cornfeld and Edwards and Sudjic (1985) as quintessential include the Mont Blanc Diplomat pen, the Swiss Army knife, the Cartier Santos watch, Dom Perignon champagne, the Polaroid SX-70 land camera, Levi's 501 jeans (see also Solomon 1986), the Zippo lighter, the American Express card, the Wham-O frisbee, the Volkswagen Beetle, Coca-Cola, and Ray Ban sunglasses. What do these products have in common? According to Cornfeld and Edwards (1983, n.p.):

> The pleasure such things offer us is wonderful and illogical; it is very like the pure joy a child feels when he unexpectedly comes into possession of something magically desirable. . . . For while we may use quintessential things for commonplace purposes, they serve as talismans and guideposts, touching our souls with souls of their own.

Sudjic (1985, p. 18) echoes this mystical totemic language.

> Caring about green wellies, or about customized Cortinas are both examples of the practice of using cult objects in a tribal way, for members to identify each other, and to exclude outsiders.

Armstrong (1971, pp. 26, 29) designates an object exhibiting such quintessential qualities as an "affecting presence."

> The . . . affecting presence (is) . . . a self-contained, perpetuating actor on the one hand and a human-perceptor related affectant on the other. . . . Ontologically, the affecting presence is a perpetuating affecting act—a near-being with its unique "personality" continuously exerting its own existence, though it is known only in transaction. It is independent of any source of "meaning" or energy external to itself; being a self-sufficient entity, it is its own "meaning" and provides its own energy.

The metaphors employed in these descriptions indicate that these are sacred objects. They are branded commodities, but give the impression that they are beyond mere commerce. This suggests that sacred objects need not be one of a kind. As with the "Chevy man," for some consumers it is the brand and model that is sacred rather than a specific, personally owned object. Sacred objects are not always singularized (Kopytoff 1986), particularistic, or unique objects. Instead, the item may be seen as unique from other brands, as with the smell of Lysol to some Irish Catholics or the flavor of Oreo cookies to their devotees. Uniqueness theory (Snyder and Fromkin 1980) recognizes a range of such individuation strategies. An example of the mysticism that may attach to such quintessential brands is the furor caused by Coca-Cola's 1985 decision to abandon its age-old formula in favor of a tastier one. Despite positive indications from taste tests, for consumers the magic and mystique were gone. As the quintessential products listed previously suggest, quintessence generally is achieved over a long period of time and is not a process that emanates exclusively from efforts by the producer.

This temporal dimension of the sacred is bound up with authenticity. While museums of art reproductions were once common, our society is currently unwilling to accept such displays as sacred. In our interviews with collectors, authenticity—discerned in various ways, including signatures, numbered prints, first editions, and items produced during a certain period of time—was a commonly cited criterion in selecting items for a collection. The quest for quintessence is a quest for authenticity—"The Real Thing" in Coca-Cola's well-chosen vocabulary. However, quintessence is seldom as universal as Coca-Cola's. It may be supported by a cult of "true believers," as with the "Chevy man" mentioned earlier. Alternatively, it may be supported by the celebration of newness in an object, as newness renders the object quintessentially perfect.

Some places were rendered quintessentially sacred by consumers' desire for authenticity. For some informants, the more commercial a place was seen as being, the more it was disparaged. The more natural, real, or authentic it was perceived as being, the more it was treated as a sacred place. Perceiving a place as real is more a matter of having it fit one's prior images or imaginative reconstructions than it is a matter of being factually, historically, or locally accurate, as noted in this field note excerpt concerning a Japanese tourist in his early twenties.

> He exhibited typical Japanese unwillingness to offend by claiming to have difficulty picking a favorite place he's been in America, but he liked the West due to the cowboy flavor of Arizona and New Mexico, and he wants to move to a smaller area of America. He doesn't like the crowded areas and said that the West is like the real America for him.

Disneyland was described by tourists as a marvelous place to bring the family. Still, a tourist at a Midwestern historical museum stressed:

> "It is important to get away from such commercial places, and learn about real history." (wm, 50s)

The type of place viewed as quintessentially sacred varies with the informant, but the function of sacred places in vacation pilgrimages remains constant. These places potentiate experience of the sacred by embodying hierophany and kratophany, by enabling communitas, and by being limned with myth by their promoters, as with Disney World (Kottak 1982).

Tourists also regarded as quintessentially sacred those places that they have visited that are exceptionally natural, uncrowded, and unspoiled by other tourists. One woman made such a discovery on her vacation with her husband, as described in this field note excerpt:

> They had not planned to go to Prince Edward Island but heard so many people in Nova Scotia say good things about it that they decided to go. In fact, it was one of their favorite parts of the trip. One 12-mile stretch of the beach was the most beautiful place she had ever been. She said it looked like "God had reached down his hand and touched it." (wf, 60s)

Such places are sacred not only because they are perceived as authentic and unspoiled; there is also some naturism or reverence for nature reflected. An emically driven interpretation is that visiting this place showed the family's resourcefulness in discovering its quintessential beauty and made the family members special and unique for having been there, further singularizing their own sacredness.

Although the intuitive feel for the condition of quintessence may be right, additional work is needed to explore fully the range of such human-object relations (e.g., Czikszentmihalyi and Rochberg-Halton 1981; van Imwagen forthcoming; Wallendorf and Arnould 1988).

In this regard, Scarry (1985) notes that apart from attachments to objects that come to represent connections to particular people (a singularized, sacred object), we also are comforted by anonymous and mass-produced objects. They are regarded in many ways as alive, as the bearers of the message, "Whoever you are, and whether or not I personally like or even know you, in at least this small way, be well" (Scarry 1985, p. 292). Quintessential objects bind us culturally, societally, and even globally to a sense of sacred uniformity, which coexists with our desires for individuation (Boorstin 1973; Breen 1988).

Sacralization through Gift-Giving. Informants identified a fourth means for sacralizing an object, namely through gift-giving. Gifts often have special meaning, and selection of gifts to give to others is clearly different from a commodity purchase. The sacred/profane distinction is evident in Malinowski's (1922) continuum with pure gifts at one end (no thought of return is involved) and pure trade at the other, and in Mauss's (1925) distinction between pure gifts and pure commodities. When informants purchased objects as gifts, they engaged in one phase of a sacralizing process. Consumers take gift objects from the profane world where they are purchased, systematically remove price markers, and decoratively wrap them (Waits 1978). They ritually exchange these gifts in a ceremony that may involve the mandatory presence of others, decorations, and special clothing (Belk 1979; Caplow 1984; Sherry 1983). These actions separate items from the profane world of commerce, singularize them (Kopytoff 1986), and turn them into gifts.

Since a gift is usually an expression of connection between people, it may take on sacred status. However, some gifts, such as the "free gifts" received in return for purchases or charge account applications, remain profane commodities. Not all gifts are sacred, and not all gifts are equally sacred.

Gifts are hallowed by connection to other sacred elements of life. Tourist sites provide consumers an opportunity to capture the sacredness of the site by buying a gift for those at home, or a souvenir for oneself. In the range of sites we sampled, gift shops were abundantly present: at cheese factories, restaurants, battlefields, castles, theatres, truck stops, recreation vehicle parks, and almost all other tourist sites encountered. Pre- or pseudo-singularized objects (i.e., mass produced artifacts ennobled by the label "gift") available at these shops were purchased and resacralized by consumers; the objects were transformed into gifts or souvenirs. To indicate where the object was obtained and to sacralize it further, the name of the site was often inscribed on it (Gordon 1986; Stewart 1984), as with t-shirts imprinted with images of the Statue of Liberty bought by two elderly informants for their grandchildren. Alternatively, metonyms—objects so closely linked with an experience that they literally embody it (Lakoff and Johnson 1980)—were selected for souvenirs, as with the inexpensive Indian jewelry bought for friends at home by a Japanese college student touring the American Southwest. This contamination by a sacred site visited on a pilgrimage enhances the sacredness of the transformed object (Kelley 1987).

Another type of gift that is often sacralized is one imbued with handwork and labor. Shortly before she died, one informant's grandmother sewed her a sampler; it is a gift that the granddaughter deeply cherishes. It is not the literal content of the poem on the sampler, which the informant could not recall from memory, but rather its symbolic content that makes it sacred for her. Because the sampler was given to her as a surprise, it is more sacred than the crafts she asks her mother to make. These latter items are closer to commodities, and she refers to these requests as "placing an order." Because she asks for them, they are not as cherished as the gift of the sampler.

In this pattern of meanings, the value-expressive, self-symbolizing character of the sacred is evident. If one of the functions of defining something as sacred is increased social cohesion (Durkheim 1915) or societal integration (Parsons and Shils 1951), then what is selected to be regarded as sacred may be value-expressive for the social group, as well as self-expressive for the individual. This multivocality gives sacred objects much of their symbolic efficacy. Such objects are different from the purely instrumental objects of the profane world. They are not uniform commodities, but are individually singularized (Kopytoff 1986) and collectively expressive. Turner (1967, p. 108) views the central cluster of sacra as the "symbolic template of the whole system of beliefs and values in a given culture."

From the data presented thus far, we might speculate that handmade gifts uniformly express the values of craft and labor. But this is not completely borne out in the rest of the data. In fact, handmade gifts were considered profane by a woman in her sixties who recalled her youth in the rural Midwest.

> She talked about how things were when she was a child. . . . The others thought she was spoiled because she got things that they didn't get to have. She got to have a "boughten" doll and they only had rag dolls. She got to have some "boughten" dresses, although most of them were made at home. She remembers one dress that she had when she was about 4 or 5 years old. It was a "boughten" dress that was very light and had a very full skirt. Her mother put it on her one time and she remembers going out after it rained and playing in the water in it and that dress floated all around her and it felt very nice. She is not sure why she remembers that, but she does.

This would have been during the time when store-bought gifts began to supplant handmade gifts, aided by advertising supporting their appropriateness as gifts (Snyder 1985; Waits 1978). The handmade dresses were profane, while those that were "boughten" in a store were, at that time, considered sacred. The informant recalled a transcendent, magical experience that occurred while wearing the purchased dress. In light of our discussion of department stores as cathedrals of consumption, it is understandable that a "boughten" gift would engender just such an experience for a rural consumer. This experience also suggests that the cultural frames for goods employed by North American consumers (described as an evolutionary sequence by Leiss et al. 1986, p. 279—idolatry, iconology, narcissism, and totemism) may be regionally as well as temporally bounded. There is often a time lag in the diffusion of cultural frames from core to periphery, as well as in adaptation of these frames to local realities. Culture change occurs on a regional basis in such multicultural settings as the contemporary United States.

Gifts indicate the value-expressive nature of the sacred. Gifts handcrafted by the giver allow the giver and recipient to celebrate the values of friendship and singularizing labor. However, when "handmade" represents everyday toil expended to meet profane needs, manufactured goods may become glorified, in part because they represent the belief that technology provides a more comfortable life for consumers. Hand labor is appreciated for specially crafted items, but is superfluous for most of our needs. Technology is valued for providing the advances that give us "boughten" goods. We observed tourists riding in air-conditioned buses arrive at a large swap meet in Amish country, ready to "visit" the land of farmers who don't use contemporary technology, "sample" the foods prepared by the farm women, and buy these "simple folk's" crafts as handmade gifts to take back home. Yet, the tourists gladly boarded the air-conditioned buses at the end of a hot summer day of shopping out-of-doors to return to their everyday lives of technology and "boughten" goods. This dialectic between self and others drives much tourism. We found that both labor and labor-saving technology are more than just core values in our secular world. They are vehicles of hierophany, commitment, and flow. The sacred status of gifts derives from their multivocal ability to express these contrasting values as well as social connections.

Gifts are kratophanous in their ability to separate us from the material world and simultaneously bind us to it. The same woman who described the "boughten" dress discussed the changing role of gifts at Christmas:

> She doesn't really remember Christmas gift giving. For her husband, a good Christmas was one when he would get 25 cents worth of candy. She thinks that perhaps Christmas was more of a family celebration then and not so much of a gift-giving time.

Gifts are not as sacred as the connections between people that they are used to signify. They provide the contemporary material basis for kindred interaction once provided by other sources, such as the "kinship work" of writing letters and making phone calls, organizing gatherings, and communal labor formerly involved in the social reproduction of intimacy (Cheal 1987). For a younger generation, however, the affiliation with the material world is seen more positively. This is true even for an Amish boy growing up in an anti-materialistic religious community.

John's favorite toy is a wooden truck which is about 18 inches long and about 10 inches high. It was given to him as a Christmas present, but he doesn't know where it came from (whether it was bought or made). What John likes most about Christmas is getting gifts. (wm, 8)

The giving and getting, rather than the gift per se—although in our Amish case, the rustic simplicity of the gift itself is telling—are especially significant (Baudrillard 1981) of the sanctity of domestic affiliations.

So gifts acquire sacred status as expressions of deeply held cultural values. Sharing these values, givers and recipients are bound together in a ritual celebration creating and reinforcing social integration. Other gift-giving instances encountered confirm our understanding of this means by which objects attain sacred status. A boy (wm, 12) on vacation at a national historic site with his extended family bought a gift for a family member who did not come on the trip, using money he had earned doing odd jobs for neighbors:

"How does it make you feel to be in a place like this; kind of fun? old?"

"Yeah, it makes me feel old; it makes me feel like going back into history. It makes you feel old. It makes you feel like you are in that time."

"What will it feel like when you wear your belt buckle?"

"I don't know. I guess it will feel (pause) make me feel like I'm a soldier or somethin' like that. Or it could give you some sort of, I can't explain. You know how you feel sort of proud? The Civil War makes you feel like you're a General or something like that; like you are in the army. . . ."

"So you will wear your belt buckle and that will kind of bring back what this place is like?"

"Well, the belt buckle's not for me."

"Oh, it's not?"

"The belt buckle's for my uncle. So he gets the belt buckle. If I were to have it, I'd probably feel proud."

This gift selection episode creates a nostalgic image of a self-reliant and patriotic boy, proud of imagined military service, enmeshed in neighborhood and familial ties. Through the gift and his adolescent description of what it evokes, he celebrates the meaning of these cultural values using the object as a projectible field (Leiss et al. 1986).

Not all gifts are meaning-laden expressions of cultural values or love. Many are profane objects bought and given in an obligatory fashion. Many such gifts are soon forgotten, put aside, or discarded. Those who are in the business of producing objects to be sold as gifts are not unaware of these issues. One informant was in the business of making and selling dolls of St. Nicholas, Santa Claus, and Father Christmas. She used antique fabric to make the doll clothing as a means of recapturing the past.

She began making these because she had always loved Christmas. She has had great success and can't keep up with the demand even though she claims to work 18 hours per day. She says she enjoys it. Despite the pressure, she has a representative and is trying to sell her work to gift stores through two major metropolitan merchandise marts. She is concerned that people won't see them as unique and handcrafted at a gift store the way they do at an antique sale (where she now sells them).

Some gift objects echo the values expressed by other kinds of sacred objects, such as the connection to the past of heirlooms, the sense of completion and mastery of collections, or the symbolism of true gifts of the self. This was often found to be the basis for the search for a gift to give on return from a trip. For this gift-giving occasion, the general expectation is that some object will be carried back from the sites visited during the pilgrimage. This ritual is a virtual reenactment of the archetypal monomyth of the heroic quest (Campbell 1949; Sherry 1987a). Buying a gift upon one's return would be inappropriate because it would not transfer any of the sacredness of the vacation to those who did not go. It would fail to allow others to participate in contamination by the sacred places and times that occurred during the vacation. Instead, it would offer them a profane commodity from their everyday world.

Sacralization through Collecting. A fifth way objects are sacralized is by inclusion in a collection (Belk et al. 1988). Even though each item may not be unique, as with one informant's collection of Hummel figurines, together they are additionally singularized by formation into a collection. Taken as a whole, collections are regarded by their owners as special, unique, and separate from the everyday items they have and use. The collection is revered and respected by collectors based on a series of superlatives most often involving its size and completeness and the energy and effort that went into assembling it.

Items that are offered for sale, even as collectibles, exist as profane commodities. Once included in a collection, an object acquires sacredness by adding to the completeness of the collection. It is ennobled by its connection to the other items and by adherence to the principles of No-Two-Alike and Unity-in-Diversity (Danet and Katriel 1987). It is also sacralized through the rituals of the hunt and enshrinement in an ordered display. The collection as a whole is sacred partially because it symbolizes attempted completeness and comprehensiveness, neither of which is ever attainable. The collector generally strives to have one perfect example of each kind of a particular item. In categories that are infinitely expansive, the collector gradually narrows the focus (e.g., all "retired" Precious Moments figurines).

Only those objects that somehow add to the completeness of the collection in the eyes of the collector are selected for this conversion. Search may assume proportions of a grail quest, indicating the scarcity of appropriate objects for inclusion. The informant who collects elephant replicas searches for them when he is on vacation, and at flea markets and garage sales, all situations with a possibility of treasure-finding. Once found for a collection, objects then take on meaning beyond their individual existence. They are now part of a set, an element in a larger scheme.

Items in collections may also attain sacred status by being bought in a state of disrepair and then transformed through labor into fine specimens. For example, one informant, an antique collector (wf, 40s), bought a table in disrepair for $3 at an auction. She planned to spend hours restoring it to its once fine condition. Through her investment of personal labor, it would be transformed into a part of a collection. Another collector did this by repairing pocketwatches. Sacredness in collections thus may derive not only from adding some completeness to the set, but also through the investment of oneself (Belk 1988b). This labor theory of value is an "elementary folk theory with deep existential roots" (Cheal 1987, p. 157).

Collectors often sacralize objects by finding and rescuing them from those who do not understand the objects' worth or value. For example, a collector of Mickey Mouse items (wm, 40s) found some original Disney display backdrops at a swap meet, where they were being used as tarps to cover and protect other merchandise that was considered valuable. He was proud to have rescued them and was now using them "appropriately" as backdrops to draw attention to the Disney items he sells. He priced the backdrops at $500 because he did not want to sell them. Folk narratives of such salvations from lucky finds are so common among collectors and swap meet habitués that the stories may be considered collectively as market mythology (Beards 1987) drawing from the theme of religious salvation and conversion.

Rather than being purchased or received in trade, some items in collections are received as gifts. This was true of all of the Hummel figurines of one collector and for some of the items owned by the elephant collector mentioned earlier. Here the object has already entered the realm of the sacred through gift-giving and remains in that realm by joining a collection. Significantly, for the elephant collector, some items were received as gifts from friends and others who had visited the museum, giving the collection a broader social significance for him. He said that he got "mushy and misty-eyed" as he thought about these gifts from museum visitors, some of whom previously had been strangers and one of whom was a movie star. The sacredness of this collection and its signification of his connection to others is enhanced by enshrinement of the gifts in the elephant museum he runs. Visitors to the museum and its related gift shop participate in further sacralization by stopping to pay homage to the significance of elephants, and by their purchases and comments. In the museum, each piece given by someone as a gift is marked with a hand-lettered sign commemorating its origin, as with donations and loans to art collections displayed in art museums. The sacralization of a collection is intensified also by drawing from the sacredness of gift-giving and museums.

Collections are often begun with objects that were given to the collector as a gift. The following excerpt from fieldnotes illustrates the way in which an object is sacralized through gift exchange:

> I talked to one woman (wf, 20s) and her mother (wf, 50s) who are looking for a particular "collectible" figurine in the Precious Moments series. She bought one last year when she was here on vacation and now is having the salesclerk see if they have a particular one in stock. She has all of the "retired" figurines (a total of about 20). She got started collecting them when her brother gave her the first one. He also started a collection for his girlfriend. As a gift, he pays for her to buy the "club selections." Sometimes she gives this type of figurine to him as a gift.

This collection began with connections to mystery, since the nature of a gift is initially not known, and ritual, since the role prescriptions incumbent on a gift recipient are observed (Caplow 1984; Sherry 1983). The starter gift nature of this collection is not unlike the friendship symbolized by starter recipes (e.g., sourdough bread, yogurt, brandied fruit) in which the original gift grows to produce more.

However, despite the sacred status of gifts and the sacredness of collections, collectors are not always pleased to receive gifts of the items they collect, as illustrated by the sentiments of a 13-year-old girl who collects Mickey Mouse figures as well as keychains:

> Her collection of Mickey Mouse items was started by someone who returned from Disneyland and brought her a gift. She can't remember who it was who gave it to her (later, off camera, her father tells her it was him). Often people will give her gifts of key chains or Mickey Mouse items. Although she appreciates the gifts, she would prefer to pick out the things for her collection herself. That way she can pick out the things that she likes. She doesn't know how to explain which ones she likes, but does know them when she sees them.

Collections may also be sacred because they are an expression of self. The personal acquisition of collectibles is an investment of self as well as a demonstration of one's hunting ability and persistence in searching for items for the collection. Since vacation travel takes people to new locales, it is often a time to search for additions to collections. Receiving items as gifts for a collection can deny one the opportunity to demonstrate hunting ability and self-expressiveness, and so such gifts may not be desired.

Some collections may be further sacralized because they are based on a more explicit expression of self, as with an informant nicknamed Bunny (wf, 30s), who also collects bunny replicas. This collection serves as a totemic representation of her individual (rather than tribal) identity. It connects the natural category of bunnies to the cultural element of an individual (Levi-Strauss 1962; Sahlins 1976). Through her collection, she simultaneously celebrates herself and nature. Similarly, other informants, women whose husbands are policemen, bought humorous-looking pig doorstops, which served to connect their husbands to a profession and to the animal kingdom. In both cases, the collection serves as a totemic expression of identity.

Finally, collectors sacralize collections by systematically labeling, arranging, and displaying the collection. This quasi-scientific or quasi-artistic activity sacralizes and legitimizes what might otherwise be seen as mere acquisitiveness by giving it a more noble apparent purpose.

Sacralization through Inheritance. Objects may achieve sacred status through inheritance as family heirlooms (Shammas, Salmon, and Dahlin 1987). Removed from the world of commerce and increasingly singularized, in part by their age, these objects gain uniqueness and contaminating sacredness by their sentimental associations with the owner's past history. Such artifacts are repositories of family continuity (Csikszentmihalyi and Rochberg-Halton 1981; Rochberg-Halton 1986). Their history helps define who the inheritors are, where they came from, and where they are going.

Heirlooms that were handmade, that were worn close to the body (such as jewelry), or that denoted ties to a native land were frequently mentioned by Odyssey informants. In the case of items worn close to the body, there is more contamination and symbolization of the self. Preservation of these closely worn items partakes of positive sacred contamination. Similarly, items from one's native land are from a sacred place, if not a sacred time as well (Belk 1988b). Thus, heirlooms move from the profane realm in which they (or their materials) were purchased into the sacred realm through connection to deceased (primarily same-sex) family members. This sacralization intensifies if accompanied by meanings connecting it to the person's physical body or the symbolic body of the person's native land, as with one informant's cameos from her mother's homeland.

Like collections, heirlooms represent completeness. They indicate that family ties have not been broken by death. In this sense, heirlooms are gifts to the living from the dead and represent the continuity of one generation to the other. Characteristic of the short histories and the nuclear family orientation of Americans, few heirlooms linked to the family longer than from the prior two generations were mentioned by informants. It is not history and long lineage that is being celebrated by heirlooms, but rather the completeness and continuation of the family—the formal celebration of which is particularly important to upper class families (Bossard and Boll 1950). Even so, as McCracken (1988) speculates, caring for family heirlooms may be decreasingly common as societies become more mobile and materialistic. The logistics of maintenance, storage, display, and dispersal may dictate less curatorial forms of familial ritual.

Sacralization through External Sanction. An object may be sacralized through sanction by an external authority. The enshrinement of a piece in a museum is one indicator of such recognition and the most common encountered during the Odyssey. That tourists bowed to the external authority of museums was evident in their quiet, reverential tones and formal conversations concerning the importance of relics on display—whether farm implements of the nineteenth century, possessions of Ellis Island immigrants, artworks and mansions of turn-of-the-century robber barons, or even elephant replicas.

In mansions of the nouveaux riches, such as those at Newport, Rhode Island, preserved furnishings showed that the former owners had sought the blessing of famous architects and artists. Often rooms and furnishings had been moved en masse from castles and chateaux. Treasures of European cathedrals and royalty had been purchased to sacralize and cleanse the often ruthlessly attained wealth of the nouveaux riches. During the owners' lives, some art treasures were further sacralized by external authorities through loans to museums and world expositions. When the mansions became public museums, heirs received the additional blessing of historical societies, art curators, and guides, who interpret these wonders for tourists.

Summary of Ways of Achieving Sacredness. In summary, sacredness adheres in certain aspects of consumption through seven different processes: ritual, pilgrimage, quintessence, gift-giving, collecting, inheritance, and external sanction. With the exceptions of quintessence and external sanction, these sacralizing processes are enacted purposively by consumers in an effort to create sacred meaning in their lives. Whether social or individual in nature, each sacralizing process separates objects, people, and experiences from the world of the profane and imbues them with precious, positive sacredness. Other processes then serve to maintain the sacred status and prevent the encroachment of the profane.

Perpetuating Sacredness

Ecstatic as one might feel upon having contact with the sacred through an object, person, place, or experience, sacred status may be lost through habituation, forgetting, or encroachment of the profane. To prevent this loss, ongoing efforts are required to maintain sacredness. Four means for maintaining sacredness in consumption that emerged from analysis of our data are separation of the sacred from the profane, performance of sustaining rituals, continuation through inheritance, and tangibilized contamination. For each, there is a related avenue of desacralization that these maintenance activities are designed to prevent.

Separation of Sacred from Profane. Often we found the sacred separated, either temporally or spatially, from the profane to minimize the likelihood of unwanted contamination. Collections were separated from other objects to reinforce their sacred, non-utilitarian status and to prevent their entrance into the profane world where they might be consumed or used. The elephant collection was in a museum adjoining a gift shop filled with elephant replicas for sale. This separation prevented any confusion that items in the collection might be for sale. As a test of this notion, we asked the collector if he ever moves anything out of the museum collection and places it for sale in the gift shop. He responded:

> "Never."
>
> "Why not?"
>
> "I wouldn't want to do that. I just don't want to do that. It would be, like, I don't know, like it would be *wrong*. It would seem wrong to me. It really would."
>
> "What would that do? What would that do to the collection; what would that do to you?"
>
> "I think it would lose some of its grandeur or something. It would not be as important if I was able to just put this elephant out in the store and sell it. People would say, 'Well, my heavens, he just sells what he wants to whenever he wants to.' But I don't want to do that. When I buy a piece, it's because I really want it for the collection. I have had people offer me some nice sums for pieces in here, I mean, at times when I really could have used a nice sum, and it was difficult to say, 'No.' But I said, 'No'; if I liked it that well and I bought it, then it must be important to the collection, so I am going to keep it there."
>
> "So once a piece joins the collection, then it stays with the collection?"
>
> ". . . it becomes the collection. It's part of it. It's going to stay there, *period.*"

This collector's behavior may be somewhat extreme, but it gives bold relief to similar separations that other people employed to preserve the sacred status of certain possessions. When an item is sacred to someone, it is regarded as beyond price and will not be sold under any circumstances (Stewart 1984). Compliance with the self-imposed rule of "never sell" applied so absolutely to sacred objects that informants were surprised we would even ask if they would consider selling them. This logic explains the behavior of a Mickey Mouse collector/dealer and an antique collector/dealer who found it unthinkable that they would use items from their collections at home as merchandise. The only collector/dealers who mixed their merchandise with their own collections were two novice dealers who each had a mental understanding, if not a spatial representation, of things that were not for sale.

Artists selling their work separated the sacred creation from the profane sale in several ways. The male sculptor mentioned in the opening vignettes did not discuss the price or sale of his work; instead, his sister handled the business end of things. The woman at a swap meet selling handcrafted dolls, which she called her "babies," used different inflection and voice tone to refer to the dolls as commodities versus the dolls as babies. She kissed the "baby" as she sold the doll (one object with two communicative voices) and personified the transaction as sending her children into the world to bring happiness to someone who would love the "baby." In so doing, she emotionally, if not physically, separated the sacred from the profane.

Similarly, a painter/sculptor (wf, 50s) was willing to sell some of her works, but regarded other pieces as part of a serial collection in which she possessed items sequentially rather than simultaneously. She didn't want to part with her work until she had enjoyed it sufficiently. To prevent premature sale, she posted prohibitive prices on certain works and raised the price if she received serious inquiries. The collector/dealer of Mickey Mouse memorabilia followed the same tactic, and each time someone showed an interest in buying one of his favorite pieces, he raised the price. This pricing structure protects the sacred by preventing its entry into the profane world of commerce. Exorbitantly high prices confirm the sacred value of these artifacts, and the sacrifice of not accepting a high price offer is a further means by which the collector/dealer pays reverence to the sacredness of these objects.

Breen (1988) shows how rituals of non-consumption in the mass consumer boycotts of English goods were instrumental both in giving American colonists a sense of nation and in precipitating the American Revolution. Boycotts serve to avoid sacralizing profane consumption objects by mixing them with sacred objects in the home. By refusing to continue to enshrine English goods in their homes and in their lives, boycotting colonists refused to accept the authority of the British Crown as either divine or legitimate to rule over them.

Home is a sacred space that provides separation from the profane everyday world, although certain areas within the home are viewed as more sacred than others (Altman and Chemers 1984). Societies differ with respect to whether communal public space or individual private space is more sacred (Tuan 1982). In contemporary Western society, the sacredness of the individual and of privacy or separation from others have gained dominance. Rochberg-Halton (1984) found that the room regarded as most special differed among three generations. About half of the children ages nine to 14 cited their bedrooms, whereas adults were likely to cite the living room where social life is enacted. Older adults (70+) cited their bedrooms, presumably because they increasingly lived their lives there. What is sacred, then, in home life is not necessarily a family gathered around the radio or hearth, as in a Norman Rockwell painting. Instead, the oldest and youngest generations in the United States are likely to harbor private treasures in their individual rooms.

Sacred possessions were separated from more functional (but similar appearing) profane objects in informants' homes. Some heirloom spoons in one home were hanging on the wall to indicate that these spoons were for viewing, not use. In another home with a bunny collection, ceramic bunny soup tureens were displayed to indicate they were not used for serving soup, at least not on ordinary occasions. Similarly, a woman who collected functional but fragile black amethyst glassware stored it on a plate rail above the kitchen cabinets, where she kept dishes that were used everyday. A grocery store owner who collected antique product packages kept them in display cases in his office, locked away from the salable grocery products that filled the shelves of the store. Collectors who sometimes used items from their collections were careful to do so only on special occasions. For example, car collectors showed these sacred possessions only at car shows or drove them in special parades and car club outings. All of these strategies maintain sacredness by separating the sacred from the profane.

Another way of maintaining object sacredness is to separate it from the profane by designating a particular space for it, creating, in effect, an enshrinement. This is evident in the elephant collection housed in a museum created for this purpose. Another informant (wf, mid-30s) preferred a separate place of honor on her bedroom wall for a sampler made by her grandmother, while non-family-made samplers could be decoratively clustered together. Fragile collections are often stored behind glass-doored cabinets in living and dining rooms that are often treated as tabernacles by adults. The items are ritually enshrined and placed in prominent areas of the house to be revered and to cast their spells on the inhabitants, while also being separated from the profane. The collector/dealer of Mickey Mouse items used to keep his collection in its own room at home, but his seven-year-old son was frightened to go into "the Mickey room," illustrating the kratophany of the sacred and acknowledging its potentially destructive power. This collector also acknowledged the "ruin and destruction" that occurs when collecting overpowers the collector and becomes addictive. By keeping the collection locked away, this kratophanous power is kept under control and separated from everyday life.

When people move from one home to another, they often become concerned about the safety of their sacred objects, which are used as vessels to transfer sacredness from one home to another. Their concern emerges, in part, because the sacredness housed in these objects must pass successfully through the profane, everyday world before reestablishment in the new home. This is reminiscent of Aeneas's flight from his home with his household gods on his back (*Aeneid,* III: 15–19). The items moved may be valuable or breakable, as with ceramic figurines and a fragile heirloom doll, or ordinary-appearing, such as an old washboard. Sometimes, people live for an interim period in a liminal house before moving into the home destination. This was the case with one couple moving out of a farmhouse to live in a small summer kitchen building for a year while a new dwelling, a reconstructed log house, was completed. The interim house was not imbued with sacredness. In fact, like another couple interviewed, they planned to keep many possessions in storage during the interim time. However, the sacred assemblage will later be brought together to transform and sacralize the newly built space. The couple was preparing for this interim period by sorting and reconsidering the status of the wide variety of objects they had acquired in their life together.

In a number of informants' homes, sacred objects were assembled together in decorative shrines, often on the mantle above the hearth, as with one young couple who noticed during the interview that all of the items displayed on the mantle had been wedding gifts. In homes without a hearth, such assemblages may be displayed in the front room on the television set. For example, one collector of native American replicas clustered an American Indian statuary lamp, family photographs, an American Indian whirligig gift, a crocheted afghan, and a crying Christ head together in the front room. Likewise, an informant who is a passionate writer/researcher and jazz collector has a room in his home that contains his jazz records, his Steinway baby grand piano, and his current writing work. Similarly, a woman who had moved across the country for a one-year period described her preservation strategy.

"Did you ship the watermelon collection out here?"
"No. Those kind of things I was kind of afraid to. That's the kind of stuff that *means* (touches heart) something to me: things we've collected, like on our honeymoon, or whatever. I would be real upset. I'd rather live without them for a year than risk having it all get busted." (wf, late 20s)

As with people who do not use sacred items for fear of breakage, this couple lived without some special things for a year rather than risk profaning them through breakage or loss. Their fears were realistic because some expensive but profane possessions, such as a microwave oven, were broken in the move.

In summary, spatial and temporal separation of the profane from the sacred was evident across contexts. There was no evidence that the sacred and profane can mix with impunity and maintain sacredness. The boundaries are permeable, but well guarded. Nevertheless, there were some instances of deliberate termination of sacred status, accomplished through mixing the sacred with the profane.

Somewhat ironically, given the elevated place of money in contemporary society, the most general way the sacred is desacralized is to turn it into a salable commodity, and thus desingularize it. This explains the exhuberance of one informant upon selling her ex-husband's left-handed golf clubs at a swap meet. She had desingularized the last remaining object that symbolized him, and converted it into a commodity. Entrance into the world of commerce through conversion to cash commodities what was previously sacred.

Our language in referring to dwellings makes this separation between (profane) housing—"a commodity . . . produced primarily for profit"—and (sacred) dwelling—which is "without economic value in any direct sense" (Saegert 1985, p. 295). Dovey (1985, pp. 53–54) also separates the profane house and the sacred home on the basis of the consideration of money:

> In the modern world, the house is a commodity involving substantial economic commitment. It is an investment of economic resources that yields profit and power. As such, the house has become increasingly similar to other products—being bought and sold, used and discarded like a car or washing machine. Home, on the other hand, involves a commitment not of money, but of time and emotion. It is the place where we invest dreams, hopes, and care. Although we can buy the props and freedom that make such an investment possible and secure, the phenomenon of home itself cannot be commoditized. . . . Yet the increasing commoditization of the house engenders a confusion between house and home because it is the image of home that is bought and sold in the marketplace.

Kopytoff (1986), like Marx (1972/orig. 1867), sees a general "drive to commoditization" in capitalist society. It is disturbing to many that everything can be bought and sold, leaving little that is sacred. However, informants were quick to point out what they would not sell. A show horse owner (wf, 20s) explained to us that her horse is "not a business," meaning that it was removed from the profane world of commerce.

Yet the language of commoditization is pervasive. Fromm (1947) argued that even people are commoditized when we market ourselves and take on "market personalities." Hyde (1983) cautions that when artists and scholars turn from presenting their work as a gift, and instead make profit a primary goal, they sow the seeds of destruction of their own creativity because no sacred soul remains in the work. Haug (1986) is among the many Marxist writers who see marketing as appropriating the sacred for selling purposes, leaving little that remains sacred after such appropriation.

The controversy attending the recent "Baby M" case, which has prompted a consideration of the propriety of commercial surrogate motherhood, illustrates the concern over commoditization (Kingsley 1987). It is difficult for many to accept that the sacred concept of motherhood is not above money. Believing that sacredness is a situational rather than absolute attribute whose boundary is inherently dangerous, van Gennep (1909) viewed *rites de passage* as protective rituals that define entrance to a new status. In a world in which surrogate mothers can be hired to bear one's children, the notion of such sacralizing and desacralizing rites is all but lost.

Although money can desacralize, this is not always the case in contemporary society. As Real (1975, p. 40) notes:

> When Duke Snider, center-fielder for the Brooklyn Dodgers, published an article in the *Saturday Evening Post* in the middle 1950s admitting "I Play Baseball for Money," there was a tremor of scandal that ran through the American public, as if a clergyman had said he did not much care for God but he liked the amenities of clerical life. But when Mercury Morris was asked on national television after the Dolphins' one-sided Super Bowl VIII victory, "Was it fun?" he replied, "It was work," and no one batted an eye.

A possible interpretation here is that the focus on money has desacralized sports. However, it appears that, like quintessential objects in the marketplace and artworks that are sacralized by a high purchase price, sports stars are no longer desacralized by high salaries and may even be sacralized by them. If players were interchangeable robots, commoditization would result and fans would no longer view them as sacred heroes.

So money is not a sufficient indicant of commoditization in contemporary Western culture. Desmonde (1962) traces the flow of sacred symbols from religious to secular contexts by showing how traditional religious symbols were transferred to one essential component of a consumption-venerating society: money. In consumer culture, "mammon" retains its etymological denotation of "that in which one places one's trust," as well as its biblical connotation of "disorder" (Haughey 1986). Money is so strongly symbolic that is presents an intriguing dialectic between good-sacred and evil-sacred. In contemporary society, money is never merely profane or ordinary; it has a kratophanous power that at alternate times serves both beneficent and evil ends. Money can singularize as well as commoditize.

Because mixing the sacred with the profane threatens to destroy the sacred, advertising is often seen as a threat, having the potential to trivialize the sacred by its copresence. For example, on commercial TV in Great Britain, the juxtaposition of advertising with broadcasts of royalty and religion are two such threats (Laski 1959). Legislation enacted in 1954 prohibits advertising within two minutes before and after any broadcast of royal occasions. With religion, as with art, advertising threatens to banish the ecstasy achieved in formerly sacred contexts. The other threat is that commodities seek to appropriate the sacredness of royalty, art, or religion through contamination. This appears to be the concern of critics such as Berger (1972), Hudson (1987), and Williamson (1986), who find it offensive that advertising should feature art masterpieces or religious figures. Outrage at the use of Beatles music in television commercials for Nike shoes echoes this concern.

Experiencing what was previously considered sacred as now mixed with the profane produces emotional reactions of loss. For example, certain actors and actresses have their names imprinted on stars on a Hollywood sidewalk, but one informant was disappointed by recent choices.

> "I was amazed at the Walk of Fame that they give stars to anyone. They had a star, I mean like Peter Frampton. I mean he was famous for like fifteen minutes. Now he's got a star for all eternity. You know, that's like real strange." (wm, late 20s)

He was disturbed because the inclusion of these supposed stars profaned what he had considered a sacred context. He lamented the loss of this illusion.

Desacralization by mixing the sacred and the profane occurs through two related phenomena: kitsch and decontextualization. Kitsch refers to decorative objects of bad taste that are popular with the masses, as with one informant's whimsical decorative pink flamingo. Discussions of kitsch imply that such objects are an offense to something sacred (e.g., Highet 1972); however, the precise nature of this offense is seldom agreed upon. In the case of religious kitsch, such as a sentimental rendering of Christ or a picture of the Virgin Mary painted on a seashell, the offense seems to be an inappropriate mixing of the sacred and the profane. Dorfles (1969) and Pawek (1969) worry that religious kitsch lead the faithful away from religion rather than toward it. In other cases, the offense seems to be the trivial nature of these pieces that makes them disposable rather than timeless (Schroeder 1977). In the case of kitsch souvenirs, the offense has been characterized as taking an object out of context inappropriately and turning it into a mere commodity (Gregotti 1969). This reflects both the commoditization discussed previously and decontextualization discussed next. Given the proprietary attitude of the upper class toward fine arts as a class marker (Lynes 1980), kitsch may represent to them a threat to desacralize fine art and may elicit an elitist fear of disenfranchisement.

Perhaps the most telling interpretation of the offense entailed in kitsch is the argument that it is inauthentic (Stewart 1984). Kitsch is charged with dealing with superficiality rather than substance (Brown 1975), with being turned out mechanically (Greenberg 1946), and with offering spurious value (Giesz 1969). The charge of inauthenticity is similar to charges of forgery or reproduction in art (see Belk 1987b) and to MacCannell's (1976) arguments concerning the "staged authenticity" experienced by the tourist. Inauthenticity charges that kitsch lacks the magic and power of the truly sacred, but pretends to sacredness through its associative representations and use.

A related desacralizing mixture of the sacred

and the profane is decontextualization. This offense against the sacred involves removing it from its context or place of origin. Arnheim (1987) speaks of sculptures and paintings being "kidnapped" by museums and "torn from (their) moorings in space and time" (Arnheim 1987, p. 682). What seems to be threatened here is the sacredness of the time and place in which the art originated rather than the sacredness of the art object per se. Putting the London Bridge in Arizona may or may not lessen the sacredness of the bridge itself, but it does threaten to lessen the sacredness of old London. The outpouring of emotion, much of it outrage, in connection with the restorative cleaning of the Sistine Chapel ceiling, which is literally shedding new light on Michelangelo's paintings (Pope-Hennessy 1987), is another example of the power of decontextualization.

Sustaining Rituals to Prevent Rationalization and Habituation. Because sacred objects may begin to seem ordinary and profane over time, ritual maintenance is sometimes needed to preserve and revivify their sacred status. Meals, holidays, vacations, and other such family rituals not only sacralize the objects they involve, they do much to maintain the sacred status of the family.

The elephant replicas collector has performed a number of rituals to preserve the sacred status of his collection. Each time he has moved, he has packed the whole collection carefully. Before he started the Elephant Museum, he kept some things in boxes, rather than risk breaking them in the unpacking. He has been through three floods and has unpacked and repacked all of the items each time with no losses. It was this packing and unpacking that convinced him to open the museum, where he could share the collection with others. He feels that he preserves the sacred status of his collection through sharing it with those who visit the museum. He mentioned that elephant families stay together for life. In a sense it is a form of eternal life that he is trying to ensure for the collection and, by extension, for himself, through these rituals.

For an informant with some monogrammed heirloom silver spoons, sacredness-maintaining rituals include cleaning, repair, and display. The soft, silver spoons had some dents that she had removed after receiving the spoons from her mother-in-law. She then had the spoons mounted and framed to hang in her dining room. Another informant had restored an heirloom quilt from her mother, as described in this fieldnote excerpt.

> The woman selling raffle tickets . . . had restored her mother's patchwork quilt and uses it in her home. It is draped over a quilt rack and used on a bed when it is needed. It had been mildewed from being packed away and a number of pieces had to be replaced. She anticipates that her daughter will take this quilt and keep it in the family.

Through her investment of labor and care in the object, she prevented it from becoming profane junk and restored its sacred status, which will be preserved by passing it on to her daughter. This fetishistic investment of labor in an object recompenses its neglect over the years. Once its sacred status is restored, it must then be preserved, having come dangerously close to vanishing. Similar levels of attention to a sacred heirloom in disrepair were reported by other informants who stripped furniture, sewed dolls back together, and oiled tools. These are not sacralizing actions, but rather are rituals that restore and maintain sacredness.

This type of restoration was described by an informant who has an heirloom that she had refinished to allow its sacred nature to shine through:

> "I have a tea wagon . . . in the dining room, . . . a little teacart that my coffee service is on, that belonged to my grandmother, that I just had refinished. It had been painted when that antiquing look was in that you painted furniture, and then you rubbed that sort of black paint over it to make it look old. And it had several layers of paint on it. I did not do the refinishing, but I decided that it is a pretty enough piece that I'd have it refinished. So that's kind of a special piece." (wf, early 30s).

Through a cleansing ritual, the once-sacred heirloom was restored. It is as if through this act of duty, the cart's glory can now shine through, as it could not when the black paint was profaning it. Oddly, for the relative who chose to put the black antiquing paint on, this was probably seen as a way of making an ugly piece more attractive. It seems odd that someone would "antique" an antique, but this too was probably done to try to resingularize the piece. This woman's refinishing of the piece restores its sacred status for her.

However, preserving sacred status in heirlooms does not always mean restoring items to their original condition. It may involve maintaining the imperfect condition of an object when imperfections serve as sacred marks of use by family members. One woman explained the logic of this approach, as noted in this fieldnote excerpt:

Rene had a commode at home that was passed down to her by her mother who got it from her mother (Rene's grandmother). It has been used by each of her children as a dresser in their rooms. Her husband refinished it and took nine coats of paint off of it. He was trying to take off the cigarette stains from when her brother had it, but she told him not to take those off because "those make it even more precious." (wf, 40s)

Maintenance of an heirloom's sacredness then does not always mean preservation in the way that a museum or seller might approach the object. Unlike the marks of a famous person, these do not increase the object's economic value. However, preserving the cigarette marks makes the object more sentimentally valuable and sacred by preserving the extended self of a family member.

The sacredness of other heirlooms is maintained by ritual prohibitions against use. To use these objects would desacralize them by making them mere utilitarian commodities. During one interview, a woman in her midthirties corrected the interviewer who mentioned some toys in the living room.

"I noticed a number of toys around. In the family room, there were toys, and in the library you called it, there were some toys. But in the *living room* there were some toys. There were some dolls . . ."

"Oh (eyebrows raised and knowing smile comes to face—emphatically), there are not. They're not toys! There should not be toys in there. They're just sort of collectibles I guess . . . There's an old piece in there; a bed in there that was his grandmother's that has a doll; a chaise bed of sorts. So that's in there, and its got some dolls on it, but they're not for play. And there are some stuffed animals in there that used to be my husband's when he was a child. So they're kind of fond favorites, I guess." (wf, mid-30s)

The items are, in fact, antique toys, but are now viewed by the informant as decorative objects removed from the profane world in which they might be used in play. Here the owners ritually comply with the self-imposed rule of "Never Use."

Some heirlooms are used, but only on ritual occasions. That is, they are separated temporally from the profane and are employed ritually. One informant (wf, mid-30s) has a lace tablecloth that was passed on to her by her grandmother. She uses it on holidays (sacred times when the family is brought together for ritual behavior) and on other "special occasions," but never for everyday use. The continuation of tradition in this way sustains the sacred status of the tablecloth as it further enhances it.

The sacredness of a place is also maintained by adherence to ritual behaviors. For example, informants at a weight loss resort were concerned about how they would be able to transfer their rituals at the resort to their home life. Many thought they would try, but would probably not be successful. They in essence admitted that the magic resides in the place and all that occurs there. They were not hopeful that they would be able to recreate this magic at home. The magical transformation that they hoped would occur was a result of their ritualistic exercise, dieting, and massages during their stay. Their daily regimen involved the abundant use of water (drinking it, swimming in it) making them feel cleansed in the transformation and intensifying their regard for the resort as a sacred place and their stay as a sacred time. For one woman, the resort "feels like home" because she has the same room each year and over time has come to know many of the others who come here. To her, the place exemplifies the American dream of achievement of one's goals, the importance of physical perfection, and stability over time. It is a place of baptism and rebirth, sacrifice and salvation. Through ritual, it maintains sacredness that is too fragile to transfer to the everyday world.

Gift-giving is a ritual that may be used not only to sacralize, as discussed earlier, but also to maintain the sacredness of personal goods, as with some informants' gifts to us intended to preserve our close connections to them. When we sometimes offered reciprocal gifts, they were refused, as they would have commoditized the interaction. We were given gifts of postcards to use as interview stimuli, candy, a handcrafted leather flyswatter, rides to get gasoline when we had run out, and dinners prepared in our honor.

The informants traveling by covered wagon had grown accustomed to being photographed by curious tourists, and a sign beside their wagon read, "Donations Appreciated for your Photos." As we had stopped, photographed them, conducted a video interview and come to know them rather well, it was unclear whether they would expect payment from us. When we mentioned that we would like to give them something for the rich insights they had given us, they refused the cash offer saying, "You don't have to do that!" When we responded by saying, "We know we don't *have* to do it, we just want to," the interaction returned to the sphere of gift-giving. The verbal exchange was a desanctifying and reconsecrating ritual to preserve the friendship while still permitting the economic transfer. Under other circumstances, no amount of ritualistic framing can excuse irreverence. Clearly, for example, one should not accept a dinner invitation from friends and then leave a cash payment. The only acceptable "payment" is a reciprocal social offering that keeps the interaction in the sacred social realm rather than in the profane, commercial realm.

Despite numerous rituals designed to maintain sacredness, habituation and rationalization constantly threaten to desacralize the sacred. In habituation, movement from the sacred to the profane occurs in a way that is gradual enough to be little noticed as some objects become worn and familiar. But time may also restore objects to a sacred status, as was explained in this fieldnote excerpt by one antique dealer/collector:

> What is interesting to her is that the nice pie safes, which are popular as living room cupboards now, used to be kitchen pieces, but many of them are now found out in chicken coops. Her business brings them back into the house.

Initially, the object loses its sacredness and is relegated to more profane areas of the home. But then, when it is old enough to become appealing to antique collectors, it moves through the world of commerce into a more sacred position than that which it initially held (Thompson 1979). We observed the same movement with other old, functional pieces, such as carpet beaters now hung on the wall as decorative items and a tramp's cupboard that hung above one informant's desk. While newness may initially sacralize an object as being quintessential, irreverence creeps in with time. Later, someone again sees the object's potential for sacredness and saves it from obscurity.

Rituals also attempt to prevent rationalization, which may desacralize the sacred in two ways. The first is that to bring rational argument to bear on the sacred is to rob it of its essential mystery and hierophanous power. For example, this was seen by Weber (1958/orig. 1904) to have occurred when science split from art, producing the "disenchantment of the world." It occurs when the scientist dissipates the beauty of the rainbow by dismissing it as light reflected and refracted in air-suspended water droplets (Belk 1986). It is the same diminution of magic thought to occur when the Santa Claus myth is exploded for the child. Such rationalized views are seldom capable of retaining the mystery, ritual, and power of former understandings and, thus, are likely to diminish sacredness.

A second way rationalization desacralizes is by offering principled excuses for ignoring, discarding, or otherwise failing to treat something with the "proper" respect. One of our informants, who raises mice to sell to pet stores or give to "good homes," rationalizes that she takes only "the mice with lousy dispositions or poor personalities" to feed to her snakes. Several small-scale pet breeders we interviewed rationalized the sale of their beloved animals by assuring us that they made sure that the animals were going only to good homes. There was undoubtedly some sincerity in this desire, but there was also an element of rationalization in turning these living beings into salable commodities. They avoided acknowledging this transformation by viewing the sale as a ritual to continue the love and affection given to the animal.

Similarly, informants discarding or selling sacred heirloom furniture or memory-laden baby clothes often suggested that someone else would make better use of them. There was an element of truth in this claim, but the need to offer such explanations suggests an element of rationalization as well. Explaining that something is the "logical thing to do under the circumstances" demystifies behavior and moves the object out of the realm of the sacred. Similarly, while the collection as a whole is sacred, some collectors are willing to convert particular items from the collection into profane, salable commodities, provided that they first find a replacement item that is "better" (e.g., a plate from a manufactured collectors' series to replace a similar, chipped plate already in the collection).

Sacred consumption may be profaned when consumers are not sufficiently reverential and do not follow prescribed rituals. MacCannell (1976, p. 43) describes tourist crowding at natural wonders as "profaning the place" in the eyes of other (presumably more serious) tourists. The burning or dragging of a flag through the streets is an act of intentional desecration of a sacred symbol, just as an overly stylized performance of the national anthem may be seen as irreverent (Rook 1984). Several informants mentioned that children weren't allowed in particular areas of their houses for fear certain items might be damaged or marred by fingerprints.

Rituals existed for some intentional desacralizations we observed. These transformation rituals are used to redefine the object's status with respect to the sacred/profane dimension. Because these rituals often preceded the disposition of formerly sacred items, they may be seen as the divestment rituals that McCracken (1986) speculated might exist. For example, a woman mentioned earlier gladly sold her ex-husband's golf clubs at a swap meet as a ritualistic way of cleansing herself of his presence in her life. By moving the golf clubs into the realm of the profane, she cleared him out of her life. She was quite cognizant of this, and she and her women friends did a little dance of joy after the sale, saying, "That's the end of him."

In summary, ritual maintains the separation between sacred and profane, ensuring that what is to remain in the sacred realm does not slip away. Other rituals transform that which was previously sacred into its now appropriate profane state, ensuring that only that which is marked by the ritual passes through the transformation.

Bequests Bequests are a third mechanism found for preserving the sacred status of certain consumption objects and experiences. Some collectors attempt to ensure the continued sacred status of their collections after their death by planning to will them to descendants as heirlooms. For example, the collector of elephant replicas plans to leave his collection to his granddaughter, who was only a year old at the time of our interview. He wants to preserve "the grandeur" of the collection by bequeathing it in such a way that it will become an heirloom. If the collection remains intact, he "imagines history will stand in awe of what he did." Through his will, he hopes to invoke wider compliance to the "Never Sell" rule mentioned earlier.

A woman in a quilt-making group believes there are bequest "rules" that protect a family's heirlooms, as mentioned in this fieldnote excerpt:

> She says that the rule is to give sons property and money and to give daughters possessions and heirlooms, because they will stay in the family and be

passed on to granddaughters that way; otherwise the son's wife may get a hold of them and this is not desirable, presumably because in case of divorce they might take them, and the family tradition would stop.

We can interpret this statement as implying that heirlooms will be passed matrilineally, whereas wealth will be passed patrilineally, an interesting hypothesis, particularly in light of the complexity of contemporary family structures. This rule also suggests that women nurture relationships and the heirloom that symbolize their relationships, as has been found in other research (e.g., Wallendorf and Arnould 1988). It also suggests the converse, namely that women, in the image of a termagant, have the power to willfully destroy family traditions through appropriation of its symbols. Thus, when sacred heirlooms are prevented from entering the profane world by keeping them in the family, the family is nurtured and preserved.

There was wide understanding and acceptance of such rules among informants. The woman whose mother had furniture made for her from walnut trees cut down at their horse farm has placed that furniture only in certain rooms of her house. A piece inscribed with her initials is in the living room, a space reserved for adults. A set of four-poster beds is used in her four-year-old daughter's room, but not in the room used by her stepdaughter when she visits. Even by their placement in the house, these objects speak of "real" family connections.

We also encountered heirloom preservation by males. When the heirloom furniture handcrafted by an informant's deceased father was damaged in a flood, he chose to work on restoring these pieces and his father's tools before reclaiming anything else in the house. An antique collector (bm, early 40s) who was also becoming a dealer, had some pieces that were heirlooms. Although he was anxious to get his business started, he said he would never sell the family heirlooms. And a man with three garages full of accumulated, usable objects to share with neighbors also had some heirloom tools that had belonged to his father. These were substantially more significant to him and would be passed on to his male heirs. Although not universal, there does appear to be a general pattern of maintaining the sacredness of connection to same-sex parents and family members through heirlooms.

The counterpart to maintaining sacredness through inheritance is losing sacred reverence for objects through lack of an appreciative heir. this was a frequent concern of collectors. The collector of elephant replicas does not want to leave his collection to his wife or daughter because he doesn't expect that either of them would carry on the museum after he dies. His fear is that the collection would be sold piece by piece on an auction block. Therefore, although the granddaughter is very young, he thinks she already enjoys elephants and hopes to bequeath the collection to her.

Why should heirs reject the responsibility of caring for the collection of a close family member? More than disinterest seems to be involved. Because collections are almost always the focus of intense attention in accumulating, classifying, maintaining, and displaying the assembled items, they normally take a great deal of the collector's time. Family members who do not share an interest in the collection may come to see it as a rival in winning their loved one's time, devotion, and attention. Resentment, perhaps unspoken, is to be expected under such conditions. Thus, to care for a deceased collector's objects of devotion may be seen as tantamount to caring for a spouse's or parent's mistress or lover.

Tangibilized Contamination. Besides rituals that allow objects to become associated with the owners and their histories, the sacredness of fleeting experiences and once-encountered places is preserved, it is hoped, through souvenirs and photographs. This is a process of tangibilizing contamination through an object. When places visited are regarded as sacred, the time spent there is also sacred (MacCannell 1976). In addition, items overtly intended as souvenirs, as well as more idiosyncratic mementos, may be regarded as sacred. They hold the contagious property of the sacred (Stewart

1984). Gordon (1986) notes five types of sacred souvenir icons:

1. Pictorial images (e.g., photographs, postcards);
2. Pieces-of-the-rock (e.g., seashells, pinecones);
3. Symbolic shorthand (e.g., miniature Eiffel Tower, toy Loch Ness monster);
4. Markers (e.g., "Grand Canyon" t-shirt, restaurant matchbook cover); and
5. Local product (e.g., olive oil from Greece, local clothing).

In each case, some logical or symbolic reminder is sought in order that the memories attached to the visit will remain vivid and "real." Evidently there is also a status motive, since such souvenirs often visibly proclaim the visit to others. We may also include in the category of tangibilized contamination the personal memento, such as pressed flowers from a suitor, wine bottle labels from a significant meal, and ticket stubs from a concert attended. Souvenirs may also represent sacred persons who touched, autographed, or owned the item. This is illuminated by home buyers in Beverly Hills who are willing to pay more for houses that formerly belonged to prominent stars, an indication that used goods are sometimes worth more than new goods and that sacredness may be reflected in price.

The experience of being in a special place, such as a vacation site, is preserved through mementoes, souvenirs, and photographs for later savoring and enjoyment. Tourists do not seem to mind that their photographs will be exactly like those of all other tourists. In fact, this duplication is viewed as a mark of authenticity, confirming the validity of the tourist's experience (MacCannell 1976). At some sites, tourists gleefully cluster with their cameras around places designated as photo opportunities.

Since we travelled to a number of tourist sites on the Odyssey, the use of photography in preserving the sacred became a recurring theme. The role of photographs in sustaining sacred experiences and relationships also was evident in photographs people carried with them or enshrined in their homes. Some consumers' houses and vehicles were so sacred to them that they carried photos of these things with them on their travels. Often photos of loved family members, pets, and favorite objects and places were enshrined in the home on mantles, bureaus, and other places of reverent display. Photos of the past were also given prominent status in historical museums, where they were a tangible link with the past these museums were sacralizing.

Two professional photographers we interviewed differed in the extent to which they see their works as preserving the sacred. One photographer sees the work in which he helped preserve others' sacred moments—wedding and bar mitzvah photos—as totally unrewarding work. He prefers taking pictures of stars like Perry Como because the subject is sacred to him and allows him to preserve the memory of his contact with such entertainment gods. The other photographer specializes in anthropological travel and nature photos, and sells prints at art shows. He has somewhat mixed feelings about selling these photographs to the public. He was pleased by one purchaser who was also a photographer and who promised that the purchased print would be hung "in a place of honor." In general, the photos themselves (i.e., his negatives) are clearly sacred to him and help preserve memories of meaningful experiences.

At a Renaissance Festival, we observed that people were able to experience the magical aspects of time travel and the romantic fantasy of being a part of another world. Through souvenir dragon-slaying swords and flowered wreaths for the hair, people attempted to transport an element of this experience back to their everyday lives. The tangible sacredness of such sites was often preserved in artifacts acquired there in the form of gifts, souvenirs, and photographs. One woman bought charms for a seldom-worn, but still cherished charm bracelet memorializing each vacation. She has a charm from Niagara Falls (from her current vacation) and one from Yellowstone Park (last year's vacation). She does not have one from her hometown. Although her own home is sacred, she feels no need symbolically to bring the hometown with her, since she is usually there. Similarly, a beauty queen representing a particular city, who is therefore herself an incarnation of that place, recalled as she looked over some souvenir pins on her sash the ethnic festival where she bought each pin, rather than the country which is supposedly symbolized by each of them. Through souvenirs and photographs, consumers tangibilize contamination of their contact with sacred consumption.

Just as the sacred can be made manifest and preserved in tangible objects, the loss of such objects threatens to desacralize. For example, collections sometimes irreverently move from the world of the sacred into the world of the profane in ways that deeply disturb people. An informant who moved across the country had a little watermelon dish broken in the move. This bothered her because she collects watermelon replicas and because her collection represents preservation and continuity, elements that are tenuous in her life at present. A man interviewed lost a $10,000 collection of books and records in a flood. A worker at a Small Business Administration Disaster Field Office talked with us about the effect of losing collections. It was her sense that young people bounce back faster than older people. Probably this is because the old have collected more and have more memories to lose.

Of course, the loss of collections or possessions in a disaster pales compared to the loss of life. The loss of a decedent's physical remains, a particularly wrenching casualty in the flood described by one informant, is more devastating still. But the loss of a collection or possessions can be unsettling nonetheless. The man who lost the books and records sustained other extensive property loss as well. He was deeply angered by these losses, even though we interviewed him six weeks after the flood. Such an occasion is disturbing because it destroys the possibility of eternal life for possessions that are closely connected to self. More important than the destruction of the items in collections is the destruction of the value that was being invested and expressed, namely continued existence of the self through the collection.

Losing a gift is another irreverent way of profaning it. Such an incident was described to us by a customer at a swap meet jewelry stand. The operators of this stand had been informants, and two of us had become close enough with them to help out with customers at their stall. As the customer looked over the wares, she explained that she once had a heart necklace that her father had given her, but its clasp broke, and she lost it. The loss was a source of great anxiety. Through such objects, one has the sacred experience of joy and connection. To lose a keepsake is irreverent and shows insufficient ritual care.

Summary of Ways of Maintaining Sacredness. Four distinct ways of preserving or maintaining the sacred status of times, places, people, things, and experiences were encountered. These were the separation of the sacred from the profane, ritual, bequests, and tangibilized contamination. In each case, we found corresponding ways that desacralization can occur. Lack of separation of the sacred from the profane, especially through commoditization, results in desacralization, and when rationalization and routinization supplant ritual, another form of desacralization occurs. Sometimes intentional divestment rituals are employed to desacralize items. And when sacred objects are lost or cannot find caring heirs, again desacralization occurs.

Interpretive Summary of Processes Involving the Sacred

We have explored the consumer behavior processes through which sacralization, preservation of sanctity, and sometimes deconsecration occur. Such rituals as contamination, gift-giving, and collecting, and various sacra such as souvenirs and heirlooms were explored in ethnographic detail to provide the reader with a feel for the many consumption settings in which sacred/profane transformations occur. Our remaining task is to provide some closure for our thesis, and to speculate upon its further significance for the field of consumer behavior research.

CONCLUSION

We have documented the properties of sacredness that consumers invest in material and experiential consumption, and have examined the ways the boundary between sacred and profane is strategically manipulated. Specifically, we have tracked the ways sacralization is initiated, sustained, and terminated. Using literatures from the social sciences and humanities, we have explored the personal, social, and cultural significance of the transformations consumers effect between sacred and profane domains of experience.

In Berman's (1984) opinion, mind or spirit has been evacuated gradually from our relationships with phenomena. The transformation of Western epistemology from participating consciousness (knowledge acquisition via merger with nature) to nonparticipating consciousness (knowledge acquisition via separation and distance from nature)—that is, from dialectical to Cartesian rationality (Wallendorf 1987a)—has deprived consumer researchers of a potentially valuable perspective. We have sought to restore some semblance of balance by employing naturalistic, interdisciplinary team research to examine a fundamental yet heretofore inaccessible consumption phenomenon.

Consumers accord sacred status to a variety of objects, places, and times that are value expressive. By expressing these values through their consumption, they participate in a celebration of their connection to the society as a whole and to particular individuals. For society, defining as sacred certain artifacts that are value-expressive provides social cohesion and societal integration. For the individual, participating in these expressions provides meaning in life and a mechanism for experiencing stability, joy, and occasionally ecstasy through connection.

There are apparent benefits to the individual from participating in the sacred as a means of giving one's life purpose. Partly for these psychological reasons, it is generally societally approved that someone should collect something, or treasure historical sites, or avidly follow sports, for such activities focus one's life and seemingly make one happy. But there are other reasons why pursuing sacred consumption is generally societally approved.

Just as Karl Marx once proclaimed that religion is the opium of the masses, sacred consumption also has the ability to channel consumer energies into a focus that may preclude revolutionary thought and action. This channeling may be dialectically cast. Homeownership has long been seen as a commitment to the community, but it may also be seen as the confinement of women to the realm of consumption to maximize economic growth in an industrialized society (Galbraith 1973). Sports fanaticism can be seen to promote community identification and spirit, but also to separate family members with differing tastes. Just as sports fans see themselves as a unified community during sacred sports moments, so do gift exchangers, heirloom-passing generations, and collectors. Acquirers of quintessential objects and souvenirs may feel a sense of community in admiring one another's consumption objects, but may be viewed as materialistic or acquisitive by others. Pet ownership may promote good citizenship by kindling emotions that allow for greater empathy with others and decrease the probability of vandalism or other antisocial behaviors. However, pet ownership also allows and fosters the expression of domination (Tuan 1984). Although we recognize the potential pathologies of self-absorption, miserliness, and narrowness that may occur within sacred consumption, we generally believe that participation in sacredness in some area of consumption is superior to a complete lack of contact with the sacred. Singularizing the self so one is not treated as a mere commodity, even if through one's possessions, involved consumers with the sacred, especially in collecting and experiences recalled through some tangible artifact.

What remains unanswered is the cultural consequence of the sacralizing processes we have examined. Sacredness exists at a cultural level to ensure the ongoing integrity of the culture itself. Through definitions of sacredness, culture hallows itself, working to compel belief. Intimations of this consequence are latent in theories of fetishism, especially in Baudrillard's (1981) critique of the "paleo-Marxist dramaturgy" that interprets commodity fetishism as mere object sanctification. Instead, the significance of fetishism is ultimately semiotic and consists in the reinforcement of cultural ideology. Through fetishism, the "closed perfection" of the system is celebrated and preserved (Baudrillard, 1981, p. 93). Through such ritualization, an individual becomes preferentially imprinted by an object while a culture simultaneously reproduces its critical structural categories. This is accomplished in large part by the sacralizing processes we have recounted in detail here.

We have chosen to adopt a clinical rather than critical perspective in describing the ways in which profane consumption is transfigured and made sacred. Divining the teleological and moral implications of secular sacralization is left to additional work adopting a theological or cultural criticism perspective. We hope such efforts will be aided by our clinical analysis. What is apparent is the capacity of consumer culture to facilitate expression of the sacred as it reproduces itself.

The behavioral complex we have described as sacralizing and desacralizing various dimensions of human experience is the ritual substratum of much consumer behavior. We have adopted the idiom of ritual to counter the "tyranny of paradigms" and the "constraining nature" of metaphors (Arndt 1985a, 1985b) characteristic of traditional consumer research. Our use of the constructs "sacred" and "profane" emerges from the interface of the subjective world and liberating paradigms described by Arndt (1985a, 1985b). By merging the phenomenological approach to consumer experience of the former paradigm with the criticistic or constructivistic orientation of the latter, a richer conceptual vocabulary for describing consumer behavior has been created.

Consider two of the metaphors that shape and reflect much inquiry in consumer research: involvement and loyalty. These two conditions or experiences suggest something of the talismanic relationship consumers form with that which is consumed. Yet, researchers have restricted their discussion of these constructs to the narrowly cognitive. Involvement has been glossed as focused activation (Cohen 1983), whether its duration is situational or enduring (Bloch and Richins 1983). Even when it has been considered as more than merely repeat purchase, loyalty is reduced to a function of decision-making, utilitarian, evaluative processes (Jacoby and Kyner 1973). Combined, these constructs deal with the arousal associated with personal meaningfulness, yet neither contends with the process of meaning investment or the cultural matrix from which that process ultimately emanates. We have described the sacred and the profane as conceptual categories that animate certain consumer behaviors. We have incorporated the spirit of these constructs into a more inclusive and culturally grounded process in which consumers routinely harness the forces of material and mental culture to achieve transcendent experience.

In his discussion of the political essence of the contemporary crisis of spirit in the Judeo-Christian tradition, Harrington (1983, p. 197) asks:

> Can Western society create transcendental common values in its everyday experience? Values which are not based upon—yet not counterposed to—the supernatural?

While the integrating consciousness affirmed by Harrington to be a potential solution to this question—namely, democratic socialism—may not appeal to many consumer researchers, certainly the question and corollary propositions he poses are of special interest. According to Harrington (1983), Western society *needs* transcendence. Like it or not, to our benefit or peril, consumption has become such a transcendental vehicle for many.

The processes used by marketers to attempt to singularize, and occasionally sacralize, a commodity so it becomes a differentiated, branded product have been described (Gardner and Levy 1955; Levitt 1984; Levy 1978). Processes that allow brands to function in unison on the social level as a constellation (Solomon and Assael 1987) to communicate status or on the cultural level as a brandscape (Sherry 1986b) to form a significant part of the built environment (Rapoport 1982) have been explored only recently.

Often quite apart from marketer efforts and considerations of brand, consumers themselves sacralize consumption objects and thereby create transcendent meaning in their lives. However, the processes used by consumers to remove an object or experience from a principally economic orbit and insert it into a personal pantheon, so that the object or experience becomes so highly infused with significance (*orenda, wakan, mana*) that it becomes a transcendental vehicle, have gone surprisingly undocumented given their frequent occurrence. While this oversight is partially a function of the impoverished technical vocabulary of traditional consumer research, it is also largely due to methodological preferences, which make the direct encounter of researcher with consumer in a naturalistic setting a rare occurrence. Participant observation and situationally appropriate depth interviews permit less restricted access to the consumer's moral economy. By laying the foundation for an understanding of the sacred in consumption, we hope we have demonstrated how rich such a direct approach can be.

REFERENCES

ACQUAVIVA, SABINO S. (1979), *The Decline of the Sacred in Industrial Society.* Oxford, England: Basil Blackwell.

ADLER, PATRICIA A., and PETER ADLER (1987), *Membership Roles in Field Research,* Qualitative Research Methods, Vol. 6. Beverly Hills, CA: Sage.

ALTMAN, IRWIN, and MARTIN M. CHEMERS (1984), *Culture and Environment.* Cambridge, England: Cambridge University Press.

APPADURAI, ARJUN (1986), "Introduction: Commodities and the Politics of Value," in *The Social Life of Things: Commodities in Cultural Perspective,* Ed. Arjun Appadurai. Cambridge, England: Cambridge University Press, 3-63.

ARMSTRONG, ROBERT P. (1971), *The Affecting Presence.* Urbana, IL: University of Illinois Press.

ARNDT, JOHAN (1985a), "The Tyranny of Paradigms: The Case for Paradigmatic Pluralism in Marketing," in *Changing the Course of Marketing: Alternative Paradigms for Widening Marketing Theory,* Eds. Nikhilesh Dholakia and Johan Arndt. Greenwich, CT: JAI, 1-25.

——— (1985b), "On Making Marketing More Scientific: The Role of Orientations, Paradigms, Metaphors, and Puzzle Solving," *Journal of Marketing,* 49 (Summer), 11-23.

ARNHEIM, RUDOLF (1987), "Art Among the Objects," *Critical Inquiry,* 13 (Summer), 677-685.

BATESON, GREGORY, and MARY C. BATESON (1987), *Angels Fear: Toward an Epistemology of the Sacred.* New York: Macmillan.

———, and MARGARET MEAD (1942), *Balinese Character: A Photographic Analysis.* New York: New York Academy of Sciences.

BAUDRILLARD, JEAN (1981), *For A Critique of the Political Economy of the Sign,* trans. Charles Levin. St. Louis, MO: Telos.

BEARDS, DICK (1987), "Antique Shop Narratives—Lost Treasure Found—and Lost," paper presented at the Popular Culture Association Annual Conference, Montreal Canada.

BEAGLEHOLE, ERNEST (1932), *Property: A Study in Social Psychology.* New York: Macmillan.

BEANE, WENDELL C. and WILLIAM C. DOTY, EDS. (1975), *Myths, Rites, and Symbols: A Mircea Eliade Reader,* Vol. 1. New York: Harper Colophon.

BECKER, HOWARD P. (1957), "Current Sacred-Secular Theory and Its Development," in *Modern Sociological Theory,* Eds. Howard Becker and Alvin Boskoff. New York: Holt, Rinehart & Winston, 133-185.

BECKER, HOWARD S. (1978), "Arts and Crafts," *American Journal of Sociology,* 83 (4), 862-889.

——— (1982), *Art Worlds,* Berkeley, CA: University of California Press.

——— (1986), *Doing Things Together.* Evanston, IL: Northwestern University Press.

BELK, RUSSELL W. (1979), "Gift Giving Behavior," in *Research in Marketing,* Vol. 2, Ed. Jagdish Sheth. Greenwich, CT: JAI, 95-126.

——— (1983), "Worldly Possessions: Issues and Criticisms," in *Advances in Consumer Research,* Vol. 10, Eds. Richard P. Bagozzi and Alice M.

Tybout. Ann Arbor, MI: Association for Consumer Research, 514–519.

——— (1986), "Art Versus Science as Ways of Generating Knowledge About Materialism," in *Perspectives on Methodology in Consumer Research,* Eds. David Brinberg and Richard Lutz. New York: Springer-Verlag, 3–36.

——— (1987a), "A Child's Christmas in America: Santa Claus as Deity, Consumption as Religion," *Journal of American Culture,* 10 (Spring), 87–100.

——— (1987b), "Symbolic Consumption of Art and Culture," in *Artists and Cultural Consumers,* Eds. Douglas V. Shaw et al. Akron, OH: Association for Cultural Economics, 168–178.

——— (1987c), "The Role of the Odyssey in Consumer Behavior and in Consumer Research," in *Advances in Consumer Research,* Vol. 14, Eds. Melanie Wallendorf and Paul Anderson. Provo, UT: Association for Consumer Research, 357–361.

——— (1988a), "Qualitative Analysis of Data from the Consumer Behavior Odyssey: The Role of the Computer and the Role of the Researcher," in *Proceedings of the Division of Consumer Psychology,* Ed. Linda Alwitt. Washington, DC: American Psychological Association, 7–11.

——— (1988b), "Possessions and the Extended Self," *Journal of Consumer Research,* 15 (September), 139–168.

———, JOHN F. SHERRY, JR., and MELANIE WALLENDORF (1988), "A Naturalistic Inquiry into Buyer and Seller Behavior at a Swap Meet," *Journal of Consumer Research,* 14 (March), 449–470.

———, MELANIE WALLENDORF, JOHN SHERRY, MORRIS HOLBROOK, and SCOTT ROBERTS (1988), "Collectors and Collections," in *Advances in Consumer Research,* Vol. 15, Ed. Michael Houston. Provo, UT: Association for Consumer Research, 548–553.

BELLAH, ROBERT N. (1967), "Civil Religion in America," *Daedalus,* 96 (1), 1–21.

———, RICHARD MADSEN, WILLIAM SULLIVAN, ANN SWIDLER, and STEVEN TIPTON (1985), *Habits of the Heart: Individualism and Commitment in American Life.* Berkeley, CA: University of California Press.

BENEDICT, BURTON, Ed. (1983), "Introduction," in *The Anthropology of World's Fairs.* Berkeley, CA: Scolar, 1–65.

BERGER, JOHN (1972), *Ways of Seeing.* London: British Broadcasting Corporation and Penguin.

BERGER, PETER L. (1967), *The Sacred Canopy: Elements of a Sociological Theory of Religion.* Garden City, NY: Anchor.

BERMAN, MORRIS (1984), *The Reenchantment of the World.* Toronto, Canada: Bantam.

BIRRELL, SUSAN (1981), "Sport as Ritual: Interpretations from Durkheim to Goffman," *Social Forces,* 60 (2), 354–376.

BLOCH, PETER H. (1981), "An Exploration into the Scaling of Consumers' Involvement with a Product Class," in *Advances in Consumer Research,* Vol. 8, Ed. Kent B. Monroe. Ann Arbor, MI: Association for Consumer Research, 61–65.

———, and MARSHA RICHINS (1983), "A Theoretical Model of the Study of Product Importance Perceptions," *Journal of Marketing,* 47 (Summer), 69–81.

BOCK, E. WILBUR (1972), "The Transformation of Religious Symbols: A Case Study of St. Nicholas," *Social Compass,* 19 (4), 537–548.

BOORSTIN, DANIEL (1973), *The Americans: The Democratic Experience.* New York: Random House.

BOSSARD, JAMES H. S., and ELEANOR S. BOLL (1950), *Ritual in Family Living: A Contemporary Study.* Philadelphia: University of Pennsylvania Press.

BOWLBY, RACHEL (1985), *Just Looking: Consumer Culture in Dreiser, Gissing and Zola.* New York: Methuen.

BREEN, T. H. (1988), " 'Baubles of Britain': The American and Consumer Revolutions of the Eighteenth Century," *Past and Present,* 119 (May), 73–104.

BRERETON, JOEL P. (1987), "Sacred Space," in *Encyclopedia of Religion,* Vol. 12, Ed. Mircea Eliade. New York: Collier-MacMillan, 526–535.

BRIGGS, CHARLES (1986), *Learning How to Ask.* Cambridge, England: Cambridge University Press.

BROWN, CURTIS F. (1975), *Star Spangled Kitsch.* New York: Universe Books.

CALDER, BOBBY J., and ALICE M. TYBOUT (1987), "What Consumer Research Is . . . ," *Journal of Consumer Research,* 14 (June), 136–140.

CAMPBELL, COLIN (1983), "Romanticism and the Consumer Ethic: Intimations of a Weber-Style Thesis," *Sociological Analysis,* 44 (4), 279–296.

——— (1987), *The Romantic Ethic and the Spirit of Modern Consumerism.* London: Basil Blackwell.

CAMPBELL, JOSEPH (1949), *The Hero With a Thousand Faces.* Princeton, NJ: Princeton University Press.

CAPLOW, THEODORE (1984), "Rule Enforcement Without Visible Means: Christmas Gift-Giving in Middletown," *American Journal of Sociology,* 89 (6), 1306–1323.

CAPRA, FRITJOF (1975), *The Tao of Physics.* Toronto, Canada: Bantam.

CHAUCER, GEOFFREY (1948), *The Canterbury Tales.* New York: Simon & Schuster.

CHEAL, DAVID (1987), " 'Showing Them You Love Them': Gift Giving and the Dialectic of Intimacy," *The Sociological Review,* 35 (February), 151–169.

CLARK, GRAHAME (1986), *Symbols of Excellence: Precious Materials as Expressions of Status.* Cambridge, England: Cambridge University Press.

CLIFFORD, JAMES (1985), "Objects and Selves—An Afterword," in *Objects and Others: Essays on Museums and Material Culture,* Vol. 3, Ed. George W. Stocking. Madison, WI: University of Wisconsin Press, 236–246.

CLODD, EDWARD (1920), *Magic in Names and in Other Things.* London: Chapman and Hall.

COHEN, ERIK (1979), "A Phenomenology of Tourist Experiences," *Sociology,* 13 (2), 179–201.

COHEN, JOEL (1983), "Involvement and You: 1000 Great Ideas," in *Advances in Consumer Research,* Vol. 10, Eds. Richard P. Bagozzi and Alice M. Tybout. Ann Arbor, MI: Association for Consumer Research, 325–328.

COLEMAN, RICHARD (1983), "The Continuing Significance of Social Class to Marketing," *Journal of Consumer Research,* 10 (December), 265–280.

COLLIER, JOHN, JR., and MALCOLM COLLIER (1986), *Visual Anthropology: Photography as a Research Tool.* Albuquerque: University of New Mexico Press.

COLPE, CARSTEN (1987), "The Sacred and the Profane," *Encyclopedia of Religion,* Vol. 12, Ed. Mircea Eliade. New York: Collier-MacMillan, 511–526.

CONNOLLY, ROBERT and ROBIN ANDERSON (1987), *First Contact: New Guinea's Highlanders Encounter the Outside World.* New York: Viking.

CORNFELD, BETTY, and OWEN EDWARDS (1983), *Quintessence: The Quality of Having It.* New York: Crown Publishers.

CSIKSZENTMIHALYI, MIHALY (1975), *Beyond Boredom and Anxiety.* San Francisco: Jossey-Bass.

———, and EUGENE ROCHBERG-HALTON (1981), *The Meaning of Things: Domestic Symbols and the Self.* New York: Cambridge University Press.

CULLER, JONATHAN (1981), "Semiotics of Tourism," *American Journal of Semiotics,* 1 (1–2), 127–140.

CUMMINGS, RONALD (1972), "The Superbowl Society," in *Heroes of Popular Culture,* Eds. Ray B. Browne et al. Bowling Green, OH: Bowling Green University Popular Press, 101–111.

CURRY, PAMELA M., and ROBERT M. JIOBU (1980), "Big Mac and *Caneton A L'Orange:* Eating, Icons and Rituals," in *Rituals and Ceremonies in Popular Culture,* Ed. Ray B. Browne. Bowling Green, OH: Bowling Green University Popular Press, 248–257.

DANET, BRENDA, and TAMAR KATRIEL (1987), "No Two Alike: The Aesthetics of Collecting," working paper, Communications Institute, Hebrew University of Jerusalem, Mount Scopus, Israel (02)883046.

DEFFONTAINES, PIERRE (1953), "The Place of Believing," *Landscape,* 2 (Spring), 22–28.

DEMERATH, N. J., III (1974), *A Tottering Transcendence: Civil vs. Cultic Aspects of the Sacred.* Indianapolis, IN: Bobbs-Merrill.

DESMONDE, WILLIAM H. (1962), *Magic, Myth, and Money: The Origin of Money in Religious Ritual.* Glencoe, IL: Free Press of Glencoe.

DORFLES, GILLO (1969), "Religious Trappings," in *Kitsch: The World of Bad Taste,* Ed. Gillo Dorfles. New York: Universe Books, 141–142.

D'ORMESSON, JEAN (1984), *Grand Hotel: The Golden Age of Palace Hotels in Architectural and Social History.* New York: Vendome.

DOVEY, KIMBERLY (1985), "Home and Homelessness," in *Home Environments,* Eds. Irwin Altman and Carol Werner. New York: Plenum, 33–63.

DUCEY, MICHAEL H. (1977), *Sunday Morning: Aspects of Urban Ritual.* New York: Free Press.

DUNCAN, JAMES S. (1985), "The House as Symbol of Social Structure: Notes on the Language of Objects Among Collectivistic Groups," in *Home Environments,* Eds. Irwin Altman and Carol M. Werner. New York: Plenum, 133–151.

DURKHEIM, EMILE (1915), *The Elementary Forms of the Religious Life.* London: Allen & Unwin.

______ (1953), *Sociology and Philosophy,* trans. D. F. Pockock. London: Cohen & West.

______ (1960), *The Division of Labor in Society,* trans. George Simpson. Glencoe, IL: Free Press of Glencoe.

______ (1975), *Durkheim on Religion: A Selection of Readings with Bibliographies and Introductory Remarks,* trans. J. Redding and W. S. F. Pickering. London: Routledge & Kegan Paul.

ELIADE, MIRCEA (1958), *Patterns of Comparative Religion.* London: Sheed & Ward.

______ (1959), *The Sacred and the Profane: The Nature of Religion,* trans. Willard R. Trask. New York: Harper & Row.

______ (1964), *Shamanism.* New York: Pantheon.

FABIEN, JOHANNES (1983), *Time and the Other: How Anthropology Makes Its Object.* New York: Columbia University Press.

FARB, PETER, and GEORGE ARMELAGOS (1980), *Consuming Passions: The Anthropology of Eating.* Boston: Houghton Mifflin.

FENN, RICHARD (1986), *Toward a Theory of Secularization,* Society for the Scientific Study of Religion Monograph Series No. 1, Orono, ME: University of Maine.

FERNANDEZ, JAMES (1986), *Persuasions and Performances: The Play of Tropes in Culture.* Bloomington, IN: Indiana University Press.

FERRAROTTI, FRANCO (1979), "The Destiny of Reason and the Paradox of the Sacred," *Social Research,* 46 (4), 648–681.

FRANKL, RAZELLE (1987), *Televangelism: The Marketing of Popular Religion.* Carbondale, IL: Southern Illinois University Press.

FROMM, ERICH (1947), *Man for Himself: An Inquiry into the Psychology of Ethics.* New York: Holt, Rinehart & Winston.

GALBRAITH, JOHN KENNETH (1973), *Economics and the Public Purpose.* New York: New American Library.

GARDNER, BURLEIGH, and SIDNEY J. LEVY (1955), "The Product and the Brand," *Harvard Business Review,* 33 (2), 33–39.

GEARY, PATRICK (1986), "Sacred Commodities: The Circulation of Medieval Relics," in *The Social Life of Things: Commodities in Cultural Perspective,* Ed. Arjun Appadurai. Cambridge, England: Cambridge University Press, 169–191.

GEERTZ, CLIFFORD (1973), *The Interpretation of Cultures.* New York: Basic Books.

GEIST, CHRISTOPHER D. (1978), "Historic Sites and Monuments as Icons," *Icons of America,* Eds. Ray B. Browne and Marshall Fishwick. Bowling Green, OH: Bowling Green University Popular Press, 57–66.

GIESZ, LUDWIG (1969), "Kitsch-man as Tourist," in *Kitsch: The World of Bad Taste,* Ed. Gillo Dorfles. New York: Universe Books, 157–174.

GLASER, BARNEY G., and ANSELM L. STRAUSS (1967), *The Discovery of Grounded Theory: Strategies for Qualitative Research.* Chicago: Aldine.

GOODMAN, PAUL (1960), *Growing Up Absurd.* New York: Vintage.

GORDON, BEVERLY (1986), "The Souvenir: Messenger of the Extraordinary," *Journal of Popular Culture,* 20 (3), 135–146.

GOULD, LEROY C., ANDREW L. WALKER, LANSING E. CRANE, and CHARLES W. LIDZ (1974), *Connections: Notes from the Heroin World.* New Haven, CT: Yale University Press.

GRABURN, NELSON H. H. (1977), "Tourism: The Sacred Journey," in *Hosts and Guests: The Anthropology of Tourism,* Ed. Valene Smith. Philadelphia: University of Pennsylvania Press.

GREELEY, ANDREW M. (1985), *Unsecular Man: The Persistence of Religion.* New York: Schocken.

GREENBERG, CLEMENT (1946), *The Partisan Reader.* New York: Dial Press.

GREGOTTI, VITTORIO (1969), "Kitsch and Architecture," *Kitsch: The World of Bad Taste,* Ed. Gillo Dorfles. New York: Universe Books, 255–276.

GUTTMANN, ALLEN (1978), *From Ritual to Record: The Nature of Modern Sports.* New York: Columbia University Press.

HARDY, ALISTER (1979), *The Spiritual Nature of Man: A Study of Contemporary Religious Experience.* Oxford, England: Clarendon.

HARRINGTON, MICHAEL (1983), *The Politics at God's Funeral: The Spiritual Crisis of Western Civilization.* New York: Penguin.

HARRIS, MARVIN (1985), *The Sacred Cow and the Abominable Pig: Riddles of Food and Culture.* New York: Simon & Schuster.

HAUG, WOLFGANG F. (1986), *Critique of Commodity Aesthetics: Appearance, Sexuality and Advertising in Capitalist Society,* trans. Robert Bock. Minneapolis, MN: University of Minnesota Press.

HAUGHEY, JOHN (1986), *The Sacred Use of Money: Personal Finance in Light of Christian Faith.* Garden City, NY: Doubleday.

HAYDEN, ILSE (1987), *Symbol and Privilege: The Ritual Context of British Royalty.* Tucson, AZ: University of Arizona Press.

HIGHET, GILBERT (1972), "Kitsch," in *The Popular Arts in America: A Reader,* Ed. William M. Hammel. New York: Harcourt Brace Jovanovich, 33-41.

HIGHWATER, JAMAKE (1981), *The Primal Mind: Vision and Reality in Indian America.* New York: New American Library.

HIRSCHMAN, ELIZABETH C. (1986), "Humanistic Inquiry in Marketing Research: Philosophy, Method, and Criteria," *Journal of Marketing Research,* 23 (August), 237-249.

———, and MORRIS HOLBROOK (1982), "Hedonic Consumption: Emerging Concepts, Methods, and Propositions," *Journal of Marketing,* 46 (Summer), 92-101.

HOBSBAWM, ERIC, and TERENCE RANGER (1983), *The Invention of Tradition.* Cambridge, England: Cambridge University Press.

HOLBROOK, MORRIS B. (1987), "From the Log of a Consumer Researcher: Reflections on the Odyssey," in *Advances in Consumer Research,* Vol. 14, Eds. Melanie Wallendorf and Paul Anderson. Provo, UT: Association for Consumer Research, 365-369.

———, and ELIZABETH HIRSCHMAN (1982), "The Experiential Aspects of Consumption: Consumer Fantasies, Feelings, and Fun," *Journal of Consumer Research,* 9 (September), 132-140.

HOMER, N.F.N. (1963), *The Odyssey,* trans. Robert Fitzgerald. Garden City, NY: Anchor.

HOPE, CHRISTINE A. (1980), "American Beauty Rituals," in *Rituals and Ceremonies in Popular Culture,* Ed. Ray B. Browne. Bowling Green, OH: Bowling Green University Popular Press, 226-237.

HOUGHTON, A. T. (1955), "Animism," in *The World's Religions,* Ed. J. N. Anderson. Grand Rapids, MI: William B. Eerdmans, 9-24.

HOUSTON, MICHAEL J., and MICHAEL L. ROTHSCHILD (1978), "Conceptual and Methodological Perspectives on Involvement," in *1978 Educators' Proceedings,* Ed. Subhash C. Jain. Chicago: American Marketing Association, 184-187.

HUBERT, HENRI, and MARCEL MAUSS (1964), *Sacrifice: Its Nature and Function.* London: Cohen & West.

HUDSON, MICHAEL D. (1987), "An Appeal from Above: The Use of Religious Figures in Advertisements," paper presented at the Popular Culture Association Annual Meeting, Montreal, Canada.

HYDE, LEWIS (1983), *The Gift: Imagination and the Erotic Life of Property.* New York: Random House.

INKELES, ALEX (1983), *Exploring Individual Modernity.* New York: Columbia University Press.

IVES, EDWARD D. (1974), *The Tape-Recorded Interview.* Knoxville, TN: University of Tennessee Press.

JACKSON, J. B. (1953), "The Place of Believing," *Landscape,* 2 (Spring), 22-28.

JACOBY, JACOB, and DAVID KYNER (1973), "Brand Loyalty vs. Repeat Purchase Behavior," *Journal of Marketing Research,* 10 (February), 1-9.

JAMES, E. O. (1962), *Sacrifice and Sacrament.* New York: Barnes & Noble.

JAMES, WILLIAM (1961), *The Varieties of Religious Experience: A Study of Human Nature.* New York: Collier.

JONES, LETHONEE (1982), "Fetishes and Fetishism in Foods and Eating," in *Objects of Special Devotion: Fetishism in Popular Culture,* Ed. Ray B. Browne. Bowling Green, OH: Bowling Green University Popular Press, 238-256.

KASSARJIAN, HAROLD H. (1987), "How We Spent Our Summer Vacation: A Preliminary Report on the 1986 Consumer Behavior Odyssey," in *Advances in Consumer Research,* Vol. 14, Eds. Melanie Wallendorf and Paul Anderson. Provo, UT: Association for Consumer Research, 376-377.

KELLER, EVELYN FOX (1985), *Reflections on Gender and Science.* New Haven, CT: Yale University Press.

KELLEY, ROBERT F. (1987), "Museums as Status Symbols: Attaining a State of Having Been," in *Advances in Nonprofit Marketing,* Vol. 2, Ed. Russell W. Belk. Greenwich, CT: JAI, 1-38.

KINGSLEY, MICHAEL (1987), "Baby M and the Moral Logic of Capitalism," *Wall Street Journal,* April 16, 27.

KIRK, G. S. (1970), *Myth.* Cambridge, England: Cambridge University Press.

KOENIG, FREDERICK (1985), *Rumor in the Marketplace: The Social Psychology of Commercial Heresay.* Dover, MA: Auburn House.

KOPYTOFF, IGOR (1986), "The Cultural Biography of Things: Commoditization as Process," in *The Social Life of Things: Commodities in Cultural Perspec-*

tive, Ed. Arjun Appadurai. Cambridge, England: Cambridge University Press, 64–91.

KOTTAK, CONRAD P. (1981), "Rituals at McDonald's," in *The American Dimension: Cultural Myths and Social Realities,* Eds. W. Arens and Susan P. Montague. Sherman Oaks, CA: Alfred, 129–136.

KOWINSKI, WILLIAM S. (1985), *The Malling of America.* New York: Atheneum.

KRON, JOAN (1983), *Home Psych: The Social Psychology of Home and Decoration.* New York: Clarkson N. Potter.

LAKOFF, GEORGE, and MARK JOHNSON (1980), *Metaphors We Live By.* Chicago: University of Chicago Press.

LASKI, MARGHANITA (1959), "Sacred and Profane," *Twentieth Century,* 165 (February), 118–129.

——— (1962), *Ecstasy: A Study of Some Secular and Religious Experiences.* Bloomington, IN: Indiana University Press.

LEACH, EDMUND R. (1961), *Rethinking Anthropology.* London: Athlone.

LEISS, WILLIAM, STEPHEN KLINE, and SUT JHALLY (1986), *Social Communication in Advertising: Persons, Products, and Images of Well-Being.* New York: Methuen.

LEVINSON, DANIEL J. (1987), "The Stages of a Woman's Life," presentation at the 1987 American Psychological Association Convention, New York.

LEVI-STRAUSS, CLAUDE (1962), *Totemism,* trans. Rodney Needham. Boston: Beacon.

——— (1965), "The Principle of Reciprocity," in *Sociological Theory,* Eds. Lewis A. Coser and Bernard Rosenberg. New York: Macmillan.

LEVITT, THEODORE (1984), "Differentiation—of Anything," in *The Marketing Imagination.* New York: Free Press, 72–93.

LEVY, SIDNEY (1978), *Marketplace Behavior—Its Meaning for Management.* New York: AMACOM.

——— (1966), "Social Class and Consumer Behavior," in *On Knowing the Consumer,* Ed. Joseph W. Newman. New York: Wiley, 146–160.

LINCOLN, YVONNA S., and EGON G. GUBA (1985), *Naturalistic Inquiry.* Beverly Hills, CA: Sage.

LIPSEY, ROGER (1984), "Participators of Sacred Things," *Parabola,* 9 (1), 16–21.

LOPES, SAL (1987), *The Wall: Images and Offerings from the Vietnam Veterans Memorial.* New York: Collins.

LUSCHEN, GUNTER, ZAHARJ STAIKOF, VERONICA STOLTE HEISKANEN, and CONOR WARD (1972), "Family, Ritual, and Secularization: A Cross-National Study Conducted in Bulgaria, Finland, Germany and Ireland," *Social Compass,* 19 (4), 519–536.

LYNES, RUSSELL (1980), *The Tastemakers: The Shaping of American Popular Taste.* New York: Dover.

MACALOON, JOHN (1984), "Olympic Games and the Theory of Spectacle in Modern Societies," in *Rite, Drama, Festival, Spectacle. Rehearsals Toward a Theory of Cultural Performance,* Ed. John MacAloon. Philadelphia, PA: Institute for the Study of Human Issues, 241–280.

MACCANNELL, DEAN (1976), *The Tourist: A New Theory of the Leisure Class.* New York: Schocken.

MCCRACKEN, GRANT (1986), "Culture and Consumption: A Theoretical Account of the Structure and Movement of the Cultural Meaning of Consumer Goods," *Journal of Consumer Goods and Activities.* Bloomington, IN: Indiana University Press, 44–53.

MALINOWSKI, BRONISLAW (1922), *Argonauts of the Western Pacific.* London: George Routledge & Sons.

——— (1954), *Magic, Science, and Religion, and Other Essays.* Garden City, NY: Doubleday.

MANN, DENNIS A. (1980), "Ritual in Architecture: The Celebration of Life," in *Rituals and Ceremonies in Popular Culture,* Ed. Ray B. Browne. Bowling Green, OH: Bowling Green University Popular Press, 61–80.

MARSH, PETER, and PETER COLLETT (1986), *Driving Passion: The Psychology of the Car.* London: Jonathan Cape.

MARTIN, BERNICE (1979), "The Sacralization of Disorder: Symbolism in Rock Music," *Sociological Analysis,* 40 (2), 87–124.

MARX, KARL (1972), "Capital: Selections," in *The Marx-Engels Reader,* Ed. Robert C. Tucker. New York: W. W. Norton, 191–318.

MASLOW, ABRAHAM (1964), *Religions, Values, and Peak-experiences.* Columbus, OH: Ohio State University Press.

MAUSS, MARCEL (1925), *The Gift.* London: Cohen & West.

MAY, LARY (1980), *Screening Out the Past: The Birth of*

Mass Culture and the Motion Picture Industry. New York: Oxford University Press.

MILES, MATTHEW B., and A. MICHAEL HUBERMAN (1984), *Qualitative Data Analysis: A Sourcebook of New Methods*. Beverly Hills, CA: Sage.

MINER, HORACE (1956), "Body Ritual Among the Nacirema," *American Anthropologist*, 58 (3), 503–507.

MOL, HANS (1976), *Identity and the Sacred: A Sketch for a New Socio-Scientific Theory of Religion*. New York: The Free Press.

——— (1983), *Meaning and Place: An Introduction to the Social Scientific Study of Religion*. New York: Pilgrim.

MOORE, ALEXANDER (1980), "Walt Disney World: Bounded Ritual Space and the Playful Pilgrimage Center," *Anthropological Quarterly*, 53 (4), 207–218.

MORRIS, WRIGHT (1948), *The Home Place*. New York: Scribner.

NASH, JEFFREY E. (1977), "Decoding the Runner's Wardrobe," in *Conformity and Conflict*, Eds. James P. Spradley and David W. McCurdy. Boston: Little, Brown, 172–185.

NAYLOR, DAVID (1981), *American Picture Palaces: The Architecture of Fantasy*. New York: Van Nostrand Reinhold.

NEAL, ARTHUR G. (1985), "Animism and Totemism in Popular Culture," *Journal of Popular Culture*, 19 (2), 15–23.

NISBET, ROBERT A. (1966), "The Sacred," in *The Sociological Tradition*. New York: Basic Books, 221–263.

O'GUINN, THOMAS C. (1987), "Touching Greatness: Some Aspects of Star Worship in Contemporary Consumption," paper presented at the American Psychological Association Convention, New York.

———, and RUSSELL W. BELK (1989), "Heaven on Earth: Consumption at Heritage Village, USA," *Journal of Consumer Research*, 16 (September), in press.

OLIVER, PAUL (1987), *Dwellings: The House Across the World*. Austin, TX: University of Texas Press.

PARSONS, TALCOTT, and EDWARD SHILS (1951), *Toward a General Theory of Action*. Cambridge, MA: Harvard University Press.

PAWEK, KARL (1969), "Christian Kitsch," in *Kitsch: The World of Bad Taste*, Ed. Gillo Dorfles. New York: Universe Books, 143–150.

PICKERING, W. S. F. (1984), *Durkheim's Sociology of Religion: Themes and Theories*. London: Routledge & Kegan Paul.

PIRSIG, ROBERT M. (1974), *Zen and the Art of Motorcycle Maintenance*. London: Bodleyhead.

PLATO, N.F.N. (1955), *The Symposium*, trans. Walter Hamilton. Harmondsworth, England: Penguin.

POPE-HENNESSY, JOHN (1987), "Storm over the Sistine Ceiling," *New York Review of Books*, October 8, 16–19.

PUNCH, MAURICE (1986), *The Politics and Ethics of Fieldwork*, Qualitative Research Methods Series, Vol. 3. Beverly Hills, CA: Sage.

RAPOPORT, AMOS (1981), "Identity and Environment: A Cross-Cultural Perspective," in *Housing and Identity: Cross-Cultural Perspectives*, Ed. James S. Duncan. London: Croom Helm, 6–35.

——— (1982), "Sacred Places, Sacred Occasions and Sacred Environments," *Architectural Design*, 52 (9/10), 75–82.

REAL, MICHAEL R. (1975), "Super Bowl: Mythic Spectacle," *Journal of Communication*, 25 (Winter), 31–43.

RHEIMS, MAURICE (1961), *The Strange Life of Objects: 35 Centuries of Art Collecting and Collectors*, trans. David Pryce-Jones. New York: Atheneum.

RICHINS, MARSHA L., and PETER H. BLOCH (1986), "After the New Wears Off: The Temporal Context of Product Involvement," *Journal of Consumer Research*, 13 (September), 280–285.

ROBERTS, KEITH A. (1984), *Religion in Sociological Perspective*. Homewood, IL: Dorsey.

ROCHBERG-HALTON, EUGENE (1984), "Object Relations, Role Models, and the Cultivation of the Self," *Environment and Behavior*, 16 (3), 335–368.

——— (1986), *Meaning and Modernity*. Chicago: University of Chicago Press.

ROOK, DENNIS W. (1984), "Ritual Behavior and Consumer Symbolism," in *Advances in Consumer Research*, Vol. 11, Ed. Thomas C. Kinnear. Provo, UT: Association for Consumer Research, 279–284.

——— (1985), "The Ritual Dimension of Consumer Behavior," *Journal of Consumer Research*, 12 (December), 251–264.

——— (1987), "Modern Hex Signs and Symbols of Security," in *Marketing and Semiotics: New Directions in the Study of Signs for Sale*, Ed. Jean Umiker-Sebeok. Berlin: Mouton de Gruyter, 239–246.

RYDELL, ROBERT W. (1984), *All the World's a Fair: Visions of Empire at American International Expositions, 1876–1916.* Chicago: University of Chicago Press.

SAEGERT, SUSAN (1985), "The Role of Housing in the Experience of Dwelling," in *Home Environments,* Eds. Irwin Altman and Carol M. Werner. New York: Plenum, 287–309.

SAHLINS, MARSHALL (1976), *Culture and Practical Reason.* Chicago: University of Chicago Press.

SANDERS, CLINTON (1985), "Tattoo Consumption: Risk and Regret in the Purchase of a Socially Marginal Service," in *Advances in Consumer Research,* Vol. 12, Eds. Elizabeth C. Hirschman and Morris B. Holbrook. Provo, UT: Association for Consumer Research, 17–22.

SCARRY, ELAINE (1985), *The Body in Pain: The Making and Unmaking of the World.* New York: Oxford University Press.

SCHROEDER, FRED E. (1977), *Outlaw Aesthetics: Arts and the Public Mind.* Bowling Green, OH: Bowling Green University Popular Press.

SCUDDER, THAYER (1982), *No Place to Go: Effects of Compulsory Relocation on Navajos.* Philadelphia, PA: Institute for the Study of Human Issues.

SERPELL, JAMES (1986), *In the Company of Animals.* Oxford, England: Basil Blackwell.

SHAMMAS, CAROLE, MARILYNN SALMON, and MICHAEL DAHLIN (1987), *Inheritance in America: From Colonial Times to the Present.* New Brunswick, NJ: Rutgers University Press.

SHARP, DENNIS (1969), *The Picture Palace and Other Buildings for the Movies.* London: Hugh Evelyn.

SHERRY, JOHN F., JR. (1983), "Gift-Giving in Anthropological Perspective," *Journal of Consumer Research,* 10 (September), 157–168.

______ (1984), "Some Implications of Consumer Oral Tradition for Reactive Marketing," in *Advances in Consumer Research,* Vol. 11, Ed. Thomas C. Kinnear. Provo, UT: Association for Consumer Research, 741–747.

______ (1986a), "Interpreting Data From the Field," paper presented at the Annual Conference of the Association for Consumer Research, Toronto, Canada.

______ (1986b), "Cereal Monogamy: Brand Loyalty as Secular Ritual in Consumer Culture," paper presented at the Annual Conference of the Association for Consumer Research, Toronto, Canada.

______ (1987a), "Keeping the Monkeys Away From the Typewriters: An Anthropologist's View of the Consumer Behavior Odyssey," in *Advances in Consumer Research,* Vol. 14, Eds. Melanie Wallendorf and Paul Anderson. Provo, UT: Association for Consumer Research, 370–373.

______ (1987b), "Advertising as a Cultural System," in *Marketing and Semiotics: New Directions in the Study of Signs for Sale,* Ed. Jean Umiker-Sebeok. Berlin: Mouton de Gruyter, 441–461.

______ (1987c), "Heresy and the Useful Miracle: Rethinking Anthropology's Contribution to Marketing," in *Research in Marketing,* Vol. 9, Ed. Jagdish Sheth. Greenwich, CT: JAI, 285–306.

______ (1988), "Market Pitching and the Ethnography of Speaking," in *Advances in Consumer Research,* Vol. 15, Ed. Michael Houston. Provo, UT: Association for Consumer Research, 543–547.

SHILS, EDWARD, and MICHAEL YOUNG (1953), "The Meaning of the Coronation," *Sociological Review,* 1 (2), 63–81.

SHINER, LARRY E. (1972), "Sacred Space, Profane Space, Human Space," *Journal of the Academy of Religion,* 40 (4), 425–436.

SLESIN, SUZANNE, STAFFORD CLIFT, and DANIEL ROZENSZTROCH (1987), *Japanese Style.* New York: Clarkson Potter.

SNOW, DAVID A., and LEON ANDERSON (1987), "Identity Work Among the Homeless: The Verbal Construction and Avowal of Personal Identities," *American Journal of Sociology,* 92 (May), 1336–1371.

SNYDER, C. R., and HOWARD FROMKIN (1980), *Uniqueness: The Human Pursuit of Difference.* New York: Plenum.

SOLOMON, MICHAEL (1986), "Deep-Seated Materialism: The Case of Levi's 501 Jeans," in *Advances in Consumer Research,* Vol. 13, Ed. Richard J. Lutz. Provo, UT: Association for Consumer Research, 619–622.

______, and HENRY ASSAEL (1987), "The Forest or the Trees? A Gestalt Approach to Symbolic Consumption," in *Marketing and Semiotics: New Directions in the Study of Signs for Sale,* Ed. Jean Umiker-Sebeok. Berlin: Mouton de Gruyter, 189–217.

SONTAG, SUSAN (1973), *On Photography.* New York: Farrar, Straus, & Giroux.

STEIN, MICHAEL (1977), "Cult and Sport: The Case of Big Red," *Mid-American Review of Sociology,* 2 (2), 29–42.

STEWART, SUSAN (1984), *On Longing: Narratives of the*

Miniature, the Gigantic, the Souvenir, the Collection. Baltimore, MD: Johns Hopkins University Press.

STIRRAT, R. L. (1984), "Sacred Models," *Man,* 19 (2), 199–215.

SUDJIC, DEYAN (1985), *Cult Objects.* London: Paladin Books.

SUSSMAN, MARVIN B., ED. (1985), *Pets and The Family.* New York: Haworth.

THOMPSON, MICHAEL (1979), *Rubbish Theory: The Creation and Destruction of Value.* Oxford, England: Oxford University Press.

TITCOMB, MARGARET (1969), *Dog and Man in the Ancient Pacific.* Honolulu, HI: Bernice P. Bishop Museum Special Publication No. 59.

TUAN, YI-FU (1978), *Space and Place: The Perspective of Experience.* Minneapolis: University of Minnesota Press.

——— (1982), *Segmented Worlds and Self: Group life and Individualism.* Minneapolis, MN: University of Minnesota Press.

——— (1984), *Dominance and Affection: The Making of Pets.* New Haven, CT: Yale University Press.

TURNER, TERENCE S. (1977), "Cosmetics: The Language of Body Adornment," in *Conformity and Conflict: Readings in Cultural Anthropology,* Eds. James P. Spradley and David W. McCurdy. Boston: Little, Brown, 162–171.

TURNER, VICTOR (1967), *The Forest of Symbols.* Ithaca, NY: Cornell University Press.

——— (1969), *The Ritual Process.* London: Routledge & Kegan Paul.

——— (1972), "Passages, Margins, and Poverty: Religious Communitas," *Worship,* 46 (7), 390–412.

——— (1977), "Variations on a Theme of Liminality," in *Secular Ritual,* Eds. Sally F. Moore and Barbara G. Myerhoff. Amsterdam, The Netherlands: Van Gorcum, 36–52.

———, and EDITH TURNER (1978), *Image and Pilgrimage in Christian Culture: Anthropological Perspectives.* Oxford, England: Basil Blackwell.

VAN GENNEP, ARNOLD (1909), *Les Rites de Passage.* Paris: E. Nourry.

VAN IMWAGEN, PETER (forthcoming), *Material Beings.* Ithaca, NY: Cornell University Press.

VOIGT, DAVID Q. (1980), "American Sporting Rituals," in *Rituals and Ceremonies in Popular Culture,* Ed. Ray B. Browne. Bowling Green, OH: Bowling Green University Popular Press, 125–140.

WAITS, WILLIAM B., JR. (1978), "The Many-Faced Custom: Christmas Gift-Giving in America, 1900–1940," unpublished dissertation, History Department, Rutgers University, New Brunswick, NJ 08903.

WALLENDORF, MELANIE (1987a), "On Intimacy," paper presented at the American Marketing Association Winter Educators' Conference, San Antonio, TX.

——— (1987b), " 'On the Road Again': The Nature of Qualitative Research on the Consumer Behavior Odyssey," in *Advances in Consumer Research,* Vol. 14, Eds. Melanie Wallendorf and Paul Anderson. Provo, UT: Association for Consumer Research, 374–375.

———, and ERIC ARNOULD (1988), " 'My Favorite Things': A Cross-Cultural Inquiry into Object Attachment, Possessiveness, and Social Linkage," *Journal of Consumer Research,* 14 (March), 531–547.

———, and RUSSELL W. BELK (1987), "Deep Meaning in Possessions: Qualitative Research from the Consumer Behavior Odyssey," video distributed by Marketing Science Institute, Cambridge, MA.

———, and DANIEL NELSON (1987), "An Archaeological Examination of Ethnic Differences in Body Care Rituals," *Psychology and Marketing,* 3 (January), 273–289.

WARNER, W. LLOYD (1959), *The Living and the Dead: A Study of the Symbolic Life of Americans.* New Haven, CT: Yale University Press.

WEBER, MAX (1958), *The Protestant Ethic and the Spirit of Capitalism.* New York: Scribner.

——— (1962), *The Sociology of Religion.* Boston: Beacon Press.

——— (1968), *On Charisma and Institution Building,* Ed. S. N. Eisenstadt. Chicago: University of Chicago Press.

WERNER, OSWALD, and G. MARK SCHOEPFLE (1987), *Systematic Fieldwork: Ethnographic Analysis and Data Management,* Vol. 1. Beverly Hills, CA: Sage.

WHETMORE, EDWARD, and DON J. HIBBARD (1978), "Paradox in Paradise: The Icons of Waikiki," in *Icons of America,* Eds. Ray B. Browne and Marshall Fishwick. Bowling Green, OH: Bowling Green University Popular Press, 241–252.

WILLIAMS, ROSALIND (1981), *Dream Worlds: Mass Consumption in Late Nineteenth Century France.* Berkeley, CA: University of California Press.

WILLIAMSON, JUDITH (1986), "Royalty and Representation," in *Consuming Passions: The Dynamics of*

Popular Culture, Ed. Judith Williamson. London: Marion Boyars, 75–89.

Wolowelsky, Joel B. (1977), "The Human Meal," *Judaism,* 26 (101), 92–96.

Zepp, Ira G., Jr. (1986), *The New Religious Image of Urban America: The Shopping Mall as Ceremonial Center.* Westminster, MD: Christian Classics.

Zerubavel, Eviatar (1981), *Hidden Rhythms: Schedules and Calendars in Social Life.* Chicago: University of Chicago Press.

29

PRIMITIVE ASPECTS OF CONSUMPTION IN MODERN AMERICAN SOCIETY*

Elizabeth C. Hirschman

This article challenges the widely held assumption that the United States of America possesses a society characterized by modern values and a secular-consumption ethic. Drawing upon concepts and techniques utilized by cultural anthropologists in the study of nonindustrialized societies, evidence is presented to support a view of U.S. consumption as an outlet for spiritual expression and the preservation of ethnic heritage. Humanistic research approaches such as participant observation are advocated.

The United States of America exhibits several characteristics associated with cultural modernity and societal development—an industrialized production base, technological innovation, labor specialization, credit markets, material affluence, and an educated, informed citizenry (Firebaugh 1983). It often is cited as the modern exemplar in cross-national comparative studies (see, for example, Firebaugh 1983; Inkeles and Smith 1974). Thus, many have assumed that American consumers would exhibit the psychological, behavioral, and social characteristics consistent with societal modernity and industrialization. For example, Spates (1983) suggests that Americans would answer the five societal value questions posed by Kluckhohn (1950) as follows:

- *What is human nature?*
  Capable of progressive improvement.
- *How should we relate to nature and the supernatural?*
  By achieving mastery and control.

*Reprinted from the *Journal of Consumer Research,* 12 (September 1985), pp. 142–154.

- *What is the nature of time?*
  Time consists of the past, present, and future, of which the future is most important.
- *What is the nature of activity?*
  Doing, not being, is the appropriate mode of activity.
- *What is the nature of our relationship to other people?*
  A focus on the gratification of the individual is the main interest in social relations (Spates 1983).

Others have forwarded similar characterizations. For example, Inkeles and Smith (1974) maintain that in industrialized societies, interpersonal relations are based upon (1) rationality, (2) formality, (3) hierarchical social stratification, and (4) achieved status. Further, consumers in such societies are depicted as possessing distinctive traits: they are seen to be more innovative relative to new products/ideas, to have more highly developed personal preferences, to exhibit higher levels of information seeking, to be more motivated toward personal achievement, to seek mastery and control over their environments, to place greater value on technology and mechanization, and to exhibit higher levels of materialism and a desire to consume (Bakan 1966; Becker 1966; McClelland 1961; Spindler and Spindler 1983).

Given this ideological orientation, it is not surprising that most conceptualizations of and conjecture about consumer behavior presuppose (1) individuals who (2) actively seek novel information and (3) make personal decisions, which lead to (4) utilitarian—or at least pragmatic—goals (see, for example, Bettman 1979; Engel, Blackwell and Kollat 1978; Howard and Sheth 1969). Further, even authors critical of the highly rational, problem-solving perspective that dominates consumer research often take as their premise the notion that consumption is most meaningfully construed as a process *centered within the individual*—as opposed to, say, the group, the tribe, or society (see, for example, Holbrook and Hirschman 1982).

In contrast to the prevailing view of the American consumer as a modern individual, I would like to present a dialectical—and likely controversial—proposition. I propose that embedded within modern American society is a variety of archaic processes, practices, and institutions that have a significant impact upon consumers' behaviors and beliefs. I suggest that personal spirituality and ancestral tradition inform many acts of consumption, that communal methods of resource distribution are actively practiced, and that ethnic group identity may dominate personal preferences in several consumption contexts. I further propose that these manifestations of the *primitive* within modern society are not antiquated anomalies, but rather vital and enduring aspects of our society.

In popular usage, the word primitive may conjure up images of blood-thirsty savages, barbaric tribal rituals, or a bare subsistence lifestyle. Conversely, to the more liberal-minded it may recall romantic images of Rousseau's noble savage, a gentle people living in harmony with nature, or a purer, less compromised mythic past for humanity. However, the lexical definition of primitive is as follows (Webster's New Collegiate Dictionary 1975):

1. assumed as a basis, primary, original;
2. of or relating to an earlier age or period, primeval;
3. closely approximating an early ancestral type, little evolved.

The sense in which the present paper uses the term "primitive" incorporates all three of these lexical meanings. I will be examining primary human processes—such as resource exchange and spirituality—and the traditions surrounding them. I will argue that many of these primary processes are little evolved from earlier periods and are directly traceable to ancestral origins.

A comprehension of these phenomena is important to the study of consumer behavior for three reasons. First, such comprehension will enable researchers to better understand how consumption may have occurred during prior historic periods (see, for example, Belk 1984a). Current research efforts are tightly focused on present-day consumption phenomena; no historically based articles have yet appeared in the

Journal of Consumer Research. This is regrettable because consumption has evolved and changed over the millennia, helping to shape and being shaped by each form of human interaction. Given the here and now orientation of most consumer research inquiries, it would appear that consumption burst forth full-blown during the latter 1960s, like Athena from the head of Zeus. How well would current theories of consumer behavior account for the consumption practices in pre-Colonial Africa or America, or even rural England in the 1800s (Braudel 1976)?

Second, despite the fact that the majority of consumer behavior investigations are conducted in industrialized countries (see, for example, Anderson and Engledow 1977; Boddewynn 1981; Douglas 1976; Ehrenberg and Goodhardt 1968), there are still several nonindustrial societies whose consumption patterns have remained largely intact. As Barnard (1983) reports, anthropological interest in contemporary hunter-gatherer societies has generated three recent conferences: "Man the Hunter" (Chicago 1966), the "International Conference on Hunting and Gathering" (Paris 1978), and the "Second International Conference on Hunting and Gathering Societies" (Quebec 1980). Although industrial development may have isolated societies such as these into the more peripheral and inaccessible regions of the earth, still it must be recognized that information-processing theories of brand choice or models of decision nets for major durables will likely shed little light on the consumption activities of the Andaman Islanders, the Australian Western Desert Aborigines, or the Kalahari Bushmen. As Geertz suggests (1983, p. 59):

> The Western conception of the person as a bounded, unique, more or less integrated motivational and cognitive universe, a dynamic center of awareness, emotion, judgment, and action organized into a distinctive whole . . . is, however, incorrigible it may seem to us, a rather peculiar idea within the context of the world's cultures.

Although anthropologists commonly incorporate the examination of consumption processes in their ethnographic analyses of non-industrialized peoples, the converse—that consumer researchers incorporate consideration of non-industrialized people's consumption processes into models of consumer behavior—does not hold. Consumer researchers appear to be blind to societies other than industrial and periods of history other than the present.

A third reason why a comprehension of primitive consumption phenomena can benefit the study of consumer behavior is found in the proposition cited at the outset—that several aspects of consumption in modern American society are primitive; that is, they arise from little-evolved, traditional, communal, and ancestral-based sources. As I will show, these phenomena are not vestigial or outmoded patterns of behavior, but rather are vital, integral components of modern-day consumers' life styles.

Perhaps the foremost proponent of these long-term social structure features is Braudel (1976, 1981), who has argued for the reconceptualization of human history as a series of layers, ranging from the deep and largely stable processes dictated by the natural environment to the more rapidly changing (and hence, more readily observable) processes of societal and personal activity. From this perspective, history is viewed as a series of "wheels within wheels" moving at graduated rates of speed; although each wheel is connected to all others, it is not reducible to or entirely determinant of the cycle of processes evolving more slowly/rapidly than itself.

In two major areas, I posit that modern-day consumption phenomena are linked to a "slowly turning wheel." These two areas are (1) the investing of products with a *spiritual significance* by modern-day consumers, and (2) the *ethnic-based* and *ancestral-based* origins of much modern-day consumption activity.

THE SPIRITUALITY OF PRODUCTS

One characteristic often attributes to primitive societies is a lack of rigid boundaries between the natural and the supernatural (see, for example, Levy-Bruhl 1966; Parsons 1979; Polanyi and Prosch 1975; Yengoyan 1979). Yengoyan observes (1979, pp. 398–399):

> One of the underlying themes in Aboriginal thought is the continuous collapsing of the natural into the supernatural and the supernatural into the natural. . . . The natural/supernatural distinction . . . has no relevance in Aboriginal culture and only divides the continuity of cultural form into arbitrary and meaningless categories. . . . For most Aboriginal cultures the terrain . . . is not only a territorial phenomenon, but also a spiritual force.

This primitive spirituality is one which permeates the physical sphere of experience, rather than being set apart from it. In modern terminology, primitive spirituality does not separate church from state, the Kingdom of God from the Kingdom of Man, or the here and now from the hereafter.

As noted in the previous discussion of modern values, it is widely assumed that such distinctions are made in modern societies—that is, that the sacred and the secular are carefully contained in separate experiential spheres to be consumed at appropriate times and in appropriate ways, much like the keeping of separate utensils for the consumption of *milchik* and *fleshik* in orthodox Jewish households. I do not believe this is the case; often, I propose, the natural and the supernatural are entwined during consumption, and to attempt to segregate them in theory—especially with the all too frequent assumption that secular interests dominate spiritual ones—is false. One could cite blatant examples of this intertwining: for instance, the refusal of some fundamentalist sects to seek medical assistance for illnesses (Ostling 1984); the inclusion of Creationism in school texts (McGrath 1984); the displaying of crucifixes or medals of saints by consumers either on their person or in their automobiles to ward off harm (Schumer 1984); or the recent concern reported in *Time* that the Olympic flame (ignited from the sun in Athens) would go out during its cross-country trek and have to be sent back to Greece for relighting—a cigarette lighter would not be suitable (Stanley 1984). But there are more subtle and perhaps more meaningful ways in which primitive spirituality suffuses consumption.

In their recent book, *The Meaning of Things,* Czikszentmihalyi and Rochberg-Halton (1982) examined consumption from a humanistic vantage point. In so doing, they arrived at a novel way of categorizing consumers and their possessions that is directly relevant to the notion of primitive spirituality. Primitive spirituality is centered around the embodiment of transcendant concepts in concrete objects (Goldwater 1967); similarly, Czikszentmihalyi and Rochberg-Halton employ the term *cultivation* to refer to the extent to which an individual invests psychic energy (i.e., spirituality) in his/her personal possessions. The more a spiritual relationship is cultivated between the consumer and the objects s/he has acquired over a lifetime, the more those objects come to transcend their constraints as a mere assemblage of physical features and to embody the ideals and recollections that the consumer holds most dear. Personal possessions, thus cultivated, become as shrines for the individual; they become the means by which personal values can be made manifest and visible. As those authors state (Czikszentmihalyi and Rochberg-Halton 1982, p. 38):

> We can now see more clearly the scope and the meaning of representations. The objects that people use, despite their incredible diversity . . . appear to be signs on a blueprint that represent the relation of man to himself, to his fellows, and to the universe.

Czikszentmihalyi and Rochberg-Halton propose a biaxial model of personal orientation that determines in large part the amount of spirituality a consumer will invest in his/her possessions. The two orthogonal axes are differentiation/integration and activity/contemplation. The differentiation and activity poles of their respective axes are associated with consumers who make little attempt to cultivate spirituality with either possessions or other people. In essence, these consumers subscribe to the modern value system that places primary emphasis on products' technical performance features and advocates separation of the individual from others and mastery over the external environment (Spindler and Spindler 1983).

Conversely, consumers oriented toward the integration and contemplation poles of the two axes experience spiritual in-dwelling (Polanyi and Prosch 1975) with the objects they have chosen to possess. These objects represent for them a path to transcendence of the material world either as objects of aesthetic contemplation or as existential linkages to family, friends, ancestors, and anticipated future generations. In essence, Czikszentmihalyi and Rochberg-Halton propose that the first type of consumer acquires possessions in order to achieve *materiality;* the second type of consumer acquires possessions to attain *ethereality*.

This second type of consumer, the one who *cultivates* possessions, evinces what I have labeled primitive spirituality in his/her consumption of products. What is especially intriguing is that the Czikszentmihalyi and Rochberg-Halton schema was developed from observation of present-day Americans—primarily families residing in and around Chicago, Illinois. Hence the integrative-contemplative consumer is alive and dwelling among us. It is also perhaps not surprising that these authors, given their humanistic personal values, advocate the generation of more such consumers. They favor the Zen rather than the Galbraithian road to affluence alluded to by Sahlins (1960).

Czikszentmihalyi and Rochberg-Halton summarize the rationale for the presence of primitive consumption spirituality in modern society more eloquently than I could; thus I let them speak for me (1982, p. 145):

> Despite a superficial veneer of modernity, the main concerns of these people are largely the same ones that have moved men and women at least since the beginnings of recorded history. It seems unlikely that the solution to their aspirations will come from technological and material advances. Despite a standard of living that is many times higher than any of the past or than that now enjoyed by most people in the world, persons in this culture are still confronted by the same fears and frustrations that have threatened the value of life since humans acquired self-consciousness.
>
> Meaning, not material possessions, is the ultimate goal in their lives, and the fruits of technology that fill the contemporary American home cannot alone provide this. People still need to know that their actions matter, that their existence forms a pattern with that of others, that they are remembered and loved, and that their individual self is part of some greater design beyond the fleeting span of mortal years.

ANCESTRY, ETHNICITY, AND CONSUMPTION

A second feature often attributed to primitive societies is the importance of kinship and ancestral traditions (Parsons 1979; Polanyi and Prosch 1975). Primitive peoples are tribal peoples; and whether nomadic or sedentary, they are organized along kinship lines (Gilmore 1981). Common ancestry, common traditions, and common 'blood' unite them (Schneider 1982). In light of this, my proposal that much consumption in modern, melting pot America occurs in similar ancestral and kin-bounded patterns may appear immediately untenable. However, despite the achieved-status values given widespread lip service in modern societies, ascribed-status realities perform a large role in shaping consumption (Glazer and Moynihan 1975).

I propose that the primitive aspects of ancestry and kinship in American culture reside in its various ethnic groups. An ethnic group possesses several structural and functional qualities of an ancestral and kin-based nature. Members of a given ethnic group (1) generally descend from common forebears (Schneider 1980), (2) tend to reside in the same locale over multiple generations—a locale that is relatively distinct from the territory occupied by another ethnic group (Patai 1977), (3) tend to marry within their own group (Elizabeth Hirschman 1983), (4) invest certain objects with meanings unique to their group across generations—i.e., have tribal totems (Caplow 1984), and (5) share a common sense of peoplehood—of kindredness (Charles Hirschman 1983). In these respects, then, an ethnic group in the United States may function as a kin-based unit bounded by common ancestry. Ethnic identity serves to bind persons together in what Czikszentmihalyi and Rochberg-Halton (1982) term "the miracle of sociability." It provides them with a common set of beliefs and values that informs many of their consumption behaviors and attitudes (Glazer and Moynihan 1975). We turn now to a discussion of the effects of ancestry and kinship on consumption practices in four American ethnic groups: Blacks, Italians, WASPs, and Jews.

Blacks

The effects of ancestry and kinship on consumption practices among Blacks is drawn primarily from Carol Stack's (1974) book, *All Our Kin,* a participant-observer ethnography of a black ghetto called The Flats. Although at the outset it may appear unfair to use a ghetto setting as the template for ethnic consumption patterns characteristic of Blacks, the harsh truth is that such a setting is the most typical one. Since Stack's analyses were written, the socio-economic status (SES) of Blacks has worsened, not improved. James McGhee, Director of Research for the National Urban League, reports that today a majority (55 percent) of black children are born to unmarried, often teen-aged mothers, whereas in 1965 only 26 percent of nonwhite newborns were illegitimate. Half of all black children have no father at home, and the median income of these single-mother households is only $7,458. Poverty accounts for a large part of this family instability; the unemployment rate among black men (16 percent) is nearly three times as high as among white men, and black family incomes are, on the average, 56 percent of white family incomes (McGhee 1984).

Despite their dire lack of material resources, these black consumers have engineered some very effective ways of coping. As the evidence provided by Stack indicates, these coping strategies are predominantly kin-based and constructed from an ancestral rationale. One's "kin" within the black community are those multigenerational relatives (and friends) to whom one may turn for help when it is needed and whose requests for help must always be met—much like Robert Frost's observation about home as the place that "when you have to go there, they have to take you in." Stack (1974, p. 29) reports:

> The (black) poor adopt a variety of tactics in order to survive. They immerse themselves in a domestic circle of kinfolk who will help them. To maintain a stable number of people who share reciprocal obligations . . . people establish socially recognized kin ties. Mothers may actively seek out their children's father's kin, consciously expanding the number of people who are intimately obligated to care for one another.

Stack notes further that "all essential resources flow from families into kin networks. . . . As people swap (goods and services), the limited supply of finished material goods in the community is perpetually redistributed among networks of kinsmen and throughout the community" (p. 33). Virtually any material resource may be incorporated within the process of reciprocal exchange: money, milk, diapers, clothing, automobiles, babysitting, laundry detergent, furniture, housing, food stamps, television sets, cigarettes, beer, and meals.

What belongs to one belongs to all in that consumer's kin network. Just as in many present or past hunting-and-gathering societies, resources are communally owned and distributed on the basis of need (Barnard 1983). For example, Brown (1978) has observed a similar pattern of resource redistribution among tribal groups in New Guinea. Similarly, Moran (1981) reports that among the Arctic Innuit food and goods are frequently distributed to poor and elderly group members, and a hunter who kills a seal shares its meat with relatives who are designated to receive particular parts. The community is thus largely egalitarian; no one is better off than his/her kin. As one resident in the Flats reported, "You not really getting ahead of nobody, you just getting better things as they go back and forth."

Barnard (1983) and Patai (1972) report that

the communal ownership and redistribution of consumption resources serve two important functions. First, they strengthen and reinforce group cohesion. The group, rather than the self, comes to be viewed as the provider of food, apparel, and other of life's necessities. Second, the distribution of products by group consensus serves to prevent, or at least reduce, the development of consumption hierarchies within the group and to promote a sense of oneness or sameness among group members.

In the conclusion of her study, Stack draws a direct analogy between modern Blacks' consumption patterns and those characterizing consumers in non-industrialized societies. She states (Stack 1974, pp. 38–39):

> The trading of goods and services among the [black] poor in complex industrial societies bears a striking resemblance to patterns of exchange organized around reciprocal giving in non-Western societies. Patterns of exchange among people living in poverty and reciprocal exchanges in cultures lacking a political state are both embedded in well-defined kinship obligations. In each type of social system strategic resources are distributed from a family base to domestic groups, and exchange transactions pervade the whole social-economic life of participants. In both of these systems a limited supply of goods is perpetually redistributed through the community.

Also in keeping with primitive societies, modern Blacks' consumption patterns appear to represent a distinct example of *specific evolution* (Sahlins 1960). Instead of gaining instrumental control over the environment and manipulating resources to achieve greater complexity, heterogeneity, and size, primitive societies evolve within their natural environmental constraints. Population and technological development grow to the point at which environmental equilibrium is achieved. Once an adaptive balance is established, further increases in complexity, size, and system heterogeneity become unnecessary and evolution ceases. Similarly, the black community studied by Stack has evolved specific adaptive strategies in response to a set of environmental constraints over which it has had little control. As Stack notes (1974, p. 125), "These highly adaptive structural features of urban Black families comprise a resilient response . . . to poverty, the inexorable unemployment of black women and men, and the access to scarce economic resources of a mother and her children."

Italians

A very thorough participant-observer study of second generation Italians was conducted by Gans (1962) in the West End Section of Boston, Massachusetts. Although Gans's study was published two decades ago and is outdated in some respects (e.g., Italian Americans now are predominately middle class in SES), the majority of Italian Americans are still of first and second generation American residency, and most continue to live in or around major cities (Nelli 1980). The consumers in Gans's study had more steady employment, and hence more material resources, than the Blacks described by Stack in the preceding section. Yet they exhibit many of the same behavior patterns. Their lives and consumption habits, recounted by Gans, echo the earlier themes of group identity and communal resource distribution along kinship lines. In fact, so much did Gans's subjects resemble those in anthropological studies of primitive peoples that he dubbed them "the urban villagers."

Among the West End Italians, communal values prevail. Gans notes, for example, that housing density in the area is very intense, such that there is little opportunity for personal privacy. This does not disturb the residents, however, who enjoy the physical closeness of others. "Hearing and seeing their neighbors' activities gave the West Enders a share in the life that went on around them, which, in turn, made them feel part of the group" (p. 21). Communal values also extend to the ways in which West Enders entertain others in their homes. Instead of trying to impress visitors (who are primarily relatives) by the conspicuous display of differentiating "status" objects in the home, West Enders tend to have similar types and amounts of material goods and to evaluate a man's hospitality "not on the basis of his housing, but on his friendliness, his moral qualities, and his abilities as a [good] host" (p. 21). Similarly, among women "material possessions are not important. . . . What matters . . . is their ability as wives, mothers, and housekeepers. For this reason, the neatness of the apartment and cooking and baking skills are of primary importance" (p. 27).

The dominant force in the life of the West End Italian consumer, according to Gans (1964), is the peer group—usually composed of relatives of the same sex and age. The individual's standing within the community is a direct function of his/her contributions to the group. The individual consumer is expected to display loyalty to the group, conform to the group's established code of conduct, and share material resources with the group. As Gans notes, "Should one mistreat a relative or friend for economic gain, or save his money for purely selfish purposes instead of benefiting family and friends, he will be evaluated negatively" (p. 27). The individual is expected to put the group's goals above his/her own, and the more resources the individual brings to the group, the higher his/her status is within it.

Ancestral traditionalism—that is, tastes and behaviors based directly upon ancestral antecedents—is also apparent among West End Italians, but it is a complex phenomenon. Gans differentiates between *acculturation*—adoption of American cultural artifacts, and *assimilation*—acceptance of and movement into the American social system. The West End Italians are highly acculturated; that is, they own television sets, refrigerators, and wear "American" clothes. Yet, they are not assimilated; the great majority of their social contacts are with other Italians, they marry Italians, and in intimate conversations, they speak Italian to one another. Hence, although they appear to be "Americanized" in a material sense, their social boundaries are largely circumscribed by ethnic identity.

Further, even material consumption is often interpreted according to ethnic traditions. As Gans notes, "A number of Italian [consumption] patterns have survived, the most visible ones being food habits. . . . Most of the women still cook only Italian dishes at home, and many of them still make their own pasta. . . . Entrees are strongly spiced, and desserts are very sweet" (p. 33). Dominant apparel trends in the outside culture are similarly adopted and adapted. "At the time of the study, Ivy League style was beginning to be seen among the young men of the West End. Their version of this style, however, bore little resemblance to that worn on the Harvard campus: flannel colors were darker, shirts and ties were much brighter, and the belt on the back of the pants was more significant in size" (p. 185). Further, even home furnishings reflect the Italian aesthetic: "When the women talked about what furniture they would like to buy . . . they looked forward to the easier to clean, simple styles of today. At the same time, they wanted bright, cheerful colors, strong textures, and enough 'body' to provide comfort" (p. 185).

WASPs

Although their access to consumption resources generally exceeds that of the Italians and Blacks described previously, White Anglo-Saxon Protestants (i.e., WASPs; Baltzell 1964) exhibit several similar ethnic consumption characteristics. For example, they place great emphasis on ancestry and kinship in resource reciprocity (termed the "old boy network," Baltzell 1964). Modern day WASPs are descendants of the English immigrants who founded the original American colonies and who subsequently formed the social and political infrastructure of the United States (Baltzell 1964). This historic fact appears to be underplayed by many scholars of social class (e.g., Coleman 1983; Fussell 1983) who, without explanation, report that members of the American upper class prefer to dress in shabby-genteel clothing; enjoy needlepoint, yachting, golf, and squash in their leisure time; send their children to private boarding schools; eat mushy, bland, overcooked foods; hang oil portraits of their ancestors on the walls; keep spaniels and setters as pets; prefer Heppelwhite, Chippendale, and Queen Anne style furniture in their houses; believe in cleanliness, promptness, and good sportsmanship; name sons after their fathers;

and use the "good silver" for everyday meals. In short, they do everything their English ancestors did (see, for example, Calvert 1984; Ransdell 1975).

That the current behavior of WASPs remains modeled so closely after that of their forebears gives testimony to the fact that they have undergone less specific evolution in their new environment than some other ethnic groups. Instead, their ancestral mores appear to have served as the template to which the behaviors of later immigrants have been expected to conform. As Charles Hirschman notes, "While the melting pot image suggests a blending of cultures, the process was essentially one of 'Angloconformity.' Immigrants were encouraged to learn English and to discard their 'foreign ways' " (1983, p. 398). Erickson describes the dominance of English ethnic customs within early colonial America (1980, p. 319):

> In 1607 people from England began settling permanently in the part of North America that became the United States. From then until the American Revolution, the dominance of English trade and capital, of English language and literature, of the English system of law and law-making, reinforced by the arrival of clergymen, lawyers, and public officials reared or trained in England, produced a culture unmistakably English.

Although the proportion of Americans of English descent had fallen to less than fifty percent by the end of the Revolutionary War period (1780–1800), they continued to dominate American cultural and business affairs and established its initial universities (e.g., Yale 1701, Harvard 1636, and Princeton 1746) and preparatory schools (e.g., Collegiate 1638; Deerfield Academy 1787; Phillips Academy (Andover) 1778; Phillips Exeter 1781), all rigorously modeled after the English system in architecture and curriculum, and continuing sources of WASP ethnic socialization (see, for example, Baltzell 1964; Randsdell 1975). It was these educational institutions that Birnbach (1980) satirized in *The Official Preppy Handbook.* A young WASP currently attending Groton preparatory school provides a caricature of the WASP consumption lifestyle (Dowd 1984, p. 50):

> We want to follow the pattern set for us. . . . We go to Groton. We go to an Ivy League college. We get a nice job. We live in New Canaan, Conn., have a Volvo and a golden retriever and send our kids to Groton. Then we go back and have tailgate parties and drink Bloody Marys.

WASP consumption patterns of the present day can be largely traced to seventeenth and eighteenth century England. For example, preferred modern WASP leisure activities appear to be derivative of skills and pastimes common to their forebears: equestrian ability (now evolved to show-jumping, dressage, polo, fox and hounds), hunting and riflery ability (now expanded to include skeet shooting, as well as the shooting of game and wild fowl), swordsmanship (now fencing), sailing (now crewing, yachting), agriculture (now gardening), fishing (now flycasting), needlepoint, and a variety of sports all having early English or Scottish origins—golf, squash, tennis, rugby, and soccer (Feeley 1983; Fussell 1983; Ransdell 1975). WASPs also adhere to English tradition by wearing neutral colored clothing composed of wool (e.g., Scottish Harris tweed suits, Shetland wool sweaters), cotton (including Indian madras, also of British colonial origin), and leather (preferably with an oiled, not lacquered, finish).[1] Apparel fits the body loosely, due to ethnic sexual mores of modesty, and is worn until it becomes unusable (see, for example, Ransdell 1975). WASPs are not style conscious and have been clothed in essentially the same costumes since the 1920s (Fussell 1983).

In terms of ethnic religious practices,

---

[1]In addition to the sources cited, these leisure and apparel characteristics are also based upon the author's observations of WASP students at Agnes Scott College and Emory University in Atlanta, Georgia, the University of Virginia, Williams College, Duke University, and Choate-Rosemary Hall preparatory school; adult WASP residents of Greenwich, Connecticut, Richmond, Virginia, Atlanta, Georgia and Charleston, South Carolina; members of the English-Speaking Union (Greenwich Chapter); and the Daughters of the American Revolution (New York City).

WASPs are not only Protestant, they are more specifically Episcopalian (i.e., Church of England) if of direct English descent, Presbyterian (i.e., Calvinist) if of direct Scottish descent, or Congregationalist (formerly Puritan) if from Massachusetts. Persons from other ethnic backgrounds wishing to be admitted to the American upper class, which is predominately WASP, are generally expected to convert to the Episcopal Church—i.e., to adopt English religious traditions (Baltzell 1964). This doesn't always succeed, though. Baltzell recounts the sad case of a young man in Larchmont, New York who was a member of the local Episcopal Church, graduated from Harvard, married the daughter of a prominent WASP family, and was still not admitted into the local country club because one of his grandparents was Jewish. Although the Episcopal priest denounced his exclusion, the directors of the Larchmont Country Club stood firm.

Two other manifestations of WASP ethnicity in consumption include the establishment of all-WASP residential communities, and the founding of several genealogical societies to preserve ancestral traditions. For example, Tuxedo Park, New York was a community conceived, designed, and constructed by Pierre Lorillard to protect the WASP ethnic elite from the incursions of foreign immigrants entering New York City during the 1880s (Baltzell 1964). To build Tuxedo Park, Lorillard "surrounded seven thousand acres with an eight-foot fence, graded some thirty miles of road, built a complete sewage and water system, a gatehouse which looked like the frontispiece of an English novel, a clubhouse staffed with imported English servants, and twenty-two casement dormered English turreted cottages. . . . Tuxedo was a complete triumph" (Baltzell 1964). Residents of Tuxedo, all taken from the (WASP) Social Register, passed their time playing tennis, croquet, golf, and squash, sailing upon the lake, and riding over its thirty miles of bridle paths.

Today, Tuxedo Park remains largely unchanged. A 1984 article in *Town and Country* provides the following description of its current WASP inhabitants, some of whom are descendants of the original residents (Insinger 1984, p. 188):

"Tuxedo is paradise regained," sighs Mrs. Dale Jenkins, overlooking the lush, formal garden from the pillared veranda of her century-old house, where nanny rules the nursery, and the restoration of the finer things—corniced ceilings, tea at five, civic duty—is a daily commitment. "You buy a way of life when you buy a house here. It is a twentieth-century Jane Austen kind of place. There are the village church, the village school, the racquet sports, and the social events around the club. . . . It isn't a chic place, but a place where the important values are lived every day. People can laugh at our security gate, but it really does keep a lot of the ugliness of the world out."

Robert Rushmore, descendant of Tuxedo's first doctor says (p. 193):

What is so extraordinary about Tuxedo is that so many of the buildings here are the same as they have always been—the gatehouse, the great houses, the church. Even the IGA in town is exactly the same as when I was a child growing up here. The sewers, the water pressure, the roads are all the same as they were in Lorillard's day. In that sense, Tuxedo has stopped time.

The article concludes with a description of the inhabitants' leisure activities (p. 262):

On the three sun-silvered lakes and through the park's untamed natural garden . . . Tuxedoites pursue the simple pleasures five minutes from their front doors. Up-to-par players and duffers swing together through the Robert Trent Jones-designed golf links. Devotees of wing and shot aim toward the hills populated with upland game and grouse. Seaworthy sybarites skim the virginal reservoir waters undisturbed by motor rat-tat-tat. Kingly court-tennis players sharpen their mental acumen on one of America's nine court-tennis courts. Wielders of hard racquets, squash raquets, tennis and paddle-tennis racquets display their mild aggressions only in the service of the sport.

Another ethnic practice of WASPs is their establishment of multiple genealogical associations to keep track of ancestral lineage, encourage interactions among group members, and preserve ethnic traditions (White 1984, p. 221). Perhaps the best known of these ancestral associations is the Daughters of the American Revolution (DAR). Founded in 1890, the DAR today has over 209,000 members in 3,150 chapters in all fifty states, the District of Columbia, England, France, and Canada ("From the Congressional Record," *DAR Magazine* 1984). To belong to the DAR, one must descend directly from a person who served as a patriot in the Revolutionary War. Because virtually all of these individuals were of British descent, the DAR's potential membership is largely limited to modern-day WASPs. An informative example of present WASP consumption values and emphasis on English ethnic origins is provided in a DAR chapter advertisement for Mrs. William G. Wilt that states (*DAR Magazine,* April 1984):

> The home of Mrs. William George Wilt is an historical landmark located on a high bank overlooking the Carquinez Straights in Benicia. The one hundred and thirteen year-old Victoria design eleven-room mansion is built of redwood on a site which was originally an Indian camping ground. It is beautifully furnished with antiques from the Perry and Martin plantations of Virginia. On the walls hang many rare portraits of Mr. and Mrs. Wilt's ancestors.
>
> Lillian Martin Wilt (Mrs. William George), a third-generation member of the Daughters of the American Revolution, was born 15 December 1890 and has been a loyal and dedicated member of DAR for 62 years. Her paternal heritage includes Cyrus and Sarah Mills, founders of the prestigious Mills College of Oakland, and from John and Sarah Roberts Martin of New Hampshire. Through this line she is related to the Presidential Adams family. Her maternal ancestry is from William Perry of England who settled in the Jamestown colony.

The emphasis upon ancestry and ancestral possessions by WASPs is a vivid manifestation of the cultivation concept suggested by Cziksszentmihalyi and Rochberg-Halton (1982). Possessions passed down through the generations recall the lifestyles and deeds of the progenitors of today's WASPs; such objects are the repositories of a form of ethnic collective unconscious. An article by Ransdell on descendants of the First Families of Virginia (F.F.V.) describes this phenomenon with some poignance. She notes (1975, p. 153):

> What we are talking about with F.F.V. encompasses two ideas. First is the reality of genealogy; second is a state of mind, an emotional tie to land, continuity, and values. . . . The values are based on a common past and a common vision of the past—of great brick houses and servants, hunt-breakfasts and debutante balls. . . . Material things take on a value beyond the monetary; the old brooch, the silver service are filled with memories, associations, ghosts.

Jews

Ethnic aspects of American Jews provide several interesting contradictions. On one hand, modern Jews follow many traditions that are ancient: the passing of an actual tribal identity (e.g., Cohen, Levi) through the paternal line; a 3,000 year-old monotheistic religious ideology; the *bris* ritual in which eight-day-old male infants are circumcised by a specialist, termed a *moel;* the *bar/bat mitzvah* ritual in which the 13-year-old Jew is declared an adult member of the group; and the marriage ritual performed under a *chuppa*—a tent-like canopy reminiscent of the group's ancestral residence. Additional atavistic features include retention in religious ceremonies of the original tribal language—Hebrew—and a few items of ancient Semitic apparel; e.g., the woven black-on-white cotton *tallis,* or prayer-shawl.

On the other hand, American Jews have exhibited very marked tendencies toward specific evolution; that is, toward altering their attitudes and improvising their behavior where such improvisation has been believed advantageous. Thus, the essential irony of current Jewish consumers is that although much of their ancient ritual remains intact, Jews as a group are perhaps the most modern of any Americans. Research has indicated that American Jews are strongly competitive, eclectic, rational, innovative, cognitively complex, individualistic, information-seeking, and achievement-oriented—the psychological hallmarks of modernity (Hirschman 1979; Patai 1977). Yet they are credited with having a stronger ethnic identity than WASPs, Italians, or Blacks (Patai 1977).

This contradictory set of influences has resulted in a dualistic set of consumption behaviors. The governing principle of Jewish consumption behavior can best be summarized as follows: in consumption behaviors externally visible to non-Jews (for example, WASPs), Jewish consumers will generally conform to prevailing social values. Since the SES of Jews is generally on a par with that of WASPs, this means that, externally, they will tend to mimic WASP consumption patterns. Conversely, in consumption behaviors not externally visible to non-Jews, such as religious ceremonies, Jews will tend to act in ways that are unique to their group. One successful young Jewish stockbroker known to the author who is employed at a Wall Street firm dominated by WASPs summarized this principle nicely—his policy, he says, has always been to "dress British; think Yiddish."

I recently conducted a participant-observer study of this phenomenon in the affluent town of Great Neck on the North Shore of Long Island, New York. Great Neck has a population of 65,000 people, approximately 80 percent of whom are second and third generation Jewish Americans. The Jewish residents are primarily professionals (e.g., lawyers, doctors) and successful business entrepreneurs. The names given the specific neighborhoods in the community symbolize the residents' achievement-motivation and desire to excel in the United States—Lake Success, Kings Point, Great Neck Estates. Normally, 85 to 90 percent of high school students attend college. Much like the Italians described by Gans, the Jews residing in Great Neck maintain aspects of their ethnic heritage in private conversations by the use of Yiddish expressions, and although few homes "keep kosher," European foods common to their countries of origin are frequently consumed—e.g., borscht, blintzes, latkes, cheesecake, lox, smoked sturgeon, as well as some of a more semitic origin—e.g., matzoh, bialys. During the Passover Seder, foods specifically associated with Jewish history—matzoh brie, bitter herbs, lamb, and honey cake—are consumed by family members in the confines of the home.

However, the public consumption of Jews in Great Neck can be characterized largely as Angloconformity. The housing styles, for example, range from Tudor to Colonial, and lawns and hedges are closely trimmed. There are public and private tennis courts, golf courses, and boating facilities. And during the Christmas season, while many of the Jewish residents observe the eight days of Hanukah by burning menorah candles in their homes, there is a lifesize Nativity creche among other Christmas decorations set up on the village green. Patai describes this external Angloconformity by Jews as follows (1977, p. 393):

> On the popular level, it has often been observed that the Jews are like the [WASP] Gentiles, only more so. . . . One almost feels as if Jews had a compulsion to outdo the [WASP] Gentiles in all those activities and behavioral features they find attractive enough to emulate. . . . Their suburban Jewish centers, synagogues, or temples with religious schools affiliated and with recreational and adult educational facilities are as a rule larger and more luxurious than the Christian churches and their appendages. . . . Having for long been excluded from [WASP] Gentile urban and country clubs, they set up such facilities as a rule with more luxurious premises.

As far as personal appearance customs are concerned, Jews again appear to be largely imitative of WASPs. Perhaps one of the most vivid and compelling examples of conformity to the WASP appearance is the frequency with which Jewish women undergo rhinoplasty to acquire English-looking noses. This is a very interesting phenomenon: an ethnic physical characteristic (and not just a purchasable material artifact) is permanently altered to make members resemble those of another group. Although to non-Jews it might seem that this topic would be a touchy subject among Jews, it is rather openly discussed. *The Official J.A.P.*[2] *Handbook,* a hu-

[2]J.A.P. means Jewish American Princess/Prince, an ethnic euphemism for an over-indulged Jewish child.

morous book about modern Jewish consumption practices recently written by a Jewish woman, has an entire section discussing "nose jobs" (Schneider 1982, p. 100):

> Of course, everyone knows about nose jobs. It's what the young female JAP gets for her sixteenth birthday. . . . These days many young male JAPs have nose jobs as well. A nose job is another Rite of Passage, in some communities as important as a bar or bat mitzvah. . . . And, big news, nose jobs are now successfully being done on twelve-year-olds!

Another point of Angloconformity among Jews is the first names given to children. There appears to be a trend among modern Jews toward anglicizing traditional Hebrew tribal names. For example, the *Official J.A.P. Handbook* suggests the following transpositions from Hebrew to English: Yehudah = Jeffrey, Baruch = Bruce, Moshe = Mitchell, Yoram = Jeremy, Avram = Allen, Golda = Jennifer, Leah = Laurie, and even Chaim = Christopher.

THEORETICAL AND METHODOLOGICAL IMPLICATIONS

Articles before this one have argued for the incorporation of an anthropological perspective within consumer research (Winick 1961) and for more emphasis on cultural tradition in generic forms of consumption (Olshavsky and Granbois 1979). Recently Levy has stated, "Does the field of marketing need anthropology, as it so evidently needs and employs mathematics, psychology, and economics? Implicitly, there can be no doubt of it" (1978, p. 557). And yet, with very few exceptions—the most notable being the work of Levy himself (cf. Boyd and Levy 1963; Gardner and Levy 1955; Levy 1969; Levy 1981)—there has been little progress toward bringing an anthropological perspective to bear upon consumption phenomena within the discipline of consumer research. (As already noted, consumption is frequently an object of study within cultural anthropology.)

The most likely explanation for this, I believe, is that consumer researchers are often emotionally and intellectually unwilling to acknowledge that anthropological processes may be operating in the lives of modern consumers (and therefore, by extension, in their own lives). We are unwilling to accept and utilize a research perspective that implies the existence of phenomena such as emotive ritual, ancestral tradition, spiritual attachment to concrete possessions, kin-based resource reciprocity, and all of those primitively based beliefs, behaviors, and bequests that we believe ourselves to have been civilized out of. Because we are unwilling to acknowledge them in ourselves, we are unwilling to perceive and examine them in other consumers.

Instead, we want to see consumers whose behaviors and attitudes are thoroughly objective and rational (as we believe our own to be), whose decisions are arrived at through logical contemplation of information gathered in a careful and consistent manner (much like our own), and who are too sophisticated, educated, and modern to be subject to ancestral taboos or preferences, to slavishly follow any tradition simply because it is there, or to embrace a ritual merely because it was beloved by their forebears. To adhere to such primitive practices, we believe, is not modern, not rational, and not scientific; so we deny their existence in ourselves and in others. We look for logical rationality only, and we find it only.

Consumer researchers are not alone in projecting scientific rationality on others like themselves. Anthropologists, also, as Levy (1978) and Winick (1961) observe, have been slow to dig in their own backyards—to observe their neighbors instead of some comfortably distant exotic culture. How much easier it is on the psyche to observe and record the tradition-bound peculiarities of some far-off tribe than to recognize in ourselves these same features. Miner once wrote a rather insightful and very witty ethnography about a tribal people now residing in the territory between Canada and

Mexico—the "Nacirema." About the Nacirema/American, he observes (1956, p. 503):

> Nacirema culture is characterized by a highly developed market economy which has evolved in a rich natural habitat. While much of the people's time is devoted to economic pursuits, a large part of the fruits of these labors and a considerable portion of the day are spent in ritual activity. The focus of this activity is the *human body,* the appearance and health of which loom as a dominant concern in the ethos of the people. While such a concern is certainly not unusual, its ceremonial aspects and associated philosophy are unique.
>
> The fundamental belief underlying the whole system appears to be that the human body is ugly and that its natural tendency is to debility and disease. Incarcerated in such a body, man's only hope is to avert these characteristic through the use of the powerful influences of ritual and ceremony. Every household has one or more shrines devoted to this purpose. The more powerful individuals in the society have several shrines in their houses and, in face, the opulence of a house is often referred to in terms of the number of such ritual centers it possesses.

Levy (1978, p. 561), comparing these same Nacirema to ethnographic accounts of other tribes, writes:

> Malinowski refers to the semicommercial and the semiceremonial aspects of the Kula exchange system; and Mauss emphasizes the pre-market and nonmarket aspects of giving and receiving. . . . In modern marketing study, it is possible to see that all "ordinary" transactions are similarly invested with significance, that a woman's bridge luncheon, a family dinner, the arrival of the new car, and so forth are as meaningful and as expressive of numerous social contracts, cultural values, and so on as the Kula and the potlatch of the Kwakiutl. Most of such transactions still await, however, their Malinowskis, Mausses, and Boases to elucidate them.

The present paper has commented on the presence of 'primitivism' in such aspects of American consumption as the spiritual cultivation of possessions, the redistribution of resources among one's kin, and the adherence to ancestral traditions in dress, food, and leisure. These are but a few examples of the kinds of phenomena that a revised view of consumer behavior could permit us to examine. These were chosen because they (1) were well documented, and (2) were believed recognizable to the reader—especially the sentimental attachments made to some possessions and the immense pull of one's ethnicity and family background. Writing about the importance of family, Brandt reiterates this last point (1984, p. 21):

> Unlike Charles, my brother, I couldn't wait to leave my hometown. I didn't have roots, and I didn't put them down. A quintessentially American attitude.
>
> Have I changed? Yes and no. I am still an itinerant, living on one coast at the moment but dreaming about the other one . . . and I still have no interest whatsoever in returning to live in the flatlands of New Jersey. But I'm older, and I understand my limits better; I know that I come from a certain family and a certain background that formed me, and that there's nothing I can do about it. I am who I am, the son of Grace Scott and Axel Brandt, grandson of Swedish American grandparents on my father's side whose first names I don't think I ever knew, nephew of numerous uncles and aunts on both sides, a cousin of cousins, and now an uncle myself and a father; and this goes on and on. I am embedded in this history, connected to all these people, flesh of their flesh. I have roots, all right, no matter where I live, and it was foolish to think otherwise. . . . These are the most powerful ties, the ones to the people who gave us birth and share our blood, and it hardly seems to matter how many years have passed, how many betrayals there may have been, how much misery in the family; we remain connected, even against our wills.

The impact of ancestry and kinship upon consumption and the spiritual meaning with which they can invigorate our possessions are important avenues for consumer research, because they are so basic—so primitive. Tucker (1967), in his insightful and intriguing volume, "Foundations for a Theory of Consumer Behavior," presented a fascinating account of the purchase of a shirt by a Mexican goat herder, Juan Navarro, as seen by anthropologist J. F. Epstein. That and other vignettes discussed by Tucker were based upon participant-observer methodology. I believe that it would be highly desirable for consumer researchers to make greater use of participant-observer methods and to approach their subject matter as an ethnographic endeavor rather than as some personally distant, objective set of empirical data. It is difficult to see how we will ever delve into the more spiritual, traditional, and primal aspects of consumers' lives if we insist on keeping them at arm's length and using sterile instrumentation in non-realistic environments. For comprehending the kinds of consumption phenomena discussed in this paper, it would appear vital for the researcher to dwell among those consumers s/he is studying both physically and psychically. Belk argues for this same proposition (1984b, pp. 9–10):

> Consumer behavior, to a greater extent than almost any other field, has an opportunity to learn via participant observation. . . . It is probably easiest to get fresh insights at the fringes of unfamiliar territory, rather than in the consumption we know best. For me, three such contexts have been Utah, with its youngest population in the U.S. and unique religious concentration, Florida with its oldest population in the U.S. and retirement communities, and Las Vegas with its unique architecture and naked hedonism.

Participant-observer methods will require not more effort on the part of consumer researchers, but rather different effort. Instead of carefully constructing and pretesting a questionnaire, the researcher would identify and then observe and participate in the consumption behaviors s/he is interested in studying. For Belk, these have included observing consumers' behavior in Las Vegas, Florida retirement communities, and the Mormon population of Utah. For this author, similar insights have come from attending D.A.R Chapter meetings, listening to lectures on British culture at the English-Speaking Union, attending Rosh Hashanah and Yom Kippur services in New York City, and celebrating Passover and Hanukah, Christmas and Easter among the faithful. We should not be afraid to use ourselves as the measuring instrument, to record through our own humanness the meaning of consumption, of possessions, and of their attendant rituals and traditions.

CONCLUSIONS

This paper has described the structural characteristics, ideologies, and consumption traits of primitive societies and of some primitive subcultures within present American society. It has been argued that current consumer-behavior theory is largely founded upon a modern normative base. This perspective may bear little resemblance to the realities of consumption in primitive societies. To the extent that modern norms operating within the consumer research production infrastructure bias investigators to see only certain outcomes and activities as consumer behavior and to interpret these outcomes and activities only within a highly rationalized framework, modern consumer research theories may have limited validity.

Only careful consideration of possible—albeit unintentional—biases in both the assumptions and findings underlying our current knowledge can reveal the extent to which it is "storybook" theory—appealingly logical, but behaviorally invalid. In the marketing literature, arguments have recently been made for a relativist, contextual approach to research (Deshpande 1983; Peter and Olson 1983). This approach stressed the subjective, phenomenological, holistic aspects of events and behaviors; it advocates the necessity of researcher empathy and in-dwelling in order to acquire understanding. The introduction of such an orientation to consumer research would likely enable us to more clearly detect the types of societies and consumers to which our current knowledge does and does not apply.

REFERENCES

ANDERSON, RONALD, and JACK ENGLEDOW (1977), "A Factor Comparison of U.S. and German Information Seekers," *Journal of Consumer Research,* 3 (March), 185–196.

BAKAN, PAUL (1966), *The Duality of Human Existence.* Chicago: Rand-McNally.

BALTZELL, E. DIGBY (1964), *The Protestant Establishment: Aristocracy and Caste in America.* New York: Random House.

BARNARD, ALAN (1983), "Contemporary Hunter-Gatherers," *Annual Review of Anthropology,* 12, 193–214.

BECKER, HOWARD (1966), "Current Sacred-Secular Theory and its Development," in *Modern Sociological Theory,* Eds. Howard Becker and Alvin Boskoff. New York: Holt, Rinehart & Winston, 140–149.

BELK, RUSSELL W. (1984a), "Against Thinking," paper presented at the National Theory Conference, American Marketing Association, Fort Lauderdale, FL.

______ (1984b), "Manifesto for a Consumer Behavior of Consumer Behavior," *Advances in Consumer Research,* Vol. 11, Ed. Thomas C. Kinnear. Provo, UT: Association for Consumer Research.

BETTMAN, JAMES R. (1979), *An Information Processing Theory of Consumer Choice.* Reading, MA: Addison-Wesley.

BIRNBACH, LISA, Ed. (1980), *The Official Preppy Handbook.* New York: Workman.

BODDEWYNN, JEAN J. (1981), "Comparative Marketing: The First Twenty-Five Years," *Journal of International Business Studies,* 12 (Spring/Summer), 61–76.

BOYD, HARPER W., and SIDNEY J. LEVY (1963), "New Dimension in Consumer Analysis," *Harvard Business Review,* November-December, 129–140.

BRANDT, ANTHONY (1984), "Bloodlines: Other Things May Change Us, But We Start and End With Family," *Esquire,* September, 21–22.

BRAUDEL, FERNAND (1976), *Capitalism and Material Life 1400–1800,* trans. Miriam Kochran. New York: Harper & Row.

______ (1981), *On History,* trans. S. Mathews. London: Weiderfeld & Nicolson.

BROWN, PAULA (1978), "New Guinea: Ecology, Society, and Culture," *Annual Review of Anthropology,* 7, 263–291.

CALVERT, CATHERINE (1984), "Christmas in Old Newport," *Town and Country,* September, 189–200.

CAPLOW, THEODORE (1982), "Christmas Gifts and Kin Networks," *American Sociological Review,* 47 (June), 383–392.

______ (1984), "Rule Enforcement without Visible Means: Christmas Gift Giving in Middletown," *American Journal of Sociology,* 86, 1306–1323.

COLEMAN, RICHARD P. (1983), "The Continuing Significance of Social Class to Marketing," *Journal of Consumer Research,* 10 (December), 265–280.

CZIKSZENTMIHALYI, MIHALY, and EUGENE ROCHBERG-HALTON (1982), *The Meaning of Things: Domestic Symbols and the Self.* Cambridge, MA: Cambridge University Press.

DESHPANDE, ROHIT (1983), "Paradigms Lost: On Theory and Method in Research in Marketing," *Journal of Marketing,* 47 (Fall), 101–110.

DOUGLAS, SUSAN P. (1976), "Cross-National Comparisons: A Case Study of Working and Non-Working Wives in the U.S. and France," *Journal of Consumer Research,* 3 (June), 12–20.

DOWD, MAUREEN (1984), "Prep Schools in Struggle to Curb Spread of Cocaine," *New York Times,* May 17, 1, 50.

EHRENBERG, A. S. C., and CHARLES J. GOODHARDT (1968), "A Comparison of American and British Repeat-Buying Habits," *Journal of Marketing Research,* 5 (February), 29–33.

ENGEL, JAMES F., ROGER D. BLACKWELL, and DAVID T. KOLLAT (1978), *Consumer Behavior* (3rd ed.). Hinsdale, IL: Dryden Press.

ERICKSON, CHARLOTTE J. (1980), "The English," in *Harvard Encyclopedia of American Ethnic Groups,* Ed. Stephan Thernstrom. Cambridge, MA: Harvard University Press, 319–336.

FEELEY, FALK (1983), *A Swarm of Wasps.* New York: Quill.

FIREBAUGH, GLENN (1983), "Scale Economy or Scale Entropy: Country Size and Rate of Economic Growth, 1950–1977," *American Sociological Review,* 48 (April), 257–269.

"From the Congressional Record," (1984), *Daughters of the American Revolution Magazine* (May), 335.

FUSSELL, PAUL (1983), *Class: A Guide Through the American Status System.* New York: Summit Books.

GANS, HERBERT J. (1962), *The Urban Villagers.* New York: The Free Press.

GARDNER, BURLEIGH, and SIDNEY J. LEVY (1955), "The Product and the Brand," *Harvard Business Review* (March/April), 33–39.

GEERTZ, CLIFFORD (1983), *Local Knowledge.* New York: Basic Books.

GILMORE, DAVID D. (1980), "Anthropology of the Mediterranean Area." *Annual Review of Anthropology,* 11, 175–205.

GLAZER, NATHAN, and DANIEL P. MOYNIHAN

(1975), *Ethnicity: Theory and Experience.* Cambridge, MA: Harvard University Press.

GOLDWATER, ROBERT (1967), *Primitivism in Modern Art.* New York: Vintage Books.

HIRSCHMAN, CHARLES (1983), "America's Melting Pot Reconsidered," *Annual Review of Sociology,* 9, 397–423.

HIRSCHMAN, ELIZABETH C. (1981), "American Jewish Ethnicity: its Relationship to Some Selected Aspects of Consumer Behavior," *Journal of Marketing,* 45 (Summer), 102–110.

——— (1983), "Religious Affiliation and Consumption Processes: An Initial Paradigm," in *Research in Marketing,* Ed. Jagdish N. Sheth. Greenwich, CT: JAI Press.

HOLBROOK, MORRIS B., and ELIZABETH C. HIRSCHMAN (1982), "The Experiential Aspects of Consumption: Consumer Fantasies, Feelings, and Fun," *Journal of Consumer Research,* 9 (September), 132–140.

HOWARD, JOHN A., and JAGDISH N. SHETH (1969), *The Theory of Buyer Behavior.* New York: Wiley.

INKELES, ALEX, and DAVID H. SMITH (1974), *Becoming Modern.* Cambridge, MA: Harvard University Press.

INSINGER, WENDY (1984), "The Greening of Tuxedo Park," *Town and Country* (May), 187–198, 261, 262.

KLUCKHOHN, FRANCES (1950), "Dominant and Substitute Profiles of Cultural Orientations," *Social Forces,* 28, 376–393.

——— (1961), *Variations in Value Orientations.* Bloomington, IN: Row, Peterson.

LEVI-STRAUSS, CLAUDE (1966), *The Savage Mind.* Chicago: University of Chicago Press.

LEVY-BRUHL, LUCIEN (1966), *The Soul of the Primitive.* New York: Praeger Press.

LEVY, SIDNEY J. (1959), "Symbols for Sale," *Harvard Business Review,* (July/August), 117, 124.

——— (1978), "Hunger and Work in a Civilized Tribe," *American Behavioral Scientist,* 21 (March/April), 557–570.

——— (1981), "Interpreting Consumer Mythology: A Structural Approach to Consumer Behavior," *Journal of Marketing,* 45 (Summer), 49–63.

LOWIE, ROBERT H. (1940), *An Introduction to Cultural Anthropology.* New York: Farrar & Rinehart.

MCCLELLAND, DAVID C. (1961), *The Achieving Society.* Princeton, NJ: D. Van Nostrand.

MCGHEE, JAMES D. (1984), "A Profile of the Black, Single, Female-Headed Household," in *The State of Black America.* New York: National Urban League.

MCGRATH, ELLIE (1984), "Texas Eases up on Evolution," *Time,* April 30, 81.

MINER, HORACE (1956), "Body Ritual among the Nacirema," *American Anthropologist,* 58, 503–507.

MOORE, WILBERT E. (1979), *World Modernization: The Limits of Convergence.* New York: Elsevier.

MORAN, EMILIO F. (1981), "Human Adaptation to Arctic Zones," *Annual Review of Anthropology,* 10, 1–25.

NELLI, HUMBERT S. (1980), "Italians," *Harvard Encyclopedia of American Ethnic Groups.* Cambridge, MA: Harvard University Press, 545–560.

OLSHAVSKY, RICHARD, and DONALD GRANBOIS (1979), "Consumer Decision Making: Fact or Fiction?" *Journal of Consumer Research,* 6 (September), 93–100.

OSTLING, RICHARD N. (1984), "Matters of Faith and Death," *Time,* April 16, 42.

PARSONS, TALCOTT (1979), *The Evolution of Societies* Englewood Cliffs, NJ: Prentice-Hall.

PATAI, RAPHAEL (1972), *The Arab Mind.* New York: Scribner.

——— (1977), *The Jewish Mind.* New York: Scribner.

PETER, J. PAUL, and JERRY C. OLSON (1983), "Is Science Marketing?" *Journal of Marketing,* 47 (Fall), 111–125.

POLANYI, MICHAEL and HARRY PROSCH (1975), *Meaning.* Chicago: University of Chicago Press.

RADIN, PAUL (1971), *The World of Primitive Man.* New York: Dutton.

RANSDELL, MARY LOUISE (1975), "Town and Country visits the Daughters of the First Families of Virginia," *Town and Country* (December), 145–153, 202, 232.

SAHLINS, MARSHALL D. (1960), "Evolution: Specific and General" in *Evolution and Culture,* Eds. M. D. Sahlins and E. R. Service. Ann Arbor, MI: University of Michigan Press, 12–44.

SCHNEIDER, ANNA M. (1982), *The Official J.A.P. Handbook.* New York: New American Library.

SCHUMER, FRAN (1984), "A Return to Religion," *New York Times Magazine,* April 15, 90–97.

SPATES, JAMES L. (1983), "The Sociology of Values," in *Annual Review of Sociology,* 9, 27–49.

SPINDLER, GEORGE D., and LOUISE SPINDLER (1983), "Anthropologists View American Culture," in *Annual Review of Anthropology,* 12, 49–78.

STACK, CAROL (1974), *All Our Kin: Strategies for Survival in a Black Community.* New York: Harper & Row.

STANLEY, ALESSANDRA (1984), "An Olympic Ideal Gets Burned," *Time,* May 14, 26.

TUCKER, WILLIAM T. (1967), *Foundations for a Theory of Consumer Behavior.* New York: Holt, Rinehart & Winston.

WHITE, ELIZABETH COX (1984), "Lineage Research," *Daughters of the American Revolution Magazine* (April), 221.

WHITE, LESLIE (1959), *The Evolution of Culture.* New York: McGraw-Hill.

WINICK, CHARLES (1961), "Anthropology's Contribution to Marketing," *Journal of Marketing,* 25 (July), 53-60.

YENGOYAN, ARAM A. (1979), "Economy, Society, and Myth in Aboriginal Australia," *Annual Review of Anthropology,* 8, 393-415.

CULTURE AND CONSUMPTION: A Theoretical Account of the Structure and Movement of the Cultural Meaning of Consumer Goods*

30

Grant McCracken

Cultural meaning in a consumer society moves ceaselessly from one location to another. In the usual trajectory, cultural meaning moves first from the culturally constituted world to consumer goods and then from these goods to the individual consumer. Several instruments are responsible for this movement: advertising, the fashion system, and four consumption rituals. This article analyzes the movement of cultural meaning theoretically, showing both where cultural meaning is resident in the contemporary North American consumer system and the means by which this meaning is transferred from one location in this system to another.

Consumer goods have a significance that goes beyond their utilitarian character and commercial value. This significance rests largely in their ability to carry and communicate cultural meaning (Douglas and Isherwood 1978; Sahlins 1976). During the last decade, a diverse body of scholars has made the cultural significance of consumer goods the focus of renewed academic study (Belk 1982; Bronner 1983; Felson 1976; Furby 1978; Graumann 1974–1975; Hirschman 1980; Holman 1980; Leiss 1983; Levy 1978; McCracken 1985c; Prown 1982; Quimby 1978; Rodman and Philibert 1985; Schlereth 1982; Solomon 1983). These scholars have established a subfield extending across the social sciences that now devotes itself with increasing clarity and thoroughness to the study of "person-object" relations. In this article, I

*Reprinted from the *Journal of Consumer Research,* 13 (June 1981), pp. 71–84.

propose to contribute a theoretical perspective to this emerging subfield by showing that the meaning carried by goods has a mobile quality for which prevailing theories make no allowance.

A great limitation of present approaches to the study of the cultural meaning of consumer goods is the failure to observe that this meaning is constantly in transit. Cultural meaning flows continually between its several locations in the social world, aided by the collective and individual efforts of designers, producers, advertisers, and consumers. There is a traditional trajectory to this movement. Usually, cultural meaning is drawn from a culturally constituted world and transferred to a consumer good. Then the meaning is drawn from the object and transferred to an individual consumer. In other words, cultural meaning is located in three places: the culturally constituted world, the consumer good, and the individual consumer, and moves in a trajectory at two points of transfer: world to good and good to individual. Figure 30.1 summarizes this relationship. In this article I propose to analyze this trajectory of meaning, taking each of its stages in turn.

Appreciating the mobile quality of cultural meaning in a consumer society should help to illuminate two aspects of consumption in modern society. First, such a perspective encourages us to see consumers and consumer goods as the way-stations of meaning. In this manner, we focus on structural and dynamic properties of consumption that have not always been emphasized. Second, the "trajectory" perspective asks us to see such phenomena as advertising, the fashion world, and consumption rituals as instruments of meaning movement. We are encouraged to acknowledge the presence of a large and powerful system at the heart of modern consumer society that gives this society some of its coherence and flexibility even as it serves as a constant source of incoherence and discontinuity. In sum, this perspective can help to demonstrate some of the full complexity of current consumption behavior and to reveal in a more detailed way just what it is to be a "consumer society."

FIGURE 30.1 Movement of Meaning

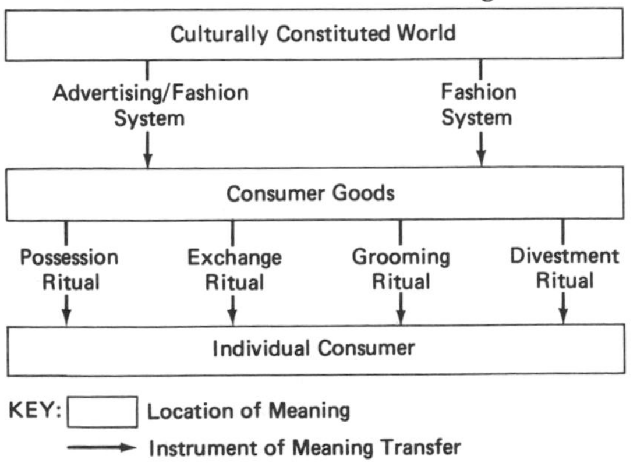

LOCATIONS OF CULTURAL MEANING: THE CULTURALLY CONSTITUTED WORLD

The original location of the cultural meaning that ultimately resides in consumer goods is the culturally constituted world. This is the world of everyday experience in which the phenomenal world presents itself to the individual's senses fully shaped and constituted by the beliefs and assumptions of his/her culture. Culture constitutes the phenomenal world in two ways. First, culture is the "lens" through which the individual views phenomena; as such, it determines how the phenomena will be apprehended and assimilated. Second, culture is the "blueprint" of human activity, determining the co-ordinates of social action and productive activity, and specifying the behaviors and objects that issue from both. As a lens, culture determines how the world is seen. As a blueprint, it determines how the world will be fashioned by human effort. In short, culture constitutes the world by supplying it with meaning. This meaning can be characterized in terms of two concepts: cultural categories and cultural principles.

Cultural Categories

Cultural categories are the fundamental co-ordinates of meaning (McCracken 1985a), representing the basic distinctions that a culture uses to divide up the phenomenal world. For instance, all cultures specify categories of time. In our culture these categories include an elaborate system that can discriminate units as fine as a "second" and as vast as a "millennium." Our culture also makes less precise but no less significant distinctions between leisure and work time, sacred and profane time, and so on. Cultures also specify categories of space. In our culture these categories include measurement and "occasion." Cultures also segment the flora, fauna, and landscape of natural and supernatural worlds into categories. Perhaps the most important categories are those that cultures create in the human community—the distinctions of class, status, gender, age, and occupation.

Cultural categories of time, space, nature, and person make up the vast body of categories, creating a system of distinctions that organizes the phenomenal world. Each culture establishes its own special vision of the world, thus rendering the understandings and rules appropriate to one cultural context preposterously inappropriate in another. A specific culture makes a privileged set of terms, within which virtually nothing appears alien or unintelligible to the individual member of the culture and outside of which there is no order, no system, no safe assumption, and no ready comprehension. In sum, by investing the world with its own particular meaning, culture "constitutes" the world. It is from a world so constituted that the meaning destined for consumer goods is drawn.

Cultural Categories in Contemporary North America

It is worth noting that cultural categories in present day North America appear to have unique characteristics. First, they possess an indeterminacy that is not normally evident in other ethnographic circumstances. For instance, cultural categories of person are marked by a persistent and striking lack of clarity, as are cultural categories of age. Second, they possess an apparent "elective" quality. Devoted as it is to the freedom of the individual, contemporary North American society permits its members to declare at their own discretion the cultural categories they presently occupy. Exercising this freedom, teenagers declare themselves adults, members of the working class declare themselves middle class, the old declare themselves young, and so on. Category membership, which in most cultures is more strictly specified and policed, is in our own society much more a matter of individual choice. In our culture, individuals are to a great extent what they claim to be, even when these claims are, by some sober sociological reckoning, implausible.

We must note a third characteristic of cultural categories in contemporary North America: they are subject to constant and rapid change. The dynamic quality of present day North American cultural categories plainly adds to their indeterminacy. More important, however, this dynamism also makes our cultural categories subject to the manipulative efforts of the individual. Social groups can seek to change their place in the categorical scheme, while marketers can seek to establish or encourage a new cultural category of person (e.g., the teenager, the "yuppie") in order to create a new market segment. Cultural categories in contemporary North America are subject to rethinking and rearrangement by several parties.

The Substantiation of Cultural Categories

Cultural categories are the conceptual grid of a culturally constituted world. They determine how this world will be segmented into discrete, intelligible parcels and how these parcels will be organized into a larger coherent system. For all their importance, however, cultural categories have no substantial presence in the world they organize. They are the scaffolding on which the world is hung and are therefore invisible. But cultural categories are constantly substantiated by human practice. Acting in conformity with the blueprint of culture, the members of a community are constantly realizing categories in the world. Individuals continually play out categorical distinctions, so that the world they create is made consistent with the world they imagine. In a sense, the members of a culture are constantly engaged in the construction—the constitution—of the world they live in.

One of the most important ways in which cultural categories are substantiated is through a culture's material objects. As we shall see in a moment, objects are created according to a culture's blueprint and to this extent, objects render the categories of this blueprint material and substantial. Thus, objects contribute to the construction of the culturally constituted world precisely because they are a vital, tangible record of cultural meaning that is otherwise intangible. Indeed, it is not too much to say that objects have a "performative" function (Austin 1963; Tambiah 1977) insofar as they give cultural meaning a concreteness for the individual that it would not otherwise have. The cultural meaning that has organized a world is made a visible, demonstrable part of that world through goods.

The process by which a culture makes its cultural categories manifest has been studied in some detail by anthropologists. Structural anthropology has supplied a theoretical scheme for this study, and several subspecialties, such as the anthropologies of art, clothing, housing, and material culture, have supplied areas of particular investigation. As a result of this work, there is now a clear theoretical understanding of the way in which linguistic and especially nonlinguistic media express cultural categories (Barthes 1967; deSaussure 1966; Levi-Strauss 1963, p. 116; Sahlins 1976). There is also a wide range of empirical investigation into the areas of spatial organization (Doxtater 1984), house form (Bourdieu 1973; Cunningham 1973), art (Fernandez 1966; Greenberg 1975), clothing (Adams 1973; McCracken 1986; Schwarz 1979), ornament (Drewal 1983), technology (Lechtman and Merrill 1977), and food (Appadurai 1981; Douglas 1971; Ortner 1978). This study of material culture has helped to show how the world is furnished with material objects that reflect and contribute to its cultural constitution—how cultural categories are substantiated.

The Substantiation of Cultural Categories in Goods

Goods may be seen as an opportunity to express the categorical scheme established by a culture. Goods are an opportunity to make culture material. Like any other species of material culture, goods allow individuals to discriminate visually among culturally specified categories by encoding these categories in the form of a set of material distinctions. Categories of person divided into parcels of age, sex, class, and occupation can be represented in a set of material distinctions by means of goods. Categories of space, time, and occasion can also be reflected in this medium of communication. Goods help substantiate the order of culture.

Several studies have examined the way in which goods serve in this substantiation. Sahlins' study (1976) of the symbolism of North American consumer goods examines food and clothing "systems" and shows their correspondence to cultural categories of person. Levy's (1981) study of the correspondence between food types and cultural categories of sex and age in American society is another excellent illustration of the way in which one can approach the demographic information carried in goods from a structuralist point of view. Both of these studies demonstrate that the order of goods is modelled on the order of culture. Both studies also demonstrate that much of the meaning of goods can be traced back to the categories into which a culture segments the world. The substantiation of class categories by consumer goods has been considered by Belk, Mayer, and Bahn (1981), Coleman (1983), Davis (1956), Form and Stone (1957), Goffman (1951), Sommers (1963), Vershure, Magel, and Sadalla (1977), and Warner and Lunt (1941). The substantiation of gender categories has been less well examined but appears to be drawing more scholarly attention (Allison et al. 1980; Belk 1982; Hirschman 1984; Levy 1959). The substantiation of age categories also appears to be receiving more attention (Disman 1984; Olson 1985; Sherman and Newman 1977–1978; Unruh 1983).

Cultural Principles

Cultural meaning also consists of cultural principles. In the case of principles, meaning resides in the ideas or values that determine how cultural phenomena are organized, evaluated, and construed. If cultural categories are the result of a culture's segmentation of the world into discrete parcels, cultural principles are the organizing ideas by which the segmentation is performed. Cultural principles are the charter assumptions that allow all cultural phenomena to be distinguished, ranked, and interrelated. As the orienting ideas for thought and action, cultural principles find expression in every aspect of social life, goods not least of all.

Cultural principles, like cultural categories, are substantiated by material culture in general and consumer goods in particular. It is worth observing that cultural categories and cultural principles are mutually presupposing, and their expression in goods is necessarily simultaneous. Therefore, goods are incapable of signifying one without signifying the other. When goods show a distinction between two cultural categories, they do so by encoding something of the principle according to which the two categories have been distinguished. Thus, the clothing that distinguishes between men and women or between high and low classes also reveals something of the nature of the differences that are supposed to exist between these categories (McCracken 1985c). Clothing communicates both the supposed "delicacy" of women and "strength" of men or both the supposed "refinement" of a higher class and "vulgarity" of a lower one. Apparently, the categories of class and sex are never communicated without this indication of how and why they are to be distinguished. The world of goods, unlike that of language, never engages in a simple signalling of difference. In fact, goods are always more forthcoming and more revealing. In the world of goods, signs are always, in a sense, more motivated and less arbitrary than in the world of language.

Cultural principles in contemporary North America have the same indeterminate, changeable, elective quality that cultural categories do. Such principles as "naturalism" can fall into disrepute in one decade, only to be rehabilitated and advanced to a new place of importance in another, as occurred in the 1950s. The principle of "disharmony" that the punk aesthetic finds so useful was once not a principle but merely the term for phenomena that had somehow escaped the successful application of another principle. The ethnographic literature on the meaning of objects as principle may be found in Adams (1973), Drewal (1983), Fernandez (1966), and McCracken (1982a). Substantive literature that shows the presence and nature of the meaning of objects as principle in contemporary North American society is not abundant. Levy (1981) makes passing reference to this question, as does Sahlins (1976), and the idea is implicitly treated in the work of Lohof (1969) on the meaning carried by the Marlboro cigarette. The idea also surfaces in the attempt of sociologists to make objects an index of status and class. For example, Laumann and House (1970) sought to establish the meaning of household furniture and resorted to the principles of "modern" and "traditional." Felson in his study of "material life styles" (1976) posited something called a "bric-a-brac factor" while Davis (1958) coined the term "Bauhaus Japanesey" to characterize a certain principle of interior design. The principle of "science" (or, more exactly, the concern for technical mastery of nature and the confidence that human affairs can be benignly transformed through technological innovation) was a favorite motif of the kitchen appliances and automobiles in 1950s and 1960s North America (Czikszentmihalyi and Rochberg-Halton 1981, p. 52). Scholars in the material culture arm of American studies and art history have made the most notable contribution here (Quimby 1978; Schlereth 1982). Prown (1980) and Cohen (1982), for instance, have examined the principles evident in American furniture.

It is plain in any case that, like cultural categories, cultural principles are substantiated by consumer goods, and these goods, so charged, help make up the culturally constituted world. Both cultural categories and principles organize the phenomenal world and the efforts of a community to manipulate this world. Goods substantiate both categories and principles and therefore enter into the culturally constituted world as both the object and objectification of this world. In short, goods are both the creations and the creators of the culturally constituted world.

INSTRUMENTS OF MEANING TRANSFER: WORLD TO GOOD

Meaning first resides in the culturally constituted world. To become resident in consumer goods, meaning must be disengaged from this world and transferred to goods. The present section proposes to examine two of the institutions that are now used as instruments of meaning transfer: advertising, and product design as practiced in the fashion system.

Advertising

Advertising works as a potential method of meaning transfer by bringing the consumer good and a representation of the culturally constituted world together within the frame of a particular advertisement. The creative director of an advertising agency seeks to conjoin these two elements in such a way that the viewer/reader glimpses an essential similarity between them. When this symbolic equivalence is successfully established, the viewer/reader attributes to the consumer good certain properties s/he knows exist in the culturally constituted world. The known properties of the culturally constituted world thus come to reside in the unknown properties of the consumer good and the transfer of meaning from world to good is accomplished.

The mechanics of such a complicated process deserve more detailed exposition. The creative director is concerned with effecting the successful conjunction of two elements, one of which is specified by a client. In most cases, the client gives the director a consumer good, the physical properties and packaging of which are fixed and not subject to manipulation. The second element, the representation of the culturally constituted world, is constrained and free in almost equal proportions. The client, sometimes drawing on marketing research and advice, will specify the properties being sought for the consumer good. Armed with these specifications, the creative director now enjoys a wide range of discretionary control. Subject only to the negative constraints of budgetary limitations and the positive constraints of a continuous brand image, the director is free to deliver the desired symbolic properties in any one of a nearly infinite number of ways.

This delivery process consists of a lengthy and elaborate series of choices (Dyer 1982; McCracken 1984; Sherry 1985; Williamson 1978). The first choice is a difficult one. The director must identify with sufficient clarity for his/her own purposes the properties that are sought for the good in question. This procedure sometimes results in a period of complicated discourse between client and director where the parties alternatively lead and follow one another into a sharpened appreciation of the properties sought for the consumer good. In any case, the advertising firm will enter into its own consultative process in order to establish clarity sufficient for its own purposes. The second choice in the delivery process is equally difficult but perhaps less consultative. The director must decide where the properties desired for the ad reside in the culturally constituted world. The director has at his/her disposal a vast array of possibilities from which to choose. Place must be selected, and the first choice here is whether the ad will have a fantasy setting or a naturalistic one. If the latter is chosen, it must be decided whether it will be an interior or an exterior setting, an urban or rural landscape, or a cultivated or untamed environment. Time of day and time of year must also be chosen. If people are to appear in the advertisement, their sex, age, class, status, and occupation must be selected and their clothing and body postures and affective states specified (Goffman 1979). These are the pieces of the culturally constituted world that can be evoked in the ad.

It must be noted that this selection process can be performed more or less well, according to the skill and training of the director. There is no simple route from the desired properties for the consumer good to the pieces of the culturally constituted world that can evoke them in the advertisement. As members of the advertising profession point out, this is a creative process where the most appropriate selections for the advertisement are not so much calculated as glimpsed. Imprecision and error in this creative process are not only possible but legion. It must also be noted that the process of selection, because it is creative, proceeds at unconscious as well as conscious levels. Directors are not always fully cognizant of how and why a selection is made, even when this selection presents itself as compelling and necessary (e.g., Arlen 1980, pp. 99, 119).

In sum, the director must choose from among alternatives that have been created by the network of cultural categories and principles that constitute a culture's world. The chosen alternatives will reflect those categories and principles that a director decides most closely approximate the meaning that the client seeks for the product. Once these two choice processes are complete, a third set of choices must be made. The director must decide just how the culturally constituted world is to be portrayed in the advertisement. This process consists of reviewing all of the objects that substantiate the selected meaning and then deciding which of these objects will be used to evoke this meaning in the advertisement. Finally, the director must decide how to present the product in its highly contrived context. Photographic and visual conventions will be exploited to give the viewer/reader the opportunity to glimpse an essential equivalence between the two elements of world and object. The director must bring these two elements into a conjunction that encourages a metaphoric identification of sameness by the would-be consumer. World and good must seem to enjoy a special harmony—must be seen to go together. When the viewer/reader glimpses this sameness (after one or many exposures to the stimuli), the process of transfer has taken place. Meaning has shifted from the culturally constituted world to the consumer good. This good now stands for a cultural meaning of which it was previously innocent.

Visual images and verbal material appear to assume a very particular relationship in this transfer process. It is chiefly the visual aspect of an advertisement that conjoins the world and the object when a meaning transfer is sought. Verbal material serves chiefly as a kind of prompt that instructs the viewer/reader in the salient properties that are supposed to be expressed by the visual part of the advertisement. Text (especially headlines) makes explicit what is already implicit in the image. Text provides instructions on how the visual part of the advertisement is to be read. The verbal component allows the director to direct the viewer/reader's attention to exactly those meaningful properties that are intended for transfer (cf. Barthes 1983, pp. 33–39; Dyer 1982, pp. 139–182; Garfinkle 1978; Moeran 1985).

All of this must now be successfully decoded by the viewer/reader. It is worth emphasizing that the viewer/reader is the final author in the process of transfer. The director brings the world and the consumer good into conjunction and then suggests their essential similarity. It is left to the viewer/reader to see this similarity and effect the transfer of meaningful properties. To this extent, the viewer/reader is an essential participant in the process of meaning transfer, as Williamson (1978, pp. 40–70) notes. The viewer/reader must complete the work of the director.

Advertising is a conduit through which meaning constantly pours from the culturally constituted world to consumer goods. Through advertising, old and new goods continually give up old meanings and take on new ones. As active participants in this process, the viewer/reader is kept informed of the present state and stock of cultural meaning that exists in consumer goods. To this extent, advertising serves as a lexicon of current cultural meanings. In large part, advertising maintains a consistency between what Sahlins calls the "order of culture" and the "order of goods" (1976, p. 178).

The Fashion System

The fashion system is less frequently observed, studied, and understood as an instrument of meaning movement, yet this system also serves as a means by which goods are systematically invested and divested of meaningful properties. The fashion system is a somewhat more complicated instrument for meaning movement than advertising. In the case of advertising, movement is accomplished by the efforts of an advertising agency to unhook meaning from a culturally constituted world and transfer it to a consumer good by means of an advertisement. In the case of the fashion system, the process has more sources of meaning, agents of transfer, and media of communication. Some of this additional complexity can be captured by noting that the fashion world works in three distinct ways to transfer meaning to goods.

In one capacity, the fashion system performs a transfer of meaning from the culturally constituted world to consumer goods that is remarkably similar in character and effect to the transfer performed by advertising. The same effort to conjoin aspects of the world and a consumer good is evident in magazines or newspapers, and the same process of glimpsed similarity is sought after. In this capacity, the fashion system takes new styles of clothing or home furnishings and associates them with established cultural categories and principles, moving meaning from the culturally constituted world to the consumer good. This is the simplest aspect of the meaning-delivery capacity of the fashion system (and ironically, the one that Barthes (1983) found so perplexing and difficult to render plain).

In a second capacity, the fashion system actually invents new cultural meanings in a modest way. This invention is undertaken by opinion leaders who help shape and refine existing cultural meaning, encouraging the reform of cultural categories and principles. These are distant opinion leaders: individuals who by virtue of birth, beauty, or accomplishment are held in high esteem. These distant opinion leaders are sources of meaning for individuals of lesser standing. In fact, it has been suggested that the innovation of meaning is prompted by the imitative appropriations of those of low standing (McCracken 1985c; Simmel 1904). Classically, the high-standing individuals come from a conventional social elite: the upper classes. These classes, for instance, originated the "preppie look" that has recently trickled down so widely and deeply. More recently, opinion leaders have come from a group of unashamedly nouveau riche characters who now dominate television in evening soap operas such as "Dallas" and "Dynasty" and who appear to have influenced the consumer and lifestyle habits of so many North Americans. Motion picture and popular music stars, revered for their status, their beauty, and sometimes their talent, also form a relatively new group of opinion-leaders. All of these new opinion leaders invent and deliver a species of meaning that has been largely fashioned from the prevailing cultural coordinates established by cultural categories and cultural principles. These opinion leaders are permeable to cultural innovations, changes in style, value, and attitude, which they then pass along to the subordinate parties who imitate them.

In a third capacity, the fashion system engages in the radical reform of cultural meanings. Some part of the cultural meaning of western industrial societies is always subject to constant and thoroughgoing change. This radical instability of meaning is due to the fact that western societies are, in the language of Claude Levi-Strauss (1966, pp. 233–234), "hot societies." Western societies willingly accept, indeed encourage, the radical changes that result from deliberate human effort and the effect of anonymous social forces (Braudel 1973, p. 323; Fox and Lears 1983; McCracken 1985d; McKendrick, Brewer, and Plumb 1982). As a result, cultural meaning in a hot, western, industrial, complex society is constantly undergoing systematic change. In contradistinction to virtually all ethnographic precedent, members of such a society live in a world that is deliberately and continually being transformed (McCracken 1985b). Indeed, it is no exaggeration to say that hot societies demand change and depend on it to drive certain economic, social, and cultural sectors in their world (cf. Barber and Lobel 1953; Fallers 1961). The fashion system serves as one of the conduits to capture and move highly innovative cultural meaning.

The groups responsible for the radical reform of cultural meaning are those existing at the margins of society, e.g., hippies, punks, or gays (Blumberg 1974; Field 1970; Meyerson and Katz 1957). Such groups invent a much more radical, innovative kind of cultural meaning than their high-standing partners in meaning-diffusion leadership. Indeed, such innovative groups represent a departure from the culturally constituted conventions of contemporary North American society. They illustrate the peculiarly western tendency to tolerate dramatic violations of cultural norms. These groups redefined cultural categories, if only through the negative process of violating such cultural categories as age and status (hippies and punks), or gender (gays). The redefined cultural categories and a number of attendant cultural principles have now entered the cultural mainstream. The innovative groups become "meaning suppliers" even when they are devoted to overturning the established order (e.g., hippies) or are determined not to allow their cultural inventions to be absorbed by the mainstream (e.g., punks; cf. Hebidge 1979; Martin 1981).

If the sources of cultural meaning are dynamic and numerous, so are the agents who gather up cultural meaning and effect its transfer to consumer goods. In the case of the fashion system, the agents form two main categories: (1) product designers, and (2) fashion journalists and social observers. Product designers may sometimes be the very conspicuous individuals who establish themselves as arbiters of clothing design in fashion centers such as Paris or Milan, and who surround themselves with a cult of personality. Other product designers, e.g., architects and interior designers, sometimes achieve a roughly comparable stature and exert an equally international influence (Kron 1983). More often, however, they are unknown outside their own industries (Clark 1976; Meikle 1979; Pulos 1983). The designers of Detroit automobiles are a case in point here, as are the product developers in the furniture and appliance industries. (Individuals such as Raymond Loewy are exceptions that prove the rule.)

The second category of agents consists of fashion journalists and social observers. Fashion journalists may belong to the print or film media and may have a high or a low profile. Social observers may be journalists who study and document new social developments—e.g., Lisa Birnbach (1980), Kennedy Fraser (1981), Tom Wolfe (1970), Peter York (1980), or they may be academics who have undertaken a roughly similar inquiry from a somewhat different point of view—e.g., Roland Barthes (1972), and Christopher Lasch (1979). Market researchers are beginning to serve in this capacity as well—e.g., John Naisbett (1982), Arnold Mitchell (1983), and possibly, John Molloy (1977).

These groups share a relatively equal division of labor. Journalists perform their part of the enterprise by serving as gate keepers of a sort. They review aesthetic, social, and cultural innovations as these first appear and then classify the innovations as either important or trivial. In this respect, journalists resemble the gatekeepers in the art (Becker 1972) and music (Hirsch 1972) worlds. Journalists are supposed to observe as best they can the whirling mass of cultural innovation and decide what is ephemeral and what will endure. After they have completed their difficult winnowing process, journalists engage in a dissemination process to make their decisions known. It must be admitted that everyone in the diffusion chain (Rogers 1983) plays a gatekeeping role and helps to influence the tastes of individuals looking for opinion leadership. Journalists are especially important because they make their influence felt even before an innovation passes to its "early adopters" (Baumgarten 1975; Meyersohn and Katz 1957; Polegato and Wall 1980).

When journalists have identified genuine innovations, product designers begin the task of drawing meaning into the mainstream and investing it in consumer goods. The product designer differs from the advertising agency director in that she/he transforms not only the symbolic properties of a consumer good but also its physical properties. Apart from fashion and trade shows (which reach only some potential consumers), the product designer does not have a meaning-giving context such as the advertisement where she/he can display the consumer good. Instead, the consumer good will leave the designer's hands and enter any context the consumer chooses. Product design is the means a designer has to convince the consumer that a specific object possesses a certain cultural meaning. The object must leave the designer's hands with its new symbolic properties plainly displayed in its new physical properties.

The designer, like the agency director, depends on the consumer to supply the final act of association and effect the meaning transfer from world to object. But unlike the agency director, the product designer does not have at his/her disposal the highly managed, rhetorical circumstances of an advertisement to encourage and direct this meaning transfer. The designer can not inform the consumer of the qualities intended for the object; these qualities must be self-evident in the object, so the consumer can effect the meaning transfer for him/herself. Therefore, it is necessary that the consumer have access to the same sources of information about new fashions in meaning that the designer has. The journalist makes this information available to the consumer so that s/he can identify the cultural significance of the physical properties of a new object. In short, the designer relies on the journalist at the beginning and then again at the very end of the meaning transfer process. The journalist supplies new meaning to the designer as well as to the recipient of the designer's work. In this way, both advertising and the fashion system are instruments for the transfer of meaning from the culturally constituted world to consumer goods. They are two of the means by which meaning is invested in the object code. It is thanks to them that the objects of our world carry such a richness, variety, and versatility of meaning and can serve us so variously in acts of self-definition and social communication.

LOCATIONS OF CULTURAL MEANING: CONSUMER GOODS

That consumer goods are the locus of cultural meaning is too well-established a fact to need elaborate demonstration here. This is what Sahlins has to say about one product category—clothing (1976, p. 179):

> Considered as a whole, the system of American clothing amounts to a very complex scheme of cultural categories and the relations between them, a veritable map—it does not exaggerate to say—of the cultural universe.

What can be said of clothing can be said of virtually all other high-involvement product categories and several low-involvement ones. Clothing, transportation, food, housing exteriors and interiors, and adornment all serve as media for the expression of the cultural meaning that constitutes our world.

That goods possess cultural meaning is sometimes evident to the consumer and sometimes hidden. Consumers may consciously see and manipulate such cultural meanings as the status of a consumer item. Just as often, however, individual consumers recognize the cultural meaning carried by consumer goods only in exceptional circumstances. For instance, consumers who have lost goods because of burglary, sudden impoverishment, or the divestment that occurs with aging evidence a profound sense of loss and even mourning (Belk 1982, p. 185). The possession rituals about to be discussed also suggest that the meaningful properties of consumer goods are not always conspicuously evident to a consumer, however much they serve to inform and control his/her action.

It was observed at the beginning of this article that the last decade has seen an outpouring of work on the cultural significance of consumer goods. Indeed, the wealth of this literature reassures us that the study of the cultural meaning carried by goods is a flourishing academic enterprise. None of this literature, however, addresses the question of the mobile quality of cultural meaning, and we may wish to make this question an operative assumption in the field. When we examine the cultural meaning of consumer goods, we may wish to determine where cultural meaning came from and how it was transferred.

INSTRUMENTS OF MEANING TRANSFER: GOOD TO CONSUMER

Thus far we have tracked the movement of cultural meaning from the culturally constituted world to consumer goods and have considered the role of two instruments in this process. We must now address how meaning, now resident in consumer goods, moves from the consumer good into the life of the consumer. In order to describe this process, a second set of instruments of meaning transfer must be discussed. These instruments appear to qualify as special instances of "symbolic action" or ritual (Munn 1973; Turner 1969). Ritual is a kind of social action devoted to the manipulation of cultural meaning for purposes of collective and individual communication and categorization. Ritual is an opportunity to affirm, evoke, assign, or revise the conventional symbols and meanings of the cultural order. To this extent, ritual is a powerful and versatile tool for the manipulation of cultural meaning. In the form of a classic rite of passage, ritual is used to move an individual from one cultural category of person to another, where she/he gives up one set of symbolic properties, e.g., those of a child, and takes up another, e.g., those of an adult (Turner 1967; Van Gennep 1960). Other forms of ritual are devoted to different social ends. Some forms are used to give "experiential reality" to certain cultural principles and concepts (Tambiah 1977). Still other forms are used to create certain political contracts (McCracken 1982b). In short, ritual is put to diverse ends in its manipulation of cultural meaning. In contemporary North America, ritual is used to transfer cultural meaning from goods to individuals. Four types of rituals are used to serve this purpose: exchange, possession, grooming, and divestment rituals. Each of these rituals represents a different stage in a more general process by which meaning is moved from consumer good to individual consumer.

Exchange Rituals

In contemporary North American exchange rituals—especially Christmas and birthday rituals—one party chooses, purchases, and presents consumer goods to another (Caplow 1982). This movement of goods is also potentially a movement of meaningful properties. Often the gift-giver chooses a gift because it possesses the meaningful properties she/he wishes to see transferred to the gift-receiver. Thus, the woman who receives a particular kind of dress is also made the recipient of a particular concept of herself as a woman (Schwartz 1967). The dress contains this concept and the giver invites the recipient to define herself in its terms. Similarly, many of the continuous gifts that flow between parents and children are motivated by precisely this notion. The gifts to the child contain symbolic properties that the parent would have the child absorb (Furby 1978, pp. 312–313).

The ritual of gift exchange establishes a potent means of interpersonal influence. Gift exchange allows individuals to insinuate certain symbolic properties into the lives of a gift recipient and to initiate possible meaning transfer. In more general terms, consumers acting as gift-givers are made agents of meaning transfer to the extent that they selectively distribute goods with specific properties to individuals who may or may not have chosen them otherwise. The study of gift exchange, well established in the social sciences (Davis 1972; Mauss 1970; McCracken 1983; Sahlins 1972), is already underway in the field of consumer research (Belk 1979) and deserves further study. Attention must be given to the choice process used by a giver to identify the gift with the cultural meanings she/he seeks to pass along to the recipient. Attention must also be given to the significance of gift wrapping and presentation as well as the context (time and place) in which gift presentations are made. These aspects of the domestic ritual of gift giving are vitally important to the meaningful properties of the goods exchanged.

Possession Rituals

Consumers spend a good deal of time cleaning, discussing, comparing, reflecting, showing off, and even photographing many of their possessions. Housewarming parties sometimes provide an opportunity for display, while the process of home "personalization" (Hirschman 1982, pp. 37–38; Kron 1983; Rapoport 1968, 1982) especially serves as the occasion for much comparison, reflection, and discussion. Though these activities have an overt functionality, they all appear to have the additional effect of allowing the consumer to claim possession as his/her own. This claiming process is not a simple assertion of territoriality through ownership. Claiming is also an attempt to draw from the object the qualities that it has been given by the marketing forces of the world of goods. This process is most conspicuous when it fails to take place. For example, occasionally a consumer will claim that a possession—a car, house, article of clothing, or other meaning-carrying good—"never really seemed to belong to me." There are certain goods that the consumer never successfully claims because she/he never successfully claims their symbolic properties. The consumer good becomes a paradox: the consumer owns it without possessing it; its symbolic properties remain immovable.

Normally, however, the individual successfully deploys possession rituals and manages to extract the meaningful properties that have been invested in the consumer good. If the cultural meaning has been transferred, consumers are able to use goods as markers of time, space, and occasion. Consumers draw on the ability of these goods to discriminate between such cultural categories as class, status, gender, age, occupation, and lifestyle. Since possession rituals allow the consumer to take possession of the meaning of a consumer good, these rituals help complete the second stage of the trajectory of the movement of cultural meaning. As we have seen, advertising agencies and the fashion world move cultural meaning from the culturally constituted world into a consumer good. Using possession rituals, individuals move cultural meaning out of their goods and into their lives.

It is worth observing that possession rituals, especially those devoted to personalizing the object, almost seem to enact on a small scale, and for private purposes, the activities of meaning transfer performed by the advertising agency. The act of personalizing is, in effect, an attempt to transfer meaning from the individual's own world to the newly obtained good. The new context in this case is the individual's complement of consumer goods, which has assumed a personal as well as public meaning. Indeed, perhaps it is chiefly in this way that an anonymous possession—manifestly the creation of a distant, impersonal mass manufacturing process—is turned into a personal possession that belongs to someone and speaks for them. Perhaps it is in this manner that individuals create a personal world of goods that reflects their own experience and concepts of self and world. The meaning that advertising transfers to goods is the meaning of the collectivity. The meaning that personal gestures transfer to goods is the meaning of the collectivity as this meaning has been inflected by the particular experience of the individual consumer.

Grooming Rituals

It is clear that some of the cultural meaning drawn from goods has a perishable nature. As a result, the consumer must draw cultural meaning out of his/her possessions on a repeated basis. When a continual process of meaning transfer from goods to consumer is necessary, the consumer will likely resort to a grooming ritual. The purpose of this ritual is to take the special pains necessary to insure that the special, perishable properties resident in certain clothes, hair styles, and looks are, as it were, "coaxed" out of their resident goods and made to live, however briefly and precariously, in the life of the individual consumer. The "going out" rituals with which one prepares for an evening out are good examples of this process. These rituals illustrate the time, patience, and anxiety with which an individual will prepare him/herself for the special public scrutiny of a gala evening or dinner party. Grooming rituals arm individuals who are "going out" with the particularly glamorous, exalted, meaningful properties that exist in their "best" consumer goods. Once captured and made resident in an individual, these meaningful properties give him/her new powers of confidence, aggression, and defense. The language with which advertisements describe certain make-up, hair-styling goods, and clothing tacitly acknowledges the meaningful properties available in goods that special grooming rituals release.

Sometimes, however, it is not the consumer but the good that must be groomed. This occurs when the consumer cultivates the meaningful properties of an object in the object rather than coaxing out the properties in him/herself. The extraordinary amounts of largely redundant time and energy lavished on certain automobiles is perhaps the best case in point here (Myers 1985, p. 562). This type of grooming ritual supercharges the object so that it, in turn, may transfer special heightened properties to an owner. Here again, the individual's role in meaning investment is evident. The importance to the consumer of cultivating consumer goods so that they can release their meaningful qualities is most strikingly highlighted by the behavior of aging individuals. Sherman and Newman report that the occupants of nursing homes who regard themselves as being "at the end of the line" engage in a process of "decathecting [removing the emotional significance from] the significant objects in their lives" (1977–1978, p. 188).

In the field of consumer research, the study of ritual has been significantly advanced by Rook (1984), who has observed how much consumption behavior is ritualized and who has noted the value of studying consumption from a ritual perspective, and by Rook and Levy (1982), who have examined grooming ritual and grooming product symbolism. It is clear that grooming rituals are one of the means by which individuals effect a transfer of symbolic properties. In grooming rituals, the meaning moves from consumer goods to the consumer. Grooming rituals help draw cultural meaning out of these goods and invest it in the consumer.

Divestment Rituals

Individuals who draw meaning out of goods come to view these meaning sources in personal terms, associating goods with their own personal properties. The possible confusion between consumer and consumer good encourages the use of the divestment ritual. Divestment rituals are employed for two purposes. When the individual purchases a good that has been previously owned, such as a house or a car, the ritual is used to erase the meaning associated with the previous owner. The cleaning and redecorating of a newly purchased home, for instance, may be seen as an effort to remove the meaning created by the previous owner. Divestment allows the new owner to avoid contact with the meaningful properties of the previous owner and to free up the meaning properties of the possession, claiming them for him/herself. The second divestment ritual takes place when the individual is about to dispense with a good, either by giving it away or selling it. The consumer will attempt to erase the meaning that has been invested in the good by association. In moments of candor, individuals suggest that they feel "a little strange about someone else wearing my old coat." In moments of still greater candor, they will confess that they fear the dispossession of personal meaning, a phenomenon that resembles the "merging of identities" that sometimes takes place between transplant donors and recipients (Simmons, Klein, and Simmons 1977, p. 68). Both rituals suggest a concern that the meaning of goods an be transferred, obscured, confused, or even lost when goods change hands (Douglas 1966). Therefore, goods must be emptied of meaning before being passed along and cleared of meaning when taken on. What looks like simple superstition is, in fact, an implicit acknowledgement of the moveable quality of the meaning with which goods are invested.

In sum, personal rituals are variously used to transfer the meaning contained in goods to individual consumers. Exchange rituals are used to direct goods charged with certain meaningful properties to those individuals the gift-giver supposes are needful of these properties. In an exchange ritual, the giver invites the receiver to partake of the properties possessed by the good. Possession rituals are practiced by an owner in order to retrieve a good's meaningful properties. Possession rituals are designed to transfer a good's properties to its owner. Grooming rituals are used to effect the continual transfer of perishable properties—properties likely to fade when possessed by the consumer. Grooming rituals allow the consumer to "freshen" the properties she/he draws from goods. These rituals can also be used to maintain and "brighten" certain of the meaningful properties resident in goods. Finally, divestment rituals are used to empty goods of meaning so that meaning-loss or meaning-contagion cannot take place. All of these rituals are a kind of microcosmic version of the instruments of meaning transfer that move meaning from world to goods, since these rituals move meaning from goods to consumer.

LOCATIONS OF CULTURAL MEANING: INDIVIDUAL CONSUMERS

Cultural meaning is used to define and orient the individual in ways that we are only beginning to appreciate. It is clear that individuals living in a contemporary Western industrial culture enjoy a wide range of choice in the meaning they may draw from goods. It was observed at the start of this article that contemporary North American culture leaves a great deal of the individual undefined. One of the ways individuals satisfy the freedom and fulfill responsibility of self-definition is through the systematic appropriation of the meaningful properties of goods. Plainly this task is not an easy one, nor is it always successful. Many individuals seek kinds of meaning from goods that do not exist there. Others seek to appropriate kinds of meaning to which they are not, by some sober sociological reckoning, entitled. Still others attempt to constitute their lives only in terms of the meaning of goods. All of these consumer pathologies are evident in modern consumption behavior and all of them illustrate how the process of meaning transfer can go wrong, to the cost of the individual and society. In normal situations, however, the individual uses goods in an unproblematical manner to constitute crucial parts of the self and the world. The logic, imperatives, and details of this process of self- and world construction through goods are enormously understudied and are only now attracting rigorous study. Our culture has studied its own beliefs and practices with a thoroughness and enthusiasm unheralded in the ethnographic record. With the same thoroughness and enthusiasm it has also made material possessions one of its most compelling preoccupations. It is therefore doubly odd and unfortunate that the study of the use of goods in the construction of self and world should have suffered such prolonged and profound neglect.

SUMMARY

Only recently has the field of "person-object" relations escaped the limitations imposed upon it by its founding father, Thorstein Veblen. The field has begun to recognize that the cultural meaning carried by consumer goods is enormously more various and complex than the Veblenian insistence on status was capable of recognizing. But now that the field has made this advance, it might consider the possibility of another. It might begin to take account of the alienable, moveable, manipulable quality of meaning. This article has sought to encourage such a development by giving a theoretical account of the structure and movement of the cultural meaning of consumer goods. It has suggested that meaning resides in three locations: the culturally constituted world, the consumer good, and the individual consumer. Advertising, the fashion system, and consumer rituals have been identified as the means by which meaning is drawn out of, and transferred between, these locations. Advertising and the fashion system move meaning from the culturally constituted world to consumer goods, while consumer rituals move meaning from the consumer good to the consumer. This is the trajectory of the movement of cultural meaning in modern developed societies.

REFERENCES

ADAMS, MARIE JEANNE (1973), "Structural Aspects of a Village Art," *American Anthropologist,* 75 (February), 265–279.

ALLISON, NEIL K., LINDA L. GOLDEN, GARY M. MULLET, and DONNA COOGAN (1980), "Sex-Typed Product Images: The Effects of Sex, Sex Role Self-Concept and Measurement Implications," in *Advances in Consumer Research,* Vol. 7, Ed. Jerry C. Olson. Ann Arbor, MI: Association for Consumer Research, 604–609

APPADURAI, ARDUN (1981), "Gastro-Politics in Hindu South Asia," *American Ethnologist,* 8 (August), 494–511.

ARLEN, MICHAEL J. (1980), *Thirty Seconds.* New York: Farrar, Straus & Giroux.

AUSTIN, J. L. (1963), *How To Do Things With Words.* New York: Oxford University Press.

BARBER, BERNARD, and LYLE LOBEL (1953), "Fashion in Women's Clothing and the American Social System," in *Class, Status and Power,* Eds. Reinhard Bendix and Seymour Martin Lipset. New York: The Free Press, 323–332.

BARTHES, ROLAND (1967), *Elements of Semiology,* trans. Annette Lavers and Colin Smith. New York: Hill and Wang.

——— (1972), *Mythologies,* trans. Annette Lavers. London: Jonathan Cape.

——— (1983), *The Fashion System,* trans. Matthew Ward and Richard Howard. New York: Hill and Wang.

BAUMGARTEN, STEVEN A. (1975), "The Innovative Communicator in the Diffusion Process," *Journal of Marketing Research,* 12 (February), 12–18.

BECKER, HOWARD S. (1982), *Art Worlds.* Berkeley, CA: University of California Press.

BELK, RUSSELL W. (1979), "Gift-Giving Behavior," in *Research in Marketing,* Vol. 2, Ed. Jagdish N. Sheth. Greenwich, CT: JAI Press, 95–126.

——— (1982), "Acquiring, Possessing, and Collecting: Fundamental Processes in Consumer Behavior," in *Marketing Theory: Philosophy of Science Perspectives,* Eds. Ronald F. Bush and Shelby G. Hunt. Chicago, IL: American Marketing Association, 185–190.

———, ROBERT MAYER, and KENNETH BAHN (1981), "The Eye of the Beholder: Individual Differences in Perceptions of Consumption Symbolism," in *Advances in Consumer Research,* Vol. 9, Ed. Andrew Mitchell. Ann Arbor, MI: Association for Consumer Research, 523–530.

BIRNBACH, LISA (1980), *The Official Preppy Handbook.* New York: Workman.

BLUMBERG, PAUL (1974), "The Decline and Fall of the Status Symbol: Some Thoughts on Status in a Post-Industrial Society," *Social Problems,* 21 (April), 480–498.

BOURDIEU, PIERRE (1973), "The Berber House," in *Rules and Meanings,* Ed. Mary Douglas. Harmondsworth, England: Penguin Books, 98–110.

BRAUDEL, FERNAND (1973), *Capitalism and Material Life 1400–1800,* trans. Miriam Kochan. London: Weidenfeld and Nicolson.

BRONNER, SIMON J. (1983), "Visible Proofs: Material Culture Study in American Folkloristics," *American Quarterly,* 35 (3), 316–338.

CAPLOW, THEODORE (1982), "Christmas Gifts and Kin Networks," *American Sociological Review,* 47 (June), 383–392.

CLARK, CLIFFORD E., JR. (1976), "Domestic Architecture as an Index to Social History: The Romantic Revival and the Cult of Domesticity in America, 1840–1870," *Journal of Interdisciplinary History,* 7 (Summer), 33–56.

COHEN, LIZABETH A. (1982), "Embellishing a Life of Labour: An Interpretation of the Material Culture of American-Class Homes, 1885–1915," in *Material Culture Studies in America,* Ed. Thomas J. Schlereth. Nashville, TN: The American Association for State and Local History, 289–305.

COLEMAN, RICHARD P. (1983), "The Continuing Significance of Social Class to Marketing," *Journal of Consumer Research,* 10 (December), 265–280.

CZIKSZENTIMIHALYI, MIHALY, and EUGENE ROCHBERG-HALTON (1981), *The Meaning of Things: Domestic Symbols and the Self.* New York: Cambridge University Press.

CUNNINGHAM, CLARK E. (1973), "Order in the Atoni House," in *Right and Left,* Ed. Rodney Needham. Chicago, IL: University of Chicago Press, 204–238.

DAVIS, J. (1972), "Gifts and the U.K. Economy," *Man,* 7 (September), 408–429.

DAVIS, JAMES (1956), "Status Symbols and the Measurement of Status Perception," *Sociometry,* 19 (September), 154–165.

——— (1958), "Cultural Factors in the Perception of Status Symbols," *The Midwest Sociologist,* 21 (December), 1–11.

DE SAUSSURE, FERDINAND (1966), *Course in General Linguistics.* New York: McGraw-Hill.

DISMAN, MILADA (1984), "Domestic Possessions as Manifestations of Elderly Immigrants' Identity," paper presented at the 13th Annual Meeting of the Canadian Association on Gerontology. Vancouver, B.C., Canada.

DOUGLAS, MARY (1966), *Purity and Danger: An Analysis of Concepts of Pollution and Taboo.* Harmondsworth, England: Penguin Books.

——— (1971), "Deciphering a Meal," in *Myth, Symbol, and Culture,* Ed. Clifford Geertz. New York: W. W. Norton, 61–81.

———, and BARON ISHERWOOD (1978), *The World of Goods: Towards an Anthropology of Consumption.* New York: W. W. Norton.

DOXTATER, DENNIS (1984), "Spatial Opposition in Non-Discursive Expression: Architecture as Ritual Process," *Canadian Journal of Anthropology,* 4 (Summer), 1–17.

DREWAL, HENRY (1983), "Body Art as an Expression of Aesthetics and Ontology Among the Yoruba," paper presented in session E-023 of the XIth International Congress of Anthropological and Ethnological Sciences. Vancouver, B.C., Canada.

DURKHEIM, EMILE, and MARCEL MAUSS (1963), *Primitive Classification,* trans. Rodney Needham. Chicago, IL: University of Chicago Press.

DYER, GILLIAN (1982), *Advertising as Communication.* New York: Methuen.

FALLERS, LLOYD A. (1961), "A Note on the Trickle Effect," in *Sociology: Progress of a Decade,* Eds. Seymour Martin Lipset and N. Smelser. Englewood Cliffs, NJ: Prentice-Hall, 501–506.

FELSON, MARCUS (1976), "The Differentiation of Material Life Styles: 1925 to 1966," *Social Indicators Research,* 3, 397–421.

FERNANDEZ, JAMES W. (1966), "Principles of Opposition and Vitality in Fang Aesthetics," *Journal of Aesthetics and Art Criticism,* 25 (Fall), 53–64.

FIELD, GEORGE A. (1970), "The Status Float Phenomenon: The Upward Diffusion of Innovation," *Business Horizons,* 13 (August), 45–52.

FORM, WILLIAM and GREGORY STONE (1957), "Urbanism, Anonymity and Status Symbolism," *American Journal of Sociology,* 62 (March), 504–514.

FOX, RICHARD WIGHTMAN and T. J. JACKSON LEARS, Eds. (1983), *The Culture of Consumption: Critical Essays in American History, 1880–1990.* New York: Pantheon Books.

FRASER, KENNEDY (1981), *The Fashion Mind.* New York: Knopf.

FURBY, LITA (1978), "Possessions: Toward a Theory of Their Meaning and Function Throughout the Life Cycle," in *Lifespan Development and Behavior,* Ed. Paul B. Baltes. New York: Academic Press, 297–336.

GARFINKLE, ANDREW D. (1978), "A Sociolinguistic Analysis of the Language of Advertising," unpublished dissertation, Department of Linguistics, Georgetown University, Washington, D.C.

GOFFMAN, ERVING (1951), "Symbols of Class Status," *British Journal of Sociology,* 2 (December), 295–304.

——— (1979), *Gender Advertisements.* Cambridge, MA: Harvard University Press.

GRAUMANN, CARL F. (1974–1975), "Psychology and the World of Things," *Journal of Phenomenological Psychology,* 4 (1), 389–404.

GREENBERG, LAURA J. (1975), "Art as a Structural System: A Study of Hopi Pottery Designs," *Studies in the Anthropology of Visual Communication,* 2 (1), 33–50.

HALL, EDWARD T. (1983), *The Dance of Life. The Other Dimension of Time.* Garden City, NY: Anchor Press.

HEBIDGE, DICK (1979), *Subculture: The Meaning of Style.* London: Methuen.

HIRSCH, PAUL M. (1972), "Processing Fads and Fashions: An Organization-Set Analysis of Cultural Industry Systems," *American Journal of Sociology,* 77 (January), 639–659.

HIRSCHMAN, ALBERT O. (1982), *Shifting Involvements.* Princeton, NJ: Princeton University Press.

HIRSCHMAN, ELIZABETH C. (1980), "Comprehending Symbolic Consumption," in *Symbolic Consumer Behavior,* Eds. Elizabeth C. Hirschman and Morris B. Holbrook. Ann Arbor, MI: Association for Consumer Research, 4–6.

——— (1984), "Leisure Motives and Sex Roles," *Journal of Leisure Research,* 16 (3), 209–223.

HOLMAN, REBECCA (1980), "Product Use as Communication: A Fresh Appraisal of a Venerable Topic," in *Review of Marketing,* Eds. Ben M. Enis and Kenneth J. Roering. Chicago, IL: American Marketing Association, 250–272.

KRON, JOAN (1983), *Home-Psych.: The Social Psychology of Home and Decoration.* New York: Clarkson N. Potter.

LASCH, CHRISTOPHER (1979), *The Culture of Narcissism.* New York: W. W. Norton.

LAUMANN, EDWARD O., and JAMES S. HOUSE (1970), "Living Room Styles and Social Attributes: The Patterning of Material Artifacts in a Modern Urban Community," *Sociology and Social Research,* 54 (April), 321–342.

LECHTMAN, HEATHER, and ROBERT S. MERRILL, Eds. (1977), *Material Culture: Styles, Organization, and Dynamics of Technology.* St. Paul, MN: West.

LEISS, WILLIAM (1983), "Things Come Alive: Economy and Technology as Modes of Social Representation in Modern Society," paper presented at Table Ronde Internationale sur les Representations. Montreal, Quebec, Canada.

LEVI-STRAUSS, CLAUDE (1966), *The Savage Mind.* Chicago, IL: University of Chicago Press.

LEVY, SIDNEY (1959), "Symbols for Sale," *Harvard Business Review,* 37 (July/August), 117–124.

———(1978), "Hunger and Work in a Civilized Tribe," *American Behavioral Scientist,* 21 (March/April), 557–570.

——— (1981), "Interpreting Consumer Mythology: A Structural Approach to Consumer Behavior," *Journal of Marketing,* 45 (Summer), 49–61.

LOHOF, BRUCE (1969), "The Higher Meaning of Marlboro Cigarettes," *Journal of Popular Culture,* 3 (3), 441–450.

MARTIN, BERNICE (1981), *A Sociology of Contemporary Cultural Change.* Oxford, England: Basil Blackwell.

MAUSS, MARCEL (1970), *The Gift.* London: Routledge & Kegan Paul.

MCCRACKEN, GRANT (1982a), "Rank and Two Aspects of Dress in Elizabethan England," *Culture.* 2 (2), 53–62.

——— (1982b), "Politics and Ritual Sotto Voce: The Use of Demeanor as an Instrument of Politics in Elizabethan England," *Canadian Journal of Anthropology,* 3 (Fall), 85–100.

——— (1983), "The Exchange of Tudor Children," *Journal of Family History,* 8 (Winter), 303-313.

——— (1984), "Anthropology and the Study of Advertising: A Critical Review of Selected Literature," Working Paper No. 84–103, Department of Consumer Studies, University of Guelph, Guelph, Ontario, Canada.

——— (1985a), "Consumer Goods and Cultural Meaning: A Theoretical Account of the Substantiation of Cultural Categories and Principles in Consumer Goods," Working Paper No. 85–102, Department of Consumer Studies, University of Guelph, Guelph, Ontario, Canada.

——— (1985b), "Consumer Goods and Cultural Change: A Theoretical Account of Change in the Cultural Meaning of Consumer Goods," Working Paper No. 85–104, Department of Consumer Studies, University of Guelph, Guelph, Ontario, Canada.

——— (1985c), "The Trickle-Down Theory Rehabilitated," in *The Psychology of Fashion,* Ed. Michael R. Solomon. Lexington, MA: Lexington Books, 39–54.

——— (1985d), "The Making of Modern Consumption Behavior: The Historical Origins and Development of the Context and Activity of Modern Consumption," Working Paper No. 85–101, Department of Consumer Studies, University of Guelph, Guelph, Ontario, Canada.

——— (1986), "Clothing as Language: An Object Lesson in the Study of the Expressive Properties of Material Culture," in *Material Anthropology: Contemporary Approaches to Material Culture,* Eds. Barrie Reynolds and Margarett Stott. New York: University Press of America, in press.

MCKENDRICK, NEIL, JOHN BREWER, and J. H. PLUMB (1982), *The Birth of a Consumer Society: The Commercialization of Eighteenth Century England.* Bloomington, IN: Indiana University Press.

MEIKLE, JEFFREY L. (1979), *Twentieth Century Limited: Industrial Design in America, 1925–1939.* Philadelphia, PA: Temple University Press.

MEYERSON, ROLF and ELIHU KATZ (1957), "Notes on a Natural History of Fads," *American Journal of Sociology,* 62 (May), 594–601.

MITCHELL, ARNOLD (1983), *The Nine American Lifestyles.* New York: Warner Books.

MOERAN, BRIAN (1985), "When the Poetics of Advertising Becomes the Advertising of Poetics: Syntactical and Semantic Paralellism in English and Japanese Advertising," *Language and Communication,* 5 (1), 29–44.

MOLLOY, JOHN T. (1977), *The Woman's Dress for Success Book.* New York: Warner Books.

MUNN, NANCY (1973), "Symbolism in a Ritual Context: Aspects of Symbolic Action," in *Handbook of Social and Cultural Anthropology,* Ed. J. L. Honigmann. Chicago, IL: Rand McNally, 579–612.

MYERS, ELIZABETH (1985), "Phenomenological Analysis of the Importance of Special Possessions: An Exploratory Study," in *Advances in Consumer Research,* Vol. 12, Eds. Elizabeth C. Hirschman and Morris B. Holbrook. Provo, UT: Association for Consumer Research, 560–565.

NAISBITT, JOHN (1982), *Megatrends.* New York: Warner Books.

NICOSIA, FRANCESCO M., and ROBERT N. MAYER (1976), "Toward a Sociology of Consumption," *Journal of Consumer Research,* 3 (September), 65–75.

OLSON, CLARK D. (1985), "Materialism in the Home: The Impact of Artifacts on Dyadic Communication," in *Advances in Consumer Research,* Vol. 12, Eds. Elizabeth C. Hirschman and Morris B. Holbrook. Provo, UT: Association for Consumer Research, 388–393.

ORTNER, SHERRY (1978), *Sherpas Through their Rituals.* Cambridge, England: Cambridge University Press.

POLEGATO, ROSEMARY, and MARJORIE WALL (1980), "Information Seeking By Fashion Opinion Leaders and Followers," *Home Economics Research Journal,* 8 (May), 327–338.

PROWN, JULES D. (1980), "Style as Evidence," *Winterthur Portfolio,* 15 (Autumn), 197–210.

——— (1982), "Mind In Matter: An Introduction to Material Culture Theory and Method," *Winterthur Portfolio,* 17 (Spring), 1–19.

PULOS, ARTHUR J. (1983), *American Design Ethic: A History of Industrial Design to 1940.* Cambridge, MA: M.I.T. Press.

QUIMBY, IAN, Ed. (1978), *Material Culture and the Study of Material Life.* New York: W. W. Norton.

RAPOPORT, AMOS (1968), "The Personal Element in Housing—an Argument for Open-Ended Design," *Journal of the Royal Institute for British Architects,* 75 (July), 300–307.

——— (1982), *Meaning of the Built Environment.* Beverly Hills, CA: Sage Publications.

ROGERS, EVERETT (1983), *Diffusion of Innovations.* New York: The Free Press.

RODMAN, MARGARET, and JEAN-MARC PHILIBERT (1985), "Rethinking Consumption: Some Problems Concerning the Practice of Objects in the Third World," paper presented at the Canadian Ethnological Society Meetings, University of Toronto, Toronto, Ontario, Canada.

ROOK, DENNIS (1984), "Ritual Behavior and Consumer Symbolism," in *Advances in Consumer Research,* Vol. 11, Ed. Thomas C. Kinnear. Provo, UT: Association for Consumer Research, 279–284.

———, and SIDNEY J. LEVY (1982), "The Psycho-Social Themes in Grooming Rituals," in *Advances in Consumer Research,* Vol. 10, Eds. Richard T. Bagozzi and Alice M. Tybout. Ann Arbor, MI: Association for Consumer Research, 329–334.

SAHLINS, MARSHALL (1972), "The Spirit of the Gift," in *Stone-Age Economics,* Ed. Marshall Sahlins. Chicago, IL: Aldine, 149–183.

——— (1976), *Culture and Practical Reason.* Chicago, IL: University of Chicago Press.

SCHLERETH, THOMAS J. (1982), "Material Culture Studies in America, 1876–1976," in *Material Culture Studies in America,* Ed. Thomas J. Schlereth. Nashville, TN: The American Association for State and Local History, 1–75.

SCHWARTZ, BARRY (1967), "The Social Psychology of the Gift," *American Journal of Sociology,* 73 (July), 1–11.

SCHWARZ, RONALD A. (1979), "Uncovering the Secret Vice: Toward an Anthropology of Clothing and Adornment," in *The Fabrics of Culture,* Eds. Justine Cordwell and Ronald Schwarz. The Hague, Netherlands: Mouton.

SHERMAN, EDWARD, and NEWMAN, EVELYN S. (1977–1978), "The Meaning of Cherished Possessions for the Elderly," *International Journal of Aging and Human Development,* 8 (2), 181–192.

SHERRY, JOHN (1985), "Advertising as a Cultural System," paper presented at the 1985 American Marketing Association Educator's Conference, Phoenix, AZ.

SIMMEL, GEORG (1904), "Fashion," *International Quarterly,* 10, 130–155.

SIMMONS, ROBERTA G., SUSAN D. KLEIN, and RICHARD L. SIMMONS (1977), *Gift of Life: The Social and Psychological Impact of Organ Donation.* New York: Wiley.

SOLOMON, MICHAEL (1983), "The Role of Products as Social Stimuli: A Symbolic Interactionism Perspective," *Journal of Consumer Research,* 10 (December), 319–329.

SOMMERS, MONTROSE (1963), "Product Symbolism and the Perception of Social Strata," in *Toward Scientific Marketing,* Ed. Stephen A. Greyser. Chicago, IL: American Marketing Association, 200–216.

TAMBIAH, STANLEY J. (1977), "The Cosmological and Performative Significance of a Thai Cult of Healing Through Mediation," *Culture, Medicine, and Psychiatry,* 1, 97–132.

TURNER, TERENCE (1969), "Tchikrin, A Central Brazilian Tribe and its Symbolic Language of Bodily Adornment," *Natural History,* 78 (October), 50–59, 80.

TURNER, VICTOR (1967), "Betwixt and Between: the Liminal Period in Rites of Passage," in *The Forest of Symbols,* Ed. Victor Turner. Ithaca, NY: Cornell University Press, 93–111.

——— (1969), "Forms of Symbolic Action," in *Forms of Symbolic Action,* Ed. Robert F. Spencer. Seattle, WA: American Ethnological Society, 3–25.

UNRUH, DAVID R. (1983), "Death and Personal History: Strategies of Identity Preservations," *Social Problems,* 30 (February), 340–351.

VAN GENNEP, ARNOLD (1960), *The Rites of Passage.* London: Routledge & Kegan Paul.

VERSHURE, BETH, STEPHEN MAGEL, and EDWARD K. SADALLA (1977), "House Form and Social Identity," in *The Behavioral Basis of Design,* Book 2, Eds. Peter Suedfeld, James A. Russell, Lawrence M. Ward, Francoise Szigeti, and Gerald Davis. Stroudsburg, PA: Dowden, Hutchinson and Ross, 273–278.

WILLIAMSON, JUDITH (1978), *Decoding Advertising.* New York: Marion Boyars.

WOLFE, TOM (1970), *Radical Chic and Mau-Mauing the Flak Catchers.* New York: Farrar, Straus & Giroux.

WARNER, LLOYD, and PAUL S. LUNT (1941), *The Social Life of a Modern Community.* New Haven, CT: Yale University Press.

YORK, PETER (1980), *Style Wars.* London: Sidgwich and Jackson.

31

BODY RITUAL AMONG THE NACIREMA*

Horace Miner

Most cultures exhibit a particular configuration or style. A single value or pattern of perceiving the world often leaves its stamp on several institutions in the society. Examples are "machismo" in Spanish-influenced cultures, "face" in Japanese culture, and "pollution by females" in some highland New Guinea cultures. Here Horace Miner demonstrates that "attitudes about the body" have a pervasive influence on many institutions in Nacireman society.

The anthropologist has become so familiar with the diversity of ways in which different peoples behave in similar situations that he is not apt to be surprised by even the most exotic customs. In fact, if all of the logically possible combinations of behavior have not been found somewhere in the world, he is apt to suspect that they must be present in some yet undescribed tribe. This point has, in fact, been expressed with respect to clan organization by Murdock. In this light, the magical beliefs and practices of the Nacirema present such unusual aspects that it seems desirable to describe them as an example of the extremes to which human behavior can go.

Professor Linton first brought the ritual of the Nacirema to the attention of anthropologists twenty years ago, but the culture of this people is still very poorly understood. They are a North American group living in the territory between the Canadian Cree, the Yaqui and Tarahumare of Mexico, and the Carib and Arawak of the Antilles. Little is known of their origin, although tradition states that they came from the east. . . .

---

*Reproduced by permission of the American Anthropological Association from *The American Anthropologist,* 58 (1956), 503–507.

Nacirema culture is characterized by a highly developed market economy which has evolved in a rich natural habitat. While much of the people's time is devoted to economic pursuits, a large part of the fruits of these labors and a considerable portion of the day are spent in ritual activity. The focus of this activity is the human body, the appearance and health of which loom as a dominant concern in the ethos of the people. While such a concern is certainly not unusual, its ceremonial aspects and associated philosophy are unique.

The fundamental belief underlying the whole system appears to be that the human body is ugly and that its natural tendency is to debility and disease. Incarcerated in such a body, man's only hope is to avert these characteristics through the use of the powerful influences of ritual and ceremony. Every household has one or more shrines devoted to this purpose. The more powerful individuals in the society have several shrines in their houses and, in fact, the opulence of a house is often referred to in terms of the number of such ritual centers it possesses. Most houses are of wattle and daub construction, but the shrine rooms of the more wealthy are walled with stone. Poorer families imitate the rich by applying pottery plaques to their shrine walls.

While each family has at least one such shrine, the rituals associated with it are not family ceremonies but are private and secret. The rites are normally only discussed with children, and then only during the period when they are being initiated into these mysteries. I was able, however, to establish sufficient rapport with the natives to examine these shrines and to have the rituals described to me.

The focal point of the shrine is a box or chest which is built into the wall. In this chest are kept the many charms and magical potions without which no native believes he could live. These preparations are secured from a variety of specialized practitioners. The most powerful of these are the medicine men, whose assistance must be rewarded with substantial gifts. However, the medicine men do not provide the curative potions for their clients, but decide what the ingredients should be and then write them down in an ancient and secret language. This writing is understood only by the medicine men and by the herbalists who, for another gift, provide the required charm.

The charm is not disposed of after it has served its purpose, but is placed in the charm-box of the household shrine. As these magical materials are specific for certain ills, and the real or imagined maladies of the people are many, the charm-box is usually full to overflowing. The magical packets are so numerous that people forget what their purposes were and fear to use them again. While the natives are very vague on this point, we can only assume that the idea in retaining all the old magical materials is that their presence in the charm-box, before which the body rituals are conducted, will in some way protect the worshipper.

Beneath the charm-box is a small font. Each day every member of the family, in succession, enters the shrine room, bows his head before the charm-box, mingles different sorts of holy water in the font, and proceeds with a brief rite of ablution. The holy waters are secured from the Water Temple of the community, where the priests conduct elaborate ceremonies to make the liquid ritually pure.

In the hierarchy of magical practitioners, and below the medicine men in prestige, are specialists whose designation is best translated "holy-mouth-men." The Nacirema have an almost pathological horror of and fascination with the mouth, the condition of which is believed to have a supernatural influence on all social relationships. Were it not for the rituals of the mouth, they believe that their teeth would fall out, their gums bleed, their jaws shrink, their friends desert them, and their lovers reject them. They also believe that a strong relationship exists between oral and moral characteristics. For example, there is a ritual ablution of the mouth for children which is supposed to improve their moral fiber.

The daily body ritual performed by everyone includes a mouth-rite. Despite the fact that these people are so punctilious about care of the mouth, this rite involves a practice which strikes the uninitiated stranger as revolting. It was reported to me that the ritual consists of inserting a small bundle of hog hairs into the mouth, along with certain magical powders, and then moving the bundle in a highly formalized series of gestures.

In addition to the private mouth-rite, the people seek out a holy-mouth-man once or twice a year. These practitioners have an impressive set of paraphernalia, consisting of a variety of augers, awls, probes, and prods. The use of these objects in the exorcism of the evils of the mouth involves almost unbelievable ritual torture of the client. The holy-mouth-man opens the client's mouth and, using the above mentioned tools, enlarges any holes which decay may have created in the teeth. Magical materials are put into these holes. If there are no naturally occurring holes in the teeth, large sections of one or more teeth are gouged out so that the supernatural substance can be applied. In the client's view, the purpose of these ministrations is to arrest decay and to draw friends. The extremely sacred and traditional character of the rite is evident in the fact that the natives return to the holy-mouth-men year after year, despite the fact that their teeth continue to decay.

It is hoped that, when a thorough study of the Nacirema is made, there will be a careful inquiry into the personality structure of these people. One has but to watch the gleam in the eye of a holy-mouth-man as he jabs an awl into an exposed nerve, to suspect that a certain amount of sadism is involved. If this can be established, a very interesting pattern emerges, for most of the population shows definite masochistic tendencies. It was to these that Professor Linton referred in discussing a distinctive part of the daily body ritual which is performed only by men. This part of the rite involves scraping and lacerating the surface of the face with a sharp instrument. Special women's rites are performed only four times during each lunar month, but what they lack in frequency is made up in barbarity. As part of this ceremony, women bake their heads in small ovens for about an hour. The theoretically interesting point is that what seems to be a preponderantly masochistic people have developed sadistic specialists.

The medicine men have an imposing temple, or *latipso,* in every community of any size. The more elaborate ceremonies required to treat very sick patients can only be performed at this temple. These ceremonies involve not only the thaumaturge but a permanent group of vestal maidens who move sedately about the temple chambers in distinctive costume and headdress.

The *latipso* ceremonies are so harsh that it is phenomenal that a fair proportion of the really sick natives who enter the temple ever recover. Small children whose indoctrination is still incomplete have been known to resist attempts to take them to the temple because "that is where you go to die." Despite this fact, sick adults are not only willing but eager to undergo the protracted ritual purification, if they can afford to do so. No matter how ill the supplicant or how grave the emergency, the guardians of many temples will not admit a client if he cannot give a rich gift to the custodian. Even after one has gained admission and survived the ceremonies, the guardians will not permit the neophyte to leave until he makes still another gift.

The supplicant entering the temple is first stripped of all his or her clothes. In everyday life the Nacirema avoids exposure of his body and its natural functions. Bathing and excretory acts are performed only in the secrecy of the household shrine, where they are ritualized as part of the body-rites. Psychological shock results from the fact that body secrecy is suddenly lost upon entry into the *latipso.* A man, whose own wife has never seen him in an excretory act, suddenly finds himself naked and assisted by a vestal maiden while he performs his natural functions into a sacred vessel. This sort of ceremonial treatment is necessitated by the fact that the excreta are used by a diviner to ascertain the course and nature of the client's sickness. Female clients, on the other hand, find their naked bodies are subjected to the scrutiny, manipulation and prodding of the medicine men.

Few supplicants in the temple are well

enough to do anything but lie on their hard beds. The daily ceremonies, like the rites of the holy-mouth-men, involve discomfort and torture. With ritual precision, the vestals awaken their miserable charges each dawn and roll them about on their beds of pain while performing ablutions, in the formal movements of which the maidens are highly trained. At other times they insert magic wands in the supplicant's mouth or force him to eat substances which are supposed to be healing. From time to time the medicine men come to their clients and jab magically treated needles into their flesh. The fact that these temple ceremonies may not cure, and may even kill the neophyte, in no way decreases the people's faith in the medicine men.

There remains one other kind of practitioner, known as a "listener." This witchdoctor has the power to exorcise the devils that lodge in the heads of people who have been bewitched. The Nacirema believe that parents bewitch their own children. Mothers are particularly suspected of putting a curse on children while teaching them the secret body rituals. The counter-magic of the witchdoctor is unusual in its lack of ritual. The patient simply tells the "listener" all his troubles and fears, beginning with the earliest difficulties he can remember. The memory displayed by the Nacirema in these exorcism sessions is truly remarkable. It is not uncommon for the patient to bemoan the rejection he felt upon being weaned as a babe, and a few individuals even see their troubles going back to the traumatic effects of their own birth.

In conclusion, mention must be made of certain practices which have their base in native esthetics but which depend upon the pervasive aversion to the natural body and its functions. There are ritual fasts to make fat people thin and ceremonial feasts to make thin people fat. Still other rites are used to make women's breasts larger if they are small, and smaller if they are large. General dissatisfaction with breast shape is symbolized in the fact that the ideal form is virtually outside the range of human variation. A few women afflicted with almost inhuman hyper-mammary development are so idolized that they make a handsome living by simply going from village to village and permitting the natives to stare at them for a fee.

Reference has already been made to the fact that excretory functions are ritualized, routinized, and relegated to secrecy. Natural reproductive functions are similarly distorted. Intercourse is taboo as a topic and scheduled as an act. Efforts are made to avoid pregnancy by the use of magical materials or by limiting intercourse to certain phases of the moon. Conception is actually very infrequent. When pregnant, women dress so as to hide their condition. Parturition takes place in secret, without friends or relatives to assist, and the majority of women do not nurse their infants.

Our review of the ritual life of the Nacirema has certainly shown them to be a magic-ridden people. It is hard to understand how they have managed to exist so long under the burdens which they have imposed upon themselves. But even such exotic customs as these take on real meaning when they are viewed with the insight provided by Malinowski when he wrote:

"Looking from far and above, from our high places of safety in the developed civilization, it is easy to see all the crudity and irrelevance of magic. But without its power and guidance early man could not have mastered his practical difficulties as he has done, nor could man have advanced to the higher stages of civilization."

NAME INDEX

SUBJECT INDEX